A Question Bank of Acupuncture

15 Sept 1339 - 1352

By

Henry C. Lu, PhD

Table of Contents

Part One: Visual Images

How to Use This Question Bank of Acupuncture / 如何使用这本针灸题库

This question bank consists of essential testing questions selected from prestigious Chinese sources; it is truly a most comprehensive question bank of its kind in any language. This Question Bank Of Acupuncture contains 3,254 Multiple-Choice Questions and 2,137 Questions of Visual Images, bringing about a total of 5,391 testing questions. The Questions Of Visual Images offers a unique opportunity for school class as well as licensing examinations in lieu of the so-called practicum examinations by which examiners conduct examinations of a single examinee, which is very time-consuming indeed. On the other hand, by using questions of visual images, pictures may be presented by a single examiner to a group of examinees for identification. This can save time and energy, what is there against it? If examinees can identify the contents of the picture, chances are that they can also identify the same thing in the clinical setting. If an examinee can identify the picture as S36 just by looking at the picture, for example, chances are that they can also identify S36 on the body, which is the real purpose of practicum examination. Again, if a student can identify the picture as the Forest Fire technique, for example, chances are that they can also apply the same technique in clinical practice. If the questions of visual images and multiple-choice questions are used in combination, it will introduce many innovative ideas to the acupuncture	这本题库刊登从中国有名书籍选出来的主要考题,真正是一本最有综合性的针灸题库. 本题库包括 3,254 选择题 以及 2,137 心象题，加起来总共有 5,391 考题. 心象题库带给教室里的考试以及针灸执照的考试唯一的机会进行测试. 通常所谓实际操作考试，是由数名考官来监考一个应考者，实在太花时间了. 另一方面，如果用心象题库来考试的话，一个考官可以把心象考题同时显示给一组的考生来辨认. 既省时间又省精力，何乐而不为? 如果考生可以辨认出心象考题的内容，说名在实际操作考试上他也可以同样做到. 举例说明一下. 如果一个考生看了图象可以辨认出是足三里，我们可以断定他也可以寻出足三里在身体的位置. 这就证实针灸心象考试和针灸实际操作考试，有异曲同工之效. 再举个例子. 如果一个考生看了图象可以辨认出是烧山火，我们可以断定在临床上他也可以操作烧山火. 如果把心象考题和选择题同时应用,对针灸考试可以带来不少的方便. 不但如此，针灸学生也

examinations. Moreover, a student can also make use of this question bank to master acupuncture and also to do well on examinations.	可以把这本针灸题库当作进修及应考成功的工具.

Part One: Questions of Visual Images 心象题库

Test 1: Meridians

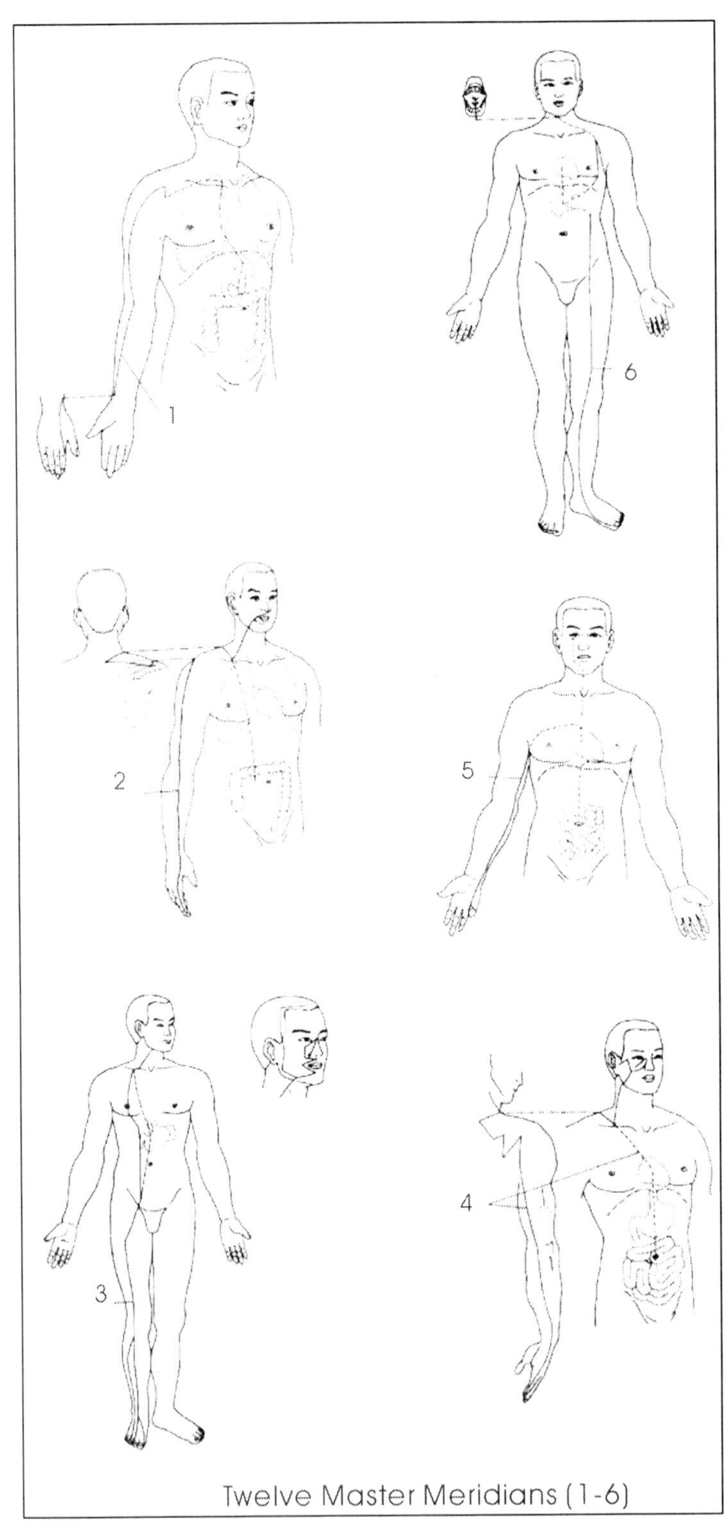

Twelve Master Meridians (1-6)

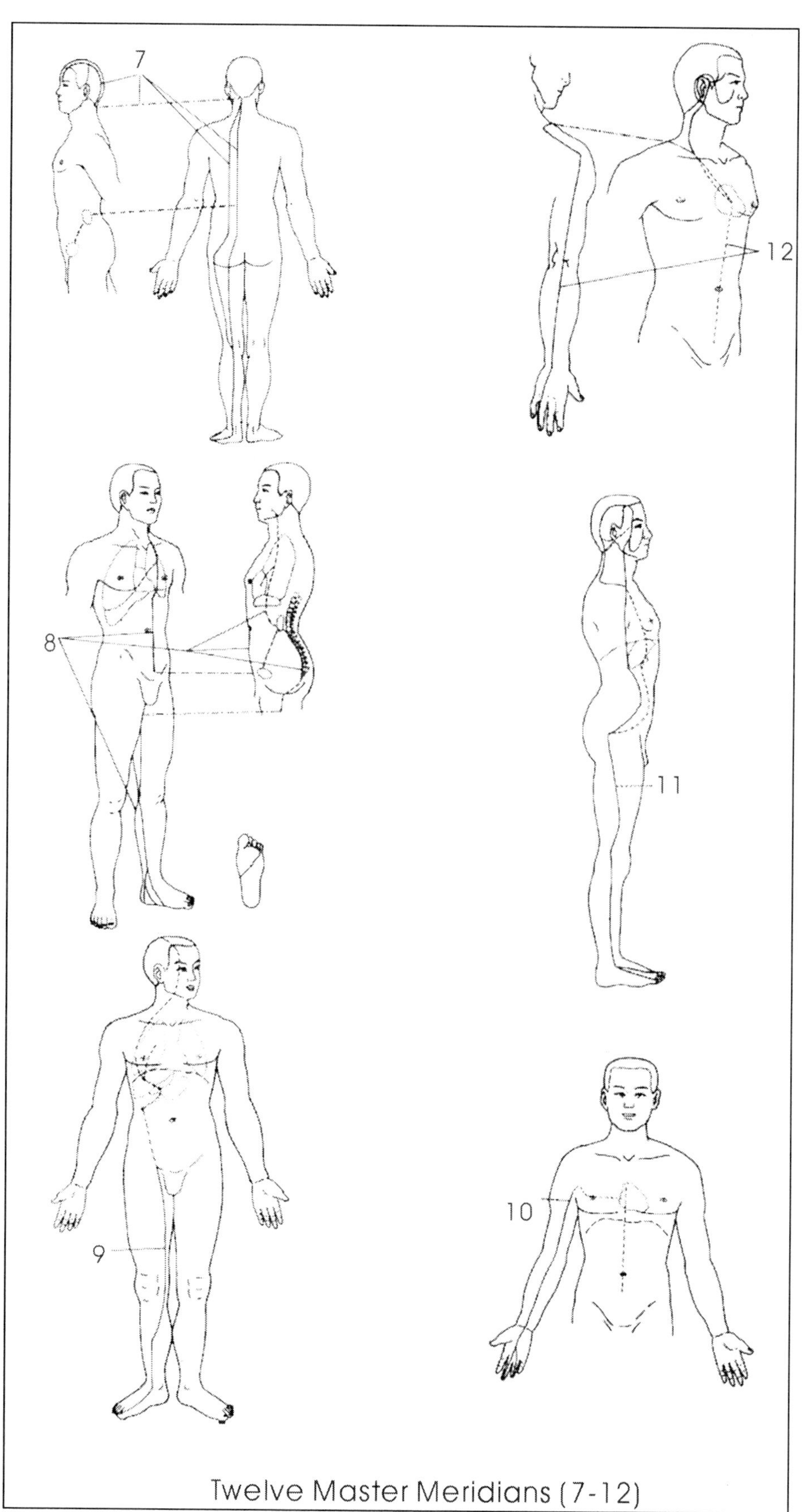

Twelve Master Meridians (7-12)

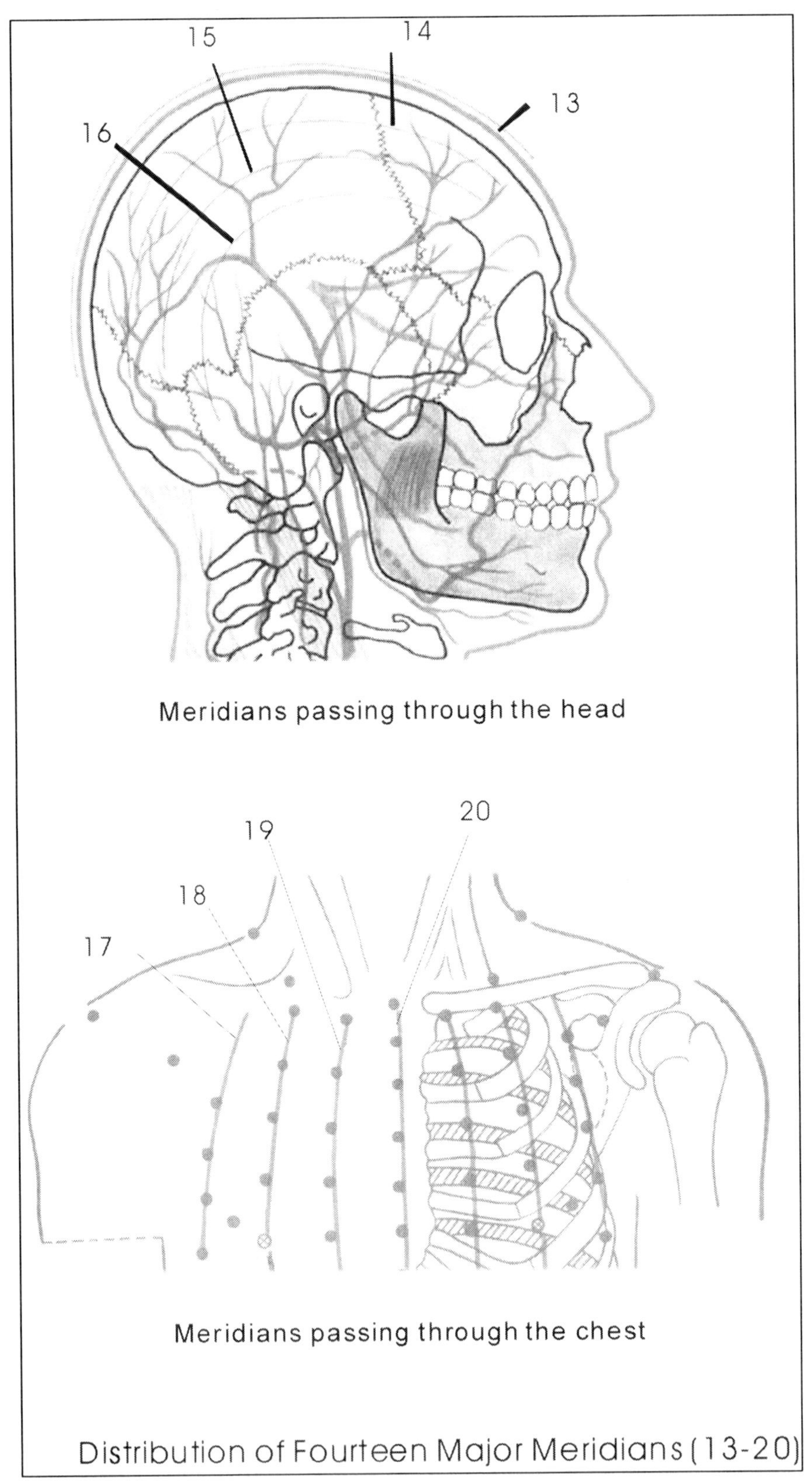

Meridians passing through the head

Meridians passing through the chest

Distribution of Fourteen Major Meridians (13-20)

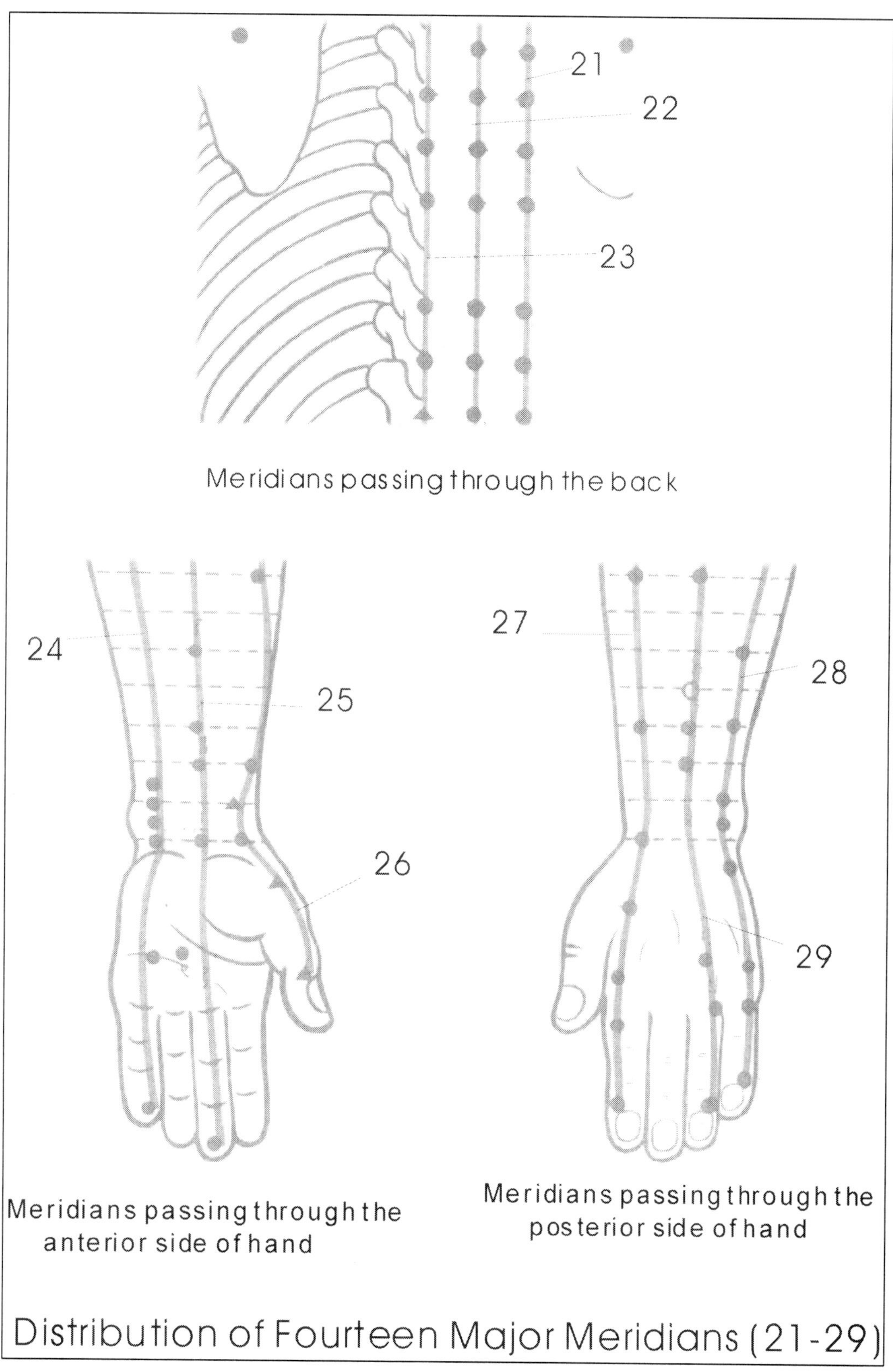

Meridians passing through the back

Meridians passing through the anterior side of hand

Meridians passing through the posterior side of hand

Distribution of Fourteen Major Meridians (21-29)

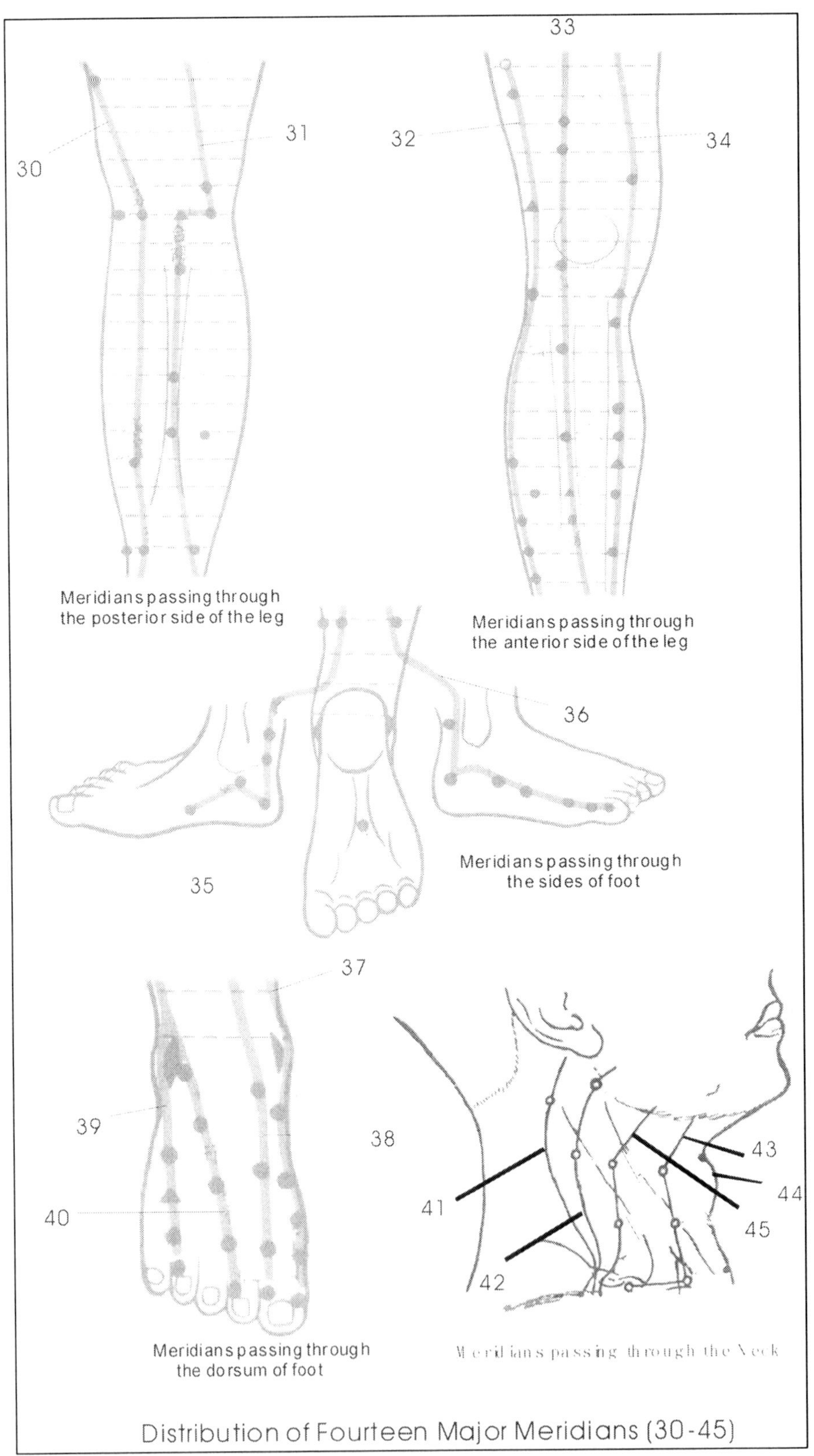

Distribution of Fourteen Major Meridians (30-45)

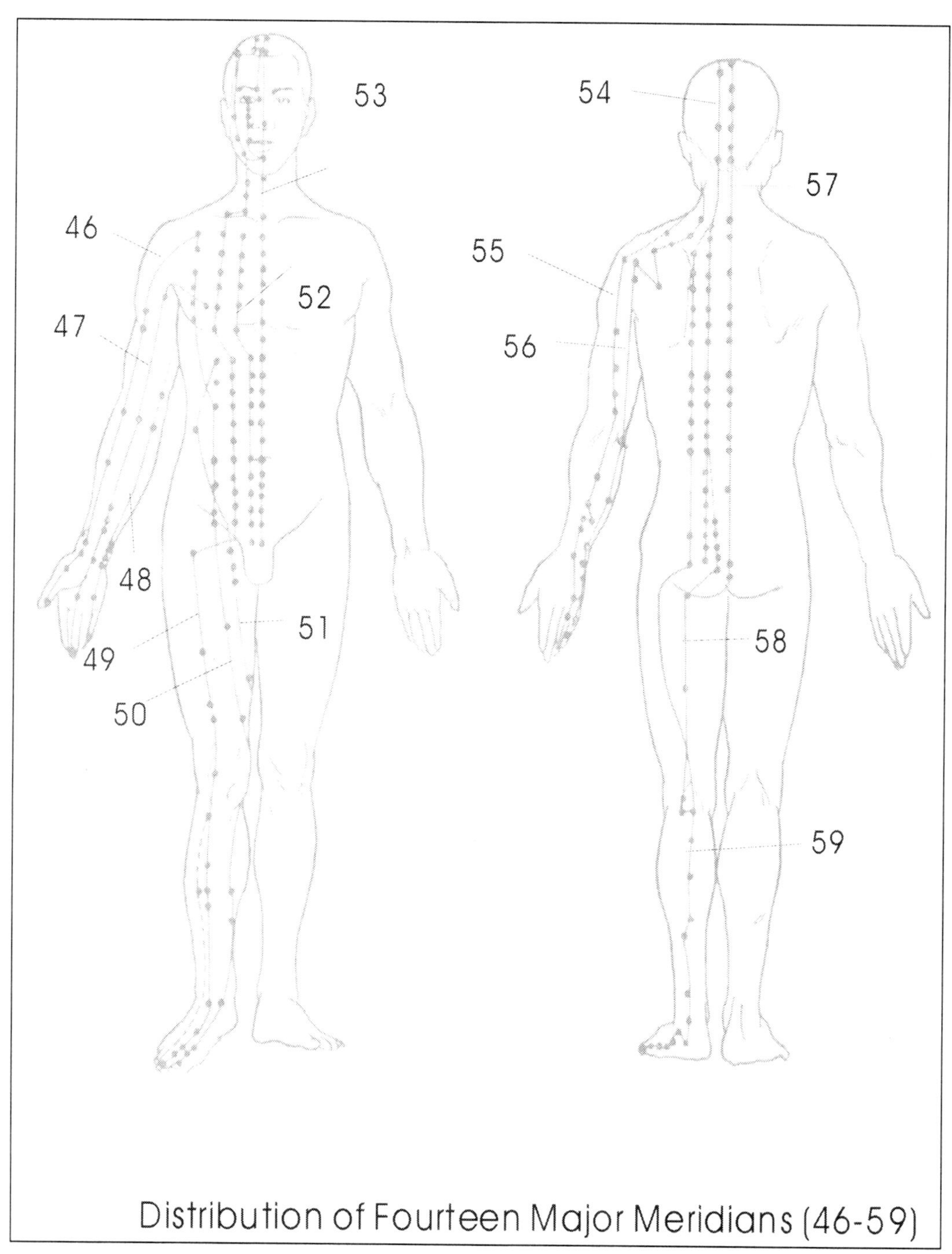

Distribution of Fourteen Major Meridians (46-59)

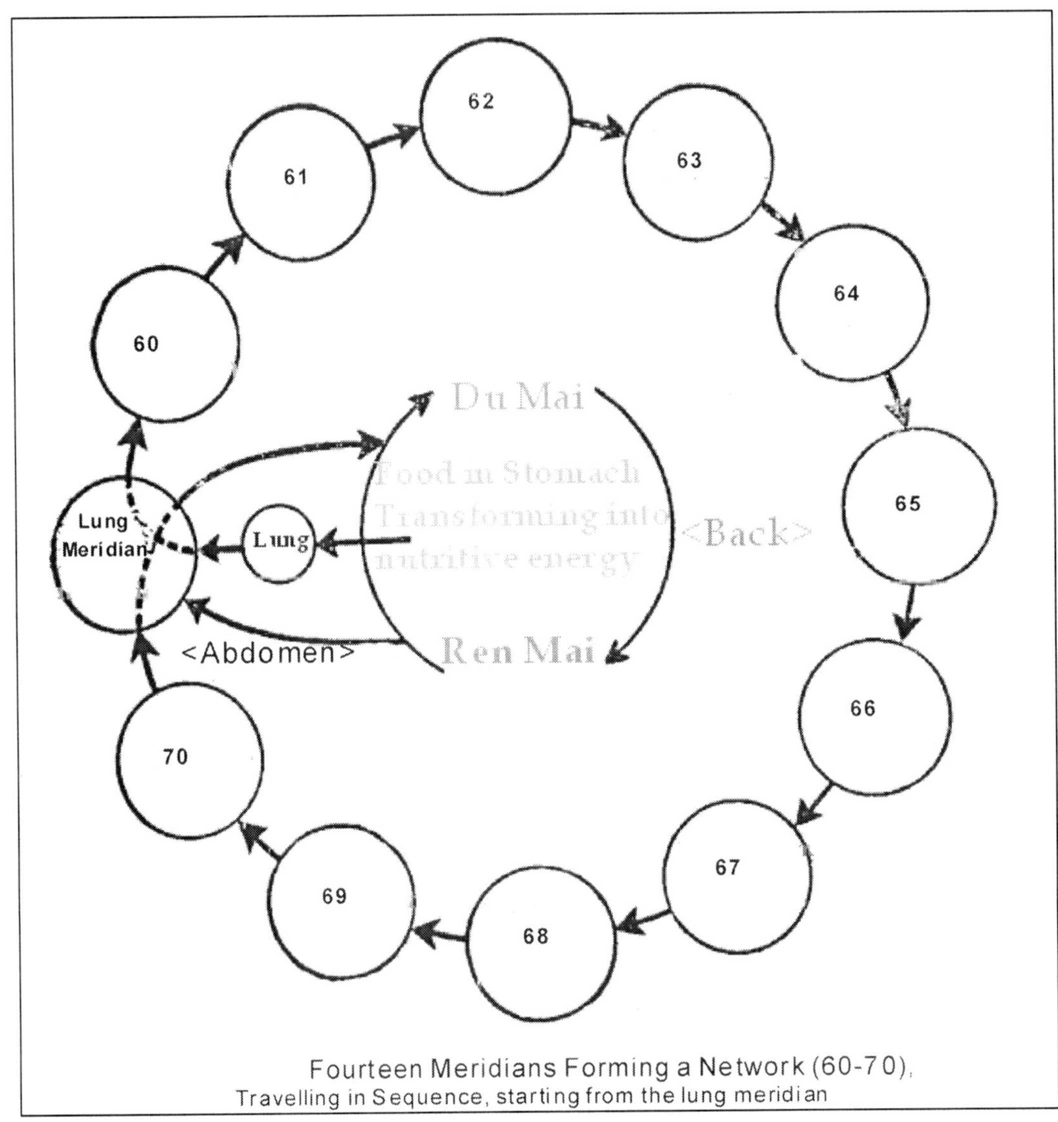

Fourteen Meridians Forming a Network (60-70),
Travelling in Sequence, starting from the lung meridian

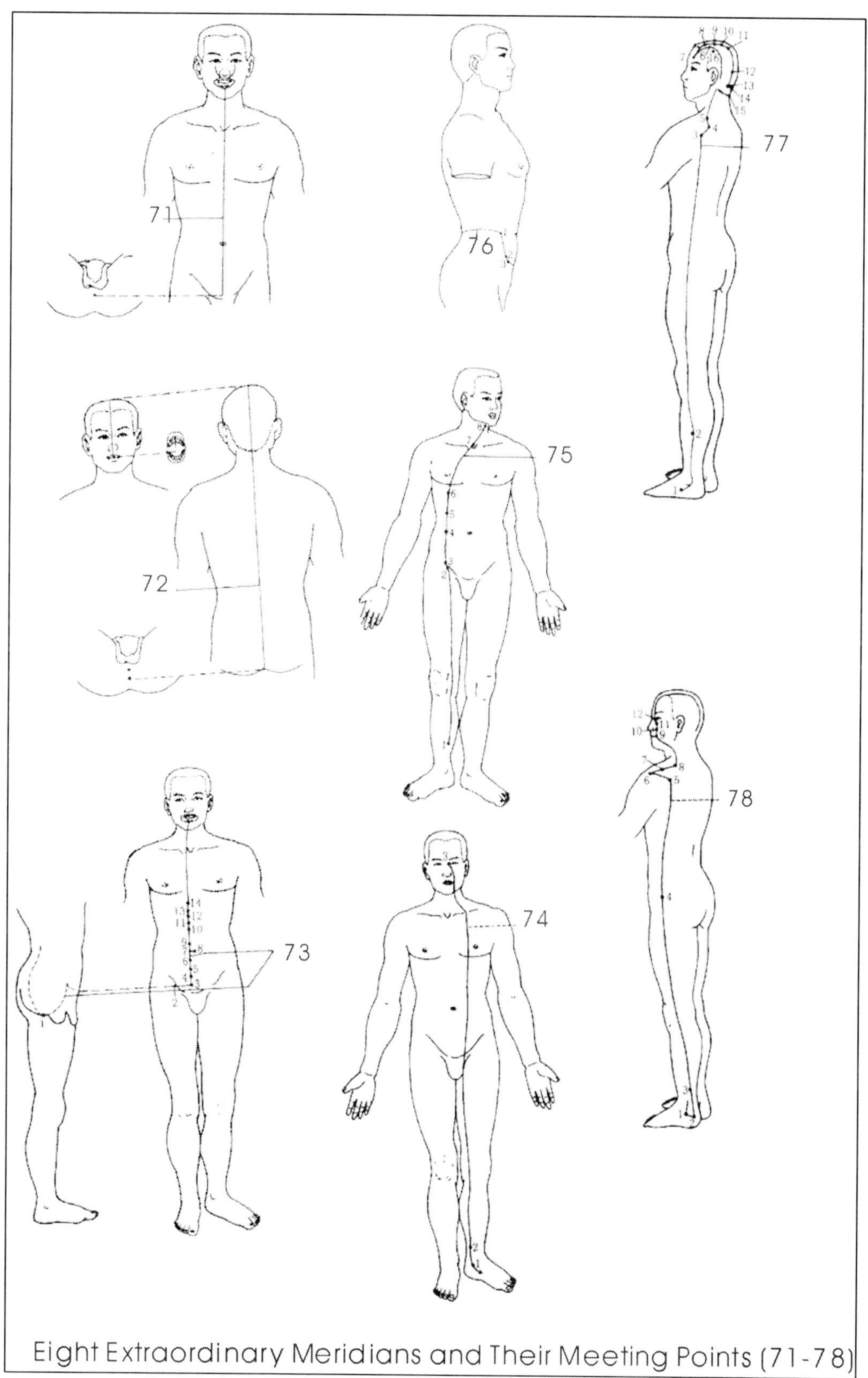

Eight Extraordinary Meridians and Their Meeting Points (71-78)

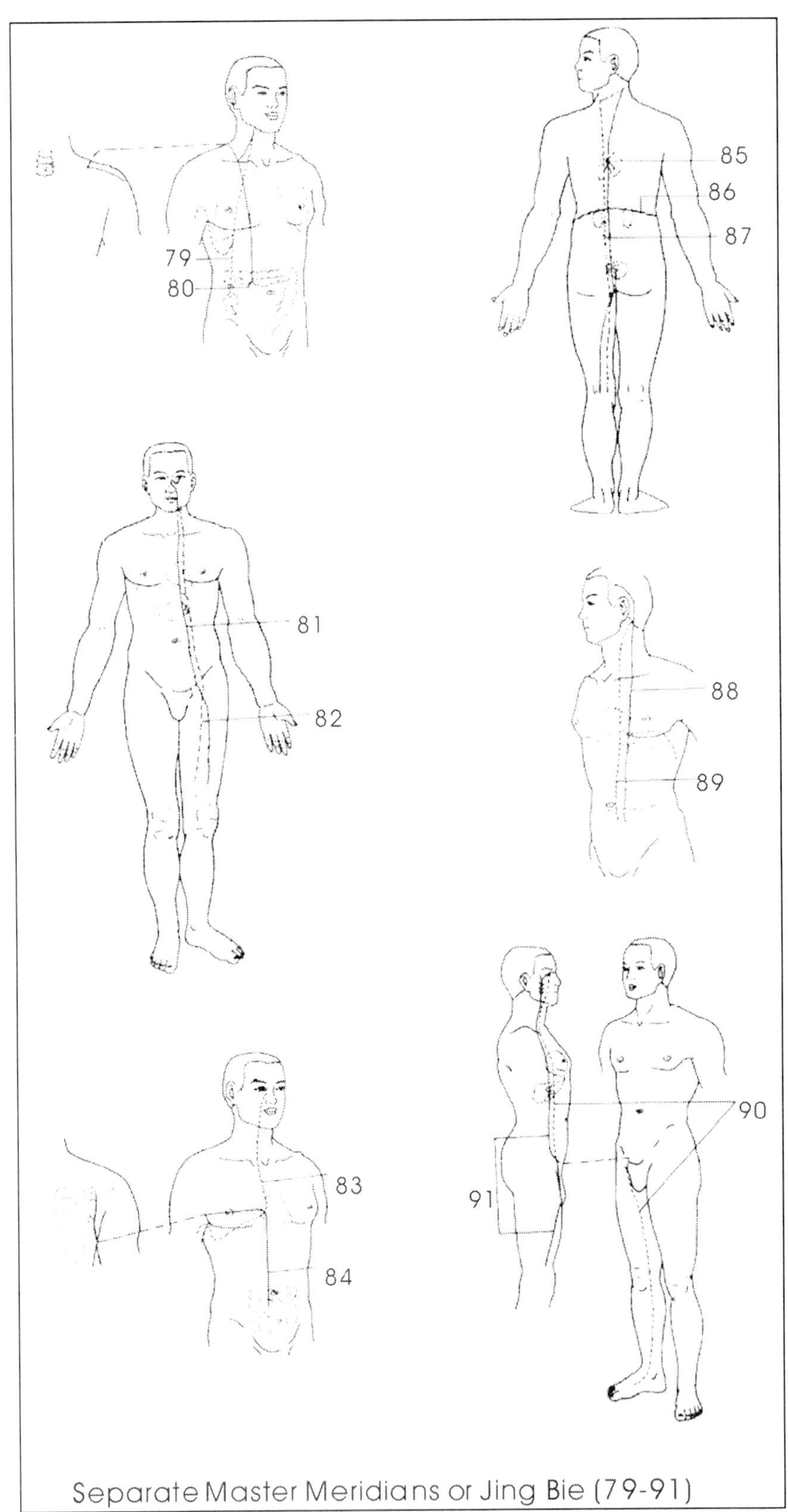

Separate Master Meridians or Jing Bie (79-91)

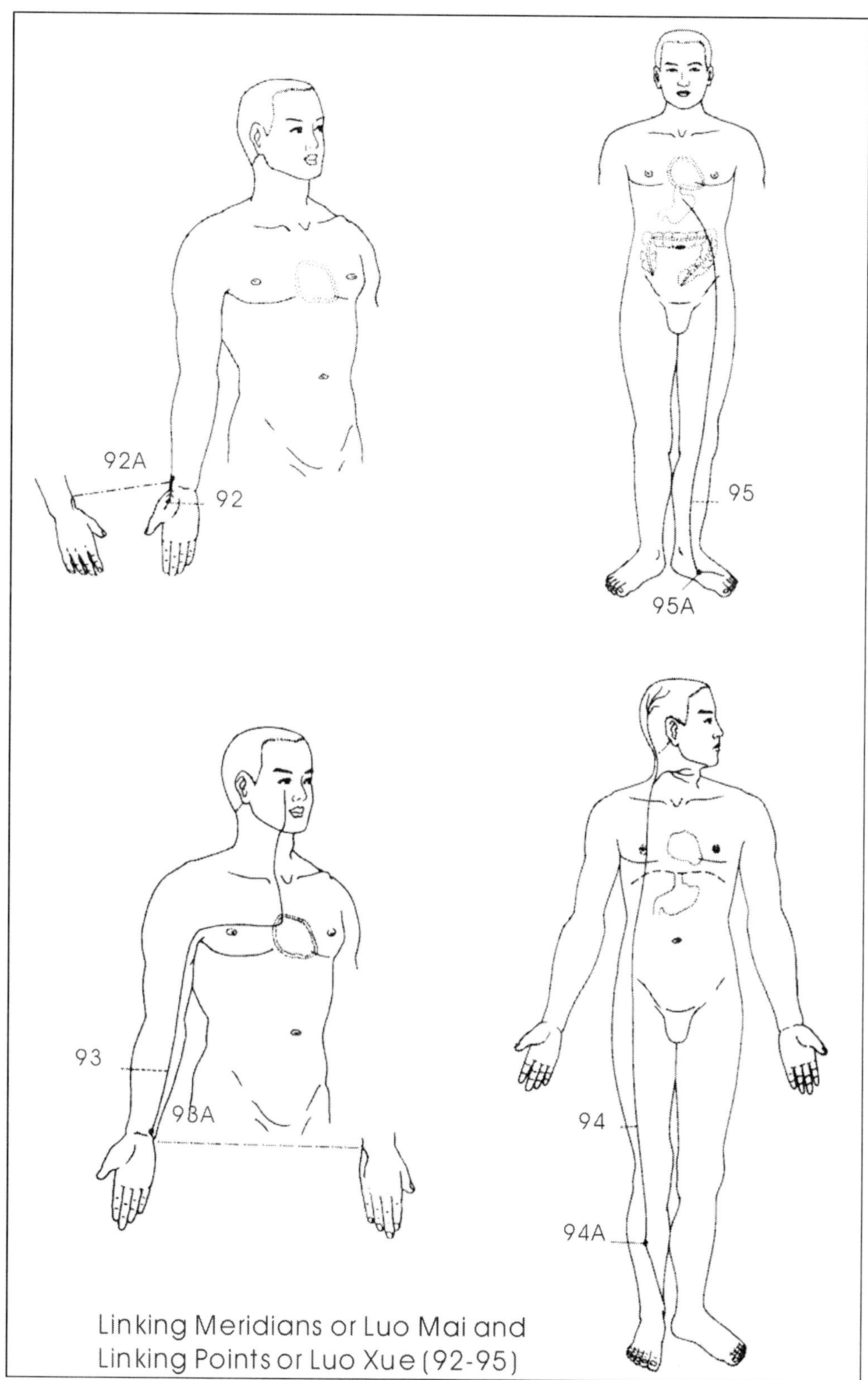

Linking Meridians or Luo Mai and Linking Points or Luo Xue (92-95)

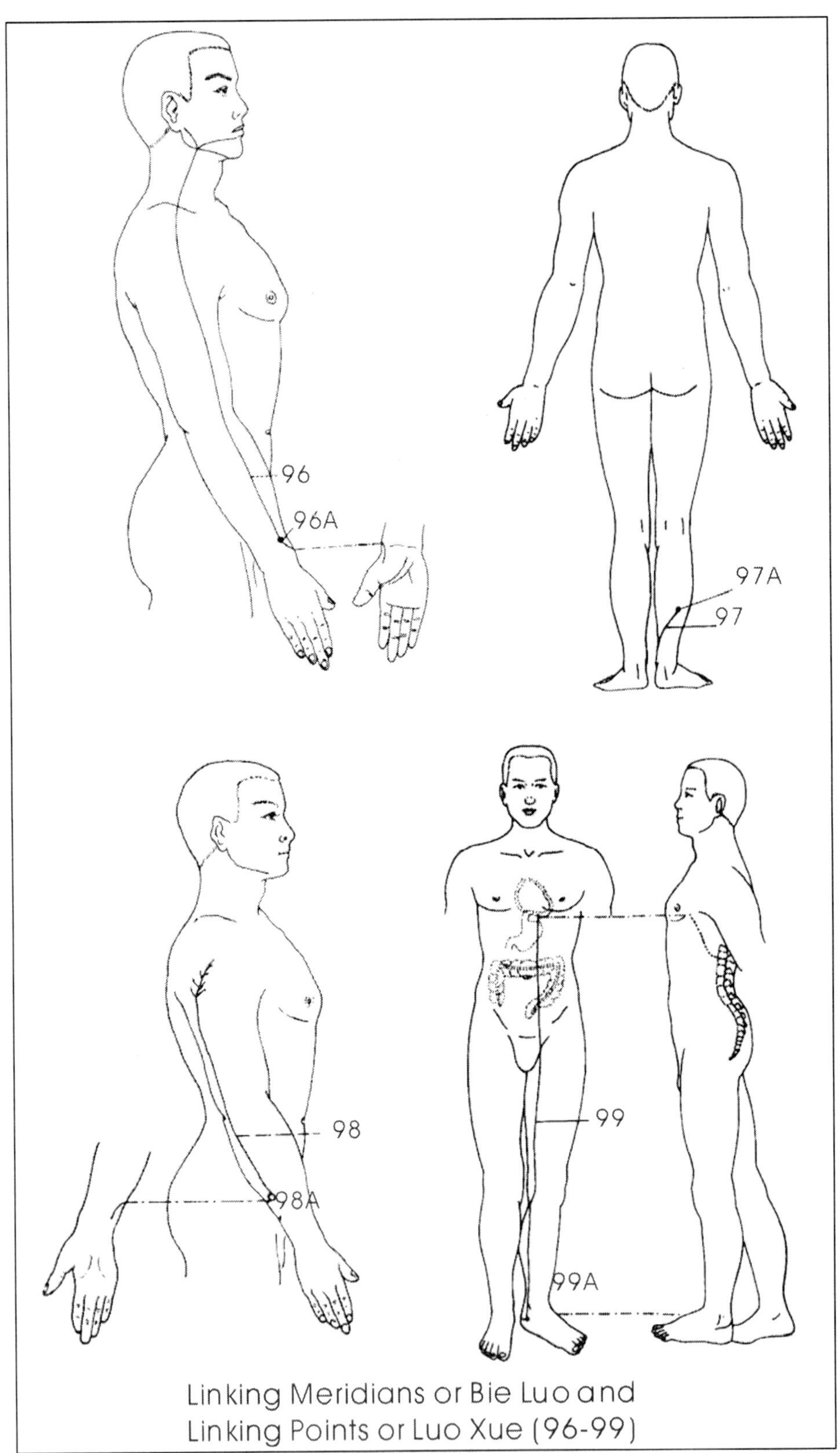

Linking Meridians or Bie Luo and
Linking Points or Luo Xue (96-99)

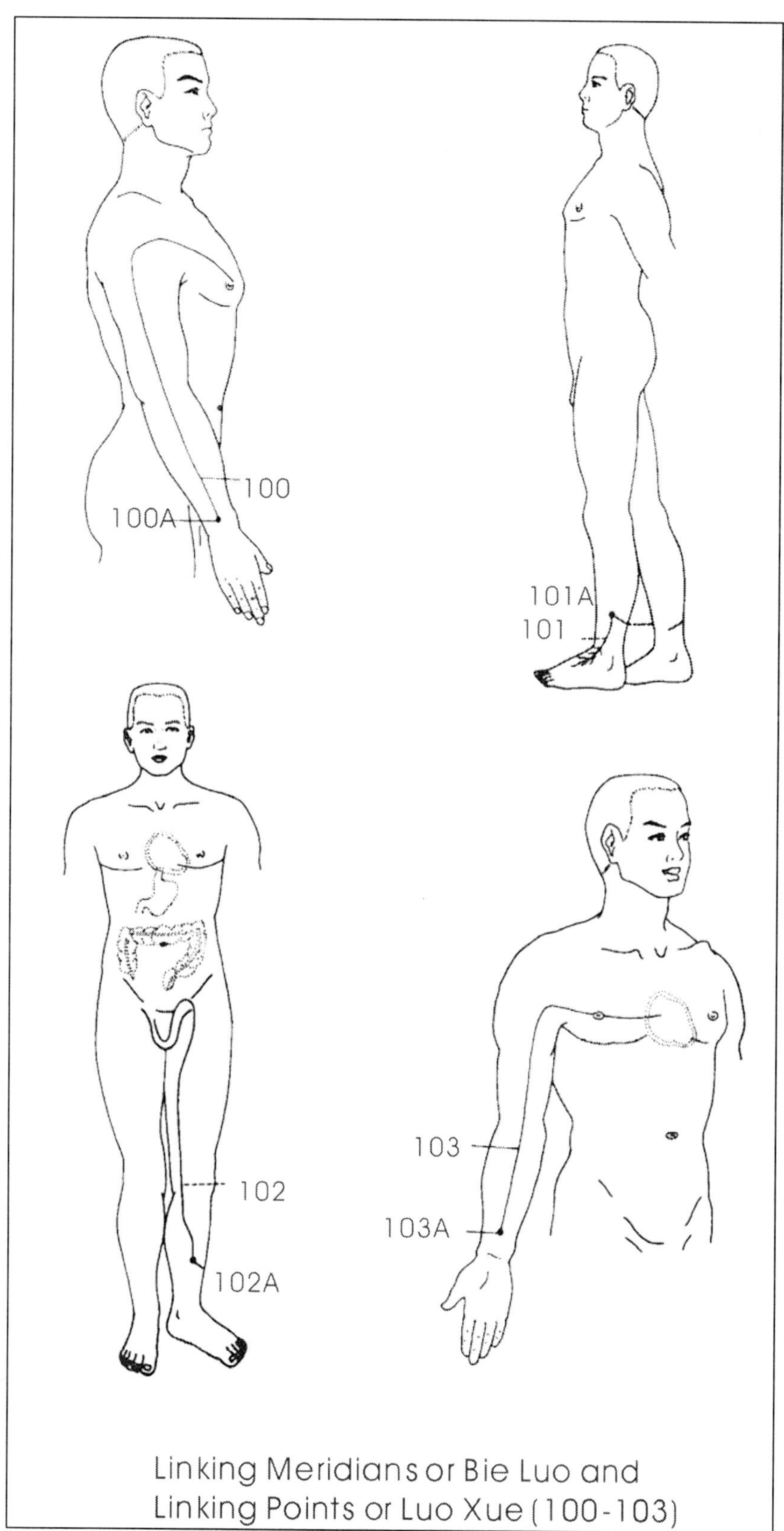

Linking Meridians or Bie Luo and
Linking Points or Luo Xue (100-103)

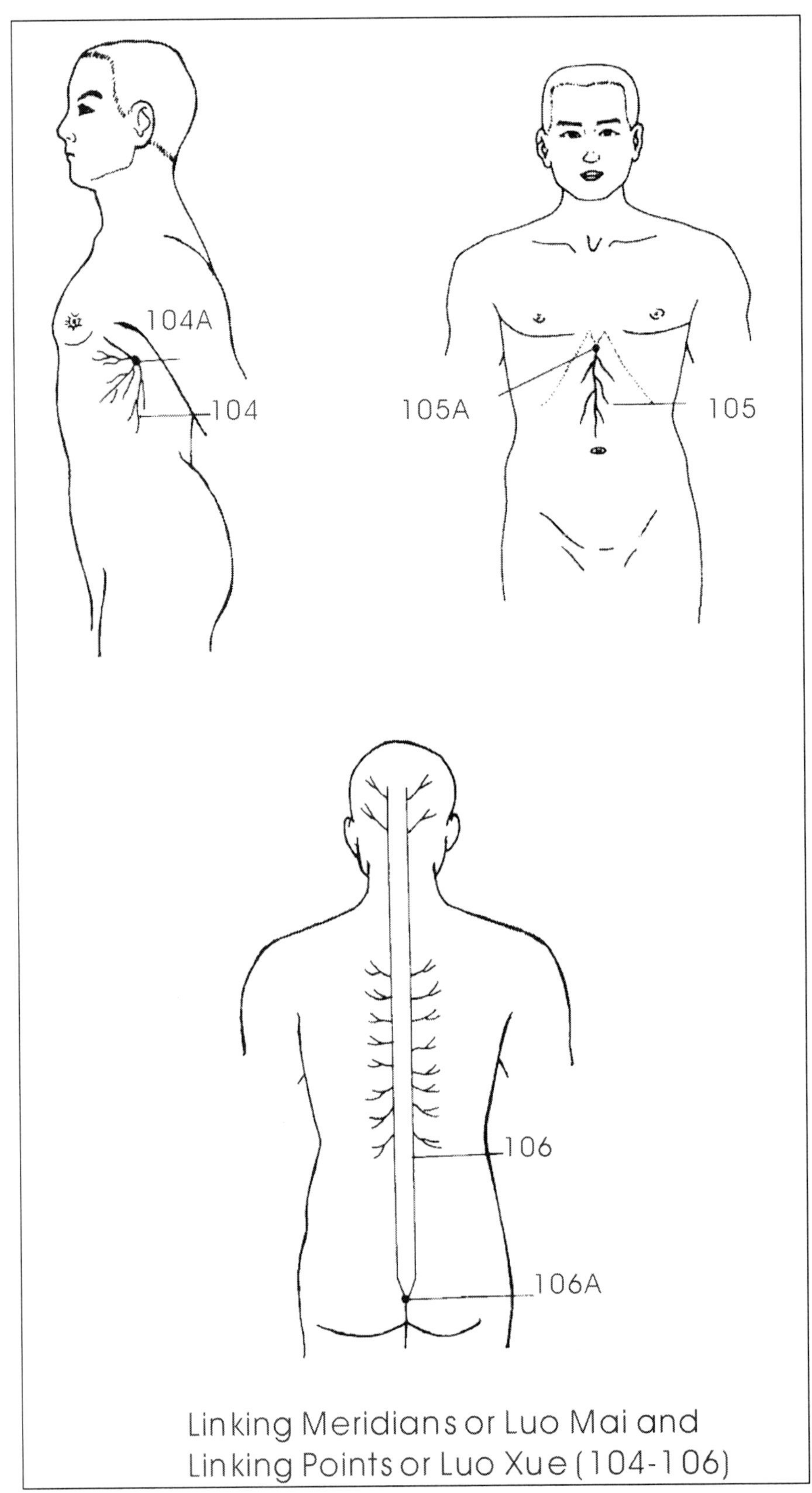

Linking Meridians or Luo Mai and
Linking Points or Luo Xue (104-106)

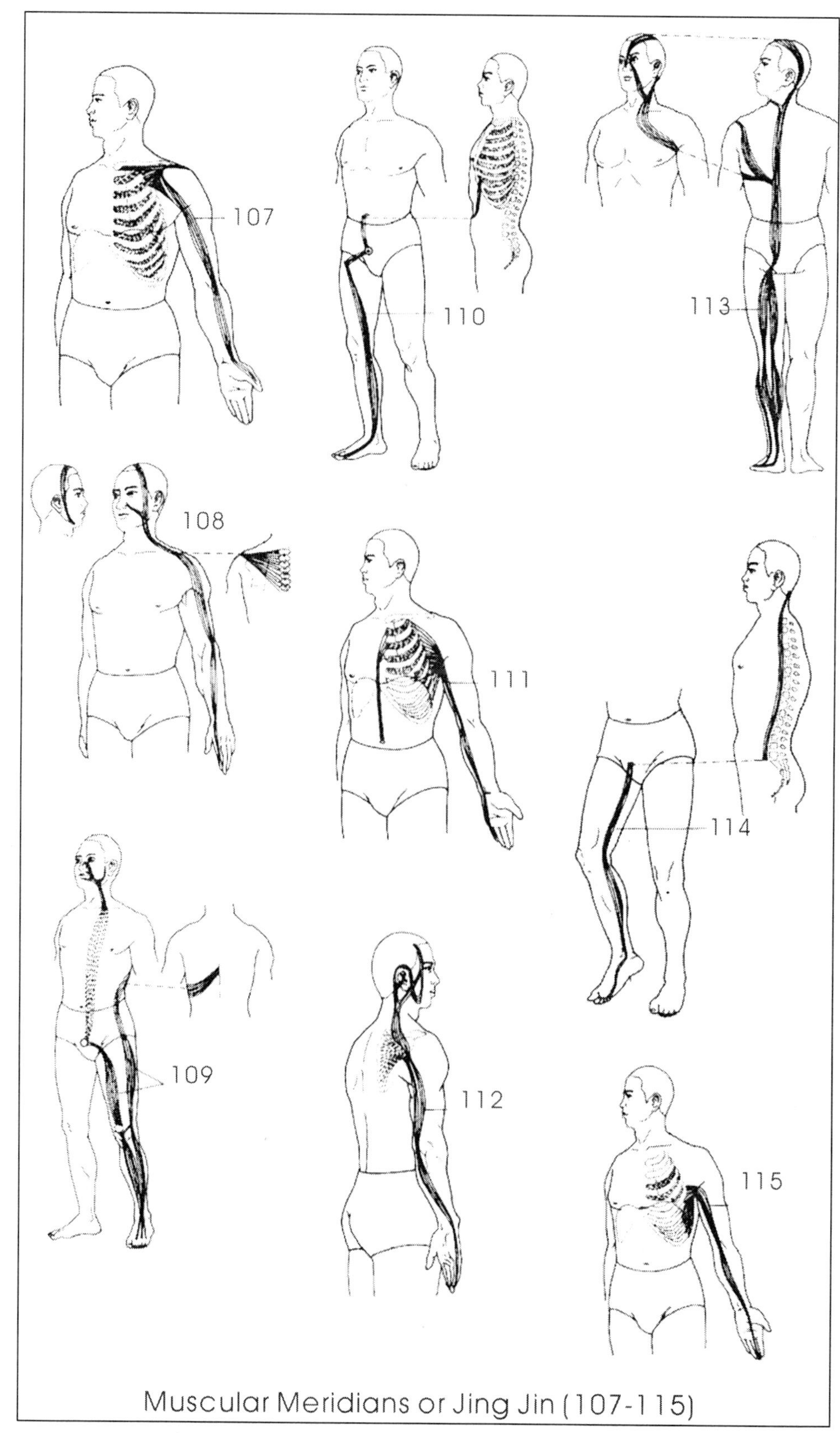

Muscular Meridians or Jing Jin (107-115)

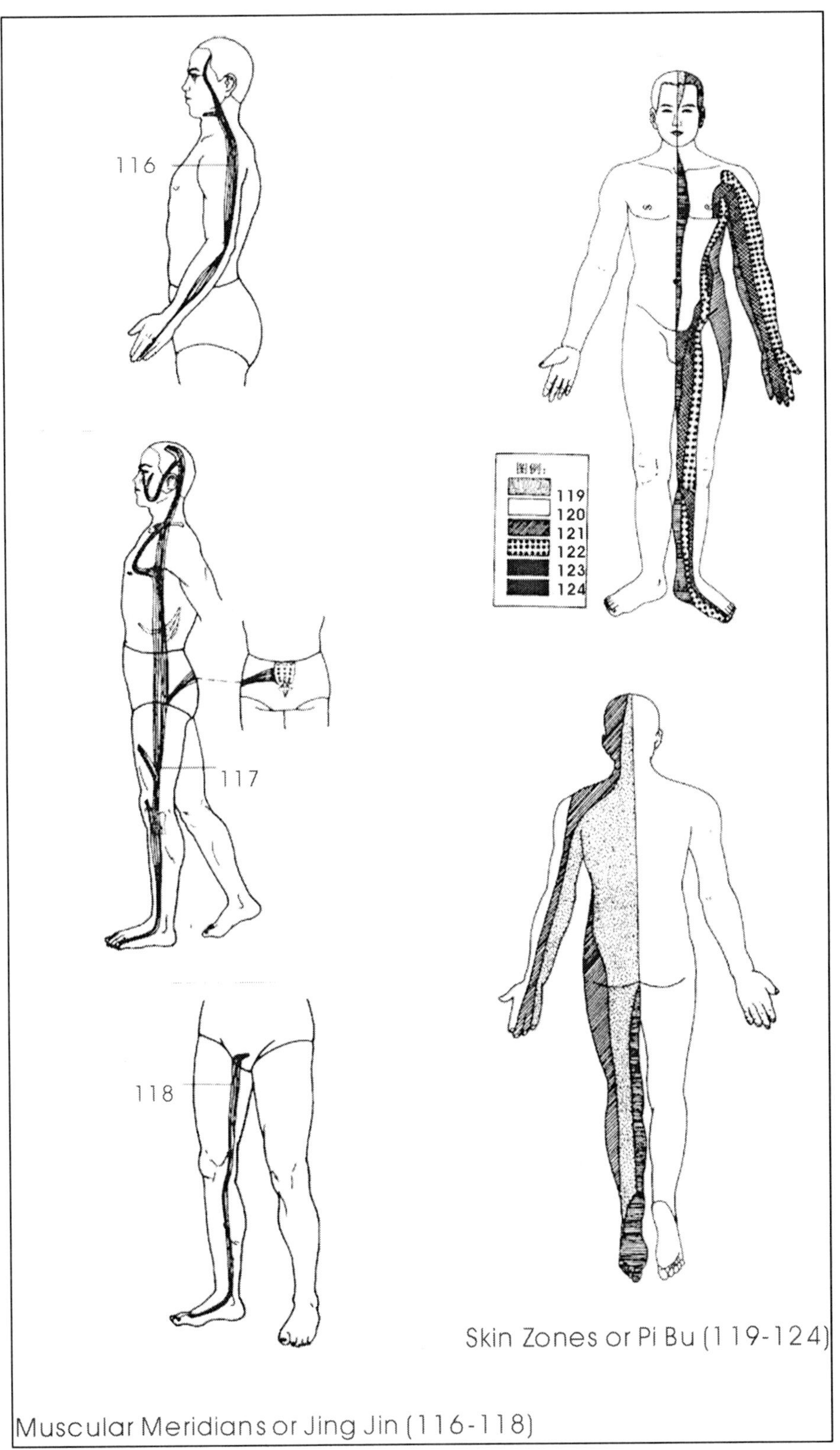
116
117
118
119
120
121
122
123
124
Skin Zones or Pi Bu (119-124)
Muscular Meridians or Jing Jin (116-118)

Test 1-8: 33 Points of Branches (Biao) and Roots (Ben)

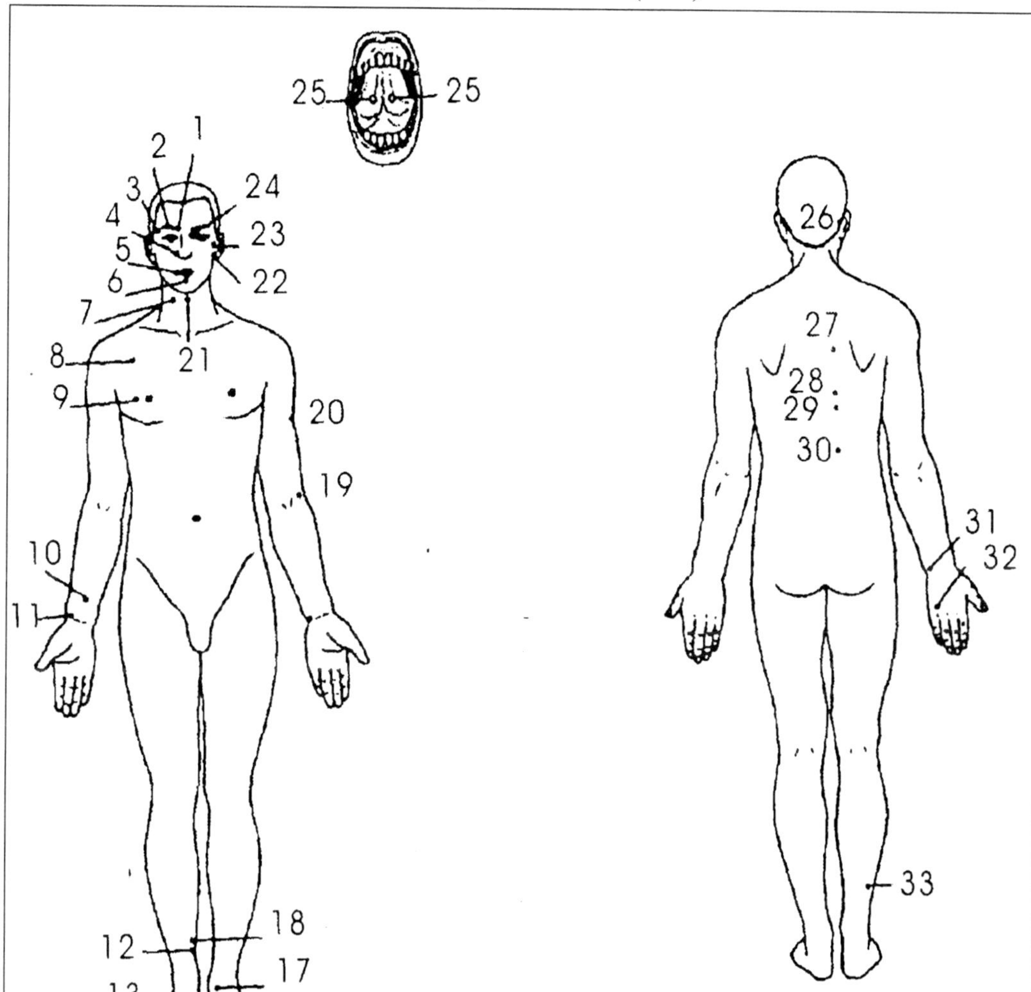

1
2
3
4
5
6
7
8
9
10
11
12
13
14
15
16
17
18
19
20
21
22
23
24
25
25
26
27
28
29
30
31
32
33

33 Points of Branches (BIAO) and Roots (BEN) (1-33)

Test 1-9: 9 Points in Four Seas (1-9)

Test 1-10: 13 Points of Roots (Gen) and Fruits (Jie) on Six Meridians of Foot (1-13)

Test 1-11: Four Energy Streets (1-4)

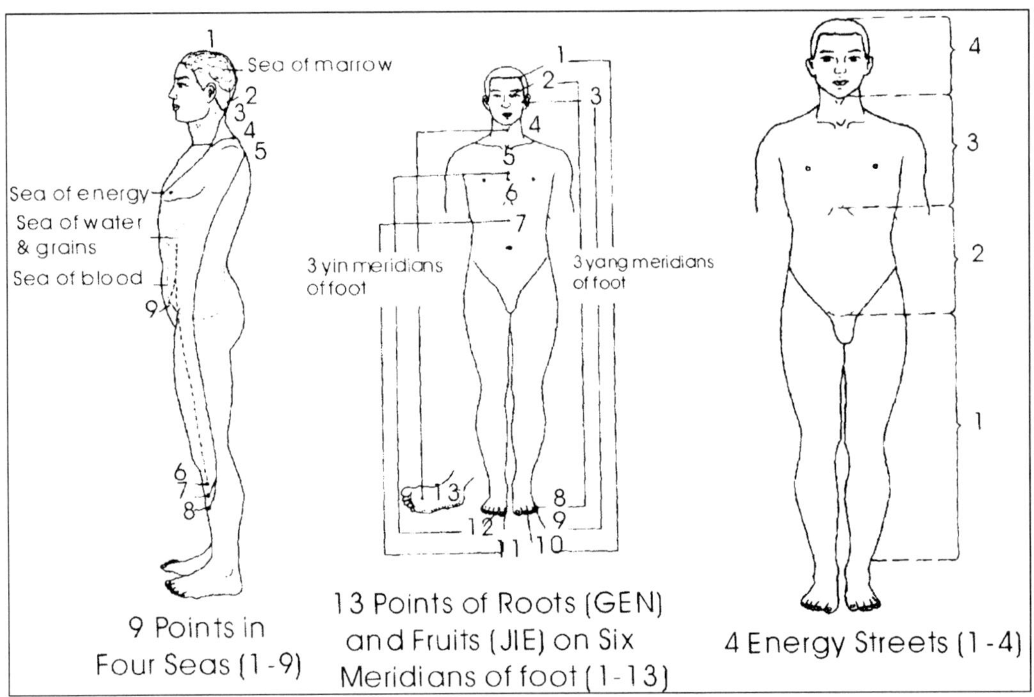

Test 1: Meridians

Test 1-1: Twelve master meridians

1		**4**		**7**		**10**	
2		**5**		**8**		**11**	
3		**6**		**9**		**12**	

Test 1-2: fourteen major meridians

13		**20**		**27**		**34**		**41**	
14		**21**		**28**		**35**		**42**	
15		**22**		**29**		**36**		**43**	
16		**23**		**30**		**37**		**44**	
17		**24**		**31**		**38**		**45**	
18		**25**		**32**		**39**		**46**	
19		**26**		**33**		**40**		**47**	

48	
49	
50	
51	
52	

53	
54	
55	
56	
57	

58	
59	
60	
61	
62	

63	
64	
65	
66	
67	

68	
69	
70	

Test 1-3: extraordinary meridians

71	
72	
73	
74	

75	
76	
77	
78	

Test 1-4: separate master meridians or Jing Bie

79	
80	
81	
82	

83	
84	
85	
[86]	

87	
88	
89	
90	

91	

Test 1-5 : linking meridians or Luo Mai

92	
93	
94	
95	

96	
97	
98	
99	

100	
101	
102	
103	

104	
105	
106	

Test 1-5A: fifteen linking points (collateral points, luò xué 絡穴)

92A	
93A	
94A	
95A	

96A	
97A	
98A	
99A	

100A	
101A	
102A	
103A	

104A	
105A	
106A	

Test 1-6 : muscular meridians

107	
108	
109	
110	

111	
112	
113	
114	

115	
116	
117	
118	

Test 1-7: skin zones 皮部

119	
120	

121	
122	

123	
124	

Test 1-8: 30 Points of Branches (Biao) and Roots (Ben)

1		8		15		22		29	
2		9		16		23		30	
3		10		17		24		31	
4		11		18		25		32	
5		12		19		26		33	
6		13		20		27			
7		14		21		28			

Test 1-9: 9 Points in Four Seas (1-9)

1		4		7	
2		5		8	
3		6		9	

Test 1-10: 13 Points of Roots (Gen) and Fruits (Jie) on Six Meridians of Foot (1-13)

1		5		9		13	
2		6		10			
3		7		11			
4		8		12			

Test 1-11: Four Energy Streets (1-4)

1		3	
2		4	

Test 2: Bone Measurements (1-67)

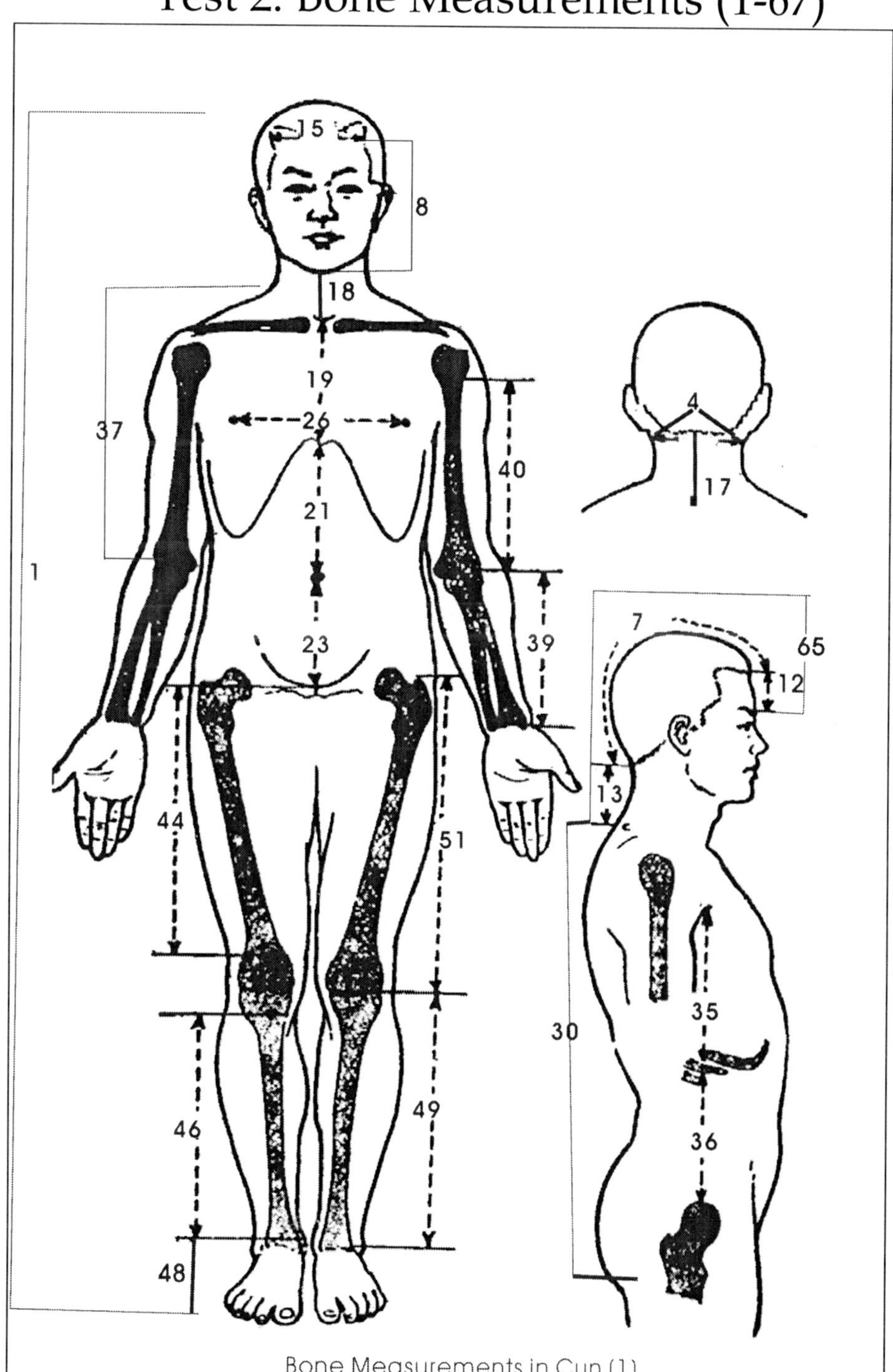

Bone Measurements in Cun (1)

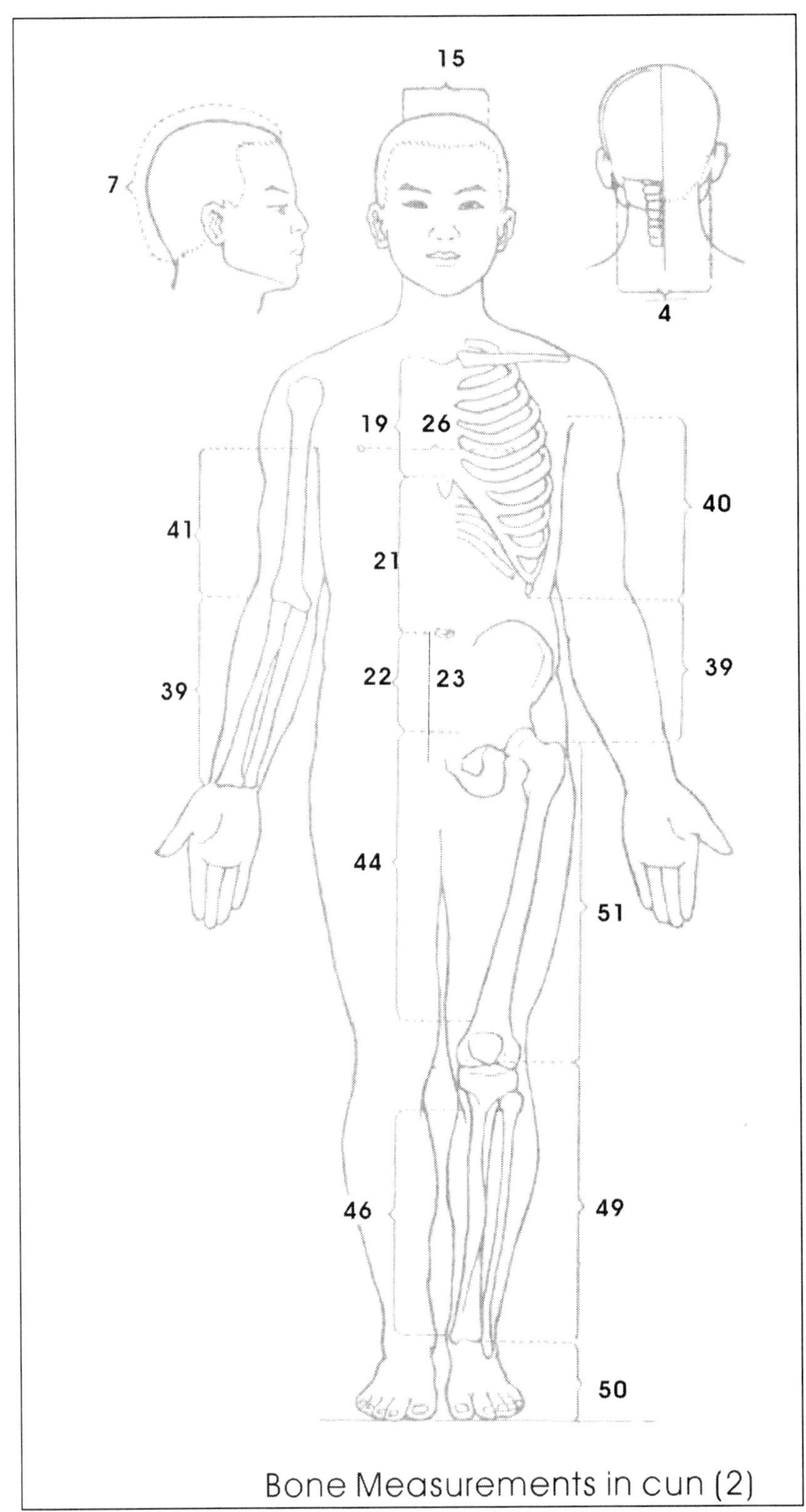

Bone Measurements in cun (2)

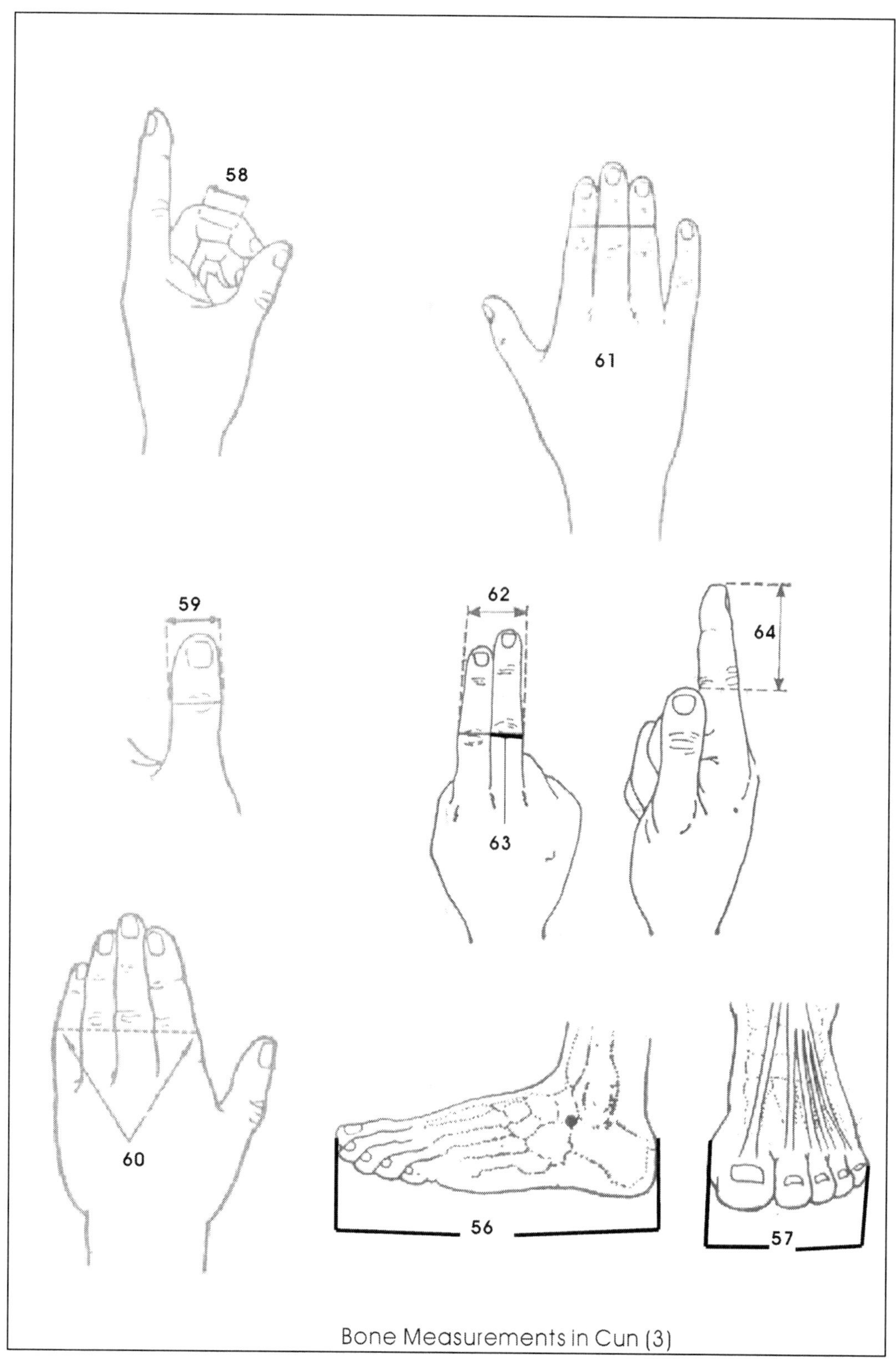

Bone Measurements in Cun (3)

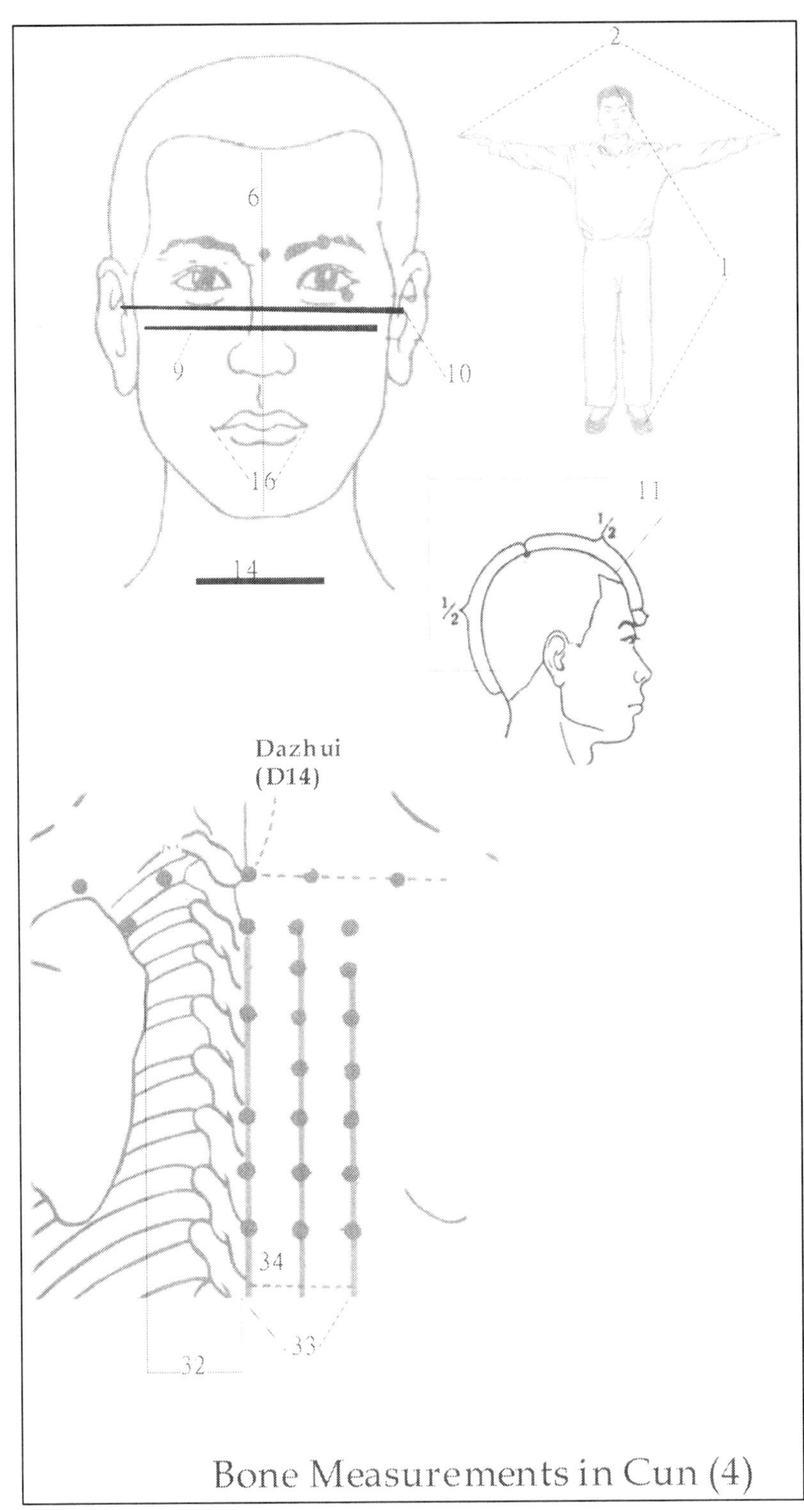

Bone Measurements in Cun (4)

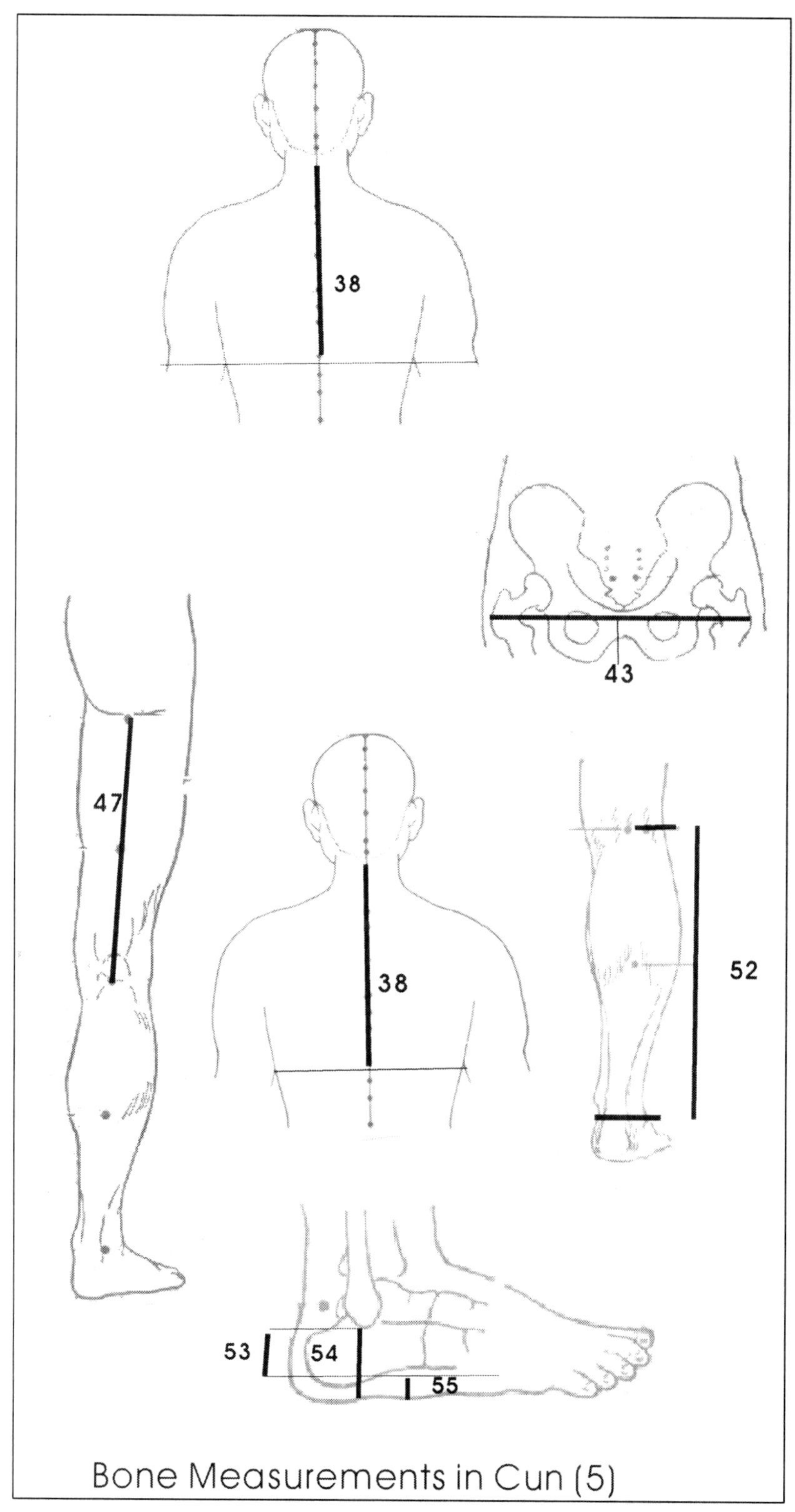

Bone Measurements in Cun (5)

Part One: Questions of Visual Images 心象题库

Q.	CUN
1	
2	
3	
4	
5	
6	
7	
8	
9	
10	
11	
12	
13	
14	
15	
16	
17	
18	
19	
20	
21	
22	
23	
24	
25	
26	
27	
28	
29	
30	
31	
32	
33	
34	
35	
36	
37	
38	
39	
40	
41	
42	
43	
44	
45	
46	
47	
48	
49	
50	
51	
52	
53	
54	
55	
56	
57	
58	
59	
60	
61	
62	
63	
64	
65	
66	
67	

Test 3: Anatomy (1-140)

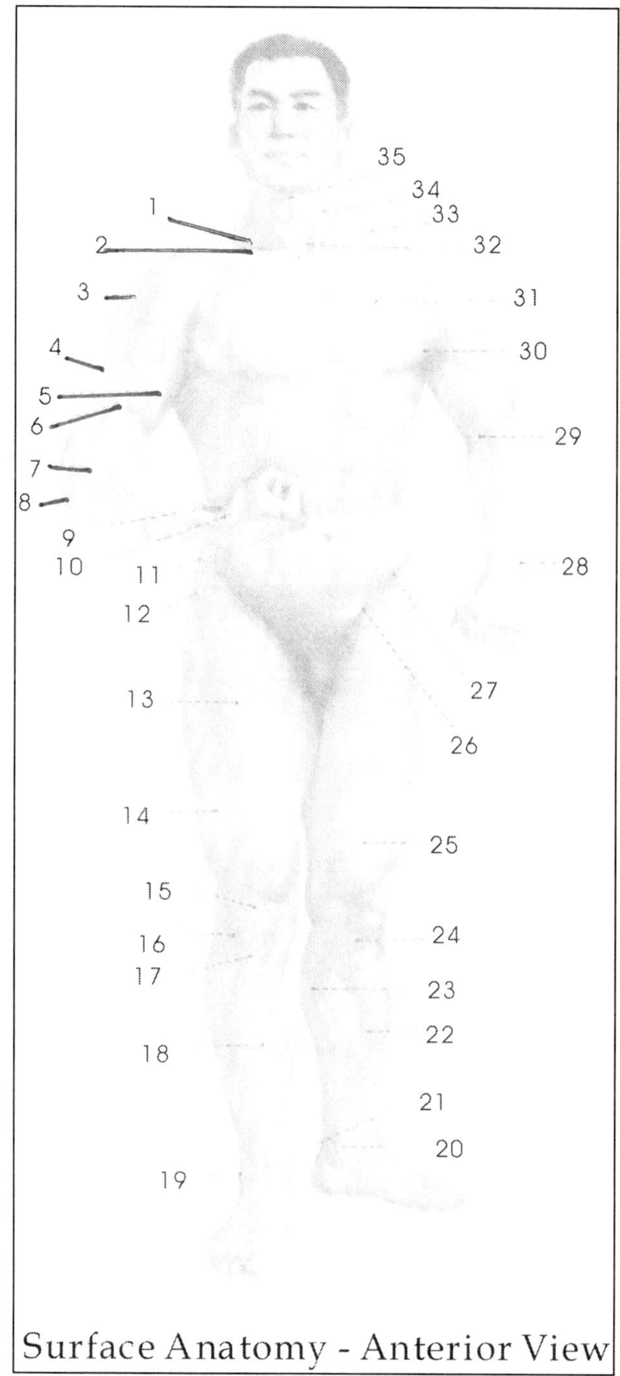

Surface Anatomy - Anterior View

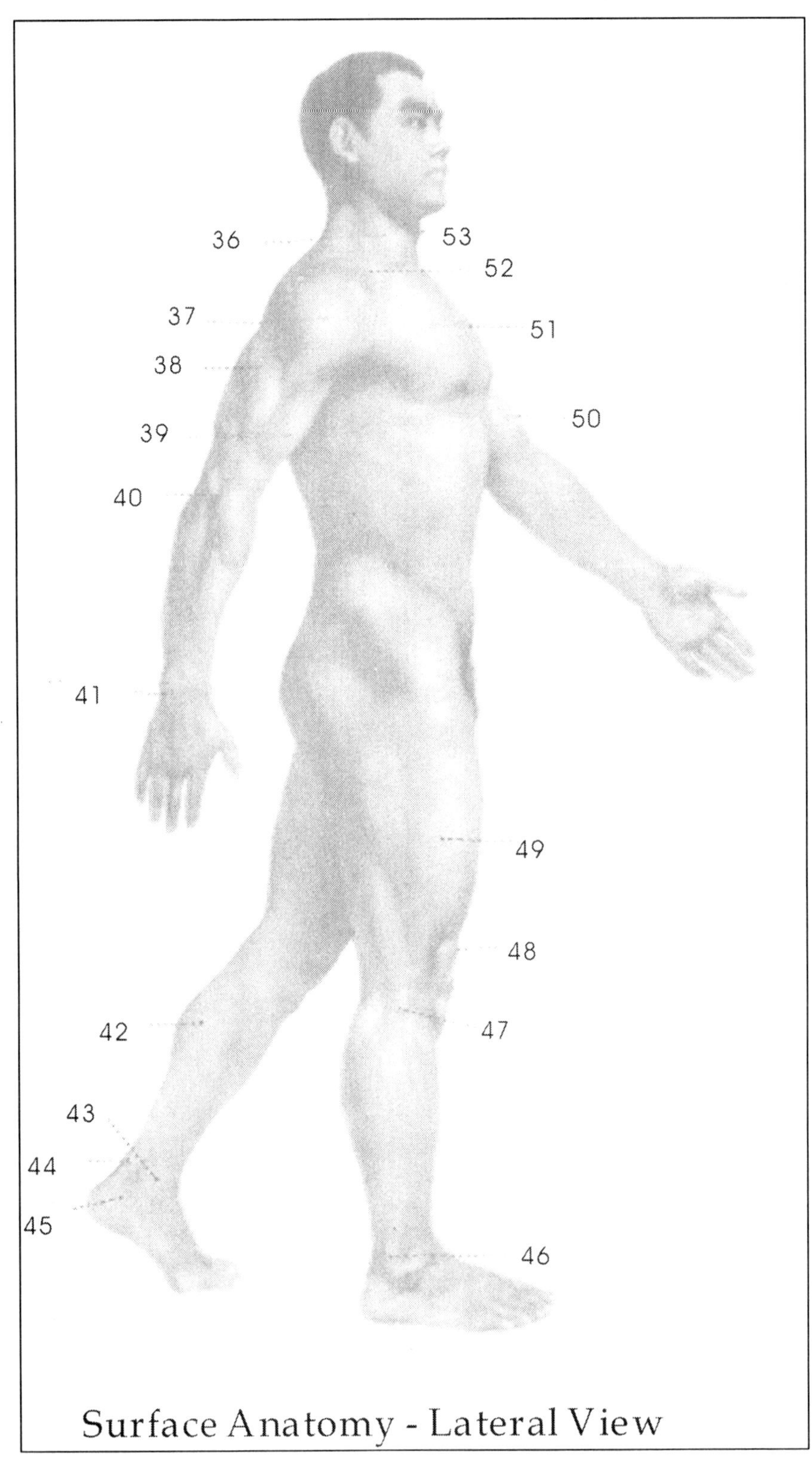

Surface Anatomy - Lateral View

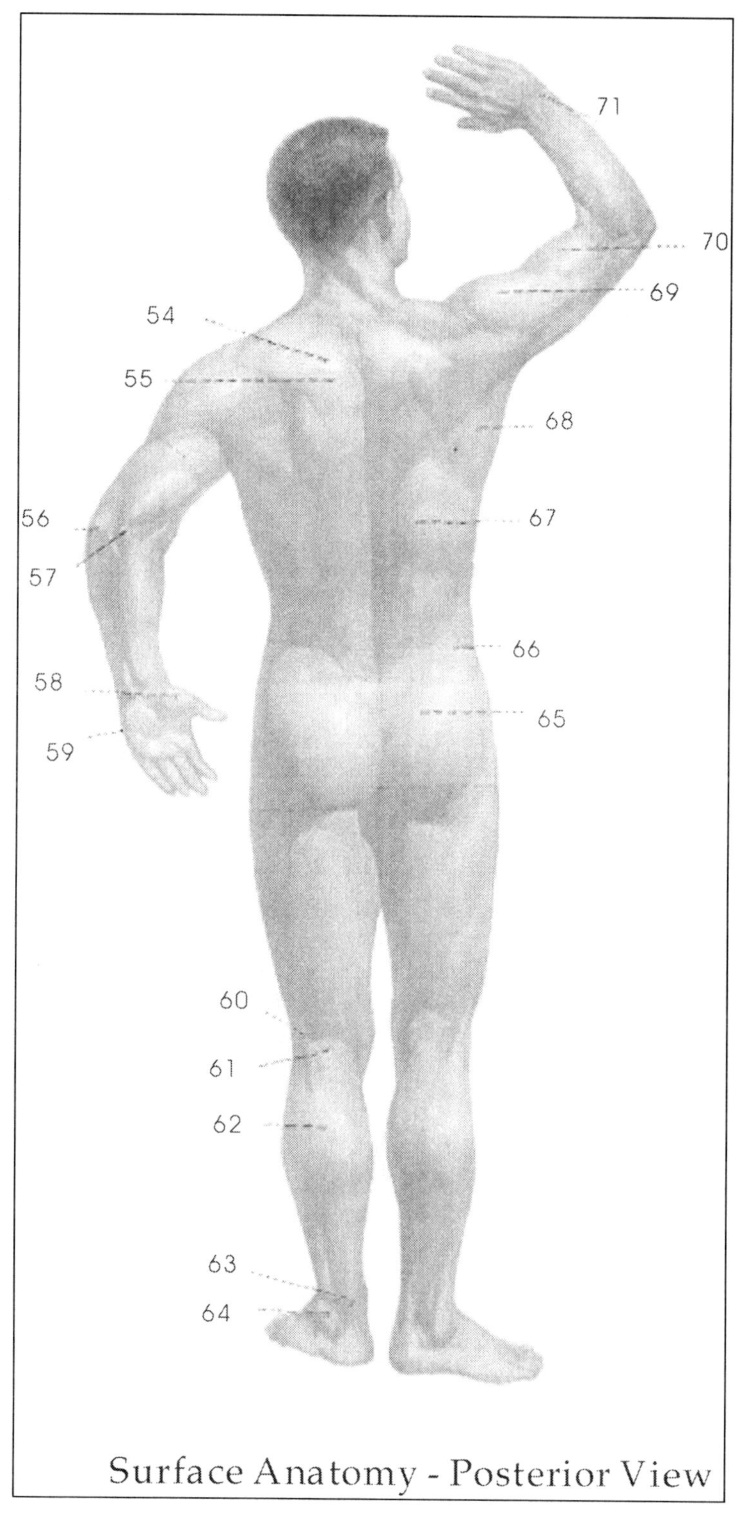

Surface Anatomy - Posterior View

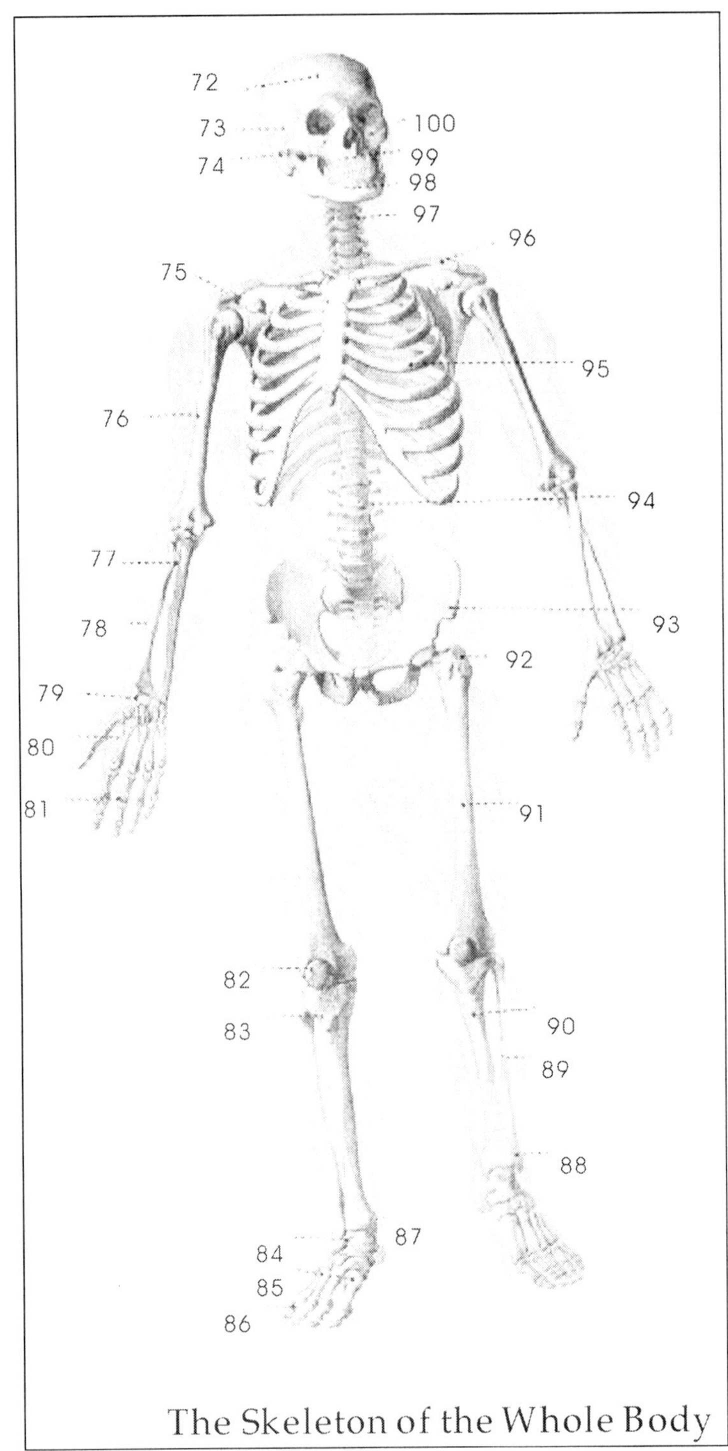

The Skeleton of the Whole Body

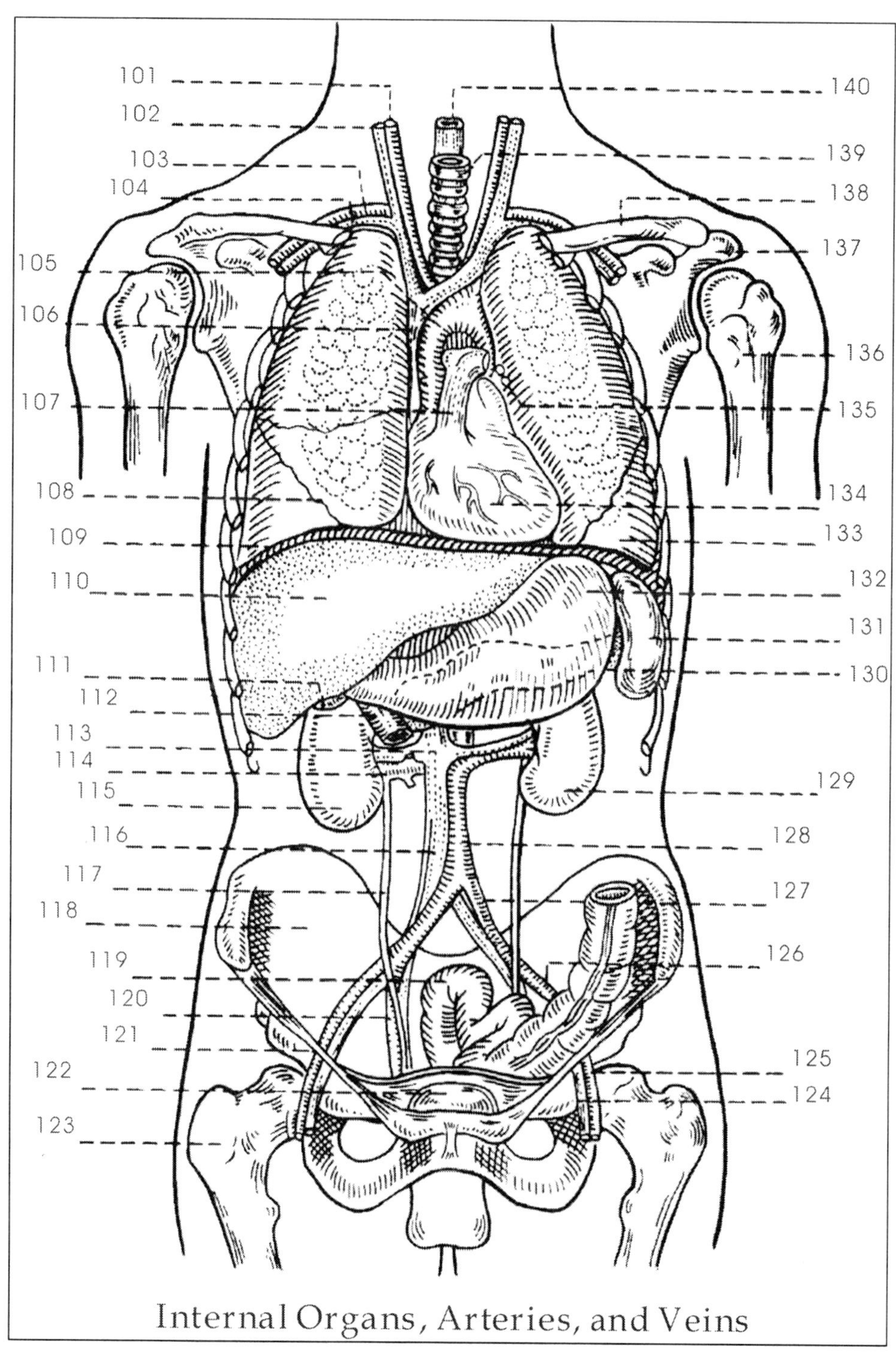

Internal Organs, Arteries, and Veins

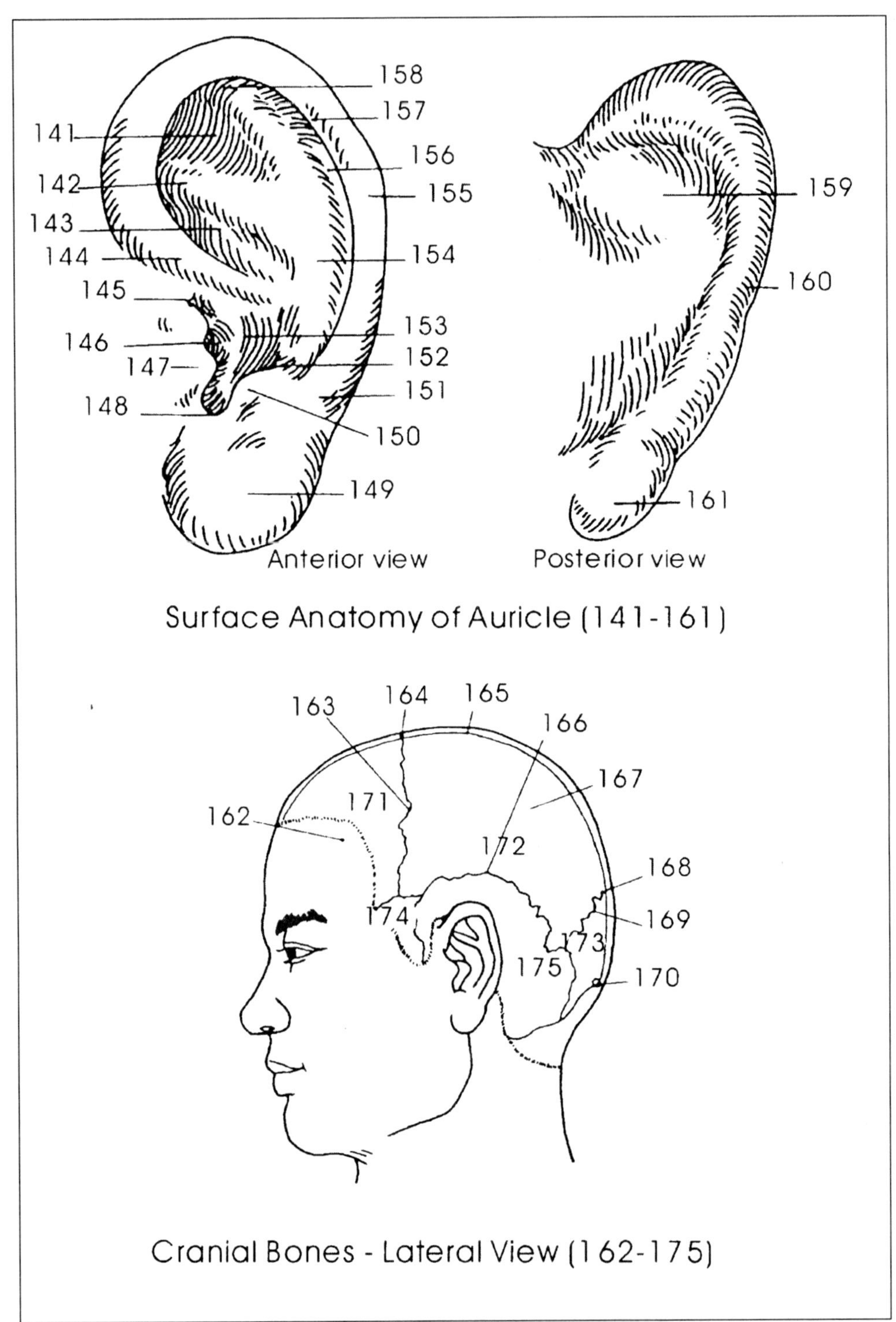

Surface Anatomy of Auricle (141-161)

Cranial Bones - Lateral View (162-175)

1		31		61		91		121		151	
2		32		62		92		122		152	
3		33		63		93		123		153	
4		34		64		94		124		154	
5		35		65		95		125		155	
6		36		66		96		126		156	
7		37		67		97		127		157	
8		38		68		98		128		158	
9		39		69		99		129		159	
10		40		70		100		130		160	
11		41		71		101		131		161	
12		42		72		102		132		162	
13		43		73		103		133		163	
14		44		74		104		134		164	
15		45		75		105		135		165	
16		46		76		106		136		166	
17		47		77		107		137		167	
18		48		78		108		138		168	
19		49		79		109		139		169	
20		50		80		110		140		170	
21		51		81		111		141		171	
22		52		82		112		142		172	
23		53		83		113		143		173	
24		54		84		114		144		174	
25		55		85		115		145		175	
26		56		86		116		146			
27		57		87		117		147			
28		58		88		118		148			
29		59		89		119		149			
30		60		90		120		150			

Test 3: Acupuncture Points on the Fourteen Meridians (1-361)

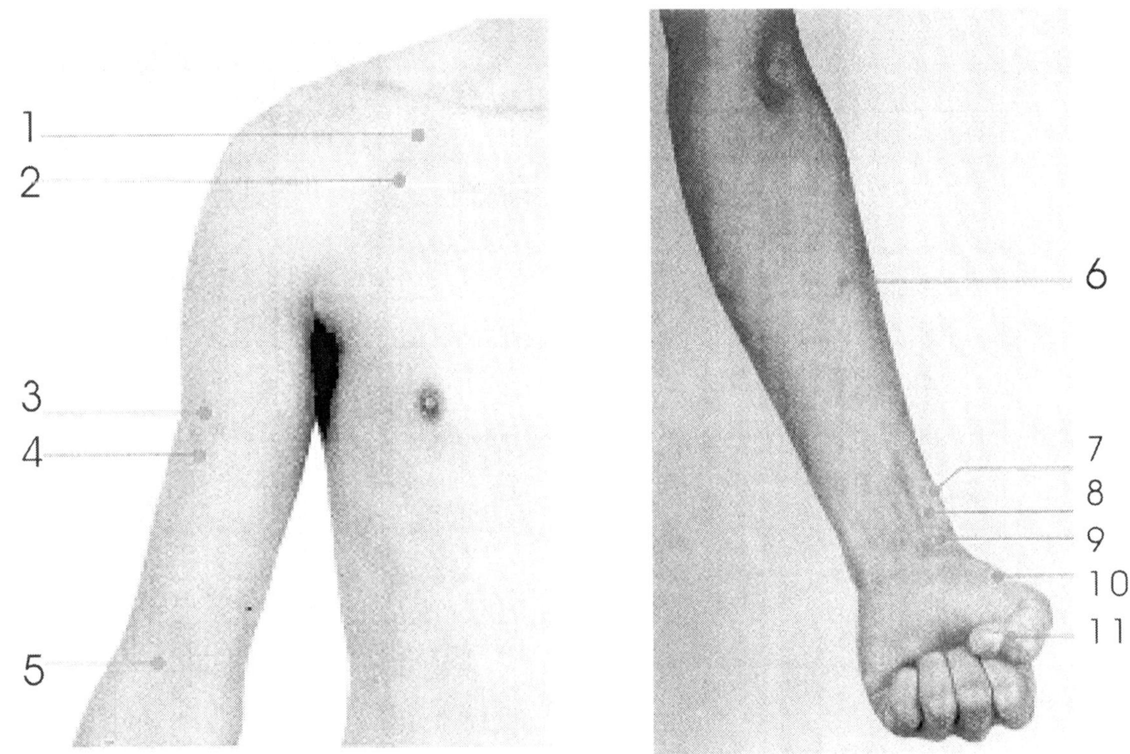

Points on the Fourteen Meridians (1)

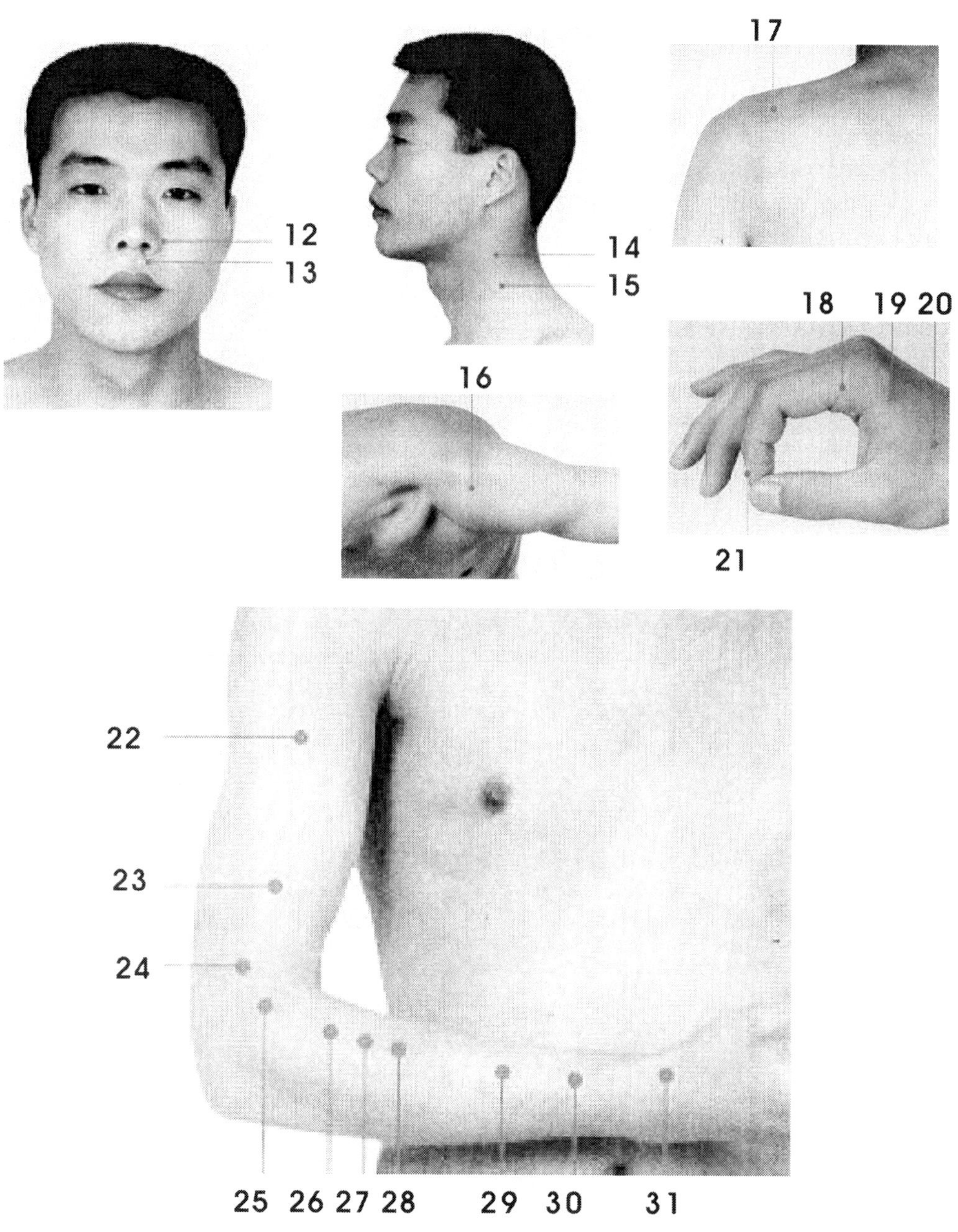

Points on Fourteen Meridians (2)

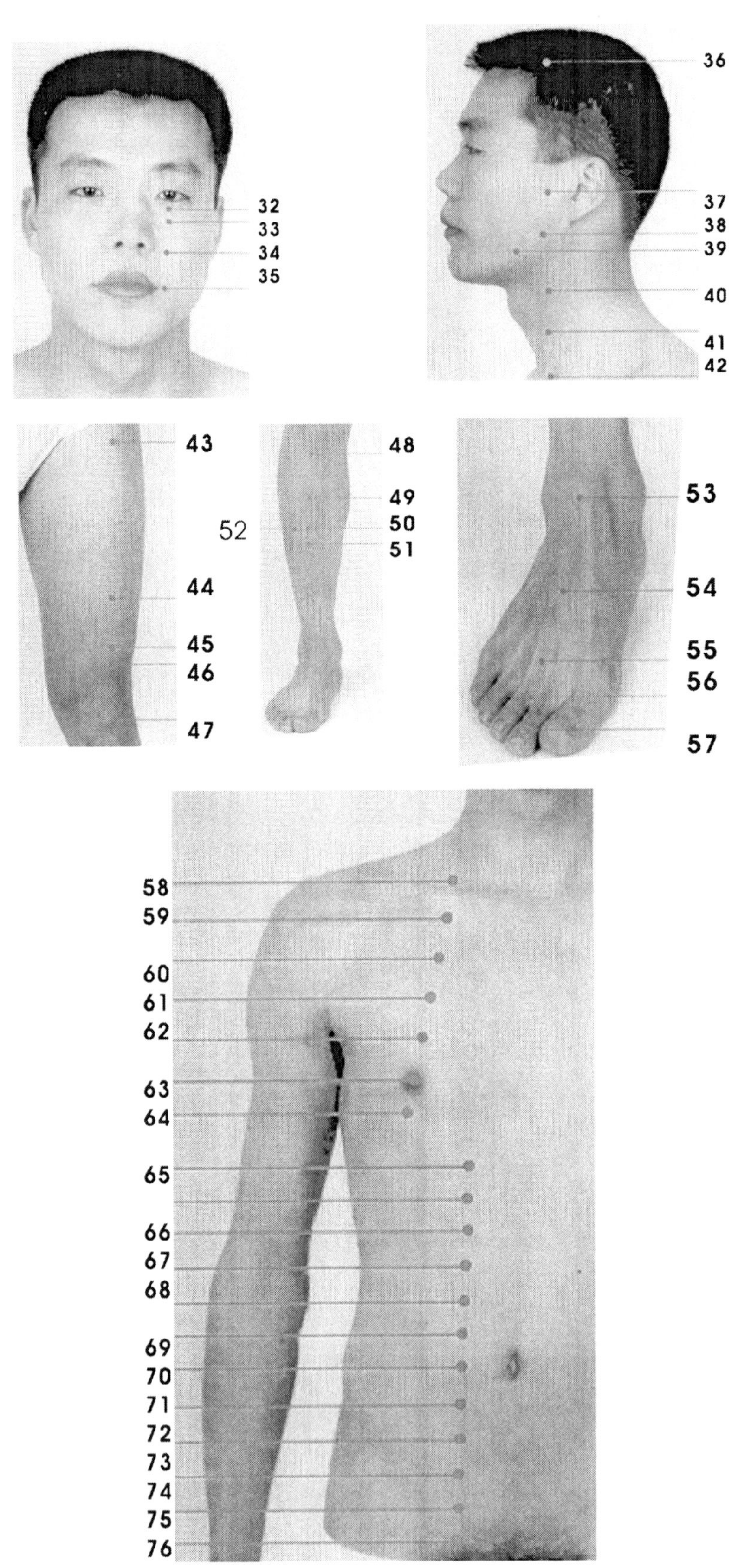

Points on Fourteen Meridians (3)

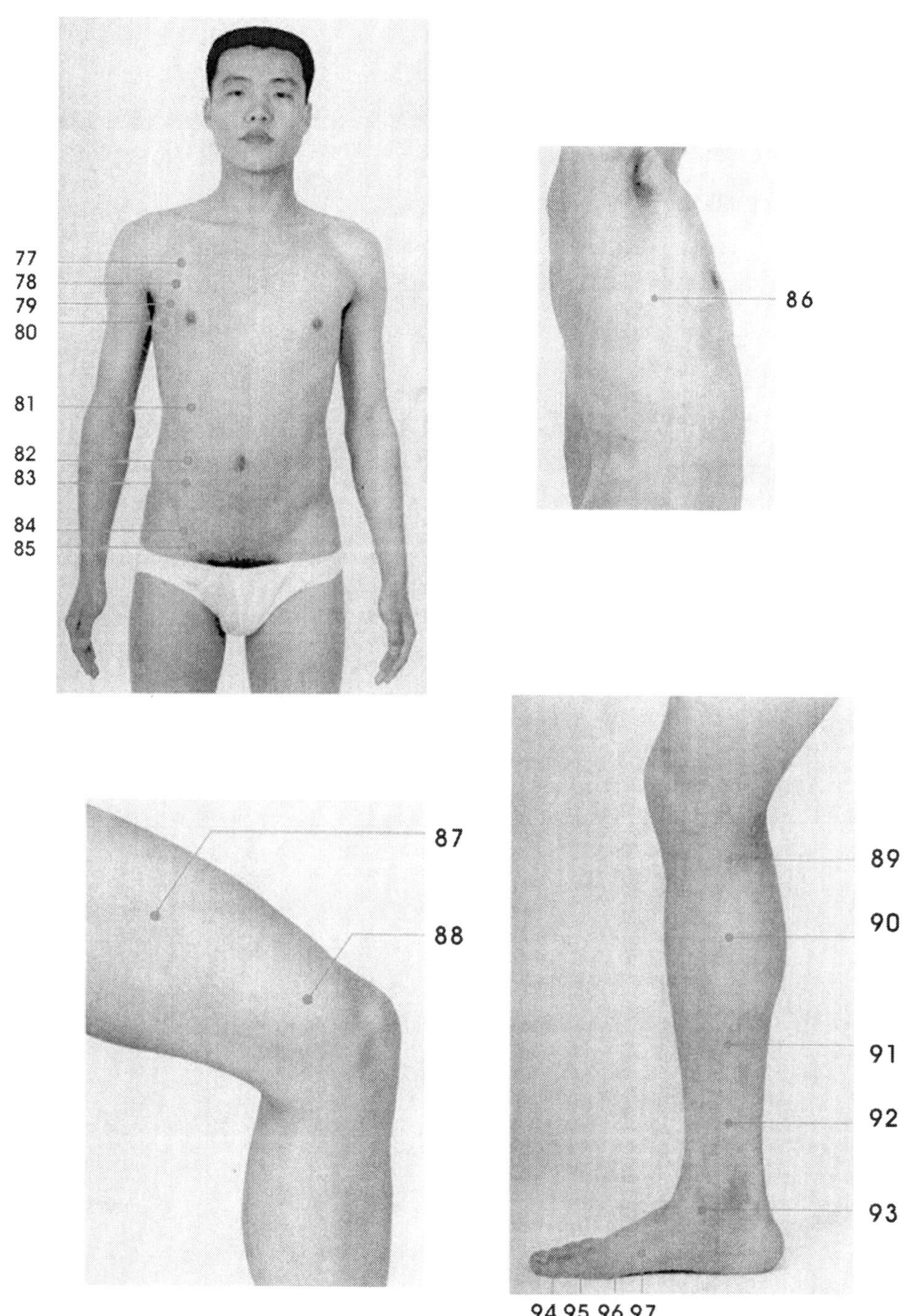

Points on Fourteen Meridians (4)

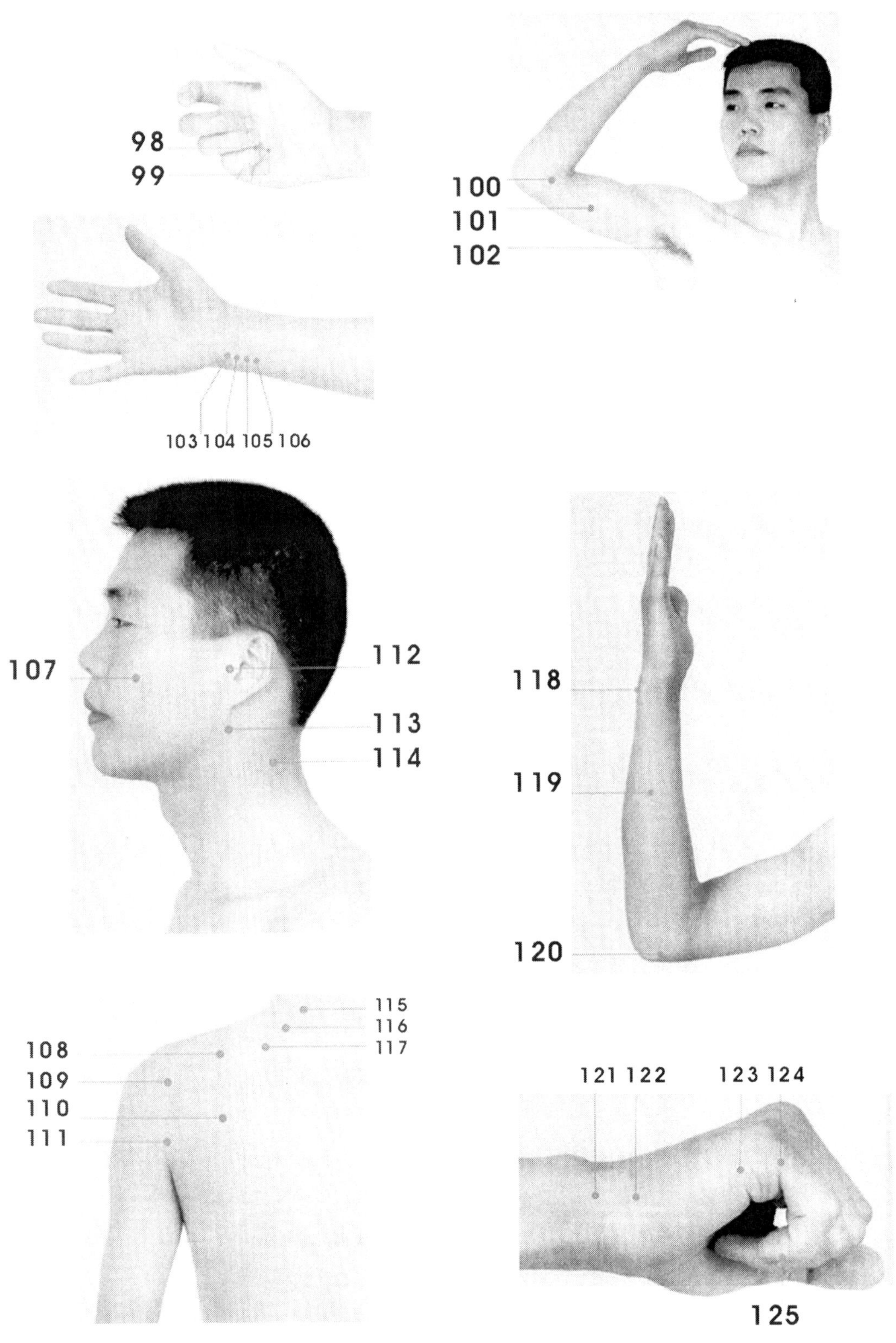

Points on Fourteen Meridians (5)

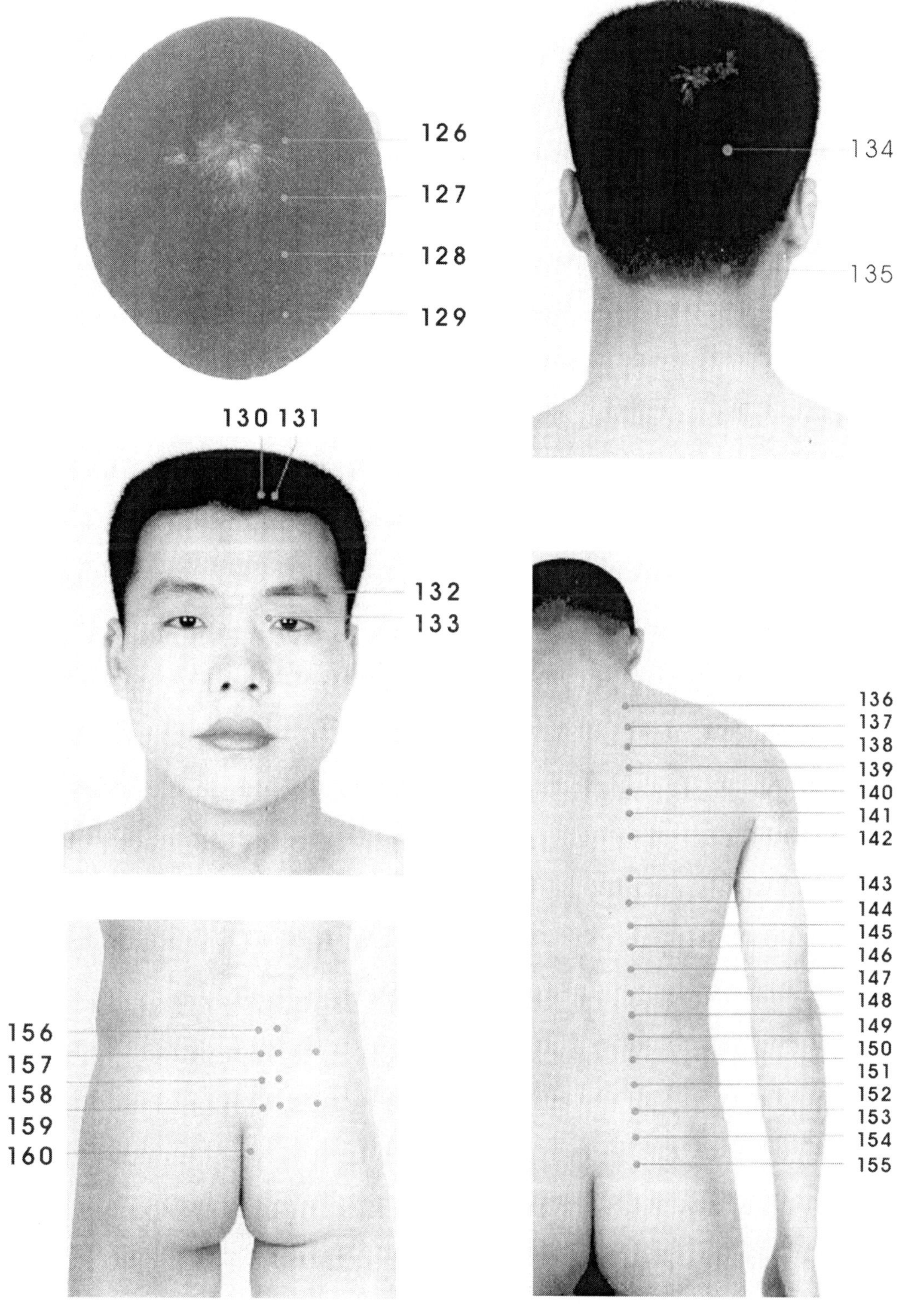

Points on Fourteen Meridians (6)

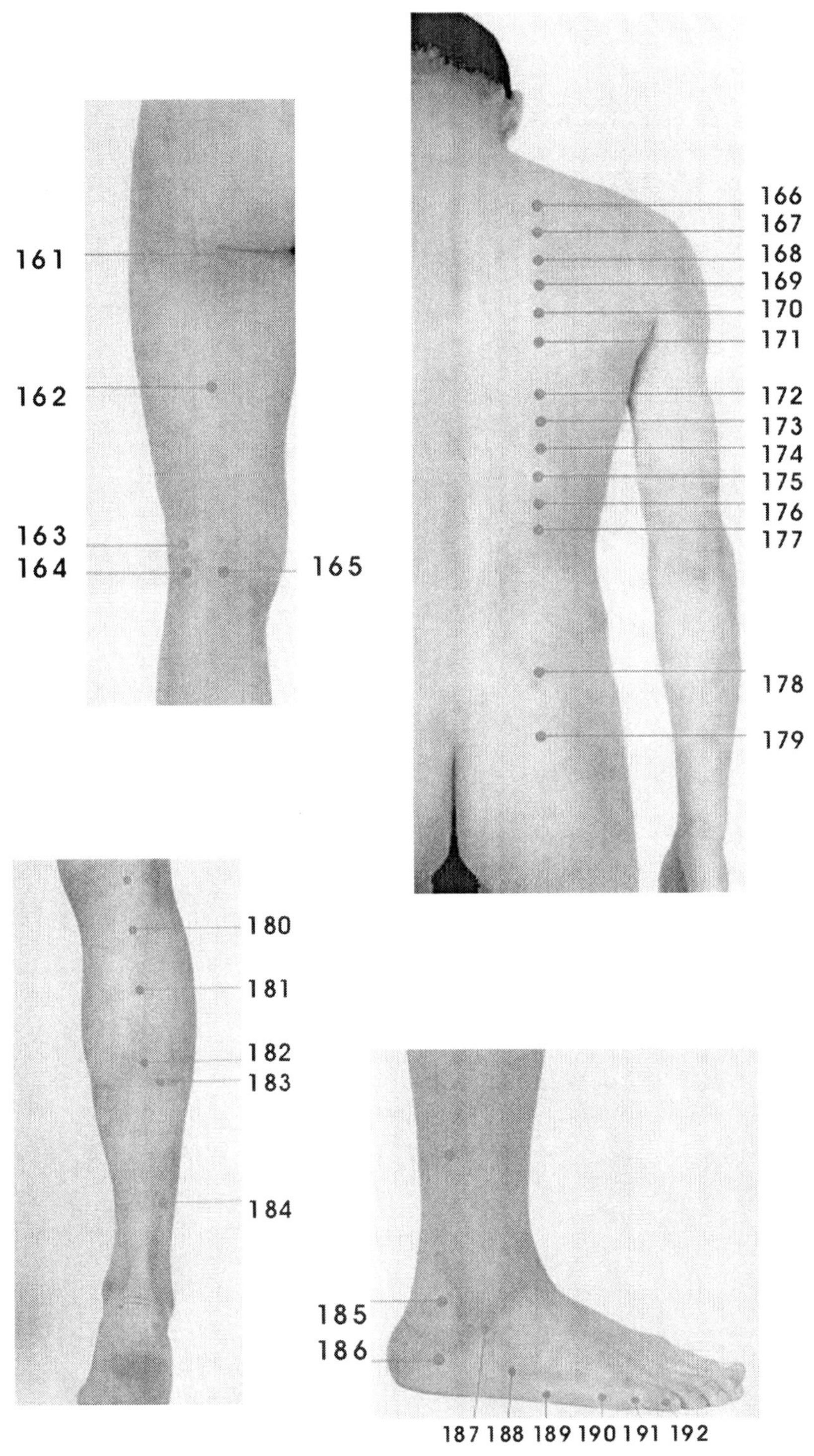

Poiints on Fourteen Meridians (7)

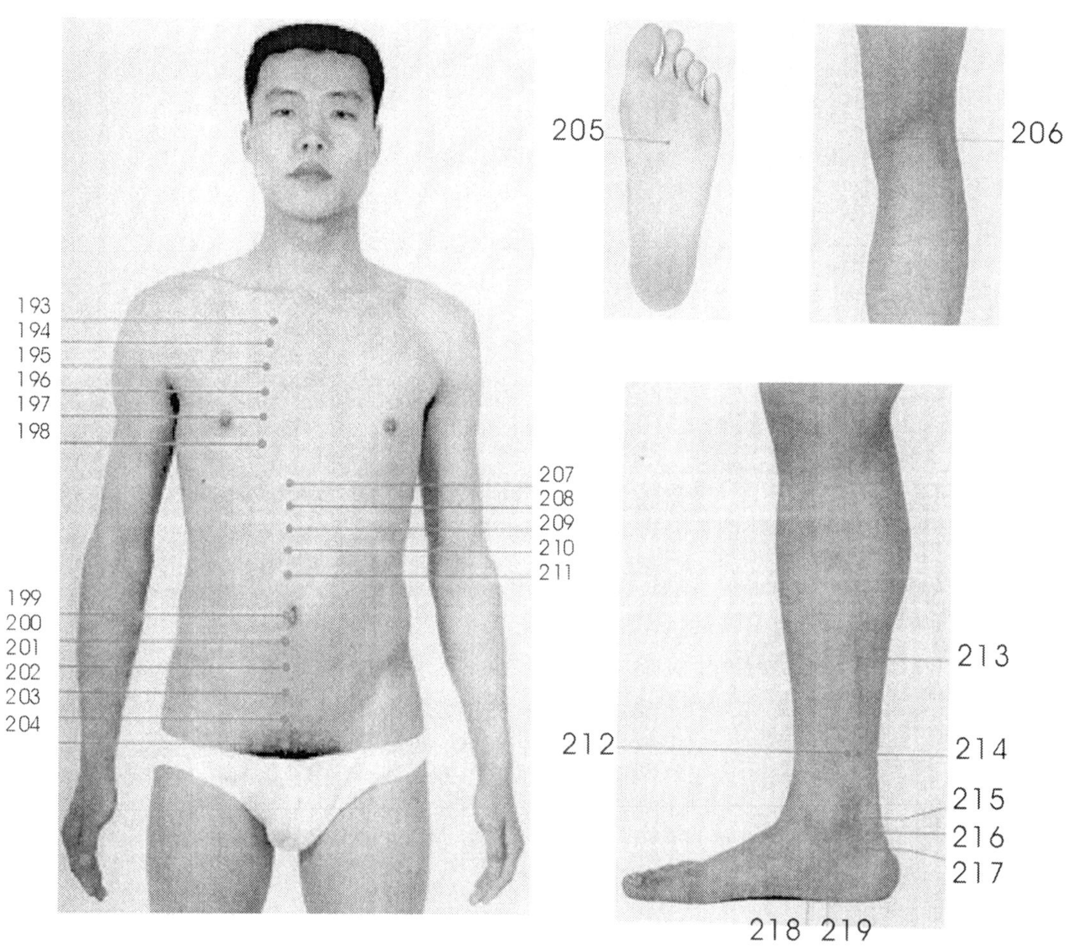

Points on the Fourteen Meridians (8)

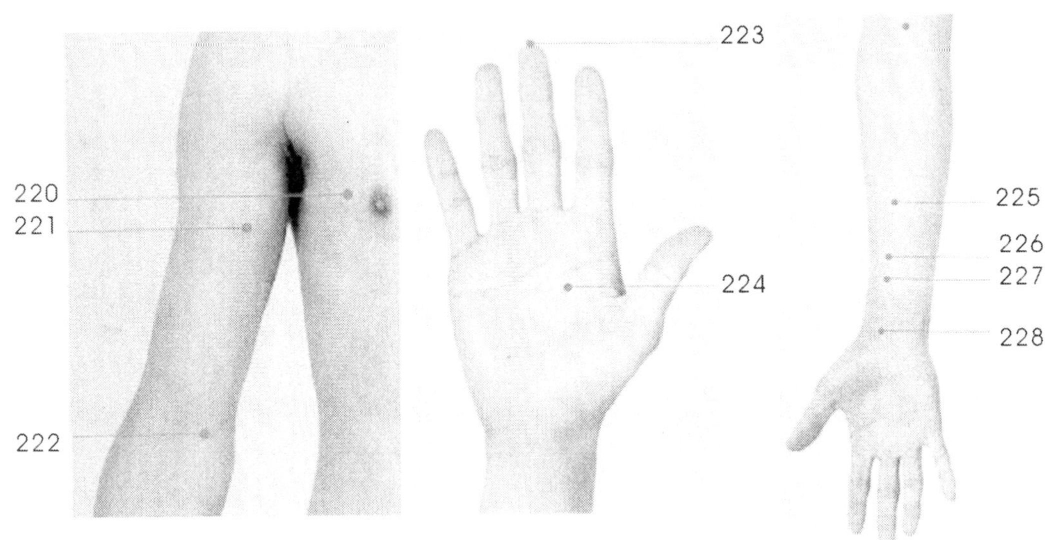

Points on the Fourteen Meridians (9)

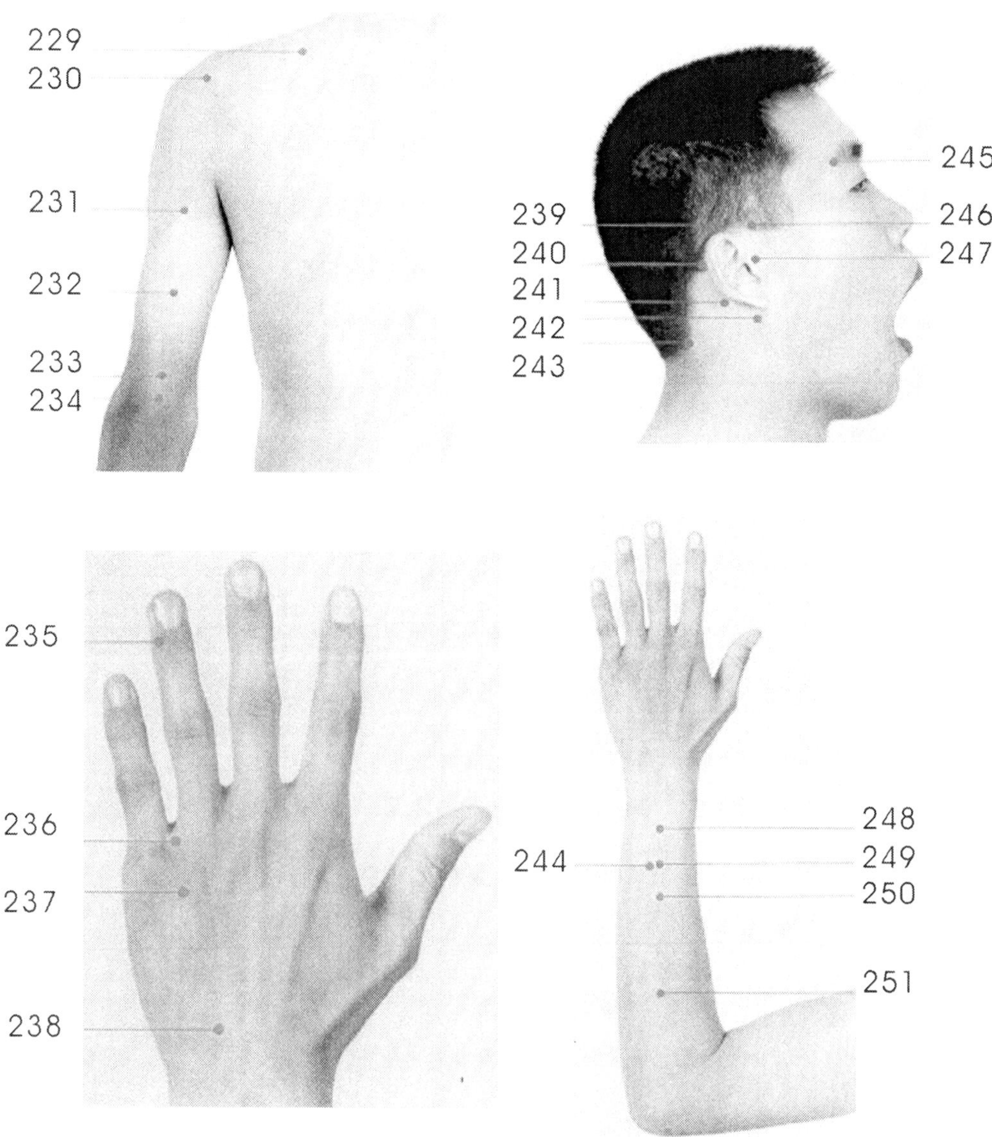

Points on the Fourteen Meridians (10)

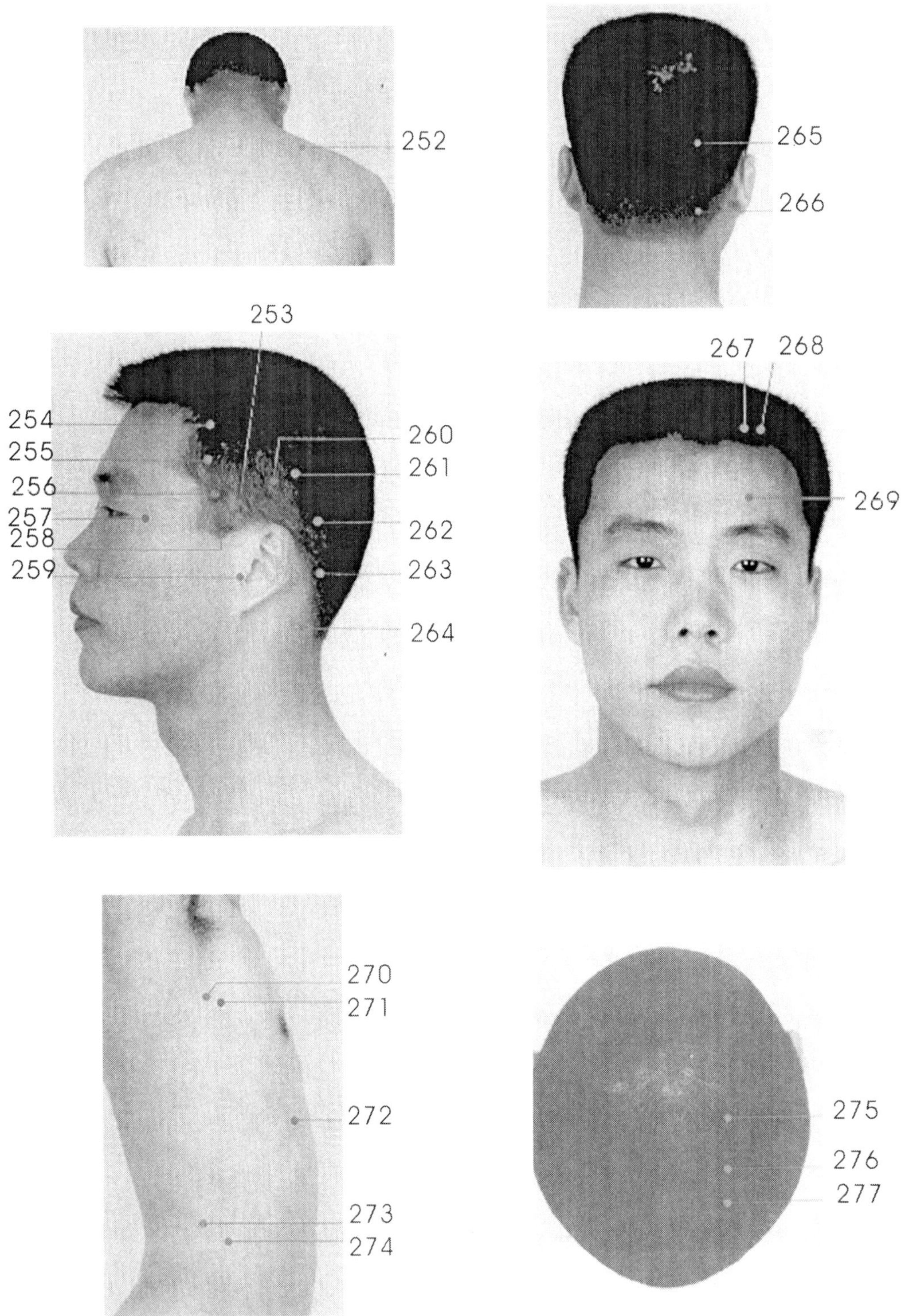

Points on Fourteen Meridians (11)

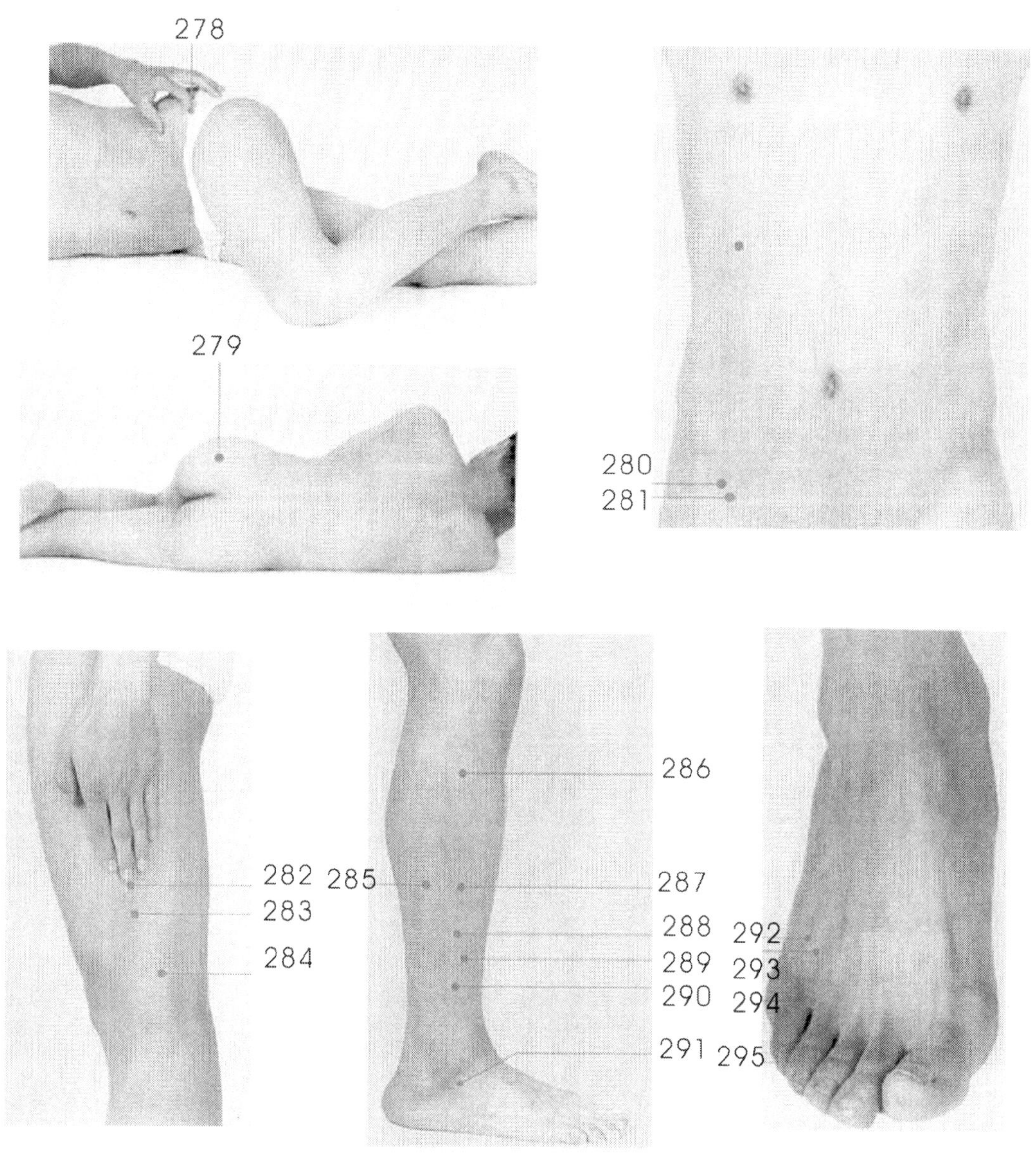

Points on Fourteen Meridians (12)

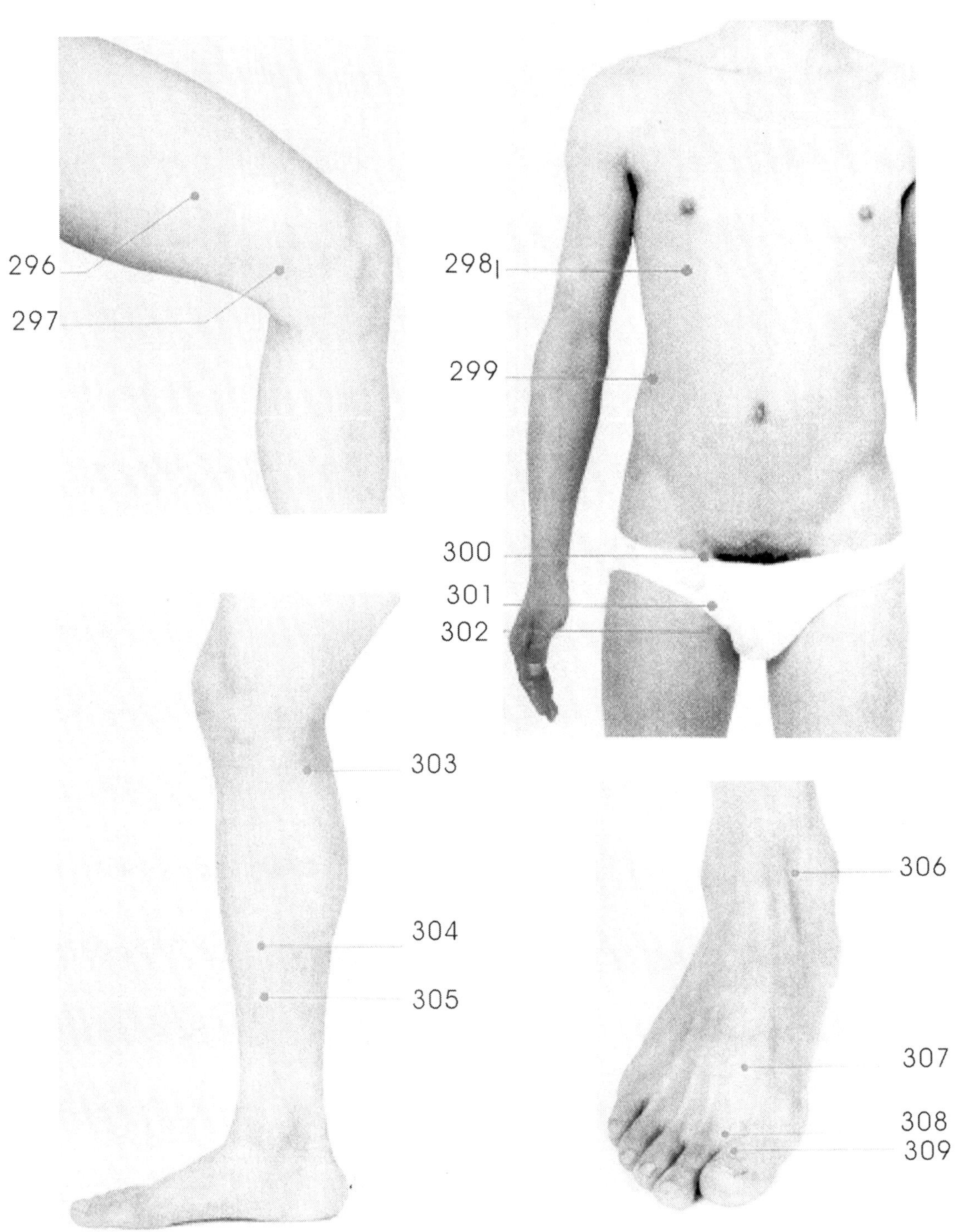

Points on the Fourteen Meridians (13)

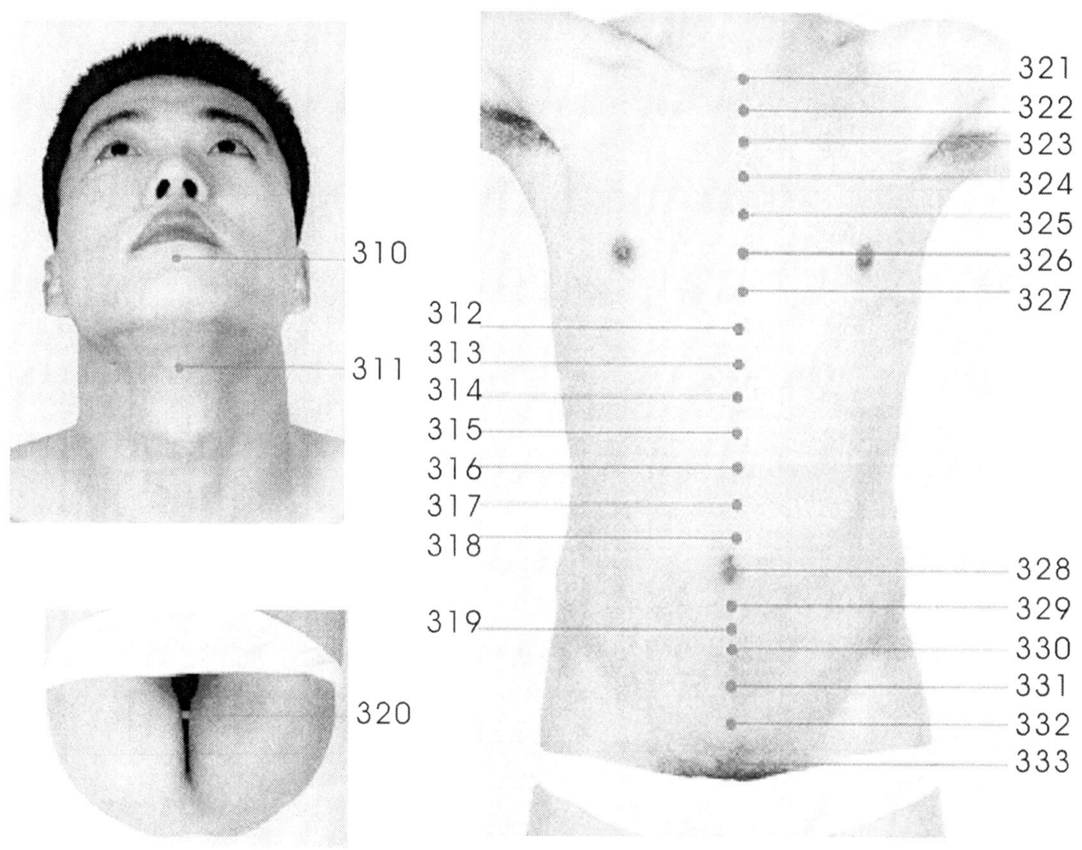

Points on the Fourteen Meridians (14)

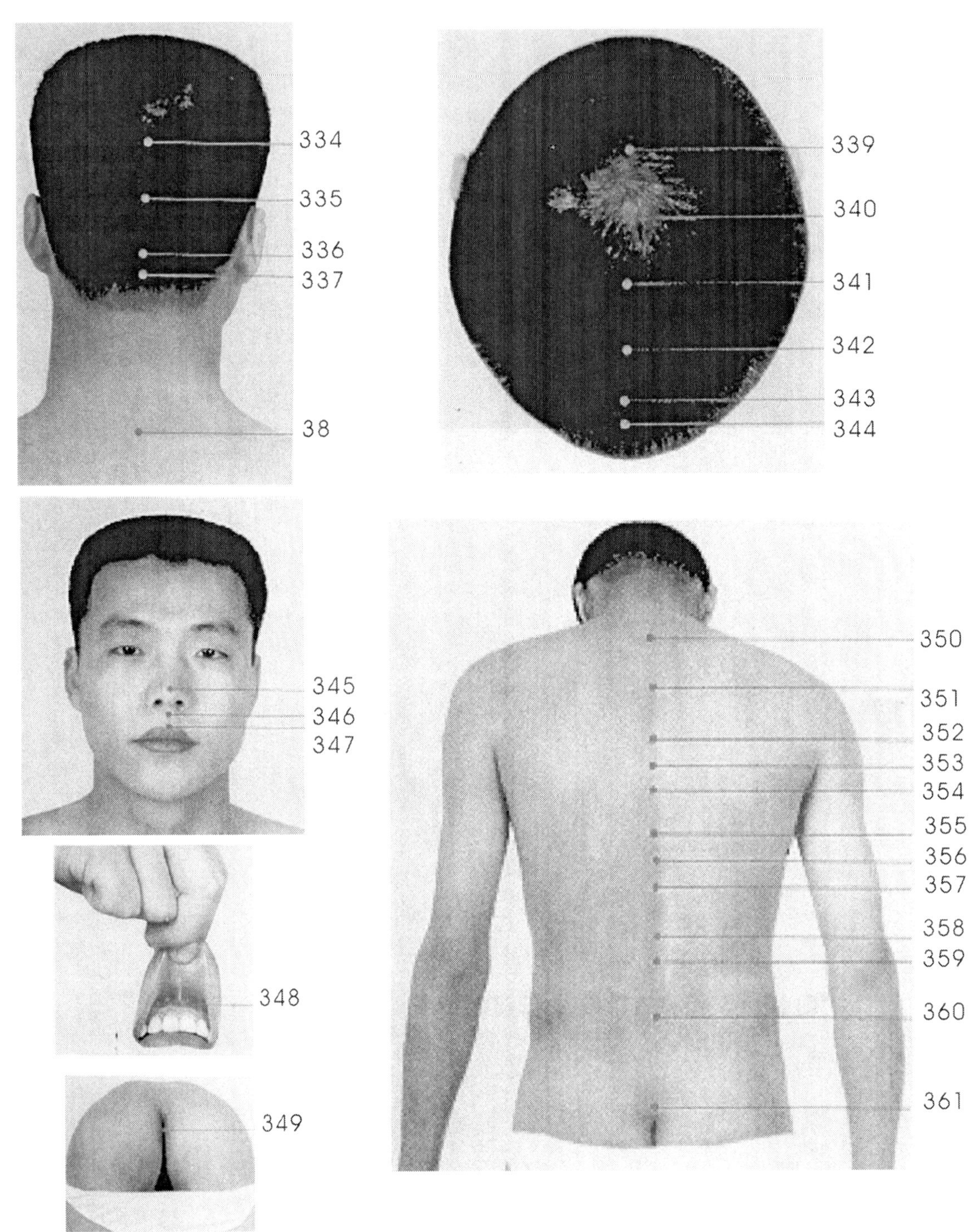

Points on the Fourteen Meridians (15)

Test 4 Acupuncture Points on the Fourteen Meridians (1-361)

1		30		59		88		117		146	
2		31		60		89		118		147	
3		32		61		90		119		148	
4		33		62		91		120		149	
5		34		63		92		121		150	
6		35		64		93		122		151	
7		36		65		94		123		152	
8		37		66		95		124		153	
9		38		67		96		125		154	
10		39		68		97		126		155	
11		40		69		98		127		156	
12		41		70		99		128		157	
13		42		71		100		129		158	
14		43		72		101		130		159	
15		44		73		102		131		160	
16		45		74		103		132		161	
17		46		75		104		133		162	
18		47		76		105		134		163	
19		48		77		106		135		164	
20		49		78		107		136		165	
21		50		79		108		137		166	
22		51		80		109		138		167	
23		52		81		110		139		168	
24		53		82		111		140		169	
25		54		83		112		141		170	
26		55		84		113		142		171	
27		56		85		114		143		172	
28		57		86		115		144		173	
29		58		87		116		145			

Test 4: Acupuncture Points on the Fourteen Meridians

174	
175	
176	
177	
178	
179	
180	
181	
182	
183	
184	
185	
186	
187	
188	
189	
190	
191	
192	
193	
194	
195	
196	
197	
198	
199	
200	
201	
202	
203	
204	

205	
206	
207	
208	
209	
210	
211	
212	
213	
214	
215	
216	
217	
218	
219	
220	
221	
222	
223	
224	
225	
226	
227	
228	
229	
230	
231	
232	
233	
234	
235	
236	

237	
238	
239	
240	
241	
242	
243	
244	
245	
246	
247	
248	
249	
250	
251	
252	
253	
254	
255	
256	
257	
258	
259	
260	
261	
262	
263	
264	
265	
266	
267	
268	

269	
270	
271	
272	
273	
274	
275	
276	
277	
278	
279	
280	
281	
282	
283	
284	
285	
286	
287	
288	
289	
290	
291	
292	
293	
294	
295	
296	
297	
298	
299	
300	

301	
302	
303	
305	
306	
306	
307	
308	
309	
310	
311	
312	
313	
314	
315	
316	
317	
318	
319	
320	
321	
322	
323	
324	
325	
326	
327	
327	
328	
330	
331	
332	

333	
334	
335	
336	
337	
338	
339	
340	
341	
342	
343	
344	
345	
346	
347	
348	
349	
350	
351	
352	
353	
354	
355	
356	
357	
358	
359	
360	
361	

Test 5: Extraordinary Points (1-48)

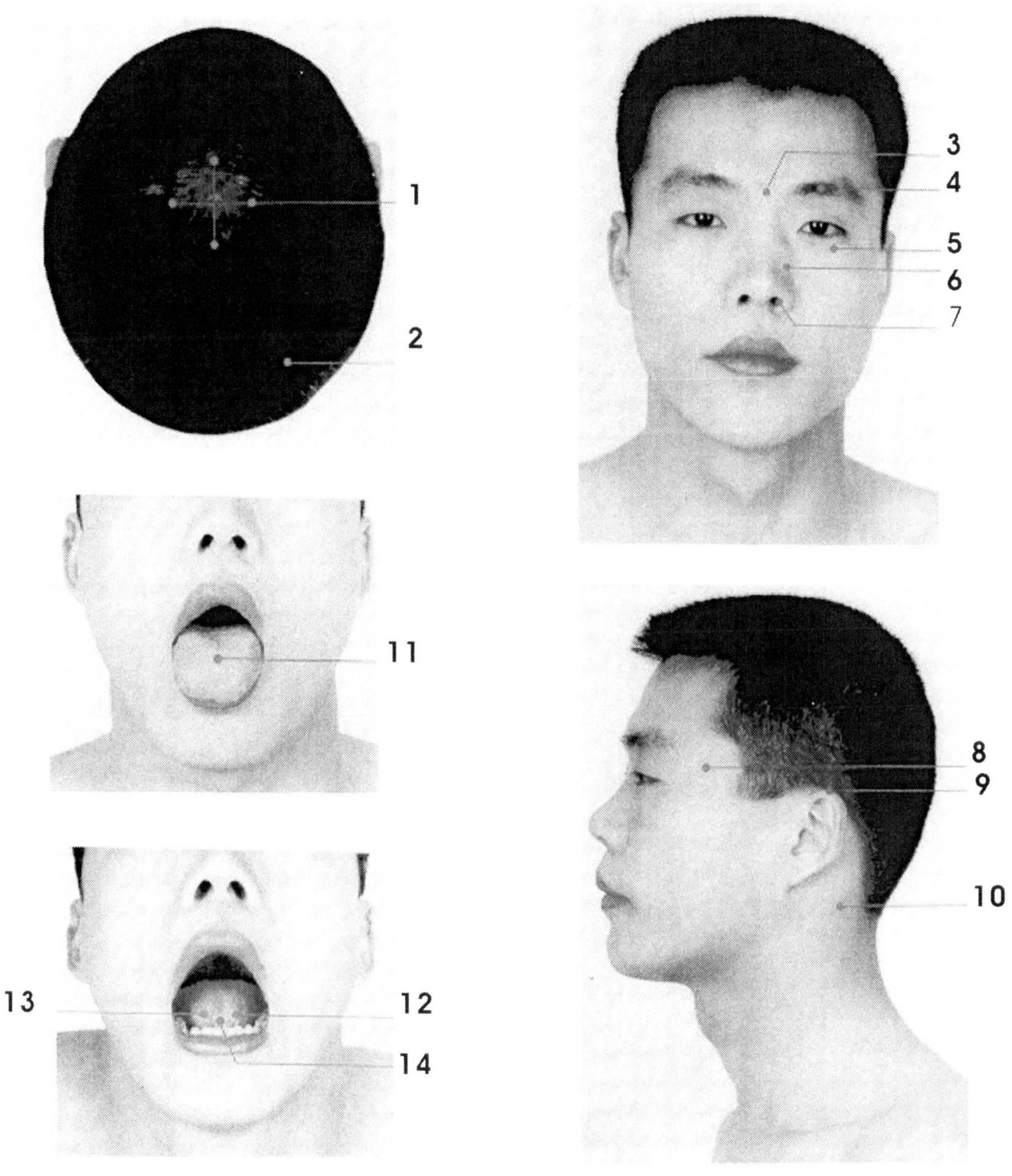

Extraordinary Points in Head and Neck Region

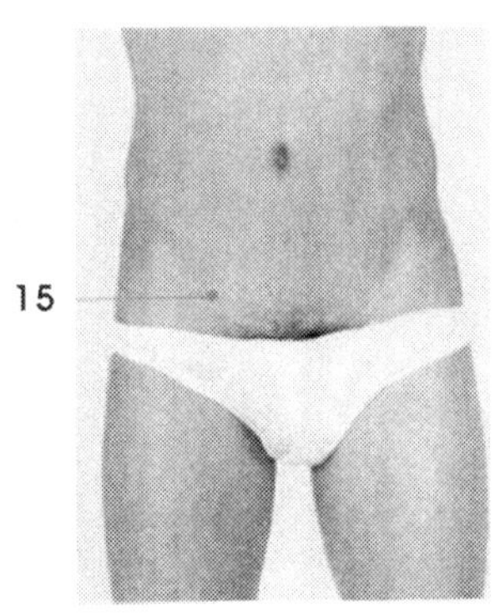

Extraordinary Point in Chest and Abdomen

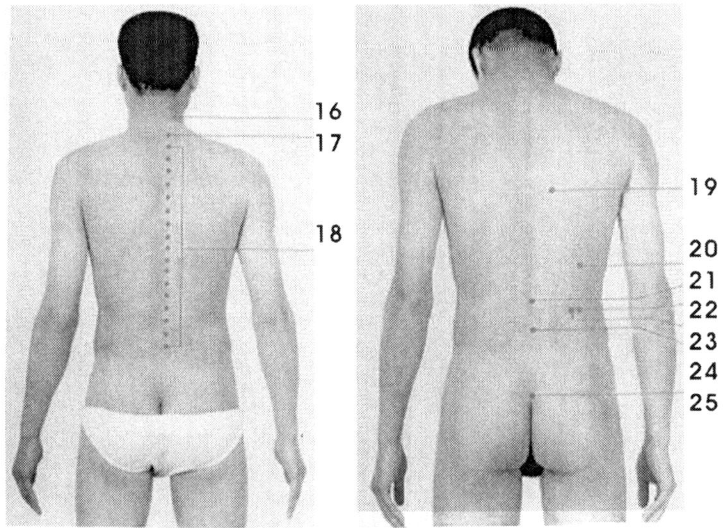

Extraordinary Points in Back Region

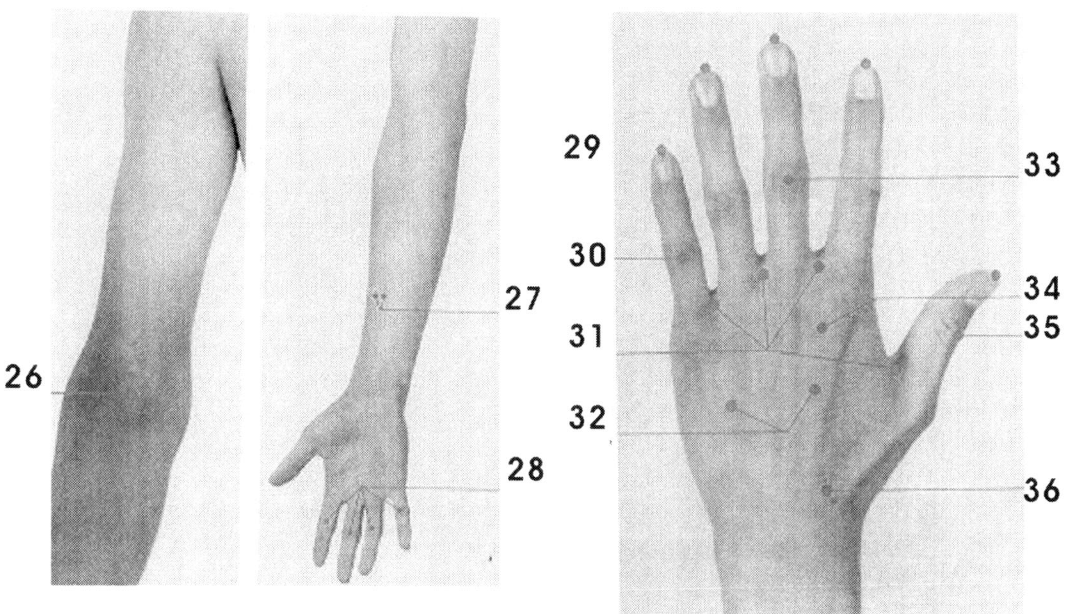

Extraordinary Points in Upper Extremities Region

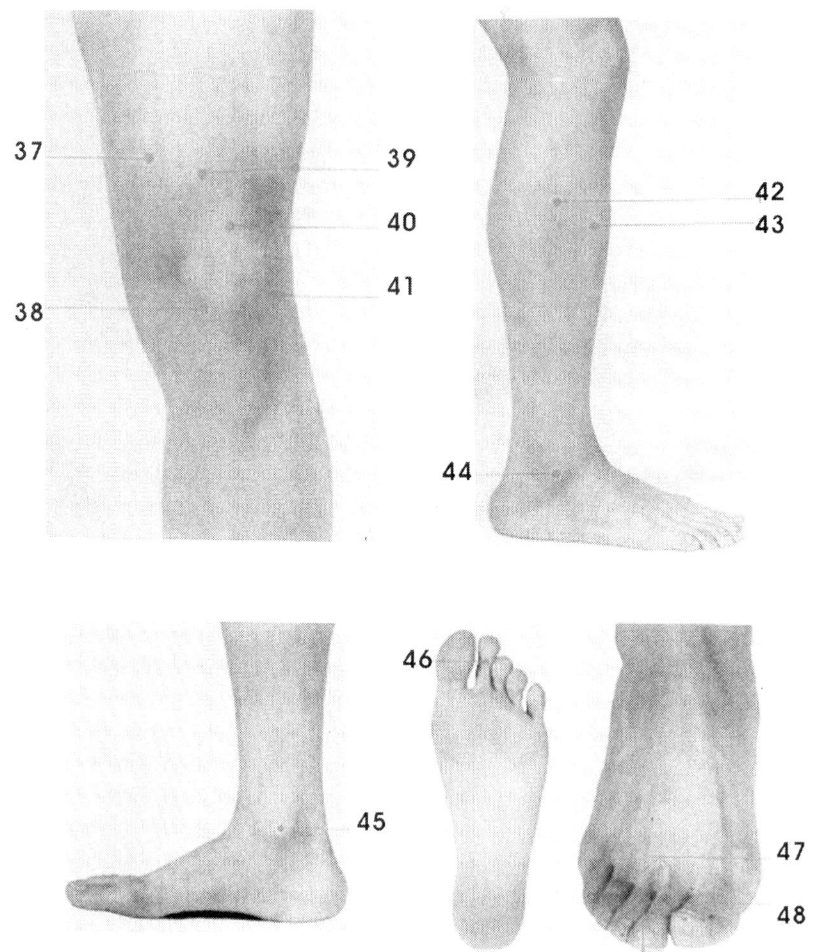

Extraordinary Points in Lower Extremities Region

Test 5: Extraordinary Points (1-48)

1		9		17		25		33		41	
2		10		18		26		34		42	
3		11		19		27		35		43	
4		12		20		28		36		44	
5		13		21		29		37		45	
6		14		22		30		38		47	
7		15		23		31		39		47	
8		16		24		32		40		48	

Test 6: Body Points (1-644)

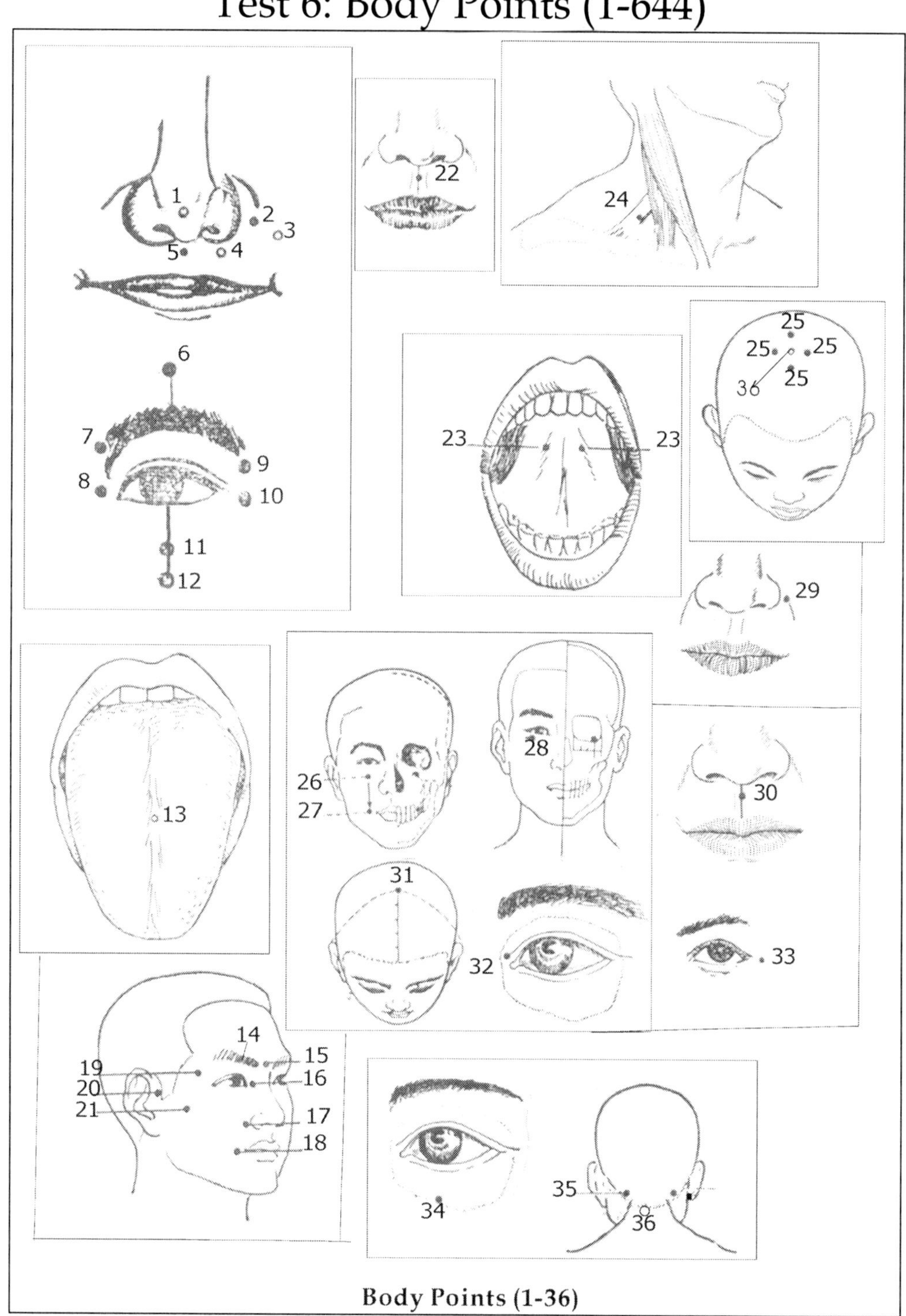

Body Points (1-36)

Test 6: Body Points

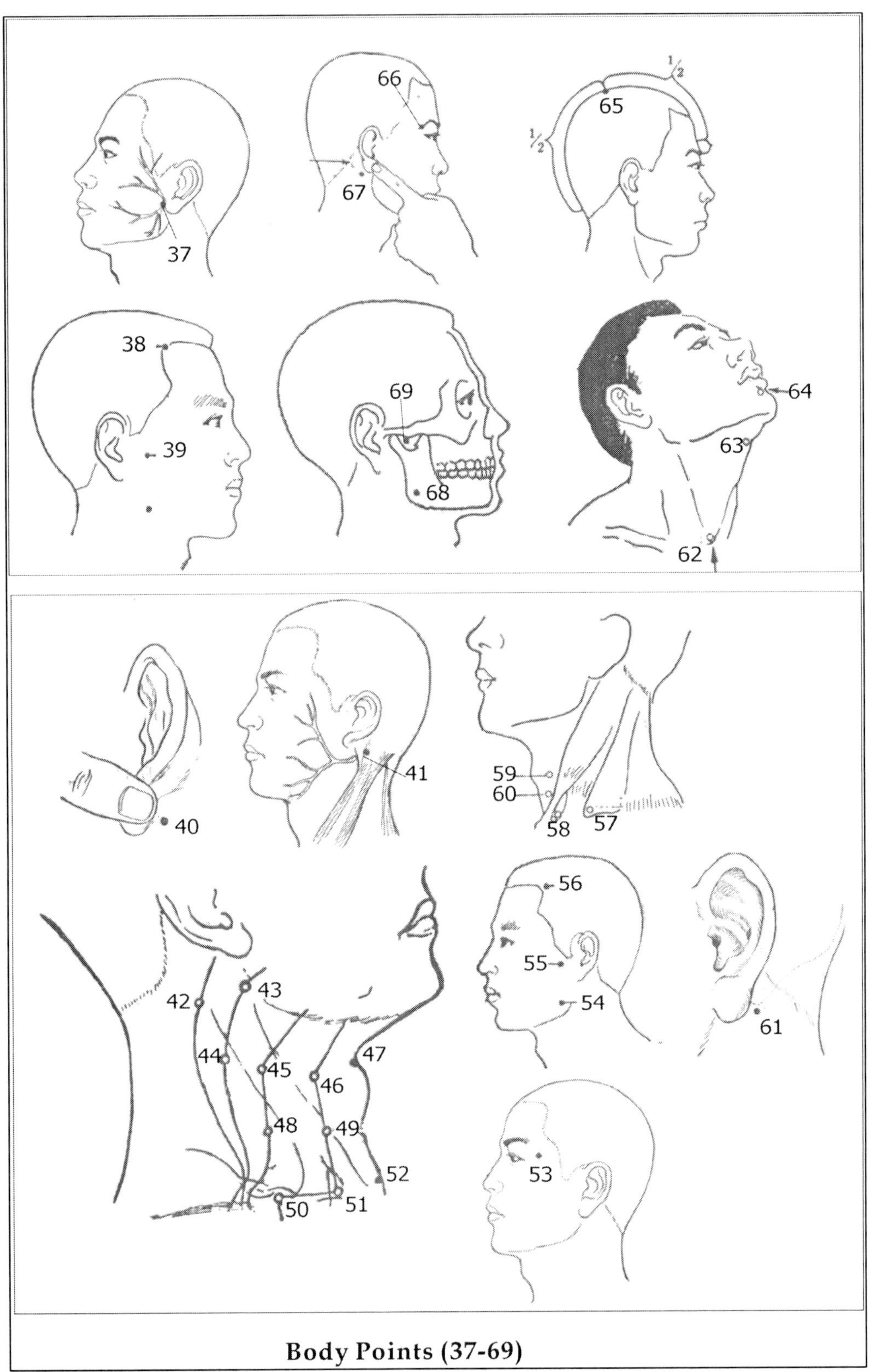

Body Points (37-69)

Test 6: Body Points

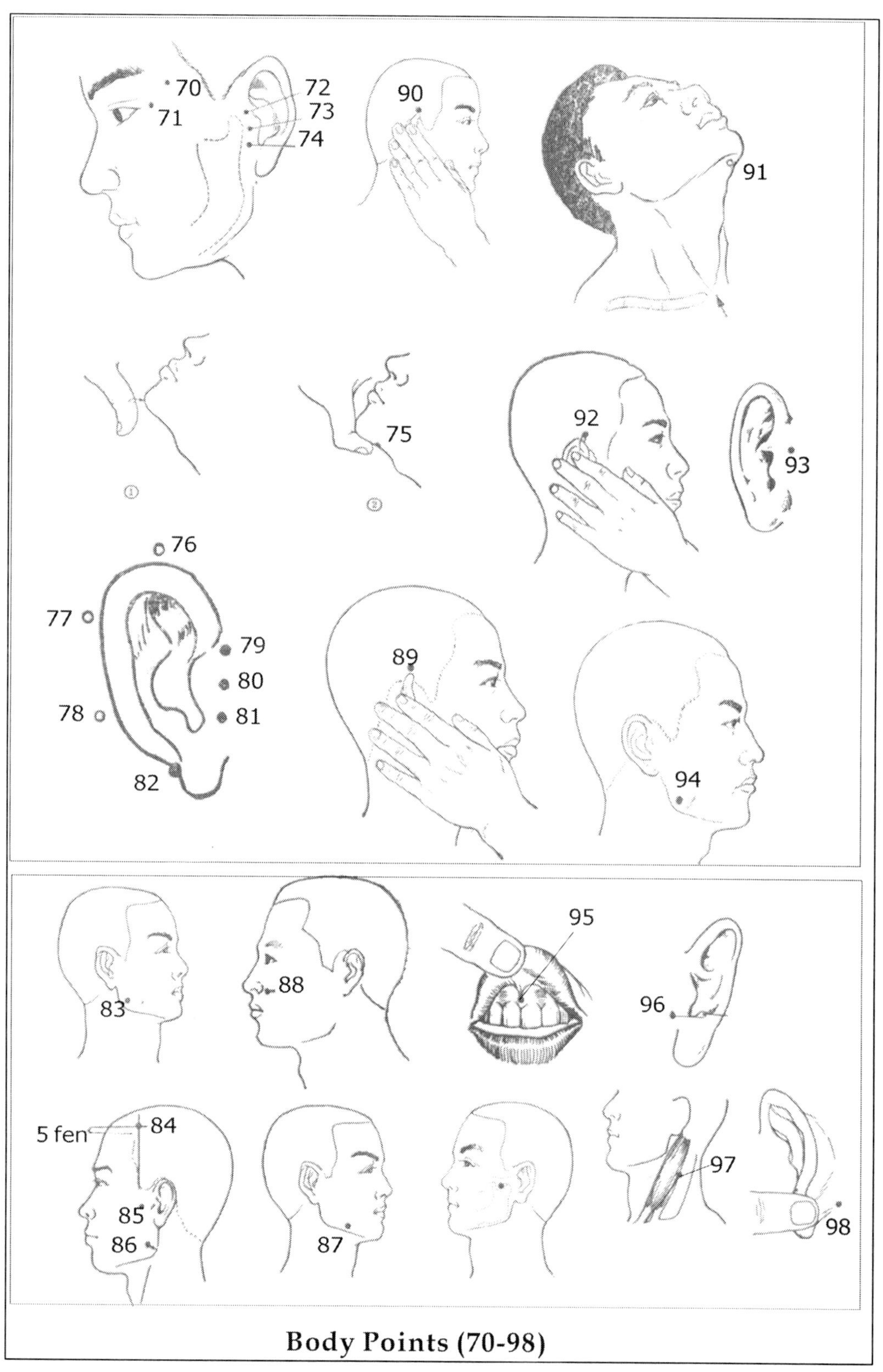

Body Points (70-98)

Test 6: Body Points

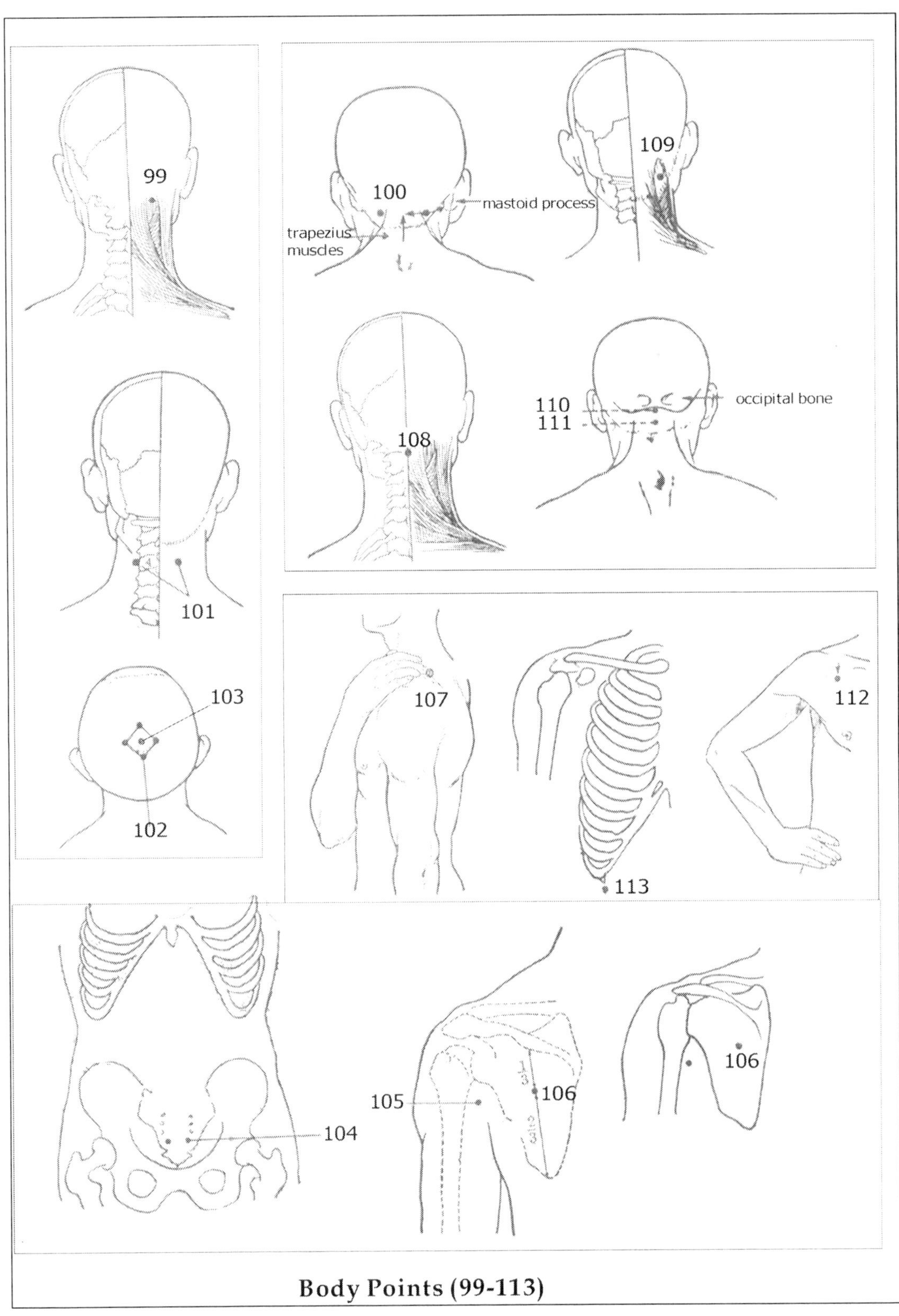

Body Points (99-113)

Test 6: Body Points

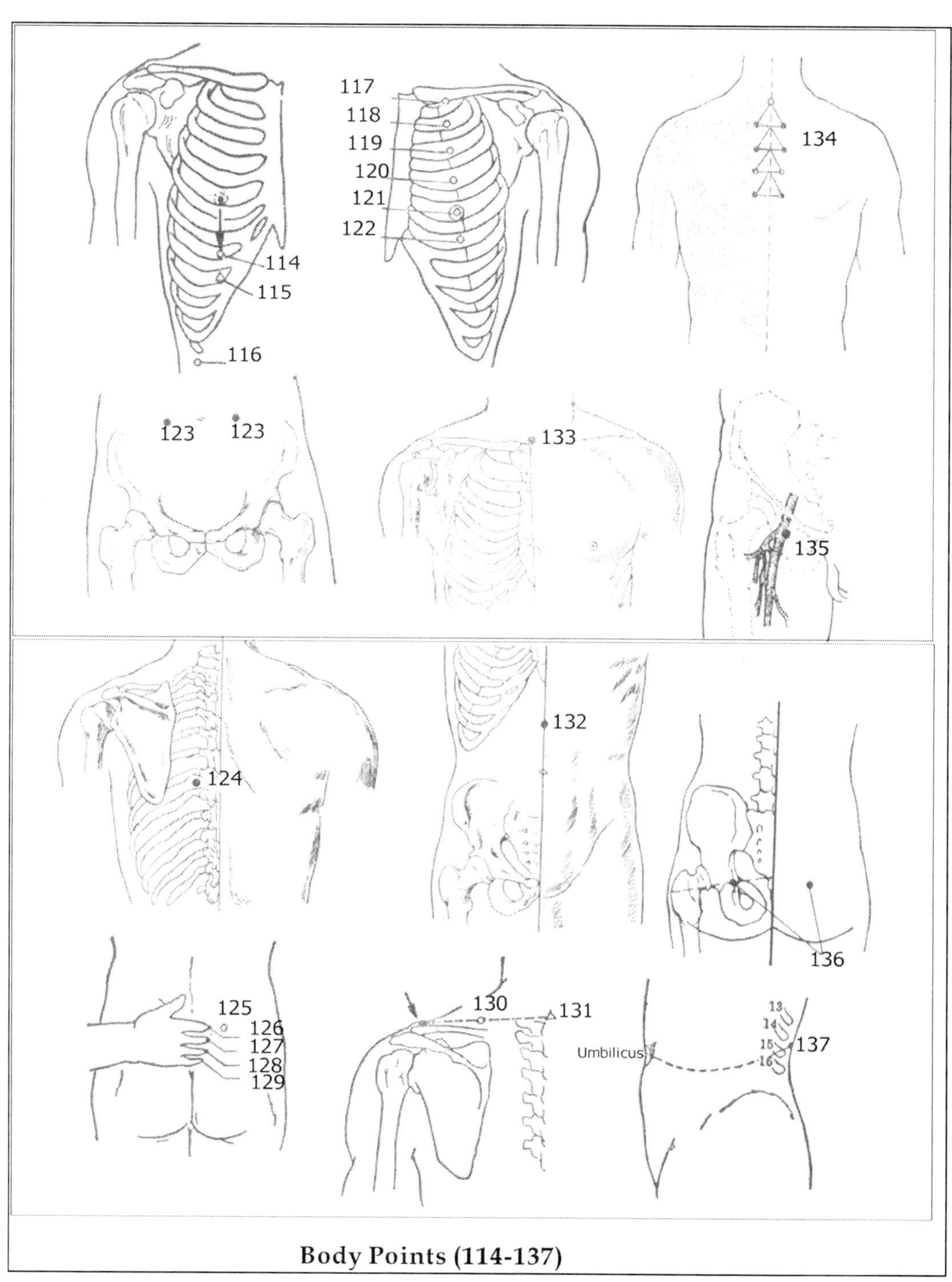

Body Points (114-137)

Test 6: Body Points

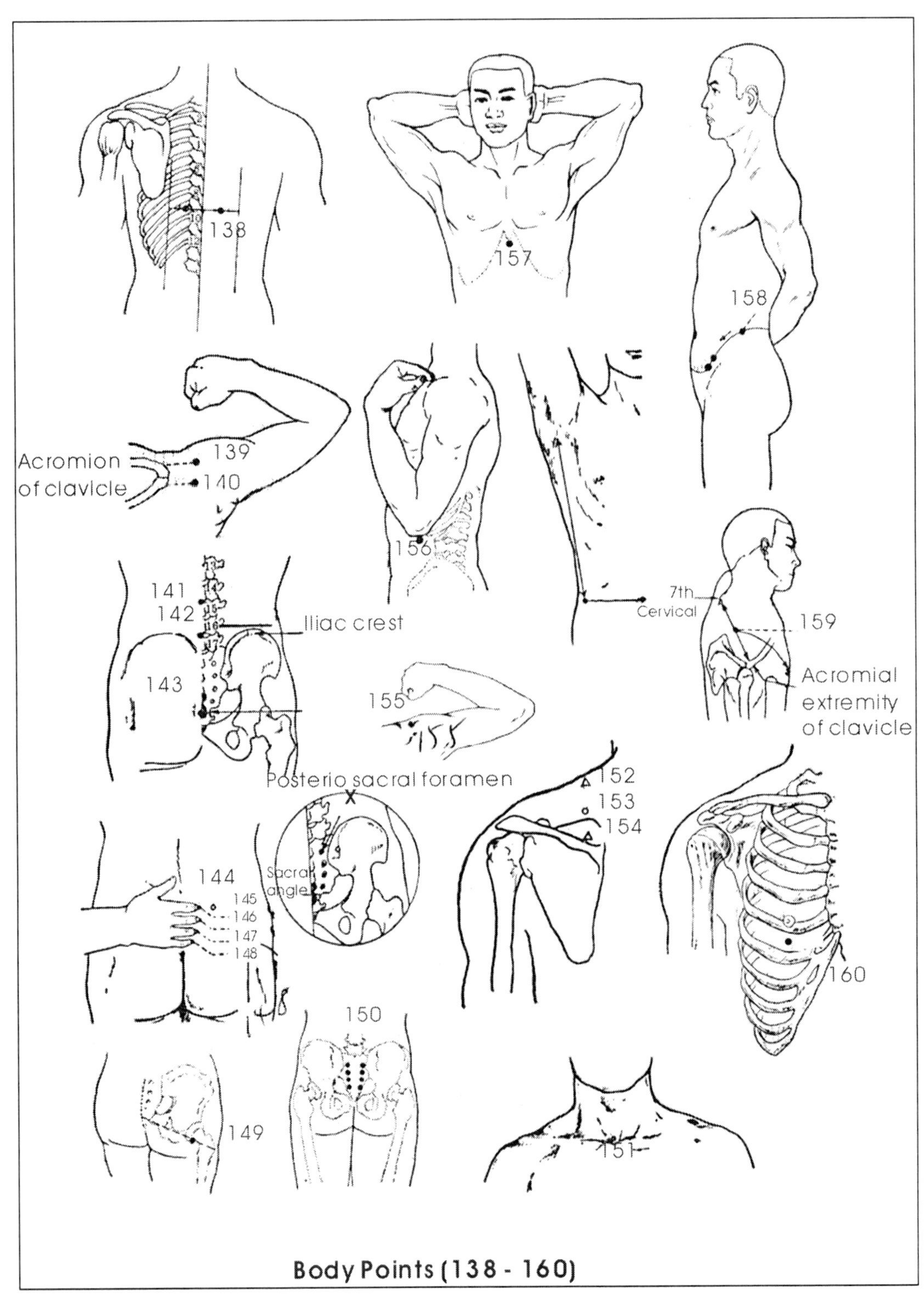

Body Points (138 - 160)

Test 6: Body Points

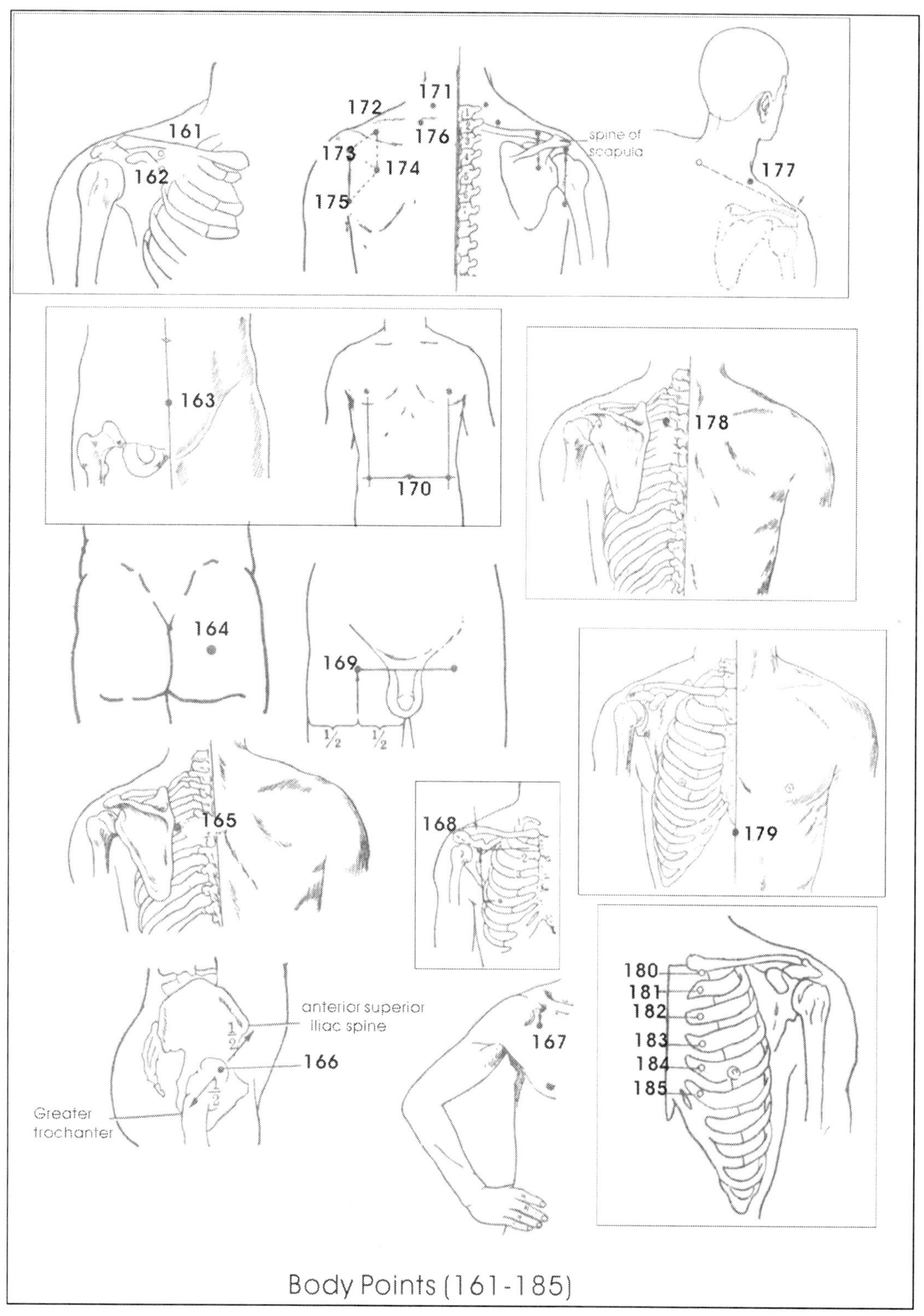

Body Points (161-185)

Test 6: Body Points

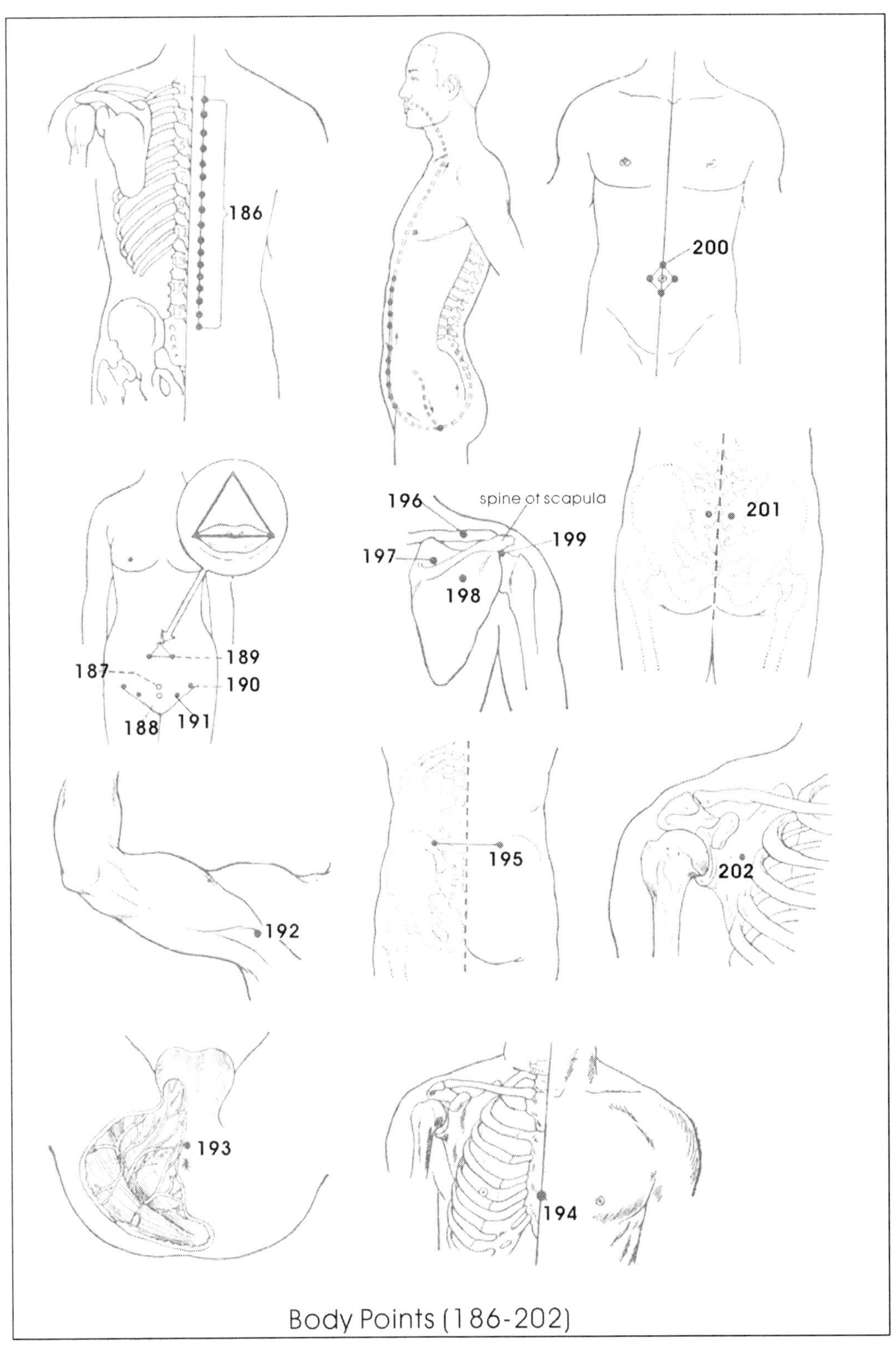

Body Points (186-202)

Test 6: Body Points

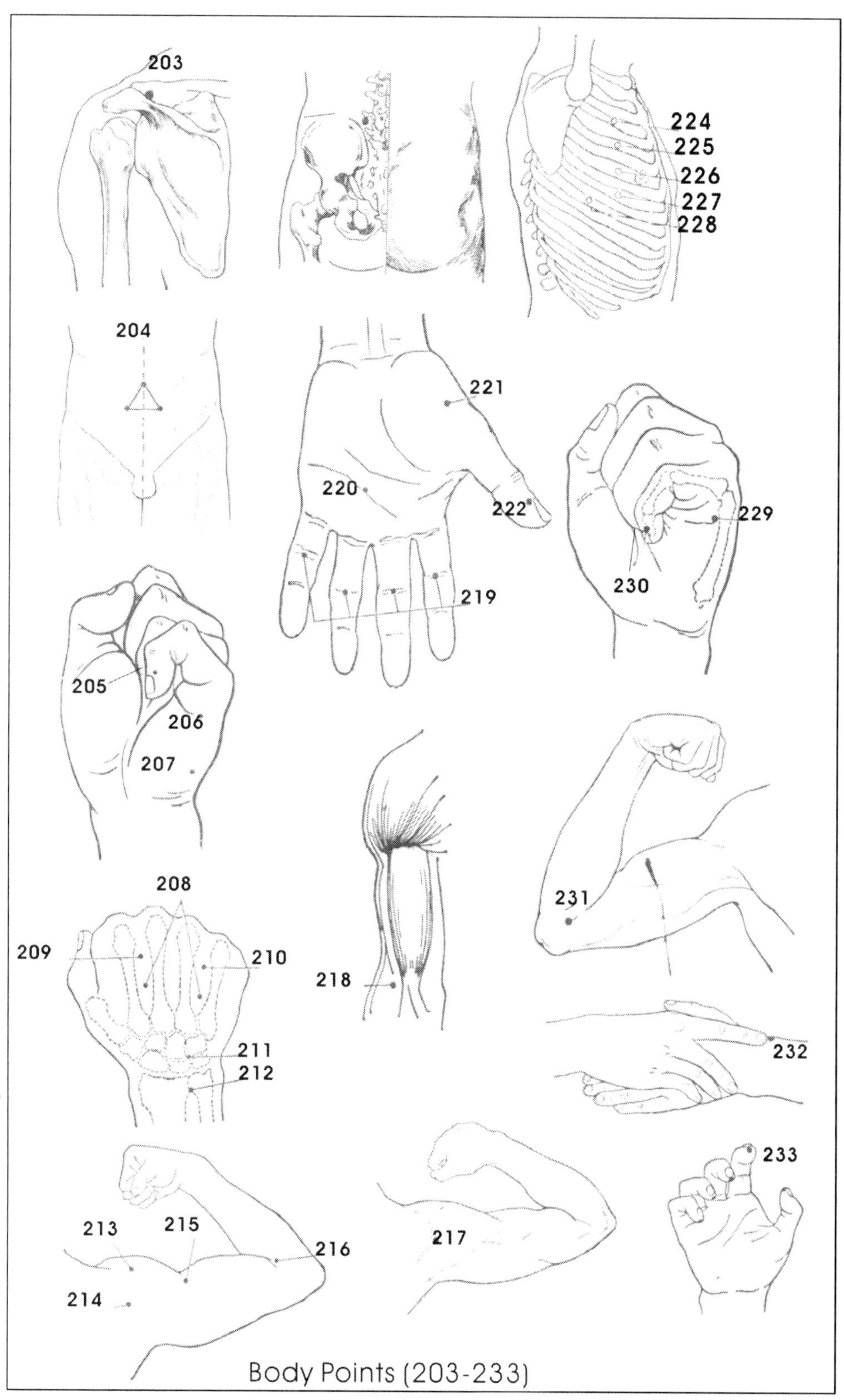

Body Points (203-233)

Test 6: Body Points

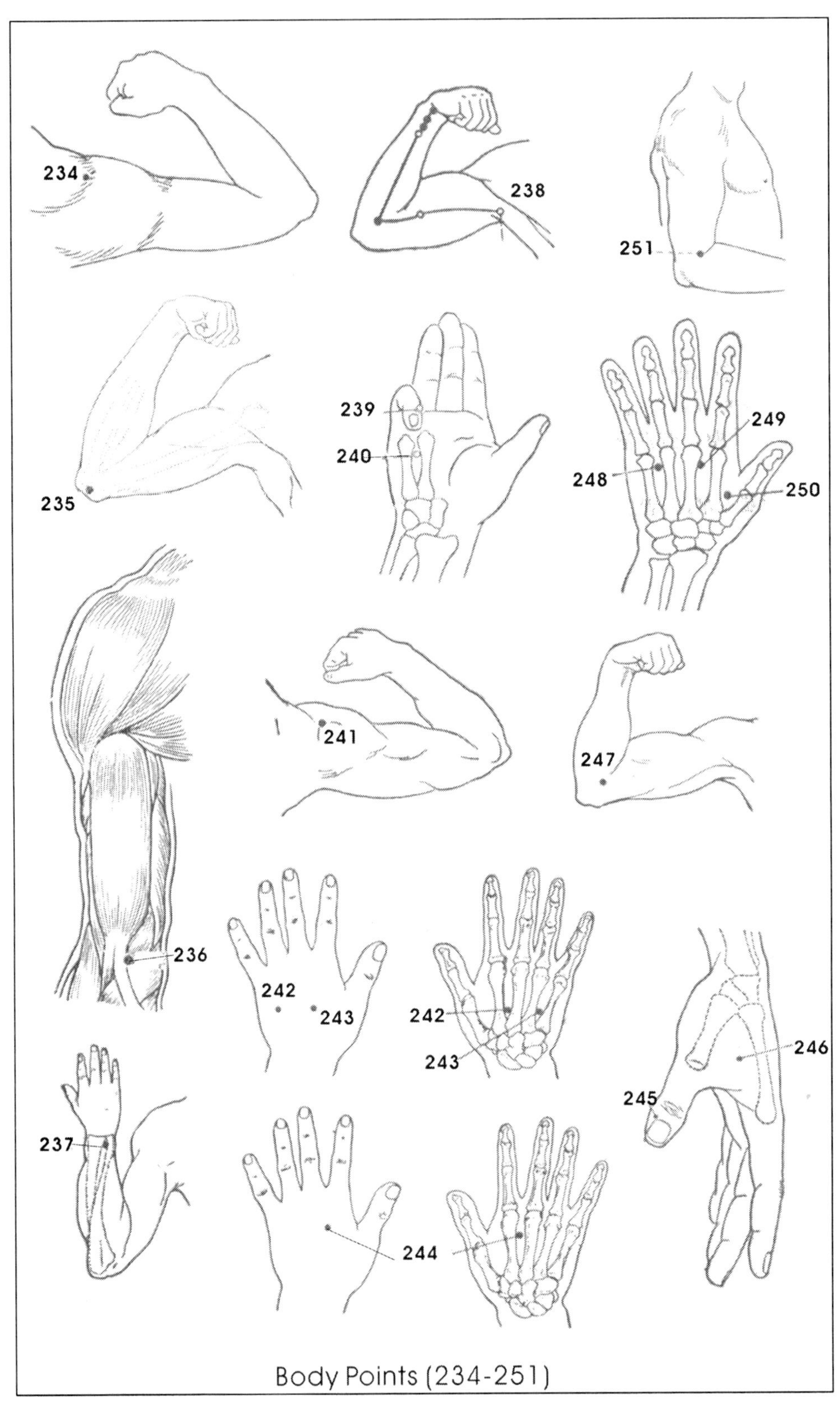

Body Points (234-251)

Test 6: Body Points

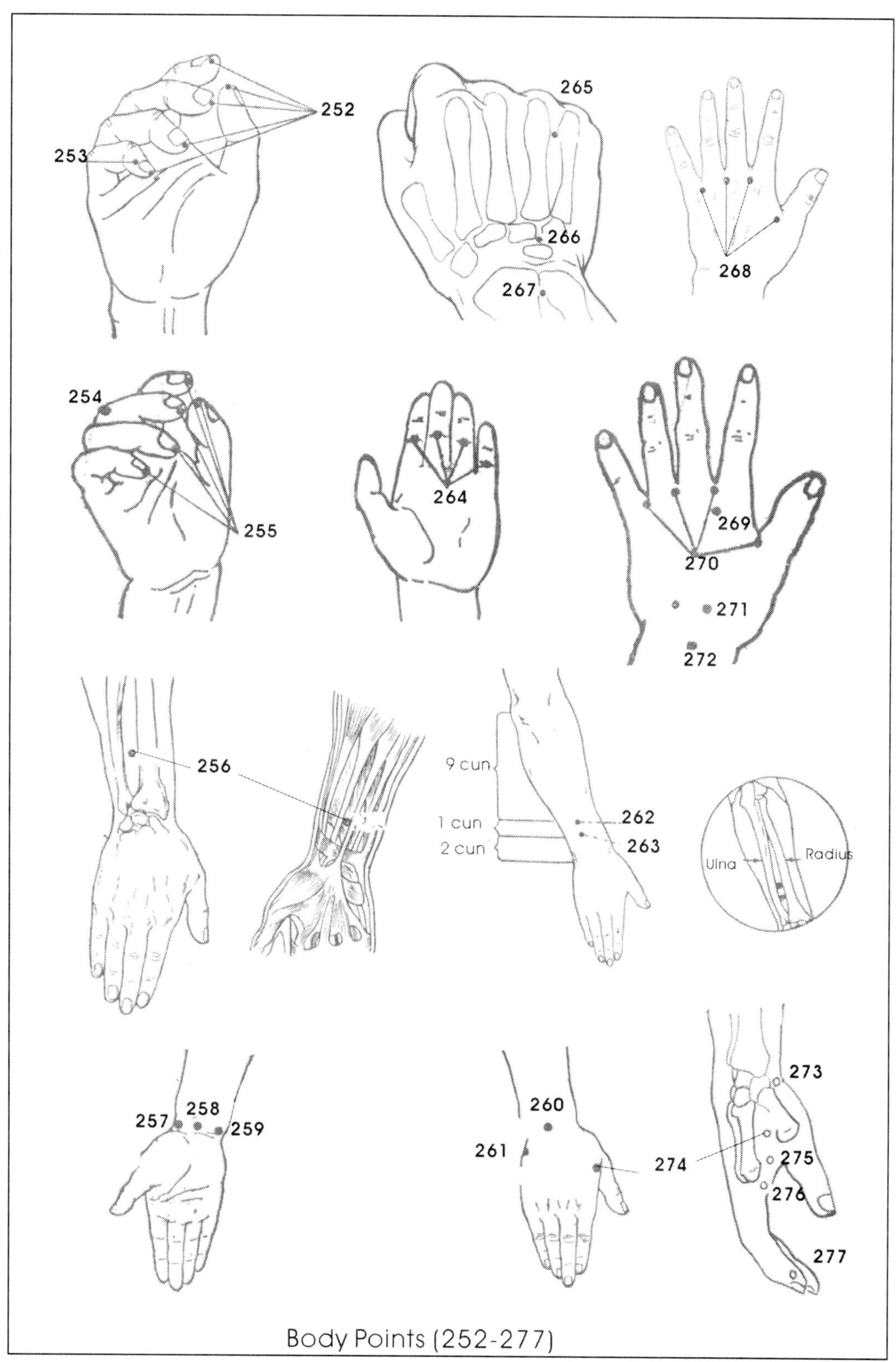

Body Points (252-277)

Test 6: Body Points

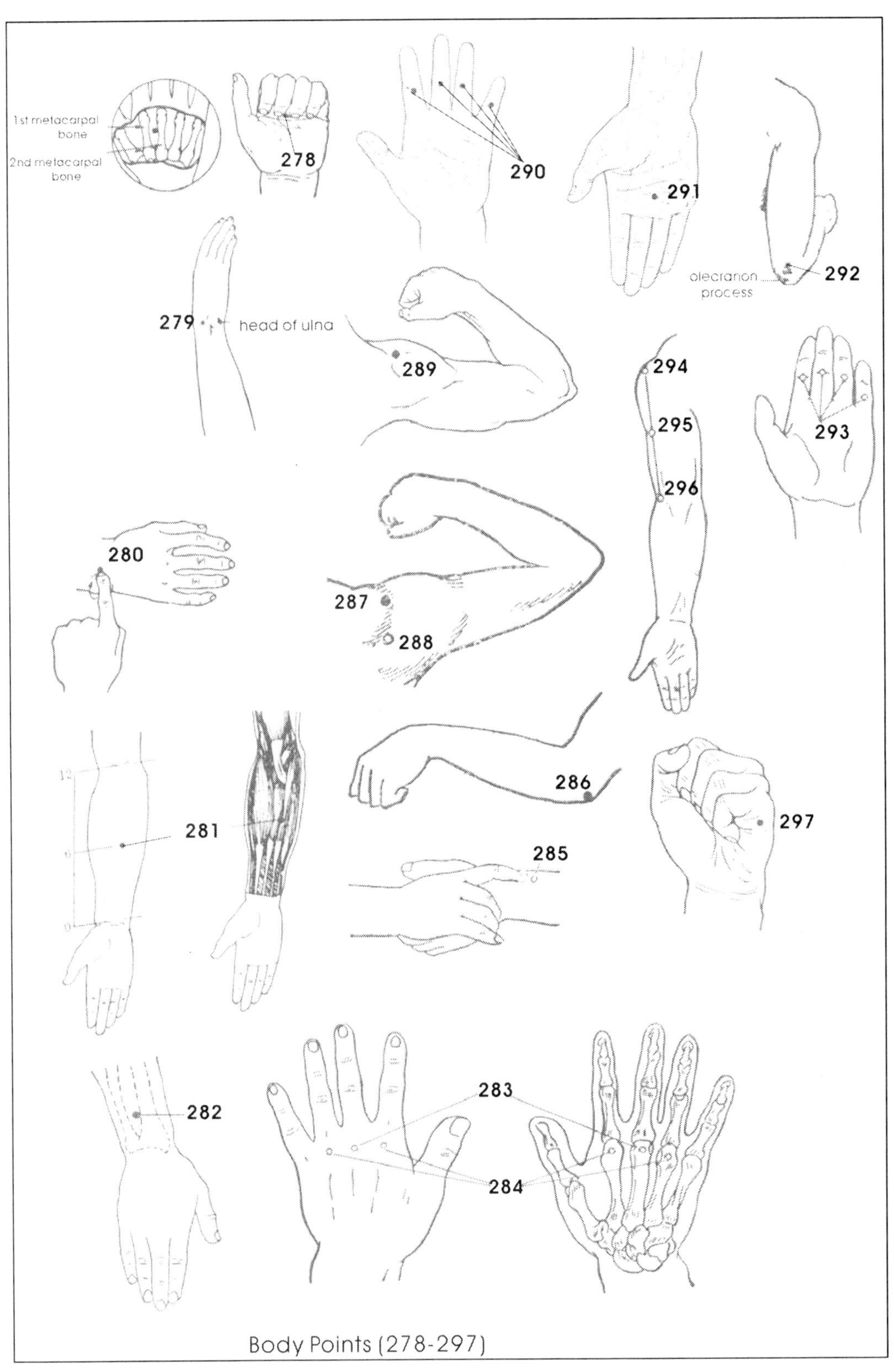

Body Points (278-297)

Test 6: Body Points

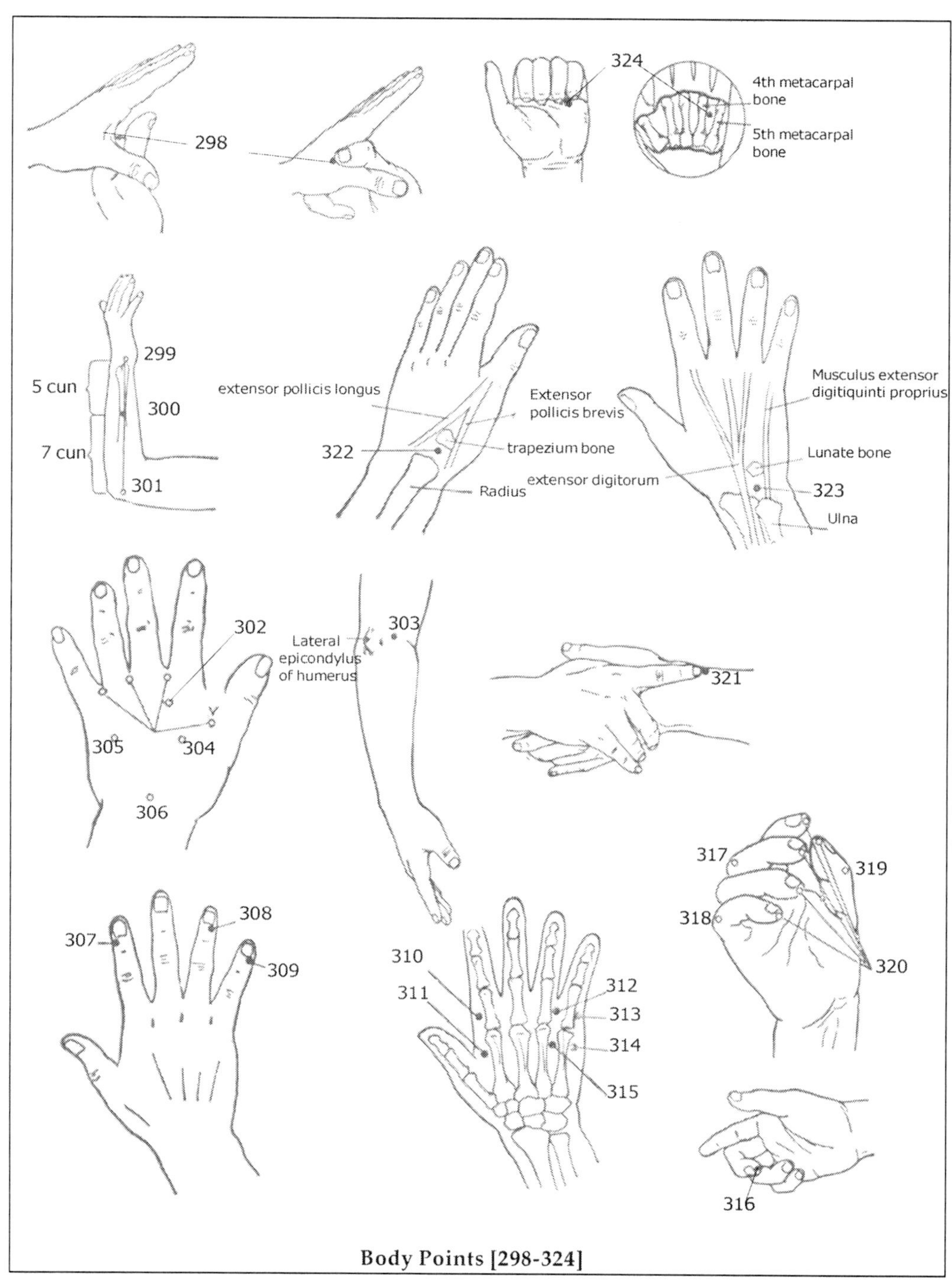

Body Points [298-324]

Test 6: Body Points

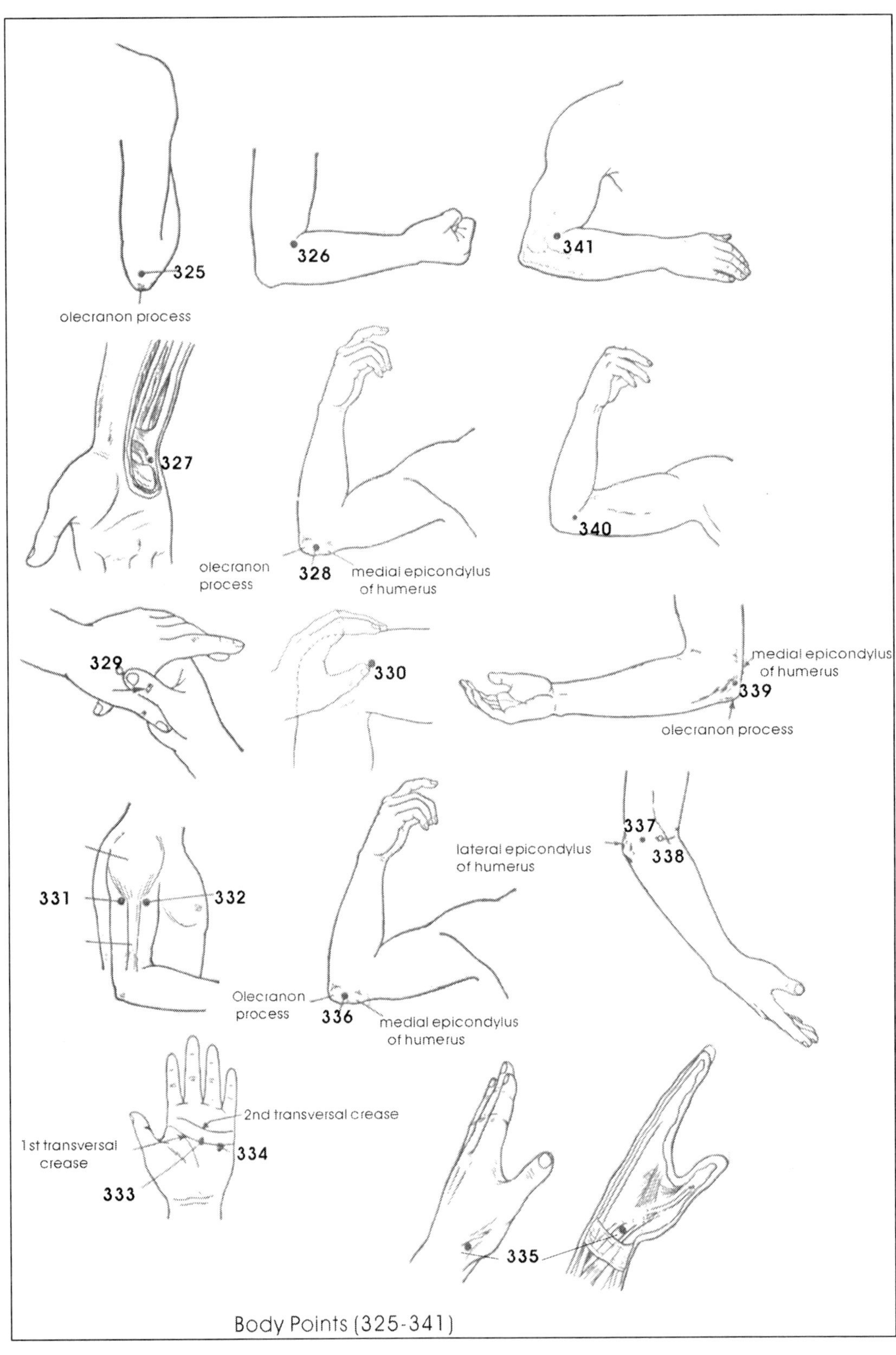

Body Points (325-341)

Test 6: Body Points

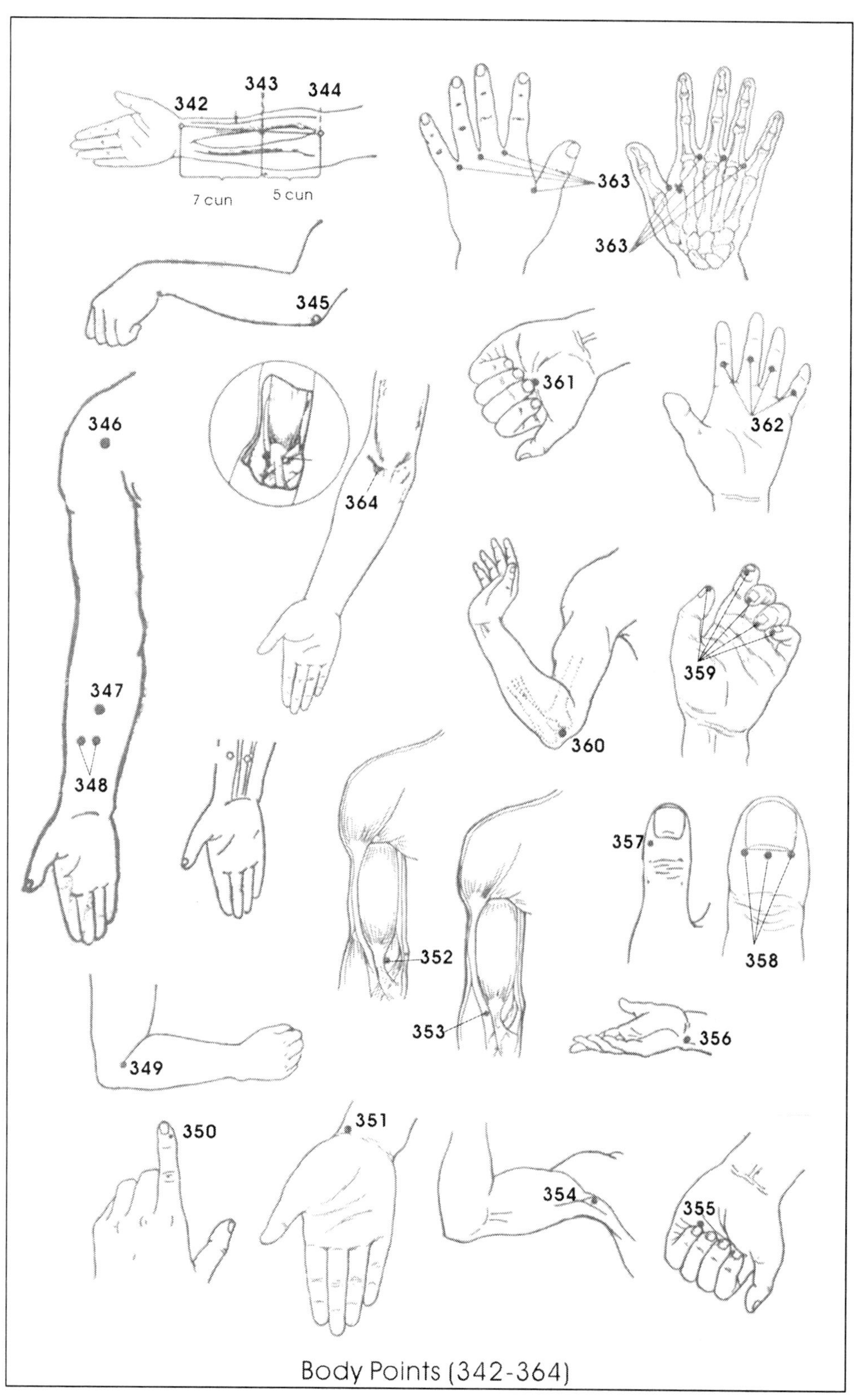

Body Points (342-364)

Test 6: Body Points

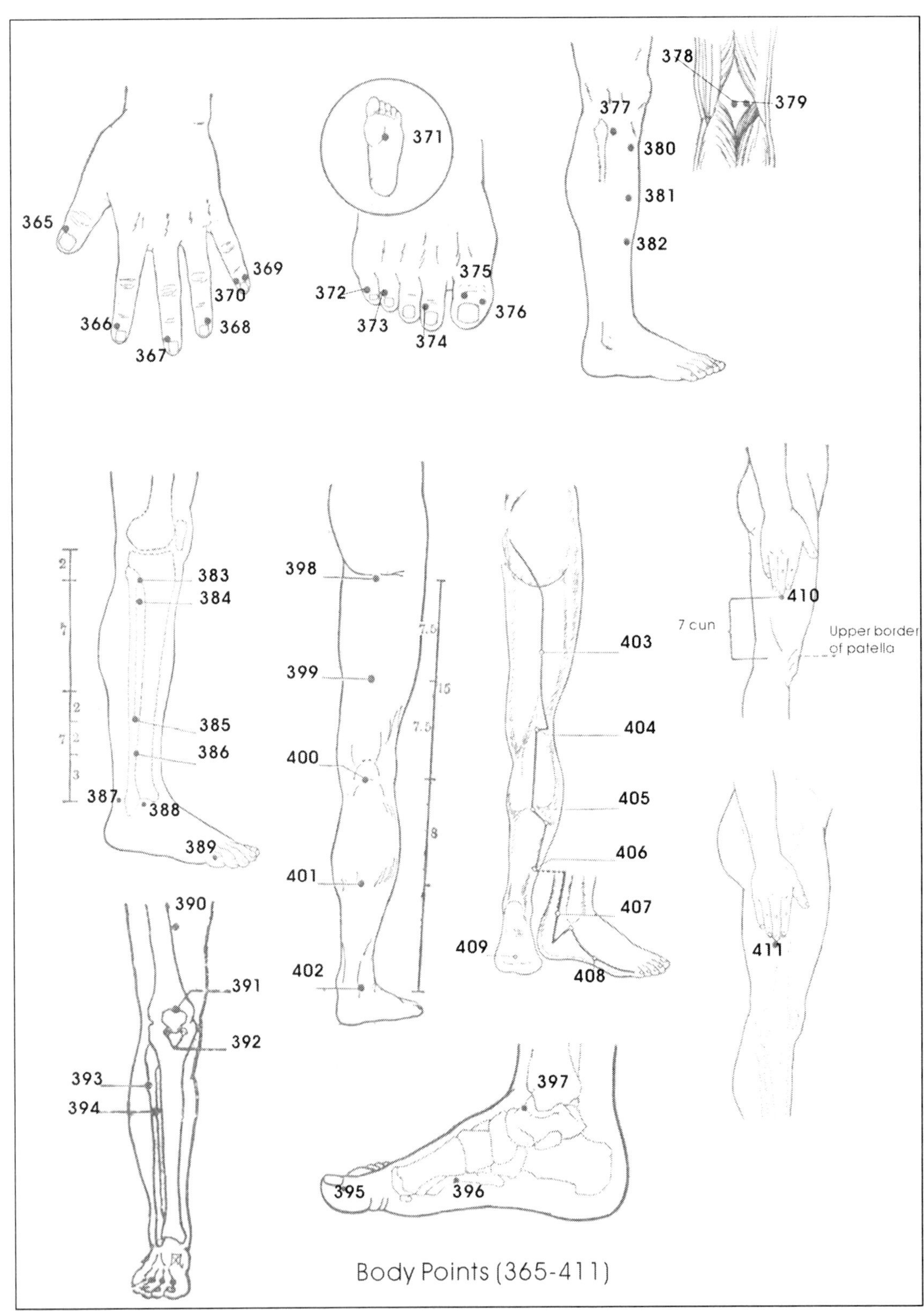

Body Points (365-411)

Test 6: Body Points

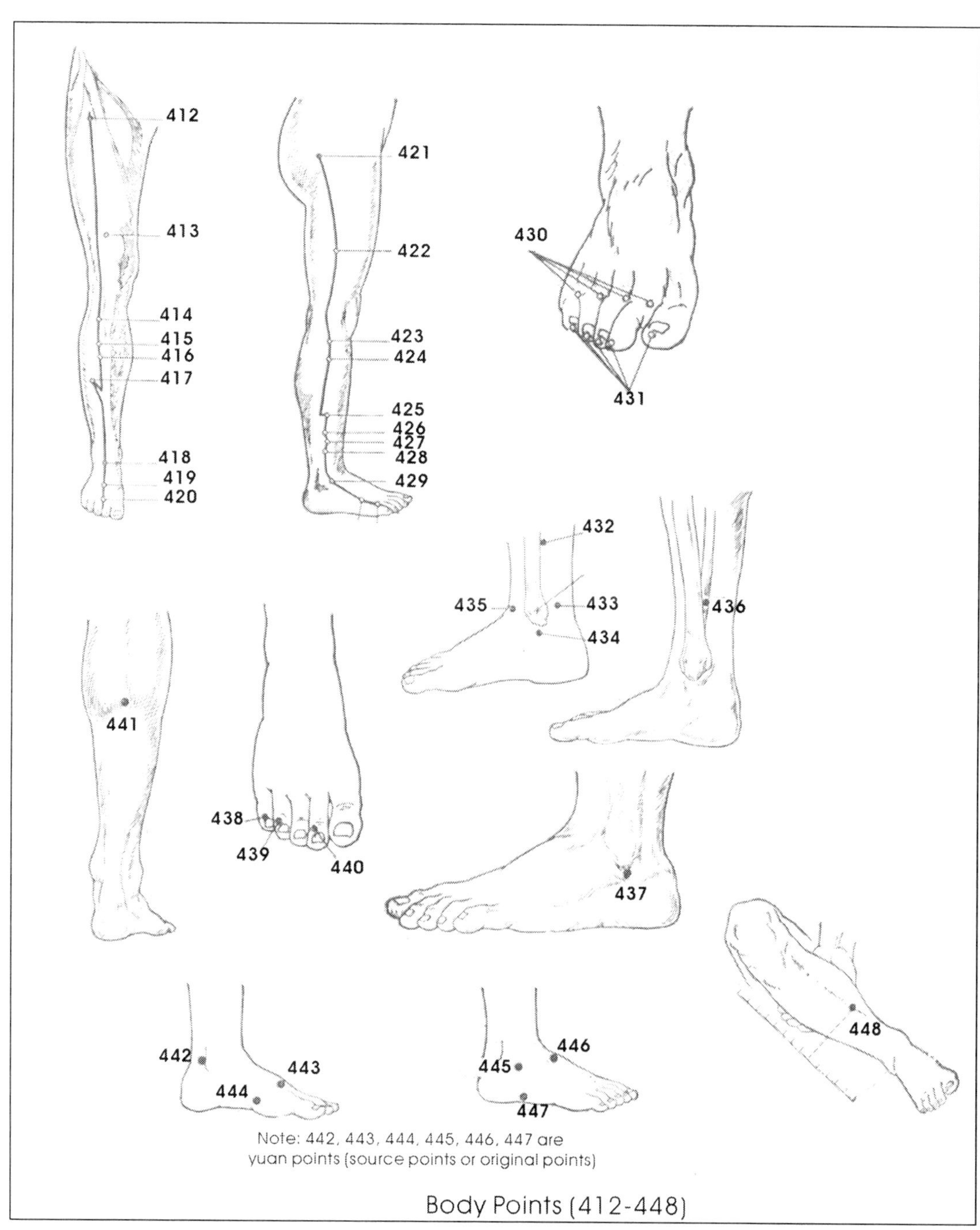

Note: 442, 443, 444, 445, 446, 447 are yuan points (source points or original points)

Body Points (412-448)

Test 6: Body Points

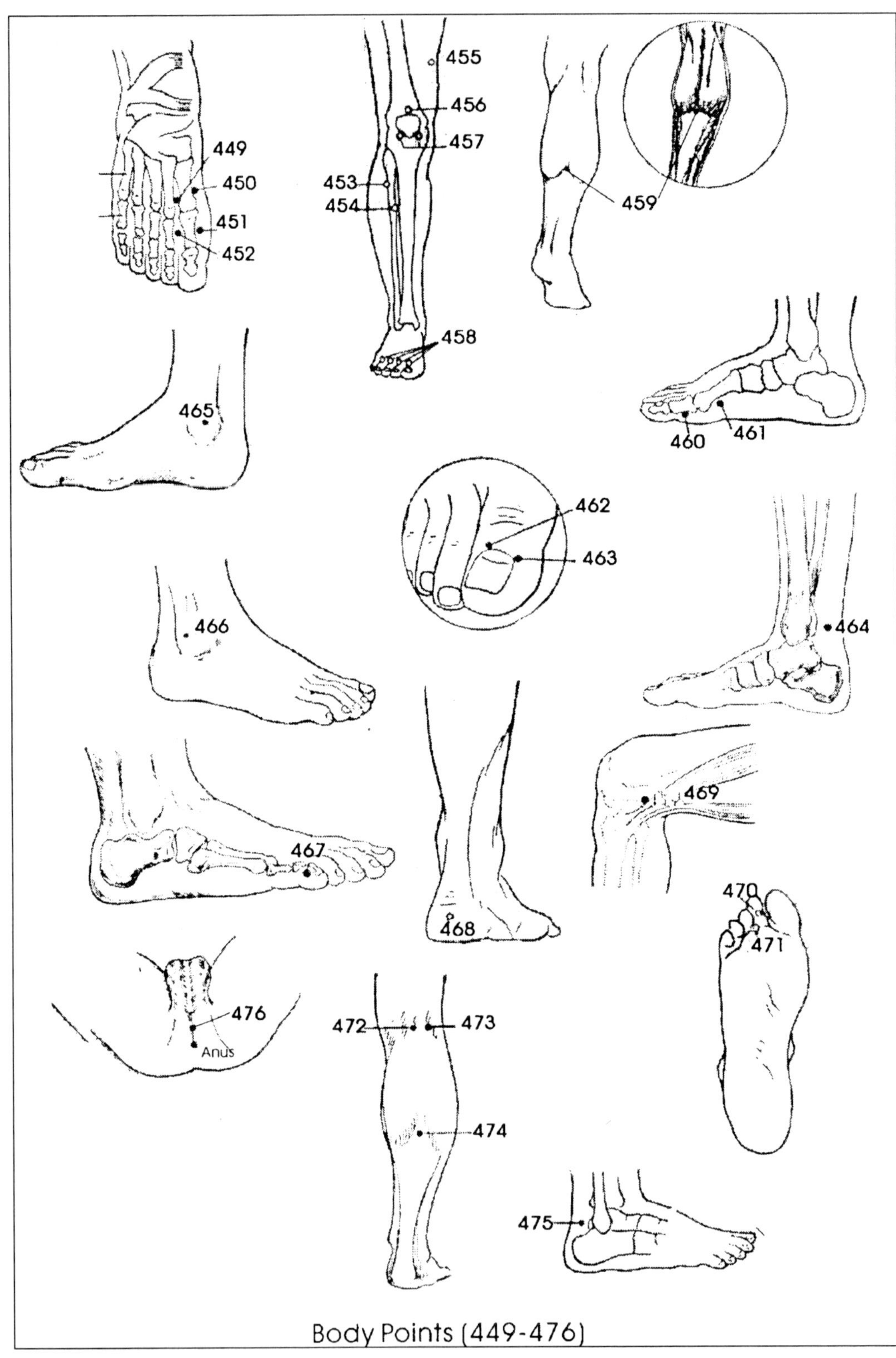

Body Points (449-476)

Test 6: Body Points

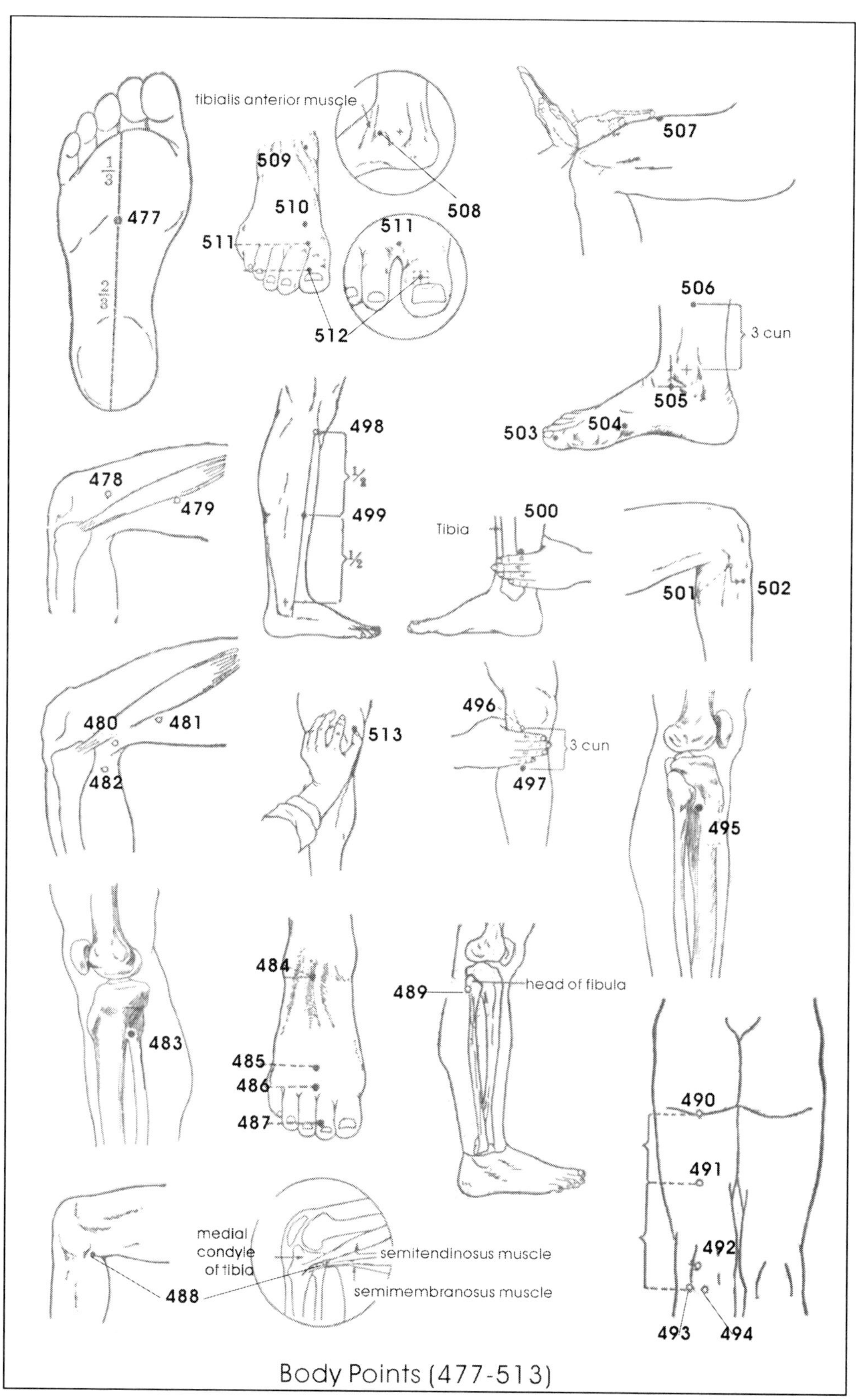

Body Points (477-513)

Test 6: Body Points

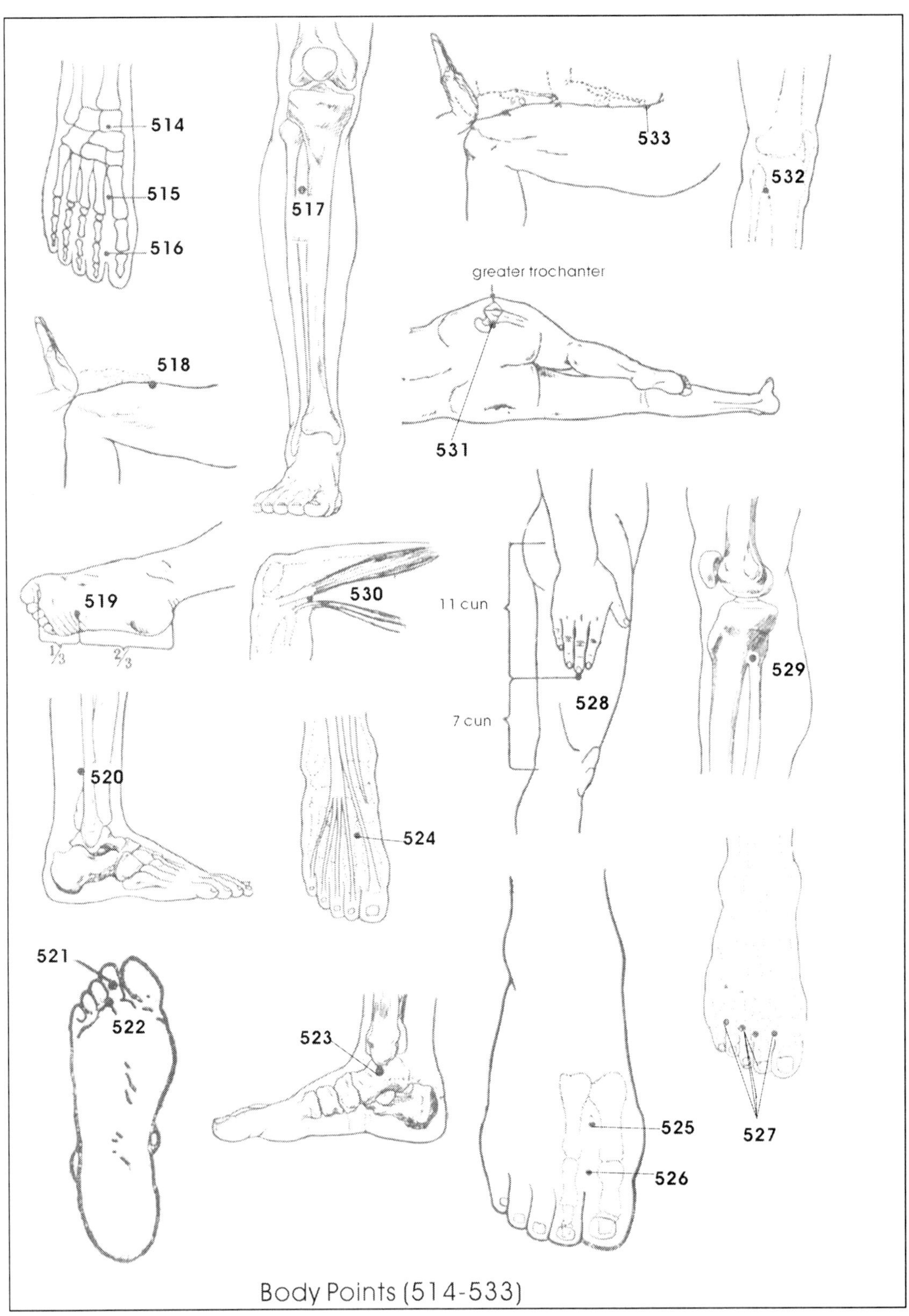

Body Points (514-533)

Test 6: Body Points

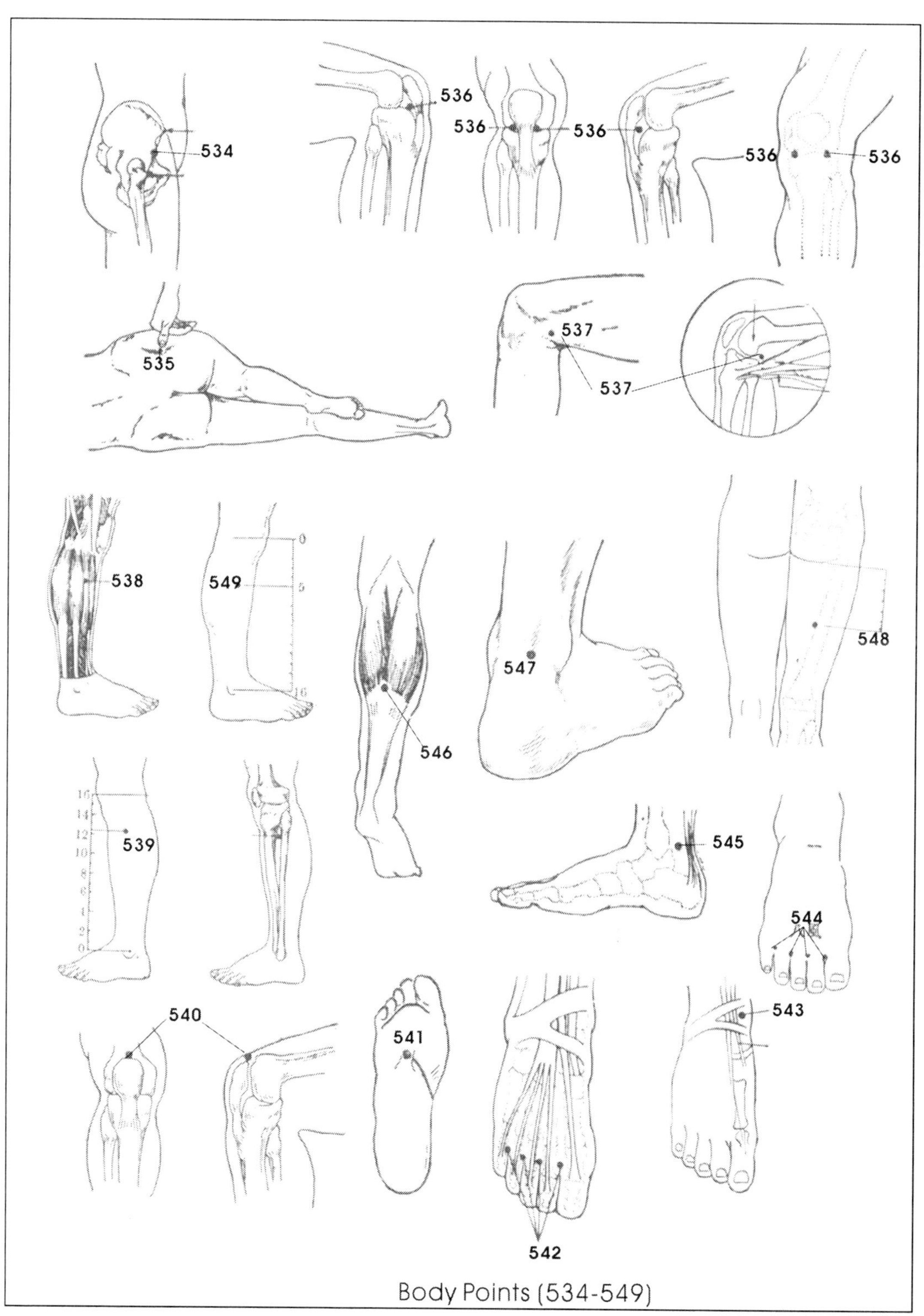

Body Points (534-549)

Test 6: Body Points

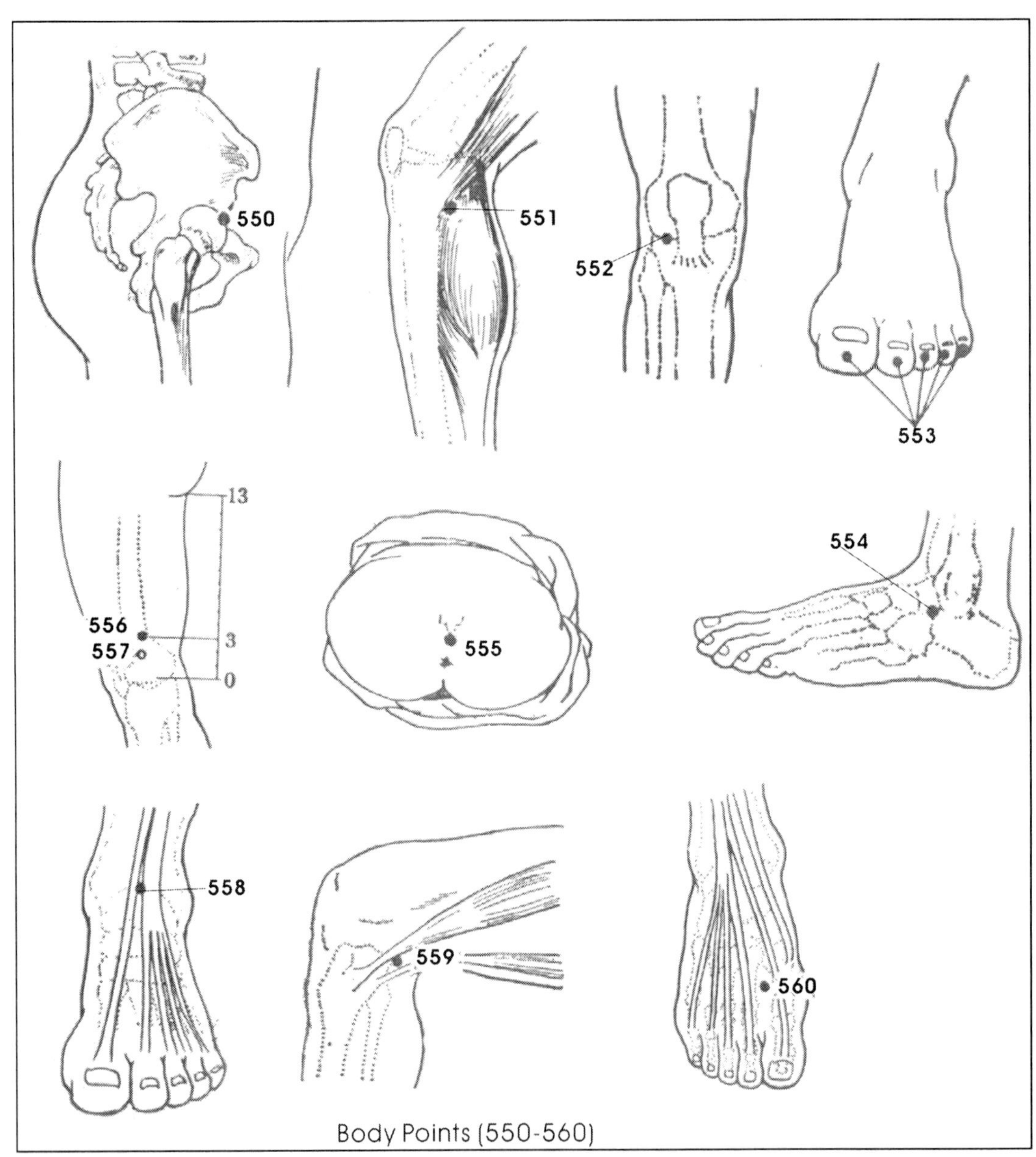

Body Points (550-560)

Test 6: Body Points

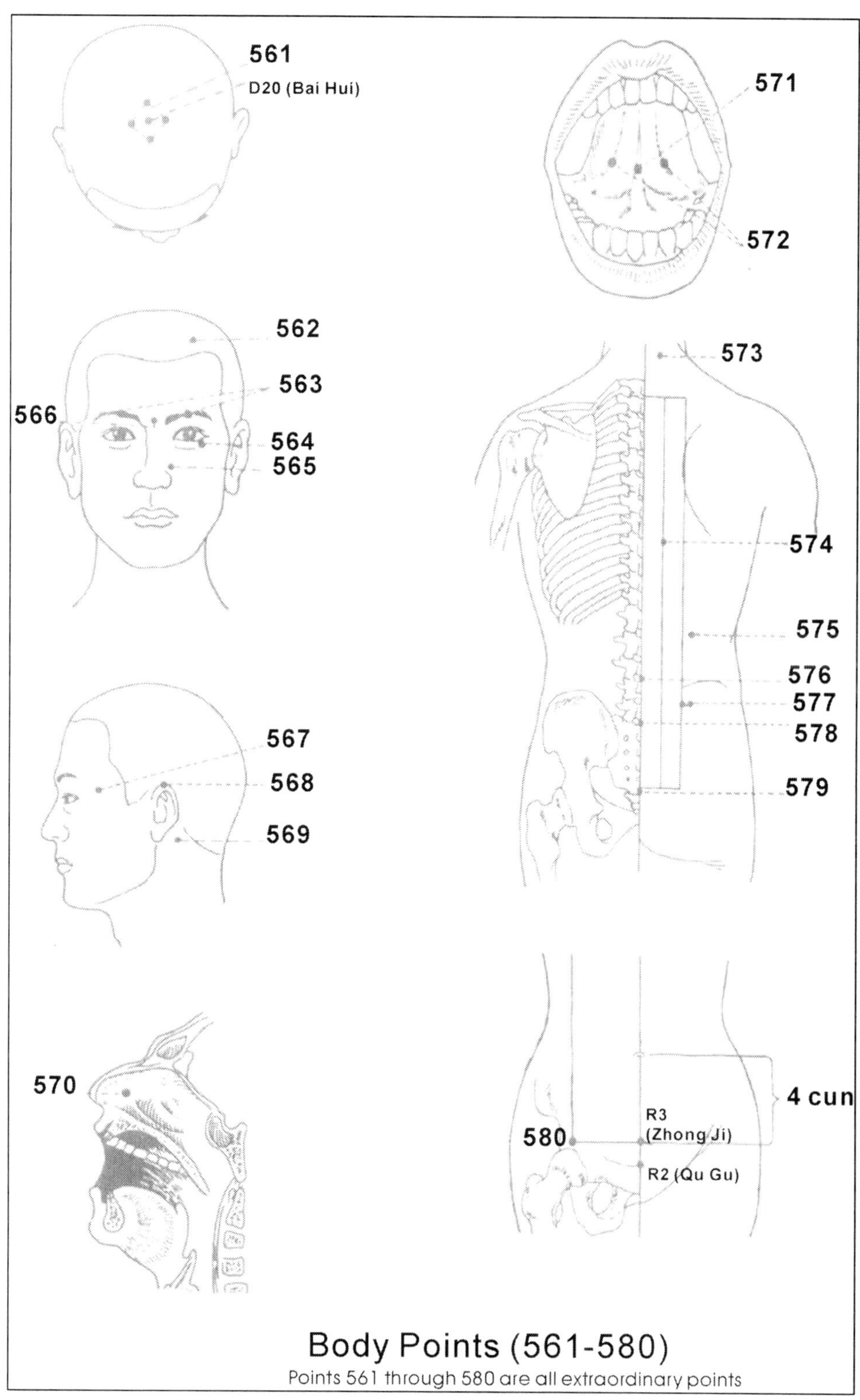

Test 6: Body Points

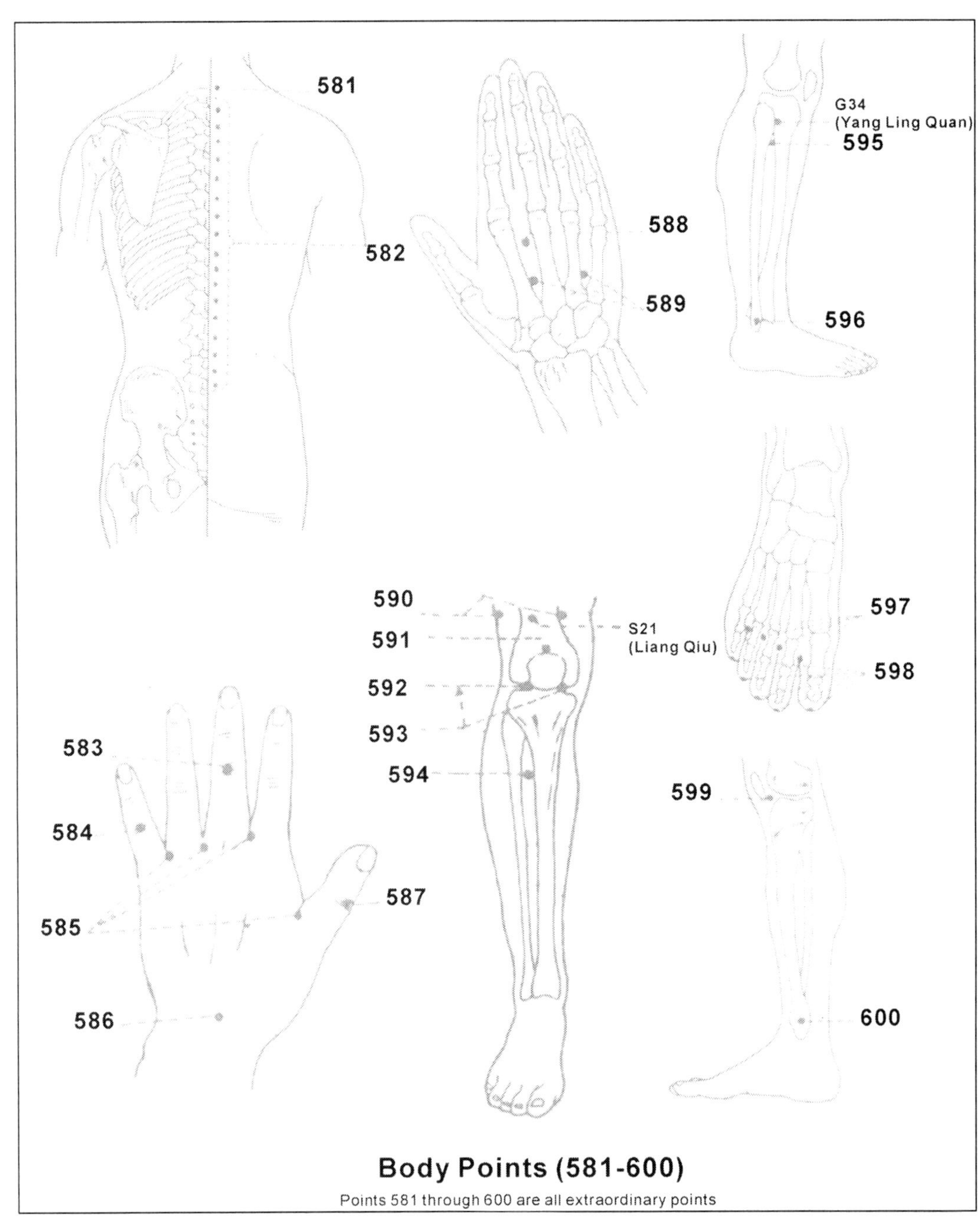

Test 6: Body Points

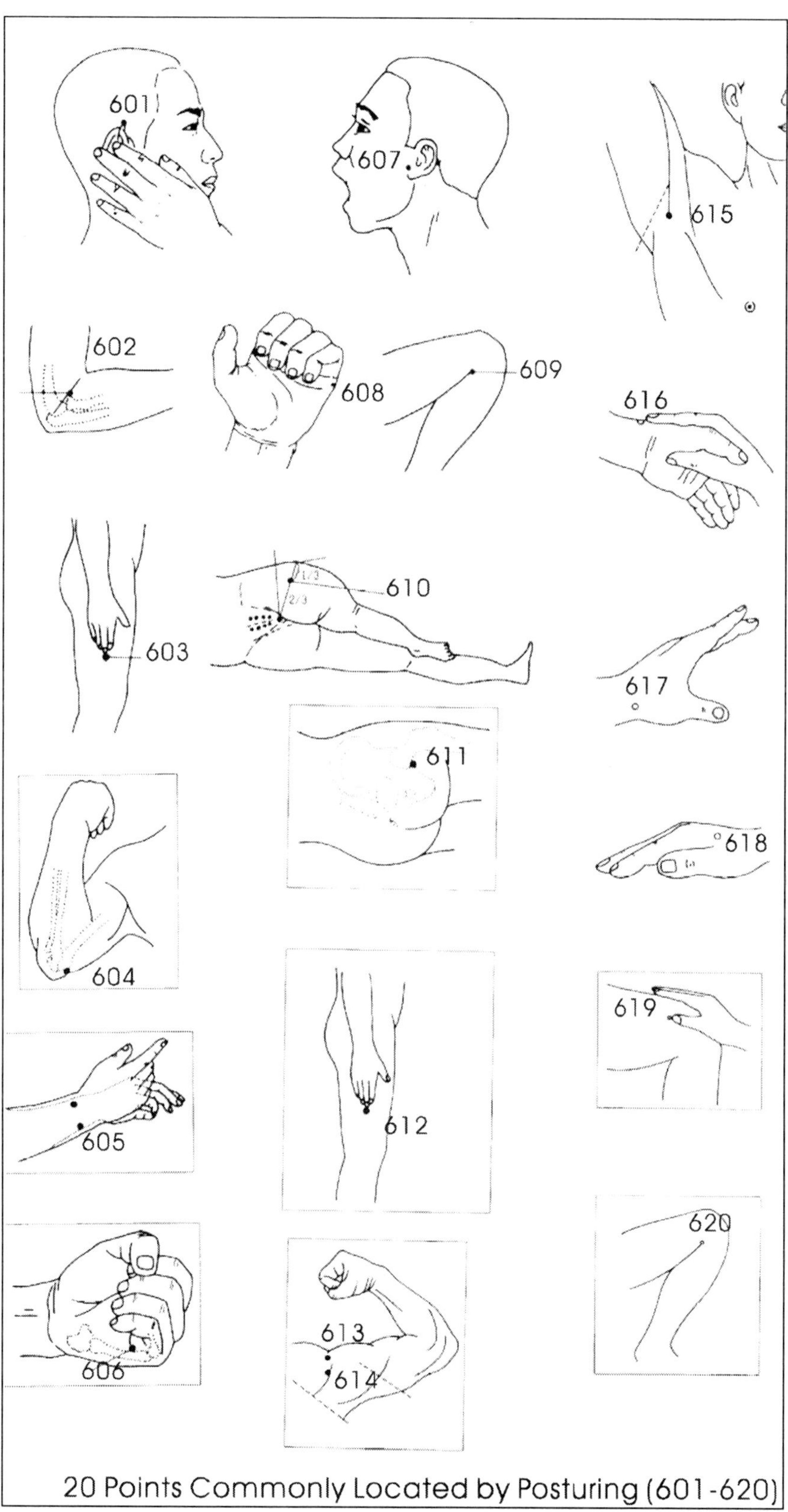

20 Points Commonly Located by Posturing (601-620)

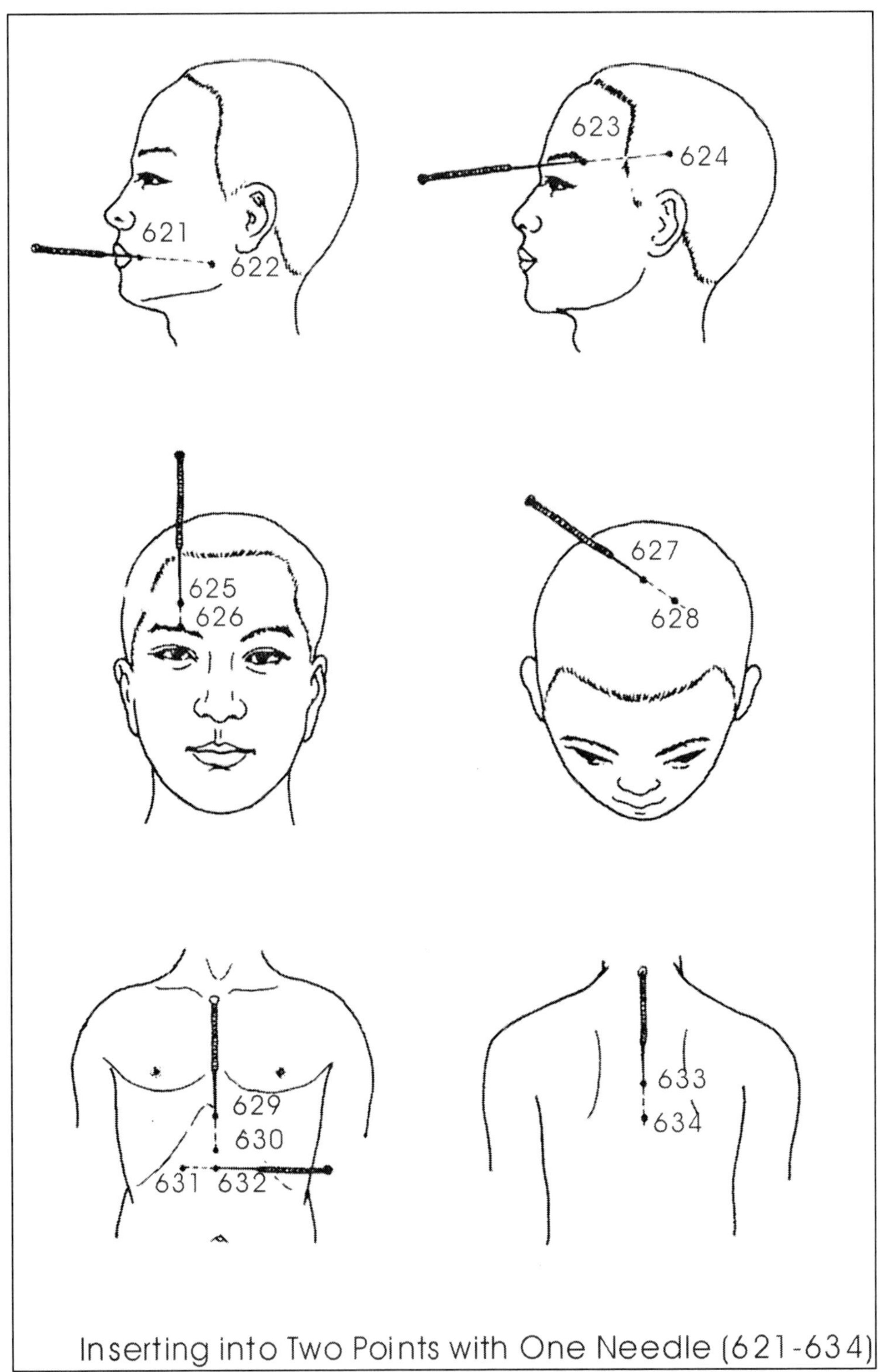

Inserting into Two Points with One Needle (621-634)

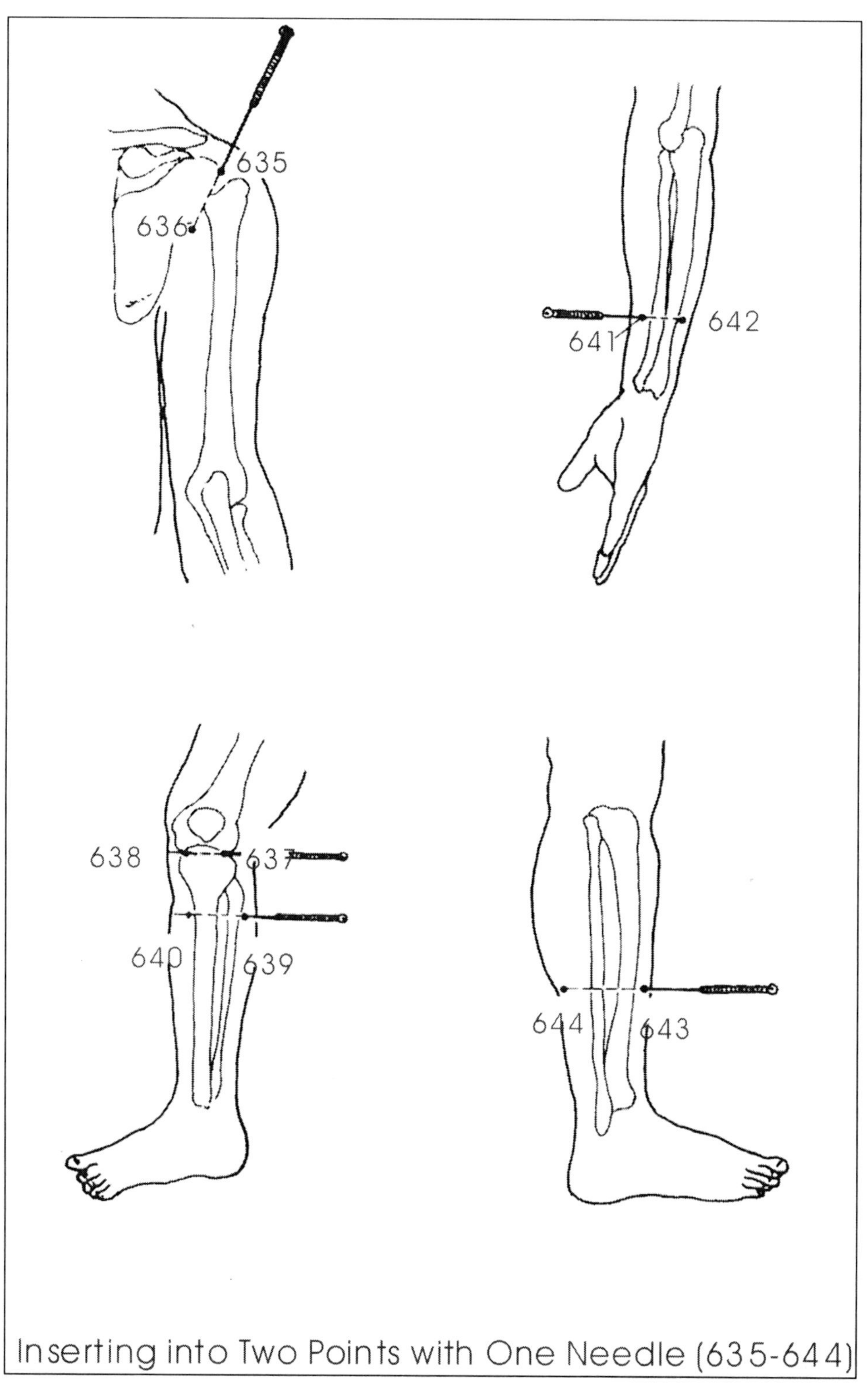

Inserting into Two Points with One Needle (635-644)

Test 5: Body Points (1-644)

1		42		83		124		165		206	
2		43		84		125		166		207	
3		44		85		126		167		208	
4		45		86		127		168		209	
5		46		87		128		169		210	
6		47		88		129		170		211	
7		48		89		130		171		212	
8		49		90		131		172		213	
9		50		91		132		173		214	
10		51		92		133		174		215	
11		52		93		134		175		216	
12		53		94		135		176		217	
13		54		95		136		177		218	
14		55		96		137		178		219	
15		56		97		138		179		220	
16		57		98		139		180		221	
17		58		99		140		181		222	
18		59		100		141		182		223	
19		60		101		142		183		224	
20		61		102		143		184		225	
21		62		103		144		185		226	
22		63		104		145		186		227	
23		64		105		146		187		228	
24		65		106		147		188		229	
25		66		107		148		189		230	
26		67		108		149		190		231	
27		68		109		150		191		232	
28		69		110		151		192		233	
29		70		111		152		193		234	
30		71		112		153		194		235	
31		72		113		154		195		236	
32		73		114		155		196		237	
33		74		115		156		197		238	
34		75		116		157		198		239	
35		76		117		158		199		240	
36		77		118		159		200		241	
37		78		119		160		201		242	
38		79		120		161		202		243	
39		80		121		162		203		244	
40		81		122		163		204		245	
41		82		123		164		205		246	

Test 6: Body Points

247		289		331		373		415		457	
248		290		332		374		416		458	
249		291		333		375		417		459	
250		292		334		376		418		460	
251		293		335		377		419		461	
252		294		336		378		420		462	
253		295		337		379		421		463	
254		296		338		380		422		464	
255		297		339		381		423		465	
256		298		340		382		424		466	
257		299		341		383		425		467	
258		300		342		384		426		468	
259		301		343		385		427		469	
260		302		344		386		428		470	
261		303		345		387		429		471	
262		304		346		388		430		472	
263		305		347		389		431		473	
264		306		348		390		432		474	
265		307		349		391		433		475	
266		308		350		392		434		476	
267		309		351		393		435		477	
268		310		352		394		436		478	
269		311		353		395		437		479	
270		312		354		396		438		480	
271		313		355		397		439		481	
272		314		356		398		440		482	
273		315		357		399		441		483	
274		316		358		400		442		484	
275		317		359		401		443		485	
276		318		360		402		444		486	
277		319		361		403		445		487	
278		320		362		404		446		488	
279		321		363		405		447		489	
280		322		364		406		448		490	
281		323		365		407		449		491	
282		324		366		408		450		492	
283		325		367		409		451		493	
284		326		368		410		452		494	
285		327		369		411		453		495	
286		328		370		412		454		496	
287		329		371		413		455		497	
288		330		372		414		456		498	

Test 6: Body Points

499		523		547		571		595		621	
500		524		548		572		596		622	
501		525		549		573		597		623	
502		526		550		574		598		624	
503		527		551		575		599		625	
504		528		552		576		600		626	
505		529		553		577		601		627	
506		530		554		578		602		628	
507		531		555		579		603		629	
508		532		556		580		604		630	
509		533		557		581		605		631	
510		534		558		582		606		632	
511		535		559		583		607		633	
512		536		560		584		608		634	
513		537		561		585		609		635	
514		538		562		586		610		636	
515		539		563		587		611		637	
516		540		564		588		612		638	
517		541		565		589		613		639	
518		542		566		590		614		640	
519		543		567		591		615		641	
520		544		568		592		616		642	
521		545		569		593		617		643	
522		546		570		594		618		644	
								619			
								620			

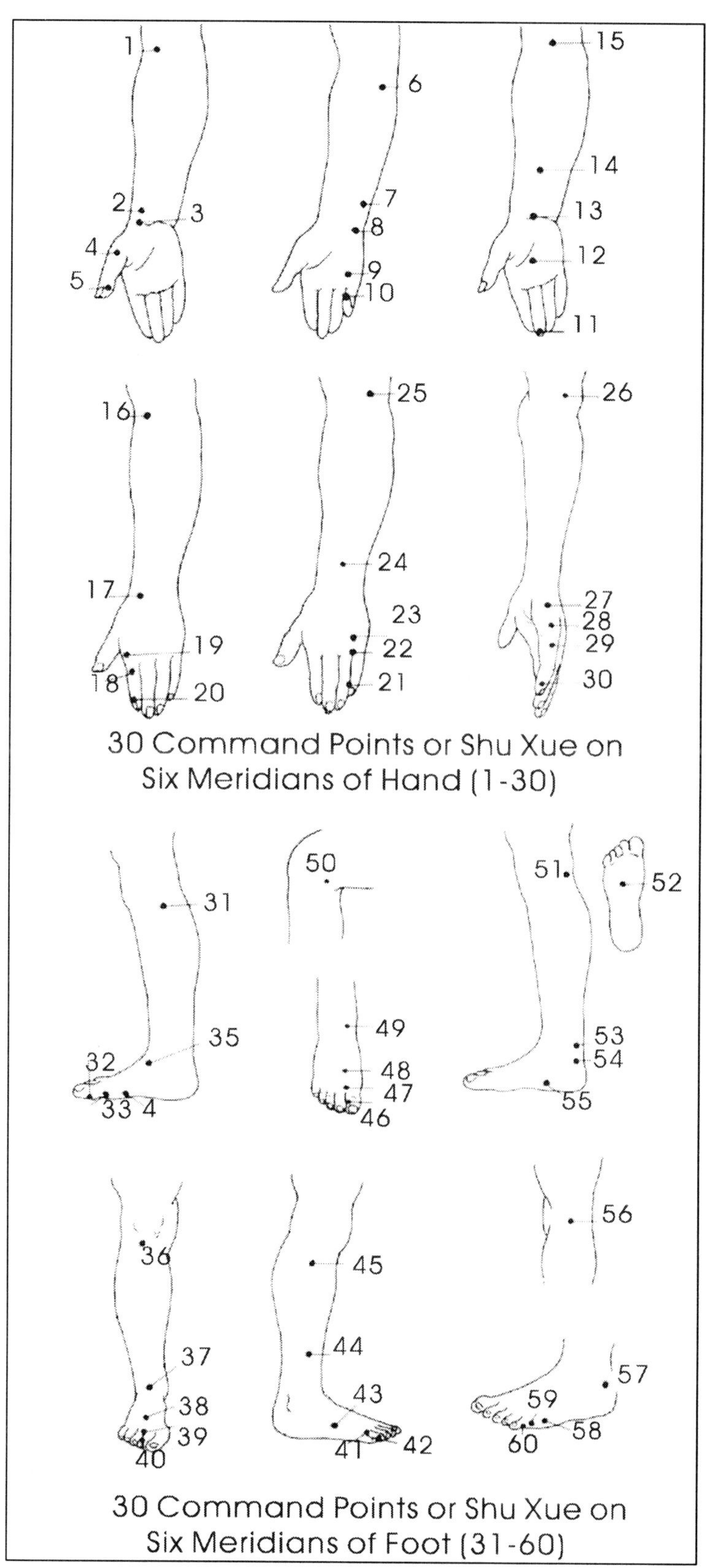

30 Command Points or Shu Xue on Six Meridians of Hand (1-30)

30 Command Points or Shu Xue on Six Meridians of Foot (31-60)

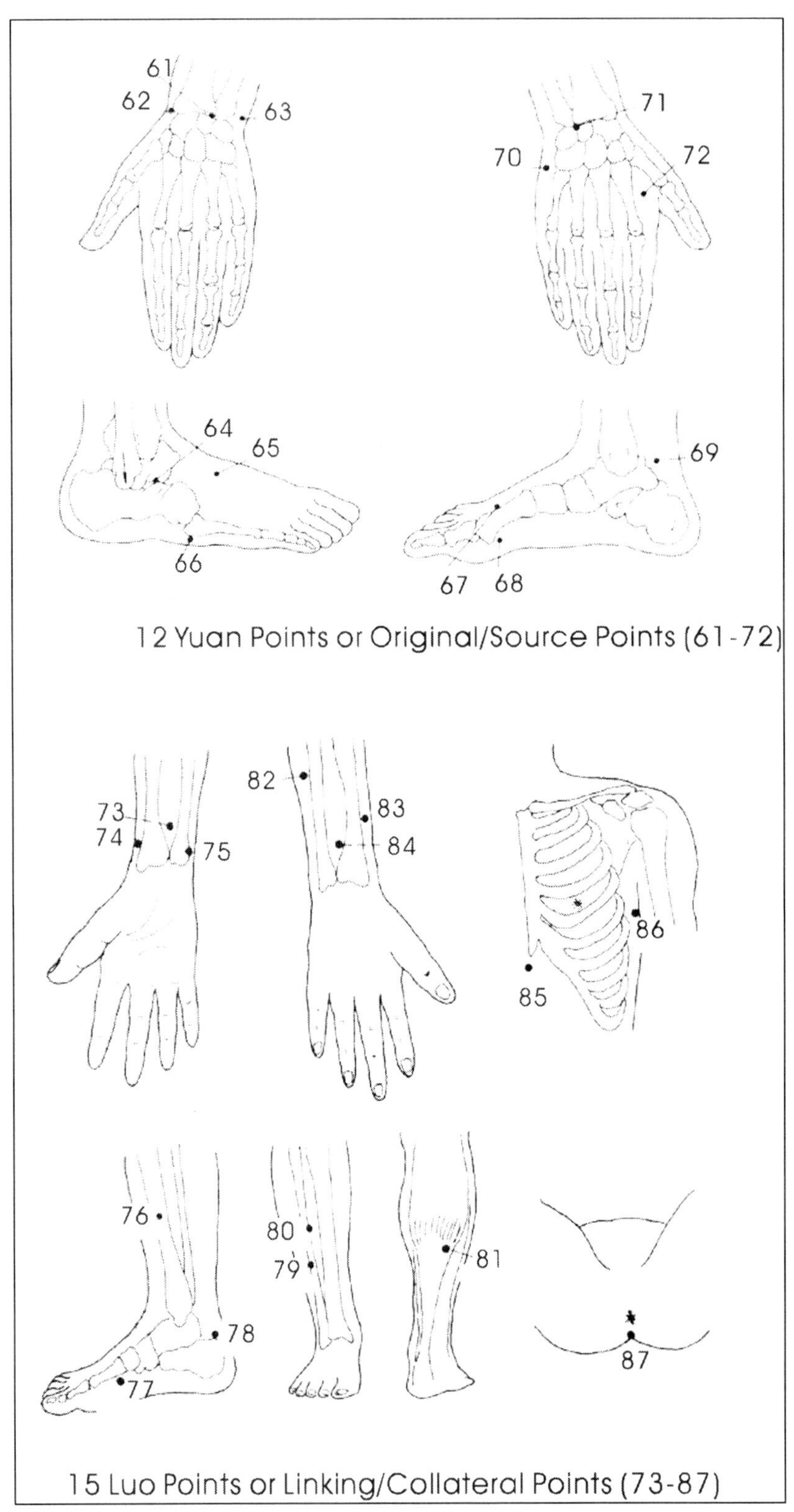

12 Yuan Points or Original/Source Points (61-72)

15 Luo Points or Linking/Collateral Points (73-87)

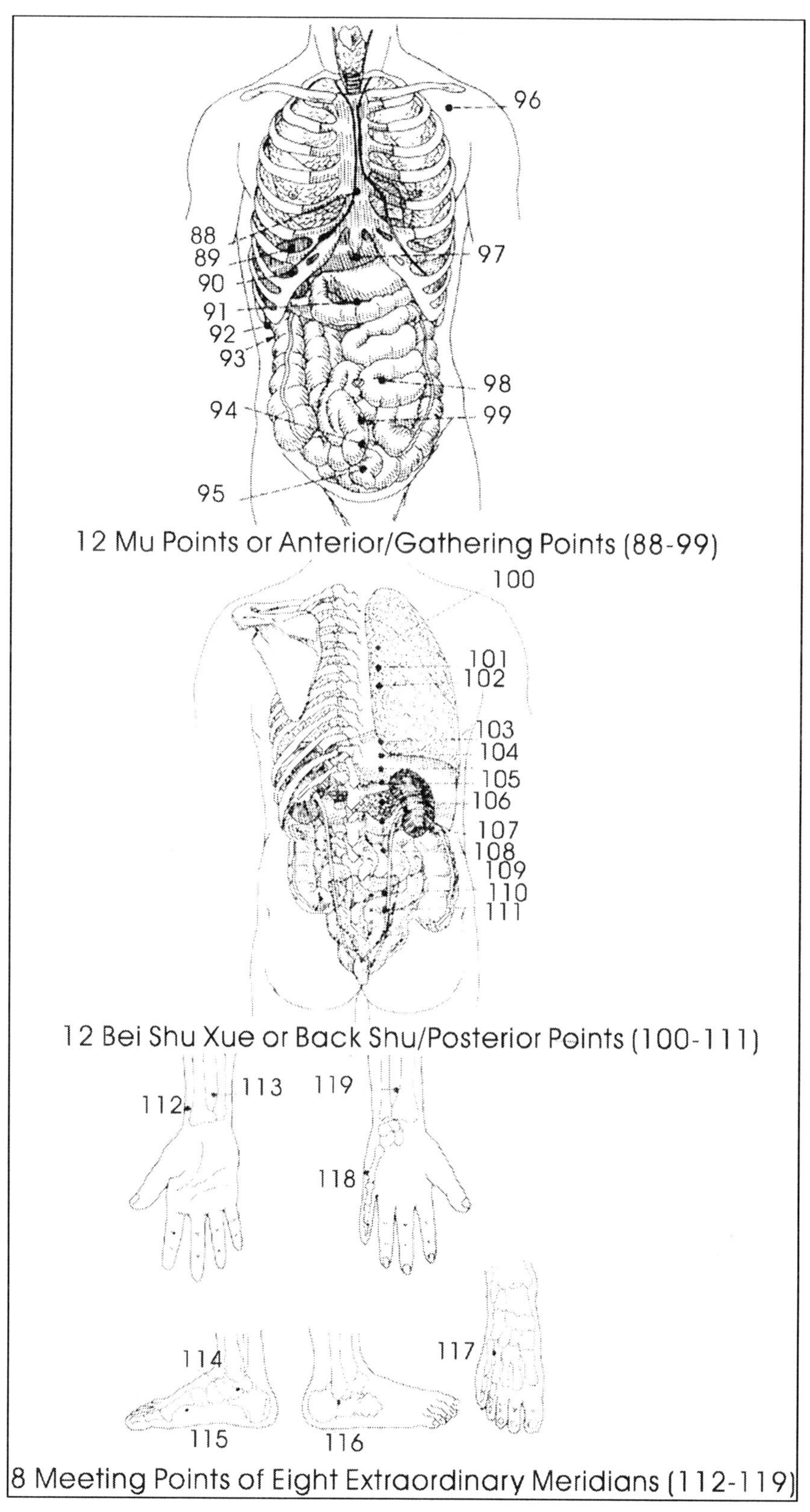
96
88
89
90
91
92
93
97
98
94
99
95
12 Mu Points or Anterior/Gathering Points (88-99)
100
101
102
103
104
105
106
107
108
109
110
111
12 Bei Shu Xue or Back Shu/Posterior Points (100-111)
113
119
112
118
117
114
115
116
8 Meeting Points of Eight Extraordinary Meridians (112-119)

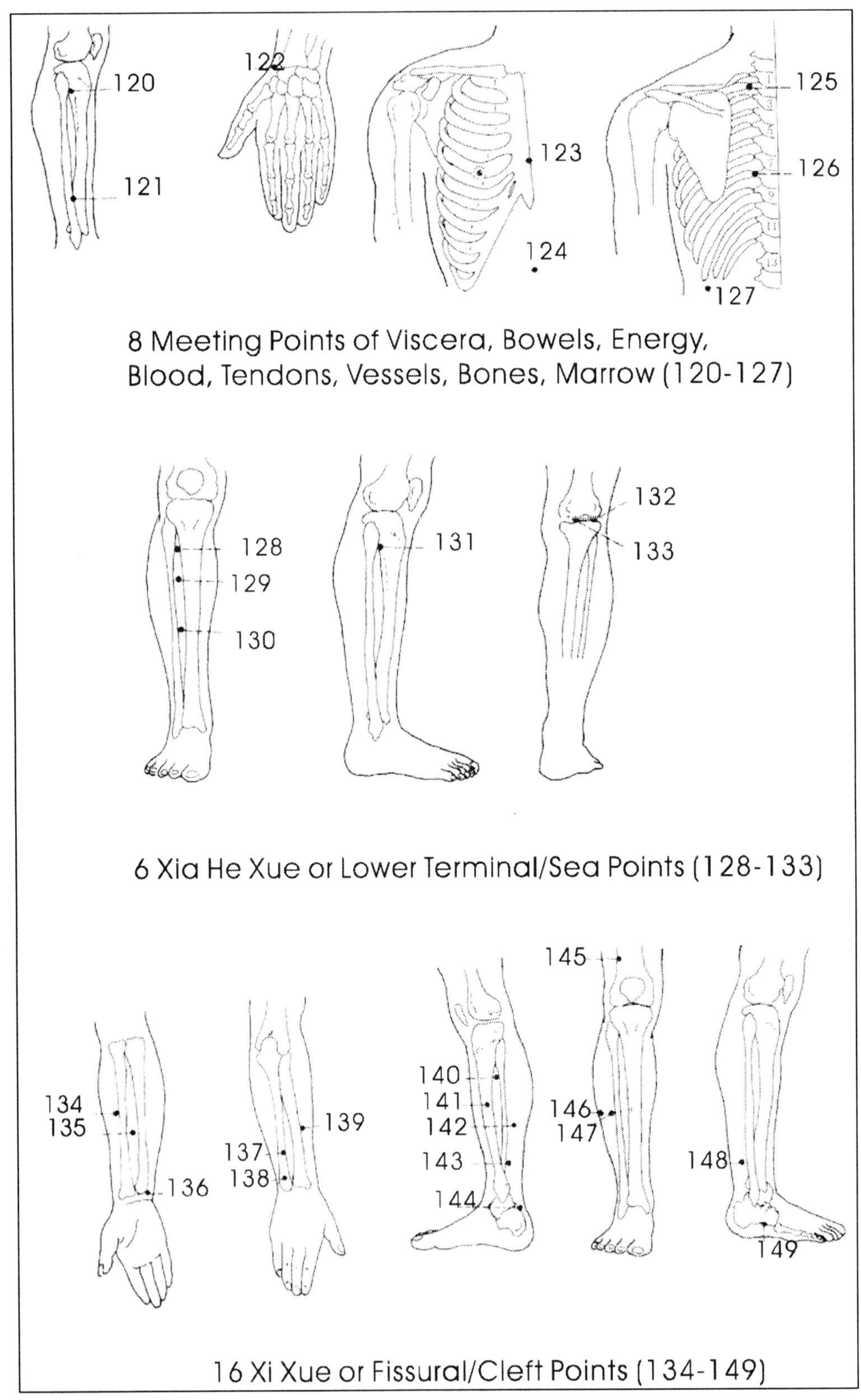
120
121
122
123
124
125
126
127
8 Meeting Points of Viscera, Bowels, Energy, Blood, Tendons, Vessels, Bones, Marrow (120-127)
128
129
130
131
132
133
6 Xia He Xue or Lower Terminal/Sea Points (128-133)
145
140
141
142
143
144
134
135
136
137
138
139
146
147
148
149
16 Xi Xue or Fissural/Cleft Points (134-149)

Test 7: Specially Designated Points

Test 7-1 Command Points or Shu Xue on Six Meridians of Hand (1-30)

1		6		11		16		21		26	
2		7		12		17		22		27	
3		8		13		18		23		28	
4		9		14		19		24		29	
5		10		15		20		25		30	

Test 7-2 Command Points or Shu Xue on Six Meridians of Foot (1-30)

1		6		11		16		21		26	
2		7		12		17		22		27	
3		8		13		18		23		28	
4		9		14		19		24		29	
5		10		15		20		25		30	

Test 7-3 Yuan Points or Source Points (1-12)

1		3		5		7		9		11	
2		4		6		8		10		12	

Test 7-4 Luo Points or Linking/Collateral Points (1-15)

1		4		7		10		13	
2		5		8		11		14	
3		6		9		12		15	

Test 7-5 Mu Points or Anterior Points (1-12)

1		3		5		7		9		11	
2		4		6		8		10		12	

Test 7-6 Bei Shu Points or Back Shu/Posterior Points (1-12)

1		3		5		7		9		11	
2		4		6		8		10		12	

Test 7-7 Meeting Points of Eight Extraordinary Meridians (1-8)

1		4		7	
2		5		8	
3		6			

Test 7-8 influential points (1-8).

1		4		7	
2		5		8	
3		6			

Test 7-9 xia he xue or Lower Sea Points (1-6)

1		3		5	
2		4		6	

Test 7-10 Xi Xue or Fissural/Cleft Points (1-16)

1		4		7		10		13		16	
2		5		8		11		14			
3		6		9		12		15			

Test 7-11 (1-12) write down the name of Mu Points / Anterior Points on the right column to pair off the Shu and Mu points / 根据俞幕配穴法在右栏写下幕穴名称.

	Bei Shu Points or Back Shu/Posterior Points	Mu Points or Anterior Points
1	B13, Fèi Shū, 肺輸	
2	B14, Jué Yīn Shū, 厥陰輸	
3	B15, Xīn Shū, 心輸	
4	B18, Gān Shū, 肝輸	
5	B19, Dăn Shū, 膽輸	
6	B20, Pí Shū, 脾輸	
7	B21, Wèi Shū, 胃俞	
8	B22, Sān Jiāo Shū, 三焦輸	
9	B23, Shèn Shū, 腎輸	
10	B25, Dà Cháng Shū, 大腸輸	
11	B27, Xiăo Cháng Shū, 小腸輸	
12	B28, Páng Guāng Shū, 膀胱輸	

Test 7-12 (1-12) write down the name of Luo Points / Linking / Collateral Points on the right column to pair off the Yuan points and Luo points / 根据原络配穴法在右栏写下络穴名称.

	Yuan Points or Source Points	Luo Points or Linking/Collateral Points
1	P7, Dà Líng 大陵	
2	Lu9, Tài Yuān 太淵	
3	H7, Shén Mén 神門	
4	G40, Qiū Xū 丘墟	
5	S42, Chōng Yáng 沖陽	
6	B64, Jīng Gŭ, 京骨	
7	Lv3, Tài Chōng 太沖	
8	Sp3, Tài Bái 太白	
9	K3, Tài Xī 太溪	
10	Si4, Wàn Gŭ 腕骨	
11	Sj4, Yáng Chí 陽池	
12	Li4, Hé Gŭ 合谷	

Test 7-13 (1-12) write down the name of Child Points on the right column to pair off the Mother points and Child points / 根据母子配穴法在右栏写下子穴名称.

	Mother points / 母穴	Child points / 子穴
1	B67, Zhì Yīn, 至陰	

2	Lv8, Qū Quán 曲泉	
3	K7, Fù Liū 復溜	
4	Sp2, Dà Dū 大都	
5	S41, Jiě Xī 解溪	
6	Lu9, Tài Yuān 太淵	
7	H9, Shào Chōng 少冲	
8	P9, Zhōng Chōng 中冲	
9	Li11, Qū Chí 曲池	
10	Sj3, Zhōng Zhǔ 中渚	
11	Si3, Hòu Xī 后溪	
12	G43, Xiá Xī 俠溪	

Test 7-14 (1-5) write down the name of northern points on the right column to pair off the southern points and northern points / 根据泻南补北配穴法在右栏写下北穴名称.

	Southern points for sedation / 南穴	Northern points for tonification / 北穴
1	H8, Shào Fǔ 少府	
2	Sp3, Tài Bái 太白	
3	Lv8, Qū Quán 曲泉	
4	Lu8, Jīng Qú 經渠	
5	Lv1, Dà Dūn 大敦	

Test 7-15 (1-11) write down the name of well points [jǐng xué] on the right column, beginning with B67, Zhì Yīn, 至陰 to complete the cycle of twelve meridians in their connecting sequences in order to induce yang from yin / 根据接经从阴引阳配穴法在右栏写下井穴名称, 从至陰开始.

	Well points [jǐng xué] / 井穴
	B67, Zhì Yīn, 至陰
1	
2	
3	
4	

5	
6	
7	
8	
9	
10	
11	

Test 7-16 (1-11) write down the name of well points [jǐng xué] on the right column, beginning with Lu11, Shǎo Shāng to complete the cycle of twelve meridians in their connecting sequences in order to induce yin from yang / 根据接经从阳引阴配穴法在右栏写下井穴名称,发从少商开始.

	Well points [jǐng xué] / 井穴		Lu11, Shǎo Shāng 少商
		1	

2		7	
3		8	
4		9	
5		10	
6		11	

Test 7-17 (1-4) write down the name of confluence points [bā mài bā huì xué] on the right column to pair off the points on two columns / 根据交经八穴配穴法在右栏写下相配的八脈交會穴名称.

1	P6, Nèi Guān 內關	
2	K6, Zhào Hăi 照海	
3	B62, Shēn Mài, 申脈	
4	G41, Zú Lín Qì, Lín Qì 足臨泣	

Test 7-18 (1-4) write down the name of influential points [bā huì xué] on the right column to pair off fissural points and influential points / 根据交经八穴配穴法在右栏写下相配的八會穴名称.

	Diseases / 疾病	fissural points, cleft points [xī xué, 郗穴];	influential points [bā huì xué, 八會穴]
1	Asthma with panting / 喘逆气急	Lu6, Kŏng Zuì 孔最	
2	Coughing out blood / 咳血	Lu6, Kŏng Zuì 孔最	
3	Acute stomachache / 胃痛剧烈	S34, Liáng Qiū 梁丘	
4	Angina pectoris / 真心痛	P4, Xī Mén 郗門	

Test 8: Acupuncture Techniques

Test 8-1 Needles and Techniques

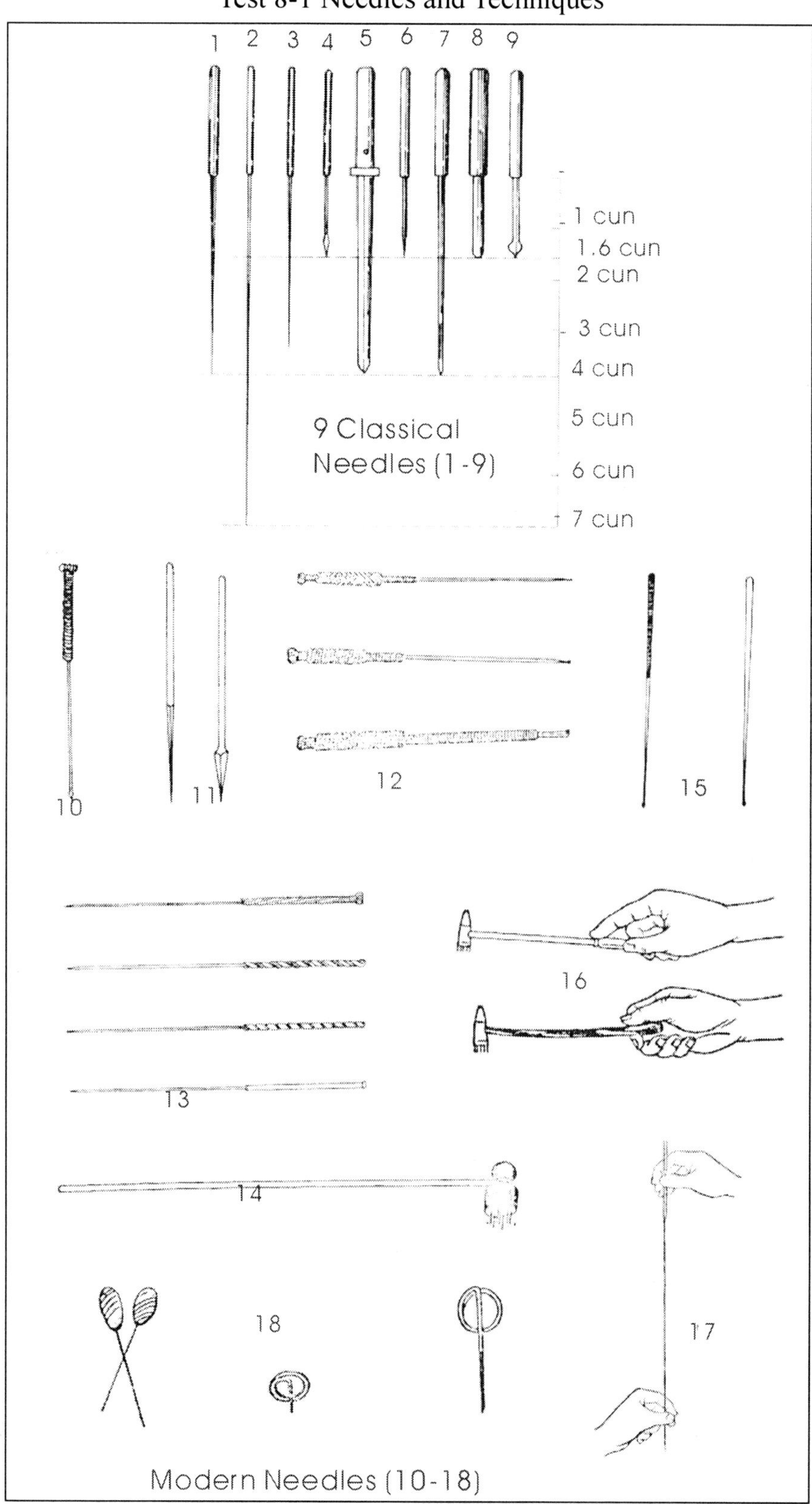

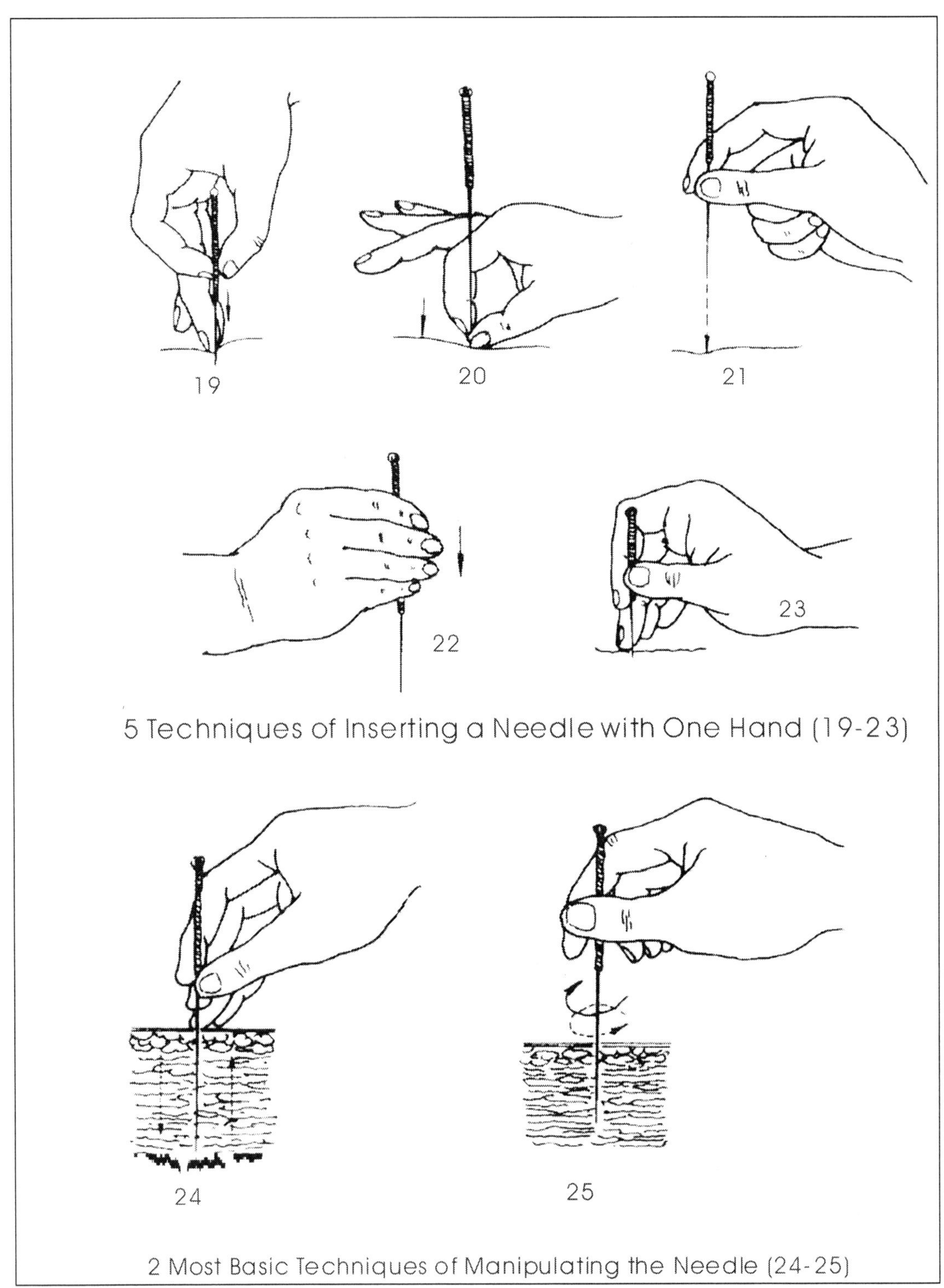

5 Techniques of Inserting a Needle with One Hand (19-23)

2 Most Basic Techniques of Manipulating the Needle (24-25)

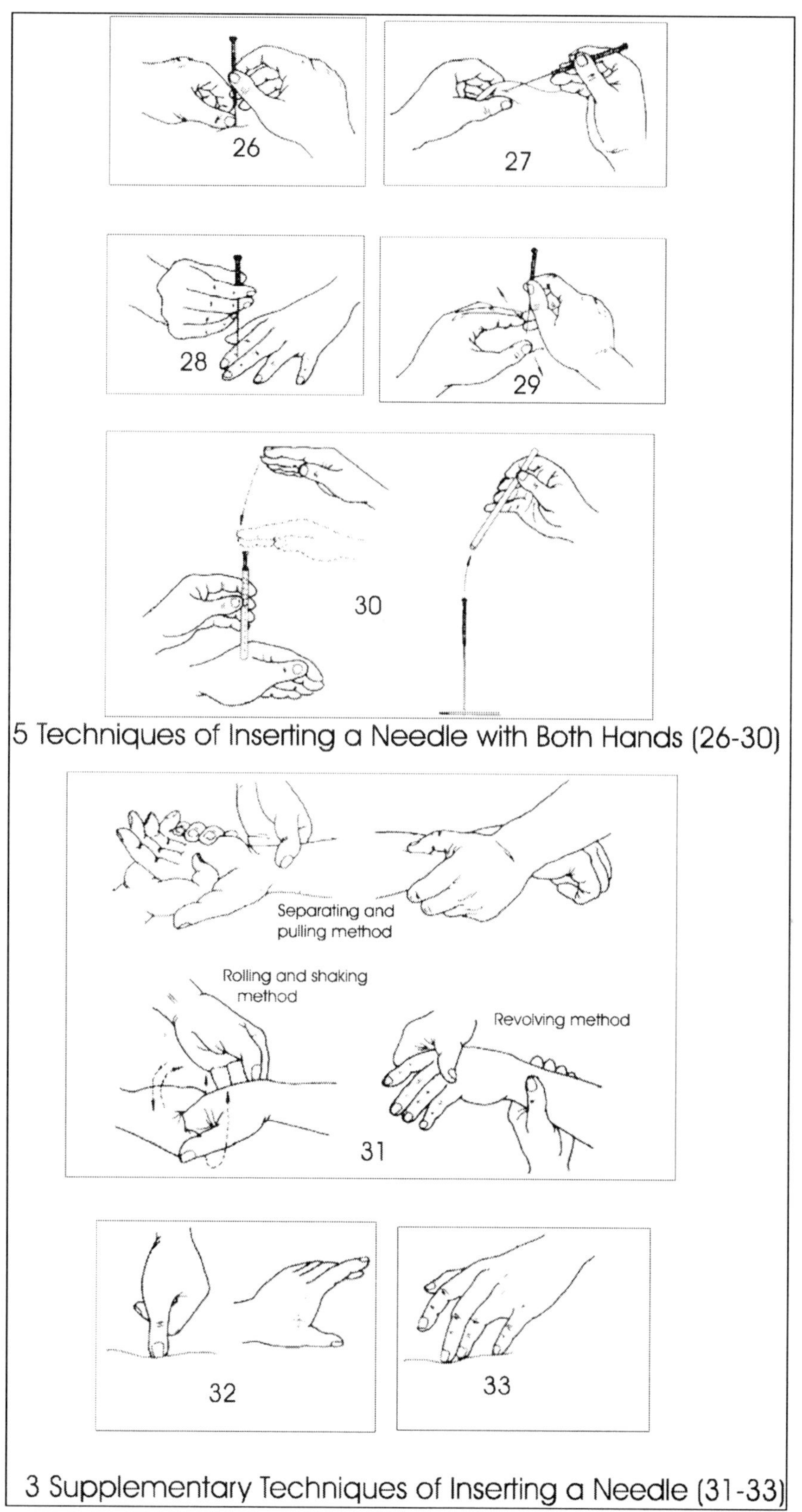

5 Techniques of Inserting a Needle with Both Hands (26-30)

3 Supplementary Techniques of Inserting a Needle (31-33)

Test 8-2 Techniques of Promoting Needling Sensations and Energy Circulation

1

2

3

4

5

6

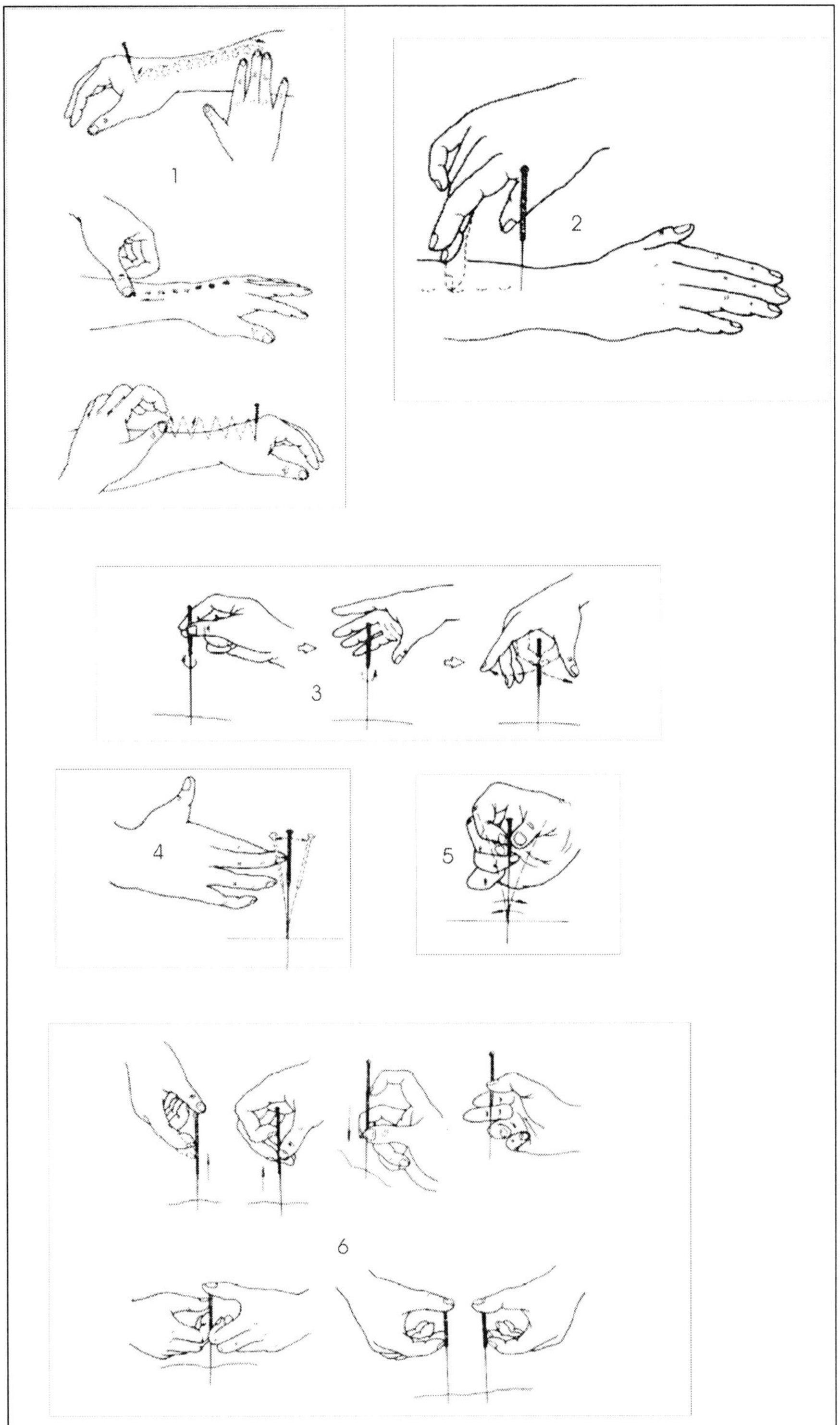

25 Techniques of Promoting Needling Sensations and Energy Circulation (1-6)

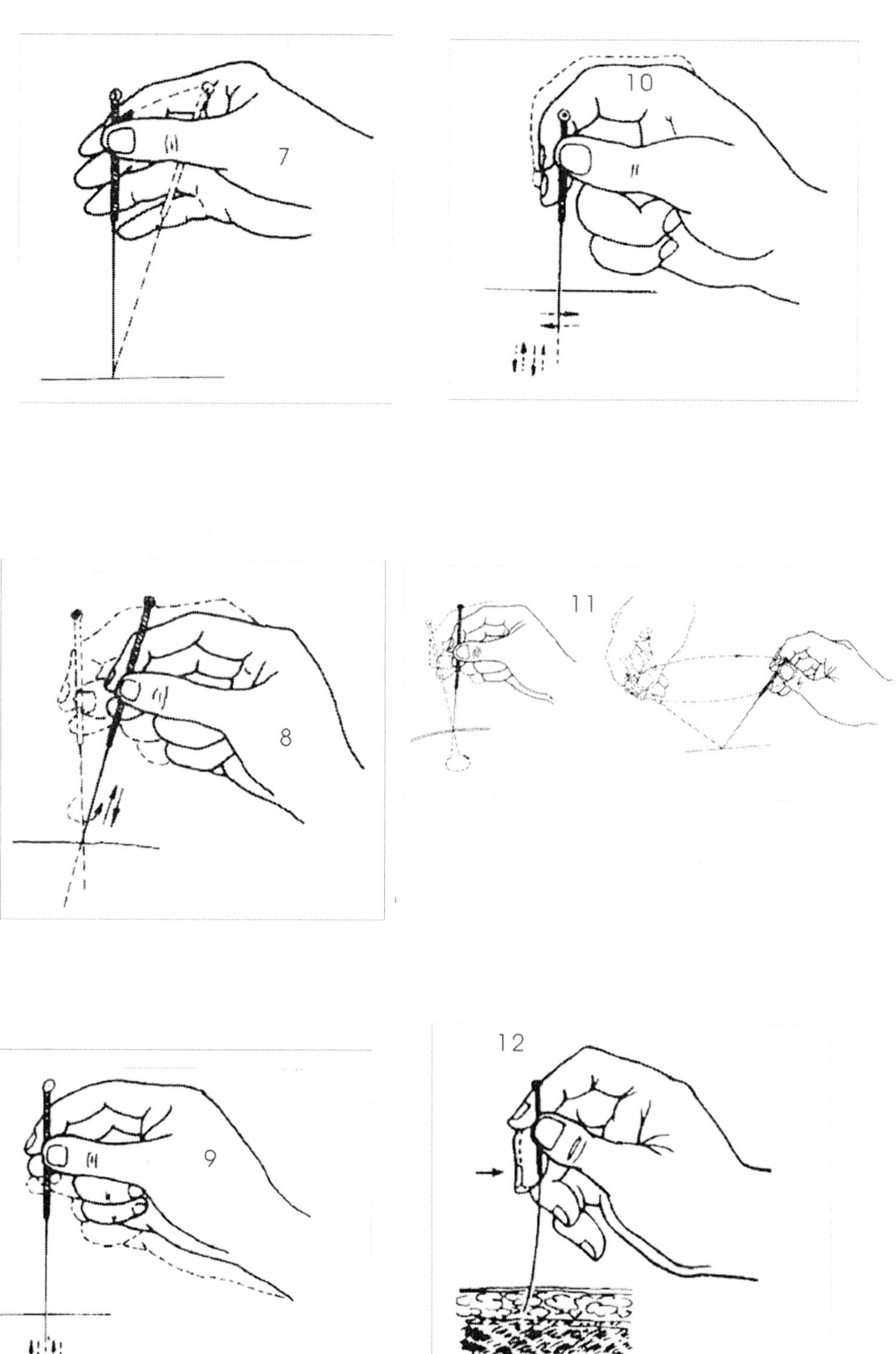

25 Techniques of Promoting Needling Sensations and Energy Circulation (7-12)

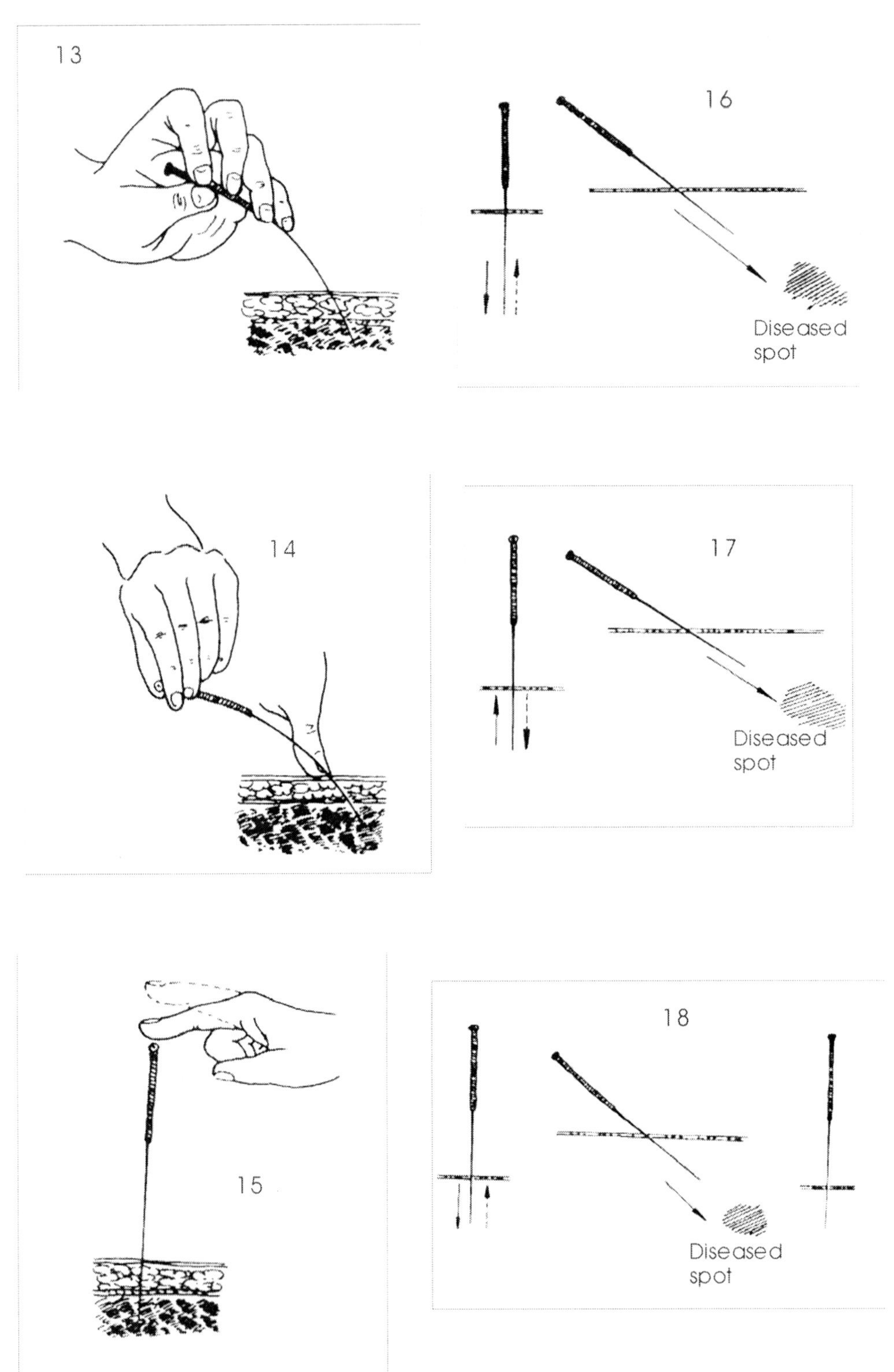

25 Techniques of Promoting Needling Sensations and Energy Circulation (13-18)

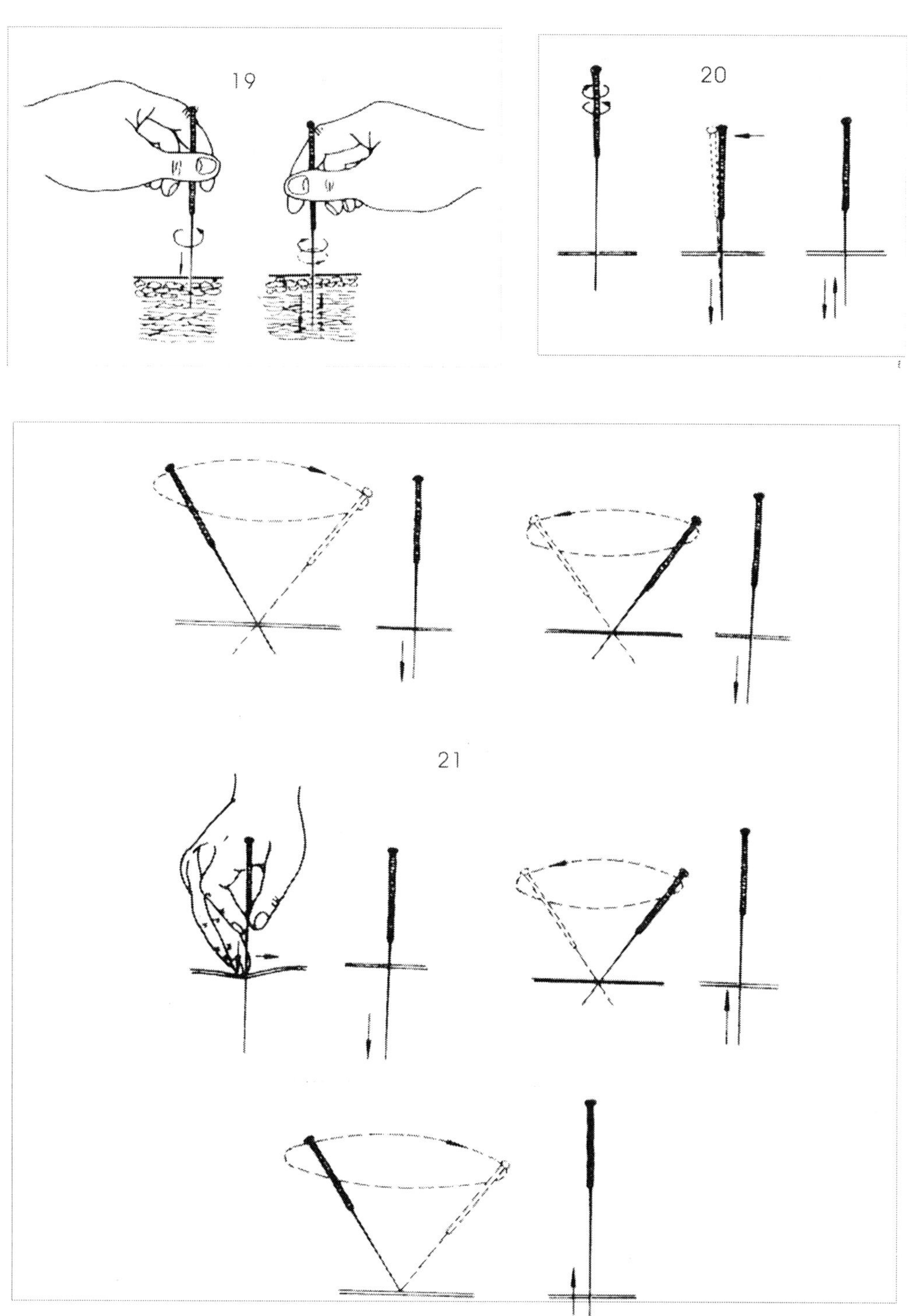

25 Techniques of Promoting Needling Sensations and Energy Circulation (19-21)

8-3 Techniques of Tonification and Sedation

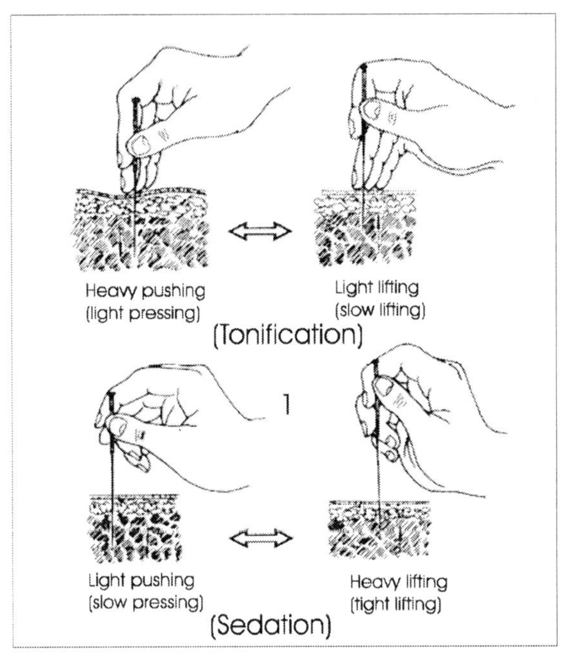

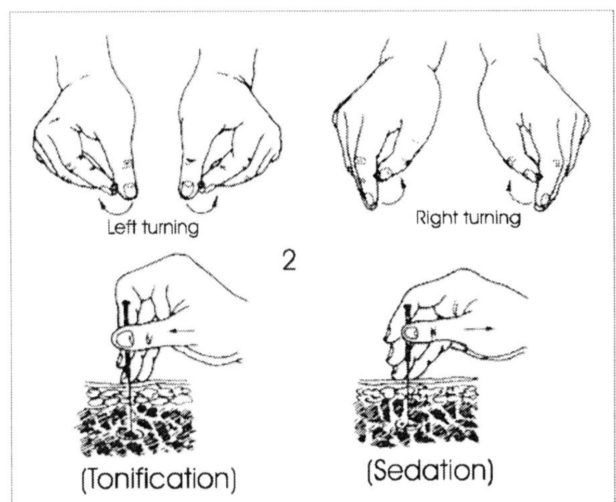

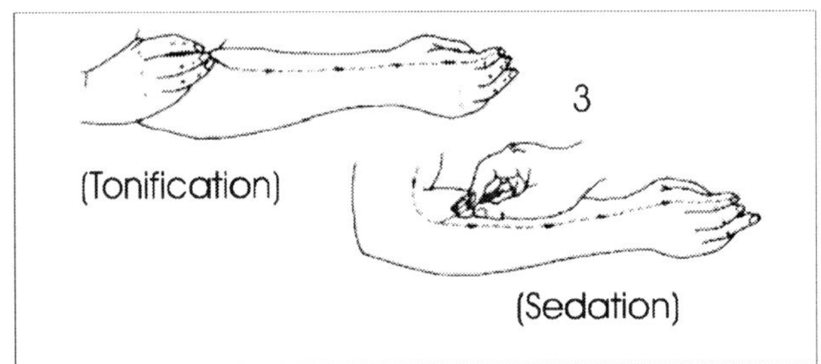

18 Techniques of Tonification and Sedation (1-3)

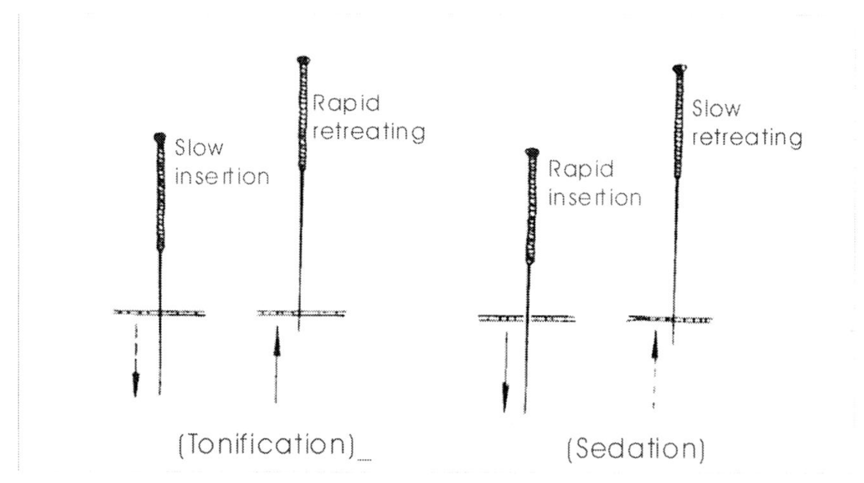

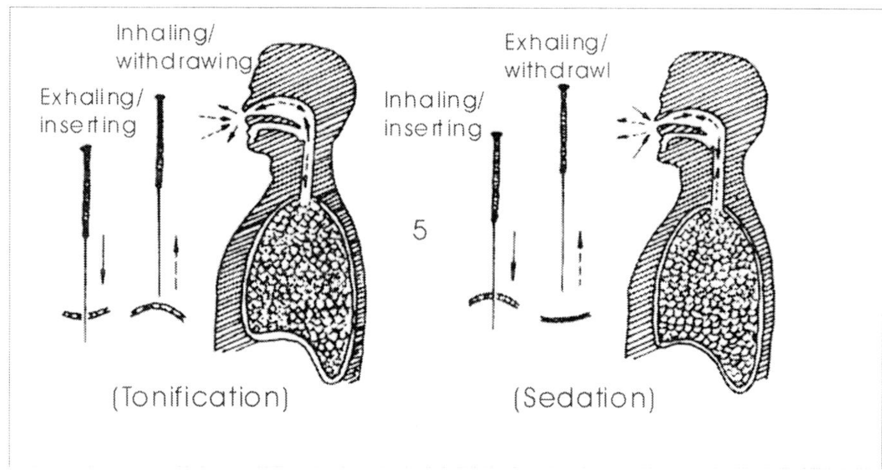

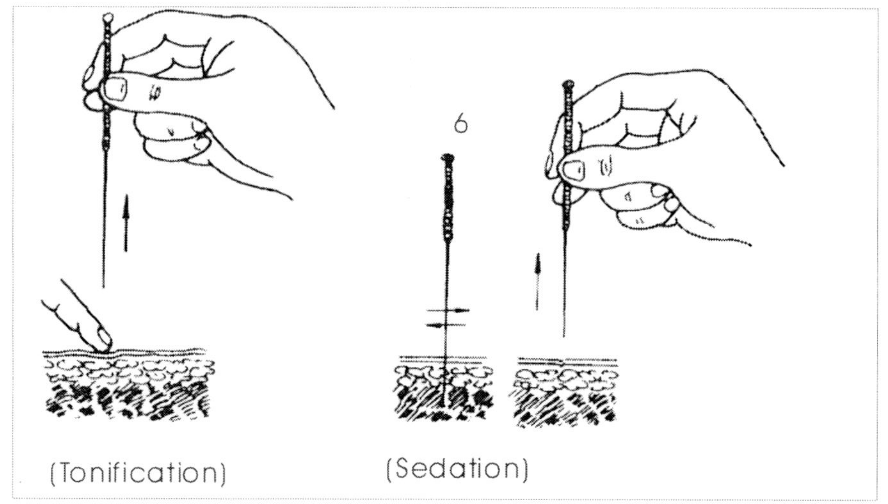

18 Techniques of Tonification and Sedation (4-6)

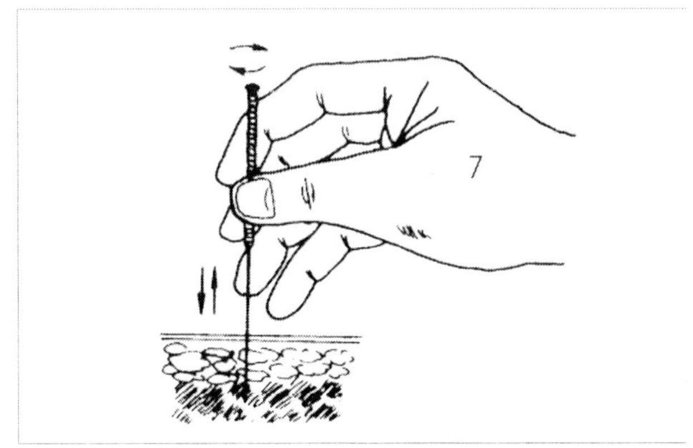

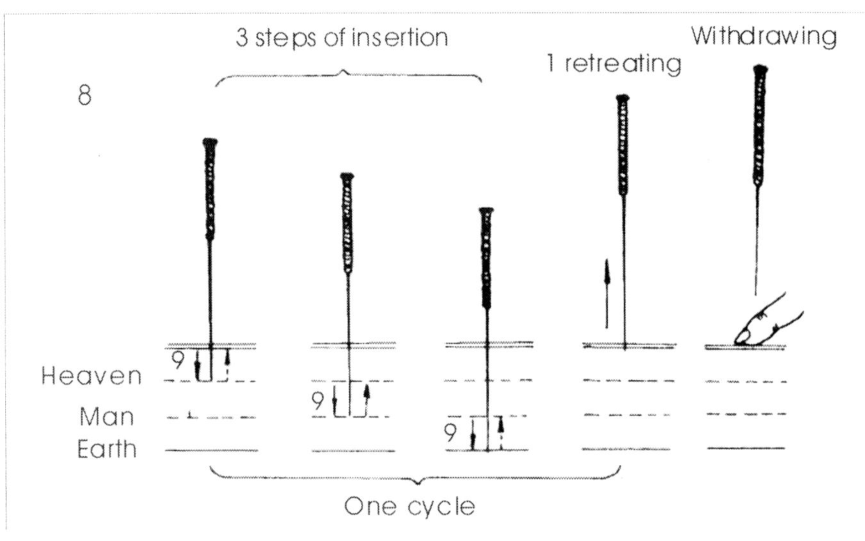

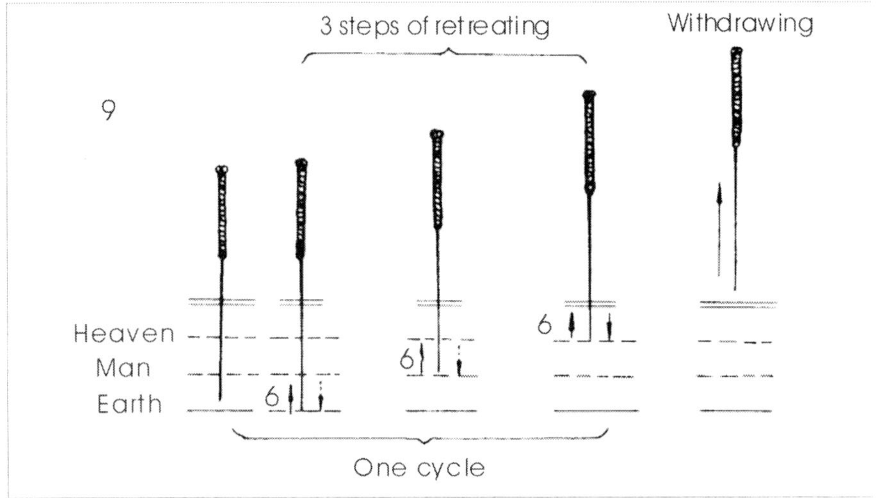

18 Techniques of Tonification and Sedation (7-9)

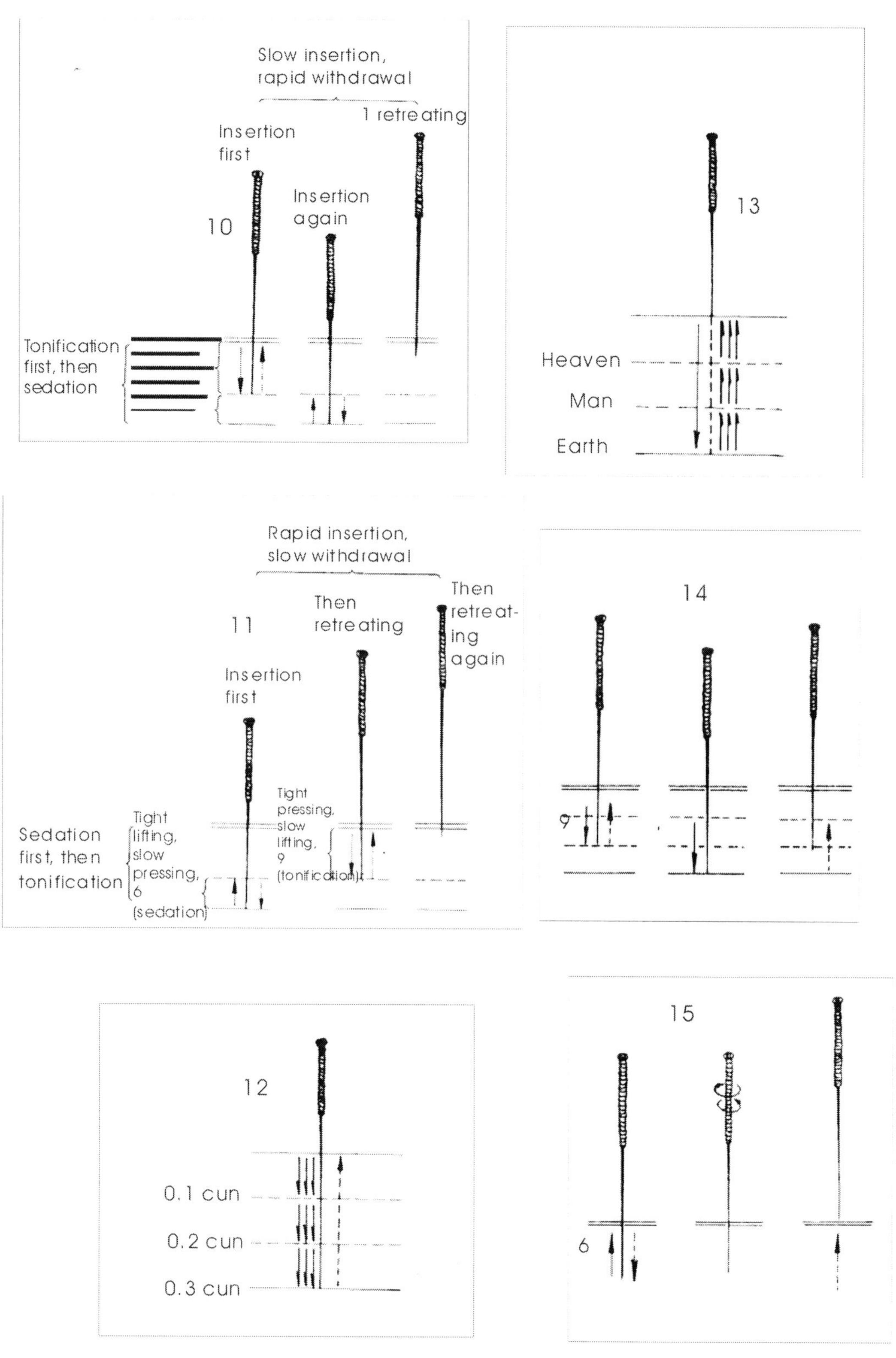

18 Techniques of Tonification and Sedation (10-15)

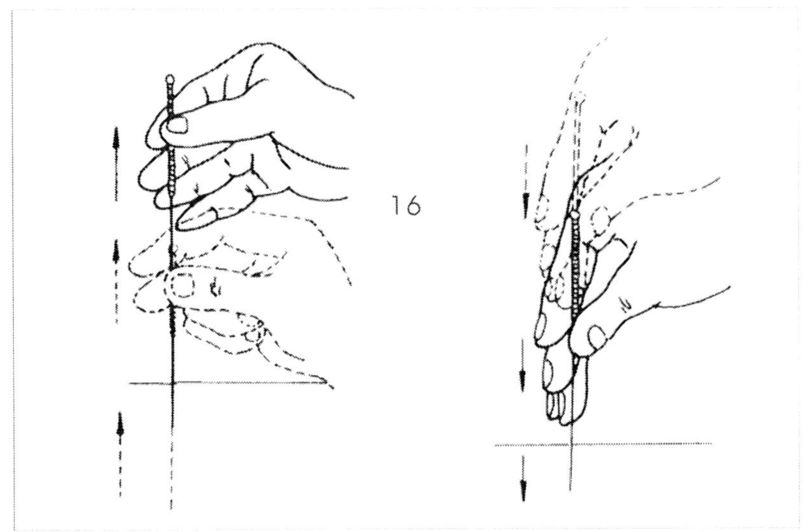

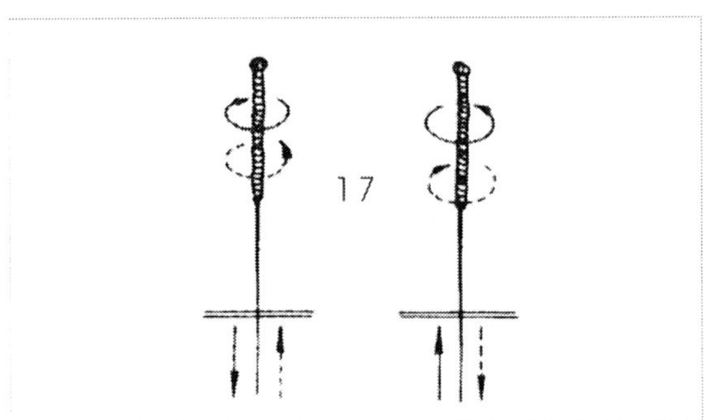

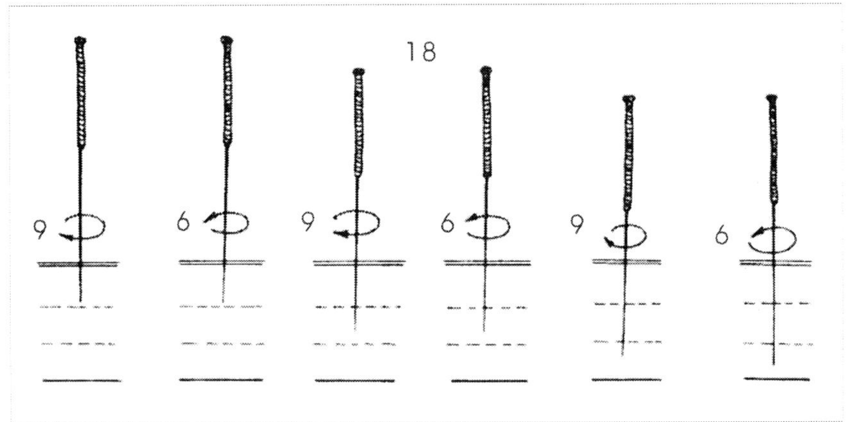

18 Techniques of Tonification and Sedation (16-18)

Test 8: Acupuncture Techniques

Test 8-1 Needles and Common Needling Techniques (1-33)

1		8		15		22		29	
2		9		16		23		30	
3		10		17		24		31	
4		11		18		25		32	
5		12		19		26		33	
6		13		20		27			
7		14		21		28			

Test 8-2 Techniques of Promoting Needling Sensations and Energy Circulation (1-25)

1		6		11		16		21	
2		7		12		17		22	
3		8		13		18		23	
4		9		14		19		24	
5		10		15		20		25	

Test 8-3 Techniques of Tonification and Sedation (1-18).

1		5		9		13		17	
2		6		10		14		18	
3		7		11		15			
4		8		12		16			

Test 9: Auricular Points (1-93)

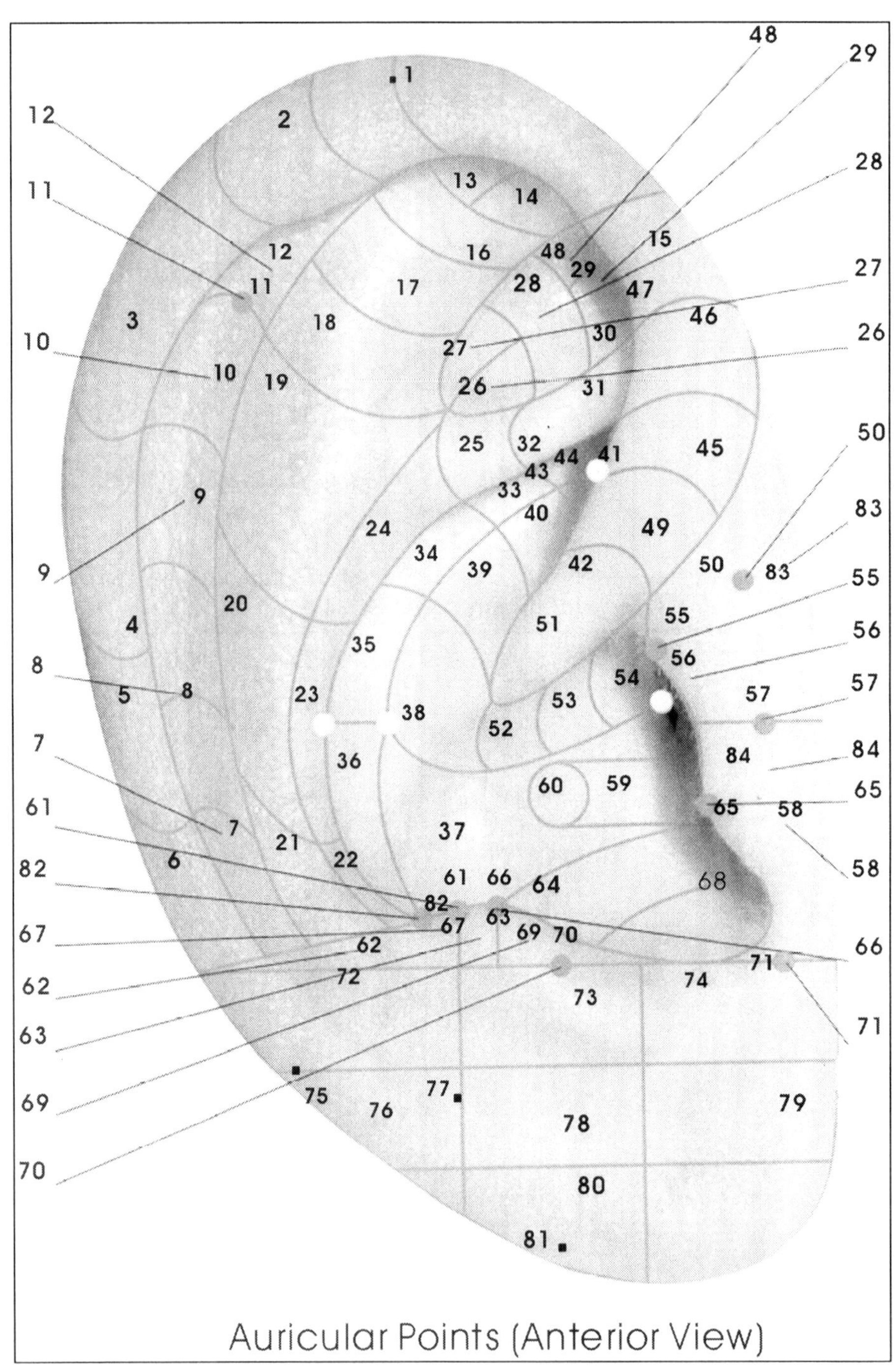

Auricular Points (Anterior View)

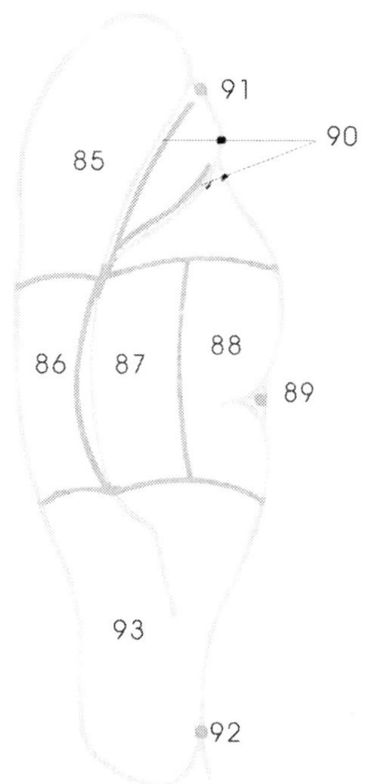

Auricular Points (Posterior View)

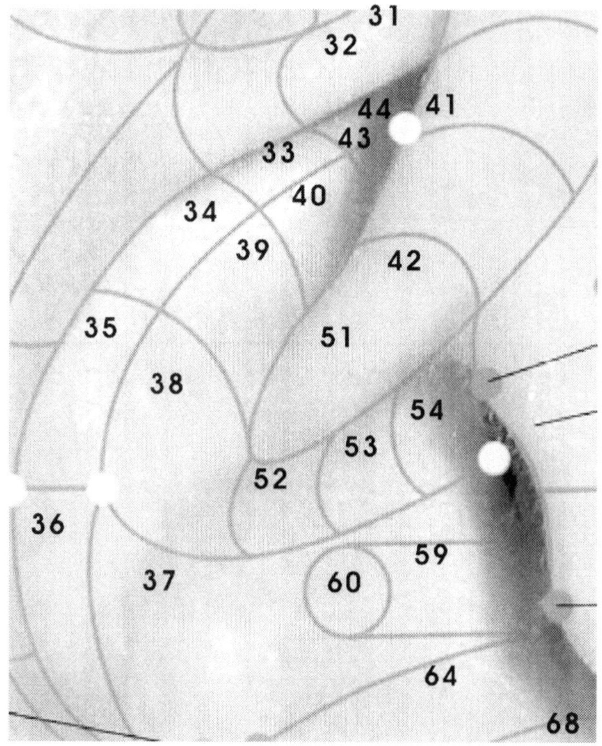

22 Auricular Points in the Concha

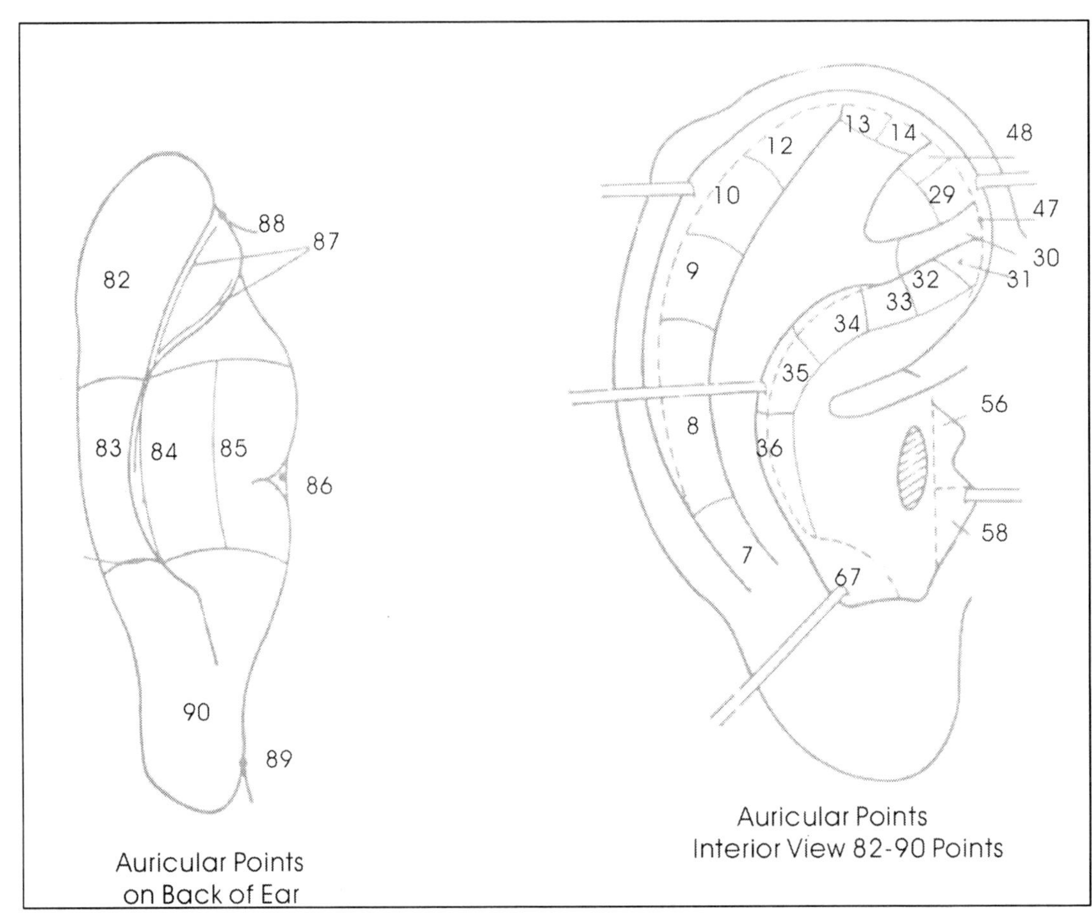

Auricular Points
on Back of Ear

Auricular Points
Interior View 82-90 Points

Test 6: Auricular Points (1-93)

1	
2	
3	
4	
5	
6	
7	
8	
9	
10	
11	
12	
13	
14	
15	
16	
17	
18	
19	

20	
21	
22	
23	
24	
25	
26	
27	
28	
29	
30	
31	
32	
33	
34	
35	
36	
37	
38	

39	
40	
41	
42	
43	
44	
45	
46	
47	
48	
49	
50	
51	
52	
53	
54	
55	
56	
57	

58	
59	
60	
61	
62	
63	
64	
65	
66	
67	
68	
69	
70	
71	
72	
73	
74	
75	
76	

77	
78	
79	
80	
81	
82	
83	
84	
85	
86	
87	
88	
89	
90	
91	
92	
93	

Test 7: Scalp Points (1-28)

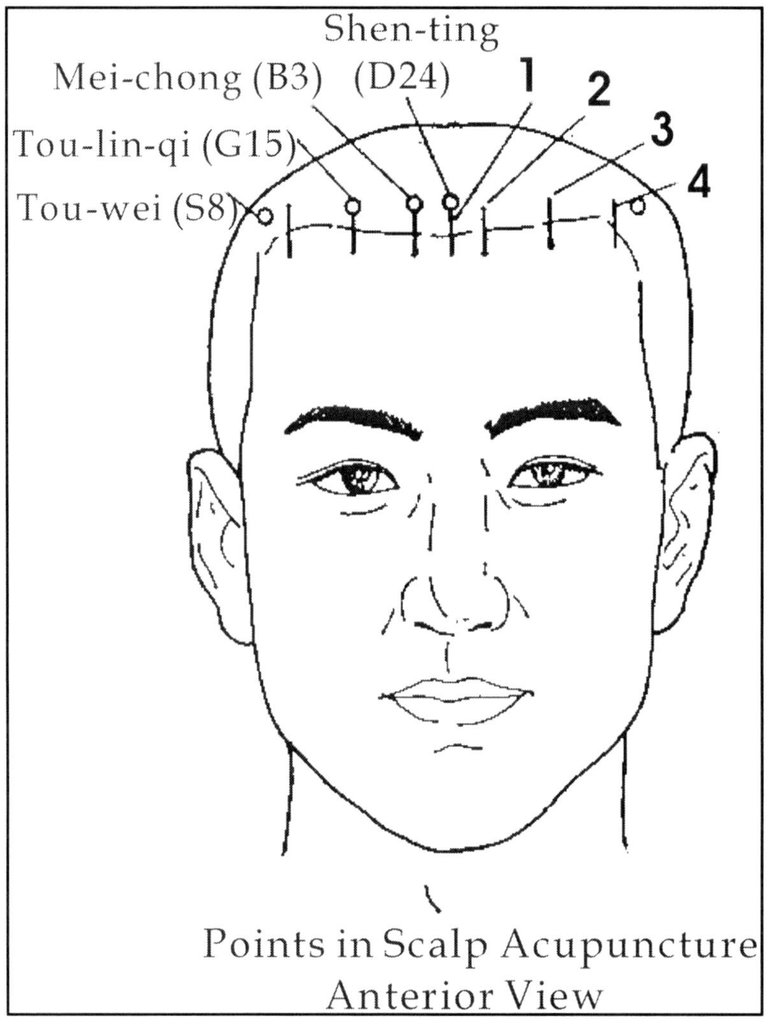

Points in Scalp Acupuncture
Anterior View

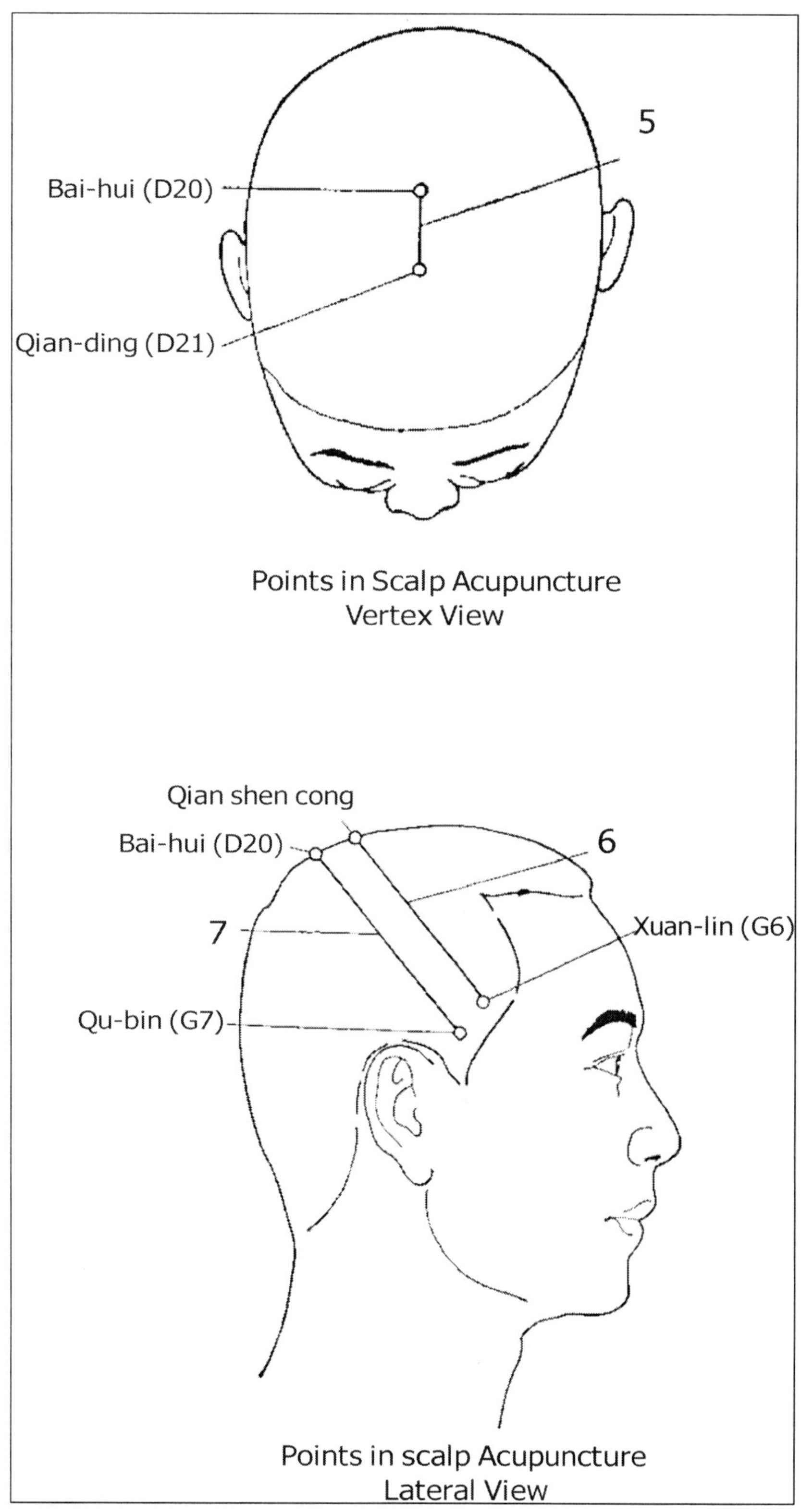

Points in Scalp Acupuncture
Vertex View

Points in scalp Acupuncture
Lateral View

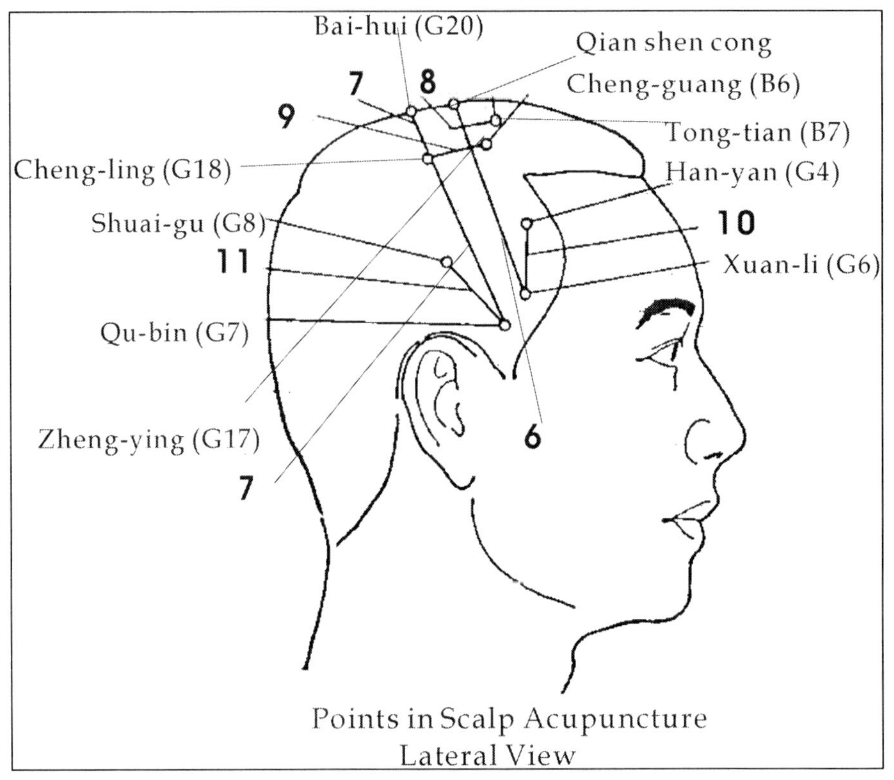

Points in Scalp Acupuncture
Lateral View

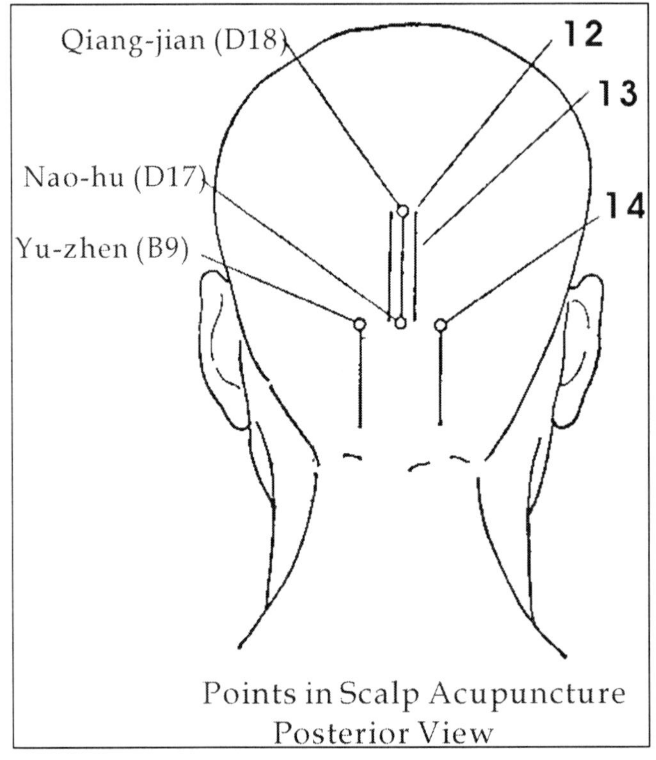

Points in Scalp Acupuncture
Posterior View

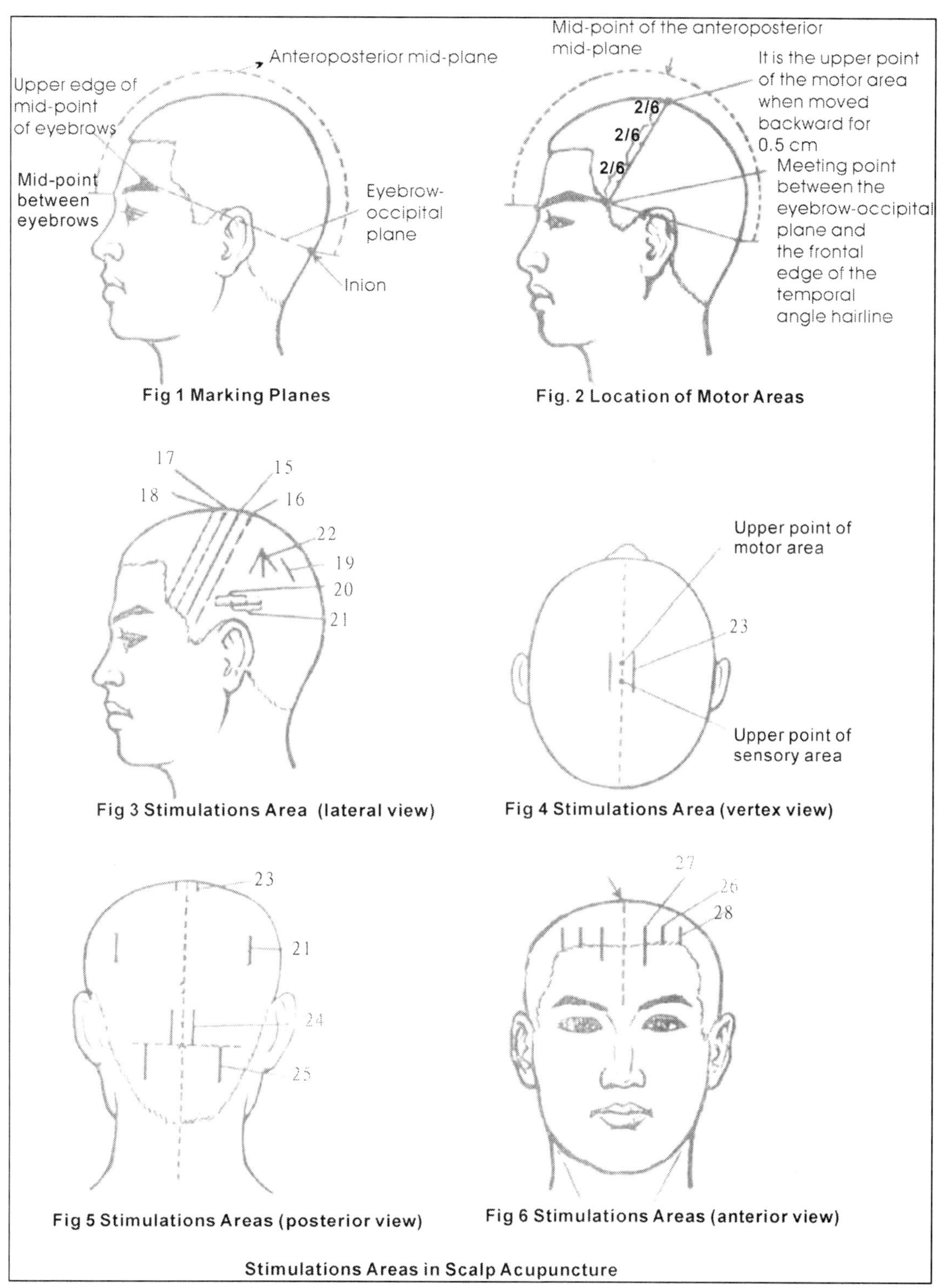

Fig 1 Marking Planes

Fig. 2 Location of Motor Areas

Fig 3 Stimulations Area (lateral view)

Fig 4 Stimulations Area (vertex view)

Fig 5 Stimulations Areas (posterior view)

Fig 6 Stimulations Areas (anterior view)

Stimulations Areas in Scalp Acupuncture

Test 10: Scalp Points (1-28)

1		
2		
3		
4		
5		
6		
7		
8		
9		
10		
11		
12		
13		
14		

15		
16		
17		
18		
19		
20		
21		
22		
23		
24		
25		
26		
27		
28		

Test 11: Regional Therapies

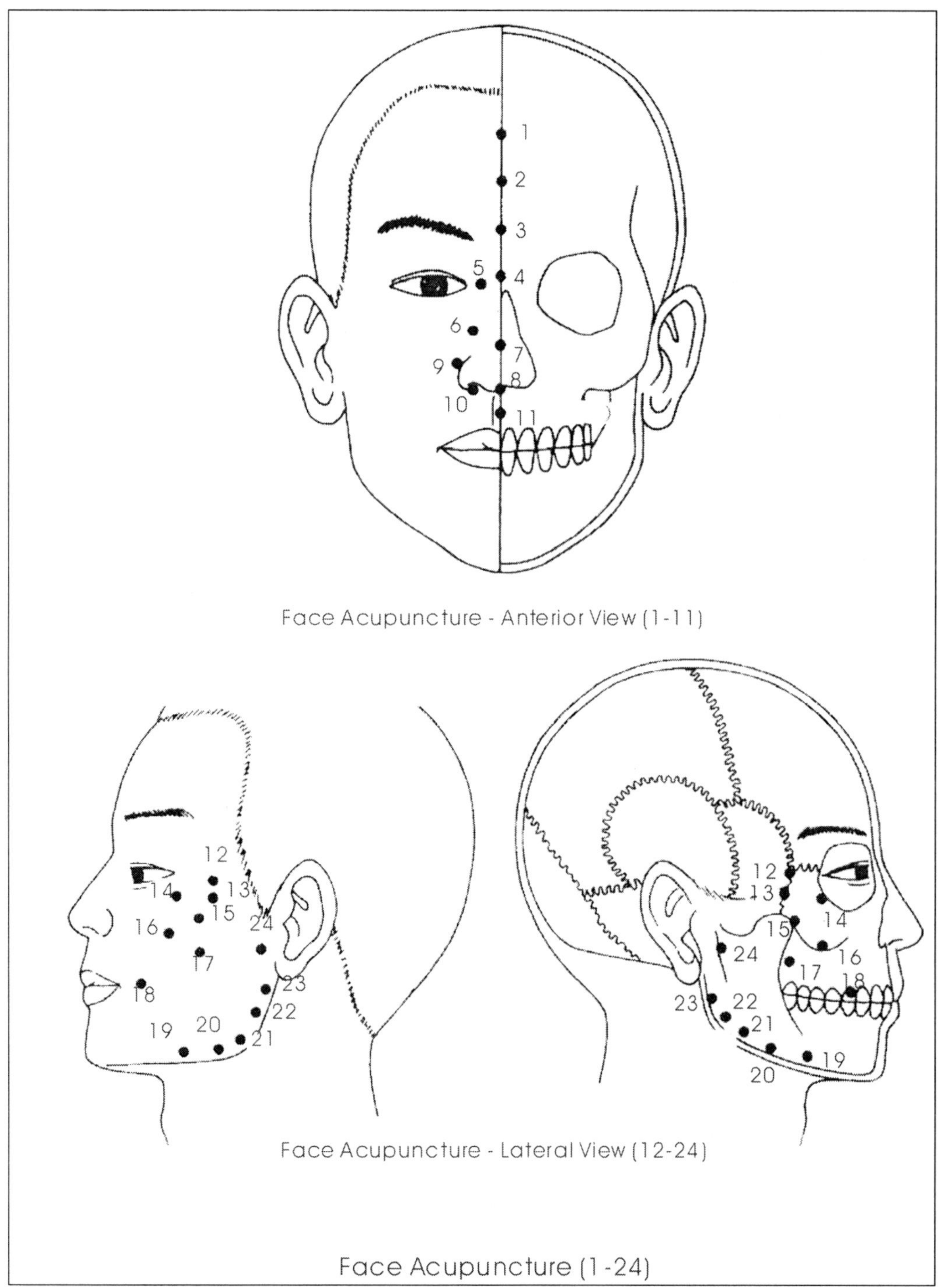

Face Acupuncture (1-24)

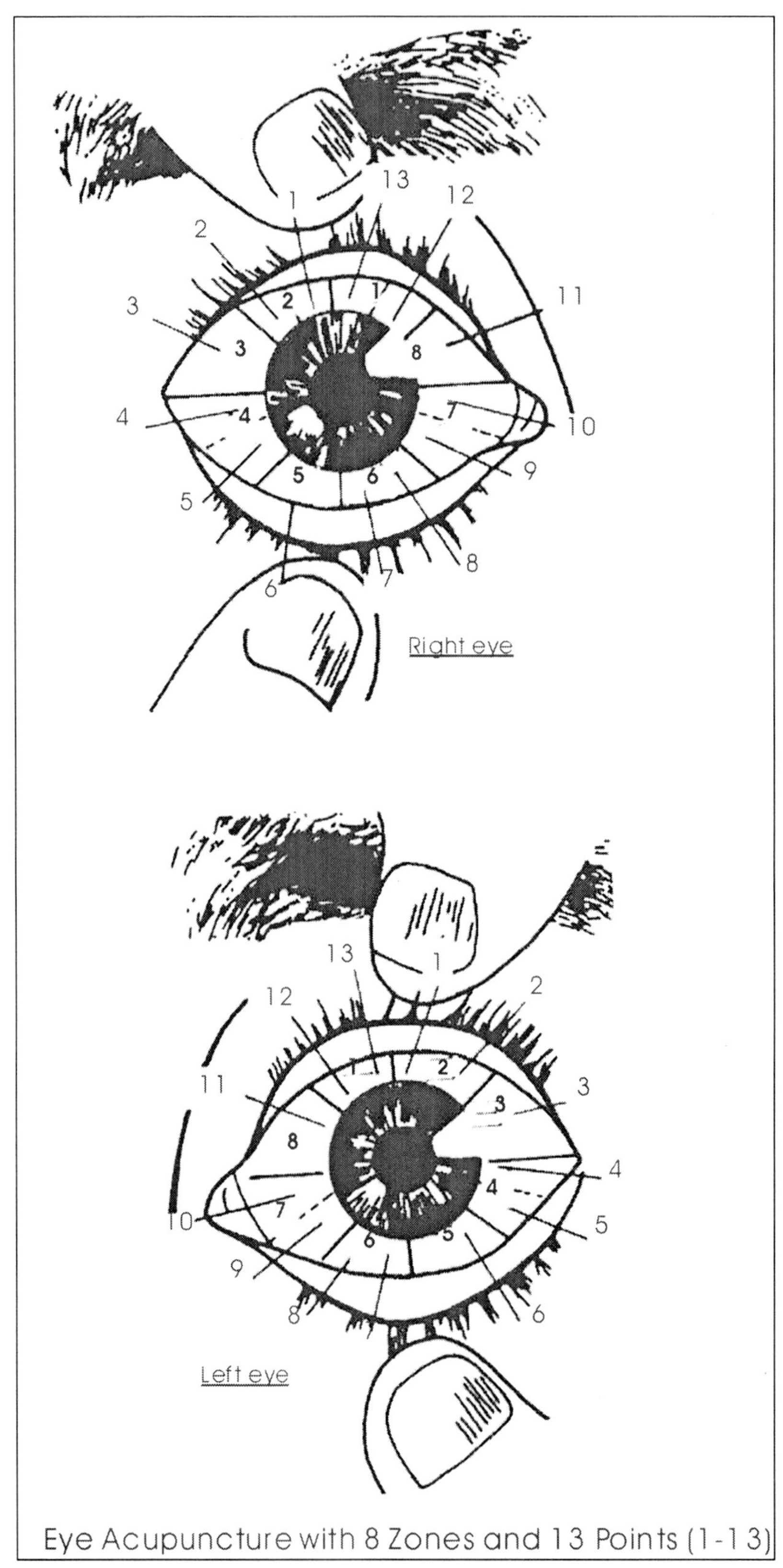

Eye Acupuncture with 8 Zones and 13 Points (1-13)

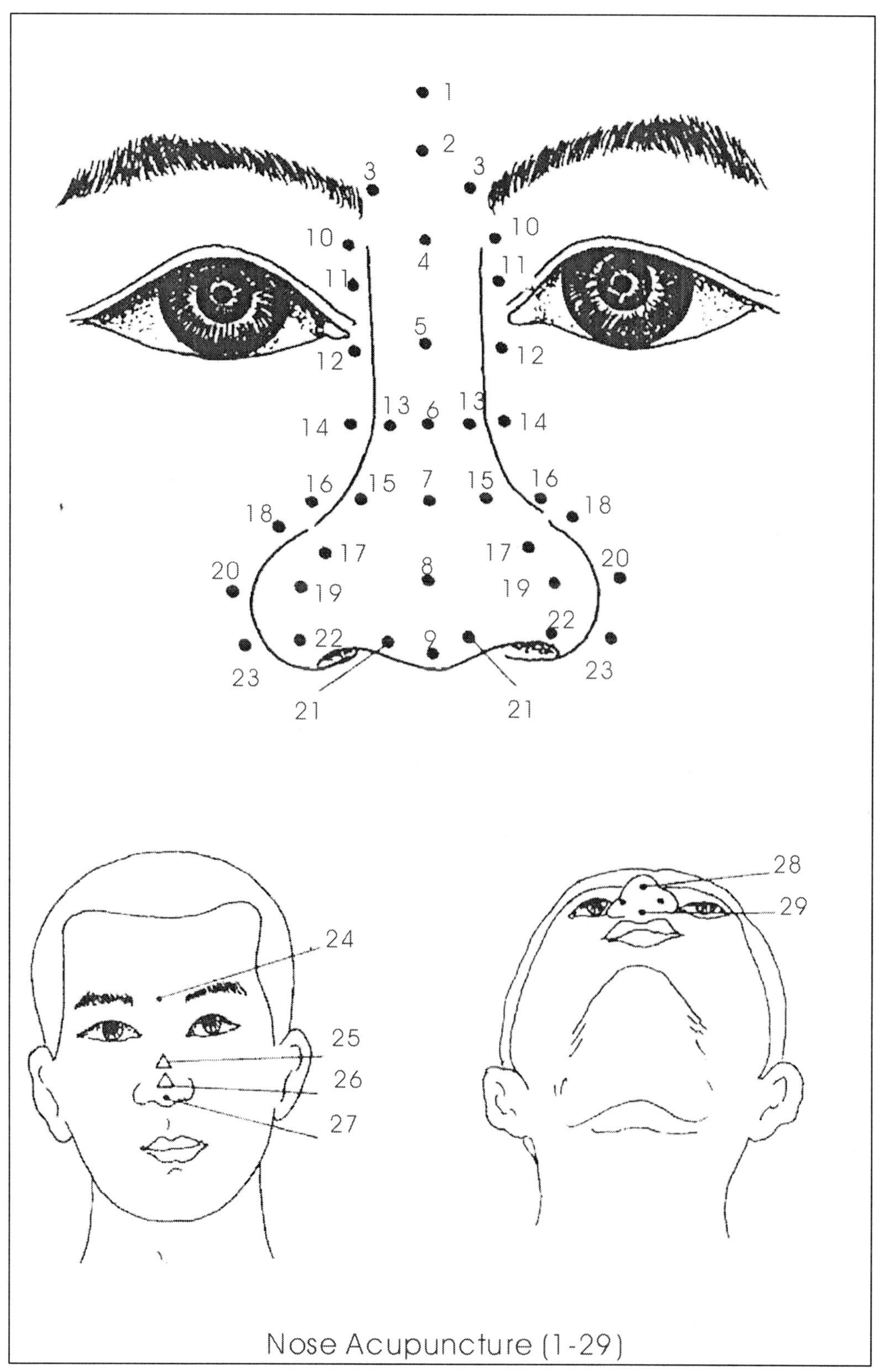

Nose Acupuncture (1-29)

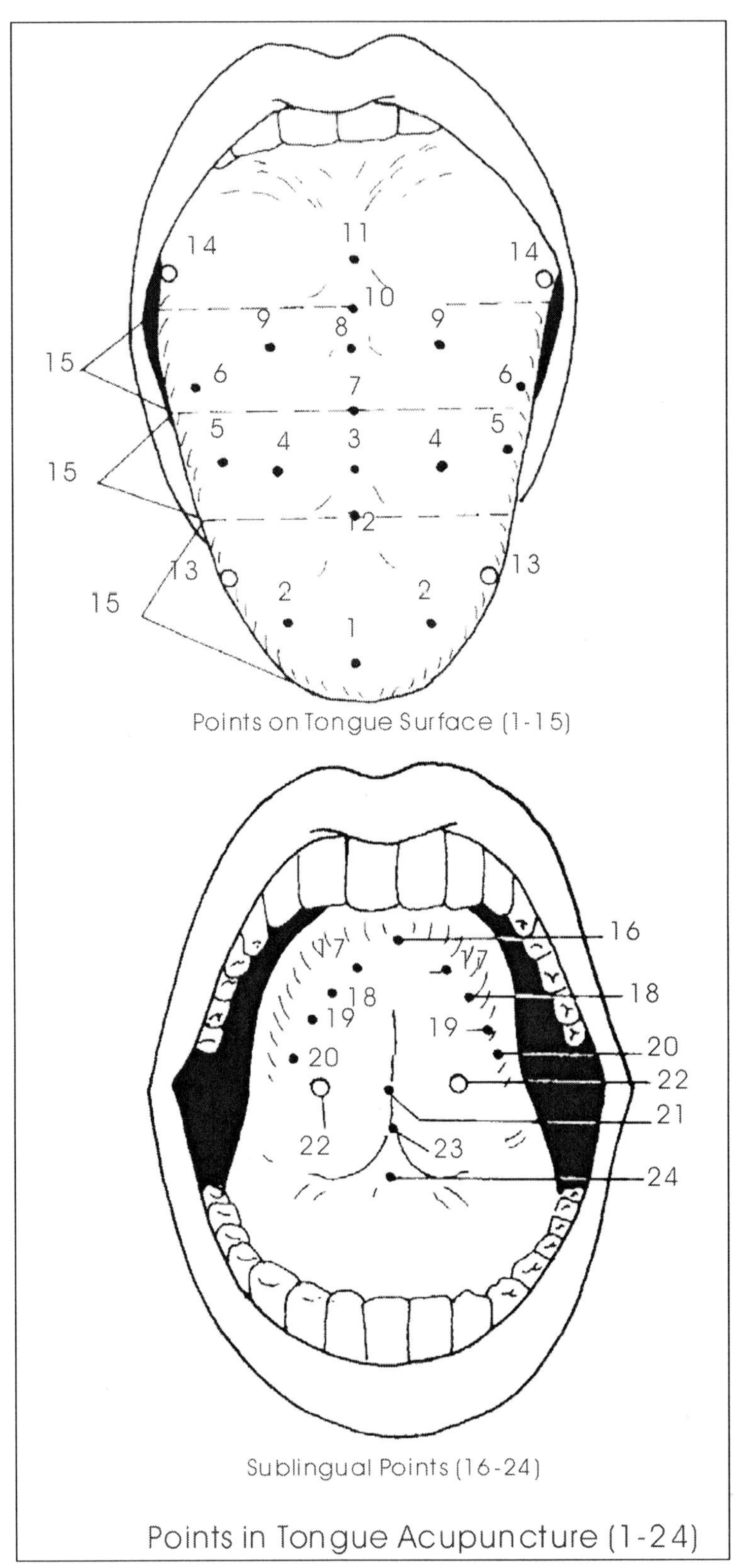

Points on Tongue Surface (1-15)

Sublingual Points (16-24)

Points in Tongue Acupuncture (1-24)

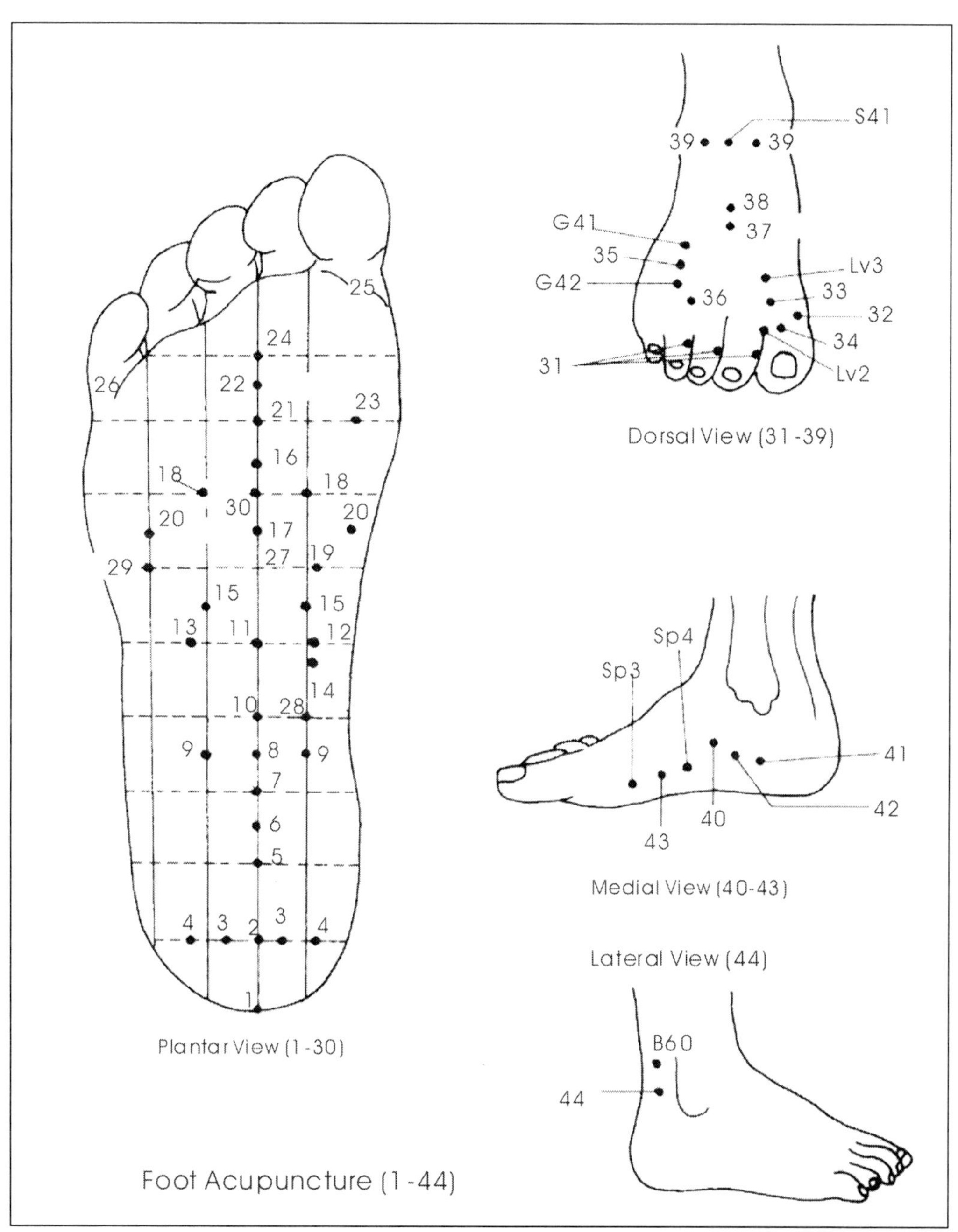

Foot Acupuncture (1-44)

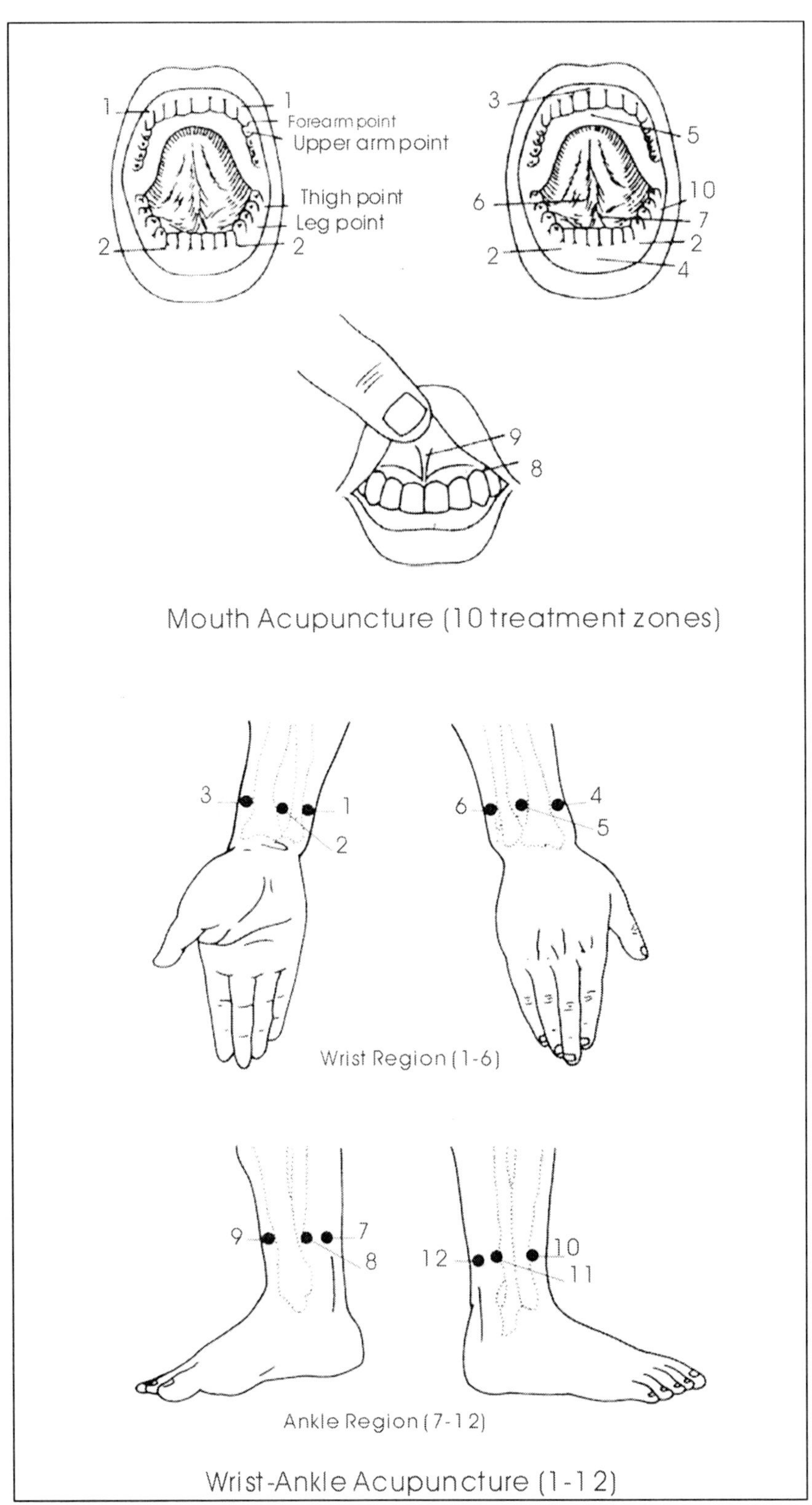

Mouth Acupuncture (10 treatment zones)

Wrist Region (1-6)

Ankle Region (7-12)

Wrist-Ankle Acupuncture (1-12)

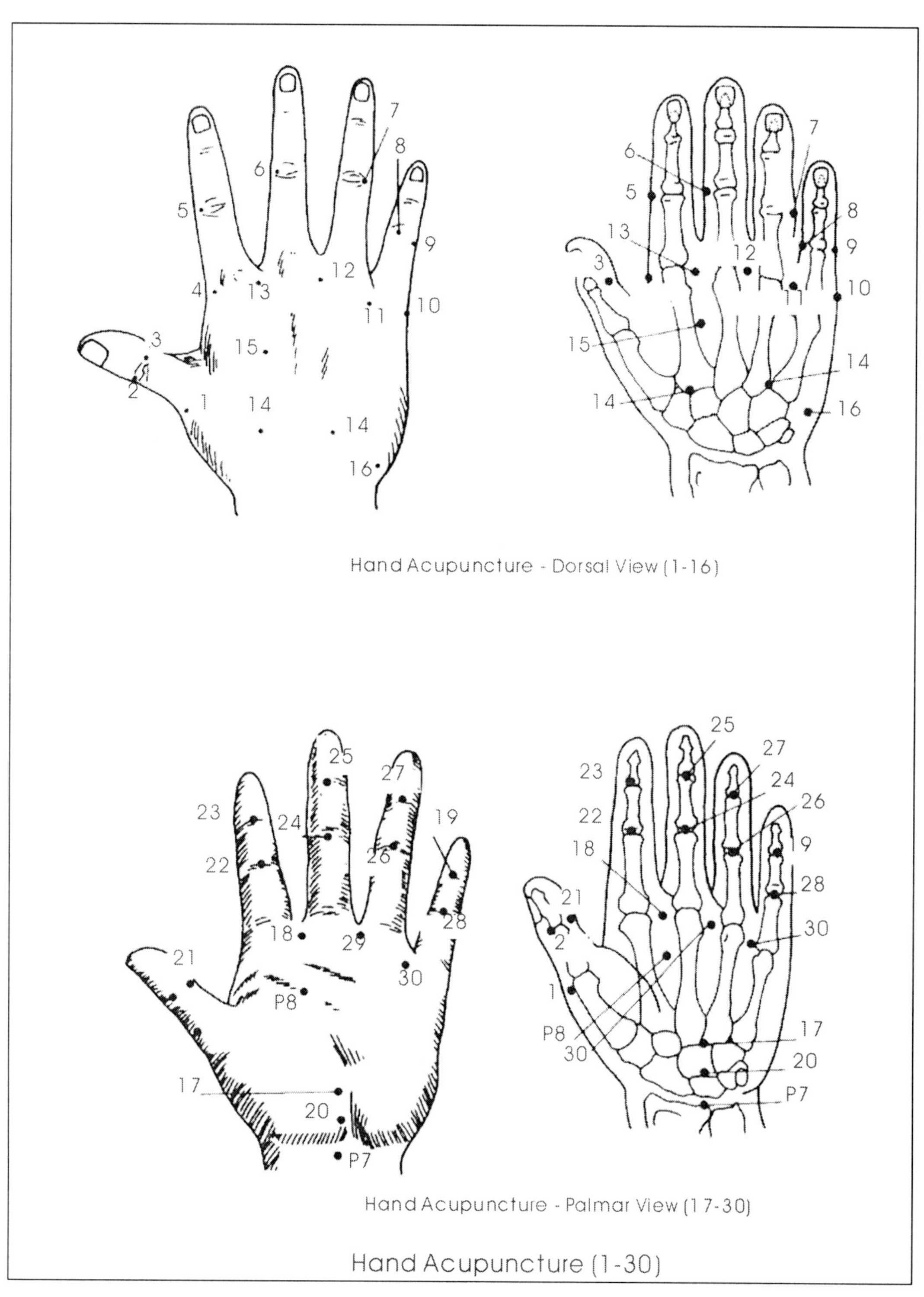

Hand Acupuncture - Dorsal View (1-16)

Hand Acupuncture - Palmar View (17-30)

Hand Acupuncture (1-30)

Test 11-1 Face Acupuncture (1-24)
Test 11-2 Eye Acupuncture with 8 zones and 13 Points (1-23)
Test 11-3 Nose Acupuncture (1-29)
Test 11-4 Tongue Acupuncture (1-24)
Test 11-5 Foot Acupuncture (1-44)
Test 11-6 Mouth Acupuncture (1-10)
Test 11-7 Wrist-Ankle Acupuncture (1-12)
Test 11-8 Hand Acupuncture (1-30)

Test 11-1 Face Acupuncture (1-24)

1	
2	
3	
4	
5	
6	
7	
8	
9	
10	
11	
12	
13	
14	
15	
16	
17	
18	
19	
20	
21	
22	
23	
24	

Test 11-2 Eye Acupuncture with 8 zones and 13 Points (1-23)

1	
2	
3	
4	
5	
6	
7	
8	
9	
10	
11	
12	
13	

Test 11-3 Nose Acupuncture (1-29)

1	
2	
3	
4	
5	
6	
7	
8	
9	
10	
11	
12	
13	
14	
15	
16	
17	
18	
19	
20	
21	
22	
23	
24	
25	
26	

27	
28	
29	

Test 11-4 Tongue Acupuncture (1-24)

1	
2	
3	
4	
5	
6	
7	
8	
9	
10	
11	
12	
13	
14	
15	
16	
17	
18	
19	
20	
21	
22	
23	
24	

Test 11-5 Foot Acupuncture (1-44)

1	
2	
3	
4	
5	
6	
7	
8	
9	
10	
11	
12	
13	
14	
15	
16	
17	
18	
19	
20	
21	
22	
23	
24	
25	
26	
27	
28	
29	
30	
31	
32	
33	
34	
35	
36	
37	
38	
39	
40	
41	
42	
43	
44	

Test 11-6 Mouth Acupuncture (1-10)

1	
2	
3	
4	
5	
6	
7	
8	
9	
10	

Test 11-7 Wrist-Ankle Acupuncture (1-12)

1	
2	
3	
4	
5	
6	
7	
8	
9	
10	
11	
12	

Test 11-8 Hand Acupuncture (1-30)

19	
1	
2	
3	
4	
5	
6	
7	
8	
9	
10	
11	
12	
13	
14	
15	
16	
17	
18	
20	
21	
22	
23	
24	
25	
26	
27	
28	
29	
30	

Test 12: Theory

Test 12-1 Five Wheels (1-5)
Test 12-2 eight contours (1-8)
Test 12-3 tongue and organs (1-4)
Test 12-4 internal organs in the face (1-12)
Test 12-5 five elements in four laws (1-5)
Test 12-6 six divisions of yin-yang (1-6)
Test 12-7 changing patterns of yin and yang (1-14)
Test 12-8 sections of pulses at wrist (1-6)
Test 12-9 pulses in the three regions symptomatic of nine symptoms (1-9)
Test 12-10 nine numerals on a turtle in a square denote nine parts of the body (1-9)
Test 12-11 nine numerals on a turtle in a square denote nine directions (1-9)
Test 12-12 nine numerals on a turtle in a square denote nine seasonal periods (1-9)
Test 12-13 nine numerals on a turtle in a square denote nine periods in a day (1-9)
Test 12-14 nine numerals on a turtle in a square denote nine internal organs (1-9)
Test 12-15 nine numerals on a turtle in a square denote trigrams (1-9)
Test 12-16 nine numerals on a turtle in a square denote nine kinds of people (1-9) Test 12-17 nine numerals on a turtle in a square denote eight acupuncture points (1-9).

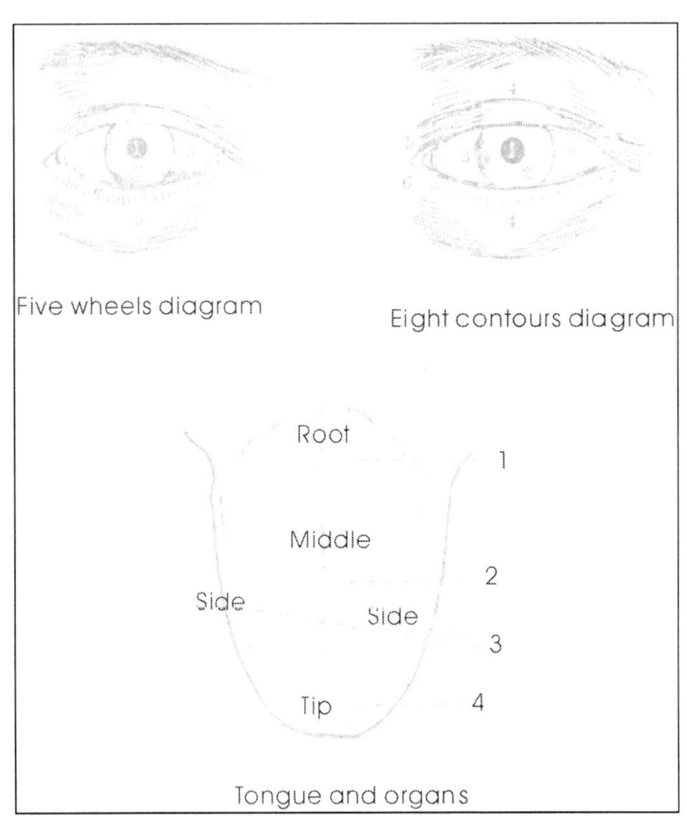

Tongue and organs

Test 12: Theory

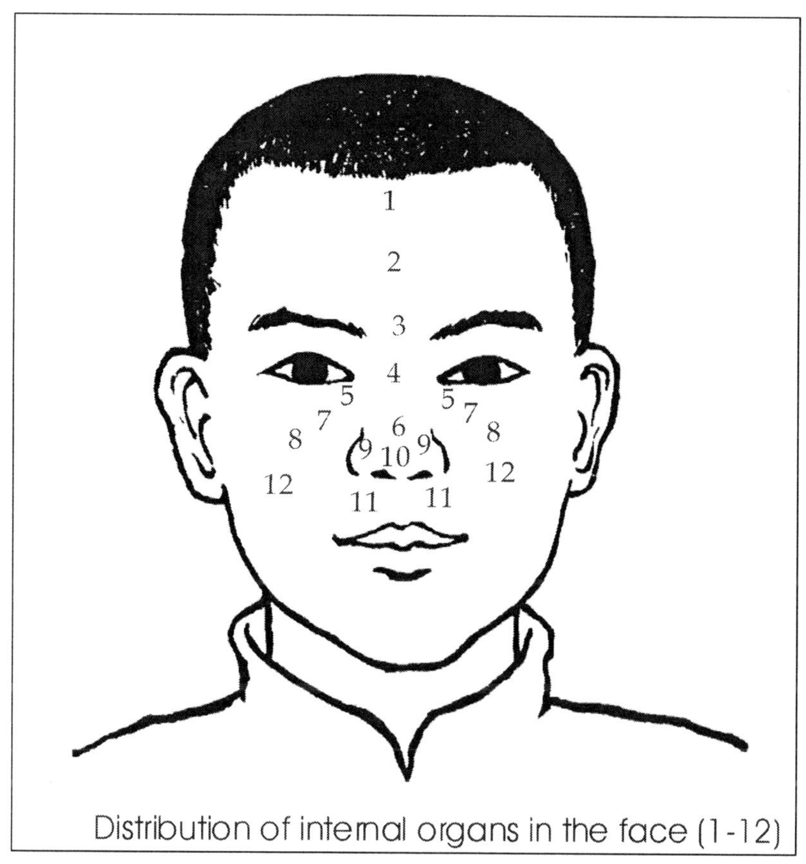

Distribution of internal organs in the face (1-12)

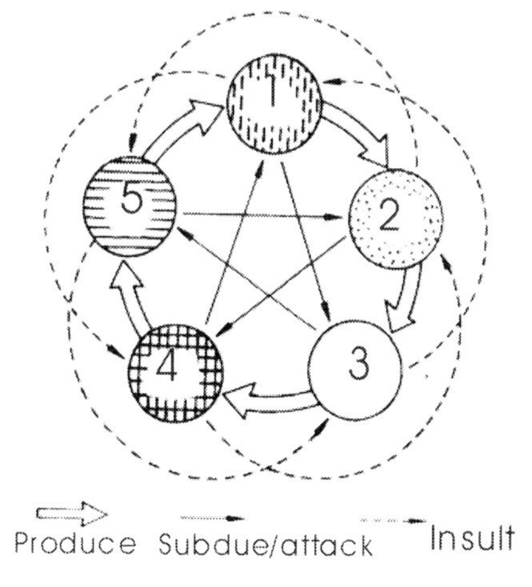

Four Laws of Five Elements (1-5)

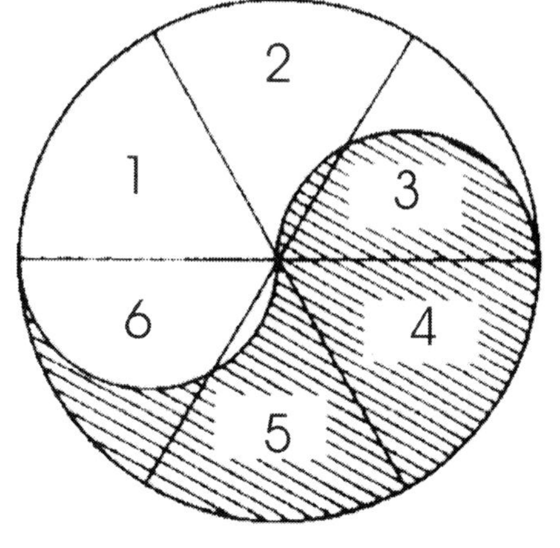

Six divisions of yin-yang (1-6)

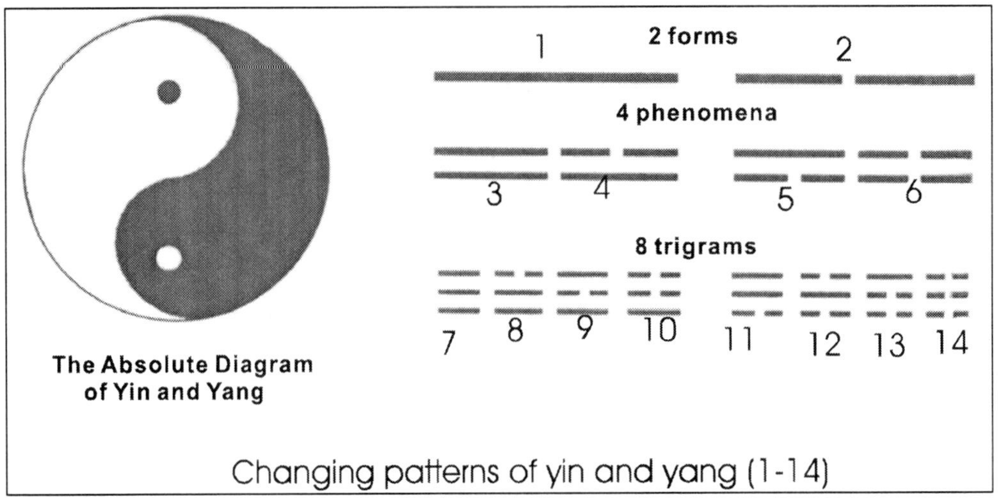

Changing patterns of yin and yang (1-14)

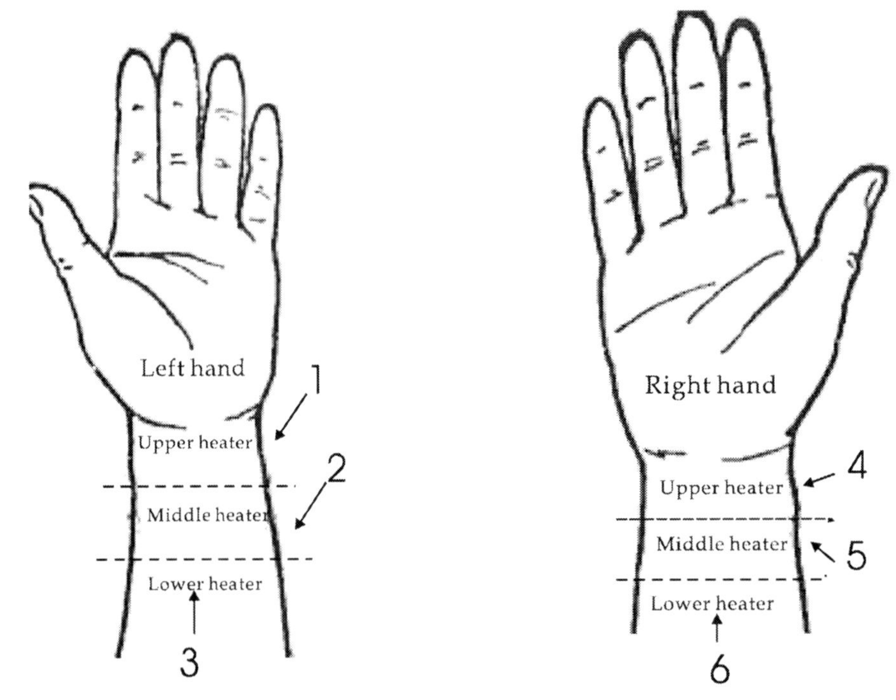

6 Sections of Pulses
Diagnostic of six Symptoms (1-6)

Test 12: Theory

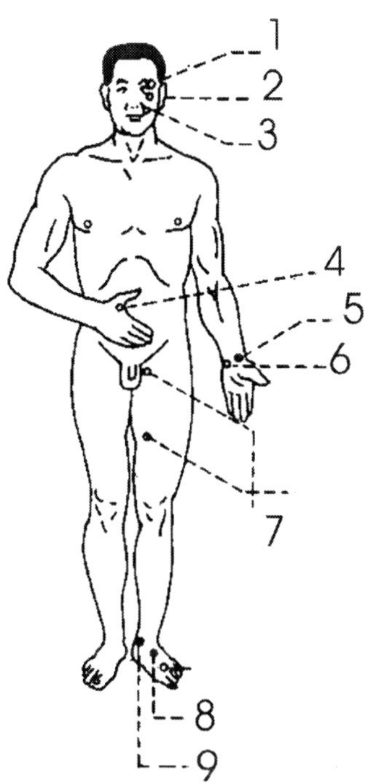

Pulses in the three regions
symptomatic of nine symptoms

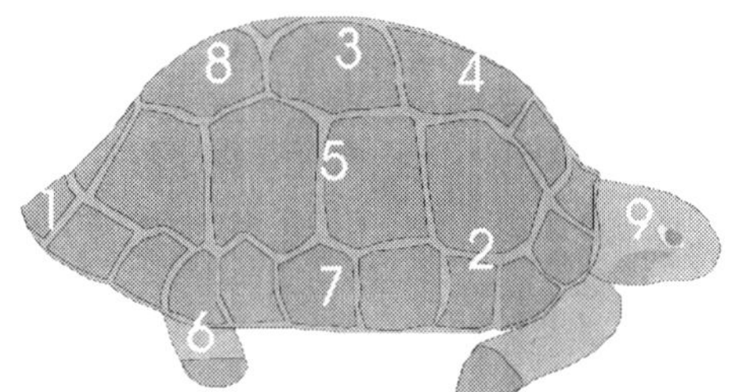

Nine numerals on a turtle in a square

4	9	2
3	5	7
8	1	6

Test 12-1 Five Wheels (1-5)

1	
2	
3	
4	
5	

Test 12-2 eight contours (1-8)

1	
2	
3	
4	
5	
6	
7	
8	

Test 12-3 tongue and organs (1-4)

1	
2	
3	
4	

Test 12-4 internal organs in the face (1-12)

1	
2	
3	
4	
5	
6	
7	
8	
9	
10	
11	
12	

Test 12-5 five elements in four laws of (1-5)

1	
2	
3	
4	
5	

Test 12-6 six divisions of yin-yang (1-6)

1	
2	
3	
4	
5	
6	

Test 12-7 changing patterns of yin and yang (1-14)

1	
2	
3	
4	
5	
6	
7	
8	
9	
10	
11	
12	
13	
14	

Test 12-8 sections of pulses at wrist (1-6)

1	
2	
3	
4	
5	
6	

Test 12-9 pulses in the three regions smptomatic of nine symptoms (1-9)

1	
2	
3	

4	
5	
6	
7	
8	
9	

Test 12-10 nine numerals on a turtle in a square denote nine parts of the body (1-9)

1	
2	
3	
4	
5	
6	
7	
8	
9	

Test 12-11 nine numerals on a turtle in a square denote nine directions (1-9)

1	
2	
3	
4	
5	
6	
7	
8	
9	

Test 12-12 nine numerals on a turtle in a square denote nine seasonal periods (1-9)

1	
2	
3	
4	
5	
6	
7	
8	
9	

Test 12-13 nine numerals on a turtle in a square denote nine periods in a day (1-9)

1	
2	
3	
4	
5	
6	
7	
8	
9	

Test 12-14 nine numerals on a turtle in a square denote nine internal organs (1-9)

1	
2	
3	
4	
5	
6	
7	
8	
9	

Test 12-15 nine numerals on a turtle in a square denote trigrams (1-9)

1	
2	
3	
4	
5	
6	
7	
8	
9	

Test 12-16 nine numerals on a turtle in a square denote nine kinds of people (1-9)

1	

2	
3	
4	
5	
6	
7	
8	
9	

Test 12-17 nine numerals on a turtle in a square denote eight acupuncture points (1-9)

1	2	
2	4	
3	8	
4	3	
5	1	
6	9	
7	7	
8	6	
9	5	

Test 13: Multiple-Choice Questions 选择题库

13-1	经络	Meridians	1-314
13-2	腧穴	Acupuncture Points	315-748
13-3	表面解剖与针灸穴位	Surface Anatomy and Acupuncture Points	749-1066
13-4	刺灸法	Techniques of Acupuncture-Moxibustion	1067-1338
13-5	针灸治疗学	Acupuncture Treatment	1339-2537
13-6	医案	Clinical Cases	2538-2642
13-7	医籍	Acupuncture Classics	2643-3062
13-8	谨慎穴位	Cautious Points	3063-3524

13-1	经络	Meridians	1-314

1	"从巅至耳上角"的经脉是: A. 足少阳胆经; B. 足太阳膀胱经 C. 督脉; D. 足厥阴肝经; E. 以上都不是	"What meridian travels from top of head to upper angle of ear"? A. foot lesser yang gallbladder meridian; B. foot greater yang bladder meridian; C. du mai / governing meridian; D. foot jue yin liver meridian; E. none of the above
2	"从耳后,入耳中,出走耳前"是哪经的支脉: A. 足少阳经; B. 足太阳经 C. 手太阳经; D. 足厥阴经; E. 手阳明经	What meridian has a branch that "travels from behind the ear, enters into the ear, and travels outward in front the ear"? A. foot lesser yang meridian / zu shao yang jing; B. foot greater yang meridian / zu tai yang jing C. hand greater yang meridian / shou tai yang jing; D. foot decreasing yin meridian / foot jue yin jing; E. hand yang ming merridian / hand bright yang meridian
3	"脊痛腰似折,髀不可以曲" 的病候属于: A 胆经; B 胃经 C. 小肠经; D 肾经; E 膀胱经.	What meridian may give rise to "pain in the spinal column; lumbago as if the waist being broken up, an inability to bend. from the hip joint"? A. gallbladder meridian; B. stomach meridian; C. small intestine meridian; D. kidney meridian E. bladder meridian.
4	"其支者,从肺出络心,注胸中"的经脉是: A 手太阴经; B 足少阴经 C. 手太阳经; D 手厥阴经; E 手少阴经.	What meridian has a. branch that starts from the lungs; and then, it moves outward to be linked. with the heart, entering into the middle point between two nipples. A. greater yin meridian of hand B. lesser yin meridian of foot C. greater yang meridian of hand D. jue yin meridian of hand E. lesser yin meridian of hand.
5	"入耳中"的经脉应是: A 手阳明经; B 足阳明经 C. 足太阳经 D 手太阳经 E 手阳明经络脉	Which meridian enters into the ear? A. Bright yang meridian of hand B. Bright yang meridian of foot C. greater yang meridian of foot; D. greater yang meridian of hand E. linking meridian of the bright yang meridian of hand
6	"上睾,结于茎"的络脉是: A 足阳明络脉;B 足太阳络脉 C. 足厥阴络脉; D 足少阴络脉; E 足少阳络脉.	What linking meridian (luo mai) "reaches the testicle, and then, goes round the penis"? A. Bright yang of foot linking meridian; B. greater yang of foot linking meridian; C. jue yin of foot linking meridian; D. lesser yin of foot linking meridian; E. lesser yang of foot linking meridian.

7	"阴脉之海"是指: A·足少阴肾经; B·足太阴脾经; C. ·足厥阴肝经; D·手少阴心经; E·任脉	"Sea of yin meridians" refers to: A. kidney meridian; B. spleen meridian; C. liver meridian; D. heart meridian; E. ren mai (conception meridian).
8	"正经"是指: A·十二经脉; B·奇经八脉 C. ·十二经别; D·十二经筋; E·十四经脉	"Orthodox meridians / zheng jing" refers to: A·twelve major meridians; B·eight extraordinary meridians; C. ·twelve separate master meridians (jing bie); D·twelve muscular meridians (jing jin); E·fourteen meridians
9	《内经》中所载多血少气的经脉是: A 阳明与太阴; B·太阳与厥阴 C. ·少阳与少阴; D·太阴与少阳; E·以上均不是.	According to (Nei Jing), what meridian has plentiful blood with scanty energy? A，bright yang / yang ming and greater yin / tai yin; B · greater yang and decreasing yin / jue yin; C. ·lesser yang / shao yang and lesser yin / shao yin; D·greater yin / tai yin and lesser yang / shao yang; E · none of the above
10	络脉中·行于浅表的部分称为: A. ·孙络; B. ·别络 C. ·支络; D. ·浮络; E. ·小络	What is the superficial part of a·luo mai / linking meridian called? A. ·sun luo / tiny linking meridian; B. ·bie luo / separate linking meridian; C. ·zhi luo / branch linking meridian; D. ·fu luo / floating linking meridian; E. ·xiao luo / small linking meridian
11	被称为 "十二经脉之海"的经脉是: A. ·冲脉; B. ·督脉 C. ·任脉; D. ·足阳明胃经; E. ·足少阴肾经	What meridian is called "the sea of the twelve master meridians"? A. ·chong mai / vigorous meridian; B. ·du mai / governing meridian; C. ·ren mai /; C. onception meridian; D. ·foot yang ming stomach meridian; E. ·foot lesser yang kidney meridian
12	病在经筋者，施治多选用: A. ·毫针; B. ·三棱针 C. ·火针; D. ·雷火神针; E. ·大针	What needle is selected to treat the diseases of muscular meridians in most cases? A. ·hao zhen (minute needle); B. ·three-edged needle C. ·fire needle; D. ·thunder fire and spiritual needle; E. ·big needle.
13	不是经络的作用： A·运行气血; B·濡养周身 C. ·抗御外邪; D·保卫机体; E·活血祛瘀	Which is not the function of meridians? A·to move energy-blood; B·to moisten and nourish the whole body; C. ·to defend against the attack of external pathogens; D·to protect the body; E·to activate bloodand remove coagulation.
14	不是十二经筋的循行走向： A·均从四肢末端走向头身; B·行于体表 C. ·不入内脏; D·结聚于关节骨骼部; E·入走体腔.	Which is NOT the travelling direction of twelve muscular meridians (jing jin)? A·all of them travel from four limbs toward the head and body; B·travelling throughout the superficial part of the body; C. ·not entering into the internal organs; D·gathering in the joints; E · entering into the cavities of the body.
15	不属于表里络属关系的是: A·手少阴—手太阳; B·足厥阴—足少阳 C. ·手阳明—手太阴; D·手少阳—手少阴; E·足太阳—足少阴.	Which pair does not form a superficial-deep relationship with each other nor the relationship of linking with, and belonging to, each other? A·hand lesser yin / shao yin—hand greater yang; B·foot decreasing yin / jue yin—foot lesser yang / shao yang; C. ·hand bright yang / yang ming—hand greater yin / tai yin; D·hand lesser yang / shao yang—hand lesser yin / shao yin; E·foot tai yang —foot lesser yin / shao yin.

16	称为"阳脉之海"的经脉是: A·任脉; B·冲脉; C·督脉; D·带脉; E·阳维脉.	What meridian is Called " sea of yang meridians "? A ·; C. onception meridian / ren mai; B ·rigorous meridian / chong mai C. ·du mai / governing meridian; D · belt meridian / dai mai E · fastener meridian of yang / yang wei mai.
17	冲脉起于: A·足跟内侧; B·足跟外侧 C. ·胞中; D·小腿内侧; E·小腿外侧.	Where is rigorous meridian / chong mai originated from? A ·medial side of heel; B ·lateral side of heel C. ·womb, D ·medial side of lower leg; E ·lateral side of lower leg.
18	冲脉为: A·十二经脉之海; B·气海 C. 阴脉之海; D·髓海; E·水谷之海.	Chong mai (vigorous meridian) is: A.sea of twelve meridians; B. sea of energy (qi hai); C. sea of blood (xue hai); D. sea of marrow (sui hai) E. sea of water and grains (shui gu zhi hai).
19	冲脉又称为: A·阳脉之海; B·阴脉之海 C. 气海; D·血海; E 髓海.	What is another name for the rigorous meridian / chong mai? A · sea of yang meridians; B · sea of yin meridians C. ·sea of energy; D · sea of blood; E · sea of marrow.
20	冲脉在腹部的分布路线与: A·任脉一致; B·胃经一致 C. ·脾经一致; D·肾经一致; E·以上均不是.	What is the distribution of rigorous meridian / chong mai in the abdominal region? A ·; C. onsistent with the; C. onception meridian / ren mai; B ·consistent with the stomach meridian; C. ·consistent with the spleen meridian; D ·consistent with the kidneys meridian; E · none of the above
21	除督脉外，还有哪一条经脉贯脊 A.足太阳膀胱经; B.足少阴肾经; C.足少阳胆经; D 足阳明胃经。	In addition to the Du Mai, what other meridian cuts across the spine? A. Bladder meridian; B. kidney meridian; C. gallbladder meridian; D. stomach meridian.
22	从肺系横出腋下，下循臑内，行少阴心主之前的经脉是指: A.手阳明大肠经; B.手太阴肺经 C. 足阳明胃经; D 手少阳三焦经.	What meridian travels from the trachea to go sideward through the larynx; and then goes along the medial region of the brachium (the upper arm) and passes in front of the heart meridian, which is the lesser yin meridian of hand? A. greater yin lung meridian of hand B. Bright yang large intestine meridian of hand C. bright yang stomach meridian of foot; D. lesser yang sanjiao (triple heater) meridian of hand
23	从四肢末端走向头身的经络，下列哪项是不正确的: A·手三阳经; B·十二经经别 C. ·十二经经筋; D，足三阴经; E·足三阳经.	What meridians do NOT travel from the tips of four limbs toward the head and body? A ·three yang meridians of hand B ·twelve separate master meridians / jing bie C. ·twelve muscular meridians / jing jin; D ·three yin meridians of foot; E ·three yang meridians of foot
24	寸口之中太渊穴处为何经之"本"? A.手少阴经; B 手太阳经 C. 手太阴经; D 手厥阴经.	In the Mouth of Pulse [CÙN KǑU] region (the radial artery of the wrist) where throbbing may be felt, Lu9 [Tài Yuān] is the root of what meridian? A. lesser yin meridian of hand (shou shao yin jing); B. greater yang meridian of hand (shou tai yang jing); C. greater yin meridian of hand (shou tai yin jing); D. decreasing yin meridian of hand (shou jue yin jing).
25	大肠经小肠经心经	What are the common symptoms treated by the large intestine

	三经是主所生病的共同病候是: A 喉痹; B 嗌肿 C. 腋肿; D 目黄; E 面赤.	meridian, the small intestine meridian, and the heart meridian? A. sore throat; B. swollen throat C. swollen armpits; D. yellowish eyes; E. reddish complexion.
26	抵小腹，挟胃的经脉是: A.足阳明胃经; B.足太阳膀胱经 C. 手太阳小肠经; D 足厥阴肝经.	What meridian reaches the lower abdominal region and travels round the stomach? A. stomach meridian; B. bladder meridian; C. small intestine meridian; D. liver meridian
27	督脉别络散布于 A.腹部; B.胸胁部 C. 头部; D 腰骶部.	Where does the separate linking meridian of du mai spread? A. abdominal region; B. chest and rib region; Chestead region; D. lumbar-sacral region.
28	督脉的生理作用是: A.调节冲任督带; B 总督奇经八脉 C. 调节阳经经气; D. 调节阴经经气.	What are the physiological functions of du mai (governing meridian)? A. regulating vigorous meridian (chōng mài),; C. onception meridian (ren mai), governing meridian (du mai), belt meridian (dai mai); B. governing the eight extraordinary meridians (qi jing bai mai); C. regulating meridian energy of yang meridians; D. regulating meridian energy of yin meridians
29	督脉又称为: A 阳脉之海; B 阴脉之海 C. 气海; D 血海; E 髓海.	What is another name for the du mai / governing meridian? A · sea of yang meridians; B · sea of yin meridians, C. sea of energy; D · sea of blood; E · sea of marrow.
30	耳后、完骨下为何经之经别出合处: A 足阳明经; B 手厥阴经 C. 手少阴经; D 足少阳经; E 手阳明.	What separate master meridian meets behind the ear and b elow mastoid process? A · bright yang meridian of foot; B ·decreasing yin meridians of hand C. ·lesser yin meridian of hand D · lesser yang meridian of foot, E ·bright yang / yang ming of hand.
31	耳前三穴耳门听宫听会由上至下分别归属于: A.三焦经小肠经胆经; B 小肠经三焦经胆经 C. 胆经小肠经三焦经; D 三焦经胆经小肠经.	Three points (Ěr Mén,Tīng Gōng, Tīng Huì) located in front of the ear, what meridian does each of them belong to, from upper to lower? A. sanjiao meridian, small intestine meridian, gallbladder meridian; B. small intestine meridian, sanjiao meridian, gallbladder meridian; C. gallbladder meridian, small intestine meridian, sanjiao meridian; D. sanjiao meridian, gallbladder meridian, small intestine meridian.
32	二条支脉在委中相合的经脉是: A.足少阳胆经; B 足阳明胃经 C. 足少阴肾经; D. 足太阳膀胱经.	What meridian has two branches to meet at popliteal fossa? A. gallbladder meridian; B. stomach meridian; C. kidney meridian; D. bladder meridian.
33	腹部经脉由任脉向外排列的顺序是: A. 任脉 脾经 肾经 胃经; B. 任脉 肾经 脾经 胃经 C. 任脉 胃经 脾经 肾经; D. 任脉 胃经 肾经 脾经; E. 任脉 肾经 胃经 脾经	The meridians in the abdominal region are arranged from ren mai /; C. onception meridian in the center and to the lateral side in the following order: A. ·ren mai /; C. onception meridian spleen meridian kidney meridian stomach meridian; B. ·ren mai /; C. onception meridian kidney meridian spleen meridian stomach meridian; C. ·ren mai /; C. onception meridian stomach meridian spleen meridian kidney meridian; D. ·ren mai /; C. onception meridian stomach

		meridian kidney meridian spleen meridian; E. ren mai /; C. onception meridian kidney meridian stomach meridian spleen meridian
34	腹部正中线旁开 0.5 寸的经脉是: A. 足太阴脾经; B. 任脉 C. 足厥阴肝经; D. 足少阴肾经;. E. 以上均不是.	Which meridian travels on the abdominal vertical plane 0.5 Cun lateral from the midline? A. spleen meridian; B. ren mai (conception meridian); C. liver meridian; D. kidney meridian E. none of the above.
35	腹部正中线旁开 2 寸的经脉是: A. 足少阴肾经; B. 足太阴脾经 C. 任脉; D. 足厥阴肝经; E 以上均不是.	Which meridian travels on the abdominal vertical plane 2 Cun lateral from the midline? A. kidney meridian; B. spleen meridian; C. ren mai (conception meridian); D. liver meridian; E. none of the above.
36	根据骨度分寸，除......外，两者间距都是 9 寸: A. 两完骨间; B. 天突至歧骨 C. 腋前纹头至肘横纹; D. 腋至季肋; E. 胸剑联合至阴交	According to the bone measurements by Cun，which of the following does NOT measure 9 Cun? A. distance between two mastoid processes; B. distance between R22 [Tiān Tū] and 7th costosternal juncture / xiphoid process C. distance between anterior axillary crease and elbow crease; D. distance between axillary and false ribs; E. distance between xiphisternal joint and R7 [Yīn Jiāo]
37	根据骨度分寸，内辅骨下廉至内踝高点为： A 18 寸; B 13 寸 C. 14 寸; D 16 寸; E 12 寸.	What is the distance between lower border of medial; C. ondyle of femur and highest point of medial malleolus (inner ankle) according to the bone measurements by Cuns? A 18 Cun; B 13 Cun; C. 14 Cun; D 16 Cun; E 12 Cun
38	根据骨度分寸，下列穴位两者间距不是 1.5 寸的是: A. 气海一神阙; B. 内关一大陵 C. 神门一灵道'; D. 灵台-督俞; E. 心俞-神堂	According to the bone measurements by Cun, which of the following does NOT measure 1.5 Cun? A. R6 [Qì Hǎi] — R8 [Shén Què]; B. P6 [Nèi Guān]— P7 [Dà Líng]; C. H7 [Shén Mén]— H4 [Líng Dào]'; D. D10 [Líng Dào] — B16 [Dū Shū]; E. B15 [Xīn Shū]— B44 [Shén Táng]
39	根据骨度分寸，以下穴位除外，两穴间距均为 0.5 寸: A. 哑门一 风府; B. 阴郄一神门 C. 经渠一太渊; D. 复溜一 交信; E. 气海一 阴交	According to the bone measurements by Cun, which of the following does NOT measure 0.5 Cun? A. D15 [Yǎ Mén] — D16 [Fēng Fǔ]; B. D16 [Fēng Fǔ] — H7 [Shén Mén]; C. Lu8 [Jīng Qú] — Lu9 [Tài Yuān]; D. K7 [Fù Liū] — K8 [Jiāo Xìn]; E. R6 [Qì Hǎi] — R7 [Yīn Jiāo]
40	根据骨度分寸法，神闕到中脘穴是: A 6 寸; B 4 寸 C. 5 寸; D 3 寸; E 1.5 寸.	What is the distance between R8 [Shén Què] and R12 / Zhōng Wǎn according to the bone measurements by Cun? A 6 Cun; B 4 Cun; C. 5 Cun; D 3 Cun; E 1 5 Cun
41	根据骨度分寸法，印堂穴至百会穴为: A. 18 寸; B. 15 寸 C. 8 寸; D. 12 寸; E. 10 寸	What is the distance between Yìn Táng and D20 [Bǎi Huì] according to the bone measurements by Cun? A. 18cun; B. 15cun; C. 8cun; D. 12cun; E. 10cun.
42	根据骨度分寸法，肘横纹至腋前横纹为： A 9 寸; B 14 寸 C. 12 寸; D 13 寸; E 8 寸.	What is the distance between elbow crease and anterior axillary crease according to the bone measurements by Cun? A 9 Cun; B 14 Cun; C. 12 Cun; D 13 Cun; E 8 Cun

43	根据骨度分寸规定,臀横纹与膝中之间的长度应是: A. ·9 寸; B. ·12 寸 C. ·14 寸; D. ·16 寸; E. ·19 寸	What is the distance between gluteal fold (gluteal-sulcus) and center of popliteal fossa according to the bone measurements by Cun? A. ·9cun; B. ·12cun; C. ·14cun; D. ·16cun; E. ·19cun
44	根据骨度规定眉心至后发际为: A.l5 寸; B. ·12 寸 C. ·18 寸; D. ·14 寸; E.16 寸	What is the distance between eyebrows and posterior hairline according to the bone measurements by Cun? A.l5cun; B. ·12cun; C. ·18cun; D. ·14cun; E.16cun
45	股骨大转子至腘横纹的骨度分寸是: A ·9 寸; B ·12 寸 C. ·13 寸; D ·16 寸; E ·19 寸	What is the distance between greater trochanter (trochanter-major) and popliteal fold according to the bone measurements by Cuns? A ·9 Cun; B ·12 Cun; C. ·13 Cun; D ·16 Cun; E ·19 Cun
46	关元穴至中脘穴间的骨度分寸是: A. ·6 寸; B. ·7 寸 C. ·7.5 寸; D. ·8 寸; E. ·8. ·5 寸	What is the distance between R4 [Guān Yuán] and R12 [Zhōng Wǎn] according to the bone measurements by Cun? A. ·6cun; B. ·7cun; C. ·7.5cun; D. ·8cun; E. ·8.5cun
47	腘横纹至外踝尖的骨度分寸是: A ·12 寸; B ·18 寸 C. ·9 寸; D ·8 寸; E ·16 寸.	What is the distance between popliteal fold and tip of the lateral malleolus according to the bone measurements by Cuns? A ·12 Cun; B ·18 Cun; C. 9 Cun; D ·8 Cun; E ·16 Cun
48	何经"标"部在头维处? A 手阳明大肠经; B 足阳明胃经 C. 手少阳三焦经: D. 足少阳胆经; E. 手太阳小肠经。	What meridian has its manifestation region [BIĀO] located on the S8（Tóu Wěi）? A. large intestine meridian; B. stomach meridian; C. sanjiao meridian; D. gallbladder meridian; E small intestine meridian.
49	还出挟口，交人中，左之右，右之左，上挟鼻孔的经脉是: A.足阳明胃经; B 手阳明大肠经 C. 足太阳膀胱经; D 足少阳胆经.	What meridian goes round the upper lip, with two branches meeting at the philtrum; the branch on the left; C. ontinues to progress toward the right, and the one on the right; C. ontinues to progress toward the left. The two branches travel along both sides of the nares? A. bright yang stomach meridian of foot; B. bright yang large intestine meridian of hand C. greater yang bladder meridian of foot; D. lesser yang gallbladder meridian of foot.
50	季肋以下至髀枢的骨度分寸是:A ·8 寸; B. ·5 寸 C. ·9 寸; D. ·13 寸; E. ·16 寸	What is the distance between lower false ribs and greater trochanter (trochanter-major) according to the bone measurements by Cun? A ·8cun; B. ·5cun; C. ·9cun; D. ·13cun; E. ·16cun
51	既称十二经之海,又称血海的是: A ·足阳明胃经; B ·足少阴肾经 C. ·足太阴脾经; D ·冲脉; E ·带脉.	Which meridian is called. “sea of twelve master meridians” and “sea of blood”? A. stomach meridian; B. kidney meridian; C. spleen meridian; D. chong mai (vigorous meridian); E. dai mai (belt meridian).
52	既循行于目内眦又循行于目外眦的经脉是: A.手太阳小肠经; B. 手少阳三焦经 C.	What meridian travels through both medial canthus and lateral canthus? A. small intestine meridian; B. sanjiao (triple heater) meridian; C. bladder meridian; D. gallbladder meridian.

	足太阳膀胱经; D 足少阳胆经.	
53	既有定位又有定名，但没定经的腧穴是: A.十四经穴; B.奇穴 C. 阿是穴; D 特定穴.	What points have a fixed name, but do not belong to a fixed. meridian? A. acupuncture points on fourteen meridians; B. extraordinary points; C. pressure points (a shi point); D. specially marked points (te ding xue).
54	交会于督脉的经脉下列何项错误的是: A.手三阳; B 足三阳 C. 阳维脉; D. 阳跷脉.	Which of the following does not meet at Du Mai (governing meridian)? A. three yang meridians of hand B. three yang meridians of foot; C. yang wei mai (fastener meridian of yang); D. yang qiao mai (heel meridian of yang).
55	经筋的分布,与何系统的关系最为密切? A 内脏系统; B 脉管系统 C. 肌肉系统; D 骨骼系统; E 皮肤.	What system is most closely related to the distribution of muscular meridians (jing jin)? A. system of internal organs; B. vascular system C. muscular system; D. skeletal system; E. skin.
56	经筋中具有总络人体诸筋作用的是: A ,足阳明经筋; B 足太阳经筋 C. 足太阴经筋; D 足少阴经筋; E 足厥阴经筋.	Which of the muscular meridians governs the functions of various muscles in the body? A. bright yang of foot muscular meridian; B. greater yang of foot muscular meridian; C. greater yin of foot muscular meridian; D. lesser yin of foot muscular meridian; E. jue yin (decreasing yin) of foot muscular meridian.
57	经络系统中，具有 "离入出合"循行分布特点的是: A 十五别络; B 十二经脉 C. 十二经筋 D 十二皮部	In the system of meridians, what meridians are characterized. by “separating from, entering into, making an exit, meeting” in their distribution? A fifteen linking meridians; B twelve master meridians; C. twelve muscular meridians; D. twelve skin zones
58	经络系统中，具有保持人体正常运动功能的是: A 十二经别；B 十二经筋； C. 十二皮部；D 阴阳跷脉。	In the system of meridians, what meridians have the function of maintaining the normal motor function in the human body? A twelve separate master meridians (jing bie); B twelve muscular meridians C. twelve skin zones; D. heel meridians of yin and yang (qiao mai)
59	经络系统中,具有约束骨骼保持人体正常运动功能的是: A 阴阳维脉：; B 阴阳跷脉： C. 十五络脉； D 十二经别； E 十二经筋	In the system of meridians, what meridians are effective in; C. ontrolling the bones and maintaining the normal exercise functions of the body? A. Fastener meridians of yin and yang (yin yang wei mai); B. heel meridians of yin and yang (yin yang qiao mai); C. fifteen linking meridians (luo mai); D. twelve separate master meridians (jing bie); E. twelve muscular meridians (jin jing).
60	经络系统中能加强表里两经在体表相互联系的主要是: A 奇经八脉；B 十五络脉；C 十二经别； D 十二经筋.	In the system of meridians, what meridians can most reinforce the; C. onnections in the body surface between superficial and deep meridians? A eight extraordinary meridians; B fifteen linking meridians C. twelve separate master meridians (jing bie); D. twelve muscular meridians.
61	经络系统中能加强表里两经在体内相互联系的主要是: A 奇经八脉; B 十五	In the system of meridians, what meridians can most reinforce the; C. onnections in the internal region between superficial and deep meridians?

	络脉 C. 十二经别; D 十二经筋.	A eight extraordinary meridians; B fifteen linking meridians C. twelve separate master meridians (jing bie); D. twelve muscular meridians.
62	经络系统中能加强表里两经之间联系的是: A.十二皮部; .B. 十二经别; C.十二经筋; D 十五络脉。	What meridians can most effectively reinforce the; C. onnection between superficial and deep meridians in the system of meridians? A. twelve skin zoners (shi er pi bu); B. twelve separate master meridians (shi er jing bie); C. twelve muscular meridians (shi er jing jin); D. fifteen linking meridians (shi wu luo mai).
63	经络系统中能加强经脉之间在浅层相互联系的主要是: A 奇经八脉; B 十五络脉 C. 十二经别; D 十二经筋; E 十二皮部.	In the system of meridians, which meridians are particularly capable of reinforcing the interconnections in the superficial region among meridians? A. eight extraordinary meridians; B. fifteen linking meridians (luo mai); C. twelve separate master meridians (jing bie); D. twelve muscular meridians (jing jin); E. twelve skin zones (pi bu).
64	经络学说中的 "血海" ,指的是: A. 足阳明胃经; B. 督脉 C. 冲脉; D. 任脉; E. 足太阴脾经	In the theory of meridians, what does "sea of blood" refer to? A. foot yang ming stomach meridian; B. du mai / governing meridian; C. chong mai / vigorous meridian; D. ren mai /; C. onception meridian; E. foot greater yin spleen meridian
65	经络学说中的"六合"是指: A 十二正经中的表里经相合; B 十二经别中的表里经别相合; C. 十二经络脉中的表里两经络脉相合; D ,十二经筋中的表里经筋相合; E 十二皮部中的表里经皮部相合.	In the system of meridians, what does "six meetings (liu he)" refer to? A. meetings of superficial and deep meridians among the twelve master meridians; B. meetings of superficial and deep meridians among the twelve separate master meridians (jing bie); C. meetings of superficial and deep meridians among the twelve linking meridians (luo mai); D. meetings of superficial and deep meridians among the twelve muscular meridians (jing jin); E. meetings of superficial and deep meridians among the twelve skin zones (pi bu).
66	经络在躯干分布的原则是"腹为阴，背为阳"，但有一条经例外，是指以下经脉中的: A 足少阳经; B 足阳明经 C. 足厥阴经; D 足少阴经; E 足太阳经.	The distribution of meridians in the trunk is based. on the principle that "abdomen is yin, back is yang". What particular meridian does not follow this principle? A. lesser yang meridian of foot; B. bright yang meridian of foot; C. decreasing yin (jue yin) meridian of foot; D. lesser yin meridian of foot; E. greater yang meridian of foot
67	经脉中，凡是六阳经的经脉分布在: A.四肢外侧; B.四肢内侧 C. 腹部; D 胸部.	What is the distribution of six yang meridians among the master meridians? A. lateral side of four limbs; B. medial side of four limbs C. abdominal region; D. chest region.
68	具有调节肢体运动和眼睑开合功能的经脉 A.督脉; B.足少阳胆经 C. 阴阳跷脉; D 阴阳维脉.	What is the meridian that regulates the movements of limbs and the opening-closing and functions of the eyelids? A. du mai; B. lesser yang gallbladder meridian of foot Chesteel meridians of yin and yang (yin and yang qiao mai); D. fastener meridians of yin and yang (yin and yang wei mai).
69	具有涵蓄十二经气血作用的经脉是:	Which meridian can accommodate and store away energy and blood of the twelve master meridians?

	A·足太阴脾经; B·足阳明胃经 C. 任脉; D·冲脉; E·以上均不是.	A. spleen meridian; B. stomach meridian; C. ren mai (conception meridian); D. chong mai (vigorous meridian); E. none of the above.
70	口、目系为何经之经别出合处: A·足阳明经; B·手厥阴经 C. 手少阴经; D·足少阳经; E·手阳明.	What separate master meridian meets at mouth and eye; C. onnectives? A·bright yang meridian of foot; B·decreasing yin meridian of hand C. ·lesser yin meridian of hand D · lesser yang meridian of foot, E·bright yang / yang ming of hand.
71	两乳头之间的骨度分寸是: A. ·8 寸; B. ·7 寸 C. ·5 寸; D. ·13 寸; E. ·12 寸	What is the distance between nipples according to the bone measurements by Cun? A. ·8 cun; B. ·7cun; C. ·5 cun; D. ·13 cun; E. ·12 cun
72	两完骨之间的骨度分寸是: A·9 寸; B·12 寸 C. ·13 寸; D·16 寸; E·19 寸.	What is the distance between mastoid processes according to the bone measurements by Cun? · A·9 Cun; B·12 Cun; C. ·13 Cun D·16 Cun E·19 Cun
73	六阳经中，除……外，均与目内眦或目外眦发生联系: A·手太阳; B·手少阳 C. ·手阳明; D·足阳明; E·足少阳.	Among the six yang meridians, which one is not; C. onnected with either medical canthus or lateral canthus? A. greater yang of hand B. lesser yang of hand C. bright yang of hand D. bright yang of foot; E. lesser yang of foot.
74	络脉最细小的部分称为: A·孙络; B. 别络 C. ·支络; D·浮络; E·小络.	What is the smallest part of the linking meridians called? A. tiny link (sun luo); B. separate link (bie luo); C. branch link (zhi luo); D. floating link (fu luo); E. small link (xiao luo).
75	面、目内眦为何经之经别出合处: A·足阳明经; B·手厥阴经 C. ·手少阴经; D·足少阳经; E·手阳明	What separate master meridian meets at face and medical canthus? A · bright yang meridian of foot; B·decreasing yin meridian of hand C. ·lesser yin meridian of hand D · lesser yang meridian of foot; E·bright yang / yang ming of hand.
76	能共同主治胸部病的经脉是: A.手三阴经; ; B.手三阳经; C. 足三阴经; D 足三阳经。	Which group of meridians has the common function of treating the diseases in the chest region? A. three yin meridians of hand B. three yang meridians of hand C. three yin meridians of foot; D. three yang meridians of foot.
77	脾之大络分出的部位的穴位是: A.丰隆; B 内关 C. 大包; D 公孙.	What point is the location where the greater linking point of spleen separate? A. S40 [Fēng Lóng]; B. P6 [Nèi Guān]; C. Sp21 [Dà Bāo]; D. Sp4 [Gōng Sūn].
78	脾之大络散布于: A·肺; B·腹 C. 胸胁; D·头; E·大肠.	Where is the greater linking point of the spleen spreading around? A·lungs; B·abdomen; C. ·chest and costal region; D·head; E·large intestine
79	其支者，别颊上(出頁)抵鼻，至目内眦的经脉是: A.足太阳膀胱经; B. 手太阳小肠经 C. 足少阳胆经; D 手少	What meridian has a branch that begins to diverge at the cheek; and then, it moves upward to regio infraorbitlis (infraorbital region); and then, it reaches the nose; and then it arrives at medial canthus? A. bladder meridian; B. small intestine meridian; C. gallbladder

	阳三焦经.	meridian; D. sanjiao (triple heater) meridian.
80	其支者，从耳后入耳中，出走耳前，过客主人前，交颊，至目锐眦的经脉是：A.手厥阴心包经; B.手少阳三焦经 C.手太阳小肠经; D 手阳明大肠经.	What meridian has a branch which travels from the region behind the ear to enter into the ear; and then, it goes outward to pass before the ear; and then, it moves through the region before Ke-Zhu-Ren (Shang-Guan, G3); and then, it meets the former branch in the cheek; and then, it reaches outer canthus (the lateral angle of eye)? A. pericardium meridian; B. sanjiao meridian; C. small intestine meridian; D. large intestine meridian.
81	其支者，从腕后直出次指内廉，出其端的经脉是：A.手阳明大肠经; B 手少阴心经 C. 手厥阴心包经; D 手太阴肺经.	What meridian has a branch that travels from the back of the wrist, passes through the medial region of the forefinger, and then goes outward to the tip of the forefinger? A. bright yang large intestine meridian of hand B. lesser yin heart meridian of hand (shao yin); C. decreasing yin (jue yin) pericardium meridian of hand D. greater yin lung meridian of hand.
82	其支者,从心系，上挟咽，系目系的经脉是：A.足厥阴肝经; B 足少阴肾经 C. 手少阴心经; D 手厥阴心包经.	What meridian has a. branch that begins to diverge at the; C. onnectives of the heart; and then, it goes upward to travel round. the throat, and is linked. with the; C. onnectives of the eye? A. decreasing yin liver meridian of foot; B. lesser yin kidney meridian of foot C. lesser yin heart meridian of hand D. decreaing yin (jue yin) pericardium meridian of hand.
83	其支者，从腰中，下挟脊贯臀入腘中的经脉是：A，足少阴肾经; B 足少阳胆经 C. 足阳明胃经; D 足太阳膀胱经.	What meridian has a branch that diverges in the lumbar region; and then, it goes downward along the spinal column; and then, it passes through the middle of gluteus maximus; and then, it goes straight to enter popliteal fossa? A. kidney meridian; B. gallbladder meridian; C. stomach meridian; D. bladder meridian.
84	其支者，循胸出胁，下腋三寸，上抵腋下，循臑内，行太阴少阴之间的经脉是：A 手太阴肺经; B.手厥阴心包经 C. ，手少阳三焦经; D 手阳明大肠经.	What meridian has a branch that travels from the middle point between the nipples; and then, it moves sideways and outward through the ribs; and then, it goes downward to the region three Cun below the armpit; and then, it turns around. and goes upward to the region below the armpit; and then, it goes along the medial region of the upper arm; and then, it travels between the greater yin meridian of hand (the lung meridian) and the lesser yin meridian of hand (the heart meridian)? A. lung meridian; B. pericardium meridian; C. sanjiao meridian; D. large intestine meridian.
85	其支者:别目锐眦，下大迎，合于手少阳抵于颇，下加颊车，下颈合缺盆的经脉是：A.手少阳三焦经; B 足太阳膀胱经 C. 足少阳胆经; D 足阳明胃经.	What meridian has a branch that diverges at outer canthus to move downward to Da-Ying (S5); and then, it meets with the meridian of the triple heater; and then, it reaches the lower part of regio infraorbitalis (infraorbital region); and then, it passes downward through the angle of mandible; and then, it travels downward to the neck; and then, it meets with the former branch at supraclavicular fossa? A. sanjiao meridian; B. bladder meridian; C. gallbladder meridian; D. stomach meridian.
86	其支者:别掌中，循小指次指出其端的经脉是：	What meridian has a branch that departs from the palm of hand to travel along the ring finger to move outward at its tip?

	脉是：A.手厥阴心包经;.B. 手太阴肺经 C. 手少阳三焦经; D 足厥阴肝经.	A. pericardium meridian; B. lung meridian; C. sanjiao meridian; D. liver meridian.
87	其支者:从巅入络脑，还出别下项，循肩膊内，挟脊，抵腰中入循膂的经脉是：A.足少阳胆经; B.足太阳膀胱经 C. 足阳明胃经; D 手太阳小肠经.	What meridian has a straight vessel that proceeds from the vertex to be linked with the brain; and then, it turns around; and then, it goes downward to pass through the neck. This vessel then travels through the region of the scapula; and then, it proceeds along the spinal column to reach the lumbar region; and then, it enters the muscles along the spinal column? A. gallbladder meridian; B. bladder meridian; C. stomach meridian; D. small intestine meridian.
88	其支者:从巅至耳上角的经脉是：A.足少阳胆经; B.足太阳膀胱经 C. 足阳明胃经; D 手太阳小肠经.	What meridian has a branch that begins to diverg at the vertex and then it arrives in the region above the apex of the ear? A. gallbladder meridian; B. bladder meridian; C. stomach meridian; D. small intestine meridian.
89	其支者:从耳后入耳中，出走耳前，至目锐眦后的经脉是：A.足少阳胆经; B 手少阻三焦经 C. 足阳明胃经; D 足太阳膀胱经.	What meridian has a branch that travels from the region behind the ear to enter into the ear; and then, it goes outward to pass through the region in front of the ear; and then, it arrives at the region behind outer canthus? A. gallbladder meridian; B. sanjiao meridian; C. stomach meridian; D. bladder meridian.
90	其支者:从肺出络心，注胸中的经脉是：A，足少阴肾经; B 下足厥阴肝经 C. 足太阴脾经; D.足阳明胃经.	What meridian has a branch that starts from the lungs; and then, it moves outward to be linked. with the heart, entering into the middle point between two nipples? A. kidney meridian; B. liver meridian; C. spleen meridian; D. stomach meridian.
91	其支者:从目系下颊里，环唇内的经脉是：A.足厥阴肝经; B.足阳明胃经 C. 足太阴脾经; D 手阳明大肠经.	What meridian has a branch that travels from the; C. onnective of the eye downward to the medial region of the cheek; and then, it goes round. the inside of the lips? A. liver meridian; B. stomach meridian; C. spleen meridian; D. large intestine meridian.
92	其支者:从缺盆循颈上颊至目锐眦，却入耳中的经脉是：A.手少阳三焦经; B. 手阳明大肠经 C. ，手太阳小肠经; D 足少阳胆经.	What meridian has a branch that begins to diverge at the supraclavicular fossa; and then, it travels along the neck; and then, it proceeds upward to the cheek to reach outer canthus; and then, it turns around. to the inside of the ear? A. lesser yang triple heater meridian of hand (san jiao meridian); B. bright yang large intestine meridian of hand C. greater yang small intestine meridian of hand D. lesser yang gallbladder meridian of foot.
93	其支者:从膻中，上出缺盆，上项，系耳后，直上出耳上角，以屈下颊至顾的经脉是：A. 足少阳胆经; B. 手太阳小肠经 C. 手阳明大肠经; D，手少阳三焦经.	What meridian has a branch which diverges in the middle region between the nipples; and then, it goes upward and then outward at supraclavicular fossa; and then, it passes upward to the back of the neck and; C. onnected with the back of the ear and then moving straight upward; and then it travels outward at the apex of the external ear; from there it zigzags downward to travel round. the Chest and to reach regio infraorbitalis

		(infraorbital region)? A. gallbladder meridian; B. small intestine meridian; C. large intestine meridian; D. sanjiao meridian.
94	其支者:复从肝别贯膈，上注肺的经脉是: A.足厥阴肝经; B.手太阴肺经 C. 足太阴脾经; D 手少阴心经.	What meridian has a branch that travels from the liver; and then, it passes through the diaphragm; and then, it goes upward to enter the lungs? A. liver meridian; B. lung meridian; C. spleen meridian; D. heart meridian.
95	其直者，从腕后直出次指内廉，出其端的经脉是: A·手阳明大肠经; B 手少阴心经 C. ·手厥阴心包经; D·手太阴肺经.	What meridian has a straight branch that travels from the back of the wrist; and then it passes through the medial region of the forefinger; and then it goes outward to the tip of the forefinger? A·hand bright yang large intestine meridian; B. hand lesser yin heart meridian; C. ·hand decreasing yin pericardium meridian; D·hand greater yin lung meridian.
96	其直者，从心系，上挟咽，系目系的经脉是: A·足厥阴肝经; B 足少阴肾经 C. ·手少阴心经; D 手厥阴心包经.	What meridian has a straight branch that diverges at the; C. onnectives of the heart; and then, it goes upward to travel round the throat; and then, it is linked with the; C. onnectives of the eye? A · foot decreasing yin liver meridian; B foot lesser yin kidney meridian; C. ·hand lesser yin heart meridian; D hand decreasing yin pericardium meridian.
97	其直者，复从心系，却上肺，下出腋下的经脉是: A.手少阴心经; B.手厥阴心包经 C. 足少阴肾经; D，足厥阴肝经.	What meridian has a straight branch that travels from the; C. onnective of the heart; and then, it goes upward to the lungs; and then, it goes downward to the armpit? A. lesser yin heart meridian of hand B. decreaing yin (jue yin) pericardium meridian of hand C. lesser yin kidney meridian of foot; D. decreasing yin liver meridian of foot.
98	其直者:从缺盆下腋循胸过季胁下合髀厌中的经脉是: A.足少阳胆经; B.手厥阴心包经 C. 足厥阴肝经; D 足太阳膀胱经.	What meridian has a straight branch that travels from the supraclavicular fossa downward to the armpit; and then, it proceeds along the chest to pass through the false ribs region; and then, it goes downward again to meet with the former branch in regio trochanterica? A. gallbladder meridian; B. pericardium meridian; C. liver meridian; D. bladder meridian.
99	其直者:从肾上贯肝膈，入肺中，循喉咙，挟舌本的经脉是: A.足太阴脾经; B，足厥阴肝经 C. 足少阴肾经; D 手太阴肺经.	What meridian has a straight branch that goes upward from the kidneys; and then, it moves upward to pass through the liver and diaphragm; and then, it enters the lungs; it then proceeds along the throat; and then, it travels round the root of tongue? A. spleen meridian; B. liver meridian; C. kidney meridian; D. lung meridian.
100	奇经八脉与十二正经不同之处，下述哪项是错误的: A·不直属脏腑; B 无表里配合 C. 没有十二正经那样的循环流注关系; D 没有	Which of the following cannot be applied to distinguish the eight extraordinary meridians from the twelve master meridians? A. eight extraordinary meridians do not directly belong to viscera. and bowels; B. correspondence between superficial and deep does not exist among eight extraordinary meridians; C.

	专属的输穴; E 其走向除带脉横行外，都是自下而上运行.	unlike the twelve master meridians, the eight extraordinary meridians do not travel and flow in regular order; D. the extraordinary meridians do not have their own acupuncture points; E. all extraordinary meridians travel from lower to upper region, except dai mai (belt meridian).
101	奇经八脉中，除督脉之外，还有何脉入脑? A. 冲脉; B. 阴阳跷脉: C. 带脉; D. 任脉; E. 阴阳维脉。	What extraordinary meridian(s) enters into the brain aside from Du Mai (governing meridian)? A. chong mai (vigorous meridian); B. yin, yang, qiao mai (heel meridians of yin and yang); C. dai mai (belt meridian); D. ren mai (conception meridian); E. yin, yang, wei mai (fastener meridians of yin and yang).
102	奇经八脉中起于季胁的是: A.冲脉; B.带脉 C. 阴维脉; D 阴跷脉.	Which of the eight extraordinary meridians is originated. from the false ribs? A. chong mai (rigorous meridian); B. dai mai (belt meridian); C. yin wei mai (fastener meridian of yin); D. yin qiao mai (heel meridian of yin).
103	奇经八脉中与脑脊柱肾有密切关系的是: A.任脉; B.冲脉 C. 督脉; D 维脉.	Among the eight extraordinary meridians, which one is most closely; C. onnected with the brain, spinal column and the kidney? A. ren mai (conception meridian); B. chong mai (vigorous meridian); C. du mai (governing meridian); D. wei mai (fastener meridian).
104	歧骨至脐中的骨度分寸是: A·12 寸; B·18 寸 C. ·9 寸; D·8 寸; E·16 寸	What is the distance between xiphoid process and middle of umbilicus according to the bone measurements by Cuns? A·12 Cun; B·18 Cun; C. 9 Cun; D·8 Cun; E·16 Cun.
105	起于鼻之交安頞中，旁纳太阳之脉，下循鼻外入上齿中的经脉是: A.足太阳膀胱经: ; B 足阳明胃经: C.手阳明大肠经: D 足少阴胆经。	What meridian starts at the root of the nose (radix nasi), accommodates the greater yang meridian of foot, proceeds downward along the lateral region of the nose, and enters into the upper gum? A. greater yang bladder meridian of foot; B. bright yang stomach meridian of foot; C. bright yang large intestine meridian of hand D. lesser yang gallbladder meridian of foot.
106	起于大指次指之端，循指上廉，出合谷两骨间，上入两筋之中，循臂上廉，入肘外廉是指: A.手少阳三焦经: ; B.手阴明大肠经: C. 手太阴肺经: D, 手厥阴心包经。	What meridian starts at the tip of forefinger, travels upward along the dorsal surface of the forefinger, and then, it travels outward to pass through an acupuncture point named He-Gu (Li4) in between the first two metacarpal bones; and then, it travels upward to enter the region between two tendons (extensor pollicis longus and extensor pollicis brevis); and then, it proceeds upward along the radial margins of the forearm to enter the lateral surface of the elbow? A. hand lesser yang triple heater meridian; B. bright yang large intestine meridian of hand C. greater yin lung meridian of hand D. decreasing yin (jue yin) pericardium meridian of hand.
107	起于大趾之端，循指内侧白肉际，上踹内的经脉是: A.足太阴脾经: ; B 足厥阴肝经: C. 足阳明胃经: D 足少阴	What meridian begins at the tip of the great toe; and then, it travels along the line separating white and dark muscles on the great toe; and then, it goes upward through gastrocnemius muscles? A. greater yin spleen meridian of foot; B. decreasing yin liver

	肾经。	meridian of foot; C. bright yang stomach meridian of foot; D. lesser yin kidney meridian of foot.
108	起于目内眦，上额交巅的经脉是： A 足少阳胆经；B.足太阳膀胱经；C.足阳明胃经； D 手少阳三焦经。	What meridian begins at medial canthus; and then, it goes upward to the forehead; the two branches of the meridian meet at the vertex? A. gallbladder meridian; B. bladder meridian; C. stomach meridian; D. sanjiao (triple heater) meridian.
109	起于目锐眦，上抵头角，下耳后，循颈行手少阳之前，至肩上，却交出手少阳之后的经脉是： A.出手少阳三焦经；；B.足少阳胆经； C.足阳明胃经； D 足太阳膀胱经。	What meridian begins at outer canthus; and then, it goes upward to reach the angle of frontal hairline; and then, it travels downward to the region behind the ear; and then, it moves along the back of neck; and then, it proceeds in front of the lesser yang meridian of hand (the meridian of the triple heater); and then, it arrives at the shoulder; and then, it meets once again with the lesser yang meridian of hand (the meridian of the triple heater); and then, it moves outward behind the latter? A. sanjiao meridian; B. gallbladder meridian; C. stomach meridian; D. bladder meridian.
110	起于内踝处照海穴的经脉是: A·冲脉；B 带脉；C.阴跷脉； D 阳跷脉；E· 阴维脉。	What meridian starts from medial malleolus at K6 (Zhào Hǎi)? A. chong mai (vigorous meridian); B. dai mai (belt meridian); C. yin qiao mai (heel meridian of yin); D. yang qiao mai (heel meridian of yang); E. yin wei mai (fastener meridian of yin).
111	起于小指次指之端，上出两指之间，循手表腕，出臂外两骨之间的经脉是： A.手阳明大肠经；；B，手少阳三焦经；C. 足少阳胆经；D 手厥阴心包经。	What meridian begins at the tip of the ring finger; and then, it goes upward; and then, it passes through the space between the ring finger and the little finger; and then, it travels along the back of the wrist; and then, it proceeds outward through the lateral region of the forearm; and then, it passes through the space between ulna and radius? A. large intestine meridian; B. sanjiao meridian; C. gallbladder meridian; D. pericardium meridian.
112	起于小指之下，斜走足心的经脉是： A.足太阳膀胱经；；B 足少阳胆经；C.足少阴肾经；D 足太阴脾经。	What meridian begins on the plantar surface of the little toe; and then, it travels sideward through the middle of the sole of foot? A. bladder meridian; B. gallbladder meridian; C. kidney meridian; D. spleen meridian.
113	起于胸中，出属心包络下膈历络三焦的经脉是： A.手少阳三焦经；B 手厥阴心包经；C.足阳明胃经； D 足少阴肾经。	What meridian begins at the middle point between the nipples; and then, it goes outward and belongs to the pericardium; and then, it goes downward to the diaphragm to pass through the triple heater in sequence? A. sanjiao meridian; B. pericardium meridian; C. stomach meridian; D. kidney meridian.
114	起于中极之下，以上毛际的经脉是： A.督脉；B.任脉； C.冲脉；D 阴跷脉。	What meridian is originated. from below R3 and travels upward through the edge of pubic hairs? A. du mai (governing meridian); B. ren mai (conception meridian); C. chong mai (vigorous meridian); D. yin qiao mai (heel meridian of yin).
115	起于中焦，下络大肠，还循胃口的经脉是：	What meridian starts from the middle heater; and then it goes downward to the large intestine; and then it turns around to pass along cardiac and pyloric orifices ?

	A.手太阴肺经；B.手阳明大肠经；C.足阳明胃经； D 手少阳三焦经。	pass along cardiac and pyloric orifices ? A. greater yin lung meridian of hand B. bright yang large intestine meridian of hand C. bright yang stomach meridian of foot; D. less yang sanjiao (triple heater) meridian of hand.
116	任脉的别络散布于: A 胸部; B ·腹部 C. ·胸腹部; D ·胸胁部; E ·以上都不是.	Where does the linking meridian (bie luo) of ren mai spread around? A. chest region; B. the abdominal region; C. chest-abdomen region; D. chest and costal region; E. none of the above.
117	任脉的生理作用主要是: A ·通调冲任; B ·调节任督 C. ·总调奇经八脉; D ·调节阴经经气; E ·总调冲任督带.	What are the primary physiological functions of ren mai (conception meridian)? A. to; C. onnect and regulate chong mai (vigorous meridian) and ren mai (conception meridian); B. to regular ren mai (conception meridian) and du mai (governing meridian); C. to regulate eight extraordinary meridians as a whole; D. to regulate meridian energy of yin meridians; E. to regulate chong mai (vigorous meridian), ren mai (conception meridian), du mai (governing meridian), and dai mei (belt meridian) as a whole.
118	任脉的终点是: A.目; B.胞中 C. 目锐眦; D 颏下.	Ren mai (conception meridian) terminates at: A. eye; B. womb C. medial canthus; D. below the chin.
119	任脉起于中极之下，止于: A. ·承浆 (颐); B. ·水沟 (人中); C. ·唇内; D. ·目下; E. ·巅顶	The ren mai /; C. onception meridian begins at below R3 [Zhōng Jí], where does it terminate? A. ·R24 [Chéng Jiàng] (lower half of cheek); B. ·D26 [Shuǐ Gōu]; C. ·inside the lips; D. ·below the eye; E. ·vertex.
120	任脉又称为: A ·阳脉之海; B ·阴脉之海 C. ·气海; D ·血海; E. 髓海.	What is another name for the; C. onception meridian / ren mai ? A · sea of yang meridians; B · sea of yin meridians C. ·sea of energy; D · sea of blood, E · sea of marrow.
121	入上齿中的经脉是: A.手太阳小肠经; B.足阳明胃经 C. 足少阳胆经; D 手少阳三焦经.	What meridian enters into the upper gums? A. greater yang small intestine meridian of hand B. bright yang stomach merdian of foot; C. less yang gallbladder meridian of foot; D. lesser yang triple heater meridian of hand (san jiao meridian).
122	入下齿中的经脉是: A ·手阳明大肠经; B ·足阳明胃经 C. ·足少阳胆经; D ·手太阳小肠经.	What meridian enters the lower gums? A ·hand bright yang large intestine meridian; B ·foot bright yang stomach meridian; C. ·Lesser yang gallbladder meridian; D · hand greater yang small intestine meridian.
123	入掌内后廉，循小指之内，出其端的经脉是： A.手阳明大肠经; B.手厥阴心包经 C. 手少阴心经; D 手太阴肺经.	What meridian enters the medial-posterior region of palm; and then, it travels along the radial margin of the little finger; and then, it goes outward at the tip of the little finger? A bright yang large intestine meridian of hand B. decreaing yin (jue yin) pericardium meridian of hand C. lesser yin heart meridian of hand D. greater yin lung meridian of hand.
124	上膈，挟咽，连舌本，散舌下的经脉是: A.足少阴肾经; B 足太阳膀胱经 C. ，足太阴脾经; D 足厥阴肝经.	What meridian goes upward to the diaphragm; and then, it travels round the throat; and then, it is linked with the root of tongue; and then, it spreads on the root of the tongue? A. lesser yin kidney meridian of foot; B. greater yang bladder meridian of foot; C. greater yin spleen meridian of foot; D. decreasing yin liver meridian of foot.

125	上膈又下肘中的经脉是： A.手阳明大肠经; B.手太阴肺经 C. 手少阴心经; D 手厥阴心包经.	What meridian moves upward to the diaphragm and later moves downward to the middle of the elbow? A. bright yang large intestine meridian of hand B. greater yin lung meridian of hand C. lesser yin heart meridian of hand D. decreasing yin (jue yin) pericardium meridian of hand.
126	下列何经行于前臂两骨之间? A 手阳明大肠经; B 手少阴心经 C. 手太阴肺经; D 少阳三焦经; E 手太阳小肠经.	What meridian passes through the space between ulna. and radius? A. large intestine meridian; B. heart meridian; C. lung meridian; D. sanjiao meridian; E. small intestine meridian.
127	下列何经行于前臂两筋之间? A 手太阴肺经; B 手少阴心经: C. 手厥阴心包经; D 手太阳小肠经; E 手少阳三焦经.	What meridian passes through the region between two tendons (flexor carpi radialis tendon and palmaris longus tendon)? A. lung meridian; B. heart meridian; C. pericardium meridian; D. small intestine meridian; E. sanjiao meridian.
128	上贯肘，循臑外，上肩，而交出足少阳之后的经脉是: A.手少阳三焦经; B 手太阳小肠经 C. ，手阳明大肠经; D 足少阳胆经.	What meridian moves upward through the elbow; and then, it travels along the lateral region of the upper arm; and then, it moves upward to the shoulder; and then, it travels outward to meet with the gallbladder meridian; and then, it proceed. behind the latter ? A. sanjiao meridian; B. small intestine meridian; C. large intestine meridian; D. gallbladder meridian.
129	上踝 8 寸，交出太阴之后，上腘内廉，循股阴入毛中，过阴器，抵小腹的经脉是: A.足阳明胃经; B.足厥阴肝经 C. 足少阴肾经; D 足太阴脾经.	What meridian goes upward to the region eight Cun above medial malleolus; and then, it meets with the greater yin meridian of foot (the spleen meridian); and then, it; C. ontinues to travel outward behind the spleen meridian; and then, it proceeds upward through the medial region of popliteal fossa; and then, it travels along the medial region of thigh; and then, it enters pubic hairs; and then, it travels round the genital organs; and then, it reaches the lower abdominal region? A. stomach meridian; B. liver meridian; C. kidney meridian; D. spleen meridian.
130	上臑外前廉，上肩，出髃骨之前廉，上出于柱骨之会上，下入缺盆的经脉是: A.手少阳三焦经; B. 手太阴肺经 C. 手阳明大肠经; D 手厥阴心包经.	What meridian moves upward to pass through the shoulder; and then it progresses outward to the anterior surface of acromion; and then it travels upward to exit above the 7th cervical; and then it travels downward to pass through the supraclavicular fossa? A. lesser yang triple heater meridian of hand (san jiao meridian); B. greater yin lung meridian of hand C. bright yang large intestine meridian of hand D. decreasing yin (jue yin) pericardium meridian of hand.
131	上入颃颡，连于目系，上出额，与督脉会于巅的经脉是: A.足厥阴肝经; B.足太阴脾经 C. ，足少阴肾经; D 足阳明胃经.	What meridian moves upward to enter into the upper aperture of maxilla. (jawbone); and then, it becomes; C. onnected with the eye; C. onnective; and then, it goes outward to the forehead; and then, it meets with the du mai at vertex?. A. liver meridian; B. spleen meridian; C. kidney meridian; D. stomach meridian.

132	上循臑外后廉，出肩解，绕肩胛，交肩上，入缺盆的经脉是：A.手少阳三焦经; B.足少阳胆经 C. 手阳明大肠经; D 手太阳小肠经.	What meridian proceeds upward along the medial-posterior region of the upper arm; and then, it moves outward at the shoulder joint; and then, it progresses round the scapula; the two branches meet at the shoulder, and each of them subsequently enters supraclavicular fossa? A.lesser yang triple heater meridian of hand (san jiao meridian); B. lesser yang gallbladder meridian of foot; C. bright yang large intestine meridian of hand D. greater yang small intestine meridian of hand.
133	上循足跗上廉，去内踝1寸，上踝8寸是：A.足少阴肾经; B.足厥阴肝经 C. 足太阴脾经; D 足阳明胃经.	What meridian goes upward along the dorsum of foot to reach the region one Cun before medial malleolus; and then, it goes upward to the region eight Cun above medial malleolus? A. kidney meridian; B. liver meridian; C. spleen meridian; D. stomach meridian.
134	上肢内侧分布的经脉是: A·手三阳经; B·手三阴经 C. ·足三阳经; D·足三阴经; E·以上都不是.	What meridians are distributed on the medial side of the upper limbs? A ·three yang meridians of hand B ·three yin meridians of hand C ·three yang meridians of foot; D.three yin meridians of foot; E · none of the above.
135	十二经别的分布特点根据其先后次序可以概括为: A.离 出 入 合; B·离 入 出 合 C. ·离 合 出 入; D 出 入 离 合; E·入 出 离 合.	The distribution of twelve separate master meridians (jing bie) is arranged. in the following order: A. to separate from, to move outward, to enter into, to join; B. to separate from, to enter into, to move outward, to join; C. to separate from, to join, to move outward, to enter into; D. to move outward, to enter into, to separate from, to join; E. to enter into, to move outward, to separate from, to join.
136	十二经络脉的走向规律是： A.阳经会合于阳经，阴经归并于阳经; B.呈网状扩散;.C.与十二经同传注; D 阴经络脉走向阳经阳经走向阴经.	What is the pattern of distribution among the twelve linking meridians (luo mai)? A. yang meridians meeting yang meridians, yin meridians returning to yang meridians; B. spreading like a net; C. same as the patterms of twelve master meridians; D. linking meridians of yin travel toward yang meridian, yang meridians travel toward yin meridians.
137	十二经脉的流注顺序: A.小肠胃; B 心包三焦胆 C. 大肠胃肺; D 肝胆肾.	What is the flowing order of the twelve master meridians? A. small intestine, stomach; B. pericardium, sanjiao, gallbladder C. large intestine, stomach, lungs; D. liver, gallbladder, kidneys.
138	十二经脉的命名主要是依据: A.阴阳五行脏腑; B.阴阳五行.手足 C. 阴阳脏腑手足; D 五行脏腑手足.	What is the basis on which twelve meridians are named? A. yin yang, five elements, viscera and bowel; B. yin yang, five elements, hand and foot; C. yin yang, viscera. and bowel, hand and foot; D. five elements, viscera. and bowels, hand and foot.
139	十二经脉的循行走向错误的是: A·手三阴经从胸走手;B·足三阳经从头走足胸 C. 手三阳经从胸走手; D·足三阴经从足走胸腹; E·手三阳经从手走头.	Which of the following is Incorrect regarding the distribution of the 'twelve meridians? A ·three yin meridians of hand travel from chest to hand B ·three yang meridians of foottravel from head to foot and chest C. three yang meridians of hand travel from chest to hand D ·three yin meridians of foot travel from foot to chest and abdomen; E ·three yang meridians of hand travel from hand to head.

	从手走头.	
140	十二经脉之气结聚于筋肉关节的体系是指: A 十五络脉; B 十二经别 C. 十二经筋; D 十二皮部; E 奇经八脉.	What meridians are the places where the energy of the twelve master meridians gathers in tendons, muscles, and joints? A. fifteen linking meridians (luo mai); B. twelve separate master meridians (jing bie); C. twelve muscular meridians (jing jin); D. twelve skin zones (pi bu); E. eight extraordinary meridians.
141	十二经脉中，肝经与肺经的交接部位在：A 肺中; B 心中 C. 肝中; D 胸中; E 胸部.	Where are liver meridian and lung meridian; C. onnected among the twelve meridians? A inside the lungs; B inside the heart; C. inside the liver; D inside the chest; E chest region.
142	十二经脉中，脾经与心经的交接部位在：A 心中; B 肺中 C. 肝中; D 胃中; E 胸中.	Where are spleen meridian and heart meridian; C. onnected among the twelve meridians? A · inside the heart; B · inside the lungs C. · inside the liver; D inside the stomach; E inside the chest.
143	十二经脉中，肾经与心包经的交接部位在： A 肺中; B 胸中 C. 心中; D 胸部; E 腹部.	Where are kidney meridian and pericardium meridian; C. onnected among the twelve meridians? A · inside the lungs; B · inside the chest; C. · inside the heart; D chest region; E abdomen region.
144	十二经脉中出入脏腑最多者为哪一经 A.足厥阴肝经; B.手少阴经心 C. 足太阴脾经; D 足少阴肾经.	Among the twelve master meridians, what meridian travels in and out of viscera. and bowels most frequently? A. liver meridian; B. heart meridian; C. spleen meridian; D. kidney meridian.
145	十二经脉中的阳经与阳经的交接在 A. 额头部; B.头面部 C. 上肢部; D 胸腹部.	Where do yang meridians meet with yang meridians among the twelve master meridians? A. forehead region; B. head and face region; C. upper limbs region; D. Chest and abdomen regions.
146	十二经中，"注心中"的经脉是: A 手厥阴经; B 手少阴经 C. 足太阴经; D 足少阴经; E 足厥阴经.	Among the twelve master meridians, which of the following enters the inside of the heart? A. jue yin of hand meridian; B. lesser yin of hand meridian; C. greater yin of foot meridian; D. lesser yin of foot meridian; E. jue yin of foot meridian.
147	十二皮部的分布区域，是以下列哪项为依据的: A 十二经脉的机能活动; B 十二经脉的循行走向 C. 十二经脉的交接规律; D 十二经脉的体表分布范围.	Which of the following is the basis of the distribution among the twelve skin zones? A the functional activities of the twelve master meridians; B the direction in the distribution of the twelve master meridians; C. the patterns in which the twelve master merdians are; C. onnected with each other; D. the area of body surface in which the twelve master meridians are distributed.
148	十五络脉中的脾之大络,散布于: A 颈项; B 腋 C. 胸肋; D 腹; E 全身.	Among the fifteen linking meridians, the greater linking meridian of the spleen spreads around: A.neck and back of neck; B. armpit; C. the chest and ribs regions; D. abdomen; E. whole body.
149	什么经脉上循足跗上廉，去内踝一寸，上踝八寸？ A 小肠经; B 膀胱经	What meridian goes upward along the dorsum of foot to reach the region one Cun before medial malleolus; and then, it goes upward to the region eight Cun above medial malleolus?

	C. ·肾经; D·胆经. E·肝经	A. small intestine meridian; B. bladder meridian; C. kidney meridian; D. gallbladder meridian; E liver meridian.
150	什么经脉有二支脉从"下廉三寸而别"？A·胃经; B·大肠经 C. ·小肠经; D·胆经; E· 任脉.	What meridian has two branches that begin to diverge at the point three Cun below the knee? A; stomach meridian; B. large intestine meridian; C. small intestine meridian; D. gallbladder meridian; E. ren mai (conception meridian).
151	什么经脉有二支脉交于承浆？A·胆经; B·大肠经 C. · 小肠经; D·胃经; E· 任脉。	What meridian has two branches meeting each other at Cheng-Jiang (R24)? A. gallbladder meridian; B. large intestine meridian; C. small intestine meridian; D. stomach meridian; E. ren mai (conception meridian).
152	什么经脉有二支脉在肩上交接？A·胃经; B·大肠经 C. ·胆经; D·小肠经; E· 膀胱经.	What meridian has two branches meeting each other at the shoulder? A. stomach meridian; B. large intestine meridian; C. gallbladder meridian; D. small intestine meridian; E. bladder meridian.
153	手厥阴心包经在何穴处分出支脉与手少阳三焦经相衔接? A 郄门; B·间使 C. 内关; D·大陵; E·劳宫.	At what point does the branch of the pericardium meridian diverge to be; C. onnected with the sanjiao meridian? A. P4, Xī Mén; B. P5, Jiān Shǐ; C. P6, Nèi Guān; D. P7, Dà Líng; E. P8, Láo Gōng.
154	手三阳经的循行走向是: A·从胸走手; B·从手上头 C. ·从头走足; D·从足走腹胸; E·从头走手.	How are three yang meridians of hand distributed? A·from chest to hand B·from hand upward o head; C. ·from head to foot; D·from foot to abdomen and chest; E. from head to hand.
155	手三阳经腧穴均可用来治疗: A 神志病; B 热病 C. 耳病 D 口齿病.	Which of the following may be treated by the points on the three yang meridians of hand? A mental diseases; B hot diseases; C. ear diseases; D. mouth and tooth diseases.
156	手三阳经在上肢外侧面的排列顺序是: A 大肠经小肠经三焦经; B·大肠经三焦经小肠经 C. ·小肠经大肠经三焦经; D·三焦经大肠经小肠经; E·小肠经三焦经大肠经	What are the sequenes in which the three yang meridians of hand are distributed on the lateral side of upper limbs? A, large intestine meridian、small intestine meridian、san jiao meridian; B·large intestine meridian, san jiao meridian、 small intestine meridian; C. ·small intestine meridian、large intestine meridian, san jiao meridian; D·san jiao meridian、large intestine meridian、 small intestine meridian; E·small intestine meridian、san jiao meridian, large intestine meridian
157	手三阴经在上肢的分布是: A.太阴在前，厥阴在中，少阴在后; B.厥阴在前，太阴在中，少阴在后 C. 太阴在前，少阴在中，厥阴在后; D 厥阴在前，少阴在中，太阴在后.	How are the three yin meridians of hand distributed in the four limbs? A. greater yin (tai yin) in the front, decreasing yin (jue yin) in the middle, lesser yin (shao yin) in the back; B. decreasing yin in the front, greater yin in the middle, lesser yin in the back; C. greater yin in the front, lesser yin in the middle, decreasing yin in the back; D. decreasing yin in the front, lesser yin in the middle, greater yin in the back.
158	手少阳经及足少阳经在:	Where are the lesser yang meridian of hand and the lesser yang meridian of foot; C. onnected?

	A·足小趾端衔接; B.目锐眦衔接 C. ·食指端衔接; D·胸中衔接; E·鼻旁衔接.	A ·they are; C. onnected at the tip of little toe; B ·they are; C. onnected at lateral canthus C. they are; C. onnected at the fingertip of forefinger; D ·they are; C. onnected at the chest; E ·they are; C. onnected at the side of the nose.
159	手少阳三焦经经过以下除 XX 以外的所有部位: A·颈前; B·缺盆 C. ·耳; D·目外眦; E·面颊部.	Which of the following does not apply to the distribution of the triple heater meridian? A. front of the neck; B. supraclavicular fossa; C. ear; D. lateral canthus; E. face and chest reigon.
160	手少阳三焦经手太阳小肠经输穴主治的共同特点是: A·主治胁肋病; B·主治肩胛病 C. ·主治神志病; D·主治耳病; E·主治口齿病.	Points on the sanjiao and points on the small intestine meridians have one treatment in common，which is: A. to treat the diseases in the costal region; B. to treat the diseases of scapular; C. to treat the diseases of spirits and emotions; D. to treat ear diseases; E. to treat mouth and tooth diseases.
161	手少阴经之属与络的脏腑为: A·心、小肠; B·肝、胆 C. ·脾、胃; D·膀胱、肾; E·大肠、肺.	The ·lesser yin meridian of hand belongs to and is linked to what organs? A ·heart and small intestine; B ·liver and gallbladder; ·C. spleen and stomach; D ·bladder and kidneys; E ·large intestine and lungs.
162	手少阴心经的穴位数是: A·20; B·9;C. ll; D·24; E·28.	How many points are on the.hand lesser yin heart meridian? A.20; B ·9 C. 11; D ·24; E ·28
163	手太阳肺经在前臂部的支脉是从下列什么穴处分出的? A·孔最; B·列缺 C. 经渠; D·鱼际.	What point is the place where the forearm branch of the hand greater yang lung meridian diverges? A Lu6 [Kǒng Zuì]; B Lu7 [Liè Quē]; C. Lu8 [Jīng Qú]; D Lu10 [Yǔ Jì].
164	手太阳经脉循行"出肘内侧两骨之间"是指: A·尺骨与桡骨; B. 第一、二指骨 C. ·第四、五指骨; D·尺骨鹰嘴与肱骨外上髁之间; E·肱骨内上髁与尺骨鹰嘴之间.	The greater yang meridian of hand travels outward in between two bones on the medial side of elbow; what are the two bones in question? A ·ulna and radius; B. 1st and 2nd phalanxes C. ·4th and th phalanxes; D · between olecranon and the lateral; C. ondyle of humerus; ·E · medial epicondylus of humerus and olecranon.
165	手太阳经循行 "出肘内侧两筋之间"的两筋是指: A·拇长伸肌腱与拇短伸肌腱; B·尺侧腕屈肌腱与尺侧腕伸肌腱 C. ·尺侧腕屈肌腱与桡侧腕屈肌腱; D·尺侧腕伸肌腱与小指短屈肌; E·肱骨内上髁与尺骨鹰嘴.	Regarding the distribution of the small intestine meridian, Nei Jing says, "it moves outward on the medial side of the elbow through 'the space between two tendons'; what do "two tendons" refer to? A. long extensor muscle of thumb and short extensor muscle of thumb; B. ulnar flexor muscle of wrist and ulnar extensor muscle of wrist; C. ulnar flexor muscle of wrist and radial flexor muscle of wrist; D. ulnar flexor muscle of wrist and short flexor muscle of little finger; E. the medial; C. ondyle of humerus and olecranon.
166	手太阴肺经起于:	Where does the lung meridian start?

	A.胸中; B 肺中 C. 上焦; D 中焦.	A. inside the chest; B. inside the lung C. upper heater (shang jiao); D. middle heater (zhong jiao).
167	手太阴肺经与手阳明大肠经的交接部位. A.拇指指端; B. 次指桡侧端 C. 头面部; D 颈项部.	Where is the meeting region between the greater yin lung meridian of hand and the bright yang large intestine meridian of hand? A. tip of the thumb; B. radial side of the tip of forefinger chest; C. head and face region; D. back of neck region.
168	手太阴肺经在上肢的循行路线是: A·上肢内侧前廉; B·上肢内侧后廉 C. ·上肢外侧前廉; D·上肢内侧中行; E·上肢外侧后廉.	What is the distribution of the lung meridian in the upper extremities? A. on the anterior-medial side of the upper extremities; B. on medial-posterior side of the upper extremities; C. on the anterior-lateral side of the upper extremities; D. on the mid-line on the lateral side of the upper extremities; E. on the posterior-lateral side of the upper extremities.
169	手太阴手少阴两经在是动所生病中都有一个共同的症状是: A 缺盆中痛; B·目黄 C. 嗌干; D·烦心; E 臂厥.	The greater yin meridian of hand and the lesser yin meridian of hand have one symptom in common due to external causes, what is this symptom? A. pain in the supraclavicular fossa; B. yellowish eyes; C. dry throat (yi gan); D. mental depression; E. upstream arms (bi jue).
170	手阳明大肠经体表循行路线，下列除哪项外，余项均错误? A 起于大指之端，循指上廉，出合谷两骨之间; B 上入两筋之中，循臂上廉，入脑 C. 上肩，出髃骨之后廉; D 从缺盆上颈，贯颊，入上齿中; E 还出挟口，交入中，左之右，右之左，上挟鼻孔。	Which of the following describes the distribution of the large intestine accurately? A. This meridian starts at the tip of thumb; and then, it travels upward along the dorsal surface of the forefinger; and then, it travels outward to pass through an acupuncture point named. He-Gu (Li4) in between the first two metacarpal bones; B. This meridian travels upward to enter the region between two tendons (extensor pollicis longus and extensor pollicis brevis); and then, it proceeds upward along the radial margins of the forearm to enter the brain; C. This meridian moves upward to pass through the shoulder; and then, it progresses outward to the posterior surface of acromion; D. This meridian moves from the supraclavicular fossa. to travel upward toward the neck; and then, it passes through the middle of the chest; and then, it enters into the upper gum; E This meridian goes round. the upper lip, and the two branches of the meridian meet at the philtrum. The branch on the left; C. ontinues to progress toward the right, and the one on the right; C. ontinues to progress toward the left. The two branches travel along both sides of the nares.
171	手阳明大肠经循行经过的部位是: A，外眼角; B·内眼角 C. 上齿; D·下齿; E·耳.	The hand bright yang large intestine meridian passes through: A ·laeral canthus; B. ·medial canthus; C. ·upper teeth; D ·lower teeth; E ·ear.
172	手阳明经及足阳明经在: A·足小趾端衔接; B.目锐眦衔接 C. ·食指端衔接; D·胸中衔接; E·鼻	Where are the bright yang / yang ming meridian and the bright yang meridian of foot; C. onnected? A ·they are; C. onnected at the tip of little toe; B ·they are; C. onnected at lateral canthus; C. ·they are; C. onnected at the finger tip of forefinger; D ·they are; C. onnected at the chest;

	旁衔接.	E ·they are; C. onnected at the side of the nose.
173	手阳明经之属与络的脏腑为: A·心、小肠; B·肝、胆 C. 脾、胃; D·膀胱、肾; E·大肠、肺.	What pair of organs does the bright yang / yang ming of hand merian belongs to and is linked to? A ·heart and small intestine; B ·liver and gallbladder; C. ·spleen and stomach; D ·bladder and kidneys; E ·large intestine and lungs.
174	手足三阳经在四肢的分布规律是: A·太阳在前 少阳在中 阳明在后; B·少阳在前 太阳在中 阳明在后 C. ，阳明在前 少阳在中 太阳在后; D，太阳在前 阳明在中 少阳在后; E·阳明在前 太阳在中 少阳在后.	What is the pattern in which the three yang meridians of hand and foot are distributed in the four limbs. A · Greater yang / tai yang in the front, lesser yang / shao yang in the middle, bright yang / yang mingin the back; B ·lesser yang / shao yang in the front, greater yang in the middle, bright yang / yang ming in the back; C. ·bright yang / yang ming in the front, lesser yang / shao yangin the middle, greater yang / tai yang in the back; D · greater yang / tai yang in the front, bright yang / yang ming in the middle, lesser yang / shao yang in the back; E ·bright yang / yang ming in the front, greater yang / tài yang in the middle, lesser yang / shao yang in the back.
175	手足三阳经在头身四肢的分布规律一般是: A·"太阳"在前，"少阳"在中(侧)，"阳明"在后; B·"太阳"在前，"阳明"在中(侧)，"少阳"在后 C. ·"阳明"在前，"太阳"在中(侧)，"少阳"在后; D·"阳明"在前，"少阳"在中(侧)，"太阳"在后; E·"少阳"在前，"阳明"在中(侧)，"太阳"在后.	How are the three yang meridians of hand and foot distributed in the head, body, and four limbs? A. greater yang in the front, lesser yang in the middle (side), bright yang in the back; B. greater yang in the front, bright yang in the middle (side), lesser yang in the back; C. bright yang in the front, greater yang in the middle (side), lesser yang in the back; D. bright yang in the front, lesser yang in the middle (side), greater yang in the back; E. lesser yang in the front, bright yang in the middle (side), greater yang in the back.
176	手足三阴经穴位所以能够治疗头面部疾病是由于: A 表里经之间的相互联系; B 依靠络脉联系 C. 根据输穴主治的特异性; D 经别与经脉之间的联系; E 阴阳经之间通过任,督二脉相互联系.	The three yin meridians of hand and foot are used to treat the diseases of the head and face, why? A. mutual; C. onnections between the superficial and deep meridians; B. depending on the; C. onnections of the linking meridians; C. unique effects of acupuncture points; D. C. onnections between the separate master meridians (jing bie) and the master meridians; E. through the yin-yang; C. onnection of ren mai (conception meridian) and du mai (governing meridian).
177	手足三阴经在四肢部的分布规律一般是: A·"太阴"在前，"厥阴"在中，"少阴"在后; B·"太阴"在前，"少阴"在中，"厥阴"在后 C. ·"少阴"在前，"厥阴"在中，"太阴"在后; D·"少阴"在前，"太阴"在中，"	How are three yin meridians of hand and foot distributed on the four limbs? A. greater yin in the front, jue yin in the middle, lesser yin in the back; B. greater yin in the front, lesser yin in the middle, jue yin in the back; C. lesser yin in the front, jue yin in the middle, greater yin in the back; D. lesser yin in the front, greater yin in the middle, jue yin in the back; E. jue yin in the front, greater yin in the middle, lesser yin in the back.

	厥阴"在后; E·"厥阴"在前，"太阴"在中，"少阴"在后.	
178	头部正中线上从眉心至大椎的骨度分寸是: A·12 寸; B·18 寸 C. ·9 寸; D·8 寸; E·16 寸.	What is the distance between midpoint of eyebrows and D14 / Dà Zhuī on the middle ·head line according to the bone measurements by Cuns? A ·12 Cun; B ·18 Cun; C. 9 Cun; D ·8 Cun; E ·16 Cun
179	外邪侵入机体,一般的传注顺序是: A·皮部 孙络 经脉 脏腑; B·皮部 浮络 络脉 脏腑 C. ·皮部 络脉 经脉 脏腑; D·皮部 孙脉 络脉 脏腑; E·皮部 经脉 络脉 脏腑.	What is the order in which external pathogens invade into the organism from outside? A. skin region, tiny links (sun luo), meridians, viscera. and bowels; B. skin region, floating links (fu luo), meridians, viscera. and bowels; C. skin region, linking meridians (luo mai), meridians, viscera. and bowels; D. skin region, tiny links (sun luo), linking meridians (luo mai), viscera. and bowels; E. skin region, meridians, linking meridians (luo mai), viscera. and bowels.
180	五脏中与足阳明胃经直接相连的是: A·脾; B·心 C. ·肝; D·肺; E·肾.	What viscus is directly; C. onnected with the foot bright yang stomach meridian? A ·spleen; B ·heart;C. ·liver D ·lungs E ·kidneys.
181	膝中至外踝尖的骨度分寸是: A. ·19 寸; B. ·16 寸 C. ·13 寸; D. ·18 寸; E. ·12 寸	What is the distance between; center of popliteal fossa and tip of lateral malleolus according to the bone measurements by Cun? A. ·19cun; B. ·16cun; C. ·13cun; D. ·18cun; E. ·12cun
182	下臂行两筋之间，入掌中，循中指，出其端的经脉是: A.手厥阴心包经; B. 手少阳三焦经 C. 足厥阴肝经; D 手太阴肺经.	What meridian moves downward to the forearm to pass through the region between two tendons (flexor carpi radialis tendon and palmaris longus tendon); and then it enters the palm; and then, it travels along the middle finger; and then, it moves outward at the tip of the ring finger? A. pericardium meridian; B. sanjiao meridian; C. liver meridian; D. lung meridian.
183	下出外踝之前，循足跗上，入小趾次趾之间是： A.足厥阴肝经; B.足太阳膀胱经 C. ，足少阳胆经; D 足阳明胃经.	What meridian travels downward; and then outward through the region before lateral malleolus; and then, it travels along the dorsum of foot to enter the space between the 4th toe and the little toe? A. liver meridian; B. bladder meridian; C. gallbladder meridian; D. stomach meridian.
184	下列何经直通于脑? A 足少阴肾经:; B 足太阳膀胱经 C. 手少阳三焦经; D 足少阳胆经; E 手太阳小肠经.	Which meridian is directly; C. onnected with the brain? A. kidney meridian; B. bladder meridian; C. sanjiao meridian; D. gallbladder meridian; E. small intestine meridian.
185	下列各经脉排列中，符合流注次序的是: A. ·胃经 大肠经」脾经; B. ·肝经胆经 肺经 C. ·心经 小肠经 大肠经; D. ·大肠经 小肠经 胃经; E. ·膀胱经 肾经 心包经	Which is the right order of meridians in which they are arranged according to their flowing sequences? A. ·stomach meridian large intestine meridian 」spleen meridian; B. ·liver meridian gallbladder meridian lung meridian; C. ·heart meridian small intestine meridian large intestine meridian; D. ·large intestine meridian small intestine meridian stomach meridian; E. ·bladder meridian kidney meridian pericardium

		meridian
186	下列各穴中，属于手厥阴心包经是： A. 天府; B 天池;.C.天髎; D 天突.	Which of the following points belongs to the pericardium meridian? A. Tiān Fŭ; B. Tiān Chí; C. Tiān Liáo; D. Tiān Tū.
187	下列各组没有按流注次序排列的 A.胆经 肝经 肺经; B.胃经 脾经 心经 C. 肾经 心包经 胆经; D.心经 小肠经 膀胱经; E.脾经 心经 小肠经	Which is NOT the right order of meridians in which they are arranged according to their flowing sequences? A. gallbladder meridian liver meridian lung meridian; B. stomach meridian spleen meridian heart meridian; C. kidney meridian pericardium meridian gallbladder meridian; D. heart meridian small intestine meridian bladder meridian; E. spleen meridian heart meridian small intestine meridian
188	下列骨度分寸错误的是:□A 每一肋骨间折作 1.4 寸; B 季胁以下至髀枢为 6 寸 C. 左右缺盆穴之间的宽度是 8 寸; D 天樞以下至横骨为 5 寸; E 由腋窝横纹到十一肋作 12 寸.	According to the bone Cun measurements (gu du fen Cun), which of the following statements is NOT Correct? A. each intercostal space measures 1.4 Cuns; B. distance between hypochondrium (12th rib) and greater trochanter measures 6 Cuns; C. distance between two points of S12 (Quē Pén) measures 8 Cuns; D. distance between tianshu (S25) and henggu (R2) measures 5 Cuns; E. distance between axilla and hypochondrium (11th rib) measures 12 Cuns.
189	下列何经从耳后，进入耳中出走耳前? A 足太阳膀胱经; B 手太阳小肠经 C. 手阳明大肠经; D 足阳明胃经; E 足少阳胆经。	Which meridian travels from behind the ear to enter into the ear and travels outward in front of the ear? A. bladder meridian; B. small intestine meridian; C. large intestine meridian; D. stomach meridian; E. gallbladder meridian.
190	下列何经绕肩胛? A 手阳明大肠经;B 手厥阴心包经: C. 手太阳小肠经; D 手少阴心经; E 手太阴肺经。	What meridian travels round the scapula? A large intestine meridian; B. pericardium meridian; C. small intestine meridian; D. heart meridian; E. lung meridian.
191	下列何经绕阴部? A 足太阴脾经;B 足阳明胃经 C. 足厥阴肝经; D 足少阳胆经; E 以上均不是。	Which meridian travels around. the genitals? A. spleen meridian; B. stomach meridian; C. liver meridian; D. gallbladder meridian; E. none of the above.
192	下列何经上连目系? A. 手厥阴心包经; B 足少阴肾经 C. 足太阴脾经: D 手少阴心经; E 以上均不是.	Which meridian is; C. onnected with the eye; C. onnective in the upper region? A. pericardium meridian; B. kidney meridian; C. spleen meridian; D. heart meridian; E. none of the above.
193	下列何经直上巅顶 A 手太阴肺经; B.足少阴贤经 C. 足厥阴肝经; D 手厥阴心包经.	Which of the following meridians travels straight upward to the vertex? A. lung meridian; B. kidney meridian; C. liver meridian; D. pericardium meridian.
194	下列何项不属胆经经穴的主治范围? A 梅核气; B 热性病及寒热往来 C. 头颞部痛; D 胸胁痛; E 髀部或腿膝外侧部	Which of the following does not belong to the treatment range of the points on the gallbladder meridian? A. neurosis of the throat (globus hystericus); B. hot diseases or alternating cold and hot; C. pain in temple; D. pain in chest and costal region; E. pain in the lateral region of thigh or leg or

	疼痛.	knee.
195	下列经别循行别入腘部的是: A·足太阳经别; B·足阳明经别 C. ·足少阳经别; D·足厥阴经别; E·足太阴经别.	Which separate master meridian (jing bie) diverges to enter into the middle of popliteal fossa? A. greater yang of foot separate master meridian; B. bright yang of foot separate master meridian; C. lesser yang of foot separate master meridian; D. jue yin of foot separate master meridian; E. greater yin of foot separate master meridian..
196	下列经别循行别入季胁部的是: A·足太阳经别; B·足阳明经别 C. ·足少阳经别; D·足厥阴经别; E·足太阴经别.	Which separate master meridian diverges to enters into the false ribs region ? A. greater yang of foot separate master meridian; B. bright yang of foot separate master meridian; C. lesser yang of foot separate master meridian; D. jue yin of foot separate master meridian; E. greater yin of foot separate master meridian.
197	下列经脉排列中,没有按照十二经脉循行流注次序的是: A·胆肝肺经; B·大肠胃脾经 C. ·心小肠肾经; D·肾心包三焦经; E·三焦胆肝.	Which of the following is not the right order in which the twelve master meridians travel and flow? A. gallbladder, liver, lung meridians; B. large intestine, stomach, spleen meridians; C. heart, small intestine, kidney meridians; D. kidney, pericardium, sanjiao meridians; E. sanjiao, gallbladder, liver meridians.
198	下列经脉循行 "挟鼻孔"的是: A·任脉; B·足阳明经 C. ·手阳明经; D·督脉; E·冲脉.	Which of the following meridians travels through the sides of the nose? A. ren mai (conception meridian); B. bright yang meridian of foot; C. bright yang meridian of hand D. du mai (governing meridian); E. chong mai (vigorous meridian).
199	下列经脉循行不经过腹腔的是: A·手太阴肺经; B·手厥阴心包经 C. ·手少阴心经; D·手少阳三焦经; E·以上都不对.	Which of the following meridians does not pass through the abdominal cavity? A. lung meridian; B. pericardium meridian; C. heart meridian; D. sanjiao meridian; E. none of the above.
200	下列经脉循行与足少阴肾经关系最为密切的是: A·督脉; B·阴跷脉 C. ·带脉; D·冲脉; E.任脉.	Which of the following meridians travels most closely along with the foot lesser yin kidney meridian? A ·du mai / governing meridian; B ·yin qiao mai / yin heel meridian; C. belt meridian / dai mai D ·rigorous meridian / chong mai; E ·; C. onception meridian / ren mai.
201	下列经脉循行中,除哪一条外都经过缺盆部: A·手阳明大肠经; B·足少阳胆经 C. ·手太阳小肠经; D·足阳明胃经; E·足太阳膀胱经.	Which of the following meridians does not travel through supraclavicula fossa region? A. large intestine meridian; B. gallbladder meridian; C. small intestine meridian; D. stomach meridian; E. bladder meridian.
202	下列经脉与阳维脉循行最为密切的是: A·足少阴肾经; B·足太阳膀胱经 C. ·足厥阴肝经; D·足少阳胆经; E·足太阴脾经.	Which of the following meridians travels most closely along with the yang wei mai (fastener meridian of yang)? A. kidney meridian; B. bladder meridian; C. liver meridian; D. gallbladder meridian; E. spleen meridian.
203	下列经脉与脏腑属	Which of the following statements is Correct in regard to

	络关系正确的是: A.手太阴经属脾络胃; B.足太阳经属脾络胃 C. 手少阴经属心络小肠; D 足少阳经属肝络胆.	"belonging to" and "linked. with"? A. greater yin meridian of hand (shou tai yin jing) belongs to the spleen and linked. to the stomach; B. greater yang meridian of foot (zu tai yang jing) belongs to the spleen and linked. to the stomach; C. lesser yin meridian of hand (shou shao yin jing) belongs to the heart and linked to the small intestine; D. lesser yang meridian of foot / zu shao yang jing belongs to the liver and linked to the gallbladder.
204	下列经脉在耳颊部没有穴位是: A·足阳明经; B·足少阳经 C. ·手少阳经; D·足太阳经; E ·手太阳经.	Which of the following meridians does not have points in the ear and chest zone? A. bright yang meridian of foot; B. lesser yang meridian of foot; C. lesser yang meridian of hand D. greater yang meridian of foot; E greater yang meridian of hand.
205	下列经脉在眼区没有穴位的是: A. ·手太阳经; B. ·足太阳经 C. ·手少阳经; D. ·足少阳经; E. ·足阳明经	Which of the following meridians does not have points in the eye zone? A. ·hand greater yang meridian / shou tai yang jing; B. ·foot greater yang meridian / zu tai yang jing; C. ·hand lesser yang meridian / hand shao yang jing; D. ·foot lesser yang meridian / zu shao yang jing; E. ·foot yang ming meridian / foot bright yang meridian.
206	下列经脉中，除....外循行均经过 "脊": A·足少阴经; B·冲脉 C. ·阳维脉; D·督脉; E·足少阳经.	Which of the following meridians does not travel through the spine? A. lesser yin meridian of foot; B. Chong mai (vigorous meridian); C. yang wei mai (fastening meridian of yang); D. du mai (governing meridian); E. lesser yang meridian of foot.
207	下列经脉中，除......外;其循行均与胃腑发生联系: A·手太阳经; B·足厥阴经 C. 任脉; D·手太阴经; E 足太阴经.	Which of the following meridians is not; C. onnected with the stomach? A. greater yang meridian of hand B. jue yin meridian of foot; C. ren mai (conception meridian); D. greater yin meridian of hand E. greater yin meridian of. foot
208	下列经脉中,除......外都经过咽喉部位? A·手太阳经脉; B·手少阴经脉 C. ·足阳明经脉; D·手阳明经脉; E·足厥阴经脉.	Which of the following meridians does not travel through the throat? A. greater yang meridian of hand B. lesser yin meridian of hand C. bright yang meridian of foot; D. bright yang meridian of hand E. jue yin meridian of foot.
209	下列经脉中，经穴数目最少的是: A·任脉; B·督脉 C. ·手阳明大肠经; D·手太阳小肠经; E·手少阳三焦经.	Among the following meridians, which has the smallest number of points on it? A. ren mai (conception meridian); B. du mai (governing meridian); C. large intestine meridian; D. small intestine meridian; E. sanjiao meridian.
210	下列经脉中，有表里关系的是: A·肝与心; B·胆与心包 C. ·肾与大肠; D·心包与三焦; E·脾与肺.	Which two of the following merdians form a superficial-deep relationship with each other? A. liver and heart; B. gallbladder and pericardium; C. kidney and large intestine; D. pericardium and sanjiao (triple heater); E. spleen and lung.
211	下列经脉中起于 "下极之输" 的是: A·任脉; B·冲脉 C. ·督脉; D·带脉;	Which meridian begins at the point located between the anus and scrotum in man or the posterior labial commissure in woman?

	E·以上均不是.	A. ren mai (conception meridian); B. chong mai (vigorous meridian); C. du mai (governing meridian); D. dai mai (belt meridian); E. none of the above.
212	下列经脉中与督脉发生联系的阴经是: A·足太阴经; B·手太阴经 C. ·足厥阴经; D·手少阴经; E·手厥阴经.	Which of the following yin meridians is; C. onnected with du mai (governing meridian)? A. greater yin meridian of foot; B. greater yin meridian of hand C. jue yin meridian of foot; D. lesser yin meridian of hand E. jue yin meridian of hand.
213	下列经脉中与阴维脉循行最为密切的是: A·足太阴脾经; B·足阳明胃经 C. ·足少阴肾经; D·足太阳膀胱经; E·足厥阴肝经.	Which of the following meridians travels most closely along with the distribution of the yin wei mai (fastening meridian of yin)? A. spleen meridian; B. stomach meridian; C. kidney meridian; D. bladder meridian; E. liver meridian.
214	下列络脉中除……以外,都是向上循行: A·手太阴经络脉; B 手太阳经络脉 C. ·手少阳经络脉; D·足厥阴经络脉; E·足太阳经络脉.	Which of the following linking meridians does not travel upward? A. greater yin of hand linking meridian; B. great yang of hand linking meridian; C. lesser yang of hand linking meridian; D. jue yin of hand linking meridian; E. greater yang of foot linking meridian.
215	下列哪项除外，其循行走向均是从四肢末端走向头身? A.十二经别; B 十二经筋 C. 手三阴经; D 手三阳经.	Which of the following meridians does not travel from the tips of four limbs toward the head and body? A. twelve separate master meridians (shi er jing bie); B. twelve muscular meridians (shi er jing jin); C. three yin meridians of hand D. three yang meridians of hand.
216	下列哪组穴不是经脉的起止穴? A.会阴承浆; B 长强兑端 C. 隐白大包; D 涌泉俞府.	Which group of points does not; C. ontain the starting and ending points of meridians? A. R1, Huì Yīn; R24, Chéng Jiàng; B. D1, Cháng Qiáng; D27, Duì Duān; C. Sp1, Yǐn Bái; Sp21, Dà Bāo; D. K1, Yǒng Quán; K27, Shū Fǔ.
217	下列有关"四海"的概念错误的是: A·血海; B·髓海 C. ·气海; D·水谷之海; E·阳脉之海.	Which of the following is not included in the “four seas”? A · sea of blood; B · sea of marrow; C. · sea of energy; D，sea of water and grains; E · sea of yang meridians.
218	下列有关冲脉描述错误的是: A·血海; B·十二经脉之海 C. ·气海; D·五脏六腑之海; E·与肾经同行.	Which of the following does not apply to Chong mai (vigorous meridian)? A. sea of blood; B. sea of twelve master meridians; C. sea of energy; D. sea of five viscera. and six bowels; E. traveling along with the kidney meridian.
219	下列有关经脉循行错误的有: A·手太阳经络心; B·冲脉上通于心 C. ·足少阴经络心; D·足太阴经注心中; E·手少阴经出属心系.	Which of the following statements is incorrect regarding the distribution of meridians? A. greater yang meridian of hand is linked. to the heart; B. Chong mai (vigorous meridian) is; C. onnected upward to the heart C. lesser yin meridian of foot is linked. to the heart; D. greater yin meridian of foot enters inside the heart; E. lesser yin meridian of hand travels outward to belong to the heart; C. onnective.

220	下列有关手太阳小肠经循行错误的是: A·出"踝"中; B·上颊 C. 出耳上角; D·至目锐眦; E·至目内眦.	Which of the following statements does not apply to the distribution of the small intestine meridian correctly? A. it goes outward at the head of ulna; B. it proceeds upward to the chest C. it moves upward at the upper angle of ear; D. it reaches lateral canthus; E. it reaches medial canthus.
221	下列有关心经的循行错误是： A，出属心系; B 上挟咽 C. 系目系; D 抵掌后锐骨之端，入掌外后廉.	Which of the following is incorrect regarding the distribution of the heart meridian? A. it moves outward to belong to the heart; C. onnective; B. it moves upward to clip the throat C. it is linked to the eye; C. onnective; D. it travels along the medial-posterior region of the arm to reach the tip of the pisiform bone; and then, it enters the medial-posterior region of palm.
222	下列脏器，除...外，均与足少阴肾经循行发生联系: A·肝脏; B·心脏 C. ·脾脏; D·肺脏; E·肾脏.	Which of the following viscera. is not; C. onnected with the distribution of the kidney meridian? A.liver; B. heart C. spleen; D. lung; E. kidney.
223	下列足太阴脾经的循行路线，哪一条符合原文? A·起于大趾内侧端; B·起于胃口 C. 起于心中; D·入腹，属脾络胃; E·上挟咽，散舌本.	Which statement about thc distribution of the spleen meridian follows the original text? A. it begins on the medial side of the big toe; B. it begins at the pyloric orifice (opening between the stomach and duodenum); C. it begins inside of the heart; D. it enters the abdomen; and then, it belongs to the spleen and is linked. with the stomach; E. it travels on both sides of the throat, spreads on the root of the tongue.
224	下面的骨度分寸不正确的是: A·前发际至后发际 12 寸; B·歧骨至脐中 8 寸 C. ·两乳头之间 8 寸; ·D·两肩胛骨脊柱缘之间 6 寸; E·膝中至外踝高点 13 寸.	Which statement about the bone measurements by Cuns is NOT Correct? A·distance between frontal hairline and posterior hairline measures 12 Cun; B·distance between xiphoid process and middle of umbilicus measures 8 Cun; C. ·distance between two nipples measures 8 Cun; ·D·distance between the medial edges of scapula measures 6 Cun; E·distance between the midpoint on the lateral side of patella and lateral malleolus measures 13 Cun.
225	下肘内，循臂内后廉，抵掌后锐骨之端的经脉是: A.手少阴心经; B 手厥阴心包经 C. 足少阴肾经; D 手太阴肺经.	What meridian goes downward to the medial region of the elbow, and travels along the medial-posterior region of the arm to reach the tip of the pisiform bone? A. lesser yin heart meridian of hand B. decreaing yin (jue yin) pericardium meridian of hand C. lesser yin kidney meridian of foot; D. greater yin lung meridian of hand.
226	循臂内上骨下廉，入寸口，上鱼，循鱼际出大指经脉是指: A.手少阳三焦经; B 手阳明大肠经 C. 手太阴肺经; D 手厥阴心包经.	What meridian passes through the medial region of the forearm below the head of radius, enters the region of the pulse at the wrist, goes upward to the thenar eminence of hand, travels along the edge of the thenar eminence of hand, and then moves outward to the tip of thumb? A. lesser yang triple heater meridian of hand (san jiao meridian); B. bright yang large intestine meridian of hand C. greater yin lung meridian of hand D. decreasing yin (jue yin)

		pericardium meridian of hand.
227	循经取穴的理论依据是: A 病在经络,内脏者可取之于皮部; B 病在上者取之下,病在下者取之上 C. 标本根结的理论; D 经脉所通，主治所及; E 四肢远端穴位可以治头面躯干及全身病.	To select points according to the distribution of meridians is based. on the principle that: A.when diseases attack the meridians and internal organs, the skin zones should be selected; B. when the diseases attack the upper region, the points in the lower region should be treated; when the diseases attack the lower region, the points in the upper region should be treated; C. based. on the the ory of primary (ben), secondary (biao), root (gen), and fruit (jie); D. the diseases within the distribution of a given meridian should be treated by the points on that meridian; E diseases of the head, face, trunk, and whole body should be treated by the distal points in the four limbs.
228	循胁里，出气街，绕毛际，横入髀厌中的经脉是: A.手太阳小肠经; B.手少阳三焦经 C.足太阳膀胱经; D 足少阳胆经.	What meridian travels along the intercostal region; and then, it moves downward and then outward to pass along the edge of rectus abdominis (abdominal rectus muscle); and then, it goes round the edge of pubic hairs; and then, it goes sideways to enter into the trochanter region? A. small intestine meridian; B. sanjiao meridian; C. bladder meridian; D. gallbladder meridian.
229	循行进入上齿中的经脉是: A 手阳明大肠经; B 足阳明胃经 C. 足少阳胆经; D 手少阳三焦经; E 足太阳膀胱经.	What meridian enters the upper teech? A hand bright yang large intestine meridian; B foot bright yang stomach meridian; C. Lesser yang gallbladder meridian D hand lesser yang triple heater meridian; E foot greater yang bladder meridian.
230	循行起于足趾，循股外上行结于面部的经筋是: A 足三阳经筋：; B 足三阴经筋： C. 手三阳经筋： D 手三阴经筋： E 以上都不是.	What muscular meridian starts from toes, travels upward along the lateral thigh to fruit in the face region? A three yang muscular meridians of foot; B three yin muscular meridians of foot C. three yang muscular meridians of hand D three yin muscular meridians of hand E · none of the above
231	循行于腹部最外侧的经脉是: A.足少阴肾经; B 足厥阴肝经; C.足太阴脾经; D 足阳明胃经。	Which of the following meridians travels through the lateral side of the abdomen furthest from the midline? A. kidney meridian; B. liver meridian; C. spleen meridian; D. stomach meridian.
232	循行在臑内后廉的经脉是: A.手太阴肺经; B.手厥阴心包经; C.手少阴心经; D, 手少阳三焦经。	What meridian travels along the medial-posterior regions of the upper arm? A. lung meridian; B. pericardium meridian; C. heart meridian; D. sanjiao meridian.
233	阳跷脉起于: A 足阳明经; B 手厥阴经;C 手少阴经; D 足少阳经; E 手阳明经.	Where is yang heel meridian / yang qiao mai originated from? A medial side of heel; B lateral side of heel; C. womb; D medial side of lower leg; E lateral side of lower leg.
234	阳跷脉起于跟中,循外踝上行，入于:	The heel meridian of yang (yang qiao mai) begins from the heel and travels along the outer ankle to enter:

	A 缺盆; B 风池 C. ·风府; D ·天柱; E · 大椎.	and travels along the outer ankle to enter: A. S12, Quē Pén; B. G20, Fēng Chí; C. D16, Fēng Fǔ; D.B10, Tiān Zhù; E. D14, Dà Zhuī.
235	腋后纹头至肘尖的骨度分寸是: A ·9 寸; B ·12 寸 C. ·13 寸; D ·16 寸; E ·19 寸.	What is the distance between posterior axillary fold and wrist crease / olecranon) according to the bone measurements by Cuns? A ·9 Cun; B ·12 Cun; C. ·13 Cun; D ·16 Cun; E ·19 Cun.
236	颐、目外眦为何经之经别出合处: A ·足阳明经; B ·手厥阴经 C. ·手少阴经; D ·足少阳经; E ·手阳明.	What separate master meridian meets at lower half of vhest, outer vanthus?: A · bright yang meridian of foot; B ·decreasing yin meridians of hand C. ·lesser yin meridian of hand, D · lesser yang meridian of foot; E ·bright yang / yang ming of hand.
237	以喉结为水平线，颈前部经脉排列从前到后的顺序是: A.任脉手阳明大肠经足阳明胃经手太阳小肠经; B 任脉足阳明胃经手太阳小肠经手阳明大场经 C. 任脉足阳明胃经手阳明大肠经手太阳小肠经; D 任脉手阳明大肠经手太阳小肠经足阳明胃经.	What is the order in which meridians are arranged on a level with laryngeal prominence? A. ren mai (conception meridian), bright yang large intestine meridian of hand, bright yang stomach meridian of foot, greater yang small intestine meridian of hand B. ren mai, bright yang stomach meridian of foot, greater yang small intestine meridian of hand, bright yang large intestine meridian of hand C. ren mai, bright yang stomach meridian of foot, bright yang large intestine meridian of hand, greater yang small intestine meridian of hand D. ren mai (conception meridian), bright yang large intestine meridian of hand, greater yang small intestine meridian of hand, bright yang stomach meridian of foot.
238	以上踹内，出腘内廉，上股内后廉，贯脊的经脉是: A.足少阴肾经; B 足太阳膀胱经 C. 足厥阴肝经; D 足太阴脾经.	What meridian goes upward through the medial region of gastrocnemius muscles; and then, it passes outward through the medial region of popliteal fossa; and then, it travels upward through the medial-posterior regions of thigh; and then, it passes through the spine? A. kidney meridian; B. bladder meridian; C. liver meridian; D. spleen meridian.
239	以下除……外,均为手阳明大肠经循行所过之处? A ·前臂; B ·上臂 C. ·食指内侧; D ·肘部内侧; E ·肩胛部.	Which of the following is outside the distribution of the large intestine meridian? A. lower arm; B. upper arm C. medial side of the forefinger; D. medial side of the elbow; E. scapular region.
240	以下贯踹内，出外踝之后，循京骨，至小趾外侧的经脉是: A.足太阴脾经; B 足少阴肾经 C. 足太阳膀胱经; D 足厥阴肝经.	What meridian moves downward to pass through gastrocnemius muscles; and then, it proceeds outward in the region behind lateral malleolus; and then, it moves along the tuberosity of the 5th metatarsal to reach the lateral region of the 5th metatarsal bone? A. spleen meridian; B. kidney meridian; C. bladder meridian; D. liver meridian..
241	以下经脉哪条的循行不与目锐眦相关 A.足少阳胆经; B.足太阳膀胱经 C. 手太阳小肠经; D 手少阳三焦经.	Which of the following meridians does not travel through medial canthus? A. gallbladder meridian; B. bladder meridian; C. small intestine meridian; D. sanjiao meridian.

242	以下经脉中，除……外都经过肺: A·手厥阴经; B·手少阴经 C. ·足厥阴经; D·足少阴经; E·手阳明经.	Which of the following meridians does not pass through the lungs? A. jue yin meridian of hand B. lesser yin meridian of hand C. jue yin meridian of foot; D. lesser yin meridian of foot; E. bright yang meridian of hand.
243	以下哪组经脉循行过气街? A.足阳明经足太阳经; B 足太阳经足少阳经 C. 足阳明经足少阳经; D 足少阳经足少阴经.	Which of the following groups of meridians travel through energy street (qi jie)? A. bright yang meridian of foot, greater yang meridian of foot; B. greater yang meridian of foot, lesser yang meridian of foot; C. bright yang meridian of foot, lesser yang meridian of foot; D. lesser yang meridian of foot, lesser yin meridian of foot.
244	以下循髀阳，出膝外廉，下外辅骨之前，直下抵绝骨之端的经脉是: A.手太阳小肠经; B. 足少阳胆经 C. 足太阳膀胱经; D 足阳明胃经.	What meridian goes downward along the lateral side of hip joint; and then, it proceeds outward in the lateral region of knee; and then, it goes downward along the frontal side of lateral; C. ondyle of femur; and then, it travels straight downward to reach the depression three Cun above lateral malleolus? A. small intestine meridian; B. gallbladder meridian; C. bladder meridian; D. stomach meridian.
245	阴经经脉同头面部的联系，主要通过: A.，奇经八脉; B. 十二经别 C. 十五络脉; D. 十二经筋; E. 十二皮部	What meridians play a major role in; C. onnecting yin meridians and head and face region? A.eight extraordinary meridians; B. twelve separate master meridians / jing bie C. fifteen luo mai / linking meridians; D. twelve muscular meridians / jing jin; E. twelve skin zones / pi bu.
246	阴经与阳经（指表里经)交接的部位在·: A·头部; B·胸腹部C.面部 ·D·手足末端 E··上肢部	Where are yin meridians and yang meridians (which form the superficial-deep relationship with each other); C. onnected? A ·head region; B ·chest and abdominal region; C. face; ·D ·tips of hand and foot; E · ·upper limbs region.
247	阴经与阴经（指手足三阴经)交接部位在： A·胸腹部;B·胸中 C. ·腹部; D.四肢部·; E. 头面部.	Where are yin meridians of hand and foot; C. onnected? A ·chest-abdominal region; B ·inside chest C. ·abdominal region D.four limbs region ·E，head-face region.
248	阴晓脉起于: A·足跟内侧; B·足跟外侧 C. ·胞中; D·小腿内侧; E·小腿外侧.	Where is the yin heel meridian / yin qiao mai originated from? A ·medial side of heel; B ·lateral side of heel C. ·womb; D ·medial side of lower leg; E ·lateral side of lower leg,
249	与冲脉交会穴最多的经脉是: A 足阳明胃经; B·任脉 C. ·足少阴肾经; D·足厥阴肝经; E·阴维脉.	Which meridian has the greatest number of meeting points with chong mai (vigorous meridian)? A. stomach meridian; B. ren mai (conception meridian); C. kidney meridian; D. liver meridian; E. yin wei mai (fastening meridian of yin).
250	与冲脉在腹部的分布路线一致的经脉是: A·任脉; B·胃经	What meridian distributes in the abdominal region in the same way as chong mai (vigorous meridian)? A. ren mai (conception meridian); B. stomach meridian; C. kidney meridian; D. spleen meridian; E. none of the above

	C. ·肾经; D·脾经; E·以上都不是.	kidney meridian; D. spleen meridian; E. none of the above.
251	与督脉发生联系的阴经是: A.足太阴脾经; B.手太阴肺经 C. 足厥阴肝经; D·手少阴心经.	Which yin meridian is; C. onnected with the Du Mai (governing meridian)? A. spleen meridian; B. lung meridian; C. liver meridian; D. heart meridian.
252	与肩胛骨下角相平的胸椎是: A.·第 5 胸椎; B.·第 6 胸椎 C. ·第 7 胸椎; D.·第 8 胸椎; E.·第 9 胸椎	What thoracic vertebrae is on a level with the superior angle of the scapula? A. ·5th thoracic vertebra; B. ·6th thoracic vertebra C. ·7th thoracic vertebra; D. ·8th thoracic vertebrae; E. ·9th thoracic vertebra.
253	与脑联络的经脉是: A·足少阴肾经; B·足太阳膀胱经 C. ·手少阳三焦经; D·足少阳胆经; E·手太阳小肠经.	What meridian is linked to the brain? A ·foot lesser yin kidney meridian; B ·foot greater yang bladder meridian; C. ·hand lesser yang triple heater meridian D foot lesser yang gallbladder meridian; E · hand greater yang small intestine meridian.
254	与手阳明大肠经在鼻旁相接的经脉是: A·肺经; B·胃经 C. ·膀胱经; D，胆经; E·小肠经.	What meridian is c; C. onnected with the hand bright yang large intestine meridian on the side of the nose? A ·lungs meridian; B ·stomach meridian; C. ·bladder meridian; ·D，gallbladder meridian; ·E. small intestine meridian.
255	与足1、2、3 趾均有联系的经脉是: A·足阳明胃经; B，足太阳膀胱经 C. ·足太阴脾经; D·足厥阴肝经; E·足少阳胆经.	What meridian isconnected with 1st, 2nd, 3rd toes? A. foot bright yang stomach meridian; B ·foot greater yang bladder meridian; C. ·foot greater yin spleen meridian ·D · foot decreasing yin liver meridian; E. lesser yang gallbladder meridian.
256	与足太阴脾经交接的是: A·心经; B·肝经 C. ·肾经; D·肺经; E·心包经.	What meridian is; C. onnected with foot greater yin spleen meridian? A ·heart meridian; B ·liver meridian; C. ·kidneys meridian; D ·lungs meridian; E ·pericardium meridian.
257	在经络系统中，除 XX 外，其循行走向均是从四肢末端走向头身: A·十二经别; B·十二经筋 C. 十二皮部; D·手三阴经; E·足三阴经.	In the system of meridians, which of the following meridians do not travel from the tips of four limbs toward the head and body? A. twelve separate master meridians (jing bie); B. twelve muscular meridians (jing jin); C. twelve skin zones (pi bu); D. three yin meridians of hand E. three yin meridians of foot.
258	在经络系统中,从十二经中离合出入的部分是指: A·奇经八脉; B·十五络脉 C. 十二经别; D·十二经筋; E·十二皮部.	In the system of meridians, the; C. oncepts of "to separate from", "to join", "to move outward", "to enter into", apply to: A. eight extraordinary meridians; B. fifteen linking meridians (luo mai; C. twelve separate master meridians (jing bie); D. twelve muscular meridians (jing jin); E twelve skin zones (pi bu).
259	在经脉病候中，手少阳三焦经主: A·津液所生病; B·脉 [illegible]	What kind of disease does the sanjiao meridian take charge of? A. symptoms associated. with body fluids; B. symptoms associated. with pulses; C. symptoms associated. with tendons;

	所生病 C. 筋所生病; D 骨所生病; E · 气所生病.	D. symptoms associated. with bones; E. symptoms associated. with energy.
260	在面部发生左右交叉的经脉是: A 大肠经; B 胃经 C. 膀胱经; D 小肠经; E 三焦经.	What meridian crosses in the face? A large intestine meridian; B stomach meridian; C. bladder meridian; D, small intestine meridian; E · san jiao meridian.
261	在奇经八脉中，司下肢运动与寝寐的是: A. 任脉; B. 督脉 C. 跷脉; D. 带脉; E. 冲脉	Which of the eight extraordinary meridians takes charge of the movements of the lower limbs and sleep? A. ren mai /; C. onception meridian; B. du mai / governing meridian; C. heel meridians / qiao mai; D. dai mai / belt meridian; E. chong mai / vigorous meridian.
262	在奇经八脉中，治疗不寐，常选用: A. 阴维脉; B. 阳维脉 C. 冲脉; D. 阴跷脉; E. 阳跷脉	Which of the eight extraordinary meridians is frequently selected to treat insomnia? A. yin wei mai / yin fastener meridian; B. yang wei mai / yang fastener meridian; C. chong mai / vigorous meridian; D. yin qiao mai / yin heel meridian; E. yang qiao mai / yang heel meridian.
263	在奇经八脉中，治疗多眠，常选用: A 阴维脉; B 阳维脉 C. 冲脉; D 阴跷脉; E 阳跷脉.	Which of the eight extraordinary meridians is often used to treat sleepiness? A. yin wei mai (fastening meridian of yin); B. yann wei mai (fastening meridian of yang); C. chong mai (vigorous meridian); D. yin qiao mai (heel meridian of yin); E. yang qiao mai (heel meridian of yang).
264	在十二经脉病候中，主骨所生病的经脉是: A 足少阴肾经; B 足太阳膀胱经 C. 足少阳胆经; D 足厥阴肝经; E 足太阴脾经.	What meridian is in; C. ontrol of the symptoms associated with bones among the twelve master meridians? A. kidney meridian; B. bladder meridian; C. gallbladder meridian; D. liver meridian; E. spleen meridian.
265	在十二经脉中, 除……外，均联系到耳: A 足阳明胃经; B 足少阳胆经 C. 足太阳膀胱经; D 手少阳三焦经; E 手阳明大肠经.	Which of the following meridians is not; C. onnected with the ear? A. stomach meridian; B. gallbladder meridian; C. bladder meridian; D. sanjiao meridian; E. large intestine meridian.
266	在十二经脉中，从缺盆上颈的经脉是: A.手阳明大肠经; B 手少阳三焦经 C. 足阳明胃经; D 手太阳小肠经.	What meridian among the twelve master meridians trevels from the supraclavicular fossa. and then, it travels upward toward the neck? A. bright yang large intestine meridian of hand B. lesser yang triple heater meridian of hand (san jiao meridian); C. bright yang stomach meridian of foot; D. greater yang small intestine meridian of hand.
267	在十二经脉中,络心循咽，下膈抵胃的经脉是: A 手阳明经; B 手太阴经 C. 手太阳经; D 手少阳经; E 足少	Which of the twelve master meridians travels along the pharynx, down to the diaphragm, and reaches the stomach? A. bright yang meridian of hand B. greater yin meridian of hand C. greater yang meridian of hand D. lesser yang meridian of hand E. lesser yang meridian of foot.

	阳经.	
268	在十二经脉中，阳经与阴经的交接部位在: A·四肢末端; B·胸部 C.·头项部; D·头面部; E·以上都不是.	In what region do yang and yin meridians meet each other among the twelve master meridians? A. tips of four limbs; B. chest region; C. head and back of neck; D. head and face; E. none of the above.
269	在十二经脉中，阴经与阴经交接的部位在: A·四肢内侧面; B·胸部 C.·腹部; D·胸腹部; E·四肢末端内侧.	In what region do yin meridians meet each other among the twelve master meridians ? A. medial side of four limbs; B. chest region; C. abdominal region; D. chest-abdominal region; E. medial side of the tips of four limbs.
270	在十二经脉中,于鼻翼旁交接的是: A·手阳明与手太阳; B·足阳明与足太阳 C.·手阳明与足阳明; D·手太阳与足太阳; E·足阳明与手少阳	Among the twelve master meridians, which two meridians meet on the side of nose wing? A. bright yang of hand and greater yang of hand B. bright yang of foot and greatr yang of foot; C. bright yang of hand and bright yang of foot; D. greater yang of hand and greater yang of foot; E. bright yang of foot and lesser yang of hand.
271	在十二经脉中,在心中相交的经脉是: A·足少阴与手厥阴; B·足少阴与手少阴 C.·足太阴与手少阴; D·足太阴与手厥阴; E·足厥阴与手少阴	Which two meridians among the twelve master meridians meet each other inside the heart? A. lesser yin of foot and jue yin of hand B. lesser yin of foot and lesser yin of hand C. greater yin of foot and lesser yin of hand D. greater yin of foot and jue yin of hand E. jue yin of foot and lesser yin of hand.
272	在十二经脉中，支脉最多的经脉是指: A.足太阳膀胱经; B.足少阳胆经 C. 足阳明胃经; D 手少阳三焦经.	What meridian has the largest number of branches among the twelve master meridians? A. greater yang bladder meridian of foot; B. less yang gallbladder meridian of foot; C. bright yang stomach merdian of foot; D. lesser yang triple heater meridian of hand (san jiao meridian).
273	在十二经脉中，注心中的经脉是: A.手厥阴心包经; B 手少阴心经 C. 足太阴脾经; D, 足少阴肾经.	What meridian enters into the heart among the twelve master meridians? A. decreaing yin (jue yin) pericardium meridian of hand B. lesser yin heart meridian of hand C. greater yin spleen meridian of foot; D. lesser yin kidney meridian of foot.
274	在十二经脉中，注胸中的经脉是: A.手厥阴心包经; B 手少阴心经 C. 足太阴脾经; D 足少阴肾经.	What meridian enters into the chest among the twelve master meridians? A. decreaing yin (jue yin) pericardium meridian of hand B. lesser yin heart meridian of hand C. greater yin spleen meridian of foot; D. lesser yin kidney meridian of foot.
275	在是动所生病中，手太阳手少阳两经的共同症候是: A·目黄; B·目锐眦痛 C. ·嗌肿痛; D·耳鸣耳聋; E· 颊痛.	The greater yang meridian of hand and the lesser yang meridian of hand have one symptom in common due to external causes, which is: A. yellowish eyes; B. pain in the medial angle of eye; C. sore throat with swelling; D. ringing in ears with deafness; E. pain in cheek.
276	在下列经脉中 ·"肝厥"属于哪经病候? A. ·足阳明胃经; B. ·足少阳三焦经 C. ·足太阴脾经;	What meridian has the symptom of "upstream energy from the region along the fibula / gan jue"? A. ·foot yang ming stomach meridian; B. ·foot lesser yang triple heater meridian; C. ·foot greater yin spleen meridian; D. ·foot

	C. ·足太阴脾经; D. ·足少阴肾经; E. ·足厥阴肝经	lesser yang kidney meridian; E. ·foot jue yin liver meridian.
277	在下列经脉中 ,"骭厥"属于哪经病候? A ·足阳明胃经; B 足少阳三焦经 C. ·足太阴脾经; D ·足少阴肾经; E ·足厥阴肝经.	What meridian is associated. with "symptoms due to upstream energy from the region along the fibula" (gu jue)? A. stomach meridian; B. sanjiao meridian; C. spleen meridian; D. kidney meridian; E. liver meridian.
278	在下列经脉中，起于中焦的是: A ·任脉; B ·督脉 C. ·冲脉; D ·手太阴肺经; E ·手少阴心经.	Which of the following meridians starts from middle heater (zhong jiao)? A. ren mai (conception meridian); B. du mai (governing meridian); C. chong mai (vigorous meridian); D. lung meridian; E. heart meridian.
279	针灸学的理论核心应是: A. ·脏象学说; B. ·阴阳学说 C. ·五行学说 D ·经络学说; E. ·子午流注学说	What is the core of acupuncture and moxibustion theory? A. ·theory of internal organs; B. ·theory of yin and yang; C. ·theory of five elements; D ·theory of meridians; E. ·zi wu liu zhu (time flowing theory).
280	正确的骨度分寸是: A ·肘横纹至腕横纹 12 寸; B ·脐中至耻骨上缘 6 寸 C. ·髀枢至膝中 16 寸; D ·臀横纹至膝中 19 寸; E ·膝中至外踝高点 13 寸.	Which of the following is correct according to the bone measurements by Cuns? A ·distance between elbow crease and wrist crease measures 12 Cun; B ·distance between middle of umbilicus and upper edge of symphysis pubis measures 6 Cun; C. ·distance between greater trochanter and midpoint of popliteal fossa measures 16 Cun; D. ·distance between gluteal fold and midpoint of popliteal fossa measures 19 Cun; E ·distance between the midpoint on the lateral side of patella and lateral malleolus measures 13 Cun
281	中府是手太阴经与何经的交会穴? A ·足厥阴; B ·手厥阴 C. ·足阳明; D ·足太阴; E ·足少阴.	Lu1 (Zhōng Fǔ) is the meeting point of the greater yin meridian of hand and: A. jue yin meridian of foot; B. jue yin meridian of hand C. bright yang meridian of foot; D. greater yin meridian of foot; E. lesser yin meridian of foot.
282	属胃络脾是什么经脉？ A ·小肠经; B ·大肠经 C. ·胃经; D ·胆经; E · 任脉	What meridian belongs to the stomach and is linked with the spleen? A; small intestine meridian; B. large intestine meridian; C. stomach meridian; D. gallbladder meridian; E. ren mai (conception meridian).
283	足厥阴肝经 "其支者，复从肝，别贯膈"下文是: A ·环唇内; B ·上入頏顙连目系 C. ·上出额与督脉会于巅; D 布胁肋; E ·上注肺.	A. branch of the liver meridian travels from the liver; and then, it passes through the diaphragm. What does it travel to next? A. it goes round the inside of the lips; B. it enters into the upper aperture of maxilla. (jawbone), and then, it becomes onnected with the eye onnective; C. it goes outward to the forehead, and then, it meets with the du mai at vertex; D. it spreads in the intercostal region; E. it goes upward to enter the lungs.
284	足厥阴肝经在内踝八寸以下部位的分布是: A.，在小腿内侧中行; B. ·在小腿内侧后廉 C. ·在小腿	How is the foot jue yin liver meridian distributed 8 Cuns below medial malleolus? A.on the midline of the medial side of lower leg; B. ·in the back of the the medial side of lower leg C. ·in the front of the the

	侧后廉 C. ·在小腿外侧前廉; D. ·在小腿外侧中行; E. ·以上均非	latera side of lower leg; D. ·on the midline of the lateral side of lower leg; E. ·none of the above.
285	足三阳经行走方向的规律是: A.从手走头; B 从胸走手 C. 从足走腹; D 从头走足.	What are the patterns of distribution as applied to the three yang meridians of foot? A. from hand toward head; B. from hest toward hand C. from foot toward abdomen; D. from head toward foot.
286	足三阳经在躯干部的排列是: A·阳明在前,少阳在侧,太阳在后; B·:少阳在前,太阳在侧,阳明在后 C.'太阳在前,·少阳在侧,阳明在后; D·阳明在前,少阳在后,太阳在侧; E·太阳在前,阳明在侧,少阳在后.	How are the three yang meridians of foot distributed in the trunk? A. ·bright yang / yang ming in the front、lesser yang / shao yang on the side、greater yang / tai yang in the back; B ·:lesser yang / shao yang in the front、greater yang on the side、bright yang / yang ming in the back; C. greater yang / tai yang in the front、·lesser yang / shao yang on the side、bright yang / yang ming in the back; D ·bright yang / yang ming in the front、lesser yang / shao yang in the back、greter yang on the side; E · greater yang / tai yang in the front、bright yang / yang ming on thc side;lesser yang / shao yang in the back.
287	足三阳经在四肢的排列是: A·阳明.少阳.太阳; ·B，少阳.太阳.阳明 C. ·太阳·:阳明.少阳; D·少阳.·阳明.·太阳; E. ·太阳.少阳.阳明.	How are the three yang meridians of foot distributed in the four limbs? A ·bright yang / yang ming、lesser yang / shao yang、greater yang; ·B，lesser yang / shao yang、 greter yang 、bright yang / y ang ming C. ·greter yang、·bright yang / yang ming、lesser yang / shao yang; D.lesser yang / shao yang、·bright yang / yang ming·、greater yang; E. greater yang lesser yang / shao yang、bright yang / yang ming.
288	足三阴经在内踝尖上 8 寸处以下分布是: A.少阴在前，太阴在中，厥阴在后; B.太阴在前，厥阴在中，少阴在后 C. 厥阴在前，少阴在中，太阴在后; D，厥阴在前，太阴在中，少阴在后.	How are the three yin meridians of foot distributed in the region 8 Cun above medial malleolus? A. lesser yin (shao yin) in the front, greater yin (tai yin) in the middle, decreasing yin (jue yin) in the back; B. greater yin in the front, decreasing yin in the middle, lesser yin in the back; C. decreasing yin in the front, lesser yin in the middle, greater yin in the back; D. decreasing yin in the front, greater yin in the middle, lesser yin in the back.
289	肺经与脾经交会于: A·章门; B.大包 C. ·云门; D·中府; E·都不对	Where do the ·lungs and spleen meridians meet? A · Lv13 / Zhāng Mén; B. Sp21 / Dà Bāo C. ·Lu2 / Yún Mén; D · Lu1 / Zhōng Fŭ; E · none of the above
290	足三阴经在内踝上八寸以上部位的排列顺序是: A. 厥阴在前、太阴在中、少阴在后; B. 太阴在前、厥阴在中、少阴在后 C. ·太阴在前、少阴在中 ·厥阴在后 D·少阴在前、厥阴在中、太阴在后; E. 厥阴在前、少阴在中、太阴	How are the three yin meridians of foot distributed in the region 8 Cuns below medical malleous? A. jue yin in the front、greater yin in the middle、lesser yin in the back; B. ·greater yin in the front、jue yin in the middle、lesser yin the back; C. ·greater yin in the front ·lesser yin in the middle、jue yin the back; D ·lesser yin in the front、jue yin in the middle、greater yin the back; E. jue yin in the front、lesser yin in the middle、··greater yin the back.

	在后	
291	足三阴经在上肢内侧面的排列顺序是: A·肺经心包经心经; B·心包经心经肺经; ·C·心经肺经心包经; D·肺经心经心包经; E·心包经肺经心经.	How are the three yin meridians of foot distributed on the medial side of upper limbs? A·lungs meridian、pericardium meridian、heart meridian; B·pericardium meridian、heart meridian、lungs meridian; · C·heart meridian、lungs meridian、pericardium meridian; D··lungs meridian、heart meridian、pericardium meridian; E·pericardium meridian、lungs meridian、heart meridian.
292	足三阴经在下肢部内踝上几寸以下，足厥阴肝经在前，足太阴脾经居中: A·4 寸; B·5 寸;C·6 寸; D·8 寸; E·7 寸.	How many Cuns below medial malleolus where the three yin meridians of foot are distributed with the foot jue yin in the front、and foot greater yin in the middle? A·4 Cun; B·5 Cun; C. ·6 Cun; D·8 Cun; E·7 Cun.
293	足少阳、足厥阴经经别的离、入、出、合 为: A·窝、肝胆、项、足少阳; B·下肢·肝胆、目、足少阳 C. ·下肢 ·肝胆 ·鼻、足少阳; D·窝、肝胆、目内眦、足少阳; E·下肢、肝胆、耳后、足少阳.	Where do "to separate from", "to join", "to move outward", "to enter into", take place as applied to the foot lesser yang / shao yang and foot jue yin separate master meridians? A · popliteal fossa liver and gallbladder, back of neck, lesser yang / shao yang; B·lower limbs liver and gallbladder eye foot lesser yang / shao yang; C. lower limbs liver and gallbladder nose foot lesser yang / shao yang; D · popliteal fossa liver and gallbladder medial canthus foot lesser yang / shao yang; E. lower limbs liver and gallbladder behind the ear foot lesser yang / shao yang.
294	足少阳胆经足跗部的支脉终止于: A·足大趾内间; B·足大趾三毛 C. ·足大趾外间; D·足第四趾内间; E·足第四趾外间.	At what point does the branch of the gallbladder meridian along the dorsum of foot terminate? A. on the medial side of the big toe; B. on the hairs on the big toe just behind the nail; C. on the lateral side of the big toe; D. on the medial side of the 4th toe; E. on the lateral side of the 4th toe.
295	足少阳胆经足跗部支脉是从何穴处分出? A·丘墟; B·足临泣 C. ·地五会; D·侠溪; E，以上均不是.	At what point does the branch of the gallbladder meridian along the dorsum of foot diverge to be; C. onnected with the sanjiao meridian? A. G40, Qiū Xū; B. G41, Zú Lín Qì; C. G42, Dì Wǔ Huì; D. G43, Xiá Xī.; E. none of the above.
296	足少阴经 "出于然骨之下" 的 "然骨"是指: A·趾骨; B·跖骨 C. ·跖趾关节; D·跖骨底; E·舟骨.	The kidney meridian proceeds outward in the region below a bone named. "Ran-Gu", which refers to: A. phalangeal bone; B. metatarsal bone; C. metatarsophalangeal joint; D. plantar metatarsal bone; E. navicular bone.
297	足少阴肾经与以下除 XX 以外的脏腑器官相联系: A·肺; B·膀胱 C. ·肝; D·胃; E·舌.	Which organ is not; C. onnected with the kidney meridian? A. lung; B. bladder; C. liver; D. stomach; E. tongue.
298	足太阳膀胱经背部第二侧线应位于: A·脊柱椎体横突外侧缘; B·脊柱正中与肩胛骨内缘连线中	The second. lateral line of the bladder meridian in the back is situated. at: A. at the lateral border of the traverse process of the spine; B. midpoint on the line connecting mid-spine and medial border of

	点处 C. 肩胛骨脊柱缘垂直线上; D·肩胛骨下角与脊柱正中连线中点处; E·以上均不是.	scapula; C. straight vertical line passing through the spinal border of scapula; D. midpoint on the line connecting the lower angle of scapula. and mid-spine; E. none of the above.
299	足太阳膀胱经的"标"为: A·跟以上 5 寸中; B·窗笼之前 C. 命门之上 1 寸; D· 两络命门; E·外踝之后.	Where is the manifestation (Biao) of the foot greater yang bladder meridian located? A·5 Cun above heel; B·in front of the ear; · C. ·1 Cun above D4 [Mìng Mén]; D·B1 / Jīng Míng;E behind lateral malleolus.
300	足太阳经及足少阴经在: A·足小趾端衔接; B.目锐眦衔接 C. ·食指端衔接; D·胸中衔接; E·鼻旁衔接.	Where are the foot greater yang meridian and the foot lesser yin meridian; C. onnected? A·connected at the tip of little toe; B·connected at lateral canthus C. ·connected at the finger tip of forefinger;. D. C. onnected at the chest; E·connected at the side of the nose.
301	足太阳经之属与络的脏腑为: A·心 小肠; B·肝、胆 C. ·脾、胃; D·膀胱、肾; E·大肠、肺.	The foot greater yang meridian belopngs to and is linked with what organs? A·heart and small intestine; B·liver and gallbladder; C. ·spleen and stomach; D·bladder and kidneys; E·large intestine and lungs.
302	足太阴脾经的起始部位是: A·脾; B·胃 C. ·心; D·足大趾内侧; E·足大趾外侧.	Where does the foot greater yin spleen meridian begin? A·spleen; B stomach; C. ·heart; D·medial side of big toe; E·lateral side of big toe.
303	足太阴脾经体表循行路线，在小腿交何经之前? A. 足少阳胆经; B. 足阳明胃经 C. 足少阴肾经; D. 足厥阴肝经; E. 以上均不是.	What meridian does the spleen meridian meet and travel outward in front of it? A. gallbladder meridian; B. stomach meridian; C. kidney meridian; D. liver meridian; E. none of the above.
304	足太阴脾经体表循行路线，在小腿交经之后，在腹部又交入何经之内侧: A 足阳明胃经; B·足厥阴肝经 C. ·足少阴肾经; D·足少阳胆经; E·以上都不是.	After the foot greater yin spleen meridian meeting in the lower leg, it meets what meridian on the medial side"? A·foot bright yang stomach meridian; B.foot decreasing yin liver meridian; C. foot lesser yin kidney meridian; D·lesser yang gallbladder meridian; E · none of the above
305	足太阴脾经直接联系的五官是: A·眼; B·耳 C. ·口; D·鼻; E·舌.	Which one of the five senses is directedly; C. onnected with the foot greater yin spleen meridian? A. ·eyes; B. ·ears C. mouth; D·nose; E. tongue.
306	足阳明胃经的起始部位是: A·鼻; B·下颌 C. ·	Where does the foot bright yang stomach meridian begin? A，nose; B·chin; C. supraclavicular fossa; D·stomach; E·toes.

	缺盆; D 胃; E 足趾.	
307	足阳明胃经的一条支脉起于胃口，下循腹里，下至气冲中而合，以下，……的部位是: A.伏兔; B.髀关 C.膝膑中; D 股外廉.	A branch of the stomach meridian starts at the pyloric orifice (opening between the stomach and duodenum), it travels along the belly to meet the straight vessel of the stomach meridian at Qi-Chong (S30). What is its next travelling region? A S32 [Fú Tù]; B S31 [Bì Guān]; C. Knee-cap; D. lateral side of thigh.
308	足阳明胃经循行不经过: A 鼻; B 齿 C. 口唇; D 下颌; E 舌.	The foot bright yang stomach meridian does not travel through: A nose; B teeth C. mouth and lips; D chin; E tongue.
309	足阳明胃经循行线上的"客主人"是指: A. 颊车穴; B. 下关穴 C. 上关穴; D. 耳门穴; E. 听宫穴	The foot yang ming stomach meridian does not travel through "Ke Zhu Ren", which refers to; A. S6 [Jiá Chē]; B. S7 [Xià Guān]; C. G3 [Shàng Guān]; D. Sj21 [Ěr Mén]; E. Si19 [Tīng Gōng].
310	足阳明胃经在腹部的腧穴距前正中线: A 0.5 寸; B 1 寸 C. 2 寸; D 4 寸; E 6 寸.	What is the distance between points on the foot bright yang stomach meridian in the abdominal region and the anterior central line? A 0.5 Cun; B 1 Cun; C. 2 Cun; D 4 Cun; E 6 Cun.
311	足阳明胃经在胸部的腧穴距前正中线: A 0.5 寸; B 1 寸 C. 2 寸; D 4 寸; E 6 寸.	What is the distance between points on the foot bright yang stomach meridian in the chest region and the anterior C. entral line? A 0.5 Cun; B 1 Cun; C. 2 Cun; D 4 Cun; E 6 Cun.
312	足阳明胃经在足跗部的支脉是从何穴处分出? A 解溪; B 冲阳 C. 陷谷; D 内庭; E 以上都不是.	A subdivision of the stomach meridian diverges at the dorsum of foot, what is this point? A S41, Jiě Xī; B S42, Chōng Yáng; C S43, Xiàn Gǔ; D S44, Nèi Tíng; E none of the above.
313	足阳明胃经足跗部的支脉入于: A 大趾; B 小趾 C. 次趾; D 中趾; E 以上均不是.	A subdivision of the stomach meridian on the dorsum of foot enters into what region? A big toe; B. little toe; C. 2nd Toe; D middle toe; E. none of the above.
314	足阳明胃经足跗部的支脉止于: A. 大趾内间; B. 大趾外间 C. 次趾外间; D. 中趾内间; E. 经上均不是	Where does the subdivision of the stomach meridian on the dorsum of foot terminate? A. medial side of big toe; B. lateral side of big toe; C. lateral side of 2nd toe; D. medial side of middle toe; E. none of the above.

13-2	腧穴	Acupuncture Points	315-748

315	"阿是穴"是指: A 经外奇穴以外的穴位; B 经穴以外的穴位 C. 病变局部	What do "A Shi Xue (pressure points or ouch points) refer to? A. points other than extraordinary points; B. points other than meridian points; C. points in the local diseased. regions; D. points in the center of local diseased regions; E. painful points

	的穴位; D·病变局部中心的穴位; E·与病变有关的压痛点.	points in the center of local diseased regions; E. painful points on pressure related to disorders.
316	"耳前三穴" (耳门 听宫 听会)，其归经由上至下分别是: A·三焦经小肠经胆经; B·小肠经胆经三焦经 C. 胆经三焦经小肠经; D·三焦经胆经小肠经; E·胆经小肠经三焦经.	"Three points in front of the ear" (Ěr Mén, Tīng Gōng, Tīng Huì) belong to what meridians respectively (from upper to lower in location)? A. triple heater, small intestine, gallbladder; B. small intestine, gallbladder, triple heater; C. gallbladder, triple heater, small intestine; D. triple heater, gallbladder, small intestine; E. gallbladder, small intestine, triple heater.
317	"合"穴是指: A·六腑之气合于下肢的腧穴; B·经气充盛且入合于脏腑的输穴 C. 两经或数经相交会的腧穴; D·精气聚会的输入; E·以上均不是.	What do "merging points / terminal points / sea points [Hé Xué] refer to? A. the points in the lower extremities where energy of six bowels merges; B ·abundant meridian energy merging into viscera and bowels; C. acupuncture points where two or more meridians meet; D ·points where pure essence gathers together; E · none of the above.
318	"经外奇穴"是指: A·经脉以外的穴位; B·十二经穴以外的穴位 C. 十二经穴以外有定名定位的穴位; D·十四经穴以外的穴位; E·经穴以外有定名定位的穴位.	What do "extraordinary points" refer to? A. points located outside the meridians; B. points other than the points on the twelve master meridians; C. points with names and locations, but outside the twelve master meridians; D. points outside the fourteen major meridians; E. points not on the meridians, but with names and locations indicated.
319	"经穴"是指: A·在经络上的穴位; B·在十二经上的穴位 C. 《内经》上的穴位; D·清代归入十四经的穴位; E·解放后归人十四经的穴位	What do "points on meridians" refer to? A ·points on master and linking meridians; B ·points on twelve master meridians; C. points mentioned in (Nei Jing); D ·points on fourteen major meridians as mentioned in Manchu dynasty; E ·points on fourteen major meridians as mentioned after the establishment of People's Republic of China.
320	"腧穴"的称呼中,下列哪种是最早出现的: A·穴位; B·穴道 C. 孔穴; D·髎穴; E·气穴.	What was the earliest name of shu xue (acupuncture points)? A. xue wei; B. xue dao; C. kong xue; D. liao xue; E. qi xue.
321	"下合穴"是指: A·膝关节以下的腧穴; B·六腑之气合于下肢的腧穴 C. 腰腹部以下的腧穴; D·手三阳经气下合于下肢的腧穴; E. 以上均不是	What do "lower merging points / lower terminal points / lower sea points [xià hé xué] refer to? A ·acupuncture points below knee joints; B ·points where energy of six bowels enters into lower extremities; C. ·acupuncture points below the lumbar and abdominal region; D. ·acupuncture points where energy of three yang meridians of hand enters into lower extremities; E. none of the above.
322	"一夫法"是将食中无名小指相并，四横指的间距为 3 寸，其量	Yi Fu Fa (one man's measurement) refers to transversal digital Cun by taking the width of four fingers together as three transversal Cuns; what is the standard of this measurement?

	取标准应按: A 食指远端指节横纹; B 中指远端指节横纹 C. 无名指远端指节横纹; D 小指近端指节横纹; E 以中指近端指节横纹为准.	A. distal crease of the forefinger; B. distal crease of the middle finger C. distal crease of the ring finger; D. proximal crease of the little finger; E. proximal crease of the middle finger.
323	"一夫法"是指: A 小指同身寸; B · 中指同身寸 C. 拇指同身寸; D 横指同身寸; E · 以上均不是.	What does Yi Fu Fa (one man's measurement) refer to? A. measurement of the little finger; B. measurement of the middle finger; C. measurement of the thumb; D. transversal measurement of four fingers; E. none of the above.
324	《内经》一书论及穴名约为 A.160 个 B. 140 个 C. 180 个, D. 200 个	About how many acupuncture points does <Nei Jing> refer to? A. 160 points; B. 140 points C. 180 points; D. 200 points.
325	按 "经脉所通,主治所及"的理论 巅顶痛最好选用: A. 太冲; B. 列缺 C. 足临泣; D. 后溪; E. 内庭	According to the theory that "a given meridian can treat diseases that occur in the region in which it is distributed", what point should be selected to treat headache in the vertex? A. Lv3 [Tài Chōng]; B. Lu7 [Liè Quē]; C. G41 [Zú Lín Qì]; D. Si3 [Hòu Xī]; E. S44 [Nèi Tíng].
326	八会穴是指哪些精气所会聚的输穴? A 气血脑髓筋脉胆女子胞; B 脏腑经脉气血阴阳 C. 脏腑气血筋脉骨髓; D 气血脑, 髓津神脉络; E · 脑髓脏腑脉胆筋骨.	What kind of pure essence gathers at the eight meeting points (eight influential points, ba hui xue)? A. energy, blood, brain, marrow, tendons, blood vessels, gallbladder, womb; B. viscera, bowels, meridians, energy, blood, yin, yang; C. viscera, bowel, energy, blood, tendons, blood vessels, bones, marrow; D. energy, blood, brain, marrow, body fluids, spirits, blood vessels, linking meridians; E. brain, marrow, viscera, bowles, blood vessels, gallbladder, tendons, bones.
327	八会穴之血会为: A 绝骨; B 大抒 C. 膈俞; D 膻中; E 章门.	What is the blood meeting point [xue hui] among the eight influential points / ba hui xue? A · G39 / Xuán Zhōng; B B11 / Dà Zhù;C. B17 / Gé Shū; D · R17 / Shān Zhōng; E · Lv13 / Zhāng Mén
328	八会穴中, 气会穴是: A 气穴; B 气海 C. 气户; D 膻中.	Which is the energy meeting point [qi hui] among the eight influential points / ba hui xue? A K13 / Qì Xué; B R6 / Qì Hăi; C. S13 / Qì Hù; D R17 / Shān Zhōng.
329	八会穴中的骨会穴是: A 绝骨; B 膻中 C. 阳陵泉; D 大杼; E 膈俞.	What is the bone meeting point [gu hui] among the eight meeting points (ba hui xue)? A. G39 (Xuán Zhōng); B. R17 (Shān Zhōng); C. G34 (Yáng Líng Quán); D.B11 (Dà Zhù); E. B17 (Gé Shū).
330	八会穴中的髓会穴是: A 百会; B 大钟 C. 绝骨(悬钟); D 完骨; E 脑户..	What is the marrow meeting point [sui hui] among the eight meeting points (ba hui xue)? A. D20 (Băi Huì); B. K4 (Dà Zhōng); C. G39 (Xuán Zhōng); D. G12 (Wán Gŭ);E D17 (Nǎo Hù).
331	八髎穴不包括: A 上髎穴; B 居髎穴 C. 次髎穴; D 中髎穴.	Which is NOT one of the eight foramen points [bā liáo xué]? A Bladder 31; B G29; C. Bladder 32; D Bladder 33.

332	八脉交会穴均分布于: A·奇经八脉循行线上; B·腕踝关节附近 C. ·肘膝关节附近; D·胸腹部; E·以上都不是.	What is the distribution of eight meeting points between eight extraordinary meridians & twelve master meridians (eight; C. onfluence points, ba mai jiao hui xue)? A. within the distribution of eight extraordinary meridians; B. around. the wrist joints and ankle joints; C. around. the elbow joints and knee joints; D. in the chest and abdomen region; E. none of the above.
333	八脉交会穴中，带脉的交会穴是: A·足临泣; B·申脉 C. ·照海; D·公孙; E·后溪.	Among the eight meridians meeting points (ba mai jiao hui xue), what is the meeting point of dai mai (belt meridian)? A. G41 (Zú Lín Qì, Lín Qì); B. B62 (Shēn Mài); C. K6 (Zhào Hǎi); D. Sp4 (Gōng Sūn); E. Si3 (Hòu Xī).
334	八脉交会穴中，申脉穴与哪条奇经脉气相通? A·督脉; B·带脉 C. ·冲脉; D·阳蹻; E·以上都不是.	Among the eight meridians meeting points (ba mai jiao hui xue), what extraordinary meridian does B62 (Shēn Mài meet? A. du mai (governing meridian); B. dai mai (belt meridian); C. chong mai (vigorous meridian); D. yang qiao mai (heel meridian of yang); E. none of the above.
335	八脉交会穴中，通于带脉与阳维的穴位是: A·照海与列缺; B·申脉与后溪 C. ·列缺与照海; D·足临泣与外关; E·足临泣与申脉.	Among the eight meridians meeting points (ba mai jiao hui xue), which two points meet dai mai (belt meridian) and yang wei mai (fastening meridian of yang)? A. K6 (Zhào Hǎi) and Lu7 (Liè Quē); B. B62 (Shēn Mài) and Si3 (Hòu Xī); C. Lu7 (Liè Quē) and K6 (Zhào Hǎi); D. G41 (Zú Lín Qì, Lín Qì) and Sj5 (Wài Guān); E. G41 (Zú Lín Qì, Lín Qì) and B62 (Shēn Mài).
336	八脉交会穴中，阳维脉通于: A·列缺; B·外关 C. ·申脉; D·临泣; E· 后溪.	Among the eight meridians meeting points (ba mai jiao hui xue), which point meets yang wei mai (fastening meridian of yang)? A. Lu7 (Liè Quē); B. Sj5 (Wài Guān); C. B62 (Shēn Mài); D. G41 (Zú Lín Qì, Lín Qì); E. Si3 (Hòu Xī).
337	八脉交会穴中,与阴蹻脉相通的穴位是: A·公孙; B·后溪 C. ·照海; D·足临泣; E·申脉.	Among the eight meridians meeting points (ba mai jiao hui xue), which point meets yin qiao mai (heel meridian of yin)? A. Sp4 (Gōng Sūn); B. Si3 (Hòu Xī); C. K6 (Zhào Hǎi); D. G41 (Zú Lín Qì, Lín Qì); E. B62 (Shēn Mài).
338	八脉交会穴中的照海与哪条奇经相通? A.阳跷脉; B 任脉 C. 带脉; D 阴跷脉.	Among the eight meeting points between eight extraordinary meridians & twelve master meridians (eight; C. onfluence points), what extraordinary meridian does K6 (Zhào Hǎi) meet? A. yang qiao mai (fastening meridian of yang); B. ren mai (conception meridian); C. dai mai (belt meridian); D. yin qiao mai (fastening meridian of yin).
339	八脉交会穴中合于胃、心、胸的是:A·冲脉 阴维脉; B·督脉 阳蹻脉 C. 阴维脉 阳蹻脉; D·带脉 阳蹻脉; E·任脉 阴维脉.	Among the eight meeting points between eight extraordinary meridians & twelve master meridians (eight; C. onfluence points), what meridians meet at stomach, heart, chest? A ·chong mai / vigorous meridian yin wei mai / yin fastener meridian; B ·du mai / governing meridian yang heel meridian; C. ·yin wei mai / yin fastener meridian yang qiao mai / yang heel meridian; D ·dai mai / belt meridian yang qiao mai / yang heel meridian; E ·ren mai /; C. onception meridian yin wei mai / yin fastener meridian.
340	八脉交会穴中与阳蹻脉相通的穴位是:	Among the eight meridians meeting points (ba mai jiao hui xue), which point meets yang qiao mai (heel meridian of yang)?

	A·申脉; B·后溪 C. ·外关; D·临泣; E·照海.	A; B62 (Shēn Mài); B. Si3 (Hòu Xī); C. Sj5 (Wài Guān); D. G41 (Zú Lín Qì, Lín Qì); E. K6 (Zhào Hǎi).
341	八脉交会穴中主治咽喉、胸膈、肺部疾患的是; A. 通督脉、任脉的腧穴; B. 通任脉、阴跷的腧穴 C. 通阴跷、阳维的腧穴; D. 通阳维、带脉的腧穴; E. 通带脉、冲脉的腧穴	Among the eight meridians meeting points (ba mai jiao hui xue), which points treat the diseases of throat, chest, diaphragm, and lungs? A. points; C. onnected with du mai / governing meridian、ren mai /; C. onception meridian; B. points; C. onnected with ren mai /; C. onception meridian、yin heel meridian; C. points; C. onnected withyin heel meridian, yang wei mai; D. points; C. onnected withyang wei mai、dai mai / belt meridian; E. points; C. onnected with dai mai / belt meridian、chong mai / vigorous meridian.
342	八下列各组穴中，除……之外，都是本经的母穴: A 肝经的曲泉; B 胆经的足临位 C. 脾经的大都; D 胃经的解溪.	Which is NOT a mother point of its own meridian? A Lv8 [Qū Quán]; B G41 [Zú Lín Qì ,Lín Qì]; C. Sp2 [Dà Dū]; D. S41 [Jiě Xī].
343	百虫窝的正确位置是: A.髌骨上缘上 2 寸; B.血海穴上 2 寸 C. ，血海穴上1寸; D 血海穴上 1.5 寸.	Where is Bǎi Chóng Wuō located? A. 2 Cun above the upper border of the patella; B. 2 Cun above Sp10 (Xuè Hǎi); C. 1 Cun above Sp10 (Xuè Hǎi); D. 1.5 Cun above Sp10 (Xuè Hǎi).
344	膀胱经的"经穴"是: A·委中; B·至阴 C. ·束骨; D·通谷; E 昆仑	What is the flowing point (jing xue, river point) of the bladder meridian? A; B40 (Wěi Zhōng); B. B67 (Zhì Yīn); C. B65 (Shù Gǔ); D. B66 (Tōng Gǔ, Zú Tōng Gǔ); E. B60 (Kūn Lún).
345	背俞穴中的厥阴俞，首见于: A·(难经》; B·《脉经》 C. ·《甲乙经》; D·《针灸资生经》; E·《千金要方》.	Among the posterior points (Back Shu Points or organ points [Bèi Shù Xué], B14 (Jué Yīn Shū) was first mentioned. in: A. <Nan Jing>; B. <Mai Jing> C. <Jia Yi Jing>; D. <Zhen Jiu Zi Sheng Jing>; E. <Qian Jin Yao Fang>.
346	不是络穴的穴位是: A·脾经—大包; B·肝经—蠡沟 C. ·胃经—丰隆; D·大肠经—合谷; E·心经—通里.	Which is NOT a linking point / luo point of the meridian listed before it? A ·spleen meridian— Sp21 / Dà Bāo; B ·liver meridian— Lv5 / Lí Gōu; C. stomach meridian— S40 / Fēng Lóng; D ·large intestine meridian— Li4 / Hé Gǔ; E ·heart meridian— H5 / Tōng Lǐ.
347	不属本经的募穴是: A·肺—中府; B·大肠—天枢 C. ·膀胱—中极; D·肝—期門; E·心—鸠尾	Which is NOT a gathering point / mu point of the meridian listed before it? A ·lungs— Lu1 / Zhōng Fǔ; B ·large intestine— S25 / Tiān Shū; C. ·bladder— R3 / Zhōng Jí; D ·liver—Lv14 [Qí Mén]; E ·heart—R15 [Jiū Wěi].
348	五行不属于木的腧穴是: A·少冲; B·少商 C. ·商阳; D·三间; E·后溪	Which point does NOT correspond to wood of five elements? A · H9 / Shào Chōng; B · Lu11 / Shǎo Shāng; C. Li1 / Shāng Yáng; D · Li3 / Sān Jiān; E · Si3 / Hòu Xī
349	五行属于金的腧穴是: A·窍阴; B·大敦 C. ·神门; D.临泣; E·丘墟	Which point does NOT correspond to metal of five elements? A ·G44 [Zú Qiào Yīn, Qiào Yīn]; B · Lv1 / Dà Dūn; C. · H7 / Shén Mén; D. G15 / Tóu Lín Qì / Lín Qì; E · G40 / Qiū Xū

350	常用清胃热的穴位有: A. 内庭; B. 冲阳 C. 丰隆; D. 胃俞; E. 梁丘	What point is frequently used to clear stomach heat? A. S44 [Nèi Tíng]; B. S42 [Chōng Yáng]; C. S40 [Fēng Lóng]; D. B21 [Wèi Shū]; E. S34 [Liáng Qiū]
351	承筋穴位于: A 委中和承山之间; B 委中下 3 寸 C. 合阳与承山之间; D 委阳与合阳之间; E 以上都不是.	Where is; B56 (Chéng Jīn) located? A. in between; B40 (Wěi Zhōng) and B57 (Chéng Shān); B. 3 Cuns below; B40 (Wěi Zhōng); C. in between; B55 (Hé Yáng) and B57 (Chéng Shān); D. in between B39 (Wěi Yáng) and B55 (Hé Yáng); E. None of the above.
352	承山治疗肛门疾患主要是通过......的内在联系。 A. 经脉; B. 络脉 C. 经别; D. 经筋; E. 皮部	What meridians play an internal role to enable B57 [Chéng Shān] to treat diseases of anus? A.master meridians; B. luo mai / linking meridians C. separate master meridians / jing bie; D. muscular meridians / jing jin; E. pi bu / skin zone.
353	除......穴之外，两穴之间的距离均为 3 寸: A 跗阳 昆仑; B 犊鼻 足三里 C. 蠡沟 中都; D 伏兔 阴市; E 阳溪 偏历.	The distance between which two points is NOT 3 Cuns? A; B59 (Fū Yáng) and B60 (Kūn Lún); B S35 (Dú Bí) and S36 (Zú Sān Lǐ); C. Lv5 (Lí Gōu) and Lv6 (Zhōng Dū); D. S32 (Fú Tù) and S33 (Yīn Shì); E. Li5 (Yáng Xī) and Li6 (Piān Lì).
354	除 xx 穴外，都由多穴点组成: A 二白; B 八邪 C. 百虫窝; D 四缝; E 腰痛点.	Which of the following; contains only one point? A. Èr Bái; B. Bā Xié C. Bǎi Chóng Wuō; D. Sì Féng; E. Yāo Tong Diǎn.
355	除哪个穴外，余穴归属督脉: A.腰俞; B 腰阳关 C. 中枢; D 神堂.	Which of the following points does not belong to Du Mai (governing meridian)? A. Yāo Shū; B. Yāo Yáng Guān; C. Zhōng Shū; D. Shén Táng.
356	除哪个穴外，余穴均归属胆经: A. 头窍陰; B.膝关 C. 阳辅; D. 五樞.	Which of the following points does not belong to the gallbladder meridian? A. Tóu Qiào Yīn; B. Xī Guān; C. Yáng Fǔ; D. Wǔ Shū.
357	大肠的下合穴是: A 下巨虚; B 足三里 C. 上巨虚; D 委阳; E 以上部不是.	What is the lower merging point (xia he xue) of the large intestine? A. S39 (Xià Jù Xū); B. S36 (Zú Sān Lǐ); C. S37 (Shàng Jù Xū); D. B39 (Wěi Yáng); E. None of the above.
358	大肠募穴属于: A 手阳明大肠经; B 手太阴肺经 C. 足阳明胃经; D 足太阳膀胱经; E 任脉.	What meridian does large intestine gathering point / mu point belong to? A hand bright yang large intestine meridian; B.hand greater yin lung meridian; C. foot bright yang stomach meridian; D foot greater yang bladder meridian; E ; C. onception meridian / ren mai.
359	大赫穴的位置在: A.脐下 5 寸，前正中线旁开 1 寸; B.脐下 4 寸，前正中线旁开 1 寸 C. 脐下 5 寸，前正中线旁开 0.5 寸; D 脐下 4 寸，前正中线旁开 0.5 寸.	Where is K12 (Dà Hè) located? A; 5 Cuns below the umbilicus (navel), and 1 Cun laterally from anterior midline; B. 4 Cuns below the umbilicus (navel), and 1 Cun laterally from anterior midline C. 5 Cuns below the umbilicus (navel), and 0.5 Cun laterally from anterior midline; D. 4 Cuns below the umbilicus (navel), and 0.5 Cun laterally from anterior midline.
360	大椎的取穴法为: A.活动标志取穴法;	What method of locating points should be used to locate D14, Dà Zhuī?

	B 肌性标志取穴法 C. 骨度折量取穴法; D 骨性标志取穴法.	Dà Zhuī? A. mobile landmarks; B. muscle landmarks C. bone and Cun measurements; D. fixed. landmarks of bones.
361	大椎与肩峰连线中点的穴位是: A 曲垣; B 天髎 C. 肩井; D 秉风; E 巨骨.	Which point is located on the midpoint of the line connecting D14 (Dà Zhuī) and acromion of scapula? A. Si13 (Qū Yuān); B. Sj15 (Tiān Liáo); C. G21 (Jiān Jǐng); D. Si12 (Bǐng Fēng); E. Li16 (Jù Gǔ).
362	胆经的"输穴"是: A 阳辅; B 丘墟 C. 侠溪; D 足临泣; E 悬钟.	What is the flowing point (shu xue or river point) of the gallbladder meridian? A. G38 (Yáng Fǔ); B. G40 (Qiū Xū); C. G43 (Xiá Xī); D. G41 (Zú Lín Qì, Lín Qì); E. G39 (Xuán Zhōng).
363	胆经的"五输穴"是: A 窍阴 侠溪 足临泣 悬钟 阳陵泉; B 窍阴 侠溪 足临泣 阳辅 阳陵泉 C. 窍阴 侠溪 足临泣 外丘 阳陵泉; D 窍阴 侠溪 丘墟 阳辅 阳陵泉; E 窍阴 侠溪 足临泣 丘墟 阳陵泉.	What are the five command points (wu shu xue) on the gallbladder meridian? A. G44 (Zú Qiào Yīn, Qiào Yīn), G43 (Xiá Xī), G41 (Zú Lín Qì, Lín Qì), G39 (Xuán Zhōng), G34 (Yáng Líng Quán); B G44 (Zú Qiào Yīn, Qiào Yīn), G43 (Xiá Xī), G41 (Zú Lín Qì, Lín Qì), G38 (Yáng Fǔ), G34 (Yáng Líng Quán); C. G44 (Zú Qiào Yīn, Qiào Yīn), G43 (Xiá Xī), G41 (Zú Lín Qì, Lín Qì), G36 (Wài Qiū), G34 (Yáng Líng Quán); D. G44 (Zú Qiào Yīn, Qiào Yīn), G43 (Xiá Xī), G40 (Qiū Xū), G38 (Yáng Fǔ), G34 (Yáng Líng Quán); E G44 (Zú Qiào Yīn, Qiào Yīn), G43 (Xiá Xī), G41 (Zú Lín Qì, Lín Qì), G40 (Qiū Xū), G34 (Yáng Líng Quán).
364	胆囊发生病变体表压痛点多发生在: A. 足三里; B. 阳陵泉 C. 上巨虚; D. 下巨虚; E. 足临泣	Where do pressure points on body surface occur when the gallbladder is diseased? A. S36 [Zú Sān Lǐ]; B. G34 [Yáng Líng Quán];C. S37 [Shàng Jù Xū]; D. S39 [Xià Jù Xū]; E. G41 [Zú Lín Qì].
365	定取背俞穴时，主要采用: A 骨度分寸定位法; B 自然标志定位法 C. 简便定位法; D 手指同身寸定位法; E 一夫法.	What primary method is used to locate posterior points / back shu points / Bèi shù xué? A bone measurements by Cuns; B natural landmarks;C. simple and C. onvenient method; D digital Cun of the middle finger E width of four fingers C. losed together.
366	督脉的经穴数日为 A.24; B.20 C. 23; D28.	How many acupuncture points on the Du Mai (governing meridian)? A. 24 points; B. 20 points; C. 23 points; D. 28 points.
367	督脉穴位中与十二经脉交会最多的是: A 百会; B 大椎 C. 风府; D 神庭; E · 水沟.	Which point on du mai (governing meridian) meets the greatest number of points on the twelve master meridians? A. D20 (Bǎi Huì); B. D14 (Dà Zhuī); C. D16 (Fēng Fǔ); D. D24 (Shén Tíng); E. D26 (Shuǐ Gōu, Rén Zhōng).
368	肝经的"五输穴"是: A 大敦 行间 太冲 中都 曲泉; B 大敦 行间 太冲 膝关 曲泉 C. 大敦 行间 太冲 中都 曲泉; D 大敦 行间 中封 膝关 曲泉; E 大敦 行间 太冲 中封 曲泉.	What are the five command points (wu shu xue) on the liver meridian? A. Lv1 (Dà Dūn), Lv2 (Xíng Jiān), Lv3 (Tài Chōng), Lv6 (Zhōng Dū), Lv8 (Qū Quán); B. Lv1 (Dà Dūn), Lv2 (Xíng Jiān), Lv3 (Tài Chōng), Lv7 (Xī Guān), Lv8 (Qū Quán); C. Lv1 (Dà Dūn), Lv2 (Xíng Jiān), Lv3 (Tài Chōng), Lv6 (Zhōng Dū), Lv8 (Qū Quán); D. Lv1 (Dà Dūn), Lv2 (Xíng Jiān), Lv4 (Zhōng Fēng) Lv7 (Xī Guān), Lv8 (Qū Quán); E Lv1 (Dà Dūn), Lv2 (Xíng Jiān), Lv3 (Tài Chōng), Lv4 (Zhōng Fēng), Lv8 (Qū Quán);.

		(Tài Chōng), Lv4 (Zhōng Fēng), Lv8 (Qū Quán);.
369	根据 "实则泻其子" 的原则，膀胱实证治疗取穴应是: A.·京骨; B.·通谷 C.·金门; D.·申脉; E.·束骨	According to the principle of "an excess syndrome should be treated by Child points"，what point should be selected to treat the excess syndrome of bladder? A. ·B64 [Jīng Gǔ]; B. ·B66 [Tōng Gǔ]; C. ·B63 [Jīn Mén]; D. ·B62 [Shēn Mài]; E. ·B65 [Shù Gǔ]
370	根据 "治风先治血" 的理论，治疗风痹选用: A.·合谷穴; B.·肝俞穴 C.·膈俞穴; D.·脾俞穴; E.·天井穴	According to the theory of "blood should be treated first in treating wind", what point should be selected to treat wind rheumatism / feng bi? A. ·Li4 [Hé Gǔ]; B. ·B18 [Gān Shū]; C. ·B17 [Gé Shū]; D. ·B20 [Pí Shū]; E. ·Sj10 [Tiān Jǐng].
371	根据骨度分寸，除……外，两者间距都是 9 寸: A·两完骨间; B·天突至中庭 C.·腋前纹头至肘横纹; D·腋窝横纹到十一肋; E·胸骨上迹至剑突.	According to the bone Cun measurements (gu du fen Cun), which of the following does NOT measure 9 Cuns? A. from mastoid process to mastoid process; B. from R22 (tiantu) to zhongting (R16); C. from anterior (or posterior) axillary fold to distal wrist crease (or olecranon); D. from anterior axillary fold to hypochondrium (11th rib); E from tiantu = R22 (suprasternal notch) to xiphoid process.
372	根据骨度分寸，下列穴位两者间距不是 1·5 寸的是: A·气海一神阙; B·内关一大陵 C.·神门一灵道; D·灵台-督俞; E·心俞-神堂.	According to the bone Cun measurements (gu du fen Cun), the distance between which two points is NOT 1.5 Cun? A; R6 (Qì Hǎi) and R8 (Shén Què); B P6 (Nèi Guān) and P7 (Dà Líng); C. H7 (Shén Mén) and H4 (Líng Dào); D. D10 (Líng Dào)B16 (Dū Shū); E. B15 (Xīn Shū) and B44 (Shén Táng).
373	根据骨度分寸，以下穴位除…外，两穴间距均为 0.5 寸: A·哑门 风府; B·阴郄 神门 C.·经渠 太渊; D·复溜 交信; E·气海 阴交.	According to the bone Cun measurements (gu du fen Cun), the distance between which two points is NOT 0.5 Cun? A. D15 (Yǎ Mén) and D16 (Fēng Fǔ); B. H6 (Yīn Xī) and H7 (Shén Mén); C. Lu8 (Jīng Qú) and Lu9 (Tài Yuān); D. K7 (Fù Liū) and K8 (Jiāo Xìn); E. R6 (Qì Hǎi) and R7 (Yīn Jiāo).
374	根据骨度分寸法，除……以外，两者间的距离都是 12 寸: A 前发际至后发际; B 肘横纹至腕横纹 C. 季肋以下至髀枢; D 腋以下至季肋.	According to the bone and Cun measurements, which of the following does not measure 12 Cuns? A. distance between frontal and posterior hairlines; B. distance between elbow crease and wrist Crease C. distance between hypochondrium (12th rib) and greater trochanter; D. distance between axilla and hypochondrium (11th rib).
375	根据骨度分寸法，下列各项中，除……以外，两者间的距离都是 9 寸: A 天突至歧骨间; B 腋以下至季肋 C. 季肋以下至髀枢; D 腋前纹头至肘横纹.	According to the bone and Cun measurements, which of the following does not measure 9 Cuns? A distance between R22 (tiantu) and xiphoid process; B distance between axilla and hypochondrium (11th rib); C. distance between hypochondrium (12th rib) and greater trochanter; D distance between axilla and elbow Crease.
376	根据骨度分寸法，印堂穴至百会穴为: A·18 寸; B·15 寸 C.·8 寸; D. 12 寸; E·10 寸	According to the bone Cun measurements (gu du fen Cun), what is the distance between Yìn Táng and D20 (Bǎi Huì)? A.18 Cuns; B.15 Cuns; C. 8 Cuns; D. 12 Cuns; E. 10 Cuns.

377	根据骨度分寸规定，臀横纹下到腘窝中点的长度应是: A·9 寸; B·12 寸 C. ·14 寸; D·16 寸; E·19 寸.	According to the bone Cun measurements (gu du fen Cun), what is the distance from gluteal fold to midpoint of popliteal fossa? A. 9 Cuns; B. 12 Cuns; C. 14 Cuns; D. 16 Cuns; E. 19 Cuns.
378	根据建筑物命名的腧穴是: A·大椎乳根腕骨颧髎; B·水沟，曲泽小海日月 C. 气海血海百会神堂; D·库房天井地仓印堂; E·光明睛明水分牵正.	Which group of points is named after buildings? A·D14 / Dà Zhuī S18 / Rŭ Gēn Si4 / Wàn Gŭ Si18 [Quán Liáo]; B · D26 / Shuǐ Gōu / Rén Zhōng，P3 / Qū Zé Si8 / Xiăo Hăi G24 / Rì Yuè; C. · R6 / Qì Hăi Sp10 / Xuè Hăi D20 / Băi Huì; B44 / Shén Táng; D. · S14 / Kù Fáng Sj10 / Tiān Jĭng S4 / Dì Cāng Yìn táng / midpoint between eyebrows / seal hall; E. ·G37 / Guāng Míng B1 / Jīng Míng R9 / Shuǐ Fēn Qiān Zèng / correction.
379	根据所在部位命名的腧穴是: A·大椎乳根腕骨颧髎; B·水沟，曲泽小海日月 C. 气海血海百会神堂; D·库房天井地仓印堂; E·光明睛明水分牵正.	Which group of points is named after their locations? A·D14 / Dà Zhuī S18 / Rŭ Gēn Si4 / Wàn Gŭ Si18 [Quán Liáo]; B · D26 / Shuǐ Gōu / Rén Zhōng，P3 / Qū Zé Si8 / Xiăo Hăi G24 / Rì Yuè; C. · R6 / Qì Hăi Sp10 / Xuè Hăi D20 / Băi Huì; B44 / Shén Táng; D · S14 / Kù Fáng Sj10 / Tiān Jĭng S4 / Dì C āng Yìn táng / midpoint between eyebrows / seal hall; E. ·G37 / Guāng Míng B1 / Jīng Míng R9 / Shuǐ Fēn Qiān Zèng / correction.
380	根据天体地貌命名的腧穴是: A·大椎乳根腕骨颧髎; B·水沟，曲泽小海日月 C. 气海血海百会神堂; D·库房天井地仓印堂; E·光明睛明水分牵正.	Which group of points is named after celestial bodies and landforms? A·D14 / Dà Zhuī S18 / Rŭ Gēn Si4 / Wàn Gŭ Si18 [Quán Liáo]; B · D26 / Shuǐ Gōu / Rén Zhōng，P3 / Qū Zé Si8 / Xiăo Hăi G24 / Rì Yuè; C. R6 / Qì Hăi Sp10 / Xuè Hăi D20 / Băi Huì; B44 / Shén Táng; D · S14 / Kù Fáng Sj10 / Tiān Jĭng S4 / Dì Cāng Yìn táng / midpoint between eyebrows / seal hall; E. ·G37 / Guāng MíngB1 / Jīng Míng R9 / Shuǐ Fēn Qiān Zèng / correction.
381	根据治疗作用命名的腧穴是: A·大椎乳根腕骨颧髎; B·水沟，曲泽小海日月 C. 气海血海百会神堂; D·库房天井地仓印堂; E·光明睛明水分牵正.	Which group of points is named after their therapeutic effects? A·D14 / Dà Zhuī S18 / Rŭ Gēn Si4 / Wàn Gŭ Si18 [Quán Liáo]; B · D26 / Shuǐ Gōu / Rén Zhōng，P3 / Qū Zé Si8 / Xiăo Hăi G24 / Rì Yuè; C. R6 / Qì Hăi Sp10 / Xuè Hăi D20 / Băi Huì; B44 / Shén Táng; D · S14 / Kù Fáng Sj10 / Tiān Jĭng S4 / Dì Cāng Yìn táng / midpoint between eyebrows / seal hall; E. ·G37 / Guāng MíngB1 / Jīng Míng R9 / Shuǐ Fēn Qiān Zèng / correction.
382	根据子母补泻法，肝经的实热证，当泻: A. ·大敦; B. ·太冲 C. ·曲泉; D. ·神门; E. ·少府	According to “the method of child-mother tonification and sedation”, what point should be selected to treat excess heat of liver meridian? A. ·Lv1 [Dà Dūn]; B. ·Lv3 [Tài Chōng]; C. ·Lv8 [Qū Quán]; D. ·H7 [Shén Mén]; E. ·H8 [Shào Fŭ].
383	根据子母补泻法，曲泉穴可用来治疗: A. ·肺经虚证; B. ·大肠经实证 C. ·肝经实证; D. ·肝经虚证; E. ·肾经实证	According to “the method of child-mother tonification and sedation”, what may be treated by Lv8 [Qū Quán]? A. ·lung meridian deficiency syndrome; B. ·large intestine meridian excess syndrome C. ·liver meridian excess syndrome; D. ·liver meridian deficiency syndrome; E. ·kidney meridian excess syndrome.
384	根据子母补泻法，肾经虚证当补: A. ·太溪; B. ·复溜 C. ·然谷; D. ·鱼际; E. ·尺泽	According to “the method of child-mother tonification and sedation”, what point should be selected to tone up kidney meridian deficiency syndrome? A. ·K3 [Tài Xī]; B. ·K7 [Fù Liū]; C. K2 [Rán Gŭ]; D. ·Lu10 [Yŭ Jì];

		E. ·Lu5 [Chǐ Zé].
385	骨度分寸法最早见于: A《内经》; B《难经》 C. ·《帛书 》; D·《甲乙经》.	What classic made mention of bone measurements by Cuns for the first time ? A·《Nei Jing》; B 《Difficult C. lassic》 C. ·《Bo Shu》; D·《Jia Yi Jing》.
386	关元穴旁开 4 寸的穴位是: A·子宫穴; B·提托 C. ·水道; D·府舍; E· 维道.	Which point is located 4 Cuns laterally away from R4 (Guān Yuán)? A. Zǐ Gōng; B. Tí Tuō; C. S28 (Shuǐ Dào); D. Sp13 (Fù Shě); E. G28 (Wéi Dào).
387	关元穴至中脘穴间的骨度分寸是: A·6 寸; B·7 寸 C. ·7·5 寸; D·8 寸; E·8·5 寸.	According to the bone Cun measurements (gu du fen Cun), what is the distance between R4 (Guān Yuán) and R12 (Zhōng Wǎn)? A. 6 Cuns; B. 7 Cuns C. 7.5 Cuns; D. 8 Cuns; E. 8.5 Cuns.
388	归属胃经的经穴有: A·期门; B·梁门 C. ·石门; D·章门; E·幽门.	Which of the following points belongs to the stomach meridian? A. Qí Mén; B. Liáng Mén; C. Shí Mén; D. Zhāng Mén; E. Yōu Mén.
389	腘横纹至外踝尖之间应折作: A.14 寸; B.16 寸 C. 18 寸; D13 寸.	What is the distance between popliteal fold and tip of lateral malleolus? A. 14 Cun; B. 16 Cun; C. 18 Cun; D. 13 Cun.
390	腘窝中点到外踝尖的骨度分寸是: A·19 寸; B·16 寸 C. ·13 寸; D·18 寸; E·12 寸.	According to the bone Cun measurements (gu du fen Cun), what is the distance from midpoint on the lateral side of patella to lateral malleolus? A. 19 Cuns; B. 16 Cuns C. 13 Cuns; D. 18 Cuns; E. 12 Cuns.
391	合谷配复溜可用于治疗: A. ·汗证; B. ·泄泻 C. ·癫狂; D. ·痫证; E. ·昏迷	What can be treated by combining Li4 [Hé Gǔ] and K7 [Fù Liū]? A. ·perspiration; B. ·diarrhea; C. ·insanity; D. ·epilepsy; E. ·fainting.
392	合谷配三阴交，其作用是: A.清热; B.安胎 C. 醒神; D 坠胎.	What is the function of the following two points combined: Li4 (Hé Gǔ) and Sp6 (Sān Yīn Jiāo); A. to clear heat; B. to secure the fetus C. to wake up the spirit; D. for abortion.
393	合谷穴在发汗止汗方面的作用与下列哪穴近似? A. ·大椎; B. ·陶道 C. ·太溪; D. ·复溜; E. ·身柱	In inducing and stopping perspiration, what point is similar to Li4 [Hé Gǔ]? A. ·D14 [Dà Zhuī]; B. ·D13 [Táo Dào]; C. ·K3 [Tài Xī]; D. ·K7 [Fù Liū]; E. ·D12 [Shēn Zhù].
394	合谷与风池相配，其治疗作用是: A. ·清热解毒; B. ·祛风解表 C. ·和解少阳; D. ·止咳平喘; E. ·平肝熄风	What is the treatment effect by combining Li4 [Hé Gǔ] and G20 [Fēng Chí]? A. ·to clear heat and dytoxify; B. ·to expel wind and relieve superficial region; C. ·to harmonize lesser yang; D. ·to stop cough and calm asthma; E. ·to calm liver and stop wind.
395	合穴是: A·商阳; B·合谷 C. ·阳溪; D·偏历; E 曲池.	Which is a hé xué / terminal-point / sea-point? A·Li1 / Shāng Yáng; B·Li4 / Hé Gǔc C. ·Li5 / Yáng Xī;D·Li6 / Piān Lì; E. Li11 / Qū Chí.
396	横向与中极相平,纵向与天枢相对的输穴是: A·归来; B·大横 C. ·水道; D·冲门;	What point is on a level with R3 (Zhōng Jí) transversally, and also facing S25 (Tiān Shū) vertically? A. S29 (Guī Lái); B. Sp15 (Dà Héng); C. S28 (Shuǐ Dào); D. Sp12 (Chōng Mén); E. K12 (Dà Hè).

	C.水道; D冲门; E大赫.	
397	喉结旁开3寸处的穴位是: A扶突; B天突 C.人迎; D水突; E以上部不是.	Which of the following points is located 3 Cuns laterally away from laryngeal prominence? A. Li18 (Fú Tū); B. R22 (Tiān Tū); C. S9 (Rén Yíng); D. S10 (Shuǐ Tū); E. None of the above.
398	后溪穴是八脉交会穴中 A.通任脉的穴位; B.通督脉的穴位 C.通冲脉的穴位; D.通带脉的穴位; E.通阳蹺脉的穴位	What meridian is Si3 [Hòu Xī]; C. onnected with among the eight meridians meeting points? A. connected with ren mai /; C. onception meridian; B. connected with du mai / governing meridian; C. connected with chong mai / vigorous meridian; D. connected with dai mai / belt meridian; E. connected with yang qiao mai / yang heel meridian.
399	季肋以下至髀枢的骨度分寸是: A8寸; B5寸 C.6寸; D13寸; E16寸.	According to the bone Cun measurements (gu du fen Cun), what is the distance between hypochondrium (12th rib) and greater trochanter? A. 8 Cuns; B. 5 Cuns; C. 6 Cuns; D. 13 Cuns; E. 16 Cuns.
400	既可治疗本经病，又可治疗奇经病的特定穴是: A.郄穴; B 八会穴 C. 络穴; D八脉交会穴.	What are specially designated points (te ding xue) which can treat the diseases of their respective meridians and also the diseases of the eight extraordinary meridians? A. xi xue (fissuralpoints or cleft-points); B. ba. hui xue (eight meeting points or eight influentialapoints); C. luo points (linking points, or collateral points); D. ba mai jiao hui xue (meeting points between eight extraordinary meridians & twelve master meridians or eight; C. onfluence points).
401	既是合穴又是下合穴的是: A委中; B委阳 C. 上巨虚; D下巨虚; E阴陵泉	Which of the following points is both a "hé xué / terminal-point" and a "lower merging point / lower sea point / xià hé xué"? A. B40 / Wěi Zhōng; B · B39 / Wěi Yáng; C. · S37 / Shàng Jù Xū; D · S39 / Xià Jù Xū; E · Sp9 / Yīn Líng Quán.
402	既是络穴，又是八脉交会穴的是: A大钟; B列缺 C. 后溪; D照海; E合谷.	Which of the following points is both a linking point (luo xue) and one of the eight merdians meeting points (ba mai jiao hui xue)? A. K4 (Dà Zhōng); B. Lu7 (Liè Quē); C. Si3 (Hòu Xī); D. K6 (Zhào Hǎi); E. Li4 (Hé Gǔ).
403	既是募穴，又是八会穴的是: A中府; B章门 C. 天枢; D气海; E石门.	Which of the following is both a gathering point (mu xue) and one of the eight meeting points (ba hui xue)? A. Lu1 (Zhōng Fǔ); B. Lv13 (Zhāng Mén); C. S25 (Tiān Shū); D. R6 (Qì Hǎi); E. R5 (Shí Mén).
404	既是募穴又是腑会穴的穴位是: A.天枢; B梁丘 C. 足三里; D中脘; E章门	What point is a gathering point / mu point and also a meeting point of bowels? A. S25 / Tiān Shū; B · S34 / Liáng Qiū; C. S36 / Zú Sān Lǐ; D · R12 / Zhōng Wǎn; E · Lv13 / Zhāng Mén
405	既为手少阴心经输穴，又为手少阴经原穴的穴位是: A极泉; B少海 C. 通里; D阴郄; E神门.	What point is on the hand lesser yin heart meridian and also the yuán xué / starting point / source-point of the same meridian? A · H1 / Jí Quán; B · H3 / Shào Hǎi; C. H5 / Tōng Lǐ; D · H6 / Yīn Xī; E · H7 / Shén Mén.

406	甲胆主气日丙子时应开：A·阳溪；B·前谷 C. ·太白；D·阴谷 ·E·大敦	What point should open during the Bǐng-Zǐ period of time on the Jiǎ gallbladder day, which takes charge of energy? A · Li5 / Yáng Xī; B · Si2 / Qián Gú; C. Sp3 / Tài Bái; D · K10 / Yīn Gǔ / ·E · Lv1 / Dà Dūn.
407	简便取穴法：垂手贴于大腿外侧，当中指端处的穴位是：A.阴市；B. 伏兔;.C. 中瀆；D 风市.	By the; C. onvenient method of locating point, with the hand straight downward and in cose touch with the lateral side of the thigh, what point is being touched by the tip of the middle finger? A. S33, Yīn Shì; B. S32, Fú Tù; C. G32, Zhōng Dū; D. G31, Fēng Shì.
408	简便取穴法：当胳膊用力时，在肩膀头下，有一块突出的、呈三角形的肌肉，叫三角肌。本穴在三角肌下端偏内侧处，当曲池与肩髃的联线上。 A 髀關；B 臂臑 C. 巨骨；D 口禾窌.	By the; C. onvenient method of locating points: When the upper arm is tense, the deltoid muscle will protrude, and this point is on the medial side of lower end of the projecting muscle. What point is being located? A S31 [Bì Guān]; B Li14; Bì Nào; C. Li16 [Jù Gǔ; D Li19 [Kǒu Hé Liáo].
409	简便取穴法：将胳膊平举，在肩关节(肩膀头)上就出现两个凹窝，本穴在前面的凹窝中，当骨缝之间(即肩峰与肱骨大结节之间)。 A 居髎；B 肩髃 C. 肩貞；D 肩中輸.	By the; C. onvenient method of locating points: When the upper arm is in a horizontal position, two depressions will occur, and locate this point in the anterior depression, in between bone sutures (in between acromion and larger tuberosity of humerus). What point is being located? A S3 [Jù Liáo]; B Li15 Jiān Yú; C. Si9 [Jiān Zhēn]; D Si15 [Jiān Zhōng Shū].
410	简便取穴法：站直，足尖着地，足跟提起，在小腿肚正中下，可出现一个"人"字形，在"人"字尖下，就是本穴。如果"人"字形不明显时，可从委中到脚后跟上与外踝尖平齐处联线的中间取穴。 A 承山；B. 承筋 C. 承扶；D. 承泣.	By the; C. onvenient method of locating point, let the patient sit straight or lie on stomach, locate this point below the belly of the gastrocnemius muscle in the depression that will occur when the foot is stretched. What point is being located? A; B57, Chéng Shān; B. B56 [Chéng Jīn]; C. B36 [Chéng Fú]; D S1 [Chéng Qì].
411	简便取穴法:胳膊下垂，在肩膀头上的高突圆骨(叫锁骨肩峰端);由高突圆骨前缘直下约二寸，当骨缝之间（即肩峰与肱骨大结节之间），就是本穴。 A 居髎；B 肩髃 C. 肩貞；D 肩中輸.	By the; C. onvenient method of locating point, with the upper arm down, at acromial extremity of clavicle (extremitas acromialis claviculae), 2 Cuns directly below the anterior border of extremitas acromialis claviculare, in between bone sutures (namely, between acrominon and larger tuberosity of humerus). What point is being located? A S3 [Jù Liáo]; B Li15 Jiān Yú; C. Si9 [Jiān Zhēn]; D Si15 [Jiān Zhōng Shū].
412	简便取穴法中，垂手贴于大腿外侧，当中指端处的穴位是：A.阴市；B. 伏兔;.C.	By the; C. onvenient method of locating point, with the hand straight downward and in close touch with the lateral side of the thigh, what point is being touched by the tip of the middle

	中瀆; D 风市.	finger? A. S33, Yīn Shì; B. S32, Fú Tù; C. G32, Zhōng Dū; D. G31, Fēng Shì.
413	交会穴中通于胃、心、胸的穴位是: A. 列缺、照海 B. 列缺、内关 C. 内关、申脉 D. 公孙、内关 E. 申脉、后溪	What meridian meeting points are; C. onnected with stomach, heart, and chest? A. Lu7 [Liè Quē] 、K6 [Zhào Hǎi]; B. Lu7 [Liè Quē] 、P6 [Nèi Guān]; C. P6 [Nèi Guān] 、B62 [Shēn Mài]; D. Sp4 [Gōng Sūn] 、P6 [Nèi Guān]; E. B62 [Shēn Mài] 、Si3 [Hòu Xī].
414	经脉属火，腧穴属木的穴位是: A 少府; B 少冲 C. 前谷; D 涌泉; E 大敦	What point belongs to wood and its meridian belongs to fire? A. H8 (Shào Fǔ); B. H9 (Shào Chōng); C. Si2 (Qián Gú); D. K1 (Yǒng Quán); E. Lv1 (Dà Dūn).
415	经脉属金，腧穴也属金的穴位是: A. 少商; B. 商阳 C. 商丘; D. 商曲; E. 以上都不是.	What point belongs to metal and its meridian also belongs to metal? A. Lu11 (Shǎo Shāng); B. Li1 (Shāng Yáng); C. Sp5 (Shāng Qiū); D. K17 (Shāng Qǔ); E. none of the above.
416	经脉属金，腧穴属水的穴位是: A 二间; B 内庭 C. 行间; D 鱼际; E 液门.	What point belongs to water and its meridian belongs to metal? A. Li2 (Èr Jiān); B. S44 (Nèi Tíng); C. Lv2 (Xíng Jiān); D. Lu10 (Yǔ Jì); E. Sj2 (Yè Mén).
417	经脉属木，腧穴属火的穴位是: A 太冲; B 中封 C. 足临泣; D 阳辅; E 丘墟	What point belongs to fire and its meridian belongs to wood? A. Lv3 (Tài Chōng); B. Lv4 (Zhōng Fēng); C. G41 (Zú Lín Qì, Lín Qì); D. G38 (Yáng Fǔ); E. G40 (Qiū Xū).
418	经脉属水, 腧穴也属水的穴位是: A 阴陵泉; B 阳陵泉 C. 足三里; D 阴谷; E 委中	Which point is a water point, which belongs to a water meridian? A. Sp9 (Yīn Líng Quán); B. G34 (Yáng Líng Quán); C. S36 (Zú Sān Lǐ); D. K10 (Yīn Gǔ); E. B40 (Wěi Zhōng).
419	经脉属水，腧穴属木的穴位是: A. 然谷; B. 太溪 C. 陷谷; D. 临泣; E. 束骨.	What point belongs to wood. and its meridian belongs to water? A. K2 (Rán Gǔ); B. K3 (Tài Xī); C. S43 (Xiàn Gǔ); D. G41 (Zú Lín Qì, Lín Qì); E. B65 (Shù Gǔ).
420	经脉属水，又是输穴的是: A. 足临泣; B. 束骨 C. 然谷; D. 大钟; E. 以上都不是	What point is a flowing point / stream point [SHÙ XUÉ], and its meridian belongs to water? A. G41 [Zú Lín Qì]; B. B65 [Shù Gǔǔ]; C. K2 [Rán Gǔ]; D. K4 [Dà Zhōng]; E. none of the above
421	井穴的五行属性是: A 阳经属金 阴经属木; B 阳经属水 阴经属火 C. 阳经属木 阴经属土; D 阳经属火 阴经属金; E 阳经属土 阴经属水.	What do well points (jing xue) correspond to? A. they belong to metal in case of yang meridians, to wood. in case of yin meridian; B. they belong to water in case of yang meridians, to fire in case of yin meridian; C. they belong to wood. in case of yang meridians, to earth in case of yin meridian; D. they belong to fire in case of yang meridians, to metal in case of yin meridian; E. they belong to earth in case of yang meridians, to water in case of yin meridian.
422	井穴是: A 隐白; B 公孙 C. 太白; D 三阴交; E 阴陵泉	Which is a jǐng xué / well point? A · Sp1 / Yīn Bái; B · Sp4 / Gōng Sūn; C. Sp3 / Tài Bái; D · Sp6 / Sān Yīn Jiāo; E. Sp9 / Yīn Líng Quán.

	E 阴陵泉.	
423	具有健脾、疏肝、益肾的穴位是: A. 阴陵泉; B. 三阴交 C. 肝俞; D. 脾俞; E. 肾俞	What point can strengthen the spleen, disperse the liver, and benefit the kidneys? A. Sp9 [Yīn Líng Quán]; B. Sp6 [Sān Yīn Jiāo]; C. B18 [Gān Shū]; D. B20 [Pí Shū]; E. B23 [Shèn Shū].
424	可以治疗各种血证的通用穴位是: A. 血海; B. 委中 C. 太白; D. 膈俞; E. 心俞	What point is normally selected to treat various kinds of blood diseases? A. Sp10 [Xuè Hǎi]; B. B40 [Wěi Zhōng]; C. Sp3 [Tài Bái]; D. B17 [Gé Shū]; E. B15 [Xīn Shū].
425	阑尾穴位于: A 天枢外开约 1.0 寸; B 天枢外开约 1.5 寸 C. 足三里直下约 1.0 寸; D 足三里直下约 1.5 寸; E 足三里直下约 2.0 寸.	The location of Lán Wěi Xué is: A. about 1 Cun lateral to S25 (Tiān Shū); B. about 1.5 Cuns lateral to S25 (Tiān Shū); C. about 1 Cun directly below S36 (Zú Sān Lǐ); D. about 1.5 Cuns below S36 (Zú Sān Lǐ); E. about 2 Cuns below S36 (Zú Sān Lǐ).
426	廉泉、照海同用，具有什么作用? A. 安神定志; B. 舒筋通络 C. 熄风化痰; D. 和胃止呕; E. 生津止渴	What are the functions of combined R23 [Lián Quán] and K6 [Zhào Hǎi]? A. to secure the spirit and fix will; B. to relax tendons and C. onnect linking meridians; C. to stop wind and transform phlegm; D. to harmonize the stomach and stop vomiting; E. to produce fluids and quench thirst.
427	两穴之间距离是 8 寸的穴位是: A 太渊至孔最; B 偏历至曲池 C. 足三里至丰隆; D 三阴交至阴陵泉; E 中极至中脘.	The distance between which two points is 8 Cuns? A. Lu9 (Tài Yuān) and Lu6 (Kǒng Zuì); B. Li6 (Piān Lì) and Li11 (Qū Chí); C. S36 (Zú Sān Lǐ); S40 (Fēng Lóng); D. Sp6 (Sān Yīn Jiāo) and Sp9 (Yīn Líng Quán); E. R3 (Zhōng Jí) and R12 (Zhōng Wǎn).
428	列缺采用何种取穴法 A.骨性标志; B. 折量法 C. 肌性标志法; D 指量法.	What method of locating points should be used to locate Lu7 / Liè Quē? A. fixed landmarks of bones; B Cun measurements C. muscle landmarks; D. digital measurements.
429	率谷穴的位置在: A.耳尖直上入发际 0.5 寸; B.耳尖直上入发际 1 寸;.C.耳尖直上入发际 1.5 寸; D 耳尖直上入发际 2 寸.	Where is G8 (Shuài Gǔ) located? A. Above the apex of ear, 0.5 Cuns above the hairline; B. Above the apex of ear, 1 Cuns above the hairline; C. Above the apex of ear, 1.5 Cuns above the hairline; D. Above the apex of ear, 2 Cuns above the hairline.
430	络穴共有: A 365 穴; B 16 穴 C. 12 穴; D 15 穴; E 10 穴.	How many linking points, / luo points altogeher? A 365 points; B.16 points; C. 12 points; D.15 points; E 10 points.
431	络穴是: A 商阳; B 合谷 C. 阳溪; D 偏历; E 曲池.	Which is a linking point / luo point? A · Li1 / Shāng Yáng; B · Li4 / Hé Gǔ; C. Li5 / Yáng Xī; D · Li6 / Piān Lì; E. Li11 / Qū Chí.
432	络穴是: A 隐白; B 公孙 C. 太白; D 三阴交; E 阴陵泉.	Which point is a linking point / luo point? A · Sp1 / Yīn Bái; B · Sp4 / Gōng Sūn; C. Sp3 / Tài Bái; D · Sp6 / Sān Yīn Jiāo; E. Sp9 / Yīn Líng Quán.

433	没有募穴分布的经脉是: A 肺经; B 脾经 C. 肝经; D 胆经; E 任脉	Which meridian has no mu xue (gathering point) on it? A. lung meridian; B. spleen meridian; C. liver meridian; D. gallbladder meridian; E. ren mai (conception meridian).
434	眉梢凹陷处的腧穴是: A. 太阳; B. 童子髎 C. 攒竹; D. 曲鬓; E. 丝竹空	What point is located in the depression on the lateral end of the eyebrow? . A. Tài Yáng [Sun / temple]; B. G1 [Tóng Zĭ Liáo]; C. B2 [Zăn Zhú]; D. G7 [Qū Bìn]; E. Sj23 [Sī Zhú Kōng]
435	募穴的正确附加名称是: A.胃经募穴; B.足阳明经募穴 C. 足阳明胃经募穴; D 胃募穴.	What is the accurate full name of mu xue (gathering points)? A. stomach meridian mu point (gathering point); B. bright yang of foot mu point; C. bright yang meridian of foot mu point; D. stomach mu point.
436	募穴共有: A 365 穴; B 16 穴 C. 12 穴; D 15 穴; E 10 穴.	How many gathering points / mu points altogether? A 365 points; B.16 points; C. 12 points; D.15 points; E 10 points.
437	募穴均位于: A 腹部; B 胸部 C. 腰部; D 背部; E 胸腹部.	Where are gathering points / mu points located? A abdominal region; B chest region; C. lumbar region; D back region; E chest-abdominal region.
438	脑户与神庭连线中点的腧穴是: A 前顶; B 后顶 C. 百会; D 囟会; E 强间	Which of the following points is located on the midpoint of the line connecting D17 (Năo Hù) and D24 (Shén Tíng)? A. D21 (Qián Dĭng); B. D19 (Hòu Dĭng); C. D20 (Băi Huì); D. D22 (Xìn Huì); E. D18 (Qiáng Jiān).
439	能主治肝胆脾胃病症的腧穴应分布在: A. 背部; B. 腰尻部 C. 肩胛部; D. 腋胁部; E. 背腰部	Where is the distribution of points capable of treating diseses of liver, gallbladder, spleen, and stomach? A. back region; B. lumbar and sacral region; C. scapular region; D. axillary and coastal region; E. back and lumbar region.
440	偏历与温溜间隔: A 1 寸; B 2 寸 C. 3 寸; D 4 寸; E 5 寸.	What is the distance between Li6 / Piān Lì and Li7 / Wēn Liū? A 1 Cun; B 2 Cun; C3 Cun; D 4 Cun; E.5 Cun.
441	奇穴 "肘尖"主要用于治疗: A 臂痛; B 上肢麻木 C. 肩周炎; D 肘关节炎; E 瘰疬.	What is the primary indication of the extraordinary point, Zhŏu Jiān? A. pain in the arm; B. numbness of the upper limbs; C. periarthritis of shoulder; D. arthritis of elbow joints; E. scrofula.
442	奇穴"安眠"...的正确位置是: A. 翳风穴与哑门穴连线的中点; B. 翳明穴与风府穴连线的中点 C. 翳风穴与风府穴连线的中点; D. 翳明穴与风池穴连线的中点; E. 翳风穴与风池穴连线的中点	Where is the accurate location of the extraordinary points named “ĀN MIÁN (good sleep)”? A. on midpoint of the line connecting Sj17 [Yì Fēng] and D15 [Yă Mén]; B. on midpoint of the line connecting Yì Míng (shelter light) and D16 [Fēng Fŭ]; C. on midpoint of the line connecting Sj17 [Yì Fēng] and D16 [Fēng Fŭ]; D. on midpoint of the line connecting Yì Míng (shelter light) and G20 [Fēng Chí]; E. on midpoint of the line connecting Sj17 [Yì Fēng] and G20 [Fēng Chí].
443	奇穴"胃上"的正确定位是:	Where is the extraordinary point, Wèi Shàng located? A. 2 Cuns below the umbilicus, 4 Cuns laterally away from the

	A·脐下2寸·旁开4寸; B·脐上4寸·旁开2寸 C. 脐上1寸·旁开4寸; D·脐上2寸·旁开4寸; E·脐上4寸·旁开4寸.	umbilicus; B. 4 Cuns above the umbilicus, 2 Cuns laterally away from the umbilicus; C. 1 Cun above the umbilicus, 4 Cuns laterally away from the umbilicus; D. 2 Cuns above the umbilicus, 4 Cuns laterally away from the umbilicus; E. 4 Cuns above the umbilicus, 4 Cuns laterally away from the umbilicus.
444	奇穴球后的正确位置是在: A. 眶上缘的外1 / 4与内3 / 4交界处; B. 眶下缘的外3 / 4与内1 / 4交界处 C. 眶上缘的内1 / 4与外3 / 4交界处; D.眶下缘的外1 / 4与内3 / 4交界处; E. 以上都不是	Where is the accurate location of the extraordinary point, qiú hòu (behind the ball)? A. on the upper edge of the orbit, 1 / 4 laterally and 3 / 4 medially; B. on the lower edge of the orbit, 1 / 4 medially and 3 / 4 laterally; C. on the upper edge of the orbit, 1 / 4 medially and 3 / 4 laterally; D. on the lower edge of the orbit, 1 / 4 laterally and 3 / 4 medially; E. none of the above.
445	奇穴四神聪位于: A.百会穴前后左右各旁开0.5寸; B.百会穴前后左右各旁开1.3寸 C. 百会穴前后左右各旁开1.5寸; D 百会穴前后左右各旁开1寸.	Where is Sì Shén Cōng (an extraordinary point) located? A. 0.5 Cun from D20 (Bǎi Huì) on the front, back, left, and right four points altogethe; B. 1.3 Cun from D20 (Bǎi Huì) on the front, back, left, and right four points altogether; C. 1.5 Cun from D20 (Bǎi Huì) on the front, back, left, and right four points altogethe; D. 1 Cun from D20 (Bǎi Huì) on the front, back, left, and right. four points altogether.
446	奇穴太阳的正确位置在: A·眉梢外开1寸; B·目外眦外开1寸 C. 眉梢与目外眦之间; D·眉梢与目外眦之间向后1寸; E·以上都不是.	Where is the extraordinary point, Tài Yáng located? A. 1 Cun laterally away from the lateral end of the eyebrow; B. 1 Cun laterally away from the lateral angle of the eye (lateral canthus); C. in between the lateral end. of the eyebrow and lateral canthus; D. in the depression 1 Cun behind the space between the lateral end. of the eyebrow and the lateral angle of the eye (lateral canthus); E. None of the above.
447	脐上3寸·旁开2寸的穴位是: A·关门; B·太乙 C. ·不容; D·承满; E·梁门.	Which of the following points is located 3 Cuns above the umbilicus and 2 Cuns lateral to the umbilicus? A. S22 (Guān Mén); B. S23 (Tài Yǐ); C. S19 (Bù Róng); D. S20 (Chéng Mǎn); E. S21 (Liáng Mén).
448	脐上4寸·旁开2寸的经穴是: A. 不容; B. 梁门 C. 幽门; D. 通谷; E. 承满	Which of the following points is located 4 Cuns above the umbilicus and 2 Cuns lateral to the umbilicus? A. S19 [Bù Róng]; B. S21 [Liáng Mén]; C. K21 [Yōu Mén]; D. B66 [Tōng Gǔ]; E. S20 [Chéng Mǎn]
449	脐上6寸·旁开2寸的穴位是: A·不容; B·关门 C. 太乙; D·承满; E·滑肉门.	Which of the following points is located 6 Cuns above the umbilicus and 2 Cuns lateral to the umbilicus? A. S19 (Bù Róng); B. S22 (Guān Mén); C. S23 (Tài Yǐ); D. S20 (Chéng Mǎn); E. S24 Huá Ròu Mén).
450	气海是指: A·胃; B·脑 C. 冲脉; D·肝; E·膻中.	What does “sea of eergy” refer to? A·stomach;B · brain; C. rigorous meridian / chong mai; D·liver; E · R17 / Shān Zhōng.
451	丘墟深刺时，可以透向: A. 然谷; B. 照海 C. 公孙; D. 解溪; E. 太溪	What is the direction of needle insertion when deep insertion is applied to G40 [Qiū Xū]? A. in the direction of K2 [Rán Gǔ]; B. in the direction of K6 [Zhào Hǎi]; C. in the direction of Sp4 [Gōng Sūn]; D. in the

		direction of S41 [Jiě Xī]; E. in the direction of K3 [Tài Xī].
452	曲差和络却穴皆属于何经？ A. 大肠经; B. 胆经 C. 膀胱经; D. 肾经; E. 心包经.	Qū Chā and Luò Què both belong to what meridian? A. large intestine meridian; B. gallbladder meridian; C. bladder meridian; D. kidney meridian; E. pericardium meridian.
453	屈肘，曲池穴外上方1寸，肱骨边缘的穴是: A 天井; B 肘髎 C. 小海; D 清冷渊.	With the elbow bent, what point is located 1 Cun above and lateral to Li11 / Qū Chí and at the border of humerus? A · Sj10 / Tiān Jǐng; B · Li12 / Zhǒu Liáo; C. · Si8 / Xiǎo Hǎi; D · Sj11 / Qīng Lěng Yuān.
454	取地仓穴常用的方法是: A 中指同身寸取穴法; B 固定标志取穴法 C. 一夫法; D 活动标志取穴法; E 骨度分寸取穴法.	What method is frequently used to locate S4 / Dì Cāng? A Digital Cun of the middle finger; B twelve muscular meridians / jing jin fixed landmarks C. width of four fingers closed together; D · locating points by mobile landmarks; E bone measurements by Cuns.
455	取环跳穴的最好体位是: A 侧卧位，两下肢平伸; B 侧卧位，屈上腿伸下腿 C. 侧卧位，屈下腿伸上腿; D 侧卧位，双下肢都弯屈; E 以上都不是.	What is the best position to locate G30 (Huán Tiào)? A. lateral recumbent position with lower limbs extended; B. lateral recumbent position with the leg on top bent and the leg at bottom stretched; C. lateral recumbent position with the leg at bottom bent and the leg on top stretched; D. lateral recumbent position with both legs bent; E. None of the above.
456	取孔最穴常用的方法是: A 中指同身寸取穴法; B 固定标志取穴法 C. 一夫法; D 活动标志取穴法; E 骨度分寸取穴法.	What method is frequently used to locate Lu6 / Kǒng Zuì? A Digital Cun of the middle finger; B fixed landmarks; C. width of four fingers closed together; D · locating points by mobile landmarks; E bone measurements by Cuns.
457	取乳根穴常用的方法是: A 中指同身寸取穴法; B 固定标志取穴法 C. 一夫法; D 活动标志取穴法; E 骨度分寸取穴法.E 骨度分寸取穴法	What method is frequently used to locate S18 / Rǔ Gēn? A Digital Cun of the middle finger; B fixed landmarks C. width of four fingers closed together; D · locating points by mobile landmarks; E bone measurements by Cuns.
458	取听宫穴常用的方法是: A 中指同身寸取穴法; B 固定标志取穴法 C. 一夫法; D 活动标志取穴法; E 骨度分寸取穴法.	What method is frequently used to locate Si19 [Tīng Gōng]? A Digital Cun of the middle finger; B fixed landmarks; C. width of four fingers closed together; D · locating points by mobile landmarks; E bone measurements by Cuns.
459	三焦的下合穴是: A.三阴交; B.委中 C. 委阳; D 足三里.	What is the “xia he xue” (lower merging point) of sanjiao (triple heater)? A; Sp6 (Sān Yīn Jiāo); B. B40 (Wěi Zhōng); C. B39 (Wěi Yáng);

		D. S36 (Zú Sān Lǐ).
460	三阴交、合谷同用，其临床效应是: A. 清热; B. 祛风 C. 救逆; D. 坠胎; E. 醒神	What is the clinical effect of combining Sp6 [Sān Yīn Jiāo] and Li4 [Hé Gǔ]? A. to clear heat; B. to expel wind; C. to rescue uprising; D. for abortion; E. to wake up the spirit.
461	三阴交穴在特定穴中属于: A.八会穴; B.交会穴 C. 八脉交会穴; D 下合穴.	What kind. of specially marked. points does Sp6 (Sān Yīn Jiāo) belong to? A. ba hui xue (eight meeting points or eight influential points); B. jiao hui xue (meridians meeting points); C. ba mai jiao hui xue (eight meeting points between eight extraordinary meridians & twelve master meridians or eight; C. onfluence points); D. xia he xie (lower merging point)
462	膻中旁开二寸是: A 神封; B 神藏 C. 步廊; D 膺窗; E 灵墟.	What point is located 2 Cuns lateral to R17 (Shān Zhōng)? A K23 (Shén Fēng); B K25 (Shén Cáng); C. K22 (Bù Láng); D. S16 (Yīng Chuāng); E K24 (Líng Xū).
463	膻中穴的作用主要是: A 宽胸理气; ; B 健脾化痰; C. 和胃止呕; D 宁心安神; E 通经活血。	What is the primary function of R17 (Shān Zhōng)? A. to expand the chest and regulate energy; B. to strengthen the spleen and transform phlegm; C. to harmonize the stomach and stop vomiting; D. to calm the heart and secure the spirit; E. to facilitate meridian flow and activate the blood.
464	善治血症的井穴是: A 足窍阴; B 少泽 C. 隐白; D 厉兑; E 关冲.	Which "well point [jing xue]" is particularly effective in the treatment of blood symptoms? A. G44 (Zú Qiào Yīn, Qiào Yīn); B. Si1 (Shào Zé); C. Sp1 (Yǐn Bái); D. S45 (Lì Duì); E. Sj1 (Guān Chōng).
465	上廉与下廉间隔: A 1 寸; B 2 寸 C. 3 寸; D 4 寸; E 5 寸.	What is the distance between Li9 / Shàng Lián and Li8 / Xià Lián? A 1 Cun; B 2 Cun; C3 Cun; D 4 Cun; E.5 Cun.
466	少府、劳宫同用，其作用是? A. 宁神志; B. 泻心火 C. 调心气; D. 止盗汗; E. 通经络	What is the function of combining H8 [Shào Fǔ] and P8 [Láo Gōng]? A. to secure the spirit and will; B. to sedate heart fire; C. to regulate heart energy; D. to stop night sweats; E. to; C. onnect master meridians and linking meridians.
467	神阙与巨阙连线中点的输穴是: A 下脘; B 中脘 C. 上脘; D 建里; E 水分.	Which point is on the midpoint of the line connecting R8 (Shén Què) and R14 (Jù Què)? A. R10 (Xià Wǎn); B. R12 (Zhōng Wǎn); C. R13 (Shàng Wǎn); D. R11 (Jiàn Lǐ); E. R9 (Shuǐ Fēn).
468	十二经脉的络穴位于: A 肘膝关节附近; B 肘膝关节以上 C. 肘膝关节以下; D.腕踝关节以下; E 腕踝关节横纹上.	Where are linking points, of.twelve master meridians located? A close to elbow joints and knee joints; B above elbow joints and knee joints; C. below elbow joints and knee joints; E above wrist and ankle joints.
469	十二井穴是: A 十二经的起始穴; B 部位于指 (趾)端 C. 五行属木; D 十二经的根穴; E 以上都不是.	What are twelve well points (jing xue)? A.starting points of twelve master meridians; B. located at the tips of fingers and toes; C. wood points in five elements; D. root points of twelve master meridians; E. none of the above.

470	石门穴位于脐下几寸? A·1 寸; B·1·5 寸 C. ·2 寸; D·2·5 寸; E·以上都不是.	How many Cuns is R5 (Shí Mén) below the umbilicus? A. 1 Cun; B. 1.5 Cuns; C. 2 Cuns; D. 2.5 Cuns; E. none of the above.
471	手厥阴心包经 "下腋3寸"指的是: A. 辄筋; B. 天池 C. 渊液; D. 天溪; E. 天泉	What point on the pericardium meridian is "3 Cun below armpit"? A. ·G23 [Zhé Jīn] ·; B. ·P1 [Tiān Chí]; C. ·G22 [Yuān Yè]; D. ·Sp18 [Tiān Xī]; E. ·P2 [Tiān Quán]
472	手三里与曲池间隔: A·1 寸; B·2 寸 C. 3 寸; D·4 寸; E·5 寸.	What is the distance between Li10 / Shǒu Sān Lǐ and Li11 / Qū Chí? A·1 Cun; B·2 Cun; ·C3 Cun; D·4 Cun; E.5 Cun.
473	手少阳三焦经的下合穴应在: A.足阳明胃经上; B 足少阳胆经 C. 足太阳膀胱经上; D 督脉经上.	Where should the merging point (xia. he xue) of the triple heater meridian be located? A. on the stomach meridian; B. on the gallbladder meridian; C. on the bladder meridian; D. on the du mai (governing meridian).
474	手少阴心经的合穴是: A 少府; B 少海 C. 小海; D·曲泽; E 尺泽.	What is the “hé xué / terminal-point / sea-point” on the hand lesser yin heart meridian? A · H8 / Shào Fǔ; B · H3 / Shào Hǎi C. Si8 / Xiǎo Hǎi; D · P3 / Qū Zé; E. Lu5 / Chǐ Zé.
475	手少阴心经的穴位数是: A·20; B 9 C. ·11; D·11; E·24.	How many points on the hand lesser yin heart meridian? A·20; B 9; C. ·11; D·11; E·24.
476	手太阴肺经在前臂的支脉所分出的穴位是: A.孔最; B 列缺 C. 经渠; D 鱼际.	What is the point where a branch of the lung meridian separates in the forearm? A. Lu6, Kǒng Zuì; B. Lu7, Liè Quē; C. Lu8, Jīng Qú; D. Lu10, Yǔ Jì.
477	手腕关节，横纹上的六个穴: A·都是原穴; B·都是输穴 C. ·屈侧的是输入,伸侧的是原穴; D·屈侧的是原穴,伸侧的是输入; E·以上都不是.	What are the six points on the tranversal crease of the wrist joints? A. all of them are starting points (source points or original points [YUÁN XUÉ]; B. all of them are flowing points (stream points [SHÙ XUÉ]; C. the points on the flexing side are flowing points (stream points [SHÙ XUÉ'], the points on the extended. side are starting points (source points or original points [YUÁN XUÉ]; D. the points on the flexing side are starting points (source points or original points [YUÁN XUÉ], the points on the extended side are flowing points (stream points [SHÙ XUÉ]; E. none of the above.
478	手阳明大肠经上出于 "柱骨之会上",穴位是: A·肩髃; B·巨骨 C. ·天柱; D·大椎; E·大杼.	What point on the large intestine meridian is located “above the meeting of spinal processes (7th cervical)”? A. Li15 (Jiān Yú); B. Li16 (Jù Gǔ); C. B10 (Tiān Zhù); D. D14 (Dà Zhuī); EB11 (Dà Zhù).
479	手指比量法又称: A. 中指同身寸法; B. 拇指同身寸法 C. 横指同身寸法; D. 指寸法; E. 一夫法.	When an acuuncturist uses the length of his / her own fingers to locate the points on patient, it is called: A. digital Cun of the middle finger; B. digital Cun of the patient's thumb; C. from one side of digital crease of middle (or distal) phalange of middle finger to the other side of digital

		crease of middle phalange of middle finger; D. digital measurements; E. width of four fingers closed. together as 3 Cuns.
480	腧穴发展的过程，一般认为历经了: A 经穴、经外奇穴、阿是穴; B 经外奇穴、阿是穴、经穴 C. 阿是穴、经外奇穴、经穴; D 阿是穴、经穴、经外奇穴; E 经穴、阿是穴、经外奇穴.	What is the sequence in which acupuncture points have been developed"? A points on meridians, extraoprdinary points ouchi points / pressure points;B · extraoprdinary points, ouchi points / pressure points, points on meridians C. ouchi points / pressure points, extraoprdinary points, points on meridians; D. ouchi points / pressure points. points on meridians, extraoprdinary points; E points on meridians, ouchi points / pressure points, extraoprdinary points.
481	腧穴分为：A 十四经穴，经外奇穴，阿是穴; B 十二经穴，经外奇穴，阿是穴; C. 十四经穴，经外奇穴，特定穴. D 十二经穴，奇穴，特定穴; E 十四经穴，特定穴，阿是穴。	Acupuncture points may be divided into: A points on 14 major meridians，extraoprdinary points，ouchi points / pressure points; B points on 12 major meridians，12 flowing points / river points / jīng xué，extraoprdinary points，ouchi points / pressure points; C. points on 14 major meridians，extraoprdinary points，specially marked points; D points on 12 major meridians，extraoprdinary points，specially marked points E points on 14 major meridians，specially marked points，ouchi points / pressure points.
482	腧穴中的"输穴"是指: A.全身所有的腧穴; B.背俞穴 C. 五输穴中第三个穴位; D 腹募穴.	What do flowing points or stream points [shù xué] designate?. A.all acupuncture points in the whole body; B. posterior points / back shu points, organ points [bèi shù xué]; C. third points among the five command points; D. gathering points / anterior points, [mù xué] in the abdomen.
483	水沟穴能治疗除 XX 以外的其他病症: A 水肿; B 癫狂 C. 昏迷; D 失眠; E 腰扭伤.	Which of the following symptoms is NOT to be treated by D26 (Shuǐ Gōu, Rén Zhōng)? A. edema; B. insanity and maniac; C. fainting; D. insomnia; E. twisting injury to the loins.
484	丝竹空穴的位置在: A 眉梢外 1 寸凹陷处; B 眉梢外 0，5 寸凹陷处 C. 眉梢凹陷处; D 目外眦旁凹陷处.	Where is Sj23 / Sī Zhú Kōng located? A · in the depression 1 Cun from lateral end of eyebrow; B in the depression 0.5 Cun from lateral end of eyebrow; C. in the depression at the lateral end of eyebrow; D · in the depression close to the lateral canthus.
485	四神聪穴位于: A 百会前后左右各开 1.3 寸; B 百会前后左右各开 1·5 寸 C. 百会前后左右各开 0·5 寸; D 百会前后左右各开 1.0 寸; E 以上部不是.	Where is Sì Shén Cōng located? A. 1.3 Cuns from D20 (Bǎi Huì) on the front, back, left, and right, four points altogether; B. 1.5 Cuns from D20 (Bǎi Huì) on the front, back, left, and right, four points altogether; C. 0.5 Cun from D20 (Bǎi Huì) on the front, back, left, and right, four points altogether; D. 1 Cun from D20 (Bǎi Huì) on the front, back, left, and right, four points altogether; E None of the above.
486	髓海是指: A 胃; B 脑; C. 冲脉; D 肝; E 膻中	What does "sea of marrow" refer to? A stomach; B · brain; C. rigorous meridian / chong mai; D liver; E · R17 / Shān Zhōng.
487	太溪穴下 1 寸的穴位是: A.复溜; B 大钟 C.	What point is located 1 Cun below K3 (Tài Xī)? A. K7, Fù Liū; B. K4, Dà Zhōng; C. K2, Rán Gǔ; D. K5, Shuǐ Quán

	然谷; D 水泉.	Quán.
488	太阳穴的正确位置在: A.眉梢外 1 寸处; B.目外眦外 1 寸处 C. 眉梢与目外眦之间; D 眉梢与目外眦之间后 1 寸.	Where is Tài Yáng located? A. 1 Cun lateral to the lateral end. of the eyebrow; B. 1 Cun lateral to the lateral angle of the eye; C. in between the lateral end of the eyebrow and the lateral angle of the eye; D. 1 Cun behind the space between the lateral end. of the eyebrow and the lateral angle of the eye.
489	特定穴是指: A. 没有归属于 "十四经", 而有特殊作用的穴位; B. 归属于" 十四经", 具有特殊治疗作用的穴位 C. 指 "十四经"中具有特殊治疗作用, 并有特殊称号的穴位; D 指对某些疾病具有特殊治疗作用的穴位;E 以上都不是。	Specially marked points (te ding xue) refer to: A. the points with special functions and outside the fourteen major meridians; B the points with special therapeutic functions and on the fourteen major meridians; C. the points on the fourteen major meridians with special therapeutic functions and also with special names; D. the points with special therapeutic functions in treating certain diseases; E. none of the above.
490	特定穴中郄穴的数目是: A.12 个; B.8 个 C. 15 个; D. 16 个.	How many fissural points / cleft points [xī xué] altogether among the specially marked points (te ding xue)?. A. 12 points; B. 8 points; C. 15 points; D. 16 points.
491	提托穴可以治疗: A 胃下垂; B 肾下垂 C. 子宫下垂; D 肝脾肿大; E · 肝肿大	Which symptom may be treated by Tí Tuō? A. gastroptosis; B. nephroptosis; C. hysteroptosis; D. hepatosplenomegaly; E. hepatomegaly.
492	替代阴经原穴的类穴是本经的: A 络穴; B 郄穴 C. 合穴; D 输穴 l E 荥穴.	What point on the yin meridians may be used to substitute for yuan xue (original or source point)? A. luo xue (linking point); B. xi xue (fissural or cleft point); C. he xue (merging point or sea point); D. shu xue (stream point); E. ying xue (spring point).
493	天柱穴的位置在: A.后发际正中直上 0.5 寸, 旁开 1.3 寸; B.后发际正中直上 1 寸, 旁开 1.5 寸 C. 后发际正中直上 2.5 寸, 旁开 1.3 寸; D 后发际正中直上 2 寸, 旁开 1.5 寸.	Where is B10 (Tiān Zhù) located? A. 0.5 Cun directly above the posterior hairline, 1.3 Cun lateral to the hairline; B. 1 Cun directly above the posterior hairline, 1.5 Cun lateral to the hairline; C. 2.5 Cun directly above the posterior hairline, 1.3 Cun lateral to the hairline; D. 2 Cun directly above the posterior hairline, 1.5 cun lateral to the hairline.
494	听宫穴属于: A 足太阳膀胱经; B 足少阳胆经 C. 手太阳小肠经; D 手少阳三焦经.	What meridian does Tīng Gōng belong to? A. bladder meridian; B gallbladder meridian; C. small intestine meridian; D triple heater meridian.
495	头部穴位中当耳尖处的发际上取: A 耳和髎; B 角孙 C. 头临泣; D 神庭.	What point among the points in the head region is located on the hairline at the tip of the ear? A Sj22 / Hé Liáo / Ěr Hé Liáo; B Sj20 / Jiǎo Sūn; C. G15 / Tóu Lín Qì; D D24 / Shén Tíng.
496	头临泣位于: A 神庭与头维连线之外 1 / 3 折点; B 神庭与头维连线之内 1	Where is G15 (Tóu Lín Qì, Lín Qì) located? A. on the line connecting D24 (Shén Tíng) and S8 (Tóu Wěi) 1 / 3 laterally; B. on the line connecting D24 (Shén Tíng) and S8

	/ 3 折点 C. 神庭穴旁开 2 寸; D 头维与神庭连线之中点; E 以上都不是.	(Tóu Wěi) 1 / 3 medially; C. 2 Cuns laterally away from D24 (Shén Tíng; D. on the midpoint of the line connecting D24 (Shén Tíng) and S8 (Tóu Wěi); E. None of the above.
497	头临泣穴和脑空穴皆属于何经？ A. 大肠经; B. 膀胱经 C. 胆经; D. 肾经; E. 心包经.	Tóu Lín Qì and Nǎo Kōng both belong to what meridian? A. large intestine meridian; B. bladder meridian; C. gallbladder meridian; D. kidney meridian; E. pericardium meridian.
498	头临泣穴至脑空穴连线上的五个腧穴排列顺序应是: A. 头临泣 正营 承灵 目窗· 脑空; B. 头临泣 承灵 目窗 正营 脑空 C 头临泣 目窗 正营 承灵 脑空; D. 头临泣 目窗 承灵 正营 脑空; E. 以上都不是	How are five points on the line connecting G15 [Tóu Lín Qì] and G19 [Nǎo Kōng] distributed? A. G15 [Tóu Lín Qì] G17 [Zhèng Yíng] G18 [Chéng Líng] G16 [Mù Chuāng] · G19 [Nǎo Kōng]; B. G15 [Tóu Lín Qì] G18 [Chéng Líng] G16 [Mù Chuāng] G17 [Zhèng Yíng] G19 [Nǎo Kōng]; C. G15 [Tóu Lín Qì] G16 [Mù Chuāng] G17 [Zhèng Yíng] G18 [Chéng Líng] G19 [Nǎo Kōng]; D. G15 [Tóu Lín Qì] G16 [Mù Chuāng] G18 [Chéng Líng] G17 [Zhèng Yíng] G19 [Nǎo Kōng]; E. none of the above
499	头维穴定位的体表解剖标志是: A 前发际; B 后发际 C. 额角发际; D 耳后发际; E 鬃发.	What body surface anatomy landmark is used to locate S8 / Tóu Wěi? A frontal hairline; B posterior hairline; C. hairline at angle of forehead; D hairline behind the ear; E. hairline on temple.
500	头维至曲鬓弧形连线上的五个腧穴排列顺序是: A. 头维 悬颅 悬厘 额厌 曲鬓; B. 头维 悬厘 额厌 悬颅 曲鬓 C. 头维 额厌 悬颅 悬厘 曲鬓; D. 头维 颁厌 悬厘 悬颅 曲鬓; E. 以上都不是	How are five points on a curve; C. onnecting S8 [Tóu Wěi] and G7 [Qū Bìn] distributed in order? A. S8 [Tóu Wěi] G5 [Xuán Lú] G6 [Xuán Lí] G4 [Hàn Yàn] G7 [Qū Bìn]; B. S8 [Tóu Wěi] G6 [Xuán Lí] G4 [Hàn Yàn] G5 [Xuán Lú] G7 [Qū Bìn]; C. S8 [Tóu Wěi] G4 [Hàn Yàn] G5 [Xuán Lú] G6 [Xuán Lí] G7 [Qū Bìn]; D. S8 [Tóu Wěi] G4 [Hàn Yàn] G6 [Xuán Lí] G5 [Xuán Lú] G7 [Qū Bìn]; E. none of the above
501	外关穴在治疗外感病方面的作用基本上与哪穴近似? A. 大杼; B. 肺俞 C. 风池; D. , 曲池; E. 印堂	In terms of treating diseases of external causes, what point is basically similar to Sj5 [Wài Guān]? A. B11 [Dà Zhù]; B. B13 [Fèi Shū]; C. G20 [Fēng Chí]; D.Li11 [Qū Chí]; E. Yìn Táng.
502	腕关节横纹上的六个穴位，在特定穴中属于: A 都是 "输穴"; B，都是 "原穴" C. 屈侧是 "输入"，伸侧是 "原穴"; D 伸侧是 "输入"，屈侧是 "原穴"; E 既有原穴又有输穴，也有经穴.	Which kind of specially marked points (te ding xue) are the six points located on the wrist crease? A. all of them are "command points (shu xue)"; B. all of them are "original points (yuan xue, source points); C. the points on the bending side are "command points", the points on the stretched. side are "original points"; D. the points on the starched side are "command points", the points on the bending side are "original points"; E. some points are original points, others are "command points", still others are "flowing points (jing xue, river points).
503	腕横纹以下 (含腕横纹一圈)哪条经脉腧穴数最多:	Which meridian has the largest number of points on it below the wrist crease (including all the points on the wrist crease in a circle)?

	A·手阳明大肠经; B·手厥阴心包经 C. 手少阳三焦经; D·手太阴肺经; E·手少阴心经.	A. large intestine meridian; B. pericardium meridian; C. triple heater meridian; D. lung meridian; E. heart meridian.
504	委中至昆仑之间应是: A·19 寸; B·16 寸 C. ·13 寸; D·18 寸; E·12 寸.	What is the distance between B40 / Wěi Zhōng and B60 / Kūn Lún? A·19 Cun; B·16 Cun; C. ·13 Cun; D·18 Cun; E·12 Cun.
505	位于侧胸部腋中线上的腧穴是: A·中府; B·膺窗 C. 大包; D 天溪; E·胸乡.	Which point is on the midaxillary line on the side of the chest? A · Lu1 / Zhōng Fǔ; B · S16 / Yīng Chuāng; C. Sp21 / Dà Bāo; D · Sp18 / Tiān Xī; E · Sp19 / Xīong Xiāng.
506	位于第一掌骨中点，赤白肉际处的穴位是: A.中渚; B.鱼际 C. 大陵; D 前谷.	What point is located at the edge of reddish and whitish muscles and at the midpoint of the first metacarpal bone? A. Sj3, Zhōng Zhǔ; B. Lu10, Yǔ Jì; C. P7, Dà Líng; D. Si2, Qián Gú.
507	位于前正中线脐上 4 寸的穴位是: A.中极; B 中府 C. 中枢; D 中脘.	Which point is located on the anterior midline 4 Cun above the umbilicus? A. R3, Zhōng Jí; B. Lu1, Zhōng Fǔ; C. D7, Zhōng Shū; D. R12, Zhōng Wǎn.
508	位于上腹部，当脐中上 4 寸，距前正中线 2 寸的腧穴是:. A 不容; B·梁门 C. ·关门; D·梁丘; E 天枢.	Which point is located in the upper abdominal region，4 Cun above middle of umbilicus，2 Cun from mid-anterior plane? A S19 / Bù Róng; B · S21 / Liáng Mén; C. S22 / Guān Mén; D · S34 / Liáng Qiū; E. S25 / Tiān Shū.
509	位于小指末节尺侧，距甲 0.1 寸的穴位是: A·少府; B·少冲 C. 少泽; D·少海; E 少商.	What point is on the ulnar side of the distal crease of little finger. 0.1 Cun behind the corner of the vallum unguis? A · H8 / Shào Fǔ; B · H9 / Shào Chōng;C. Si1 / Shào Zé; D · H3 / Shào Hǎi; E · Lu11 / Shǎo Shāng.
510	位于掌后腕横纹桡侧，桡动脉的桡侧凹陷中的穴位是: A.神门; B·大陵 C. ·太渊; D.阳池.	What point is located on the radial side of wrist crease in the depression on the radial side of radial artery / arteria radialis? A. H7 / Shén Mén; B · P7 / Dà Líng; C. Lu9 / TàiYuān; D. Sj4 / Yáng Chí
511	位于足太阳膀胱经的穴位是: A.心俞; B.神门 C. 阴郄; D 郄门.	Which of the following points is on the bladder meridian? A. Xīn Shū; B. Shén Mén; C. Yīn Xī; D. Xī Mén.
512	位置都在肘横纹处的输穴是: A·肘髎 曲池; B·少海 尺泽 C. ·天井 五里; D·小海 支正; E· 曲泽 天井.	Which two points are located on the elbow crease? A. Li12 (Zhǒu Liáo) and Li11 (Qū Chí); B. H3 (Shào Hǎi) and Lu5 (Chǐ Zé); C. Sj10 (Tiān Jǐng) and Li13 (Shǒu Wǔ Lǐ); D. Si8 (Xiǎo Hǎi) and Si7 (Zhi Zhèng); E. P3 (Qū Zé) and Sj10 (Tiān Jǐng).
513	胃经的郄穴是: A·丰隆; B·条口 C. 阴市; D·梁丘; E·解溪.	What is the xi xue (fissural or cleft point) of the stomach meridian? A. S40 (Fēng Lóng); B. S38 (Tiáo Kǒu); C. S33 (Yīn Shì); D. S34 (Liáng Qiū); E. S41 (Jiě Xī).
514	五输穴分属五行始于:	What medical classic made mention of the correspondence between five command points (wu shu xue) and five elements

	A·《内经》; B·《难经》 C. ·《针灸甲乙经》; D·《脉经》; E.《子午流注针经》.	for the first time? A. <Nei Jing>; B. <Nan Jing>; C. <Zhen Jiu Jia Yi Jing>; D. <Mai Jing>; E. <Zi Wu Liu Zhu Zhen Jing>.
515	五输穴中的"荣"穴分布在: A.掌指或跖趾关节之后; B.掌指或跖趾关节之前 C. 肘膝关节附近 D 前臂足部	What is the distribution of "ying points (spring points) among the five command points? A. behind metacarpophalangeal joints or metatarsophalangeal joints; B. in front of metacarpophalangeal joints or metatarsophalangeal joints; C. near elbow or knee joints; D. forearms and knee regions.
516	五输穴中以所注为输所溜为: A·井; B·荣 C. ·输; D·经; E 合.	Among the five command points (wu shu xue), the points at which energy stream flows into a pool of inert energy are called. stream points (shu xue); what are the points at which energy stream flows copiously? A. well points (jing xue); B spring points (ying xue);C. stream points (shu xue); D. flowing points (or river points, jing xue); E. merging points (sea points, he xue).
517	五输穴中治疗 "体重节痛"的是: A·荣穴; B·输穴 C. ·井穴; D·经穴; E·合穴.	What point may be selected to treat "heaviness of the body and pain in the joints" among the five command points (wu shu xue)? A. ying xue (spring point); B. shu xue (stream point); C. jing xue (well point); D. jing xue (flowing point, river point); E. he xue (merging point or sea point).
518	五行属水,而所属经脉属木的荣穴是: A·劳宫; B·少府 C. ·然谷; D·侠溪; E·行间.	Which is a spring point (ying xue),and belongs to a wood meridian? A. P8 (Láo Gōng); B. H8 (Shào Fǔ); C. K2 (Rán Gǔ); D. G43 (Xiá Xī); E. Lv2 (Xíng Jiān).
519	郄穴大部分都分布于: A 肘膝关节以下; B 肘膝关节以上 C. ·肘膝关节附近; D·腕踝关节附近; E·肘膝关节以下.	Where are most of the fissural points / cleft point / xi point distributed? A·below elbow joints and knee joints; B·above elbow joints and knee joints C. ·close to elbow joints and knee joints; D·close to wrist and ankle joints; E · none of the above
520	郄穴共有: A 8 个; B·12 个 C. ·14 个; D·16 个; E·18 个.	How many fissural points / cleft point / xi points altogether? A·8 points; B·12 points; C. ·14 points; D·16 points; E·18 points.
521	下合穴的主治与下列哪类穴位的主治近似? A. ·(背)俞穴; B. ·募穴 C. ·络穴; D. ·郄穴; E. ·原穴	In terms of function, what points are similar to xia he xue / lower sea point / lower terminal point? A. ·Posterior Points / Back Shu Points / Organ Points [BÈI SHÙ XUÉ]; B. ·Gathering Points / Anterior Points, Front Mu Point [MÙ XUÉ]; C. · linking points, / Collateral Points [LUÒ XUÉ]; D. ·xi xue / fissural or cleft points; E. ·yuan xue / source points / original points.
522	下巨虚是: A.胃经的络穴; B. ·胃经的郄穴 C. ·八脉交会穴; D. ·大肠下合穴; E. ·以上都不是	S39 [Xià Jù Xū] belongs to: A.stomach meridian linking points, / Collateral Points [LUÒ XUÉ]; B. ·stomach meridian xi xue / fissural or cleft point C. ·eight meridians meeting points; D. large intestine xia he xue / lower sea point / lower terminal point; E. ·none of the above.
523	下列不是郄穴的是:	Which point is not a xi point (fissural point or cleft point)?

	A.合谷; B 阴郄 C. 地机; D 梁丘.	A Li4 (Hé Gǔ); B H6 (Yīn Xī); C. Sp8 (Dì Jī); D. S34 (Liáng Qiū).
524	下列不属于胆经的穴位是: A·头窍阴; B·头临泣 C. 足临泣; D·角孙; E· 率谷	Which of the following points does NOT belong to the gallbladder meridian? A. Tóu Qiào Yīn; B. Tóu Lín Qì C. Zú Lín Qì; D. Jiăo Sūn; E. Shuài Gŭ.
525	下列除哪个穴外，均是手阳明大肠经穴? A.商阳; B 阳溪 C. 阳池; D 口禾髎.	Which of the following points does not belong to the large intestine meridian? A. Shāng Yáng; B. Yáng Xī; C. Yáng Chí; D. Kŏu Hé Liáo.
526	下列各经脉中，有郄穴的是: A.阴阳维脉; B.任督脉 C. 冲脉; D 带脉.	Which of the following meridians has xi point (fissural point or cleft points on it? A. fastensing meridian of yin and yang (yin, yang wei mai); B. ren and du mai (conception and governing meridians); C. chong mai (vigorous meridian); D. dai mai (belt meridian).
527	下列各项，属俞募配穴的是: A.·肺俞、列缺; B.，肺俞、中府 C. ·肺俞、膻中; D.·肺俞、气户; E.·肺俞、天池	Which of the following is a combination of shu point and mu point (back shu point and anterior mu point)? A. ·B13 [Fèi Shū], Lu7 [Liè Quē]; B. B13 [Fèi Shū], Lu1 [Zhōng Fŭ; C. B13 [Fèi Shū], R17 [Shān Zhōng]; D. ·B13 [Fèi Shū], S13 [Qì Hù]; E. ·B13 [Fèi Shū], P1 [Tiān Chí].
528	下列各穴， 属·于八会穴的是: A.公孙; B.内关 C. ·列缺; D. ·后溪; E. ·以上都不是	Which of the following is a "ba hui xue / eight meeting point"? A.Sp4 [Gōng Sūn]; B.P6 [Nèi Guān]; C. ·Lu7 [Liè Quē]; D. ·Si3 [Hòu Xī]; E. ·none of the above
529	下列各穴，不是特定穴的是: A·中府; B·中脘 C. ·地机; D 合谷; E 犊鼻.	Which of the followig point is NOT a specially marked. point (te ding xue)? A. Lu1 (Zhōng Fŭ); B. R12 (Zhōng Wăn); C. Sp8 (Dì Jī); D. Li4 (Hé Gŭ); E. S35 (Dú Bí).
530	下列各穴，除……外，都属小肠经。 A·天窗; B·天容 C. ·天髎; D·天宗; E·天府.	Which of the following points does NOT belong to the small intestine meridian? A. Tiān Chōng; B. Tiān Róng; C. Tiān Liáo; D. Tiān Zōng; E. Tiān Fŭ.
531	下列各穴，五行属火，又为荥穴的是: A·前谷; B·通谷 C. ·侠溪; D·少府; E 以上都不是.	Which point is both a fire point and a spring point (ying xue)? A. Si2 (Qián Gú); B. B66 (Tōng Gŭ, Zú Tōng Gŭ); C. G43 (Xiá Xī); D. H8 (Shào Fŭ); E. none of the above.
532	下列各穴，主治便秘较好的是: A. ·公孙 丰隆; B. ·中脘 下巨虚 C. ·水分 上巨虚; D. ·支沟 天枢; E. ·下脘 陷谷	Which two points are more effective in treating; C. onstipation? A. ·Sp4 [Gōng Sūn] S40 [Fēng Lóng]; B. ·R12 [Zhōng Wăn] S39 [Xià Jù Xū]; C. ·R9 [Shuĭ Fēn] S37 [Shàng Jù Xū]; D. ·Sj6 [Zhi Gōu] S25 [Tiān Shū]; E. ·R10 [Xià Wăn] S43 [Xiàn Gŭ]
533	下列各穴，属 "荥" 穴的是: A·厉兑; B·陷谷 C. ·内庭; D 解溪; E·足三里.	Which point is a spring point (ying xue)? A. S45 (Lì Duì); B. S43 (Xiàn Gŭ); C. S44 (Nèi Tíng); D. S41 (Jiě Xī); E. S36 (Zú Sān Lĭ).
534	下列各穴，属 "原" 穴的是: A·曲泉; B·行间	Which point is an original point (yuan xue, source point)? A. Lv8 (Qū Quán); B. Lv2 (Xíng Jiān); C. Lv4 (Zhōng Fēng); D. Lv3 (Tài Chōng); E. Lv1 (Dà Dūn).

	C. ·中封; D ·太冲; E ·大敦·.	
535	下列各穴，属于八会穴的是: A ·公孙; B 内关 C. ·列缺; D ·后溪; E ·章门.	Which point belongs to the category of eight meeting points (ba hui xue)? A. Sp4 (Gōng Sūn); B. P6 (Nèi Guān); C. Lu7 (Liè Quē); D. Si3 (Hòu Xī); E. Lv13 (Zhāng Mén).
536	下列各穴，属于胆经的是: A ·期门; B ·章门 C. ·京门; D ·石门; E ·梁门.	Which of the following points belongs to the gallbladder meridian? A Qí Mén; B Zhāng Mén; C. Jīng Mén; D. Shí Mén; E. Liáng Mén.
537	下列各穴，属于心包经 "合"穴"的是: A. ·劳宫; B. ·间使 C. ·大陵; D. ·曲泽; E. ·郄门	Which of the following points belongs to the pericadium meridian? A. ·P8 [Láo Gōng]; B. ·P5 [Jiān Shǐ]; C. ·P7 [Dà Líng]; D. ·P3 [Qū Zé]; E. ·P4 [Xī Mén].
538	下列各穴 除 ·...外 ·都属于八脉交会穴: A.头临泣; B.公孙 C. ·内关; D. ·后溪; E. ·列缺	Which of the following is NOT an "eight meridians meeting point"? A.G15 [Tóu Lín Qì]; B.Sp4 [Gōng Sūn]; C. ·P6 [Nèi Guān]; D. ·Si3 [Hòu Xī]; E. Lu7 [Liè Quē].
539	下列各穴 除 ·...外都是募穴: A.中府; B. 鸠尾 C. ·章门; D. ·期门; E. ·石门	Which of the following is NOT a "gathering points / anterior points, front mu point [mù xué]? A.Lu1 [Zhōng Fǔ]; B.R15 [Jiū Wěi]; C. ·Lv13 [Zhāng Mén]; D. ·Lv14 [Qí Mén]; E. ·R5 [Shí Mén].
540	下列各穴中，不归属足太阳膀胱的是: A 会阳; B.合阳 C. 冲阳; D 委阳.	Which of the following points does not belong to the bladder meridian? A. Huì Yáng; B. Hé Yáng;C. Chōng Yáng; D. Wěi Yáng;
541	下列各穴中，不是募穴的为: A 章门; B 期门 C. 云门; D 石门.	Which of the following points is not a gathering point / mu point? A Lv13 / Zhāng Mén; B Lv14 / Qí Mén; C. Lu2 / Yún Mén; D R5 / Shí Mén.
542	下列各穴中，除......外，既是络穴，又是经脉交会穴: A 列缺; B 照海 C. 内关; D 外关.	Which of the following points is neither a linking point / luo point, nor a meridian meeting point? A Lu7 / Liè Quē; B K6 / Zhào Hǎi; C. P6 / Nèi Guān; D Sj5 / Wài Guān.
543	下列各穴中，除......外，均是郄穴: A 梁丘; B 阳池 C. 水泉; D 养老.	Which point is not a fissural point / cleft point / xi point? A S34 / Liáng Qiū; B Sj4 / Yáng Chí;C. K5 / Shuǐ Quán; D Si6 / Yǎng Lǎo.
544	下列各穴中，既是胃之募穴，又是腑的会穴的是: A 中脘; B 章门 C. 期门; D 膻中.	Which of the following points is both a stomach gathering point / stomach mu point, and at the same time, also a meeting point of bowels? A R12 / Zhōng Wǎn; B Lv13 / Zhāng Mén; C. Lv14 / Qí Mén; D R17 / Shān Zhōng.
545	下列各穴中，既是原穴又是八会穴的是: A 合谷; B 太渊 C. 阳陵泉; D 绝骨.	Which point is a yuán xué / starting-points / source-point and also one of the eight influential points / ba hui xue? A Li4 / Hé Gǔ; B Lu9 / TàiYuān; C. G34 / Yáng Líng Quán; D G39 / Xuán Zhōng.
546	下列各穴中，止呕作用较好的是: A 足三里; B 中脘 C.	Which is a more effective point to stop vomiting? A S36 / Zú Sān Lǐ; B R12 / Zhōng Wǎn; C. P6 / Nèi Guān; D. B21 / Wèi Shū.

	内关; D 胃俞.	
547	下列各穴中，属于胆经的穴位是: A·风池; B·耳门 C. ·翳风; D·天牖; E·角孙.	Which of the following points belongs to the gallbladder meridian? A. Fēng Chí; B. Ěr Mén; C. Yì Fēng; D. Tiān Yǒu E Jiǎo Sūn.
548	下列各穴中，属于三焦经的穴位是: A·率谷; B·听宫 C. ·听会; D·完骨; E·翳风.	Which of the following points belongs to the triple heater meridian? A. Shuài Gǔ; B. Tīng Gōng C. Tīng Huì; D. Wán Gǔ; E. Yì Fēng.
549	下列各穴中，属于胃经的穴位是: A·禾髎; B·巨髎 C. ·素髎; D，颧髎; E. ·瞳子髎.	Which of the following points belongs to the stomach meridian? A. Hé Liáo (Ěr Hé Liáo); B. Jù Liáo; C. Sù Liáo; D. Quán Liáo; E. Tóng Zǐ Liáo.
550	下列各穴中，属于足阳明胃经是: A.禾髎; B 巨髎 C. 颧髎; D·素髎.	Which of the following points belongs to foot bright yang stomach meridian? A. Kǒu Hé Liáo; B Jù Liáo; C. Quán Liáo; D · Sù Liáo.
551	下列各穴中不属于手太阴肺经的是: A.天府; B 侠白 C. 经渠; D 肩髃.	Which of the following points does not belong to the lung meridian? A. Lu3, Tiān Fǔ; B. Lu4, Xiá Bái; C. Lu8, Jīng Qú; D. Li15, Jiān Yú.
552	下列各穴中不属于郄穴的是: A 筑宾; B·交信 C. ·支正; D 跗阳; E· 郄门.	Which of the following points is NOT a xi xue / fissural or cleft point? A. K9 (Zhú; Bīn); B. K8 (Jiāo Xìn); C. Si7 (Zhi Zhèng); D. B59 (Fū Yáng);E P4 (Xī Mén).
553	下列各穴中不属于原穴的是: A. ·腕骨; B. ·合谷 C. ·阳池; D. ·陷谷; E. ·丘墟	Which of the following points is NOT a yuan xue / source point / original point? A. ·G12 [Wán Gǔ]; B. ·Li4 [Hé Gǔ];C. ·Sj4 [Yáng Chí]; D. ·S43 [Xiàn Gǔ]; E. ·G40 [Qiū Xū].
554	下列各穴中与经外奇穴八风同位的是: A·太冲; B·陷谷 C. ·侠溪; D·地五会; E·通谷.	Which of the following points is located in the same region as the extraordinary point named Bā Fēng? A. Lv3 (Tài Chōng); B. S43 (Xiàn Gǔ); C. G43 (Xiá Xī); D. G42 (Dì Wǔ Huì); E. B66 (Tōng Gǔ, Zú Tōng Gǔ).
555	下列各穴中与经外奇穴八邪同位的是: A·三间; B·中渚 C. 液门; D·前谷; E·合谷.	Which of the following points is located in the same region as the extraordinary point named Bā Xié? A. Li3 (Sān Jiān); B. Sj3 (Zhōng Zhǔ); C. Sj2 (Yè Mén); D. Si2 (Qián Gú); E. Li4 (Hé Gǔ).
556	下列各穴中属于脾经的穴位是: A·商丘; B·丘墟 C. ·中封; D 解溪; E·太溪.	Which of the following points belongs to the spleen meridian? A. Shāng Qiū; B. Qiū Xū; C. Zhōng Fēng; D. Jiě Xī; E. Tài Xī.
557	下列各穴属于心包经 "合穴"的是: A·劳宫; B·间使 C. ·大陵; D·曲泽; E·郄门.	Which point is the merging point (he xue) of the pericardium meridian? A. P8 (Láo Gōng); B. P5 (Jiān Shǐ); C. P7 (Dà Líng); D. P3 (Qū Zé); E. P4 (Xī Mén).
558	下列各组，具有和胃止呕作用的是: A. ·脾	Which points can harmonize the stomach and stop vomiting? A. ·B20 [Pí Shū] R13 [Shàng Wǎn]; B. ·B21 [Wèi Shū] Li4 [Hé

	俞 上脘; B. ·胃俞 合谷 C. ·中脘 内关; D. ·公孙 建里; E. ·下脘 阴陵泉	Gǔ]; C. ·R12 [Zhōng Wǎn] P6 [Nèi Guān]; D. ·Sp4 [Gōng Sūn] R11 [Jiàn Lǐ]; E. ·R10 [Xià Wǎn] Sp9 [Yīn Líng Quán]
559	下列各组，具有祛风解表的是: A. ·外关 阳池; B. ·曲池 丰隆 C. ·陶道 足三里 D ·风池 合谷 E 风市 风门	Which points can expel wind and relax the superficial region? A. ·Sj5 [Wài Guān] Sj4 [Yáng Chí]; B. ·Li11 [Qū Chí] S40 [Fēng Lóng]; C. ·D13 [Táo Dào] S36 [Zú Sān Lǐ]D ·G20 [Fēng Chí] Li4 [Hé Gǔ]; EG31 [Fēng Shì] B12 [Fēng Mén]
560	下列各组八脉交会穴，其中错误的是: A ·公孙通于冲脉; B ·内关通于阴跷脉 C. ·后溪通于督脉; D ·列缺通于任脉; E ·临泣通于带脉.	Among the eight meridians meeting points (ba mai jiao hui xue), which of the following statements is NOT correct? A. Sp4 (Gōng Sūn) meets chong mai (vigorous meridian); B. P6 (Nèi Guān) meets yin qiao mai (heel meridian of yin); C. Si3 (Hòu Xī) meets du mai (governing meridian; D. Lu7 (Liè Quē) meets ren mai (conception meridian); E. G41 (Zú Lín Qì, Lín Qì) meets dai mai (belt meridian).
561	下列各组不属俞、募配穴的是: A. ·天枢 大肠俞; B. ·巨阙 心俞 C. ·京门 胆俞; D. ·期门 肝俞; E. ·章门 脾俞	Which is NOT a combination of shu point and mu point (back shu point and anterior mu point)? A. ·S25 [Tiān Shū] B25 [Dà Cháng Shū]; B. ·R14 [Jù Què] B15 [Xīn Shū]; C. ·G25 [Jīng Mén] B19 [Dǎn Shū]; D. ·Lv14 [Qí Mén] B18 [Gān Shū]; E. ·Lv13 [Zhāng Mén] B20 [Pí Shū]
562	下列各组穴不全为五输穴的是: A.涌泉 然谷 太溪 复溜阴谷; B.商阳 二间 三间 阳溪曲池 C. 少泽 前谷 后溪 阳谷小海; D 至阴 通谷 束骨 京骨 委中.	Which of the following groups; C. ontains point or points which do not belong to the category of five command points (wu shu xue)? A. K1 (Yǒng Quán); K2 (Rán Gǔ); K3 (Tài Xī); K7 (Fù Liū); K10 (Yīn Gǔ). B Li1 (Shāng Yáng); Li2 (Èr Jiān): Li3 (Sān Jiān); Li5 (Yáng Xī); Li11, Qū Chí. C. Si1 (Shào Zé); Si2 (Qián Gú); Si3 (Hòu Xī); Si5 (Yáng Gǔ); Si8 (Xiǎo Hǎi). D; B67 (Zhì Yīn); B66 (Tōng Gǔ); B65 (Shù Gǔ); B64 (Jīng Gǔ); B40 (Wěi Zhōng)
563	下列各组穴中，除……外，均是原络配穴: A 太渊 偏历; B 冲阳 丰隆 C. 阳池 内关; D 太溪 飞扬.	Which does not belong to the combination of source-point and collateral-point [yuan luo pei xue]? A Lu9 / TàiYuān Li6 / Piān Lì; B S42 / Chōng Yáng S40 / Fēng Lóng; C. Sj4 / Yáng Chí P6 / Nèi Guān; D K3 / Tài Xī; B58 / Feī Yáng.
564	下列各组穴中，哪组是原络配穴? A 太白 公孙; B 腕骨 支正 C. 合谷 列缺; D 阳池 外关.	Which belongs to the combination of source-point and collateral-point [yuan luo pei xue]? A Sp3 / Tài Bái Sp4 / Gōng Sūn; B Si4 / Wàn Gǔ Si7 / Zhi Zhèng; C. Li4 / Hé Gǔ Lu7 / Liè Quē; D Sj4 / Yáng Chí Sj5 / Wài Guān.
565	下列各组中，不是俞募配穴的是: A. ·厥阴俞 巨阙; B. ·肝俞 期门 C. ·小肠俞 关元; D. ·肾俞 京门; E. ·肺俞 中府	Which does not belong to the combination of shu point and mu point (back shu point and anterior mu point / shu mu pei xue)? A. ·B14 [Jué Yīn Shū] R14 [Jù Què]; B. ·B18 [Gān Shū] Lv14 [Qí Mén]; C. ·B27 [Xiǎo Cháng Shū] R4 [Guān Yuán]; D. ·B23 [Shèn Shū] G25 [Jīng Mén]; E. ·B13 [Fèi Shū] Lu1 [Zhōng Fǔ]
566	下列各组中，除哪组外全是五输穴? A.少商鱼际.太渊经渠尺泽; B.少海灵道神门少府少冲 C. 头窍阴地五会头临泣丘墟悬钟; D 小海	Which of the following groups; C. ontains point or points which do not belong to the category of five command points (wu shu xue)? A Lu11 (Shǎo Shāng), Lu10 (Yǔ Jì), Lu9 (Tài Yuān), Lu8 (Jīng Qú), Lu5 (Chǐ Zé); B H3 (Shào Hǎi), H4 (Líng Dào), H7 (Shén Mén), H8（Shào Fǔ）, H9 (Shào Chōng); C. G11 (Tóu Qiào Yīn);

	阳谷后溪前谷少泽	G42 (Dì Wǔ Huì), G15 (Tóu Lín Qì, Lín Qì), G40 (Qiū Xū),G39 (Xuán Zhōng); D. Si8 (Xiǎo Hǎi); Si5 (Yáng Gǔ), Si3 (Hòu Xī), Si3 (Hòu Xī),Si2 (Qián Gú) ,Si1 (Shào Zé).
567	下列各组中均为原穴的是: A.大陵太白灵道太冲神门; B.太白太冲太渊灵道商丘 C. 太渊太白太冲太溪大陵; D 太冲太白行间大陵神门.	Which group of the following; C. ontains the points all of which are yuan points (source points, original points)? A。 P7 (Dà Líng); Sp3 (Tài Bái); H4 (Líng Dào); Lv3 (Tài Chōng); H7 (Shén Mén). B. Sp3 (Tài Bái); H4 (Líng Dào); Lv3 (Tài Chōng); Lu9 (Tài Yuān) Sp5 (Shāng Qiū). C. Lu9 (Tài Yuān); P7 (Dà Líng); Sp3 (Tài Bái); Lv3 (Tài Chōng); K3 (Tài Xī). D. P7 (Dà Líng); Sp3 (Tài Bái); Lv3 (Tài Chōng) H7 (Shén Mén); Lv2 (Xíng Jiān).
568	下列关于中脘穴的描述错误的是: A. 属任脉经穴; B. 位于脐上4寸 C. 八会穴中的腑会穴; D. 主要治疗脾胃病证; E. 脾的募穴	Which of the following is an incorrect description of [Zhōng Wǎn]? A. it belongs to ren mai /; C. onception meridian; B. it is located 4cun above umbilicus; C. it is a fu hui / meeting point of viscera among the ba hui xue / eight meeting points; D. it is primarily used to treat diseases of spleen and stomach; E. it is a spleen gathering point / anterior point, front mu point [mù xué].
569	下列经脉中，除……以外，其郄穴均位于膝关节以下: A 足阳明胃经; B 足太阴脾经 C. 足少肾经; D 足太阳膀胱经.	Which meridian has xi xue (fissural or cleft point) which is not located below the knee joint? A. kidney meridian; B. liver meridian; C. spleen meridian; D. stomach meridian; E. gallbladder meridian.
570	下列经脉中，经穴数目最少的是: A.手太阳小肠经; B 足阳明胃经 C. 手阳大肠经; D 手少阳三焦经.	Which of the following meridians has the smallest number of points on it? A. small intestine meridian; B. stomach meridian; C. large intestine meridian; D. triple heater meridian.
571	下列井穴位于指甲角尺侧约 0·1 寸处的是: A 商阳; B 少商 C. 中冲; D 关冲; E 少冲.	Which of the following points is a well point (jing xue) located about 0.1 Cun on the ulnar side of the angle of nail? A. Shāng Yáng; B. Shǎo Shāng; C. Zhōng Chōng; D. Guān Chōng; E. Shào Chōng.
572	下列井穴中，治疗疝气应首选: A. 涌泉; B. 隐白 C. 大敦; D.足窍阴; E. 至阴	Which of the following well points [jǐng xué] should be selected to treat hernia and a few external diseases of the male genitals on a priority basis? A. K1 [Yǒng Quán]; B. Sp1 [Yǐn Bái]; C. Lv1 [Dà Dūn]; D.G44 [Zú Qiào Yīn]; E. B67 [Zhì Yīn]
573	下列井穴中具有催乳作用的是: A 关冲; B 少冲 C. 少泽; D 少商.	Which of the following well points [jǐng xué] can promote milk secretion? A. Sj1 [Guān Chōng]; B. H9 [Shào Chōng]; C.. Si1 Shào Zé]; D. Lu11 [Shǎo Shāng].
574	下列哪个除外，均为手太阳小肠经穴? A.阳溪; B.后溪 C. 肩中俞; D 肩外俞.	Which of the following points does not belong to the small intestine meridian? A. Yáng Xī; B. Hòu Xī; C. Jiān Zhōng Shū; D. Jiān Wài Shū.
575	下列哪个穴除外，均为手少阳三焦经穴: A.耳门; B.耳和髎	Which of the following points does not belong to triple heater meridian? A. Ěr Mén; B. Ěr Hé Liáo; C. Jiǎo Sūn; D. Shuài Gǔ.

	C. ，角孙; D 率谷.	
576	下列哪个穴组两穴之间间距最长: A·耳门一听宫; B·通里一阴郄 C. ·章门一带脉; D·支沟一会宗; E 听会一耳门.	Which two points have the greatest distance between them? A. Sj21 (Ěr Mén)— Si19 (Tīng Gōng); B. H5 (Tōng Lǐ)— H6 (Yīn Xī); C. Lv13 (Zhāng Mén)— G26 (Dài Mài); D. Sj6 (Zhi Gōu)— Sj7 (Huì Zōng); E. G2 (Tīng Huì)— Sj21 (Ěr Mén).
577	下列哪条经脉循行线上没有募穴? A.胆经; B.肝经 C. 脾经; D 肺经.	Which of the following meridians does not have a point to serve as mu point (gathering point)? A. gallbladder meridian; B. liver meridian; C. spleen meridian; D. lung meridian.
578	下列哪一条经脉腧穴数目最多: A.足太阴膀胱经; B. 足阳经胃经 C. 足少阳胆经; D 手阳明大肠经.	Which of the following meridians has the largest number of points on it? A. bladder meridian; B. stomach meridian; C. gallbladder meridian; D. large intestine meridian.
579	下列哪组八脉交会穴主治肺系、咽喉、胸膈等疾患? A. ·后溪 申脉; B. ·内关 公孙 C. ·外关 临泣; D. ·列缺 照海; E. ·以上都不是	Which of the following eight meridians meeting points [ba mai jiao hui xue] can treat diseases of lung; C. onnectives, throat, chest and diaphragm, etc.? A. ·Si3 [Hòu Xī] B62 [Shēn Mài]; B. ·P6 [Nèi Guān] Sp4 [Gōng Sūn]; C. ·Sj5 [Wài Guān] G41 [Zú Lín Qì]; D. ·Lu7 [Liè Quē] K6 [Zhào Hǎi]; E. ·none of the above
580	下列哪组不全是五输穴? A·涌泉 然谷 太溪 复溜 阴谷; B. 商阳 二间 三间 阳溪 曲池 C. 关冲 液门 中渚 支沟 天井; D·少泽 前谷 后溪 阳谷 小海; E·至阴 通谷 束骨 京骨 委中.	Which group of points has one or more points that are NOT among the five command points [wu shu xue)? A. K1 (Yǒng Quán), K2 (Rán Gǔ), K3 (Tài Xī) K7 (Fù Liū), K10 (Yīn Gǔ); B. Li1 (Shāng Yáng), Li2 (Èr Jiān), Li3 (Sān Jiān), Li5 (Yáng Xī), Li11 (Qū Chí); C. Sj1 (Guān Chōng), Sj2 (Yè Mén), Sj3 (Zhōng Zhǔ), Sj6 (Zhi Gōu), Sj10 (Tiān Jǐng); D. Si1 (Shào Zé), Si2 (Qián Gú), Si3 (Hòu Xī), Si5 (Yáng Gǔ), Si8 (Xiǎo Hǎi); E. B67 (Zhì Yīn);B66 (Tōng Gǔ, Zú Tōng Gǔ);B65 (Shù Gǔ);B64 (Jīng Gǔ);B40 (Wěi Zhōng).
581	下列哪组不是经脉的起止经穴? A·会阴 承浆; B·长强 兑端 C. ·隐白 大包; D. 承泣 厉兑; E·涌泉 俞府.	Which two points in the following groups are neither the beginnings nor the endings of meridians? A. R1 (Huì Yīn), R24 (Chéng Jiàng); B. D1 (Cháng Qiáng); D27 (Duì Duān); C. Sp1 (Yǐn Bái); Sp21 (Dà Bāo); D. S1 (Chéng Qì) S45 (Lì Duì); E. K1 (Yǒng Quán). K27 (Shū Fǔ).
582	下列哪组均是原穴? A 太渊 太白 太冲 太溪 大陵; B 太渊 太溪 C. 太白 太冲 行间 大陵 神门; D 太白 灵道 太冲 神门 大陵.	Which group of points all belong to yuán xué / starting-points / source-points? A.Lu9 / TàiYuān Sp3 / Tài Bái Lv3 / Tài Chōng K3 / Tài Xī P7 / Dà Líng; B Lu9 / TàiYuān K3 / Tài Xī; C. Sp3 / Tài Bái Lv3 / Tài Chōng Lv2 / Xíng Jiān P7 / Dà Líng H7 / Shén Mén; D Sp3 / Tài Bái D10 / Líng Dào Lv3 / Tài Chōng H7 / Shén Mén P7 / Dà Líng.
583	下列哪组全是五输穴: A 中冲 劳宫 大陵 间使 曲泽; B 商阳 二间 三间 合谷 曲池 C. 关冲 液门 中诸 阳池 天井; D 少泽 前谷 后溪 阳谷 腕骨.	Which group of points all belong to five command points [wu shu xue)?? A P9 / Zhōng Chōng P8 / Láo Gōng P7 / Dà Líng P5 / Jiān Shǐ P3 / Qū Zé; B Li1 / Shāng Yáng Li2 / Èr Jiān Li3 / Sān Jiān Li4 / Hé Gǔ Li11 / Qū Chí; C. Sj1 [Guān Chōng], Sj2 [Yè Mén], Sj3 [Zhōng Zhǔ], Sj4 / Yáng Chí Sj10 / Tiān Jǐng; D Si1 / Shào Zé Si2 / Qián Gú Si3 / Hòu Xī Si5 / Yáng Gǔ Si4 / Wàn Gǔ

584	下列哪组腧穴的间距不相等: A·肩井一天髎一曲垣; B·神阙一天枢一大横 C. ·人迎一水突一气舍; D·头维一颔厌一悬颅; E· 三阴交一漏谷一地机.	Which three points have unequal distances between them? A. G21 (Jiān Jǐng)— Sj15 (Tiān Liáo)— Si13 (Qū Yuān); B. R8 (Shén Què)— S25 (Tiān Shū)— Sp15 (Dà Héng); C. S9 (Rén Yíng)— S10 (Shuǐ Tū)— S11 (Qì Shě); D. S8 (Tóu Wěi)— G4 (Hàn Yàn)— G5 (Xuán Lú); E. Sp6 (Sān Yīn Jiāo)— Sp7 (Lòu Gǔ)— Sp8 (Dì Jī).
585	下列那组都是原穴? A·太渊 大陵 灵道 太白 太冲; B·太渊 神门 商丘 太冲 太溪 C. ·太渊 大陵 神门 太白 行间; D·太渊 神门 太白 太冲 太溪; E·以上都不是.	Which of the following groups; C. ontains points all of which are original points (yuan xue or source points)? A. Lu9 (Tài Yuān), P7 (Dà Líng), H4 (Líng Dào), Sp3 (Tài Bái), Lv3 (Tài Chōng); B. Lu9 (Tài Yuān); H7 (Shén Mén) Sp5 (Shāng Qiū) Lv3 (Tài Chōng), K3 (Tài Xī); C. Lu9 (Tài Yuān), P7 (Dà Líng); H7 (Shén Mén) Sp3 (Tài Bái), Lv2 (Xíng Jiān); D. Lu9 (Tài Yuān), H7 (Shén Mén)Sp3 (Tài Bái), Lv3 (Tài Chōng); K3 (Tài Xī); E. none of the above.
586	下列配穴，除......外，都是俞募配穴: A. ·心俞 巨阙; B. ·肝俞 期门 C. ·脾俞 章门; D. ·肺俞 膻中; E. ·肾俞 京门	Which is NOT a combination of shu point and mu point (back shu point and anterior mu point)? A. ·B15 [Xīn Shū] R14 [Jù Què]; B. ·B18 [Gān Shū] Lv14 [Qí Mén]; C. ·B20 [Pí Shū] Lv13 [Zhāng Mén]; D. ·B13 [Fèi Shū] R17 [Shān Zhōng]; E. ·B23 [Shèn Shū] G25 [Jīng Mén].
587	下列配穴，除......外，都是主客配穴: A. ·太白 丰隆; B. ·太冲 蠡沟 C. ·太溪 飞扬; D. ·大陵 外关; E. ·合谷 列缺	Which is NOT a combination of host and guest [zhu ke]? A. ·Sp3 [Tài Bái] S40 [Fēng Lóng]; B. ·Lv3 [Tài Chōng] Lv5 [Lí Gōu]; C. ·K3 [Tài Xī] B58 [Feī Yáng]; D. ·P7 [Dà Líng] Sj5 [Wài Guān]; E. ·Li4 [Hé Gǔ] Lu7 [Liè Quē]
588	下列配穴，除......外，均属俞募配穴? A·膻中 心俞; B·章门 脾俞 C. ·关元 小肠俞; D·京门 肾俞; E·石门 三焦俞.	Which of the following is NOT a combination of shu xue (back shu point) and mu xue (gathering point)? A. R17 (Shān Zhōng);B15 (Xīn Shū); B. Lv13 (Zhāng Mén);B20 (Pí Shū); C. R4 (Guān Yuán);B27 (Xiǎo Cháng Shū); D. G25 (Jīng Mén);B23 (Shèn Shū); E. R5 (Shí Mén);B22 (Sān Jiāo Shū).
589	下列配穴中，除......外，都是原络配穴: A. ·太冲 光明; B. ·太白 丰隆 C. ·神门 支正; D. ·阳池 内关; E. ·太溪 大钟	Which does NOT belong to the combination of source-point and collateral-point [yuan luo pei xue]? A. ·Lv3 [Tài Chōng] G37 [Guāng Míng]; B. ·Sp3 [Tài Bái] S40 [Fēng Lóng]; C. ·H7 [Shén Mén] Si7 [Zhi Zhèng]; D. ·Sj4 [Yáng Chí] P6 [Nèi Guān]; E. ·K3 [Tài Xī] K4 [Dà Zhōng].
590	下列任脉穴组与足三阴经交会的是: A·会阴 阴交; B·中极 关元 C. ·石门 中脘; D·神阙 鸠尾; E·上脘 膻中.	Which two points on ren mai (conception meridian) are meeting with the three yin meridians of foot? A. R1 (Huì Yīn), R7 (Yīn Jiāo); B. R3 (Zhōng Jí), R4 (Guān Yuán); C. R5 (Shí Mén), R12 (Zhōng Wǎn); D. R8 (Shén Què), R15 (Jiū Wěi); E. R13 (Shàng Wǎn), R17 (Shān Zhōng).
591	下列荥穴中，与五行相配属火，而所属经脉属水的是: A.然谷; B 大都 C. 前谷; D 劳宫.	Among the following ying points (outpouring points), which point belongs to fire and its meridian belongs to water? A. K2 [Rán Gǔ]; B. Sp2 [Dà Dū]; C. Si2 [Qián Gú]; D. P8 [Láo Gōng].
592	下列手太阳小肠经穴按顺序哪个在最先:	Which of the following points on the small intestine meridian should;ome first in the proper order?

	A·曲垣; B·肩中俞 C. ·秉风; D·天宗; E·肩外俞.	A. (Qū Yuān); B. (Jiān Zhōng Shū); C. (Bǐng Fēng); D. (Tiān Zōng); E. (Jiān Wài Shū)
593	下列输穴中，除……外，都是本经的母穴? A.肺经的太渊;.B肝经的曲泉 C.心经的少冲; D 脾经的太白.	Which of the following points is not a mother point on its own meridian? A Lu9 (Tài Yuān); B Lv8 (Qū Quán); C. H9 (Shào Chōng); D. Sp3 (Tài Bái).
594	下列输穴属经错误的是: A·天鼎属手阳明大肠经; B·天窗属手少阳三焦经 C. ·天容属手太阳小肠经; D·天牖属手少阳三焦经; E·天突属任脉经.	Which of the following is an incorrect statement? A. Tiān Dǐng belongs to the large intestine meridian; B Tiān Chuāng belongs to the san jiao meridian; C. Tiān Róng belongs to the small intestine meridian; D. Tiān Yǒu belong to san jiao meridian; E. Tiān Tū belongs to ren mai (conception meridian).
595	下列腧穴除 ~ 外都是郄穴 A·孔最; B·郄门 C. ·中渚; D·跗阳; E·阳交.	Which of the following points is NOT a xi xue (fissural point)? A. Lu6 (Kǒng Zuì); B. P4 (Xī Mén); C. Sj3 (Zhōng Zhǔ); D. B59 (Fū Yáng); E. G35 (Yáng Jiāo).
596	下列腧穴除 ~外,都是络穴? A·丰隆; B·光明 C. ·飞扬; D·大钟; E·商丘.	Which point is NOT a linking point (luo xue)? A. S40 (Fēng Lóng); B. G37 (Guāng Míng); C. B58 (Feī Yáng); D. K4 (Dà Zhōng); E. Sp5 (Shāng Qiū).
597	下列腧穴除……外，都是络穴: A·公孙; B·通里 C. ·支正; D，内关; E·太溪	Which point is NOT a linking point (luo xue)? A. Sp4 (Gōng Sūn); B. H5 (Tōng Lǐ); C. Si7 (Zhi Zhèng); D. P6 (Nèi Guān); E. K3 (Tài Xī).
598	下列腧穴除……外，都是五输穴的内容: A·井穴; B·荥穴 C. ·背俞穴; D·经穴; E·合穴.	Which of the following does NOT belong to five command points (wu shu xue)? A. jing xue (flowing point, river point); B. ying xue (spring point); C. back shu point (bei shu xue); D.jing xue (flowing point, river point); E.he xue (merging point or sea point).
599	下列腧穴除……外，既是络穴又是八脉交会穴: A·列缺; B·内关 C. ·公孙; D·外关; E·水泉.	Which of the following point is neither a linking point (luo xue) nor one of the eight merdians meeting points (ba mai jiao hui xue)? A. Lu7 (Liè Quē); B. P6 (Nèi Guān); C. Sp4 (Gōng Sūn); D. Sj5 (Wài Guān); E. K5 (Shuǐ Quán).
600	下列腧穴除……外都是郄穴 A.孔最; B.郄门 C. ·中渚; D.跗阳; E.阳交	Which of the following points is NOT a xi xue / fissural or cleft point ? A. ·Lu6 [Kǒng Zuì]; B. ·P4 [Xī Mén]; C. ·Sj3 [Zhōng Zhǔ]; D. ·B59 [Fū Yáng]; E. ·G35 [Yáng Jiāo].
601	下列腧穴除……以外，均属足少阴肾经: A·太溪; B·照海 C. ·复溜; D·中封; E·阴谷.	Which of the following points does NOT belong to the kidney meridian? A. Tài Xī; B. Zhào Hǎi; C. Fù Liū; D. Zhōng Fēng E Yīn Gǔ.
602	下列腧穴定位有错误的是:	Which of the following statements is NOT correct? A. Zhōng Quán is on the back of the wrist, on the midpoint of

	A·中泉穴在手腕背侧阳溪与阳池穴连线的中点; B·安眠穴在翳风与风池连线的中点 C. ·环中穴在环跳与腰俞连线中点; D·水沟穴在人中沟的中点; E· 手逆注在尺桡骨间，肘横纹与腕横纹连线的中点.	the line connecting Li5 (Yáng Xī) and Sj4 (Yáng Chí); B. Ān Mián is on the midpoint of the line connecting Sj17 (Yì Fēng) and G20 (Fēng Chí); C. Huán Zhōng is on the midpoint between G30 (Huán Tiào) G30 and D2 (Yāo Shū) D2; D. D26 (Shuǐ Gōu, Rén Zhōng) is in the middle of philtrum; E. Shǒu Nì Zhu is in between ulna and radius, on the midpoint of the line connecting elbow crease and wrist crease.
603	下列腧穴中，哪组不在同一水平上: A·大赫一中极; B·脊中一脾俞 C. ·郄门一四渎; D·筑宾一蠡沟; E·会宗一间使.	Which two points among the following groups are NOT on a level with each other? A. K12 (Dà Hè)— R3 (Zhōng Jí); B. D6 (Jǐ Zhōng)— B20 (Pí Shū); C. P4 (Xī Mén)— Sj9 (Sì Dú); D. K9 (Zhú; Bīn)— Lv5 (Lí Gōu); E. Sj7 (Huì Zōng)— P5 (Jiān Shǐ).
604	下列腧穴中，孕妇禁针的是: A. ·曲池; B. ·肩井 C. ·肩贞; D. ·大椎; E. ·足三里	Which point is a forbidden point for treating pregnant women? A. ·Li11 [Qū Chí]; B. ·G21 [Jiān Jǐng]; C. ·Si9 [Jiān Zhēn]; D. ·D14 [Dà Zhuī]; E. ·S36 [Zú Sān Lǐ]
605	下列特定穴中，除……外基本上部位于肘膝关节以下? A·八脉交会穴; B·五输穴 C. 络穴; D·八会穴; E· 原穴.	Among the following specially marked. points (te ding xue), which are NOT located below the elbow or knee joints? A. eight meridians eight meeting points (ba mai jiao hui xue); B. five command points (wu shu xue); C. linking points, (luo xue); D. eight meeting points (ba hui xue); E. original points (souce points, yuan xue).
606	下列特定穴中，治疗急性病症应首选: A. ·原穴; B. ·俞穴 C. ·八会穴; D. ·八脉交会穴; E. ·郄穴	Among the following specially marked points (te ding xue), which should be selected to treat acute diseases? A. ·yuan xue / source points / original points; B. ·Posterior Points / Back Shu Points / Organ Points [BÈI SHÙ XUÉ]; C. ·ba hui xue / eight meeting points; D. ·eight meridians meeting points; E. ·xi xue / fissural or c left points.
607	下列头面部输穴中，应合口而取的是: A·听会; B·下关 C. ·耳门; D·听宫; E·以上都不是.	Which point in the head and face region should be located with the mouth closed? A G2 (Tīng Huì); B S7 (Xià Guān); C. Sj21 (Ěr Mén); D. Si19 (Tīng Gōng); E. None of the above.
608	下列五输穴，除……外，都是本经的子穴: A·大肠经的二间; B·小肠经的小海 C. 胃经的厉兑; D·胆经的辅阳; E·膀胱经的通谷.	Which is NOT the child point (zi xue) of its own meridian? A. Li2 (Èr Jiān); B. Si8 (Xiǎo Hǎi); C. S45 (Lì Duì); D. G38 (Yáng Fǔ); E. B66 (Tōng Gǔ, Zú Tōng Gǔ).
609	下列五输穴中，除……以外，都是本经的母穴: A 大肠经的三间; B 小肠经的小海 C. 包经的大陵 D 脾经的商丘	Among the following five command points [wu shu xue], which is not the mother point of its own meridian? A Li3 / Sān Jiān on large intestine meridian; B Si8 / Xiǎo Hǎi on small intestine meridian; C. P7 / Dà Líng on pericardium meridian; D. Sp5 / Shāng Qiū on spleen meridian.
610	下列五输穴中，除…外，均不是本经的子穴: A.肾经的涌泉; B 肝经的太冲 C. 胃	Which of the following points is a child point on its own meridian? A K1 (Yǒng Quán); B Lv3 (Tài Chōng); C. S44 (Nèi Tíng); D. Li5

	肝经的太冲 C. 胃经的内庭; D 大肠经的阳.	(Yáng Xī).
611	下列穴名中带 "阴" 字的何穴不归属于阴经: A 阴谷; B 阴郄 C. 会阴; D 阴市; E 阴交.	All the points below have " Yīn" as part of their names, which point does NOT belong to a yin meridian? A. Yīn Gǔ; B. Yīn Xī; C. Huì Yīn; D. Yīn Shì; E. Yīn Jiāo.
612	下列穴位，不属于膀胱经的是: A 脑空; B 天柱 C. 会阳; D 合阳 E 委阳.	Which of the following points does NOT belong to the bladder meridian? A. Nǎo Kōng; B. Tiān Zhù; C. Huì Yáng; D. Hé Yáng; E. Wěi Yáng.
613	下列穴位，不属于胃经的是: A 水突; B 伏兔 C. 扶突; D 髀关; E · 丰隆.	Which of the following points does not belong to the stomach meridian? A. Shuǐ Tū; B. Fú Tū; C. Fú Tù; D. Bì Guān; E. Fēng Lóng.
614	下列穴位，除……外，均与神庭穴相平? A 头临泣; B 头维 C. 五处; D 本神; E 眉冲.	Which of the following points is on a level with D24 (Shén Tíng)? A. G15 (Tóu Lín Qì， Lín Qì); B. S8 (Tóu Wěi); C. B5 (Wǔ Chù); D. G13 (Běn Shén); E. B3 (Méi Chōng).
615	下列穴位名称中，除……外，都是络穴: A 飞扬; B 蠡沟 C. 支正; D 复溜; E 光明.	Which of the following points is NOT a linking point (luo xue)? A; B58 (Feī Yáng); B. Lv5 (Lí Gōu); C. Si7 (Zhi Zhèng); D. K7 (Fù Liū); E. G37 (Guāng Míng).
616	下列穴位位置错误的是: A 素髎位于鼻尖正中; B 神庭位于前发际正中直上 0.5 寸 C. 气海位于脐下 1.5 寸; D 犊鼻位于髌韧带外侧曲陷中; E 风府位于后发际直上 1.5 寸.	Which of the following statements is NOT correct? A. D25 (Sù Liáo) is the tip of the nose; B. D24 (Shén Tíng) is 0.5 Cun above the middle of the frontal hairline; C. R6 (Qì Hǎi) is 1.5 Cuns below umbilicus; D. S35 (Dú Bí) is located in the depression on the lateral side of the patella ligament with the knee bent; E. D16 (Fēng Fǔ) is 1.5 Cuns directly above the posterior hairline.
617	下列穴位中，不是募穴的为: A.期门; B.石门 C. 京门; D 梁门.	Which of the following points is not a mu point (gathe ring point)? A Lv14 (Qí Mén); B R5 (Shí Mén); C. G25 (Jīng Mén); D. S21 (Liáng Mén).
618	下列穴位中，除……外，既是络穴，又是八脉交会穴的是: A.外关; B 公孙 C. 照海; D 列缺.	Which of the following points is neither a luo xue (linking point), nor a meeting point between eight extraordinary meridians & twelve master meridians (a; C. onfluence point)? A Sj5 (Wài Guān); B Sp4 (Gōng Sūn); C. K6 (Zhào Hǎi); D. Lu7 (Liè Quē).
619	下列穴位中，除……以外，均属督脉: A 腰俞; B 兑端 C. 腰奇; D 腰阳关.	Which point does not belong to du mai / governing meridian? A Yāo Shū; B Duì Duān; C. Yāo qí (waist miracle); D Yāo Yáng Guān.
620	下列穴位中，肝的募穴是:	What is the liver mu xue (liver gathering point)? A. R5 (Shí Mén); B. Lv14 (Qí Mén); C. Lv13 (Zhāng Mén); D.

	A 石门; B 期门 C. 章门; D 京门; E 以上都不是.	G25 (Jīng Mén); E. none of the above.
621	下列穴位中，既是胃之募穴,又是腑之会穴的是: A 中脘; B 章门 C. 期门; D 巨阙; E 以上都不是.	Which of the following poins is both the stomach mu xue (stomach gathering point) and the meeting of bowels? A. R12 (Zhōng Wǎn); B. Lv13 (Zhāng Mén); C. Lv14 (Qí Mén); D. R14 (Jù Què); E. None of the above.
622	下列穴位中，具有舒筋作用的是: A 期门; B 日月 C. 丘墟; D 阳陵泉; E 悬钟.	Which of the following points can relax tendons? A Lv14 (Qí Mén); B. G24 (Rì Yuè); C. G40 (Qiū Xū); D. G34 (Yáng Líng Quán); E. G39 (Xuán Zhōng).
623	下列穴位中，具有醒神开窍作用的是: A 少商; B 水沟 C. 劳宫; D 丰隆; E. 内关.	Which of the following points can wake up the spirit and open the cavities? A. Lu11 (Shǎo Shāng); B. D26 (Shuǐ Gōu, Rén Zhōng); C. P8 (Láo Gōng); D. S40 (Fēng Lóng); E. P6 (Nèi Guān).
624	下列穴位中，可以应用口寸(两口角间的长度)取穴的是: A 子宫穴; B 三角灸 C. 提托穴; D 痞根穴; E 胃管下俞.	Which of the following points may be located by mouth Cun (from angle of mouth to angle of mouth)? A. Zǐ Gōng; B. San Jiao Jiu; C. Tí Tuō; D. Pǐ Gēn; E. Wèi Guān Xià Shū.
625	下列穴位中，位于颏孔者是: A 颊车; B 大迎 C. 挟承浆(頦髎); D 承浆; E 以上都不对.	Which of the following points is located on the foramen mentale of the mandible? A. S6 (Jiá Chē); B. S5 (Dà Yíng); C. Jiā Chéng Jiàng (Kē Liáo); D. R24 (Chéng Jiàng); E none of the above.
626	下列穴位中，位于眶外的是: A 承泣; B 瞳子髎 C. 精明; D 球后; E 以上都不是.	Which point is located outside of orbit? A. S1 (Chéng Qì); B. G1 (Tóng Zǐ Liáo); C. B1 (Jīng Míng); D. Qiú Hòu; E. None of the above.
627	下列穴位中，位于腋中线上的是: A 天池; B 輒筋 C. 日月; D 大包; E 期门.	Which of the following points is located on the midaxillary line? A. P1 (Tiān Chí); B. G23 (Zhé Jīn); C. G24 (Rì Yuè); D. Sp21 (Dà Bāo); E. Lv14 (Qí Mén).
628	下列穴位中，与五行相配属金，其所属经脉也属金的: A.商丘; B.经渠 C. 中封; D 阳谷.	Which point belongs to metal and its meridian also belongs to metal? A. Sp5 (Shāng Qiū); B. Lu8 (Jīng Qú); C. Lv4 (Zhōng Fēng); D. Si5 (Yáng Gǔ).
629	下列穴位中不是郄穴的是: A 中都; B 筑宾 C. 交信; D 照海; E 跗阳.	Which of the following points is NOT a xi xue (fissural or cleft point)? A. Lv6 (Zhōng Dū); B. K9 (Zhú; Bīn); C. K8 (Jiāo Xìn); D. K6 (Zhào Hǎi); E. B59 (Fū Yáng).
630	下列穴位中不属募穴的是: A 巨阙; B 章门 C. 中极; D 气海; E 日月.	Which of the following points is NOT a mu xue (gathering point)? A. R14 (Jù Què); B. Lv13 (Zhāng Mén); C. R3 (Zhōng Jí); D. R6 (Qì Hǎi); E. G24 (Rì Yuè).
631	下列穴位中除......	Which point does NOT belong to du mai (governing meridian)?

	外均属督脉穴: A 腰俞; B 腰阳关 C. 腰奇; D 命门; E 兑端.	A. Yāo Shū; B. Yāo Yáng Guān; C. Yāo Qí; D. Mìng Mén; E. Duì Duān.
632	下列穴位中既是原穴又是八会穴的是: A.合谷; B. 公孙 C. 内关; D. 列缺; E. 太渊.	Which of the following points is both an original point (yuan xue or source point) and one of the eight meeting points (ba hui xue)? A. Li4 (Hé Gǔ); B. Sp4 (Gōng Sūn); C. P6 (Nèi Guān); D. Lu7 (Liè Quē); E. Lu9 (Tài Yuān).
633	下列穴位中间距为 2 寸的是: A 外关 三阳络; B 上廉 下廉 C. 阳溪 偏历; D 大陵 间使; E 以上都不是.	The distance between which two points is 2 Cuns? A. Sj5 (Wài Guān) and Sj8 (Sān Yáng Luò); B. Li9 (Shàng Lián) and Li8 (Xià Lián); C. Li5 (Yáng Xī) and Li6 (Piān Lì); D. P7 (Dà Líng) and P5 (Jiān Shǐ); E. None of the above.
634	下列穴位中间距为 4 寸的是: A 玉堂 灵墟; B 库房 华盖 C. 神封 膻中; D 乳根 步廊; E 以上都不是	The distance between which two points is 4 Cuns? A. R18 (Yù Táng) and H4 (Líng Dào); B. S14 (Kù Fáng) and R20 (Huá Gài); C. K23 (Shén Fēng) and R17 (Shān Zhōng); D. S18 (Rǔ Gēn) and K22 (Bù Láng); E. none of the above.
635	下列穴位中与关元穴不在一条水平线上是: A.水道; B.子户 C. 子宫; D 提托.	Which of the following points is not on a level with R4 (Guān Yuán)? A S28, Shuǐ Dào; B. Zǐ Hù; C, Zǐ Gōng; D. Tí Tuō.
636	下列穴组，除。。。外，都是原络穴: A. 阳池 内关; B. 太白 丰隆 C. 丘墟 蠡沟; D. 大钟 京骨; E. 偏历 列缺	Which of the following points is neither a yuan point [source points] nor a linking point / collateral point [luò xué]? A. Sj4 [Yáng Chí] P6 [Nèi Guān]; B. Sp3 [Tài Bái] S40 [Fēng Lóng]; C. G40 [Qiū Xū] Lv5 [Lí Gōu]; D. K4 [Dà Zhōng] B64 [Jīng Gǔ]; E. Li6 [Piān Lì] Lu7 [Liè Quē].
637	下列穴组与任脉中极穴相平的是: A 气穴; B 大巨 C. 大赫; D 水道; E 府舍.	Which point is on a level with R3 (Zhōng Jí)? A. K13 (Qì Xué); B S27 (Dà Jù); C. K12 (Dà Hè); D. S28 (Shuǐ Dào); E. Sp13 (Fù Shě).
638	下列穴组与任脉中脘穴相平的是: A 梁门 幽门; B 石关 关门 C. 商曲 太乙; D 承满 四满; E 以上都不是.	Which two points are on a level with R12 (Zhōng Wǎn)? A S21 (Liáng Mén) and K21 (Yōu Mén); B. K18 (Shí Guān) and S22 (Guān Mén); C. K17 (Shāng Qǔ) and S23 (Tài Yǐ); D. S20 (Chéng Mǎn) and K14 (Sì Mǎn); E. None of the above.
639	下列穴组中，两穴都与脐相平的是: A. 天枢 章门; B. 肓門 京门 C. 天枢 京门; D. 大横 带脉; E. 肓俞 章门	Which two points are on a level with umbilicus? A. S25 [Tiān Shū] Lv13 [Zhāng Mén]; B. B51 [Huāng Mén] G25 [Jīng Mén]; C. S25 [Tiān Shū] G25 [Jīng Mén]; D. Sp15 [Dà Héng] dai mai / belt meridian; E. K16 [Huāng Shū] Lv13 [Zhāng Mén].
640	下列有关会阴穴的说法错误的是: A 任脉经穴的起始穴; B 是络穴 C. 是任督冲三脉交会穴; D 位于两阴之间; E 针法灸法都可使用.	Which of the following statements about R1 (Huì Yīn) is NOT Correct? A. it is the beginning point of ren mai (conception meridian); B. it is a linking point (luo xue); C. it is a meeting point of ren mai (conception meridian), du mai (governing meridian), and chong mai (vigorous meridian); D. it is located in between the genitals and the anus; E. it may be treated by either acupuncture or

		moxibusiton.
641	下列有关募穴描述错误的是: A·是脏腑经气汇聚的地方; B·均位于胸腹部 C. 分布与内脏的高下部位相应; D·在各脏腑所属的经脉循行线上; E· 腑病取之，有 "阳病引阴"之意.	Which of the following is NOT an accurate description of Mu Xue (gathering points)? A. gathering points are the gathering places of viscera, bowels, and meridian energy; B gathering points are all locted in the chest and abdomen region; C. gathering points are distributed in the regions on a level with their corresponding organs; D. gathering points are all located on the meridians of their respective organs; E. gathering points may be used to treat the disease of bowels, because "yin should be brought in to treat yang diseases".
642	下列俞募穴的组合，有错误的是: A. 肺俞 中府 B 肾俞 京门 C. 肝俞 章门; D. 胆俞 日月; E. 三焦俞 石门	Which group is NOT a combinaion of a gathering point / anterior points, front mu point [mù xué] and a merging point / terminal point\, sea points [hé xué]? A. B13 [Fèi Shū] Lu1 [Zhōng Fǔ] BB23 [Shèn Shū] G25 [Jīng Mén]; C. B18 [Gān Shū] Lv13 [Zhāng Mén]; D. B19 [Dǎn Shū] G24 [Rì Yuè]; E. B22 [Sān Jiāo Shū] R5 [Shí Mén].
643	下列针灸配方中，称为"开 四关"的穴组是: A. 内关 外关; B. 关冲 关门 C. 上关 下关; D. 腰阳关 膝阳关; E. 合谷 太冲	Which of the following groups of points is called, "opening of four gates"? A. P6 [Nèi Guān] Sj5 [Wài Guān]; B. Sj1 [Guān Chōng] S22 [Guān Mén]; C. G3 [Shàng Guān] S7 [Xià Guān]; D. D3 [Yāo Yáng Guān] G33 [Yáng Guān, Xī Yáng Guān]; E. Li4 [Hé Gǔ] Lv3 [Tài Chōng].
644	下列诸脉,除……外,都有郄穴 A 阴维脉; B 阴跷脉 C. 阳维脉; D 阳跷脉; E 冲脉.	Which of the following meridians does NOT have a xi xue (fissural or cleft point)? A. yin wei mai (fastening meridian of yin); B. yin qiao mai (heel meridian of yin); C. yang wei mai (fasening meridian of yang); D. yang qiao mai (heel meridian of yang); E. chong mai (vigorous meridian).
645	下列诸脉中，有郄穴的是: A 任脉; B 督脉 C. 冲脉; D 带脉; E 阴维脉.	Which of the following meridians has a xi xue (fissural or ceft point)? A. ren mai (conception meridian); B. du mai (governing meridian); C. chong mai (vigorous meridian); D. dai mai (belt meridian); E. yin wei mai (fastening meridian of yin).
646	下列属原络配穴的是: A.丘墟 光明; B. 太溪 大钟 C. 腕骨 支正; D. 太渊 偏历; E. 大陵 内关	Which of the following is a combination of yuan point and luo point (source point and linking point)? A.G40 [Qiū Xū] G37 [Guāng Míng]; B. K3 [Tài Xī] K4 [Dà Zhōng]; C. G12 [Wán Gǔ] Si7 [Zhi Zhèng]; D. Lu9 [Tài Yuān] Li6 [Piān Lì]; E. P7 [Dà Líng] P6 [Nèi Guān].
647	下列足厥阴肝经特定穴正确的是: A 膝关是 "合穴"; B 中都是"络穴 " C. 中封是"郄穴"; D 蠡沟是"经穴"; E 中都是 "郄穴".	Which of the following statements about the specially marked. points (te ding xue) on the liver meridian is accurate? A. Lv7 (Xī Guān) is a merging point (sea point); B. Lv6 (Zhōng Dū) is a linking point (luo xue); C. Lv4 (Zhōng Fēng) is a fissural point (cleft point, xi xue); D. Lv5 (Lí Gōu) is a flowing point (jing xue, river point); E. Lv6 (Zhōng Dū) is a fissural point (cleft point, xi xue).
648	下列足太阳膀胱经穴，除……外均位于背部距督脉 3 寸的经线上:	Which of the points on the bladder meridian is NOT located in the back, 3 Cuns laterally away from du mai (governing meridian)? A; B42 (Pò Hù); B. B48 (Yáng Gāng); C. B12 (Fēng Mén); D. B52

	A 魄户; B 阳纲 C. 风门; D 志室; E 胞肓.	(Zhì Shì); E. B53 (Bāo Huāng).
649	下列足太阳膀胱经穴，除外均位于背部距督脉 1.5 寸的经线上: A 膈俞; B 督俞 C. 厥阴俞; D 膏肓俞; E 气海俞.	Which of the points on the bladder meridian is NOT located in the back, 1.5 Cuns laterally away from du mai (governing meridian)? A.B17 (Gé Shū); B.B16 (Dū Shū); C. B14 (Jué Yīn Shū); D. B43 (Gāo Huāng Shū); E. B24 (Qì Hǎi Shū).
650	现定十四经穴名计数为: A 349 穴; B.359 穴 C. 360 穴; D 361 穴; E 365 穴.	At present, how many points are there on the 14 major meridians? A 349 points; B.359 points; C. 360 points; D.361 points; E 365 points.
651	现有经穴数目是: A 360; B 361 C. 362; D 354	At present, how many points are there on the twelve master meridians altogether ? A 360; B 361; C. 362; D 354.
652	小肠下合穴是: A 小海; B 少海 C. 下巨虚; D 上巨虚; E 委阳.	Which is the lower merging point [xia he xue] of the small intestine? A · Si8 / Xiǎo Hǎi; B · H3 / Shào Hǎi; · C. S39 / Xià Jù Xū; D S37 / Shàng Jù Xū; E · B39 / Wěi Yáng.
653	小腹部病症，妇科病症，在远端取穴中最常用的经穴是: A. 脾经穴; B. 胃经穴 C. 胆经穴; D. 膀胱经穴; E. 以上都不是	According to distal selection of points, which is the point most commonly selected to treat diseases of lower abdomen and gynecopathy ? A. points on spleen meridian; B. points on stomach meridian; C. points on gallbladder meridian; D. points on bladder meridian; E. none of the above.
654	心的募穴是: A 膻中; B 日月 C. 巨阙; D 京门; E 中脘.	What is the heart mu xue (heart gathering point)? A. R17 (Shān Zhōng); B. G24 (Rì Yuè); C. R14 (Jù Què); D. G25 (Jīng Mén); E. R12 (Zhōng Wǎn).
655	胸骨上迹至剑突之间的骨度分寸是: A 6 寸; B 6.5 寸 C. 7 寸; D 8 寸; E 9 寸	According to the bone Cun measurements (gu du fen Cun), what is the distance between tiantu = R22 (suprasternal notch) and xiphoid process? A. 6 Cuns; B. 6.5 Cuns; C. 7 Cuns; D. 8 Cuns; E. 9 Cuns.
656	悬钟穴的位置是: A. 外踝下缘直下 7 寸，腓骨后缘; B. 外踝上缘直上 7 寸，腓骨后缘 C. 商丘穴直上 3 寸 腓骨后缘; D. 外踝尖直上 3 寸，腓骨后缘; E. 外踝尖直上 3 寸 腓骨前缘.	Where is G39 [Xuán Zhōng] located? A. 7 Cuns directly below lower edge of lateral malleolus, at the posterior edge of fibula; B. 7 Cuns directly above lower edge of lateral malleolus, at the posterior edge of fibula; C. 3 Cuns directly above Sp5 [Shāng Qiū], at the posterior edge of lateral malleolus; D. 3 Cuns directly above the tip of of lateral malleolus, at the posterior edge of fibula; E. 3 Cuns directly above the tip of of lateral malleolus, at the anterior edge of fibula
657	穴大体上分为三类，指的是 A 十四经穴、经外奇穴、特定穴; B，十四经穴、经外奇穴、阿是穴 C. 经穴、奇穴、阿是穴;	What do “three broad categoriesof points” refer to? A points on 14 major meridians, extraoprdinary points, specially marked points; B points on 14 major meridians, extraoprdinary points, pressure points [ouch points]; C. flowing points / river points / jīng xué, extraoprdinary points, ouchi points / pressure points; D. flowing points / river

	D 经穴、络穴、阿是.	points / jīng xué, linking points, / luo points, ouchi points / pressure points.
658	穴的正确附加名称正确的是: A·胃募穴; B·胃经募穴 C. 阳明经募穴 D·足阳明募穴; E· 以上均通用.	What is the proper name of gathering point / mu point? A ·stomach gathering point / wei mu point; B ·stomach meridian gathering point / wei jing mu point; C. ·bright yang meridian / yang ming meridian gathering point / yang ming jing mu point; D ·foot bright yang / yang ming gathering point / zu yang ming mu point; E， none of the above.
659	血海是指: A·胃;B·脑 C. 冲脉; D·肝; E 膻中.	What does "sea of blood" refer to? A ·stomach; B · brain; C. ·rigorous meridian / chong mai; D ·liver; E · R17 / Shān Zhōng.
660	阳白采用何种取穴法 A 骨度折量取穴法; B.肌性标志取穴法 C. 骨性标志取穴法;D 指寸法.	What method of locating points should be used to locate G14, Yáng Bái? A. bone and Cun Measurements; B. muscle landmarks C. fixed. landmarks of bones; D. digital measurements.
661	阳白穴位于瞳孔直上，当眉上: A·0·5 寸处; B·1 寸处 C. ·1·5 寸处; D·2 寸处; E·入发际处	G14 (Yáng Bái) is located directly above the pupil, how far is it above the eyebrow? A. 0.5 Cun; B. 1 Cun; C. 1.5 Cuns; D. 2 Cuns; E. inside the hairline.
662	阳交穴是: A. 阳维脉的郄穴; B. 阳跷脉的郄穴 C. ·胆经的郄穴; D. ·膀胱经的郄穴; E. ·以上都不是	What does G35 [Yáng Jiāo] belong to? A. ·a xi xue / fissural or cleft point of yang wei mai / yang fastener meridian; B. ·a xi xue / fissural or cleft point of yang qiao mai / yang heel meridian; C. ·a xi xue / fissural or cleft point of gallbladder meridiant; D. ·a xi xue / fissural or cleft point of bladder meridian; E. ·none of the above
663	阳经五输穴所属五行顺序是: A·木火土金水; B·金水木火土 C. ·金木水火土; D·木水金火土; E·以上都不是.	Five command points (wu shu xue) belong to five elements in the following order: A. wood, fire, earth, metal, water; B. metal, water, wood, fire, earth; C. metal, wood, water, fire, earth; D. wood, water, metal, fire, earth; E. none of the above.
664	阳跷脉的郄穴是: A·外丘; B·金门 C. 跗阳; D·阳交; E·梁丘.	What is the xi xue (fissural or cleft point) of yang qiao mai (heel meridian of hang)? A. G36 (Wài Qiū); B. B63 (Jīn Mén); C; B59 (Fū Yáng); D. G35 (Yáng Jiāo); E. S34 (Liáng Qiū).
665	阳维脉的郄穴是: A 筑宾; B 跗阳 C. 金门; D·水泉; E·阳交.	What is the xi xue (fissural or cleft point) of yang wei mai (fastening meridian of yang)? A. K9 (Zhú; Bīn); B. B59 (Fū Yáng); C. B63 (Jīn Mén); D. K5 (Shuǐ Quán); E. G35 (Yáng Jiāo).
666	阳溪与偏历间隔: A·1 寸; B·2 寸;C 3 寸; D·4 寸; E·5 寸.	What is the distance between Li5 / Yáng Xī and Li6 / Piān Lì? A ·1 Cun; B ·2 Cun; ·C3 Cun; D ·4 Cun; E.5 Cun.
667	腋前横纹头至肘横纹的骨度分寸是: A·6 寸; B·7 寸 C. ·7·5 寸; D·8 寸; E. 9 寸.	What is the distance between anterior axillary fold and elbow crease in the bone Cun measurements? A. 6 Cuns; B. 7 Cuns C. 7.5 Cuns; D. 8 Cuns; E. 9 Cuns.
668	以两手虎口交叉取列缺，属于: A·动作标志取穴法; B·食指同身寸法 C·简便取穴法; D·	With a clasp of two hands, and the forefinger of one hand pressing against the styloid process of radius of the other hand, to locate Lu7 (Liè Quē); what method of locating points is being used?

	C. 简便取穴法; D·小指同身寸法; E·骨度分寸取穴法.	A. mobile landmarks; B. measurement of the forefinger; C. simple and C. onvenient method; D. measurement of the little finger; E. bone Cun measurements.
669	以下八会穴, 哪个是错误的: A·腑会中脘; B·骨会大椎 C. 髓会绝骨(悬钟); D·筋会阳陵泉; E·脏会章门.	Concerning the eight meeting points (ba hui xue), which of the following statemens is NOT Correct? A. meeting of bowels → R12 (Zhōng Wǎn); B. meeting of bone → D14 (Dà Zhuī); C. meeting of marrow→ G39 (Xuán Zhōng); D. meeting of tendons → G34 (Yáng Líng Quán); E. meeting of viscera → Lv13 (Zhāng Mén).
670	以下八脉交会穴，除...外都是错误的? A·内关通阴跷; B·申脉通阳维 C. ·外关通带脉; D·公孙通冲脉; E· 后溪通任脉	Among the eight meridians meeting points (ba mai jiao hui xue), which of the following statements is Correct? A. P6 (Nèi Guān) meets yin qiao (heel meridian of yin); B. B62 (Shēn Mài) meets yang wei (fastening meridian of yang); C. Sj5 (Wài Guān) meets dai mai (belt meridian); D. Sp4 (Gōng Sūn) meets chong mai (vigorous meridian); E. Si3 (Hòu Xī) meets ren mai (conception meridian).
671	以下不属于特定穴的是: A¨商阳; B·阳溪; · C. 合谷; D 曲池; E 肩髃.	Which point is not one of the specially marked points [te ding xue]? A¨ Li1 / Shāng Yáng; B · Li5 / Yáng Xī; · C. · Li4 / Hé Gǔ; D · Li11 / Qū Chí;E Li15 / Jiān Yú.
672	以下不属于天枢穴主治病证的是: A 便秘; B·腹泻 C. ·月经不调; D·水肿; E·目赤肿痛	Which is NOT the indication of S25 / Tiān Shū? A · Cconstipation; B · diarrhea; C. irregular menstruation; D ·edema; E ·pink eye with swelling and pain.
673	以下除。...外，都属俞募配合: A. 肺俞中府; B. ·心俞 膻中 C. ·脾俞 京门; D. ·胆俞 日月; E. ·肾俞 京门	Which group is NOT a combinaion of a gathering point / anterior point / front mu point [mù xué] and a merging point / terminal point / sea points [hé xué]? A. ·B13 [Fèi Shū] Lu1 [Zhōng Fǔ]; B. ·B15 [Xīn Shū] R17 [Shān Zhōng]; C. ·B20 [Pí Shū] G25 [Jīng Mén]; D. ·B19 [Dǎn Shū] G24 [Rì Yuè]; E. ·B23 [Shèn Shū] G25 [Jīng Mén].
674	以下除……外,各穴都与脐相平: A·腹哀; B·带脉 C. ·肓俞; D·大横; E. 天枢.	Which of the following points is NOT on a level with the umbilicus? A. Sp16 (Fù Āi); B. G26 (Dài Mài); C. K16 (Huāng Shū); D. Sp15 (Dà Héng); E. S25 (Tiān Shū).
675	以下配穴，除 ~外都是俞募配穴: A·大肠俞 天枢; B 脾俞 章门 C. ·心俞 巨阙; D·胆俞 日月; E·肝俞 京门.	Which of the following is NOT pairing of shu xue (back shu point) and mu xue (gathering point)? A. B25 (Dà Cháng Shū); S25 (Tiān Shū); B. B20 (Pí Shū); Lv13 (Zhāng Mén); C. B15 (Xīn Shū); R14 (Jù Què); D.B19 (Dǎn Shū) G24 (Rì Yuè); E. B18 (Gān Shū), G25 (Jīng Mén).
676	以下腧穴不针不灸的是: A 缺盆; B 承泣 C. 人迎; D 乳中; E 乳根.	Which point cannot be treated by acupuncture nor by moxibustion? A ·S12 [Quē Pén]; B · S1 / Chéng Qì; C. S9 / Rén Yíng; D ·S17 / Rǔ Zhōng; E · S18 / Rǔ Gēn.
677	以下腧穴不属于大肠经的是: A·合谷; B·阳谷 C. ·阳溪; D·手三里; E 臂臑.	Which point is not on the large intestine meridian? A · Hé Gǔ; B · Yáng Gǔ; C. ·Yáng Xī; D · Shǒu Sān Lǐ; E. ·Bì Nào.

678	以下腧穴不属于足太阴脾经的是: A·隐白; ·B·太白 C. ·侠白; D·大都; E·大包	Which point is not on the foot greater yin spleen meridian? A · Yǐn Bái; ·B · Tài Bái; C. Xiá Bái; D · Dà Dū; E · Dà Bāo
679	以下腧穴不属于足阳明胃经的是: A·下关; B 迎香 C. ·缺盆; D·下关; E·条口.	Which point is not on the foot bright yang stomach meridian? A ·Xià Guān; B. Yíng Xiāng; C. ·Quē Pén; D / Xià Guān; E ·Tiáo Kǒu.
680	以下腧穴既可治疗咳嗽，又可治疗中风昏迷的是: A·尺泽; B·孔最 C. ·太渊; D·鱼际; E 少商.	What point can treat cough and can also treat coma in stroke? A · Lu5 / Chǐ Zé; B · Lu6 / Kǒng Zuì; C. Lu9 / TàiYuān; D · Lu10 / Yǔ Jì; E · Lu11 / Shǎo Shāng.
681	以下腧穴均为特定穴的是: A·少商商阳列缺; B·二间上廉合谷 C. ·尺泽曲池肩髃; D·经渠温溜,足三里; ·E.偏历太渊迎香.	Which group of points all belong to specially marked points? A · Lu11 / Shǎo Shāng Li1 / Shāng Yáng Lu7 / Liè Quē; B · Li2 / Èr Jiān Li9 / Shàng Lián Li4 / Hé Gǔ; C. Lu5 / Chǐ Zé Li11 / Qū Chí Li15 / Jiān Yú; D · Lu8 / Jīng QúLi7 / Wēn Liū, S36 / Zú Sān Lǐ; ·E. Li6 / Piān Lì Lu9 / TàiYuān ·Li20 / Yíng Xiāng
682	以下腧穴均位于前臂部的是: A·偏历列缺; B·合谷臂臑 C. ·天府孔最; D·商阳少商; E·侠白肩髃.	Which group of points are located in the upper arm region?: A · Li6 / Piān Lì Lu7 / Liè Quē; B · Li4 / Hé Gǔ Li14 / Bì Nào; C. Lu3 / Tiān Fǔ Lu6 / Kǒng Zuì; D · Li1 / Shāng Yáng Lu11 / Shǎo Shāng; E · Lu4 / Xiá Bái,Li15 / Jiān Yú.
683	以下腧穴中距肘横纹 2 寸的是: A 手三里; B 手五里 C. 肘髎; D 上廉; E·偏历.	What point is located two cuns from elbow crease? A · Li10 / Shǒu Sān Lǐ; B · Li13 / Shǒu Wǔ Lǐ; C. Li12 / Zhǒu Liáo; D ·Li9 / Shàng Lián; E · Li6 / Piān Lì.
684	以下腧穴中与鼻翼下缘相平的是: A·迎香; B·巨髎 C. ·地仓; D·下关; E·颊车.	Which point is on a level with the inferior border of the nose wing (ala nasi)? · A. Li20 / Yíng Xiāng; B · S3 / Jù Liáo; C. S4 / Dì Cāng; D · S7 / Xià Guān; E · S6 / Jiá Chē.
685	以下腧穴中属于手太阴肺经的是: A 风门; B·期门 C. ·神门; D·天池; E·云门.	What point belongs to the hand greater yin lung meridian? A Fēng Mén; B · Qí Mén; C. · Shén Mén; D Tiān Chí; E ·Yún Mén.
686	以下穴位除……外，都是募穴: A 章门; B·期门 C. ·京门; D·石门; E·云门.	Which point is NOT a gathering point (a mu xue)? A. Lv13 (Zhāng Mén); B. Lv14 (Qí Mén); C. G25 (Jīng Mén); D. R5 (Shí Mén); E. Lu2 (Yún Mén).
687	以下有关阳陵泉穴在归属上的错误是: A八会穴; B·五输穴 C. ·具有舒筋作用; D·下合穴; E·八脉交会穴.	Which of the following statements about G34 (Yáng Líng Quán) is NOT correct? A. it is one of the eight meeting points (ba hui xue); B. it is one of the five command points (wu shu xue); C. it can relax tendons; D. it is a lower merging point (xia he xue); E. it is one of the eight meridians meeting points (ba mai jiao hui xue).

688	以下有关中脘穴在归属上的错误是: A·募穴; B·八脉交会穴 C. ·在脐上4寸; D·八会穴; E· 交会穴.	Which of the following statements about R12 (Zhōng Wăn) is NOT correct? A. it is a mu xue (gathering point); B. it is one of the ba mai jiao hui xue (eight meridians meeting points); C. it is 4 Cuns above the umbilicus; D. it is one of ba hui xue (eight meeting points); E. it is a meeting point.
689	以下属手太阳小肠经的穴位是: A·听会; B·听宫 C. ·耳门; D·上关; E·下关.	Which of the following points belongs to the small intestine meridian? A. Tīng Huì; B. Tīng Gōng; C. Ěr Mén; D. Shàng Guān; E. Xià Guān.
690	阴经的郄穴多治疗: A. ·有关气方面的病证; B. ·有关血方面的病证 C. ·有关痰方面的病证; D. ·有关神志方面的病证; E. ·有关运动方面的病证	What diseases are treated by xi xue / fissural / cleft points on yin meridians? A. ·diseases involving energy; B. ·diseases involving blood; C. ·diseases involving phlegm; D. ·diseases involving spirits and will; E. ·diseases involving mobility.
691	阴经没有单独列原穴，使用时，什么穴可以代之? A 络穴; B 郄穴 C. 合穴; D 输穴.	Yin meridians have no independent yuán xué / starting-points / source-points，which points may be used as substitutes in clinical practice? A linking points, / luo points; B fissural point / cleft point / xi point; C. hé xué / terminal-points / sea-points points; D flowing points / stream points [shù xué].
692	阴蹻脉的郄穴是: ·A 阳交; B. ·交信 C. ·梁丘; D. ·外丘; E. ，以上部不是	What is the xi xue / fissural or cleft point of the yin heel meridian? A ·G35 [Yáng Jiāo]; B. ·K8 [Jiāo Xìn]; C. S34 [Liáng Qiū]; D. ·G36 [Wài Qiū]; E. none of the above.
693	殷门穴的位置在: A.承扶与委中的连线上，委中穴上5寸; B.承扶与委中的连线上，委中穴上8寸 C. 承扶与委中的连线上，委中穴上7寸; D 承扶与委中的连线上，委中穴下6寸.	Where is B37 (Yīn Mén) located? A. on the line connecting B36 [Chéng Fú] and B40 [Wěi Zhōng], 5 Cun above B40 [Wěi Zhōng]; B. on the line connecting B36 [Chéng Fú] and B40 [Wěi Zhōng], 8 Cun above B40 [Wěi Zhōng]; C. on the line connecting B36 [Chéng Fú] and B40 [Wěi Zhōng], 7 Cun above B40 [Wěi Zhōng]; D. on the line connecting B36 [Chéng Fú] and B40 [Wěi Zhōng], 6 Cun below B40 [Wěi Zhōng].
694	印堂穴以何种取穴法定位比较正确? A·骨度折量法; B·指量法 C. 一夫法; D·固定标志法; E·活动标志法.	How to locate "Yìn táng / midpoint between eyebrows / seal hall" more accurately? A ·by bone Cun measurements; B · by digital measurements; C. ·by one man's measurement; D ·by fixed landmarsk; E ·by mobile landmarks.
695	迎香的定位正确的是: A·鼻翼下缘"，鼻唇沟中; B·鼻翼外缘中点旁，鼻唇沟中 C. ·鼻翼旁，平鼻翼下缘; D·鼻孔外缘，鼻唇沟中; E·鼻翼上缘，鼻唇沟中.	What is the accurate location of Li20 / Yíng Xiāng? A. below the lower border of ala nasi (nose wing), in the nasolabial sulcus; B. laterally from the midpoint of lateral border of ala nasi (nose wing), in the nasolabial sulcus; C. on the side of ala nasi (nose wing), on a level with lower border of ala nasi (nose wing); D. on the side of nostril, in the nasolabial sulcus; E. at the upper border of ala nasi (nose wing), in the nasolabial sulcus.
696	用五输穴治疗 "心下	What point may be selected to treat "fullness below the heart

	满"，应该选用: A·输穴; B·经穴 C. ·荥穴; D·井穴; E 合穴.	(xin xia man)"? A. shu xue (stream point); B. jing xue (flowing point, river point); C. ying xue (spring point); D. jing xue (well point); E. he xue (merging point or sea point).
697	用子母补泻法治疗肾经实证应取: A. 阴谷; B.·然谷 C. ·太溪; D.·复溜; E.·涌泉	According to the child mother tonification sedation method, what point should be selected to treat kidney meridian excess syndrome? A. ·K10 [Yīn Gǔ]; B. ·K2 [Rán Gǔ]; C. ·K3 [Tài Xī]; D. ·K7 [Fù Liū]; E. ·K1 [Yǒng Quán]
698	用子母补泻法治疗肾经虚证应取: A. 阴谷; B.·然谷 C. ·太溪; D.·复溜; E.·涌泉	According to the child mother tonification sedation method, what point should be selected to treat kidney meridian deficiency syndrome? A. ·K10 [Yīn Gǔ]; B. ·K2 [Rán Gǔ]; C. ·K3 [Tài Xī]; D. ·K7 [Fù Liū]; E. ·K1 [Yǒng Quán].
699	用子母补泻法治疗心经实证应取: A. ·少海; B.·少府 C. ·少冲; D.·灵道; E.·神门	According to the child mother tonification sedation method, what point should be selected to treat heart meridian excess syndrome? A. ·H3 [Shào Hǎi]; B. ·H8 [Shào Fǔ]; C. ·H9 [Shào Chōng]; D. ·H4 [Líng Dào]; E. ·H7 [Shén Mén]
700	用子母补泻法治疗心经虚证应取: A. ·少海; B.·少府 C. ·少冲; D.·灵道; E.·神门	According to the child mother tonification sedation method, what point should be selected to treat heart meridian deficiency syndrome? A. ·H3 [Shào Hǎi]; B. ·H8 [Shào Fǔ]; C. ·H9 [Shào Chōng]; D. ·H4 [Líng Dào]; E. ·H7 [Shén Mén]
701	原穴共有: A·365 穴; B·16 穴 C. ·12 穴; D·15 穴; E·10 穴.	How many yuán xué / starting-points / source-points are there altogether? A ·365 points; B.16 points; C. ·12 points; D.15 points; E ·10 points.
702	原穴是: A·商阳; B·合谷 C. ·阳溪; D·偏历; E 曲池.	Which is a yuán xué / starting-point / source-point? A · Li1 / Shāng Yáng; B · Li4 / Hé Gǔ; C. Li5 / Yáng Xī; D · Li6 / Piān Lì; E. Li11 / Qū Chí.
703	原穴是: A·隐白; B·公孙 C. ·太白; D·三阴交; E 阴陵泉.	Which point is a yuán xué / starting-point / source-point? A · Sp1 / Yǐn Bái; B · Sp4 / Gōng Sūn; C. Sp3 / Tài Bái; D · Sp6 / Sān Yīn Jiāo; E. Sp9 / Yīn Líng Quán.
704	在督脉经穴中，除交会穴外，唯一的特定穴是: A 俞穴; B 八会穴 C. 络穴; D 原穴.	Aside from the meeting points, what is the only specially marked point [te ding xue] the du mai / governing meridian has? A flowing point / river point; B. eight influential point / ba hui xue; C. linking point / luo point; D yuán xué / starting-point / source-point
705	在华佗夹脊穴中，治疗腹部疾患的是: A·胸 1-12 夹脊; B·胸 1-腰 4 夹脊 C. ·胸 6-12 夹脊; D·胸 12-腰 4 夹脊; E 胸 6-腰 4 夹脊.	Which is effective in treating the symptoms of the abdomen among Huá Tuó Jiā Jí? A. the spinous processes of the 1-2 thoracic vertebrae; B. the spinous process of the 1 thoracic vertebra downward to the 4th lumbar vertebra; C. the spinous processes of the 6-12 thoracic vertebrae; D. the spinous process of the 12th thoracic vertebra downward to 4th lumbar vertebra; E. the spinous process of the 6th thoracic vertebra downward to 4th lumbar vertebra.
706	在华佗夹脊穴中，治	Which is effective in treating the symptoms of the upper limbs

	疗上肢疾患的是: A 胸 1-2 夹脊; B 胸 1-3 夹脊 C. 胸 1-4 夹脊; D 胸 1-5 夹脊; E 胸 1-7 夹脊.	among Huá Tuó Jiā Jí? A. the spinous processes of the 1-2 thoracic vertebrae; B. the spinous processes of the 1-3 thoracic vertebrae C. the spinous processes of the 1-4 thoracic vertebrae; D. the spinous process of the 1-5 thoracic vertebrae; E. the spinous processes of the 1-7 thoracic vertebrae.
707	在华佗夹脊穴中，治疗下肢疾患的应是: A 胸 10-腰 2 夹脊; B 胸 11-腰 3 夹脊 C. 胸 12-腰 4 夹脊; D 胸 1-腰 4 夹脊; E. 腰 2-腰 4 夹脊.	Which is effective in treating the symptoms of the lower limbs among Huá Tuó Jiā Jí? A. the spinous processes of the 10th thoracic vertebra downward to 2nd lumbar vertebra; B. the spinous processes of the 11th thoracic vertebra downward to 3rd lumbar vertebra; C. the spinous processes of the 12th thoracic vertebra downward to 4th lumbar vertebra; D. the spinous processes of the 1st thoracic vertebra downward to 4th lumbar vertebra E the spinous processes of the 2nd. thoracic vertebra downward to 4th lumbar vertebra.
708	在华佗夹脊穴中，治疗胸部疾患的是: A 胸 1-7 夹脊; B 胸 1-8 夹脊 C. 胸 1-9 夹脊; D 胸 1-10 夹脊; E 胸 1-12 夹脊.	Which is effective in treating the symptoms of the chest among Huá Tuó Jiā Jí? A. the spinous processes of the 1-7 thoracic vertebrae; B. the spinous processes of the 1-8 thoracic vertebrae C. the spinous processes of the 1-9 thoracic vertebrae; D. the spinous processes of the 1-10 thoracic vertebrae; E. the spinous processes of the 1-12 thoracic vertebrae.
709	在肩部，肩髃后方，当臂外展时，于肩峰后下方呈现凹陷处穴是： A.肩外俞; B 肩貞 C. 肩中俞; D 肩髎.	What point is located in the shoulder on the posterior side of Li15 [Jiān Yú], in the depression that occurs on the posterior inferior side of the acromion when the arm extends laterally? A. Si14, Jiān Wài Shū; B. Si9, Jiān Zhēn; C. Si15, Jiān Zhōng Shū; D. Sj14, Jiān Liáo.
710	在颈部与喉结相平，胸锁乳突肌前缘的穴位是: A. 水突; B. 天突 C. 扶突; D. 人迎; E. 大迎	What point is located in the neck, on a level with the laryngeal prominence, at the anterior edge of sternocleidomastoid muscle? A. S10 [Shuǐ Tū] B. R22 [Tiān Tū]; C. Li18 [Fú Tū]; D. S9 [Rén Yíng]; E. S5 [Dà Yíng].
711	在手太阴肺经中，治疗头项强痛应首选: A，中府; B 尺泽 C. 列缺 D.太渊 E 鱼际	What point on the hand greater yin lung meridian should be selected as the primary point to treat stiffness and pain in the back of neck? A，Lu1 / Zhōng Fǔ; B · Lu5 / Chǐ Zé; C. Lu7 / Liè Quē D. Lu9 / TàiYuān E · Lu10 / Yǔ Jì
712	在特定穴中，膈俞穴属于: A. 八会穴; B. 络穴 C. 郄穴; D. 原穴; E. 五输穴	Among the te ding xue / specially designated points, what does B17 [Gé Shū] belong to? A. a ba hui xue / eight meeting point; B. a linking point / collateral point [luò xué]; C. a xi xue / fissural or cleft point; D. a yuan xue / source point / original point; E. one of the five shu points / five command points.
713	在特定穴中，列缺属于: A 八会穴; B 络穴	Among the specially marked. points (te ding xue), Lu7 (Liè Quē) is: A. one of the eight meeting points (ba hui xue); B. one of the

	C. 郄穴; D 经穴; E 以上都不是.	linking points, (luo xue); C. one of the fissural points (cleft points, xi xue); D. one of the flowing points [Jīng Xué); E. none of the above.
714	在特定穴中，六腑病变往往反应于: A 输穴; B 募穴 C. 郄穴; D 原穴; E 络穴.	What specially marked. points (te ding xue) may often be used to detect the disorders of six bowels? A. shu xue (stream points); B. mu xue (gathering points); C. xi xue (fissural or cleft points); D. yuan xue (original or source points); E. luo xue (linking points,).
715	在特定穴中，下巨虚是: A 大肠的下合穴; B 小肠的下合穴 C. 胃的下合穴; D 胆的下合穴; E 三焦的下合穴.	What is the category of S39 (Xià Jù Xū) among the specially marked points (te ding xue)? A. lower merging point (xia he xue) of the large intestine; B. lower merging point (xia he xue) of the small intestine; C. lower merging point (xia he xue) of the stomach; D. lower merging point (xia he xue) of the gallbladder; E. lower merging point (xia he xue) of the san jiao (triple heater).
716	在特定穴中，治疗腑病多选用 A. 原穴; B. 经穴 C. 背俞穴; D. 下合穴; E. 郄穴	What points among the te ding xue / specially designated points should be selected to treat diseases of bowels? A. yuan xue / source points / original points; B. flowing points / river points [jīng xué]; C. posterior points / back shu points / bèi shù xué; D. xia he xue / lower sea points / lower terminal points; E. xi xue / fissural or cleft points.
717	在特定穴中，治疗急性病一般选用: A. 原穴; B.络穴 C. 郄穴; D. 合穴; E. 俞穴	What points among the te ding xue / specially designated points should be selected to treat acute diseases? A. yuan xue / source points / original points; B. linking points, / collateral points [luò xué]; C. xi xue / fissural or cleft points; D. merging points / terminal points / sea points [hé xué]; E. posterior points / back shu points / bèi shù xué.
718	在头足部有同名的穴位是: A 阳关; B 三里 C. 通谷; D 五里; E 临泣.	Which of the following has one point on the head and one point on the foot by the same name? A. Yáng Guān; B. Sān Lǐ C. Tōng Gǔ; D. Wǔ Lǐ; E. Lín Qì.
719	在五输穴中，以所出为: A 井穴; B 荥穴 C. 输穴; D 经穴; E 合穴.	Among the five command points [wu shu xue]，which moves outward?: A jǐng xué / well points; B yíng xué / outpouring-points / spring-points; C. flowing points / stream points / shù xué; D flowing points / river points / jīng xué; E · hé xué / terminal-points / sea-points.
720	在五输穴中，以所行为: A 井穴; B 荥穴 C. 输穴; D 经穴; E 合穴.	Among the five command points [wu shu xue]，which flows through?: A jǐng xué / well points; B yíng xué / outpouring-points / spring-points; C. flowing points / stream points / shù xué; D flowing points / river points / jīng xué; E · hé xué / terminal-points / sea-points.
721	在五输穴中，治疗腑病的主要是: A 井穴; B 荥穴 C. 输穴; D 经穴; E 合穴.	Which of the five command points (wu shu xue) may be used to treat the diseases of bowels? A jǐng xué / well points; B yíng xué / outpouring-points / spring-points C. flowing points / stream points / shù xué; D flowing points / river points / jīng xué; E · hé xué / terminal-points / sea-points.

722	在下列各穴，除……外，都是募穴: A·中府; B·鸠尾 C. ·章门; D·期门; E·石门.	Which is NOT a gathering point (mu xue)? A. Lu1 (Zhōng Fǔ); B. R15 (Jiū Wěi); C. Lv13 (Zhāng Mén); D. Lv14 (Qí Mén); E. R5 (Shí Mén).
723	在下列络穴中，治疗癫痫的首选穴是: A.·长强 蠡沟 C. ·大包; D. ·公孙; E. ·蠡沟	Among the following linking points, / Collateral points [luò xué] 中，what should be selected to treat epilepsy? A. ·D1 [Cháng Qiáng] ·Lv5 [Lí Gōu]; C. ·Sp21 [Dà Bāo]; D. ·Sp4 [Gōng Sūn]; E. ·Lv5 [Lí Gōu]
724	在下列特定穴中，治疗腑病一般多选用: A. ·俞穴; B. ·络穴 C. ·原穴; D. ·井穴; E. ·募穴	Among the te ding xue / specially designated points, what should be selected to treat diseases of bowels? A. ·posterior points / back shu points / bèi shù xué; B. · linking points, / collateral points [luò xué]; C. ·yuan xue / source point / original point; D. ·well points [jǐng xué]; E. ·gathering points / anterior points, front mu point [mù xué].
725	在下列特定穴中，治疗腑痛宜选用: A·输穴; B·络穴 C. ·八会穴; D·下合穴; E·郄穴.	Among the following specially marked points，what may be selected to treat pain in the bowels? A·lake-points / stream-points; B·linking points, / luo points; C. ·eight influential points / ba hui xue; D·lower merging point; E·fissural point / cleft point / xi point.
726	在下列五输穴中，除……外，都是本经的母穴: A·大肠经的曲池; B·小肠经的后溪 C. ·胃经的解溪; D·胆经的临泣; E·膀胱经的至阴.	Which is NOT the mother point (mu xue) of its own meridian? A. Li11 (Qū Chí); B. Si3 (Hòu Xī); C. S41 (Jiě Xī); D. G41 (Zú Lín Qì, Lín Qì); E. B67 (Zhì Yīn).
727	在下列穴位中，对心率具有双向调整作用的主要是: A. ·足三里; B. ·内关 C. ·合谷; D. ·巨阙; E. ·神门	Which point has a dual regultion of heart rates? A. ·S36 [Zú Sān Lǐ]; B. ·P6 [Nèi Guān]; C. ·Li4 [Hé Gǔ]; D. ·R14 [Jù Què]; E. ·H7 [Shén Mén]
728	在下列穴位中，与关元穴不在一条水平线上的穴位是: A·水道; B·子户 C. ·胞门; D·子宫; E·提托.	Which of the following points is NOT on a level with R4 (Guān Yuán)? A. S28 (Shuǐ Dào); B. Zǐ Hù; C. Bāo Mén; D. Zǐ Gōng; E. Tí Tuō.
729	在下列穴组中，除……外，均为主客配穴: A. ·太渊 偏历; B. ·冲阳 公孙 C. ·京骨 大钟; D. ·神门 支正; E. ·丘墟 光明	Which is NOT a combination of host and guest [zhu ke]? A. ·Lu9 [Tài Yuān] Li6 [Piān Lì]; B. ·S42 [Chōng Yáng] Sp4 [Gōng Sūn]; C. ·B64 [Jīng Gǔ] K4 [Dà Zhōng]; D. ·H7 [Shén Mén] Si7 [Zhi Zhèng]; E. ·G40 [Qiū Xū] G37 [Guāng Míng]
730	在阳溪与曲池穴的连线上，曲池穴下2寸处的穴位是: A·偏历; B·温溜 C. ·下廉; D·上廉; E·手三里.	Draw a line connecting Li5 (Yáng Xī) and Li11 (Qū Chí), what point is located 2 Cuns below Li11 (Qū Chí)? A. Li6 (Piān Lì); B. Li7 (Wēn Liū); C. Li8 (Xià Lián); D. Li9 (Shàng Lián); E. Li10 (Shǒu Sān Lǐ).
731	在针刺操作过程中，不可向内深刺以免刺伤肺脏的肺经腧穴是:	What point on the lung meridian cannot be inserted into too deeply to avoid inserting into the lungs? A Lu1 / Zhōng Fǔ; ·; B · Lu3 / Tiān Fǔ; C. S12 [Quē Pén]; D Sp21

	穴是: A 中府; B 大府 C. 缺盆; D 大包; E 天池.	/ Dà Bāo; E · P1 / Tiān Chí.
732	针刺治疗青光眼，能使眼压下降的最好穴位是: A. 太冲; B. 行间 C. 足临泣; D. 侠溪; D.光明	What point may best be selected to treat glaucoma and also to reduce eye pressure? A. ·Lv3 [Tài Chōng]; B.Lv2 [Xíng Jiān]; C. ·G41 [Zú Lín Qì]; D. ·G43 [Xiá Xī]; D.G37 [Guāng Míng].
733	指出下面哪个俞募配穴是错误的: A. 肺俞中府; B. 肝俞期门 C. 脾俞中脘; D. 肾俞京门; E. 胆俞日月	Which is NOT a combination of shu point and mu point (back shu point and anterior mu point)? A. ·B13 [Fèi Shū] Lu1 [Zhōng Fǔ]; B. ·B18 [Gān Shū]Lv14 [Qí Mén]; C. ·B20 [Pí Shū] R12 [Zhōng Wǎn]; D. ·B23 [Shèn Shū]G25 [Jīng Mén]; E. ·B19 [Dǎn Shū]G24 [Rì Yuè]
734	治疗表里经病应首选: A ·原穴; B 络穴 C. ·八会穴; D ·募穴; E ·郄穴	Which of the following should be selected to treat the meridians forming a deep-superficial relationship with each other? A. yuan xue (original or source points); B. luo xue (linking points,); C. ba hui xue (eight meeting points); D. mu xue (gathering points); E. xi xue (fissural or C. left points).
735	治疗胎位不正应首选: A. ·足窍阴; B. ·中冲 C. ·至阴; D. ·少冲; E. ·厉兑	Which of the following should be selected to treat fetus in wrong position? A. ·G44 [Zú Qiào Yīn]; B. ·P9 [Zhōng Chōng]; C. ·B67 [Zhì Yīn]; D. ·H9 [Shào Chōng]; E. ·S45 [Lì Duì]。
736	治疗胃、心、胸病症，公孙宜配: A. 足三里; B. 中脘 C. 内关; D. 神门; E. 膻中	What point should be used in combination with Sp4 [Gōng Sūn] to treat diseases of stomach, heart, and chest? A. ·S36 [Zú Sān Lǐ]; B. ·R12 [Zhōng Wǎn];C. ·P6 [Nèi Guān]; D. ·H7 [Shén Mén]; E. ·R17 [Shān Zhōng]
737	中府是手太阴经与何经的交会穴? A. 足厥阴; B. 手厥阴 C. ，足阳明; D. 足太阴; E. 足少阴	Lu1 [Zhōng Fǔ] is a meeting point between the hand greater yin meridian / hand tai yin meridian and waht meridian? A. ·decreasing yin of foot [zu jue yin]; B. ·decreasing yin of hand [shou jue yhin]; C. bright yang of foot [zu yang ming]; D. ·greater yin of foot [zu tai yin]; E. ·lesser yin of foot [zu shao yin].
738	中极穴旁开 3 寸的穴位是: A 提托; B 维胞 C. 子宫; D 水道; E 归来.	Which point is located 3 Cuns laterally away from R3 (Zhōng Jí)? A. Tí Tuō; B. Wéi; Bāo; C. Zǐ Gōng; D. S28 (Shuǐ Dào); E. S29 (Guī Lái).
739	肘横纹中，肱二头肌腱尺侧缘的腧穴是: A. 少海; B. 小海 C. 曲泽; D. 尺泽; E. 曲池	What point is located on the elbow crease, at the edge of the ulnar side of tendons of the biceps brachii muscle? A. ·H3 [Shào Hǎi]; B. ·Si8 [Xiǎo Hǎi]; C. ·P3 [Qū Zé]; D. ·Lu5 [Chǐ Zé]; E. ·Li11 [Qū Chí]
740	筑宾在特定穴中属于: A 络穴; B 经穴 C. ·郄穴; D ，原穴; E ·八会穴.	What specially marked point does K9 (Zhú; Bīn) belong to? A. luo xue (linking point); B. jing xue (flowing point, river point); C. xi xue (fissural or cleft point); D. yuan xue (original or source point); E. ba hui xue (eight meeting points).
741	足三阳经输穴主治病症相同的是: A 神志病; B 胃肠病 C. 眼病; D 咽喉病; E 前阴病.	What are the common therapeutic effects among the points on the three yang meridians of foot? A. emotional and mental disorders; B. gastrointestinal disorders; C. eye disorders; D. throat disorders; E. gential disorders.

742	足少阳胆经的率谷穴,位于耳尖直上的哪个部位? A·与发际交界处; B·入发际 0.5 寸; C. ·入发际 1 寸; D·入发际 1·5 寸; E·入发际 2 寸.	In what region directly above the apex of ear is G8 (Shuài Gŭ) located? A. on the border of hairline; B. 0.5 Cun inside the hairline; C. 1 Cun inside the hairline; D. 1.5 Cuns inside the hairline; E. 2 Cuns inside the hairline.
743	足少阳胆经阳交穴的位置是: A·外踝上 7 寸，腓骨前缘; B·外踝上 7 寸，外丘穴后 1 寸处 C. ·外踝尖直上 7 寸; D·外踝上 7 寸，外丘穴前 1 寸处; E·以上都不是.	Where is G35 (Yáng Jiāo) located? A. 7 Cuns above lateral malleolus, on the anterior border of fibula; B. 7 Cuns above lateral malleolus, 1 Cun behind G36 (Wài Qiū); C. 7 Cuns directly above the tip of lateral malleolus; D. 7 Cuns above lateral malleolus, 1 Cun in front of G36 (Wài Qiū); E. none of the above.
744	足太阳膀胱经的下合穴为: A·下巨虚; B·委阳 C. ·委中 D·阳陵泉 E·上巨虚	What is the lower merging point on the foot greater yang bladder meridian? A · S39 / Xià Jù Xū; B39 / Wĕi Yáng; C. B40 / Wĕi Zhōng; D · G34 / Yáng Líng Quán; E · S37 / Shàng Jù Xū.
745	足太阳膀胱经的原穴是: A 足通谷; B 束骨 C. ·昆仑; D 京骨; E 委中.	Which is the yuán xué / starting-point / source-point of the foot greater yang bladder meridian? A. B66 / Tōng Gŭ / Zú Tōng Gŭ; B. B65 / Shù Gŭ; C. B60 / Kūn Lún; D. B64 / Jīng Gŭ; E. B40 / Wĕi Zhōng.
746	足太阳膀胱经位于后头部的腧穴是: A.五处; B 承光 C. 通天; D 络却.	Which of the following points on the foot greater yang bladder meridian is located in the back of head? A. B5 / Wŭ Chestù; B. B6 / Chéng Guāng; C. B7 / Tōng Tiān; D. B8 / Luò Què.
747	足阳明胃经循行线上的 "客主人"是指: A·颊车穴; B·下关穴 C. ·上关穴; D·耳门穴; E. 听宫穴	It is said that the stomach meridian passes through Ke-Zhu-Ren, what point does Ke-Zhu-Ren refer to? A. S6 (Jiá Chē); B. S7 (Xià Guān); C. G3 (Shàng Guān); D. Sj21 (Ĕr Mén); E. Si19 (Tīng Gōng).
748	足阳明胃经在大腿部的腧穴均位于: A 股骨大转子与股骨外上髁的连线上; B·股骨大转子与髌底外侧端的连线上 C. 髂前上棘与髌底外侧端的连线上; D 耻骨联合上缘与股骨内上髁的连线上; E 耻骨联合上缘与髌底内侧端的连线上.	How are the points on the foot bright yang stomach meridian distributed in the thigh region? A. they are distributed on the line connecting greater trochantera and lateral epicondyle of femur; B. they are distributed on the line connecting greater trochanter and the lateral side of patella; C. they are distributed on the line connecting anterior superior iliac spine and the lateral side of patella; D. they are distributed on the line connecting upper edge of pubic symphysis and medial epicondyle of femur; E. they are distributed on the line connecting upper edge of pubic symphysis and the medial side of patella.

13-3	表面解剖与针灸穴位	Surface Anatomy and Acupuncture Points	749-1066

749	白环俞内侧 1 寸，当第四骶后孔中，是取何穴位？A. B33 [中髎]; B. B32 [次髎]; C. B35 [会附]; D. D1 [長強]; E. B34 [下髎].	On the medial side of B30 [Bái Huán Shū] and 1 Cun away from it, inside the 4th posterior sacral foramen. What is this point? A. B33 [Zhōng Liáo]; B. B32 [Cì Liáo]; C. B35 [Huì Ang]; D. D1 [Cháng Qiáng]; E. B34 [Xià Liáo].
750	膀胱俞内侧 0.8 寸，当第二骶散后孔中，是取何穴位？A. B33 [中髎]; B. B32 [次髎]; C. B35 [会附]; D. D1 [長強]; E. B34 [下髎]	On the medial side of; B29 (pangguangshu), 0.8 Cun from it; inside the 2nd posterior sacral foramen. What is this point? A. B33 [Zhōng Liáo]; B. B32 [Cì Liáo]; C. B35 [Huì Ang]; D. D1 [Cháng Qiáng]; E. B34 [Xià Liáo]
751	鼻尖端正中，是取何穴位？A. S1 [承泣]; B. D25 [素髎]; C. S3 [巨髎]; D. Li20 [迎香]; E. S2 [四白].	In the middle of the tip of the nose. What is this point? A. S1 [Chéng Qì]; B. D25 [Sù Liáo]; C. S3 [Jù Liáo]; D. Li20 [Yíng Xiāng]; E. S2 [Sì Bái].
752	鼻翼旁 0.5 寸，在与鼻翼外缘中点平齐的鼻唇沟中，是取何穴位？A. S1 [承泣]; B. D25 [素髎]; C. S3 [巨髎]; D. Li20 [迎香]; E. S2 [四白].	0.5 Cun (5 fens) laterally from the ala nasi (nose wing), in the nasolabial sulcus; on a level with the midpoint of the lateral side of ala nasi. What is this point? A. S1 [Chéng Qì]; B. D25 [Sù Liáo]; C. S3 [Jù Liáo]; D. Li20 [Yíng Xiāng]; E. S2 [Sì Bái].
753	鬓发前缘直上平神庭旁开 4.5 寸，是取何穴位？A. G13 [本神]; B. G15 [頭臨泣]C. B3 [眉冲]; D. B4 [曲差]; E. S8 [頭維]	Directly above the anterior edge of hair on temple, on a level with D24 (shenting) and 4.5 Cun laterally away from D24. What is this point? A. G13 [Běn Shén]; B. G15 [Tóu Lín Qì];C. B3 [Méi Chōng]; D. B4 [Qū Chestā]; E. S8 [Tóu Wěi]
754	承光后 1.5 寸，是取何穴位？A; B9 [玉枕]; B. B8 [絡却]; C. B6 [承光]; D. B5 [五處]; E. B7 [通天]	1.5 Cuns behind, Chengguang (B6). What is this point? A. B9 [Yù Zhěn]; B. B8 [Luò Què]; C. B6 [Chéng Guāng]; D. B5 [Wǔ Chestù]; E. B7 [Tōng Tiān]
755	承泣直下 0.3 寸，眶下孔处，是取何穴位？A. S1 [承泣]; B. D25 [素髎]; C. S3 [巨髎]; D. Li20 [迎香]; E. S2 [四白].	0.3 Cun below S1 (chengqi), in the infraorbital foramen. What is this point? A. S1 [Chéng Qì]; B. D25 [Sù Liáo]; C. S3 [Jù Liáo]; D. Li20 [Yíng Xiāng]; E. S2 [Sì Bái].
756	承山外側斜下 1 寸，腓肠肌外側（与阳交。外丘相平)，是取何穴位？A; B57 [承山]; B. B56 [承筋]; C. G39 [懸鍾]; D. Sp6 [三陰交]; E. B58 [飛揚].	7 Cuns above Kunlun (B60), on the lateral side of the gastrocnemius muscle. What is this point? A; B57 [Chéng Shān]; B. B56 [Chéng Jīn]; C. G39 [Xuán Zhōng]; D. Sp6 [Sān Yīn Jiāo]; E. B58 [Feī Yáng].
757	尺骨鹰嘴上 1 寸凹陷中，是取何穴位？A. Sj10 [天井]; B. Si8 [小海]; C. Lu7 [列缺]; D. Lu8 [經渠]; E. Li11 [曲池]	In the depression 1 Cun above the olecranon. What is this point? A. Sj10 [Tiān Jǐng]; B. Si8 [Xiǎo Hǎi]; C. Lu7 [Liè Quē]; D. Lu8 [Jīng Qú]; E. Li11 [Qū Chí].
758	尺骨鹰嘴与肱骨内上髁之间，是取何穴位？A. Sj10 [天井]; B. Si8 [小海]; C. Lu7 [列缺]; D. Lu8 [經渠]; E. Li11 [曲池]	In between the ulnar olecranon and the medial epicondyle of humerus. What is this point? A. Sj10 [Tiān Jǐng]; B. Si8 [Xiǎo Hǎi]; C. Lu7 [Liè Quē]; D. Lu8 [Jīng Qú]; E. Li11 [Qū Chí]
759	尺骨鹰嘴直上 2 寸(天井上 1 寸)，是取何穴位？A. Li14 [臂臑]; B. Sj12 [消濼]; C. G28 [維道]; D. Sj11 [清冷淵]; E. Sj13 [臑會]	2 Cuns directly above the tip of the olecranon (1 Cun above Tianjing=Sj10). What is this point? A. Li14 [Bì Nào]; B. Sj12 [Xiāo Luò]; C. G28 [Wéi Dào]; D. Sj11 [Qīng Lěng Yuān]; E. Sj13 [Nǎo Huì]

760	除哪个穴外，余穴均与脐相平 A.腹结; B.带脉 C.，大横 D 天枢	Which of the following points is NOT on a level with the umbilicus? A. Sp14 (Fù Jié); B. G26 (Dài Mài); C. Sp15 (Dà Héng); D. S25 (Tiān Shū).
761	垂臂合腋，腋后皺襞直上 1 寸，是取何穴位？A. Sj16 [天牖]; B. Si9 [肩貞]; C. Si11 [天宗]; D. Si17 [天容]; E. Si10 [臑輸].	With arms down and armpit closed, 1 Cun above the posterior axillary fold. What is this point? A. Sj16 [Tiān Yǒu]; B. Si9 [Jiān Zhēn]; C. Si11 [Tiān Zōng]; D. Si17 [Tiān Róng]; E. Si10 [Nào Shū].
762	次髎穴刺入骶后孔时，刺中的结构是: A 第2骶神经干和第2骶神经后支; B 第2骶神经干和第2骶神经前支 C. 第3骶神经干和第3骶神经后支 D 第3骶神经干和第3骶神经前支	What nerve is being inserted into when we insert a needle at B32 [Cì Liáo] to reach posterior sacral foramen? A. 2nd sacral nerve trunk and posterior branch of 2nd sacral nerve; B 2nd sacral nerve trunk and anterior branch of 2nd sacral nerve; C. 3rd sacral nerve trunk and posterior branch of 3rd sacral nerve; D 3rd sacral nerve trunk and anterior branch of 3rd sacral nerve.
763	大腿后側中央承扶下 6 寸，是取何穴位？A. G32 [中瀆]; B. G30 [環跳]; C. B37 [殷門]; D. G31 [風市]; E. B38 [浮郄]	6 Cuns below Chengfu (B36), in the center of the back of thigh, on the line connecting the gluteal fold and the popliteal fold; what is this point? A. G32 [Zhōng Dū]; B. G30 [Huán Tiào]; C. B37 [Yīn Mén]; D. G31 [Fēng Shì]; E. B38 [Fú Xī]
764	大腿外側中间，膕横紋水平线上 7 寸，是取何穴位？A. G32 [中瀆]; B. G30 [環跳]; C. B37 [殷門]; D. G31 [風市]; E. B36 [承扶]	On the lateral side of thigh, 7 Cuns above the patella (with distance between greater trochanter & knee joint as 19 Cuns). On the line connecting the anterior superior iliac spine and the head of fibula, it can be reached by the tip of middle finger when the hand is down. What is this point? A. G32 [Zhōng Dū]; B. G30 [Huán Tiào]; C. B37 [Yīn Mén]; D. G31 [Fēng Shì]; E. B36 [Chéng Fú]
765	大椎旁开 2 寸，是取何穴位？A. Si13 [曲垣]; B. Si15 [肩中輸]; C. Si12 [秉風]; D. G21 [肩井]; E. Si14 [肩外輸]	2 Cuns laterally from D14 (dazhui). What is this point? A. Si13 [Qū Yuān]; B. Si15 [Jiān Zhōng Shū]; C. Si12 [Bǐng Fēng]; D. G21 [Jiān Jǐng]; E. Si14 [Jiān Wài Shū]
766	大椎穴位于: A 第7颈椎棘突之上方; B 第7颈椎棘突之尖端 C. 第7胸椎棘突下方 D 第7颈椎棘突下方.	Where is D14 [Dà Zhuī] located? A. above the spinous process of 7th cervical vertebra; B at the tip of the spinous process of 7th cervical vertebra; C. below the spinous process of 7th thoracic vertebra; D below the spinous process of 7th cervical vertebra.
767	地机直下寸，当三阴交上 3 寸，是取何穴位？A. Sp7 [漏谷]; B. Lv5 [蠡溝]; C. S38 [條口]; D. K9 [筑賓]; E. Lv6 [中都]	With the distance between the tip of medial malleolus (inner ankle) and Yinlingquan=Sp9 as 13 Cuns, this point is located 6 Cuns above the medial malleolus. What is this point? A. Sp7 [Lòu Gǔ]; B. Lv5 [Lí Gōu]; C. S38 [Tiáo Kǒu]; D. K9 [Zhú; Bīn]; E. Lv6 [Zhōng Dū]
768	第二腰椎棘突下，旁开 3 寸的穴位是: · A 气海俞; B 大肠俞 C. 肾俞; D 志室; E 三焦俞.	What point is located 3 Cuns laterally from the lower end of the spinous process of the 2nd. lumbar vertebra? A; B24 (Qì Hǎi Shū); B. B25 (Dà Cháng Shū); C. B23 (Shèn Shū); D. B52 (Zhì Shì); E. B22 (Sān Jiāo Shū).
769	第五胸椎棘突下，旁开 3 寸的穴位是:	What point is located 3 Cuns laterally from the lower end. of the spinous process of the 5th thoracic vertebra?.

	A 神道; B 神堂 C. 灵台; D 心俞; E. 厥阴俞.	A. D11 (Shén Dào); B. B44 (Shén Táng); C. D10 (Líng Tái); D.B15 (Xīn Shū); EB14 (Jué Yīn Shū).
770	第一腰椎棘下，旁开 3 寸的穴位是: A 肓门; B 悬枢 C. 三焦俞; D 意舍; E 胃仓.	What point is located 3 Cuns laterally from the lower end of the spinous process of the 1st lumbar vertebra? A; B51 (Huāng Mén); B. D5 (Xuán Shū);C. B22 (Sān Jiāo Shū); D. B45 (Yì Xī); E. B50 (Wèi Cāng).
771	第一跖骨基底部前下缘白肉际，是取何穴位？A. Sp4 [公孫]; B. B64 [京骨]; C. S42 [沖陽]; D. B63 [金門]; E. G41 [足臨泣]	At the juncture of the white and dark muscles on the anterior inferior border of the base of 1st metatarsal bone. What is this point? A. Sp4 [Gōng Sūn]; B. B64 [Jīng Gǔ]; C. S42 [Chōng Yáng]; D. B63 [Jīn Mén]; E. G41 [Zú Lín Qì ,Lín Qì]
772	定取腰部穴位标志的髂嵴间平线，相当于: A 12 椎; B 13 椎 C. 14 椎; D 15 椎; E. 16 椎	The inter-iliac-crest line, which is used as a landmark to locate the points in the lumbar region，is on a level with: A. 12th vertibra; B. 13th vertibra; C. 14th vertibra; D. 15th vertibra; E. 16th vertibra.
773	犊鼻下 3 寸，是取何穴位？A. S37 [上巨虛]; B. S36 [足三里]; C. S40 [丰隆]; D. S39 [下巨虛]; E. S38 [條口]	3 Cuns below Dubi=S35 (there are 16 Cuns between S35 & Jiexi=S41), 1 Cun laterally from the anterior border of tibia. What is this point? A. S37 [Shàng Jù Xū]; B. S36 [Zú Sān Lǐ]; C. S40 [Fēng Lóng]; D. S39 [Xià Jù Xū]; E. S38 [Tiáo Kǒu]
774	耳尖正上方，颞颥部入发际处，是取何穴位？A. D23 [上星]; B. Sj20 [角孫]; C. Sj19 [顱息]; D. Sj18 [瘛脈]; E. D24 [神庭]	In the temple region, inside the hairline and directly above the apex of auricle. What is this point? A. D23 [Shàng Xīng]; B. Sj20 [Jiǎo Sūn]; C. Sj19 [Lú Xī]; D. Sj18 [Chì Mài]; E. D24 [Shén Tíng]
775	耳屏正中前方凹陷中，是取何穴位？A. Sj21 [耳門]; B. G2 [聽會]; C. S5 [大迎]; D. Sj17 [翳風]; E. Si19 [聽宮]	In the depression in front of the tragus. What is this point? A. Sj21 [Ěr Mén]; B. G2 [Tīng Huì]; C. S5 [Dà Yíng]; D. Sj17 [Yì Fēng]; E. Si19 [Tīng Gōng]
776	耳前方，颧弓与下颌切迹所形成的凹陷中的穴位是: A 承泣 B 四白 C 地仓 D 颊车 E 下关	What point is in front the ear, in the depression between the inferior border of the zygomatic arch and the mandibular notch? A · S1 / Chéng Qì; B · S2 / Sì Bái; C. · S4 / Dì Cāng D · S6 / Jiá Chē; E · S7 / Xià Guān.
777	耳前顴弓上缘，下关直上，是取何穴位？A. G3 [上關]; B. S6 [頰車]; C. R24 [承漿]; D. S7 [下關]; E. Si18 [顴髎]	In front of the ear, on the upper border of the zygomatic arch, directly above Xiaguan=S7. What is this point? A. G3 [Shàng Guān]; B. S6 [Jiá Chē]; C. R24 [Chéng Jiàng]; D. S7 [Xià Guān]; E. Si18 [Quán Liáo]
778	腓骨小头前下方凹陷中，是取何穴位？A. G34 [陽陵泉]; B. G33 [膝陽關]; C. S35 [犢鼻]; D. B39 [委陽]; E. B40 [委中]	With the knee joint half bent, in the depression on the anterior-inferior side of the highest projection of the head of fibula, (capitulum fibulae), at the tibiofibular joint (articulatio tibiofibularis). What is this point? A. G34 [Yáng Líng Quán]; B. G33 [Xī Yáng Guān]; C. S35 [Dú Bí]; D. B39 [Wěi Yáng]; E. B40 [Wěi Zhōng]
779	肺俞穴位于: A 第2胸椎棘突下，旁开0.5寸; B 第2胸椎棘突下，旁开1.5寸 C. 第3胸椎棘突下，旁开0.5寸; D 第3胸椎棘突下，旁开1.5寸.	Where is B13 [Fèi Shū] located? A below the process of 2nd thoraci vertebra，0.5 Cun lateral to it; B below the process of 2nd thoraci vertebra,1.5 Cun lateral to it; C. below the process of 3rd thoraci vertebra，0.5 Cun lateral to it; D below the process of 3rd thoracic vertebra，1.5 Cun lateral to it.
780	分布于风池穴处的皮神	What cutaneous nerve is distributed at G20 [Fēng

	经是: A 第1颈神经的后支; B 第2颈神经的后支 C. 枕小神经; D 耳大神经.	Chí]? A posterior branch of 1st cervical nerve; B posterior branch of 2nd cervical nerve; C. lesser occipital nerve; D. great auricular nerve.
781	分布于合谷穴处的皮神经是: A 尺神经手背支; B 桡神经浅支 C. 正中神经; D 前臂外侧皮神经.	What cutaneous nerve is distributed at Li4 [Hé Gǔ]? A back of hand branch of ulnar nerve; B superficial branch of radial nerve; C. median nerve; D. cutaneous nerve of lateral side of forearm.
782	分布于肩髃穴处的皮神经是: A 前臂外侧皮神经; B 锁骨上神经 C. 肩胛上神经; D 前肩胛下神经.	What cutaneous nerve is distributed at Li15 [Jiān Yú]? A cutaneous nerve of lateral side of forearm; B supraclavicular nerve; C. suprascapular nerve; D anterior subscapular nerve.
783	分布于睛明穴处的皮神经是: A动眼神经; B 视神经 C. 三叉神经; D 面神经.	What cutaneous nerve is distributed at B1 [Jīng Míng]? A. oculomotor nerve; B optic nerve (2nd; cranial); C. trigeminal nerve; D facial nerve
784	分布于内关穴处的皮神经是: A. 正中神经的分支; B 前臂内侧皮神经 C. 前臂外侧皮神经; D 前臂内侧皮神经和前臂外侧皮神经.	What cutaneous nerve is distributed at P6 [Nèi Guān]? A. branch of median nerve; B cutaneous nerve of medial forearm C. cutaneous nerve of lateral forearm; D. cutaneous nerve of medial and lateral forearm.
785	分布于三阴交穴的皮神经是: A. 腓肠内侧皮神经; B 腓肠外侧皮神经 C. 隐神经; D 股后皮神经.	What cutaneous nerve is distributed at Sp6 [Sān Yīn Jiāo]? A cutaneous nerve of medial gastrocnemius muscle (calf); B cutaneous nerve of lateral gastrocnemius muscle (calf); C. saphenous nerve; D. cutaneous nerve in the back of femur.
786	分布于听宫穴处的皮神经是: A 眼神经; B 上颌神经 C. 下颌神经; D 耳大神经.	What cutaneous nerve is distributed at Si19 [Tīng Gōng]? A. ophthalmic branch of the trigeminus nerve; B maxillary branch of the trigeminus nerve; C. mandibular branch of the trigeminus nerve; D great auricular nerve.
787	分布于委中穴处的皮神经是: A 坐骨神经; B 胫神经 C. 闭孔神经; D 股后皮神经.	What cutaneous nerve is distributed at B40 [Wěi Zhōng]? A. sciatic nerve; B tibial nerve cobturator nerve D; cutaneous nerve in the back of femur.
788	分布于中髎穴的皮神经是: A臀上神经; B 臀上皮神经 C. 臀中皮神经; D 臀下皮神经.	What cutaneous nerve is distributed at B33 [Zhōng Liáo]? A superior gluteal nerve; B superior gluteal cutaneous nerve; C. middle gluteal cutaneous nerve; D inferior gluteal cutaneous nerve.
789	分布于中脘穴的皮神经为: A第4对肋间神经; B 第6对肋间神经 C. 第8对肋间神经; D 第10对肋间神经.	What cutaneous nerve is distributed at R12 [Zhōng Wǎn]? A. 4th pair of Intercostal Nerve; B 6th pair of Intercostal Nerve; C. 8th pair of Intercostal Nerve; D 10th pair of Intercostal Nerve.
790	分布于足三里穴的皮神	What cutaneous nerve is distributed at S36 [Zú Sān

	经是: A 腓肠内侧皮神经; B 腓肠外侧皮神经 C. 隐神经; D 腓浅神经.	Lǐ]? A cutaneous nerve of medial gastrocnemius muscle (calf); B. cutaneous nerve of lateral gastrocnemius muscle (calf); C. saphenous nerve; D. Superficial Peroneal Nerve
791	风池穴位于: A 隆椎棘突和肩峰连线之中点; B 耳垂和乳突之间，平枕外隆凸之下 C. 斜方肌和胸锁乳突肌之间，平枕外隆凸之下; D 斜方肌和肩胛提肌之间，平枕外隆凸之下.	Where is G20 [Fēng Chí] located? A. midpoint of the line connecting spinous process of prominent vertebra and acromion of scapula; B in between ear lobe and mastoid process，on a level with inferior border of external occipital protuberance; C. in between trapezius muscles and sternocleidomastoid muscle, on a level with inferior border of external occipital protuberance; D in between trapezius muscles and levator muscle of scapula，on a level with inferior border of external occipital protuberance.
792	风市下 2 寸，是取何穴位？A. G32 [中瀆]; B. G30 [環跳]; C. B37 [殷門]; D. B38 [浮郄]; E. B36 [承扶]	5 Cuns above the patella, 2 Cuns below Fengshi=G31, on the line connecting the anterior superior iliac spine and the head of fibula. What is this point? A. G32 [Zhōng Dū]; B. G30 [Huán Tiào]; C. B37 [Yǐn Mén]; D. B38 [Fú Xī]; E. B36 [Chéng Fú]
793	扶突下 1 寸，胸锁乳突肌后缘，是取何穴位？A. R23 [廉泉]; B. S10 [水突]; C. Li17 [天鼎]; D. Si17 [天容]; E. Si16 [天窗]	1 Cun below Li18 (futu), on the posterior border of the sternocleidomastoideus. What is this point? A. R23 [Lián Quán]; B. S10 [Shuǐ Tū]; C. Li17 [Tiān Dǐng]; D. Si17 [Tiān Róng]; E. Si16 [Tiān; Chuāng]
794	复溜前约 0.5 寸，与胫骨后缘之间，是取何穴位？A. K6 [照海]; B. K8 [交信]; C. Lv4 [中封]; D. Sp5 [商丘]; E. B59 [跗陽]	In front of Fuliu=K7, 5 fens before Fuliu=K7, 2 Cuns above medial malleolus (inner ankle), on the medial border of tibia, 1 Cun below Sanyinjiao=Sp6 slightly behind it. What is this point? A. K6 [Zhào Hǎi]; B. K8 [Jiāo Xìn]; C. Lv4 [Zhōng Fēng]; D. Sp5 [Shāng Qiū]; E. B59 [Fū Yáng]
795	股二头肌腱内缘，委阳上 1 寸，是取何穴位？A. Sp9 [陰陵泉]; B. B38 [浮郄]; C. Lv8 [曲泉]; D. K10 [陰谷]; E. Lv7 [膝關].	On the lateral side of the popliteal fossa, 1 Cun above Weiyang (B39), close to the medial border of the biceps femoris. What is this point? A. Sp9 [Yīn Líng Quán]; B. B38 [Fú Xī]; C. Lv8 [Qū Quán]; D. K10 [Yīn Gǔ]; E. Lv7 [Xī Guān].
796	关于肺俞穴的正确说法是: A属于手太阴肺经; B 属于督脉穴位 C. 为第3、4胸神经前支分布区域; D 为第3、4胸神经后支分布区域.	Which is an accurate description of Fèi Shū? A a point on lung meridian; B a point on du mai [governing meridian]; C. in the distribution zone of the 3rd and 4th anterior branches of thoracic nerve; D. in the distribution zone of the 3rd and 4th posterior branches of thoracic nerve.
797	光明下 1 寸(外踝高点上 4 寸)稍前处，是取何穴位？A. G35 [陽交]; B. B58 [飛揚]; C. G38 [陽輔]; D. G36 [外丘]; E. B55 [合陽].	4 Cuns above lateral malleolus (outer ankle), in front of the fibula. What is this point? A. G35 [Yáng Jiāo]; B. B58 [Feī Yáng]; C. G38 [Yáng Fǔ]; D. G36 [Wài Qiū]; E. B55 [Hé Yáng].
798	腘窝中央，当股二头肌腱与半膜肌腱的中央，是取何穴位？A. G34 [陽陵泉]; B. G33 [膝陽關]; C. S35 [犢	In the middle of popliteal fossa. What is this point? A. G34 [Yáng Líng Quán]; B. G33 [Xī Yáng Guān]; C. S35 [Dú Bí]; D. B39 [Wěi Yáng]; E. B40 [Wěi Zhōng]

	鼻]; D. B39 [委陽]; E. B40 [委中]	
799	合谷穴在手背第1、2掌骨之间，约平: A 第1掌骨底; B 第2掌骨底 C. 第2掌骨中点; D 第2掌骨头	Li4 [Hé Gǔ] is located between 1st and 2nd metacarpal bones on the back of hand, about on a level with: A base of 1st metacarpal bone; B base of 2nd metacarpal bone; C. midpoint of 2nd metacarpal bone; D. head of 2nd metacarpal bone.
800	合阳与承山之间，腓肠肌肌腹的中央，是取何穴位？A. K7 [復溜]; B. B56 [承筋]; C. G39 [懸鍾]; D. Sp6 [三陰交]; E. B58 [飛揚].	In between Heyang (B55) and Chengshan (B57), in the middle of belly of the gastrocnemius. What is this point? A. K7 [Fù Liū]; B. B56 [Chéng Jīn]; C. G39 [Xuán Zhōng]; D. Sp6 [Sān Yīn Jiāo]; E. B58 [Feī Yáng].
801	和玉枕、脑户相平，下对风池，是取何穴位？A. G19 [腦空]; B. G18 [承靈]; C. G16 [目窗]; D.B10 [天柱]; E. G17 [正營]	On a level with inion and D17 (Naofu), directly above G20 (fengchi). What is this point? A. G19 [Nǎo Kōng]; B. G18 [Chéng Líng]; C. G16 [Mù Chuāng];D.B10 [Tiān Zhù]; E. G17 [Zhèng Yíng].
802	喉结旁开 1.5 寸，是取何穴位？A. R22 [天突]; B. S11 [氣舍]; C. S9 [人迎]; D. S12 [缺盆]; E. G20 [風池]	1.5 Cun laterally away from laryngeal prominence. What is this point? A. R22 [Tiān Tū]; B. S11 [Qì Shě]; C. S9 [Rén Yíng]; D. S12 [Quē Pén]; E. G20 [Fēng Chí]
803	喉结旁开 1.5 寸，胸锁乳突肌前缘颈总动脉应手处，是取何穴位？A. R22 [天突]; B. S11 [氣舍]; C. S9 [人迎]; D. S12 [缺盆]; E. G20 [風池]	1.5 Cun laterally away from the laryngeal prominence, on the anterior side of the sternocleidomastoideus, on the throbbing spot of arteria carotis communis. What is this point? A. R22 [Tiān Tū]; B. S11 [Qì Shě]; C. S9 [Rén Yíng]; D. S12 [Quē Pén]; E. G20 [Fēng Chí].
804	喉结旁开 3.5 寸;当扶突斜上方约 0.5 寸胸锁乳突肌后缘，是取何穴位？A. R23 [廉泉]; B. S10 [水突]; C. Li17 [天鼎]; D. Li18 [扶突]; E. Si16 [天窗]	3.5 Cuns laterally from the laryngeal prominence, slantingly 0.5 Cun above Li18 (futu), on the posterior border of the sternocleidomastoideus. What is this point? A. R23 [Lián Quán]; B. S10 [Shuǐ Tū]; C. Li17 [Tiān Dǐng]; D. Li18 [Fú Tū]; E. Si16 [Tiān Chuāng]
805	喉结旁开 3 寸(人迎后 1.5 寸)，当胸锁乳突肌两头之间，是取何穴位？A. R23 [廉泉]; B. S10 [水突]; C. Li17 [天鼎]; D. Li18 [扶突]; E. Si16 [天窗]	3 Cuns laterally from the center of Adam's apple (1.5 Cun behind S9 (renying), in between two heads of sternocleidomastoid muscle (sternum head and clavicle head). What is this point? A. R23 [Lián Quán]; B. S10 [Shuǐ Tū]; C. Li17 [Tiān Dǐng]; D. Li18 [Fú Tū]; E. Si16 [Tiān Chuāng]
806	喉结旁开 3 寸，胸锁乳突肌的胸骨头与锁骨头之间的穴位是: A.扶突; B.水突 C. 人迎; D 大迎.	What point is located 3 Cuns on the lateral side of laryngeal prominence in between the two heads of the sternocleidomastoid muscle (sternum head and clavicle head) A. Li18 (Fú Tū); B. S10 (Shuǐ Tū); C. S9 (Rén Yíng); D. S5 (Dà Yíng).
807	華佗夹脊穴的定位方法是: A 第一胸椎至第四骶椎各椎棘突下旁开 0.5 寸; B 第一胸椎至第五腰椎各椎棘突下旁开 0.5 寸 C. 第一胸椎至第十二胸椎各椎棘突下旁开 0.5 寸; D 第七颈椎至第十二胸椎各椎棘突下	Where is Huá Tuó Jiā Jí located? A. situated. 5 fens laterally away from the region below the spinous process, from the spinous process of the 1st thoracic vertebra downward to the spinous process of the 4th sacral vertebra; B. situated 5 fens laterally away from the region below the spinous process, from the spinous process of the 1st thoracic vertebra downward to the

	旁开 0·5 寸; E 第一颈椎至第五腰椎各椎棘突下旁开 0·5 寸.	spinous process of the 5th lumbar vertebra; C. situated 5 fens laterally away from the region below the spinous process, from the spinous process of the 1st thoracic vertebra downward to the spinous process of the 12th thoracic vertebra; D. situated. 5 fens laterally away from the region below the spinous process, from the spinous process of the 7th cervical vertebra downward to the spinous process of the 12th thoracic vertebra; E. situated. 5 fens laterally away from the region below the spinous process, from the spinous process of the 1st cervical vertebra downward to the spinous process of the 5th lumbar vertebra.
808	环跳穴位于股骨大转子与何解剖位置连线上？ A 股骨大转子与骶角连线的外 2 / 3 与内 1 / 3 交界处; B 股骨大转子与骶角连线的外 1 / 3 与内 2 / 3 交界处 C. 股骨大转子与尾骨连线的中点 D 股骨大转子与骶管裂孔连线的外 2 / 3 与内 1 / 3 交界处 E 股骨大转子与骶管裂孔连线的外 1 / 3 与内 2 / 3 交界处	G30 (Huán Tiào) is located on the line connecting greater trochanter and what anatomical landmark? A. on the line connecting greater trochanter and sacral angle, lateral 2 / 3 and medial 1 / 3; B. on the line connecting greater trochanter and sacral angle, lateral 1 / 3 and medial 2 / 3; C. on the midpoint of the line connecting greater trochanter and coccyx; D. on the line connecting greater trochanter and sacral hiatus, lateral 2 / 3 and medial 1 / 3; E. on the line connecting greater trochanter and sacral hiatus, lateral 1 / 3 and medical 2 / 3.
809	间使上 2 寸，是取何穴位？ A. P6 [內關]; B. P4 [郄門]; C. H6 [陰郄 D. H4 [靈道]; E. Lu6 [孔最]	2 Cun above P5 (jianshi). What is this point? A. P6 [Nèi Guān]; B. P4 [Xī Mén]; C. H6 [Yīn Xī]; D. H4 [Líng Dào]; E. Lu6 [Kǒng Zuì]
810	肩井与曲垣连线的中点，当肩胛骨的内上角端，是取何穴位？A. Li16 [巨骨]; B. B31 [上髎]; C. Sj14 [肩髎]; D. Li15 [肩髃]; E. Sj15 [天髎]	At the superior-medial angle of the scapula, on the midpoint of the line connecting Jianjing=g21 and Quyuan=Si13. What is this point? A. Li16 [Jù Gǔ]; B. B31 [Shàng Liáo]; C. Sj14 [Jiān Liáo]; D. Li15 [Jiān Yú]; E. Sj15 [Tiān Liáo]
811	肩外俞的位置在: A.第一胸椎棘突下，旁开 2 寸; B.第一胸椎棘突下，旁开 3 寸 C.第七胸椎棘突下，旁开 3 寸 D，第七胸椎棘突下，旁开 2 寸	Where is Si14 (Jiān Wài Shū) located? A. below the spinous process of 1st thoracic vertebra, 2 Cuns laterally away from it; B. below the spinous process of 1st thoracic vertebra, 3 Cuns laterally away from it; C. below the spinous process of 7th thoracic vertebra, 3 Cuns laterally away from it; D. below the spinous process of 7th thoracic vertebra, 2 Cuns laterally away from it.
812	肩贞直上，肩胛岗下缘凹陷中，是取何穴位？A. Sj16 [天牖]; B. Si13 [曲垣]; C. Si11 [天宗]; D. Si17 [天容]; E. Si10 [臑輸].	Directly above Jianzhen=Si9, in the depression below the inferior edge of the spine of the scapula. What is this point? A. Sj16 [Tiān Yǒu]; B. Si13 [Qū Yuān]; C. Si11 [Tiān Zōng]; D. Si17 [Tiān Róng]; E. Si10 [Nào Shū].
813	简便取穴法中，垂手贴腿当中指端处的穴位是: A. 伏兔; B. 阴市 C. 中渚; D. 膝阳关; E. 风市	By the; C. onvenient method of locating point, let the patient stand straight with hands down and attached to the thigh, this point is the resting place of the tip the middle finger. What is this point? A. S32 [Fú Tù]; B. S33 [Yīn Shì]; C. Sj3 [Zhōng Zhǔ]; D. G33 [Yáng Guān, Xī Yáng Guān]; E. G31 [Fēng Shì]

814	解溪穴位于足背踝关节横纹中央，当在: A.踇长与趾长伸肌腱之间; B.踇长与趾总伸肌腱之间 C. 踇长与趾短伸肌腱之间 D 趾长与趾总伸肌腱之间	S41 (Jiě Xī) is located in the middle of the crease of the ankle joint on the dorusm of foot, in between: A. extensor hallucis longus and extensor digitorum longus; B. extensor hallucis longus and common extensor muscle of toe; C. extensor hallucis longus and short exensor muscle of toe; D. long extensor muscle of toe and common extensor muscle of toe.
815	由池穴的正确定位是: A 肘横纹上，肱二头肌腱的桡侧缘; B 肘横纹上，肱二头肌腱的尺侧缘 C. 肘横纹外侧端，肱二头肌腱的桡侧缘与肱骨外上髁连线中点; D 肘横纹内侧端，肱二头肌腱的尺侧缘与肱骨内上髁连线中点; E 肘横纹外侧端，肱二头肌腱的桡侧缘与尺骨鹰嘴连线中点.	Where is the accurate location of Li11 [Qū Chí]? A on the elbow crease，on the radial side of triceps brachii (lateral head of triceps brachii); B on the elbow crease，on the ulnar side of triceps brachii (lateral head of triceps brachii); C. on the lateral end of elbow crease，on midpoint of the line connecting radial edge of triceps brachii (lateral head of triceps brachii) and lateral epicondylus of humerus; D.on the medial end of elbow crease, on the midpoint of the line connecting ulnar edge of the radial side of triceps brachii (lateral head of triceps brachii) and medial epicondylus of humerus; E on the lateral end of the elbow crease, on the midpoint of the line connecting radial end of ulnar edge of the radial side of triceps brachii (lateral head of triceps brachii) and olecranon process.
816	睛明穴位于: A眼内眦上0.1寸; B 眼外眦上0.1寸 C. 眉头上0.1寸D 眉梢上0.1寸	Where is B1 [Jīng Míng] located? A. 0.1 Cun above medial canthus; B 0.1 Cun above outer canthus; C. 0.1 Cun above medial end of eyebrows; D. 0.1 Cun above lateral end of eyebrows.
817	睛明穴正确针刺，入针后可以刺中: A. 视神经; B 动眼神经 C 滑车神经D 展神经	When a needle is inserted into B1 [Jīng Míng] with accuracy, what nerve may be inserted? A. Optic Nerve (2nd cranial); B Oculomotor Nerve; C. Trochlear Nerve; D. Abducent Nerve.
818	胫骨内侧髁下缘凹陷中，是取何穴位？A. Sp9 [陰陵泉]; B. B38 [浮郄]; C. Lv8 [曲泉]; D. K10 [陰谷]; E. Lv7 [膝關].	In the depression directly below the medial; C. ondyle of tibia, on a level with the lower border of tuberosity of tibia, vis-a-vis Yanglingquan (G34), 1 Cun higher than G34.. What is this point? A. Sp9 [Yīn Líng Quán]; B. B38 [Fú Xī]; C. Lv8 [Qū Quán]; D. K10 [Yīn Gǔ]; E. Lv7 [Xī Guān].
819	胫骨内侧面中央。内踝高点上 5 寸，是取何穴位？A. Sp7 [漏谷]; B. Lv5 [蠡溝]; C. Sp8 [地機]; D. K9 [筑賓]; E. Lv6 [中都]	5 Cuns above the medial malleolus (inner ankle), on the medial border of tibia. What is this point? A. Sp7 [Lòu Gǔ]; B. Lv5 [Lí Gōu]; C. Sp8 [Dì Jī]; D. K9 [Zhú; Bīn]; E. Lv6 [Zhōng Dū]
820	胫骨内侧面中央。内踝高点上 7 寸，是取何穴位？A. Sp7 [漏谷]; B. Lv5 [蠡溝]; C. Sp8 [地機]; D. K9 [筑賓]; E. Lv6 [中都]	7 Cuns above the medial malleolus (inner ankle), on the medial border of tibia., 2 Cuns directly above Ligou = Lv 5. What is this point? A. Sp7 [Lòu Gǔ]; B. Lv5 [Lí Gōu]; C. Sp8 [Dì Jī]; D. K9 [Zhú; Bīn]; E. Lv6 [Zhōng Dū]
821	頦唇沟正中凹陷处，是取何穴位？A. G3 [上關]; B. S6 [頰車]; C. R24 [承漿]; D.	In the depression in the middle of the mentolabial sulcus. What is this point? A. G3 [Shàng Guān]; B. S6 [Jiá Chē]; C. R24 [Chéng Jiàng]; D. S7 [Xià Guān]; E. Si18 [Quán

	S7 [下關]; E. Si18 [顴髎]	C. R24 [Chéng Jiàng]; D. S7 [Xià Guān]; E. Si18 [Quán Liáo]
822	口角外侧，上对瞳孔，是取何穴位？A. S4 [地倉]; B. D26 [水溝]; C. Li19 [口禾髎]; D. D28 [齦交].	On the lateral side of the angle of mouth, directly below the pupil. What is this point? A. S4 [Dì Cāng]; B. D26 [Shuǐ Gōu]; C. Li19 [Kǒu Hé Liáo]; D.D28 [Yín Jiāo].
823	口角外侧，上直对瞳孔的穴位是: A·承泣 B·四白 C·地仓 D·颊车 E·下关	What point is on the lateral side of the angle of mouth, directly below the pupil? A · S1 / Chéng Qì; B · S2 / Sì Bái; C. · S4 / Dì Cāng D · S6 / Jiá Chē E · S7 / Xià Guān.
824	昆仑直下，当跟骨凹陷中赤白肉际，是取何穴位？A; B63 [金門]; B. B61 [仆參]; C. K2 [然谷]; D. B62 [申脈]; E. G40 [丘墟]	In the depression below the heel, 1.5 Cuns directly below Kunlun (B60). What is this point? A; B63 [Jīn Mén]; B. B61 [Pū Cān]; C. K2 [Rán Gǔ]; D. B62 [Shēn Mài]; E. G40 [Qiū Xū]
825	蠡沟穴的正确位置是: A·内踝上 5 寸，胫骨内侧面的前缘; B·内踝上 5 寸，胫骨内侧面的中央 C. ·内踝上 5 寸，胫骨内侧面的后缘 D·内踝上 5 寸，胫骨内侧面后缘后 0·5 寸 E·以上都不是	Where is Lv5 (Lí Gōu) located? A. 5 Cuns above the medial malleolus (inner ankle), in front of the medial border of tibia; B. 5 Cuns above the medial malleolus (inner ankle), in the middle of the medial border of tibia; C. 5 Cuns above the medial malleolus (inner ankle), in the middle of the posterior border of tibia; D. 5 Cuns above the medial malleolus (inner ankle), 0.5 Cun behind the posterior border of tibia; E none of above.
826	两肾在体内的位置是: A. 右肾在肝之上，左肾在脾之上; B. 右肾在肝之下，左肾在脾之下 C. 右肾在肝之下，左肾在脾之上; D. 右肾在肝之上，左肾在脾之下; E. 右肾在心之下，左肾在脾之上.	Where are the two kidneys located? A. the right kidney lies above the liver, while the left kidney is situated. above the spleen; B. the right kidney lies below the liver, while the left kidney is situated. below the spleen; C. the right kidney lies below the liver, while the left kidney is situated. above the spleen; D. the right kidney lies above the liver, while the left kidney is situated. below the spleen; E. the right kidney lies below the heart, while the left kidney is situated. above the spleen.
827	两手虎口交叉，一手食指按在桡骨茎突上，当指尖尽处陷中的穴位是: A. 经渠; B. 列缺 C. 阳溪; D. 偏历; E. 以上都不是	With a clasp of two hands, and the forefinger of one hand pressing against the styloid process of radius of the other hand, this point may be located in the depression that can be reached by the tip of forefinger. What is this point? A. ·Lu8 [Jīng Qú]; B. ·Lu7 [Liè Quē]; C. ·Li5 [Yáng Xī]; D. ·Li6 [Piān Lì]; E. ·none of the above
828	眉梢外端陷中，是取何穴位？A; B2 [攢竹]; BB1 [睛明]; C. G14 [陽白]; D. G1 [童子髎]; E. Sj23 [絲竹空].	In the depression on the lateral side of the eyebrow. What is this point? A; B2 [Zǎn Zhú]; B. B1 [Jīng Míng]; C. G14 [Yáng; Bái]; D G1 [Tóng Zǐ Liáo]; E. Sj23 [Sī Zhú Kōng].
829	眉头内侧端眶上切迹处，是取何穴位？A; B2 [攢竹]; BB1 [睛明]; C. G14 [陽白]; D. G1 [童子髎]; E. Sj23 [絲竹空].	On the medial end of the eyebrow where wrinkle occurs; on the supraorbital notch. What is this point? A; B2 [Zǎn Zhú]; B. B1 [Jīng Mín]; C. G14 [Yáng; Bái]; D G1 [Tóng Zǐ Liáo]; E. Sj23 [Sī Zhú Kōng].
830	面部瞳孔直下，眶下孔凹陷	Which point is directly below the pupil in the face, in the

	处的穴位是: A·承泣 B·四白 C·地仓 D·颊车 E·下关	depression on the infra-orbital foramen? A · S1 / Chéng Qì; B. · S2 / Sì Bái / C. · S4 / Dì Cāng; D. · S6 / Jiá Chē E · S7 / Xià Guān
831	拇指桡侧爪甲角旁 0.1 寸，是取何穴位？A. Si4 [腕骨]; B. Li4 [合谷]; C. Li1 [商陽]; D. P9 [中沖]; E. Lu11 [少商]	In the depression on the radial side of thumb about 0.1 Cun from vallum unguis. What is this point? A. Si4 [Wàn Gǔ]; B. Li4 [Hé Gǔ]; C. Li1 [Shāng Yáng]; D. P9 [Zhōng Chōng]; E. Lu11 [Shǎo Shāng]
832	目窗后 1 寸，是取何穴位？A. G19 [腦空]; B. G18 [承靈]; C. G20 [風池]; D.B10 [天柱]; E. G17 [正營]	1 Cun behind Muchuang (G16). What is this point? A. G19 [Nǎo Kōng]; B. G18 [Chéng Líng]; C. G20 [Fēng Chí]; D.B10 [Tiān Zhù]; E. G17 [Zhèng Yíng]
833	目内眦角上方 0.1 寸处，是取何穴位？A; B2 [攢竹]; BB1 [睛明]; C. G14 [陽白]; D. G1 [童子髎]; E. Sj23 [絲竹空].	1 fen above the medial angle of the eye (inner Canthus). What is this point? A; B2 [Zǎn Zhú]; B. B1 [Jīng Mín]; C. G14 [Yáng; Bái]; D G1 [Tóng Zǐ Liáo]; E. Sj23 [Sī Zhú Kōng].
834	目外眦角直下，顴骨下缘凹陷中，是取何穴位？A. G3 [上關]; B. S6 [頰車]; C. R24 [承漿]; D. S7 [下關]; E. Si18 [顴髎]	Directly below the lateral angle of the eye (outer canthus), in the depression at the lower edge of the zygomatic bone. What is this point? A. G3 [Shàng Guān]; B. S6 [Jiá Chē]; C. R24 [Chéng Jiàng]; D. S7 [Xià Guān]; E. Si18 [Quán Liáo]
835	内关上 1 寸，是取何穴位？A. H4 [靈道]; B. P4 [郄門]; C. H6 [陰郄 D. P5 [間使]; E. Lu6 [孔最]	1 Cun above P6 (neiguan). What is this point? A. H4 [Líng Dào]; B. P4 [Xī Mén]; C. H6 [Yīn Xī]; D. P5 [Jiān Shǐ]; E. Lu6 [Kǒng Zuì]
836	内关穴位于: A前臂掌侧腕横纹上2寸，于掌长肌和桡侧腕屈肌腱之间; B 前臂掌侧腕横纹上3寸，于掌长肌和桡侧腕屈肌腱之间 C. 腕背横纹上2寸，于尺、桡骨之间 D 腕背横纹上3寸，于尺，桡骨之间	Where is P6 (neiguan) located? A. 2 Cun above palmar side of wrist crease, in between long palmar muscle and radial side of flexor muscle of wrist; B. 3 Cun above palmar side of wrist crease, in between long palmar muscle and radial side of flexor muscle of wrist; C. 2 Cun above wrist crease on back of hand， in between ulna and radius; D. 3 Cun above wrist crease on back of hand， in between ulna and radius.
837	内踝高点向后，与跟腱之间凹陷处，是取何穴位？A. K3 [太溪]; B. K6 [照海]; C. K4 [大鍾]; D. S41 [解溪]; E. K5 [水泉]	Behind the medial malleolus, in the depression above the calcaneus (calcaneum), on a level with the projection of the medial malleolus, on the midpoint between the posterior border of the medial malleolus and the medial side of the heel. What is this point? A. K3 [Tài Xī]; B. K6 [Zhào Hǎi]; C. K4 [Dà Zhōng]; D. S41 [Jiě Xī]; E. K5 [Shuǐ Quán]
838	内踝高点直上 3 寸，胫骨后缘，是取何穴位？A; B57 [承山]; B. B56 [承筋]; C. G39 [懸鍾]; D. Sp6 [三陰交]; E. B58 [飛揚].	3 Cuns above the projection of the medial malleolus, behind the tibia (with distance between Yinlingquan=Sp9 and the medial malleolus as 13 Cuns), on the medial-posterior border of tibia. A. B57 [Chéng Shān]; B. B56 [Chéng Jīn]; C. G39 [Xuán Zhōng]; D. Sp6 [Sān Yīn Jiāo]; E. B58 [Feī Yáng].
839	内踝前1寸，当胫骨前肌腱之内侧缘，在解溪与商丘之间，是取何穴位？A. K7 [復溜]; B. K8 [交信]; C. Lv4 [中封]; D. K6 [照海]; E	1 Cun from the anterior-inferior side of the medial malleolus (inner ankle), in front of Shangqiu=Sp5 and behind Jiexi=S41, in between the extensor hallucis longus and the tibialis anterior. What is this point? A. K7 [Fù

	[中封]; D. K6 [照海]; E. B59 [跗陽]	Liū]; B. K8 [Jiāo Xìn]; C. Lv4 [Zhōng Fēng]; D. K6 [Zhào Hǎi]; E. B59 [Fū Yáng]
840	内踝前下方凹陷，，是取何穴位？A. K7 [復溜]; B. K8 [交信]; C. Lv4 [中封]; D. Sp5 [商丘]; E. B59 [跗陽]	In the depression on the antero-inferior side of the medial malleolus, in between the medial malleolus. What is this point? A. K7 [Fù Liū]; B. K8 [Jiāo Xìn]; C. Lv4 [Zhōng Fēng]; D. Sp5 [Shāng Qiū]; E.; B59 [Fū Yáng]
841	内踝正下方，当内踝下缘约 0.4 寸，是取何穴位？A. K3 [太溪]; B. K6 [照海]; C. K4 [大鍾]; D. S41 [解溪]; E. K5 [水泉]	In the depression directly below the medial malleolus. What is this point? A. K3 [Tài Xī]; B. K6 [Zhào Hǎi]; C. K4 [Dà Zhōng]; D. S41 [Jiě Xī]; E. K5 [Shuǐ Quán]
842	脑户旁开 1.3 寸，是取何穴位？A; B9 [玉枕]; B. B8 [絡却]; C. B6 [承光]; D. B5 [五處]; E. B7 [通天]	1.3 Cuns laterally away from D17 (naohu). What is this point? A. B9 [Yù Zhěn]; B. B8 [Luò Què]; C. B6 [Chéng Guāng]; D. B5 [Wǔ Chestù]; E. B7 [Tōng Tiān]
843	臑会与清冷渊连线的中点，是取何穴位？A. Li14 [臂臑]; B. Sj12 [消濼]; C. G28 [維道]; D. Li12 [肘髎]; E. Sj13 [臑會]	On the midpoint of the line connecting Qinglengyuan=Sj11 and Naohui=Sj13. What is this point? A. Li14 [Bì Nào]; B. Sj12 [Xiāo Luò]; C. G28 [Wéi Dào]; D. Li12 [Zhǒu Liáo]; E. Sj13 [Nǎo Huì]
844	皮肤感觉不受脊神经后支管理的是: A. 风池穴; B 大椎穴 C. 肺俞穴 D 上髎穴	Posterior branch of spinal nerves does not; C. ontrol skin sensations at what point? A. G20 [Fēng Chí]; B. D14 [Dà Zhuī]; C. B13 [Fèi Shū]; D. B31 [Shàng Liáo].
845	偏历上 2 寸，是取何穴位？A. Sj5 [外關]; B. H5 [通里]; C. Li7 [溫溜]; D. Sj8 [三陽絡]; E. H4 [靈道]	2 Cuns above Li6 (pianli). What is this point? A. Sj5 [Wài Guān]; B. H5 [Tōng Lǐ]; C. Li7 [Wēn Liū]; D. Sj8 [Sān Yáng Luò]; E. H4 [Líng Dào]
846	平第二骶后孔，督脉旁开 1.5 寸的穴位是: A 小肠俞;; B 膀胱俞; C. · 中膂俞; D 胞肓; E · 秩边.	Which point is on a level with the second posterior sacral foramen, 1.5 Cuns laterally away from du mai (governing meridian)? A; B27 (Xiǎo Cháng Shū); B. B28 (Páng Guāng Shū); C. B29 (Zhōng Lu Shū); D. B53 (Bāo Huāng); E; B54 (Zhì biān).
847	平劳官，于无名指与小指之间，即当第四、五掌骨间，是取何穴位？A. Si5 [陽谷]; B. H8 [少府]; C. Lu10 [魚際]; D. Sj4 [陽池]; E. Li4 [合谷]	On a level with P8 (laogong), in between ring finger and little finger, namely, between the 4th and 5th metacarpal bones which can be reached by the tip of the little finger when the fist is clenched. What is this point? A. Si5 [Yáng Gǔ,]; B. H8 H8 [Shào Fǔ]; C. Lu10 [Yǔ Jì]; D. Sj4 [Yáng Chí]; E. Li4 [Hé Gǔ]
848	平三阴交下 1 寸向后即太溪直上 2 寸，跟腱前缘，是取何穴位？A. K7 [復溜]; B. K8 [交信]; C. Lv4 [中封]; D. Sp5 [商丘]; E. B59 [跗陽]	On the midpoint between the medial border of tibia and the Achilles tendon, 2 Cuns above Taixi=K3. A. K7 [Fù Liū]; B. K8 [Jiāo Xìn]; C. Lv4 [Zhōng Fēng]; D. Sp5 [Shāng Qiū]; E. B59 [Fū Yáng]
849	平悬钟向后，昆仑直上 3 寸，是取何穴位？A. K7 [復溜]; B. K8 [交信]; C. Lv4 [中封]; D. Sp5 [商丘]; E. B59 [跗陽]	3 Cuns above Kunlun (B60) or above the lateral malleolus. A. K7 [Fù Liū]; B. K8 [Jiāo Xìn]; C. Lv4 [Zhōng Fēng]; D. Sp5 [Shāng Qiū]; E. B59 [Fū Yáng]

850	屏上切迹前方凹陷中，是取何穴位？A. Sj21 [耳門]; B. G2 [聽會]; C. S5 [大迎]; D. Sj17 [翳風]; E. Si19 [聽宮]	In the depression in front of the incisura supratragica, (tuberculum supratragicum). What is this point? A. Sj21 [Ěr Mén]; B. G2 [Tīng Huì]; C. S5 [Dà Yíng]; D. Sj17 [Yì Fēng]; E. Si19 [Tīng Gōng]
851	期门穴的位置是: A 锁骨中线上，当第四肋间隙处; B 锁骨中线上，当第五肋间隙处； C. 锁骨中线上，当第六肋间隙处； D 锁骨中线上，当第七肋间隙处； E 以上都不是. with the patient lying on back, this point is directly 1 Cun above the interaction of medial 1 / 3 and lateral 2 / 3 of C. lavicle	Where is Lv14 (Qí Mén) located? A. On the mid-line, in the 4th intercostal space; B. On the mid-line, in the 5th intercostal space; C. on the mid-line, in the 6th intercostal space; D. On the mid-line, in the 7th intercostal space； E. none of the above.
852	奇穴 "颈臂"的正确位置是 A 锁骨内 1 / 3 与外 2 / 3 交界处; B 锁骨外 1 / 3 与内 2 / 3 交界处 C. 锁骨中点处; D ,锁骨内 1 / 3 与外 2 / 3 交界处直上 1 寸; E 锁骨外 1 / 3 与内 2 / 3 交界处直上 1 寸.	Where is the extraordinary point, Jǐng bi [neck arm] located? A; at the intersection of medial 1 / 3 and lateral 2 / 3 of clavicle; B. at the intersection of lateral 1 / 3 and medial 2 / 3 of clavicle; C. midpoint of clavicle; D. this point is directly 1 Cun above the intersection of medial 1 / 3 and lateral 2 / 3 of clavicle; E. this point is directly 1 Cun above the intersection of lateral 1 / 3 and medial 2 / 3 of clavicle.
853	奇穴球后的正确位置是在: A 眶上缘的外 1 / 4 与内 3 / 4 交界; B. 眶下缘的内 3 / 4 与外 1 / 4 交界 C. 眶上缘的内 1 / 4 与外 3 / 4 交界; D. 眶下缘的外 1 / 4 与内 3 / 4 交界; E 以上都不是	What is the Correct location of the extraordinary point, Qiú Hòu? A. Located below the upper border of the orbit, 1 / 4 laterally and 3 / 4 medially; B. Located below the lower border of the orbit, 3 / 4 laterally and 1 / 4 medially; C. Located below the upper border of the orbit, 3 / 4 laterally and 1 / 4 medially; D. Located below the lower border of the orbit, 1 / 4 laterally and 3 / 4 medially; E. none of the above.
854	气冲直下 2 寸，是取何穴位？A. Sj1 [關沖]; B. H9 [少沖]; C. Si1 [少澤]; D. Lv10 [足五里]; E. Lv11 [陰廉]	On the medial side of thigh, 2 Cuns below Qichong=S30. What is this point? A. Sj1 [Guān Chōng]; B. H9 [Shào Chōng]; C. Si1 [Shào Zé]; D. Lv10 [Zú Wǔ Lǐ, Wǔ Lǐ]; E. Lv11 [Yīn Lián]
855	气舍旁开，锁骨上缘中点下对锁骨中线，是取何穴位？A. R22 [天突]; B. Si16 [天窗]; C. S9 [人迎]; D. S12 [缺盆]; E. G20 [風池]	Laterally away from S11 (qishe), on the midpoint of the superior border of the clavicle, facing the mammary line below. What is this point? A. R22 [Tiān Tū]; B. Si16 [Tiān Chuāng]; C. S9 [Rén Yíng]; D. S12 [Quē Pén]; E. G20 [Fēng Chí]
856	髂前上棘前缘，约与关元相平处，是取何穴位？A. Lv13 [章門]; B. G24 [日月]; C. G27 [五樞]; D. G26 [帶脈]; E. G25 [京門]	On the anterior border of the anterior superior iliac spine (spina iliac anterior superior), on a level with R4 (guanyuan). What is this point? A. Lv13 [Zhāng Mén]; B. G24 [Rì Yuè]; C. G27 [Wǔ Shū]; D. G26 [Dài Mài]; E. G25 [Jīng Mén]
857	髂前上棘且与股骨大轉子连线的中点，是取何穴位？A. G29 [居髎]; B. S31 [髀關]; C. Sp11 [箕門]; D.	On the midpoint of the line connecting the anterior superior iliac spine and the projection of trochanter major, 3 Cuns behind Weidao=G28. What is this point? A. G29

	Sp10 [血海]; E. Lv9 [陰包]	[Ju Liao']; B. S31 [Bì Guān]; C. Sp11 [Jī Mén]; D. Sp10 [Xuè Hǎi]; E. Lv9 [Yīn; Bāo]
858	前发际上 5 寸、后发际上 7 寸，约在两耳尖连线的中点，是取何穴位？A. D16 [風府]; B. D20 [百會]; C. D22 [囟會]; D. D21 [前頂]; E. D15 [啞門]	Five Cuns from the frontal and seven Cuns from the posterior hairline, on the midpoint of the line connecting the apex of two earlobes. What is this point? A. D16 [Fēng Fǔ]; B. D20 [Bǎi Huì]; C. D22 [Xìn Huì]; D. D21 [Qián Dǐng]; E. D15 [Yǎ Mén]
859	前发际正中直上 0.5 寸，是取何穴位？A. D23 [上星]; B. Sj20 [角孫]; C. Sj19 [顱息]; D. Sj18 [瘈脈]; E. D24 [神庭]	In the middle of the frontal hairline, 5 fens above the hairline. What is this point?. A. D23 [Shàng Xīng]; B. Sj20 [Jiǎo Sūn]; C. Sj19 [Lú Xī]; D. Sj18 [Chì Mài]; E. D24 [Shén Tíng]
860	曲差直上 0.5 寸，平上星，是取何穴位？A; B9 [玉枕]; B. B8 [絡却]; C. B6 [承光]; D. B5 [五處]; E. B7 [通天]	0.5 Cun above Qucha (B4), on a level with D23 (shangxing). What is this point? A; B9 [Yù Zhěn]; B. B8 [Luò Què]; C. B6 [Chéng Guāng]; D. B5 [Wǔ Chestù]; E. B7 [Tōng Tiān]
861	曲池外上方约1寸，当肱骨外上髁的上方，是取何穴位？A. Li12 [肘髎]; B. H3 [少海]; C. Li13 [手五里]; D. P3 [曲澤]; E. Lu5 [尺澤]	On the superior-lateral side of Quchi=Li11, 1 Cun away from Li11, above lateral epicondylus of humerus. What is this point? A. Li12 [Zhǒu Liáo]; B. H3 [Shào Hǎi]; C. Li13 [Shǒu Wǔ Lǐ]; D. P3 [Qū Zé]; E. Lu5 [Chǐ Zé]
862	曲池穴深刺时，除可刺中桡神经分支外，还可刺中：A. 尺神经的分支；; B 正中神经的分支； C. 肌皮神经的分支； D 腋神经的分支。	What nerve may be inserted into in addition to branches of radial nerve, when a deep insertion is applied to Li11 (Qū Chí)? A branches of Ulnar Nerve; B branches of Median Nerve; C. branches of musculocutaneous Nerve; D. branches of Axilliary Nerve.
863	曲池直上 3 寸，是取何穴位？A. Li12 [肘髎]; B. H3 [少海]; C. Li13 [手五里]; D. P3 [曲澤]; E. Lu5 [尺澤]	3 Cuns above Quchi=Li11. What is this point? A. Li12 [Zhǒu Liáo]; B. H3 [Shào Hǎi]; C. Li13 [Shǒu Wǔ Lǐ]; D. P3 [Qū Zé]; E. Lu5 [Chǐ Zé]
864	屈肘，曲池穴外上方 1 寸，肱骨边缘的穴是：A.天井；; B.肘髎； C. 小海； D 清冷渊。	With the elbow bent, which point is located 1 Cun above and lateral to Li11 (Qū Chí) on the border of humerus? A. Sj10 (Tiān Jǐng); B. Li12 (Zhǒu Liáo); C. Si8 (Xiǎo Hǎi); D. Sj11 (Qīng Lěng Yuān)。
865	屈膝，髌骨内缘上 2 寸，是取何穴位？A. G29 [居髎]; B. S31 [髀關]; C. Sp11 [箕門]; D. Sp10 [血海]; E. Lv9 [陰包]	With knee bent, 2 Cuns from & on medial side of the patella (18 Cuns between superior border of knee and pubic bone), on the anterior-inferior side of the medial side of thigh. What is this point? A. G29 [Ju Liao']; B. S31 [Bì Guān]; C. Sp11 [Jī Mén]; D. Sp10 [Xuè Hǎi]; E. Lv9 [Yīn; Bāo]。
866	屈膝，当膝内侧横纹头后上方凹陷中，是取何穴位？A. Sp9 [陰陵泉]; B. B38 [浮郄]; C. Lv8 [曲泉]; D. K10 [陰谷]; E. Lv7 [膝關].	With the knee bent, this point is on the medial end of the popliteal fold, in front of the semimembranosus, below the femur. What is this point? A. Sp9 [Yīn Líng Quán]; B. B38 [Fú Xī]; C. Lv8 [Qū Quán]; D. K10 [Yīn Gǔ]; E. Lv7 [Xī Guān].
867	屈膝，在膕窝内侧，半腱肌腱与半膜肌腱之间的穴位是:	With the knee bent, what point is located on the medial side of popliteal fossa, in between musculus semimembranosus and semitendinosus?

	A委中；B委阳； C. 阴谷； D阴陵泉； E曲泉。	semimembranosus and semitendinosus? A; B40 (Wěi Zhōng); B. B39 (Wěi Yáng); C. K10 (Yīn Gŭ); D. Sp9 (Yīn Líng Quán); E. Lv8 (Qū Quán).
868	屈肘当肘横纹的尺(内)侧端，是取何穴位？A. Li12 [肘髎]; B. H3 [少海]; C. Li13 [手五里]; D. P3 [曲澤]; E. Lu5 [尺澤]	At the medial end of the elbow crease when the elbow is flexed. What is this point? A. Li12 [Zhǒu Liáo]; B. H3 [Shào Hǎi]; C. Li13 [Shǒu Wŭ Lĭ]; D. P3 [Qū Zé]; E. Lu5 [Chĭ Zé]
869	屈肘当肘横纹的外侧端凹陷处与少海内外相对，是取何穴位？A. Sj10 [天井]; B. Si8 [小海]; C. Lu7 [列缺]; D. Lu8 [經渠]; E. Li11 [曲池]	With the elbow bent, this point is located in the depression on the lateral end of elbow crease, this point and H3 (shaohai) are face to face. What is this point? A. Sj10 [Tiān Jĭng]; B. Si8 [Xiǎo Hǎi]; C. Lu7 [Liè Quē]; D. Lu8 [Jīng Qú]; E. Li11 [Qū Chí]
870	屈肘以掌向胸，当尺骨小头桡侧缘凹陷中，是取何穴位？A. Sj8 [三陽絡]; B. Sj9 [四瀆]; C. Si6 [養老]; D. Sj6 [支溝]; E. Sj7 [會宗]	With the palm of hand facing the chest, this point is located at the seam on the radial side of head of ulna. What is this point? A. Sj8 [Sān Yáng Luò]; B. Sj9 [Sì Dú]; C. Si6 [Yǎng Lǎo]; D. Sj6 [Zhi Gōu]; E. Sj7 [Huì Zōng]
871	顴弓与下颔切迹之间凹陷处，是取何穴位？A. G3 [上關]; B. S6 [頰車]; C. R24 [承漿]; D. S7 [下關]; E. Si18 [顴髎]	In the depression between the inferior border of the zygomatic arch and the mandibular notch. What is this point? A. G3 [Shàng Guān]; B. S6 [Jiá Chē]; C. R24 [Chéng Jiàng]; D. S7 [Xià Guān]; E. Si18 [Quán Liáo]
872	人迎与气舍之间，当胸锁乳突肌前缘，是取何穴位？A. R23 [廉泉]; B. S10 [水突]; C. Li17 [天鼎]; D. Li18 [扶突]; E. Si16 [天窗]	In between Renying=S9 and Qishe=S11, on the anterior border of the sternocleidomastoideus. What is this point? A. R23 [Lián Quán]; B. S10 [Shuĭ Tū]; C. Li17 [Tiān Dĭng]; D. Li18 [Fú Tū]; E. Si16 [Tiān Chuāng]
873	人迎直下锁骨上缘，胸锁乳突肌的两头之间，是取何穴位？A. R22 [天突]; B. S11 [氣舍]; C. Si16 [天窗]; D. S12 [缺盆]; E. G20 [風池]	Directly below S9 (renying), on the superior border of the clavicle, in between two heads of sternocleidomastoid muscle (sternum & clavicle heads). What is this point? A. R22 [Tiān Tū]; B. S11 [Qì Shě]; C. Si16 [Tiān Chuāng]; D. S12 [Quē Pén]; E. G20 [Fēng Chí]
874	人中沟 1 / 3 处，是取何穴位？A. S4 [地倉]; B. D26 [水溝]; C. Li19 [口禾髎]; D. D27 [兌端].	In the philtrum, 1 / 3 distance from the upper end of philtrum. What is this point? A. S4 [Dì Cāng]; B. D26 [Shuĭ Gōu]; C. Li19 [Kǒu Hé Liáo]; D. D27 [Duì Duān].
875	日月穴的位置在： A.乳头直下，第 7 肋间隙；；B 乳头直下，第 6 肋间隙；C. 第 11 肋游离端的下方；D 第 12 肋游离端的下方。	Where is G24 (Rì Yuè) located? A. directly below the nipple, in the 7th intercostals space; B. directly below the nipple, in the 6th intercostals space; C. on the lower border of the tip of the 11th rib; D. On the lower border of the tip of the 12th rib.
876	乳头直下，第六肋间隙的穴位是： A.京门；B.期门； C. 内庭；D 日月。	Which point is located directly below the nipple and in the 6th intercostal space? A. G25 (Jīng Mén); B. Lv14 (Qí Mén); C. S44 (Nèi Tíng); D. G24 (Rì Yuè)。
877	乳突后下方，与下颔角相平，胸锁乳突肌后缘，是取何穴位？A. Sj16 [天牖]; B. Si9 [肩貞]; C. Si11 [天宗]; D. Si17 [天容]; E. Si10 [臑輸].	Behind and below mastoid process, on a level with angle of mandible, on the posterior border of the sternocleidomastoideus. What is this point? A. Sj16 [Tiān Yǒu]; B. Si9 [Jiān Zhēn]; C. Si11 [Tiān Zōng]; D. Si17 [Tiān Róng]; E. Si10 [Nào Shū].
878	乳突前下方，耳垂后缘凹陷	In front of and below the mastoid process, in the

	中，是取何穴位？A. Sj21 [耳門]; B. G2 [聽會]; C. S5 [大迎]; D. Sj17 [翳風]; E. Si19 [聽宮]	depression behind the lobule of the auricle. What is this point? A. Sj21 [Ěr Mén]; B. G2 [Tīng Huì]; C. S5 [Dà Yíng]; D. Sj17 [Yì Fēng]; E. Si19 [Tīng Gōng]
879	乳中直下三肋(期门下一肋)当第七肋间隙，是取何穴位？A. Lv13 [章門]; B. G24 [日月]; C. G27 [五樞]; D. G26 [帶脈]; E. G25 [京門]	Three ribs directly below the nipple (1 rib below Lv4=qimen), in the 7th intercostal space. What is this point? A. Lv13 [Zhāng Mén]; B. G24 [Rì Yuè]; C. G27 [Wǔ Shū]; D. G26 [Dài Mài]; E. G25 [Jīng Mén]
880	三角肌后下缘与肱骨交点处，肩髎直下 3 寸，是取何穴位？A. Li14 [臂臑]; B. Sj12 [消濼]; C. G28 [維道]; D. Sj11 [清冷淵]; E. Sj13 [臑會]	At the meeting point between the posterior lower border of the deltoid muscle and humerus, 3 Cuns below Jianliao=Sj14. What is this point? A. Li14 [Bì Nào]; B. Sj12 [Xiāo Luò]; C. G28 [Wéi Dào]; D. Sj11 [Qīng Lěng Yuān]; E. Sj13 [Nǎo Huì]
881	三角肌前下缘与肱骨交点处，曲池直上 7 寸，是取何穴位？A. Li14 [臂臑]; B. Sj12 [消濼]; C. G28 [維道]; D. Sj11 [清冷淵]; E. Sj13 [臑會]	At the meeting point between the anterior lower border of the deltoid muscle and humerus, 7 Cuns above Quchi=Li11. What is this point? A. Li14 [Bì Nào]; B. Sj12 [Xiāo Luò]; C. G28 [Wéi Dào]; D. Sj11 [Qīng Lěng Yuān]; E. Sj13 [Nǎo Huì]
882	三阳络上3寸即肘尖下5寸，是取何穴位？A. Lu9 [太淵]; B. Sj9 [四瀆]; C. Si6 [養老]; D. Sj6 [支溝]; E. Sj7 [會宗]	3 Cun above Sj9 (sanyangluo), namely, 5 Cuns below the olecranon. What is this point? A. Lu9 [Tài Yuān]; B. Sj9 [Sì Dú]; C. Si6 [Yǎng Lǎo]; D. Sj6 [Zhi Gōu]; E. Sj7 [Huì Zōng]
883	上臂外展至水平位时，肩锁关节外部出现两个凹陷.，后方凹陷中，是取何穴位？A. Li16 [巨骨]; B. B31 [上髎]; C. Sj14 [肩髎]; D. Li15 [肩髃]; E. Sj15 [天髎]	With the upper arms extended on the horizontal level, two depressions will occur in the lateral region of acromioclavicular joint. This point is in the depression behind (in the back). What is this point? A. Li16 [Jù Gǔ]; B. B31 [Shàng Liáo]; C. Sj14 [Jiān Liáo]; D. Li15 [Jiān Yú]; E. Sj15 [Tiān Liáo]
884	上臂外展至水平位时，肩锁关节外部出现两个凹陷.前方凹陷中，是取何穴位？A. Li16 [巨骨]; B. B31 [上髎]; C. Sj14 [肩髎]; D. Li15 [肩髃]; E. Sj15 [天髎]	With the upper arms extended on the horizontal level, two depressions will occur in the lateral region of acromioclavicular joint. This point is in the depression in the front. What is this point? A. Li16 [Jù Gǔ]; B. B31 [Shàng Liáo]; C. Sj14 [Jiān Liáo]; D. Li15 [Jiān Yú]; E. Sj15 [Tiān Liáo]
885	上唇尖端，人中沟与口唇相接处，是取何穴位？A. S4 [地倉]; B. D26 [水溝]; C. Li19 [口禾髎]; D. D28 [齦交]; E. D27 [兌端].	At the tip of the upper lip, at the junction between the philtrum and the upper lip. What is this point? A. S4 [Dì Cāng]; B. D26 [Shuǐ Gōu]; C. Li19 [Kǒu Hé Liáo]; D. D28 [Yín Jiāo]; E. D27 [Duì Duān].
886	上唇系带与齿齦的连接处，是取何穴位？A. S4 [地倉]; B. D26 [水溝]; C. Li19 [口禾髎]; D. D28 [齦交]; E. D27 [兌端].	At the junction of upper frenum and gum. What is this point? A. S4 [Dì Cāng]; B. D26 [Shuǐ Gōu]; C. Li19 [Kǒu Hé Liáo]; D. D28 [Yín Jiāo]; E. D27 [Duì Duān].
887	上巨虚下 2 寸，即犊鼻下 8 寸，是取何穴位？A. G37 [光明]; B. S36 [足三里]; C. S40 [丰隆]; D. S39 [下巨虛]; E. S38 [條口]	In the middle of the anterior-lateral side of the lower leg, on the midpoint of the line connecting Dubi=S35 and Jiexi=S41, between tibia & fibula, 8 Cuns below Dubi=S35. What is this point? A. G37 [Guāng Míng]; B. S36 [Zú Sān Lǐ]; C. S40 [Fēng Lóng]; D. S39 [Xià Jù Xū];

		E. S38 [Tiáo Kǒu]
888	上巨虛下 3 寸，是取何穴位？A. G37 [光明]; B. S36 [足三里]; C. S40 [丰隆]; D. S39 [下巨虛]; E. S38 [條口]	9 Cuns below Dubi=S35, 1 Cun below Tiaokou=S38, 1 Cun below the middle of the anterior-lateral side of the lower leg, in between the tibia & fibula, 0.5 Cun away from anterior border of tibia. What is this point? A. G37 [Guāng Míng]; B. S36 [Zú Sān Lǐ]; C. S40 [Fēng Lóng]; D. S39 [Xià Jù Xū]; E. S38 [Tiáo Kǒu]
889	深刺合谷穴时，刺中的结构是： A桡神经浅支；B 尺神经分支；C 正中神经分支；D 桡神经深支。	What nerve is inserted when a deep insertion is applied to Li4 [Hé Gǔ]? A. superficial branch of Radial Nerve; B. branches of Ulnar Nerve C. branches of Median Nerve; D deep branches of Radial Nerve.
890	深刺肩髃穴，除可以刺中腋神经分支外。还可刺中： A 肩胛下神经; B 肩胛上神经; C 肩胛背神经; D 胸背神经.	When a deep insertion is appliedto Li15 [Jiān Yú], in addition to branches of axillary nerve, what other nevers may also be inserted into? A. Subscapular Nerve; B Suprascapular Nerve C. Dorsal Nerve of Scapula; D Thoradorsal Nerve.
891	深刺内关穴，可以刺中的神经干是: A 尺神经; B 正中神经 C. 桡神经; D 肌皮神经.	What nerve trunk may be inserted into when a deep insertion is applied to P6 [Nèi Guān]? A.Ulnar Nerve; B. Median Nerve C. Radial Nerve; D. cutaneous Nerve
892	深刺三阴交穴时，可以刺中的神经是: A胫神经分支; B 隐神经 C. 腓深神经; D 腓总神经.	What nerve may be inserted into when deep insertion is applied to Sp6 [Sān Yīn Jiāo]? A. branches of Tibial Nerve; B Saphenous Nerve; C. Deep Peroneal Nerve; D. Common Peroneal Nerve.
893	神门上 0.5 寸，是取何穴位？A. P6 [內關]; B. P4 [郄門]; C. H6 [陰郄]; D. P5 [間使]; E. Lu6 [孔最]	0.5 Cuns above Shenmen=H7. What is this point? A. P6 [Nèi Guān]; B. P4 [Xī Mén]; C. H6 [Yīn Xī]; D. P5 [Jiān Shǐ]; E. Lu6 [Kǒng Zuì]
894	神门上 1.5 寸与列缺相平，是取何穴位？A. Sj5 [外關]; B. H5 [通里]; C. Li7 [溫溜]; D. Li6 [偏歷]; E. H4 [靈道]	1.5 Cuns above Shemen=H7, on a level with Lu7 (lieque). What is this point? A. Sj5 [Wài Guān]; B. H5 [Tōng Lǐ]; C. Li7 [Wēn Liū]; D. Li6 [Piān Lì]; E. H4 [Líng Dào]
895	神门上 1 寸与经渠相平，是取何穴位？A. Sj5 [外關]; B. H5 [通里]; C. Li7 [溫溜]; D. Li6 [偏歷]; E. H4 [靈道]	1 Cun above Shenmen=H7, on a level with Lu8 (jingqu). What is this point? A. Sj5 [Wài Guān]; B. H5 [Tōng Lǐ]; C. Li7 [Wēn Liū]; D. Li6 [Piān Lì]; E. H4 [Líng Dào]
896	神庭旁开 1.5 Cun，当神庭与本神的中点，是取何穴位？A. G13 [本神]; B. G15 [頭臨泣]; C. B3 [眉沖]; D. B4 [曲差]; E. S8 [頭維]	1.5 Cun lateral from D24 (shenting), on the midpoint of the line connecting D24 and G13 (benshen). What is this point? A. G13 [Běn Shén]; B. G15 [Tóu Lín Qì]; C. B3 [Méi Chōng]; D. B4 [Qū Chestā]; E. S8 [Tóu Wěi]
897	神庭旁开 3 寸，即神庭与头维连线的外 1 / 3 处，是取何穴位？A. G13 [本神]; B. G15 [頭臨泣]; C. B3 [眉沖]; D. B4 [曲差]; E. S8 [頭維]	3 Cun lateral from D24 (shenting), namely, lateral 1 / 3 when the distance between D24 and Touwei=S8 is divided into 3 equal parts. What is this point? A. G13 [Běn Shén]; B. G15 [Tóu Lín Qì]; C. B3 [Méi Chōng]; D. B4 [Qū Chestā]; E. S8 [Tóu Wěi]
898	神庭上 0.5 寸，是取何穴位？A. D23 [上星]; B. Sj20	5 fens above D24 (shenting). What is this point? A. D23 [Shàng Xīng]; B. Sj20 [Jiāo Sūn]; C. Sj19 [Lú Xī]; D. Sj18

	[角孫]; C. Sj19 [顱息]; D. Sj18 [瘈脈]; E. D24 [神庭]	[Chì Mài]; E. D24 [Shén Tíng]
899	神庭至百会的连线之上 1 / 3 (百会前 1.5 寸)，是取何穴位？A. D16 [風府]; B. S8 [頭維]; C. D22 [囟會]; D. D21 [前頂]; E. D15 [啞門]	At the upper 1 / 3 of the line connecting D24 (shenting) and D20 (baihui), 1.5 Cuns in front of baihui (D20). What is this point? A. D16 [Fēng Fǔ]; B. S8 [Tóu Wěi]; C. D22 [Xìn Huì]; D. D21 [Qián Dǐng]; E. D15 [Yǎ Mén]
900	神庭至百会的连线之下 1 / 3 (在百会前 3 寸)，是取何穴位？A. D16 [風府]; B. G13 [本神]; C. D22 [囟會]; D. D21 [前頂]; E. D15 [啞門]	At the lower 1 / 3 of the line connecting D24 (shenting) and D20 (baihui), 3 Cuns in front of baihui (D20). What is this point? A. D16 [Fēng Fǔ]; B. G13 [Běn Shén]; C. D22 [Xìn Huì]; D. D21 [Qián Dǐng]; E. D15 [Yǎ Mén]
901	十二肋端下际，是取何穴位？A. Lv13 [章門]; B. G24 [日月]; C. G27 [五樞]; D. G26 [帶脈]; E. G25 [京門]	On the lower border of the tip of the 12th rib. What is this point? A. Lv13 [Zhāng Mén]; B. G24 [Rì Yuè]; C. G27 [Wǔ Shū]; D. G26 [Dài Mài]; E. G25 [Jīng Mén]
902	十一浮肋端下际，是取何穴位？A. Lv13 [章門]; B. G24 [日月]; C. G27 [五樞]; D. G26 [帶脈]; E. G25 [京門]	On the lower border of the tip of 11th rib. What is this point? A. Lv13 [Zhāng Mén]; B. G24 [Rì Yuè]; C. G27 [Wǔ Shū]; D. G26 [Dài Mài]; E. G25 [Jīng Mén]
903	十一肋游离端的穴位是: A 京门; B 章门: C. 期门: D 关门; E 带脉.	Which point is located on the free end of the 11th rib? A. G25 (Jīng Mén); B. Lv13 (Zhāng Mén); C. Lv14 (Qí Mén); D. S22 (Guān Mén); E. G26 (Dài Mài).
904	十一肋游离端直下与脐相平的穴位是: A 京门; B 章门: C. 期门: D 带脉; E 关门.	Which point is directly below the free end of the 11th rib and on a level with the umbilicus? A. G25 (Jīng Mén); B. Lv13 (Zhāng Mén); C. Lv14 (Qí Mén); D. G26 (Dài Mài); E.S22 (Guān Mén).
905	食指桡侧爪甲角旁 0.1 寸，是取何穴位？A. Si4 [腕骨]; B. Li4 [合谷]; C. Li1 [商陽]; D. P9 [中沖]; E. Lu11 [少商]	1 fen behind the corner of the vallum unquis on the radial side of the forefinger. What is this point? A. Si4 [Wàn Gǔ]; B. Li4 [Hé Gǔ]; C. Li1 [Shāng Yáng]; D. P9 [Zhōng Chōng]; E. Lu11 [Shǎo Shāng]
906	手背尺側，第五掌骨基底部与三角骨之间凹陷中，是取何穴位？A. Si4 [腕骨]; B. Li4 [合谷]; C. Li1 [商陽]; D. P9 [中沖]; E. Lu11 [少商]	On the ulnar side of the back of hand, in the depression between the 5th metacarpal bone & triangular bone. What is this point? A. Si4 [Wàn Gǔ]; B. Li4 [Hé Gǔ]; C. Li1 [Shāng Yáng]; D. P9 [Zhōng Chōng]; E. Lu11 [Shǎo Shāng]
907	手背桡侧第一.二掌骨之间，约当第二掌骨桡侧之中点，是取何穴位？A. Si4 [腕骨]; B. Li4 [合谷]; C. Li1 [商陽]; D. P9 [中沖]; E. Lu11 [少商]	In between the midpoint of the 1st & 2nd metacarpal bones, on the midpoint of the radial side of the 2nd metacarpal bone. What is this point? A. Si4 [Wàn Gǔ]; B. Li4 [Hé Gǔ]; C. Li1 [Shāng Yáng]; D. P9 [Zhōng Chōng]; E. Lu11 [Shǎo Shāng].
908	手厥阴心包经的两筋是指: A.拇短伸肌腱和拇长伸肌腱; B 尺骨与桡骨 C. 桡侧腕屈肌腱和尺侧腕屈肌腱; D 掌长肌腱和桡侧腕屈肌腱之间.	The pericardium meridian passes through two tendons, which are: A. extensor pollicis brevis and extensor hallucis longus; B. ulna and radius; C. flexor carpi radialis and flexor carpi ulnaris; D. palmaris longus tendon and flexor carpi radialis tendon).
909	手太阳小肠经的腕骨穴，位	Si4 (Wàn Gǔ) is located in the back of hand on the ulnar

	于手背尺侧，当尺骨茎突: A.尺骨茎突前凹陷中; B.豌豆骨凹陷中 C. 三角骨凹陷中; D 三角骨前缘凹陷中.	side, at styloid process of ulna: A. in the depression in front of styloid process of ulna; B. in the depression of pisiform bone (os pisiforme); C. in the depression of triquetral bone; D. in the depression on the anterior border of of triquetral bone.
910	水沟(督脉)旁 0.5 寸，鼻翼外缘直下，是取何穴位？A. S4 [地倉]; B. D26 [水溝]; C. Li19 [口禾髎]; D. D28 [齦交] E. D27 [兌端].	5 fens (0.5 Cun) laterally away from Renzhong=D25, below the lateral margin of nostril. What is this point? A. S4 [Dì Cāng]; B. D26 [Shuǐ Gōu]; C. Li19 [Kǒu Hé Liáo]; D. D28 [Yín Jiāo]; E. D27 [Duì Duān].
911	丝竹空向下，目外眦外 0.5 寸，是取何穴位？A; B2 [攢竹]; BB1 [睛明]; C. G14 [陽白]; D. G1 [童子髎]; E. S1 [承泣].	5 fens away from the outer canthus, below Sj23 (sizhukong). What is this point? A. B2 [Zǎn Zhú]; B. B1 [Jīng Mín]; C. G14 [Yáng; Bái]; D. G1 [Tóng Zǐ Liáo]; E. S1 [Chéng Qì].
912	四缝穴的正确位置是： A. 在二三四五指掌面，近端指关节横纹中点; B.在二三四五指掌面，远端指节横纹中点 C. 在四指掌面，远端指节中点; D 在第五指掌侧，远端指节中点.	Where is Sì Féng located? A. on the palmar side, on the 1st interphalangeal joints (proximal) of four fingers (forefinger, middle finger, index finger, and little finger); B. on the palmar side, on the 2nd interphalangeal joints (distal) of four fingers (the forefinger, middle finger, index finger, and little finger); C. on the palmar side, on the proximal joint of the forefinger; D. on the palmar side, on the midpoint of the distal joint of the little finger.
913	锁骨肩峰端与肩胛岗结合部之间凹陷处，是取何穴位？A. Li16 [巨骨]; B. B31 [上髎]; C. Sj14 [肩髎]; D. Li15 [肩髃]; E. Sj15 [天髎]	In the depression above the acromioclavicular joint, and in between the extremitas acromialis claviculae and the combining site of spina scapulae. What is this point? A. Li16 [Jù Gǔ]; B. B31 [Shàng Liáo]; C. Sj14 [Jiān Liáo]; D. Li15 [Jiān Yú]; E. Sj15 [Tiān Liáo]
914	锁骨中线直上，当大椎和肩峰连线的中点，是取何穴位？A. Si13 [曲垣]; B. Si15 [肩中輸]; C. Si12 [秉風]; D. G21 [肩井]; E. Si14 [肩外輸]	Directly above clavicle, on the midpoint of the line connecting the spinous process of the 7th cervical vertebra (or D14) and the acromion. What is this point? A. Si13 [Qū Yuān]; B. Si15 [Jiān Zhōng Shū]; C. Si12 [Bǐng Fēng]; D. G21 [Jiān Jǐng]; E. Si14 [Jiān Wài Shū]
915	太溪与水泉的中点，稍向后约 0.5 寸跟腱内缘，是取何穴位？A; B60 [崑崙]; B. K6 [照海]; C. K4 [大鍾]; D. S41 [解溪]; E. B61 [仆參].	In front of and above the tendo calcaneus, on the postero-inferior side of Taixi=K3, 5 Cuns below Taixi=K3 but slightly behind it, at the intersection between the medial border of the tendo calcaneus and the heel. What is this point? A. B60 [Kūn Lún]; B. K6 [Zhào Hǎi]; C. K4 [Dà Zhōng]; D. S41 [Jiě Xī]; E. B61 [Pū Cān].
916	太溪直上 5 寸。当腓肠肌内侧肌腹下端，与蠡沟相平，是取何穴位？A. Sp7 [漏谷]; B. S38 [條口]; C. Sp8 [地機]; D. K9 [筑賓]; E. Lv6 [中都]	5 Cuns above Taixi=K3, on the medial-inferior border of the gastrocnemius and below it belly. What is this point? A. Sp7 [Lòu Gǔ]; B. S38 [Tiáo Kǒu]; C. Sp8 [Dì Jī]; D. K9 [Zhú; Bīn]; E. Lv6 [Zhōng Dū]
917	太溪直下 1 寸，当跟骨结节内侧前上部凹陷中，是取何穴位？A; B60 [崑崙]; B. K6 [照海]; C. K4 [大鍾]; D. S41 [解溪]; E. K5 [水泉]	1 Cun below Taixi=K3, straight below the posterior border of the medial malleolus, in the depression on the antero-superior side of the tuberosity of calcaneus. What is this point? A. B60 [Kūn Lún]; B. K6 [Zhào Hǎi]; C. K4 [Dà Zhōng]; D. S41 [Jiě Xī]; E. K5 [Shuǐ Quán]

918	陶道旁开 3 寸，肩胛骨内上方，是取何穴位？A. Si13 [曲垣]; B. Si15 [肩中輸]; C. Si12 [秉風]; D. G21 [肩井]; E. Si14 [肩外輸]	3 Cuns laterally from D13 (taodao), on the superior-medial side of scapula. What is this point? A. Si13 [Qū Yuān]; B. Si15 [Jiān Zhōng Shū]; C. Si12 [Bǐng Fēng]; D. G21 [Jiān Jǐng]; E. Si14 [Jiān Wài Shū]
919	天牖穴位于: A 扶突下 1 寸,胸锁乳突肌后缘; B 结喉旁开 3 寸 C. 乳突后下方，胸锁乳突肌后缘，约平下颌角处; D 结喉旁开 4 寸; E 下颌角后，胸锁乳突肌前缘.	Where is Sj16 (Tiān Yǒu) located? A. 1 Cun below Li18 (Fú Tū), on the posterior border of sternocleidomastoideus; B. 3 Cuns laterally away from laryngeal prominence; C. on the posterior-inferior side of mastoid process, on the posterior border of sternocleidomastoideus, approximately on a level with the angle of mandible; D. 4 Cuns laterally away from laryngeal prominence; E. behind the angle of mandible, on the anterior border of sternocleidomastoideus.
920	条口外开一横指，是取何穴位？A. S37 [上巨虛]; B. S36 [足三里]; C. S40 [丰隆]; D. S39 [下巨虛]; E. G37 [光明]	8 Cuns away from the lateral malleolus, 1 digital Cun lateral to tiaokou (S38), 1.5 Cuns lateral to the anterior border of tibia, between tibia & fibula. What is this point? A. S37 [Shàng Jù Xū]; B. S36 [Zú Sān Lǐ]; C. S40 [Fēng Lóng]; D. S39 [Xià Jù Xū]; E. G37 [Guāng Míng]
921	听宫下方屏间切迹前方凹陷中，是取何穴位？A. Sj21 [耳門]; B. G2 [聽會]; C. S5 [大迎]; D. Sj17 [翳風]; E. Si19 [聽宮].	In the depression on the anterior-inferior side of the tragus, directly below Tinggong (Si19). What is this point? A. Sj21 [Ěr Mén]; B. G2 [Tīng Huì]; C. S5 [Dà Yíng]; D. Sj17 [Yì Fēng]; E. Si19 [Tīng Gōng]
922	听宫穴位于: A耳屏与下颌关节之间; B 耳屏上切迹与下颌关节之间 C. 颧弓与下颌切迹之间; D 耳垂与颧颞骨乳突之间.	Where is Si19 [Tīng Gōng] located? A. between Tragus and Mandibular Articulation; B between incisura supratragica and Mandibular Articulation; C. between Head of Mandible and Mandibular Notch; D. between Ear Lobe and Mastoid Process of zygomaticotemporal process.
923	听宫穴针刺时，可以刺中的神经是: A上颌神经; B 面神经颞支 C. 耳大神经; D 耳颞神经.	What nerve may be inserted into when deep insertion is applied to Si19 [Tīng Gōng]? A. Maxillary Nerve; B temporal branch of Facial Nerve; C. Great Auricular Nerve; D. Auriculotemporal Nerve.
924	通天后 1.5 寸，是取何穴位？A; B9 [玉枕]; B. B8 [絡却]; C. B6 [承光]; D. B5 [五處]; E. B7 [通天]	1.5 Cuns behind Tongtian (B7). What is this point? A; B9 [Yù Zhěn]; B. B8 [Luò Què]; C. B6 [Chéng Guāng]; D. B5 [Wǔ Chestù]; E. B7 [Tōng Tiān]
925	瞳孔正中直下，眼眶与眶下缘之间，是取何穴位？A. S1 [承泣]; B. D25 [素髎]; C. S3 [巨髎]; D. Li20 [迎香]; E. S2 [四白].	When the eyes look straight, this point is directly below the pupil in between the eyeball & the inferior border of the orbit. What is this point? A. S1 [Chéng Qì]; B. D25 [Sù Liáo]; C. S3 [Jù Liáo]; D. Li20 [Yíng Xiāng]; E. S2 [Sì Bái].
926	瞳孔直上，在眉毛中央上 1 寸处，是取何穴位？A; B2 [攢竹]; BB1 [睛明]; C. G14 [陽白]; D. G1 [童子髎]; E. Sj23 [絲竹空].	1 Cun above the middle of the eyebrow, directly above the pupil. What is this point? A; B2 [Zǎn Zhú]; B. B1 [Jīng Míng]; C. G14 [Yáng; Bái]; D. G1 [Tóng Zǐ Liáo]; E. Sj23 [Sī Zhú Kōng].
927	瞳孔直下，平鼻翼下缘处，是取何穴位？A. S1 [承泣]; B. D25 [素髎]; C. S3 [巨	Directly below the middle of the eye, on a level with the inferior border of the nose wing (ala nasi). What is this point? A. S1 [Chéng Qì]; B. D25 [Sù Liáo]; C. S3 [Jù

	髎]; D. Li20 [迎香]; E. S2 [四白].	Liáo]; D. Li20 [Yíng Xiāng]; E. S2 [Sì Bái].
928	头临泣后 1 寸，是取何穴位？A. G19 [腦空]; B. G18 [承靈]; C. G16 [目窗]; D.B10 [天柱]; E. G17 [正營]	1 Cun behind Linqi=G15. What is this point? A. G19 [Nǎo Kōng]; B. G18 [Chéng Líng]; C. G16 [Mù Chuāng]; D. B10 [Tiān Zhù]; E. G17 [Zhèng Yíng]
929	臀下横纹正中，是取何穴位？A. G32 [中瀆]; B. G30 [環跳]; C. B37 [殷門]; D. G31 [風市]; E. B36 [承扶]	In the middle of the gluteal sulcus (gluteal fold). What is this point? A. G32 [Zhōng Dū]; B. G30 [Huán Tiào]; C. B37 [Yīn Mén]; D. G31 [Fēng Shì]; E. B36 [Chéng Fú]
930	外关上 1 寸与偏历相平，是取何穴位？A. Sj8 [三陽絡]; B. Sj9 [四瀆]; C. Si6 [養老]; D. Sj6 [支溝]; E. Sj7 [會宗]	1 Cun above Sj5 (waiguan), on a level with Li6 (pianli). What is this point? A. Sj8 [Sān Yáng Luò]; B. Sj9 [Sì Dú]; C. Si6 [Yǎng Lǎo]; D. Sj6 [Zhi Gōu]; E. Sj7 [Huì Zōng]
931	外踝高点上 7 寸，与下巨虛相平，在腓骨后缘，是取何穴位？A. G35 [陽交]; B. G37 [光明]; C. G38 [陽輔]; D. G36 [外丘]; E. B55 [合陽].	In between Yanglingquan (G34) and the lateral malleolus, 7 Cuns above the lateral malleolus (the distance between the lower border of knee and the lateral malleolus is divided into 16 Cuns), on the posterior border of fibula on a level with B58. What is this point? A. G35 [Yáng Jiāo]; B. G37 [Guāng Míng]; C. G38 [Yáng Fǔ]; D. G36 [Wài Qiū]; E. B55 [Hé Yáng].
932	外踝高点上 7 寸，与下巨虛相平，在腓骨前缘，是取何穴位？A. G35 [陽交]; B. G37 [光明]; C. G38 [陽輔]; D. G36 [外丘]; E. B55 [合陽].	In between Yanglingquan (G34) and the lateral malleolus, on the anterior border of fibula, in front of Yangjiao (G35), 7 Cuns above the lateral malleolus, in front of fibula (on the midpoint between Yanglingquan (G34) and the outer ankle). What is this point? A. G35 [Yáng Jiāo]; B. G37 [Guāng Míng]; C. G38 [Yáng Fǔ]; D. G36 [Wài Qiū]; E. B55 [Hé Yáng].
933	外踝高点向后，与跟腱之间凹陷处，是取何穴位？A; B60 [崑崙]; B. B61 [仆參]; C. K2 [然谷]; D. B62 [申脈]; E. G40 [丘墟]	In the depression in front of the tendo calcaneus behind the lateral malleolus, in between the lateral malleolus and the Achilles tendon What is this point?. A; B60 [Kūn Lún]; B. B61 [Pū Cān]; C. K2 [Rán Gǔ]; D. B62 [Shēn Mài]; E. G40 [Qiū Xū]
934	外踝高点直上 3 寸，腓骨前缘，是取何穴位？A; B57 [承山]; B. B56 [承筋]; C. G39 [懸鍾]; D. Sp6 [三陰交]; E. B58 [飛揚].	3 Cuns above the lateral malleolus (outer ankle), on the anterior border of fibula. What is this point? A; B57 [Chéng Shān]; B. B56 [Chéng Jīn]; C. G39 [Xuán Zhōng]; D. Sp6 [Sān Yīn Jiāo]; E. B58 [Feī Yáng].
935	外踝高点直上 5 寸腓骨前缘，是取何穴位？A. G35 [陽交]; B. G37 [光明]; C. G38 [陽輔]; D. G36 [外丘]; E. B55 [合陽].	5 Cuns above the lateral malleolus, in front of the fibula. What is this point? A. G35 [Yáng Jiāo]; B. G37 [Guāng Míng]; C. G38 [Yáng Fǔ]; D. G36 [Wài Qiū]; E. B55 [Hé Yáng].
936	外踝前下方，趾长伸肌腱外侧凹陷中，是取何穴位？A; B60 [崑崙]; B. B61 [仆參]; C. K2 [然谷]; D. B62 [申脈]; E. G40 [丘墟]	In the depression on the frontal-lower side of the lateral malleolus, on the extended line passing through the 4th digital space. What is this point? A; B60 [Kūn Lún]; B. B61 [Pū Cān]; C. K2 [Rán Gǔ]; D. B62 [Shēn Mài]; E. G40 [Qiū Xū]
937	外踝正下方凹陷中，是取何穴位？A; B60 [崑崙]; B. B61 [仆參]; C. K2 [然谷];	In the depression below the center of the lateral malleolus. What is this point? A; B60 [Kūn Lún]; B. B61 [Pū Cān]; C. K2 [Rán Gǔ]; D. B62 [Shēn Mài]; E. G40 [Qiū Xū]

	D. B62 [申脈]; E. G40 [丘墟]	
938	腕骨穴位于第5掌骨基底与何骨之间? A. 尺骨茎突; B. 三角骨 C. 豌豆骨; D. 钩骨; E. 以上都不是	G12 [Wán Gŭ] is locted between base of 5th metacarpal bone and what bone? A. styloid process of ulna; B. triquetral bone; C. pisiform bone; D. hamate bone; E. none of the above.
939	腕横纹尺侧，尺侧腕屈肌的桡侧凹陷中的穴位是: A 大陵; B 神门 C. 太渊; D 解溪; E 劳宫.	Which point is on the ulnar side of the elbow Crease, in the depression on the radial side of flexor Carpi ulnaris? A · P7 / Dà Líng; B · H7 / Shén Mén; C. · Lu9 / TàiYuān; D · S41 / Jiě Xī; E. P8 / Láo Gōng.
940	腕横纹上1.5寸，桡骨茎突上方，是取何穴位？A. Sj10 [天井]; B. Si8 [小海]; C. Lu7 [列缺]; D. Lu8 [經渠]; E. Li11 [曲池]	1.5 Cuns above the distal wrist crease, above the styloid process of the radius. What is this point? A. Sj10 [Tiān Jĭng]; B. Si8 [Xiăo Hăi]; C. Lu7 [Liè Quē]; D. Lu8 [Jīng Qú]; E. Li11 [Qū Chí]
941	腕横纹上1寸，桡动脉桡侧凹陷中，是取何穴位？A. Sj10 [天井]; B. Si8 [小海]; C. Lu7 [列缺]; D. Lu8 [經渠]; E. Li11 [曲池]	1 Cun above the distal wrist crease, in the depression on the lateral border of the radial artery. What is this point? A. Sj10 [Tiān Jĭng]; B. Si8 [Xiăo Hăi]; C. Lu7 [Liè Quē]; D. Lu8 [Jīng Qú]; E. Li11 [Qū Chí]
942	腕横纹上5寸在阳谷与小海的连线上当尺骨掌侧缘，与温溜相平，是取何穴位？A. Lu9 [太淵]; B. H7 [神門]; C. P7 [大陵]; D. Si7 [支正]; E. Li5 [陽溪]	5 Cuns above wrist, on the line connecting Si5 (yanggu) and Si8 (xiaohai), at the border on the palmar side of radius, on a level with Li7 (wenliu). What is this point? A. Lu9 [Tài Yuān]; B. H7 [Shén Mén]; C. P7 [Dà Líng]; D. Si7 [Zhi Zhèng]; E. Li5 [Yáng Xī]
943	腕横纹上7寸，尺泽与太渊之间，是取何穴位？A. P6 [內關]; B. P4 [郄門]; C. H6 [陰郄 D. P5 [間使]; E. Lu6 [孔最]	7 Cuns above the distal wrist crease, in between Lu5 (chize) and Lu9 (Taiyuan). What is this point? A. P6 [Nèi Guān]; B. P4 [Xī Mén]; C. H6 [Yīn Xī]; D. P5 [Jiān Shĭ]; E. Lu6 [Kŏng Zuì]
944	腕横纹中央，掌长肌腱与桡侧腕屈肌腱之间的穴位是: A 大陵; B 内关 C. 间使; D 阳溪; E 阳谷.	In the middle of distal wrist crease in between two tendons (palmaris longus & flexor carpi radialis)? A. P7 (Dà Líng); B. P6 (Nèi Guān); C. P5 (Jiān Shĭ); D. Li5 (Yáng Xī); E. Si5 (Yáng Gŭ).
945	尾骨尖端与肛门中点，是取何穴位？A. B33 [中髎]; B. B32 [次髎]; C. B35 [会阳]; D. D1 [長強]; E. B34 [下髎]	In the depression between the tip of coccyx and the anus.What is this point? A. B33 [Zhōng Liáo]; B. B32 [Cì Liáo]; C. B35 [Huì Ang]; D. D1 [Cháng Qiáng]; E. B34 [Xià Liáo]
946	委阳穴位于腘横纹外端与何肌腱内缘的交点处? A 股二头肌腱; B 股四头肌腱 C. 缝匠肌肌腱 D 半腱肌肌腱; E 半膜肌肌腱.	B39 (Wĕi Yáng) is located on the lateral side of the popliteal fossa, on the medial border of what muscle? A. biceps femoris muscle; B. quadriceps muscle of thigh (m. quadriceps femoris); C. sartorius muscle (tailor's muscle); D. semitendinosus muscle; E. semimembranosus muscle (musculus emimenbranosus).
947	委中外开一寸，股二头肌腱内缘，是取何穴位？A. G34 [陽陵泉]; B. G33 [膝陽關]; C. S35 [犢鼻]; D. B39 [委陽]; E. Sp7 [漏谷]	At the lateral angle of the popliteal fossa, on the medial border of the biceps femoris muscle. What is this point? A. G34 [Yáng Líng Quán]; B. G33 [Xī Yáng Guān]; C. S35 [Dú Bí]; D. B39 [Wĕi Yáng]; E. Sp7 [Lòu Gŭ]
948	委中穴深刺，可以刺中的神经干是:	What nerve trunk may be inserted into when deep insertion is applied to B40 [Wĕi Zhōng]? A Sciatic

	A坐骨神经; B 腓浅神经 C. 腓深神经; D 胫神经.	insertion is applied to B40 [Wĕi Zhōng]? A.Sciatic Nerve; B Superficial Peroneal Nerve; C. Deep Peroneal Nerve; D Tibial Nerve.
949	委中穴位于：A腘窝横纹中点; B 腘窝横纹外侧端 C. 腘窝横纹内侧端; D 臀沟中点.	Where is Weizhong (B40) located? A. midpoint of transverse crease of Popliteal Fossa; B lateral end of Transverse crease of Popliteal Fossa C. medial end of Transverse crease of Popliteal Fossa; D. midpoint of Gluteal Fold.
950	委中直下 2 寸，腓肠肌内、外侧头之间，是取何穴位？A. G35 [陽交]; B. G37 [光明]; C. G38 [陽輔]; D. G36 [外丘]; E. B55 [合陽].	2 Cuns below Weizhong (B40) when the distance between B40 and Kunlun (B60) is divided into 16 Cuns, in between the two heads of gastrocnemius (medial and lateral heads). What is this point? A. G35 [Yáng Jiāo]; B. G37 [Guāng Míng]; C. G38 [Yáng Fŭ]; D. G36 [Wài Qiū]; E. B55 [Hé Yáng].
951	委中直下 8 寸，腓肠肌肌腹的下方，是取何穴位？A; B57 [承山]; B. B56 [承筋]; C. G39 [懸鍾]; D. Sp6 [三陰交]; E. B58 [飛揚].	In the depression below the belly of the gastrocnemius that occurs while the foot is stretched. What is this point? A; B57 [Chéng Shān]; B. B56 [Chéng Jīn]; C. G39 [Xuán Zhōng]; D. Sp6 [Sān Yīn Jiāo]; E. B58 [Feī Yáng].
952	位于背部第七胸椎棘突下，旁开 3 寸的穴是：A.膈关; B.膈俞 C. 至阳; D 督俞.	Which point is located 3 Cuns laterally away from the lower end. of the spinous process of the 7th thoracic vertebra? A; B46 (Gé Guān); B.B17 (Gé Shū); C. D9 (Zhì Yáng); D.B16 (Dū Shū).
953	位于骶管裂孔的输穴是: A·下髎; B 腰奇 C. 腰俞; D 会阴; E 腰阳关.	What point is located in the sacral hiatus? A. B34 (Xià Liáo); B. Yāo Qí C. D2 (Yāo Shū); D. R1 (Huì Yīn); E. D3 (Yāo Yáng Guān).
954	位于第 2 腰椎棘突下，旁开 1.5 寸的穴位是: A·肾俞; B·三焦俞 C. ·命门; D·关元俞; E·腰阳关.	What point is below the spinous process of the 2nd lumbar vertebra, 1.5 Cuns laterally from it? A. B23 / Shèn Shū; B. B22 / Sān Jiāo Shū C. · D4 / Mìng Mén; D. B26 / Guān Yuán Shū; E · D3 / Yāo Yáng Guān.
955	位于第 8 胸椎棘突下，旁开 3 寸的穴位是: A 噫嘻; B 膈俞 C. 心俞; D·膈关; E 没有穴位	What point is located below the spinous process of 8th thoracic vertebra, 3 Cun laterally from it? A. B45 / Yì Xī; B. ·B17 / Gé Shū C. ·B15 / Xīn Shū; D. B46 / Gé Guān; E. ·No point located there.
956	位于第八胸椎棘突下，旁开 3 寸的穴位是: A·噫嘻; B·膈俞 C. ·魂门; D·膈关; E·没有穴位.	What point is located below the spinous process of the 8th thoracic vertebra, 3 Cuns laterally away from it? A; B45 (Yì Xī); B. B17 (Gé Shū); C. B47 (Hún Mén); D. B46 (Gé Guān); E. No such point.
957	位于第三胸椎棘突下，旁开 1.5 寸的穴位是：A.风门; B.厥阴俞 C. 心俞; D 肺俞.	Which point is located 1.5 Cuns laterally away from the lower end. of the spinous process of 3rd thoracic vertebra? A.B12 (Fēng Mén); B. B14 (Jué Yīn Shū); C. B15 (Xīn Shū); D. B13 (Fèi Shū).
958	位于腹部前正中线旁开 0.5 寸的经脉是: A.足太阴脾经; B.足少阴肾经 C. 足阳明胃经; D 足厥阴肝经.	Which meridian is located 0.5 Cun laterally away from the mid-abdominal line? A. spleen meridian; B. kidney meridian; C. stomach meridian; D. liver meridian.
959	位于结喉旁开 3·5 寸，胸锁乳突肌后缘的穴位是:	What point is located 3.5 Cun laterally from laryngeal prominence, at the posterior edge of

	A. 天容; B. 天窗 C. 天牖; D. 天鼎; E. 以上都不是	sternocleidomastoid muscle? A. Si17 [Tiān Róng]; B. Si16 [Tiān Chuāng]; C. Sj16 [Tiān Yǒu]; D. Li17 [Tiān Dǐng]; E. none of the above
960	位于面部，目外眦直下，颧骨下缘凹陷处穴: A.口禾髎; B.和髎 C. 巨髎; D 颧髎.	Which point is located in the face, directly below the lateral angle of eye (outer canthus), in the depression on the lower order of the zygomatic bone? A. Li19 (Kǒu Hé Liáo); B. Sj22 (Hé Liáo (Ěr Hé Liáo); C. S3 (Jù Liáo); D. Si18 (Quán Liáo).
961	位于拇长伸肌腱与拇短伸肌腱之间凹陷中的穴位是: A.大陵; B.腕骨 C. 阳溪; D 阳谷.	What point is located in the depression between extensor pollicis brevis & extensor pollicis longus? A. P7 (Dà Líng); B. Si4 (Wàn Gǔ); C. Li5 (Yáng Xī); D. Si5 (Yáng Gǔ).
962	位于拇短伸肌腱与拇长伸肌腱之间凹陷中的穴位是: A. 大陵; B. 腕骨 C. 阳溪; D. 阳谷; E. 合谷	What point is located in the depression between short extensor muscle of thumb and long extensor muscle of thumb? A. P7 [Dà Líng]; B. G12 [Wán Gǔ]; C. Li5 [Yáng Xī]; D. Si5 [Yáng Gǔ]; E. Li4 [Hé Gǔ]
963	位于前臂背侧，腕背横纹上3寸，尺骨与桡骨之间 A.支沟;.B.会宗 C. 三阳络; D 外关.	Which point is located on the back of forearm, 3 Cuns above the dorsal carpal crease, in between ulnar and radius? A. Sj6 (Zhi Gōu); B. Sj7 (Huì Zōng); C. Sj8 (Sān Yáng Luò); D. Sj5 (Wài Guān).
964	位于人体后正中线上的穴位是: A 风池穴; B 大椎穴 C. 肺俞穴; D 下髎穴.	Which point is located on the posterior midline of the body? A. G20 [Fēng Chí]; B. D14 [Dà Zhuī]; C. B13 [Fèi Shū]; D. B34 [Xià Liáo].
965	位于手背第一二掌骨之间约平第二掌骨中点处的穴位是: A 中渚; B 劳宫 C. 鱼际; D 合谷; E 后溪.	What point is located on the midpoint of 1st & 2nd. metacarpal bones, about on a level with 2nd. metacarpal? A. Sj3 (Zhōng Zhǔ); B. P8 (Láo Gōng); C. Lu10 (Yǔ Jì); D. Li4 (Hé Gǔ); E. Si3 (Hòu Xī).
966	位于腕掌侧横纹尺侧端，尺侧腕屈肌腱的桡侧凹陷处的穴位是: A.太渊; B.腕骨 C. 大陵; D 神门.	Which point is located on the ulnar side of the palmar carpal crease, in the depression on the radial side of the flexor carpi ulnaris muscle? A. Lu9 (Tài Yuān); B. Si4 (Wàn Gǔ); C. P7 (Dà Líng); D. H7 (Shén Mén).
967	位于小腿外侧，外踝尖上5寸，腓骨前缘穴是： A.悬钟; B 光明 C. 阳辅 D 外丘.	Which point is located on the lateral side of the lower leg, 5 Cuns above the lateral malleolus, on the anterior; border of fibula? A. G39 (Xuán Zhōng); B. G37 (Guāng Míng); C. G38 (Yáng Fǔ); D. G36 (Wài Qiū).
968	位于掌后腕横纹桡侧，桡动脉的桡侧凹陷中的穴位是: A 神门; B.大陵 C. 太渊; D 阳池.	Which point is located on radial side of the distal wrist crease, in the depression on the radial border of the radial artery? A. H7 (Shén Mén); B. P7 (Dà Líng); C. Lu9 (Tài Yuān); D. Sj4 (Yáng Chí).
969	位于肘横纹中，当肱二头肌腱的尺侧缘穴是： A.尺泽; B.曲池 C. 曲泽; D 小海.	Which point is located on the elbow crease, on the ulnar border of tendons of the biceps brachii muscle A. Lu5 (Chǐ Zé); B. Li11 (Qū Chí); C. P3 (Qū Zé); D. Si8

		(Xiǎo Hǎi).
970	位于足背第一二跖骨结合部之前凹陷处是: A.内庭; B.行间 C. 太冲; D 侠溪.	Which point is located in the depression in front of the combining site of the first and second metatarsal bones? A. S44 (Nèi Tíng); B. Lv2 (Xíng Jiān); C. Lv3 (Tài Chōng); D. G43 (Xiá Xī).
971	位于足底部，第二趾远端趾间关节横纹中点的穴位是: A ·独阴穴; B ·里内庭 C. ·四强穴; D ·内至阴; E 以上都不是.	Which point is located underside of foot, at the distal crease of interdigital joint of the second toe? A. Dú Yīn; B. Lǐ Nèi Tíng; C. Sì Qiáng; D. Nèi Zhì Yīn; E. None the above.
972	位于足第一跖骨基底部前缘凹陷处的穴位是: A. ·京骨; B. ·束骨 C. ·太白; D. ·大都; E. ·公孙	What point is located in the depression at the anterior edge of the base of 1st metatarsal bone? A. ·B64 [Jīng Gǔ]; B. ·B65 [Shù Gǔ]; C. ·Sp3 [Tài Bái]; D. ·Sp2 [Dà Dū]; E. ·Sp4 [Gōng Sūn].
973	握拳，手背侧，第三掌骨小头高点处的经外奇穴是: A ·大骨空; B ·中魁 C. ·小骨空; D ·五虎; E ·拳尖.	What extraordinary point is located at the peak of the head of the third metacarpal bone on the back of your fist? A. Dà Gǔ Kōng; B. Zhōng Kuí; C. Xiǎo Gǔ Kōng; D. Wǔ Hǔ; E. Quán Jiān.
974	握拳，中指尖着掌处，当第二、三掌指关节后偏于第三掌骨的梡侧, 是取何穴位？A. Si5 [陽谷]; B. H8 [少府]; C. Lu10 [魚際]; D. Sj4 [陽池]; E. P8 [勞宮]	In between the 2nd & 3rd metacarpal bones on the proximal transversal crease of the palm which may be touched by the tip of the middle finger when the fist is clenched. What is this point? A. Si5 [Yáng Gǔ,]; B. H8 H8 [Shào Fǔ]; C. Lu10 [Yǔ Jì]; D. Sj4 [Yáng Chí]; E. P8 [Láo Gōng]
975	无名指尺侧爪甲角旁 0.1 寸, 是取何穴位？A. Sj1 [關冲]; B. H9 [少冲]; C. Si1 [少澤]; D. Lv10 [足五里]; E. Lv11 [陰廉]	About 0.1 Cun (1 fen) behind the vallum unquis on the ulnar side of the ring finger. What is this point? A. Sj1 [Guān Chōng]; B. H9 [Shào Chōng]; C. Si1 [Shào Zé]; D. Lv10 [Zú Wǔ Lǐ, Wǔ Lǐ]; E. Lv11 [Yīn Lián]
976	五处后 1.5 寸, 是取何穴位？A; B9 [玉枕]; B. B8 [絡却]; C. B6 [承光]; D. B5 [五處]; E. B7 [通天]	1.5 Cuns behind Wuchu (B5). What is this point? A; B9 [Yù Zhěn]; B. B8 [Luò Què]; C. B6 [Chéng Guāng]; D. B5 [Wǔ Chestù]; E. B7 [Tōng Tiān]
977	五枢前斜 0.5 寸.髂前上棘前下方, 是取何穴位？A. Li14 [臂臑]; B. Sj12 [消濼]; C. G28 [維道]; D. Sj11 [清冷淵]; E. Sj13 [臑會]	5 fens slantingly below Wushu=G27, on the inferior-medial side of the anterior superior iliac spine,. What is this point? A. Li14 [Bì Nào]; B. Sj12 [Xiāo Luò]; C. G28 [Wéi Dào]; D. Sj11 [Qīng Lěng Yuān]; E. Sj13 [Nǎo Huì]
978	膝关节外侧面，髌骨下缘外膝眼, 是取何穴位？A. G34 [陽陵泉]; B. G33 [膝陽關]; C. S35 [犢鼻]; D. B39 [委陽]; E. B40 [委中]	With the knee bent, this point is located in the depression on the lateral side of the patella ligament, on the inferior border of the patella. What is this point? A. G34 [Yáng Líng Quán]; B. G33 [Xī Yáng Guān]; C. S35 [Dú Bí]; D. B39 [Wěi Yáng]; E. B40 [Wěi Zhōng]
979	膝关节向后，屈膝膕窝横纹内侧，当半膜肌腱和半腱肌腱之间, 是取何穴位？A. Sp9 [陰陵泉]; B. B38 [浮郄]; C. Lv8 [曲泉]; D. K10 [陰谷]; E. Lv7 [膝關].	With the knee half bent, this point is on the medial side of the popliteal fossa in between the semitendinosus and the semimembranosus, behind the medial condyle of tibia, on the medial end of the transverse crease of knee-bend on a level with B40. What is this point? A. Sp9 [Yīn Líng Quán]; B. B38 [Fú Xī]; C. Lv8 [Qū Quán]; D. K10 [Yīn Gǔ]; E. Lv7 [Xī Guān].

980	下颌角后下方，胸锁乳突肌前缘，是取何穴位？A. Sj16 [天牖]; B. Si9 [肩貞]; C. Si11 [天宗]; D. Si17 [天容]; E. Si10 [臑輸].	Behind the angle of the mandible, in the depression at the frontal edge of the sternocleidomastoid muscle. What is this point? A. Sj16 [Tiān Yǒu]; B. Si9 [Jiān Zhēn]; C. Si11 [Tiān Zōng]; D. Si17 [Tiān Róng]; E. Si10 [Nào Shū].
981	下颌角前上方，咬肌高点，是取何穴位？A. G3 [上關]; B. S6 [頰車]; C. R24 [承漿]; D. S7 [下關]; E. Si18 [顴髎]	In front of and above the angle of the mandible, on the projection of the masseteric muscle. What is this point? A. G3 [Shàng Guān]; B. S6 [Jiá Chē]; C. R24 [Chéng Jiàng]; D. S7 [Xià Guān]; E. Si18 [Quán Liáo]
982	下颌角前下 1.3 寸，咬肌附着部前缘凹陷处，是取何穴位？A. Sj21 [耳門]; B. G2 [聽會]; C. S5 [大迎]; D. Sj17 [翳風]; E. Si19 [聽宮]	1.3 Cun below and in front of the angle of the mandible, in the depression at the frontal edge of masseteric muscle attached to the mandible. What is this point? A. Sj21 [Ěr Mén]; B. G2 [Tīng Huì]; C. S5 [Dà Yíng]; D. Sj17 [Yì Fēng]; E. Si19 [Tīng Gōng]
983	下髎下 1 寸许，尾骨下端督脉旁开 0.5 寸，是取何穴位？A. B33 [中髎]; B. B32 [次髎]; C. B35 [会阳]; D. D1 [長強]; E. G24 [日月]	About 1 Cun below B34 (xialiao), on the lateral side of du mai on the lower border of coccyx, 5 fens away from it. What is this point? A. B33 [Zhōng Liáo]; B. B32 [Cì Liáo]; C. B35 [Huì Ang]; D. D1 [Cháng Qiáng]; E. G24 [Rì Yuè]
984	下列除哪个穴外，其余穴位均在前臂内侧掌长肌腱与桡侧腕屈肌腱之间: A 大陵; B.通里 C. 内关; D 间使.	Which of the following is NOT located on the medial side of forearm, between palmaris longus & flexor carpi radialis? A. P7 (Dà Líng); B. H5 (Tōng Lǐ); C. P6 (Nèi Guān); D. P5 (Jiān Shǐ).
985	下列除哪个穴外，余穴的平于第四肋间隙? A.天池; B 乳中 C. 神堂; D 神封.	Which point is NOT on a level with the 4th intercostal space? A. P1 (Tiān Chí); B. S17 (Rǔ Zhōng); C. B44 (Shén Táng); D. K23 (Shén Fēng).
986	下列各组穴位中，与脐下 4 寸相平的穴 A.气穴腹结; B 大巨四满 C. 大赫归来; D 府舍冲门.	Which two points are on a level with 4 Cuns below the umbilicus? A. K13 (Qì Xué), Sp14 (Fù Jié); B. S27 (Dà Jù), K14 (Sì Mǎn); C. K12 (Dà Hè), S29 (Guī Lái); D. Sp13 (Fù Shě), Sp12 (Chōng Mén).
987	下列腧穴的定位错误的是: A. 承泣-目正视，瞳孔直下，当眶下缘与眼球之间; B 四白-目正视，瞳孔直下，当眶下孔凹中 C. 巨髎-目正视，瞳孔直下，平鼻翼上缘处; D. 地仓-口角旁 0.4 寸，巨髎而直下; 颊车-下颌角前上方-横指凹陷中，咀嚼时咬肌隆起最高点处.	Which of the following point locations is NOT correct? A. S1 (Chéng Qì)–When eyes look straight, this point is directly below pupil, in between the eyeball & the inferior border of the orbit; B. S2 (Sì Bái) –When eyes look straight, this point is directly below pupil, in the depression on the infra-orbital foramen; C. S3 (Jù Liáo) –Directly below the middle of the eye, on a level with the superior border of the nose wing (ala nasi); D. S4 (Dì Cāng) –A distance of 0.4 Cuns laterally away from the angle of mouth, on the medial side of the nasolabial sulcus; E. S6 (Jiá Chē) –one transversal finger width in front of, and above, the angle of the mandible, on the highest point of the masseteric muscle while biting.
988	下列穴位，哪一个不在副神经分布区域: A 风池穴; B 大椎穴 C. 肺俞穴; D 肩髃穴.	What point is not located in the distribution of accessory nerve? A. G20 [Fēng Chí]; B. D14 [Dà Zhuī]; C. B13 [Fèi Shū]; D. Li15 [Jiān Yú]

		D Li15 [Jiān Yú].
989	下列穴位中，位于腋中线上的是: A. ·天池; B. ·辄筋 C. ·日月; D. ·大包; E. ·日月	Which point is located on the midaxillary line? A. ·P1 [Tiān Chí]; B. ·G23 [Zhé Jīn]; C. ·G24 [Rì Yuè]; D. ·Sp21 [Dà Bāo]; E. ·G24 [Rì Yuè]
990	项后入发际 0.5 寸，平耳垂,是取何穴位？A. D16 [風府]; B. D20 [百會]; C. D22 [囟會]; D. D21 [前頂]; E. D15 [啞門]	In the center of the back of the neck, below inion, 5 fens above the posterior hairline, on a level with the earlobe, in between the spinous processes. What is this point? A. D16 [Fēng Fǔ]; B. D20 [Bǎi Huì]; C. D22 [Xìn Huì]; D. D21 [Qián Dǐng]; E. D15 [Yǎ Mén]
991	小肠俞内侧 0.7 寸，当第一骶后孔中, 是取何穴位？A. Li16 [巨骨]; B. B31 [上髎]; C. Sj14 [肩髎]; D. Li15 [肩髃]; E. Sj15 [天窌]	0.7 Cun on the medial side of; B27 (xiaochangshu), inside the 1st posterior sacral foramen (foramina sacralia posteriora). What is this point? A. Li16 [Jù Gǔ]; B. B31 [Shàng Liáo]; C. Sj14 [Jiān Liáo]; D. Li15 [Jiān Yú]; E. Sj15 [Tiān Liáo]
992	小指尺侧爪甲角旁 0.1 寸,是取何穴位？A. Sj1 [關沖]; B. H9 [少沖]; C. Si1 [少澤]; D. Lv10 [足五里]; E. Lv11 [陰廉]	About 0.1 Cun behind the corner of the vallum unguis on the ulnar side of the little finger. What is this point? A. Sj1 [Guān Chōng]; B. H9 [Shào Chōng]; C. Si1 [Shào Zé]; D. Lv10 [Zú Wǔ Lǐ, Wǔ Lǐ]; E. Lv11 [Yīn Lián]
993	小指桡侧爪甲角旁 0.1 寸,是取何穴位？A. Sj1 [關沖]; B. H9 [少沖]; C. Si1 [少澤]; D. Lv10 [足五里]; E. Lv11 [陰廉]	About 0.1 Cun behind the corner of the vallum unguis on the radial side of the little finger. What is this point? A. Sj1 [Guān Chōng]; B. H9 [Shào Chōng]; C. Si1 [Shào Zé]; D. Lv10 [Zú Wǔ Lǐ, Wǔ Lǐ]; E. Lv11 [Yīn Lián]
994	悬钟穴的位置是: A ·外踝下缘直上 3 寸，腓骨后缘; B ·外踝上缘直上 3 寸，腓骨后缘 C. ·商丘穴直上 3 寸，腓骨后缘; D ·外踝尖直上 3 寸,腓骨后缘; E ·外踝尖直上 3 寸,腓骨骨缘	Where is G39 (Xuán Zhōng) located? A. 3 Cuns directly above the inferior border of lateral malleolus, on the posterior border of fibula; B. 3 Cuns directly above the superior border of lateral malleolus, on the posterior border of fibula; C. 3 Cuns directly above Sp5 (Shāng Qiū), on the posterior border of fibula; D. 3 Cuns directly above the tip of lateral malleolus (outer ankle), on posterior border of fibula; E. 3 Cuns directly above the tip of lateral malleolus (outer ankle), on anterior border of fibula.
995	血海上 6 寸, 是取何穴位？A. G29 [居髎]; B. S31 [髀關]; C. Sp11 [箕門]; D. G32 [中瀆]; E. Lv9 [陰包]	6 Cuns directly above Xuehai=Sp10。 What is this point? A. G29 [Ju Liao']; B. S31 [Bì Guān]; C. Sp11 [Jī Mén]; D. G32 [Zhōng Dū]; E. Lv9 [Yīn; Bāo]
996	哑门上 0.5 寸，枕骨粗隆下缘, 是取何穴位？A. D16 [風府]; B. D20 [百會]; C. D22 [囟會]; D. D21 [前頂]; E. D23 [上星]	0.5 Cun above D15 (yamen), at the lower border of external occipital protuberance. What is this point? A. D16 [Fēng Fǔ]; B. D20 [Bǎi Huì]; C. D22 [Xìn Huì]; D. D21 [Qián Dǐng]; E. D23 [Shàng Xīng]
997	哑门外开 1.3 寸，当斜方肌外侧缘, 是取何穴位？A. G19 [腦空]; B. G18 [承靈]; C. G16 [目窗]; D.B10 [天柱]; E. G17 [正營]	1.3 Cun laterally away from D15 (yamen), on the lateral side of the origin of the trapezius muscle. What is this point? A. G19 [Nǎo Kōng]; B. G18 [Chéng Líng]; C. G16 [Mù Chuāng]; D.B10 [Tiān Zhù]; E. G17 [Zhèng Yíng]
998	阳白直上，曲差与本神之间,是取何穴位？A. G13 [本神]; B. G15 [頭臨泣]; C. B3 [眉沖]; D. B4 [曲差]E. S8 [頭維]	Directly above Yangbai=G14, in between B4 (qucha) and G13 (benshen). What is this point? A. G13 [Běn Shén]; B. G15 [Tóu Lín Qì]; C. B3 [Méi Chōng]; D. B4 [Qū Chestā]E. S8 [Tóu Wěi]

	S8 [頭維]	
999	阳陵泉上 3 寸，是取何穴位？A. Sp7 [漏谷]; B. G33 [膝陽關]; C. S35 [犢鼻]; D. B39 [委陽]; E. B40 [委中]	3 Cuns above G34 [Yáng Líng Quán]. What is this point? A. Sp7 [Lòu Gǔ]; B. G33 [Xī Yáng Guān]; C. S35 [Dú Bí]; D. B39 [Wěi Yáng]; E. B40 [Wěi Zhōng]
1000	阳陵泉穴位于: A腓骨头前上方凹陷处; B 腓骨头前下方凹陷处 C. 腓骨头后上方凹陷处; D 腓骨头后下方凹陷处.	Where is G34 [Yáng Líng Quán] located? A. in the depression in the front of and above head of fibula; B in the depression in the front of and below head of fibula; C. in the depression in the back of and above head of Fibula; D. in the depression in the back of and below head of fibula.
1001	阳陵泉穴针刺时 不能刺中: A 腓肠外侧皮神经; B 腓肠内侧皮神经 C. 腓浅神经; D 腓深神经.	What nerve should not be inserted into when needling G34 [Yáng Líng Quán]? A. cutaneous nerve on the lateral side of gastrocnemius muscle; B cutaneous nerve on the medial side of gastrocnemius muscle; C. Superficial Peroneal Nerve; D Deep Peroneal Nerve.
1002	阳溪上 3 寸，是取何穴位？A. Sj5 [外關]; B. H5 [通里]; C. Li7 [溫溜]; D. Li6 [偏歷]; E. H4 [靈道]	3 Cuns above Yangxi=Li5. What is this point? A. Sj5 [Wài Guān]; B. H5 [Tōng Lǐ]; C. Li7 [Wēn Liū]; D. Li6 [Piān Lì]; E. H4 [Líng Dào]
1003	仰卧，于喉结与下颔骨之间，当舌骨体上缘中点，是取何穴位？A. R23 [廉泉]; B. S10 [水突]; C. Li17 [天鼎]; D. Li18 [扶突]; E. Si16 [天窗]	Lying on back, this point is in between laryngeal prominence and mandible, on the midpoint of the upper edge of hyoid bone. What is this point? A. R23 [Lián Quán]; B. S10 [Shuǐ Tū]; C. Li17 [Tiān Dǐng]; D. Li18 [Fú Tū]; E. Si16 [Tiān Chuāng]
1004	仰掌，第一掌指关节后近第一掌骨中部赤白肉际，是取何穴位？A. Si5 [陽谷]; B. H8 [少府]; C. Lu10 [魚際]; D. Sj4 [陽池]; E. P8 [勞宮]	With the palm facing upward, behind 1st metacarpophalangeal joint, close to the middle of the 1st metacarpal bone, on the border of dark-red muscles. What is this point? A. Si5 [Yáng Gǔ,]; B. H8 H8 [Shào Fǔ]; C. Lu10 [Yǔ Jì]; D. Sj4 [Yáng Chí]; E. P8 [Láo Gōng]
1005	翳风和角孙沿耳轮的连线之中、下 1 / 3，是取何穴位？ A. D23 [上星]; B. Sj20 [角孫]; C. Sj19 [顱息]; D. Sj18 [瘈脈]; E. D24 [神庭]	Draw a curve along the root of the ear to connect Sj17 and Sj20; lower 1 / 3 of the curve. What is this point? A. D23 [Shàng Xīng]; B. Sj20 [Jiǎo Sūn]; C. Sj19 [Lú Xī]; D. Sj18 [Chì Mài]; E. D24 [Shén Tíng]
1006	翳风和角孙沿耳轮的连线之中上 1 / 3，是取何穴位？A. D23 [上星]; B. Sj20 [角孫]; C. Sj19 [顱息]; D. Sj18 [瘈脈]; E. D24 [神庭]	Draw a curve along the root of the ear to connect Sj17 and Sj20; upper 1 / 3 of the curve. What is this point? A. D23 [Shàng Xīng]; B. Sj20 [Jiǎo Sūn]; C. Sj19 [Lú Xī]; D. Sj18 [Chì Mài]; E. D24 [Shén Tíng]
1007	阴廉下 1 寸，是取何穴位？A. Sj1 [關沖]; B. H9 [少沖]; C. Si1 [少澤]; D. Lv10 [足五里]; E. Sp10 [血海]	On the medial side of thigh, 3 Cuns below Qichong=S30, on the lateral side of the adductor muscles. On the medial side of the superficial branch of the medial femoral artery. What is this point? A. Sj1 [Guān Chōng]; B. H9 [Shào Chōng]; C. Si1 [Shào Zé]; D. Lv10 [Zú Wǔ Lǐ, Wǔ Lǐ]; E. Sp10 [Xuè Hǎi]
1008	阴陵泉斜后一寸，当胫骨内侧髁后下方，是取何穴位？A. G34 [陽陵泉]; B. B38 [浮郄]; C. Lv8 [曲泉]; D. K10 [陰谷]; E. Lv7 [膝關]	On the postero-inferior side of the medial condyle of tibia, 1 Cun behind Yinlingquan=Sp8. What is this point? A. G34 [Yáng Líng Quán]; B. B38 [Fú Xī]; C. Lv8 [Qū Quán]; D. K10 [Yīn Gǔ]; E. Lv7 [Xī Guān].

	K10 [陰谷]; E. Lv7 [膝關].	
1009	阴陵泉直下 3 寸，是取何穴位？A. Sp7 [漏谷]; B. Lv5 [蠡溝]; C. Sp8 [地機]; D. K9 [筑賓]; E. Lv6 [中都]	On the medial side of tibia, 3 Cuns directly below Yinlingquan=Sp9, 4 Cuns above Lougu=Sp7. What is this point? A. Sp7 [Lòu Gǔ]; B. Lv5 [Lí Gōu]; C. Sp8 [Dì Jı]; D. K9 [Zhú; Bīn]; E. Lv6 [Zhōng Dū]
1010	与肩胛骨下角相平的胸椎是: A 第 5 胸椎; B 第 6 胸椎 C. 第 7 胸椎; D 第 8 胸椎; E 第 9 胸椎.	Which thoracic vertibra is on a level with the inferior angle of the scapula? A. 5th thoracic vertibra; B. 6th thoracic vertibra; C. 7th thoracic vertibra; D. 8th thoracic vertibra; E. 9th thoracic vertibra.
1011	在尺侧端，尺侧腕屈肌腱的桡侧凹陷中，是取何穴位？A. Lu9 [太淵]; B. H7 [神門]; C. P7 [大陵]; D. Si7 [支正]; E. Li5 [陽溪]	Along the distal wrist crease, in the depression on the radial side of the flexor carpi ulnaris muscle. What is this point? A. Lu9 [Tài Yuān]; B. H7 [Shén Mén]; C. P7 [Dà Líng]; D. Si7 [Zhi Zhèng]; E. Li5 [Yáng Xī]
1012	在尺骨和桡骨之间，腕背横纹上 2 寸，是取何穴位？A. Sj5 [外關]; B. H5 [通里]; C. Li7 [溫溜]; D. Li6 [偏歷]; E. H4 [靈道]	In between ulna and radius, 2 Cuns above dorsal carpal crease. What is this point? A. Sj5 [Wài Guān]; B. H5 [Tōng Lǐ]; C. Li7 [Wēn Liū]; D. Li6 [Piān Lì]; E. H4 [Líng Dào]
1013	在第五跖骨小头后下方，是取何穴位？A. Sp2 [大都]; B. Sp3 [太白]; C. Sp1 [隱白]; D. B65 [束骨]; E. B66 [足通谷].	Behind and below the head of the 5th metatarsal bone. What is this point? A. Sp2 [Dà Dū]; B. Sp3 [Tài Bái]; C. Sp1 [Yǐn Bái]; D. B65 [Shù Gǔ]; E. B66 [Zú Tōng Gǔ].
1014	在第五跖趾关节外侧的前下方，是取何穴位？A. Sp2 [大都]; B. Sp3 [太白]; C. Sp1 [隱白]; D. B65 [束骨]; E. B66 [足通谷].	On the lateral side of the 5th metatarsophalangeal joint, on the anterior and inferior side. What is this point? A. Sp2 [Dà Dū]; B. Sp3 [Tài Bái]; C. Sp1 [Yǐn Bái]; D. B65 [Shù Gǔ]; E. B66 [Zú Tōng Gǔ].
1015	在第一跖趾关节的后下方，是取何穴位？A. Sp2 [大都]; B. Sp3 [太白]; C. Sp1 [隱白]; D. B65 [束骨]; E. B66 [足通谷].	On the medial side of the 1st metatarsophalangeal joint, on the posterior and inferior side. What is this point? A. Sp2 [Dà Dū]; B. Sp3 [Tài Bái]; C. Sp1 [Yǐn Bái]; D. B65 [Shù Gǔ]; E. B66 [Zú Tōng Gǔ].
1016	在第一跖趾关节内侧的前下方，是取何穴位？A. Sp2 [大都]; B. Sp3 [太白]; C. Sp1 [隱白]; D. B65 [束骨]; E. B66 [足通谷].	On the medial side of the 1st metatarsophalangeal joint, on the anterior-inferior side. What is this point? A. Sp2 [Dà Dū]; B. Sp3 [Tài Bái]; C. Sp1 [Yǐn Bái]; D. B65 [Shù Gǔ]; E. B66 [Zú Tōng Gǔ].
1017	在耳垂后方，当乳突与下颌角之间凹陷处是： A.天牖; B.天容 C. 瘛脉; D 翳风.	Which point is located behind the lobule of the auricle, in the depression between the mandible and the mastoid process? A. Sj16 (Tiān Yǒu); B. Si17 (Tiān Róng); C. Sj18 (Chì Mài); D. Sj17 (Yì Fēng).
1018	在风池穴正确针刺时，针尖应刺向: A对侧眼内眦; B 对侧眼外眦 C. 同侧眼内眦; D 同侧眼外眦.	When inserting into G20 [Fēng Chí] accurately, what direction should the tip of the needle face? A. facing Medial Canthus on the opposite side; B facing Outer Canthus on the other side; C. facing Medial Canthus on the same side; D facing Outer Canthus on the same side.
1019	在股骨大转子与骶管裂孔连线的外 1 / 3 与内 2 / 3 的交点，是取何穴位？A. G32	In the center of the triangle formed by the greater trochanter, iliac crest, and ischial tuberosity, behind greater trochanter, 1 / 3 distance from the greater

	[中瀆]; B. G30 [環跳]; C. B37 [殷門]; D. G31 [風市]; E. B36 [承扶]	greater trochanter, 1 / 3 distance from the greater trochanter when the distance between the greater trochanter and the sacral hiatus is divided into 3 equal parts. What is this point? A. G32 [Zhōng Dū]; B. G30 [Huán Tiào]; C. B37 [Yīn Mén]; D. G31 [Fēng Shì]; E. B36 [Chéng Fú]
1020	在横纹中央，掌长肌腱与桡侧腕屈肌腱之间，是取何穴位？A. Lu9 [太淵]; B. H7 [神門]; C. P7 [大陵]; D. Si7 [支正]; E. Li5 [陽溪]	In the middle of the distal wrist crease in between two tendons (palmaris longus & flexor carpi radialis). What is this point? A. Lu9 [Tài Yuān]; B. H7 [Shén Mén]; C. P7 [Dà Líng]; D. Si7 [Zhi Zhèng]; E. Li5 [Yáng Xī]
1021	在肩胛冈上窝正中处的穴位是： A.秉风;.B.天宗 C. 曲垣; D 肩中俞.	Which point is located in the middle of the supraspinatous fossa? A. Si12 (Bǐng Fēng); B. Si11 (Tiān Zōng); C. Si13 (Qū Yuān); D. Si15 (Jiān Zhōng Shū).
1022	在肩胛骨岗上窝的内侧端，约当臑俞与第二胸椎连线的中点，是取何穴位？A. Si13 [曲垣]; B. Si15 [肩中輸]; C. Si12 [秉風]; D. G21 [肩井]; E. Si14 [肩外輸]	On the medial side of the supraspinatous fossa, on the midpoint of the line connecting Si10 (naoshu) and 2nd thoracic vertebra. What is this point? A. Si13 [Qū Yuān]; B. Si15 [Jiān Zhōng Shū]; C. Si12 [Bǐng Fēng]; D. G21 [Jiān Jǐng]; E. Si14 [Jiān Wài Shū]
1023	在肩胛骨岗下窝中央，是取何穴位？A. Sj16 [天牖]; B. Si9 [肩貞]; C. Si11 [天宗]; D. Si17 [天容]; E. Si10 [臑輸].	In the infraspinatous fossa. What is this point? A. Sj16 [Tiān Yǒu]; B. Si9 [Jiān Zhēn]; C. Si11 [Tiān Zōng]; D. Si17 [Tiān Róng]; E. Si10 [Nào Shū].
1024	在髂前上棘直下，与臀沟平齐的交点，和承扶相对，是取何穴位？A. G29 [居髎]; B. S31 [髀關]; C. Sp11 [箕門]; D. Sp10 [血海]; E. Lv9 [陰包]	With the thigh bent, this point is directly below the spina iliaca anterior superior, in the depression between the lateral border of the sartorius & the medial border of the tensor fasciae latae, on a level with the gluteal fold, vis-à-vis B36 (cheng-fu). What is this point? A. G29 [Ju Liao']; B. S31 [Bì Guān]; C. Sp11 [Jī Mén]; D. Sp10 [Xuè Hǎi]; E. Lv9 [Yīn; Bāo]
1025	在前臂掌面桡恻，桡骨茎突与挠动脉之间凹陷处，腕横纹上 1 寸的穴位是: A·列缺; B 经渠 C. ·太渊; D·鱼际; E 少商.	What point is located on the radial side of the palm of forearm，in the depression between styloid process of the radius andradial artery，1 Cun above the wrist crease? A·Lu7 / Liè Quē; B. · Lu8 / Jīng Qú; C. · Lu9 / TàiYuān; D. · Lu10 / Yǔ Jì; E. · Lu11 / Shǎo Shāng.
1026	在桡侧端，桡动脉桡侧凹陷中，是取何穴位？A. Lu9 [太淵]; B. H7 [神門]; C. P7 [大陵]; D. Si7 [支正]; E. Li5 [陽溪]	At the tip of the radial side of the distal wrist crease, in the depression on the radial side of the radial artery. What is this point? A. Lu9 [Tài Yuān]; B. H7 [Shén Mén]; C. P7 [Dà Líng]; D. Si7 [Zhi Zhèng]; E. Li5 [Yáng Xī]
1027	在手掌心，当第 23 掌骨之间偏于第 3 掌骨，握拳屈指时中指尖处: A.少府; B.鱼际 C. 后溪; D 劳宫.	Which point is located in the palm of hand, between 2nd. & 3rd metacarpal bones, closer to the 3[rD.] metacarpal bone, and it may be touched by tip of middle finger when fist is clenched? A. H8 (Shào Fǔ); B. Lu10 (Yǔ Jì); C. Si3 (Hòu Xī); D. P8 (Láo Gōng).
1028	在天宗直上，肩胛岗中点上缘凹陷中，是取何穴位？A. Si13 [曲垣]; B. Si15 [肩中	Directly above Si11 (tianzong), in the depression on the superior border of the midpoint of the infraspinatous fossa. What is this point? A. Si13 [Qū Yuān]; B. Si15

	輸]; C. Si12 [秉風]; D. G21 [肩井]; E. Si14 [肩外輸]	[Jiān Zhōng Shū]; C. Si12 [Bǐng Fēng]; D. G21 [Jiān Jǐng]; E. Si14 [Jiān Wài Shū]
1029	在头部，当攒竹直上入发际0.5寸，神庭与曲差连线之间的穴位是： A.头临泣; B 头维 C. 上星; D 眉冲.	Which point is located in the head region, directly above B2 (Zǎn Zhú), 0.5 Cun inside the hairline, on the line connecting D24 (Shén Tíng) and B4 (Qū Chestā)? A. G15 (Tóu Lín Qì，Lín Qì); B. S8 (Tóu Wěi); C. D23 (Shàng Xīng); D. B3 (Méi Chōng).
1030	在外侧胸锁乳突肌后缘扶突穴后与喉结相平的穴位是： A.天容; B.天窗 C. 天鼎; D 天髎.	Which point is located on the lateral side, on the posterior border of sternocleidomastoideus, behind Li18 (Fú Tū), on a level with the laryngeal prominence? A. Si17 (Tiān Róng); B. Si16 (Tiān Chuāng); C. Li17 (Tiān Dǐng); D. Sj15 (Tiān Liáo).
1031	在腕背横纹桡侧端，取穴时拇指翘起.当拇长、短伸肌腱之间凹陷中，是取何穴位？A. Lu9 [太淵]; B. H7 [神門]; C. P7 [大陵]; D. Si7 [支正]; E. Li5 [陽溪]	On the radial side of dorsal carpal crease. With the thumb up, this point is in the depression named the anatomical snuffbox, in the depression between two tendons (extensor pollicis brevis & extensor pollicis longus). What is this point? A. Lu9 [Tài Yuān]; B. H7 [Shén Mén]; C. P7 [Dà Líng]; D. Si7 [Zhì Zhèng]; E. Li5 [Yáng Xī]
1032	在腕背横纹中，指总伸肌腱尺侧缘凹陷中，是取何穴位？A. Si5 [陽谷]; B. H8 [少府]; C. Lu10 [魚際]; D. Sj4 [陽池]; E. P8 [勞宮]	On the radial side of dorsal carpal crease. In the depression on the ulnar side of the extensor digitorum communis muscle. What is this point? A. Si5 [Yáng Gǔ,]; B. H8 H8 [Shào Fǔ]; C. Lu10 [Yǔ Jì]; D. Sj4 [Yáng Chí]; E. P8 [Láo Gōng]
1033	在腕关节尺侧、当三角骨与尺骨茎突之间凹陷中，是取何穴位？A. Si5 [陽谷]; B. H8 [少府]; C. Lu10 [魚際]; D. Sj4 [陽池]; E. P8 [勞宮]	On the ulnar side of the ulnocarpal joint, in the depression between the styloid process of ulna & the triangular bone (triquetrum). What is this point? A. Si5 [Yáng Gǔ,]; B. H8 H8 [Shào Fǔ]; C. Lu10 [Yǔ Jì]; D. Sj4 [Yáng Chí]; E. P8 [Láo Gōng]
1034	在五里与曲泉的连线上，股骨内上髁上4寸，缝匠肌后缘，是取何穴位？A. G29 [居髎]; B. S31 [髀關]; C. Sp11 [箕門]; D. Sp10 [血海]; E. Lv9 [陰包]	4 Cuns above the medial epicondyle of femur (or Ququan=Lv8) in between the sartorius muscle and vastus medialis muscle. What is this point? A. G29 [Ju Liao']; B. S31 [Bì Guān]; C. Sp11 [Jī Mén]; D. Sp10 [Xuè Hǎi]; E. Lv9 [Yīn; Bāo]
1035	在翳风和风府连线的中点，适当胸鎖乳突肌和斜方肌之间的凹陷处，是取何穴位？A. R22 [天突]; B. S11 [氣舍]; C. S9 [人迎]; D. S12 [缺盆]; E. G20 [風池]	On the midpoint of the line connecting Sj17 (yifeng) and D16 (fengfu), in the depression in between sternocleidomastoid muscle and musculus trapezius. What is this point? A. R22 [Tiān Tū]; B. S11 [Qì Shě]; C. S9 [Rén Yíng]; D. S12 [Quē Pén]; E. G20 [Fēng Chí]
1036	在掌长肌腱和桡侧腕屈肌腱之间，腕横纹上2寸，是取何穴位？A. P6 [內關]; B. P4 [郄門]; C. H6 [陰郄 D. P5 [間使]; E. Lu6 [孔最]	2 Cuns above the distal wrist crease or Daling=P7, in between two tendons (palmaris longus & flexor Carpi radialis). What is this point? A. P6 [Nèi Guān]; B. P4 [Xī Mén]; C. H6 [Yīn Xī]; D. P5 [Jiān Shǐ]; E. Lu6 [Kǒng Zuì]
1037	在舟骨粗隆前下缘凹陷处的穴位是: A·太白; B·公孙 C. ·京骨; D·然谷; E· 冲阳.	What point is located in the depression on the anterior inferior border of the tuberosity of the navicular bone? A. Sp3 (Tài Bái); B. Sp4 (Gōng Sūn); C. B64 (Jīng Gǔ); D. K2 (Rán Gǔ); E. S42 (Chōng Yáng).
1038	攒竹直上，神庭与曲差之间(神庭旁开0.5寸)，是取何穴位？A. G13 [本神]; B.	Directly above B2 (zanzhu), in between D24 (shenting) and B4 (qucha), 0.5 Cun lateral to D24. What is this point? A. G13 [Běn Shén]; B. G15 [Tóu Lín Qì]; C. B3 [Méi

	G15 [頭臨泣]; C. B3 [眉沖]; D. B4 [曲差]E. S8 [頭維]	A. G13 [Běn Shén]; B. G15 [Tóu Lín Qì]; C. B3 [Méi Chōng]; D. B4 [Qū Chestā]E. S8 [Tóu Wěi]
1039	章门穴直下平脐，是取何穴位？A. Lv13 [章門]; B. G24 [日月]; C. G27 [五樞]; D. G26 [帶脈]; E. G25 [京門]	Directly below Lv13 (zhangmen), on a level with the navel. What is this point? A. Lv13 [Zhāng Mén]; B. G24 [Rì Yuè]; C. G27 [Wǔ Shū]; D. G26 [Dài Mài]; E. G25 [Jīng Mén]
1040	针刺下髎穴时，可刺中的神经是: A臀上神经; B 臀下神经 C. 坐骨神经; D 阴部神经.	What nerve may be inserted into when needling B34 [Xià Liáo]? A. Superio Gluteal Nerve; B Inferior Gluteal Nerve; C. Sciatic Nerve; D. pudendal nerve.
1041	正确针刺中脘穴时，当针尖刺过皮下组织后可达的结构为: A 腹直肌; B 腹横筋膜 C. 腹膜; D 白线.	In needling R12 [Zhōng Wǎn] with accuracy, what structure may be inserted into after the tip of needle passes subcutaneous tissue? A. Abdominal Rectus Muscle; B. Transverse Fascia; C. Peritoneum; D linea alba (white line).
1042	正营后 1.5 寸，是取何穴位？A. G19 [腦空]; B. G18 [承靈]; C. G16 [目窗]; D.B10 [天柱]; E. G20 [風池]	1.5 Cuns behind Zhengying (G17). What is this point? A. G19 [Nǎo Kōng]; B. G18 [Chéng Líng]; C. G16 [Mù Chuāng]; D.B10 [Tiān Zhù]; E. G20 [Fēng Chí]
1043	支沟尺侧外开 1 寸，是取何穴位？A. Sj8 [三陽絡]; B. Sj9 [四瀆]; C. Si6 [養老]; D. Lu9 [太淵]; E. Sj7 [會宗]	On the ulnar side of Zhigou=Sj6, and 1 digital Cun (namely, one tendon distance) from Sj6. What is this point? A. Sj8 [Sān Yáng Luò]; B. Sj9 [Sì Dú]; C. Si6 [Yǎng Lǎo]; D. Lu9 [Tài Yuān]; E. Sj7 [Huì Zōng]
1044	支沟上 1 寸当阳池至尺骨鹰嘴连线的下 1 / 3 处，是取何穴位？A. Sj8 [三陽絡]; B. Sj9 [四瀆]; C. Si6 [養老]; D. Lu9 [太淵]; E. Sj7 [會宗]	1 Cun above Sj6 (zhigou), at the lower 1 / 3 of the line connecting Sj4 (yangchi) and olecranon process. What is this point? A. Sj8 [Sān Yáng Luò]; B. Sj9 [Sì Dú]; C. Si6 [Yǎng Lǎo]; D. Lu9 [Tài Yuān]; E. Sj7 [Huì Zōng]
1045	至阳穴位于: A 第 3 胸椎棘突下间; B 第 5 胸椎棘突下间 C. 第 6 胸椎棘突下间; D 第 7 胸椎棘突下间; E 第 9 胸椎棘突下间.	Where is D9 (Zhì Yáng) located? A. below the spinous process of the 3rd thoracic vertebra; B. below the spinous process of the 5th thoracic vertebra; C. below the spinous process of the 6th thoracic vertebra; D. below the spinous process of the 7th thoracic vertebra; E. below the spinous process of the 9th thoracic vertebra.
1046	中膂俞内侧 0.9 寸，当第三骶后孔中，是取何穴位？A. B33 [中髎]; B. B32 [次髎]; C. B35 [会阳]; D. D1 [長強]; E. B34 [下髎]	Inside the 3rd posterior sacral foramen, on the medial side of and 9 fens away from B29 (zhonglushu). What is this point? A. B33 [Zhōng Liáo]; B. B32 [Cì Liáo]; C. B35 [Huì Ang]; D. D1 [Cháng Qiáng]; E. B34 [Xià Liáo]
1047	中脘穴位于: A 脐上4寸; B 脐上2寸 C. 脐中间; D 脐下4寸.	Where is R12 [Zhōng Wǎn] located? A. 4 Cuns above umbilicus; B. 2 Cuns above umbilicus C. middle of umbilicus; D. 4 Cuns below umbilicus.
1048	中指尖端，是取何穴位？A. Si4 [腕骨]; B. Li4 [合谷]; C. Li1 [商陽]; D. P9 [中沖]; E. Lu11 [少商]	About 0.1 Cun above the corner of the vallum unquis on the radial side of the middle finger. What is this point? A. Si4 [Wàn Gǔ]; B. Li4 [Hé Gǔ]; C. Li1 [Shāng Yáng]; D. P9 [Zhōng Chōng]; E. Lu11 [Shǎo Shāng]

1049	舟骨粗隆下缘凹陷中，是取何穴位？A; B60 [崑崙]; B. B61 [仆參]; C. K2 [然谷]; D. B62 [申脈]; E. G40 [丘墟]	In the depression at the lower border of the tuberosity of the navicular bone. What is this point? A; B60 [Kūn Lún]; B. B61 [Pū Cān]; C. K2 [Rán Gŭ]; D. B62 [Shēn Mài]; E. G40 [Qiū Xū]
1050	肘横纹中，肱二头肌腱的尺侧，是取何穴位？A. Li12 [肘髎]; B. H3 [少海]; C. Li13 [手五里]; D. P3 [曲澤]; E. Lu5 [尺澤]	On the elbow crease on the ulnar side of the biceps brachii muscle. What is this point? A. Li12 [Zhŏu Liáo]; B. H3 [Shào Hăi]; C. Li13 [Shŏu Wŭ Lĭ]; D. P3 [Qū Zé]; E. Lu5 [Chĭ Zé]
1051	肘横纹中，肱二头肌腱的桡侧，是取何穴位？A. Li12 [肘髎]; B. H3 [少海]; C. Li13 [手五里]; D. P3 [曲澤]; E. Lu5 [尺澤]	On the elbow crease in the depression on the radial side of the biceps brachii muscles. What is this point? A. Li12 [Zhŏu Liáo]; B. H3 [Shào Hăi]; C. Li13 [Shŏu Wŭ Lĭ]; D. P3 [Qū Zé]; E. Lu5 [Chĭ Zé]
1052	足背踝关节前横纹中点，当趾长伸肌腱与拇长伸肌腱之间，与外踝高点平齐处，是取何穴位？A. K3 [太溪]; B. K6 [照海]; C. K4 [大鍾]; D. S41 [解溪]; E. K5 [水泉]	On the transversal crease at the intersection of the lower leg and the dorsum of foot, in the center of the ligamentum cruciatum, in between the extensor digitorum longus and the extensor hallucis longus. What is this point? A. K3 [Tài Xī]; B. K6 [Zhào Hăi]; C. K4 [Dà Zhōng]; D. S41 [Jiě Xī]; E. K5 [Shuĭ Quán]
1053	足次趾趾甲根的外侧角旁 0.1 寸，是取何穴位？A. S45 [歷兌]; B. G44 [足竅陰]; C. Lv1 [大敦]; D. K1 [涌泉]; E. B67 [至陰]	1 fen to the lateral angle of the toenail root of the 2nd toe. What is this point? A. S45 [Lì Duì]; B. G44 [Zú Qiào Yīn]; C. Lv1 [Dà Dūn]; D. K1 [Yŏng Quán]; E. B67 [Zhì Yīn]
1054	足大趾趾甲根的内侧角旁 0.1 寸，是取何穴位？A. Sp2 [大都]; B. Sp3 [太白]; C. Sp1 [隱白]; D. B65 [束骨]; E. B66 [足通谷].	About 1 fen behind the corner of the vallum unquis on the medial side of the big toe. What is this point? A. Sp2 [Dà Dū]; B. Sp3 [Tài Bái]; C. Sp1 [Yĭn Bái]; D. B65 [Shù Gŭ]; E. B66 [Zú Tōng Gŭ].
1055	足大趾趾趾甲根的外 1 / 4 与内 3 / 4 的交点，是取何穴位？A. S45 [歷兌]; B. G44 [足竅陰]; C. Lv1 [大敦]; D. K1 [涌泉]; E. B67 [至陰]	At the intersection between lateral 1 / 4 and medial 3 / 4 of the toenail of the big toe. What is this point? A. S45 [Lì Duì]; B. G44 [Zú Qiào Yīn]; C. Lv1 [Dà Dūn]; D. K1 [Yŏng Quán]; E. B67 [Zhì Yīn]
1056	足跗上第四，五跖骨结合部前方凹陷中，当小趾伸肌腱的外侧，是取何穴位？A. Sp4 [公孫]; B. B64 [京骨]; C. S42 [沖陽]; D. B63 [金門]; E. G41 [足臨泣]	In the depression anterior to the combining side of the 4th and 5th metatarsal bones, on the lateral side of the extensor muscle of the little toe. What is this point? A. Sp4 [Gōng Sūn]; B. B64 [Jīng Gŭ]; C. S42 [Chōng Yáng]; D. B63 [Jīn Mén]; E. G41 [Zú Lín Qì ,Lín Qì]
1057	足跗上解溪下 1.5 寸，当第二、三跖骨与楔状骨之间的凹陷处，是取何穴位？A. Sp4 [公孫]; B. B64 [京骨]; C. S42 [沖陽]; D. B63 [金門]; E. G41 [足臨泣]	In the depression in between 2nd and 3rd metatarsal bones and the cuneiform bone,. What is this point? A. Sp4 [Gōng Sūn]; B. B64 [Jīng Gŭ]; C. S42 [Chōng Yáng]; D. B63 [Jīn Mén]; E. G41 [Zú Lín Qì ,Lín Qì]
1058	足跗上外踝前缘申脉前下方，当骰骨外側凹陷中，是取何穴位？A. Sp4 [公孫]; B. B64 [京骨]; C. S42 [沖陽]; D. B63 [金門]; E. G41 [足臨泣]	In the depression on the lateral side of the cuboid bone, on the anterior-inferior side of B62 (shenmai), which is on the anterior border of lateral malleolus on dorsum of foot. What is this point? A. Sp4 [Gōng Sūn]; B. B64 [Jīng Gŭ]; C. S42 [Chōng Yáng]; D. B63 [Jīn Mén]; E. G41 [Zú Lín Qì ,Lín Qì]

1059	足跗外側第五跖骨粗隆下赤白肉际，是取何穴位？A. Sp4 [公孫]; B. B64 [京骨]; C. S42 [沖陽]; D. B63 [金門]; E. G41 [足臨泣]	In the juncture of the dark and white muscles below the tuberosity of the 5th metatarsal bone on the lateral side of the dorsum of foot. What is this point? A. Sp4 [Gōng Sūn]; B. B64 [Jīng Gǔ]; C. S42 [Chōng Yáng]; D. B63 [Jīn Mén]; E. G41 [Zú Lín Qì ,Lín Qì]
1060	足三里下 3 寸，是取何穴位？A. S37 [上巨虛]; B. G37 [光明]; C. S40 [丰隆]; D. S39 [下巨虛]; E. S38 [條口]	6 Cuns below Dubi=S35, 3 Cuns below Zusanli=S36, on the tibialis anterior, in between tibia and fibula, on the lateral side of tibia. What is this point? A. S37 [Shàng Jù Xū]; B. G37 [Guāng Míng]; C. S40 [Fēng Lóng]; D. S39 [Xià Jù Xū]; E. S38 [Tiáo Kǒu]
1061	足三里穴刺穿小腿骨间膜后，可刺中: A 腓肠外侧皮神经; B 腓浅神经 C. 腓深神经; D 胫神经.	In needling Zusanli=S36, what nerve may be inserted into after the needle penetrates through interosseous membrane of the lower leg? A. cutaneous nerve of lateral gastrocnemius muscle; B superficial peroneal nerve; C. deep peroneal nerve; D. tibial nerve -
1062	足三里穴位于: A股骨外上髁直下3寸，于胫骨前缘旁1横指凹陷处; B 胫骨外侧髁直下3寸。于胫骨前缘旁1横指凹陷处 C. 腓骨头直下3寸，于胫骨前缘旁1横指凹陷处; D 犊鼻穴(外膝眼)直下3寸，于胫骨前缘旁1横指凹陷处.	Where is S36 [Zú Sān Lǐ] located? A. 3 Cun directly below External Epicondyle of Femur, in the depression 1 transverse digit lateral from the frontal edge of tibia; B. 3 Cun directly below lateral condyle of tibia in the depression 1 transverse digit lateral from the frontal edge of tibia; C. 3 Cun directly below head of fibula, in the depression 1 transverse digit lateral from the frontal edge of tibia; D 3 Cun directly below S35 [Dú Bí], in the depression 1 transverse digit lateral from the frontal edge of tibia.
1063	足少阳胆经的居髎穴，位于: A 髂前上棘与股骨大转子连线的上 1 / 3 与 2 / 3 交界处; B 髂脊最高点与股骨大转子连线的中点处 C. 髂前上棘与股骨大转子连线的中点处; D 髂脊最高点与股骨大转子连线的 1 / 3 与下 2 / 3 交界处; E 以上均不是	Where is G29 (Jū Liáo) located? A. on the upper 1 / 3 and 2 / 3 of the line connecting anterior superior iliac spine (spina illiaca anterior superior) and greater trochanter; B. On the midpoint of the line connecting highest point of iliac crest and greater trochanter; C. on the midpoint of the line connecting anterior superior iliac spine (spina illiaca anterior superior) and greater trochanter; D. on the 1 / 3 and lower 2 / 3 of the line connecting highest point of iliac crest and greater trochanter; E. none of the above.
1064	足四趾趾甲根的外側角旁 0.1 寸，是取何穴位？A. S45 [歷兌]; B. G44 [足竅陰]; C. Lv1 [大敦]; D. K1 [涌泉]; E. B67 [至陰]	1 fen to the lateral angle of the toenail root of the 4th toe (about 1 fen behind the lateral corner of the vallum unguis). What is this point? A. S45 [Lì Duì]; B. G44 [Zú Qiào Yīn]; C. Lv1 [Dà Dūn]; D. K1 [Yǒng Quán]; E. B67 [Zhì Yīn]
1065	足小趾趾甲根的外側角旁 0.1 寸，是取何穴位？A. S45 [歷兌]; B. G44 [足竅陰]; C. Lv1 [大敦]; D. K1 [涌泉]; E. B67 [至陰]	1 fen to the lateral angle of the toenail root of the little toe. What is this point? A. S45 [Lì Duì]; B. G44 [Zú Qiào Yīn]; C. Lv1 [Dà Dūn]; D. K1 [Yǒng Quán]; E. B67 [Zhì Yīn]
1066	足掌心，蹺足时呈现的凹陷处取，是取何穴位？A. S45 [歷兌]; B. G44 [足竅陰]; C. Lv1 [大敦]; D. K1 [涌泉]; E. B67 [至陰]	In the center of sole of foot where a depression occurs when the foot is raised. What is this point? A. S45 [Lì Duì]; B. G44 [Zú Qiào Yīn]; C. Lv1 [Dà Dūn]; D. K1 [Yǒng Quán]; E. B67 [Zhì Yīn]

13-4	刺灸法	Techniques of Acupuncture-Moxibustion	1067-1338

13-4 刺灸法 / Techniques of Acupuncture-Moxibustion

1067	"刺浮痹皮肤也"是指: A.半刺; B 扬刺 C. 毛刺; D. 赞刺.	"A needle is inserted into the superficial skin in order to disperse floating rheumatism in the skin" is called: A halved. Needling; B. scattered. Needling; C. hairy needling; D. supplemental needling.
1068	"催气手法"最早由谁提出? A.何若愚; B.窦汉卿 C. 陈会; D 徐之才.	Who first put forward the method of "expediting arrival of energy"? A He Ruo Yu (12th C. entury); B. Dou Han Qing (1196-1280); C. Chesten Hui (1368-1425?); D. Xu Zhi Cai (492-572).
1069	"得气"也称: A 经气传导; B 气至病所 C. 循经感传; D 针刺反应; E 针感.	What is another name for De Qi (gaining energy)? A. transmission of meridian energy; B. arrival of energy in the diseased spot; C. transmission of sensations along meridian; D. response of needle insertion; E. needling sensations.
1070	"火补火泻"是指: A."大补大泻"; B 毫针补泻 C. 火针补泻; D 烧山火 透天凉; E 艾炷直接灸的补泻法.	What is meant by "fire tonificaion fire sedation"? A. tonfication and sedation on a large scale; B. tonfication and sedation by a minute needle; C. tonfication and sedation by a fire needle; D. forest fire technique and cool heaven technique; E. tonfication and sedation with direct moxibustion by moxa.
1071	"九针"其中有: A 大针.长针火针; B. 长计梅花针毫针 C. 馋针圆针, 鍉针; D. 锋针粗针鈹针; E. 以上都不是.	Which of the following groups lists the needles all of which are among the "Nine Needles"? A big needle, long needle, fire needle; B. long needle, plum blossom needle, minute needle (hao zhen); C. Scooping needle (chan zhen), round needle (yuan zhen), key-shaped needle (ti zhen); D. Sharp-edged needle (feng zhen), rough needle (cu zhen), Sword-shaped needle (pi zhen); E. none of the above.
1072	"浅内而疾发针, 无针伤内, 如拔毛状, 以取皮气"是指: A.半刺; B.扬刺 C. 毛刺; D 赞刺.	"The shallow insertion and immediate withdrawal, without harming inside by a needle, not unlike removal of a fine hair to obstain skin energy" is called: A halved. Needling; B. scattered. Needling; C. hairy needling; D. supplemental needling.
1073	"烧山火"和"透天凉"最早出现在哪部书中: A.《内经》; B《针经指南》 C. 《针灸大成》; D《针灸大全》.	What TCM Classic recorded "forest fire" and "cool-heaven-technique" for the first time? A.Yellow Emperor's Cclassics (Nei Jing); B. <Zhen Jing Zhi Nan> by Dou Han Qing (1196-1280); C. Compendium of Acupuncture and Moxibustion (1601), Zhen Jiu Da Cheng by Yang Ji Zhou (1522-1620); D. Zhen Jiu Da Quan,1439.
1074	"头为精明之府"语出: A《素问》; B·《灵枢》 C. 《针灸甲乙经》; D·《针灸大成》.	What Classic says, "head is the residence of essence and spirits"? A《Su Wen》; B·《Ling Shu》 C. 《Zhen Jiu Jia Yi Jing》; D·《Zhen Jiu Da Cheng》.
1075	"正内, 傍内四而浮	"The needles are inserted at five points, which are scattered

	之，以治寒气之博大者也。是指：A.半刺; B.扬刺 C.毛刺; D 赞刺.	around it on four sides, with one in the middle and the four others scattered around on four sides to treat old Rheumatism in the superficial region that involves a wider area" is called: A halved. Needling; B. scattered. Needling; C. hairy needling; D. supplemental needling.
1076	"肺主声，令耳闻声。"语出: A《素问》; B《灵枢》; C.《难经》; D《证治准绳》.	What Classic maintains that "the lungs are in charge of sounds; thus, the ears can hear sounds"? A《Su Wen》; B《Ling Shu》 C. 《Difficult C. lassic》 D《Zheng Zhi Zhun Sheng (1602)》
1077	"九针"最早被记述在哪部著作中: A.马王堆 《帛书》; B《内经》 C.《甲乙经》; D《针灸大成》.	Which Classic first recorded "nine needles"? A《ma wang dui》《Bo Shu》; B《Nei Jing》 C. 《Jia Yi Jing》 D《Zhen Jiu Da Chesteng》
1078	"扬刺者，正内一，傍内四而浮之，以治寒气之博大者也"。语出: A《素问》; B《灵枢》 C. 《难经》; D《甲乙经》.	Which Classic mentioned the following: "scattered needling in which one is in the middle with the four others scattered around it on four sides by a shallow insertion for the treatment of cold rheumatism in the superficial region that involves a wider area"? A《Su Wen》; B《Ling Shu》 C. 《Difficult C. lassic》; D《Jia Yi Jing》.
1079	《灵枢·经脉》所说"以经取之"的治疗原则适用于: A 虚证; B 实证 C. 不盛不虚之证; D 寒证; E 热证.	What disease should be treated by "the points on the diseased meridian" according to Ling shu, Chapter 10? A deficient diseases; B. excess diseases; C. diseases which are neither excessive nor deficient; D. cold diseases; E. hot diseases.
1080	提插补泻法中的补法是: A. 先插后提; B. 重插轻提 C. 速匀提插; D. 提插都重; E. 提插都轻	What is tonification in the "lifting and pushing-in technqiues of tonification andsedation"? A. pushing before lifting; B. heavy pushing light lifting' C. lifting and pushing evenly; D. heavy pushing and lifting; E. light lifting and pushing.
1081	1 寸毫针的法定计量针身长度为: A.15 mm;.25 mm;.40 mm; D45mm.	How long is the minute needle (hao zhen) which measures 1 Cun? A.15 mm; B.25 mm; C. 40 mm; D45 mm.
1082	30 号毫针的直径为: A.0.38 mm; B. 0.34 mm C. 0.32 mm; D 0.30 mm.	What is the diameter of the No.30 minute needle? A.0.38 mm; B.0.34 mm; C. 0.32 mm; D 0.30 mm.
1083	艾条灸法包括: A. 瘢痕灸、无瘢痕灸; B. 隔姜灸、隔蒜灸 C. ，隔盐灸、隔附子饼灸; D. 温和灸、雀啄灸; E. 太乙针灸，雷火针灸	Moxiustion by moxa sticks (moxa torches) includes: A. scar moxibustion, no-scar moxibustion; B. Moxibustion with ginger in between moxa and skin、Moxibustion with garlic in between moxa and skin; C. Moxibustion with salt in between moxa and skin、Moxibustion with cake of radix aconiti praeparata in between moxa and skin; D. warm and harmonious moxibustion、Sparrow pecking moxibustion; E. Taiyi medicated acupuncture and moxibustion，thunder fire medicated acupuncture and moxibusition.
1084	按《耳穴名称与部位》耳郭上有穴位: A.81	How many auricular points are there according to <Names and Locations Of Auriuclar Points>?

	个; B.91 个 C. 78 个; D88 个.	and Locations Of Auriuclar Points>? A. 81 points; B.91 points; C. 78 points; D88 points.
1085	拔罐法古代最早用于治疗: A.肺结核; B 疮疡 C. 风湿病; D 痛经.	What disease was cupping initially used to treat? A.pulmonary tuberculosis; B. carbuncle and ulcer; C. rheumatism; D. period pain.
1086	拔罐法早期称为: A 吮血疗法; B 排脓疗法 C. 排气疗法; D 闪罐法; E. 以上都不是.	What was the name for cupping at the earlier stage? A blood-sucking therapy (shun xue liao fa); B. drain-off-pus therapy (pai nong liao fa); C. exhaust therapy (pai qi liao fa); D. flashing cupping therapy (shan guan fa); E.none of the above.
1087	白芥子灸属于: A, 直接灸; B 天灸 C. 温和灸 D, 悬灸	Which does “moxibustion by semen sinapis albae (bai jie zi jiu) fall within? A direct moxibusiton; B. medicated. moxibustion to cause blisters; C. warm and harmonious moxibustion; D. hanging moxibustion (xuan jiu).
1088	病在经筋者，施治多选用: A 毫针; B 三棱针 C. 火针; D 雷火神针; E 大针.	Which technique is mostly selected in treating the disease in the meridian tendon region? A minute needle (hao zhen); B three-edged needles (san leng zhen); C. fire needle (huo zhen); D. thunder fire and spiritual needle (lei huo shen zhen); E.big needle (da zhen).
1089	不适宜拔罐的疾病为: A.高热抽搐; B.慢性病 C. 急性病; D 疼痛性疾病.	What disease should NOT be treated by cupping? A. high fever and twitching; B. Chronic diseases C. acute diseases; D. painful diseases;
1090	不宜用三棱针点刺法进行治疗的病证是: A 高热惊厥; B 中风脱证 C. 中暑昏迷; D 急性腰扭伤; E 喉蛾.	What disease should NOT be treated by dotting insertion with a three-edged needle? A. high fever and convulsion; B. wind stroke with prolapse C. sun stroke and fainting; D. acue lumbar sprain; E. tonsillitis.
1091	产后泌乳不足可取耳穴为: A.胸椎; B.肾上腺 C. 交感; D 神门.	What auricular point may be used to treat postnatal hypogalactia? A.thoracic vertebrae; B. adrenal gland; C. sympathetic; D. divine door (spiritual door).
1092	长针的进针宜采用哪种进针法: A.指切进针法; B.挟持进针法 C. 提捏进针法; D 舒张进针法.	How to insert a long needle? A.Nail-cutting method; B. holding the needle method; C. Needle insertion by pushing-up; D. spreading method
1093	常用于十宣十二井穴和耳尖部位放血的操作方法是: A.点刺法; B 散刺法 C. 刺络法; D 挑刺法.	What technique is most frequently used for bloodletting at Shí Xuān / ten statements [ten expansions], twelve well points, and Ěr Jiān / tip of ear? A. pointed insertion with a three-edged. needle; B. scattered insertion with a three-edged. needle; C. cupping with bloodletting; D. Incision needling with a prismatic needle.
1094	常用于止痛、镇静、针麻的电针波形是: A. 密波; B. 疏波 C. 疏密波; D. 断续波; E.，锯齿波	What wave should be used in electro acupuncture for pain relief, sedation, and anesthesia? A. · Dense wave; B. · Sparse wave C. · Sparse-dense wave; D. · Intermittent wave; E.serrated wave.
1095	承泣穴的正确刺灸方	What is the right method of treating S1 / Chéng Qì by

	法是: A·快速进针; B·大幅度提插捻转 C. 多用灸法 ·少用针刺; D·紧靠眼球直刺; E·紧靠眶下缘直刺 0·5 寸.	acupuncture and moxibustion? A ·rapid needle insertion; B ·lifting, pushing and twirling on a large scale; C. more moxibustion and less needling; D ·perpendicular insertion tightly close to the pupil; E. perpendicular insertion for 0.5 Cun tightly close to infraorbital margin.
1096	除 XX 外，均为三棱针常用的刺法 A. 挑刺; B. 刺络 C. ·点刺; D. 毛刺; E. 散刺	Which is NOT the technique of insertion with a three-edged needle? A. · Incision needling; B. ·insrting into linking meridians C. ·dotted needling; D. ·Hairy needling; E. · Spreading needling.
1097	除 xx 穴外 ·都常用灸法来防病保健: A·足三里; B·神门; G 身柱; D·大椎; E·涌泉.	Which point is NOT treated by moxibustion to prevent diseases and maintain good health? A. S36 [Zú Sān Lǐ]; B. H7 [Shén Mén]; C. D15 [Yǎ Mén]; D. D14 [Dà Zhuī]; E. K1 [Yǒng Quán].
1098	除 XX 穴外，均宜平刺或斜刺: A·印堂; B·列缺 C. 哑门; D·风门; E·中都.	Which point should NOT be treated by level insertion or slanting insertion? A ·YÌN TÁNG (midpoint between eyebrows, seal hall); B. Lu7 [Liè Quē]; C. D15 [Yǎ Mén]; D. G20 [Fēng Chí]; E. G32 [Zhōng Dū].
1099	刺血疗法可以在以下除什么穴以外的穴位进行? A. 十宣; B. 耳尖 C. 委中; D. 经渠; E. 瘛脉。	Which of the following should not be treated by bloodletting? A. SHÍ XUĀN (ten statements, ten expansions); B. Tip of Ear; C. B40 [Wěi Zhōng]; D. Lu8 [Jīng Qú]; E. Sj18 [Chì Mài].
1100	从胆经头临泣穴向前引一直线，长 1 寸为: A.额旁 1 线; B.额旁 2 线 C. 额旁 3 线; D 顶旁 2 线.	Draw a straight line forward from G15 (Tóu Lín Qì，Lín Qì) for 1 Cun, what is this line? A.1st lateral plane on forehead; B. 2nd. Lateral plane on forehead; C. 3[rD]. lateral plane on forehead; D. 2[nd.] Lateral vertex plane.
1101	从督脉百会穴至前顶穴之段被称为: A.顶颞前斜线; B. 颞前线 C. 枕上正中线; D 顶中线.	What plane is the line connecting D20 (Bǎi Huì) and D21 (Qián Dǐng)? A.vertex temoral anterior slanting plane; B. frontal temporal plane; C. mid-occipital upper plane; D. mid-vertex plane
1102	从督脉神庭穴向前引一直线，长 1 寸为: A.顶中线; B.颞前线 C. 枕上正中线; D 额中线.	Draw a straight line forward from D24 (Shén Tíng) for 1 Cun, what is this line? A mid-vertex plane; B. frontal temporal plane; C. mid-occipital upper plane; D. mid-forehead plane.
1103	催气手法，最早由谁提出: A·何若愚; B·窦汉卿 C. 陈会; D·徐大椿.	Who first mentioned “expediting arrival of energy / cui qi fa”? A ·He Ruo Yu in Jin Dynasty; B. ·Dou Han Qing 1196-1280); C. · Chen Hui in Ming Dynasty; D ·Xu Da Chun (1693-1771).
1104	大椎穴的正确操作法是: A. 直刺 0.5-0.8寸; B 向上斜刺0.5 ·0.8 寸 C. 向下斜刺0.5 ·0.8寸; D 向两侧斜刺 0.5 ·0·8寸.	What is the right technique to treat D14 [Dà Zhuī]? A. perpendicular insertion for 0.5-0.8 Cun; B upward slanting insertion for 0.5 ·0.8 Cun; C. downward slanting insertion for 0.5 ·0.8 Cun; D slanting insertion toward both sides for 0.5 ·0·8 Cun.

1105	灯火灸治疗下列疾病有良好疗效: A. 乳痈; B. 疔疮 C. 痄腮; D. 麦粒肿; E. · 落枕	Which may be treated by rush fire moxibustion with good results? A. · carbuncle in the breast (acute mastitis); B. · furuncle; C. ·mumps; D. · stye, hordeolum; E. neck pain with stiffness.
1106	癫痫和精神失常应取: A.额旁 1 线 B.额旁 2 线 C. 额旁 3 线 D 额中线	Which should be used to treat epilepsy and mental disorders? A. 1st lateral plane on forehead; B. 2nd. lateral plane on forehead; C. 3rD. lateral plane on forehead; D. mid-forehead plane.
1107	电针法的通电时间一般为: A.5min; B.5-l0min; C. 5-20min; D20-30min.	How long should electricity be connected to the needle in elector acupuncture in general? A. 5min; B.5-l0min; C. 5-20min; D. 20-30min.
1108	电针治疗淋证，具体取穴是: A. · 中极 行间; B. 曲骨 中封 C. 膀胱俞 委中; D. 肾俞 三阴交; E. 关元 太溪	What points should be selected to treat "lin" condition (urinary strains, strangury) by electro acupuncture? A.R3 [Zhōng Jí] Lv2 [Xíng Jiān]; B. ·R2 [Qū Gǔ] Lv4 [Zhōng Fēng]; C. ·B28 [Páng Guāng Shū] B40 [Wěi Zhōng]; D. ·B23 [Shèn Shū] Sp6 [Sān Yīn Jiāo]; E. ·R4 [Guān Yuán] K3 [Tài Xī].
1109	电针治疗最适宜的电流强度应在: A.感觉阈; B 痛阈 C. 感觉阈和痛阈之间; D 低于感觉阈.	What is the best current intensity in electro acupuncture? A.sense threshold; B. pain threshold; C. in between sense threshold and pain threshold; D. lower than sense threshold.
1110	顶颞后斜线的下 2 / 5 主治: A·上肢感觉异常; B·头面部感觉异常 C. ·上肢瘫痪; D·运动性失语.	What does lower 2 / 5 vertex temporal posterior slanting plane treat? A ·abnormal sensation in the upper limbs; B ·abnormal sensation in the head-face region; C. paralysis of the upper limbs; D · aphemia.
1111	顶颞前斜线的中 2 / 5 主治: A·对侧下肢瘫痪; B·对侧躯干瘫痪 C. ·上肢瘫痪; D·中枢性面瘫.	What does middle 2 / 5 vertex temporal posterior slanting plane treat? A ·paralysis of lower limbs on the opposite side; B ·paralysis of trunk on the opposite side; C. paralysis of the upper limbs; ·D. central paralysis of face.
1112	顶旁 2 线是从正营到承灵穴之间，督脉旁开: A.0.75 寸; B.1.5 寸 C. 0.5 寸; D 2.25 寸.	On the 2nd. lateral vertex plane, how far is the line between G17 (Zhèng Yíng) and G18 (Chéng Líng) laterally away from du mai? A.0.75 Cun; B.1.5cun; C. 0.5cun; D 2.25cun.
1113	督脉旁 1.5 寸，从膀胱经通天穴向后引一直线，长 1.5 寸为: A.顶旁 l 线; B.顶旁 2 线 C. 枕上旁线; D 枕下旁线.	What is the line that is1.5 Cun lateral to du mai and drawn from B7 (Tōng Tiān) backward for 1.5 Cun in length? A.1st lateral vertex plane; B. 2nd. lateral vertex plane; C. mid-occipital lateral plane; D. mid-occipital lower plane.
1114	短刺是针刺在: A. 皮肤; B. 肌肉 C. 筋; D. 脉; E. 骨.	In applying the technique of slow-paced needling (duan ci), which of the following is needled? A. skin; B. muscles; C. tendons; D. blood vessels; E. needle reaching bones.
1115	短针的进针宜采用哪种进针法? A. 指切进针法; B.挟	How to insert a short needle? A Nail-cutting method; B. holding the needle method;C. Needle insertion by pushing up; D. spreading method

	持进针法 C. 提捏进针法; D 舒张进针法.	Needle insertion by pushing-up; D. spreading method.
1116	对耳屏内侧面的耳穴是: A.交感; B 艇角 C. 内分泌; D 皮质下.	What auricular point is located On the medial side of antetragus? A.sympathetic; B. C. ymba angle (ting jiao); C. internal secretion, (endocrine); D. subcortex.
1117	额旁 1 线是从何穴向前引一直线，长 1 寸: A.头临泣; B.眉冲 C. 头维; D 通天.	Draw a straight line forward from what point for 1 Cun is the 1st lateral forehead plane? A.G15 (Tóu Lín Qì， Lín Qì); B. B3 (Méi Chōng); C. S8 (Tóu Wěi); D. B7 (Tōng Tiān).
1118	额旁 3 线是从何处向下引一直线，长 1 寸? A.头临泣; B.头维 C. 头维穴内侧 0.75 寸; D 头维穴内侧 2.25 寸.	Draw a straight line forward from what point for 1 Cun is the 3rd. lateral forehead plane? A.G15 (Tóu Lín Qì， Lín Qì); B. 0.75 Cun medial to S8 (Tóu Wěi); C. S8 (Tóu Wěi); D. 2.25 Cun medial to S8 (Tóu Wěi).
1119	耳垂正面中央部的耳穴是: A.舌; B 面颊 C. 眼; D 扁桃体.	What auricular point is located in the center on the anterior side of earlobe (lobule of the auricle)? A.tongue; B. face and Chest C. eye; D. tonsil.
1120	耳甲腔正中凹陷处的耳穴是: A.肝; B.心 C. 胃; D 肺.	What auricular point is located in the depression in the middle of cavum conchae auriculae? A. liver; B. heart C. stomach; D. lungs.
1121	耳轮脚消失处的耳穴是: A 胃; B 肺 C. 神门; D 肝.	What auricular point is locted in the disappearing spot of crus helicis? A stomach; B. lungs; C. divine door (spiritual door); D. liver.
1122	耳轮与对其轮之间的凹沟称为: A.耳甲; B 三角窝 C. 耳甲腔; D 耳舟.	What is the depression between helix and anthelix? A.conchae auriculae; B. triangular fossa; C. cavum conchae auriculae; D. scapha.
1123	耳脉最早记载在: A·《阴阳十一脉灸经》; B·《素问》 C. 《灵枢》; D·《针灸甲乙经》.	Which Classic recorded auricular meridian for the first time?: A·《Eleven Moxibustion Meridians of Yin and Yang》; B·《Su Wen》 C. 《Ling Shu》; D·《Zhen Jiu Jia Yi Jing》.
1124	耳鸣耳聋眩晕应取: A 枕下旁线; B.枕上旁线 C. 颞后线; D 颞前线.	Which should be used to treat ringing in ears, deafness, and vertigo? A mid-occipital lower plane; B. mid-occipital lateral plane; C. posterior temporal plane; D. frontal temporal plane.
1125	耳屏和对耳屏之间的凹陷处称为: A.屏上切迹; B 屏间切迹 C. 轮屏切迹; D 耳舟.	What is the depression between tragus and antetragus? A. incisura supratragica; B. incisura intertragica; C. helix-tragic notch; D. scapha.
1126	耳屏游离缘下部尖端的耳穴是: A.外鼻; B.肾上腺 C. 外耳; D 皮质下.	What auricular point is located at the tip of the lower region of the free end of tragus? A.external nose; B. adrenal gland; C. external ear; D. subcortex.
1127	耳穴 “耳迷根”与下列分部在同一水平线的是: A·耳轮脚; B·对耳轮下脚 C. ·耳屏上缘;	The auricular point, “arnold’s nerve root” is on a level with which of the following? A. crus helicis; B. crus anthelicis inferior; C. upper border of tragus; D. lower border of tragus; E. outlet of the external

	D ·耳屏下缘; E ·外耳道口.	auditory canal.
1128	耳穴 "高血压点"位于: A ·肾上腺与目 1 穴中点稍前; B ·肾上腺与目 1 穴中点稍后 C. ·内鼻与目 1 穴中点稍前; D ·内鼻与目 1 穴中点稍后; E ·外鼻与目 1 穴中点稍前.	Where is the auricular point "hypertension point" located? A. slightly in front of the midpoint between adrenal gland and eye 1; B. slightly in the back of the midpoint between adrenal gland and eye 1; C. slightly in front of the midpoint between internal nose and eye 1; D. slightly in the back of the midpoint between internal nose and eye 1; E. slightly in front of the midpoint between external nose and eye 1.
1129	耳穴 "交感" 的位置在: A ·对耳轮下脚外 1 / 2 处; B ·对其轮下脚内 1 / 2 处 C. ·对耳轮下脚中点; D ·对耳轮下脚与耳轮内侧交界处; E ·对耳轮下脚的内上角. at the lower edge of antihelicis in the 1 / 3 intersection laterally.	Where is the auricular point, "sympathetic" located? A; laeral ½ of c rus anthelicis inferior; B. medial ½ crus anthelicis inferior C; midpoint of crus anthelicis inferior D. intersection between; crus anthelicis inferior and medial side of helix; E. medial-upper anger of crus anthelicis inferior.
1130	耳穴 "神门" 的正确位置在: A ·在对其轮上脚的下中 1 / 3 交界外; B ·在对耳轮上脚的上中 1 / 3 交界处; C. ·在对耳轮的 1 / 2 交界处; D ·在对其轮下脚的下中 1 / 3 交界处; E ·在对其轮下脚的上中 1 / 3 交界处.	What is the accurate location of the auricular point "Shén Mén [spiritual door]"? A. at the lower middle edge of antihelicis in the 1 / 3 intersection laterally; B. at the upper middle edge of antihelicis in the 1 / 3 intersection; C. at the 1 / 2 intersection of antihelices; D. at the lower middle edge of antihelicis in the 1 / 3 intersection; E. at the upper middle edge of antihelicis in the 1 / 3 intersection.
1131	耳穴 "胃"的位置在: A. ·耳轮脚下方内侧 1 / 3 处 C. ·耳轮脚下方外侧 1 / 3 处 C. ·在口与贲门之间; D. ·耳轮脚消失处; E. ·对耳轮下脚的内上角.	Where is the auricular point "stomach" located? A. ·below crus helices 1 / 3 medially; B. below crus helices 1 / 3 laterrally; C. ·in between mouth and cardiac orifice; D. on the spot where cruris helicis disappears; E. ·medial upper angle of crus anthelicis inferior.
1132	耳穴脑点在: A. 对耳屏的尖端; B 对耳屏的内侧面 C. 对耳屏尖与轮屏切迹间的中点; D 对耳屏外侧面的后上方; E 对耳屏外面的后下方。	Where is the auricular point "brain point" located? A. at the tip of antetragus; B. on the medial side of antetragus; C. midpoint between tip of antetragus and Helix tragus notch; D. behind and above the lateral side of antetragus; E. behind and below the lateral side of antetragus.
1133	耳穴皮质下的位置是在: A ·对耳屏的内侧面; B ·屏间切迹底部 C. ·轮屏切迹正中处;	Where is the auricular point "Subcortex" located? A. on the medial side of antetragus; B. in the base of incisura intertragica; C. in the middle of Helix tragus notch; D. at the lateral edge below tragus; E. in front of and below incisura

	C. 轮屏切迹正中处; D·耳屏下部外侧缘; E·屏间切迹前下方.	intertragica.
1134	耳穴诊断疾病，最早见于: A.·马王堆出土《帛书》; B.·《黄帝内经》 C.·《千金要方》; D.·《外台秘要》; E.·《肘后备急方》	What was the earliest discovery of diagnosis of diseases by auricular points? A. ·Ma Wang dui <classics on silk and bamboo slips>; B.·《Huang Di Nei Jing 》 C. ·《Thousand Gold Essential Formulae for Acute Symptoms (652)》; D.·《Wai Tai Mi Yao 752》; E.·《Zhou Hou Bei Ji Fang》
1135	耳针法所用毫针的规格为: A.26-30 号 0.3 ·0.5 寸长; B.30-32 号 0.5 ·0.8 寸长 C. 26 ·30 号 0.5 ·0.8 寸长; D 30-32 号 0.3-0.5 寸长.	What is the specification of the minute needle used in auricular therapy? A.No.26-30, 0.3 ·0.5 Cun in length; B. No. 30-32, 0.5 ·0.8 Cun in length; C. No. 26-30, 0.5 ·0.8 Cun in length; D. No. 30-32, 0.3-0.5 Cun in length.
1136	耳针疗法中不可用: A.·电针法; B.·刺血法 C.·温灸法; D.·灯火灸法; E.·以上都不是	Which should not be applied in auricular acupuncture therapy? A. ·electro acupuncture; B. ·cupping with bloodletting C. ·warm moxibustion; D. ·Rush fire moxibustion; E. ·none of the above
1137	耳针治疗便秘，除取直肠下段与大肠外，还可加用: A.·皮质下; B.·内分泌 C.·交感; D.·肾上腺; E.·神门	In addition to lower section of rectum and large intestine, what other auricular point may be added to treat constipation by auricular acupuncture? A. ·subcortex; B. ·internal secretion; C. sympathetic; D. ·adrenal gland; E. ·Shén Mén [divine door].
1138	耳针治疗发热、高血压、炎症应取: A.降压沟; B.·高血压点 C.·耳尖; D.·神门; E.·肾上腺	What point should be selected to treat fever, hypertension, and inflammation, in auricular acupuncture? A. ·Hypotensor Groove (Depressor Groove); B. ·Hypertension Point C. tip of ear; D. ·Shén Mén [divine door]; E. ·adrenal gland.
1139	耳针治疗中暑，下列穴组中应选: A.·肺 神门 心 脑干; B.·心 枕 肾上腺 皮质下 C.·交感 内分泌 肾; D.·耳炎 脑点 三焦; E.·以上均不是	What group of points should be selected to treat sunstroke in auricular therapy? A. ·lungs, Shén Mén [divine door], heart, brain stem; B. ·heart occiput adrenal gland subcortex; C. ·sympathetic internal secretion kidneys; D. ·ear inflammation brain stem san jiao (triple heater); E. ·none of the above.
1140	风池穴操作的错误者为: A 向前直刺 0.8 ·1.2 寸; B.向眉心方向斜刺 0.8 ·1.2 寸 C. 向鼻尖方向斜刺 0.8 ·1.2 寸; D，向下颌方向斜刺 0.8 ·1.2 寸.	What is the wrong technique applied to G20 (Fēng Chí)? A straight forward perpendicular insertion for 0.8-1.2 Cuns; B. slanting insertion toward the region between eyebrows for 0.8-1.2 Cuns; C. slanting insertion toward the tip of nose for 0.8-1.2 Cuns; D. slanting insertion toward the chin for 0.8-1.2 Cuns.
1141	敷涌泉或神阙穴治小儿口腔炎的灸法为 A.细辛灸; B 天南星灸 C. 白芥子灸 D 蒜泥灸	What kind.of topical application with herbs to K1 (Yǒng Quán) or R8 (Shén Què) may be applied to treat stomatitis in children? A.moxibustion with Herba Asari; B. moxibustion with Rhizoma Arisaematis; C. moxibustion with Semen Sinapis

		Albae; D. moxibustion with garlic paste.
1142	敷涌泉穴治疗咯血衄血的灸法为: A.细辛灸;.B 天南星灸 C. 白芥子灸; D 蒜泥灸.	What kind of topical application with herbs to K1 (Yǒng Quán) may be applied to treat discharge of blood from the mouth and nosebleed? A. moxibustion with Herba Asari; B. moxibustion with Rhizoma Arisaematis; C. moxibustion with Semen Sinapis Albae; D. moxibustion with garlic paste.
1143	敷于颊车颧髎穴治疗面神经麻痹的灸法为: A.细辛灸; B 天南星灸 C. 白芥子灸; D 蒜泥灸.	What kind of topical application with herbs to S6 (Jiá Chē), Si18 (Quán Liáo) may be applied to treat numbness of facial nerve? A. moxibustion with Herba Asari; B. moxibustion with Rhizoma Arisaematis; C. moxibustion with Semen Sinapis Albae; D. moxibustion with garlic paste.
1144	附子饼的制作，一般是用附子粉末和何物混合制作成? A.麻油; B 盐水 C. 黄酒; D 陈醋; E 以上都不是.	What ingredient is used to mix with powder of radix aconiti praeparata to make cake of radix aconiti praeparata? A. sesame oil; B. salt water; C. yellow wine; D. old vinegar; E. none of the above.
1145	腹中积块及未溃疮疡最适宜的间接灸为: A 隔姜灸; B 隔蒜灸 C. 隔盐灸; D 隔附子灸.	What is the best direct moxibustion to treat lumpy accumulations in the abdomen and ulcers prior to ulceration? A indirect moxa; C. moxibustion with ginger in between; B. Moxibustion with garlic in between moxa and skin; C. moxibustion with salt in between; D. Moxibustion with cake of Radix Aconiti Praeparata in between moxa and skin
1146	隔姜灸的确切作用是: A.清热解毒杀虫; B 主温肾壮阳 C. 温中散寒扶阳固脱; D 防病保健; E 解表散寒温中.	What is precise function of moxibustion with ginger in between moxa and skin? A to clear heat, dexoxify, and destroy worms; B to warm kidneys and tone up yang; C. to warm the middle region, disperse cold, support yang, and fix prolapse; D. to prevent diseases and maintain health; E. to relax the superficial region, disperse cold, and warm the middle region.
1147	隔盐灸可用来治疗: A.虚寒性呕吐; B 哮喘 C. 脐风; D 肺痨; E 疮疡.	What can moxibustion with salt in between moxa and skin treat? A. deficient and cold vomiting; B. asthma; C. tetanus neonatorium; D. lung exhaustion / tuberculosis / consumptive disease; E. sores and carbuncles.
1148	根据《灵枢 经脉》记载，对"不盛不虚"的病证，应该采取: A 补之; B 泻之 C. 除之; D 以经取之; E 留之.	How to treat the diseases which are neither excessive nor deficient according to Ling Shu Chapter 10? A twelve muscular meridians / jing jin tonification; B. by sedation; C. by removing pathogens; D. by the points on the diseased meridians; E. by retention of needle in the body.
1149	古代针法的"青龙摆尾"指的是: A.弹柄法; B.循法 C. 摇柄法; D 震颤法.	What is the ancient needling technique called, "green dragon wagging its tail"? A. flicking the handle of the needle; B. manipulating the inserted needle by tracing the meridian; C. shaking the handle of the needle; D. shaking the needle to cause trembling.
1150	古代最早的针具为: A 砭石; B 骨针 C.	What was the earliest ancient needle instruement?

	竹针; D ·青铜针.	A · stone needle; B ·bone needle; C. bamboo needle; D ·bronze needle.
1151	骨科手术针麻，选用耳穴"肾"的根据是: A. ·耳穴的神经支配; B. ·中医脏象学说 C. ·经络学说; D. ·参照肾区的生理作用; E. ·肾区与手术部位相应	What is the basis of selecting the auricular point "kidneys" for anaesthesia in orthopaedic operations? A. ·controlling nerve in the auricular point; B. ·TCM theory of internal organs; C. ·theory of meridians; D. ·physiological function of kidney zone; E. ·correspondence between kidney zone and operation region.
1152	横刺适用于: A.骨骼边缘的腧穴; B.血管部位 C. 瘢痕部位; D 皮肤浅薄处的腧穴.	Transveral needle insertion may be applied to: A. points on the border of bones; B. region with blood vessels; C. region with scars; D. region with a shallow and thin skin and flesh.
1153	后人用作火针治疗瘰疬痈肿的是: A. 鈹针; B 大针 C. 员针; D. 鍉針.	What is the fire needle subsequently used to treat scrofula and swelling of carbuncle? A.Sword-shaped needle; B. big needle; C. round-sharp needle; D. key-shaped needle.
1154	呼吸补泻法中的补法是: A 呼气时捻转，吸气时提插; B 呼气时提插，吸气时捻转 C. 呼气时出针 ·吸气时进针; D 呼气时进针 ·吸气时出针; E 呼气时提插，吸气时出针	What is tonification in "the technique of breathing tonification sedation"? A. Twirling the needle on expiration, Lifting and pushing on inspiration; B. Lifting and pushing on expiration, Twirling the needle on inspiration; C. Pulling out the needle on expiration, Inserting the needle on inspiration; D. Inserting the needle on expiration, Pulling out the needle on inspiration; E. Lifting and pushing on expiration, Pulling out the needle on inspiration.
1155	呼吸补泻法中的泻法是: A 吸气时提插，呼气时捻转; B 吸气时捻转 ·呼气时提插 C. ，吸气时进针，呼气时出针; D 吸气时出针，呼气时进针; E 吸气时出针，呼气时提插.	What is sedation in "the technique of breathing tonification sedation"? A. Lifting and pushing on inspiration, Twirling the needle on expiration; B. Twirling the needle on inspiration, Lifting and pushing on expiration; C. Inserting the needle on inspiration, Pulling out the needle on expiration; D. Pulling out the needle on inspiration, Inserting the needle on expiration; E. Pulling out the needle on inspiration, Lifting and pushing on expiration.
1156	化脓灸时，艾火烧灼皮肤可产生剧痛，此时应: A 迅速去掉艾火; B 疾吹其火 ·加速燃烧，以缩短疼痛时间 C. 用手在施灸穴位周围轻轻拍打，以缓解疼痛; D 不予理采 ·让其火自灭.	In performing the treatment of "Burning the skin to leave scars", what do you do when moxa heat burns the patient's skin to cause acute pain? A. extinguish the fire quickly; B. increase the fire to shorten the duration of suffering; C. slapping the surrounding area of treatment points to relieve pain; D. no action should be taken, and let fire extinguish by itself.
1157	患者肌力、肌张力基本正常，但不能解钮扣，拾硬币，若用头针治疗，宜刺: A. 运动区上 1 / 5; B. 运动区中 2 / 5 C. 运动区下 2 / 5; D. 运用区;	The patient has normal muscular tension, but cannot unbutton or pick up coins; what area should be treated by scalp acupuncture? A. ·upper 1 / 5 of motor area of cerebrum; B. ·middle 2 / 5 of motor area of cerebrum 2 / 5; C. lower 2 / 5 of ·motor area of cerebrum 2 / 5; D. ·Intricate movements (application) area;

	E. ·平衡区	E. ·Equilibrium area.
1158	回阳、救逆，固脱，宜选用: A. 隔蒜灸; B. 隔姜灸 C. 隔盐灸; D. 隔附子饼灸; E. 隔韭灸	How to restore yang, rescue uprising, and fix collapse? A. ·Moxibustion with garlic in between moxa and skin; B. ·Moxibustion with ginger in between moxa and skin; C. ·Moxibustion with salt in between moxa and skin; D. ·Moxibustion with cake of semen sojae praeparatum in between moxa and skin; E. ·Moxibustion with Chinese chive in between moxa and skin.
1159	疾徐补泻法中的补法是: A 进针快少捻针出针慢; B ·进针慢少捻针出针快 C. 进针慢多捻针出针快; D ·进针快多捻针出针慢; E ·进针慢多捻针出针慢.	What is tonification in the "technique of slow-and-quick tonification sedation"? A. quick insertion, little twirling, slow withdrawal of needle; B. slow insertion, little twirling, quick withdrawal of needle; C. slow insertion, twirling a lot, quick withdrawal of needle; D. quick insertion, twirling a lot, slow withdrawal of needle; E. slow insertion, twirling a lot, slow withdrawal of needle.
1160	疾徐补泻法中的泻法是: A. 进针快，出针慢; B. 进针慢，出针快 C. ·进针快而重插，出针慢而轻提; D. ·进针快而轻插，出针慢而重提; E. 进针快，出针时摇大针孔 Located at the upper tip of the auricle which may be located by folding the auricle;	What is sedation in the "technique of slow-and-quick tonification sedation"? A. ·quick insertion, slow withdrawal of needle; B. ·slow insertion, quick withdrawal of needle; C. ·quick insertion with heavy pushing, slow withdrawal of needle with light lifting; D. ·quick insertion with light pushing, slow withdrawal of needle with heavy lifting; E. ·quick insertion, shaking to enlarge needle holes in withdrawing the needle.
1161	将耳轮向耳屏对折时，可取何耳穴: A ·指; B 趾 C. ·耳尖; D ·耳迷根; E ·内耳.	What auricular point may be located by bending the ear toward tragus? A finger; B. toes C. tip of ear; D. Arnold's Nerve Root; E. internal ear.
1162	九针中，形如剑锋的针具是 A 鑱針; B ·锋针 C. ·员针; D ·员利针; E 鈹针.	Which of the "nine needles" resembles the tip of a sword in shape? A Scooping needle (chan zhen); B Sharp-edged needle (feng zhen); C. round needle (yuan zhen); D round-sharp needle (yuan li zhen); E. Sword-shaped needle (pi zhen).
1163	九针中那种针可治急病? A 鍉针; B.鈹针 C. 锋针; D 员利针.	Which of the nine needles may be used to treat acute diseases? A key-shaped needle; B. Sword-shaped needle; C. Sharp-edged needle; D. round-sharp needle.
1164	九针中三面有棱的针是: A. 鍉针; B ·铍针 C. ·锋针; D ·员利针.	Which of the nine needles has an edge on three sides? A. Key-shaped needle; B ·Sword-shaped needle; C. ·Sharp-edged needle; D ·Round-sharp needle.
1165	九针中用于按摩的针具是: A 鑱針; B 鍉针 C. ·员针; D ·员利针; E 鈹针.	Which of the "nine needles" is used in massage? A ·Scooping needle (chan zhen); B. key-shaped needle (ti zhen); C. round needle (yuan zhen); D. round-sharp needles (yuan li zhen); E. Sword-shaped needle (pi zhen).
1166	灸疮化脓，一般在灸后多少时间? A ·2 天左右; B ·3 天左	How long does it take for carbuncle caused by moxibustion to postulate after moxibustion treatment? A. about 2 days; B. about 3 days; C. about 5 days; D. about 7

	右 C. ·5 天左右; D·7 天左右; E·10 天左右.	days; E. about 10 days.
1167	灸疮自行痊愈脱落，一般在灸后: A·2-3 周左右; B·3-4 周左右 C. ·4-5 周左右; D·5-6 周左右; E·6-7 周左右.	How long does it take for carbuncle caused by moxibustion to heal after moxibustion treatment? A. about 2-3 weeks; B. about 3-4 weeks; C. about 4-5 weeks; D. about 5-6 weeks; E. about 6-7 weeks.
1168	据文献记载，最早制作火罐的材料是: A·牛角; B·竹筒 C. 陶土; D·土簋; E·木钵.	According to historical documents, what was fire cup made of initially? A. horn; B. tube section of bamboo; C. potter's clay; D. earth vessel; E. wood bowl.
1169	距离枕外粗隆 3·5 厘米，向下引平行于前后中线的 4 厘米长的直线刺激区是: A. ·胃区; B. ·视区 C. ·平衡区; D. ·足运感区; E. ·胸腔区	Draw a 4-cm downward line from the point 3.5 cm away from external occipital protuberance, parallel to the front-back midline; what is this line called? A. ·Stomach area; B. ·Visual area; C. ·Equilibrium area; D. ·Foot-motor sensory area; E. ·Thoracic cavity area.
1170	开阖补泻法中的补法是: A·出针前轻轻揉按针孔周围; B·出针时摇大针孔 C. ·出针后不按针孔; D·出针后揉按针孔; E·以上都不是.	What is tonification in the "opening and closing technique for tonification and sedation"? A. lightly pressing the surrounding of needle hole before pulling out the needle; B. leave the needle hole wide open by forcefully shaking the needle while it is being pulled out; C. pull out the needle without pressing the neele hole; D. press the needle hole right after the needle is pulled out; E. none of the above.
1171	开阖补泻法中的泻法是: A·出针时摇大针孔; B·出针后揉按针孔 C. ·出针后轻轻叩打针孔; D·出针时不闭针孔; E·以上都不是.	What is sedation in the "opening and closing technique for tonification and sedation"? A; leave the needle hole wide open by forcefully shaking the needle while it is being pulled out; B. press the needle hole right after the needle is pulled out; C. lightly knocking the needle hole after the needle is pulled out; D. pull out the needle out without closing the neele hole; E. none of the above.
1172	开阖补泻是指: A. ·按子午流注中的开穴、闭穴进行补泻; B. ·开是泻法、阖是补法 C. ·阖是泻法、开是补法; D. ·开针孔是补法，闭针孔是泻法; E. ·闭针孔是补法，开针孔是泻法	What is the opening and closing technique for tonification and sedation? A. ·to administer tonification and sedation according to opening points and closing points in energy-flowing Acupuncture [ZǏ WǓ LIÚ ZHÙ]; B. ·opening is sedation, closing is tonification; C. ·closing is sedation, opening is tonification; D. ·tonification is to open up the needle hole, sedation is to close it; E. ·tonification is to close the needle hole, sedation is to open it.
1173	可以治疗更年期综合征的耳穴是: A.交感; B.脑干 C. 内分泌; D 缘中.	Which auricular point may be used to treat menopause syndrome? A. sympathetic; B. brain stem (nao gan); C. internal secretion (endocrine); D. mid-edge / brain point (yuan zhong, nao dian).
1174	雷火神针是: A.一种火针; B 一种温针 C. 一种特制的	What is "Thunder fire and spiritual needle" ? A. it is a kind of fire needle; B. it is a warm needle; C. it is a specially made minute needle; D. it is a technique used in

	毫针; D 一种配合符咒的针法; E 一种特制的艾条.	specially made minute needle; D. it is a technique used in combination of magic incantations; E. a specially made moax stick.
1175	链霉素中毒可选耳穴是: A 屏尖; B.神门 C.皮质下; D.肾上腺.	What auricular point may be selected for streptomycin poisoning? A tip of tragus; B. divine door (spiritual door); C. subcortex; D. adrenal gland.
1176	临床常用的留罐时间为: A.3-5 分钟; B.5-10 分钟 C. l0-15 分钟; Dl5-30 分钟.	In; clinical practice, how long should; cupping last? A.3-5 minutes; B. 5-10 minutes; C. 10-15 minutes; D. 15-30 minutes.
1177	临床治疗脑溢血, 除……外，均不宜用头针治疗: A 急性期; B 并发高热 C. 并发心衰; D 有急性炎症; E 并发头痛.	Under what condition, cerebral hemorrhage may be treated by scalp acupuncture? A · acute stage; B. accompanied by fever C. accompanied by heart failure; D. presence of acute inflammation; E. accompanied by headache.
1178	留针可起到: A 得气的作用; B 行气的作用 C. 催气的作用; D 候气的作用; E 以上都不是.	What effects may be produced by retention of needle (let needle stay in)? A · to promote energy response (de qi); B. to promote energy flowing; C. to speed up arrival of energy; D. to wait for arrival of energy; E. none of the above.
1179	率谷穴向下至曲鬓穴之间的连线称为: A. 颞前线; B.项颞前斜线 C. 颞后线 D 项颞后斜线.	What is the line connecting G8 (Shuài Gŭ) and G7 (Qū; Bìn)? A. frontal temporal plane; B. vertex temporal anterior slanting plane; C. posterior temporal plane; D. vertex temporal posterior slanting plane.
1180	泌尿生殖系统疾病应取: A.额中线; B.额旁 1 线 C. 额旁 2 线; D 额旁 3 线.	Which should be used to treat the diseases of the urinary-reproductive systems? A. mid-forehead plane; B. 1st lateral plane on forehead; C. 2nd. lateral plane on forehead; D. 3rd. lateral plane on forehead.
1181	命门火衰最适宜的间接灸为: A 隔姜灸; B 隔蒜灸;.C 隔盐灸; D 隔附子灸.	What is the best direct moxibustion to treat life door fire in decline (ming men huo shuai)? A. moxibustion with ginger in between moxa and skin; B. moxibustion with garlic in between moxa and skin; C. moxibustion with salt in between moxa and skin; D. moxibustion with cake of RADIX ACONITI PRAEPARATA in between moxa and skin.
1182	哪种操作方法常用于曲泽委中等穴，治急性吐泻中暑发热等? A.点刺法; B 散刺法 C. 刺络法; D 挑刺法.	Which technique is frequently applied to P3 (Qū Zé); B40 (Wěi Zhōng), etc. for the treatment of acute vomiting and diarrhea, sunstroke with fever, etc.? A. pointed insertion with a three-edged needle; B. scattered insertion with a three-edged needle; C. cupping with bloodletting (ci luo fa); D. incision needling with a prismatic needle.
1183	哪种操作方法多用于局部瘀血血肿或水肿,顽癣等? A.点刺法; B 散刺法 C. 刺络法; D 挑刺	What technique is mostly used to treat local blood coagulation, anasarca due to blood stasis, edema, chronic tinea? A. pointed insertion with a three-edged needle; B. scattered

	法.	insertion with a three-edged needle; C. cupping with bloodletting (ci luo fa); D. incision needling with a prismatic needle.
1184	哪种疾病不适于瘢痕灸: A.哮喘; B 瘰疬 C. 糖尿病; D 慢性胃肠病.	Which should NOT be treated by the technique of "burning the skin to leave scars"? A.asthma; B. scrofula; C. diabetes mellitus; D. chronic gastrointestinal diseases.
1185	哪种三棱针法又叫豹纹刺: A.点刺法; B 散刺法 C. 刺络法; D 挑刺法.	Which method of inserting a three-edged. needle is also called, "leopard-needling"? A.pointed insertion with a three-edged. needle; B. scattered insertion with a three-edged needle; C. cupping with bloodletting; D. incision needling with a prismatic needle.
1186	脑血管意外后遗症患者，理解语言能力障碍，答非所问，若用头针治疗，宜刺: A.·言语一区; B.·言语二区 C. ·言语三区; D.·晕听区; E.·运用区	How to treat a patient with after-effects of cerebrovasacular accident, unable to understand language, or to answer questions, by scalp acupuncture? A. ·Speech area No1; B. ·Speech area No2; C. ·Speech area No3; D. ·Vertigo-auditory area; E. ·Intricate movements (application) area.
1187	能刺激膈神经做人工电动呼吸抢救呼吸衰竭的电流波型是: A.锯齿波; B 密波 C. 疏密波; D 断续波. A.锯齿波; B.密波 C. 疏密波; D 断续波.	What electric waveform should be used to rescue a patient of respiratory failure by stimulating phrenic nerve to perform artificial electric respiration? A. zigzag wave; B. dense wave C. sparse-dense wave; D. intermittent wave.
1188	能降低神经应激功能的电流波型是：A.锯齿波; B 密波 C. 疏密波; D 断续波.	What waveform can reduce the function of nerve in copping with excitation? A. zigzag wave; B. dense wave; C. sparse-dense wave; D. intermittent wave.
1189	捻转补泻法中的补法是: A 捻转角度大，频率慢，用力轻; B 捻转角度小，频率快，用力重 C. 捻转角度大，频率快，用力重; D 捻转角度小，频率慢，用力轻; E，捻转角度小，频率慢，用力重.	What is tonification in the technique of "tonification and sedation by twirling"? A. twirling on a larger scale, slower in frequency, with less force; B. twirling on a smaller scale, quicker in frequency, with greater force; C. twirling on a larger scale, quicker in frequency, with greater force; D. twirling on a smller scale, slower in frequency, with less force; E. twirling on a smaller scale, slower in frequency, with greater force.
1190	捻转补泻法中的泻法是: A 捻转角度小，频率快，用力轻; B 捻转角度大，频率慢，用力轻; C 捻转角度小，频率慢，用力轻; D 捻转角度大，频率慢，用力重; E 捻转角度大，频率快，用力重.	What is sedation in the technique of "tonification and sedation by twirling"? A; twirling on a smaller scale, quicker in frequency, with less force; B. twirling on a larger scale, slower in frequency, with less force; C. twirling on a smaller scale, slower in frequency, with less force; D. twirling on a larger scale, slower in frequency, with greater force; E. twirling on a larger scale, quicker in frequency, with greater force;
1191	颞前线是颔厌穴至何处之间的连线? A. 正营; B.悬厘 C.	Frontal temporal plane connects G4 (Hàn Yàn) and what point?

	率谷; D 曲鬓.	A.G17 (Zhèng Yíng); B. G6 (Xuán Lí); C. G8 (Shuài Gŭ); D. G7 (Qū; Bìn).
1192	皮层性视力障碍白内障近视眼应取： A. 枕下旁线；B.枕上旁线；C.颞前线； D 颞后线。	Which should be used to treat cortical disorder of vision, cataract, myopia (nearsightedness)? A. mid-occipital lower plane; B. mid-occipital lateral plane; C. frontal temporal plane; D. posterior temporal plane。
1193	皮肤针的叩击法主要是运用: A. 腕力; B. 肘部的力量 C. 指力; D. 肩部的力量; E. 前臂的力量。	In applying a skin needle, the force of knocking should primarily come from: A. force of wrist; B. force of elbow; C. force of fingers; D. force of shoulders;　E. force of forearm.
1194	皮肤针是"九针"中...基础上发展而来的: A. 圆利针; B. 鍉针 C. 圆针; D 锋针; E. 馋针.	Which of the nine needles developed to become skin needle? A. round-sharp needles (yuan li zhen); B. key-shaped needle (ti zhen); C. round needle (yuan zhen); D. sharp-edged needle (feng zhen); E.scooping needle (chan zhen)。
1195	皮内针法又称: A 埋针法; B 角法 C. 毛刺法; D 放血疗法.	What is another name for intradermal needle? A neede-embedding therapy; B horn; cupping; C. hairy needling; D. bloodletting therapy.
1196	皮内针留针期间，可每隔多久用手按压埋针处，以加强刺激? A.lh; B.2h; C.3h; D。4h。	What is the interval of pressing an embedded intradermal needle in the body to reinforce the stimulation? A. lh; B. 2h; C. 3h; D. 4h。
1197	皮内针留针期间，每次用于按压埋针处时间应为：A. l-2 min; B 2-3 min; C. 3-4 min;D. 0.5 min。	How long may the embedded intradermal needle be pressed each time? A. l-2 min; B 2-3 min; C. 3-4 min; D. 0.5 min。
1198	皮内针留针时间一般为: A 4h ; ; B 1~2d;C 1~3d ; D 3~5d 。	About how long should an intradermal needle be retained in general? A 4h ; ; B 1~2d;C 1~3d ; D 3~5d 。
1199	皮内针在何处不宜埋针 A，背俞穴; B.四肢部腧穴 C. 关节附近腧穴 D 耳穴	What region of the body should NOT have an intradermal needle embedded? A. back shu points (posterior transport points); B. points in the four extremities C. points C. lose to the joints; D. auricular points.
1200	平补平泻法是: A 既有补法成份，也有泻法成分; B 既不是补法，也不是泻法 C. 以补为主，兼有泻法; D 以泻为主，兼有补法; E 进针后均匀提插捻转，得气后出针.	What is Tonification and sedation by neutral technique (ping bu ping xie)? A. it; C. ontains some tonification and also some sedation; B. neither tonification nor sedaton; C. it is primarily tonification with some sedation; D. it is primarily sedation with some tonification; E. Insert the needle, and then manipulate the needle by lifting, pushing in, and twirling harmoniously, and pull out the needle after the arrival of meridian energy.
1201	平刺时，针身与皮肤的夹角为: A.90°; B.45° C. 30°; D15°.	What degree between the body of the needle and the skin in tranversal insertion? A.90°; B.45° C. 30°; D15°.
1202	丘墟深刺时，可以透	In applying a deep insertion to G40 [Qiū Xū], toward what

	向: A ·然谷; B ·照海 C. ·公孙; D ·解溪; E ·太溪.	point the needle should face? A ·K2 [Rán Gǔ]; B. K6 [Zhào Hǎi]; C. Sp4 [Gōng Sūn]; D. S41 [Jiě Xī]; E. K3 [Tài Xī].
1203	取头面颈胸腹部以及下肢前面的腧穴体位是: A 仰卧位; B 侧卧位 C. 俯卧位; D 仰靠坐位.	What is the patient's position in locating points on head, in the face, neck, Chest, abdomen and anterior lower limbs? A horizontal position with feet slightly bent; B. the lateral recumbent position; C. prone position; D. sitting position with head supported from behind.
1204	取头项、背、腰、臀部以及下肢后面的腧穴应选择的体位是: A. ·仰卧位; B. ·侧卧位 C. ·俯卧位; D. ·仰靠坐位; E. ·俯伏坐位	What posture should be assumed by the patient when points on head and back of neck, back, waist, and hip regions are engaged? A. ·horizontal position with feet slightly bent; B. ·Lateral recumbent position; C. ·Prone position; D. ·Sitting position with head supported from behind; E. ·Sitting position with face resting on table.
1205	雀啄灸多用于灸治: A. ·虚证; B. ·实证 C. ·寒证; D. ·急性病; E. ·慢性病	What disease is sparrow pecking moxibustion mostly used to treat? A. ·deficient syndrome; B. ·excess syndrome C. ·cold syndrome; D. ·acute diseases; E. ·chropnic disease.
1206	若天气炎热，皮内针留针时间应为: A.4h; B.l-2h C. 1-3h; D3-5h.	What is the duration of embedding an intradermal needle in the body when the weather is hot? A.4h; B.l-2h C. 1-3h; D3-5h.
1207	三个月以上的孕妇，除禁刺一些通经活血穴外，也不宜针刺: A. ·头面 ·颈项部腧穴; B. ·胸、背部腧穴 C. ·腹、腰髓部腧穴; D. ·上、下肢阴经腧穴; E. ·上、下肢阳经腧穴	After a woman is pregnant for three months or longer, some points that Can; C. onnect meridians and activate blood are forbidden points; which of the following are also forbidden points? A. ·acupuncture points on head, in face and back of neck region; B. ·acupuncture points in; Chest, back regions C. ·acupuncture points in the abdomen and lumbar region; D. ·acupuncture points on yin meridians in the lower limbs; E. ·acupuncture points on yang meridians in the upper and lower limbs.
1208	三棱针刺法相当于古代的: A. 齐刺; B. 经刺 C. 半刺; D. 络刺; E. 扬刺。	Which of the following ancient techniques Corresponds to the method of inserting a three-edged needle? A. Simultaneous needling (qi C. i); B. meridian-needling (jig C. i) Chestalved-needling (ban; C. i); D. reticular-needling (luo C. i); E.scattered-needling (yang C. i).
1209	三棱针古称: A.大针; B.锋针 C. 员针; D 员利针.	What were three-edged needles Called. In ancient China? A. big needles; B. Sharp-edged. Needles C. round. Needle; D. round-sharp needles.
1210	三棱针散刺法适用于: A ·急性腰扭伤; B ·高热惊厥 C. ·中风昏迷; D ·丹毒; E ·咽喉肿痛.	What C. am be treated by the spreading needling / scattered insertion with a three-edged needle? A. acute lumbar sprain; B. high fever and shock C. wind stroke and fainting; D. erysipelas; E. sore throat with swelling.
1211	三棱针又称: A.巨针; B.大针 C. ·馋针; D. ·锋针; E. ·鈹针	What is another name for three-edged needle? A.big needle; B.big needle C. ·Scooping needle; D. ·Sharp-edged needle; E. ·Sword-shaped needle.
1212	三棱针在操作时，右	In applying a three-edged. Needle, use the right hand to

	手持针，用拇次两指捏住针柄，中指指腹紧靠针身下端，针尖露出: A.1-3mm; B. l-2mm C. 3-5mm;D2-3mm.	□old. The needle, with the thumb and the forefinger grasping the handle tightly, and the ball of the middle finger very C. lose to the lower part of the needle with the tip of needle exposed; how long should be the tip of the needle exposed outside? A.1-3mm; B.l-2mm C. 3-5mm D2-3mm.
1213	三棱针治疗时，如需出血量多时，每周宜治: A.l-2 次; B2-3 次 C. 3-4 次; D4-5 次.	In administering treatment by three-edged. Needles, how many treatments should be administered. Per week when a larger quantity of bleeding is desired? A.1-2 times; B. 2-3 times C. 3-4 times; D. 4-5 times.
1214	三棱针治疗时，一般每次出血量以数滴至: A.1-3m1; B 2ml C. 2-3m1; D3-5ml	In administering treatment by three-edged. Needles, bleeding should range from a few drops to: A.1-3m1; B 2ml C. 2-3m1; D3-5ml.
1215	施灸程序应该是: A.先上后下，先阴后阳; B 先上后下 先阳后阴 C. 先中后上 先阴后阳; D 先中后下 先阳后阴; E 先腹后背 先阴后阳.	What is the proper sequence of moxibustion? A. upper first then lower, yin first then yang; B. upper first then lower, yang first then yin; C. midde first then upper, yin first then yang; D. middle first then lower, yang first then yin; E. abdomen first then back, yin first then yang.
1216	适用于皮肉浅薄部位的毫针进针方法是: A 指切进针法; B 挟持进针法 C. 提捏进针法; D 舒张进针法; E 套管进针法.	What technique should be used to insert into the superficial region at the skin and flesh level with a minute needle [hao zhen]? A. Nail-cutting method; B. Needle insertion by holding the needle C. Needle insertion by pushing-up; D. Needle insertion by spreading / spreading method; E. Needle insertion with a tube.
1217	舒张进针法适用于 A.长针的进针; B.短针的进针 C. 皮肉浅薄部位的进针; D 皮肤松弛部位的进针.	The spreading method of inserting a needle may be applied to: A. inserting a long needle; B. inserting a short needle C. inserting a needle into the region with a shallow and thin skin and flesh; D. inserting a needle into the region with relaxed. Skin.
1218	太乙神针和雷火神针的不同之处是: A. 制作方法; B 主治病证 C. 施灸方法; D 药物处方.	What is the difference between “tai-yi star needle” and “thunder fire and spiritual needle”? A. in the method Of manufacturing; B. in treatment indications C. in the technique of applying moxibustion; D. in the herbs to be applied
1219	提捏进针法可用于: A 百会; B 头维 C. 阳白; D 上星.	What point may be treated by the needle insertion by pushing-uptechnique? A D20 / Bǎi Huì; B S8 / Tóu Wěi C. G14 / Yáng; Bái; D D23 / Shàng Xīng.
1220	提捏进针法适用于: A.长针的进针; B 短针的进针 C. 皮肉浅薄部位的进针; D 皮肤松弛部位的进针.	The method Of inserting a needle by “pushing-up” may be applied to: A.inserting a long needle; B. inserting a short needle C. inserting a needle into the region with a shallow and thin skin and flesh; D. inserting a needle into the region with relaxed. Skin.
1221	同时取用面部、下腹部及足背部穴位，最	What posture should be assumed by the patient when points in the face, lower abdomen and back of foot are to be engaged

	适宜的体位是: A. ·侧卧位; B. ·俯卧位 C. ·仰卧位; D. ·仰靠坐位; E. ·俯伏坐位	in the face, lower abdomen and back of foot are to be engaged simultaneously? A. ·Lateral recumbent position; B. ·Prone position; C. ·horizontal position with feet slightly bent; D. ·Sitting position with head supported from behind; E. ·Sitting position with face resting on table.
1222	同一耳穴，因左右耳而异名的是: A·平喘; B·脑干 C. ·卵巢; D·胰; E·肝.	What auricular point has one identical point on each side, but the two point have two different names? A. Panting Tranquilizer; B·Brain Stem C. ·ovary; D. ·Pancreas; E. liver.
1223	头部晕听区中点向后引 4 厘米长的水平线是: A. ·言语二区; B. ·言语三区 C. ·运用区; D. ·视区; E. ·足运感区	Draw a 4 C. m horizontal line backward from the midpoint of vertigo-auditory area; what is this point? A. ·Speech area No2; B. ·Speech area No3 C. ·Intricate movements (application) area; D. ·Visual area; E. Foot-motor sensory area.
1224	头针"言语二区"的主治症是: A. ·运动性失语; B. ·命名性失语 C. ·感觉性失语; D. ·失用症; E. ·以上都不是	What Can be treated by "Speech area No2 " in scalp acupuncture? A. ·aphemia; B. ·aphasia C. ·sensory aphasia; D. ·apraxia; E. ·none of the above
1225	头针"言语三区"的主治症是: A. ·感觉性失语; B. ·失用症 C. ·命名性失语; D. ·运动性失语; E. ·以上都不是	What Can be treated by "Speech area No3 "in scalp acupuncture? A. ·sensory aphasia; B. ·apraxia C. ·aphasia; D. ·aphemia; E. ·none of the above
1226	头针"言语一区"的主治症 A. ·失用症; B. ·眩晕症 C. ·感觉性失语; D. ·命名性失语; E. ·运动性失语	What Can be treated by "Speech area No1"in scalp acupuncture? A. ·apraxia; B. ·vertigo; C. ·sensory aphasia; D. ·aphasia; E. ·aphemia.
1227	头针操作时持转速度为: A·150 次左右; B·200 次左右 C. ·250 次左右; D·100 次左右.	What is the speed at which a needle should be twirled in scalp acupuncture? A about ·150 times; B · about 200 times;C. ·about250times; D ·about 100 times.
1228	头针操作时每次捻针时间为: A.1-2min; B. 3-4min; C. 2-3min; D 4-5min.	In scalp acupuncture, how a long a needle should be twirled? A.1-2min; B. 3-4min; C. 2-3min; D4-5min.
1229	头针操作所采用的进针手法,一般采用: A·指切进针法; B·提捏进针法 C. ·挟持进针法; D·舒张进针法; E·以上都不是.	What is the common technique of inserting a needle in scalp acupuncture? A ·Nail-cutting method; B. Needle insertion by pushing up the skin at the point C. needle insertion by holding the needle; D. spreading method; E. none of the above.
1230	头针的捻转速度要求每分钟达: A. ·50 次左右; B. ·100 次左右 C. ·150 次左右; D. ·180 次左右; E. ·200 次左右	What is the speed of twirling a needle every minute in scalp acupuncture? A. ·about 50 times; B. ·about 100 times C. ·about 150 times; D. ·about 180 times; E. ·about 200 times.

1231	头针感觉区的位置在: A. 运动区向前移0·5 厘米; B. 运动区向前移 1·0 厘米 C. 运动区向后移0·5 厘米; D. 运动区向后移 1·0 厘米; E. 运动区向后移 1·5 厘米	Where is "sensory area" located in scalp acupuncture? A. ·moving forward 0.5 cm from motor area of cerebrum; B. ·moving forward 1.0 cm from motor area of cerebrum; C. moving backward 0.5 cm from motor area of cerebrum; D. · moving backward 1.0 cm from motor area of cerebrum; E. · moving backward 1.5 cm from motor area of cerebrum.
1232	头针疗法所用毫针的规格为: A.28-30 号长 1.5-3 寸; B, 28-30 号长 0.5-1.5 寸 C. 30-32 号长 1.5-3 寸; D30-32 号长 0.5-1.5 寸.	What is the specification of a minute needle in scalp acupuncture? A. 28-30, 1.5-3cun in length; B.28-30, 0.5-1.5 Cun in length; C. 30-32, 1.5-3 Cun in length; D. 30-32, 0.5-1.5 Cun in length.
1233	头针前后正中线的标定线是: A. ·从前发际至后发际线; B. ·从眉间至后发际线 C. ·从眉间至枕外粗隆线; D. ·从前发际至枕外粗隆线; E. ·以上都不是	What is the standard line of "Anterior-posterior midline" in scalp acupuncture? A. ·from anterior hairline to posterior hairline; B. ·from midpoint between eyebrows to posterior hairline; C. from midpoint between eyebrows to external occipital protuberance line; D. ·from anterior hairline to external occipital protuberance line; E. ·none of the above
1234	头针视区主要用来治疗: A. ·青光眼; B. ·目赤肿痛 C. ·色盲; D. ·夜盲; E. ·皮层性视力障碍	What disease is the primary indication of "Visual area" in scalp acupuncture? A. ·glaucoma; B. ·pink eyes with swelling and pain; C. ·color blindness; D. ·night blindness; E. ·cortical visul disturbance.
1235	头针运针的特点是: A. 快提插; B. 快捻转 C. 慢进针; D. 慢捻转; E. 轻提插.	What is the characteristic of manipulating the needle in scalp acupuncture? A. quick lifting-pushing of the needle; B. quick twirling of the needle; C. slow insertion of the needle; D. slow twirling of the needle; E.quick lifting-pushing of the needle.
1236	头针针刺要求针与头皮的夹角呈: A·10 度; B·15 度 C. ·20 度; D·30 度; E·45 度.	In scalp acupuncture, what degree should be formed. by the inserted needle and the scalp? A. ·10 degrees; B. ·15 degrees; C. ·20 degrees; D. ·30 degrees; E. ·45 degrees.
1237	头针治疗失用症应选: A. 运动区; B. ·感觉区 C. ·足运感区; D. ·晕听区; E. 运用区	Which should be selected to treat apraxia in scalp acupuncture? A. ·motor area of cerebrum; B. ·Sensory area C. ·Foot-motor sensory area; D. ·Vertigo-auditory area; E. ·Intricate movements (application) area
1238	头针治疗小脑共济失调，宜取: A. 运动区; B. ·舞蹈震颤控制区 C. 运用区; D. ·足运感区; E. ·平衡区	Which should be selected to treat cerebellar ataxia in scalp acupuncture? A. ·motor area of cerebrum; B. ·Area of controlling St Vitus dance and tremor C. ·Intricate movements (application) area; D. ·Foot-motor sensory area; E. ·Equilibrium area.
1239	头针主要治疗: A·神经性疾病; B·脑源性疾病 C. ·全身性疾病; D·血液的疾病; E·四肢的疾病.	What are the primary indications of scalp acupuncture? A ·nervous diseases; B diseases of brain origin; C. diseases of the whole body; D. blood diseases; E. diseases of four limbs.
1240	为便于取穴，耳垂被	For the sake of locating auricular points more easily, how

	分为: A.6 区; B.8 区 C. 9 区; Dl2 区.	many zones is the ear lobe divided into? A. 6 zones; B. 8 zones; C. 9 zones; D. 12 zones.
1241	位于对耳轮上下脚分叉处的耳穴是: A·子宫; B·神门 C. ·精宫; D·盆腔; E·膝.	What auricular point separates crus antihelicis superior and crus antihelicis inferior? A·uterus; B. divine door (spiritual door); C. semen palace (jing gong); D. pelvic cavity; E. knees.
1242	位于对耳屏的内侧面的耳穴是: A·肾上腺; B·三焦 C. ·皮质下; D·内分泌; E·平喘.	What auricular point is on the medial side of antetragus? A·Adrenal Gland; B. ·Triple Burning (Sanjiao); C. ·Subcortex; D. ·Internal Secretion (Endocrine); E. ·Panting Tranquilizer.
1243	舞蹈震颤控制区上点在: A. 前后正中线中点前 1 厘米; B. 前后正中线中点后 1 厘米 C. ·感觉区前 1·5·厘米; D. ·感觉区后 1·5 厘米; E. ·运动区后 1·5 厘米	Where is the upper point of "Area of; controlling St Vitus dance and tremor"? A. ·1 cm in front of the midpoint of the anterior-posterior midline; B. ·1 cm in the back of the midpoint of the anterior-posterior midline; C. 1.5 cm in front of sensory area; D. ·1.5 cm behind sensory area; E. ·1.5 cm behind motor area of cerebrum.
1244	吸筒法指的是: A.皮肤针法; B 角法 C. 灸法; D 穴位注射法.	What is bamboo sucking technique? A.technique of applying skin needle; B. techique of cupping; C. technique of moxibustion; D. technique of point injection.
1245	下列病症中，适宜于隔蒜灸的是: A·外感表症; B·虚寒性呕吐 C. 阳萎早泄; D·瘰疬; E·漏肩风.	Which of the following may be effectively treated by "moxibustion with garlic in between moxa and skin"? A. superficial symptoms of external causes; B. deficient and cold vomiting; C. impotence and premature ejaculation; D. scrofula; E. omalgia (neuralgia of shoulder).
1246	下列治法中，治疗痔疮宜选用: A·挑治; B·拔罐 C. ·电针; D·皮肤针; E·艾灸.	Which of the following should be used to treat haemorrhoids? A·pricking therapy; B·cupping; C. ·electroacupuncture; D. ·skin-needle therapy; E·moxibustion.
1247	下列耳穴，除……之外，均在"三焦"区周围? A·口; B·鼻 C. ·肺; D·皮质下; E 内分泌.	Which of the following auricular points is NOT in the surrounding of "triple burning (sanjiao)"? A · mouth; B. nose; C. lungs; D. subcortex E. internal secretion (endocrine).
1248	下列耳穴中，定位有错误的是: A."扁桃体"在耳垂 8 区正中; B·"眼"在耳垂 5 区的中央 C. ·"内耳"在耳垂 5 区正中; D·"上颌"在耳垂 3 区正中处; E·"牙痛点 2"在耳垂 4 区的中央.	Which is NOT a correct description of an auricular point? A. "tonsil" in the middle of earlobe (lobule of the auricle) zone 8; B. "eye" in the middle of earlobe (lobule of the auricle) zone 5; C. "internal ear" in the middle of earlobe (lobule of the auricle) zone 5; D. "Upper Jaw" in the middle of earlobe (lobule of the auricle) zone 3; E. "Toothache Point" in the middle of earlobe (lobule of the auricle) zone 4.
1249	下列各项，除…外，都是拔罐法的治疗作用: A·温经通络; B·祛湿逐寒 C. 行气活血; D·补益气血; E·消肿	Which is NOT the function of cupping? A. to warm meridians and connect linking meridians; B. to expel dampness and cold; C. to promote energy flow and activate blood; D. to tone up energy and blood; E. to heal swelling and relieve pain.

	止痛.	
1250	下列各项，哪些应慎用灸法? A. 寒邪束表; B. 阳虚暴脱 C. 瘀血阻络; D. 寒滞经络; E. 阴虚发热	Which of the following should be treated by moxibustion with great care? A. cold pathogen restricting the superficialregion; B. yang deficiency with sudden collapse; C. blood coagulation obstructing linking meridians; D. coldness freezing meridians; E. yin deficiency with fever.
1251	下列灸法中，治疗中风脱证宜选用: A 隔盐灸; B 隔豆鼓饼灸 C. 隔附子饼灸; D 隔蒜灸.	What kind of moxibustion should be selected to treat prolapsed type of wind stroke? A. Moxibustion with salt in between moxa and skin; B. Moxibustion with cake of SEMEN SOJAE PRAEPARATUM in between moxa and skin; C. Moxibustion with cake of RADIX ACONITI PRAEPARATA in between moxa and skin; D. Moxibustion with garlic in between moxa and skin.
1252	下列疗法除……外都是皮部理论的临床应用: A. 药物敷贴; B. 梅花针叩刺 C. 灸法; D. 穴位注射; E. 埋针	Which is NOT a clinical application of thetheory of pi bu / skin zone? A. Sticking on medicated herbs (using non-heating materials of fire); B. needle insertion by tapping with a plum blossom needle; C. moxibustion; D. Acupuncture Points Injection Therapy; E. neddle embedding.
1253	下列名称中，除……外，均是皮肤针的别名: A 梅花针; B 罗汉针 C. 微针; D 七星针; E 小儿针.	Which of the following does not refer to skin needle? A. plum blossom needle; B. luo han zhen; C. tiny needle; D. seven star needle; E.children needle.
1254	下列哪个穴组不宜用电针治疗? A 肾俞 大肠俞; B 风府 风池 C. 乳根 期门; D 命门 肾俞; E 腰俞 次髎.	Which group of points should not be treated by electro acupuncture? A. B23 [Shèn Shū] B25 [Dà Cháng Shū]; B. D16 [Fēng Fǔ] G20 [Fēng Chí]; C. S18 [Rǔ Gēn] Lv14 [Qí Mén]; D. D4 [Mìng Mén] B23 [Shèn Shū]; E. D2 [Yāo Shū] B32 [Cì Liáo].
1255	下列哪项不是耳穴处方原则? A 按疾病的相应部位选穴; B 循经选穴 C. 按中医理论选穴; D 按现代医学知识选穴; E 根据临床经验选穴.	Which is NOT the principle of selecting auricular points? A. selecting points according to the corresponding region of disease; B. selecting points according to the distribution of meridians; C. selecting points according to the theory of Chinese medicine; D. selecting points according to the knowledge of modern medicine; E. selecting points according to clinical experience.
1256	下列哪项不是晕针的原因? A 精神紧张; B 针具选择不合适 C. 体位不合适; D，针刺手法过重; E 患者体质虚弱	Which is NOT the cause of needle sickness (symptoms during treatment)? A. mental tension; B. inadequate instruments; C. improper posture; D. excessively strong technique; E. deficient and weak state of the patient.
1257	下列哪项不宜用耳针治疗? A 习惯性流产的孕妇; B 高血压 C. 动脉硬化; D 冠心病; E 以上都不是.	Which should NOT be treated by auricular acupuncture? A.pregnant women with habitual miscarriage; B. hypertension; C. arteriosclerosis; D. coronary heart disease; E. none of the above.
1258	下列哪项不属于三棱	Which is NOT "acupuncture with a three-edged needle"?

	针刺法: A. ·点刺; B. 散刺 C. ，挑刺; D. ·刺络; E. ·输刺	A. ·dotted-needling; B. ·spreading needling; C. incision needling; D. ·reticular needling; E. ·transportable-needling.
1259	下列哪一组穴位可用仰靠坐位？ A·风池 风府 曲池 血海; B·百会 哑门 足三里 C. ·廉泉 列缺 照海; D·人中 腰阳关 委中; E·风池 腰阳关 环跳 阳陵泉.	Which group of points may be treated with the patient in the sitting position with head supported from behind? A ·G20 [Fēng Chí], D16 [Fēng Fǔ], Li11 [Qū Chí], Sp10 [Xuè Hǎi]; B. D20 [Bǎi Huì], D15 [Yǎ Mén], S36 [Zú Sān Lǐ]; C. R23 [Lián Quán], Lu7 [Liè Quē], K6 [Zhào Hǎi]; D. D26 [Shuǐ Gōu [Rén Zhōng], D3 [Yāo Yáng Guān];B40 [Wěi Zhōng]; E. G20 [Fēng Chí], D3 [Yāo Yáng Guān], G30 [Huán Tiào], G34 [Yáng Líng Quán].
1260	下列哪种疾病不宜使用三棱针疗法? A.高热; B 久痹 C. 顽癣; D 中风脱证.	Which of the following diseases should NOT be treated by three-edged needles? A.high fever; B. chronic rheumatism C. chronic tinea; D. stroke with prolapse.
1261	下列哪种情况可以针刺: A 皮肤感染的部位; B 皮肤有溃疡的部位 C. 皮肤有肿瘤的部位; D 皮肤有疮疹的部位.	Which of the following can be needled? A. region of skin infection; B. region of skin ulcer; C. region of skin tumor; D. region of skin sores and carbuncles.
1262	下列哪组腧穴适用于侧卧位? A 头维下关肩髃外关陽陵泉; B.百会风府大椎委中承扶 C. 上星印堂天突曲池肩髃; D 印堂百会膻中中脘足三里.	Which group of points is better located with the patient in the lateral recumbent position? A S8 (Tóu Wěi), S7 (Xià Guān), Li15 (Jiān Yú), Sj5 (Wài Guān), G34 (Yáng Líng Quán); B D20 (Bǎi Huì), D16 (Fēng Fǔ), D14 (Dà Zhuī);B40 (Wěi Zhōng);B36 (Chéng Fú); C. D23 (Shàng Xīng), Yìn Táng, R22 (Tiān Tū), Li11 (Qū Chí), Li15 (Jiān Yú); D. Yìn Táng, D20 (Bǎi Huì), R17 (Shān Zhōng), R12 (Zhōng Wǎn), S36 (Zú Sān Lǐ).
1263	下列哪组腧穴适用于俯卧位: A.头维下关肩髃外关陽陵泉; B 百会风府大椎委中承扶;C.上星印堂天突曲池肩髃; D 印堂百会膻中中脘足三里.	Which group of points should use prone position? A. S8 [Tóu Wěi], S7 [Xià Guān], Li15 [Jiān Yú], Sj5 [Wài Guān], G34 [Yáng Líng Quán]; B D20 [Bǎi Huì], D16 [Fēng Fǔ], D14 [Dà Zhuī];B40 [Wěi Zhōng];B36 [Chéng Fú]; C. D23 [Shàng Xīng], YÌN TÁNG (midpoint between eyebrows, seal hall), R22 [Tiān Tū], Li11 [Qū Chí], Li15 [Jiān Yú]; D. YÌN TÁNG (midpoint between eyebrows, seal hall), D20 [Bǎi Huì], R17 [Shān Zhōng], R12 [Zhōng Wǎn], S36 [Zú Sān Lǐ].
1264	下列哪组腧穴适用于仰靠坐位: A.头维下关肩髃外关陽陵泉; B.百会风府大椎委中承扶 C. 上星印堂天突曲池肩髃; D. 印堂百会膻中胃俞足三里.	Which group of points is better located with the patient in the sitting position with head supported from behind? A S8 (Tóu Wěi), S7 (Xià Guān), Li15 (Jiān Yú), Sj5 (Wài Guān), G34 (Yáng Líng Quán); B D20 (Bǎi Huì), D16 (Fēng Fǔ), D14 (Dà Zhuī);B40 (Wěi Zhōng);B36 (Chéng Fú); C. D23 (Shàng Xīng), Yìn Táng, R22 (Tiān Tū), Li11 (Qū Chí), Li15 (Jiān Yú); D. Yìn Táng, D20 (Bǎi Huì), R17 (Shān Zhōng), R12 (Zhōng Wǎn), S36 (Zú Sān Lǐ).
1265	下列头针刺激区中，除。。。。外，都平行于前后正中线。 A. ·视区; B. ·言语二区 C. ·足运感区; D. ·言语三区; E. ·生殖区	Which is not in parallel to the anterior-posterior midline in scalp acupuncture? A. ·Visual area; B. ·Speech area No2 C. ·Foot-motor sensory area; D. ·Speech area No3; E. ·Reproduction area.

1266	下列穴位中除……外，经常用以刺血治病: A 十宣; B 印堂 C. 委中; D 经渠; E 耳尖.	Which is NOT normally needled for blooletting? A. SHÍ XUĀN (ten statements, ten expansions); B. ·Yìn Táng; C. B40 [Wĕi Zhōng]; D. ·Lu8 [Jīng Qú]; E. ·Ĕner jian (tip of ear).
1267	下列晕针处理方法错误的是: A. ·患者平卧·头部垫高; B.注意通风·保暖 C. ·予饮温开水或糖开水; D. ·可指掐或针刺人中·素髎·内关·足三里等穴; E. ·可灸百会·关元·气海	Which is NOT the proper way of dealing with needle sickness? A. let the patient lie on back with head on high pillow; B. paying attention of ventilation and keeping warm; C. ·let the patient drink warm water or sugar water; D. ·use a finger to knead or apply acupuncture to D26 [Shuĭ Gōu [Rén Zhōng] ·D25 [Sù Liáo] ·P6 [Nèi Guān] ·S36 [Zú Sān Lĭ], etc; E. ·apply moxibustion to D20 [Băi Huì] ·R4 [Guān Yuán] ·R6 [Qì Hăi]
1268	下列属于间接灸的是: A 无瘢痕灸; B 隔附子饼灸 C. 太乙针灸; D. 温灸器灸; E. 瘢痕灸.	Which of the following belongs to Indirect Moxibustion [JIĀN JIĒ JIŬ]? A Moxibustion without burning the skin (moxibustion without scars); B. Moxibustion with cake of RADIX ACONITI PRAEPARATA in between moxa and skin; C. Tai-yi star needle and moxibustion (Tai yi zhen jiu); D. warm moxibustion with container (wen jiu qi jiu); E.burning the skin to leave scars (scar moxibutoin).
1269	下述八卦配属八脉八穴有错误的是: A. 坎"1"联申脉; B. 震"3"属后溪 C. 乾"6"是公孙; D. 艮"8"属内关; E. 离 9"列缺	Which is NOT correct about the way a trigram is linked to one of the eight meridian eight points? A. ·kăn "1" linked to B62 [Shēn Mài]; B. ·zhèn "3" linked to Si3 [Hòu Xī]; C. ·qiān "6" linked to Sp4 [Gōng Sūn]; D. ·gĕn "8" linked to P6 [Nèi Guān]; E. ·lí 9"linked to Lu7 [Liè Quē].
1270	下述脑血管病例中，可用头针言语二区治疗的是: A. ·称呼"名称"能力障碍; B. ·理解语言能力障碍 C. 能理解语言 ·但失去了语言能力; D. 统治一切语言障碍; E. ·以上均不是	Which of the following cases of cerebrovascular diseases may be treated by Speech area No2 in scalp acupuncture? A. ·disturbance of calling a name; B. ·disturbance of understanding language C. ·able to understand language with loss of speech; D. ·all kinds of language disturbances may be treated; E. ·none of the above.
1271	下述针麻选穴中，哪一种是根据神经分布选穴的? A. ·头颈部手术选合谷; B. ·胃大部切除术选足三里 C. 拔牙选颊车、颧髎; D. ·剖腹产选带脉; E. ·甲状腺手术选扶突	Which of the following is selected for acupuncture anaesthesia according to nerve distribution? A. ·select Li4 [Hé Gŭ] for operations in the head and neck region; B. ·select S36 [Zú Sān Lĭ] for major gastrectomy; C. ·select S6 [Jiá Chē] ·Si18 [Quán Liáo] for tooth extraction; D. ·select G26 [Dài Mài] for cesarean section; E. ·select Li18 [Fú Tū] for thyroid gland operation.
1272	消化系统疾病应取: A.额旁 1 线; B.额旁 2 线 C. 额旁 3 线; D 额中线.	Which should be used to treat the diseases of the digestive system? A. 1st lateral plane on forehead; B. 2nd. lateral plane on forehead; C. 3rD. lateral plane on forehead; D. mid-forehead plane.
1273	小儿痄腮最适宜的灸法为:	What kind. of moxibustion may be applied to treat mumps in children?

	A.天灸; B.灯火灸 C. 太乙针灸; D 雀啄灸.	A. medicated moxibustion to cause blisters; B. Rush fire moxibustion; C. Tai-yi star needle moxibustion; D. Sparrow pecking moxibustion.
1274	小海穴针刺或穴位注射不当，可以损伤: A. 尺神经; B. 正中神经 C. 桡神经; D. 腋神经; E. 前臂内侧皮神经	What nerve will be damaged when Si8 [Xiǎo Hǎi] is improperly needled or treated by injection therapy improperly? A. groove of the ulnar nerve (sulcus nervi ulnaris); B. median nerve (n medianus); C. radialis nerve; D. axillary nerve; E. Cutaneous Nerve of medial forearm..
1275	小脑疾病引起的平衡障碍应取: A.枕上正中线; B.颞后线 C. 枕上旁线; D 枕下旁线.	Loss of balance in movement due to diseases of the cerebellum should be treated by: A. mid-occipital upper plane; B. Posterior temporal plane; C. mid-occipital lateral plane; D. mid-occipital lower plane.
1276	蝎蜂等虫毒咬伤 宜用: A 瘢痕灸; B 雀啄灸 C. 隔姜灸; D 隔蒜灸; E 温筒灸.	How to treat insect bites such as by scorpio [Quán Xiē] and wasps? A scar moxib ustion; B Sparrow pecking moxibustion C. Moxibustion with ginger in between moxa and skin; D. Moxibustion with garlic in between moxa and skin; E. mobibustion by bamboo tube.
1277	斜刺，针身与皮肤表面所形成的夹角是: A. 15°角左右; B. 30°角左右 C. 45°角左右; D. 50°角左右; E. 75°角左右	In slanting insertion, what is the angle formed by the body of needle and the skin? A. about 15°; B. about 30°; C. about 45°; D. about 50°; E. about 75°.
1278	斜刺的角度应为: A 10 °左右; B 15 ° 左右 C. 30 °左右; D 45 °左右; E 60 °左右.	What is the angle of slanting insertion? A. about 10°; B. about 15°; C. about 30°; D. about 45°; E:about 60°.
1279	心血管呼吸系统疾病应取 A.额旁 1 线 B. 额旁 2 线 C. ，额旁 3 线 D 额中线	Which should be used to treat the diseases of the cardio-vascular systems? A. 1st lateral plane on forehead; B. 2nd. lateral plane on forehead; C. 3rd. lateral plane on forehead; D. mid-forehead plane.
1280	行针的基本手法是: A. 提插法; D. 循法 C. 平补平泻; D. 提插补泻法; E. 以上都不是.	What is the basic technique of manipulating an inserted needle? A. lifting and pushing in technique (ti Cha fa); B. Manipulating the inserted needle by tracing the meridian (xun fa); C. neutral technique (ping bu ping xie); D. Lifting-pushing technique for tonificationa and sedation [TÍ CHĀ BǓ XIÈ].
1281	穴位注射法用于四肢部的剂量为：A.0.lml; B. 0.3 – 0.5ml; C.l-2ml; D2 — 0.5ml。	What is the dose of point injection therapy as applied to the four limbs? A. 0.lml; B. 0.3 – 0.5ml; C. l-2ml; D. 2 — 0.5ml.
1282	扬刺法是: A. 正入一傍入一; B. 正入一，傍入二 C. 正入一傍入三; D. 正入一傍入四; E. 以上	What is scattered needling (yang ci fa)? A. one needle inserted in the middle and another needle inserted on the side; B. one needle inserted in the middle and two needles inserted around it; C. one needle inserted in

	入一傍入四; E. 以上都不是.	the middle and three needles inserted around it; D. one needle inserted in the middle and four needles inserted around it; E.none of the above.
1283	药罐的负压产生方法为: A.闪火法; B 煮罐法 C. 抽气罐法; D 滴酒法.	In medicated cupping, how to produce negative pressure? A. Flashing paper stick cupping; B. boiling cupping; C. air pumping cupping; D. wine dripping technique.
1284	依循行定针刺的方向，其所达到的目的为: A.气至病所; B 迎随补泻 C. 针刺安全; D 尽快得气.	What is the objective of inserting a needle according to the direction of meridian energy flow? A. to bring energy to the affected region; B. the needle is twirled in the same direction as the flow of energy streams in the meridians for tonification, the needle is twirled in the opposite direction for sedation; C. to be secure in needle insertion; D. to speed up energy response as quickly as possible.
1285	以金属针替代砭石，在什么时代已基本完成? A 战国; B 秦 C. 西汉; D 东汉; E 三国.	When was the stone needle completely replaced by the metal needle? A Warring States Period (475-221; BC); B. Qin Dynasty (221-206; BC); C. Western Han Dynasty (206; BC-AD 24); D. Eastern Han Dynasty (25-220 AD); E Three Kingdoms Period (220-280 AD).
1286	以下部位除......以外都应禁止直接灸? A. 眼睛; B. 胸腹部 C. 颜面部; D. 浅表血管部; E. 腋窝正中.	Which of the following may be treated by direct moxibustion? A. eye region; B. chest-abdomen region; C. face region; D. shallow and superficial blood vessels region; E. armpit region.
1287	以下除...以外可适当增加留针时间? A 急性病; B 顽固性疾病 C. 疼痛性疾病; D 虚性疾病; E 寒性疾病.	Which of the following should NOT be treated with prolonged retention of needle in the body? A acute diseases; B. chronic diseases; C. painful diseases; D. deficient diseases; E. cold diseases.
1288	以下手法除什么法以外均是行针辅助手法? A. 循法; B. 刮柄法 C. 震颤法; D. 捻转法; E. 搓柄法.	Which of the following is NOT called, supplementary methods of manipulating the inserted needle (Xing zhen fu zhu shou fa)? A. Technique of pushing with the balls of fingers; B. scraping technique; C. shaking the needle to cause trembling; D. technique of twirling the needle; E. rolling the needle
1289	以下头针刺激区可治命名性失语的是: A. 言语三区; B. 言语二区 C. 运用区; D. 晕听区; E. 感觉区.	What point in scalp acupuncture may be used to treat aphasia? A. Speech area No3; B. Speech area No2; C. Intricate movements (application) area; D. Vertigo-auditory area; E. Sensory area.
1290	以下针刺手法除。。。外，都属于补法: A. 进针快、出针慢; B. 出针后按闭针孔 C. 先浅后深，重插轻提; D. 呼气进针，吸气出针; E. 得气后，均匀提插捻转	Which of the following is NOT tonification? A. rapid insertion, slow withdrawal; B. close the needle hole after pulling out the needle; C. shallow first and then deep, heavy pushing and light lifting; D. inserting the needle on expiration, pulling out needle on inspiration; E. even lifting, even pushing, and even twirling after energy responses.

1291	用1%普鲁卡因注射次髎三阴交可以治疗: A 腰痛; B 遗尿 C. 遗精; D 阳痿; E 慢性泄泻.	What may be treated by injecting 1% novocaine into B32 [Cì Liáo] and Sp6 [Sān Yīn Jiāo]? A. lumbago; B. enuresis; C. seminal emission; D. impotence; E. chronic diarrhea.
1292	用耳针治疗输液反应，应取: A 肾内分泌; B 眼肝耳尖 C. 肾肝眼神门; D 肾上腺平喘; E 神门皮质下.	What auricular point may be selected to treat transfusion reaction? A. kidney, internal secretion; B. eye, liver, tip of ear; C. kidney, liver, eye, divine door; D. adrenal gland, calm asthma; E. divine door, subcortex.
1293	用皮肤针治疗面瘫，一般可叩刺: A. 睛明 攒竹 地仓 颊车; B. 阳白 丝竹空 承浆 下关 C. 合谷 地仓 颊车 承泣; D. 牵正 阳白 太阳 四白; E. 风池 合谷 太冲 地仓	When facial paralysis is to be treated by a cutaneous needle, what points may be inserted by tapping? A. B1 [Jīng Míng] B2 [Zǎn Zhú] S4 [Dì Cāng] S6 [Jiá Chē]; B. G14 [Yáng Bái] Sj23 [Sī Zhú Kōng] R24 [Chéng Jiàng] S7 [Xià Guān]; C. Li4 [Hé Gǔ] S4 [Dì Cāng] S6 [Jiá Chē] S1 [Chéng Qì]; D. Qian Zhèng [pulling and Correcting] G14 [Yáng Bái] Tài Yáng [Sun / temple] S2 [Sì Bái]; E. G20 [Fēng Chí] Li4 [Hé Gǔ] Lv3 [Tài Chōng] S4 [Dì Cāng]
1294	用少量维生素B，或当归注射液注射关元、中极二穴，可治疗: A. ，遗尿; B. 癃闭 C. 脱肛; D. 遗精; E. 石淋	What may be treated by injecting a little vitamin B or Radix angelicae Sinensis injection [Dāng Guī] into R4 [Guān Yuán] 、and R3 [Zhōng Jí]? A.enuresis; B. suppression of urination; C. prolapse of anus; D. seminal emission; E. stony strangury.
1295	用天灸治疗阴疽痰核，一般宜选: A 毛茛灸; B 斑蝥灸 C. 旱莲草灸; D 蒜泥灸; E 白芥子灸.	In general, what type of "medicated moxibustion to cause blisters" may be used to treat " yin; cellulitis and subcutaneous nodule"? A Herba et radix ranunculus moxibution; B MYLABRIS moxibustion; C. Herba ecliptae moxibustion; D garlic moxibustion; E. SEMEN SINAPIS ALBAE moxibusiotn.
1296	用于缓解肌肉和血管痉挛的电针电流波型应选择: A.锯齿波; B.密波 C. 疏密波; D 断续波.	What waveform should be used for relaxing the muscles and spasm of the blood vessels? A. zigzag wave; B. dense wave; C. sparse-dense wave; D. intermittent wave.
1297	用于泻血，治痈肿热病的针具是: A 鈹针; B 锋针 C. 圆利针; D 长针; E 大针.	Which acupuncture needle is used to sedate blood in the treatment of carbuncle swelling and hot diseases? A · Sword-shaped needle (pi zhen); B. Sharp-edged needle (feng zhen); C. round-sharp needles (yuan li zhen); D. long needle (chang zhen); E. big needle (da zhen).
1298	用左手拇、食两指将所刺腧穴部位的皮肤向两侧撑开，使皮肤绷紧，右手持针于两指的中间刺人的进针法是: A. 指切进针法; B. 夹持进针法 C. 舒张进针法; D. 提捏进针法; E. 以上都不是	With the left five fingers extending straight, and the forefinger and middle finger slightly apart to be placed on the point, use the right hand to hold the needle and insert into the skin in between the left forefinger and middle fingers; what is this technique called? A. Nail-cutting method; B. Needle insertion by holding the needle; C. Needle insertion by spreading / spreading method; D. Needle insertion by pushing-up; E. none of the above
1299	有关耳穴"睾丸"的概念错误是:	Which of the following is NOT a correct statement about the auricular point, "Testicles"?

	A·本穴区又称 "卵巢"; B·在对耳屏的内侧前下方 C. ·是内分泌穴区的一部分; D·主治生殖系统疾病; E·以上都不是.	A. ·this zone is also called, "ovary"; B. it is located in the anterior-lower region of the medial side of antetragus; C. it is part of the zone of internal secretion (endocrine); D. it is primarily used to treat the diseases of the reproductive system; E. none of the above.
1300	有宁心安神作用的耳穴是: A·枕; B·心 C. ·交感; D·脑; E·降压沟.	What auricular point has the function of calming the heart and secure the spirit? A. occiput; B. heart; C. sympathetic; D. brain; E. hypotensor groove (depressor groove).
1301	右下肢瘫痪，头针刺激区当取: A. 右运动区下 2 / 5; B. 左运动区下 2 / 5 C. 右运动区中 2 / 5; D. 左运动区上 1 / 5; E. 左运动区下 1 / 5.	What zone of scalp acupuncture may be selected to treat paralysis of lower limbs? A. 2 / 5 below right motor area of cerebrum; B. 2 / 5 below left motor area of cerebrum; C. middle 2 / 5 of right motor area of cerebrum; D. 1 / 5 above left motor area of cerebrum; E. 1 / 5 below left motor area of cerebrum.
1302	与内脏相应的耳穴集中在: A.耳甲; B.耳舟 C. 对耳轮; D 耳垂.	The auricular points corresponding to the internal organs are concentrated in: A.; conchae auriculae; B.scapha canthelix; D. earlobe (lobule of the auricle).
1303	与躯干相应的耳穴分布在: A.耳垂; B.耳舟 C. 对耳轮体 D 对耳轮上下脚	The auricular points corresponding to the trunk are located in: A. earlobe (lobule of the auricle); B. scapha C. corpus antehelix; D. crus antihelicis superior and crus antihelicis inferior.
1304	与上肢相应的耳穴分布在: A.耳垂; B 耳舟 C. 对耳轮体; D 对其轮上下脚.	Where are the auricular points corresponding to upper limbs located? A. earlobe (lobule of the auricle); B. scapha C. corpus antehelix; D. crus antihelicis superior and crus antihelicis inferior.
1305	与头面相应的耳穴分布在: A.耳垂; B 耳舟 C. 对耳轮体; D 耳甲.	Where are the auricular points corresponding to head and face located? A.earlobe (lobule of the auricle); B. scapha C. corpus antehelix; D. conchae auriculae.
1306	与下肢相应的耳穴分布在: A.耳甲; B.耳舟 C. 对其轮体; D 对耳轮上下脚.	The auricular points corresponding to the lower limbs are located in: A.; conchae auriculae; B. scapha; C. corpus antehelix; D. crus antihelicis superior and crus antihelicis inferior.
1307	在对耳轮上，与对耳轮下脚下缘同水平高的耳穴是: A. ·颈; B. 胸 C. 腹; D. 股; E. 膝	What auricular point is on the anthelix, on a level with the lower edge of crus anthelicis inferior? A. ·neck; B. ·chest; C. ·abdomen; D. ·thigh; E. ·knee.
1308	在对耳轮上，与屏上切迹同水平高的耳穴是: A·腹; B·胸 C. ·颈; D·脊椎; E·肩关节.	What auricular point is on the anthelix, on a level with the incisura supratragica? A ·abdomen; B ·chest; C. ·neck; D ·vertebra; E ·shoulder joints.
1309	在对其轮上，与对耳轮下脚下缘同水平高的耳穴是: A·颈; B·胸 C. ·腹;	What auricular point is located on anthelix, on a level with the lower border of crus anthelicis inferior? A ·neck; B. chest; C. abdomen; D. thigh.

	D 股.	
1310	在耳甲腔中心最凹陷处的耳穴是: A 肺; B 大肠 C. 胃; D 肝; E 心.	What auricular point is located in the lowest depression in the center of cavum conchae auriculae? A lung; B large intestine; C. stomach; D liver; E heart.
1311	在耳穴 "肝""肾"之间的耳穴是: A 脾; B 胰 C. 肾上腺; D 十二指肠; E 胃.	What auricular point is situated in between two auricular points, "liver" and "kidneys"? A spleen; B. pancreas; C. adrenal gland; D. duodenum; E. stomach.
1312	在耳穴分区中，与头面部相应的穴位全分布在: A. 耳垂; B. 耳屏 C. 对耳屏; D. 屏间切迹; E. 耳垂，对耳屏，耳屏上都有	In the dividing zones of auricular points, where are points corresponding to the head and face region distributed? A. lobulu auriculae; B. tragus; C. antetragus; D. incisura intertragica; E. lobulu auriculae，antetragus，tragus.
1313	在九针中，长 4 寸，针身粗圆的针具是: A 圆针; B 鍉针 C. 长针; D 大针. E 鑱针	Which of the "nine needles" measures 4 Cuns in length with a rough and round body? A. round needle (yuan zhen); B. key-shaped needle (ti zhen); C. long needle (chang zhen); D. big needle (da zhen); E.Scooping needle (chan zhen).
1314	在下列灸法中 治疗霍乱最好选用: A.隔蒜灸; B 豆豉灸 C. 胡椒灸; D 附子灸; E 隔盐灸.	What is the best way to treat cholera by moxibustion? A. Moxibustion with garlic in between moxa and skin; B Moxibustion with semen sojae praeparatum in between moxa and skin; C. Moxibustion with pepper in between moxa and skin; D Moxibustion with radix aconiti praeparata in between moxa and skin; E. Moxibustion with salt in between moxa and skin.
1315	在下列天灸法中 具有收敛止血及发泡作用的是: A.毛茛灸; B 斑蝥灸 C. 白芥子灸; D 旱莲草灸; E 大蒜灸.	Which kind of"medicated moxibustion to cause blisters" can constrict and stop bleeding and cause vesiculation? A. Herba et radix ranunculus moxibustion; B. mylabris; C. Semen sinapis albae; D. Herba ecliptae moxibustion; E garlic moxibustion.
1316	在针刺手法上，眼眶内的经穴应: A 直入直出; B 斜刺轻捻 C. 向眶尖方向捻转刺入; D 可作中等度提插; E 先捻转后提插	What technique of needle insertion should be applied to needle the points in the socket of eyeball or orbit? A · insert the needle straight in and withdraw it straight out; B. slanting insertion with light twirling; C. insert the needle by twirling in the direction of the angle of the orbit; D. medium inserting and twirling the needle; E.twirl the needle first, and then lift and push in the needle.
1317	在针灸治则中，对于脱肛子宫脱垂等症，最好选用: A 平补平泻法; B 补多泻少法 C. 灸法; D 针法; E 留针法.	According to the principles of acupuncture and moxibustion treatment, what is the best technique of treating proctoptosis (prolapse of anus) and hysteroptosis (prolapse of uterus)? A neutral technique; B. more tonification than sedation; C. by moxibustion; D. by acupuncture; E. by retention of needle in the body.
1318	针刺基本手法包括: A. 捻转法 提插法; B. 捻转法 刮柄法 C. 提插法 弹柄法; D. 刮柄法 弹柄法;	The basic techniques of acupuncture include: A. twirling lifing and pushing; B. twirling scrapping the handle; C. lifting and pushing and flicking the needle; D. scrapping the handle, flicking the needle; E. rolling the

	E. 搓柄法 摇柄法	needle, shaking the needle.
1319	针刺麻醉时，电针法的电流波型应采用: A 密波; B 疏波 C. 疏密波; D 断续波.	In acupuncture anesthesia, what current wave form should be used in electro acupuncture? A dense wave; B loose wave C. loose-dense wave; D interrupted wave.
1320	针刺胸椎棘突下间的穴位，应采用: A 直刺; B 斜刺 C. 向上斜刺; D 向下斜刺; E 平刺.	What technique of needle insertion should be applied to needle the points in between the spinous processes of thoracic vertebrae? A straight insertion; B. slanting insertion; C. slanting insertion with the needle facing upward; D. slanting insertion with the needle facing downward; E. level insertion.
1321	针刺治疗热病的手法，应用 A. 呼进吸出; B. 速刺速出 C. 重插轻提; D. 留针; E. 灸法	How to treat hot diseases by acupuncture? A.pushing on expiration, pulling out on inspiration; B. quick insertion and quick pulling out; C. heavy pushing and light lifting; D. retention of needle; E. moxibustion.
1322	针法的原始工具是: A 铁针; B 铜针 C. 砭石; D 金针; E 银针.	What was the primitive instrument used in ancient acupuncture? A iron needle; B. bronze needle; C. stone needle; D. gold needle; E. silver needle.
1323	针灸的治疗原则，"寒"则应该采取: A 补之; B 徐之 C. 泄之; D 留之; E 灸之.	According to the principles of acupuncture and moxibustion treatment, what is the best technique of treating "cold diseases"? A · by tonification; B. by removing it; C. by sedation; D. by retention of needle in the body; E. by moxibustion.
1324	针灸的治疗原则，"热"则应该采取: A 补之; B 徐之 C. 泄之; D 留之; E 疾之.	According to the principles of acupuncture and moxibustion treatment, what is the best technique of treating "hot diseases"? A twelve muscular meridians / jing jin tonification; B. by removing it; C. by sedation; D. by retention of needle in the body; E. pulling out the needle very shortly.
1325	针麻辅助用药，特别需要慎重使用的是: A. 镇静药; B. 镇痛药 C. 局麻药; D. 肌肉松弛剂; E. 抗胆碱药	What supplementary drug should be used most carefully in acupuncture anaesthesia? A. sedative; B. analgesic; C. local anaesthesia; D. muscle relaxant; E. anticholinergic.
1326	针身与针柄成一直线的皮内针具为: A 麦粒型; B.揿钉型 C. 图钉型; D 梅花型.	What kind of intradermal needle has its body and handle forming a straight line? A grain-of-wheat type ; B. drawing-pin type; C. thumbtack type; D cloveleaf type.
1327	针身与针柄呈垂直状的皮内针具为: A 颗粒型; B 麦粒型 C. 揿钉型; D.梅花型.	What kind of intradermal needle has its body and handle at a right angle to each other? A granular (pellet) type; B grain-of-wheat type; C. thumbtack type; D. cloveleaf type
1328	枕上正中线与枕上旁线之间距离: A. 1.5寸; B. 0.75寸 C. 0.5寸; D 2.25寸.	What is the distance between mid-occipital upper plane and mid-occipital lateral plane? A. 1.5 Cun; B. 0.75 Cun; C. 0.5 Cun; D. 2.25 Cun.

1329	枕下旁线是从何穴向下引一长2寸的直线? A.玉枕; B.脑户 C.,强间; D 百会.	Mid-occipital lateral plane refers to the line that starts from a point and downward for 2 Cuns; what is this point? A; B9 (Yù Zhěn); B. D17 (Nǎo Hù); C. D18 (Qiáng Jiān); D. D20 (Bǎi Huì).
1330	正确的行针辅助手法是: A 提插法 捻转法 震颤法; B 提插法 捻转法 弹针法 C. 提插法 捻转法 刮柄法; D 震颤法 弹针法 刮柄法; E 提插法 刮柄法 震颤法.	What are the supplementary techniques of acupuncture" A ·lifting and pushing in technique twirling shaking the needle to cause trembling; B ·lifting and pushing in technique twirling flicking the needle; C. ·lifting and pushing in technique twirling scrapping the handle; D. ·shaking the needle to cause trembling. flicking the needle scrapping the handle; E ·lifting and pushing in technique scrapping the handle shaking the needle to cause trembling.
1331	治疗低血压的耳穴应首选: A ·皮质下; B ·神门 C. ·交感; D ·肾上腺; E ·内分泌.	What auricular point should be selected to treat hypotension? A. subcortex; B. divine door; C. sympathetic; D. adrenal gland; E. internal secretion.
1332	治疗皮层性多尿、夜尿,用头针治疗可选: A. ·足运感区; B. ·晕听区 C. ·平衡区; D. ·生殖区; E.躯干运动区	What area of scalp acupuncture may be selected to treat cortical diuresis、bed wetting? A. ·Foot-motor sensory area; B. ·Vertigo-auditory area; C. ·Equilibrium area; D. ·Reproduction area; E. motor area of trunk.
1333	治疗热痹可用: A.刮柄法; B.弹柄法 C. 烧山火; D 透天凉.	How to treat hot rheumatism? A. scrapping the handle; B. flicking the needle; C. forest fire; D. cool heaven technique.
1334	子午流注 (纳甲法)的时间周期为: A. ·5天; B. ·10 天 C. ·12天; D. ·15 天; E. ·以上都不是	What is the time-cycle in energy-flowing acupuncture [ZǏ WǓ LIÚ ZHÙ (combination of 12 meridians and 10 stems)? A. ·5 days; B. ·10 days; C. 12 days; D. ·15 days; E. ·none of the above.
1335	最初的拔罐用具是: A. 竹筒; B. 陶罐 C. 兽角; D. 铜罐; E. 以上都不是.	What is the earliest instrument used in cupping? A. bamboo cup; B. ceramic cup; C. animal horn; D. copper cup; E. none of the above.
1336	最原始的针具是: A. 骨针; B 竹针; C. 铜针; D. 铁针; E. 砭石.	What is the most primitive needle? A. bone needle; B bamboo needle; C. copper needle; D. iron needle; E. stone needle.
1337	最早的记载拔罐法的古医籍是: A.《灵枢》; B.《甲乙经》 C. 《五十二病方》 D《针灸大成》	Which Classic recoreded cupping for the first time? A.Ling Shu Jing 403-221; BC; B..Zhen Jiu Jia Yi Jing; C. fifty-two formulas for diseases (unearthed in 1973); D. Zhen Jiu Da Chesteng (1601).
1338	左取右,右取左,左右交叉取穴,刺在络者是: A. 巨刺; B. 缪刺 C. 经刺; D. 络刺; E. 输刺.	To treat a disease by inserting a needle into the linking meridian and when the disease occurs on the right side the points on the left side should be engaged, and vice versa; what is this technique called? A. opposite needling (ju ci); B. reverse technique of needling (miao ci); C. Meridian needling (jing ci); D. reticular-needling (luo ci); E. transportable needling (shu ci).

13-5	针灸治疗学	Acupuncture Treatment	1339-2537

13-5 针灸治疗学 / Acupuncture Treatment

1339	在华佗夹脊穴中，治疗下肢疾患的应是: A·胸10-腰2夹脊; B·胸11-腰3夹脊 C. ·胸12-腰4夹脊; D·胸1-腰4夹脊; E·腰2-腰4夹脊	Among points in HUÁ TUÓ JIĀ JÍ (Dr. Huatuo's clippings of spine), which can treat diseases of lower extremities? A. ·clipping Chest10-lumbar2 spines; B. ·clipping Chest11-lumbar3 spines C. ·clipping Chest12-lumbar4 spines; D. ·clipping Chest1-lumbar4 spines.
1340	下列奇穴中主治目疾的是: A·拳尖; B·五虎 C. ·中魁; D·虎口; E·威灵	Which of the following extraordinary points / qi xue can treat eye diseases? A. ·Quán Jiān [tip of fist]; B. ·Wu Hu [five tigers]; C. ·Zhōng Kuí [middle head / middle leader]; D. ·Hu Kou [mouth of tiger]; E. ·Wēi Líng [majestic soul / fantastic effects]
1341	下列奇穴中治疗呕吐的是: A·拳尖; B·二白 C. ·女膝; D·精灵; E·中魁	Which of the following extraordinary points / qi xue can treat vomiting? A. ·Quán Jiān [tip of fist]; B. ÈR BÁI (two whites); C. ·Nu Xī [female knee]; D. ·Jīng Líng [pure sou / [pure effects]; E. ·Zhōng Kuí [middle head / middle leader]
1342	除xx穴外，均可治疗水肿: A·归来; B·水分 C. ·膀胱俞; D·阴陵泉; E·委阳	Which of the following cannot treat edema? A. ·S29 [Guī Lái]; B. ·R9 [Shuǐ Fēn]; C. ·B28 [Páng Guāng Shū]; D. ·Sp9 [Yīn Líng Quán]; E. ·B39 [Wěi Yáng]
1343	用五输穴治疗 "心下满"，应该选用: A·输穴; B·经穴 C. ·荥穴; D·井穴; E·合穴	In using “the five shu points / five command points” to treat "fullness below the heart"，what should be selected? A. ·flowing points / stream points [SHÙ XUÉ]; B. ·Flowing Points / River Points [JĪNG XUÉ]; C. ·Outpouring Points / Spring Points [YÍNG XUÉ]; D. ·Well Points [JǏNG XUÉ]; E. ·merging point / terminal point / sea points [HÉ XUÉ].
1344	五输穴中治疗 "体重节痛" 的是: A·荥穴; B·输穴 C. ·井穴; D·经穴; E·合穴	In using “the five shu points / five command points” to treat " heaviness of the body and pain in the joints"，what should be selected? A. ·Outpouring Points / Spring Points [YÍNG XUÉ]; B. ·flowing points / stream points [SHÙ XUÉ]; C. ·Well Points [JǏNG XUÉ]; D. ·Flowing Points / River Points [JĪNG XUÉ]; E. ·merging point / terminal point / sea points [HÉ XUÉ].
1345	治疗 "逆气而泄"，在五输穴中最好选用: A·合穴; B·经穴 C. ·输穴; D·荥穴; E·井穴	In using “the five shu points / five command points” to treat " uprising energy and diarrhea "，what should be selected? A. ·merging point / terminal point / sea points [HÉ XUÉ]; B. ·Flowing Points / River Points [JĪNG XUÉ]; C. ·flowing points / stream points [SHÙ XUÉ]; D. ·Outpouring Points / Spring Points [YÍNG XUÉ]; E. ·Well Points [JǏNG XUÉ]
1346	"喘咳寒热"之证，用五输穴治疗，最好选用: A·井穴; B·荥穴 C. ·输穴; D·经穴; E·合穴	In using “the five shu points / five Command points” to treat " asthma cough chills heat"; what should be selected?

		A. ·Well Points [JǏNG XUÉ]; B. ·Outpouring Points / Spring Points [YÍNG XUÉ]; C. ·flowing points / stream points [SHÙ XUÉ]; D. ·Flowing Points / River Points [JĪNG XUÉ]; E. ·merging point / terminal point / sea points [HÉ XUÉ].
1347	在五输穴中·治疗腑病的主要是：A.井穴；B·荥穴 C. 输穴; D·经穴; E·合穴	In using "the five shu points / five command points" to treat " viscera and bowels "， what should be selected? A.Well Points [JǏNG XUÉ]; B. ·Outpouring Points / Spring Points [YÍNG XUÉ]; C. ·flowing points / stream points [SHÙ XUÉ]; D. ·Flowing Points / River Points [JĪNG XUÉ]; E. ·merging point / terminal point / sea points [HÉ XUÉ].
1348	中风闭证昏迷的主要处方是: A·水沟 中冲 丰隆 太冲 劳宫; B·下关 颊车 合谷 风池 C. 中冲 太冲 丰隆 合谷; D·合谷 百会 颊车 太冲; E·丰隆 涌泉 大椎 少冲	Which prescription of points should be selected to treat closed type of wind stroke with fainting? A. ·D26 [Shuǐ Gōu] P9 [Zhōng Chōng] S40 [Fēng Lóng] Lv3 [Tài Chōng] P8 [Láo Gōng]; B. ·S7 [Xià Guān] S6 [Jiá Chē] Li4 [Hé Gǔ] G20 [Fēng Chí]; C. P9 [Zhōng Chōng] Lv3 [Tài Chōng] S40 [Fēng Lóng] Li4 [Hé Gǔ]; D. ·Li4 [Hé Gǔ] D20 [Bǎi Huì] S6 [Jiá Chē] Lv3 [Tài Chōng]; E. ·S40 [Fēng Lóng] K1 [Yǒng Quán] D14 [Dà Zhuī] H9 [Shào Chōng]
1349	凡年高形盛气虚之人，常针灸风市、足三里二穴，其作用是: A·养生保健; B·防治感冒 C. ·调养脾胃; D·预防中风; E·以上都不是	G31 [Fēng Shì] and S36 [Zú Sān Lǐ] are often selected to treat the elderly in strong physical; condition with energy deficiency by acupuncture and moxibustion? What is the function of the two points in question? A. ·to nourish life and maintain good health; B. ·to prevent and treat the common cold; C. ·to regulate and nourish spleen and stomach; D. ·to prevent wind stroke; E. ·none of the above
1350	治疗肾虚泄泻，除取主穴外，还可加用: A·肾俞 太溪; B·中脘 天枢 C. ·命门 关元; D·神阙 照海; E·以上都不是	In addition to primary points, what other points may be added to treat kidney deficiency diarrhea? A. ·B23 [Shèn Shū] K3 [Tài Xī]; B. ·R12 [Zhōng Wǎn] S25 [Tiān Shū]; C. ·D4 [Mìng Mén] R4 [Guān Yuán]; D. ·R8 [Shén Què] K6 [Zhào Hǎi]; E. ·none of the above
1351	治疗滑精的主要处方是: A·委中 风府 环跳 肾俞 太溪; B·肾俞 脾俞 委中 阿是穴 C. ·百会 照海·关元 阿是穴; D·肾俞 委中 百会 水沟 中极; E·太溪 肾俞 关元 志室	What is the primary prscription of points to treat sliding seminal emission? A. ·B40 [Wěi Zhōng] D16 [Fēng Fǔ] G30 [Huán Tiào] B23 [Shèn Shū] K3 [Tài Xī]; B. ·B23 [Shèn Shū] B20 [Pí Shū] B40 [Wěi Zhōng] pressure point [ouch point]; C. ·D20 [Bǎi Huì] K6 [Zhào Hǎi] ·R4 [Guān Yuán] pressure point [ouch point]; D. ·B23 [Shèn Shū] B40 [Wěi Zhōng] D20 [Bǎi Huì] D26 [Shuǐ Gōu] R3 [Zhōng Jí]; E. ·K3 [Tài Xī] B23 [Shèn Shū] R4 [Guān Yuán] B52 [Zhì Shì]
1352	惊悸属于痰火内动者，治疗时除用主方外，还可加用: A·膈俞 脾俞 足三里; B·厥阴俞 肾俞 太溪 C. ·脾俞 三焦俞 气海俞; D·内关 尺泽 丰隆; E·丰隆 膏肓俞	In addition to primary points, what other points may be added to treat palpitation and shock due to phlegm fire disturbing internally? A. ·B17 [Gé Shū] B20 [Pí Shū] S36 [Zú Sān Lǐ]; B. ·B14 [Jué Yīn Shū] B23 [Shèn Shū] K3 [Tài Xī]; C. ·B20 [Pí

	太渊	Shū] B22 [Sān Jiāo Shū] B24 [Qì Hǎi Shū]; D. P6 [Nèi Guān] Lu5 [Chǐ Zé] S40 [Fēng Lóng]; E. S40 [Fēng Lóng] B43 [Gāo Huāng Shū] Lu9 [Tài Yuān]
1353	选心俞、膈俞、间使、足三里、三阴交诸穴，用25毫克--50毫克氯丙嗪行穴位注射，可治疗: A 癫证; B 狂证 C. 痫证; D 不寐; E 以上均不是	What may be treated by selecting B15 [Xīn Shū]、B17 [Gé Shū]、P5 [Jiān Shǐ]、S36 [Zú Sān Lǐ]、Sp6 [Sān Yīn Jiāo], etc for point injection of 25 mg to 50 mg of wintermin? A. insanity; B. maniac psychosis C. epilepsy; D. insomia; E. none of the above.
1354	治疗水肿的主要处方是: A 水分 气海 三焦俞 足三里 三阴交; B 关元 归来 大冲 阴陵泉 三阴交 C. 胆俞 阳陵泉 阴陵泉 内庭 大冲; D 风池 肝俞 肾俞 行间 侠溪; E 以上部不是	What is the primary prscription of points to treat edema? A. R9 [Shuǐ Fēn] R6 [Qì Hǎi] B22 [Sān Jiāo Shū] S36 [Zú Sān Lǐ] Sp6 [Sān Yīn Jiāo]; B. R4 [Guān Yuán] S29 [Guī Lái] Lv3 [Tài Chōng] Sp9 [Yīn Líng Quán] Sp6 [Sān Yīn Jiāo]; C. B19 [Dǎn Shū] G34 [Yáng Líng Quán] Sp9 [Yīn Líng Quán] S44 [Nèi Tíng] Lv3 [Tài Chōng]; D. G20 [Fēng Chí] B18 [Gān Shū] B23 [Shèn Shū] Lv2 [Xíng Jiān] G43 [Xiá Xī]; E. none of the above.
1355	脚气冲心的危候 除针刺主穴之外 还可加用: A.中极 间使 大陵; B 石门 神门 少海 C. 郄门 巨阙 内关; D 天枢 中脘 鸠尾; E 膻中 阴陵泉 太冲	In addition to primary points, what other points may be added to treat the critical symptoms of cardiac beriberi? A.R3 [Zhōng Jí] P5 [Jiān Shǐ] P7 [Dà Líng]; B.R5 [Shí Mén] H7 [Shén Mén] H3 [Shào Hǎi]; C. P4 [Xī Mén] R14 [Jù Què] P6 [Nèi Guān]; D. S25 [Tiān Shū] R12 [Zhōng Wǎn] R15 [Jiū Wěi]; E. R17 [Shān Zhōng] Sp9 [Yīn Líng Quán] Lv3 [Tài Chōng]
1356	治疗行痹，除取主穴外，宜加用: A 大椎 曲池; B 膈俞 血海 C. 肾俞 三阴交; D 曲池 阳陵泉; E 风池 风门	In addition to primary points, what other points may be added to treat migratory rheumatism? A. D14 [Dà Zhuī] Li11 [Qū Chí]; B. B17 [Gé Shū] Sp10 [Xuè Hǎi]; C. B23 [Shèn Shū] Sp6 [Sān Yīn Jiāo]; D. Li11 [Qū Chí] G34 [Yáng Líng Quán]; E. G20 [Fēng Chí] B12 [Fēng Mén]
1357	治疗痿证取穴的主要法则是取: A 足太阴经; B 足厥阴经 C. 阳明经; D 少阳经; E 太阳经	What meridian should be selected to treat flaccid syndrome according to the primary principle of treatment? A. foot greater yin meridian; B. foot decreasing yin meridian / foot jue yin jing C. bright yang meridians; D. lesser yang meridians; E. greater yang meridians.
1358	以中极、合谷、血海、三阴交、行间诸穴组成处方，可用于治疗: A 痛经实证; B 经行先期 C. 经行先后无定期; D 血枯经闭; E 血滞经闭	What disease may be treated by a combination of the following points: R3 [Zhōng Jí]、Li4 [Hé Gǔ]、Sp10 [Xuè Hǎi]、Sp6 [Sān Yīn Jiāo]、Lv2 [Xíng Jiān]? A. excess syndrome of period pain; B. premature menstruation; C. irregular menstruation; D. suppression of menstruation due to poor blood conditions; E. suppression of menstruation due to blood congestion.
1359	徐文伯与宋废帝同诊双胎，用针刺哪两条经脉的穴位胎儿应针而下? A 泻足太阳，补手太阴; B 泻足厥阴，补手阳明 C. 泻足阳明，补手厥阴; D 泻足太阴，补手	Xu Wen Bo and Emperor Song made diagnosis of twins together and applied acupuncture, which induced instant birth. Which two meridians are needled? A. sedate food greater yang and tone up hand greater meridians; B. sedate foot decreasing yin, tone up hand

	阳明; E·泻足少阴，补手少阳	bright yang meridians; C. sedate foot bright yang, tone up hand decreasing yin meridians; D. ·sedate foot greater yin, tone up hand bright hand meridians; E. ·sedate foot lesser yin, tone up hand lesser yang meridians.
1360	痄腮若兼睾丸肿大，治疗应在主方的基础上加用: A·中极 三阴交 B·归来 蠡沟 C. ·气冲 太冲 D·太冲 曲泉 E·曲泉 三阴交	In addition to primary points, what other points may be added to treat mumps with swollen testicles? A. ·R3 [Zhōng Jí] Sp6 [Sān Yīn Jiāo]; B. ·S29 [Guī Lái] Lv5 [Lí Gōu]; C. ·S30 [Qì Chōng] Lv3 [Tài Chōng]; D. ·Lv3 [Tài Chōng] Lv8 [Qū Quán]; E. ·Lv8 [Qū Quán] Sp6 [Sān Yīn Jiāo]
1361	治疗痔疮不宜选用: A·皮肤针; B·拔罐 C. ·电针; D·挑治; E·头针	Which should not be used to treat hemorrhoids? A. · skin needle; B. ·cupping C. ·electro acupuncture; D. · pricking therapy; E. ·scalp acupuncture.
1362	阳虚型咽喉肿痛的主要处方是: A·少商 尺泽 合谷; B·合谷 颊车 内庭 C. ·太溪 照海 鱼际; D·合谷 内庭 行间; E·以上都不是	What is the prescription of points for yang deficiency type of sore throat with swelling? A. ·Lu11 [Shǎo Shāng] Lu5 [Chǐ Zé] Li4 [Hé Gǔ]; B. ·Li4 [Hé Gǔ] S6 [Jiá Chē] S44 [Nèi Tíng]; C. ·K3 [Tài Xī] K6 [Zhào Hǎi] Lu10 [Yǔ Jì]; D. ·Li4 [Hé Gǔ] S44 [Nèi Tíng] Lv2 [Xíng Jiān]; E. ·none of the above.
1363	治疗不寐的针灸主方是: A·神门 内关; B，神门 三阴交 C. ·内关 三阴交; D·心俞 肾俞; E·心俞 脾俞	What is the primary prescription of points to treat insomnia? A. ·H7 [Shén Mén] P6 [Nèi Guān]; B.， H7 [Shén Mén] Sp6 [Sān Yīn Jiāo]; C. ·P6 [Nèi Guān] Sp6 [Sān Yīn Jiāo]; D. ·B15 [Xīn Shū] B23 [Shèn Shū]; E. ·B15 [Xīn Shū] B20 [Pí Shū]
1364	治疗热痹宜取: A·血海 曲池; B·大椎 血海 C. ·大椎 曲池; D·膈俞 血海; E·太溪 曲池	What points should be selected to treat hot rheumatism? A. ·Sp10 [Xuè Hǎi] Li11 [Qū Chí]; B. ·D14 [Dà Zhuī] Sp10 [Xuè Hǎi]; C. ·D14 [Dà Zhuī] Li11 [Qū Chí]; D. ·B17 [Gé Shū] Sp10 [Xuè Hǎi]; E. ·K3 [Tài Xī] Li11 [Qū Chí]
1365	治疗面瘫远道取穴，常用: A·合谷 足三里; B·合谷 内关 C. ·合谷 三阴交; D·合谷 太冲; E·合谷 内庭	What points should be selected to treat facial paraysis? A. ·Li4 [Hé Gǔ] S36 [Zú Sān Lǐ]; B. ·Li4 [Hé Gǔ] P6 [Nèi Guān]; C. ·Li4 [Hé Gǔ] Sp6 [Sān Yīn Jiāo]; D. ·Li4 [Hé Gǔ] Lv3 [Tài Chōng]; E. ·Li4 [Hé Gǔ] S44 [Nèi Tíng]
1366	治疗癔病失语，宜在主方基础上加: A·哑门 通里; B·哑门 神门 C. ·哑门 廉泉; D，哑门 天突; E·哑门 百会	In addition to primary points, what other points may be added to treat hysterical aphasia? A. ·D15 [Yǎ Mén] H5 [Tōng Lǐ]; B. ·D15 [Yǎ Mén] H7 [Shén Mén]; C. ·D15 [Yǎ Mén] R23 [Lián Quán]; D. D15 [Yǎ Mén] R22 [Tiān Tū]; E. ·D15 [Yǎ Mén] D20 [Bǎi Huì]
1367	治疗风寒感冒宜取: A·列缺 合谷 大椎 风池; B·列缺 合谷 曲池 风池 C. ·列缺 合谷 外关 鱼际; D·列缺 风门 风池 合谷; E·列缺 风门 鱼际 风府	What points should be selected to treat wind-cold type of the common cold? A. ·Lu7 [Liè Quē] Li4 [Hé Gǔ] D14 [Dà Zhuī] G20 [Fēng Chí]; B. ·Lu7 [Liè Quē] Li4 [Hé Gǔ] Li11 [Qū Chí] G20 [Fēng Chí]; C. ·Lu7 [Liè Quē] Li4 [Hé Gǔ] Sj5 [Wài Guān] Lu10 [Yǔ Jì]; D. ·Lu7 [Liè Quē] B12 [Fēng Mén] G20 [Fēng Chí] Li4 [Hé Gǔ]; E. ·Lu7 [Liè Quē] B12 [Fēng Mén] Lu10 [Yǔ Jì] D16 [Fēng Fǔ]
1368	治疗哮喘实证，宜取: A·膻	What points should be selected to treat asthma?

	中 列缺 肺俞 尺泽; B·膻中 肺俞 中府 太渊 C. ·膻中 气海 肺俞 中府; D·膻中 尺泽 中府 肺俞; E. 膻中 气海 丰隆 足三里	A. ·R17 [Shān Zhōng] Lu7 [Liè Quē] B13 [Fèi Shū] Lu5 [Chǐ Zé]; B. ·R17 [Shān Zhōng] B13 [Fèi Shū] Lu1 [Zhōng Fǔ] Lu9 [Tài Yuān]; C. ·R17 [Shān Zhōng] R6 [Qì Hǎi] B13 [Fèi Shū] Lu1 [Zhōng Fǔ]; D. ·R17 [Shān Zhōng] Lu5 [Chǐ Zé] Lu1 [Zhōng Fǔ] B13 [Fèi Shū]; E.R17 [Shān Zhōng] R6 [Qì Hǎi] S40 [Fēng Lóng] S36 [Zú Sān Lǐ]
1369	治疗肝气犯胃所致呕吐，宜在主方基础上加: A·阳陵泉 太冲; B·阳陵泉 支沟 C. ·太冲 合谷; D·太冲 章门; E·阳陵泉 肝俞	In addition to primary points, what other points may be added to treat vomiting due to liver energy offending the stomach? A. ·G34 [Yáng Líng Quán] Lv3 [Tài Chōng]; B. ·G34 [Yáng Líng Quán] Sj6 [Zhi Gōu]; C. ·Lv3 [Tài Chōng] Li4 [Hé Gǔ]; D. ·Lv3 [Tài Chōng] Lv13 [Zhāng Mén]; E. ·G34 [Yáng Líng Quán] B18 [Gān Shū].
1370	治疗脾胃虚寒型胃痛，宜取: A·脾经、胃经穴位为主; B·督脉经穴为主 C. ·胃经穴位为主; D·任脉经穴为主; E·背俞、任脉经穴为主	What points should be selected to treat stomachache due to spleen-stomach deficiency and cold? A. ·primrily points on the spleen meridian、stomach meridian; B. · primrily points on the du mai / governing meridian; C. · primrily points on the stomach meridian; D. · primrily points on the ren mai / conception meridian; E. ·back shu points (posterior points)、and points on ren mai / conception meridian.
1371	治疗饮食停滞所致腹痛，除取中脘、天枢、气海、足三里外，还取经验效穴: A·二白; B·曲池 C. ·四白; ·D·里内庭; E·中魁	What points should be selected to treat abdominal pain caused by food stoppage in addition to R12 [Zhōng Wǎn]、S25 [Tiān Shū]、R6 [Qì Hǎi] 、S36 [Zú Sān Lǐ]? A. ·ÈR BÁI (two whites); B. ·Li11 [Qū Chí]; C. ·S2 [Sì Bái] ·D ·Lǐ Nèi Tíng [medial inner yard]; E. ·Zhōng Kuí [middle head / middle leader]
1372	治疗热结便秘，在主方基础上配: A·大椎 内庭; B·大椎 合谷 C. ·合谷 曲池; D·曲池 公孙; E·内关 公孙	In addition to primary points, what other points may be added to treat hot constipation? A. ·D14 [Dà Zhuī] S44 [Nèi Tíng]; B. ·D14 [Dà Zhuī] Li4 [Hé Gǔ]; C. ·Li4 [Hé Gǔ] Li11 [Qū Chí]; D. ·Li11 [Qū Chí] Sp4 [Gōng Sūn]; E. ·P6 [Nèi Guān] Sp4 [Gōng Sūn].
1373	治气虚崩漏，宜在主方基础上配: A·脾俞 足三里; B·百会 气海 C. ·气海 膻中; D·关元 气海; E·百会 脾俞	In addition to primary points, what other points may be added to treat bleeding from the uterus / metrorrhagia metrostaxis? . A. ·B20 [Pí Shū] S36 [Zú Sān Lǐ]B ·D20 [Bǎi Huì] R6 [Qì Hǎi]; C. ·R6 [Qì Hǎi] R17 [Shān Zhōng]; D. ·R4 [Guān Yuán] R6 [Qì Hǎi]; E. ·D20 [Bǎi Huì] B20 [Pí Shū].
1374	治疗疟疾的常用处方是: A·大椎 百会 间使; B·大椎 百会 后溪 C. ·陶道 间使 后溪; D·大椎 外关 后溪; E·大椎 后溪 间使	What is the common prescription for malaria? A. ·D14 [Dà Zhuī] D20 [Bǎi Huì] P5 [Jiān Shǐ]; B. ·D14 [Dà Zhuī] D20 [Bǎi Huì] Si3 [Hòu Xī]; C. ·D13 [Táo Dào] P5 [Jiān Shǐ] Si3 [Hòu Xī]; D. ·D14 [Dà Zhuī] Sj5 [Wài Guān] Si3 [Hòu Xī]; E. ·D14 [Dà Zhuī] Si3 [Hòu Xī] P5 [Jiān Shǐ]
1375	脱肛一症，取下列哪条经穴治疗 A·督脉; B·任 C. ·膀胱经; D·带脉; E·大肠经	What meridian points should be selected to treat prolapse of anus? A. ·du mai / governing meridian; B. ·ren mai / conception meridian; C. ·bladder meridian; D. ·dai mai / belt

		meridian; E. ·large intestine meridian.
1376	治疗遗精的常用水针取穴是: A·关元 气海; · B·关元 中极 C. ·肾俞 关元; D·气海 中极; E·肾俞 膀胱俞	What meridian points should be selected to treat seminal emission by point injection therapy? A. ·R4 [Guān Yuán] R6 [Qì Hǎi] ·; B. ·R4 [Guān Yuán] R3 [Zhōng Jí]; C. ·B23 [Shèn Shū] R4 [Guān Yuán]; D. ·R6 [Qì Hǎi] R3 [Zhōng Jí]; E. ·B23 [Shèn Shū] B28 [Páng Guāng Shū].
1377	治疗痛经的经验效穴是: A·三阴交; B·足三里 C. ·合谷; D·次髎; E·地机	What is the effective experience point to treat period pain? A. ·Sp6 [Sān Yīn Jiāo]; B. ·S36 [Zú Sān Lǐ]; C. ·Li4 [Hé Gǔ]; D. ·B32 [Cì Liáo]; E. ·Sp8 [Dì Jī]
1378	治疗产后乳汁不足的井穴是: A·少商; B·商阳 C. ·少泽; D·大敦; E·隐白	What well points [JǏNG XUÉ] may be selected to treat galactostasis (scanty breast milk)? A. ·Lu11 [Shǎo Shāng]; B. ·Li1 [Shāng Yáng]; C. ·Si1 Shào Zé]; D. ·Lv1 [Dà Dūn]; E. ·Sp1 [Yǐn Bái].
1379	治疗风疹，以取下列经穴为主? A·手阳明 足太阴; B·手阳明 足阳明 C. ·足太阳 足阳明; D·足阳明 足太阴; E·手太阳 手阳明	What meridian points should be selected as primary points to treat rubella? A. ·hand bright yang, foot greater yin meridians; B. ·hand bright yang, foot bright yang meridians; C. foot greater yang, foot bright yang meridians; D. ·foot bright yang, foot greater yin meridians; E. ·hand greaer yang and hand bright yang meridians.
1380	防治痔疾最常用的穴位是: A·承扶; B·承满 C. ·承筋; D·承泣; E·承山	What are common points for hemorrhoids? A. ·B36 [Chéng Fú]; B. ·S20 [Chéng Mǎn]; C. ·B56 [Chéng Jīn]; D. ·S1 [Chéng Qì]; E. ·B57 [Chéng Shān].
1381	胃脘病，属腑气上逆者，取募、合穴: A·中脘 上巨虚; B·中脘 足三里 C. ·天枢 上巨虚; D·中极 足三里; E·关元 下巨虚	What “gathering points / anterior points, Front Mu Point [MÙ XUÉ] and merging point / terminal point / sea points [HÉ XUÉ]” may be selected to treat stomach diseases that belong to bowel energy uprising? A. ·R12 [Zhōng Wǎn] S37 [Shàng Jù Xū]; B. ·R12 [Zhōng Wǎn] S36 [Zú Sān Lǐ]; C. ·S25 [Tiān Shū] S37 [Shàng Jù Xū]; D. ·R3 [Zhōng Jí] S36 [Zú Sān Lǐ]; E. ·R4 [Guān Yuán] S39 [Xià Jù Xū].
1382	汗出肢冷、拟回阳救逆，当取: A·气海 膻中; B·中脘 足三里 C. ·神阙 关元; D·关元 三阴交; E·神阙 三阴交	What points should be selected to treat perspiration with cold limbs by restoring yang and rescue uprising? A. ·R6 [Qì Hǎi] R17 [Shān Zhōng]; B. ·R12 [Zhōng Wǎn] S36 [Zú Sān Lǐ]; C. ·R8 [Shén Què] R4 [Guān Yuán]; D. ·R4 [Guān Yuán] Sp6 [Sān Yīn Jiāo]; E. ·R8 [Shén Què] Sp6 [Sān Yīn Jiāo].
1383	治疗久泻脱肛的常用穴位是: A·百会; B·筋缩 C. ·足三里; D·气海; E·天枢	What is the common point to treat chronic diarrhea with prolapse of anus? A. ·D20 [Bǎi Huì]; B. · D8 [Jīn Suō]; C. ·S36 [Zú Sān Lǐ]; D. ·R6 [Qì Hǎi]; E. ·S25 [Tiān Shū].
1384	下列穴位中治疗心悸胸闷宜选用: A·神门; B·内关 C. ·足三里; D·三阴交; E·合谷	What points should be selected to treat palpitation with chest congestion? A. ·H7 [Shén Mén]; B. ·P6 [Nèi Guān]; C. ·S36 [Zú Sān Lǐ]; D. ·Sp6 [Sān Yīn Jiāo]; E. ·Li4 [Hé Gǔ]

1385	肾精亏虚型眩晕当取 A·百会 悬钟 肾俞 足三里；B·悬钟 肾俞 太溪 百会 C. ·太溪 三阴交 百会 肾俞；D·肾俞 足三里 百会 太溪；E·百会 肾俞 关元 命门	What points should be selected to treat kidney essence deficiency syndrome of vertigo? A. ·D20 [Bǎi Huì] G39 [Xuán Zhōng] B23 [Shèn Shū] S36 [Zú Sān Lǐ]; B. ·G39 [Xuán Zhōng] B23 [Shèn Shū] K3 [Tài Xī] D20 [Bǎi Huì]; C. ·K3 [Tài Xī] Sp6 [Sān Yīn Jiāo] D20 [Bǎi Huì] B23 [Shèn Shū]; D. ·B23 [Shèn Shū] S36 [Zú Sān Lǐ] D20 [Bǎi Huì] K3 [Tài Xī]; E. ·D20 [Bǎi Huì] B23 [Shèn Shū] R4 [Guān Yuán] D4 [Mìng Mén].
1386	"纳甲法"中戊配属何脏：A·心；B.·心包 C. ·胃；D·肺；E·肾.	In the system of "selecting points according to daily stem", what organ; corresponds to Wù? A. ·heart; B. ·pericardium; C. stomach; D. ·lungs; E. ·kidneys
1387	"纳子法"地支配属脏腑、经脉规律，酉时应配：A·心；B·肝 C. ·脾；D·肺；E·肾.	In the system of "selecting points according to hourly branch", what organ; corresponds to Yǒu hours in the pattern of "combining earthly branches and viscera and bowels"? A·heart; B·liver; C. ·spleen; D·lungs; E·kidneys
1388	"逆气而泄"之证以五输穴治疗，最好选用：A·井穴；B·荥穴 C. ·输穴；D·经穴；E·合穴.	Which of the five command points may be used to treat "uprising denergy with diarrhea"? A · jǐng xué / well points; B · outpouring-points / spring-points C. · command points; D. ·flowing points / river points / jīng xué; E · hé xué / terminal points / sea points.
1389	"逆气里急"是何经的病候：A·任脉；B·督脉 C. ·冲脉；D·带脉；E·阴维脉.	What meridian may develop the symptom of "uprising energy from the abdomen with abdominal pain"? A. ·conception meridian / ren mai; B ·du mai / governing meridian; C. ·rigorous meridian / chong mai; D · belt meridian / dai mai; E. · fastener merdian of yin / yin wei mai.
1390	"阳缓阴急"属于哪一条脉的主病：A·阳维；B·阴维 C. ·阳跷；D·阴跷；E·督脉.	Which meridian may display "a relazation of yang side and a tightening of yin side " ? A ·fastener meridian of yang / yáng wéi mài; B ·fastener meridian of yin / yin wéi mài;C. ·heel meridian of yang / yang qiao mai; ·D ·heel meridian of yin / yin qiao mai; E ·du mai / governing meridian.
1391	针灸治疗暴盲，其基本处方除可取睛明、瞳子髎、风池、光明外，可再加：A·太溪；B·太阳 C. ·太冲；D·太白；E·太渊.	What point may be added to the basic prescription of points to treat sudden blindness by acupuncture therapy, in addition to B1 / Jīng Míng、 G1 / Tóng Zǐ Liáo、 G20 / Fēng Chí，G37 / Guāng Míng? A · K3 / Tài Xī; B · Tài yáng / sun / temple C. · Lv3 / Tài Chōng; D. · Sp3 / Tài Bái; E. · Lu9 / TàiYuān.
1392	针灸治疗麦粒肿的治则为：A·只灸不针；B·只针不灸 C. 针灸并用；D·宣肺解表 E·清热明目.	What is the treatment principle to treat hordeolum / stye by acupuncture therapy? A · moxibustion without acupuncture; B · acupuncture without moxibustion; C. both acupuncture and moxibustiond; D ·to expand the lungs and relax the superficial region; E. to ·clear heat and sharpen vision.

1393	艾条灸的符号是：A·Δ; B↓ C. x; D ▯; E↑	What symptom represents ·mugwort stick moxibustion? A·Δ; B↓ C. x; D ▯; E↑
1394	按"经脉所通，主治所及"的理论，巅顶痛最好选用: A·太冲 ; B·列缺 C. ·足临泣 ; D·后溪 ; E·内庭	According to the theory, "The points of meridians may be selected to for treat the diseases that occur in their distribution", which point should be selected to treat pain in the vertex? A. Lv3 (Tài Chōng); B. Lu7 (Liè Quē); C. G41 (Zú Lín Qì, Lín Qì); D. Si3 (Hòu Xī); E S44 (Nèi Tíng).
1395	按八会穴主治，阳陵泉适宜于治疗：A·筋病；B·脉病 C. ·骨病；D·髓病；E·均不对	According to the therapeutic functions of eight influential points / ba hui xue, what can G34 / Yáng Líng Quán treat? A. ·tendon disease; B. ·meridian disease C. bone disease D. ·marrow disease; E. ·none of the above
1396	按八会穴主治，瘀血证宜取：A·气海; B·血海 C. ·膈俞; D·太渊; E·都不对	According to the therapeutic functions of eight influential points / ba hui xue, what should be selected to treat blood coagulation? A. · point R6 / Qì Hǎi; B. ·Sp10 / Xuè Hǎi; C. ·B17 / Gé Shū; D. · Lu9 / TàiYuān; E. · none of the above
1397	按八脉交会穴的应用，列缺配照海的主治范围是：A·眼病; B·牙病 C. ·耳病; D 咽喉病; E，舌体病	According to the therapeutic functions of eight influential points / ba hui xue, what is the primary therapeutic scope of combining Lu7 / Liè Quē with K6 / Zhào Hǎi ? A. ·eye disease; B. ·tooth disease; C. ear disease; D. throat disease; E. the body of tongue disease.
1398	按辨位归经，偏头痛属于：A·阳明头痛; B·太阳头痛 C. ·少阳头痛; D·厥阴头痛; E·少阴头痛	What does migraine headache belong to in terms of meridian distribution?：A·bright yang / yang ming headache; B · Tài yáng / sun / temple headache C. ·lesser yang / shao yang headache; D·decreasing yin headache; E·lesser yin / shao yin headache.
1399	按异经子母补泻法，大肠虚证应取：A·曲池; B·二间 C. ·三阴交; D·足三里; E·上巨墟	According to the principle of sedating child points and toning mother points on different meridians, which point may be used to treat heart meridian in excess syndrome? A · Li11 / Qū Chí; B · Li2 / Èr Jiān; C. · Sp6 / Sān Yīn Jiāo; D · S36 / Zú Sān Lǐ; E · S37 / Shàng Jù Xū.
1400	按俞募配穴法，胃病应取：A·梁门、胃俞; B·中脘、胃俞 C. ·中脘、脾俞; D·胃仓、中脘; E·以上都不是	According to the principle of combinging back shu points and mu points, which of the following should be selected to treat stomach disease? A · S21 / Liáng Mén，B21 / Wèi Shū; B · R12 / Zhōng Wǎn，B21 / Wèi Shū C. R12 / Zhōng Wǎn，B20 / Pí Shū; D. B50 / Wèi Cāng，R12 / Zhōng Wǎn; E · none of the above
1401	按主客配穴法，脾经先病，胃经后病应取：A·太白、丰隆; B·冲阳、丰隆 C. ·太白、冲阳; D.公孙、丰隆; E.均不是	According to the principle of host-guest combination, what points should be selected if the spleen meridian is diseased first, followed by the disease of the stomach meridian? A · Sp3 / Tài Bái，S40 / Fēng Lóng; B · S42 / Chōng Yáng，S40 / Fēng Lóng C. Sp3 / Tài Bái，S42 / Chōng Yáng; D. Sp4 / Gōng Sūn，S40 / Fēng Lóng; E. none of the above

1402	八脉交会穴中，后溪通：A·任脉; B·督脉 C. ·阳维脉; D·阳跷脉 E·都不对	Among the meeting points of eight meridians，what does Si3 / Hòu Xī connect? A. conception meridian / ren mai; B ·du mai / governing meridian; C. fastener meridian of yang / yang wei mai; D. ·yang heel meridian / yang qiao mai E. · none of the above
1403	八脉交会穴中，与阴维脉相通的是：A列缺；B·内关 C. ·照海; D·公孙 E·中脘	Among the meeting points of eight meridians, what point connects the fastener merdian of yin / yin wei mai? A. Lu7 / Liè Quē; B · P6 / Nèi Guān; C. K6 / Zhào Hăi; D · Sp4 / Gōng Sūn; E · R12 / Zhōng Wăn.
1404	八脉交会穴中的照海与哪条奇经相通: A ·阳跷脉; B 任脉 C. ·带脉; D ·阴跷脉	Which extraordinary meridian is connected with K6 / Zhào Hăi which is one of the meeting points of eight meridians? A ·yang heel meridian / qiao mai of yang; B; conception meridian / ren mai; C. belt meridian / dai mai; D. ·yin heel meridian / qiao mai of yin
1405	八脉交会穴中与列缺相交会于任脉的穴是：A·公孙；B·外关 C. ·后溪；D·申脉 E照海	Among the eight ·meeting points of eight meridians, what point meets Lu7 / Liè Quē at the conception meridian / ren mai? A · Sp4 / Gōng Sūn; B · Sj5 / Wài Guān; C. Si3 / Hòu Xī; D. B62 / Shēn Mài; E. K6 / Zhào Hăi.
1406	八脉交会穴中主治咽喉胸膈肺部疾患的是; A·通督脉任脉的腧穴 ; B·通任脉阴跷的腧穴 C. ·通阴跷阳维的输穴 ; D·通阳维带脉的腧穴 E，通带脉冲脉的腧穴	Which of the eight extraordinary meridians eight meeting points (ba mai jiao hui xue) can treat the disorders of the throat, chest,diagphram, and lungs? A; point connected with du mai / governing meridian; B. point connected with ren mai (conception meridian); C. point connected with yin heel meridian and yang fastner meridian (yang wei mai); D. point connected with belt meridian / dai mai; E. point connected with vigorous meridian (chong mai).
1407	拔牙术针麻效果以拔( )时最好：A·上牙；B·下牙 C. ·前牙；D·后牙；E·上前牙	What teeth may undergo tooth extraction by acupuncture anaesthesia with good result? A ·upper teeth; B ·lower teeth; C. ·frontal teeth; D ·back teeth; E ·upper frontal teeth.
1408	百会、长强、足三里治痔疮属什么配穴法：A·局部；B·远端 C. ·上下；D·三部；E·前后	Which kind of combination is being applied when D20 / Băi Huì, D1 / Cháng Qiáng，S36 / Zú Sān Lĭ are combined to treat hemorrhoid? A. ·local; B ·distal; C. upper and lower; D. ·three regions; E. ·anterior and posterior.
1409	百会气海肝俞肾俞脾俞合谷足三里等穴组成处方，用于治疗哪种头痛: A·风袭经络，巅顶疼痛 ; B·肝阳亢逆，头晕头痛 C. ·头风久病，顽固难愈 ; D·气血不足，头目昏重 ; E·头痛势急，如锥如刺	Which type of headache may be treated by the combination of the following points: D20 (Băi Huì), R6 (Qì Hăi);B18 (Gān Shū);B23 (Shèn Shū);B20 (Pí Shū), Li4 (Hé Gŭ), S36 (Zú Sān Lĭ)? A. wind attacking meridians, pain in vertex; B. liver yang uprising, dizziness and headache; C. chronic disease of head wind, difficult to recover; D. insufficient energy and blood, dizziness of head and eyes with blurred vision and heaviness; E. acute headache as if being hit and pricked.
1410	百会穴主治除下列什么证以外的各症? A中风昏厥；;	Which of the following is NOT to be treated by D20 (Băi Huì)?

	B. 头痛头晕 C. 惊悸健忘; D. 阴挺.久泻脱肛; E. 便秘腹胀。	A. wind stroke with sudden fainting; B. headache and dizziness; C. palpitation due to fright, and forgetfulness; D. hysteroptosis, chronic diarrhea, prolaspe of anus; E. constipation and abdominal swelling.
1411	鼻炎风邪外袭、风寒为主型的针灸治则是：A·只针不灸; B·针灸并用 C. ·只灸不针; D·以针为主; E·以灸为主	What is the principle of treating rhinitis with external attack of pathogenic wind and wind cold as the primary causes? A. · acupuncture without moxibustion; B. · both acupuncture and moxibustion; C. · moxibustion without acupuncture; D. ·primarily by acupuncture; E. ·primarily by moxibustion
1412	鼻炎风邪外袭、风热为主型的针灸治则是：A·只针不灸; B·针灸并用 C. ·只灸不针; D·以针为主; E·以灸为主	What is the principle of treating rhinitis with external attack of pathogenic wind and wind heat as the primary causes? A · acupuncture without moxibustion; B · both acupuncture and moxibustion; C · moxibustion without acupuncture; D ·primarily by acupuncture; E ·primarily by moxibustion
1413	鼻渊的治法，应取何经穴为主? A·手足太阴 ; B，手足阳明 C. ·手太阴足阳明 ; D·手太阴手阳明 ; E·足太阴手阳明	Which meridian points should be selected to treat nasal pool? A. greater yin meridians of hand and foot; B. bright yang meridians of hand and foot; C. greater yin meridian of hand, bright yang meridians of foot; D. greater yin meridian of hand, bright yang meridian of hand; E greater yin meridian of foot, bright yang meridian of hand.
1414	鼻渊的治法为: A 温肺散寒通利鼻窍; B 清热宣肺.通利鼻窍 C. 肃降肺气通利鼻窍; D 疏风解表通利鼻窍; E 以上都不是。	How to treat nasal pool (bi yuan)? A. to warm the lungs, disperse cold, facilitate nasal cavities; B. to clear heat and expand the lungs, facilitae nasal cavities C. to constrict and bring down lung energy, facilitae nasal cavities; D. to disperse wind, relax superficial region, and facilitae nasal cavities; E. none of the above.
1415	扁桃体摘除术针麻可选用：A·支沟; B·四白 C. ·合谷; D·下关; E·风市	What point may be selected for tonsillectomy by acupuncture anaesthesia? A · Sj6 / Zhi Gōu; B · S2 / Sì Bái / C. · Li4 / Hé Gǔ; D · S7 / Xià Guān; E · G31 / Fēng Shì
1416	便秘的病位在：A·脾；B·胃 C. ·肠; D·肾; E·肝	What is the diseased region in constipation? A ·spleen ·; B ·stomach; C. ·intestines; D ·kidneys; E ·liver.
1417	不仅能治疗局部病，而且还能治疗本经循行所过的远隔部位的脏腑组织器官病证是：A.近治作用; B 特异性作用 C. ，远治作用; D 双向良性调整作用	Not only capable of treating local symptoms, it can also treat the symptoms in the distribution of the affected. meridian where viscera and bowels and tissues are located; what function is involved? A. therapeutic function of treating local diseases; B. special and specific therapeutic function; C. therapeutic function of treating distal diseases; D. therapeutic function of regulating and striking a balance between two extreme.
1418	不能用于昏迷急救的穴位是：A.膻中; B.会阴 C. 素髎; D 神阙	Which point should NOT be used to treat acute cases of fainting? A. R17 (Shān Zhōng); B. R1 (Huì Yīn); C. D25 (Sù Liáo);

		D. R8 (Shén Què).
1419	不能用于虚脱急救的穴位是：A.神阙; B.气海 C. 关元; D 石门	Which point should NOT be used to treat acute cases of deficient prolapse? A. R8 (Shén Què); B. R6 (Qì Hǎi); C. R4 (Guān Yuán); D. R5 (Shí Mén).
1420	不属八脉交会组穴的是：A 内关、公孙; B·合谷、太冲 C. 列缺、照海; D·后溪、申脉E·外关、足临泣	Which group of points does not belong to the meeting points of eight meridians? A P6 / Nèi Guān，Sp4 / Gōng Sūn; B · Li4 / Hé Gǔ，Lv3 / Tài Chōng; C. Lu7 / Liè Quē、 K6 / Zhào Hǎi; D · Si3 / Hòu Xī，B62 / Shēn Mài; E · Sj5 / Wài Guān 、G41 / Zú Lín Qì / Lín Qì
1421	不属于: "宛陈则除之"治则的病症是：A·扭伤 ·B·毒虫咬伤 C. ·癃闭; D·小儿疳证; E·腱鞘囊肿	Which should not be treated by the principle, "chronic clots should be removed"? A ·twisting injuries; ·B ·poisonous insect bites;C. suppression of urination; D ·malnutrition in children; E ·thecal cyst
1422	不属于阳黄的临床表现的是：A·眼白和皮肤黄色鲜明; B.发热 C. ·小便黄赤，大便秘结; D·神疲乏力; E·苔黄腻，脉滑数	What clinical manifestion will determine that it does not belong to yang jaundice? A. clear signs of fresh yellowishness in the white of eyes and skin; B.fever; C. ·yellowish-reddish urine，constipation; D ·fatigue and lack of energy; E · yellowish and greasy coating on the tongue，slippery and rapid pulse.
1423	产后乳少而浓稠，乳房胀满而痛，伴胃脘胀闷，可在基本处方的基础上再加：A·气海、血海; B¨足三里、中脘 C. ·内关、期门; D·行间、三阴交; E·公孙、内关	What points may be added to the basic prescription of points to treat galactostasis / scanty breast milk after birth with thick milk, and swollen and painful breasts, accompanied by swollen and dull stomach? A · R6 / Qì Hǎi，Sp10 / Xuè Hǎi; B¨ S36 / Zú Sān Lǐ，R12 / Zhōng Wǎn; C. · P6 / Nèi Guān，Lv14 / Qí Mén; D · Lv2 / Xíng Jiān，Sp6 / Sān Yīn Jiāo; E · Sp4 / Gōng Sūn，P6 / Nèi Guān
1424	产后乳少清稀，·乳房柔软无胀感，伴神疲食少，可在基本处方的基础上再加：A·关元、气海; B¨足三里、三阴交 C. ·内关、期门; D. 太冲、行间; E·血海、膈俞	What points may be added to the basic prescription of points to treat galactostasis / scanty breast milk after birth with clearand thin milk, soft breasts without swelling sensation, accompanied by fatigue and poor appetite? A · R4 / Guān Yuán，R6 / Qì Hǎi; B¨ S36 / Zú Sān Lǐ，Sp6 / Sān Yīn Jiāo; C. · P6 / Nèi Guān，Lv14 / Qí Mén; D. Lv3 / Tài Chōng, Lv2 / Xíng Jiān; E · Sp10 / Xuè Hǎi, B17 / Gé Shū.
1425	常用清胃热的穴位有：A·内庭; B·冲阳 C. ·丰隆; D·胃俞; E·梁丘	Which point is frequently used to clear stomach heat? A · S44 / Nèi Tíng; B · S42 / Chōng Yáng C. · S40 / Fēng Lóng; D ·; B21 / Wèi Shū; E · S34 / Liáng Qiū
1426	常用于治疗鼻病的穴位是：A.百会; B.大椎 C. 陶道; D 上星	What point is frequently used to treat diseases of the nose? A. D20 (Bǎi Huì); B. D14 (Dà Zhuī); C. D13 (Táo Dào); D. D23 (Shàng Xīng).
1427	承山治疗肛门疾患主要是	Which of the following meridians is being involved when

	通过什么经脉的内在联系。A 经脉; B 络脉 C. 经别; D 经筋; E 皮部.	B57 (Chéng Shān) is used to treat the symptoms of the anus? A. master meridian; B.linking meridian; C. separate master meridian (jing bie); D. muscular meridians; E. skin zones.
1428	尺泽、鱼际、少商可用于治疗下列哪一型发热: A 风寒束表型; B 风热壅盛型 C. 热在气分型; D 热入营血型; E 疫毒熏蒸型	What type of high fever can be treated by Lu5 / Chǐ Zé, Lu10 / Yǔ Jì、and Lu11 / Shǎo Shāng? A · wind cold constricting the superficial region type; B · wind heat in abundance type; C. ·heat at the energy level type; D ·heat entering into nutritive and blood levels type; E ·toxic pestilence steaming type.
1429	除 xx 穴外，均可治疗水肿: A 归来; B 水分 C. 膀胱俞; D 阴陵泉; E 委阳	Which of the following points may NOT be selected to treat edema? A. S29 (Guī Lái); B. R9 (Shuǐ Fēn); C; B28 (Páng Guāng Shū); D. Sp9 (Yīn Líng Quán); E B39 (Wěi Yáng).
1430	除下列哪脏腑外均与黄疸病变有关? A. 脾; B. 胃 C. 肺; D. 肝; E. 胆。	Which organ is NOT related. to the symptoms of jaundice? A. spleen; B. stomach C. lungs; D. liver; E. gallbladder.
1431	除下列什么穴外均可治实证胁痛? A 期门; B 支沟;C 阳陵泉;D 太冲;E 少冲。	Which of the following points should NOT be selected to treat the excess type of lumbago? A Lv14 [Qí Mén]; B Sj6 [Zhi Gōu]; C G34 [Yáng Líng Quán]; D Lv3 [Tài Chōng]; E H9 [Shào Chōng].
1432	大椎穴治疗震颤麻痹，下列刺灸方法除 ( ) 外均多选用: A 重灸; B 拔罐 C. 浅刺; D 针感向四肢放射; E 刺血	Which technique of acupuncture and moxibustion is not appled to treat Parkinsonism at D14 / Dà Zhuī? A ·heavy moxibusiton; B · cupping C. ·shallow insertion; D ·radiation of needling sensation toward the four limbs; E. ·bloodletting.
1433	带下病在治疗时应取下列哪组穴位为佳? A. 带脉白环俞足三里三阴交; B. 带脉白环俞三阴交关元 C. 带脉白环俞三阴交中极; ; D. 带脉白环俞三阴交.气海; E. 带脉白环俞.次髎关元。	Which group of points should best be selected to treat vaginal discharge? A. G26 / Dài Mài B30 / Bái Huán Shū S36 / Zú Sān Lǐ Sp6 / Sān Yīn Jiāo; B. G26 / Dài Mài B30 / Bái Huán Shū Sp6 / Sān Yīn Jiāo R4 / Guān Yuán; C. G26 / Dài Mài B30 / Bái Huán Shū Sp6 / Sān Yīn Jiāo R3 / Zhōng Jí; D. G26 / Dài Mài B30 / Bái Huán Shū Sp6 / Sān Yīn Jiāo.R6 / Qì Hǎi; E. G26 / Dài Mài B30 / Bái Huán Shū. B32 / Cì Liáo R4 / Guān Yuán 。
1434	带状疱疹多由湿热火毒所致，病位涉及少阳、阴经脉，应取: A 期门; B 阴陵泉、支沟 C. 行间; D 夹脊穴; E 皮损局部	Herpes zoster is mostly due to damp heat and toxic fire, with symptoms affecting the lesser yang / shao yang、yin meridians; what point should be used to treat it? A · Lv14 / Qí Mén; B · Sp9 / Yīn Líng Quán，Sj6 / Zhi Gōu; C. Lv2 / Xíng Jiān; D · Huá tuó jiā jí / Dr Huatuo's clippings of spine; E ·local region of skin injury
1435	胆囊发生病变体表压痛点多发生在: A 足三里; B 阳陵泉 C. 上巨虚; D 下巨虚; E 足临泣	Which point is most frequently the pressure point on body surface when the gallbadder is diseased? A. S36 (Zú Sān Lǐ); B. G34 (Yáng Líng Quán); C. S37 (Shàng Jù Xū); D. S39 (Xià Jù Xū); E.G41 (Zú Lín Qì, Lín Qì).
1436	低血压病患者宜常年灸:	What point should regularly be treated by moxibustion

	A·百会; B·关元 C. 气海; D·足三里; E·命门	for hypotension? A · D20 / Bǎi Huì; B · R4 / Guān Yuán; C. R6 / Qì Hǎi; D · S36 / Zú Sān Lǐ; E · D4 / Mìng Mén
1437	低血压病见有神志恍惚，甚则晕厥多见于：A 心阳不振证; B·中气不足证 C. ·心肾阳虚证; D.脾肾阳虚证; E· 阳气虚脱证	Which syndrome accounts for hypotension with unclear consciousness，and fainting in severe cases? A syndrome of heart yang in decline; B ·middle energy in deficiency syndrome C. ·heart kidneys yang deficiency syndrome; D. yang deficiency of spleen and kidneys syndrome; E · yang energy deficiency with prostration.
1438	低血压病失眠健忘者治疗应在基本处方中再加: A·头维; B·四神聪 C. ·安眠; D 神门; E·内关	What points may be added to the basic prescription of points to treat hypotension with insomnia and forgetfulness? A · S8 / Tóu Wěi; B · Sì shén Cōng / four spiritual intelligences; C. Ān mián / good sleep; D H7 / Shén Mén; E · P6 / Nèi Guān
1439	低血压病四肢不温者治疗可在基本处方中再灸: A·神阙、大椎; B·关元、命门 C. ·大椎、命门; D·关元、太溪; E·百会、气海	What points for moxibustion may be added to the basic prescription of points to treat hypotension with cold limbs? A · R8 / Shén Què 、D14 / Dà Zhuī; B · R4 / Guān Yuán, D4 / Mìng Mén; C. ·D14 / Dà Zhuī、 D4 / Mìng Mén; D · R4 / Guān Yuán，K3 / Tài Xī; E · D20 / Bǎi Huì，R6 / Qì Hǎi
1440	低血压病头晕头痛者治疗可在基本处方中再加: A·印堂、太阳; B·印堂、百会 C. ·太阳、风池; D·四神聪; E·印堂、风府	What points may be added to the basic prescription of points to treat hypotension with dizziness and headache? A · Yìn táng / midpoint between eyebrows / seal hall，Tài yáng / sun / temple; B · Yìn táng / midpoint between eyebrows / seal hall，D20 / Bǎi Huì; C. · Tài yáng / sun / temple，G20 / Fēng Chí; D · Sì shén Cōng / four spiritual intelligences; E · Yìn táng / midpoint between eyebrows / seal hall，D16 / Fēng Fǔ
1441	低血压病心阳不振者治疗可在基本处方中再加: A·大椎、命门; B·内关、太溪 C. ·神阙、关元; D·膻中、厥阴俞; E·内关、足三里	What point may be added to the main prescription of points to treat hypotension of heart yang in decline? A ·D14 / Dà Zhuī、 D4 / Mìng Mén; B · P6 / Nèi Guān，K3 / Tài Xī; C. · R8 / Shén Què，R4 / Guān Yuán; D · R17 / Shān Zhōng，B14 / Jué Yīn Shū; E · P6 / Nèi Guān，S36 / Zú Sān Lǐ
1442	地机是哪一类特定穴: A·络穴; B·合穴 C. ·郄穴; D·下合穴; E·交会穴	What kind of specially marked points is Sp8 / Dì Jī? A ·linking points, / luo points; B · hé xué / terminal-points sea-points points; C. ·fissural point / cleft point / xi point; D ·lower merging point; E · meridian-meeting point.
1443	地机穴在治疗痛经时，是取其: A. 行血祛瘀的作用; B. 清泻血分之热的作用 C. 调经祛痰，使血有所归的作用; D. 健脾利湿，调血通经的作用; E 以上都不是.	Why is Sp8 (Dì Jī) an effective point for treating period. pain? A. it can promote blood circulation, expel coagulation; B. it can clear and sedate heat at the blood level; C. it can regulate menstruation and expel phlegm, so that blood can return to its original source; D. it can strenthen the spleen and benefit dampness, regulate blood and facilitate menstruation; E. none of the above.
1444	癫病见有淡漠少语，面色萎	What syndrome accounts for depressive psychosis with

	黄，大便稀溏，舌淡，脉弱等症状者分型多为：A 痰气郁结型；B·气虚痰结型 C. 心脾两虚型；D·阴虚火旺型；E·气滞血於型	indifferent expression, withered and yellowish complexion, discharge of watery stools, pale tongue, weak pulse? A·phlegm energy congestion type; B·energy deficiency with phlegm congestion type; C. heart spleen deficiency simultaneously; D · yin deficiency with abundant fire; E·energy congestion and blood coagulation type.
1445	癫病见有神志呆钝，胸闷泛恶，喜叹息，忧虑多疑，苔腻，脉滑者分型多为：·A 痰气郁结型；B·气虚痰结型 C. ·心脾两虚型；D·阴虚火旺型；E·气滞血瘀型	What syndrome accounts for depressive psychosis with idiotic spirits, congested chest, belching, love of sighing, worry and suspecious, greasy coating, slipper pulse? A·phlegm energy congestion type; B·energy deficiency with phlegm congestion type; C. heart spleen deficiency simultaneously; D · yin deficiency with abundant fire; E · energy congestion and blood coagulation type.
1446	癫证的治疗原则是： A.豁痰开窍理气解郁；B 清心泄火醒脑开窍 C. 清心泻热理气解郁；D 豁痰开窍清心泻火	What treatment principle should be applied to treat depressive psychosis (dian zheng)? A. to expel phlegm and open cavities, regulate energy and relieve inhibition; B. to clear heat and sedate fire, wake up the brain and open cavities; C. to clear the heart and sedate heat, regulate energy and relieve inhibition; D. to expel phlegm and open cavities, clear the heart and sedate fire.
1447	电针治疗淋证，宜用高频脉冲电作较强刺激，具体取穴是: A 中极 行间; B·曲骨 中封 C. 膀胱俞 委中; D·肾俞 三阴交 ; E·关元 太溪	In treating lin syndrome (stranguria syndrome) by electro acupuncture, high frequency pulse current should be used to generate stronger stimulation; which group of points should be selected in concrete application? A. R3 (Zhōng Jí); Lv2 (Xíng Jiān); B. R2 (Qū Gŭ); Lv4 (Zhōng Fēng); C; B28 (Páng Guāng Shū); B40 (Wěi Zhōng); D; B23 (Shèn Shū); Sp6 (Sān Yīn Jiāo); E R4 (Guān Yuán). K3 (Tài Xī).
1448	头痛发作的初期可用 "四关穴"通关达窍，并加用：A·阴陵泉；B·足三里 C. ·涌泉；D·阳陵泉 ·E。百会	At the initial stage of headache, “four gates points” may be used to connect the gates and open cavities; what additional point may be added? A · Sp9 / Yīn Líng Quán; B · S36 / Zú Sān Lĭ C. · K1 / Yŏng Quán; D · G34 / Yáng Líng Quán; ·E. D20 / Băi Huì
1449	对外伤性截瘫的治疗，其总的治疗原则是：A·祛邪散寒、通经活络；B·清热祛邪、疏通经络 C. ··补益肝肾、通利小便；D·疏通督脉、调和气血；E·宣通阳气、活血化瘀	What is the overall principle of treating traumatic paraplegia? A·to drive out pathogens and disperse cold, connect meridians and activate linking meridians; B·clear heat and expel pathogens, dispers and connect meridians; C. to tone and benefit liver and kidneys、promote urination; D·to disperse and connect du mai / governing meridian、regulate and harmonize energy and blood; E·to expand and connect yang energy、activate blood and transform coagulation
1450	对于痹证中的热痹，除了根据发病部位的局部取穴外，还应配: A.大椎曲池; B.外关合谷 C. 曲池外关; D 大椎合谷	In treating hot rheumatism (re bi), which group of points should be selected along with local points? A. D14 (Dà Zhuī), Li11 (Qū Chí); B. Sj5 (Wài Guān), Li4 (Hé Gŭ); C. Li11 (Qū Chí); Sj5 (Wài Guān); D. D14 (Dà

		Zhuī) Li4 (Hé Gŭ).
1451	对于风寒感冒，临床中应选取 A.大椎外关合谷; B.大椎风门肺俞 C. 肺俞列缺尺泽; D 大椎风门列缺	In clinical practice, which group of points should be selected to treat wind-cold type of the common cold? A. D14 (Dà Zhuī) Sj5 (Wài Guān); Li4 (Hé Gŭ); B. D14 (Dà Zhuī)B12 (Fēng Mén)B13 (Fèi Shū); C. B13 (Fèi Shū); Lu7 (Liè Quē) Lu5 (Chǐ Zé); D. D14 (Dà Zhuī)B12 (Fēng Mén) Lu7 (Liè Quē).
1452	对于经脉经筋四肢关节等部位的红肿疼痛或麻木等症，一般多选用: A·对证取穴;; B·远道取穴 C. 近部取穴; D·经验取穴; E·原络取穴.	Which principle of selecting points should be applied to treat red swelling and pain in meridians, muscular meridians, and joints of four limbs? A. selecting points to treat various syndromes; B. selecting distant (distal) points for treatment; C. selecting local points for treatment; D. selecting experience points for treatment; E. combination of a Yuan point (original point) and a Luo point (linking point).
1453	对于内伤咳嗽除取肺俞三阴交外，还应选取 A.太渊; B.太溪 C. 太冲; D 太白	What point should be selected to treat cough of internal injury in addition to B13 (Fèi Shū) and Sp6 (Sān Yīn Jiāo)? A. Lu9 (Tài Yuān); B. K3 (Tài Xī); C. Lv3 (Tài Chōng); D. Sp3 (Tài Bái).
1454	对于疝气中的寒症主穴处方是： A，关元三角灸气海大教; B 关元三阴交气海中极 C. 关元三阴交大敦气海; D 关元中极大敦气海	Which group of points should be selected as the primary points to treat cold hernia? A，R4 [Guān Yuán] triangular moxibustion R6 [Qì Hǎi] Lv1 [Dà Dūn]; B R4 [Guān Yuán] Sp6 [Sān Yīn Jiāo] R6 [Qì Hǎi] R3 [Zhōng Jí]; C. R4 [Guān Yuán] Sp6 [Sān Yīn Jiāo] Lv1 [Dà Dūn] R6 [Qì Hǎi]; D R4 [Guān Yuán] R3 [Zhōng Jí] Lv1 [Dà Dūn] R6 [Qì Hǎi]
1455	呃逆病位在： A·胃; B 肝 C. ·肺; D·肾; E·膈	What region is diseased in hiccups? A·stomach; B liver; C. ·lungs; D·kidneys; E·diaphragm.
1456	恶露不绝气虚失摄证宜在基本方基础上再加：A·膻中; B足三里 C. ·百会; D·太冲; E·地机	What points may be added to the basic prescription of points to treat energy deficiency with loss of constriction type of lochiorrhea / persistent lochia? A · R17 / Shān Zhōng; B S36 / Zú Sān Lǐ;C. · D20 / Bǎi Huì; D · Lv3 / Tài Chōng; E · Sp8 / Dì Jī
1457	恶露不绝气虚失摄证宜在基本方基础上再加：A·中极 ·B·百会 C. ·地机; D·足三里; E·归来	What points may be added to the basic prescription of points to treat energy deficiency with loss of constriction type of lochiorrhea / persistent lochia? A · R3 / Zhōng Jí; ·B · D20 / Bǎi Huì; C. Sp8 / Dì Jī; D · S36 / Zú Sān Lǐ; E · S29 / Guī Lái.
1458	恶露不绝血热内扰证宜在基本方基础上再加: A·足三里; B·百会 C. ·中极; D·地机; E·膈俞	What points may be added to the basic prescription of points to treat the internal disturbance of blood heat type of lochiorrhea / persistent lochia? A · S36 / Zú Sān Lǐ; B · D20 / Bǎi Huì; C. ·R3 / Zhōng Jí; D · Sp8 / Dì Jī; E ·B17 / Gé Shū.
1459	耳针治疗鼻渊，一般选用: A·肺 鼻 肾上腺 枕; B，肾 额 肺 脑点 C. ·肾上腺 额 内鼻 肺; D·内鼻 下屏尖 额 肺	Which group of auricular points should be selected to treat nasal pool? A. lungs, nose, adrenal gland, occiput; B. kidneys, forehead, lung, brain point; C. adrenal gland, forehead,

	; E 肺 皮质下 肾上腺 内鼻'	internal nose, lung; D. inernal nose lower tip of tragus, forehead, lung; E. lung, subcortex, adrenal gland, internal nose.
1460	耳针治疗便秘，除取直肠下段与大肠外，还可加用: A 皮质下; B 内分泌 C. · 交感; D 肾上腺; E 神门	In addition to Lower Section of Rectum and Large Intestine, what auricular point should be selected to treat constipation by auricular acupuncture? A. subcortex; B. internal secretion (endocrine); C. sympathetic; D. adrenal gland; E. divine door (spiritual door).
1461	耳针治疗发热高血压炎症应取: A 降压沟; B 高血压点 C. 耳尖; D 神门;; E 肾上腺.	Which group of auricular points should be selected to treat fever? A. hypotensor groove (depressor groove); B. hypertension point; C. tip of ear; D. divine door; E. adrenal gland.
1462	耳针治疗胃脘痛，除选用胃脾以外，还可选用: A 交感 神门 皮质下; B 枕 大肠 肝 C. 交感 大肠 肝; D 皮质下 口 枕; E 神门 小肠 皮质下	In treating stomachache by auricular acupuncture, which group of points should be selected in addition to stomach, spleen? A. sympathetic, divine door (spiritual door) subcortex; B. occiput; large intestine, liver; C. sympathetic, large intesitne, liver; D. subcortex, mouth, occiput; E; divine door (spiritual door), small intestine, subcortex.
1463	耳针治疗中暑，下列穴组中应选: A 肺 神门 心 脑干; B 心 枕 肾上腺 皮质下 C. ，交感 内分泌 肾; D 耳炎 脑点 三焦; E 以上均不是	Which group of auricular points should be selected to treat sunstroke? A. lungs, divine door, heart, brain stem; B. heart, occiput, adrenal gland, subcortex; C. sympathetic, inernal secretion, kidneys; D. ear inflammaton, brain point, triple heater; E. none of the above.
1464	二尖瓣分离术针麻可选用: A 睛明、合谷; B 合谷、内关 C. 合谷、内关、臂臑 D 足三里、内关、E切口旁压痛敏感点 E 脊中、命门	What points may be selected to perform mitral commissurotomy by acupuncture anaesthesia? A·B1 / Jīng Míng，Li4 / Hé Gǔ; B · Li4 / Hé Gǔ，P6 / Nèi Guān; C. · Li4 / Hé Gǔ，P6 / Nèi Guān，Li14 / Bì Nào; D · S36 / Zú Sān Lǐ，P6 / Nèi Guān 、pressure pain and sensitive points on the side of incision; E · D6 / Jǐ Zhōng, D4 / Mìng Mén.
1465	肺痨盗汗者，除用主方外，还可加用: A 哑门 阴郄; B 通里 复溜 C. 肺俞 合谷; D 阴郄 复溜; E 合谷 足三里	In addition to major points, which group of points should be selected to treat tuberculosis of the lungs and night sweats? A. D15 (Yǎ Mén); H6 (Yīn Xī); B. H5 (Tōng Lǐ); K7 (Fù Liū); C.B13 (Fèi Shū) Li4 (Hé Gǔ); D. H6 (Yīn Xī) K7 (Fù Liū); E Li4 (Hé Gǔ), S36 (Zú Sān Lǐ)
1466	风火牙痛的主要处方是: A 尺泽 少商 合谷 陷谷 关冲; B 合谷 颊车 内庭 下关 外关 风池 C. 鱼际 太溪 照海; D 合谷 内庭 颊车 下关 行间 太溪; E 以上皆不可	Which group of points should be selected to treat wind fire toothache? A; Lu5 (Chǐ Zé), Lu11 (Shǎo Shāng), Li4 (Hé Gǔ), Sj1 (Guān Chōng); B. Li4 (Hé Gǔ), S6 (Jiá Chē), S44 (Nèi Tíng); S7 (Xià Guān), Sj5 (Wài Guān), G20 (Fēng Chí); C. Lu10 (Yǔ Jì); K3 (Tài Xī) K6 (Zhào Hǎi); D. Li4 (Hé Gǔ), S44 (Nèi Tíng), S6 (Jiá Chē), S7 (Xià Guān), Lv2 (Xíng Jiān), K3 (Tài Xī); E none of the above.
1467	风热感冒的治疗原则是:	What treatment principle should be applied to treat

	A.祛风散寒解表宣肺; B.疏散风热清肃肺气 C. 祛风清热宣肺止咳; D 疏散风热解表宣肺	wind-hot type of the common cold? A. to expel wind and disperse cold, relax the superficial region and expand the lungs; B. to disperse wind heat, clear and constrict lung energy; C. to expel wind and clear heat, expand the lungs and relieve cough; D. to disperse wind heat, relax the superficial reigon and expand the lungs.
1468	风热型目赤肿痛，在主方的基础上还可加用: A·风池 曲池; B·风池 阳池 C. ·合谷 外关; D·少商 上星; E 太阳 二间.	In addition to the major prescription, which group of points should be selected to treat the wind heat type of pink eyes with swelling and pain? A. G20 (Fēng Chí); Li11 (Qū Chí); B. G20 (Fēng Chí); Sj4 (Yáng Chí); C. Li4 (Hé Gǔ); D. Lu11 (Shǎo Shāng) D23 (Shàng Xīng); E Tài Yáng, Li2 (Èr Jiān).
1469	风痰阻络型中风可在基本处方上再加: A·曲池、内庭、丰隆; B·丰隆、合谷 C. ·足三里、气海; D·太溪、风池; E·太冲、太溪	What points may be added in addition to the basic prescription of acupuncture and moxibustion to treat wind stroke that belongs to the wind phlegm obstructing linking meridian type? A · Li11 / Qū Chí, S44 / Nèi Tíng, S40 / Fēng Lóng; B · S40 / Fēng Lóng, Li4 / Hé Gǔ; C. · S36 / Zú Sān Lǐ, R6 / Qì Hǎi; D · K3 / Tài Xī, G20 / Fēng Chí; E · Lv3 / Tài Chōng, K3 / Tài Xī
1470	风邪窒壅遏经络造成耳聋耳穴外还可加用: A. 风池 风府; B. 风池 曲池 C. 曲池 外关; D. 外关 合谷; E. 合谷 大椎.	In addition to auricular points, which group of points may be selected to treat deafness due to pathogenic wind obstructing meridians? A. G20 (Fēng Chí); D16 (Fēng Fǔ); B. G20 (Fēng Chí); Li11 (Qū Chí); C. Li11 (Qū Chí); Sj5 (Wài Guān); D. Sj5 (Wài Guān), Li4 (Hé Gǔ); E Li4 (Hé Gǔ). D14 (Dà Zhuī).
1471	肝病用俞募配穴法可选: A·肝俞 章门; B·肝俞 期门 C. ·肝俞 石门; D·肝俞 京门; E·肝俞 关元	Which group of points is NOT a combination of anterior mu point and posterior transport (back shu) point? A. B18 (Gān Shū); Lv13 (Zhāng Mén); B. B18 (Gān Shū); Lv14 (Qí Mén); C. B18 (Gān Shū); R5 (Shí Mén); D. B18 (Gān Shū); G25 (Jīng Mén); E B18 (Gān Shū); S22 (Guān Mén).
1472	肝胆火盛型耳聋耳鸣，除针刺主穴之外，还可加用: A·行间 阳纲; B·肝俞 至阳 C. ·太冲 丘墟; D·中都 中封; E，以上都不是	In addition to needling major points, which group of points should be selected to treat deafness and ringing in the ears due to excessive fire of the liver and gallbladder? A. Lv2 (Xíng Jiān); B48 (Yáng Gāng); B. B18 (Gān Shū); D9 (Zhì Yáng); C. Lv3 (Tài Chōng); G40 (Qiū Xū); D. Lv6 (Zhōng Dū) Lv4 (Zhōng Fēng); E none of the above.
1473	肝气犯胃所致呕吐，治疗时宜取用: A·中脘 内关 足三里 胃俞 外关 合谷; B·中脘 内关 足三里 胃俞 上脘 肾俞 C. ·中脘 内关 足三里 胃俞 膻中 丰隆; D·中脘 内关 足三里 胃俞 阳陵泉 太冲; E·中脘 内关 足三里 胃俞 脾俞 章门.	Which group of points should be selected to treat vomiting due to liver energy offending the stomach? A. R12 (Zhōng Wǎn), P6 (Nèi Guān), S36 (Zú Sān Lǐ), B21 (Wèi Shū), Sj5 (Wài Guān), Li4 (Hé Gǔ); B. R12 (Zhōng Wǎn), P6 (Nèi Guān), S36 (Zú Sān Lǐ);B21 (Wèi Shū); R13 (Shàng Wǎn); B23 (Shèn Shū); C. R12 (Zhōng Wǎn), P6 (Nèi Guān), S36 (Zú Sān Lǐ);B21 (Wèi Shū) R17 (Shān Zhōng); S40 (Fēng Lóng); D. R12 (Zhōng Wǎn), P6 (Nèi Guān), S36 (Zú Sān Lǐ);B21 (Wèi Shū) G34 (Yáng Líng Quán) Lv3 (Tài Chōng); E R12 (Zhōng Wǎn), P6 (Nèi Guān), S36 (Zú Sān Lǐ);B21 (Wèi Shū); B20 (Pí Shū),

		Lv13 (Zhāng Mén)
1474	肝气犯胃型呕吐可在基本方的基础上加：A·太冲、期门；B·丰隆、公孙 C. ·天枢、梁门；D·外关、大椎；E·脾俞、三阴交	What points may be added to the basic prescription of points to treat the liver energy offending the stomach type of vomiting? A · Lv3 / Tài Chōng，Lv14 / Qí Mén; B · S40 / Fēng Lóng，Sp4 / Gōng Sūn; C. ·S25 / Tiān Shū，S21 / Liáng Mén; D · Sj5 / Wài Guān 、D14 / Dà Zhuī; E ·; B20 / Pí Shū，Sp6 / Sān Yīn Jiāo.
1475	肝阳暴亢型中风可在基本处方上再加：A·足三里、气海；B·太溪、三阴交 C. ·丰隆、合谷；D·风池、完骨；E·太冲、太溪	What points may be added in addition to the basic prescription of acupuncture and moxibustion to treat wind stroke that belongs to acute liver yang uprising? A · S36 / Zú Sān Lǐ，R6 / Qì Hǎi; B · K3 / Tài Xī，Sp6 / Sān Yīn Jiāo; C. · S40 / Fēng Lóng，Li4 / Hé Gǔ; D · G20 / Fēng Chí 、mastoid process; E · Lv3 / Tài Chōng，K3 / Tài Xī
1476	肝阳上亢型眩晕的主要处方是: A·脾俞 肾俞 关元 足三里；B·百会 气海 血海 内关 中脘 C. 风池 肝俞 肾俞 行间 侠溪；D·中脘 内关 丰隆 解溪 头维；E·神门 肾俞 内关 关元 足三里.	Which group of points should be selected to treat vertigo due to liver yang uprising? A; B20 (Pí Shū); B23 (Shèn Shū) R4 (Guān Yuán) S36 (Zú Sān Lǐ); B. D20 (Bǎi Huì); R6 (Qì Hǎi) Sp10 (Xuè Hǎi) P6 (Nèi Guān) R12 (Zhōng Wǎn); C. G20 (Fēng Chí)B18 (Gān Shū); B23 (Shèn Shū) Lv2 (Xíng Jiān) G43 (Xiá Xī); D. R12 (Zhōng Wǎn) P6 (Nèi Guān) S40 (Fēng Lóng) S41 (Jiě Xī) S8 (Tóu Wěi); E H7 (Shén Mén); B23 (Shèn Shū) P6 (Nèi Guān) R4 (Guān Yuán) S36 (Zú Sān Lǐ).
1477	高热以选下列哪组穴位为佳? A 大椎足三里复溜合谷，B. 大椎陶道.神门合谷 C. 大椎风池内关合谷; D. 大椎曲池少商，合谷; E. 以上都不是。	Which group of points should best be selected to treat high fever? A. D14 [Dà Zhuī], S36 [Zú Sān Lǐ], K7 [Fù Liū] Li4 [Hé Gǔ]; B. D14 [Dà Zhuī], D13 [卜áo Dào], H7 [Shén Mén], Li4 [Hé Gǔ]; C. D14 [Dà Zhuī], G20 [Fēng Chí], P6 [Nèi Guān], Li4 [Hé Gǔ]; D. D14 [Dà Zhuī], Li11 [Qū Chí], Lu11 [Shǎo Shāng], Li4 [Hé Gǔ]; E None of the above
1478	膏肓;大椎治疗白细胞减少症多选用的刺灸方法是：A·针刺泻法；B·刺血法 C. ·重灸法；D·拔罐法；E·电针	What technique of acupuncture-moxbustion is applied when B43 / Gāo Huāng Shū, D14 / Dà Zhuī are selected to treat liukopenia? A · needling sedation; B ·blood-letting C. ·heavy moxibusiton; D · cupping; E ·electro acupuncture.
1479	根据 "纳甲法"开穴规律，甲日于甲戌时开胆经足窍阴，那么乙日应于乙酉时开：A·行间；B·大敦 C. ·涌泉；D¨隐白；E·太冲	By the rule of "selecting points according to 10 stems", G44 [Zú Qiào Yīn, Qiào Yīn] should open for treatment during the Jiǎ-Xu period (7-9 pm) on Jiǎ day; what point should open for treatment during the Yǐ Yǒu period (5-7 pm) on Yǐ day? A · Lv2 / Xíng Jiān; B · Lv1 / Dà Dūn; C. · K1 / Yǒng Quán; D¨ Sp1 / Yǐn Bái; E · Lv3 / Tài Chōng
1480	根据 "纳支法"之"补母泻子取穴法"，心经病变属实者应配：A·少冲；B·少府 C. ·神门；D·灵道；E·少海	By the rule of "selecting points according to branches" for toification and sedation by child point and mother point, what point should be selected to treat excess syndrome of heart meridian disorder? A · H9 / Shào Chōng; B · H8 / Shào Fǔ; C. H7 / Shén Mén;

		D · D10 / Líng Dào; E · H3 / Shào Hǎi Dì Zhi.
1481	根据 "纳支法"之按时循经取穴法，胃经病变应在( )选取胃经有关腧穴：A·午未; B·巳午 C. ·辰巳; D·子丑; E·酉戌	By the rule of "selecting points according to branches", which is to select hourly points according to flowing sequences of meridians, when should the points on stomach meridian be selected to treat disorders of stomach meridian? A. ·Wǔ-Wè; B. ·Sì-Wǔ; C. ·Chén-Sì; D. ·Zǐ-Chǒu; E ·Yǒu-Xū
1482	根据"实则泻其子"的原则，膀胱实证治疗取穴应是: A·京骨; B·通谷 C. ·金门; D·申脉;; E·束骨	According to "sedating the child in excess", what point should be selected to treat excess of the bladder meridian? A; B64 (Jīng Gǔ); B. B66 (Tōng Gǔ, Zú Tōng Gǔ); C. B63 (Jīn Mén); D. B62 (Shēn Mài); E. B65 (Shù Gǔ).
1483	根据"阳进阴退"的原则，丁日丁未时开心经井穴少冲，戊日应( )时开井穴厉兑：A·甲戌; B·丙申 C. ·戊午; D·己巳; E·壬寅	According to the principle of "yang advancing while yin retreating", the jǐng xué / well point, H9 / Shào Chōng, will open during the Dīng-Wè hour on Dīng day, when will the jǐng xué / well point, S45 / Lì Duì, open on Wù day? A ·Jiǎ -Xū· B ·Bǐng-Shēn; C. ·Wù -Wǔ; D ·Jǐ -Sì; E ·Rén-Yín
1484	根据《灵枢·经脉》篇提出的针灸治疗原则，寒则：A·除之; B·疾之 C. ·补之; D·泻之; E·留之	According to the principle of acupuncture therapy put forward in 《Ling Shu Chestapter 10》， what should be done with cold? A ·removing it; B ·rapid insertion of needle; C. ·twelve muscular meridians / jing jin tonfication; D ·twelve muscular meridians / jing jin sedation; E ·longer retention of needle.
1485	根据本经子母补泻法，治疗心经实证应取：A·少海; B·少府 C. ·少冲; D·少泽; E·都不是	According to the principle of sedating child points and toning mother points of the same meridian, which point may be used to treat heart meridian in excess syndrome? A · H3 / Shào Hǎi; B · H8 / Shào Fǔ; C. · H9 / Shào Chōng; D · Si1 / Shào Zé; E · none of the above.
1486	根据五输穴的主病，治疗 "体重节痛"应取：A荥穴; B·输穴 C. ·井穴; D·经穴; E·合穴	According to the therapeutic functions of five command points, which of the following can treat " heaviness of the body and pain in joint"? A outpouring points / spring points; B ·flowing points / stream points / shù xué; C. · jǐng xué / well points; D ·flowing points / river points / jīng xué; E · hé xué / terminal-points / sea-points points.
1487	根据现代研究，具有降低眼压作用的主要穴位是: A·睛明; B·光明 C. ·臂臑; D·太阳; E·行间	According to modern research, which point is the major point to reduce eye pressure? A.B1 (Jīng Míng); B. G37 (Guāng Míng); C. Li14 (Bì Nào); D. Tài Yáng; E. Lv2 (Xíng Jiān).
1488	根据子母补泻法，肝经的实热证，当泻: A·大敦; B·太冲 C. ·曲泉; D·神门; E·少府	According to "tonification and sedation by mother and child points", what point should be sedated. to treat excessive heat in the liver meridian? A. Lv1 (Dà Dūn); B. Lv3 (Tài Chōng); C. Lv8 (Qū Quán); D. H7 (Shén Mén); E. H8 (Shào Fǔ).
1489	根据子母补泻法，曲泉穴可用来治疗: A·肺经虚证; B·大肠经实	According to "tonification and sedation by mother and child points", what can Lv8 (Qū Quán) treat? A. deficiency syndrome of lung meridian; B. excess

	证 C. 肝经实证; D 肝经虚证; E 肾经实证	syndrome of large intestine meridian; C. excess syndrome of liver meridian; D. deficiency syndrome of liver meridian; E. excess syndrome of kidney meridian.
1490	根据子母补泻法，肾经虚证当补: A 太溪; B 复溜 C. 然谷; D 鱼际; E 尺泽	According to "tonification and sedation by mother and child points", what point should be sedated. to treat deficiency of the kidney meridian? A. K3 (Tài Xī); B. K7 (Fù Liū); C. K2 (Rán Gǔ); D. Lu10 (Yǔ Jì); E. Lu5 (Chǐ Zé).
1491	关于冷秘的针刺治疗错误的是：A.针灸并用; B 补法 C. 可在基本方的基础上加神阙、关元; D 可用温针灸; E 可用隔姜灸	What is erroneous in treating cold constpation by acupuncture? A. both acupuncture and moxibustion should be used; B · tonfication; C. add R8 / Shén Què, R4 / Guān Yuán to the basic prescription; D use warm acupuncture and moxibustion ; E Moxibustion with ginger in between moxa and skin / indirect moxa.
1492	关于气秘的针灸治疗正确的是：A 只针不灸，补法; B 只灸不针，补法 C. 只针不灸，泻法; D 只灸不针，泻法; E 针灸并用，补泻兼施	Which is the right method of acupuncture therapy in treating energy type of constipation? A · acupuncture without moxibustion , tonfication; B · moxibustion without acupuncture , tonfication; C. · acupuncture without moxibustion , sedation; D · moxibustion without acupuncture , sedation; E · both acupuncture and moxibustion are applied, both tonification and sedation are applied
1493	关于热秘的针刺治疗错误的是：A 通调腑气、润肠通便 。B 针灸并用 C. 只针不灸D 泻法; E. 可加曲池、合谷清泻腑热	What is erroneous in treating hot constipation by acupuncture? A. to facilitate and regulate bowel energy, lubricate intestines and promote bowel movement; B. · both acupuncture and moxibustion should be used; C. acupuncture without moxibustion; D · sedation; E. add Li11 / Qū Chí, Li4 / Hé Gǔ to clear and sedate bowel heat.
1494	关元配三阴交治痛经是因为: A 双向调节; B 局部作用 C. 远治作用; D 全身作用; E 足三阴经与任脉汇通	Why is the combination of R4 / Guān Yuán and Sp6 / Sān Yīn Jiāo capable of period pain? A bidirectional regulation; B local function; C. distala funciton; D whole body function; E. combined function of three yin meridians of foot and conception meridian / ren mai
1495	关元三阴交肝俞三穴所组成的处方，是用于治疗 A. 月经先期; B 月经后期 C. 月经先后不定期; D 痛经	What disease is to be treated by the prescription of points, which include R4 (Guān Yuán), Sp6 (Sān Yīn Jiāo), and B18 (Gān Shū)? A. premature menstruation; B. overdue menstruation; C. irregular menstruation; D. period. pain.
1496	关元穴是: A 三焦的募穴; B 三焦经的募穴; C. 大肠经的募穴; D 小肠的募穴; E 小肠经的募穴	What is the nature of R4 / Guān Yuán? A sanjiao / triple heater gathering point / mu point; B · san jiao meridian gathering point / mu point; C. large intestine meridian gathering point / mu point; D · small intestine gathering point / mu point; E · small intestine meridian gathering point / mu point.

1497	光明、肝俞、太溪治疗色盲，属：A·标本兼治; B.治标为主 C. 治本为主; D·加强调补肝肾、濡养目窍的作用; E·随症配穴	What is the treatment principle of using G37 / Guāng Míng，B18 / Gān Shū、K3 / Tài Xī to treat color blindness? A·to treat symptoms and roots simultaneously; B·treating symptoms as the primary principle; C. ·treating roots as the primary principle; D·enhancing the regulation and tonfication of liver and kidneys、lubricating and nourishing eye cavities; E·combination of points according to symptoms.
1498	合谷颊车内庭下关外关风池六穴配合应用，可主治: A·三叉神经痛; B·阴虚牙痛 C. 咽喉肿痛; D·风火牙痛; E·口眼歪斜	Which disease may be treated by the combination of the following points: Li4 (Hé Gŭ), S6 (Jiá Chē), S44 (Nèi Tíng), S7 (Xià Guān), Sj5 (Wài Guān), G20 (Fēng Chí)? A. trigeminal neuralgia; B. yin deficiency toothache; C. sore throat with swelling; D. wind fire toothache; E. wry eyes and mouth.
1499	合谷配复溜可用于治疗: A·汗证; B·泄泻 C. ·癫狂; D·痫证; E·昏迷	What can be treated by combining Li4 (Hé Gŭ) and K7 (Fù Liū)? A·perspiration syndrome; B·diarrhea C. ·insanity; D. epilepsy syndrome; E·fainting.
1500	合谷穴在发汗止汗方面的作用与下列哪穴近似? A·大椎; B，陶道 C. ·太溪; D·复溜; E·身柱	Which of the following points has the similar effect as Li4 (Hé Gŭ) in inducing and checking perspiration? A·D14 / Dà Zhuī; B， D13 / Táo Dào; C. · K3 / Tài Xī; D · K7 / Fù Liū; E · D12 / Shēn Zhù.
1501	合谷与风池相配，其治疗作用是: A·清热解毒; B·祛风解表 C. ·和解少阳; D·止咳平喘; E·平肝熄风	What is the therapeutic function of combinging Li4 (Hé Gŭ) and G20 (Fēng Chí)? A·to clear heat and detoxify; B·to expel wind and relax superficial region; C. ·to harmonize lesser yang; D·to stop cough and calm asthma; E·to calm liver and stop wind.
1502	患者两膝关节疼痛，局部热肿，痛不可近，关节活动障碍并兼有发热口渴，苔黄燥，脉滑数。治疗时可取用: A·阳陵泉 犊鼻 梁丘 膈俞 血海; B 犊鼻 梁丘 大椎 曲池 阳陵泉 膝阳关 C. 阳陵泉 膝阳关 犊鼻 肾俞 关元; D·足三里 商丘 犊鼻 梁丘 阳陵泉; E· 环跳 悬钟 阳陵泉 犊鼻 膝阳关	Which group of points should be selected to treat the following symptoms: pain in both knee joints, hot swelling in the local region, pain that Ccannot be touched, restricted movements of joints with fever and thirst, yellowish and dry coating on the tongue, a slippery and rapid. pulse? A. G34 (Yáng Líng Quán); S35 (Dú Bí) S34 (Liáng Qiū)B17 (Gé Shū) Sp10 (Xuè Hăi); B. S35 (Dú Bí); S34 (Liáng Qiū) D14 (Dà Zhuī) Li11 (Qū Chí) G34 (Yáng Líng Quán); G33 (Yáng Guān, Xī Yáng Guān); C. G34 (Yáng Líng Quán); G33 (Yáng Guān, Xī Yáng Guān) S35 (Dú Bí); B23 (Shèn Shū) R4 (Guān Yuán); D. S36 (Zú Sān Lĭ) Sp5 (Shāng Qiū) S35 (Dú Bí) S34 (Liáng Qiū) G34 (Yáng Líng Quán); E. G30 (Huán Tiào) G39 (Xuán Zhōng)G34 (Yáng Líng Quán); G33 (Yáng Guān, Xī Yáng Guān)..
1503	患者证见声音嘶哑，喉燥咽干，口干鼻干，兼见干咳. 气逆舌红脉小数，辨证应属: A. 肺阴虚损; B. 内热袭肺 C. 痰热壅肺; D. 肺燥伤津; E. 肺肾阴虚.	A patient with hoarseness, dry throat, dry mouth and dry nose, accompanied. by dry cough, uprising energy, red. tongue, a small and rapid pulse; what is the syndrome involved? A. lung yin deficiency and deprivation; B. internal heat invading the lungs; C. phlegm heat accumulated in the lungs; D. lung dryness harming fluids; E. yin deficiency of

		lungs and kidneys.
1504	黄疸甚者应在基本方的基础上加： A·中脘; B·腕骨 C. ·内关; D·天枢; E·大椎	What points may be added to the basic prescription of points to treat severe Cases of jaundice? A · R12 / Zhōng Wǎn; B · Si4 / Wàn Gǔ; C. P6 / Nèi Guān; D · S25 / Tiān Shū; E ·D14 / Dà Zhuī
1505	回阳固脱苏厥救逆是针对什么病而设立的治则: A.中风; B 虚脱 C. 高热; D 气厥	What disease is to be treated by the principles, "to restore yang and rescue collapse' and "to wake up and rescue uprising"? A. wind stroke; B. deficiency prolpase; C. high fever; D. energy uprising.
1506	火盛伤阴型狂病治疗可在基本处方上加：A·三阴交、大钟; B·合谷、·太冲 C. ·血海、膈俞; D·中脘、神门; E·合谷、血海	What points may be added in addition to the basic prescription of acupuncture and moxibustion to treat the flaming fire harming the yin type of maniac psychosis? A · Sp6 / Sān Yīn Jiāo， K4 / Dà Zhōng; B · Li4 / Hé Gǔ 、 · Lv3 / Tài Chōng; C. · Sp10 / Xuè Hǎi，B17 / Gé Shū; D · R12 / Zhōng Wǎn，H7 / Shén Mén; E · Li4 / Hé Gǔ，Sp10 / Xuè Hǎi.
1507	火针治疗腱鞘囊肿的操作部位在：A·外关; B·阳溪 C. ·囊肿局部; D·后溪; E曲池	In treating thecal cyst, what region should fire needling therapy applied to? A · Sj5 / Wài Guān; B · Li5 / Yáng Xī; C. ·local cyst; D · Si3 / Hòu Xī; E. Li11 / Qū Chí
1508	急性痛症可选用：A·原穴; B·郄穴 C. ·下合穴; D·输穴; E 阿是穴	What point may be selected to treat acute pain? A · yuán xué / starting-points / source-points; B ·fissural point / cleft point / xi point; C. ·lower merging point; D · command points; E ·ouchi points / pressure points
1509	急性泄泻的主要处方是: A·中脘 天枢 上巨虚 阴陵泉 ; B·脾俞 中脘 章门 足三里 C. ·足三里 天枢 命门 关元 ; D·脾俞 章门 上巨虚 下巨虚 ; E·太溪 肾俞 足三里 天枢	Which group of points should be selected to treat acute diarrhea? A. R12 (Zhōng Wǎn, S25 (Tiān Shū), S37 (Shàng Jù Xū), Sp9 (Yīn Líng Quán); B. B20 (Pí Shū), R12 (Zhōng Wǎn), Lv13 (Zhāng Mén), S36 (Zú Sān Lǐ); C. S36 (Zú Sān Lǐ) S25 (Tiān Shū), D4 (Mìng Mén), R4 (Guān Yuán); D. B20 (Pí Shū), Lv13 (Zhāng Mén); E..K3 (Tài Xī);B23 (Shèn Shū), S36 (Zú Sān Lǐ), S25 (Tiān Shū), S25 (Tiān Shū),
1510	甲状腺手术、乳腺癌根治术针麻都可选用：A 睛明、合谷; B·合谷、内关 C. ·合谷、内关、臂臑; D·足三里、内关、切口旁压痛敏感点; E·脊中、命门	What point should be selected for acupuncture anaesthesia in thyroidectomy and mammary cancer radical operation? A. ·B1 / Jīng Míng， Li4 / Hé Gǔ; B. · Li4 / Hé Gǔ， P6 / Nèi Guān; C. · Li4 / Hé Gǔ， P6 / Nèi Guān， Li14 / Bì Nào; D. · S36 / Zú Sān Lǐ， P6 / Nèi Guān 、 pressure pain and sensitive points on the side of incision; E. · D6 / Jǐ Zhōng， D4 / Mìng Mén
1511	脚气冲心的危候，除针刺主穴之外，还可加用: A，中极 间使 大陵; B·石门 神门 少海 C. ·郄门 巨阙 内关; D·天枢 中脘 鸠尾; E·膻中 阴陵泉 太冲	In addition to needling major points, which group of points should be selected to treat beriberi hitting the heart (jiao qi chong xin)? A. R3 (Zhōng Jí); P5 (Jiān Shǐ) P7 (Dà Líng); B. R5 (Shí Mén); H7 (Shén Mén) H3 (Shào Hǎi); C. P4 (Xī Mén); R14

		(Jù Què) P6 (Nèi Guān); D. S25 (Tiān Shū) R12 (Zhōng Wǎn) R15 (Jiū Wěi); E. R17 (Shān Zhōng). Sp9 (Yīn Líng Quán) Lv3 (Tài Chōng).
1512	戒酒综合征兼见腹痛、腹泻，可在基本处方的基础上加：A·足三里、三阴交；B·天枢、上巨虚 C. ·脾俞、胃俞；D·脾俞、章门；E·太冲、太白	What points may be added to the basic prescription of points to treat alcohol withdrawal syndrome accompanied by abdominal pain and diarrhea? A · S36 / Zú Sān Lǐ，Sp6 / Sān Yīn Jiāo; B · S25 / Tiān S hū，S37 / Shàng Jù Xū C. B20 / Pí Shū，B21 / Wèi Shū; D. B20 / Pí Shū，Lv13 / Zhāng Mén; E. · Lv3 / Tài Chōng，Sp3 / Tài Bái.
1513	戒烟综合征兼见肌肉抖动，可在基本处方的基础上加：A.太冲、合谷；B·脾俞、足三里 C. ·水沟、太冲；D·列缺、丰隆；E·神门、三阴交	What points may be added to the basic prescription of points to treat smoking withdrawal syndrome accompanied by muscular shivering? A. Lv3 / Tài Chōng，Li4 / Hé Gǔ; B. B20 / Pí Shū，S36 / Zú Sān Lǐ; C. D26 / Shuǐ Gōu / Rén Zhōng、Lv3 / Tài Chōng;; D·Lu7 / Liè Quē、 S40 / Fēng Lóng; E · H7 / Shén Mén，Sp6 / Sān Yīn Jiāo.
1514	戒烟综合征兼见胸闷、气促、痰多，可在基本处方的基础上加： A·膻中、内关；B·合谷、太冲 C. 曲池、大椎；D·脾俞、足三里；E·神门、内关.	What points may be added to the basic prescription of points to treat smoking withdrawal syndrome accompanied by dull chest, rapid breathing, plentiful phlegm? A · R17 / Shān Zhōng, P6 / Nèi Guān; B · Li4 / Hé Gǔ, Lv3 / Tài Chōng; C. Li11 / Qū Chí, D14 / Dà Zhuī; D. B20 / Pí Shū, S36 / Zú Sān Lǐ; E · H7 / Shén Mén, P6 / Nèi Guān.
1515	进行耳针治疗带状疱疹应取：A·肝；B·肾 C. ·膀胱；D·胃；E·胆	What point should be used to treat herpes zoster by auricular acupuncture? A ·liver; B ·kidneys; C. ·bladder; D ·stomach; E ·gallbladder
1516	惊悸怔忡时宜取下列哪组穴位为最佳? A 厥阴俞神堂.少府内关;B 内关通里.太溪照海;C 少海少府少冲中冲;D.心俞.肝俞，肾输.神门，E 郄門.神门心俞巨阙.	Which group of points should be selected to treat palpitation and nervousness? .A. B14 / Jué Yīn Shū; B44 / Shén Táng.H8 / Shào Fǔ P6 / Nèi Guān; B. P6 / Nèi Guān H5 / Tōng Lǐ.K3 / Tài Xī K6 / Zhào Hǎi; C. H3 / Shào Hǎi H8 / Shào Fǔ H9 / Shào Chōng P9 / Zhōng Chōng; D. B15 / Xīn Shū.B18 / Gān Shū ， B23 / Shèn Shū.H7 / Shén Mén; E. P4 / Xī Mén.H7 / Shén MénB15 / Xīn Shū R14 / Jù Què.
1517	惊悸属于痰火内动者，治疗时除用主方外，还可加用: A·膈俞 脾俞 足三里 ；B·厥阴俞 肾俞 太溪 C. 脾俞 三焦俞 气海俞 ；D·内关 尺泽 丰隆 ；E·丰隆 膏肓俞 太渊	In addition to major points, which group of points may be selected to treat palpitaiton due to internal disturbance of phlegm fire? A. B17 (Gé Shū); B20 (Pí Shū); S36 (Zú Sān Lǐ); B. B14 (Jué Yīn Shū); B23 (Shèn Shū) K3 (Tài Xī);.C. B20 (Pí Shū); B22 (Sān Jiāo Shū); B24 (Qì Hǎi Shū);. D. P6 (Nèi Guān) Lu5 (Chǐ Zé) S40 (Fēng Lóng);.E. S40 (Fēng Lóng); B43 (Gāo Huāng Shū). Lu9 (Tài Yuān).
1518	睛明、瞳子髎、风池治色盲属：A·标本兼治；B·治标为主 C. ·治本为主；D·加强调补肝肾、濡养目窍的作用；E·随症配穴	What is the treatment principle of using B1 / Jīng Míng，G1 / Tóng Zǐ Liáo、G20 / Fēng Chí to treat color blindness? A ·to treat symptoms and roots simultaneously; B ·treating symptoms as the primary principle;

		C. ·treating roots as the primary principle; D·enhancing the regulation and tonfication of liver and kidneys、lubricating and nourishing eye C. avities; E·combination of points according to symptoms
1519	睛明太冲太阳合谷是治疗什么病的主穴处方: A.目赤肿痛; B 耳鸣耳聋 C. ，牙痛; D 三叉神经痛	What disease is to be treated by the prescription, which includes the following as the primary points: B1 (Jīng Míng), Lv3 (Tài Chōng), Tài Yáng, Li4 (Hé Gǔ)? A.pink eye with swelling and pain; B. ringing in ears and deafness; C. toothache; D. trigeminal neuralgia.
1520	井穴不适于：A·心下满；B·泻热开窍 C. ·镇痉宁神；D·肢端麻木; E·益气养血	Jǐng xué / well points are not the right points to treat which disease? A. ·fullness below the heart; B. ·to sedate heat and open cavities; C. calm spasm and secure the spirit; D. numbness at the tip of limbs; E. ·benefit energy and nourish blood
1521	九宫中与三相配的是：A·公孙; B·外关 C. ·后溪 D·申脉 E照海	What point corresponds to 3 among the nine palaces? A · Sp4 / Gōng Sūn; B · Sj5 / Wài Guān; C. ·Si3 / Hòu Xī; D. B62 / Shēn Mài; E. K6 / Zhào Hǎi.
1522	久痢脱肛者应在基本方的基础上加：·A·公孙; B·内关 C. ·内庭; D·百会; E.关元	What points may be added to the basic prescription of points to treat chronic diarrhea and proctoptosis / prolapse of anus? · A · Sp4 / Gōng Sūn; B · P6 / Nèi Guān; C. S44 / Nèi Tíng; D · D20 / Bǎi Huì; E. R4 / Guān Yuán
1523	久泄、久痢以致脱肛宜用：A·实则泻之; B·宛陈则除之 C. ·陷下则灸之; D·不盛不虚以经取之; E·都不对	How to treat proctoptosis / prolapse of anus due to chronic diarrhea and chronic dysentery? A·to sedate in case of excess; B·chronic clots should be removed; C. a depressed disease should be treated by moxibustion D · If the symptoms belong neither to excess nor to deficiency, they should be treated by the points on the meridian; E · none of the above
1524	具有健脾疏肝益肾的穴位是: A·阴陵泉; B·三阴交 C. ·肝俞 D·脾俞; E，肾俞.	Which point can strengthen the spleen, disperse the liver, and benefit the kidneys? A · Sp9 / Yīn Líng Quán; B · Sp6 / Sān Yīn Jiāo; C. ·B18 / Gān Shū; D. B20 / Pí Shū; E，B23 / Shèn Shū.
1525	具有解表清热，退热作用的穴位是： A.大椎; B.哑门 C. 列缺; D 风门	What point has the effect of relaxing the superficial region and clearing heat, reducing fever? A. D20 (Bǎi Huì); B. D15 (Yǎ Mén); C. Lu7 (Liè Quē); D.B12 (Fēng Mén).
1526	咳嗽咯痰色黄身热头痛口干，咽喉肿痛，脉浮数，舌苔薄黄，针刺治疗可用: A·肺俞 列缺 合谷 大椎 外关; B. 尺泽 少商 合谷 肺俞 列缺 C. 肺俞 太渊 章门 太白 丰隆; D·肺俞 尺泽 阳陵泉 太冲; E·肺俞 中府 列缺 膻中 丰隆	Which group of points should be selected to treat cough with discharge of yellowish phlegm, hot sensations in the body, headache, dry mouth, swollen and sore throat, a superficial and rapid. pulse, a thin layer of yellowish coating? A.B13 (Fèi Shū), Lu7 (Liè Quē), Li4 (Hé Gǔ), D14 (Dà Zhuī), Sj5 (Wài Guān); B. Lu5 (Chǐ Zé); Lu11 (Shǎo Shāng) Li4 (Hé Gǔ)B13 (Fèi Shū) Lu7 (Liè Quē); C. B13 (Fèi Shū); Lu9 (Tài Yuān) Lv13 (Zhāng Mén) Sp3 (Tài Bái) S40 (Fēng Lóng); D.B13 (Fèi Shū) Lu5 (Chǐ Zé); G34 (Yáng Líng Quán) Lv3 (Tài Chōng); E. B13 (Fèi Shū) Lu1

		(Zhōng Fǔ). Lu7 (Liè Quē); R17 (Shān Zhōng) S40 (Fēng Lóng).
1527	可以治疗各种血证的穴位是: A·血海; B·委中 C. ·太白; D·膈俞; E·心俞	Which point can treat various kinds of bleeding? A · Sp10 / Xuè Hǎi; B. B40 / Wěi Zhōng; C. · Sp3 / Tài Bái; D·B17 / Gé Shū; E. ·B15 / Xīn Shū.
1528	可用拇指尖重掐至局部酸胀，适宜于治疗落枕初始的是: A·风府; B·承山 C. ·风池; D·天柱; E·肩外俞·	In treating the initial stage of "falling off the pillow / neck pain with stiffnes", what point may be strongly pinched with the tip of thumb until local soring and swelling? A · D16 / Fēng Fǔ; B. B57 / Chéng Shān; C. G20 / Fēng Chí; D. ·B10 / Tiān Zhù; E. · Si14 / Jiān Wài Shū ·
1529	狂病发病年龄多见于: A·婴幼儿; B·儿童 C. ·青少年; D·中年; E·老年	What kind of people are more subject to the attack of maniac psychosis? A ·infants and babies; B ·children; C. ·youths; D ·middle age; E ·old age.
1530	狂病见有彻夜不眠、头痛躁狂、两目怒视等症状者辨证分型多属于: A·痰火扰神型 ·B·火盛伤阴型 C. ·气血瘀滞型; D·肝肾阴虚型; E·心脾两虚型	What syndrome accounts for maniac psychosis with sleeplessness all night, headache, jumpiness, both eyes with an angry look? A ·phlegm fire disturbing the spirit type; ·B ·flaming fire harming yin type; C. congestion and and blood coagulation type; D · yin deficiency of liver and kidneys type; E · heart and spleen deficiency type.
1531	狂病见有躁扰不安，恼怒多言，甚则登高而歌等症状者辨证分型多属于: A·痰火扰神; B·火盛伤阴 C. ·气血瘀滞; D·肝肾阴虚; E·心脾两虚	What syndrome accounts for maniac psychosis with jumpiness and anxiety, anger and excessive talking, climbing high mountains and singing? A. ·phlegm fire disturbing the spirit; B. ·flaming fire harming the yin; C. ·energy congestion and blood coagulation; D. yin deficiency of liver and kidneys; E. ·heart and spleen deficiency
1532	狂病治疗多选用: A·针灸并用; B·只灸不针 C. ·只针不灸; D·以针为主; E，·以灸为主 ·	How is maniac psychosis mostly treated? A. · both acupuncture and moxibustion; B. · moxibustion without acupuncture C. acupuncture without moxibustion; D. ·primarily by acupuncture; E，primarily by moxibustion ·
1533	阑尾切除术针麻可选用: A·睛明、合谷; B·合谷、内关 C. ·合谷、内关、臂臑; D·足三里、内关、切口旁压痛敏感点; E·脊中、命门	What points may be selected to perform appendectomy by acupuncture anaesthesia? A ·B1 / Jīng Míng，Li4 / Hé Gǔ; B · Li4 / Hé Gǔ，P6 / Nèi Guān; C. Li4 / Hé Gǔ，P6 / Nèi Guān，Li14 / Bì Nào; D · S36 / Zú Sān Lǐ，P6 / Nèi Guān 、pressure pain and sensitive points on the side of incision; E. D6 / Jǐ Zhōng, D4 / Mìng Mén.
1534	廉泉照海同用，具有什么作用? A·安神定志 ; B·舒筋通络 C. ·熄风化痰 ; D·和胃止呕 ; E·生津止渴	What is the function of combining R23 (Lián Quán) and K6 (Zhào Hǎi)? A. to secure the spirit and fix the will; B. to relax tendons and connect linking meridians; C. to stop wind and transform phlegm; D. to harmonize the stomach and stop vomiting; E to generate fluids and quench thirst.

1535	列缺、照海、鱼际、太溪、肺俞组成的处方适宜治疗：A·阴虚火旺之咽喉肿痛；B·肺阴不足之慢性咽喉炎 C. 痰瘀互结之慢性咽喉炎；D·风热壅肺之咽喉肿痛 E·肾阴亏虚之慢性咽喉炎	What can be treated by the prescription of points consisting of Lu7 / Liè Quē、 K6 / Zhào Hǎi，Lu10 / Yǔ Jì、K3 / Tài Xī，B13 / Fèi Shū? A · the yin deficiency with abundant fire type of swollen and painful throat; B ·the lungs yin deficiency with chronic laryngopharyngitis; C. the phlegm coagulation mixed with each other type of chronic laryngopharyngitis; D. · wind heat accumulated in the lungs type of swollen and painful throat; E. ·the kidney yin deprivation and deficiency type of chronic laryngopharyngitis.
1536	列缺穴与八卦中的( )相配：A·乾；B·坤 C. 坎；D·离；E 震	Lu7 / Liè Quē corresponds to which of the eight trigrams? A ·Qīan (1st trigram); B ·Kūn (8th trigram); C. Kǎn (6th trigram); D ·Lí (3rd trigram); E. Zhèn (4th trigram)
1537	列缺属什么特定穴：A·原穴；B·络穴 C. 郄穴；D·八会穴；E·交会穴	What kind of specially marked points does Lu7 / Liè Quē belong to? A · yuán xué / starting-points / source-points; B ·linking points, / luo points; C. fissural point / cleft point / xi point; D. ·eight influential points / ba hui xue; E ·meridian-meeting point
1538	临床痫证发作时，针刺可取：A.印堂间使太冲；B 百会水沟后溪 C. 百会太冲后溪；D 百会水沟太溪	In clinical practice, what points should be needled to deal with the attack of epilepsy? A. Yìn Táng; P5 (Jiān Shǐ) Lv3 (Tài Chōng); B. D20 (Bǎi Huì); D26 (Shuǐ Gōu, Rén Zhōng) Si3 (Hòu Xī); C. D20 (Bǎi Huì); Lv3 (Tài Chōng) Si3 (Hòu Xī); D. D20 (Bǎi Huì); D26 (Shuǐ Gōu, Rén Zhōng) K3 (Tài Xī).
1539	临床用于昏迷急救的穴位是：A.龈交；B，兑端 C. 水沟；D 神庭	In clinical practice, which point is used to treat acute cases of fainting? A. D28 (Yín Jiāo); B. D27 (Duì Duān); C. D26 (Shuǐ Gōu, Rén Zhōng); D. D24 (Shén Tíng).
1540	临床治疗外感咳嗽，针刺除选用肺俞尺泽外，还应选取 A.足三里；B 三阴交 C. 列缺；D 曲泽	In clinical practice, what other point should be selected to treat cough of external causes in addition to:B13 (Fèi Shū) and Lu5 (Chǐ Zé)? A. S36 (Zú Sān Lǐ); B. Sp6 (Sān Yīn Jiāo); C. Lu7 (Liè Quē); D. P3 (Qū Zé).
1541	临床中取颊车地仓合谷内庭太冲穴治疗 A.半身不遂 B.口眼歪斜 C. 闭证 D 脱证	In clinical practice, what disease is treated by the following points: S6 (Jiá Chē), S4 (Dì Cāng), Li4 (Hé Gǔ), S44 (Nèi Tíng), Lv3 (Tài Chōng)? A. hemiplegia; B. wry mouth and eyes; C. closed type; D. prolapsped type.
1542	流行性腮腺炎一般多流行于：A·冬季；B·夏季· C. ·冬、春季；D·秋、冬季，E·夏、秋季	In what season does epedemic parotitis mostly attack? A ·winter; B ·summer; C. ·winter, spring; D. ·autumn, winter; E. ·summer autumn
1543	梅核气治疗配穴可用：A·通里、三阴交；B·太溪、肾俞 C. ·列缺、照海；D·四白、光明；E·曲池、足三里	How to combine points to treat neurosis of the throat / globus hystericus? A · H5 / Tōng Lǐ，Sp6 / Sān Yīn Jiāo; B · K3 / Tài Xī，B23 / Shèn Shū; C. ·Lu7 / Liè Quē、 K6 / Zhào Hǎi; D · S2 / Sì Bái / ，G37 / Guāng Míng; E · Li11 / Qū Chí，S36 / Zú Sān

		Lǐ.
1544	梦遗除取关元大赫志室外，还可加用: A·心俞 小肠俞 内关; B·肾俞 三阴交 足三里' C. ·神门 ·心俞 内关; D·太溪 行间 中极; E·以上均不是.	In addition to R4 (Guān Yuán), K12 (Dà Hè), and B52 (Zhì Shì), which group of points should be selected to treat seminal emission with erotic dreams? A.B15 (Xīn Shū), P6 (Nèi Guān); B. B23 (Shèn Shū), Sp6 (Sān Yīn Jiāo), S36 (Zú Sān Lǐ); C. H7 (Shén Mén) B15 (Xīn Shū), P6 (Nèi Guān); D. K3 (Tài Xī) Lv2 (Xíng Jiān) R3 (Zhōng Jí); E. None of the above.
1545	某患者大便秘结欲便不得，嗳气频作，脘腹痞满，时有疼痛，纳食减少. 苔薄，脉弦，治宜选择: A. 支沟天枢.太冲; B. 支沟，气海上巨虚 C. 支沟大横上巨虚; D. 支沟.期门太冲; E. 以上都不是。	A patient suffers from constipation, with a desire for bowel movements but unable to do so, frequent bleching, congestion and fullness in the stomach and abdomen, occasional pain, poor appetite, thin, coating of the tongue, a wiry pulse; which group of points should be selected for treatment? A. Sj6 / Zhi Gōu S25 / Tiān Shū.Lv3 / Tài Chōng; B. Sj6 / Zhi Gōu ，R6 / Qì Hǎi S37 / Shàng Jù Xū; C. Sj6 / Zhi Gōu Sp15 / Dà Héng S37 / Shàng Jù Xū; D. Sj6 / Zhi Gōu.Lv14 / Qí Mén Lv3 / Tài Chōng; E. none of the above
1546	哪一种 "经络现象"不属于经穴压诊范畴: A·敏感; B·麻木 C. ·结节; D·丘疹; E·凹陷	Which “meridian phenomenon” does not fall within the scope of point pressing diagnopsis? A·oversensitivity; B·numbness; C. nodule; D·papule; E·depressed symptom.
1547	内伤头痛的肝阳上亢型，除取百会风池太溪外，还应取 A.太阳; B.太白 C. 太冲; D 太渊	In treating liver yang uprising type of vertigo due to internal injury, what other point should be selected in addition to D20 (Bǎi Huì), G20 (Fēng Chí), K3 (Tài Xī)? A. Tài Yáng; B. Sp3 (Tài Bái); C. Lv3 (Tài Chōng); D. Lu9 (Tài Yuān).
1548	内庭、十二井、支沟可用于治疗下列哪一型发热: A·风寒束表型; B·风热壅盛型 C. ·热在气分型; D·热入营血型; E·疫毒熏蒸型	What type of high fever may be treated by S44 / Nèi Tíng 、twelve well points、 and Sj6 / Zhi Gōu? A · wind cold constricting the superficial region type; B·accumulated wind heat in abundance type; C. ·heat at the energy level type; D. ·heat entering into nutritive and blood levels type; E. toxic pestilence steaming type.
1549	能治疗肺系疾病的穴位是: A·公孙; B·内关 C. ·外关; D·照海; E·后溪	What point can treat the diseases of the lungs system? A · Sp4 / Gōng Sūn; B · P6 / Nèi Guān; C. · Sj5 / Wài Guān; D · K6 / Zhào Hǎi; E · Si3 / Hòu Xī.
1550	能主治肝胆脾胃病症的输穴应分布在: A·背部; B·腰尻部 C. ·肩胛部; D·腋胁部; E·背腰部.	What is the distribution of points, which can be used to treat the diseases of the liver, gallbladder, spleen, and stomach? A·back region; B·lumbar-sacral region; C. shoulder and scapular regions; D axillary and costal region; E·back and lumbar region.
1551	年高形盛气虚之人，常针灸风市足三里二穴，其作用是: A·养生保健; B·防治感冒 C. ·调养脾胃; D·预防中风 E·以上都不是	What objective may be achieved. in treating “the elderly with strong body and deficient energy” at G31 (Fēng Shì) and S36 (Zú Sān Lǐ) by acupuncture and moxibustion among? A. to nourish the body and take measures to stay healthy;

		B. to prevent and treat the common cold; C. to regulate and nourish the spleen and stomach; D. to prevent wind stroke; E none of the above.
1552	扭伤的取穴原则，一般多采用：A·远部取穴法; B·辨证取穴法 C. 俞募配穴法; D·上下配穴法 ·E·，近部取穴法	What is the common principle of selecting points to treat sprain inhury? A ·Principles of selecting distal points; B ·Principles of selecting points according to syndrome; C. Methods of pairing off Bèi Shù Xué and Mù Xué; D ·Methods of pairing off upper and lower points; ·E. ·Principles of selecting neighboring points.
1553	疟疾的刺治最好时机是: A·疟疾发作前 1 日; B·疟疾发作前 2-3 小时 C. 疟疾发作前 1-2 小时; D·疟疾发作前半小时; E·疟疾发作时	When is the best time to treat malaria by acupuncture? A. one day prior to the appearance of symptoms; B. 2-3 hours prior to the appearance of symptoms; C. 1-2 hours prior to the appearance of symptoms; D. half an hour prior to the appearance of symptoms; E. during the appearance of symptoms.
1554	呕吐的针灸治疗原则不正确的是：A·虚证用补法; B·实证用泻法 C. ·胃阴不足者可用灸法； D·肝气犯胃者用泻法; E·胃阴不足者平补平泻	What principle of acupuncture therapy should not be applied to treat vomiting? A · use tonfication to treat deficiency syndrome; B · use sedation to treat excess syndrome C. ·use moxibustio to treat stomach yin deficiency ·; D. use sedation to treat ·liver energy offending the stomach; E · use neutral technique to treat stomach yin deficiency
1555	呕吐偏于痰饮者，除取主穴之外，还可加用: A·膻中 丰隆; B·脾俞 章门 C. ·下脘 璇玑; D·上脘 胃俞; E·阳陵泉 太冲.	In addition to major points, which group of points should be added to in treat vomiting with prodominent watery mucus in the stomach and intestines? A. R17 (Shān Zhōng); S40 (Fēng Lóng); B; B20 (Pí Shū); Lv13 (Zhāng Mén); C. R10 (Xià Wǎn); R21 (Xuán Jī); D. R13 (Shàng Wǎn); B21 (Wèi Shū); E G34 (Yáng Líng Quán). Lv3 (Tài Chōng).
1556	脾病用俞募配穴法可选: A，脾俞 期门; B·脾俞 京门 C. ·脾俞 中脘; D·脾俞 日月; E·脾俞 章门.	Using the combination of anterior mu point and posterior transport (back shu) point, which group of points may be selected to treat spleen disease? A; B20 (Pí Shū) Lv14 (Qí Mén); B; B20 (Pí Shū); G25 (Jīng Mén); C; B20 (Pí Shū); R12 (Zhōng Wǎn); D; B20 (Pí Shū) G24 (Rì Yuè); E. B20 (Pí Shū) Lv13 (Zhāng Mén).
1557	脾经湿热型带状疱疹可在基本处方基础上再加 （ ）以健脾运湿: A·外关; B·三阴交 C. ·上巨虚; D·曲泉; E·阳陵泉	What point may be added to the basic prescription of points to treat the spleen deficiency with damp heat type of herpes zoster to strengthen the spleen and mobilize dampness? A · Sj5 / Wài Guān; B · Sp6 / Sān Yīn Jiāo; C. · S37 / Shàng Jù Xū; D · Lv8 / Qū Quán; E · G34 / Yáng Líng Quán.
1558	脾虚痰瘀所致的扁平疣的治则是：A·三棱针点刺出血; B·只针不灸 C. 针灸并用，泻法; D·针刺为主，平补平泻; E·只灸不针，补法	What treatment principle may be applied to treat the spleen deficiency and phlegm coagulation type of flat wart? A · three-edged needles to let blood by dotted-needling; B · acupuncture without moxibustion; C. both acupuncture and moxibustion are applied，sedation; D · primarily by needling with neutral technique; E · moxibustion without acupuncture ， tonfication.

1559	脾俞胃俞关元肾俞合谷天枢上巨虚等穴组成处方，可以治疗：A·湿热痢; B·寒湿痢 C.·休息痢; D·噤口痢; E·以上均不是.	What can be treated by the combination of following points:; B20 (Pí Shū);B21 (Wèi Shū), R4 (Guān Yuán);B23 (Shèn Shū), Li4 (Hé Gǔ), S25 (Tiān Shū), S37 (Shàng Jù Xū)? A. damp heat dysentery; B. cold dampness dysentery; C. recurrent dysentery; D. fasting dysentery; E. none of the above.
1560	贫血的肾阴亏虚证型宜选用的治法是：A·只针不灸; B·只灸不针 C.·针灸并用; D·泻法; E，针补并灸	What method of treatment should be applied to treat anemia that belongs to kidneys yin deficiency syndrome? A.·· acupuncture without moxibustion; B.· moxibustion without acupuncture C. ·both acupuncture and moxibustion; D· sedation; E. acupuncture by tonfication with moxibustion.
1561	贫血兼两颧潮红者治疗可在基本处方上加：A·太阳 B·百会 C.·风池; D 太溪; E·风府	What points may be added to the basic prescription of points to treat anemia with pink cheeks? A · Tài yáng / sun / temple; ·B · D20 / Bǎi Huì; C. G20 / Fēng Chí; D K3 / Tài Xī; E;· D16 / Fēng Fǔ.
1562	贫血兼心悸者治疗可在基本处方上加：A·大椎; B·内关 C.·关元; D·膻中; E·足三里	What points may be added to the basic prescription of points to treat anemia with palpitation? A·D14 / Dà Zhuī; B · P6 / Nèi Guān; C. R4 / Guān Yuán; D · R17 / Shān Zhōng; E · S36 / Zú Sān Lǐ.
1563	贫血见有五心烦热可加（ ）清热除烦：A·心俞; B·内关 C.·关元; D·三阴交; E·劳宫	In treating anemia characterized by hot sensations in five hearts (chest, two palms, and two soles), what point should be added to clear heat and remove depression? A. ·B15 / Xīn Shū; B. · P6 / Nèi Guān; C. R4 / Guān Yuán; D. · Sp6 / Sān Yīn Jiāo; E. · P8 / Láo Gōng
1564	贫血见有遗精阳痿、畏寒自汗的证型属于：A·心脾两虚证; B·脾胃虚弱证 C.·脾肾阳虚证；D·肾阴亏虚证; E·以上都不是	What syndrome accounts for anemia with seminal emission, impotence, fear of cold and excessive perspiration? A ·heart-spleen deficiency syndrome; B · spleen-stomach deficiency and weakness syndrome; C. ·spleen kidneys yang deficiency syndrome; D. ·kidneys yin deficiency syndrome; E · none of the above.
1565	奇穴腰痛点主治是：A.慢性腰痛; B.急性腰痛 C. 肾虚腰痛; D 急性腰扭伤	What is the indication of the extraordinary point, Yāo Tòng Xué? A. chronic lumbago; B. acute lumbago; C. lumbago due to kidney deficiency; D. acute lumbar twisting injury.
1566	脐下腹痛宜取：A·下脘; B·天枢·C.·大横，D·上巨虚; E·关元	What point should be selected to treat abdominal pain below the umbilicus? A · R10 / Xià Wǎn; B · S25 / Tiān Shū; · C. · Sp15 / Dà Héng; D · S37 / Shàng Jù Xū; E · R4 / Guān Yuán.
1567	脐周腹痛宜取：A·中脘; B·大横 C.·天枢; D·气海; E·关元	What point should be selected to treat abdominal pain around the umbilicus? A · R12 / Zhōng Wǎn; B · Sp15 / Dà Héng; C. · S25 / Tiān Shū; D · R6 / Qì Hǎi; E · R4 / Guān Yuán.
1568	气血虚弱型眩晕的治则应是：A.平肝熄风滋水涵木; B.运脾和中除湿涤痰 C. 调理脾胃补益气血；D 补肾	In treating the energy and blood deficiency type of vertigo, what treatment principle should be applied? A. to calm the liver and stop wind, water and nourish

	调理脾胃补益气血; D 补肾益精培元固本	wood; B. to mobilize the spleen and harmonize the middle region, remove dampness and expel phlegm; C. to regulate the spleen and stomach, tone and benefit energy and blood; D. to tone the kidney and benefit essence, develop original energy and solidify the root.
1569	曲池治疗瘰疬时针刺方法为: A 直刺:B 斜刺;C 平刺向臂臑透刺;D 艾灸;E 放血.	What technique of insertion should be used to needle Li11 (Qū Chí) in the treatment of scrofula? A Perpendicular needle insertion (90 degrees): B Oblique needle insertion (40 to 60 degrees,); C. horizontal needle insertion all the way through upper arm; D. moxibustion; E. bloodletting..
1570	取百会心俞脾俞足三里穴可治疗 A.血虚头痛; B.痰浊头痛 C. 瘀血头痛; D 肝阳上亢头痛	What disease is treated by the following points: D20 (Bǎi Huì);B15 (Xīn Shū);B20 (Pí Shū), S36 (Zú Sān Lǐ)? A. blood deficiency headache; B. turbid phlegm headache; C. blood coagulation headache; D. liver yang uprising headache.
1571	取气海三阴交肾俞足三里等腧穴治疗 A.崩漏实证; B 崩漏虚证 C. 痛经实证; D 痛经虚证	What disease may be treated by the prescription, which includes: R6 (Qì Hǎi), Sp6 (Sān Yīn Jiāo);B23 (Shèn Shū), S36 (Zú Sān Lǐ), etc.? A. excessive syndrome of bleeding from the uterus / metrorrhagia and metrostaxis; B. deficiency syndrome of bleeding from the uterus / metrorrhagia and metrostaxis; C. excessive syndrome of (painful menstruation / dysmenorrhea); D. deficiency syndrome of (painful menstruation / dysmenorrhea).
1572	取心经、心包经和督脉穴为主可用于: A 心气不足证; B 心血亏虚证 C. 心火亢盛证; D 痰蒙心窍证; E 心脉瘀阻证	What can be treated by combining primary points on the heart, pericardium, and du mai / governing meridians? A heart energy deficiency syndrome; B heart blood deficiency syndrome; C. heart fire abundance syndrome; D phlegm blocking heart cavity syndrome; E syndrome of heart merdian blood coagulation.
1573	取翳风听会侠溪中渚为主穴主要治疗 A.牙痛; B 三叉神经痛 C. 目赤肿痛; D 耳聋耳鸣	What disease is to be treated by the prescription, which includes the following as the primary points: Sj17 (Yì Fēng), G2 (Tīng Huì), G43 (Xiá Xī), Sj3 (Zhōng Zhǔ)? A.toothache; B. trigeminala neuralgia; C. pink eyes with swelling and pain; D. ringing in ears and deafness.
1574	取足三里、太冲、肾俞治疗色盲, 属: A 标本兼治; B. 治标为主 C. 治本为主; D 加强调补肝肾、濡养目窍的作用; E 随症配穴	What is the treatment principle of using S36 / Zú Sān Lǐ, Lv3 / Tài Chōng, B23 / Shèn Shū to treat color blindness? A to treat symptoms and roots simultaneously; B treating symptoms as the primary principle; C. treating roots as the primary principle; D enhancing the regulation and tonfication of liver and kidneys、lubricating and nourishing eye cavities; E combination of points according to symptoms.
1575	热痹的治疗除在病变局部选, 穴外, 可再加: A 肾俞、关元; B 大椎、曲池 C. 内关、合谷; D 膈俞、血海; E 阴陵泉、足三里	In addition to selection of local points, what points may be added to treat hot rheumatism? A. B23 / Shèn Shū, R4 / Guān Yuán; B D14 / Dà Zhuī、Li11 / Qū Chí; C. P6 / Nèi Guān, Li4 / Hé Gǔ; D B17 / Gé

		Shū，Sp10 / Xuè Hǎi; E · Sp9 / Yīn Líng Quán，S36 / Zú Sān Lǐ
1576	热邪内蕴，多食即吐，呕吐酸苦热臭，口渴，喜寒恶热，大便秘结，脉数苔黄。除针刺主穴外，还可加用: A·上脘 胃俞 ; B·膻中 丰隆 C. 合谷 金津 玉液 ; D·大陵 中脘 ; E·内关 阳陵泉	In addition to needling major points, which group of points should be added to treat the following: hidden pathogenic heat, vomiting on excessive eating, vomiting food with a sour and bitter taste and a hot and offensive smell, thirst, fondness of chills and aversion to heat, constipation, a rapid pulse and yellowish coating? A; B23 (Shèn Shū) R13 (Shàng Wǎn); B. R17 (Shān Zhōng); S40 (Fēng Lóng); C. Li4 (Hé Gǔ); Jīn Jīn Yù Yè; D. P7 (Dà Líng) R12 (Zhōng Wǎn); E. P6 (Nèi Guān), G34 (Yáng Líng Quán).
1577	热证腹痛的治疗原则是: A.清热导滞行气止痛 B 温经散寒缓急止痛 C.通调气血缓急止痛 D 温运脾阳行气止痛	What treatment principle should be applied to treat hot abdominal pain? A. to clear heat and direct flow of congestion, promote energy flow and relieve pain; B. to warm meridians and disperse cold, slow down acute symptom and relieve pain; C. to connect and regulate energy and blood, slow down acute symptom and relieve pain; D. to warm and mobilize spleen yang, promote energy flow and relieve pain.
1578	妊娠呕吐加用三阴交、丰隆的治疗作用是：A·健脾和胃; B·补益脾胃 C. ·健脾化痰; D·开胃进食; E·清头明目	What is the function of adding Sp6 / Sān Yīn Jiāo，S40 / Fēng Lóng in treating morning sickness? A · to strengthen the spleen and stomach; B ·to tone and benefit spleen and stomach C. to strengthen the spleen and transform phlegm; D ·to improve appetite; E ·to clear the head and sharpen vision.
1579	妊娠呕吐选基本处方加灸中脘、天枢、针里内庭是治疗：A·脾胃虚弱者; B·痰饮阻滞者 C. ·肝胃不和者; D·伴神倦嗜卧者; E·伴厌食较重者	In treating morning sickness, moxibustion is applied to R12 / Zhōng Wǎn and S25 / Tiān Shū 、and acupuncture is applied to Lǐ nèi ting / medial inner yard, in addition to the basic prescription of points; what kind of patients is such additional measure intended to treat? A · patients with spleen-stomach deficiency and weakness; B · patients with watery phlegm obstruction and stagnation; C. ·patients with liver-stomach disharmony; D ·patients with fatigued spirits and love of lying down; E ·patients with more serious symptoms of anorexia / loss of appetite
1580	乳腺炎好发于：A 怀孕期; B·月经期 C. ·产后哺乳期; D·经前期; E·分娩期·	When does mastitis mostly attack? A during pregnancy; B ·during menstruation; C. ·Postnatal breast feeding period; D. ·premenstrual period; E ·during labor. ·
1581	乳腺增生病治疗所取主穴属：:A手少阳经穴; B··足阳明经穴 ·C·手阳明经穴; D·足少阴经穴; E，任脉穴.	To what meridian do primary points for treating hyperplasia of mammary glands belong? · A. points on the hand lesser yang meridians; B. ·points on the foot bright yang meridians; ·C · points on the hand bright yang meridians; D. · points on the foot lesser yin meridians; E.conception meridian / ren mai.
1582	乳汁不足乳房胀痛，应选用哪组处方?	Which group of points may be selected to treat galactostasis (scanty breast milk) and swollen pain in the

	A·膻中 乳根 少冲; B·中脘 乳根 少泽 C. ·期门 章门 足三里; D·膻中 乳根 少泽 期门; E·期门 膻中 足三里 脾俞.	breasts? A. R17 (Shān Zhōng), S18 (Rŭ Gēn), H9 (Shào Chōng); B. R12 (Zhōng Wăn), S18 (Rŭ Gēn) Si1 (Shào Zé); C. Lv14 (Qí Mén); Lv13 (Zhāng Mén) S36 (Zú Sān Lĭ); D. R17 (Shān Zhōng) S18 (Rŭ Gēn) Si1 (Shào Zé) Lv14 (Qí Mén); E. Lv14 (Qí Mén);. R17 (Shān Zhōng) S36 (Zú Sān Lĭ); B20 (Pí Shū).
1583	三叉神经第三支疼痛，局部取穴宜选: A·夹承浆; B·颧髎 C. ·迎香; D·翳风; E·以上均不是	Which point should be selected to treat trigeminal neuralgia of the 3rd. branch? A. Jiā Chéng Jiàng; B. Si18 (Quán Liáo); C. Li20 (Yíng Xiāng); D. Sj17 (Yì Fēng); E. None of the above.
1584	三焦的下合穴是: A·三阴交; B·委中 C. ·委阳; D·足三里	Which is the lower merging point on sanjiao / triple heate? A · Sp6 / Sān Yīn Jiāo; B. B40 / Wĕi Zhōng; C. B39 / Wĕi Yáng; D. · S36 / Zú Sān Lĭ.
1585	三阴交、阴陵泉可治疗下列哪一型胆绞痛: A·肝胆湿热型; B·肝胆气滞型 C. ·饮食积滞型; D·蛔虫妄动型 E·肝血不足型	What type of colic of gallbladder can Sp6 / Sān Yīn Jiāo, Sp9 / Yīn Líng Quán treat? A·liver allbladder damp heat type; B·liver and gallbladder energy; congestion type; C. ·accumulated and congested food type; D·disturbance of roundworm type; E · liver blood deficiency type.
1586	三阴交合谷同用，其临床效应是: A·清热; B·祛风 C. ·救逆; D·坠胎 E·醒神.	What is the c linical effect of combining Sp6 (Sān Yīn Jiāo) and Li4 (Hé Gŭ)? A. to clear heat; B·to expel wind; C. ·to rescue uprising; D·for abortion; E·to wake the spirit.
1587	色盲的针灸治则为: A·针灸并用; B·以针为主 C. ·以灸为主; D·只针不灸; E·只灸不针	What is the principle of treating color blindness by acupuncture-moxibustion? A · both acupuncture and moxibustion; B·primarily by acupuncture; C. ·primarily by moxibustion; D · acupuncture without moxibustion; E · moxibustion without acupuncture.
1588	疝修补术针麻应选用: A·足三里、中都; B·足三里、维道 C. ·足三里、上巨虚、D·足三里、带脉; E. 足三里、合谷	What points should be selected for acupuncture anaesthesia to perform repair of hernia? A · S36 / Zú Sān Lĭ, Lv6 / Zhōng Dū; B · S36 / Zú Sān Lĭ, G28 / Wéi Dào; C. · S36 / Zú Sān Lĭ, S37 / Shàng Jù Xū; D · S36 / Zú Sān Lĭ, G26 / Dài Mài; E. S36 / Zú Sān Lĭ, Li4 / Hé Gŭ.
1589	少府劳宫同用，其作用是? A·宁神志; B·泻心火 C. ·调心气; D·止盗汗; E·通经络.	What is the function of combining H8 (Shào Fŭ) and P8 (Láo Gōng)? A. to secure the spirit and will power; B·to sedate heart fire. C. ·to regulate heart energy; D. ·to stop night sweats; E. ·to connect master and linking meridians.
1590	少商放血主治: A目赤肿痛:B鼻衄不止:C牙痛咽喉肿痛;D小便不利;马便秘腹胀。	What disease may be treated by bloodletting at Lu11 (Shăo Shāng)? A. pink eyes with swelling and pain: B. incessant nosebleed: C. toothache and sore throat with swelling and pain; D. diminished urination; E. constipation and abdominal swelling.

1591	申脉与八脉交会穴中的( )相配：A·列缺；B·后溪 C. ·公孙; D·内关; E·照海	B62 / Shēn Mài may be paired with which of the meeting points of eight meridians? A ·Lu7 / Liè Quē; B · Si3 / Hòu Xī; C. Sp4 / Gōng Sūn; D · P6 / Nèi Guān; E · K6 / Zhào Hǎi.
1592	深刺易引起流产的穴位是:A 内关:B 至阴:C 太冲:D 合谷;E 关元。	What point can easily cause miscarriage by a deep insertion? A P6 / Nèi Guān; B. B67 / Zhì Yīn; C Lv3 / Tài Chōng;D Li4 / Hé Gŭ;E R4 / Guān Yuán.
1593	神门治痴呆症时刺法应该是: A 浅刺;B 深刺强刺；C 平刺:D 斜刺;E 雀啄刺。	What technique of insertion should be used to needle H7 (Shén Mén) in the treatment of idiocy? A. shallow insertion;B. deep and strong insertion; C. horizontal insertion: D. oblique insertion; E. sparrow pecking insertion.
1594	肾虚性耳鸣耳聋，治疗时除选主穴外，还可加用: A·少商 上星 ；B，肾俞 关元 C. ·外关 合谷 ；D·太冲 丘墟 ；E·以上都不是	In addition to needling major points, which group of points should be selected to treat deafness and ringing in the ears due to deficiency of the kidneys? A. Lu11 (Shǎo Shāng), D23 (Shàng Xīng); B. B23 (Shèn Shū); R4 (Guān Yuán); C. Sj5 (Wài Guān), Li4 (Hé Gŭ); D. Lv3 (Tài Chōng); G40 (Qiū Xū); E none of the above.
1595	肾虚引起的痛经主要表现为： A. 经期小腹冷痛，按之痛甚; B. 经前小腹隐痛，按之痛减 C. 经前小腹胀痛，胀甚于痛; D. 经后小腹胀痛，胀甚于痛; E.以上均不是。	What are the symptoms of period. pain due to kidney deficiency? A. Cold pain in lower abdomen during menstruation，pain getting worse on pressure; B. hidden pain in the lower abdomen before menstruation，pain getting better on pressure; C. swelling in the lower abdomen before menstruation，more swelling than pain; D. swelling in the lower abdomen after menstruation，more swelling than pain; E. none of the above。
1596	肾阳亏虚型崩漏的治则是：A·只针不灸，泻法; B·针灸并用，平补平泻 C. 只针不灸，补法; D·只针不灸，平补平泻; E，针灸并用，补法	What treatment principle may be applied to treat the kidney yang deprivation and deficiency type of bleeding from the uterus / metrorrhagia and metrostaxis? A · acupuncture without moxibustion ，sedation; B · both acupuncture and moxibustion are applied，neutral technique; C. acupuncture without moxibustion，tonfication; D · acupuncture without moxibustion，neutral technique; E.both acupuncture and moxibustion are applied，tonfication.
1597	十二经脉之气与奇经八脉相汇通的穴称：A·奇穴; B·八会穴 C. ·交会穴; D·八脉交会穴 E·十四经穴	What is the name of points on the twelve meridians, which connect the energy of twelve meridians with that of the eight extraordinary meridians? A · extraoprdinary points; B ·eight influential points / ba hui xue; C. ·meridian meeting points; D ·meeting points of eight meridians; E ·points on the fourteen meridians.
1598	实证便秘除取支沟天枢穴外，还应选取 A.大肠俞上巨虚 B 曲池内庭 C. ，上巨虚下巨虚; D 足三里中脘	Which group of points should be selected to treat the excess type of constipation in addition to Sj6 (Zhi Gōu) and S25 (Tiān Shū)? A; B25 (Dà Cháng Shū); S37 (Shàng Jù Xū); B. Li11 (Qū Chí); S44 (Nèi Tíng); C. S37 (Shàng Jù Xū); S39 (Xià Jù

		Xū); D. S36 (Zú Sān Lǐ) R12 (Zhōng Wǎn).
1599	实证便秘的治疗原则是：A.清热理气温中通便; B 健脾益气通导肠腑 C. 清热利湿通导肠腑; D. 清热理气通导肠腑	What treatment principle should be applied to treat the excess type of constipation? A. to clear heat and regulate energy, warm the middle reigon and promote bowel movements; B. to strengthen the spleen and benefit energy, direct the flow of congested. bowel of intestine; C. to clear heat and benefit dampness, direct the flow of congested. bowel of intestine; D. to clear heat and regulate energy, direct the flow of congested. bowel of intestine.
1600	实证胁痛应选用 A.章门 期门; B 期门，太冲 C. 太冲 阳陵泉; D 期门 阳陵泉	Which group of points should be selected to treat the excess type of hypochondriac pain? A. Lv13 (Zhāng Mén), Lv14 (Qí Mén); B. Lv14 (Qí Mén), Lv3 (Tài Chōng); C. Lv3 (Tài Chōng), G34 (Yáng Líng Quán); D. Lv14 (Qí Mén), G34 (Yáng Líng Quán).
1601	视网膜色素变性的针灸治则是：A·只针不灸; B·只灸不针 C. 针灸并用; D·先针后灸; E先灸后针	What is the treatment principle of treating pigmentary degeneration of retina by acupuncture-moxibustion? A · acupuncture without moxibustion; B · moxibustion without acupuncture; C. both acupuncture and moxibustion; D. acupuncture followed by moxibustion; E. moxibustion followed by acupuncture.
1602	适宜于胃阴不足证的是：A·针灸并用; B·重用灸法 C. ·针补加灸; D·泻法; E·平补平泻	How to treat stomach yin deficiency? A · simultaneous application of acupuncture-moxibustion; B ·intense moxibustion; C. ·acupuncture tonification supplemented by moxibusiotn; D · sedation; E · neutral technique
1603	手太阴肺经穴位中，治疗头项强痛当首选 A.中府; B. 尺泽 C. 列缺; D 鱼际	What is the best point on the lung meridian to treat stiffness and pain in the back of head and neck? A. Lu1 (Zhōng Fǔ); B Lu5 (Chǐ Zé); C. Lu7 (Liè Quē); D. Lu10 (Yǔ Jì).
1604	水沟、百会、内关、大椎、中冲宜用于治疗：A·气厥; B·血厥 C. ·痰厥; D·寒厥; E·热厥	What can be treated by the following points: D26 / Shuǐ Gōu / Rén Zhōng、 D20 / Bǎi Huì，P6 / Nèi Guān 、D14 / Dà Zhuī、 · P9 / Zhōng Chōng? A · energy uprising; B ·blood uprising C. ·phlegm uprising; D ·cold uprising; E ·heat uprising.
1605	水肿小便不利常选合穴: A·三阴交; B，阴陵泉 C. ·阳陵泉; D·委阳; E·水分	Which hé xué / terminal-point / sea-point is often selected to treat edema and decreased urination? A. · Sp6 / Sān Yīn Jiāo; B. Sp9 / Yīn Líng Quán; C. G34 / Yáng Líng Quán; D. · B39 / Wěi Yáng; E. · R9 / Shuǐ Fēn.
1606	髓病用八会穴治疗，应取: A·悬钟; B 阳陵泉 C. ·大杼; D·太渊; E·以上都不是.	Which of the following eight meeting points (ba hui xue) may be selected to treat the disease of marrow? A. G39 (Xuán Zhōng); B. G34 (Yáng Líng Quán); C. B11 (Dà Zhù); D. Lu9 (Tài Yuān); E. none of the above.
1607	所属经脉属水，"五行输"也属水的穴是：A·涌泉; B·昆仑 C. ·然谷; D·阴谷; E·委中	What meridian belongs to water, and its “flowing points / stream points / shu xue” among the five command points also belong to water? A · K1 / Yǒng Quán; B. B60 / Kūn Lún; C. K2 / Rán Gǔ; D. · K10 / Yīn Gǔ /; E. B40 / Wěi Zhōng.
1608	胎位不正时应艾灸: A·大	What point should be treated by moxibustion in case of

	敦; B 隐白 C. ·至阴; D·三阴交	fetus in wrong position? A · Lv1 / Dà, Dūn; B Sp1 / Yǐn Bái; C. 67 / Zhì Yīn; D · Sp6 / Sān Yīn Jiāo.
1609	太冲是何经的原穴：A·脾经; B·肝经 C. ·肾经; D·胃经; E·胆经	Tài Chōng is the “yuán xué / starting point / source point” of what meridian? A. ·spleen meridsian; B. ·liver meridian; C. ·kidneysmeridian; D. ·stomach meridian; E. · gallbladder meridian.
1610	太渊是八会穴中的：A.气会; B·血会 C. ·筋会; D·脉会; E·脏会	What kind of eight influential points / ba hui xue · does Lu9 / TàiYuān belong to?：A. energy meeting point; B ·blood meeting point; C. ·tendon meeting point; D. ·meridian meeting point; E ·viscera meeting point.
1611	痰火扰神型狂病治疗可在基本处方上加：A·神门、大钟; B·合谷、太冲 C. ·血海、膈俞; D 中脘、·神门·E·大钟。·三阴交	What point may be added to treat the phlegm fire disturbing the spirit type of maniac psychosis in addition to the basic prescription? A · H7 / Shén Mén，K4 / Dà Zhōng; B · Li4 / Hé Gǔ，Lv3 / Tài Chōng; C. Sp10 / Xuè Hǎi，B17 / Gé Shū; D R12 / Zhōng Wǎn 、H7 / Shén Mén; ·E · K4 / Dà Zhōng · Sp6 / Sān Yīn Jiāo.
1612	痰气郁结型癫病针灸治疗多用：A·以针为主; B·以灸为主 C. ·只针不灸; D·只灸不针; E·刺血为主	What therapy is applied to treat depressive psychosiskind of phlegm energy, congestion type? A ·primarily by acupuncture; B ·primarily by moxibustion; C. acupuncture without moxibustion; D · moxibustion without acupuncture; E ·primarily by bloodletting.
1613	痰湿中阻的眩晕症应选取哪一经的合穴: A.足阳明胃经; B·足厥阴肝经 C. ·足少阴肾经; D·足太阴脾经	Which meridian’s “hé xué / terminal point / sea point” should be selected to treat dizziness (giddiness / vertigo) due to phlegm dampness obstructing the middle region? A. foot bright yang stomach meridian; B. · foot decreasing yin liver meridian; C. ·foot lesser yin kidney meridian; D ·foot greater yin spleen meridian.
1614	提托穴可以治疗 A.胃下垂; B.肾下垂 C. 疝气; D 泄泻	What can Tí Tuō treat? A. gastroptosis; B. nephroptosis; C. hernia; D. diarrhea.
1615	天枢合谷上巨虚,中脘内庭内关同用，主要用于治疗: A·湿热痢; B·寒湿痢 C. 噤口痢; D·休息痢; E·以上均不是.	What can be treated by the combination of following points: S25 (Tiān Shū), Li4 (Hé Gǔ), S37 (Shàng Jù Xū), R12 (Zhōng Wǎn), S44 (Nèi Tíng), P6 (Nèi Guān)? A. damp heat dysentery; B. cold dampness dysentery; C. recurrent dysentery; D. fasting dysentery; E. none of the above.
1616	痛痹的治疗除在病变局部选穴外，可再加：A·阴陵泉、足三里; B·风池、风府，C·大椎、曲池; D·肾俞、关元; E·膈俞、血海	In addition to selection of local points，what points may be added to treat painful rheumatism? A. · Sp9 / Yīn Líng Quán，S36 / Zú Sān Lǐ; B. · G20 / Fēng Chí，D16 / Fēng Fǔ; C. ·D14 / Dà Zhuī、 Li11 / Qū Chí; D. B23 / Shèn Shū，R4 / Guān Yuán; E. ·B17 / Gé Shū，Sp10 / Xuè Hǎi.
1617	头痛，肢楚，鼻塞流涕，咽痒咳嗽，咯稀痰，恶寒无汗，脉浮紧，舌苔薄白。治疗取穴宜用: A·大椎 曲池 合谷 十宣;	Which group of points should be selected to treat the following: headache, pain in the limbs, nasal; congestion and discharge, itchy throat and cough, discharge of thin phlegm, aversion to chills and absence of perspiration, a

	B·大椎 曲池 合谷 外关 C. ·列缺 风池 合谷 风门; D·迎香 风池 外关 丰隆; E·太阳 肺俞 陶道 丰隆.	superficial and tight pulse, a thin layer of white coating on the tongue? A. D14 (Dà Zhuī) Li11 (Qū Chí) Li4 (Hé Gŭ) Shí Xuān; B. D14 (Dà Zhuī) Li11 (Qū Chí) Li4 (Hé Gŭ) Sj5 (Wài Guān); C. Lu7 (Liè Quē) G20 (Fēng Chí) Li4 (Hé Gŭ)B12 (Fēng Mén); D. Li20 (Yíng Xiāng) G20 (Fēng Chí) Sj5 (Wài Guān) S40 (Fēng Lóng); E. Tài Yáng;B13 (Fèi Shū), D13 (Táo Dào) S40 (Fēng Lóng).
1618	头痛、目痛急剧发作时，可在:( )穴点刺出血：A·迎香;B·太阳 C. ·少商; D·迎香;E·太冲	What point may be treated by dotted-needling to let blood for acute attack of headache and eye pain? A · Li20 / Yíng Xiāng; B · Tài yáng / sun / temple; C. Lu11 / Shăo Shāng; D · Li20 / Yíng Xiāng; E · Lv3 / Tài Chōng
1619	头晕目眩而兼四肢乏力面色恍白心悸失眠脉微细者，治疗时以选用哪组穴位最为合适? A·中脘 内关 解溪 丰隆; B·风池 肝俞 行间 侠溪 C. 脾俞 肾俞 气海 百会; D·百会 前顶 风池 曲池; E·百会 太阳 风池 列缺.	Which group of points should be selected to treat the following symptoms: dizziness and vertigo with weak four limbs, pale complexion, palpitation and insomnia, a feeble and fine pulse? A. R12 (Zhōng Wăn) P6 (Nèi Guān) S41 (Jiĕ Xī) S40 (Fēng Lóng); B. G20 (Fēng Chí)B18 (Gān Shū) Lv2 (Xíng Jiān) G43 (Xiá Xī); C. B20 (Pí Shū) B23 (Shèn Shū) R6 (Qì Hăi) D20 (Băi Huì); D. D20 (Băi Huì) D21 (Qián Dĭng) G20 (Fēng Chí) Li11 (Qū Chí); E. D20 (Băi Huì) Tài Yáng G20 (Fēng Chí) Lu7 (Liè Quē).
1620	头针治疗眩晕可取： A·额中线、额旁1线; B·顶中线、额旁1线 C. ·顶中线、枕下旁线; D·顶中线、枕上旁线;E·枕上正中线、枕下旁线	Which of the following should be selected to treat vertigo by scalp acupuncture? A · mid-forehead plane、 1st lateral plane on forehead; B · mid-vertex plane，1st lateral plane on forehead; C. · mid-vertex plane，lower-occipital lateral plane; D · mid-vertex plane，mid-occipital lateral plane; E · mid-occipital upper plane、 lower-occipital lateral plane.
1621	脱肛的治疗原则是： A.升提中气; B.益气固脱 C. 升提固脱; D 益气健脾	What treatment principle should be applied to treat prolapse of the anus? A. to elevate middle energy; B. to benefit energy and stabilize prolapse; C. to lift and stabilize prolapse; D. to benefit energy and strengthen the spleen.
1622	外感咳嗽兼有咽喉肿痛时，除取主穴外，宜加: A·鱼际 孔最; B·少商 尺泽 C. ，廉泉 太渊; D·天突 列缺; E·以上均不是	In addition to major points, which group of points should be added to treat cough with swelling and pain in the throat due to external causes? A · Lu10 / Yŭ Jì Lu6 / Kŏng Zuì; B · Lu11 / Shăo Shāng Lu5 / Chĭ Zé; C. R23 / Lián Quán Lu9 / TàiYuān; D · R22 / Tiān Tū Lu7 / Liè Quē; E · none of the above.
1623	外感咳嗽应选取: A·肺俞、尺泽、列缺; B·大椎、风门、尺泽 C. 肺俞、风门、列缺; D.大椎、肺俞、列缺	Which group of points should be selected to treat cough due to external cause? A. ·B13 / Fèi Shū ，Lu5 / Chĭ Zé Lu7 / Liè Quē; B. ·D14 / Dà Zhuī ·B12 / Fēng Mén ·Lu5 / Chĭ Zé; C. ·B13 / Fèi Shū ·B12 / Fēng Mén ·Lu7 / Liè Quē; D. D14 / Dà Zhuī 、B13 / Fèi Shū Lu7 / Liè Quē.
1624	外关穴与九宫中的()相配: A·一; B 二 C. 三; D·四; E·五	What number vorrespond to Sj5 / Wài Guān among the nine palaces? A 1; B 2 C. 3; D ·4; E ·5

1625	外关穴在治疗外感病方面的作用基本上与哪穴近似? A·大杼; B·肺俞 C. ·风池; D·曲池; E·印堂	Which of the following points has a similar effect as Sj5 (Wài Guān) in treating the diseases caused by external pathogens? A. B11 (Dà Zhù); B. B13 (Fèi Shū); C. G20 (Fēng Chí); D. Li11 (Qū Chí); E. Yìn Táng.
1626	委中穴主治除下列什么证以外的各症: A 急慢性腰痛;B 崩漏带下: C. 丹毒疔疮: D 腹痛吐泻; E 无汗癫疾。	Which of the following is NOT to be treated by B40 (Wěi Zhōng)? A. acute and chronic lumbago; B. vaginal bleeding with discharges; C. erysipelas and furuncle; D. abdominal pain with vomiting and diarrhea; E. depressive psychosis with no perspiration.
1627	痿证以肢体逐渐痿软无力，下肢为重，·微肿而麻木不仁，或足胫热感，小便赤涩，舌红、苔黄腻，脉滑数为主症，针灸治疗选穴在基本选穴的基础上，再配: A·脾俞、胃俞、章门、中脘; B·肝俞、肾俞、太冲、太溪 C. ·阴陵泉、中极; D·大椎、尺泽、肺俞、二间; E·内关、合谷、脾俞、胃俞	What points may be added in addition to the basic prescription of points for paralysis of limbs, lower limbs in particular, with light swelling, numbness, or hot sensation in the tibia, with red urine and difficult urination, red tongue，yellowish and greasy coating on the tongue，slippery and rapid pulse as major symptoms? A. B20 / Pí Shū，B21 / Wèi Shū，Lv13 / Zhāng Mén，R12 / Zhōng Wǎn; B. ·B18 / Gān Shū, B23 / Shèn Shū, Lv3 / Tài Chōng，K3 / Tài Xī; C. · Sp9 / Yīn Líng Quán，R3 / Zhōng Jí; D. ·D14 / Dà Zhuī、 Lu5 / Chǐ Zé，B13 / Fèi Shū，Li2 / Èr Jiān; E. · P6 / Nèi Guān，Li4 / Hé Gǔ，B20 / Pí Shū, B21 / Wèi Shū
1628	痿症肺热所致配穴时以下列哪组穴位为主? A 孔最中府劳宫;B 尺泽肺俞;C 尺泽.孔最列缺;D 中府.大椎少府;E 曲池尺泽，肺俞。	Which group of points should be selected to treat the hot lung type of paralysis? A. Lu6 [Kǒng Zuì] Lu1 [Zhōng Fǔ] P8 [Láo Gōng]; B Lu5 [Chǐ Zé] B13 [Fèi Shū]; C. Lu5 [Chǐ Zé]. Lu6 [Kǒng Zuì] Lu7 [Liè Quē]; D. Lu1 [Zhōng Fǔ] D14 [Dà Zhuī] H8 [Shào Fǔ]; E. Li11 [Qū Chí] Lu5 [Chǐ Zé] B13 [Fèi Shū]。
1629	胃肠积热之风疹，治法为：A·直接灸法; B·毫针泻法 C. ·平补平泻法; D·穴位注射法; E·三棱针点刺法	How to treat rubella due to gastroenteristic heat accumulation? A ·direct moxibustion; B · sedation by a minute needle; C. ·neutral technique of tonification and sedation; D · acupuncture points injection therapy; E · three-edged needles dotted-needling.
1630	胃大部切除术针麻应选用: A·足三里、中都; B·足三里、维道 C. ·足三里、上巨虚、D·足三里、带脉; E. 足三里、合谷	What points should be selected for acupuncture anaesthesia in subtotal amputation of the stomach? A · S36 / Zú Sān Lǐ，Lv6 / Zhōng Dū; B · S36 / Zú Sān Lǐ, G28 / Wéi Dào C. ·S36 / Zú Sān Lǐ，S37 / Shàng Jù Xū; D · S36 / Zú Sān Lǐ，G26 / Dài Mài; E. S36 / Zú Sān Lǐ, Li4 / Hé Gǔ.
1631	胃痛以中脘足三里为主穴的主要原因是: A. 中脘属局部取穴，足三里属循经远端取穴; B. 中脘属胃之募穴，足三里是:胃经之合穴 C. 中脘是足阳明经的交会穴，足三里是:胃经的合土穴; D. 中脘为腑之会穴，足三里是:胃之下合穴;	What is the primary rationale behind the practice of treating stomachache by R12 (Zhōng Wǎn) and S36 (Zú Sān Lǐ)? A. R12 / Zhōng Wǎn belongs to a local selection, S36 / Zú Sān Lǐ belongs to selection along the meridian, a distal selection; B. R12 / Zhōng Wǎn is the gathering point / mu point of the stomach, S36 / Zú Sān Lǐ is the hé xué / terminal-point / sea-point of the stomach; C. R12 / Zhōng

	E. 中脘是胃之募穴，足三里是:胃之下合穴。	Wăn is the meeting point of the bright yang meridian of foot，S36 / Zú Sān Lǐ is the terminal-point / sea-point and earth point; D. R12 / Zhōng Wăn is a meeting point of bowels，S36 / Zú Sān Lǐ is the lower merging point of stomach; E. R12 / Zhōng Wăn is the gathering point / mu point of stomach，S36 / Zú Sān Lǐ is the lower merging point of the stomach。
1632	胃下垂兼见嗳气、喜叹息者可在基本方的基础上加：A·期门; B·气海 C. ·足三里; D·百会; E·公孙	What method may be used to treat gastroptosis with belching and love of sighing? · A. Lv14 / Qí Mén; B · R6 / Qì Hăi; C. S36 / Zú Sān Lǐ; D. · D20 / Băi Huì; E. · Sp4 / Gōng Sūn
1633	胃下垂症见恶心者可在基本方的基础上加：A·太冲; B·脾俞 C. ·足三里; D·内关; E·胃俞	What method may be used to treat gastroptosis with nausea? A · Lv3 / Tài Chōng; B ·; B20 / Pí Shū; C. S36 / Zú Sān Lǐ; D · P6 / Nèi Guān; E. B21 / Wèi Shū.
1634	胃阴不足型胃痛一般采用：A·针灸并用; B·只针不灸 C. ·只灸不针; D·针灸皆可; E·针灸皆不宜	What method is normally used to treat the stomach yin deficiency type of stomachache? A · both acupuncture and moxibustion; B · acupuncture without moxibustion; C. moxibustion without acupuncture; D · either acupuncture or moxibustion; E · neither acupuncture nor moxibustion
1635	胃俞足三里神门三阴交四穴同用，可以治疗哪一类型的失眠? A·心脾亏损型 ; B·肾气不足型 C. ·心胆气虚型 ; D·脾胃不和型 ; E，肝阳上扰型	Which type of insomnia may be treated by the combination of the following four points:; B21 (Wèi Shū), S36 (Zú Sān Lǐ), H7 (Shén Mén), Sp6 (Sān Yīn Jiāo)? A. deficiency of heart and spleen; B. insufficient kidney energy; C. energy deficiency of heart and gallbladder; D. disharmony between spleen and stomach E liver yang disturbing upward.
1636	无脉症宜选: A·尺泽 B·孔最 C·列缺 D·太渊 E·鱼际	What point should be selected to treat pulselessness? A · Lu5 / Chǐ Zé; B · Lu6 / Kŏng Zuì; C. ·Lu7 / Liè Quē; D. · Lu9 / TàiYuān; E. · Lu10 / Yŭ Jì.
1637	郄会配穴治哮喘的组穴是：A·膻中、中府; B¨膻中、孔最 C. ·肺俞、膻中; D·中府、肺俞; E·均不是	Which group of points should be selected to treat asthma according to the principle of ·combining a fissural point / cleft point / xī xué with an eight meeting point / eight influential point / bā huì xué? A · R17 / Shān Zhōng，Lu1 / Zhōng Fŭ; B¨ R17 / Shān Zhōng，Lu6 / Kŏng Zuì; C. ·B13 / Fèi Shū，R17 / Shān Zhōng; D · Lu1 / Zhōng Fŭ，B13 / Fèi Shū; E ·none of the above
1638	下合穴的主治与下列哪类穴位的主治近似? A·(背)俞穴; B·募穴 C. ·络穴; D·郄穴; E·原穴	Which of the following has a similar therapeutic function as the lower merging points (xia he xue)? A. back shu points (bei shu xue); B. gathering points (mu xue); C. linking points, (luo xue); D. fissural points (xi xue) E original points (yuan points or source points).
1639	下列不属于低血压病治则的是：A·活血化瘀; B·补益心脾 C. ·调和气血; D·补肾充髓 E，温阳化气	Which treatment principle should not be applied to treat hypotension? A ·to activate blood and transform coagulation; B to tone

		and benefit heart and spleen; C. ·to regulate and harmonize energy and blood; D ·to tone kidneys and fill marrow; E，to warm yang and transform energy.
1640	下列不属于胃火上逆型呃逆的临床表现的是：A·呃声洪亮有力，冲逆而出；B·口臭烦渴，喜冷饮 C. ·呃声低沉无力；D·尿赤便秘 E·苔黄燥， ·脉滑数	Which symptom does not belong to the clinical manifestion of stomach fire uprising type of hiccups? A ·hiccups produing a high-pitched and quick noise; B ·bad breath, depression, thirst，love of cold drink; C. ·hiccups producing a lowand weak noise; D ·reddish urine with constipation E · yellowish and dried coating on the tongue slippery and rapid pulse.
1641	下列不属于胃下垂的症状为：A·面色无华；B·腹部坠胀不适 C. ·食少乏力；D·两颧潮红 E·形体消瘦	Which is not a symptom of gastroptosis? A ·dull complexion; B ·falling and distension and discomfort in the abdominal region; C. ·poor appetite and lack of energy; D ·reddish cheeks; E. ·skinny body
1642	下列不属俞募配穴的是：A·肝俞、期门；B·心俞、·巨阙 C. ·厥阴俞、膻中 ·D. 脾俞、中脘 E·以下都不是	Which of the following does not fall within the principle of combinging back shu points and mu points? A. ·B18 / Gān Shū，Lv14 / Qí Mén; B. ·B15 / Xīn Shū R14 / Jù Què; C. ·B14 / Jué Yīn Shū，R17 / Shān Zhōng; ·D. B20 / Pí Shū，R12 / Zhōng Wǎn; E. · none of the above.
1643	下列不属原络配穴的是：A·太冲、光明；B·太溪、大钟 C. ·神门、支正；D·太渊、偏历 E.阳池、内关	Which of the following does not belong to the principle of combining a “starting point / source point / original point / yuán xué” with “a linking point / luo point”? A · Lv3 / Tài Chōng，G37 / Guāng Míng; B · K3 / Tài Xī，K4 / Dà Zhōng; C. H7 / Shén Mén，Si7 / Zhi Zhèng; D · Lu9 / TàiYuān，Li6 / Piān Lì; E. Sj4 / Yáng Chí，P6 / Nèi Guān
1644	下列除（）外，都可用于治疗阴虚火旺型遗精： A·会阴；B·关元 C. ·肾俞；D·阴陵泉；E·太溪	Which of the following cannot treat the yin deficiency with abundant fire type of seminal emission? A · R1 / Huì Yīn; B · R4 / Guān Yuán; C. ·B23 / Shèn Shū; D · Sp9 / Yīn Líng Quán; E. · K3 / Tài Xī
1645	下列除（ ）外均为针刺治疗呃逆的基本处方用穴：A·膈俞；B·足三里 C. ·太冲；D·天突；E·膻中	Which point does not belong to the basic prescription of points to treat hiccups? A. ·B17 / Gé Shū; B. · S36 / Zú Sān Lǐ; C. ·Lv3 / Tài Chōng; D. · R22 / Tiān Tū; E. · R17 / Shān Zhōng
1646	下列除（）外针麻效果好：A·头面部；B·颈部 C. ·胸部；D·会阴部；E·五官	What regions of points cannot produce good effect of acupuncture anaesthesia? A ·head-face region; B ·neck region; C. ·chest region; D · perineum region; E. ·region of five senses
1647	下列耳穴中除（）外，都可用于治疗慢性疲劳综合征：A·心、肾；B·肝、脾 C. ·脑、皮质下；D·肺、气管；E·神门、交感	Which auricular point cannot treat chronic fatigue syndrome? A ·heart、kidneys; B ·liver、spleen; C. · brain，subcortex; D ·lungs、 trachea; E · H7 / Shén Mén，sympathetic
1648	下列耳穴中除（）外，都可治疗戒毒综合征：A·肺 ·B·口 C. ·脾；D·皮质下；E·神门	What auricular point cannot treat abstinence syndrome? A ·lungs; ·B · mouth; C. ·spleen; D · subcortex; E · H7 / Shén Mén
1649	下列耳穴中除（）外，都可治疗戒毒综合征出现腹痛、	What auricular point cannot treat abstinence syndrome with abdominal pain and diarrhea?

	腹泻者：A·大肠；B·胃 C. ·腹; D·交感; E·肺	A ·large intestine; B ·stomach; C. ·abdomen; D · sympathetic; E ·lungs
1650	下列干支按阴阳相合的规律应是：A·丙未; B·庚子 C. ·甲丑; D·丁亥 E·辛酉	Which is a correct combination of yin-yang combination of stem-branch? A. ·Bǐng-Weì; B. ·Gēng-Zǐ; C. ·Jiǎ-Chǒu; D. ·Dīng-Hài; E ·Xīn-Yǒu.
1651	下列干支中不配属夏的是：A·丙; B·丁·C. ·己; D·巳 E午	Which stem or branch does not correspond to summer? A. ·Bǐng; B. ·Dīng; · C. ·Jǐ; D. ·Sì; E. Wǔ
1652	下列各项除（）外均可治疗胃下垂：A·公孙; B·内关 C. ·足三里; D·大陵; E·百会	Which point cannot treat gastroptosis? A · Sp4 / Gōng Sūn; B · P6 / Nèi Guān; C. · S36 / Zú Sān Lǐ; D · P7 / Dà Líng; E · D20 / Bǎi Huì
1653	下列各项中，除（）外，都能治疗阴虚火旺型失眠：A·关元; B·太溪 C. ·安眠; D·太冲; E·涌泉	Which of the following cannot treat insomenia due to abundant deficiency fire? A · R4 / Guān Yuán; B · K3 / Tài Xī; C. Ān mián / good sleep; D · Lv3 / Tài Chōng; E · K1 / Yǒng Quán.
1654	下列各项中除（）外，都能治疗心肾阳虚之哮喘：A·肺俞; B大椎 C. ·中府; D·列缺; E·关元	Which cannot treat asthma that belongs to treat asthma due to heart-kidneys yang deficiency? A ·B13 / Fèi Shū; BD14 / Dà Zhuī; C. · Lu1 / Zhōng Fǔ; D ·Lu7 / Liè Quē; E · R4 / Guān Yuán.
1655	下列各项中除（）外，·都能用于痰浊中阻型痴呆的治疗：A·足三里 ，B 大钟 C. ·悬钟 ·D·委中 ; E·中脘	Which point is not used to treat idiocy due to turbid phlegm obstruction? A. · S36 / Zú Sān Lǐ; B. K4 / Dà Zhōng; C. ·G39 / Xuán Zhōng ·D. B40 / Wěi Zhōng ·; E · R12 / Zhōng Wǎn
1656	下列各项中除（）外，都可清热利湿通淋：A·中极; B·气海 C. ·委阳; D·肾俞; E·京门	What point cannot clear heat, benefit dampness, and treat stranguria? A · R3 / Zhōng Jí; B · R6 / Qì Hǎi; C. B39 / Wěi Yáng; D. B23 / Shèn Shū; E · G25 / Jīng Mén
1657	下列各项中除（）外，都可应用于抗衰老：A·足三里; B·合谷 C. ·关元; D·百会; E·肾俞	What point cannot be applied to antiaging? A. · S36 / Zú Sān Lǐ; B. · Li4 / Hé Gǔ; C. ·R4 / Guān Yuán; D. · D20 / Bǎi Huì; E. B23 / Shèn Shū
1658	下列各项中除（）外，都可应用于抗衰老：A·皮肤针; B·耳针 C. ·隔药饼灸; D·穴位注射; E·三棱针	What type of therapy cannot be applied for antiaging? A · skin acupuncture; B · auricular acupuncture; C. moxibustion with herbs and cake in between skin and moxa stick; D · acupuncture points injection therapy; E · three-edged needles.
1659	下列各项中除（）外，都能补益肝肾：A·三阴交; B·太溪 C. ·阳陵泉; D·肝俞; E·肾俞	What point cannot tone and benefit liver and kidneys? A. · Sp6 / Sān Yīn Jiāo; B. · K3 / Tài Xī; C. ·G34 / Yáng Líng Quán; D. ·B18 / Gān Shū; E. B23 / Shèn Shū
1660	下列各项中除（）外，都能补益气血，用于治疗气血不足型眩晕：A·气海; B·足三里 C. ·血海 D·脾俞; E·合谷	Which point cannot tone energy and blood in the treatment of vertigo-dizziness due to treat yin deficiency of liver and kidneys? A. · R6 / Qì Hǎi; B. · S36 / Zú Sān Lǐ; C. Sp10 / Xuè Hǎi; D. B20 / Pí Shū; E. · Li4 / Hé Gǔ
1661	下列各项中除（）外，都能疏肝理气：A·行间; B·肝俞	What point cannot disperse the liver and regulate energy?

	C. ·日月; D·太冲; E. 关元	A. · Lv2 / Xíng Jiān; B. ·B18 / Gān Shū; C. G24 / Rì Yuè; D. · Lv3 / Tài Chōng; E. R4 / Guān Yuán
1662	下列各项中除 () 外，都能用于治疗尿失禁：A·中极；B·膀胱俞 C. ·肾俞；D·中府E·三阴交	Which point cannot treat incontinence of urination: A. · R3 / Zhōng Jí; B. · B28 / Páng Guāng Shū; C. B23 / Shèn Shū; D. · Lu1 / Zhōng Fŭ; E. · Sp6 / Sān Yīn Jiāo
1663	下列各项中除 () 外，都能治疗 黄褐斑 ：A·迎香；B·阴陵泉 C. ·颧髎；D·血海；E·三阴交	What point cannot treat chloasma (skin turning brown)? A. · Li20 / Yíng Xiāng; B. · Sp9 / Yīn Líng Quán; C. · Si18 / Quán Liáo; D. · Sp10 / Xuè Hăi; E. · Sp6 / Sān Yīn Jiāo
1664	下列各项中除 () 外，都能治疗抽搐：A·筋缩；B·阳辅 C. ·合谷；D·阳陵泉；E·劳宫	What point cannot treat twitching? A ·D8 / Jīn Suō; B · G38 / Yáng Fŭ; C. · Li4 / Hé Gŭ; D · G34 / Yáng Líng Quán; E · P8 / Láo Gōng.
1665	下列各项中除 () 外，都能治疗带状疱疹：A·支沟；B·阴陵泉 C. ·行间；D·夹脊穴；E·风市	Which is not the point to treat herpes zoster: A · Sj6 / Zhi Gōu; B · Sp9 / Yīn Líng Quán; C. · Lv2 / Xíng Jiān; D · Huá tuó jiā jí / Dr Huatuo's clippings of spine; E · G31 / Fēng Shì
1666	下列各项中除 () 外，都能治疗单纯性肥胖症：A·风池；B·曲池 C. ·上巨虚；D·阴陵泉；E·合谷	Which point cannot treat simple obesity? A · G20 / Fēng Chí; B · Li11 / Qū Chí; C. ·S37 / Shàng Jù Xu; D · Sp9 / Yīn Líng Quán; E · Li4 / Hé Gŭ
1667	下列各项中除 () 外，都能治疗风寒感冒：A·风池；B·大椎 C. ·尺泽；D·列缺；E合谷·	Which point cannot be used to treat wind; cold type of the common; Cold? A · G20 / Fēng Chí; B ·D14 / Dà Zhuī; C. · Lu5 / Chĭ Zé; D ·Lu7 / Liè Quē; E. Li4 / Hé Gŭ ·
1668	下列各项中除 () 外，都能治疗风寒咳嗽：A·肺俞；B·中府 C. ·尺泽；D·列缺；E·风门	·Which point cannot treat wind-cold type of cough? A ·B13 / Fèi Shū; B · Lu1 / Zhōng Fŭ; C. · Lu5 / Chĭ Zé; D ·Lu7 / Liè Quē; E ·B12 / Fēng Mén
1669	下列各项中除 () 外，都能治疗肝肾阴虚型痫病：A·肝俞 ；B·太冲 C. ·太溪；D·肾俞；E·合谷	Which of the following points cannot treat epilepsy due to yin deficiency of liver and kidneys? A ·B18 / Gān Shū ·; B. · Lv3 / Tài Chōng; C. · K3 / Tài Xī; D. B23 / Shèn Shū; E · Li4 / Hé Gŭ
1670	下列各项中除 () 外，都能治疗肝郁型失眠： A·安眠；B·行间 C. ·尺泽；D·风池；E·太冲	Which of the following cannot treat insomenia of liver congestion syndrome? A · Ān mián / good sleep; B · Lv2 / Xíng Jiān; C. Lu5 / Chĭ Zé; D · G20 / Fēng Chí; E · Lv3 / Tài Chōng
1671	下列各项中除 () 外，都能治疗感冒：A. 合谷；B. 风门 C. 外关；D. 肩贞；E. 足三里	Which point cannot be used to treat the common cold? A. Li4 / Hé Gŭ; B.B12 / Fēng Mén; C. Sj5 / Wài Guān; D. Si9 / Jiān Zhēn; E. S36 / Zú Sān Lĭ
1672	下列各项中除 () 外，都能治疗高热：A·合谷；B·大椎 C. ·外关；D·内关；E·曲池	What point cannot treat high fever? A · Li4 / Hé Gŭ; B ·D14 / Dà Zhuī; C. · Sj5 / Wài Guān; D · P6 / Nèi Guān; E · Li11 / Qū Chí
1673	下列各项中除 () 外，都能治疗寒厥：A·神阙；B·关元 C. ·合谷；D·百会 ·E·水沟	What point cannot treat cold uprising? A · R8 / Shén Què; B · R4 / Guān Yuán; C. · Li4 / Hé Gŭ; D · D20 / Băi Huì; ·E · D26 / Shuĭ Gōu / Rén Zhōng
1674	下列各项中除 () 外，都能治疗惊恐伤肾型阳痿：A·中极；B·肾俞 C. ·三阴交；	Which of the following cannot treat shock and fear harming the kidney type of impotence?

	D·神门; E·阴陵泉	A·R3 / Zhōng Jí; B. B23 / Shèn Shū C. ·Sp6 / Sān Yīn Jiāo; D·H7 / Shén Mén; E·Sp9 / Yīn Líng Quán
1675	下列各项中除 () 外，都能治疗竞技紧张综合征：A·百会; B·四神聪 C. ·神门; D·内关; E·关元	What point cannot treat competitive tension syndrome? A·D20 / Bǎi Huì; B·Sì shén Cōng / four spiritual intelligences; C. ·H7 / Shén Mén; D·P6 / Nèi Guān; E·R4 / Guān Yuán
1676	下列各项中除 () 外，都能治疗咳嗽：A.太渊; B·列缺 ...C·尺泽; D·内关 ·E·肺俞	Which point cannot treat cough? A. Lu9 / TàiYuān; B·Lu7 / Liè Quē; C·Lu5 / Chǐ Zé; D·P6 / Nèi Guān; ·E·B13 / Fèi Shū
1677	下列各项中除 () 外，都能治疗气血不足型闭经：A·血海; B·气海 C. ·大椎; D·三阴交; E·脾俞 ·	What point cannot treat the energy-blood deficiency type of Suppression of Menstruation / Amenorrhea? A·Sp10 / Xuè Hǎi; B·R6 / Qì Hǎi C. ·D14 / Dà Zhuī; D·Sp6 / Sān Yīn Jiāo; E·; B20 / Pí Shū
1678	下列各项中除 () 外，都能治疗气血虚弱型抽搐：A·三阴交; B·气海 C. ·合谷; D·阳陵泉; E·劳宫	What point cannot treat the blood deficiency and weakness type of twitching? A·Sp6 / Sān Yīn Jiāo; B·R6 / Qì Hǎi; C. ·Li4 / Hé Gǔ; D·G34 / Yáng Líng Quán; E·P8 / Láo Gōng
1679	下列各项中除 () 外，都能治疗雀斑：A·迎香; B·印堂 C. ·合谷; D·关元; E·三阴交	What point cannot treat freckle? A·Li20 / Yíng Xiāng; B·Yìn táng / midpoint between eyebrows / seal hall; C. Li4 / Hé Gǔ; D·R4 / Guān Yuán; E·Sp6 / Sān Yīn Jiāo
1680	下列各项中除 () 外，都能治疗热厥：A·大椎; B·关元 C. ·中冲; D·百会; E·水沟	What point cannot treat heat uprising? A·D14 / Dà Zhuī; B·R4 / Guān Yuán; C. ·P9 / Zhōng Chōng; D·D20 / Bǎi Huì; E·D26 / Shuǐ Gōu / Rén Zhōng
1681	下列各项中除 ( ) 外，都能治疗乳腺炎：A¨膻中; B·肩井 C. ··期门; D·孔最; E·乳根	Which point cannot treat mastitis? A¨ R17 / Shān Zhōng; B·G21 / Jiān Jǐng; C. ·Lv14 / Qí Mén; D·Lu6 / Kǒng Zuì; E·S18 / Rǔ Gēn
1682	下列各项中除 ( ) 外，都能治疗乳腺增生病：A·内关; B·太冲 C. **乳根**; D·屋翳; E·少府'	Which of the following points cannot treat hyperplasia of mammary glands? A·P6 / Nèi Guān; B·Lv3 / Tài Chōng; C. S18 / Rǔ Gēn; D·S15 / Wū Yì; E·H8 / Shào Fǔ '
1683	下列各项中除 () 外，都能治疗肾绞痛：A·肾俞; B·膀胱俞 C. ·三阴交; D·梁丘; E，京门	What point cannot treat renal colic? A. B23 / Shèn Shū; B. B28 / Páng Guāng Shū; C. Sp6 / Sān Yīn Jiāo; D·S34 / Liáng Qiū; E，G25 / Jīng Mén
1684	下列各项中除 () 外，都能治疗湿热浸淫型eczema：A·曲池; B·三阴交 C. ·脾俞 D·肺俞; E·膈俞	What point cannot treat the spleen deficiency with hidden dampness type of eczema? A·Li11 / Qū Chí; B·Sp6 / Sān Yīn Jiāo; C. ·B20 / Pí Shū; D·B13 / Fèi Shū; E·B17 / Gé Shū
1685	下列各项中除 () 外，都能治疗脱肛：A·百会; B.大肠俞 C. ·长强; D·合谷; E·承山	Which point cannot treat proctoptosis / prolapse of anus? A·D20 / Bǎi Huì; B. B25 / Dà Cháng Shū; C. D1 / Cháng Qiáng; D·Li4 / Hé Gǔ; E·; B57 / Chéng Shān
1686	下列各项中除 () 外，都能治疗胃痉挛：A·孔最; B·中脘 C. ·足三里; D·天枢; E·神阙	Which point cannot treat gastrospasm? A·Lu6 / Kǒng Zuì; B·R12 / Zhōng Wǎn; C. ·S36 / Zú Sān Lǐ; D·S25 / Tiān Shū; E·R8 / Shén Què
1687	下列各项中除 () 外，都能治疗心绞痛：A·内关; B·郄门 C. ·阴郄; D·命门; E·后	Which point cannot treat angina pectoris? A·P6 / Nèi Guān; B·P4 / Xī Mén; C. ·H6 / Yīn Xī; D·D4 /

	门 C. ·阴郄; D ·命门; E ·巨阙	Mìng Mén; E · R14 / Jù Què
1688	下列各项中除 () 外，都能治疗心绞痛心脾两虚者：A. 心俞、脾俞; B ·中极、阳陵泉 C. ·阴郄、足三里; D ·巨阙、内关; E ·郄门、膻中	Which point cannot treat the heart and spleen deficiency type of angina pectoris? A.B15 / Xīn Shū，B20 / Pí Shū; B · R3 / Zhōng Jí，G34 / Yáng Líng Quán; C. · H6 / Yīn Xī，S36 / Zú Sān Lǐ; D · R14 / Jù Què，P6 / Nèi Guān; E · P4 / Xī Mén，R17 / Shān Zhōng
1689	下列各项中除 () 外，都能治疗心绞痛心肾阳虚者：A ·心俞、肾俞; B ·厥阴俞、阴郄 C. ·关元、足三里; D ·巨阙、内关; E ·郄门、膻中	Which point cannot treat the heart and kidneys yang deficiency type of angina pectoris? A ·B15 / Xīn Shū，B23 / Shèn Shū; B ·B14 / Jué Yīn Shū，H6 / Yīn Xī; C. R4 / Guān Yuán，S36 / Zú Sān Lǐ; D · R14 / Jù Què，P6 / Nèi Guān; E · P4 / Xī Mén，R17 / Shān Zhōng
1690	下列各项中除 () 外，都能治疗虚脱汗出肢冷：·A ·神阙; B ·关元 C. ·合谷; D ·百会; E ·命门	What point cannot treat deficient prostration with perspiration and cold limbs? · A · R8 / Shén Què; B · R4 / Guān Yuán; C. · Li4 / Hé Gǔ; D · D20 / Bǎi Huì; E · D4 / Mìng Mén
1691	下列各项中除 () 外，都能治疗血栓闭塞性脉管炎：A ·中脘; B ·阴陵泉 ·C ·气海; D ·关元; E ·膈俞	Which point cannot treat thrombo-embolia angitis? A · R12 / Zhōng Wǎn; B · Sp9 / Yīn Líng Quán; ·C · R6 / Qì Hǎi; D · R4 / Guān Yuán; E ·B17 / Gé Shū
1692	下列各项中除 () 外，都能治疗血虚风燥型神经性皮炎：A ·合谷; B ·曲池 C. ·血海; D 委中; E ·大椎	Which point cannot treat the blood deficiency and wind dryness type of neurodermatitis? A · Li4 / Hé Gǔ; B · Li11 / Qū Chí; C. · Sp10 / Xuè Hǎi; D. B40 / Wěi Zhōng; E ·D14 / Dà Zhuī
1693	下列各项中除 () 外，都能治疗牙痛：A ·太阳; B ·下关 C. 颊车; D 内庭; E ·合谷	Which point cannot treat toothache? A · Tài yáng / sun / temple; B · S7 / Xià Guān; C. S6 / Jiá Chē; D S44 / Nèi Tíng; E · Li4 / Hé Gǔ
1694	下列各项中除 () 外，都能治疗瘿病气阴两虚证：A ·天突、膻中; B ·合谷、足三里 C. ·三阴交、丰隆; D ·太冲、内关; E ·瘿肿局部	Which of the following cannot treat goiter due to deficiency of energy and yin? A · R22 / Tiān Tū，R17 / Shān Zhōng; B · Li4 / Hé Gǔ，S36 / Zú Sān Lǐ; C. · Sp6 / Sān Yīn Jiāo，S40 / Fēng Lóng; D · Lv3 / Tài Chōng，P6 / Nèi Guān; E ·local goiter swelling.
1695	下列各项中除 () 外，都能治疗瘀浊阻塞型癃闭：A ·关元; B ·膀胱俞 C. ·血海; D ·膈俞; E ·太溪	Which of the following cannot treat the coagulation and turbid obstruction type of suppression of urination? A · R4 / Guān Yuán; B ·; B28 / Páng Guāng Shū; C. · Sp10 / Xuè Hǎi; D ·B17 / Gé Shū; E · K3 / Tài Xī
1696	下列各项中除 () 外，都能治疗中耳炎：A ·听宫; B ·合谷 C. ·外关; D ·翳风; E ·少商	What point cannot treat otitis media? A · Si19 / Tīng Gōng; B · Li4 / Hé Gǔ; C. · Sj5 / Wài Guān; D · Sj17 / Yì Fēng; E · Lu11 / Shǎo Shāng
1697	下列各项中除 () 外，都能治疗中暑：A ·大椎 ·B ·内关 C. ·合谷; D ·曲泽 ·E ·阳辅	What point cannot treat sunstroke? A ·D14 / Dà Zhuī ·B · P6 / Nèi Guān; C. · Li4 / Hé Gǔ; D · P3 / Qū Zé ·E · G38 / Yáng Fǔ
1698	下列各项中除 () 外，都能治疗中暑神志昏迷：A ·曲泽; B ·内关 C. ·阳陵泉; D ·水沟; E ·十宣	What point cannot treat sunstroke with coma? A · P3 / Qū Zé; B · P6 / Nèi Guān; C. · G34 / Yáng Líng Quán; D · D26 / Shuǐ Gōu / Rén Zhōng; E · Shí xuān / ten statements / ten expansions

1699	下列各项中除（）外，都是耳针治疗白细胞减少症用穴：A·脾、胃；B·内分泌 C.¨耳尖；D·肾；E·皮质下	Which auricular point is not used to treat liukopenia? A·spleen、stomach; B · Internal Secretion / Endocrine; C. tip of ear; D ·kidneys; E · subcortex
1700	下列各项中除（）外，都是慢性疲劳综合征的治则：A·疏肝理脾；B·温阳散寒 C. ·补益肝肾；D·健脑养神；E·消除疲劳	Which treatment principle is not applicable to the treatment of chronic fatigue syndrome? A ·to disperse the liver and regulate the spleen; B · to warm yang and disperse cold; C. ·to tone and benefit liver and kidneys; D ·to strengthen the brain and nourish the spirit; E ·to relieve fatigue
1701	下列各项中除（）外，都是气郁化火型癔病的基本治则：A·理气解郁；B·养心安神 C. ·清泻肝火；D·解郁和胃；E·宽胸解郁	·Which treatment principle cannot be applied to treat hysteria of energy inhibition transforming into fire ? A ·to regulat energy and relieve inhibition; B ·to nourish the heart and secure the spirit; C. ·to clear and sedate liver fire; D. ·to relieve inhibition and harmonize stomach; E ·to expand the chest and relieve inhibition
1702	下列各项中除（）外，都是针灸治疗痴呆的基本处方用穴：A·足三里；B·大钟 C. ·悬钟；D·太溪；E·中脘	Which point does not belong to the basic prescription of points to treat idiocy? A · S36 / Zú Sān Lǐ; B · K4 / Dà Zhōng; C. ·G39 / Xuán Zhōng; D · K3 / Tài Xī; E · R12 / Zhōng Wǎn
1703	下列各项中除（）外，都是治疗白细胞减少症基本处方用穴：A·足三里；B·内关 C. ·膏肓；D·大椎；E·肾俞	Which point does not belong to the basic prescription of points for treating liukopenia? A · S36 / Zú Sān Lǐ; B · P6 / Nèi Guān; C. ·B43 / Gāo Huāng Shū; D ·D14 / Dà Zhuī; E ·; B23 / Shèn Shū
1704	下列各项中除（）外，都是治疗癫病的基本处方用穴：A·脾俞；B·丰隆 C. ·心俞；D·神门；E·合谷	Which does not belong to the basic prescription of points to treat depressive psychosis? Ac B20 / Pí Shū; B. · S40 / Fēng Lóng; C. B15 / Xīn Shū; D. · H7 / Shén Mén; E. · Li4 / Hé Gǔ
1705	下列各项中除（）外，都是治疗癫病气虚痰凝型的处方用穴：A·脾俞；B·中脘 C. ·足三里；D·神门；E·太冲	Which does not belong to the basic prescription of points to treat depressive psychosis of energy deficiency with phlegm congestion? A.; B20 / Pí Shū; B. · R12 / Zhōng Wǎn; C. S36 / Zú Sān Lǐ; D. · H7 / Shén Mén; E · Lv3 / Tài Chōng
1706	下列各项中除（）外，都是治疗近视的基本处方：A·睛明、承泣；B·风池、承泣 C. ·四白、太阳；D·风池、合谷；E·风池、光明	Which group of points does not belong to the major points to treat myopia? A ·B1 / Jīng Míng, S1 / Chéng Qì; B · G20 / Fēng Chí， S1 / Chéng Qì; C. · S2 / Sì Bái / ， Tài yáng / sun / temple; D · G20 / Fēng Chí， Li4 / Hé Gǔ; E · G20 / Fēng Chí， G37 / Guāng Míng
1707	下列各项中除（）外，都是治疗失眠处方主穴： A·神门；B·内关 C. ·安眠 ·D百会；E·涌泉	Which of the following points is not a primary point to treat insomnia? A · H7 / Shén Mén; B · P6 / Nèi Guān; C. · Ān mián / good sleep ·D D20 / Bǎi Huì; E · K1 / Yǒng Quán
1708	下列各项中除（）外，都为治疗带状疱疹的治则：A·清热利湿；B.活血通络 C. ·只针不灸；D·针灸并用；E·泻法	What treatment principle may not be applied to treat herpes zoster? A ·to clear heat, benefit dampness; B.to actiave blood and connect linking meridians; C. acupuncture without moxibustion; D · both acupuncture and moxibustion; E · sedation

1709	下列各项中除（）外，都用于治疗肝肾阴虚型眩晕：A·肝俞；B·肾俞 C.·太溪；D·大敦；E·绝骨	Which point is not used to treat vertigo-dizziness due to yin deficiency of liver and kidneys? A·B18 / Gān Shū; B·; B23 / Shèn Shū; C. ·K3 / Tài Xī; D·Lv1 / Dà Dūn; E·G39 / Xuán Zhōng
1710	下列各项中除（）外，都用于治疗痰热内扰型失眠：A·中脘；B·安眠 C.·外关；D·内庭 ·E·丰隆	Which of the following cannot treat insomenia due to phlegm heat disturbing internally? A·R12 / Zhōng Wǎn; B·Ān mián / good sleep; C. ·Sj5 / Wài Guān; D·S44 / Nèi Tíng; ·E·S40 / Fēng Lóng
1711	下列各项中除（）外，均可用于治疗阴虚火旺型早泄：A·关元；B·阴陵泉 C.·三阴交；D·太溪；E·照海	Which of the following cannot treat yin deficiency with abundant fire type of premature ejaculation? A·R4 / Guān Yuán; B·Sp9 / Yīn Líng Quán; C. ·Sp6 / Sān Yīn Jiāo; D·K3 / Tài Xī; E·K6 / Zhào Hǎi
1712	下列各项中除（）外，均属治疗各类型扁平疣的腧穴：A·合谷；B·三阴交 C.·太冲；D·商丘；E·曲泽	What point cannot treat various types of flat wart? A·Li4 / Hé Gǔ; B·Sp6 / Sān Yīn Jiāo; C. ·Lv3 / Tài Chōng; D·Sp5 / Shāng Qiū; E·P3 / Qū Zé
1713	下列各项中除（）外，一般不用于治疗胃肠痉挛：A·中府；B·阴陵泉 C.·梁丘；D·丰隆；E·委中	Which point is generally not used to treat gastrointestinal spasm? A·Lu1 / Zhōng Fǔ; B·Sp9 / Yīn Líng Quán; C. ·S34 / Liáng Qiū; D·S40 / Fēng Lóng; E·; B40 / Wěi Zhōng
1714	下列各项中除（）外都不能治疗颈椎病上肢及手指麻痛：A·曲池、合谷、外关；B·曲池、内关、阳谷 C.·尺泽、太渊、肩髃；D·内关、合谷、孔最；E·外关、合谷、阳谷	Which group of points can treat numbness and pain of upper limbs and fingers in cervical spondylopathy? A·Li11 / Qū Chí，Li4 / Hé Gǔ，Sj5 / Wài Guān; B·Li11 / Qū Chí，P6 / Nèi Guān，Si5 / Yáng Gǔ; C. ·Lu5 / Chǐ Zé，Lu9 / TàiYuān，Li15 / Jiān Yú; D·P6 / Nèi Guān，Li4 / Hé Gǔ，Lu6 / Kǒng Zuì; E·Sj5 / Wài Guān，Li4 / Hé Gǔ，Si5 / Yáng Gǔ
1715	下列各项中除（）外都能治疗风寒痹阻型颈椎病：A·风门；B·风府 C.·后溪；D·天柱E·内关	Which point cannot treat the wind cold rheumatic obstruction type of cervical spondylopathy? A·B12 / Fēng Mén; B·D16 / Fēng Fǔ; C. ·Si3 / Hòu Xī; D·B10 / Tiān Zhù; E·P6 / Nèi Guān
1716	下列各项中除（）外都能治疗肝肾亏虚型颈椎病：A·足三里；B·大椎 C.·天柱；D·颈椎夹脊；E.地机	What point cannot treat the the liver and kidney deprivation and deficiency type of cervical spondylopathy? A·S36 / Zú Sān Lǐ; B·D14 / Dà Zhuī; C. ·B10 / Tiān Zhù; D jǐng zhuī jiā jí / cervical vertebra clippings of spine; E. Sp8 / Dì Jī
1717	下列各项中除（）外都能治疗寒湿凝滞型痛经：A·水道；B·地机 C.关元；D·合谷；E·三阴交	Which point cannot treat the cold dampness congestion type of period pain? A·S28 / Shuǐ Dào; B·Sp8 / Dì Jī; C. R4 / Guān Yuán; D·Li4 / Hé Gǔ; E·Sp6 / Sān Yīn Jiāo
1718	下列各项中除（）外都能治疗落枕：A·后溪；B·悬钟 C.阿是穴；D·委中；E·落枕穴	Which point cannot treat “falling off the pillow / neck pain with stiffness”? A·Si3 / Hòu Xī; B·G39 / Xuán Zhōng; C. ·Ouchi points / pressure points; D·; B40 / Wěi Zhōng; E·Luò zhěn / falling

		off the pillow / neck pain point.
1719	下列各项中除（ ）外皆为治疗百日咳的常用穴：A·列缺；B·肺俞 C. ·风门；D·天枢；E·丰隆	Which point is not commonly used to treat whooping cough / pertusis? A ·Lu7 / Liè Quē; B ·B13 / Fèi Shū; C. ·B12 / Fēng Mén; D · S25 / Tiān Shū; E · S40 / Fēng Lóng
1720	下列各项中除（ ）外均可用于颞下颌关节功能紊乱综合征的治疗：A·电针；B·指针 C. ·耳针；D·走罐；E穴位注射	What technique cannot be applied to treat the syndrome of temporalmandibular joint functional disorder? A ·electro acupuncture; B ·finger-pressure; C. auricular acupuncture; D ·Running cupping; E. acupuncture points injection therapy
1721	下列各项中除（ ）外均可治疗颞下颌关节功能紊乱综合征：A·听宫；B·下关 C. ·翳明；D.颊车；E·合谷	Which point cannot treat the syndrome of temporalmandibular joint functional disorder? A · Si19 / Tīng Gōng; B · S7 / Xià Guān; C. · Yì míng / shelter light; D. S6 / Jiá Chē; E · Li4 / Hé Gŭ
1722	下列各项中除（ ）外均可治疗外伤性截瘫：A·委中；B·三阴交 C. ·悬钟；D.风池；E·足三里	What point cannot treat traumatic paraplegia? A. B40 / Wĕi Zhōng; B. · Sp6 / Sān Yīn Jiāo; C. · G39 / Xuán Zhōng; D. G20 / Fēng Chí; E. · S36 / Zú Sān Lĭ
1723	下列各项中除（ ）外均可治疗足跟痛血瘀型：A·肝俞、承山；B·昆仑、申脉 C. ·膈俞、阿是穴；D·太冲、太溪；E，悬钟、照海	Which of the following points cannot treat the blood coagulation type of painful heels? A. ·B18 / Gān Shū，B57 / Chéng Shān; B. B60 / Kūn Lún，B62 / Shēn Mài; C. ·B17 / Gé Shū 、Ouchi points / pressure points; D. · Lv3 / Tài Chōng，K3 / Tài Xī; E. G39 / Xuán Zhōng，K6 / Zhào Hăi
1724	下列各项中除（ ）外均为颞下颌关节功能紊乱综合征的治则：A·补法；B·泻法 C. ·平补平泻；D·祛风散寒；E舒筋活络	Which treatment principle is not applicable to the syndrome of temporalmandibular joint functional disorder? A · tonfication; B · sedation; C. neutral technique; D ·to expel wind and disperse cold; E. to relax tendons and activate linking meridians.
1725	下列各项中除（ ）外均为治疗肩关节周围炎的基本穴位：A·肩三针；B·阿是穴 C. ·阳陵泉；D·天府；E·中平穴	What point is not a basic point to treat scapulohumeral periarthritis? A ·Jiān sān zhēn / shoulder three needles / three needles on the shoulders; B ·Ouchi points / pressure points; C. · G34 / Yáng Líng Quán; D · Lu3 / Tiān Fŭ; E · Zhōng pīng xué
1726	下列各项中除（ ）外均为治疗肘劳的基本穴位：A·曲池；B·肘髎 C. ·手三里；D·手五里；E·内关	Which is not a basic point to treat elbow fatigue / zhou lao? A · Li11 / Qū Chí; B · Li12 / Zhŏu Liáo; C. · Li10 / Shŏu Sān Lĭ; D · Li13 / Shŏu Wŭ Lĭ; E · P6 / Nèi Guān
1727	下列各项中除（）·外，都能止哮平喘：A·膻中；B.天突 C. 定喘；D·复溜；E·中府	Which point cannot calm sputum noise in the throat and stop panting and short breath? A · R17 / Shān Zhōng; B. R22 / Tiān Tū; C. Dìng Chuăn / fix panting / stop panting / panting tranquillizer; D · K7 / Fù Liū; E · Lu1 / Zhōng Fŭ
1728	下列各项中除（）·外，都能治疗中暑手足抽搐：A·太	What point cannot treat sunstroke with twitching of hand and foot?

	冲; B·二间 C. ·合谷; D·阳陵泉; E·百会。	A · Lv3 / Tài Chōng; B · Li2 / Èr Jiān; C. · Li4 / Hé Gŭ; D · G34 / Yáng Líng Quán; E · D20 / Băi Huì 。
1729	下列各项中除 ()·外，都是癔病的基本辨证分型：A·肝气郁结型; B·气郁化火型 C. 心脾两虚型; D·气滞血瘀型; E·阴虚火旺型	Which of the following syndromes basically does not account for hysteria? A · liver energy congestion type; B ·energy inhibition transforming into fire type; C. heart spleen deficiency simultaneously; D · energy congestion and blood; coagulation type; E · yin deficiency with abundant fire
1730	下列各项中除 （ ）外，都能治疗丹毒：A·太溪; B·合谷 ·C·委中; D·血海; E·曲池	Which point cannot treat erysipelas? A · K3 / Tài Xī; B · Li4 / Hé Gŭ; ·C ·; B40 / Wĕi Zhōng; D · Sp10 / Xuè Hăi; E · Li11 / Qū Chí
1731	下列各项中除 （ ）外，都是治疗颈部扭伤的基本处方：A·大椎; B·天柱 C. ·风府; D·风池; E·后溪	Which is not a basic point to treat neck sprain? A ·D14 / Dà Zhuī; B ·B10 / Tiān Zhù; C. · D16 / Fēng Fŭ; D · G20 / Fēng Chí; E · Si3 / Hòu Xī
1732	下列各项中除 ( )之外，都能治疗皮肤瘙痒症：A·曲池; B·心俞 C. ·风市; D·血海; E膈俞	Which point cannot treat skin tich? A · Li11 / Qū Chí; B ·B15 / Xīn Shū; C. ·G31 / Fēng Shì; D · Sp10 / Xuè Hăi; EB17 / Gé Shū
1733	下列各项中除 (·) 外，都能治疗阳脱：A.曲池; B·关元 C. ·足三里; D·百会; E·气海	What point cannot treat yang prostration? A. Li11 / Qū Chí; B · R4 / Guān Yuán; C. S36 / Zú Sān Lĭ; D · D20 / Băi Huì; E · R6 / Qì Hăi
1734	下列各项中除 (·)·外，都能开窍启闭，治疗牙关紧闭：A.下关; B·关元 C. ·合谷; D·百会; E·水沟	What point cannot open up cavities and closure in the treatment of lockjaw? A. S7 / Xià Guān; B · R4 / Guān Yuán; C. · Li4 / Hé Gŭ; D · D20 / Băi Huì; E · D26 / Shuĭ Gōu / Rén Zhōng
1735	下列各项中除 (·) 外，都能治疗血热型月经不调：A·行间; B 地机 C. ·血海; D·三阴交; E·曲池	Which point cannot treat the blood heat type of irregular menstruation? A · Lv2 / Xíng Jiān; B Sp8 / Dì Jī; C. · Sp10 / Xuè Hăi; D · Sp6 / Sān Yīn Jiāo; E · Li11 / Qū Chí
1736	下列各项中除 (·) 外，均为治疗目赤肿痛的基本处方用穴：A·瞳子髎; B·太阳 C. ·风池; D·合谷; E太冲	Which does not belong to the major points to treat pink eye with swelling and pain? A · G1 / Tóng Zĭ Liáo; B · Tài yáng / sun / temple; C. G20 / Fēng Chí; D · Li4 / Hé Gŭ; E. Lv3 / Tài Chōng
1737	下列各项中除 ( ) 外 都能治疗痔疮：A·长强; B·百会 C. ·承山; D·委中; E·二白	Which point cannot treat hemorrhoid / pile? A. · D1 / Cháng Qiáng; B. · D20 / Băi Huì; C. B57 / Chéng Shān; D. B40 / Wĕi Zhōng; E. · Èr Bái / two whites
1738	下列各项中除 ( ) 外，都能治疗乳腺炎的初期：A·膻中; B·肩井 C. ·期门; D·大椎; E·合谷	Which point cannot treat the initial stage of mastitis? A · R17 / Shān Zhōng; B · G21 / Jiān Jĭng; C. · Lv14 / Qí Mén; D ·D14 / Dà Zhuī; E · Li4 / Hé Gŭ
1739	下列各项中除( ) 外，都能治疗肾阴亏虚型中耳炎：A·耳门]; B·风池 C. ·翳风; D·太溪; E·肾俞·	What point cannot treat the kidney yin deprivation and deficiency type of otitis media? A ·Sj21 / Ĕr Mén]; B · G20 / Fēng Chí; C. · Sj17 / Yì Fēng; D · K3 / Tài Xī; E ·; B23 / Shèn Shū ·
1740	下列各项中除 ( ) 外都能拔罐治疗落枕：A·大椎; B·肩井 C. ·肩外俞; D·阿是穴; E·风池	Which point cannot treat "falling off the pillow / neck pain with stiffness" by cupping ? A ·D14 / Dà Zhuī; B · G21 / Jiān Jĭng; C. · Si14 / Jiān Wài

	是穴; E·风池	Shū; D·Ouchi points / pressure points; E · G20 / Fēng Chí
1741	下列各项中除()外，都能治疗单纯性肥胖症？ A·风池; B·曲池 C. ·上巨虚; D·阴陵泉; E. 合谷	Which point cannot treat simple obesity? A · G20 / Fēng Chí; B · Li11 / Qū Chí; C. · S37 / Shàng Jù Xū; D · Sp9 / Yīn Líng Quán; E. Li4 / Hé Gǔ
1742	下列各项中除（ ）外，都是治疗踝部扭伤的基本处方：A·解溪; B·委中 C. ·昆仑; D·申脉; E·丘墟	Which is not a basic point to treat ankle sprain? A. · S41 / Jiě Xī; B.; B40 / Wěi Zhōng; C. B60 / Kūn Lún; D. B62 / Shēn Mài; E · G40 / Qiū Xū
1743	下列各项中除（ ）外，都是治疗膝部扭伤的基本处方：A·膝眼; B·鹤顶 C. ·风市; D·梁丘; E·阳陵泉	Which is not a basic point to treat knee sprain? A. · Xī yǎn / knee eye; B. · Hè dǐng / top of a crane; C. G31 / Fēng Shì; D. · S34 / Liáng Qiū; E. · G34 / Yáng Líng Quán
1744	下列各项中除（ ）外，都是治疗腰部扭伤的基本处方：A·肾俞；B·腰阳关 C. ·腰奇穴; D·委中; E·阿是穴	Which is not a basic point to treat lumbar sprain? A. B23 / Shèn Shū; B. · D3 / Yāo Yáng Guān; C. ·Yāo qí / waist miracle point; D. B40 / Wěi Zhōng; E. ·Ouchi points / pressure points
1745	下列各项中除（ ）外皆为治疗急惊风的常用穴：A·水沟; B·中冲 C. ·合谷; D·太冲; E·关元	Which of the following is not a common point to treat acute infantile convulsion? A · D26 / Shuǐ Gōu / Rén Zhōng; B · P9 / Zhōng Chōng; C. · Li4 / Hé Gǔ; D · Lv3 / Tài Chōng; E · R4 / Guān Yuán
1746	下列各项中除（ ）外，都是治疗癫病痰气郁结型的处方用穴：A·脾俞; B·肝俞 C. ·太溪; D·神门; E·太冲	Which does not belong to the basic prescription of points to treat depressive psychosis due to phlegm energy congestion? A ·; B20 / Pí Shū; B ·B18 / Gān Shū; C. · K3 / Tài Xī; D · H7 / Shén Mén; E · Lv3 / Tài Chōng
1747	下列各项中除（ ）外，都能温阳救逆：A.下关; B·关元 C. ·命门; D·百会; E·气海·	What point vannot warm yang and rescuer uprising? A. S7 / Xià Guān; B · R4 / Guān Yuán; C. · D4 / Mìng Mén; D · D20 / Bǎi Huì; E · R6 / Qì Hǎi ·
1748	下列各项中除C）外，都能治疗胆绞痛：A·太冲; B·阴陵泉 C. ·气海; D·日月; E·中脘	What point vannot treat volic of gallbladder? A · Lv3 / Tài Chōng; B · Sp9 / Yīn Líng Quán; C. · R6 / Qì Hǎi; D · G24 / Rì Yuè; E · R12 / Zhōng Wǎn
1749	下列各项中除取主穴外，可用于治疗目赤肿痛风热外袭型的是：A·合谷、太冲; B·侠溪、行间 C. ·风池、曲池; D·风池、太冲; E·侠溪、曲池	What points may be added to the basic prescription of points to treat the external attack of wind heat type of pink eye with swelling and pain? A · Li4 / Hé Gǔ，Lv3 / Tài Chōng; B · G43 / Xiá Xī，Lv2 / Xíng Jiān; C. G20 / Fēng Chí，Li11 / Qū Chí; D · G20 / Fēng Chí，Lv3 / Tài Chōng; E · G43 / Xiá Xī，Li11 / Qū Chí
1750	下列各项中除取主穴外，可用于治疗目赤肿痛热毒炽盛型的是：A·合谷、太冲; B·侠溪、行间 C. ·风池、曲池; D·风池、太冲; E·侠溪、曲池·	What points may be added to the basic prescription of points to treat the abundant toxic heat type of pink eye with swelling and pain? A · Li4 / Hé Gǔ，Lv3 / Tài Chōng; B · G43 / Xiá Xī，Lv2 / Xíng Jiān; C. · G20 / Fēng Chí，Li11 / Qū Chí; D · G20 / Fēng Chí，Lv3 / Tài Chōng; E · G43 / Xiá Xī，Li11 / Qū Chí ·
1751	下列各项中属腱鞘囊肿治疗处方的是：A·阳陵泉; B·悬钟 C. 阴陵泉; D·囊肿	Which point can treat thecal cyst? A · G34 / Yáng Líng Quán; B · G39 / Xuán Zhōng; C. Sp9 / Yīn Líng Quán; D·local cyst; E · Li4 / Hé Gǔ

	局部E·合谷	D·local cyst; E · Li4 / Hé Gŭ
1752	下列各穴，主治便秘较好的是: A·公孙，丰隆; B·中脘，下巨虚 C. ·水分 上巨虚; D·支沟 天枢 E·下脘 陷谷	Which group of points can better be selected to treat constipation? A. Sp4 (Gōng Sūn); S40 (Fēng Lóng); B. R12 (Zhōng Wăn); S39 (Xià Jù Xū); C. R9 (Shuĭ Fēn); S37 (Shàng Jù Xū); D. Sj6 (Zhi Gōu) S25 (Tiān Shū); E R10 (Xià Wăn), S43 (Xiàn Gŭ)
1753	下列各穴除（ ）外都常用于治疗胃痛: A·公孙; B·梁丘 C. ·风池; D 足三里·; E. 内关	Which of the following points is not used to treat stomachache normally? A · Sp4 / Gōng Sūn; B · S34 / Liáng Qiū; C. · G20 / Fēng Chí; D S36 / Zú Sān Lĭ ·; E. P6 / Nèi Guān
1754	下列各穴除（ ）外均可温胃散寒: A·太冲; B·足三里 C. ·胃俞; D·脾俞; E·中脘	Which of the following points cannot warm the stomach and disperse cold? A · Lv3 / Tài Chōng; B · S36 / Zú Sān Lĭ; C. ·; B21 / Wèi Shū; D ·; B20 / Pí Shū; E · R12 / Zhōng Wăn
1755	下列各穴除（·）外都常用于治疗胃痛: A·公孙; B·梁丘 C. ·风池·; D足三里; E. 内关	Which of the following points cannot treat stomachache? A · Sp4 / Gōng Sūn; B · S34 / Liáng Qiū; C. · G20 / Fēng Chí ·; D S36 / Zú Sān Lĭ; E. P6 / Nèi Guān
1756	下列各穴中，按 "经脉所通，主治所及"的理论，治疗上齿痛最好选用: A·太冲; B·劳宫 C. ·足临泣; D·内庭; E·少泽.	According to the theory, "The points of meridians may be selected to treat the diseases that occur on their distribution", which point should be selected to treat toothache? A. Lv3 (Tài Chōng); B. P8 (Láo Gōng); C. G41 (Zú Lín Qì, Lín Qì); D. S44 (Nèi Tíng); E. Si1 (Shào Zé).
1757	下列各穴中，除...外，均可用来治疗丹毒: A，合谷 曲池; B·足三里 解溪 C. 阴陵泉 血海; D·委中; E·金津 玉液	Which of the following group of points should NOT be selected to treat erysipelas? A. Li4 (Hé Gŭ); Li11 (Qū Chí); B. S36 (Zú Sān Lĭ); S41 (Jiĕ Xī); C. Sp9 (Yīn Líng Quán); Sp10 (Xuè Hăi); D. B40 (Wĕi Zhōng); E. Jīn Jīn Yù Yè.
1758	下列各穴中，治疗痔疾最有效的是: A·侠白; B 隐白 C. ·四白; D·二白; E· 浮白	Which of the following is a most effective point to treat hemorrhoids? A. Lu4 (Xiá Bái); B. Sp1 (Yĭn Bái); C. S2 (Sì Bái); D. Èr Bái; E. G10 (Fú Bái).
1759	下列各穴中除 () 外，均可采用点刺出血法治疗目赤肿痛: A·瞳子髎; B·太阳 C. ·攒竹; D·太冲; E·风池	Which of the following points should not be treated by dotted-needling to let blood for treating pink eye with swelling and pain? A. · G1 / Tóng Zĭ Liáo; B. · Tài yáng / sun / temple; C. B2 / Zăn Zhú; D. · Lv3 / Tài Chōng; E. · G20 / Fēng Chí.
1760	下列各穴中只有（ ）时朝鼻根方向透刺: A·印堂; B·水沟 C. ·素髎; D·上星; E·迎香	Which of the following points may be inserted all the way through (tou ci) in the direction of the nose root? A · Yìn táng / midpoint between eyebrows / seal hall; B · D26 / Shuĭ Gōu / Rén Zhōng; C. · D25 / Sù Liáo; D · D23 / Shàng Xīng; E · Li20 / Yíng Xiāng
1761	下列各组，具有和胃止呕作用的是: A·脾俞 上脘; B·胃俞 合谷 C. ·中脘 内关; D·公孙 建里 ; E·下脘 阴陵泉.	Which group of points may be selected to harmonize the stomach and relieve vomiting? A; B20 (Pí Shū); R13 (Shàng Wăn); B; B21 (Wèi Shū); Li4 (Hé Gŭ); C. R12 (Zhōng Wăn); P6 (Nèi Guān); D. Sp4 (Gōng Sūn) R11 (Jiàn Lĭ); E R10 (Xià Wăn). Sp9 (Yīn Líng Quán)

1762	下列各组，具有祛风解表的是: A. 外关 阳池; B. 曲池 丰隆 C. 陶道 足三里; D. 风池 合谷; E. 风市 风门.	Which group of points can expel wind and relax the superficial region? A. Sj5 (Wài Guān); Sj4 (Yáng Chí); B. Li11 (Qū Chí) S40 (Fēng Lóng); C. D13 (Táo Dào); S36 (Zú Sān Lǐ); D. G20 (Fēng Chí) Li4 (Hé Gǔ); E. G31 (Fēng Shì).B12 (Fēng Mén).
1763	下列各组不属俞募配穴的是: A. 天枢 大肠俞; B. 巨阙 心俞 C. 京门 胆俞; D. 期门 肝俞; E. 章门 脾俞.	Which group of points is NOT a combination of anterior mu point and posterior transport (back shu) point? A. S25 (Tiān Shū); B25 (Dà Cháng Shū); B. R14 (Jù Què)B15 (Xīn Shū); C. G25 (Jīng Mén)B19 (Dǎn Shū); D. Lv14 (Qí Mén)B18 (Gān Shū); E. Lv13 (Zhāng Mén); B20 (Pí Shū).
1764	下列各组中，不是俞募配穴的是: A.厥阴俞 巨阙; B.肝 俞 期门 C. 小肠俞 关元; D.肾 俞 京门; E.肺 俞 中府	Which group of points is NOT a combination of anterior mu point and posterior transport (back shu) point? A. B14 (Jué Yīn Shū); R14 (Jù Què); B. B18 (Gān Shū); Lv14 (Qí Mén); C. B27 (Xiǎo Cháng Shū); R4 (Guān Yuán); D. B23 (Shèn Shū) G25 (Jīng Mén); E. B13 (Fèi Shū) Lu1 (Zhōng Fǔ).
1765	下列关于腱鞘囊肿治则不正确的是：A.针刺为主; B.泻法 C. .行气活血; D.化瘀散结E补法	Which is inaccurate in treating thecal cyst? A. primarily by needling; B. sedation; C. to promote energy flow and activate blood; D. to transform coagulation and disperse congestion; E. tonfication.
1766	下列关于腱鞘炎的针灸治则正确的是：A.艾灸为主; B.泻法 C. .补法; D.软坚散结; E.疏筋活络	Which of the following is an accurate principle to treat tenoosynovitis by acupuncture-moxibustion ? A. primarily by moxibustion; B. sedation; C. . tonfication; D. to soften hardness and disperse congestion; E. to disperse tendons and activate linking meridians
1767	下列关于目赤肿痛治疗方法的叙述，哪项是正确的：A.先针后灸; B.先灸后针 C. .只灸不针; D.只针不灸; E.以上均不是	What treatment method should be applied to treat pink eye with swelling and pain? A. acupuncture followed by moxibusiton; B moxibustion followed by acupuncture C. moxibustion without acupuncture; D. acupuncture without moxibustion; E. none of the above
1768	下列关于针灸治疗斜视的治疗原则的叙述，哪项是正确的：A.祛风通络、补益肝肾; B.牵正明目、补益肝肾 C. .祛风通络、调和肝脾; D.养血明目、调和肝脾; E.调养气血、补益肝肾	Which is the correct treatment principle to treat squint? A. to expel wind and connect linking meridians、tone and benefit liver and kidneys; B. to correct squint and sharpen vision、tone and benefit liver and kidneys; C. to expel wind and connect linking meridians、to adjust and harmonize liver and spleen; D. to nourish blood and sharpen vision、to adjust and harmonize liverspleen; E. to adjust and nourish energy and blood、to tone and benefit liver and kidneys
1769	下列既能治疗崩漏，又能治疗疝气的穴位是：A.隐白; B.大敦 C. 归来; D.横骨	Which of the following points can treat vaginal bleeding and hernia simulataneously? A. Sp1 (Yǐn Bái); B. Lv1 (Dà Dūn); C. S29 (Guī Lái); D. K11 (Héng Gǔ).
1770	下列居于远部取穴是: A.昏迷取素髎水沟; B.久痢	Which falls within the method of selecting distal points? A. Coma treated by D25 (Sù Liáo), D26 (Shuǐ Gōu, Rén

	脱肛取百会 C. 血病取膈俞; D 胃痛取中脘梁门	Zhōng); B. Chronic diarrhea and prolaspe of anus treated by D20 (Bǎi Huì); C. blood disease treated by B17 (Gé Shū); D. stomachache treated by R12 (Zhōng Wǎn) S21 (Liáng Mén).
1771	下列哪个井穴，止血作用较强 A.商阳; B.至阴 C. 大敦; D 隐白	Which of the following well points (jing xue) can stop bleeding most effectively? A. Li1 (Shāng Yáng); B. B67 (Zhì Yīn); C. Lv1 (Dà Dūn); D. Sp1 (Yǐn Bái).
1772	下列哪个腧穴是针灸治疗痔疮的经验用穴：A·长强; B·百会 C. ·承山; D·会阳; E·二白	Which is an experience point to treat hemorrhoids / pile? A · D1 / Cháng Qiáng; B · D20 / Bǎi Huì; C. ·; B57 / Chéng Shān; D · B35 / Huì Yáng; E · Èr Bái / two whites
1773	下列哪项不属于胃痛的基本处方用穴：A·中脘; B·内关 C. ·足三里; D·公孙; E·神阙	Which point does not belong to the basic prescription of points to treat stomachache? A · R12 / Zhōng Wǎn; B · P6 / Nèi Guān; C. · S36 / Zú Sān Lǐ; D · Sp4 / Gōng Sūn; E · R8 / Shén Què
1774	下列哪些病因一般不会导致黄疸的形成：A·感受疫毒湿热; B·脾胃虚弱 C. ·肺气不宣; D·肝胆湿热; E·饮食所伤	Which of the following is not likely to cause jaundice? A ·under the attack of damp heat epidemics poison; B · spleen-stomach deficiency and weakness; C. ·lungs energy not expanding; D ·liver gallbladder damp heat; E ·damage by food
1775	下列哪一个不属治疗鼻出血的基本处方用穴：A·迎香; B·上星 C. ·水沟; D·印堂; E·合谷	Which point does not belong to the basic prescription of points to treat nosebleed? A · Li20 / Yíng Xiāng; B · D23 / Shàng Xīng; C. · D26 / Shuǐ Gōu / Rén Zhōng; D · Yìn táng / midpoint between eyebrows / seal hall; E · Li4 / Hé Gǔ
1776	下列哪种病的治则为清心泻热，醒脑定志: A.癫证; B·痫证 C. ·狂证; D·闭证	Which disease should be treated by the treatment principle of clearing heart and sedating heat, , waking up the brain and fixing emotions? A. depressive psychosis; B ·epilepsy C. ·insanity; D · blockage syndrome.
1777	下列哪组八脉交会穴可治疗肺系、咽喉、胸膈等疾患: A·外关、足临泣; B·后溪、申脉·C. ·公孙、内关; D·列缺、照海	Which group of "meeting points of eight meridians"can treat the disease of the lungs system, throat, chest and diaphragm, etc? A · Sj5 / Wài Guān 、G41 [Zú Lín Qì ,Lín Qì]; B · Si3 / Hòu Xī , B62 / Shēn Mài; · C. · Sp4 / Gōng Sūn , P6 / Nèi Guān; D ·Lu7 / Liè Quē 、 K6 / Zhào Hǎi
1778	下列哪组腧穴既属于八脉交会穴，又属于治疗咽喉肿痛基本处方中的腧穴: A·列缺、公孙; B·列缺、照海 C. ·内关、照海; D·后溪、照海; E·列缺、申脉	·What group of points belongs to the meeting points of eight meridians, and at the same time, it also belongs to the basic prescription of points to treat swollen and painful throat? A ·Lu7 / Liè Quē、 Sp4 / Gōng Sūn; B ·Lu7 / Liè Quē、 K6 / Zhào Hǎi; C. · P6 / Nèi Guān, K6 / Zhào Hǎi; D · Si3 / Hòu Xī, K6 / Zhào Hǎi; E ·Lu7 / Liè Quē、; B62 / Shēn Mài
1779	下列那项配穴法的可治肺病咳嗽？ A.中府尺泽太渊; B.内关足三里 C. 行间太溪; D 百会长强	Which of the following combinations of points can treat lung disease with cough? A. Lu1 (Zhōng Fǔ), Lu5 (Chǐ Zé) Lu9 (Tài Yuān); B. P6 (Nèi Guān), S36 (Zú Sān Lǐ); C. Lv2 (Xíng Jiān), K3 (Tài Xī); D. D20 (Bǎi Huì), D1 (Cháng Qiáng).

1780	下列那项配穴法的可治胃病？A.中府尺泽太渊; B.内关足三里 C. 行间太溪; D 百会长强	Which of the following combinations of points can treat stomach disease? A. Lu1 (Zhōng Fǔ), Lu5 (Chǐ Zé) Lu9 (Tài Yuān); B. P6 (Nèi Guān), S36 (Zú Sān Lǐ); C. Lv2 (Xíng Jiān), K3 (Tài Xī); D. D20 (Bǎi Huì), D1 (Cháng Qiáng).
1781	下列那项配穴法的可治牙痛？A.中府尺泽太渊; B.内关足三里 C. 行间太溪; D 百会长强	Which of the following combinations of points can treat toothache? A. Lu1 (Zhōng Fǔ), Lu5 (Chǐ Zé) Lu9 (Tài Yuān); B. P6 (Nèi Guān), S36 (Zú Sān Lǐ); C. Lv2 (Xíng Jiān), K3 (Tài Xī); D. D20 (Bǎi Huì), D1 (Cháng Qiáng).
1782	下列那项配穴法的可治子宫脱垂？A.中府尺泽太渊; B.内关足三里 C. 行间太溪; D 百会长强.	Which of the following combinations of points can treat prolapse of the uterus? A. Lu1 (Zhōng Fǔ), Lu5 (Chǐ Zé) Lu9 (Tài Yuān); B. P6 (Nèi Guān), S36 (Zú Sān Lǐ); C. Lv2 (Xíng Jiān), K3 (Tài Xī); D. D20 (Bǎi Huì), D1 (Cháng Qiáng).
1783	下列配穴，除……外，都是俞募配穴: A·心俞 巨阙; B·肝俞 期门 C. ·脾俞 章门; D·肺俞 膻中; E·肾俞 京门.	Which group of points is NOT a combination of anterior mu point and posterior transport (back shu) point? A.B15 (Xīn Shū); R14 (Jù Què); B.B18 (Gān Shū); Lv14 (Qí Mén); C. B20 (Pí Shū), Lv13 (Zhāng Mén); D.B13 (Fèi Shū) R17 (Shān Zhōng); E. B23 [Shèn Shū] G25 [Jīng Mén].
1784	下列配穴，除……外，都是主客配穴: A·太白 丰隆; B·太冲 蠡沟 C. ·太溪 飞扬; D·大陵 外关; E·合谷 列缺	Which group of points is NOT a host-guest combination? A. Sp3 (Tài Bái); S40 (Fēng Lóng); B. Lv3 (Tài Chōng); Lv5 (Lí Gōu); C. K3 (Tài Xī); B58 (Feī Yáng); D. P7 (Dà Líng) Sj5 (Wài Guān); E Li4 (Hé Gǔ). Lu7 (Liè Quē)
1785	下列配穴中，除…·外，都是原络配穴？ A·太冲 光明; B·太白 丰隆 C. 神门 支正; D·阳池 内关; E·太溪 大钟.	Which group of points is NOT the combination of a Yuan point (original point) and a Luo point (linking point)? A. Lv3 (Tài Chōng); G37 (Guāng Míng); B. Sp3 (Tài Bái); S40 (Fēng Lóng); C. H7 (Shén Mén); Si7 (Zhi Zhèng); D. Sj4 (Yáng Chí) P6 (Nèi Guān); E. K3 (Tài Xī). K4 (Dà Zhōng).
1786	下列奇穴中，主治痔疾的是: A.提托; B 二白 C. 中泉; D 里内庭	Which extraordinary point among the following can treat hemorrhoids most effectively? A. Tí Tuō; B. Èr Bái; C. Zhōng Quán; D. Lǐ Nèi Tíng.
1787	下列奇穴中治疗呕吐的是: A·拳尖; B·二白 C. ，女膝; D·精灵; E·中魁	Which of the following extraordinary points may be selected to treat vomiting? A. Quán Jiān; B. Èr Bái; C. Nǚ Xī; D. Jīng Líng; E. Zhōng Kuí.
1788	下列奇穴中主治目疾的是: A·拳尖; B·五虎 C. ·中魁; D·虎口; E·威灵	Which of the following extraordinary points may be selected to treat eye diseases? A. Quán Jiān; B. Wǔ Hǔ; C. Zhōng Kuí; D. Hǔ Kǒu; E. Wēi Líng.
1789	下列时间与午时吻合的是: A·7—9时; B·9—11时 C. ·11—13时; D·13—15时; E·15—16时	Which period of time correspond to Wǔ among the 12 branches? A·7—9; B·9—11; C. ·11—13; D·13—15; E·15—16.
1790	下列腧穴除（)之外，都是络穴：A·通里；B·偏历 C. ·长强; D·鸠尾; E，支沟	Which of the following acupuncture points is not a linking point / luo point? A · H5 / Tōng Lǐ; B · Li6 / Piān Lì; C. D1 / Cháng Qiáng; D · R15 / Jiū Wěi; E，Sj6 / Zhi Gōu

1791	下列腧穴除（)之外，都是俞募配穴法：A·膻中、心俞；B·章门、脾俞 C.·关元、小肠俞；D·京门、肾俞；E·石门、三焦俞	Which of the following does not fall within the principle of combinging back shu points and mu points? A · R17 / Shān Zhōng，B15 / Xīn Shū; B · Lv13 / Zhāng Mén, B20 / Pí Shū; C. · R4 / Guān Yuán, B27 / Xiǎo Cháng Shū; D · G25 / Jīng Mén, B23 / Shèn Shū; E · R5 / Shí Mén, B22 / Sān Jiāo Shū
1792	下列腧穴除（)之外，其余均为治疗咽喉肿痛的基本处方用穴：A·列缺; B·天容 C.·照海; D·外关 E·合谷	What point does not belong to the basic prescription of points to treat swollen and painful throat? A·Lu7 / Liè Quē; B · Si17 / Tiān Róng; C. · K6 / Zhào Hǎi; D · Sj5 / Wài Guān; ·E · Li4 / Hé Gǔ
1793	下列腧穴中( )不是郄穴：A·阴郄; B·大都 C.·阳交; D·交信; E·孔最	Which of the following is not a fissural point / cleft point / xi point? A · H6 / Yīn Xī; B · Sp2 / Dà Dū; C. · G35 / Yáng Jiāo; D ·K8 / Jiāo Xìn; E · Lu6 / Kǒng Zuì
1794	下列腧穴中，除（)穴外都是原穴：A·合谷; B·大陵 C.·外关; D 丘墟; E·冲阳	Which of the following acupuncture points is not a yuán xué / starting-points / source-points? A · Li4 / Hé Gǔ; B · P7 / Dà Líng; C. · Sj5 / Wài Guān; D G40 / Qiū Xū; E · S42 / Chōng Yáng
1795	下列腧穴中，孕妇禁针的是: A·曲池; B·肩井 C.·肩贞; D·大椎; E·足三里	Which point is a forbidden point in treating pregnant women by acupuncture? A. Li11 (Qū Chí); B. G21 (Jiān Jǐng); C. Si9 (Jiān Zhēn); D. D14 (Dà Zhuī); E. S36 (Zú Sān Lǐ).
1796	下列腧穴中通阴维脉又善治胃、心、胸疾病的穴位是：A·公孙·; B·列缺 C.·内关; D·照海; E·申脉	What point is connected with the fastener merdian of yin / yin wei mai, and also an effective point to treat the symptoms of the stomach, heart, and chest? A · Sp4 / Gōng Sūn ·; B ·Lu7 / Liè Quē; C. · P6 / Nèi Guān; D · K6 / Zhào Hǎi; E. B62 / Shēn Mài
1797	下列腧穴中治疗鼻病的要穴是：A·印堂；B·迎香 C.·水沟; D·上星; E·合谷	Which point is an important point to treat nose disease? A · Yìn táng / midpoint between eyebrows / seal hall; B · Li20 / Yíng Xiāng; C. · D26 / Shuǐ Gōu / Rén Zhōng; D. · D23 / Shàng Xīng; E · Li4 / Hé Gǔ
1798	下列特定穴中，治疗急性病症应首选: A·原穴; B·俞穴 C.·八会穴; D·八脉交会穴; E·郄穴	Which of the following specially marked. points (te ding xue) should be used to treat acute diseases? A. original points (yuan points or source points); B. stream points (shu points); C. eight meeting points (ba hui xue); D. eight meridians eight meeting points (ba mai jiao hui xue); E. fissural points (xi xue).
1799	下列五输穴除（)之外，都是本经的母穴：A·曲池; B·后溪 C.·解溪; D·行间 E·至阴	Amopng the following five command points, which is not a mother point on its meridian? A · Li11 / Qū Chí; B · Si3 / Hòu Xī; C. · S41 / Jiě Xī; D · Lv2 / Xíng Jiān E ·; B67 / Zhì Yīn
1800	下列五输穴除（)之外，都是本经的子穴: A·二间; B·小海 C.·厉兑; D.阳辅 E·足通谷	Amopng the following five command points, which is not a child point on its meridian? A · Li2 / Èr Jiān; B · Si8 / Xiǎo Hǎi; C. · S45 / Lì Duì; D. G38 / Yáng Fǔ E ·; B66 / Tōng Gǔ / Zú Tōng Gǔ
1801	下列郄穴中经脉从属错误的是:	Which of the following is NOT correct regarding the connection between fissural point / cleft point / xi point

	A 阴维脉交信; B 手少阴心经阴郄 C. ·足太阴脾经地机; D ·足阳明胃经梁丘	connection between fissural point / cleft point / xi point and its associated meridian? A · fastener merdian of yin / yin wei mai and K8 [Jiāo Xìn]; B hand lesser yin heart meridian and H6 / Yīn Xī; C. ·foot greater yin spleen meridian and Sp8 / Dì Jī; D ·foot bright yang stomach meridian and S34 / Liáng Qiū
1802	下列穴位除（）外，都是治疗眩晕的基本处方用穴：A·百会; B·风池 C. ·头维; D·大敦 E 绝骨	Which point does not belong to the basic prescription of points to treat vertigo-dizziness? A · D20 / Bǎi Huì; B · G20 / Fēng Chí; C. · S8 / Tóu Wěi; D · Lv1 / Dà Dūn E · G39 / Xuán Zhōng
1803	下列穴位除（）外，均是治疗震颤麻痹的基本用穴：A·四神聪; B·风池 C. ·阳陵泉; D·百会 E·阴陵泉	Which point is not a basic point to treat Parkinsonism? A · Sì shén Cōng / four spiritual intelligences; B · G20 / Fēng Chí; C. · G34 / Yáng Líng Quán; D · D20 / Bǎi Huì E · Sp9 / Yīn Líng Quán
1804	下列穴位除哪项外，均为针刺治疗三叉神经痛的基本处方穴位：A·攒竹; B·下关 C. ·太溪; D合谷 E·内庭	Which point is not used in the basic prescription of points to treat trigerminal neuralgia? A ·; B2 / Zǎn Zhú; B · S7 / Xià Guān; C. · K3 / Tài Xī; D Li4 / Hé Gǔ E · S44 / Nèi Tíng
1805	下列穴位在治疗高热症中能宣达三焦气机、疏散风热的为：A·大椎; B·曲池 C. ·合谷; D·外关 E·风池	In treating high fever, what point can promote the mechanism of sanjiao / triple heater、and disperse wind heat? A ·D14 / Dà Zhuī; B · Li11 / Qū Chí; C. · Li4 / Hé Gǔ; D · Sj5 / Wài Guān E · G20 / Fēng Chí.
1806	下列穴位中，与五行相配属金，其所属经脉也属金的是: A·商丘; B 经渠 C. ·中封; D 阳谷	Which of the following points corresponds to metal among five elements，and its associated meridian also corresponds to metal? A · Sp5 / Shāng Qiū; B · Lu8 / Jīng Qú; C. ·Lv4 / Zhōng Fēng; D · Si5 / Yáng Gǔ
1807	下列穴位中，治疗胎位不正应首选: A 足窍阴; B 至阴 C. 少泽; D 少冲	Which should be selected as the primary point to treat fetus in wrong position? A G44 / Zú Qiào Yīn / Qiào Yīn; B. B67 / Zhì Yīn; C. Si1 / Shào Zé ·; D H9 / Shào Chōng
1808	下列穴位中，治疗消渴病可以配用: A·胃管下俞; B 崇骨穴 C. ·百劳穴; D·痞根穴 E·中泉穴	Which point may be selected in combination to treat xiao ke or diabetes-like condition (elimination and thirst)? A. Wèi Guān Xià Shū; B. Chestóng Gǔ; C. Bǎi Láo; D. Pǐ Gēn; E. Zhōng Quán.
1809	下列穴位中，主治便秘较好的穴位是: A 公孙丰隆; B 中脘下巨虚; C 下脘上巨虚; D 天枢支沟	Which points are more effective for constipation? A Sp4 / Gōng Sūn S40 / Fēng Lóng; B R12 / Zhōng Wǎn S39 / Xià Jù Xū; C. R10 / Xià Wǎn S37 / Shàng Jù Xū; D S25 / Tiān Shū Sj6 / Zhi Gōu
1810	下列穴位中;对心率有双向调整作用的是: A 神门; B 内关 C. 少冲; D 少府	Which point has a dual-directional regulation of heart beats? A H7 / Shén Mén; B P6 / Nèi Guān; C. H9 / Shào Chōng; D H8 / Shào Fǔ
1811	下列穴位中能宣散一身阳热之气的穴位为: A·大椎; B.曲池 C. ·合谷; D·外关 E·风池	What point can spread the energy of yang heat in the whole body? A ·D14 / Dà Zhuī; B. Li11 / Qū Chí; C. · Li4 / Hé Gǔ; D · Sj5

		/ Wài Guān E · G20 / Fēng Chí.
1812	下列穴位中治疗咳血应首选: A·孔最; B·列缺 C. ·太渊; ·D 鱼际; E 中府	Which of the following linking points, (luo xue) may best be selected to treat "coughing out blood"? A ·Lu6 [Kǒng Zuì]; B ·Lu7 [Liè Quē]; C. ·Lu9 [Tài Yuān]; ·D Lu10 [Yǔ Jì]; E. Lu1 [Zhōng Fǔ].
1813	下列荥穴中，与五行相配属火，而所属经脉居水的是: A·然谷; B 大都 C. ·前谷; D·劳宫	Which of the following outpouring points / spring points corresponds to fire among five elements, and its associated meridian corresponds to water? A · K2 / Rán Gǔ; B Sp2 / Dà Dū; C. · Si2 / Qián Gú; D · P8 / Láo Gōng
1814	下列俞募穴的组合，有错误的是: A. 肺俞 中府; B. 肾俞 京门 C. 肝俞 章门; D. 胆俞 日月; E. 三焦俞 石门.	Which group of points is NOT a combination of anterior mu point and posterior transport (back shu) point? A.B13 (Fèi Shū); Lu1 (Zhōng Fǔ); B; B23 (Shèn Shū); G25 (Jīng Mén); C.B18 (Gān Shū); Lv13 (Zhāng Mén); D.B19 (Dǎn Shū) G24 (Rì Yuè); E; B22 (Sān Jiāo Shū). R5 (Shí Mén)
1815	下列与 "热则疾之"无关的是: A·浅刺疾出; B·热病可灸 C. ·少留针; D·泻法 E·点刺出血	Which of the following has nothing to do with " the needle should be pulled out shortly in case of heat"? A ·shallow insertion with quick withdrawl of needle; B ·hot diseases treated by moxibustion; C. ·short retention of needle; D · sedation; E · dotted-needling to let blood
1816	下列晕针处理方法中哪一条是错误的? A. 立即起针; B. 卧床时头部抬高 C. 饮适量温水或糖水; D. 指捏或针刺人中穴; E 苏醒后当天不能再行针刺.	Which of the following is NOT the proper way of dealing with needle sickness (dizziness or fainting during acupuncture treatment)? A. pulling out the needle right away; B. put the patient's head in a higher position while lying down; C. drink some warm water or sugar water; D. kneed or needle D26 [Shuǐ Gōu [Rén Zhōng]; E. no more needling the same day after the patient wakes up.
1817	下列针灸方法适宜于肝肾阴虚型眩晕的是: A·只针不灸，泻法; B·针灸并用，泻法 C. ·针灸并用，补法; D·以针为主，平补平泻; E·以灸为主，平补平泻	Which of the following treatment principles of acupuncture-moxibustion should be applied to treat vertigo-dizziness of the yin deficiency of liver and kidneys type? A · acupuncture without moxibustion and by sedation; B · both acupuncture and moxibustion by sedation; C. · both acupuncture and moxibustion by tonfication; D ·mainly by acupuncture with a neutral technique; E ·mainly by moxibusiton with a neutral technique
1818	下列针灸配方中，称为 "开四关"的穴组是: A·内关 外关; B·关冲 关门 C. ·上关 下关; D·腰阳关 膝阳关; E·合谷 太冲	Which group of points is called, "opening four gates"? A · P6 / Nèi Guān Sj5 / Wài Guān; B · Sj1 / Guān Chōng S22 / Guān Mén; C. · G3 / Shàng Guān S7 / Xià Guān; D · D3 / Yāo Yáng Guān G33 / Yáng Guān / Xī Yáng Guān; E · Li4 / Hé Gǔ Lv3 / Tài Chōng
1819	下列治疗鼻炎的腧穴不属基本处方用穴的是: A.迎香; B·鼻通 C. ·印堂; D·上星; E·合谷	Which points does not belong to the basic prescription of points to treat rhinitis by acupuncture? A. Li20 / Yíng Xiāng; B ·Bí tōng / smooth passage of the nose / nose open passage; C. · Yìn táng / midpoint between eyebrows / seal hall; D · D23 / Shàng Xīng; E · Li4 / Hé Gǔ

1820	下列治疗肾精亏虚型耳鸣，耳聋的治则中，哪一项是错误的：A·补肾填精；B·只针不灸 C. ·针灸并用；D·补法；E·平补平泻	Which treatment principle is incorrect in treating the kidney essence deficient and derivation type of tinnitus and deafness? A. ·tone kidneys and fill essence; B. · acupuncture without moxibustion; C. · both acupuncture and moxibustiond; D. tonfication; E. · neutral technique
1821	下列治疗实证耳鸣、耳聋的治则中，哪一项是错误的：A·疏风泻火；B·化痰通腑 C. ·化痰开窍；D.以针为主；E·泻法	Which treatment principle is incorrect in treating the excess type of tinnitus anddeafness? A·dispersing wind and sedating fire; B·transform phlegm and connect bowels; C. ·transform phlegm and open up cavities; D.primarily by acupuncture; E · sedation
1822	下列治则除（）外，均是治疗震颤麻痹的基本治则：A·补益肝肾；B·益气养血 C. ·补中益气；D·熄风止痉；E·化痰通络	Which treatment principle cannot be applied to treat Parkinson's disease? A·to tone and benefit liver and kidneys; B·to benefit energy and nourish blood; C. ·to tone middle region and benefit energy; D·to stop wind and relieve spasm; E·to transform phlegm and connect linking meridians
1823	下列属本经配穴法的是：A·肺病咳嗽取中府、尺泽、太渊；B·胃病取内关、足三里 C. ·牙痛取行间、太溪；D·子宫脱垂取百会、长强	Which of the following groups of points combines the points on the same meridian to treat the disease of that meridian? A·Lu1 / Zhōng Fǔ，Lu5 / Chǐ Zé，Lu9 / TàiYuān for cough in lungs disease; B·P6 / Nèi Guān，S36 / Zú Sān Lǐ for stomach disease; C. ·Lv2 / Xíng Jiān，K3 / Tài Xī for toothacheī; D. ·D20 / Bǎi Huì，D1 / Cháng Qiáng for prostration of uterus.
1824	下列属表里配穴的是：A·中府、尺泽；B·孔最、列缺 ·C·内关、外关；D·合谷、太冲；E·太溪、太冲	Which of the following is a combination of superficial-deep points? A. Lu1 / Zhōng Fǔ，Lu5 / Chǐ Zé; ·B · Lu6 / Kǒng Zuì、Lu7 / Liè Quē; ·C · P6 / Nèi Guān，Sj5 / Wài Guān; D · Li4 / Hé Gǔ，Lv3 / Tài Chōng; E · K3 / Tài Xī，Lv3 / Tài Chōng
1825	下列属前后配穴法的是：A.前内关后外关；B.前中极后膀胱俞 C. 前大陵后阳池；D，前太溪后昆仓	Which group of points falls within the principle of "selectin anterior and posterior points in pairs to treat diseases"? A. P6 (Nèi Guān) in the front, Sj5 (Wài Guān) in the back; B. R3 (Zhōng Jí) in the front, B28 (Páng Guāng Shū) in the back; C. P7 (Dà Líng) in the front, Sj4 (Yáng Chí) in the back; D. K3 (Tài Xī) in the front, B60 (Kūn Lún) in the back.
1826	下列属上下配穴法的是：A.公孙内关治胃心病；B.中府太渊治肺病 C. 口喎取地仓合谷；D 腿痛取环跳悬钟	Which group of points falls within the principle of "selecting upper and lower points in pairs to treat diseases"? A. to treat the diseases of the stomach and the heart by Sp4 (Gōng Sūn) and P6 (Nèi Guān); B. to treat lung diseases by Lu1 (Zhōng Fǔ) and Lu9 (Tài Yuān); C. to treat wry mouth by S4 (Dì Cāng) and Li4 (Hé Gǔ); D. to treat pain in the legs by G30 (Huán Tiào) and G39 (Xuán Zhōng).
1827	下列属随症选穴的是：A·肝阳上亢取太冲；B·发热针曲	Which of the following is based on selection of points according to symptoms?

	池 C. ·心肾不交灸神门; D·五更泄灸命门; E·脾虚腹泻针足三里	according to symptoms? A ·select Lv3 / Tài Chōng to treat liver yang uprising; B ·select Li11 / Qū Chí for fever; C. ·select H7 / Shén Mén for absence of communication between heart and kidneys; D ·select D4 / Mìng Mén by moxibustion to treat diarrhea before dawn; E ·sedate S36 / Zú Sān Lǐ to treat diarrhea due to spleen deficiency.
1828	下列属于对症取穴是： A. 鼻病取迎香; B.胃痛取足三里 C. 癃闭取关元; D 失眠多梦取神门	Which of the following is a symptomatic treatment? A. diseases of the nose treated by Li20 (Yíng Xiāng); B. stomachache treated by S36 (Zú Sān Lǐ); C. suppression of urination treated by R4 (Guān Yuán); D. insomnia with many dreams treated by H7 (Shén Mén).
1829	下列属于近部取穴是： A. 高热取大椎陶道; B.目赤肿痛取行间 C. 口喎取颊车地仓; D 气病胸闷取膻中.	Which falls within the method of selecting local points? A. high fever treated by D14 (Dà Zhuī), D13 (Táo Dào); B. pink and swollen eyes treated by Lv2 (Xíng Jiān); C. wry mouth treated by S6 (Jiá Chē), S4 (Dì Cāng); D. energy disease and dull chest treated by R17 (Shān Zhōng).
1830	下列属于阴阳(表里)配穴法的是： A.胃病取中脘梁门; B.昏迷取合谷太冲 C. 邪在肾，取涌泉，昆仑.D 心病取心俞膻中	Which group of points falls within the principle of "selectin points on yin and yang (superficial and deep) meridians in pairs to treat disease"? A. to treat stomach diseases by R12 (Zhōng Wǎn), S21 (Liáng Mén); B. to treat coma by Li4 (Hé Gǔ), Lv3 (Tài Chōng); C. when pathogens attack the kidney, select K1 (Yǒng Quán), B60 (Kūn Lún); D. to treat heart diseases by B15 (Xīn Shū), R17 (Shān Zhōng).
1831	下列属于远部取穴是: A·昏迷取素髎、水沟; B 久痢脱肛取百会 C. ·血病取膈俞; D·胃痛取中脘、梁门	Which of the following belongs to the method of selecting a distal point for treatment? A D25 / Sù Liáo 、 D26 / Shuǐ Gōu / Rén Zhōng for ·coma; B D20 / Bǎi Huì for chronic diarrhea and proctoptosis / prolapse of anus; C. ·B17 / Gé Shū for blood disease; D ·R12 / Zhōng Wǎn ，S21 / Liáng Mén for stomachache.
1832	下列属于针灸治疗原则的是：A·扶正祛邪; B·虚则补之 C. ·子母补泻; D·调和阴阳; E·都不是	Which belongs to the principle of acupuncture therapy? A to support body energy and expel pathogen; B ·to tone up deficiency; C. · applying tonfification and sedation to child and mother; D · to regulate yin and yang; E · none of the above
1833	下列属原络配穴的是: A·丘墟 光明; B·太溪 大钟 C. ·腕骨 支正; D·太渊 偏历; E·大陵 内关.	Which group of points is a combination of a Yuan point (original point) and a Luo point (linking point)? A. G40 (Qiū Xū)G37 (Guāng Míng); B. K3 (Tài Xī). K4 (Dà Zhōng); C. Si4 (Wàn Gǔ); Si7 (Zhi Zhèng); D. Lu9 (Tài Yuān) Li6 (Piān Lì); E. P7 (Dà Líng). P6 (Nèi Guān).
1834	下列足阳明经的特定穴正确的是：A·荥穴内庭; B.合穴丰隆 C. ·络穴解溪; D·郄穴阴市; E·都不对	Which of the following is an accurate statement about the "specially marked points (te ding xue)" on the foot bright yang meridian? A · S44 / Nèi Tíng is an outpouring point / spring point; B. S40 / Fēng Lóng is a hé xué / terminal-point / sea-point; C. · S41 / Jiě Xī is a linking point / luo point; D · S33 / Yīn Shì is a fissural point / cleft point / xi point; E · none of the above

1835	痫病发则卒然昏仆，·目睛上视，口吐白沫，手足抽搐多为: A·痰火扰神 ·B·血虚风动 C. ·瘀阻脑络; D·风痰闭窍; E·心脾两虚	What syndrome mostly accounts for epilepsy with sudden fainting, eyes looking up, vomiting of white bubbles, twitching of hands and feet? A·phlegm fire disturbing the spirit; ·B · blood deficiency with disturbing wind; C. ·coagulation blocking brain links; D·wind phlegm blocking the cavities; E·heart and spleen deficiency.
1836	痫证在针灸治疗中的主要治法是: A·清心宁神; B·豁痰开窍 C. ·疏肝理气; D·健运脾气; E·通腑泄热	How to treat epilepsy by acupuncture and moxibustion? A. to clear the heart and secure the spirit; B. to remove phlegm and open cavities; C. to disperse the liver and regulate energy; D. to strengthen and mobilize spleen energy; E. to connect the bowels and sedate heat.
1837	现代新发现的治疗肩关节周围炎的经验效穴是: A·中平穴; B·手三里 C. ·太溪; D·昆仑; E尺泽	What is a modern discovery of experience point to treat scapulohumeral periarthritis? A · Zhōng pīng xué (middle horizontal point); B · Li10 / Shǒu Sān Lǐ; C. · K3 / Tài Xī; D ·; B60 / Kūn Lún; E. Lu5 / Chǐ Zé
1838	小便淋沥不爽，排尿无力，面色恍白，神气怯弱，舌质淡，脉沉细而尺弱者，治疗时宜取: A·膀胱俞 中极 阳陵泉 行间; B. 膀胱俞 中极 阳陵泉三阴交 阴谷 肾俞 三焦俞 气海 委阳 D·中极 三阴交 曲骨 大赫 归来 E 以上均不是	Which group of points should be selected to treat the following: dribbling urination, weak urination, whitish complexion, poor spirit, pale color of the tongue, a deep and fine pulse with weak proximal pulse? A; B28 (Páng Guāng Shū); R3 (Zhōng Jí) G34 (Yáng Líng Quán) Lv2 (Xíng Jiān); B. B28 (Páng Guāng Shū); R3 (Zhōng Jí) G34 (Yáng Líng Quán) Sp6 (Sān Yīn Jiāo); C. K10 (Yīn Gǔ);B23 (Shèn Shū); B22 (Sān Jiāo Shū) R6 (Qì Hǎi) B39 (Wěi Yáng); D. R3 (Zhōng Jí) Sp6 (Sān Yīn Jiāo) R2 (Qū Gǔ) K12 (Dà Hè) S29 (Guī Lái); E. None of the above.
1839	小便频数，淋沥刺痛，尿中时挟砂石，除选用主穴外，还可加用: A·肾俞 照海; B·照海 三阴交 C. ·曲泉; D·委阳 然谷; E·百会 气海.	In addition to major points, which group of points should be selected to treat the following: frequent urination, dribbling urination with pricking pain, sandy stones in urine? A; B23 (Shèn Shū); K6 (Zhào Hǎi); B. K6 (Zhào Hǎi); Sp6 (Sān Yīn Jiāo); C. Lv8 (Qū Quán); D. B39 (Wěi Yáng) K2 (Rán Gǔ); E. D20 (Bǎi Huì), R6 (Qì Hǎi).
1840	小儿脑炎后遗证出现痴呆，可选取: A·哑门 廉泉 关冲 合谷; B·大椎 哑门 风池 百会 C. ·合谷 天突 廉泉 颊车; D·内关 神门 三阴交 安眠; E·大椎 安眠 合谷 阳陵泉	Which group of points should be selected to treat idocy as the aftereffect of encephalitis? A. D15 (Yǎ Mén); R23 (Lián Quán) Sj1 (Guān Chōng) Li4 (Hé Gǔ); B. D14 (Dà Zhuī); D15 (Yǎ Mén); G20 (Fēng Chí) D20 (Bǎi Huì); C. Li4 (Hé Gǔ); R22 (Tiān Tū) R23 (Lián Quán) S6 (Jiá Chē); D. P6 (Nèi Guān) H7 (Shén Mén) Sp6 (Sān Yīn Jiāo) Ān Mián; E. D14 (Dà Zhuī), Ān Mián, Li4 (Hé Gǔ), G34 (Yáng Líng Quán).
1841	小儿遗尿，其选穴治疗主要应以: A·任脉; B·任脉及背俞穴 C. ·任督二脉; D·膀胱经背俞穴; E·任脉及足阳明胃经	Which meridian points may be selected to treat enuresis in children? A. ren mai (conception meridian); B. ren mai (conception meridian) and back shu points (transport points in the back); C. ren mai (conception meridian) and du mai (governing meridian); D. bladder meridian and back shu

		points (transport points in the back); E. ren mai (conception meridian) and stomach meridian.
1842	小腹部病症，妇科病症，在远端取穴中最常用的经穴是: A·脾经穴; B·胃经穴 C. 胆经穴; D·膀胱经穴; E·以上都不妥	What meridian points are most frequently selected as distant points to treat the disorders in the lower abdomen region and in women's disases? A. points on spleen meridian; B. points on stomach meridian; C. points on gallbladder meridian; D. points on bladder meridian; E. none of the above.
1843	小海穴针刺或注射不当，可以损伤: A.正中神经; B 桡神经 C. 腋神经; D 尺神经	Improper needling or injecting at Si8 (Xiǎo Hǎi) may cause damages to: A. median nerve; B. radial nerve C. axillary nerve; D. ulnar nerve
1844	泄泻病位在: ·A·脾; B 胃 C. 肠; D·肝; E·肾	Where is the diseased region in diarrhea? · A·spleen; B stomach; C. intestines; D·liver; E·kidneys
1845	泄泻的病机主要在于: A·肝气郁滞; B.肾阳亏虚 C. 食滞胃脘; D·脾胃功能障碍; E·湿热积滞	What is the primary pathogenesis of diarrhea? A·liver energy inhibition; B. kidney yang deprivation and deficiency; C. ·food stagnation in the stomach; D·functional disturbance of spleen and stomach; E · damp heat accumulation and stagnation
1846	心包的募穴是: A·膻中; B·巨阙 C. ·鸠尾; D·中庭; E·天池	What is the pericardium gathering point / mu point? A · R17 / Shān Zhōng; B · R14 / Jù Què; C. · R15 / Jiū Wěi; D · R16 / Zhōng Tíng; E · P1 / Tiān Chí
1847	心悸急性发作者针刺可用: A·补法; B·泻法 · C. 平补平泻法; D。禁用针刺; E·刺血法	What technique of acupuncture should be applied to treat an acute attack of papitation? A. · tonfication; B. · sedation; · C. neutral technique; D. no acupuncture treatment; E. ·bloodletting
1848	心脾两虚型癫病针灸治疗多用: A·以针为主; B·以灸为主 C. ·只针不灸; D·只灸不针; E·针灸并用	What acupuncture therapy is applied to treat depressive psychosiskind of heart and spleen deficiency type? A·primarily by acupuncture; B·primarily by moxibustion; C. acupuncture without moxibustion; D · moxibustion without acupuncture; E · both acupuncture and moxibustion
1849	心血不足型惊悸，除取主穴之外，可加用: A·心俞 中脘; B·脾俞 足三里 C. ·脾俞 膈俞; D·尺泽 内关; E·以上都不是	In addition to major points, which group of points may be selected to treat the heart blood deficiency type of palpitation? A.B15 (Xīn Shū); R12 (Zhōng Wǎn); B. B20 (Pí Shū); S36 (Zú Sān Lǐ); C. B20 (Pí Shū)B17 (Gé Shū); D. Lu5 (Chǐ Zé) P6 (Nèi Guān); E. none of the above.
1850	辛亥日乙丑时应开穴: A·公孙; B·申脉 C. ·内关; D·外关; E·临泣	What point opens during the Yǐ-Chǒu period of time on Xīn-Hài day? A · Sp4 / Gōng Sūn; B ·B62 / Shēn Mài; C. · P6 / Nèi Guān; D · Sj5 / Wài Guān; E · G15 / Tóu Lín Qì / Lín Qì
1851	行痹的治疗除在病变局部选穴外，可再加: A·膈俞、血海; B·阴陵泉、足三里 C. ·大椎、曲池; D·肾俞、关元; E·风池、百会 ·	In addition to selection of local points, what points may be added to treat migratory rheumatism? A·B17 / Gé Shū, Sp10 / Xuè Hǎi; B · Sp9 / Yīn Líng Quán, S36 / Zú Sān Lǐ; C. ·D14 / Dà Zhuī、 Li11 / Qū Chí; D · B23 / Shèn Shū, R4 / Guān Yuán; E · G20 / Fēng Chí, D20 / Bǎi

		Huì. ·
1852	行间诸穴组成处方，可用于治疗: A·痛经实证; B 经行先期 C. 经行先后无定期; D·血枯经闭; E·血滞经闭	Which disease may be treated by a prescription that includes Lv2 (Xíng Jiān), etc.? A. excess syndrome of period pain; B. premature menstruation; C. irregular menstruation; D. suppression of menstruation due to withered blood; E. suppression of menstruation due to blood coagulation.
1853	虚证胃痛的治疗原则应采取 A.和胃降逆行气止呕 B 疏通瘀滞和胃止痛 C. 和胃止痛行气止呕; D 温中健脾和胃止痛	What treatment principle should be used to treat the deficiency type of stomachache? A. to harmonize the stomach and bring down uprising, promote energy flow and stop vomiting; B. to disperse and move coagulation and congestion, harmonize the stomach and relieve pain; C. to harmonize the sotmach and relieve pain, promote energy flow and relieve vomiting; D. to warm the middle region and strengthen the spleen, harmonize the stomach and relieve pain.
1854	选心俞膈俞间使足三里三阴交诸穴，用 25 毫克-50 毫克氯丙嗪行穴位注射，可治疗: A·癫证; B·狂证 C. ·痫证; D·不寐;; E·以上均不是	Which disease may be treated by injecting 25-50 mg of wintermine into the following points: B15 (Xīn Shū);B17 (Gé Shū), P5 (Jiān Shǐ), S36 (Zú Sān Lǐ), Sp6 (Sān Yīn Jiāo)? A. psychosis (dian); B. maniac (kuang); C. epilepsy; D. insomnia; E. none of the above.
1855	选择天枢上巨虚三阴交治疗 A.便秘; B.泄泻 C. ，痢疾; D 脱肛	What disease may be treated by selecting S25 (Tiān Shū), S37 (Shàng Jù Xū), Sp6 (Sān Yīn Jiāo)? A. constipation; B. diarrhea; C. dysentery; D. prolapse of the anus.
1856	眩晕治疗基本处方中除（ ）外，都为近部取穴，疏调头部气机以治疗眩晕：A,百会; B 绝骨 C. ·风池; D·头维; E·太阳	Which point is not a local point to disperse and regulate energy machinery in the head region for the treatment of vertigo-dizziness? A, D20 / Bǎi Huì; B · G39 / Xuán Zhōng C. · G20 / Fēng Chí; D · S8 / Tóu Wěi; E · Tài yáng / sun / temple
1857	穴取关元、足三里、下巨虚，针灸并用、施行补法适宜于：A·大肠虚证; B·大肠寒证 C. ·小肠虚寒证; D·小肠气滞证; E·都不对	What can be treated by applying acupuncture-moxibustion with tonfication to R4 / Guān Yuán，S36 / Zú Sān Lǐ，S39 / Xià Jù Xū ? A ·large intestine deficiency syndrome; B ·cold large intestine syndrome; C. ·small intestine cold-deficiency syndrome; D ·small intestine energy; C. ongestion syndrome; E · none of the above
1858	穴位贴敷及穴位注射治疗腱鞘炎的穴位是：A·外关; B·涌泉 C. ·阿是穴; D·后溪; E·曲池	What point should be used to treat tenoosynovitis by “point herb application” and “acupuncture points injection” therapy? A · Sj5 / Wài Guān; B · K1 / Yǒng Quán; C. ·Ouchi points / pressure points; D · Si3 / Hòu Xī; E · Li11 / Qū Chí
1859	穴位注射治疗白细胞减少症可选用：A·大椎、绝骨; B·公孙、内关 C. ·足三里、血海; D·气海、丰隆; E·中脘、关元	What acupuncture points should be selected for injection therapy in the treatment of leukopenia? A ·D14 / Dà Zhuī、 G39 / Xuán Zhōng; B · Sp4 / Gōng Sūn，P6 / Nèi Guān; C. · S36 / Zú Sān Lǐ, Sp10 / Xuè Hǎi; D · R6 / Qì Hǎi, S40 / Fēng Lóng; E¨ R12 / Zhōng Wǎn, R4 / Guān Yuán

1860	血海属足太阴经穴，有养血凉血之功，与( )相配寓"治风先治血，血行风自灭"之意： A·曲池；B·三阴交 C. ·风门；D·膈俞；E·合谷	Sp10 / Xuè Hǎi is on the foot greater yin meridian, and it can nourish blood and cool blood; what point should it be combined with in order to act on the principle, “it is necessary to treat blood in order to treat wind, and when blood gets going, wind will disappear all by itself”? A · Li11 / Qū Chí; B · Sp6 / Sān Yīn Jiāo; C. ·B12 / Fēng Mén; D ·B17 / Gé Shū; E · Li4 / Hé Gǔ
1861	血枯闭经一般选用: A·脾俞 肾俞 气海 足三里；B·中极 合谷 血海 三阴交 行间 C. 血海 膈俞 太冲 行间 足三里；D·脾俞 命门 关元 三阴交 地机；E·以上都不是	Which group of points may be selected to treat suppression of menstruation with withered blood? A. B20 (Pí Shū) B23 (Shèn Shū) R6 (Qì Hǎi) S36 (Zú Sān Lǐ); B. R3 (Zhōng Jí) Li4 (Hé Gǔ) Sp10 (Xuè Hǎi) Sp6 (Sān Yīn Jiāo) Lv2 (Xíng Jiān); C. Sp10 (Xuè Hǎi)B17 (Gé Shū) Lv3 (Tài Chōng) Lv2 (Xíng Jiān) S36 (Zú Sān Lǐ); D. B20 (Pí Shū); D4 (Mìng Mén) R4 (Guān Yuán) Sp6 (Sān Yīn Jiāo) Sp8 (Dì Jī); E. None of the above.
1862	血热内扰型崩漏的治则是: A·只针不灸，泻法；B·针灸并用，平补平泻 C. 只针不灸，补法；D·只针不灸，平补平泻；E，针灸并用，补法	What treatment principle may be applied to treat the the internal disturbance of blood heat type of bleeding from the uterus / metrorrhagia and metrostaxis? A · acupuncture without moxibustion ， sedation; B · both acupuncture and moxibustion are applied， neutral technique; C. acupuncture without moxibustion ， tonfication; D · acupuncture without moxibustion ， neutral technique; E. both acupuncture and moxibustion are applied， tonfication
1863	血栓闭塞性脉管炎属于中医学什么范畴：A·丹毒；B·痹证 C. ·痿证；D·中风；E·消渴	Which does thrombo-embolia angitis correspond to in traditional Chestinese medicine? A · erysipelas; B · bi syndrome / rheumatic syndrome; C. paralysis syndrome; D ·wind stroke / zhong feng; E ·elimination and thirst / xiao ke
1864	牙痛，局部肿痛，口臭而渴，大便秘，脉洪数，苔黄。治疗取穴应首选: A. 合谷 颊车 外关 风池; B. 合谷 颊车 内庭 下关 C. 合谷 太溪 行间 下关; D. 合谷 颊车 大迎 颧髎; E. 合谷 外关 上关 大迎.	Which group of points should be selected to treat toothache, local swelling and pain, bad breath with thirst, constipation, a forceful and rapid pulse, yellowish coating on the tongue? A. Li4 (Hé Gǔ) S6 (Jiá Chē) Sj5 (Wài Guān) G20 (Fēng Chí); B. Li4 (Hé Gǔ) S6 (Jiá Chē) S44 (Nèi Tíng); S7 (Xià Guān); C. Li4 (Hé Gǔ) K3 (Tài Xī) Lv2 (Xíng Jiān) S7 (Xià Guān); D. Li4 (Hé Gǔ) S6 (Jiá Chē); E. Li4 (Hé Gǔ) Sj5 (Wài Guān) G3 (Shàng Guān) S5 (Dà Yíng).
1865	阳经经脉五输穴中输穴的五行属性为: A·木; B·火 C. 水; D·金; E·土	What element do the flowing points / stream points / shu xue among the five command points on yang meridians correspond to? A. ·wood; B. ·fire; C. water; D. ·metal; E. earth
1866	阳虚型咽喉肿痛的主要处方是: A·少商 尺泽 合谷; B·合谷 颊车 内庭 C. ·太溪 照海 鱼际; D·合谷 内庭 行间; E·以上都不是	Which group of points should be selected to treat the yang deficiency type of sore throat with swelling? A. Lu11 (Shǎo Shāng); Lu5 (Chǐ Zé) Li4 (Hé Gǔ); B. Li4 (Hé Gǔ); S6 (Jiá Chē) S44 (Nèi Tíng); C. K3 (Tài Xī); K6 (Zhào Hǎi) Lu10 (Yǔ Jì); D. Li4 (Hé Gǔ); S44 (Nèi Tíng)Lv2 (Xíng Jiān); E. none of the above.

1867	腰痛偏于劳损型者，除取委中肾俞等主穴以外，还可加用: A·脾俞 志室; B·胃俞 腰阳关 C. ·膈俞 次髎; D·大杼 腰俞; E·以上都不是	In addition to B40 (Wěi Zhōng) and B23 (Shèn Shū), which group of points should be selected to treat the predominantly fatigued and impaired. type of lumbago? A; B20 (Pí Shū); B52 (Zhì Shì); B. B21 (Wèi Shū) D3 (Yāo Yáng Guān); C. B17 (Gé Shū) B32 (Cì Liáo); D.B11 (Dà Zhù) D2 (Yāo Shū); E. None of the above.
1868	腰痛证宜取哪组穴位为佳?A肝俞.肾俞 悬钟 照海;B肾俞委中 夹脊 阿是穴;C秩边 环跳.肾俞 足临泣; D委中 委阳 太溪 太冲; E以上均不是。	Which group of points should best be selected to treat lumbago? A. B18 / Gān Shū. B23 / Shèn Shū G39 [Xuán Zhōng] K6 [Zhào Hǎi]; B. B23 / Shèn Shū B40 / Wěi Zhōng Dr. Huatuo's clippings of spine pressure point [ouch point]; C. B54 [Zhì Biān] G30 [Huán Tiào]. B23 / Shèn Shū G41 [Zú Lín Qì ,Lín Qì]; D. B40 / Wěi Zhōng B39 [Wěi Yáng] K3 [Tài Xī] Lv3 [Tài Chōng]; E. none of the above.
1869	腰痛属于寒湿型者，除取主穴外，还可加用: A，大椎 命门; B·志室 脾俞 C. ·风府 腰阳关; D·腰俞 脾俞; E·腰俞 三阴交	In addition to major points, which group of points should be selected to treat the cold dampness type of lumbago? A. D14 (Dà Zhuī) D4 (Mìng Mén); B. B52 (Zhì Shì); B20 (Pí Shū); C. D16 (Fēng Fǔ); D3 (Yāo Yáng Guān); D. D2 (Yāo Shū); B20 (Pí Shū); E. D2 (Yāo Shū) Sp6 (Sān Yīn Jiāo).
1870	要求针灸并用并强调重用灸法的是：A·气虚证; B·气滞证 C. ·气逆证; D·气陷证; E·都不是	Which of the following requires treatment by acupuncture-moxibustion with emphasis on moxibustioln? A ·energy deficiency syndrome; B ·energy congestion syndrome; C. · energy uprising syndrome; D ·energy cave-in syndrome; E · none of the above
1871	腋下瘰疬，尚未化脓，不红不热，按之移动，当选: A·翳风 天井 足临泣; B·臂臑 手三里 大迎 C. ·肩井 少海 阳辅; D·极泉 肩髃 少海; E·肩贞 肩髎 曲池	Which group of points should be selected to treat scrofula prior to suppuration, neither red nor hot, and moving on pressure? A. Sj17 (Yì Fēng) Sj10 (Tiān Jǐng) G41 (Zú Lín Qì, Lín Qì); B. Li14 (Bì Nào); Li10 (Shǒu Sān Lǐ) S5 (Dà Yíng); C. G21 (Jiān Jǐng); H3 (Shào Hǎi) G38 (Yáng Fǔ); D. H1 (Jí Quán) Li15 (Jiān Yú) H3 (Shào Hǎi); E. Si9 (Jiān Zhēn) Sj14 (Jiān Liáo) Li11 (Qū Chí)
1872	·般不用于休息痢的腧穴是：· A·天枢; B·脾俞 C. ·神阙; D·中冲; ·E·足三里	What acupuncture point is not normally used to treat recurrent dysentery? · A · S25 / Tiān Shū; B. B20 / Pí Shū; C. ·R8 / Shén Què; D · P9 / Zhōng Chōng; ·E · S36 / Zú Sān Lǐ.
1873	·治疗气血两虚诱发的斑秃，可在基本处方的基础上再加： A·肝俞; B·通天 C. ·足三里; D·风池; E·后溪.	What points may be added to the basic prescription of points to treat the simultaneous deficiency of energy and blood type of alopecia areata? A ·B18 / Gān Shū; B. B7 / Tōng Tiān; C. S36 / Zú Sān Lǐ; D · G20 / Fēng Chí; E · Si3 / Hòu Xī
1874	乙肝主气日癸已时应开： A·阳溪; B·前谷 C. ·太白; D·阴谷 ·E·大敦	What point open during the Guǐ-Jǐ period of time when Yǐ liver takes charge of energy? A · Li5 / Yáng Xī; B · Si2 / Qián Gú; C. · Sp3 / Tài Bái; D · K10 / Yīn Gǔ; ·E · Lv1 / Dà Dūn
1875	乙肝主气日同时开： A·阳溪; B·前谷 C. ·太白;	The day when Yǐ liver takes charge of energy, which point will open simultaneously?

	D·阴谷; ·E·大敦.	A · Li5 / Yáng Xī; B · Si2 / Qián Gú C. · Sp3 / Tài Bái; D · K10 / Yīn Gǔ; E · Lv1 / Dà Dūn
1876	以"苦心痛"为主症的奇经八脉是：A·任脉；B·督脉 C. 冲脉；D·阳维脉；E·阴维脉	Which of eight extraordinary meridians may display "heart pain" as its primary symptom? A. conception meridian / ren mai; B ·du mai / governing meridian; C. rigorous meridian / chong mai; D · fastener meridian of yang / yang wei mai; E · fastener merdian of yin / yin wei mai
1877	以大椎风门少商组合成处方，其主要作用为: A·祛风平喘; B·通经止痛 C. 宣肺解表; D·清热解毒; E·温经散寒	What is the primary function of combining D14 (Dà Zhuī), B12 (Fēng Mén), and Lu11 (Shǎo Shāng)? A. to expel wind and calm asthma; B. to connect meridians and relieve pain; C. to expand the lungs and relax the superficial region; D. to clear heat and detoxicate; E. to warm meridians and disperse cold.
1878	以上与肩关节周围炎的治疗无关的穴位是：A·中平穴; B·手三里 C. ·太溪; D·昆仑; E尺泽	Which point has nothing to do with the treatment of scapulohumeral periarthritis? A · Zhōng pīng xué; B · Li10 / Shǒu Sān Lǐ; C. K3 / Tài Xī; D. B60 / Kūn Lún; E. Lu5 / Chǐ Zé
1879	以下除……穴外，孕妇均应禁针: A 合谷; B 肩井 C. 阴陵泉; D 至阴	Which point may be selected to treat pregnant women? A Li4 / Hé Gǔ; B G21 / Jiān Jǐng; C. Sp9 / Yīn Líng Quán; D. B67 / Zhì Yīn
1880	以下除哪证禁忌外均为治疗疔疮的禁忌? A 疔疮初起应注意保暖，勿受风寒;B 疔疮初起，切忌挤压针挑;C 红肿发硬时，忌手术切开;D 疔疮初起，患部不宜针刺拔罐; E 治疗时，忌食鱼腥，虾蟹等发物。	Which of the following is NOT a forbidden measure in treating furuncle? A. at the beginning of furuncle, it is necessary to keep warm, avoiding wind cold; B.at the beginning of furuncle, it is necessary to avoid squeezing, pressing, and using a prismatic needle; C. when red swelling becomes hard, avoid cutting it open; D. at the beginning of furuncle, it is necessary to avoid needling or cupping; E. in the course of treatment, avoid fish, prawns, crabs.
1881	以下具有强壮作用的腧穴是: ·A·犊鼻; B·足三里 C·上巨虚; D·下巨虚; E·丰隆	Which point can boost up body strength? · A · S35 / Dú Bí; B · S36 / Zú Sān Lǐ; C. S37 / Shàng Jù Xū; D · S39 / Xià Jù Xū; E · S40 / Fēng Lóng
1882	以下哪组穴位一般不用于治疗坐骨神经痛? A·肾俞 大肠俞 腰4夹脊; B·秩边 环跳 殷门 C. 委中 承山; D·伏兔 足三里; E·阳陵泉 绝骨	Which group of points may NOT ,in general, be selected to treat sciatica? A; B23 (Shèn Shū) B25 (Dà Cháng Shū) Huá Tuó Jiā Jí (4th Lumbar vertebra); B. B54 (Zhì biān) G30 (Huán Tiào) B37 (Yīn Mén; C. B40 (Wěi Zhōng); B57 (Chéng Shān); D. S32 (Fú Tù) S36 (Zú Sān Lǐ); E. G34 (Yáng Líng Quán) G39 (Xuán Zhōng)
1883	以下配穴，除……以外均是俞募配穴 A.肝俞京门; B. 心俞巨阙 C. ，大肠俞天枢; D 胆俞日月	Which group of points does NOT fall within the principle o "selecting anterior Mu points and posterior back shu point in pairs to treat diseases"? A.B18 (Gān Shū), G25 (Jīng Mén); B.B15 (Xīn Shū), R14 (Jù Què); C. B25 (Dà Cháng Shū), S25 (Tiān Shū); D.B19 (Dǎn Shū), G24 (Rì Yuè).
1884	以下腧穴中长于治疗汗证的腧穴是： A·商阳 ·B·合谷 C. ·曲池 ；D·手三里 E·肩髎	Which point is particularly effective for perspiration? A · Li1 / Shāng Yáng; ·B · Li4 / Hé Gǔ; C. · Li11 / Qū Chí; D · Li10 / Shǒu Sān Lǐ; ·E ·Sj14 / Jiān Liáo

	里·E·肩髎	
1885	以下穴位用于治疗颈部扭伤的是：A·后溪；B·委中 C. ·阳陵泉 ·D·合谷；E·阳池	Which point can treat neck sprain? A. · Si3 / Hòu Xī; B. B40 / Wěi Zhōng; C. ·G34 / Yáng Líng Quán; ·D. · Li4 / Hé Gŭ; E. · Sj4 / Yáng Chí
1886	以下穴位用于治疗腕部扭伤的是：A·后溪；B·委中 C. ·阳陵泉 ·D·合谷；E·阳池	Which point can treat wrist sprain? A · Si3 / Hòu Xī; B ·; B40 / Wěi Zhōng; C. G34 / Yáng Líng Quán; ·D · Li4 / Hé Gŭ; E · Sj4 / Yáng Chí
1887	以下穴位用于治疗膝部扭伤的是：A·后溪；B·委中 C. ·阳陵泉 ·D·合谷；E·阳池	Which point can treat knee sprain? A. · Si3 / Hòu Xī; B. B40 / Wěi Zhōng C. · G34 / Yáng Líng Quán; ·D. · Li4 / Hé Gŭ; E · Sj4 / Yáng Chí
1888	以治疗心痛和热病为主的穴位是: A·极泉; B·少海·C·灵道 D·阴郄; E·少冲	Which point should be selected as the primary point to treat heart pain and hot diseases? A. · H1 / Jí Quán; B. · H3 / Shào Hăi; ·C. · D10 / Líng Dào; D. · H6 / Yīn Xī; E. · H9 / Shào Chōng
1889	以中脘足三里内关治疗失眠症，适用于: A·心脾亏损型; B·阴虚火旺型 C. ·胃腑失和型; D·心胆气虚型; E·肝阳上扰型	Which type of insomnia may be treated by the combination of the following points: R12 (Zhōng Wăn), S36 (Zú Sān Lĭ), P6 (Nèi Guān)? A. deficiency of heart and spleen; B. yin deficiency with abundant fire; C. loss of stomach harmony; D. energy deficiency of heart and gallbladder; E. liver yang disturbing upward.
1890	阴黄的针刺治疗下列叙述不正确的是: A·以清利湿热为治则; B·针灸并用 C. ·泻法; D·平补平泻; E·用温针灸	What treatment principle in acupuncture should not be used to treat the yin type of jaundice? A ·to clear damp heat as the treatment principle; B · both acupuncture and moxibustion; C · sedation; D · neutral technique; E ·use warm acupuncture-moxibustion
1891	阴经经脉五输穴五行属性正确的是: A·木火土金水 。B·金水木火土 ，C·金木水火土; D·木火金水土 ，E，土木金火水	Which is a correct sequence of five elements to correspond to five command points on yin meridians? A. ·wood fire earth metal water; B. metal, water, wood, fire, earth; C. · metal, wood, water, fire, earth; D. ·wood, fire, metal, water, earth; E. earth, wood, metal, fire, water
1892	阴证水肿在治疗时，除取水分气海三焦俞足三里外，还应酌选: A·肺俞 大杼 水道; B·合谷 水沟 水分 C. ·偏历 中脘 太白; D·阴陵泉 关元 足三里; E·脾俞 肾俞 阴陵泉	Which group of points should be selected to treat the yin type of edema in addition to the following points: R9 (Shuĭ Fēn), R6 (Qì Hăi); B22 (Sān Jiāo Shū), S36 (Zú Sān Lĭ)? A. B13 (Fèi Shū) B11 (Dà Zhù) S28 (Shuĭ Dào); B. Li4 (Hé Gŭ) D26 (Shuĭ Gōu, Rén Zhōng) R9 (Shuĭ Fēn); C. Li6 (Piān Lì) R12 (Zhōng Wăn) Sp3 (Tài Bái); D. Sp9 (Yīn Líng Quán) R4 (Guān Yuán) S36 (Zú Sān Lĭ); E. B20 (Pí Shū); B23 (Shèn Shū) Sp9 (Yīn Líng Quán).
1893	饮食停滞型呕吐可在基本方的基础上加: A·太冲。期门; B·丰隆、公孙 C. ·天枢、梁门; D·外关、大椎; E·脾俞、三阴交	What points may be added to the basic prescription of points to treat the food stagnation type of vomiting? A · Lv3 / Tài Chōng 。 Lv14 / Qí Mén; B · S40 / Fēng Lóng, Sp4 / Gōng Sūn; C. · S25 / Tiān Shū, S21 / Liáng Mén; D · Sj5 / Wài Guān 、 D14 / Dà Zhuī; E B20 / Pí Shū, Sp6 /

		Sān Yīn Jiāo
1894	饮食停滞之腹痛脘腹胀满痛处拒按，选用下列哪组穴位最佳? A. 中脘，.天枢 关元 足三里; B. 中脘，天枢 气海 足三里，C. 中脘 大横 章门 足三里; D. 下脘 章门 天枢 阴陵泉; E. 上脘 建里 关元 足三里。	Which group of points may be selected to treat abdominal pain due to food. stoppage and congestion, with swelling and fullness in the stomach and abdomen, pain with aversion to pressure? A. R12 [Zhōng Wǎn] S25 [Tiān Shū] R4 [Guān Yuán] S36 [Zú Sān Lǐ]; B. R12 [Zhōng Wǎn] S25 [Tiān Shū] R6 [Qì Hǎi] S36 [Zú Sān Lǐ]; C. R12 [Zhōng Wǎn] Sp15 [Dà Héng] Lv13 [Zhāng Mén] S36 [Zú Sān Lǐ]; D. R10 [Xià Wǎn] Lv13 [Zhāng Mén] S25 [Tiān Shū] Sp9 [Yīn Líng Quán]; E. R13 [Shàng Wǎn] R11 [Jiàn Lǐ] R4 [Guān Yuán] S36 [Zú Sān Lǐ]
1895	荥穴主治：A·心下满; B·体重节痛 C. ·逆气而泄; D.身热; E··喘咳寒热	What disease can be treated by the outpouring points / spring points? A·fullness below the heart; B heaviness of the body and pain in joints; C. ·uprising denergy with diarrhea; D. body heat; E··asthma, cough, chills and fever.
1896	痈证夜间发作时针刺照海穴主要是山于: A 照海为八脉交会穴之一; B 病在阴跷;C 照海可清热宁神;D 照海可滋阴益肾;E 以上均不是。	What is the main rationale for treating the onset of carbuncle at night by needling K6 (Zhào Hǎi)? A. K6 (Zhào Hǎi) is one of meeting points between eight extraordinary meridians & twelve master meridians / confluence points [bā mài bā huì xué]; B. yin qiao [yin heel meridian] is diseased; C. K6 (Zhào Hǎi) can clear heat and secure the spirit; D. K6 (Zhào Hǎi) can water yin and benefit kidneys; E. none of the above.
1897	用灸法矫正胎位成功率最高的妊娠月份是: A·妊娠 8 个月以上; B·妊娠 7 个月 C. ·妊娠 6 个月; D·妊娠 5 个月; E·妊娠 3-4 个月	During what month of pregnancy may moxibustion be applied to correct fetus poisition with a best chance of success? A. over 8th month of pregancy; B. 7th month of pregnancy; C. 6th month of pregancy; D. 5th month of pregnancy; E. 3rd ---4th month of pregancy.
1898	用皮肤针治疗面瘫，一般可叩刺: A·睛明 攒竹 地仓 颊车; B·阳白 丝竹空 承浆 下关 C. ·合谷 地仓 颊车 承泣; D·牵正 阳白 太阳 四白; E·风池 合谷 太冲 地仓	In skin needle therapy, in general, which group of points should be needled. by tapping? A.B1 (Jīng Míng); B2 (Zǎn Zhú) S4 (Dì Cāng) S6 (Jiá Chē); B. G14 (Yáng; Bái); Sj23 (Sī Zhú Kōng) R24 (Chéng Jiàng) S7 (Xià Guān); C. Li4 (Hé Gǔ); S4 (Dì Cāng) S6 (Jiá Chē) S1 (Chéng Qì); D. qiān zhèng, G14 (Yáng; Bái) Tài Yáng S2 (Sì Bái); E. G20 (Fēng Chí). Li4 (Hé Gǔ); Lv3 (Tài Chōng) S4 (Dì Cāng).
1899	用少量维生素 B，或当归注射液注射关元中极二穴，可治疗: A·遗尿; B·癃闭 C. ·脱肛; D·遗精; E·石淋	What disease can be treated by injecting a small amount of vitamin B or radix angelicae sinensis injection solution into R4 (Guān Yuán) and R3 (Zhōng Jí)? A. enuresis; B. suppression of urination; C. prolapse of the anus; D. seminal emission; E. Stony strangury.
1900	用水针治疗鼻衄，应首选: A·二间 合谷; B·内庭 迎香 C. ·曲池 风池; D 迎香 合谷; E·上星 合谷	In point injection therapy, which group of points should be selected to treat nosebleed? A. Li2 (Èr Jiān) Li4 (Hé Gǔ); B. S44 (Nèi Tíng); Li20 (Yíng Xiāng); C. Li11 (Qū Chí) G20 (Fēng Chí); D. Li20 (Yíng Xiāng) Li4 (Hé Gǔ); E. D23 (Shàng Xīng) Li4 (Hé Gǔ).

1901	用穴位埋线法治疗咳嗽，除取大椎定喘肺俞外，还可加用: A·天突 膻中; B·廉泉 足三里 C. ·心俞 膈俞; D·膏肓俞 肾俞; E·以上均不是	In point catgut implantation therapy, which group of points should be selected to treat cough in addition to: D14 (Dà Zhuī), Dìng Chuǎn;B13 (Fèi Shū)? A. R22 (Tiān Tū) R17 (Shān Zhōng); B. R23 (Lián Quán) S36 (Zú Sān Lǐ); C. B15 (Xīn Shū) B17 (Gé Shū); D. B43 (Gāo Huāng Shū) B23 (Shèn Shū); E. None of the above.
1902	用子母补泻法治疗肾经实证应取: A·阴谷; B·然谷 C. 太溪; D·复溜; E·涌泉	What point should be treated according to the principle of mother-child tonification and sedation? A. K10 (Yīn Gǔ); B. K2 (Rán Gǔ); C. K3 (Tài Xī); D. K7 (Fù Liū); E. K1 (Yǒng Quán).
1903	用子母补泻法治疗心经实证应取: A·少海; B·少府 C. ·少冲; D·灵道; E·神门	According to "tonification and sedation by mother and child points", what point should be selected to treat excess of the heart meridian? A. H3 (Shào Hǎi); B. H8 (Shào Fǔ;) C. H9 (Shào Chōng); D. H4 (Líng Dào); E. H7 (Shén Mén).
1904	用子母补泻法治疗心经虚证应取: A·少海; B·少府 C. ·少冲; D·灵道; E·神门	According to "tonification and sedation by mother and child points", what point should be selected to treat deficiency of the heart meridian? A. H3 (Shào Hǎi); B. H8 (Shào Fǔ); C. H9 (Shào Chōng); D. H4 (Líng Dào); E. H7 (Shén Mén).
1905	由中风所致的口眼㖞斜，除取地仓颊车合谷内庭外，宜加用: A·人中; B·翳风 C. ·外关; D·太冲; E·商丘	What point should be used to treat wry eyes and mouth in addition to S4 (Dì Cāng), S6 (Jiá Chē), Li4 (Hé Gǔ), S44 (Nèi Tíng)? A. D26 (Shuǐ Gōu, Rén Zhōng); B. Sj17 (Yì Fēng); C. Sj5 (Wài Guān); D. Lv3 (Tài Chōng); E. Sp5 (Shāng Qiū).
1906	有和解少阳、清热泻火、疏通少阳经气之功的手少阳经穴是：A¨耳门; B·听会 C. ·中渚; D·太阳; E·外关	What point on the hand lesser hang meridian can harmonize and relieve lesser yang / shao yang、clear heat and sedate fire、disperse and conecti energy of lesser yang meridians? A¨ Sj21 / Ěr Mén; B · G2 / Tīng Huì; C. Sj3 / Zhōng Zhǔ; D · Tài yáng / sun / temple; E · Sj5 / Wài Guān
1907	有和胃解痉作用的一组穴位是：A·神门、关元; B·丰隆、下巨虚 C. ·伏兔、上巨虚; D·内关、梁门; E·阴陵泉、下巨虚	What point can relieve stomach spasm? A · H7 / Shén Mén，R4 / Guān Yuán ; B · S40 / Fēng Lóng，S39 / Xià Jù Xū; C. · S32 / Fú Tù，S37 / Shàng Jù Xū; D · P6 / Nèi Guān，S21 / Liáng Mén; E · Sp9 / Yīn Líng Quán，S39 / Xià Jù Xū
1908	鱼际部位割治，可治疗: A·腕部腱鞘囊肿; B 腕关节狭窄性腱鞘炎 C. ·哮喘; D·小儿疳疾; E·咽肿喉痹	What can be treated by point cutting therapy applied to thenar eminence region? A. in the wrist thecal cyst; B. tenocynovitis in the writ joint; C. asthma; D. malnutrition in children; E. swelling and rheumatism in the throat.
1909	与颞下颌关节功能紊乱综合征的治疗无关的是: A·听宫、下关; B·肝俞、肾俞 C. ·太阳、风池; D·合谷、颊车; E·地仓、大迎	Which points are not related to the treatment of the syndrome of temporalmandibular joint functional disorder? A · Si19 / Tīng Gōng，S7 / Xià Guān; B ·B18 / Gān Shū，B23 / Shèn Shū; C. · Tài yáng / sun / temple，G20 / Fēng Chí; D · Li4 / Hé Gǔ，S6 / Jiá Chē; E · S4 / Dì Cāng，S5 / Dà

		Yíng
1910	与心相配的天干是：A·甲；B·己 C. ·丙；D·丁；E·壬	What stem corresponds to heart? A. Jiă; B. Jĭ; C. Bĭng; D. Dīng; E. Rén
1911	与阳维相通的穴位是：A·公孙；B·内关 C. ·外关；D·照海；E·后溪	What point is in communication with the fastener meridian of yang / yáng wéi mài? A · Sp4 / Gōng Sūn; B · P6 / Nèi Guān; C. Sj5 / Wài Guān; D · K6 / Zhào Hăi; E · Si3 / Hòu Xī
1912	与阴维相通的穴位是：A·公孙；B·内关 C. ·外关；D·照海；E·后溪	What point is in communication with the fastener meridian of yin / yin wéi mài? A · Sp4 / Gōng Sūn; B · P6 / Nèi Guān; C. · Sj5 / Wài Guān; D · K6 / Zhào Hăi; E · Si3 / Hòu Xī
1913	月经不调，一般分为：A·经漏，经迟 经早；B经早'经迟 经乱 C. 经乱痛经经早；D 经迟;经闭经乱；E 经早经闭经迟	In general, menoxenia may be divided into: A · leaking menstruation，overdue menstruation、premature menstruation; B premature menstruation、overdue menstruation、irregular menstruation; C. irregular menstruation、 period pain 、premature menstruatio; D overdue menstruation, suppression of menstruation、irregular menstruation; E premature menstruation、suppression of menstruation、overdue menstruation
1914	月经先期的治疗原则是：A.清热解毒调和气血；B 温经散寒和血调经 C. 调补肝肾；D，清热调经	What treatment principle should be applied to treat premature menstruation? A. to clear heat and detoxicate, regulate and harmonize energy and blood; B. to warm meridians and disperse cold, harmonize blood and regulate menstruation; C. to regulate and tone up the liver and kidneys; D. to clear heat and regumate menstruation.
1915	晕厥以选下列哪组穴位为佳? A 百会神庭.印堂太阳；B 百会囟会人中承浆 C. 通天四神聪神门液门；D 人中合谷.三阴交内关；E 人中合谷，足三里，中冲。	Which group of points should best be selected to treat syncope [yun jue]? A. D20 [Băi Huì], D24 [Shén tíng], YÌN TÁNG, TÀI YÁNG; B. D20 [Băi Huì], D22 [Xìn Huì], D26 (Renzhong ,Shuigou), R24 [Chéng Jiàng]; C. B7 [Tōng Tiān], SÌ SHÉN, H7 [Shén Mén], Sj2 [Yè Mén]; D. D26 (Renzhong Shuigou), Li4 [Hé Gŭ], Sp6 [Sān Yīn Jiāo], P6 [Nèi Guān]; E. D26 (Renzhong Shuigou), Li4 [Hé Gŭ], S36 [Zú Sān Lĭ], P9 [Zhōng Chōng]
1916	在阿是穴点刺出血治疗的头痛类型是：A·痰浊上扰证；B·肝阳上亢证 C. 气血不足证；D·外感风邪证；E 风热袭络证	What type of headache may be treated by ouchi points / pressure points with dotted-needling to let blood? A turbid phlegm disturbing upward syndrome; B liver yang uprising syndrome; C. energy-blood deficiency syndrome; D attack of external pathogenic wind syndrome; E. wind heat attacking linking meridian syndrome
1917	在耳周有疏利少阳、行气通窍作用的足少阳经穴是：A¨耳门；B·听会 C. ·中渚；D·太阳；E·外关	What point around the ear and on the foot lesser yang meridian can promote energy circulation and connect cavities?：A¨ Sj21 / Ĕr Mén; B · G2 / Tīng Huì; C. · Sj3 / Zhōng Zhŭ; D · Tài yáng / sun / temple; E · Sj5 / Wài Guān
1918	在华佗夹脊穴中，治疗下腹	Among Huá Tuó Jiā Jí, which points can treat the

	疾患的是：A.胸 12—腰 1; B.胸 10—腰 4 C. 腰 1—腰 5; D. 胸 12—腰 5	diseases of the lower abdomen? A. thoracic 12—lumbar 1; B. thoracic 10—lumbar 4; C. lumbar 1—lumbar 5; D. thoracic 12—lumbar 5.
1919	在手太阴肺经穴位中，治疗头项病痛可以选用: A·中府; B·尺泽 C. ·列缺; D·太渊; E·鱼际	Which of the following points may be selected to treat headache and pain in the back of neck? A · Lu1 / Zhōng Fǔ; B · Lu5 / Chǐ Zé; C. ·Lu7 / Liè Quē; D · Lu9 / TàiYuān; E · Lu10 / Yǔ Jì
1920	在特定穴中，急性病痛一般选用: A 原穴; B 络穴 C. 郄穴; D 合穴	Among the specially marked points, which is normally selected to treat acute disease and pain? A yuán xué / starting-points / source-points; B. blinking points, / luo points; C. fissural point / cleft point / xi point; D hé xué / terminal-points / sea-points points
1921	在特定穴中，能主治 "五脏六腑之有疾"的是: A·输穴; B·合穴 C. ·原穴; D·下合穴; E·郄穴	Which of the following specially marked. points (te ding xue) may be selected to treat the disorders of the five viscera and six bowels? A. · lake-points / stream-points / Shù Xué; B. · hé xué / terminal-points / sea-points points; C. yuán xué / starting-points / source-points; D. ·lower merging points / xia he xue; E. ·fissural points / cleft points / xi point.
1922	在下列"井"穴中，具有催乳作用的穴位是：A.少泽; B. 少商 C. 商阳; D，少冲	Which of the following well points (jing xue) van promote milk secretion most effectively? A. Si1 (Shào Zé); B. Lu11 (Shǎo Shāng); C. Li1 (Shāng Yáng); D. H9 (Shào Chōng)
1923	在下列"井"穴中，治疗胎位不正应首选 A.中冲; B 大教 C. 至阴; D 历兑	Which of the following well points (jing xue) is best to treat fetus in wrong position? A. P9 (Zhōng Chōng); B. Lv1 (Dà Dūn); C. B67 (Zhì Yīn); D. S45 (Lì Duì).
1924	在下列各穴中，治疗口疮口臭，最好选用: A·条口; B·劳宫 C. ·合谷; D·地仓; E·迎香	Which group of points should be selected to treat mouth vanker and bad breath? A. S38 (Tiáo Kǒu); B. P8 (Láo Gōng); C. Li4 (Hé Gǔ); D. S4 (Dì Cāng); E. Li20 (Yíng Xiāng).
1925	在下列各穴中，治疗眼底病变一般应首选: A·太阳; B·球后 C. ·鱼腰; D·印堂; E· 睛明	Which point should be selected to treat the disorder of eyeground? A. Tài Yáng; B. Qiú Hòu; C. Yú Yāo; D. Yìn Táng; EB1 (Jīng Míng).
1926	在下列经外奇穴中，主治痔疮脱肛的穴位主要是: A·中魁; B·外劳宫 C. ·二白; D·中泉; E·八邪	Which of the following extraordinary points may be selected to treat hemorrhoids and prolapse of the anus? A. Zhōng Kuí; B. Wài Láo Gōng; C. Èr Bái; D. Zhōng Quán; E. Bā Xié.
1927	在下列络穴中，治疗癫痫的首选穴是: A·长强; B·鸠尾 C. ·大包; D·公孙; E· 蠡沟.	Which of the following linking points, (luo xue) may best be selected to treat epilepsy? A. D1 [Cháng Qiáng]; B. R15 [Jiū Wěi]; C. Sp21 [Dà Bāo]; D. Sp4 [Gōng Sūn]; E.Lv5 [Lí Gōu]
1928	在下列特定穴中，治疗腑病应首选: A·五输穴; B·原穴 C. ·络穴; D·下合穴; E·郄穴	Which of the following specially marked. points (te ding xue) should be used to treat the diseases of bowels? A. five command points (wu shu xue); B. original points (yuan points or source points); C. linking points, (luo xue); D. lower merging points (xia he xue); E. fissural points (xi xue).
1929	在下列穴位中，对心率具有	Which of the following points can regulate heart beats in

	双向调整作用的主要是: A·足三里; B·内关 C. ·合谷; D·巨阙; E·神门	both ways? A. S36 (Zú Sān Lǐ); B. P6 (Nèi Guān); C. Li4 (Hé Gǔ); D. R14 (Jù Què); E. H7 (Shén Mén).
1930	在下列穴位中,孕妇可用: A·关元; B·气海 C. ·血海; D·腰阳关; E·昆仑	Which point may be applied to treat pregnant women? A. R4 (Guān Yuán); B. R6 (Qì Hǎi); C. Sp10 (Xuè Hǎi); D. D3 (Yāo Yáng Guān); E. B60 (Kūn Lún).
1931	在下列穴位中，治疗肝脾肿大可以选用: A·腰眼穴; B·腰奇穴 C. ·三角灸; D·痞根穴; E·十七椎	Which point may be selected to treat hepatosplenomegaly? A. Yāo Yǎn; B. Yāo Qí; C. San Jiao Jiu; D. Pǐ Gēn; E. Shí Qī Zhuī.
1932	在下列穴组中，除……外，均为主客配穴: A·太渊 偏历; B·冲阳 公孙 C. ·京骨 大钟; D·神门 支正; E·丘墟 光明	Which group of points is NOT a host-guest combination? A. Lu9 (Tài Yuān) Li6 (Piān Lì); B. S42 (Chōng Yáng) Sp4 (Gōng Sūn); C. B64 (Jīng Gǔ) K4 (Dà Zhōng); D. H7 (Shén Mén) Si7 (Zhi Zhèng); E. G40 (Qiū Xū). G37 (Guāng Míng).
1933	在治疗带状疱疹的处方中具有疏肝泻热作用并为荥穴的是: A·期门; B·阴陵泉、支沟 C. ·行间; D·夹脊穴; E·皮损局部	In the prescription of points to treat herpes zoster, what yíng xué / outpouring point / spring point can disperse the liver and sedate heat? A · Lv14 / Qí Mén; B · Sp9 / Yīn Líng Quán, Sj6 / Zhi Gōu; C. · Lv2 / Xíng Jiān; D · Huá tuó jiā jí / Dr Huatuo's clippings of spine; E ·local region of skin injury
1934	在治疗带状疱疹时胸胁部皮疹加: A·期门; B·阴陵泉、支沟 C. ·行间; D·夹脊穴; E·皮损局部	What point should be added to treat herpes zoster with skin rash in the chest and costal regions? A · Lv14 / Qí Mén; ·B Sp9 / Yīn Líng Quán, Sj6 / Zhi Gōu; C. Lv2 / Xíng Jiān; D · Huá tuó jiā jí / Dr Huatuo's clippings of spine; E ·local region of skin injury.
1935	在治疗高热的处方中能宣肺解表、清泻阳明实热的穴位为: A·大椎; B·曲池 C. ·内关; D·外关; E·风池	In the prescription of points to treat high fever, what point can expand the lungs and relieve the superficial region,clear and sedate bright yang / yang ming excess heat? A ·D14 / Dà Zhuī; B · Li11 / Qū Chí; C. · P6 / Nèi Guān; D · Sj5 / Wài Guān; E · G20 / Fēng Chí
1936	在治疗胃肠痉挛中，专治急性发作性痛症的穴位是: A·中脘 ·B·足三里 C. ·合谷; D·梁丘; E·天枢	What point is specialized in treating acute pain of gastrointestinal spasm? A · R12 / Zhōng Wǎn; ·B · S36 / Zú Sān Lǐ; C. Li4 / Hé Gǔ; D ·S34 [Liáng Qiū]; E · S25 / Tiān Shū.
1937	在治疗胁痛的针灸处方中，有"见肝之病，当先实脾"之意的腧穴是: A·期门; B·阳陵泉 C. ·足三里; D·支沟; E·太冲	It is said in the prescription of points to treat hypochondriac pain, that "when the liver is diseased, it is necessary to tone up the spleen", what point does it refer to? A · Lv14 / Qí Mén; B · G34 / Yáng Líng Quán; C. · S36 / Zú Sān Lǐ; D · Sj6 / Zhi Gōu; E · Lv3 / Tài Chōng
1938	在治疗癔病的基本处方中具有宽胸解郁作用的穴位是: A.神门; B·内关 C. ·期门; D·心俞; E. 太冲	In the basic prescription of points to treat hysteria, what points can expand the chest and relieve inhibition? A. H7 / Shén Mén; B · P6 / Nèi Guān; C. · Lv14 / Qí Mén; D ·B15 / Xīn Shū ·; E. Lv3 / Tài Chōng
1939	在治疗癔病的基本处方中具有疏肝理气解郁作用的	In the basic prescription of points to treat hysteria, what combination of points can disperse the liver and regulate

	穴组是：A·内关配合谷；B·太冲配期门 C. ·内关配心俞；D·合谷配神门；E·心俞配内关	energy and relieve inhibition? A · P6 / Nèi Guān combined with Li4 / Hé Gŭ; B · Lv3 / Tài Chōng combined with Lv14 / Qí Mén; C. · P6 / Nèi Guān; combined with B15 / Xīn Shū; D · Li4 / Hé Gŭ combined with H7 / Shén Mén; E ·B15 / Xīn Shū combined with P6 / Nèi Guān.
1940	脏腑病远端取穴应首选：A·头面；B·胸腹 C. ·腰背；D·四肢肘、膝关节以上；E·四肢肘、膝关节以下.	What distal points should be selected first to treat diseases of ·viscera and bowels? A · head and face; B ·chest and abdomen; C. ·waist and back; D ·four limbs, elbow、 and above knee joints; E ·four limbs, elbow、 and below knee joints
1941	痄腮流行多见于 A.冬季；B.夏季 C. 秋季；D 冬春季	In what season does mumps occur mostly? A. winter; B. summer; C. autumn; D. winter and spring.
1942	痄腮若兼睾丸肿大，治疗应在主方的基础上加用：A·中极 三阴交；B·归来 蠡沟 C. 气冲 太冲；D·太冲 曲泉；E·曲泉 三阴交	Which group of points should be selected to treat mumps with swollen and enlarged testes in addition to major points? A. R3 (Zhōng Jí); Sp6 (Sān Yīn Jiāo); B. S29 (Guī Lái); Lv5 (Lí Gōu); C. S30 (Qì Chōng); G9 (Tiān; Chōng); D. G9 (Tiān; Chōng) Lv8 (Qū Quán); E. Lv8 (Qū Quán). Sp6 (Sān Yīn Jiāo).
1943	痄腮治疗时除取合谷外关颊车翳风外，还应取 A，太冲；B.关冲 C. 少冲；D 中冲 E 以上都不是。	What point should be selected to treat mumps in addition to: Li4 (Hé Gŭ), Sj5 (Wài Guān), S6 (Jiá Chē), Sj17 (Yì Fēng)? A.Lv3 / Tài Chōng; B. Sj1 / Guān Chōng; C. H9 / Shào Chōng; D P9 / Zhōng Chōng; E..none of the above.
1944	照海穴与八卦中的( )相配：A·乾；B·艮 C. ·坤；D·坎；E·兑	K6 / Zhào Hăi is paired wih which of the eight trigrams? A ·Qīan (1st trigram); B ·Gěn (7th trigram); C. ·Kūn (8th trigram); D ·Kăn (6th trigram); E ·Duì (2nd trigram)
1945	照海治大便秘结时常配：A 水泉;B 四渎;C 支沟; D. 水分:E 水道。	What point should be selected to combine with K6 (Zhào Hăi) in the treatment of constipation? A. K5 [Shuĭ Quán]; B. Sj9 [Sì Dú]; C. Sj6 [Zhi Gōu]; D. R9 [Shuĭ Fēn]; E. S28 [Shuĭ Dào].
1946	针刺麻醉时捻针的频率为每分钟几次：A.50 ·100; B.100 ·200 C. ·150 ·250; D·200 ·300; E·250 ·300	What is the frequency of twirling the needle each minute in acupuncture anesthesia? A.50—100; B.100—200 C. ·150—250; D ·200—300; E ·250 —300
1947	针刺面瘫的选穴和配穴原则是：A·少阳经穴为主，阳明太阳经穴为辅；B·太阳经穴为主，阳明少阳经穴为辅 C. ，足少阳经穴为主，手少阳足阳明经穴为辅；D·足阳明经穴为主，手阳明足少阳经穴为辅；E. 阳明经穴为主，少阳经穴为辅	Which should be the principle of selecting points and combining points to treat facial paralysis? A. points on lesser yang meridians as primary points, points on bright yang and greater yang meridians as combining points; B. points on greater yang meridians as primary points, points on bright yang and lesser yang meridians as combining points; C. points on lesser yang meridian of foot as primary points, points on bright yang meridian of foot as combining points; D. points on bright yang meridian of foot as primary points, points on bright yang meridian of hand and lesser yang meridian of foot as combining points; E. points on bright yang meridians

		as primary points, points on lesser yang meridians as combining points.
1948	针刺治疗风寒阻络型面肌痉挛加: A·内庭; B·太溪 C. ·大椎; D·风池; E·翳风。	What point may be added to treat spasm of facial muscles that belongs to wind cold obstructing linking meridian? A · S44 / Nèi Tíng; B · K3 / Tài Xī; C. ·D14 / Dà Zhuī; D · G20 / Fēng Chí; E · Sj17 / Yì Fēng 。
1949	针刺治疗呕吐不宜选用 A. 足三里; B，内关 C. 外关; D 中脘	What point should NOT be selected to treat vomiting? A. S36 (Zú Sān Lǐ); B. P6 (Nèi Guān); C. Sj5 (Wài Guān); D. R12 (Zhōng Wǎn).
1950	针刺治疗青光眼，能使眼压下降的最好穴位是: A·太冲; B·行间 C. ·足临泣; D·侠溪; E·光明	Which point may best be selected to lower eye pressure in treating glaucoma? A. Lv3 (Tài Chōng); B. Lv2 (Xíng Jiān); C. G41 (Zú Lín Qì, Lín Qì); D. G43 (Xiá Xī); E. G37 (Guāng Míng).
1951	针刺治疗痄腮，应选何经穴为主? A·手足少阳; B·手足阳明 C. ·手阳明; D·手少阳; E·足阳明	What meridian points should be selected as major points to treat mumps? A. lesser yang meridians of hand and foot; B. bright yang meridians of hand and foot; C. bright yang meridian of hand D. lesser yang meridian of hand; E. bright yang meridian of foot.
1952	针灸并用、补法适用于: A·肺气上逆证 ·B·胃气上逆证 ·C·肝气上逆证; D·肾不纳气证; E·都不对	Which can be treated by acupuncture and moxibustion with tonfication? A ·lungs energy uprising syndrome; B ·stomach energy uprising syndrome; ·C ·liver energy uprising syndrome; D ·kidneys unable to absorb energy syndrome; E · none of the above
1953	针灸并用、泻法适宜于: A·肝血不足证; B·肝脉寒滞证 C. ·肝阳上亢证; D·肝气郁结证; E·肝风内动证	Which can be treated by acupuncture and moxibustion with sedation? A ·liver blood deficiency syndrome; B ·liver meridian cold and congestion syndrome C. ·liver yang uprising syndrome; D · liver energy congestion syndrome; E ·internal liver wind disturbing syndrome.
1954	针灸抗衰老，脾气虚弱型可在基本处方的基础上加: A·脾俞、胃俞; B·脾俞、肾俞 C. ·气海、脾俞; D·肾俞、肝俞; E·肾俞、大肠俞	What points may be added to the basic prescription of points for antiaging that belongs to the spleen energy deficiency and weakness type? A. B20 / Pí Shū，B21 / Wèi Shū; B. B20 / Pí Shū，B23 / Shèn Shū; C. R6 / Qì Hǎi，B20 / Pí Shū; D. B23 / Shèn Shū，B18 / Gān Shū; E. B23 / Shèn Shū，B25 / Dà Cháng Shū
1955	针灸抗衰老，心肺气虚型可在基本处方的基础上加: A·神门、尺泽; B·肺俞、神门 C. ·心俞、太渊; D·心俞、肺俞; E，列;缺、太渊	What points may be added to the basic prescription of points for antiaging that belongs to the heart and lung energy deficiency type? A. · H7 / Shén Mén，Lu5 / Chǐ Zé; B. ·B13 / Fèi Shū，H7 / Shén Mén; C. ·B15 / Xīn Shū，Lu9 / TàiYuān; D. ·B15 / Xīn Shū，B13 / Fèi Shū; E. Lu7 / Liè Quē，Lu9 / TàiYuān
1956	针灸治疗鼻出血的操作中，下列哪个腧穴宜斜向上透刺鼻通穴: A.迎香; B·鼻通 C. ·印堂; D·上星; E·合谷	In treating nosebleed by acupuncture therapy, which point should be inserted slantingly upward all the way until the needle reaches Bí tōng / smooth passage of the

		nose? A. Li20 / Yíng Xiāng; B ·Bí tōng / smooth passage of the nose; C. Yìn táng / midpoint between eyebrows / seal hall; ·D23 / Shàng Xīng; E · Li4 / Hé Gǔ
1957	针灸治疗扁平疣脾湿痰瘀型，可在基本处方的基础上再加：A·曲池；B·尺泽 C. ·阴陵泉；D·太冲；E·内庭	In acupuncture therapy, what point may be added to the basic prescription of points to treat the spleen dampness with phlegm coagulatiopn type of flat wart? A · Li11 / Qū Chí; B · Lu5 / Chǐ Zé; C. · Sp9 / Yīn Líng Quán; D · Lv3 / Tài Chōng; E · S44 / Nèi Tíng
1958	针灸治疗不孕症之气滞血瘀证，可在基本方基础上再加：A·气海、血海；B·太冲、膈俞 C. 三阴交·关元；D·次髎、中极；E·归来、行间	What points may be added to the basic prescription of points to treat the energy; congestion and blood coagulation type of infertility in women? A · R6 / Qì Hǎi，Sp10 / Xuè Hǎi; B · Lv3 / Tài Chōng，B17 / Gé Shū; C. Sp6 / Sān Yīn Jiāo ·R4 / Guān Yuán; D · B32 / Cì Liáo，R3 / Zhōng Jí; E · S29 / Guī Lái，Lv2 / Xíng Jiān
1959	针灸治疗不孕症之痰湿阻滞证，可在基本方基础上再加：A公孙、内关，B合谷、三阴交C 丰隆，阴陵泉；D·中脘、足三里；E·中极、肺俞	What points may be added to the basic prescription of points to treat the phlegm dampness obstruction type of infertility in women? A. Sp4 / Gōng Sūn，P6 / Nèi Guān; B. Li4 / Hé Gǔ，Sp6 / Sān Yīn Jiāo; C. S40 / Fēng Lóng ，Sp9 / Yīn Líng Quán; D. · R12 / Zhōng Wǎn，S36 / Zú Sān Lǐ; E. · R3 / Zhōng Jí，B13 / Fèi Shū
1960	针灸治疗丹毒取穴以( )为主：A·皮损局部和手阳明经腧穴；B·皮损局部 C. ·手阳明经腧穴；D·足阳明经腧穴 ·E·督脉腧穴	What should be selected as primary in acupuncture therapy of erysipelas? A ·local damaged skin region and acupuncture points on hand bright yang / yang ming meridian; B ·local damaged skin region; C. ·acupuncture points on hand bright yang / yang ming meridian; D ·acupuncture points on hand bright yang meridian of foot; ·E ·acupuncture points on du mai / governing meridian
1961	针灸治疗丹毒湿热蕴结型可在基本处方上加：A·水沟；B·合谷 C. ·委中；D·血海；E·阴陵泉	What points may be added to the basic prescription of points to treat the hidden damp heat type of erysipelas? A · D26 / Shuǐ Gōu / Rén Zhōng; B · Li4 / Hé Gǔ; C. B40 / Wěi Zhōng; D · Sp10 / Xuè Hǎi; E · Sp9 / Yīn Líng Quán
1962	针灸治疗丹毒胎火蕴毒型可在基本处方上加：A·水沟；B·合谷 C. ·委中；D·血海；E. 曲池	What points may be added to the basic prescription of points to treat the hidden toxin infantile fire type of erysipelas? A · D26 / Shuǐ Gōu / Rén Zhōng; B · Li4 / Hé Gǔ; C. B40 / Wěi Zhōng; D · Sp10 / Xuè Hǎi; E. Li11 / Qū Chí
1963	针灸治疗胆石症肝胆气滞型，可在基础方上再加：A·内关透外关；B·内关透支沟·C·支沟透偏历；D·合谷透三间；E·阳陵泉透阴陵泉	What points may be added to the basic prescription of points to treat the liver-gallbladder energhy congestion type of Cholelithiasis? A · P6 / Nèi Guān inserted all the way through Sj5 / Wài Guān; B · P6 / Nèi Guān inserted all the way through Sj6 / Zhi Gōu; ·C · Sj6 / Zhi Gōu inserted all the way through Li6 / Piān Lì; D · Li4 / Hé Gǔ inserted all the way through Li3 / Sān Jiān; E · G34 / Yáng Líng Quán inserted all the

		way through Sp9 / Yīn Líng Quán
1964	针灸治疗胆石症以哪组选穴最佳：A·以肝、胆的背俞穴为主；B·以肝、胆的募穴为主C·以肝、胆的下合穴为主；D·以肝、胆的原穴为主；E·以肝、胆的背俞穴、募穴、下合穴为主	In treating Cholelithiasis by acupuncture therapy, which group is the best selection of points? A ·selecting liver and gallbladder posterior points / back shu points / Bèi shù xué as primary points; B ·selecting liver、gallbladder gathering point / mu point as primary points; C. ·selecting liver、gallbladder lower merging point as primary points; D ·selecting liver、gallbladder yuán xué / starting-points / source-points as primary points; E ·selecting posterior points / back shu points / bèi shù xué 、gathering points / mu points、lower merging points of the liver and gallbladder as primary points
1965	针灸治疗肺经热盛之鼻出血宜在基本处方的基础上加：A·少商、风池；B·内庭、厉兑 C. ·太冲、侠溪；D·太溪、太冲；E·足三里、三阴交	What points may be added to the basic prescription of points to treat the lungs meridian with abundant heat type of nosebleed? A · Lu11 / Shǎo Shāng，G20 / Fēng Chí; B · S44 / Nèi Tíng，S45 / Lì Duì; C. · Lv3 / Tài Chōng，G43 / Xiá Xī; D · K3 / Tài Xī, Lv3 / Tài Chōng; E · S36 / Zú Sān Lǐ，Sp6 / Sān Yīn Jiāo
1966	针灸治疗肺胃热盛之咽喉肿痛可在基本处方的基础上加：A·尺泽、曲池、内庭；B·尺泽、外关、少商 C. ·太溪、涌泉、三阴交；D·少商、太溪、曲池；E·以上都不对	What points may be added to the basic prescription of points to treat the lung and stomach with abundant heat type of swollen and painful throat? A. · Lu5 / Chǐ Zé，Li11 / Qū Chí，S44 / Nèi Tíng; B. · Lu5 / Chǐ Zé，Sj5 / Wài Guān，Lu11 / Shǎo Shāng; C. · K3 / Tài Xī，K1 / Yǒng Quán，Sp6 / Sān Yīn Jiāo; D. · Lu11 / Shǎo Shāng，K3 / Tài Xī，Li11 / Qū Chí; E. none of the above
1967	针灸治疗风热外袭型麦粒肿可在基本处方的基础上再加： A·合谷、风池；B·曲池、行间·C. ·三阴交、阴陵泉；D·风门、肺俞；E·中脘、合谷	What points may be added to the basic prescription of points to treat hordeolum / stye due to the external attack of wind heat? A · Li4 / Hé Gǔ，G20 / Fēng Chí; B · Li11 / Qū Chí，Lv2 / Xíng Jiān; · C. Sp6 / Sān Yīn Jiāo，Sp9 / Yīn Líng Quán; D ·B12 / Fēng Mén，B13 / Fèi Shū; E · R12 / Zhōng Wǎn，Li4 / Hé Gǔ
1968	针灸治疗肝火上逆之鼻出血宜在基本处方的基础上加：A·少商、风池；B·内庭、厉兑 C. ·太冲、侠溪；D·太溪、太冲；E·足三里、三阴交	What points may be added to the basic prescription of points to treat the liver fire uprising type of nosebleed? A · Lu11 / Shǎo Shāng，G20 / Fēng Chí; B · S44 / Nèi Tíng，S45 / Lì Duì; C. · Lv3 / Tài Chōng，G43 / Xiá Xī; D · K3 / Tài Xī, Lv3 / Tài Chōng; E · S36 / Zú Sān Lǐ，Sp6 / Sān Yīn Jiāo
1969	针灸治疗肝经湿热型阴痒的处方是：A·蠡沟、太冲、行间、曲骨；B·肾俞、太溪、中极、足三里 C. ·血海、三阴交、命门、太冲；D·三阴交、脾俞、足三里、肾俞；E·三阴交、行间、脾俞、太溪	What is the prescripion of points to treat the liver meridian damp heat type of yin itch? A · Lv5 / Lí Gōu, Lv3 / Tài Chōng, Lv2 / Xíng Jiān, R2 / Qū Gǔ; B. B23 / Shèn Shū，K3 / Tài Xī，R3 / Zhōng Jí，S36 / Zú Sān Lǐ; C. · Sp10 / Xuè Hǎi，Sp6 / Sān Yīn Jiāo，D4 / Mìng Mén，Lv3 / Tài Chōng; D · Sp6 / Sān Yīn Jiāo，B20 /

	溪	Pí Shū, S36 / Zú Sān Lǐ, B23 / Shèn Shū; E · Sp6 / Sān Yīn Jiāo, Lv2 / Xíng Jiān, B20 / Pí Shū, K3 / Tài Xī
1970	针灸治疗肝阳上亢所致的眩晕除取风池，肝俞行间外，还应选 A.太溪; B.阳溪 C. 侠溪; D 后溪	In treating the liver yang uprising type of vertigo by acupuncture and moxibustion, what other point should be selected in addition to G20 (Fēng Chí), B18 (Gān Shū), Lv2 (Xíng Jiān)? A. K3 (Tài Xī); B. Li5 (Yáng Xī); C. G43 (Xiá Xī); D. Si3 (Hòu Xī).
1971	针灸治疗寒疝可在基本处方上加神阙及：A·气海; B·下巨虚 C. ·关元; D·水分; E·阴谷	In addition to R8 / Shén Què, what point may be added to the basic prescription of points to treat cold hernia? A · R6 / Qì Hǎi; B · S39 / Xià Jù Xū; C. · R4 / Guān Yuán; D · R9 / Shuǐ Fēn; E · K10 / Yīn Gǔ.
1972	针灸治疗寒湿阻络型血栓闭塞性脉管炎，可在基本处方上加：A·阴陵泉; B·太冲 C. 气海; D·曲池; E·八风	What points may be added to the basic prescription of points to treat the cold dampness obstructing linking meridians type of thrombo-embolia angitis? A. · Sp9 / Yīn Líng Quán; B. · Lv3 / Tài Chōng; C. R6 / Qì Hǎi; D · Li11 / Qū Chí; E. Bā fēng / eight winds
1973	针灸治疗狐疝可在基本处方上加三角灸及：·A上巨虚; B·下巨虚 C. ·维道; D·中极; E·公孙	In addition to “triangular moxibustion (san jiao jiu)”, what point may be added to the basic prescription of points to treat fox hernia / inguinal hernia? · A S37 / Shàng Jù Xū; B · S39 / Xià Jù Xū; C. · G28 / Wéi Dào; D · R3 / Zhōng Jí; E · Sp4 / Gōng Sūn
1974	针灸治疗急惊风的常用方法为：A·补法; B·泻法 C. ·可以用补法，也可以用泻法; D·补法与泻法交替运用; E·平补平泻	What is the most common method of treating acute infantile convulsion? A · tonfication; B · sedation; C. ·twelve muscular meridians / jing jin tonfication or by sedation; D · alternating tonfication and sedation; E · neutral technique
1975	针灸治疗腱鞘囊肿常取穴位是：A·外关; B·阳溪 C. ·囊肿局部; D·后溪; E曲池	What point is frequently selected to treat thecal cyst? A · Sj5 / Wài Guān; B · Li5 / Yáng Xī; C. ·local cyst; D · Si3 / Hòu Xī; E. Li11 / Qū Chí
1976	针灸治疗噤口痢除用基本处方外，还应加用：A·关元、三阴交; B·曲池、内庭 C. ·大椎、中冲 ·D·内关、中脘; E·脾俞、神阙	What points may be added to the basic prescription of points to treat fasting dysentery? A. · R4 / Guān Yuán, Sp6 / Sān Yīn Jiāo; B. · Li11 / Qū Chí, S44 / Nèi Tíng; C. ·D14 / Dà Zhuī、 P9 / Zhōng Chōng; ·D. · P6 / Nèi Guān, R12 / Zhōng Wǎn; E. B20 / Pí Shū, R8 / Shén Què
1977	针灸治疗痢疾，以下各穴除( )外均可通调大肠腑气：A·合谷; B·阴陵泉 ·C·天枢; D·上巨虚; E·大肠俞··	In treating dysentery by acupuncture therapy, which point cannot facilitate and regulate bowel energy of the large intestine? A · Li4 / Hé Gǔ; B · Sp9 / Yīn Líng Quán; ·C · S25 / Tiān Shū; D · S37 / Shàng Jù Xū; E. B25 / Dà Cháng Shū.
1978	针灸治疗面瘫的基本处方为: A·阳白、四白、颊车、地仓、翳风、颧髎; B·翳风、颧髎、合谷、太冲、丰隆 C. ·阳白、四白、颊车、地仓、翳风、列缺; D·颊车、	What is the basic prescription of points in acupuncture therapy to treat facial paralysis? A. · G14 / Yáng; Bái、 S2 / Sì Bái / , S6 / Jiá Chē, S4 / Dì Cāng, Sj17 / Yì Fēng, Si18 / Quán Liáo; B. · Sj17 / Yì Fēng, Si18 / Quán Liáo, Li4 / Hé Gǔ, Lv3 / Tài Chōng, S40 /

	地仓、翳风、颧髎、大陵；E·阳白、四白、颊车、地仓、翳风、颧髎、合谷	Fēng Lóng; C. G14 / Yáng; Bái, S2 / Sì Bái / , S6 / Jiá Chē, S4 / Dì Cāng, Sj17 / Yì Fēng 、Lu7 / Liè Quē; D. · S6 / Jiá Chē, S4 / Dì Cāng, Sj17 / Yì Fēng, Si18 / Quán Liáo, P7 / Dà Líng; E. · G14 / Yáng; Bái, S2 / Sì Bái / , S6 / Jiá Chē, S4 / Dì Cāng, Sj17 / Yì Fēng, Si18 / Quán Liáo, Li4 / Hé Gǔ
1979	针灸治疗命门火衰型阳痿，可在基本处方上再加：A·命门、志室、气海；B·命门、心俞、阴陵泉 C. 心俞、脾俞、足三里；D·命门、百会、神门；E·命门、阴陵泉透阳陵泉	What points may be added to the basic prescription of points to treat the life door in decline type of impotence? A. · D4 / Mìng Mén, B52 / Zhì Shì, R6 / Qì Hǎi; B. · D4 / Mìng Mén, B15 / Xīn Shū, Sp9 / Yīn Líng Quán; C. ·B15 / Xīn Shū, B20 / Pí Shū, S36 / Zú Sān Lǐ; D. · D4 / Mìng Mén, D20 / Bǎi Huì, H7 / Shén Mén; E. · D4 / Mìng Mén, Sp9 / Yīn Líng Quán inserted all the way through G34 / Yáng Líng Quán
1980	针灸治疗内直肌麻痹可加：A·睛明、印堂；B·承泣、四白 C. 瞳子髎、太阳；D·上明、攒竹；E·丝竹空、上明	What points may be added to treat musculus rectus medialis paralysis? A. ·B1 / Jīng Míng, Yìn táng / midpoint between eyebrows / seal hall; B. · S1 / Chéng Qì, S2 / Sì Bái; C. G1 / Tóng Zǐ Liáo, Tài yáng / sun / temple; D. · Shàng míng / upper brightness / upper bright vision, B2 / Zǎn Zhú; E. · Sj23 / Sī Zhú Kōng, Shàng míng / upper brightness / upper bright vision
1981	针灸治疗脾虚气弱型眼睑下垂，可在基本处方的基础上再加：A.足三里、支正；B·尺泽、百会、脾俞 C. 。足三里、脾俞、百会；D·足三里、百会、风门；E. 中脘、脾俞	What points may be added to the basic prescription of points to treat the spleen deficiency and weak energy type of eyelid dropping? A. S36 / Zú Sān Lǐ, Si7 / Zhi Zhèng; B. · Lu5 / Chǐ Zé, D20 / Bǎi Huì, B20 / Pí Shū; C. S36 / Zú Sān Lǐ, B20 / Pí Shū, D20 / Bǎi Huì; D. · S36 / Zú Sān Lǐ, D20 / Bǎi Huì, B12 / Fēng Mén; E. R12 / Zhōng Wǎn, B20 / Pí Shū
1982	针灸治疗脾虚湿蕴型eczema，可在基本处方的基础上再加：A·水道；B·足三里 C. ·阴陵泉；D·脾俞；E·曲池	In acupuncture therapy, what points may be added to the basic prescription of points to treat the spleen deficiency with hidden dampness type of eczema? A. · S28 / Shuǐ Dào; B. · S36 / Zú Sān Lǐ; C. Sp9 / Yīn Líng Quán; D. B20 / Pí Shū; E. · Li11 / Qū Chí
1983	针灸治疗脾虚湿滞型胎位不正宜在基本方基础上再加：A·足三里、太冲；B·阴陵泉、丰隆 C. 脾俞、阳陵泉；D·中脘、气海；E·脾俞、肾俞	What points may be added to the basic prescription of points to treat fetus in wrong position due to spleen deficiency with dampness stagnation? A. · S36 / Zú Sān Lǐ, Lv3 / Tài Chōng; B. · Sp9 / Yīn Líng Quán, S40 / Fēng Lóng; C. B20 / Pí Shū, G34 / Yáng Líng Quán; D. · R12 / Zhōng Wǎn, R6 / Qì Hǎi; E. B20 / Pí Shū 、B23 / Shèn Shū.
1984	针灸治疗贫血取用悬钟意在：A·气血双补；B·调理脾胃 C. 滋养心脾；D·养髓补血；E·益气补血	What is the acupuncture therapy rationale of using G39 / Xuán Zhōng to treat anemia? A. ·toning energy-blood; B. ·regulating spleen and stomach; C. ·watering and nourishg heart and spleen; D. ·nourishing marrow and toning blood; E. ·benefit energy and tone blood.

1985	针灸治疗气滞血瘀型的痔疮，可在基本处方上再加：A·气海; B·白环俞 C. ·阴陵泉; D··飞扬; E·孔最	What point may be added to the basic prescription of points to treat the energy; congestion and blood coagulation type of hemorrhoidc / pile? A. · R6 / Qì Hǎi; B. · B30 / Bái Huán Shū; C. · Sp9 / Yīn Líng Quán; D. B58 / Feī Yáng; E. · Lu6 / Kǒng Zuì
1986	针灸治疗气滞血瘀型血栓闭塞性脉管炎，可在基本处方上加：A·阴陵泉; B·太冲 C. ·气海; D·曲池; E·八风	What points may be added to the basic prescription of points to treat the energy; congestion and blood coagulation type of thrombo-embolia angitis? A. · Sp9 / Yīn Líng Quán; B. · Lv3 / Tài Chōng; C. · R6 / Qì Hǎi; D. · Li11 / Qū Chí; E. Bā fēng / eight winds
1987	针灸治疗青光眼实证多采用：A·针灸并用; B.只灸不针 C. ·只针不灸; D·先针后灸; E·先灸后针	What technique of acupuncture therapy is used to treat the excess syndrome of glaucoma? A. · both acupuncture and moxibustion; B. moxibustion without acupuncture; C. · acupuncture without moxibustion; D. ·acupuncture followed by moxibustion; E. ·moxibustion followed by acupuncture
1988	针灸治疗青光眼实证宜：A·清热泻火、化痰通络; B·补益肝肾、明目止痛 C. ·化痰熄风、清肝明目; D·健脾化湿、清肝明目; E·平降肝阳、熄风明目	How to treat the excess syndrome of glaucoma by acupuncture therapy? A. ·to cear heat and sedate fire、transform phlegm and connect linking meridians; B. ·to tone and benefit liver and kidneys、sharpen vision, relieve pain; C. ·to transform phlegm, stop wind、clear liver, sharpen vision; D. ·to strengthen the spleen and transform dampness、clear liver, sharpen vision; E. ·to calm and bring down liver yang、stop wind, sharpen vision
1989	针灸治疗青光眼虚证多采用：A·先灸后针; B·先针后灸 C. ·只针不灸; D·只灸不针; E，以针为主	How to treat deficiency syndrome of glaucoma by acupuncture therapy? A ·moxibustion followed by acupuncture; B ·acupuncture followed by moxibustion; C. acupuncture without moxibustion; D · moxibustion without acupuncture; E.primarily by acupuncture
1990	针灸治疗青光眼虚证宜：A·清热泻火、化痰通络; B·补益肝肾、明目止痛 C. ·化痰熄风、清肝明目; D·健脾化湿、清肝明目; E·平降肝阳、熄风明目	How to treat the deficiency syndrome of glaucoma by acupuncture therapy? A. ·to clear heat and sedate fire、transform phlegm and connect linking meridians; B. ·to tone and benefit liver and kidneys、sharpen vision, relieve pain; C. to transform phlegm, stop wind、clear liver, sharpen vision; D. ·to strengthen the spleen and transform dampness、clear liver, sharpen vision; E. ·to calm and bring down liver yang、stop wind, sharpen vision
1991	针灸治疗肾精亏虚型男性不育症，可在基本处方上再加：A. 神门; B. 内关 C. 太溪、D. 中极; E. 太冲	What points may be added to the basic prescription of points to treat the kidney essence deprivation and deficiency type of male infertility? A. H7 / Shén Mén; B. P6 / Nèi Guān; C. K3 / Tài Xī; D. R3 / Zhōng Jí; E. Lv3 / Tài Chōng
1992	针灸治疗肾气不固型尿失	What points may be added to the basic prescription of

	禁，·可在基本处方的基础上再加： A·关元、命门；B·肺俞、脾俞 C. ·足三里、脾俞；D。阴棱泉、行间；E·次髎、太冲	points to treat incontinence of urination due to kidney energy not solid? A. · R4 / Guān Yuán，D4 / Mìng Mén; B. ·B13 / Fèi Shū，B20 / Pí Shū; C. · S36 / Zú Sān Lǐ，B20 / Pí Shū; D. Sp9 / Yīn Líng Quán i，Lv2 / Xíng Jiān; E. · B32 / Cì Liáo，Lv3 / Tài Chōng
1993	针灸治疗肾虚不固型遗精，可在基本处方的基础上加：A·志室、太溪；B·心俞、脾俞 C. ·太溪、神门；D·中极、阴陵泉；E·太溪、阴陵泉	What points may be added to the basic prescription of points to treat the kidney deficiency and not solid type of seminal emission? A. B52 / Zhì Shì，K3 / Tài Xī; B. ·B15 / Xīn Shū，B20 / Pí Shū; C. · K3 / Tài Xī，H7 / Shén Mén; D. · R3 / Zhōng Jí，Sp9 / Yīn Líng Quán; E. · K3 / Tài Xī，Sp9 / Yīn Líng Quán
1994	针灸治疗肾虚不固型早泄，可在基本处方上再加：A·命门、太溪；B 心俞、脾俞 C. ·太溪、照海；D·命门、脾俞；E·脾俞、太溪	What points may be added to the basic prescription of points to treat premature ejaculation due to kidney deficiency with unsolid condition? A. · D4 / Mìng Mén，K3 / Tài Xī; B. B15 / Xīn Shū，B20 / Pí Shū; C. · K3 / Tài Xī，K6 / Zhào Hǎi; D. · D4 / Mìng Mén，B20 / Pí Shū; E. B20 / Pí Shū，K3 / Tài Xī
1995	针灸治疗肾虚寒凝型胎位不正宜在基本方基础上再加：A·肾俞、气海；B·命门、阴陵泉 C. ·期门、太冲；D·阴陵泉，丰隆；E·肾俞、肝俞	What points may be added to the basic prescription of points to treat fetus in wrong position due to kidney deficiency with cold congestion? A. B23 / Shèn Shū，R6 / Qì Hǎi; B. · D4 / Mìng Mén，Sp9 / Yīn Líng Quán; C. Lv14 / Qí Mén，Lv3 / Tài Chōng; D. · Sp9 / Yīn Líng Quán ，S40 / Fēng Lóng; E. B23 / Shèn Shū，B18 / Gān Shū
1996	针灸治疗肾阳不足型男性不育症，可在基本处方上再加：A. 太溪、B. 神阙 C. 太溪、D. 中极；E. 太冲	What points may be added to the basic prescription of points to treat the kidneys yang deficiency type of male infertility? A. K3 / Tài Xī; B. R8 / Shén Què; C. K3 / Tài Xī; D. R3 / Zhōng Jí; E. Lv3 / Tài Chōng
1997	针灸治疗湿热浸淫型可在基本处方的基础上再加：A·肝俞；B·太白 C. ·水道；D·血海；E·胃俞	In acupuncture therapy, what points may be added to the basic prescription of points to trea the damp heat invading type of eczema? A. ·B18 / Gān Shū; B. · Sp3 / Tài Bái; C. · S28 / Shuǐ Dào; D. · Sp10 / Xuè Hǎi; E. B21 / Wèi Shū
1998	针灸治疗湿热瘀滞型的痔疮，可在基本处方上再加：A·气海；B·白环俞 C. ·阴陵泉；D··飞扬；E·孔最	What points may be added to the basic prescription of point to treat the damp heat congestion type of hemorrhoids / pile? A. · R6 / Qì Hǎi; B. B30 / Bái Huán Shū; C. Sp9 / Yīn Líng Quán; D. B58 / Feī Yáng; E. · Lu6 / Kǒng Zuì
1999	针灸治疗湿热瘀滞型的痔疮基本处方上再加阴陵泉及：A·秩边；B·阳陵泉 C. ·三阴交；D. 白环俞；E·气海	In addition to Sp9 / Yīn Líng Quán, what point may be added to the basic prescription of points to treat the damp heat congestion type of hemorrhoidc / pile? A. B54 / Zhì biān; B. · G34 / Yáng Líng Quán; C. · Sp6 / Sān Yīn Jiāo; D. B30 / Bái Huán Shū; E · R6 / Qì Hǎi
2000	针灸治疗视神经萎缩肝气郁结型除取基本处方外，可	What points may be added to the basic prescription of points to treat the liver energy congestion type of optic

	配：A·合谷、膈俞；B·风池、太冲 C. ·行间、·侠溪；D·行间、膈俞；E·风池、光明	atrophy? A. · Li4 / Hé Gǔ，B17 / Gé Shū; B. · G20 / Fēng Chí，Lv3 / Tài Chōng; C. · Lv2 / Xíng Jiān 、· G43 / Xiá Xī; D. · Lv2 / Xíng Jiān，B17 / Gé Shū; E. · G20 / Fēng Chí，G37 / Guāng Míng
2001	针灸治疗视神经萎缩肝气郁结型可加：A·行间，侠溪；B·肾俞、太溪 C. ·合谷、膈俞；D·风池、太冲；E·肝俞、合谷	What points may be added to the basic prescription of points to treat the liver energy congestion type of optic atrophy? A. · Lv2 / Xíng Jiān ，G43 / Xiá Xī; B. B23 / Shèn Shū，K3 / Tài Xī; C. · Li4 / Hé Gǔ，B17 / Gé Shū; D. · G20 / Fēng Chí，Lv3 / Tài Chōng; E. ·B18 / Gān Shū，Li4 / Hé Gǔ
2002	针灸治疗视神经萎缩气血瘀滞型 、除取基本处方外，可配：A·合谷、膈俞；B·风池、太冲 C. ·行间、光明；D 行间、膈俞；E风池、光明	What points may be added to the basic prescription of points to treat the energy congestion and blood coagulation type of optic atrophy? A. · Li4 / Hé Gǔ，B17 / Gé Shū; B. G20 / Fēng Chí，Lv3 / Tài Chōng; C. Lv2 / Xíng Jiān 、 G43 / Xiá Xī; D. · Lv2 / Xíng Jiān，B17 / Gé Shū; E. · G20 / Fēng Chí，G37 / Guāng Míng
2003	针灸治疗视网膜色素变性肝肾阴虚 一者可加：A·攒竹、承泣、肝俞、太溪；B·肾俞、肝俞、太溪 C. ·肾俞、命门、关元；D·风池、足三里、太冲；E·脾俞、三阴交、太溪	What points may be added to the basic prescription of points to treat the yin deficiency of liver and kidneys type of pigmentary degeneration of retina? A. B2 / Zǎn Zhú，S1 / Chéng Qì，B18 / Gān Shū，K3 / Tài Xī; B. B23 / Shèn Shū，B18 / Gān Shū，K3 / Tài Xī; C. B23 / Shèn Shū，D4 / Mìng Mén，R4 / Guān Yuán; D. G20 / Fēng Chí，S36 / Zú Sān Lǐ，Lv3 / Tài Chōng; E. B20 / Pí Shū，Sp6 / Sān Yīn Jiāo，K3 / Tài Xī
2004	针灸治疗视网膜色素变性基本处方除取睛明、球后、翳明、养老外，还可取：A·攒竹、承泣、肝俞、太溪；B·肾俞、肝俞、太溪 C. ·肾俞、命门、关元；D·风池、足三里、太冲；E·脾俞、三阴交、太溪	In treating pigmentary degeneration of retina by acupuncture therapy, what other points may be selected in addition to B1 / Jīng Míng 、Qiú hòu / behind the ball，Yì míng / shelter light，Si6 / Yǎng Lǎo? A. B2 / Zǎn Zhú，S1 / Chéng Qì，B18 / Gān Shū，K3 / Tài Xī; B. B23 / Shèn Shū，B18 / Gān Shū，K3 / Tài Xī; C. B23 / Shèn Shū，D4 / Mìng Mén，R4 / Guān Yuán; D. · G20 / Fēng Chí，S36 / Zú Sān Lǐ，Lv3 / Tài Chōng; E. B20 / Pí Shū，Sp6 / Sān Yīn Jiāo，K3 / Tài Xī
2005	针灸治疗视网膜色素变性脾气虚弱者，除基本处方外，可加：A·足三里、三阴交；B·足三里、脾俞 C. ·足三里、风池；D·脾俞、三阴交；E·承泣、三阴交	What points may be added to the basic prescription of points to treat the spleen energy deficiency and weakness type of pigmentary degeneration of retina? A. S36 / Zú Sān Lǐ，Sp6 / Sān Yīn Jiāo; B. · S36 / Zú Sān Lǐ，B20 / Pí Shū; C. ·S36 / Zú Sān Lǐ，G20 / Fēng Chí; D. B20 / Pí Shū，Sp6 / Sān Yīn Jiāo; E. S1 / Chéng Qì，Sp6 / Sān Yīn Jiāo
2006	针灸治疗视网膜色素变性肾阳不足者可加：A·攒竹、承泣、肝俞、太溪；B·肾俞、肝俞、太溪 C. ·肾俞、命门、关元；D·风池、足三里、太冲；E·脾俞、三阴交、太溪	What points may be added to the basic prescription of points to treat the kidney yang deficiency type of pigmentary degeneration of retina? A. B2 / Zǎn Zhú，S1 / Chéng Qì，B18 / Gān Shū，K3 / Tài Xī; B. B23 / Shèn Shū，B18 / Gān Shū，K3 / Tài Xī; C. B23 / Shèn Shū，D4 / Mìng Mén，R4 / Guān Yuán; D. G20 / Fēng Chí，S36 / Zú Sān Lǐ，Lv3 / Tài Chōng; E. B20 / Pí

		Shū，Sp6 / Sān Yīn Jiāo，K3 / Tài Xī
2007	针灸治疗脱肛的脾虚气陷证可在基本处方基础上再加：A·下巨虚；B·肾俞 C. ·足三里；D·大敦；E·曲池	What point may be added to the basic prescription of points to treat the spleen deficiency with energy cave-in type of proctoptosis / prolapse of anus? A. S39 / Xià Jù Xū; B. B23 / Shèn Shū; C. S36 / Zú Sān Lǐ; D. Lv1 / Dà Dūn; E. · Li11 / Qū Chí
2008	针灸治疗脱肛的肾气不固证可在基本处方基础上再加：A·阴陵泉；B·气海 C. ·足三里；D·大敦；E·肝俞	What points may be added to the basic prescription of points to treat the kidneys energy not solid type of proctoptosis / prolapse of anus? A. Sp9 / Yīn Líng Quán; B. R6 / Qì Hǎi; C. ·S36 / Zú Sān Lǐ; D. Lv1 / Dà Dūn; E. ·B18 / Gān Shū
2009	针灸治疗脱肛的湿热下注证，可在基本处方基础上再加：A·阴陵泉；B·气海 C. ·足三里；D·大敦；E·曲池	What points may be added to the basic prescription of points to treat the damp heat flowing downward type of proctoptosis / prolapse of anus? A. Sp9 / Yīn Líng Quán; B. R6 / Qì Hǎi; C. S36 / Zú Sān Lǐ; D. Lv1 / Dà Dūn; E. · Li11 / Qū Chí
2010	针灸治疗胃肠痉挛兼恶心呕吐可在基础方上加：A·公孙；B.关元 C. ·梁门；D·膈俞；E·天枢	What points may be added to the basic prescription of points to treat gastrointestinal spasm accompanied by nausea and vomiting? A. · Sp4 / Gōng Sūn; B. R4 / Guān Yuán; C. · S21 / Liáng Mén; D. ·B17 / Gé Shū; E. · S25 / Tiān Shū
2011	针灸治疗胃肠痉挛之寒客胃肠证可在基础方上加灸( )以温寒止痛：A·公孙；B.关元 C. ·梁门；D·膈俞；E·天枢	What point may be added, for moxibustion, to the basic prescription of points to treat gastrointestinal spasm that belongs to the cold residing in the stomachand intestine type in order to warm up coldness and relieve pain? A. Sp4 / Gōng Sūn; B. R4 / Guān Yuán; C. S21 / Liáng Mén; D. ·B17 / Gé Shū; E. · S25 / Tiān Shū
2012	针灸治疗胃痉挛者可在基础方上加（)以和胃解痉：A·公孙；B.关元 C. ·梁门；D·膈俞；E·天枢	What points may be added to the basic prescription of points to treat gastrospasm in order to harmonize the stomach and relieve spasm? A. Sp4 / Gōng Sūn; B. R4 / Guān Yuán; C. S21 / Liáng Mén; D. ·B17 / Gé Shū; E. · S25 / Tiān Shū
2013	针灸治疗下焦瘀滞型尿失禁，可在基本处方的基础上再加：A·关元、命门；B·脾俞、足三里 C. ·肺俞、足三里；D.次髎、太冲；E·阴陵泉、行间	What points may be added to the basic prescription of points to treat incontinence of urination due to lower heater coagulation and congestion? A. R4 / Guān Yuán，D4 / Mìng Mén; B. B20 / Pí Shū，S36 / Zú Sān Lǐ; C. B13 / Fèi Shū，S36 / Zú Sān Lǐ; D. B32 / Cì Liáo，Lv3 / Tài Chōng; E. Sp9 / Yīn Líng Quán，Lv2 / Xíng Jiān
2014	针灸治疗下斜肌麻痹可加：A·睛明、印堂；B·承泣、四白 C. 瞳子髎、太阳；D·上明、攒竹；E·丝竹空、上明	What points may be added to treat inferior oblique muscle paralysis? A. ·B1 / Jīng Míng，Yìn táng / midpoint between eyebrows / seal hall; B. · S1 / Chéng Qì，S2 / Sì Bái; C. G1 / Tóng Zǐ Liáo，Tài yáng / sun / temple; D. · Shàng míng / upper brightness / upper bright vision，B2 / Zǎn Zhú; E. · Sj23 / Sī Zhú Kōng，Shàng míng / upper brightness / upper bright vision

2015	针灸治疗下直肌麻痹可加：A 睛明、印堂；B 承泣、四白 C. 瞳子髎、太阳；D 上明、攒竹；E 丝竹空、上明	What points may be added to treat muculus rectus inferior paralysis? A. B1 / Jīng Míng，Yìn táng / midpoint between eyebrows / seal hall; B. · S1 / Chéng Qì，S2 / Sì Bái; C. G1 / Tóng Zǐ Liáo，Tài yáng / sun / temple; D. · Shàng míng / upper brightness / upper bright vision，B2 / Zǎn Zhú; E. · Sj23 / Sī Zhú Kōng，Shàng míng / upper brightness / upper bright vision
2016	针灸治疗眼睑颤动的治则是： A 以灸为主；B 补法 C. 以针为主；D 泻法；E 针灸并用	What is the principle of treating flickering eyelid by acupuncture and moxibustion? A primarily by moxibustion; B · tonfication; C. primarily by acupuncture; D · sedation; E · both acupuncture and moxibustion are applied
2017	针灸治疗阳水可在基本处方的基础上再加：A 肺俞、列缺、脾俞；B 肺俞、列缺、合谷 C. 肺俞、合谷、三阴交；D 列缺、合谷、足三里；E 合谷、足三里、三阴交	What points may be added to the basic prescription of points to treat yang water? A. B13 / Fèi Shū 、Lu7 / Liè Quē、; B20 / Pí Shū; B. B13 / Fèi Shū 、Lu7 / Liè Quē、 Li4 / Hé Gǔ; C. B13 / Fèi Shū，Li4 / Hé Gǔ，Sp6 / Sān Yīn Jiāo; D. Lu7 / Liè Quē、 Li4 / Hé Gǔ，S36 / Zú Sān Lǐ; E. · Li4 / Hé Gǔ，S36 / Zú Sān Lǐ，Sp6 / Sān Yīn Jiāo
2018	针灸治疗阴水属脾虚者，可在基本处方的基础上再加：A 肺俞、列缺、脾俞；B 列缺、脾俞、足三里 C. 脾俞、足三里、三阴交；D 足三里、三阴交、合谷；E 三阴交、太冲，合谷	What points may be added to the basic prescription of points to treat yin water that belongs to spleen deficiency? A. B13 / Fèi Shū 、Lu7 / Liè Quē、; B20 / Pí Shū; B. Lu7 / Liè Quē、; B20 / Pí Shū，S36 / Zú Sān Lǐ; C. B20 / Pí Shū，S36 / Zú Sān Lǐ，Sp6 / Sān Yīn Jiāo; D. · S36 / Zú Sān Lǐ，Sp6 / Sān Yīn Jiāo，Li4 / Hé Gǔ; E. · Sp6 / Sān Yīn Jiāo，Lv3 / Tài Chōng ，Li4 / Hé Gǔ
2019	针灸治疗阴水属肾虚者，可在基本处方的基础上再加：A 肺俞、肾俞、关元；B 肾俞、关元、足三里 C. 关元、足三里、阳陵泉；D 足三里、阳陵泉、列缺；E 阳陵泉、列缺、合谷	What points may be added to the basic prescription of points to treat yin water that belongs to kidneys deficiency? A. B13 / Fèi Shū，B23 / Shèn Shū，R4 / Guān Yuán; B. B23 / Shèn Shū，R4 / Guān Yuán，S36 / Zú Sān Lǐ; C. R4 / Guān Yuán，S36 / Zú Sān Lǐ，G34 / Yáng Líng Quán; D. · S36 / Zú Sān Lǐ，G34 / Yáng Líng Quán 、Lu7 / Liè Quē; E. · G34 / Yáng Líng Quán 、Lu7 / Liè Quē、 Li4 / Hé Gǔ
2020	针灸治疗阴挺时,应采用什么手法？ A 补法，B 泻法;C 平补平泻；D 补法并灸；E 泻法并灸。	What technique should be used in treating hysteroptosis (prolapse of the uterus) by acupuncture and moxibustion? A. tonification; B. sedation; C. neutral technique; D. tonification and moxibusiton; E. sedation and moxibution.
2021	针灸治疗阴虚火旺之鼻出血宜在基本处方的基础上加：A 少商、风池；B 内庭、厉兑 C. 太冲、侠溪；D 太溪、太冲；E 足三里、三阴交	What points may be added to the basic prescription of points to treat the yin deficiency with abundant fire type of nosebleed? A. · Lu11 / Shǎo Shāng，G20 / Fēng Chí; B. · S44 / Nèi Tíng，S45 / Lì Duì; C. · Lv3 / Tài Chōng，G43 / Xiá Xī; D. · K3 / Tài Xī，Lv3 / Tài Chōng; E. · S36 / Zú Sān Lǐ，Sp6 / Sān Yīn Jiāo

2022	针灸治疗饮食积滞之胃肠痉挛可在基础方上加: A·公孙; B.关元 C. ·梁门; D·膈俞; E·天枢	What points may be added to the basic prescription of points to treat the accumulated and congested food type of gastrointestinal spasm? A. · Sp4 / Gōng Sūn; B. R4 / Guān Yuán; C. · S21 / Liáng Mén; D. ·B17 / Gé Shū; E. · S25 / Tiān Shū
2023	针灸治疗饮食积滞之胃肠痉挛可在基础方上加用: A·建里、公孙; B·关元、神阙 C. ·公孙、内关; D·上巨虚、下巨虚; E·筋缩、阳陵泉	What points may be added to the basic prescription of points to treat the accumulated and congested food type of gastrointestinal spasm? A. · R11 / Jiàn Lǐ, Sp4 / Gōng Sūn; B. · R4 / Guān Yuán, R8 / Shén Què; C. Sp4 / Gōng Sūn, P6 / Nèi Guān; D. · S37 / Shàng Jù Xū, S39 / Xià Jù Xū; E. ·D8 / Jīn Suō、 G34 / Yáng Líng Quán
2024	针灸治疗原则为 A.标本缓急 B.调和阴阳 C. 疏通经络 D 扶正祛邪	What is the principle of treatment in acupuncture and moxibustion? A. treating primary and secondary; onditions, acute and chronic symptoms differently; B. regulate yin and yang; C. relax and facilitate flow of meridian energy; D. support body energy and expel pathogens.
2025	针灸治疗原则中, "寒则留之"是指: A·艾灸时间长; B·艾灸量大 C. ·寒证留针时间长; D·坐罐; E都不是·	In acupuncture therapy, what is meant by the principle that "withdrawal of needle should be delayed in case of cold"? A · promonged moxibustion; B · heavy moxibustion; C. · prlonged retention of needle in case of cold syndorme; D ·Prolonged cupping; E. none of the above ·
2026	针灸治疗原则中, "热则疾之"是指: A·施灸壮数多; B急吹其火 C. ·拔罐速度快; D·拔罐火力强; E·毫针点刺疾出少留或不留针	What is meant by the principle of acupuncture therapy that "the needle should be pulled out shortly in case of heat"? A ·using more moxa sticks; B fire extinguished quickly; C. quick cupping; D. · cupping with stronger fire; E · dotted-needling by a minute needle, which should be pulled out shortly or right away.
2027	针灸治疗滞产气血虚弱型宜在基本处方的基础上再加: A·血海; B·足三里 C. ·膈俞; D.内关; E·气冲	What points may be added to the basic prescription of points to treat the blood deficiency type of prolonged labor? A · Sp10 / Xuè Hǎi; B · S36 / Zú Sān Lǐ; C. ·B17 / Gé Shū; D. P6 / Nèi Guān; E · S30 / Qì Chōng
2028	针灸治疗滞产气血虚弱型宜在基本处方的基础上再加: A·足三里; B·内关 C. ·气冲; D·太冲; E·地机	What points may be added to the basic prescription of points to treat the energy and blood deficiency type of prolonged labor? A. · S36 / Zú Sān Lǐ; B. · P6 / Nèi Guān; C. · S30 / Qì Chōng; D. · Lv3 / Tài Chōng; E. · Sp8 / Dì Jī
2029	针灸治疗滞产气滞血瘀型, 宜在基本处方的基础上再加: A·太冲; B·气冲 C. ·内关; D·气海; E, 足三里	What points may be added to the basic prescription of points to treat the energy; congestion and blood coagulation type of prolonged labor? A. · Lv3 / Tài Chōng; B. · S30 / Qì Chōng; C. · P6 / Nèi Guān; D. · R6 / Qì Hǎi; E, S36 / Zú Sān Lǐ
2030	针灸治疗中耳炎, 在操作时刺翳风穴要选较细的针、只	A fine needle should be selected to needle Sj17 [Yì Fēng] to treat otitis media, without lifting and pushing

	捻转不提插是为了：A 防止症状加重；B.防止刺伤耳膜 C. 防止刺伤面神经；D 防止出血；E 防止疼痛	to treat otitis media, without lifting and pushing manipulation, only twirling of needle; why is that? A to prevent symptoms from getting worse; B.to prevent inserting into and harming ear drum; C. to prevent inserting into and harming facial nerve; D to prevent bleeding; E to prevent causing pain
2031	针灸治疗中耳炎伴头痛甚者可在基本处方上加：A 耳门；B 听会 C. 中渚；D 太阳；E 外关	What point may be added to the basic prescription of points to treat otitis media accompanied by severe headche? A. Sj21 / Ěr Mén; B. G2 / Tīng Huì; C. Sj3 / Zhōng Zhǔ; D. Tài yáng / sun / temple; E. Sj5 / Wài Guān
2032	针灸治疗中风闭证时，除取十二井水沟太冲外，还应取 A.天突；B.曲池 C. 外关；D 丰隆	In treating the closed. type of wind stroke, what other point should be selected in addition to twelve well points (shi er jing xue), D26 (Shuǐ Gōu, Rén Zhōng), and Lv3 (Tài Chōng)? A. R22 (Tiān Tū); B. Li11 (Qū Chí); C. Sj5 (Wài Guān); D. S40 (Fēng Lóng).
2033	针灸治疗中暑出现呕吐者，可在基础方上再加：A 三阴交、胆俞；B 太白、太溪 C. 关元、气海；D 公孙、中脘 E 内庭、陷谷	What points may be added to the basic prescription of points to treat sunstroke with vomiting? A. Sp6 / Sān Yīn Jiāo，B19 / Dǎn Shū; B. Sp3 / Tài Bái，K3 / Tài Xī; C. R4 / Guān Yuán，R6 / Qì Hǎi; D. Sp4 / Gōng Sūn，R12 / Zhōng Wǎn E. S44 / Nèi Tíng 、S43 / Xiàn Gǔ
2034	针灸治疗中暑汗出肢冷、脉微欲绝者，可在基础方上再加：A.关元、气海；B 头维、太阳 C. 中脘、公孙；D 劳宫、涌泉；E 曲池、委中	What points may be added to the basic prescription of points to treat sunstroke with perspiration, cold limbs, a feeble pulse about to exhaust? A. R4 / Guān Yuán，R6 / Qì Hǎi; B. S8 / Tóu Wěi 、Tài yáng / sun / temple; C. R12 / Zhōng Wǎn，Sp4 / Gōng Sūn; D. P8 / Láo Gōng，K1 / Yǒng Quán; E. Li11 / Qū Chí，B40 / Wěi Zhōng
2035	针灸治疗中暑头晕头痛者，可在基础方上再加：A.关元、气海；B 头维、太阳 C. 中脘、公孙；D 劳宫、涌泉；E 曲池、委中	What points may be added to the basic prescription of points to treat sunstroke with dizziness and headache? A. R4 / Guān Yuán，R6 / Qì Hǎi; B. S8 / Tóu Wěi 、Tài yáng / sun / temple; C. R12 / Zhōng Wǎn，Sp4 / Gōng Sūn; D. P8 / Láo Gōng，K1 / Yǒng Quán; E. Li11 / Qū Chí，B40 / Wěi Zhōng
2036	针灸治疗中暑阴证，可在基础方上再加：A.关元、气海；B 头维、太阳 C. 中脘、公孙；D 劳宫、涌泉；E 曲池、委中	What point may be added to the basic prescription of points to treat the yin type of sunstroke? A. R4 / Guān Yuán，R6 / Qì Hǎi; B. S8 / Tóu Wěi 、Tài yáng / sun / temple; C. R12 / Zhōng Wǎn，Sp4 / Gōng Sūn; D. P8 / Láo Gōng，K1 / Yǒng Quán; E. Li11 / Qū Chí，B40 / Wěi Zhōng
2037	针灸治疗中心性视网膜炎初期，其治则为：A 活血通络、调和气血；B 活血通络、养血明目 C. 活血通络、补益肝肾；D 补益肝肾、养血明目；E 调和气血、养血明目	What principle of acupuncture therapy should be applied to treat the initial stage of central retinitisthe? A. activate blood and connect linking meridians、to adjust and harmonize energy-blood; B. activate blood and connect linking meridians、to nourish blood and sharpen vision; C. to activate blood and connect linking

		meridians、to tone and benefit liver and kidneys; D. to tone and benefit liver and kidneys、to nourish blood and sharpen vision; E. to adjust and harmonize energy-blood、to nourish blood and sharpen vision·
2038	针灸治疗中心性视网膜炎后期，其治则为: A 活血通络、调和气血; B 活血通络、养血明目 C. 活血通络、补益肝肾; D 补益肝肾、养血明目; E 调和气血、养血明目	What principle of acupuncture therapy dshould be applied to treat the late stage of central retinitisthe? A. activate blood and connect linking meridians、to adjust and harmonize energy-blood; B. activate blood and connect linking meridians、to nourish blood and sharpen vision; C. to activate blood and connect linking meridians、to tone and benefit liver and kidneys; D. to tone and benefit liver and kidneys、to nourish blood and sharpen vision; E. to adjust and harmonize energy-blood、to nourish blood and sharpen vision·
2039	针灸治疗肘劳下臂旋后受限者可在基本处方的基础上加: A. 下廉; B·少海 C. ·尺泽; D·天井; E·阿是穴	What point may be added to the basic prescription of points to treat elbow fatigue with difficulty in turning the lower arms backward? A. Li8 / Xià Lián; B。 · H3 / Shào Hǎi; C. Lu5 / Chǐ Zé; D。 · Sj10 / Tiān Jǐng; E。 Ouchi points / pressure points
2040	针灸治疗肘劳下臂旋前受限者可在基本处方的基础上加: A·下廉; B·少海 C. ·尺泽; D·天井; E·阿是穴	What point may be added to the basic prescription of points to treat elbow fatigue with difficulty in turning the lower arms forward? A. Li8 / Xià Lián; B。 · H3 / Shào Hǎi; C. Lu5 / Chǐ Zé; D。 · Sj10 / Tiān Jǐng; E。 Ouchi points / pressure points。
2041	针灸治疗肘劳肘尖疼痛者可在基本处方的基础上加: A·下廉; B·少海 C. ·尺泽; D·天井; E·阿是穴	What points may be added to the basic prescription of points to treat elbow fatigue with pain at the elbow tip? A. · Li8 / Xià Lián; B. · H3 / Shào Hǎi; C. · Lu5 / Chǐ Zé; D. · Sj10 / Tiān Jǐng; E. Ouchi points / pressure points
2042	针灸治疗肘劳肘内侧疼痛者可在基本处方的基础上加: A·下廉; B·少海 C. ·尺泽; D·天井; E·阿是穴	What points may be added to the basic prescription of points to treat elbow fatigue with pain on the medial sidie of the elbow? A. · Li8 / Xià Lián; B. · H3 / Shào Hǎi; C. · Lu5 / Chǐ Zé; D. · Sj10 / Tiān Jǐng; E. Ouchi points / pressure points
2043	针灸治疗作用是: A 补虚泻实; B 扶正祛邪 C.标本兼治 D 三因制宜	What is the therapeutic function of acupuncture therapy? A. to tone deficiency and sedate excess; B. to support righteous energy and expel pathogens; C.to treat symptoms and roots simultaneously; D. Treatment adjusted to three distinct circumstances
2044	只针不灸、平补平泻的针灸方法多用于何型失眠的治疗: A 痰热内扰; B 肝郁化火 C. ·阴虚火旺; D 心脾两虚; E. 心虚胆怯	What type of insomnia is mostly treated by acupuncture without moxibustion, by the neutral technique? A. internal disturbance of phlegm heat; B. · liver inhibition transforming into fire; C. yin deficiency with abundant fire; D. heart-spleen deficiency; E. deficient heart with timid gallbladder
2045	指出下面哪个俞募配穴是错误的: A，肺俞 中府	Which group of points is NOT a combination of anterior mu point and posterior transport (back shu) point?

	;B·肝俞 期门 C. ·脾俞 中脘 ;D·肾俞 京门 ;E·胆俞 日月	A. B13 (Fèi Shū); Lu1 (Zhōng Fǔ); B. B18 (Gān Shū); Lv14 (Qí Mén); C. B20 (Pí Shū); R12 (Zhōng Wǎn); D. B23 (Shèn Shū) G25 (Jīng Mén); E. B19 (Dǎn Shū). G24 (Rì Yuè).
2046	治疗百日咳初咳期，可在基本处方的基础上再加：A·合谷、外关；B·天突、孔最 C. ·太渊、太白；D·脾俞、足三里；E，内关、内庭	What points may be added to the basic prescription of points to treat whooping cough / pertusis at its initial coughing stage? A. Li4 / Hé Gǔ，Sj5 / Wài Guān; B. R22 / Tiān Tū，Lu6 / Kǒng Zuì; C. Lu9 / TàiYuān，Sp3 / Tài Bái; D. B20 / Pí Shū，S36 / Zú Sān Lǐ; E. P6 / Nèi Guān，S44 / Nèi Tíng
2047	治疗胞衣不下，应首选： A·里内庭；B·气端 C. ·独阴；D·八风；E·女膝	Which point may be selected to treat retention of placenta? A. Lǐ Nèi Tíng; B. Qì Chuǎn; C. Dú Yīn; D. Bā Fēng; E. Nu Xī.
2048	治疗暴盲肝阳化风证的治则为：A·行气活血、养血明目；B·行气活血、化瘀通络 C. ·平肝熄风、养血明目；D·平肝熄风、清肝明目；E·补益气血、养血明目	What treatment principle should be applied to treat the liver yang transforming into wind type of sudden blindness? A. to promote energy circulation, activate blood、nourish blood and sharpen vision; B. to promote energy circulation, activate blood、transform coagulation connecting linking meridians; C. to calm the liver and stop wind、to nourish blood and sharpen vision; D. to calm the liver and stop wind、to clear the liver and sharpen visione to tone and benefit energy-blood、to nourish blood and sharpen vision; E. to tone up and benefit energy and blood, nourish blood and sharpen vision.
2049	治疗暴盲气血两虚证的治则为：A·行气活血、养血明目；B·行气活血、化瘀通络 C. ·平肝熄风、养血明目；D·平肝熄风、清肝明目；E·补益气血、养血明目	What treatment principle should be a[pplied to treat the energy-blood deficiency type of sudden blindness? A to promote energy circulationactivate blood、nourish blood and sharpen vision; B to promote energy circulation, activate blood、transform coagulation, connect linking meridians; C. to calm the liver and stop wind、nourish blood and sharpen vision; D to calm the liver and stop wind、clear the liver and sharpen visione; E. to tone and benefit energy-blood、nourish blood and sharpen vision
2050	治疗暴盲气滞血瘀证的治则为：A·行气活血、养血明目；B·行气活血、化瘀通络 C. ·平肝熄风、养血明目；D·平肝熄风、清肝明目；E·补益气血、养血明目	What treatment principle should be applied to treat the energy congestion and blood coagulation type of sudden blindness? A to promote energy circulationactivate blood、nourish blood and sharpen vision; B to promote energy circulation, activate blood、transform coagulation, connect linking meridians; C. to calm the liver and stop wind、nourish blood and sharpen vision; D to calm the liver and stop wind、clear the liver and sharpen visione; E. to tone and benefit energy-blood、nourish blood and sharpen vision

2051	治疗背脊部痛痹，应取用: A·环跳 居髎 悬钟 血海 膈俞 夹脊; B·水沟 身柱 腰阳关 肾俞 关元 夹脊 C. ·大推 曲池 肾俞 阳陵泉 悬钟 夹脊; D·足三里 商丘 脾俞 昆仑 丘墟 夹脊; E·阳陵泉 外关 阳池 血海 阳溪 夹脊	Which group of points should be selected to treat painful rheumatism that attacks the back and spine region? A. G30 (Huán Tiào) G29 (Jū Liáo) G39 (Xuán Zhōng) Sp10 (Xuè Hǎi) B17 (Gé Shū) Huá Tuó Jiā Jí; B. D26 (Shuǐ Gōu, Rén Zhōng) D12 (Shēn Zhù) D3 (Yāo Yáng Guān) B23 (Shèn Shū) R4 (Guān Yuán) Huá Tuó Jiā Jí; C. D14 (Dà Zhuī) Li11 (Qū Chí) B23 (Shèn Shū) G34 (Yáng Líng Quán) G39 (Xuán Zhōng) Huá Tuó Jiā Jí; D. S36 (Zú Sān Lǐ) Sp5 (Shāng Qiū); B20 (Pí Shū); B60 (Kūn Lún) G40 (Qiū Xū) Huá Tuó Jiā Jí; E. G34 (Yáng Líng Quán). Sj5 (Wài Guān) Sj4 (Yáng Chí) Sp10 (Xuè Hǎi) Li5 (Yáng Xī) Huá Tuó Jiā Jí.
2052	治疗崩漏的主穴是：A·太冲、膻中、三阴交、关元; B. 脾俞、太溪、三阴交、足三里 C. ·关元、三阴交、血海、膈俞; D·丰隆、太冲、血海、三阴交; E·中脘、太溪、足三里、膻中	What are the primary points to treat bleeding from the uterus / metrorrhagia and metrostaxis? A. · Lv3 / Tài Chōng，R17 / Shān Zhōng，Sp6 / Sān Yīn Jiāo，R4 / Guān Yuán; B. B20 / Pí Shū，K3 / Tài Xī，Sp6 / Sān Yīn Jiāo，S36 / Zú Sān Lǐ; C. ·R4 / Guān Yuán，Sp6 / Sān Yīn Jiāo，Sp10 / Xuè Hǎi，B17 / Gé Shū; D. · S40 / Fēng Lóng，Lv3 / Tài Chōng，Sp10 / Xuè Hǎi，Sp6 / Sān Yīn Jiāo; E. · R12 / Zhōng Wǎn，K3 / Tài Xī，S36 / Zú Sān Lǐ，R17 / Shān Zhōng
2053	治疗崩漏首选: A·隐白; B·大都 C. ·三阴交; D·公孙; E·阴陵泉	What point may be selected as the primary point to treat bleeding from the uterus / metrorrhagia and metrostaxi? A. · Sp1 / Yǐn Bái; B. · Sp2 / Dà Dū; C. ·Sp6 / Sān Yīn Jiāo; D. · Sp4 / Gōng Sūn; E. · Sp9 / Yīn Líng Quán
2054	治疗闭经的肝肾亏虚证除基本处方外可加: A·肝俞、太溪; B·归来，命门 C. 太冲、期门; D·行间、地机 E. 气海，血海.	What points may be added to the basic prescription of points to treat the liver and kidney deprivation deficiency syndromof suppression of menstruation / Amenorrhea? A. ·B18 / Gān Shū，K3 / Tài Xī; B. · S29 / Guī Lái ，D4 / Mìng Mén; C. Lv3 / Tài Chōng，Lv14 / Qí Mén; D. · Lv2 / Xíng Jiān，Sp8 / Dì Jī; E. R6 / Qì Hǎi ，Sp10 / Xuè Hǎi.
2055	治疗闭经的气血不足证除基本处方外可加：A·肝俞、太溪; B·归来，命门 C. 太冲、期门; D·行间、地机; E 气海，血海	What points may be added to the basic prescription of points to treat the energy and blopod deficiency type of suppression of menstruation / amenorrhea? A. ·B18 / Gān Shū，K3 / Tài Xī; B. · S29 / Guī Lái ，D4 / Mìng Mén; C. Lv3 / Tài Chōng，Lv14 / Qí Mén; D. · Lv2 / Xíng Jiān，Sp8 / Dì Jī; E. R6 / Qì Hǎi ，Sp10 / Xuè Hǎi
2056	治疗闭经的气滞血瘀证除基本处方加: A·肝俞、太溪; B·归来，命门 C. 太冲、期门; D·行间、地机; E气海，血海	What points may be added to the basic prescription of points to treat the energy congestion and blood coagulation type of suppression of menstruation / amenorrhea? A. ·B18 / Gān Shū，K3 / Tài Xī; B. · S29 / Guī Lái ，D4 / Mìng Mén; C. Lv3 / Tài Chōng，Lv14 / Qí Mén; D. · Lv2 / Xíng Jiān，Sp8 / Dì Jī; E. R6 / Qì Hǎi ，Sp10 / Xuè Hǎi
2057	治疗扁平疣的基本方中，合谷配何穴称为 "四关"，可调和气血、疏肝理气：A·少冲; B·太冲 C. ·少泽; D·中	Among the points in the basic prescription to treat flat wart, the " four gates" refer to Li4 / Hé Gǔ in.ombination with what point to regulate and harmonize energy and

	冲; E·关冲	blood, disperse liver and regulate energy? A. · H9 / Shào Chōng; B. · Lv3 / Tài Chōng; C. · Si1 / Shào Zé; D. · P9 / Zhōng Chōng; E. · Sj1 / Guān Chōng
2058	治疗便血应首选: A·隐白 B·公孙 C·三阴交 D·阴陵泉 E 大横	Which point should be selected as the primary point to treat discharge of blood from anus? A. · Sp1 / Yǐn Bái; B. · Sp4 / Gōng Sūn; C. · Sp6 / Sān Yīn Jiāo; D. · Sp9 / Yīn Líng Quán; E. Sp15 / Dà Héng
2059	治疗肠胃实热型荨麻疹，可在基本处方的基础上再加: A·足三里; B·三阴交 C. ·肺俞; D·列缺; E肾俞	What points may be added to the basic prescription of points to treat the excess heat in the intestines and stomach type of urticaria? A. · S36 / Zú Sān Lǐ; B. · Sp6 / Sān Yīn Jiāo; C. ·B13 / Fèi Shū; D. ·Lu7 / Liè Quē; E. B23 / Shèn Shū
2060	治疗肠痈，一般多选用: A·曲池 合谷 天枢 内庭; B·曲池 上巨虚 大横 内庭 C. ·足三里 曲池 天枢 阑尾; D·阑尾 天枢 大肠俞 小肠俞; E·以上均不是	Which group of points should be selected to treat intestinal carbuncle? A. Li11 (Qū Chí) Li4 (Hé Gǔ) S25 (Tiān Shū); S44 (Nèi Tíng); B. Li11 (Qū Chí); S37 (Shàng Jù Xū) Sp15 (Dà Héng) S44 (Nèi Tíng); C. S36 (Zú Sān Lǐ); Li11 (Qū Chí); S25 (Tiān Shū); Lán Wěi Xué; D. Lán Wěi Xué S25 (Tiān Shū); B25 (Dà Cháng Shū); B27 (Xiǎo Cháng Shū); E. none of the above
2061	治疗冲任失调型痤疮，可在基本处方的基础上再加: A·丰隆; B·血海 C. ·足三里; D·命门; E，尺泽	What points may be added to the basic prescription of points to treat the loss of balance in the rigorous and conception meridians type of acne? A. · S40 / Fēng Lóng; B. · Sp10 / Xuè Hǎi; C. · S36 / Zú Sān Lǐ; D. · D4 / Mìng Mén; E. Lu5 / Chǐ Zé
2062	治疗冲任失调型痤疮，可在基本处方的基础上再加: A·少商; B·风门 C. ·阴陵泉; D·足三里; E. 膈俞	What point may be added to the basic prescription of points to treat the loss of balance in the rigorous and c onception meridians type of acne? A. · Lu11 / Shǎo Shāng; B. ·B12 / Fēng Mén; C. · Sp9 / Yīn Líng Quán; D. · S36 / Zú Sān Lǐ; E. B17 / Gé Shū
2063	治疗冲任血虚型不孕症，可在基本方基础上再加: A 肾俞、神阙: ; B·阴陵泉、丰隆; C. ·气海，血海; D·太冲、膈俞; E·中脘、足三里.	What points may be added to the basic prescription of points to treat infertility in women with blood deficiency in chong mai / vigorous meridian and ren mai / conception meridian? A. B23 / Shèn Shū， R8 / Shén Què; B. · Sp9 / Yīn Líng Quán，S40 / Fēng Lóng; C. · R6 / Qì Hǎi ，Sp10 / Xuè Hǎi; D. · Lv3 / Tài Chōng 、 ·B17 / Gé Shū; E. · R12 / Zhōng Wǎn，S36 / Zú Sān Lǐ.
2064	治疗抽搐风邪甚者，可在基础方上再加: A·足三里; B·太白 C. ·风府; D·三阴交; E·气海	What points may be added to the basic prescription of points to treat severe twitching with pathogenic wind? A. · S36 / Zú Sān Lǐ. B. · Sp3 / Tài Bái; C. D16 / Fēng Fǔ; D. · Sp6 / Sān Yīn Jiāo; E · R6 / Qì Hǎi
2065	治疗唇疔，可在基本处方的基础上再加: ( )、内庭穴。A·身柱; B三棱针点刺出血 C. ·曲泽; D·隐白; E·委中·	In treating lip furuncle, what point may be added to the basic prescription of points, in addition to S44 / Nèi Tíng? A · D12 / Shēn Zhù; B dotted-needling with a three-edged needle to let blood; C. P3 / Qū Zé; D · Sp1 / Yǐn Bái; E ·; B40 / Wěi Zhōng ·

2066	治疗带下病的主穴是：A·膻中、三阴交、气海、关元；B·脾俞、太溪、三阴交、足三里、膻中 C·带脉、关元、三阴交、白环俞；D·太冲、血海、三阴交、脾俞、肝俞；E·中脘、太溪、足三里、膻中	What are the primary points to treat vaginal discharges? A. · R17 / Shān Zhōng，Sp6 / Sān Yīn Jiāo，R6 / Qì Hǎi，R4 / Guān Yuán; B. B20 / Pí Shū，K3 / Tài Xī，Sp6 / Sān Yīn Jiāo，S36 / Zú Sān Lǐ，R17 / Shān Zhōng; ·C. G26 / Dài Mài，R4 / Guān Yuán，Sp6 / Sān Yīn Jiāo，B30 / Bái Huán Shū; D. · Lv3 / Tài Chōng，Sp10 / Xuè Hǎi，Sp6 / Sān Yīn Jiāo，B20 / Pí Shū，B18 / Gān Shū; E. · R12 / Zhōng Wǎn，K3 / Tài Xī，S36 / Zú Sān Lǐ，R17 / Shān Zhōng
2067	治疗单纯性肥胖症中的脾胃虚弱证，可在基本处方的基础上再加：A·合谷；B·足三里 C. ·血海；D·膻中；E·照海	What points may be added to the basic prescription of points to treat simple obesity due to deficiency of spleen and stomach? A. · Li4 / Hé Gǔ; B. · S36 / Zú Sān Lǐ; C. · Sp10 / Xuè Hǎi; D. · R17 / Shān Zhōng; E. · K6 / Zhào Hǎi
2068	治疗单纯性肥胖症中的真元不足证，可在基本处方的基础上再加：A·合谷；B·太白 C. ·血海；D·膻中；E·关元	What points may be added to the basic prescription of points to treat the deficient true energy type of simple obesity? A. · Li4 / Hé Gǔ; B. · Sp3 / Tài Bái; C. · Sp10 / Xuè Hǎi; D. · R17 / Shān Zhōng; E. · R4 / Guān Yuán
2069	治疗胆绞痛伴恶心呕吐者，可在基础方上加用：A·支沟、外关；B·三阴交、阴陵泉·C. ·百生窝、迎香；D·内关、足三里；E··至阳、肝俞	What points may be added to the basic prescription of points to treat colic of gallbladder accompanied by nausea and vomiting? A. · Sj6 / Zhi Gōu，Sj5 / Wài Guān; B. · Sp6 / Sān Yīn Jiāo，Sp9 / Yīn Líng Quán; C. · Bǎi Chóng wuō / nest of hundred insects，Li20 / Yíng Xiāng; D. · P6 / Nèi Guān，S36 / Zú Sān Lǐ; E. ·· D9 / Zhì Yáng，B18 / Gān Shū
2070	治疗胆绞痛伴见发热寒战者，可在基础方上加用：A·支沟、外关；B·三阴交、阴陵泉 C. ·百虫窝、迎香；D·内关、足三里；E·至阳、肝俞	What points may be added to the basic prescription of points to treat colic of gallbladder accompanied by fever and chills? A. · Sj6 / Zhi Gōu，Sj5 / Wài Guān; B. · Sp6 / Sān Yīn Jiāo，Sp9 / Yīn Líng Quán; C. Bǎi Chóng wuō / nest of hundred insects，Li20 / Yíng Xiāng; D. · P6 / Nèi Guān，S36 / Zú Sān Lǐ; E. · D9 / Zhì Yáng，B18 / Gān Shū
2071	治疗胆绞痛由蛔虫妄动引起者，可在基础方上加用：A·太冲、侠溪；B·三阴交、阴陵泉 C. 内关、足三里；D·百虫窝、迎香；E·以上都不对	What points may be added to the basic prescription of points to treat the disturbance of roundworm type of colic of gallbladder? A. · Lv3 / Tài Chōng，G43 / Xiá Xī; B. · Sp6 / Sān Yīn Jiāo，Sp9 / Yīn Líng Quán; C. P6 / Nèi Guān，S36 / Zú Sān Lǐ; D. Bǎi Chóng wuō / nest of hundred insects，Li20 / Yíng Xiāng; E. none of the above
2072	治疗胆绞痛之恶心呕吐者，·可在基础方上加用：A·太冲；B·阴陵泉 C. ·内关；D 百虫窝；E·天枢	What points may be added to the basic prescription of points to treat colic of gallbladder accompanied by nausea and vomiting? A. · Lv3 / Tài Chōng; B. · Sp9 / Yīn Líng Quán; C. · P6 / Nèi Guān; D. Bǎi Chóng wuō / nest of hundred insects; E. · S25 / Tiān Shū
2073	治疗胆绞痛之肝胆气滞者，	What point may be added to the basic prescription of

	可在基础方上加用：A·太冲; B·阴陵泉 C. ·内关; D 百虫窝; E·天枢	points to treat the liver and gallbladder energy congestion type of colic of gallbladder? A. · Lv3 / Tài Chōng; B. · Sp9 / Yīn Líng Quán; C. P6 / Nèi Guān; D. Bǎi Chóng wuō / nest of hundred insects; E. · S25 / Tiān Shū
2074	治疗胆绞痛之肝胆湿热者，可在基础方上加用：A·太冲; B·阴陵泉 C. ·内关; D 百虫窝; E·天枢	What point may be added to the basic prescription of points to treat the liver and gallbladder damp heat type of colic of gallbladder? A. · Lv3 / Tài Chōng; B. · Sp9 / Yīn Líng Quán; C. P6 / Nèi Guān; D. Bǎi Chóng wuō / nest of hundred insects; E. · S25 / Tiān Shū
2075	治疗胆绞痛之蛔虫妄动者，可在基础方上加用：A·太冲; B·阴陵泉 C. ·内关; D 百虫窝; E·天枢	What point may be added to the basic prescription of points to treat the disturbance of roundworm type of colic of gallbladder? A · Lv3 / Tài Chōng; B · Sp9 / Yīn Líng Quán; C. · P6 / Nèi Guān; D. Bǎi Chóng wuō / nest of hundred insects; E · S25 / Tiān Shū
2076	治疗癫狂病的十三鬼穴，首先由谁提出? A·張介賓; B·孙思邈 C. ，張景岳; D·杨上善; E，張志聰	Who first made mention of thirteen ghost points to treat depressive-psychosis (dian) and maniac-psychosis (kuang)? A. Zhang Jie bin (1563-1640); B. Sun Si Miao (581-682); C. Zhang Jing Yue (1563-1640); D. Yang Shang Shan (6th To 7th century); E. Zhang Zhi Cong (1610-1695).
2077	治疗癫证，其主要处方是: A·心俞 肝俞 脾俞 神门 丰隆; B· 大椎 水沟 风府 内关 丰隆 C. ·脾俞 肾俞 关元 足三里; D·风池 肝俞 肾俞 行间 侠溪; E·中脘 内关 丰隆 解溪	Which group of points may be selected to treat depressive-psychosis (dian)? A. B15 (Xīn Shū) B18 (Gān Shū) B20 (Pí Shū) H7 (Shén Mén) S40 (Fēng Lóng); B. D14 (Dà Zhuī) D26 (Shuǐ Gōu, Rén Zhōng) D16 (Fēng Fǔ) P6 (Nèi Guān) S40 (Fēng Lóng); C. B20 (Pí Shū); B23 (Shèn Shū) R4 (Guān Yuán) S36 (Zú Sān Lǐ); D. G20 (Fēng Chí)B18 (Gān Shū); B23 (Shèn Shū) Lv2 (Xíng Jiān); E.. R12 (Zhōng Wǎn). P6 (Nèi Guān) S40 (Fēng Lóng) S41 (Jiě Xī).
2078	治疗疔疮所取主穴属专：A·任脉穴; B·手少阳经穴 C. ·督脉穴; D·足太阳经穴; E·足阳明经穴	To what meridian do the primary points to treat furuncle belong? A. conception meridian / ren mai; B. · points on the hand lesser yang meridians; C. ·du mai / governing meridian; D. · foot Tài yáng / sun / temple flowing points / river points / jīng xué; E. · points on the foot bright yang meridians
2079	治疗呃逆，宜取: A·天突 肺俞 合谷 足三里 ; B·膻中 中脘 膈俞 内关 C. ·巨阙 膈俞 内关 足三里 ; D·膈俞 中脘 气海 太冲 ; E. 以上均不是	Which group of points should be selected to treat hiccups? A. R22 (Tiān Tū)B13 (Fèi Shū) Li4 (Hé Gǔ) S36 (Zú Sān Lǐ); B. R17 (Shān Zhōng); R12 (Zhōng Wǎn)B17 (Gé Shū) P6 (Nèi Guān); C. R14 (Jù Què) B17 (Gé Shū) P6 (Nèi Guān) S36 (Zú Sān Lǐ); D. B17 (Gé Shū); R12 (Zhōng Wǎn) R6 (Qì Hǎi) Lv3 (Tài Chōng); E. none of the above.
2080	治疗耳鸣、耳聋取中渚、侠溪是属于：A·辨证配穴; B 临近配穴 C. 局部配穴;	In treating tinnitus、deafness, when Sj3 / Zhōng Zhǔ, G43 / Xiá Xī are selected, the selection belongs to:

	B·临近配穴 C. ·局部配穴; D·循经远取; E·以上都不是	A. combining points according to differential diagnosis; B. ·combining local points and distal points; C. ·combining local points; D. ·combining local points along meridians; E. · none of the above
2081	治疗耳鸣、耳聋时轻时重，遇劳加重，休息则减，伴神疲乏力，食少腹胀，大便易溏，舌淡，苔薄白，脉细弱者治疗宜：A·疏风清热，通利耳窍; B·清泻肝胆，泻火开窍 C. ·豁痰泻火，通利耳窍; D·补肾填精，上荣耳窍; E·补益脾胃，濡养耳窍	What should be done in treating the following case: tinnitus、deafness, sometimes lighter and sometimes more severe， getting worse when fatigued, getting better after rest, accompanied by fatigue, lack of energy， poor appetite , and abdominal swelling，discharge of watery stools easily，pale tongue，a thin layer of tongue coating and whitish，a fine and weak pulse? A. · to disperse wind and clear heat ， connect and smooth out ear cavities; B. ·to clear and sedate liverallbladder， sedating fireopen up cavities; C. ·to remove phlegm, sedate fire，connect and smooth out ear cavities; D. ·to tone up kidneys, fill essence ， nourish ear cavities in the upper region; E. ·to tone and benefit spleen-stomach， moitsen and nourish ear cavities
2082	治疗耳鸣如蝉，耳内闭塞如聋，伴头晕目眩，胸闷痰多，舌红，苔黄腻，脉弦滑者治疗宜：A·疏风清热，通利耳窍; B·清泻肝胆，泻火开窍 C. ·豁痰泻火，通利耳窍; D·补肾填精，上荣耳窍; E·补益脾胃，濡养耳窍	What should be done in treating the following case: ringing in the ears like the sound of a cicada，blockage inside the ear as if deafness，accompanied by dizziness with whirling sensations，congested chest and plentiful phlegm，red tongue ，yellowish coating on the tongue and greasy，wiry, and slippery pulse? A. · to disperse wind and clear heat ， connect and smooth out ear cavities; B. ·to clear and sedate liver-gallbladder， sedate fire, open up cavities; C. ·to remove phlegm, sedate fire，connect and smooth out ear cavities; D. ·to tone kidneys, fill essence，nourish ear cavities in the upper region; E. ·to tone and benefit spleen-stomach，moitsen and nourish ear cavities.
2083	治疗肺经风热型痤疮，可在基本处方上再加：A·足三里; B·三阴交 C. ·尺泽; D·列缺; E·手三里	What point may be added to the basic prescription of points to treat the wind heat in the lung meridian type of acne? A. · S36 / Zú Sān Lǐ; B. · Sp6 / Sān Yīn Jiāo; C. · Lu5 / Chǐ Zé; D. ·Lu7 / Liè Quē; E. · Li10 / Shǒu Sān Lǐ
2084	治疗肺经热盛型鼻出血宜：A·针灸并用; B·只灸不针 C. ·攻补兼施; D·只针不灸; E·补法	How to treat nosebleed due to abundant heat in the lungs meridian? A. · both acupuncture and moxibustion; B. · moxibustion without acupuncture; C. · simultaneous treatment by attacking and tonification; D. · acupuncture without moxibustion; E. · tonfication
2085	治疗肺痨潮热，除用主方外，还可加用: A·鱼际 劳宫; B·大椎 太溪 C. ·大椎 合谷; D·关元 足三里; E·中府 尺泽	In addition to major points, which group of points should be selected to treat tuberculosis of the lungs and tidal fever? A. Lu10 (Yǔ Jì), P8 (Láo Gōng); B. D14 (Dà Zhuī); K3 (Tài Xī); C. D14 (Dà Zhuī) Li4 (Hé Gǔ); D. R4 (Guān Yuán) S36 (Zú Sān Lǐ); E. Lu1 (Zhōng Fǔ). Lu5 (Chǐ Zé)

2086	治疗肺痨咯血，应在主方的基础上加用: A·中府足三里; B·云门 尺泽 C. ·鱼际 经渠; D·膈俞 中府; E·膈俞 鱼际	In addition to major points, which group of points should be selected to treat tuberculosis of the lungs and discharge of blood from the mouth? A. Lu1 (Zhōng Fǔ); S36 (Zú Sān Lǐ); B. Lu2 (Yún Mén) Lu5 (Chǐ Zé); C. Lu10 (Yǔ Jì); Lu8 (Jīng Qú); D.B17 (Gé Shū) Lu1 (Zhōng Fǔ); E. B17 (Gé Shū). Lu10 (Yǔ Jì).
2087	治疗肺热引起的痿证，除取主穴外，还应加用: A·鱼际 孔最 曲池; B·肺俞 尺泽 大椎 C. 列缺 合谷 少商; D·少商 二间 大椎; E·以上均不是	In addition to major points, which group of points should be selected to treat paralysis due to hot lungs? A. Lu10 (Yǔ Jì) Lu6 (Kǒng Zuì) Li11 (Qū Chí); B. B13 (Fèi Shū); Lu5 (Chǐ Zé) D14 (Dà Zhuī); C. Lu7 (Liè Quē); Li4 (Hé Gǔ) Lu11 (Shǎo Shāng); D. Lu11 (Shǎo Shāng) Li2 (Èr Jiān) D14 (Dà Zhuī); E. None of the above.
2088	治疗肺胃热盛之咽喉肿痛宜: A·疏泄肝胆; B·清热化痰 C. ·滋阴降火; D·疏风清热; E·清泻热邪	How to treat swollen and painful throat due to abundant heat in the lungs and stomach? A. ·to disperse and sedate liver and gallbladder; B. to·clear heat, transform phlegm; C. ·to water yin and bring down fire; D. · to disperse wind and clear heat; E. ·to clear and sedate pathogenic heat
2089	治疗风寒感冒，可在基本处方的基础上再加: A·少商; B·尺泽 C. ·鱼际; D·风门; E·中脘	What points may be added to the basic prescription of points to treat the common cold of a wind-cold type? A. · Lu11 / Shǎo Shāng; B. · Lu5 / Chǐ Zé; C. · Lu10 / Yǔ Jì; D ·B12 / Fēng Mén; E. · R12 / Zhōng Wǎn
2090	治疗风寒咳嗽，可在基本处方的基础上再加: A·少商; B·尺泽 C. ·鱼际; D·风门; E. 孔最	What point may be added to the basic prescription of points to treat the wind.old type of cough? A. · Lu11 / Shǎo Shāng; B. · Lu5 / Chǐ Zé; C. Lu10 / Yǔ Jì; D. ·B12 / Fēng Mén; E. Lu6 / Kǒng Zuì
2091	治疗风寒束表型荨麻疹，可在基本处方的基础上再加: A·足三里; B·三阴交 C. ·肺俞; D·列缺; E肾俞	What points may be added to the basic prescription of points to treat urticaria due to wind cold constricting the superficial region? A. · S36 / Zú Sān Lǐ; B. · Sp6 / Sān Yīn Jiāo; C. ·B13 / Fèi Shū; D. ·Lu7 / Liè Quē; E. B23 / Shèn Shū
2092	治疗风寒头痛除基本处方外，下列穴组还当选: A·曲池、合谷、大椎; B·风门、大椎、风池 c·合谷、三阴交、内庭; D·足三里、三阴交、丰隆; E·足三里、膈俞、血海	Which group of points may be selected to treat wind cold headache in addition to the basic prescription of points? A. · Li11 / Qū chí, Li4 / Hé Gǔ 、D14 / Dà Zhuī; B. ·B12 / Fēng Mén 、D14 / Dà Zhuī、 G20 / Fēng Chí; C. · Li4 / Hé Gǔ, Sp6 / Sān Yīn Jiāo 、·S44 / Nèi Tíng; D. · S36 / Zú Sān Lǐ, Sp6 / Sān Yīn Jiāo, S40 / Fēng Lóng; E. · S36 / Zú Sān Lǐ, B17 / Gé Shū, Sp10 / Xuè Hǎi
2093	治疗风火牙痛可在基本处方的基础上再加: A·翳风、风池; B·太溪、照海; C·尺泽、少商; D·厉兑、二间; E·足三里、三阴交	What point may be added to the basic prescription of points to treat the wind fire type of toothache? A. · Sj17 / Yì Fēng, G20 / Fēng Chí; B. · K3 / Tài Xī, K6 / Zhào Hǎi; C. · Lu5 / Chǐ Zé, Lu11 / Shǎo Shāng; D. · S45 / Lì Duì, Li2 / Èr Jiān; E. · S36 / Zú Sān Lǐ, Sp6 / Sān Yīn Jiāo
2094	治疗风热犯表型荨麻疹，可在基本处方的基础上再加: A·曲池; B·血海; C·三阴交; D·大椎E·内关	What point may be added to the basic prescription of points to treat the wind heat offending the superficial region type of urticaria?

		A. · Li11 / Qū chí; B. · Sp10 / Xuè Hǎi; C. Sp6 / Sān Yīn Jiāo; D. ·D14 / Dà Zhuī P6 / Nèi Guān
2095	治疗风热头痛，可在基本处方上加用：A·风池; B·曲池; C·三阴交; D·膈俞; E·足三里	Which point may be selected to treat wind heat headache in addition to the basic prescription of points? A. · G20 / Fēng Chí; B. · Li11 / Qū chí; C. Sp6 / Sān Yīn Jiāo; D. ·B17 / Gé Shū; E. · S36 / Zú Sān Lǐ
2096	治疗风热型目赤肿痛，除选主穴外，还可加用: A·肾俞 命门; B·关元 太溪 C，行间 侠溪; D·脾俞 阴陵泉; E·少商 上星	In adition to major points, which group of points should be selected to treat pink eyes with swelling and pain due to wind heat? A; B23 (Shèn Shū), D4 (Mìng Mén); B. R4 (Guān Yuán); K3 (Tài Xī); C. Lv2 (Xíng Jiān). G43 (Xiá Xī); D. B20 (Pí Shū) Sp9 (Yīn Líng Quán); E. Lu11 (Shǎo Shāng), D23 (Shàng Xīng).
2097	治疗风热壅肺之咽喉肿痛宜：A·疏泄肝胆; B·清热化痰 C·滋阴降火; D·疏风清热; E·清泻热邪	How to treat the wind heat accumulated in the lungs type of swollen and painful throat? A. ·dispersing and sedating liver and gallbladder; B. ·clear heat and transform phlegm; C. ·to water yin and bring down fire; D. · to disperse wind and clear heat; E. ·to clear and sedate pathogenic heat
2098	治疗风热蕴阻型神经性皮炎，可在基本处方的基础上再加：A·行间; B·太溪; C·脾俞; D·外关; E·委中	What point may be added to the basic prescription of points to treat the wind heat obstruction type of neurodermatitis? A. · Lv2 / Xíng Jiān; B. · K3 / Tài Xī; C. B20 / Pí Shū; D. · Sj5 / Wài Guān; E. B40 / Wěi Zhōng
2099	治疗风湿头痛，可在基本处方的基础上加用：A·丰隆; B·内廷; C· 风府; D 足三里; E. 三阴交	Which point may be selected to treat wind-damp headache in addition to the basic prescription of points? A. · S40 / Fēng Lóng; B. · S44 / Nèi Tíng; C. · D16 / Fēng Fǔ; D. S36 / Zú Sān Lǐ; E. Sp6 / Sān Yīn Jiāo
2100	治疗风邪袭络型眼睑下垂，可在基本处方的基础上再加：A·太溪、命门、肾俞; B·足三里、脾俞、尺泽; C·足三里、脾俞、百会; D·太溪、肾俞。·风门; E¨·合谷、风池	What points may be added to the basic prescription of points to treat the pathogenic wind attacking linking meridians type of eyelid dropping? A. · K3 / Tài Xī，D4 / Mìng Mén，B23 / Shèn Shū; B. · S36 / Zú Sān Lǐ，B20 / Pí Shū，Lu5 / Chǐ Zé; C. · S36 / Zú Sān Lǐ，B20 / Pí Shū，D20 / Bǎi Huì; D. · K3 / Tài Xī，B23 / Shèn Shū 。·B12 / Fēng Mén; E¨. · Li4 / Hé Gǔ，G20 / Fēng Chí
2101	治疗风阳上扰型眩晕，可在基本处方的基础上再加：A·行间、·太冲、太溪; B·内关、中脘、丰隆; C·气海、血海、足三里; D·肝俞、肾俞、太溪; E·合谷、曲池、太阳	What point may be added to the main prescription of points to treat vertigo due to wind yang disturbing upward? A. · Lv2 / Xíng Jiān 、 · Lv3 / Tài Chōng，K3 / Tài Xī; B. · P6 / Nèi Guān，R12 / Zhōng Wǎn，S40 / Fēng Lóng; C. · R6 / Qì Hǎi，Sp10 / Xuè Hǎi，S36 / Zú Sān Lǐ; D. ·B18 / Gān Shū，B23 / Shèn Shū，K3 / Tài Xī; E. · Li4 / Hé Gǔ，Li11 / Qū Chí，Tài yáng / sun / temple
2102	治疗肝胆火盛引起的目赤肿痛，除取主穴外，还可加用: A·肝俞 魂门; B·风市 曲泉; C·风池 侠溪; D·肩井 中都; E·以上部不是	In adition to major points, which group of points should be selected to treat pink eyes with swelling and pain due to excess fire in the liver and gallbladder? A. B18 (Gān Shū); B47 (Hún Mén); B. G31 (Fēng Shì); Lv8 (Qū Quán); C. G20 (Fēng Chí); G43 (Xiá Xī); D. G21 (Jiān Jǐng) Lv6 (Zhōng Dū); E. none of the above.

2103	治疗肝火亢盛型高血压，可在基本处方的基础上再加：A·太溪、风池；B·膈俞、风池；C·行间、风池；D·血海、风池；E·肝俞、风池	In treating hypertension due to abundant liver fire, what points may be added to the basic prescription of points? A. · K3 / Tài Xī，G20 / Fēng Chí; B. ·B17 / Gé Shū，G20 / Fēng Chí; C. · Lv2 / Xíng Jiān，G20 / Fēng Chí; D. · Sp10 / Xuè Hǎi，G20 / Fēng Chí; E. ·B18 / Gān Shū，G20 / Fēng Chí
2104	治疗肝火上逆型鼻出血宜：A·针灸并用；B·只灸不针；C·攻补兼施；D·只针不灸；E·补法	How to treat nosebleed due to liver fire uprising? A. · both acupuncture and moxibustion; B. · moxibustion without acupuncture; C. · simultaneous treatment by attack and tonification; D. · acupuncture without moxibustion; E. · tonfication
2105	治疗肝火烁肺型咳嗽的主要处方是：A·肝俞 鱼际 侠溪 行间；B·肺俞 尺泽 阳陵泉 太冲；C·中府 丰隆 肺俞 太渊；D·列缺 合谷 行间 章门；E·肝俞 肺俞 太渊 章门	Which group of points should be selected to treat cough due to liver fire burning the lungs? A. B18 (Gān Shū); Lu10 (Yǔ Jì) G43 (Xiá Xī) Lv2 (Xíng Jiān); B. B13 (Fèi Shū) Lu5 (Chǐ Zé) G34 (Yáng Líng Quán); Lv3 (Tài Chōng); C. Lu1 (Zhōng Fǔ); S40 (Fēng Lóng)B13 (Fèi Shū) Lu9 (Tài Yuān); D. Lu7 (Liè Quē) Li4 (Hé Gǔ) Lv2 (Xíng Jiān) Lv13 (Zhāng Mén); E. B18 (Gān Shū);.B13 (Fèi Shū) Lu9 (Tài Yuān) Lv13 (Zhāng Mén)
2106	治疗肝气犯胃型胃痛的主要处方是：A. 中脘 足三里 内关 期门 阳陵泉；B. 中脘 足三里 神阙 关元 公孙；C·中脘 足三里 胃俞 气海 章门；D·中脘 足三里 胃俞 内关 章门 E 中脘 足三里 气海 天枢 里内庭	Which group of points should be selected to treat stomachache due to liver energy offending the stomach? A. R12 (Zhōng Wǎn); S36 (Zú Sān Lǐ) P6 (Nèi Guān) Lv14 (Qí Mén) G34 (Yáng Líng Quán); B. R12 (Zhōng Wǎn); S36 (Zú Sān Lǐ); R8 (Shén Què) R4 (Guān Yuán) Sp4 (Gōng Sūn); C. R12 (Zhōng Wǎn); S36 (Zú Sān Lǐ); B21 (Wèi Shū) R6 (Qì Hǎi) Lv13 (Zhāng Mén); D. R12 (Zhōng Wǎn); S36 (Zú Sān Lǐ); B21 (Wèi Shū) P6 (Nèi Guān) Lv13 (Zhāng Mén); E. R12 (Zhōng Wǎn); S36 (Zú Sān Lǐ). R6 (Qì Hǎi) S25 (Tiān Shū) Lǐ Nèi Tíng.
2107	治疗肝气郁结型胎位不正，应在基本方基础上再加：A·中脘、关元；B·肾俞、气海；C·阴陵泉、丰隆；D·脾俞、行间；E·期门、太冲	What points may be added to the basic prescription of points to treat the liver energy congestion type of fetus in wrong position? A. · R12 / Zhōng Wǎn，R4 / Guān Yuán; B. B23 / Shèn Shū，R6 / Qì Hǎi; C. · Sp9 / Yīn Líng Quán，S40 / Fēng Lóng; D. B20 / Pí Shū，Lv2 / Xíng Jiān; E. · Lv14 / Qí Mén，Lv3 / Tài Chōng
2108	治疗肝肾不足诱发的斑秃，可在基本处方的基础上再加：A·太冲 ·B·气海；C·申脉 ·D¨风池；E·太溪	What point may be added to the basic prescription of points to treat the deficient liver and kidneys type of alopecia areata? A. · Lv3 / Tài Chōng; B. · R6 / Qì Hǎi; C. B62 / Shēn Mài; ·D.¨ G20 / Fēng Chí; E. · K3 / Tài Xī
2109	治疗肝肾不足诱发的斑秃，可在基本处方的基础上再加：A·中封；B·太冲；C·头维；D·合谷；E·命门	What point may be added to the basic prescription of points to treat the deficient liver and kidneys type of alopecia areata? A ·Lv4 / Zhōng Fēng; B · Lv3 / Tài Chōng C · S8 / Tóu Wěi; D · Li4 / Hé Gǔ; E · D4 / Mìng Mén
2110	治疗肝肾亏虚型闭经，可在	What additional points may be added to treat the liver

	基本处方的基础上再加：A·中脘、足三里；B·太溪、肝俞；C·膈俞、血海；D·脾俞、太冲；E·太冲、期门	and kidney deprivation and deficiency type of suppression of menstruation / amenorrhea? A. · R12 / Zhōng Wǎn，S36 / Zú Sān Lǐ; B. · K3 / Tài Xī，B18 / Gān Shū; C. ·B17 / Gé Shū，Sp10 / Xuè Hǎi; D. B20 / Pí Shū，Lv3 / Tài Chōng; E. · Lv3 / Tài Chōng，Lv14 / Qí Mén
2111	治疗肝肾亏虚型近视，可在基本处方的基础上再加：A·心俞、膈俞、足三里、三阴交；B·心俞、膈俞、内关、神门；C·脾俞、胃俞、内关、三阴交；D·脾俞、胃俞、足三里、三阴交；E·肝俞、肾俞、太冲、太溪	What points may be added to the basic prescription of points to treat the liver and kidney deprivation and deficiency type of myopia? A. ·B15 / Xīn Shū，B17 / Gé Shū，S36 / Zú Sān Lǐ，Sp6 / Sān Yīn Jiāo; B. ·B15 / Xīn Shū，B17 / Gé Shū，P6 / Nèi Guān，H7 / Shén Mén; C. B20 / Pí Shū，B21 / Wèi Shū，P6 / Nèi Guān，Sp6 / Sān Yīn Jiāo; D. B20 / Pí Shū，B21 / Wèi Shū，S36 / Zú Sān Lǐ，Sp6 / Sān Yīn Jiāo; E. ·B18 / Gān Shū，B23 / Shèn Shū，Lv3 / Tài Chōng，K3 / Tài Xī
2112	治疗肝肾亏虚型皮肤瘙痒症，可在基本处方的基础上再加：A·太溪；B·肺俞；C·大椎；D·气海；E·阴郄	What point may be added to the basic prescription of points to treat the liver and kidney deficiency type of skin itch? A. · K3 / Tài Xī; B. ·B13 / Fèi Shū; C. ·D14 / Dà Zhuī; D. · R6 / Qì Hǎi; E. · H6 / Yīn Xī
2113	治疗肝肾阴虚型抽搐，可在基础方上再加：A·肾俞；B·涌泉；C·风府；D·劳宫；E·气海	What point may be added to the basic prescription of points to treat the liver and kidney yin deficiency type of twitching? A. B23 / Shèn Shū; B. · K1 / Yǒng Quán; C. · D16 / Fēng Fǔ; D. · P8 / Láo Gōng; E. · R6 / Qì Hǎi
2114	治疗肝肾阴虚型阴痒，可在基本处方的基础上再加：A·曲泉、太溪，照海；B·太溪、照海、命门；C·膈俞、血海 中极；D·脾俞、足三里、三阴交；E太冲，肝俞、曲泉 ，	What points may be added to the basic prescription of points to treat the yin deficiency of liver and kidneys type of yin itch? A. · Lv8 / Qū Quán，K3 / Tài Xī ，K6 / Zhào Hǎi; B. · K3 / Tài Xī，K6 / Zhào Hǎi，D4 / Mìng Mén; C. ·B17 / Gé Shū，Sp10 / Xuè Hǎi R3 / Zhōng Jí; D. B20 / Pí Shū，S36 / Zú Sān Lǐ，Sp6 / Sān Yīn Jiāo; E. Lv3 / Tài Chōng ，B18 / Gān Shū，Lv8 / Qū Quán ，
2115	治疗肝肾阴虚型震颤麻痹可在基本处方上再加：A·太冲、阳陵泉；B·足三里、三阴交；C·肝俞、肾俞；D·气海、血海；E·肾俞、太溪	What points may be added to the basic prescription of points to treat Parkinsonism that belongs to liver kidney yin deficiency type? · A. · Lv3 / Tài Chōng，G34 / Yáng Líng Quán; B. · S36 / Zú Sān Lǐ，Sp6 / Sān Yīn Jiāo; C. ·B18 / Gān Shū，B23 / Shèn Shū; D. · R6 / Qì Hǎi，Sp10 / Xuè Hǎi; E. B23 / Shèn Shū，K3 / Tài Xī
2116	治疗肝胃不和型妊娠呕吐，可在基本方基础上再加：A·三阴交、丰隆；B·百会、气海 ；C.脾俞、胃俞；D·神门、心俞；E·期门，太冲	What points may be added to the basic prescription of points to treat the liver and stomach disharmony type of morning sickness? A. · Sp6 / Sān Yīn Jiāo，S40 / Fēng Lóng; B. · D20 / Bǎi Huì，R6 / Qì Hǎi; C. B20 / Pí Shū，B21 / Wèi Shū; D. · H7 / Shén Mén，B15 / Xīn Shū; E. · Lv14 / Qí Mén ，Lv3 / Tài Chōng
2117	治疗肝阳亢逆型头痛的主	Which group of points should be selected to treat

	要处方是: A·百会 通天 行间 阿是穴; B·上星 头维 合谷 阿是穴; C·后顶 天柱 昆仑 阿是穴; D·风池 百会 悬颅 侠溪 行间; E·百会 气海 肝俞 脾俞 肾俞 合谷 足三里	headache due to liver yang uprising? A. D20 (Bǎi Huì), B7 (Tōng Tiān), Lv2 (Xíng Jiān); B. D23 (Shàng Xīng); S8 (Tóu Wěi) Li4 (Hé Gǔ), a shi xue (ouch point or tender point); C. D19 (Hòu Dǐng)B10 (Tiān Zhù); B60 (Kūn Lún) a shi xue (ouch point or tender point); D. G20 (Fēng Chí) D20 (Bǎi Huì) G5 (Xuán Lú) G43 (Xiá Xī) Lv2 (Xíng Jiān); E. D20 (Bǎi Huì). R6 (Qì Hǎi)B18 (Gān Shū); B20 (Pí Shū); B23 (Shèn Shū) Li4 (Hé Gǔ) S36 (Zú Sān Lǐ).
2118	治疗肝阳上亢的眩晕症，应选取的背俞穴是: A.肝俞肾俞; B 肝俞胆俞; C，脾俞胃俞; D，肺俞肾俞	In treating the liver yang uprising type of vertigo, which back shu points (bei shu xue) should be selected? A. B18 (Gān Shū);B23 (Shèn Shū); B. B18 (Gān Shū) B19 (Dǎn Shū); C. B20 (Pí Shū);B21 (Wèi Shū); D. B13 (Fèi Shū),B23 (Shèn Shū).
2119	治疗肝郁化火型神经性皮炎，可在基本处方的基础上再加: A·脾俞、血海; B·太溪、血海; C·风市、阴陵泉; D·侠溪、行间; E·合谷、外关	What points may be added to the basic prescription of points to treat the liver inhibition transforming into fire type of neurodermatitis? A. B20 / Pí Shū，Sp10 / Xuè Hǎi; B. · K3 / Tài Xī，Sp10 / Xuè Hǎi; C. · G31 / Fēng Shì，Sp9 / Yīn Líng Quán; D. · G43 / Xiá Xī，Lv2 / Xíng Jiān; E. · Li4 / Hé Gǔ，Sj5 / Wài Guān
2120	治疗疳证兼有虫积者，可在基本处方的基础上再加: A·三阴交; B·百虫窝; C·天枢; D·章门; E·胃俞	What point may be added to the basic prescription of points to treat mulnutrition in children with parasitic infestation? A. · Sp6 / Sān Yīn Jiāo; B. Bǎi chóng wuō / nest of hundred insects; C. · S25 / Tiān Shū; D. · Lv13 / Zhāng Mén; E. B21 / Wèi Shū
2121	治疗疳证如用穴位割治的方法，一般取: A·外关; B. 八邪; C·八风; D·大鱼际; E·小鱼际	What point should be used in point cutting therapy to treat mulnutrition in children? A. · Sj5 / Wài Guān; B. Bā xié / eight evils; C. Bā fēng / eight winds; D. Dà Yǔ Jì; E. Xiǎo Yǔ Jì
2122	治疗感冒以列缺合谷为主穴，其原因主要为: A. 病在肺; B. 病在太陽阳明; C. 病在表; D. 病在肺卫; E. 以上部不是.	What is the primary rationale behind the practice of treating the common cold by Lu7 (Liè Quē) and Li4 (Hé Gǔ)? A. disease in the lungs; B. disease in the greater yang and bright yang; C. disease in the superficial region; D. disease in the lung defense energy; E. none of the above.
2123	治疗高热见神昏瞻语者可在基础方上再加（ ）以开窍泻热: A·风池; B·尺泽; C·内庭; D·素髎; E·外关	What points may be added to the basic prescription of points to treat high fever with and unclear consciousness and delirium? A. · G20 / Fēng Chí ; B. · Lu5 / Chǐ Zé; C. · S44 / Nèi Tíng; D. · D25 / Sù Liáo; E. · Sj5 / Wài Guān
2124	治疗高热因于风寒者可在基础方上再加: A·风池; B·尺泽; C·内庭; D·素髎; E·外关	What points may be added to the basic prescription of points to treat the wind cold type of high fever? A. · G20 / Fēng Chí ; B. · Lu5 / Chǐ Zé; C. · S44 / Nèi Tíng; D. · D25 / Sù Liáo; E. · Sj5 / Wài Guān
2125	治疗高热因于风热者可在	What point may be added to the basic prescription of

	基础方上再加：A·风池；B·尺泽；C·内庭；D·素髎；E·外关	points to treat the wind heat type of high fever? A. · G20 / Fēng Chí; B. · Lu5 / Chǐ Zé; C. · S44 / Nèi Tíng; D. · D25 / Sù Liáo; E. · Sj5 / Wài Guān
2126	治疗高热因于气分热盛者可在基础方上再加（ ）以通腑泻热：A·风池；B·尺泽；C·内庭；D·素髎；E·外关	In treating high fever due to abundant heat at the energy level, what point may be added to the basic prescription of points in order to connect bowels and sedate heat? A. · G20 / Fēng Chí ·; B. · Lu5 / Chǐ Zé; C. · S44 / Nèi Tíng; D. · D25 / Sù Liáo; E. · Sj5 / Wài Guān
2127	治疗高血压首选：A·商阳；B·合谷；C·阳溪；D·手三里；E·曲池	What point should be selected as the primary point to treat hypertension? A. · Li1 / Shāng Yáng; B. · Li4 / Hé Gǔ; C. · Li5 / Yáng Xī; D. · Li10 / Shǒu Sān Lǐ; E. · Li11 / Qū Chí
2128	治疗高血压在基本处方中具疏肝理气、平降肝阳作用的腧穴是：A·百会；B·合谷；C·三阴交；D·太冲；E·曲池	Among the basic prescription of points to treat hypertension, what point can disperse the liver and regulate energy, calm and bring down liver yang? A. · D20 / Bǎi Huì; B. · Li4 / Hé Gǔ; C. · Sp6 / Sān Yīn Jiāo; D. · Lv3 / Tài Chōng; E ·. Li11 / Qū Chí
2129	治疗更年期综合征的基本处方中，除肾俞、太溪、三阴交外，还包括：A·足三里、气海；B·神门、内关；C·太冲、风池；D·关元、百会；E·丰隆、中脘	What point, in addition to B23 / Shèn Shū, K3 / Tài Xī, and Sp6 / Sān Yīn Jiāo， may be added to the basic prescription of points to treat menopause syndrome? A. · S36 / Zú Sān Lǐ， R6 / Qì Hǎi; B. · H7 / Shén Mén， P6 / Nèi Guān; C. · Lv3 / Tài Chōng， G20 / Fēng Chí; D. · R4 / Guān Yuán， D20 / Bǎi Huì; E. · S40 / Fēng Lóng， R12 / Zhōng Wǎn
2130	治疗更年期综合征脾肾阳虚型应在基本方基础上再加：A·气海、足三里、脾俞；B·涌泉、太冲、风池；C·中脘、丰隆、公孙；D·期门、肝俞、行间；E·神门、内关、心俞	What points may be added to the basic prescription of points to treat the spleen and kidney yang deficiency type of menopause syndrome? A. · R6 / Qì Hǎi， S36 / Zú Sān Lǐ， B20 / Pí Shū; B. · K1 / Yǒng Quán， Lv3 / Tài Chōng， G20 / Fēng Chí; C. · R12 / Zhōng Wǎn， S40 / Fēng Lóng， Sp4 / Gōng Sūn; D. · Lv14 / Qí Mén， B18 / Gān Shū， Lv2 / Xíng Jiān; E. · H7 / Shén Mén， P6 / Nèi Guān， B15 / Xīn Shū
2131	治疗更年期综合征心肾不交型应在基本方基础上再加：A·气海、足三里、脾俞；B·涌泉、太冲、风池；C·中脘、丰隆、公孙；D·期门、肝俞、行间；E·神门、内关、心俞	What points may be added to the basic prescription of points to treat the no communication between heart and kidneys type of menopause syndrome? A. · R6 / Qì Hǎi， S36 / Zú Sān Lǐ， B20 / Pí Shū; B. · K1 / Yǒng Quán， Lv3 / Tài Chōng， G20 / Fēng Chí; C. · R12 / Zhōng Wǎn， S40 / Fēng Lóng， Sp4 / Gōng Sūn; D. · Lv14 / Qí Mén， B18 / Gān Shū， Lv2 / Xíng Jiān; E. · H7 / Shén Mén， P6 / Nèi Guān， B15 / Xīn Shū
2132	治疗寒厥可在基础方上再加：A·行间；B·神阙；C·风府；D·丰隆；E·气海	What point may be added to the basic prescription of points to treat cold uprsing? A. · Lv2 / Xíng Jiān; B. · R8 / Shén Què; C. · D16 / Fēng Fǔ; D. · S40 / Fēng Lóng; E. · R6 / Qì Hǎi
2133	治疗寒疟，可在基本处方的基础上再加：A·至阳、期门；B·中脘、足三里；C·风门、太冲D·曲池、十宣；E、内	What points may be added to the basic prescription of points to treat cold malaria? A. · D9 / Zhì Yáng， Lv14 / Qí Mén; B. · R12 / Zhōng Wǎn，

	太冲D·曲池、十宣; E，·内关、尺泽	S36 / Zú Sān Lǐ; C. ·B12 / Fēng Mén Lv3 / Tài Chōng; D. · Li11 / Qū Chí，Shí xuān / ten statements / ten expansions; E. · P6 / Nèi Guān，Lu5 / Chǐ Zé
2134	治疗寒湿痢，除用主穴外，还可加用: A·中脘 气海; B·梁门 内庭; C·内关 曲池; D·关元 神阙; E. 中极 肾俞	In addition to needling major points, which group of points should be added to treat damp-cold dysentery? A. R12 (Zhōng Wǎn), R6 (Qì Hǎi); B. S21 (Liáng Mén),S44 (Nèi Tíng); C. P6 (Nèi Guān); Li11 (Qū Chí); D. R4 (Guān Yuán) R8 (Shén Què); E R3 (Zhōng Jí);B23 (Shèn Shū)
2135	治疗寒湿凝滞型痛经的处方是: ·A·关元、三阴交、地机、十七椎、水道; B·关元、三阴交、合谷、太冲、次髎; C·关元、三阴交、足三里、胃俞、命门; D 关元、三阴交、足三里，太冲、肾俞; E. 关元、血海、三阴交、足三里、脾俞	What is the prescription of points to treat the cold dampness congestion type of period pain? · A. · R4 / Guān Yuán，Sp6 / Sān Yīn Jiāo，Sp8 / Dì Jī 、17th vertebra、 S28 / Shuǐ Dào; B. · R4 / Guān Yuán，Sp6 / Sān Yīn Jiāo，Li4 / Hé Gǔ，Lv3 / Tài Chōng，B32 / Cì Liáo; C. · R4 / Guān Yuán，Sp6 / Sān Yīn Jiāo，S36 / Zú Sān Lǐ，B21 / Wèi Shū，D4 / Mìng Mén; D. R4 / Guān Yuán，Sp6 / Sān Yīn Jiāo，S36 / Zú Sān Lǐ ，Lv3 / Tài Chōng，B23 / Shèn Shū; E. R4 / Guān Yuán，Sp10 / Xuè Hǎi，Sp6 / Sān Yīn Jiāo，S36 / Zú Sān Lǐ，B20 / Pí Shū
2136	治疗寒湿偏盛的带下病，除取主穴之外，还可加用: A·阳陵泉 行间; B·中极 三阴交; C·关元 足三里; D·次髎 中极; E·肾俞 阴陵泉	In addtion to the major points, which group of points may be selected to treat vaginal discharge with cold dampness in excess? A. G34 (Yáng Líng Quán) Lv2 (Xíng Jiān); B. R3 (Zhōng Jí); Sp6 (Sān Yīn Jiāo); C. R4 (Guān Yuán); S36 (Zú Sān Lǐ); D. B32 (Cì Liáo) R3 (Zhōng Jí); E. B23 (Shèn Shū). Sp9 (Yīn Líng Quán).
2137	治疗寒湿腰痛在基本处方的基础上再加: A·膈俞; B·肾俞; C·大肠俞; D 大椎; E·委中	What point may be added to treat cold-dampness lumbago in addition to the basic prescription? A. ·B17 / Gé Shū; B. B23 / Shèn Shū; C. B25 / Dà Cháng Shū; D. D14 / Dà Zhuī; E. B40 / Wěi Zhōng
2138	治疗寒邪内积型腹痛的主要处方是: A. 中脘 足三里 内关 章门 脾俞 胃俞; B.中脘 足三里 章门 气海 脾俞 胃俞; C·中脘 足三里 神阙 关元 公孙; D·中脘 足三里 气海 天枢 里内庭; E. 中脘 足三里 内关 期门 阳陵泉.	Which group of points should be selected to treat abdominal pain due to internal accumulation of cold pathogens? A. R12 (Zhōng Wǎn); S36 (Zú Sān Lǐ). P6 (Nèi Guān)Lv13 (Zhāng Mén); B20 (Pí Shū)B21 (Wèi Shū); B. R12 (Zhōng Wǎn); S36 (Zú Sān Lǐ0, Lv13 (Zhāng Mén) R6 (Qì Hǎi); B20 (Pí Shū)B21 (Wèi Shū); C. R12 (Zhōng Wǎn); S36 (Zú Sān Lǐ); R8 (Shén Què) R4 (Guān Yuán) Sp4 (Gōng Sūn); D. R12 (Zhōng Wǎn); S36 (Zú Sān Lǐ) R6 (Qì Hǎi) S25 (Tiān Shū) Lǐ Nèi Tíng; E. R12 (Zhōng Wǎn); S36 (Zú Sān Lǐ) P6 (Nèi Guān) Lv14 (Qí Mén) G34 (Yáng Líng Quán)..
2139	治疗寒证腹痛应选用 A.中脘内关足三里; B，中脘上巨虚足三里; C.中脘神阙足三里; D 内关中脘神阙	Which group of points should be selected to treat cold abdominal pain? A. R12 (Zhōng Wǎn) P6 (Nèi Guān) S36 (Zú Sān Lǐ); B. R12 (Zhōng Wǎn) S36 (Zú Sān Lǐ); C. R12 (Zhōng Wǎn) R8 (Shén Què) S36 (Zú Sān Lǐ); D. P6 (Nèi Guān) R12 (Zhōng Wǎn) R8 (Shén Què).
2140	治疗狐疝的主要处方是: A·气冲 阳陵泉 太溪; B，关元 三阴交 大敦; C·关元	Which group of points should be selected to treat fox hernia (Inguinal hernia)?

	三角灸 大敦; D·关元 归来 太冲 三阴交 阴陵泉; E·以上均不是	A. S30 (Qì Chōng) G34 (Yáng Líng Quán) K3 (Tài Xī); B. R4 (Guān Yuán) Sp6 (Sān Yīn Jiāo) Lv1 (Dà Dūn); C. R4 (Guān Yuán) Sān Jiāo Jiǔ Lv1 (Dà Dūn); D. R4 (Guān Yuán) S29 (Guī Lái) Lv3 (Tài Chōng) Sp6 (Sān Yīn Jiāo) Sp9 (Yīn Líng Quán); E. None of the above.
2141	治疗滑精，除用主穴之外，还可加用: A·心俞 神门 内关; B，肾俞 关元 内关; C·肾俞 太溪 足三里; D·中极 三阴交 神门; E·心俞 肾俞 中极	In addition to major points, which group of points should be selected to treat sliding seminal emission? A. B15 (Xīn Shū) H7 (Shén Mén) P6 (Nèi Guān); B. B23 (Shèn Shū) R4 (Guān Yuán) P6 (Nèi Guān); C; B23 (Shèn Shū) K3 (Tài Xī) S36 (Zú Sān Lǐ); D. R3 (Zhōng Jí) Sp6 (Sān Yīn Jiāo) H7 (Shén Mén); E. B15 (Xīn Shū) B23 (Shèn Shū) R3 (Zhōng Jí)
2142	治疗黄疸首选: A·隐白 B·公孙 C·三阴交 D·阴陵泉 E·大横	Which point should be selected as the primary point to treat jaundice? A. · Sp1 / Yǐn Bái; B. · Sp4 / Gōng Sūn; C. · Sp6 / Sān Yīn Jiāo; D. · Sp9 / Yīn Líng Quán; E. Sp15 / Dà Héng
2143	治疗火毒炽盛之疔疮，可在基本处方的基础上再加:（ ）、大椎以泻火解毒。A·身柱; B三棱针点刺出血; C·曲泽; D·隐白; E·委中·	In treating the flaming toxic fire type of furuncle, what point may be added to the basic prescription of points, in addition to D14 / Dà Zhuī, to sedate fire and counteract toxic effect? A. · D12 / Shēn Zhù; B. dotted-needling with three-edged needles to let blood; C. · P3 / Qū Zé; D. · Sp1 / Yǐn Bái; E. B40 / Wěi Zhōng ·
2144	治疗火毒入营型的疔疮，可在基本处方的基础上再加: A·所属经脉之荥穴; B所属经脉之郄穴; C·所属经脉之合穴; D·所属经脉之井穴 ·E·所属经脉之下合穴	What points may be added to the basic prescription of points to treat the toxic fire entering into the nutritive level type of furuncle?: A. ·outpouring-points / spring-points of the affected meridian; B. fissural point / cleft point / xi point of the affected meridian; C. ·hé xué / terminal-points / sea-points of the affected meridian; D. jǐng xué / well points of the affected meridian; ·E. ·lower merging point of the affected meridian
2145	治疗火毒蕴结的流行性腮腺炎，可在基本处方上再加: A翳风; B·水沟; C·足临泣; D·大椎; E·关冲	What points may be added to the basic prescription of points to treat epedemic parotitis due to hidden congestion of toxic fire? A. Sj17 / Yì Fēng; B. · D26 / Shuǐ Gōu / Rén Zhōng; C. ·G41 / Zú Lín Qì / Lín Qì; D. ·D14 / Dà Zhuī; E. · Sj1 / Guān Chōng
2146	治疗急惊风暴受惊恐证，可在基本处方的基础上再加: A·中脘、丰隆; B·外关、风池; C·印堂、承浆; D·足三里、三阴交; E·飞扬、承山	What points may be added to the basic prescription of points to treat acute infantile convulsion with acute attack of shock and fear? A. · R12 / Zhōng Wǎn，S40 / Fēng Lóng; B. · Sj5 / Wài Guān，G20 / Fēng Chí; C. · Yìn táng / midpoint between eyebrows / seal hall，R24 / Chéng Jiàng; D. · S36 / Zú Sān Lǐ，Sp6 / Sān Yīn Jiāo; E. B58 / Feī Yáng，B57 / Chéng Shān
2147	治疗急惊风不宜采用的刺灸方法是: A.毫针浅刺; B	What technique of acupuncture and moxibustion should NOT be applied to treat acute infantile convulsion?

	疾出针不留针; C.施用针刺泻法; D 施用灸法	A. shallow insertion with a minute needle; B. pulling out the needle quickly without retention of the needle in the body; C. acupuncture by sedation; D. by moxibustion.
2148	治疗急惊风兼有高热时，可在基本处方的基础上再加: A·中脘; B·大椎; C·印堂; D.气海; E·足三里	What point may be added to the basic prescription of points to treat acute infantile convulsionwith high fever? A. · R12 / Zhōng Wǎn; B. ·D14 / Dà Zhuī; C. · Yìn táng / midpoint between eyebrows / seal hall; D. R6 / Qì Hǎi; E. · S36 / Zú Sān Lǐ
2149	治疗急性的胃痛应选用 A.内关; B.外关; C.中极; D 梁丘	What point should be selected to treat acute stomachache? A. P6 (Nèi Guān); B. Sj5 (Wài Guān); C. R3 (Zhōng Jí); D. S34 (Liáng Qiū)
2150	治疗急性泄泻应选取哪一经募穴 A.手阳明大肠经 B.手太阳小肠经; C.足阳明胃经; D 足少阳胆经	The mu point (gathering point) of which meridian should be selected to treat acute diarrhea? A. large intestine meridian; B. small intestine meridian; C. stomach meridian; D. gallbladder meridian
2151	治疗肩关节周围炎病属太阴经者，可在基本处方的基础上加: A·尺泽、阴陵泉; B.承山、手三里; C·阳陵泉、后溪; D·手三里、阳陵泉; E·曲池、阳陵泉	What points may be added to the basic prescription of points to treat scapulohumeral periarthritis that belongs to the greater yin meridian? A. · Lu5 / Chǐ Zé，Sp9 / Yīn Líng Quán; B. B57 / Chéng Shān，Li10 / Shǒu Sān Lǐ; C. · G34 / Yáng Líng Quán，Si3 / Hòu Xī; D. · Li10 / Shǒu Sān Lǐ，G34 / Yáng Líng Quán; E. · Li11 / Qū Chí，G34 / Yáng Líng Quán
2152	治疗肩周炎病属阳明经者除取主穴外，还应取: A·条口; B.肩贞; C·阳陵泉; D·中平; E 手三里	What point may be added to the basic prescription of points to treat scapulohumeral periarthritis that belongs to the bright yang (yang ming) meridians? A. · S38 / Tiáo Kǒu; B. Si9 / Jiān Zhēn; C. · G34 / Yáng Líng Quán; D. · Zhōng pīng xué; E. Li10 / Shǒu Sān Lǐ
2153	治疗肩周炎能起疏筋活络、通络止痛作用的穴是: A·条口; B.肩贞; C·阳陵泉; D·中平; E手三里	What point can disperse tendons and activate linking meridians, connect meridians and relieve pain in the treatment of scapulohumeral periarthritis? A. · S38 / Tiáo Kǒu; B. Si9 / Jiān Zhēn; C. · G34 / Yáng Líng Quán; D. · Zhōng pīng xué; E. Li10 / Shǒu Sān Lǐ
2154	治疗肩周炎时所取的"肩三针"指的是肩髃、肩前和: A·条口; B.肩贞; C·阳陵泉; D·中平; E手三里	“Jiān sān zhēn / shoulder three needles / three needles on the shoulders " used to treat scapulohumeral periarthritis include Li15 / Jiān Yú 、Jiān qián / anterior shoulder, and: A. · S38 / Tiáo Kǒu; B. Si9 / Jiān Zhēn; C. · G34 / Yáng Líng Quán; D. · Zhōng pīng xué; E. Li10 / Shǒu Sān Lǐ
2155	治疗肩周炎痛在阳明、太阳经采用透穴法时应取( )透承山: A·条口; B.肩贞; C·阳陵泉; D·中平; E手三里	In treating scapulohumeral periarthritis with pain in the bright yang / yang ming and greater yang meridians, when the method of “inserting into one point until the needle reaches another point” is to be used, what point should be inserted until the needle reaches B57 / Chéng Shān? A. · S38 / Tiáo Kǒu; B. Si9 / Jiān Zhēn; C. · G34 / Yáng Líng Quán; D. · Zhōng pīng xué; E. Li10 / Shǒu Sān

		Lǐ
2156	治疗腱鞘炎不能用的方法是：A·艾灸；B·针刺; C·拔罐; D·穴位贴敷; E·穴位注射	What therapy should not be applied to treat tenoosynovitis? A. · moxibustion; B. · needling; C. · cupping; D. · Point herb application; E. · acupuncture points injection therapy
2157	治疗腱鞘炎的基本处方取穴有：A·外关; B·内关; C·阳谷; D·列缺; E·神门	What is the basic point to treat tenoosynovitis? A. · Sj5 / Wài Guān; B. · P6 / Nèi Guān; C. · Si5 / Yáng Gǔ; D. ·Lu7 / Liè Quē; E. · H7 / Shén Mén
2158	治疗腱鞘炎的基本处方取穴有：A·外关; B·涌泉; C·阿是穴; D·后溪; E·曲池	What is the basic point to treat tenoosynovitis? A. · Sj5 / Wài Guān; B. · K1 / Yǒng Quán; C. ·Ouchi points / pressure points; D. · Si3 / Hòu Xī; E. · Li11 / Qū Chí
2159	治疗戒毒综合征兼见烦躁惊厥可加：A 天枢、上巨虚; B·脾俞、足三里 ·C·中冲、涌泉; D·太冲、合谷; E·心俞、肾俞·	What point may be added to treat abstinence syndrome accompanied by depression with jumpiness? A. S25 / Tiān Shū，S37 / Shàng Jù Xū; B. B20 / Pí Shū，S36 / Zú Sān Lǐ; ·C. · P9 / Zhōng Chōng，K1 / Yǒng Quán; D. · Lv3 / Tài Chōng，Li4 / Hé Gǔ; E. ·B15 / Xīn Shū，B23 / Shèn Shū ·
2160	治疗戒毒综合征兼见腹痛、腹泻可加：A 天枢、上巨虚; B·脾俞、足三里 ·C·中冲、涌泉; D·太冲、合谷; E·心俞、肾俞·	What point may be added to treat abstinence syndrome accompanied by abdominal pain and diarrhea? A. S25 / Tiān Shū，S37 / Shàng Jù Xū; B. B20 / Pí Shū，S36 / Zú Sān Lǐ; ·C. · P9 / Zhōng Chōng，K1 / Yǒng Quán; D. · Lv3 / Tài Chōng，Li4 / Hé Gǔ; E. ·B15 / Xīn Shū，B23 / Shèn Shū ·
2161	治疗戒酒综合征兼见烦躁不安、抑郁，可在基本处方的基础上加：A·心俞、内关; B·脾俞、胃俞; C·脾俞、足三里; D·中冲、涌泉; E·合谷、三阴交	What points may be added to the basic prescription of points to treat alcohol withdrawal syndrome accompanied by depression with jumpiness, insecurity, and mental inhibition? A. ·B15 / Xīn Shū，P6 / Nèi Guān; B. B20 / Pí Shū，B21 / Wèi Shū; C. B20 / Pí Shū，S36 / Zú Sān Lǐ; D. · P9 / Zhōng Chōng，K1 / Yǒng Quán; E. · Li4 / Hé Gǔ，Sp6 / Sān Yīn Jiāo
2162	治疗戒烟综合征兼见精神萎靡，可在基本处方的基础上加：A·心俞、内关; B·脾俞、胃俞; C·脾俞、足三里; D·中冲、涌泉; E·合谷、三阴交	What points may be added to the basic prescription of points to treat smoking withdrawal syndrome with poor spirits? A. ·B15 / Xīn Shū，P6 / Nèi Guān; B. B20 / Pí Shū，B21 / Wèi Shū; C. B20 / Pí Shū，S36 / Zú Sān Lǐ; D. · P9 / Zhōng Chōng，K1 / Yǒng Quán; E. · Li4 / Hé Gǔ，Sp6 / Sān Yīn Jiāo
2163	治疗经前期紧张综合征的主穴是：A·神门、百会、太冲、膻中、三阴交; B·脾俞、太溪、三阴交、足三里、膻中; C·肾俞、神门、百会、太冲、血海; D·丰隆、百会、太冲、血海、三阴交; E·中脘、太溪、三阴交、气海、膻中	What are the primary points to treat premenstrual syndrome? A. · H7 / Shén Mén，D20 / Bǎi Huì，Lv3 / Tài Chōng，R17 / Shān Zhōng，Sp6 / Sān Yīn Jiāo; B. B20 / Pí Shū，K3 / Tài Xī，Sp6 / Sān Yīn Jiāo，S36 / Zú Sān Lǐ，R17 / Shān Zhōng; C. B23 / Shèn Shū，H7 / Shén Mén，D20 / Bǎi Huì，Lv3 / Tài Chōng，Sp10 / Xuè Hǎi; D. · S40 / Fēng Lóng，D20 / Bǎi Huì，Lv3 / Tài Chōng，Sp10 / Xuè Hǎi，Sp6 / Sān

		Yīn Jiāo; E. · R12 / Zhōng Wǎn，K3 / Tài Xī，Sp6 / Sān Yīn Jiāo，R6 / Qì Hǎi，R17 / Shān Zhōng
2164	治疗经水先期的主方是: A·气海 三阴交 肾俞 脾俞; B·气海 三阴交 血海 归来; C·气海 三阴交 交信 足三里; D·气海 三阴交 太冲 太溪; E·气海 三阴交 关元 大赫	Which group of points may be selected to treat premature menstruation? A.. R6 (Qì Hǎi), Sp6 (Sān Yīn Jiāo) B23 (Shèn Shū); B20 (Pí Shū); B. R6 (Qì Hǎi), Sp6 (Sān Yīn Jiāo); Sp10 (Xuè Hǎi); S29 (Guī Lái); C. R6 (Qì Hǎi), Sp6 (Sān Yīn Jiāo); K8 (Jiāo Xìn) S36 (Zú Sān Lǐ); D. R6 (Qì Hǎi), Sp6 (Sān Yīn Jiāo); Lv3 (Tài Chōng) K3 (Tài Xī); E. R6 (Qì Hǎi), Sp6 (Sān Yīn Jiāo);. R4 (Guān Yuán) K12 (Dà Hè).
2165	治疗经行不畅，少腹胀痛，胸胁满闷，脉弦，主要处方是: A·中极 血海 行间 足三里; B·血海 太溪 大敦 关元; C·脾俞 肝俞 膈俞 肾俞; D·中极 地机 次髎 行间; E·命门 肾俞 关元 太冲	Which group of points may be selected to treat difficult menstruation, swelling and pain in the lower abdomen, fullness and dullness in the chest and hypochondriac region, wiry pulse? A. R3 (Zhōng Jí) Sp10 (Xuè Hǎi) Lv2 (Xíng Jiān) S36 (Zú Sān Lǐ); B. Sp10 (Xuè Hǎi); K3 (Tài Xī) Lv1 (Dà Dūn) R4 (Guān Yuán); C. B20 (Pí Shū)B18 (Gān Shū)B17 (Gé Shū); B23 (Shèn Shū); D. R3 (Zhōng Jí) Sp8 (Dì Jī) B32 (Cì Liáo) Lv2 (Xíng Jiān); E. D4 (Mìng Mén) B23 (Shèn Shū) R4 (Guān Yuán) Lv3 (Tài Chōng)
2166	治疗惊悸的主要处方是: A·膈俞 脾俞 足三里 心俞; B·郄门 神门 心俞 巨阙 C·厥阴俞 肾俞 太溪 三阴交; D·脾俞 三焦俞 气海俞 心俞; E·肺俞 尺泽 丰隆 心俞	Which group of points may be selected as the major prescription to treat palpitation? A. B17 (Gé Shū) B20 (Pí Shū) S36 (Zú Sān Lǐ) B15 (Xīn Shū); B. P4 (Xī Mén) H7 (Shén Mén)B15 (Xīn Shū) R14 (Jù Què); C. B14 (Jué Yīn Shū) H7 (Shén Mén); D. B20 (Pí Shū); B22 (Sān Jiāo Shū); B24 (Qì Hǎi Shū) B15 (Xīn Shū); E. B13 (Fèi Shū), Lu5 (Chǐ Zé) S40 (Fēng Lóng);B15 (Xīn Shū).
2167	治疗颈椎病劳损血瘀者可在基本处方的基础上再加: A·膈俞、合谷、太冲; B·天宗、条口、合谷; C·百会、风池、太阳; D·曲池、合谷、外关; E·风府、风门、天宗	What points may be added to the basic prescription of points to treat cervical spondylopathy with internal injury, overstrain, and blood coagulation;? A. ·B17 / Gé Shū，Li4 / Hé Gǔ，Lv3 / Tài Chōng; B. · Si11 / Tiān Zōng，S38 / Tiáo Kǒu，Li4 / Hé Gǔ; C. · D20 / Bǎi Huì，G20 / Fēng Chí，Tài yáng / sun / temple; D. · Li11 / Qū Chí，Li4 / Hé Gǔ，Sj5 / Wài Guān; E. · D16 / Fēng Fǔ，B12 / Fēng Mén，Si11 / Tiān Zōng
2168	治疗颈椎病上肢及手指麻痛者可在基本处方的基础上再加: A·膈俞、合谷、太冲; B·天宗、条口、合谷; C·百会、风池、太阳; D·曲池、合谷、外关; E·风府、风门、天宗	What points may be added to the basic prescription of points to treat cervical spondylopathy with numbness and pain in the upper limbs and fingers? A. ·B17 / Gé Shū，Li4 / Hé Gǔ，Lv3 / Tài Chōng; B. · Si11 / Tiān Zōng，S38 / Tiáo Kǒu，Li4 / Hé Gǔ; C. · D20 / Bǎi Huì，G20 / Fēng Chí，Tài yáng / sun / temple; D. · Li11 / Qū Chí，Li4 / Hé Gǔ，Sj5 / Wài Guān; E. · D16 / Fēng Fǔ，B12 / Fēng Mén，Si11 / Tiān Zōng
2169	治疗颈椎病头晕目眩者可在基本处方的基础上再加: A·膈俞、合谷、太冲; B·天宗、条口、合谷; C·百会、风池、太阳; D·曲池、合谷、	What points may be added to the basic prescription of points to treat cervical spondylopathy with dizziness and whirling sensations? A. ·B17 / Gé Shū，Li4 / Hé Gǔ，Lv3 / Tài Chōng; B. · Si11 /

	外关; E·风府、风门、天宗	Tiān Zōng, S38 / Tiáo Kǒu, Li4 / Hé Gǔ; C. · D20 / Bǎi Huì, G20 / Fēng Chí, Tài yáng / sun / temple; D. · Li11 / Qū Chí, Li4 / Hé Gǔ, Sj5 / Wài Guān; E. · D16 / Fēng Fǔ, B12 / Fēng Mén, Si11 / Tiān Zōng
2170	治疗竞技紧张综合征的其他疗法中除（ ）外均可选用：A·头针; B·火针; C·电针; D·耳针; E·皮肤针	What type of acupuncture should not be used to treat competitive tension syndrome? A. · scalp acupuncture; B. · fire acupuncture; C. electro acupuncture; D. · auricular acupuncture; E. · skin acupuncture
2171	治疗竞技紧张综合征兼见书写困难，视力模糊，可在基本处方的基础上加：A·素髎、水沟; B·风池、百会; C·大椎、人迎; D·三阴交、太溪; E·太冲、合谷	What points may be added to the basic prescription of points to treat competitive tension syndrome accompanied by difficulty in writing, and blurred vision? A. · D25 / Sù Liáo, D26 / Shuǐ Gōu / Rén Zhōng; B. · G20 / Fēng Chí, D20 / Bǎi Huì; C. ·D14 / Dà Zhuī、 S9 / Rén Yíng; D. · Sp6 / Sān Yīn Jiāo, K3 / Tài Xī; E. · Lv3 / Tài Chōng, Li4 / Hé Gǔ
2172	治疗竞技紧张综合征兼见血压升高，可在基本处方的基础上加：A·素髎、水沟; B·风池、百会; C·大椎、人迎; D·三阴交、太溪; E·太冲、合谷	What points may be added to the basic prescription of points to treat competitive tension syndrome accompanied by hypertension? A. · D25 / Sù Liáo, D26 / Shuǐ Gōu / Rén Zhōng; B. · G20 / Fēng Chí, D20 / Bǎi Huì; C. ·D14 / Dà Zhuī、 S9 / Rén Yíng; D. · Sp6 / Sān Yīn Jiāo, K3 / Tài Xī; E. · Lv3 / Tài Chōng, Li4 / Hé Gǔ
2173	治疗竞技紧张综合征兼见晕厥可刺：A·太冲、合谷; B·神门、内关; C·关元、中极; D·素髎、水沟; E，足三里、三阴交	What point may be punctured to treat competitive tension syndrome accompanied by fainting? A. · Lv3 / Tài Chōng, Li4 / Hé Gǔ; B. · H7 / Shén Mén, P6 / Nèi Guān; C. · R4 / Guān Yuán, R3 / Zhōng Jí; D. · D25 / Sù Liáo, D26 / Shuǐ Gōu / Rén Zhōng; E.S36 / Zú Sān Lǐ, Sp6 / Sān Yīn Jiāo
2174	治疗咳嗽、咯血、潮热，当首选：A·尺泽; B 中府; C·列缺; D·少商	What point should be selected first in order to treat cough, discharge of blood from the mouth, and tidal fever? A. · Lu5 / Chǐ Zé; B. Lu1 / Zhōng Fǔ; C. ·Lu7 / Liè Quē; D. · Lu11 / Shǎo Shāng
2175	治疗咳嗽痰黄，质稠难咯，口干咽痛，身热头痛，苔薄黄，脉浮数者，可在基本处方的基础上再加：A·太溪; B·尺泽; C·足三里; D¨风门; E·脾俞	What point may be added to the basic prescription of points to treat cough with yellowish phlegm, sticky and difficult to cough out, dried mouth and sore throat, hot sensation in the body and headache, a thin layer of yellowish coating, a superficial and rapid pulse? A. · K3 / Tài Xī; B. · Lu5 / Chǐ Zé; C. · S36 / Zú Sān Lǐ; D.¨B12 / Fēng Mén; E. B20 / Pí Shū
2176	治疗口疮当首选的穴位是：A 二间; B 液门; C 劳宫; D 少府 ·	What point should be selected as the primary point to treat mouth canker? A. Li2 / Èr Jiān; B. Sj2 / Yè Mén; C. P8 / Láo Gōng; D. H8 / Shào Fǔ
2177	治疗口角㖞斜以取：A 面部穴为主;B 手足阳明经穴为主;C 足太阳经穴为主;D 足阳明经穴为主; E 辨	What points should be selected as primary points to treat wry mouth? A. primarily points in the face region; B primarily points

	证取穴为主。	on the foot and hand bright yang meridians; C. primarily points in the foot greater yang meridian; D primarily points on the foot bright yang meridian; E. primarily selecting points according to differential diagnosis.
2178	治疗口渴引饮，口唇干燥，下列诸穴中宜选: A·内关; B·金津玉液; C·廉泉; D·口禾髎; E·劳宫	Which point should be selected to treat thirst with heavy drinking of water, dry mouth and lips? A. P6 (Nèi Guān); B. Jīn Jīn Yù Yè; C. R23 (Lián Quán); D. Li19 (Kǒu Hé Liáo); E. P8 (Láo Gōng).
2179	治疗口舌生疮当首选 A.二间; B.液门; C.劳宫; D 少府	Which point should be selected to treat canker in the mouth and tongue? A. Li2 (Èr Jiān); B. Sj2 (Yè Mén); C. P8 (Láo Gōng); D. H8 (Shào Fǔ).
2180	治疗口喎远部取穴的首选穴位是: A. 地仓; B. 颊车; C. 合谷; D. 足三里; E. 丰隆.	Which distal point should be selected to treat wry mouth? A. S4 (Dì Cāng); B. S6 (Jiá Chē); C. Li4 (Hé Gǔ); D. S36 (Zú Sān Lǐ); E. S40 (Fēng Lóng).
2181	治疗口眼歪斜首选: A·商阳 ·B·阳溪; C·合谷; D·曲池; E·手三里·	What point should be selected as the primary point to treat wry mouth and eyes? A. · Li1 / Shāng Yáng; ·B. Li5 / Yáng Xī; C. · Li4 / Hé Gǔ; D. · Li11 / Qū Chí; E. · Li10 / Shǒu Sān Lǐ
2182	治疗狂证的主要处方是: A·鸠尾 大椎 腰奇 间使 足三里 丰隆; B·少商 隐白 水沟 风府 大陵 曲池 丰隆; C·风池 肝俞 肾俞 行间 侠溪 心俞; D·中脘 内关 丰隆 解溪 神门; E·脾俞 肾俞 关元 足三里 百会	Which group of points may be selected to treat maniac-psychosis (kuang)? A. R15 (Jiū Wěi) D14 (Dà Zhuī) Yāo Qí P5 (Jiān Shǐ) S36 (Zú Sān Lǐ) S40 (Fēng Lóng); B. Lu11 (Shǎo Shāng) Sp1 (Yǐn Bái) D26 (Shuǐ Gōu, Rén Zhōng) D16 (Fēng Fǔ) P7 (Dà Líng) Li11 (Qū Chí) S40 (Fēng Lóng); C. G20 (Fēng Chí) B18 (Gān Shū) B23 (Shèn Shū) Lv2 (Xíng Jiān) G43 (Xiá Xī) B15 (Xīn Shū); D. R12 (Zhōng Wǎn) P6 (Nèi Guān) S40 (Fēng Lóng) S41 (Jiě Xī) H7 (Shén Mén); E. B20 (Pí Shū) B23 (Shèn Shū) R4 (Guān Yuán) S36 (Zú Sān Lǐ) D20 (Bǎi Huì)
2183	治疗阑尾炎的气滞血瘀型，可在基本处方上再加: A·阑尾穴; B·上巨虚; C·中脘; D·大肠俞; E支沟	What points may be added to the basic prescription of points to treat the energy congestion and blood coagulation type of appendicitis? A. ·Lán wěi / appendix point; B. · S37 / Shàng Jù Xū; C. · R12 / Zhōng Wǎn; D. B25 / Dà Cháng Shū; E. Sj6 / Zhi Gōu
2184	治疗阑尾炎的瘀滞化热型，可在基本处方上再加: A·阑尾穴; B·上巨虚; C·中脘; D·大肠俞; E支沟	What point may be added to the basic prescription of points to treat the coagulation and congestion transforming into heat type of appendicitis? A. ·Lán wěi / appendix point; B. · S37 / Shàng Jù Xū; C. · R12 / Zhōng Wǎn; D. B25 / Dà Cháng Shū; E. Sj6 / Zhi Gōu
2185	治疗阑尾炎适宜的手法是: A·补法; B·泻法; C·疾出针不留针; D·平补平泻; E. 三棱针点刺	What is the right technique of treating appendicitis? A. · tonfication; B. · sedation; C. rapid withdrawl of needle without needle retention; D. · neutral technique; E. three-edged needles dotted-needling
2186	治疗阑尾炎所取主穴属: A·手阳明经穴; B·足阳明经	To what meridians do the primary points of treating appendicitis belong?

	穴; C·手足阳明经穴; D·手少阳经穴 ·E·足少阳经穴	A. · points on the hand bright yang meridian; B · points on the foot bright yang meridian; C · points on the hand and foot bright yang meridians; D · points on the hand lesser yang meridian; ·E · points on the foot lesser yang meridian
2187	治疗痢疾便秘肠痈常选用: A·承泣; B·头维; C·天枢; D·归来; E·伏兔	Which point is frequently selected to treat dysentery, constipation, and periappendicular abscess? A. · S1 / Chéng Qì; B. · S8 / Tóu Wěi; C. · S25 / Tiān Shū; D. · S29 / Guī Lái; E · S32 / Fú Tù
2188	治疗六腑痛症宜选：A·井穴; B·原穴; C·络穴; D·俞穴; E·募穴	Which of the following should be selected to treat pain in the six bowels? A. · jǐng xué / well points; B. · yuán xué / starting-points / source-points; C. ·linking points, / luo points; D. ·posterior points / back shu points / bèi shù xué; E. ·gathering points / mu points
2189	治疗聋哑，在听力有所改善而言语不清情况下，可以配用: A. 外关 合谷 少商; B. 太冲 丘墟 上星; C. 哑门 天突 合谷; D. 通里 哑门 大陵; E. 廉泉 通里 哑门	In treating deaf-mutism when the patient has shown improvement in hearing with no clear speech, which group of points should be selected for treatment? A. Sj5 (Wài Guān), Li4 (Hé Gǔ) Lu11 (Shǎo Shāng); B. Lv3 (Tài Chōng) G40 (Qiū Xū) D23 (Shàng Xīng); C. D15 (Yǎ Mén) R22 (Tiān Tū) Li4 (Hé Gǔ); D. H5 (Tōng Lǐ) D15 (Yǎ Mén) P7 (Dà Líng); E. R23 (Lián Quán) H5 (Tōng Lǐ) D15 (Yǎ Mén).
2190	治疗落枕病及督脉、太阳经者，可在基本处方上再加: A·风池、风市、肩井; B·肩井、肩外俞、风市; C·肩外俞、·风府、天柱; D·风市、风池、风府; E·风府、肩井、风池	In treating "falling off the pillow / neck pain with stiffness" that affects the du mai / governing meridian、and the greater yang meridians, what points may be added to the basic prescription of points? A. · G20 / Fēng Chí，G31 / Fēng Shì，G21 / Jiān Jǐng; B. · G21 / Jiān Jǐng, Si14 / Jiān Wài Shū，G31 / Fēng Shì; C. · Si14 / Jiān Wài Shū 、 · D16 / Fēng Fǔ，B10 / Tiān Zhù; D. · G31 / Fēng Shì，G20 / Fēng Chí，D16 / Fēng Fǔ; E. · D16 / Fēng Fǔ, G21 / Jiān Jǐng，G20 / Fēng Chí
2191	治疗落枕病及少阳经者，可在基本处方上再加：A·风府; B·承山; C·风池; D·天柱; E·肩外俞·	In treating "falling off the pillow / neck pain with stiffness" that affects the lesser yang (shao yang) meridians, what point may be added to the basic prescription of points? A. · D16 / Fēng Fǔ; B. B57 / Chéng Shān; C. · G20 / Fēng Chí; D. ·B10 / Tiān Zhù; E. · Si14 / Jiān Wài Shū ·
2192	治疗落枕时，.宜取何经经穴为主? A 督脉 足少阳经; B. 督脉 手少阳经; C. 督脉 手太阳经; D. 督脉 足太阳经; E 督脉 手足太阳经。	The points on what meridian should be selected as primary points to treat neck pain (also called falling off the pillow)? A. du mai [governing meridian] foot lesser yang meridian; B. du mai [governing meridian] hand lesser yang meridian; C. du mai [governing meridian] hand greater yang meridian; D. du mai [governing meridian] foot greater yang meridian; E. du mai [governing meridian] hand and foot greater yang meridians.
2193	治疗落枕应选取手太阳小	What point on small intestine meridian should be

	肠经的: A·后溪; B·太溪; C·阳溪; D·阳池	selected to treat luò zhěn / falling off the pillow / neck pain? A. · Si3 / Hòu Xī; B. · K3 / Tài Xī; C. · Li5 / Yáng Xī; D. · Sj4 / Yáng Chí
2194	治疗泌尿系结石伴恶心呕吐者，可在基础方上加用：A·命门; B·阴陵泉; C·水道; D·足三里; E·天枢	What points may be added to the basic prescription of points to treat urinary stone accompanied by nausea and vomiting? A. · D4 / Mìng Mén; B. · Sp9 / Yīn Líng Quán; C. · S28 / Shuǐ Dào; D. · S36 / Zú Sān Lǐ; E. · S25 / Tiān Shū
2195	治疗泌尿系结石肾气不足者，可在基础方上加用：A·命门; B·阴陵泉; C·水道; D·足三里; E·天枢	What point may be added to the basic prescription of points to treat the kidney energy deficiency type of urinary stone? A. · D4 / Mìng Mén; B. · Sp9 / Yīn Líng Quán; C. · S28 / Shuǐ Dào; D. · S36 / Zú Sān Lǐ; E. · S25 / Tiān Shū
2196	治疗泌尿系结石湿热甚者，可在基础方上加用（ ）以清利湿热：A·命门; B·阴陵泉；C·水道；D·足三里；E·天枢	What point may be added to the basic prescription of points to treat the severe damp heat type of urinary stone by clearing damp heat? A. · D4 / Mìng Mén; B. · Sp9 / Yīn Líng Quán; C. · S28 / Shuǐ Dào; D. · S36 / Zú Sān Lǐ; E. · S25 / Tiān Shū
2197	治疗泌尿系结石小便淋沥不畅者加用（ ）以利尿通淋: A·命门; B·阴陵泉; C·水道; D·足三里; E·天枢	What point may be added to treat urinary stone with dribbling and difficult urination to promote urination and treat stranguria? A. · D4 / Mìng Mén; B. · Sp9 / Yīn Líng Quán; C. · S28 / Shuǐ Dào; D. · S36 / Zú Sān Lǐ; E. · S25 / Tiān Shū
2198	治疗面瘫，下列穴位中最常用的是： A.外关; B.内关; C.天容; D 翳风	What point is most frequently used to treat facial paralysis? A. Sj5 (Wài Guān); B. P6 (Nèi Guān); C. Si17 (Tiān Róng); D. Sj17 (Yì Fēng).
2199	治疗面瘫常选用: A·地仓颊车下关; B·梁丘足三里; C·犊鼻足三里条口; D·伏兔下关阴市 E·缺盆鹰窗	Which points are frequently selected to treat facial paralysis ? A. S4 / Dì Cāng S6 / Jiá Chē S7 / Xià Guān; B. · S34 / Liáng Qiū S36 / Zú Sān Lǐ; C. · S35 / Dú Bí S36 / Zú Sān Lǐ S38 / Tiáo Kǒu; D. · S32 / Fú Tù S7 / Xià Guān S33 / Yīn Shì; E. ·S12 Quē Pén S16 / Yīng Chuāng
2200	治疗面瘫下列哪个穴位不应取: A·合谷; B·太阳; C·太溪; D·颊车	Which point should NOT be used to treat facial parslysis? A. · Li4 / Hé Gǔ; B. · Tài yáng / sun / temple; C. · K3 / Tài Xī; D. · S6 / Jiá Chē
2201	治疗面肿虚浮的主要穴位是: A·承浆; B·水沟; C 印堂; D·地仓; E·迎香	Which point should be selected to treat swollen face with puffiness? A. R24 (Chéng Jiàng); B. D26 (Shuǐ Gōu, Rén Zhōng); C. Yìn Táng; D. S4 (Dì Cāng); E.Li20 (Yíng Xiāng).
2202	治疗目赤肿痛除清热解毒外，还应 A，疏风; B 利湿; C.益气明目; D 散郁止痛	Which treatment principle should be applied to treat pink eyes with swelling in addition to “clearing heat and detoxicating”? A. to disperse wind; B. to benefit dampness; C. to benefit energy and sharpen vision; D.to disperse inhibition and relieve pain.
2203	治疗目赤肿痛既有疏通局部经络而明目，又有疏泻肝	What point can disperse and connect local meridians, sharpen vision, and also disperse and sedate fire of liver

	胆之火作用的腧穴是：A·风池、曲池；B·侠溪、行间；C·攒竹、瞳子髎；D·太阳、合谷；E·合谷、太冲	and gallbladder in the treatment of pink eye with swelling and pain? A. · G20 / Fēng Chí，Li11 / Qū Chí; B. · G43 / Xiá Xī，Lv2 / Xíng Jian; C. B2 / Zǎn Zhú，G1 / Tóng Zǐ Liáo; D. · Tài yáng / sun / temple，Li4 / Hé Gǔ; E. · Li4 / Hé Gǔ，Lv3 / Tài Chōng
2204	治疗目赤肿痛以下列哪组穴位为佳？A 阳白鱼腰睛明球后；B 四白丝竹空睛明.太阳；C 合谷太冲睛明太阳；D 合谷太冲肝俞印堂；E 以上都不是。	Which group of points should best be selected to treat pink eyes with swelling? A. G14 [Yáng Bái] Yú Yāo (fish waist) B1 / Jīng Míng Qiú hòu / behind the ball; B S2 / Sì Bái / Sj23 / Sī Zhú KōngB1 / Jīng Míng.Tài yáng / sun / temple; C. Li4 / Hé Gǔ Lv3 / Tài Chōng B1 / Jīng Míng Tài yáng / sun / temple; D. Li4 / Hé Gǔ Lv3 / Tài Chōng B18 / Gān Shū Yìn táng / midpoint between eyebrows / seal hall; E. none of the above
2205	治疗目内眦、头项、腰背病症常用申脉配：A·外关；B·内关；C·后溪；D·委中；E·足临泣	What point is often combined with B62 / Shēn Mài to treat the disease of medial canthus、head and back of neck、waist and back disease? A. · Sj5 / Wài Guān; B. · P6 / Nèi Guān; C. · Si3 / Hòu Xī; D. B40 / Wěi Zhōng; E. ·G41 / Zú Lín Qì / Lín Qì
2206	治疗颞下颌关节功能紊乱综合征耳鸣耳聋者，可在基本处方的基础上加：A·风池、肝俞；B·翳风、耳门；C·听宫、翳明；D·大迎、翳明；E·太阳、百会	What points may be added to the basic prescription of points to treat the syndrome of temporalmandibular joint functional disorder with ringing in ears and deafness? A. · G20 / Fēng Chí，B18 / Gān Shū; B. · Sj17 / Yì Fēng，Sj21 / Ěr Mén; C. · Si19 / Tīng Gōng，Yì míng / shelter light; D. · S5 / Dà Yíng，Yì míng / shelter light; E. · Tài yáng / sun / temple，D20 / Bǎi Huì
2207	治疗颞下颌关节功能紊乱综合征头昏头痛者，可在基本处方的基础上加：A·风池、太阳；B·听会、太阳；C·听会、百会；D大迎、翳明；E·翳明、听会	What points may be added to the basic prescription of points to treat the syndrome of temporalmandibular joint functional disorder with dizziness and headache? A. · G20 / Fēng Chí，Tài yáng / sun / temple; B. · G2 / Tīng Huì，Tài yáng / sun / temple; C. · G2 / Tīng Huì，D20 / Bǎi Huì; D S5 / Dà Yíng，Yì míng / shelter light; E. · Yì míng / shelter light，G2 / Tīng Huì
2208	治疗女性经期风疹伴月经不调，可在基本处方的基础上再加：A·风门；B·大椎；C·关元；D·内关；E·足三里	What points may be added to the basic prescription of points to treat rubella in women during menstruation accompanied by irregular menstruation? A. ·B12 / Fēng Mén; B. ·D14 / Dà Zhuī; C. · R4 / Guān Yuán; D. · P6 / Nèi Guān; E. · S36 / Zú Sān Lǐ
2209	治疗呕吐首选：A·隐白 B·公孙 C·三阴交 D·阴陵泉 E 大横	Which point should be selected as the primary point to treat vomiting? A. · Sp1 / Yǐn Bái; B. · Sp4 / Gōng Sūn; C. · Sp6 / Sān Yīn Jiāo; D. · Sp9 / Yīn Líng Quán; E. Sp15 / Dà Héng
2210	治疗脾气下陷型泄泻可在基本方的基础上加：A·公孙；B.百会；C·建里；D·太冲；E·太溪	What point may be added to the basic prescription of points to treat diarrhea of the spleen energy cave-in type? A. · Sp4 / Gōng Sūn; B. D20 / Bǎi Huì; C. · R11 / Jiàn Lǐ; D. · Lv3 / Tài Chōng; E. · K3 / Tài Xī

2211	治疗脾气虚弱型白细胞减少症，可在基本处方的基础上再加：A·关元、命门；B·气海、丰隆；C·公孙、内关；D·中脘、胃俞；E·大椎、绝骨·	What points may be added to the basic prescription of points to treat leukopenia due to spleen energy deficiency and weakness? A. · R4 / Guān Yuán，D4 / Mìng Mén; B. · R6 / Qì Hǎi，S40 / Fēng Lóng; C. · Sp4 / Gōng Sūn，P6 / Nèi Guān; D. · R12 / Zhōng Wǎn，B21 / Wèi Shū; E. ·D14 / Dà Zhuī、·G39 / Xuán Zhōng ·
2212	治疗脾胃虚寒型胃痛的主要处方是：A. 中脘 足三里 内关 期门 阳陵泉；B. 中脘 足三里 神阙 关元 公孙；C·中脘 足三里 胃俞 气海 章门；D·中脘 足三里 气海 天枢 里内庭；E. 中脘 足三里 内关 章门 脾俞 胃俞	Which group of points should be selected to treat stomachache due to deficient and cold spleen and stomach? A. R12 (Zhōng Wǎn); S36 (Zú Sān Lǐ) P6 (Nèi Guān) Lv14 (Qí Mén) G34 (Yáng Líng Quán); B. R12 (Zhōng Wǎn); S36 (Zú Sān Lǐ); R8 (Shén Què) R4 (Guān Yuán) Sp4 (Gōng Sūn); C. R12 (Zhōng Wǎn); S36 (Zú Sān Lǐ); B21 (Wèi Shū) R6 (Qì Hǎi) Lv13 (Zhāng Mén); D. R12 (Zhōng Wǎn); S36 (Zú Sān Lǐ) R6 (Qì Hǎi) S25 (Tiān Shū) Lǐ Nèi Tíng; E. R12 (Zhōng Wǎn); S36 (Zú Sān Lǐ). P6 (Nèi Guān)Lv13 (Zhāng Mén); B20 (Pí Shū)B21 (Wèi Shū).
2213	治疗脾胃虚弱型妊娠呕吐，可在基本方基础上再加：A·三阴交、丰隆；B·百会、气海 ·；C.脾俞、胃俞；D·神门、心俞；E·期门，太冲	What points may be added to the basic prescription of points to treat the spleen-stomach deficiency and weakness type of morning sickenss? A · Sp6 / Sān Yīn Jiāo，S40 / Fēng Lóng; B. · D20 / Bǎi Huì，R6 / Qì Hǎi ·; C. B20 / Pí Shū，B21 / Wèi Shū; D. · H7 / Shén Mén，B15 / Xīn Shū; E. · Lv14 / Qí Mén ，Lv3 / Tài Chōng
2214	治疗脾胃虚弱型小儿厌食，可在基本处方的基础上再加：A·内关、合谷；B·三阴交、太冲；C·太冲、太白；D·脾俞、胃俞；E·肾俞、关元	What points may be added to the basic prescription of points to treat the spleen-stomach deficiency and weakness type of anorexia in children? A. · P6 / Nèi Guān，Li4 / Hé Gǔ; B. · Sp6 / Sān Yīn Jiāo，Lv3 / Tài Chōng; C. · Lv3 / Tài Chōng，Sp3 / Tài Bái; D. B20 / Pí Shū，B21 / Wèi Shū; E. B23 / Shèn Shū，R4 / Guān Yuán
2215	治疗脾虚气弱型近视，可在基本处方的基础上再加：A·心俞、膈俞、足三里、三阴交；B·心俞、膈俞、内关、神门；C·脾俞、胃俞、内关、三阴交；D·脾俞、胃俞、足三里、三阴交；E·肝俞、肾俞、太冲、太溪	What points may be added to the basic prescription of points to treat the spleen deficiency and weak energy type of myopia? A. ·B15 / Xīn Shū，B17 / Gé Shū，S36 / Zú Sān Lǐ，Sp6 / Sān Yīn Jiāo; B. ·B15 / Xīn Shū，B17 / Gé Shū，P6 / Nèi Guān，H7 / Shén Mén; C. B20 / Pí Shū，B21 / Wèi Shū，P6 / Nèi Guān，Sp6 / Sān Yīn Jiāo; D. B20 / Pí Shū，B21 / Wèi Shū，S36 / Zú Sān Lǐ，Sp6 / Sān Yīn Jiāo; E. ·B18 / Gān Shū，B23 / Shèn Shū，Lv3 / Tài Chōng，K3 / Tài Xī
2216	治疗脾虚湿困型 黄褐斑 ，可在基本处方的基础上加：A·脾俞、胃俞；B·脾俞、足三里；C·脾俞、阴陵泉；D·阴陵泉、三阴交；E·肾俞、阴陵泉	What points may be added to the basic prescription of points to treat the spleen deficiency with disturbing dampness type of chloasma? A. B20 / Pí Shū，B21 / Wèi Shū; B. B20 / Pí Shū，S36 / Zú Sān Lǐ; C. B20 / Pí Shū，Sp9 / Yīn Líng Quán; D. · Sp9 / Yīn Líng Quán，Sp6 / Sān Yīn Jiāo; E. B23 / Shèn Shū，

		Sp9 / Yīn Líng Quán
2217	治疗脾虚湿困型带下病除主穴外可加用：A·太溪；B·足三里；C·太冲；D 行间；E·中极	What points may be added to the basic prescription of points to treat the spleen deficiency with disturbing dampness type of vaginal discharges? A. · K3 / Tài Xī; B. · S36 / Zú Sān Lǐ; C. · Lv3 / Tài Chōng; D. Lv2 / Xíng Jiān; E. · R3 / Zhōng Jí
2218	治疗脾虚湿热型麦粒肿，可在基本处方的基础上再加：A·三阴交、阴陵泉；B·风门、肺俞；C·合谷、风池；D·风门、合谷；E·曲池、行间	What points may be added to the basic prescription of points to treat the spleen deficiency and damp heat type of hordeolum / stye? A. · Sp6 / Sān Yīn Jiāo，Sp9 / Yīn Líng Quán; B. ·B12 / Fēng Mén，B13 / Fèi Shū; C. · Li4 / Hé Gǔ，G20 / Fēng Chí; D. ·B12 / Fēng Mén，Li4 / Hé Gǔ; E. · Li11 / Qū Chí，Lv2 / Xíng Jiān
2219	治疗脾虚湿蕴型eczema，可在基本处方的基础上再加：A·肝俞；B·胃俞；C·水道；D·十宣；E·命门	What point may be added to the basic prescription of points to treat the spleen deficiency with hidden dampness type of eczema? A. ·B18 / Gān Shū; B. B21 / Wèi Shū; C. · S28 / Shuǐ Dào; D. · Shí xuān / ten statements / ten expansions; E. · D4 / Mìng Mén
2220	治疗脾虚湿滞型胎位不正，应在基本方基础上再加：A·中脘、关元；B·肾俞、气海；C·阴陵泉、丰隆；D·脾俞、行间；E·期门、太冲	What points may be added to the basic prescription of points to treat the spleen deficiency with dampness stagnation type of fetus in wrong position? A. · R12 / Zhōng Wǎn，R4 / Guān Yuán; B. B23 / Shèn Shū，R6 / Qì Hǎi; C. · Sp9 / Yīn Líng Quán，S40 / Fēng Lóng; D. B20 / Pí Shū，Lv2 / Xíng Jiān; E. · Lv14 / Qí Mén，Lv3 / Tài Chōng
2221	治疗脾虚卫弱型皮肤瘙痒症，可在基本处方的基础上再加：A·肝俞；B·脾俞；C·太溪；D·大椎；E·合谷	What points may be added to the basic prescription of points to treat the spleen deficiency with weak defense energy type of skin itch? A. ·B18 / Gān Shū; B. B20 / Pí Shū; C. · K3 / Tài Xī; D. ·D14 / Dà Zhuī; E. · Li4 / Hé Gǔ
2222	治疗脾虚卫弱型皮肤瘙痒症，可在基本处方的基础上再加：A·太溪；B·肺俞；C·大椎；D·气海；E·阴郄	What points may be added to the basic prescription of points to treat the spleen deficiency with weak defense energy type of skin itch? A. · K3 / Tài Xī; B. ·B13 / Fèi Shū; C. ·D14 / Dà Zhuī; D. · R6 / Qì Hǎi; E. · H6 / Yīn Xī
2223	治疗气厥实证可在基础方上再加：A·行间；B·神阙；C·风府；D·丰隆；E·气海	What points may be added to the basic prescription of points to treat the excess type of energy uprising (qi jue)? A. · Lv2 / Xíng Jiān; B. · R8 / Shén Què; C. · D16 / Fēng Fǔ; D. · S40 / Fēng Lóng; E. · R6 / Qì Hǎi
2224	治疗气厥实证可在基础方上再加：A·足三里；B·太白；C·太冲；D·三阴交；E·气海	What points may be added to the basic prescription of points to treat the excess type of energy uprising (qi jue)? A. · S36 / Zú Sān Lǐ; B. · Sp3 / Tài Bái; C. · Lv3 / Tài Chōng; D. · Sp6 / Sān Yīn Jiāo; E. · R6 / Qì Hǎi
2225	治疗气淋，可在基本处方的基础上再加：A·膀胱俞、昆仑；B·脾俞、太白；C·肾俞、	What points may be added to the basic prescription of points to treat energy type of lin condition (urinary strains, strangury)?

	太溪; D·足三里、陷谷; E·肝俞、太冲	A. B28 / Páng Guāng Shū, B60 / Kūn Lún; B. B20 / Pí Shū, Sp3 / Tài Bái; C. B23 / Shèn Shū, K3 / Tài Xī; D. · S36 / Zú Sān Lǐ, S43 / Xiàn Gǔ; E. ·B18 / Gān Shū, Lv3 / Tài Chōng
2226	治疗气虚邪滞型鼻炎宜: A·只针不灸; B·针灸并用; C·只灸不针; D·以针为主; E·以灸为主	What is the method of treating the energy deficiency and pathogenic congestion type of rhinitis? A. · acupuncture without moxibustion; B. · both acupuncture and moxibustion; C. · moxibustion without acupuncture; D. ·primarily by acupuncture; E. ·primarily by moxibustion
2227	治疗气虚型崩漏,除取主穴外,还可加用: A气海 胃俞; B脾俞 足三里; C膻中 内关; D百会 中极; E血海 水泉	In addtion to the major points, which group of points may be selected to treat the energy deficiency type of vaginal bleeding? A. R6 (Qì Hǎi); B21 (Wèi Shū); B. B20 (Pí Shū); S36 (Zú Sān Lǐ); C. R17 (Shān Zhōng); P6 (Nèi Guān); D. D20 (Bǎi Huì) R3 (Zhōng Jí); E. Sp10 (Xuè Hǎi); K5 (Shuǐ Quán).
2228	治疗气虚型月经不调的针灸处方是: A·中脘、血海、三阴交、足三里、太冲; B·膈俞、太溪、交信、足三里、归来; C.血海、三阴交、足三里、胃俞、命门; D·血海、阴交、足三里、太冲、肾俞; E·关元、血海、三阴交、足三里、脾俞	What is the prescription of acupuncture points to treat the energy deficiency type of irregular menstruation? A. · R12 / Zhōng Wǎn, Sp10 / Xuè Hǎi, Sp6 / Sān Yīn Jiāo, S36 / Zú Sān Lǐ, Lv3 / Tài Chōng; B. ·B17 / Gé Shū, K3 / Tài Xī 、K8 / Jiāo Xìn、 S36 / Zú Sān Lǐ, S29 / Guī Lái; C. Sp10 / Xuè Hǎi, Sp6 / Sān Yīn Jiāo, S36 / Zú Sān Lǐ, B21 / Wèi Shū, D4 / Mìng Mén; D. · Sp10 / Xuè Hǎi, R7 / Yīn Jiāo, S36 / Zú Sān Lǐ, Lv3 / Tài Chōng, B23 / Shèn Shū; E. · R4 / Guān Yuán, Sp10 / Xuè Hǎi, Sp6 / Sān Yīn Jiāo, S36 / Zú Sān Lǐ, B20 / Pí Shū
2229	治疗气血不足型经前期紧张综合征,除针刺主穴外,还应加用: A·脾俞; B·太溪; C·肾俞; D·丰隆; E·中脘	In addition to needling main points, what point should be added to treat premenstrual syndrome that belongs to deficiency energy and blood type? A. B20 / Pí Shū; B. · K3 / Tài Xī; C. B23 / Shèn Shū; D. · S40 / Fēng Lóng; E. · R12 / Zhōng Wǎn
2230	治疗气血不足型头痛的主要处方是: A·百会 气海 肝俞 脾俞 肾俞 合谷 足三里; B·百会 通天 行间 阿是穴; C·上星 头维 合谷 阿是穴; D·后顶 天柱 昆仑 阿是穴; E·风池 百会 悬颅 侠溪 行间	Which group of points should be selected to treat headache due to deficient energy and blood? A. D20 (Bǎi Huì). R6 (Qì Hǎi)B18 (Gān Shū); B20 (Pí Shū) B23 (Shèn Shū) Li4 (Hé Gǔ) S36 (Zú Sān Lǐ); B. D20 (Bǎi Huì) B7 (Tōng Tiān), Lv2 (Xíng Jiān) a shi xue (ouch point or tender point); C. D23 (Shàng Xīng) S8 (Tóu Wěi) Li4 (Hé Gǔ), a shi xue (ouch point or tender point); D. D19 (Hòu Dǐng) B10 (Tiān Zhù); B60 (Kūn Lún) a shi xue (ouch point or tender point); E. G20 (Fēng Chí) D20 (Bǎi Huì) G5 (Xuán Lú) G43 (Xiá Xī) Lv2 (Xíng Jiān).
2231	治疗气血两播型皮肤瘙痒症,可在基本处方基础上再加: A·太溪; B·肺俞; C·大椎; D·气海; E·阴郄	What points may be added to the basic prescription of points to treat the heat at the energy and blood levels type of skin itch? A. · K3 / Tài Xī; B. ·B13 / Fèi Shū; C. ·D14 / Dà Zhuī; D. · R6 / Qì Hǎi; E · H6 / Yīn Xī
2232	治疗气血两虚引起的斑秃,	What points may be added to the basic prescription of

	可在基本处方的基础上再加：A·太冲·B·气海；C·申脉 ·D¨风池；E·太溪	points to treat the simultaneous deficiency of energy and blood type of alopecia areata? A. · Lv3 / Tài Chōng ··B. · R6 / Qì Hǎi; C. B62 / Shēn Mài ·D.¨ G20 / Fēng Chí; E. · K3 / Tài Xī
2233	治疗气血虚弱所致的眩晕症不必用的穴位有 A.百会；B.脾俞；C，胃俞；D 太溪	In treating the energy and blood deficiency type of vertigo, what point need NOT be selected? A. D20 (Bǎi Huì); B. B20 (Pí Shū); C. B21 (Wèi Shū); D. K3 (Tài Xī).
2234	治疗气血虚弱型，可在基本处方的基础上再加：A少商；B·鱼际；C·风门；D·气海；E·中脘	What points may be added to the basic prescription of points to treat idiocy due energy and blood deficiency? A. Lu11 / Shǎo Shāng; B. · Lu10 / Yǔ Jì; C. ·B12 / Fēng Mén; D. · R6 / Qì Hǎi; E. · R12 / Zhōng Wǎn
2235	治疗气血虚弱型震颤麻痹可在基本处方上再加：A·足三里、三阴交；B·中脘、太白；C·脾俞、胃俞；D·大包、期门；E·气海·血海	What points may be added to the basic prescription of points to treat Parkinsonism that belongs to the energy and blood deficiency type? · A. · S36 / Zú Sān Lǐ，Sp6 / Sān Yīn Jiāo; B. · R12 / Zhōng Wǎn，Sp3 / Tài Bái; C. B20 / Pí Shū，B21 / Wèi Shū; D. · Sp21 / Dà Bāo，Lv14 / Qí Mén; E. · R6 / Qì Hǎi ·Sp10 / Xuè Hǎi
2236	治疗气血瘀滞型痛经，可在基本处加用： A 中脘、脾俞、足三里；B·合谷、太冲、次髎；C·膈俞、脾俞、气海·D 关元、脾俞、三阴交·E 太冲、太溪、命门	What additional points may be added to treat the energy congestion and blood coagulation type of period pain? A. R12 / Zhōng Wǎn，B20 / Pí Shū，S36 / Zú Sān Lǐ; B. · Li4 / Hé Gǔ，Lv3 / Tài Chōng，B32 / Cì Liáo; C. ·B17 / Gé Shū，B20 / Pí Shū，R6 / Qì Hǎi; ·D. R4 / Guān Yuán，B20 / Pí Shū，Sp6 / Sān Yīn Jiāo ·E Lv3 / Tài Chōng，K3 / Tài Xī，D4 / Mìng Mén
2237	治疗气滞型便秘，除取用大肠俞天枢支沟上巨虚外，还可加用： A·合谷 曲池；B·中脘 行间；C 脾俞 胃俞；D 气海 神阙；E·关元 命门.	In treating the energy congestion type of; constipation, which group of points should be selected in addition to B25 (Dà Cháng Shū), S25 (Tiān Shū), Sj6 (Zhi Gōu), S37 (Shàng Jù Xū)? A. Li4 (Hé Gǔ); Li11 (Qū Chí); B. R12 (Zhōng Wǎn) Lv2 (Xíng Jiān); C. B20 (Pí Shū); B21 (Wèi Shū); D. R6 (Qì Hǎi) R8 (Shén Què); E. R4 (Guān Yuán), D4 (Mìng Mén).
2238	治疗气滞血瘀型 黄褐斑，可在基本处方的基础上加：A·太冲、膈俞；B·太冲、合谷；C·血海、肾俞；D·肝俞、肾俞；E·足三里、三阴交	What points may be added to the basic prescription of points to treat the energy congestion and blood coagulation type of chloasma? A. · Lv3 / Tài Chōng，B17 / Gé Shū; B. · Lv3 / Tài Chōng，Li4 / Hé Gǔ; C. · Sp10 / Xuè Hǎi 、B23 / Shèn Shū; D. ·B18 / Gān Shū，B23 / Shèn Shū; E. · S36 / Zú Sān Lǐ，Sp6 / Sān Yīn Jiāo
2239	治疗气滞血瘀型经前期紧张综合征，除针刺主穴外加用：A·脾俞；B·膈俞；C·肾俞；D·期门	In addition to needling main points, what point should be added to treat premenstrual syndrome that belongs to energy congestion and lood coagulation type? A. B20 / Pí Shū; B. ·B17 / Gé Shū; C. B23 / Shèn Shū; D. ·Lv14 / Qí Mén
2240	治疗热毒炽盛型麦粒肿，可在基本处方的基础上再加：	What points may be added to the basic prescription of points to treat the toxic heat in abundance type of

	A·三阴交、阴陵泉; B·风门、肺俞; C·合谷、风池; D·风门、合谷; E·曲池、行间	hordeolum / stye? A. · Sp6 / Sān Yīn Jiāo, Sp9 / Yīn Líng Quán; B. ·B12 / Fēng Mén, B13 / Fèi Shū; C. · Li4 / Hé Gŭ, G20 / Fēng Chí; D. ·B12 / Fēng Mén, Li4 / Hé Gŭ; E. · Li11 / Qū Chí, Lv2 / Xíng Jiān
2241	治疗热毒攻心的流行性腮腺炎可在基本处方上再加: A翳风; B·水沟; C·足临泣; D·大椎; E·关冲	What points may be added to the basic prescription of points to trea the toxic heat attacking the heart type of epedemic parotitis? A. Sj17 / Yì Fēng; B. · D26 / Shuĭ Gōu / Rén Zhōng; C. ·G41 / Zú Lín Qì / Lín Qì; D. ·D14 / Dà Zhuī; E. · Sj1 / Guān Chōng
2242	治疗热淋, 可在基本处方的基础上再加: A·行间; B. 委中; C·大椎; D·曲池; E·昆仑	What points may be added to the basic prescription of points to treat hot type of lin condition (urinary strains, strangury)? A. · Lv2 / Xíng Jiān; B. B40 / Wĕi Zhōng; C. ·D14 / Dà Zhuī; D. · Li11 / Qū Chí; E. B60 / Kūn Lún
2243	治疗热壅盛型抽搐, 可在基础方上再加: A·肾俞; B·涌泉; C·风府; D·劳宫; E·气海	What points may be added to the basic prescription of points to treat the accumulated heat in abundance type of twitching? A. B23 / Shèn Shū; B. · K1 / Yŏng Quán; C. · D16 / Fēng Fŭ; D. · P8 / Láo Gōng; E. · R6 / Qì Hăi
2244	治疗妊娠呕吐伴眩晕重者, 可在基本方的基础上再加: A·百会、气海; B·百会、风池; C·太冲、期门; D·神门、心俞; E·三阴交、丰隆	What points may be added to the basic prescription of points to treat morning sickness accompanied by vertigo and dizziness? A. · D20 / Băi Huì, R6 / Qì Hăi; B. · D20 / Băi Huì, G20 / Fēng Chí; C. · Lv3 / Tài Chōng, Lv14 / Qí Mén D. · H7 / Shén Mén, B15 / Xīn Shū; E. · Sp6 / Sān Yīn Jiāo, S40 / Fēng Lóng
2245	治疗乳房疾病以什么配穴方式最为常用? A 俞募配穴; B 表里经配穴; C 同名经配穴; D 上下配穴; E 远近配穴。	What combination of points is most common in treating the diseases of breasts? A. Methods of pairing off Bèi Shù Xué and Mù Xué; B. Methods of pairing off points on meridians forming a deep-superficial relationship; C. Methods of pairing off points on the meridians with similar yin-yang classification; D.Methods of pairing off upper and lower points; E Methods of pairing off distal and local points.
2246	治疗乳少、乳痈应首选: A. 曲池、外关、太冲; B 膻中、少泽、太冲; C·膻中、少泽、乳根; D·天泉、膻中、气海	What point should be selected to treat scanty milk secretion and carbuncle in the breast (acute mastitis)? A. Li11 / Qū Chí ,Sj5 / Wài Guān ,Lv3 / Tài Chōng; B. R17 / Shān Zhōng , Si1 / Shào Zé 、 Lv3 / Tài Chōng; C. · R17 / Shān Zhōng , Si1 / Shào Zé 、 S18 / Rŭ Gēn; D. · Tiān Quán , R17 / Shān Zhōng , R6 / Qì Hăi
2247	治疗乳腺炎的经验穴是: A·足三里; B.梁丘; C·期门; D·内关; E·肩井	What is the experience point to treat mastitis? A. · S36 / Zú Sān Lĭ; B. S34 / Liáng Qiū; C. · Lv14 / Qí Mén; D. · P6 / Nèi Guān; E. · G21 / Jiān Jĭng
2248	治疗乳腺增生病之冲任失	What points may be added to the basic prescription of

	调型，可在基本处方上再加：A·丰隆；B·三阴交；C屋翳…D太冲；E·中脘	points to treat hyperplasia of mammary glands that belongs to the loss of balance in the rigorous and conception meridians type? A. · S40 / Fēng Lóng; B. · Sp6 / Sān Yīn Jiāo; C. S15 / Wū Yì; D. Lv3 / Tài Chōng; E. · R12 / Zhōng Wǎn
2249	治疗乳腺增生病之肝郁气滞型，可在基本处方上再加： A·太冲；B·三阴交；C·足三里；D·内关；E·章门·	What points may be added to the basic prescription of points to treat hyperplasia of mammary glands that belongs to the liver energy congestion type? A. · Lv3 / Tài Chōng; B. · Sp6 / Sān Yīn Jiāo; C. · S36 / Zú Sān Lǐ; D. · P6 / Nèi Guān; E. · Lv13 / Zhāng Mén ·
2250	治疗乳腺增生病之痰湿阻络型，可在基本处方上再加：A·丰隆；B·三阴交；C屋翳…D. 太冲；E·中脘	What point may be added to the basic prescription of points to treat hyperplasia of mammary glands that belongs to the phlegm dampness obstructing linking meridians type? A. · S40 / Fēng Lóng; B. · Sp6 / Sān Yīn Jiāo; C. S15 / Wū Yì; D. Lv3 / Tài Chōng; E. · R12 / Zhōng Wǎn
2251	治疗三叉神经痛应选用:A.合谷 太冲；B 曲池 外关；C，百会 四神聪.D 头维 太阳.	What points should be selected to treat trigeminal neuralgia? A. Li4 [Hé Gǔ] Lv3 / Tài Chōng; B. Li11 [Qū Chí] Sj5 [Wài Guān]; C.D20 [Bǎi Huì] four spiritual intelligences; D. S8 [Tóu Wěi] TÀI YÁNG (the sun, the temple).
2252	治疗疝气常用的穴位是；A 大敦；B 行间；C 内庭；D 陷谷	Which is the commonly used point to treat hernia? A. Lv1 / Dà Dūn; B. Lv2 / Xíng Jiān; C. S44 / Nèi Tíng; D. S43 / Xiàn Gǔ
2253	治疗上胞振跳，可在基本处方的基础上再加：A·心俞、脾俞；B·血海、肝俞；C·睛明、鱼腰；D·承泣、下关；E·下关、足三里	What points may be added to the basic prescription of points to treat flickering upper eyelid? A. ·B15 / Xīn Shū，B20 / Pí Shū; B. · Sp10 / Xuè Hǎi，B18 / Gān Shū; C. ·B1 / Jīng Míng，Yú yāo / fish waist; D. · S1 / Chéng Qì，S7 / Xià Guān; E. · S7 / Xià Guān，S36 / Zú Sān Lǐ
2254	治疗上消证，可在基本处方的基础上再加：A·中脘、内庭；B.太渊、少府；C·太冲、照海；D·阴谷、气海；E·命门、至阳	What points may be added to the basic prescription of points to treat diabetes-like condition (elimination and thirst / xiao ke) characterized by excessive drink called "upper elimination"? A · R12 / Zhōng Wǎn，S44 / Nèi Tíng; B. Lu9 / TàiYuān，H8 / Shào Fǔ; C. · Lv3 / Tài Chōng，K6 / Zhào Hǎi; D. · K10 / Yīn Gǔ / ，R6 / Qì Hǎi; E. · D4 / Mìng Mén，D9 / Zhì Yáng
2255	治疗蛇丹时选用太冲穴，而不选行间穴是因为：A. 太冲是输穴；B 太冲可以疏肝；C 太冲可以泻肝胆之热；D 太冲可以养血；E 以上都不是。	Lv3 (Tài Chōng), but NOT Lv2 (Xíng Jiān) is often selected to treat herpes zoster, why is that? A. Lv3 / Tài Chōng is a lake-point / stream-point / shu xue; B. Lv3 / Tài Chōng can disperse the liver; C. Lv3 / Tài Chōng can sedate heat of liver and gallbladder; D Lv3 / Tài Chōng can nourish blood; E. none of the above。
2256	治疗神经性皮炎的基本处方中，( ) 既可疏风清热，又能清血分之郁热：A·风池；B·大椎；C·曲池；D·委中；E·膈俞	In the prescription of basic points to treat neurodermatitis, which point can disperse wind and clear heat, and clear inhibited heat at blood level? A. · G20 / Fēng Chí; B. ·D14 / Dà Zhuī; C. · Li11 / Qū Chí; D. B40 /

	中; E·膈俞	Wěi Zhōng; E. ·B17 / Gé Shū
2257	治疗肾绞痛伴尿血者，可在基础方上加用：A·命门、气海；B·内关、足三里；C·曲骨、阴陵泉；D·委阳、次髎；E·膈俞、血海	What points may be added to the basic prescription of points to treat renal colic accompanied by blood in urine? A. · D4 / Mìng Mén，R6 / Qì Hǎi; B. · P6 / Nèi Guān，S36 / Zú Sān Lǐ; C. · R2 / Qū Gǔ，Sp9 / Yīn Líng Quán; D. · B39 / Wěi Yáng，B32 / Cì Liáo; E. ·B17 / Gé Shū，Sp10 / Xuè Hǎi
2258	治疗肾绞痛伴尿中砂石者，可在基础方上加用：A·命门、气海；B·内关、足三里 C·曲骨、阴陵泉；D·委阳、次髎；E·膈俞、血海	What points may be added to the basic prescription of points to treat renal colic with sandy stones in urine? A. · D4 / Mìng Mén，R6 / Qì Hǎi; B. · P6 / Nèi Guān，S36 / Zú Sān Lǐ; ·C. · R2 / Qū Gǔ，Sp9 / Yīn Líng Quán; D. · B39 / Wěi Yáng，B32 / Cì Liáo; E. ·B17 / Gé Shū，Sp10 / Xuè Hǎi
2259	治疗肾绞痛湿热甚者，可在基础方上加用：A·命门、气海；B·内关、足三里；C·曲骨、阴陵泉；D·委阳、次髎；E·膈俞、血海	What points may be added to the basic prescription of points to treat the severe damp heat type of renal colic? A. · D4 / Mìng Mén，R6 / Qì Hǎi; B. · P6 / Nèi Guān，S36 / Zú Sān Lǐ; C. · R2 / Qū Gǔ，Sp9 / Yīn Líng Quán; D. · B39 / Wěi Yáng，B32 / Cì Liáo; E. ·B17 / Gé Shū，Sp10 / Xuè Hǎi
2260	治疗肾精亏损所致的头痛应选取 A.百会悬钟肾俞太溪；B.百会气海肝俞 太溪 C.头维百会悬钟肾俞；D 百会肝俞胆俞太溪	In treating the kidney essence deficiency type of headache, which group of points should be selected? A. D20 (Bǎi Huì), G39 (Xuán Zhōng) B23 (Shèn Shū), K3 (Tài Xī); B. D20 (Bǎi Huì), R6 (Qì Hǎi);B18 (Gān Shū), K3 (Tài Xī); C. S8 (Tóu Wěi), D20 (Bǎi Huì), G39 (Xuán Zhōng);B23 (Shèn Shū); D. D20 (Bǎi Huì);B18 (Gān Shū);B19 (Dǎn Shū), K3 (Tài Xī).
2261	治疗肾气不足型遗尿，可在基本处方的基础上再加：A·脾俞、肾俞；B·关元、肾俞；C·心俞、肺俞；D·胆俞、肝俞；E·大肠俞、小肠俞	What points may be added to the basic prescription of points to treat the kidneys energy deficiency type of enuresis? A. B20 / Pí Shū，B23 / Shèn Shū; B. · R4 / Guān Yuán，B23 / Shèn Shū; C. ·B15 / Xīn Shū，B13 / Fèi Shū ·; D. ·B19 / Dǎn Shū，B18 / Gān Shū; E. B25 / Dà Cháng Shū，B27 / Xiǎo; Cháng Shū
2262	治疗肾虚胞寒型不孕症，可在基本方基础上再加：A 肾俞、神阙，B·阴陵泉、丰隆；C·气海，血海；D·太冲、·膈俞；E·中脘、足三里	What points may be added to the basic prescription of points to treat the kidney deficiency and cold womb type of infertility in women? A. B23 / Shèn Shū，R8 / Shén Què; B. · Sp9 / Yīn Líng Quán，S40 / Fēng Lóng; C. · R6 / Qì Hǎi ，Sp10 / Xuè Hǎi; D. · Lv3 / Tài Chōng 、 ·B17 / Gé Shū; E. · R12 / Zhōng Wǎn，S36 / Zú Sān Lǐ
2263	治疗肾虚肝亢型注意力缺陷多动症，可在基本处方的基础上再加：A·足三里、解溪；B.合谷、曲池；C·肾俞、行间；D·风池、外关，E·关元、中极	What points may be added to the basic prescription of points to treat restless syndrome with lack of attention that belongs to the kidney deficiency liver excess type? A. · S36 / Zú Sān Lǐ，S41 / Jiě Xī; B. Li4 / Hé Gǔ，Li11 / Qū Chí; C. B23 / Shèn Shū，Lv2 / Xíng Jiān; D. · G20 / Fēng Chí，Sj5 / Wài Guān; E. · R4 / Guān Yuán，R3 / Zhōng Jí
2264	治疗肾虚头痛的治则是：A，平肝潜阳；B 滋阴补肾；C.健脾补气；D 滋阴降火	What treatment principle should be applied to treat kidney deficiency headache? A. to calm the liver and suppress yang; B. to water yin

		and tone the kidney; C. to strengthen the spleen and tone energy; D. to water yin and bring down fire.
2265	治疗肾虚泄泻，除取脾俞天枢足三里三阴交外，还应配用 A.肾俞命门; B 肾俞太溪 C，神阙照海; D. 命门中脘	Which group of points should be selected to treat the kidney deficiency type of diarrhea in addition to B20 (Pí Shū), S25 (Tiān Shū), S36 (Zú Sān Lǐ), Sp6 (Sān Yīn Jiāo)? A. B23 (Shèn Shū) D4 (Mìng Mén); B. B23 (Shèn Shū) K3 (Tài Xī); C. R8 (Shén Què); K6 (Zhào Hǎi); D. D4 (Mìng Mén) R12 (Zhōng Wǎn).
2266	治疗肾虚泄泻，除取主穴外，还可加用: 。 A·肾俞 太溪; B·中脘 天枢; C 命门 关元; D·神阙照海; E 以上都不是	In addition to needling major points, which group of points should be added in treating kidney deficiency diarrhea? A. B23 (Shèn Shū); K3 (Tài Xī); B. R12 (Zhōng Wǎn); S25 (Tiān Shū); C. D4 (Mìng Mén); R4 (Guān Yuán); D. R8 (Shén Què); E. none of the above.
2267	治疗肾阳亏虚型崩漏，除针刺主穴外可再加：A·气海、命门；B·膈俞、中脘；C·肾俞、太溪；D·期门，肝俞；E·足三里、脾·俞	What points may be added to the basic prescription of points to treat the kidney yang deprivation and deficiency type of bleeding from the uterus / metrorrhagia and metrostaxis? A. · R6 / Qì Hǎi，D4 / Mìng Mén; B. ·B17 / Gé Shū，R12 / Zhōng Wǎn; C. B23 / Shèn Shū，K3 / Tài Xī; D. · Lv14 / Qí Mén ，B18 / Gān Shū; E. · S36 / Zú Sān Lǐ，B20 / Pí Shū
2268	治疗失眠的要穴是: A·极泉; B·少海; C 通里 D·阴郄，E·神门	Which point should be selected as the primary point to treat insomnia? : A. · H1 / Jí Quán; B. · H3 / Shào Hǎi; C. H5 / Tōng Lǐ; D. · H6 / Yīn Xī，E. · H7 / Shén Mén
2269	治疗失眠首选: A·隐白 B·公孙 C·三阴交 D·阴陵泉 E 大横	Which point should be selected as the primary point to treat insomnia? A. · Sp1 / Yǐn Bái; B. · Sp4 / Gōng Sūn; C. · Sp6 / Sān Yīn Jiāo; D. · Sp9 / Yīn Líng Quán; E. Sp15 / Dà Héng
2270	治疗失眠引起的头痛，宜选用: A. 人中 合谷 太冲; B. 心俞 脾俞 内关; C. 肝俞 太冲 太溪; D. 安眠 神门 三阴交; E. 大迎 承浆 下关	Which group of points should be selected to treat headache due to insomnia? A. D26 (Shuǐ Gōu, Rén Zhōng). Li4 (Hé Gǔ) Lv3 (Tài Chōng); B. B15 (Xīn Shū); B20 (Pí Shū) P6 (Nèi Guān); C. B18 (Gān Shū) Lv3 (Tài Chōng) K3 (Tài Xī); D. Ān Mián H7 (Shén Mén) Sp6 (Sān Yīn Jiāo); E. S5 (Dà Yíng). R24 (Chéng Jiàng) S7 (Xià Guān).
2271	治疗失眠症应选取 A.神门大陵太渊; B 神门内关三阴交; C.神门内关太冲; D 太冲合谷三阴交	Which group of points should be selected to treat insomnia? A. H7 (Shén Mén) P7 (Dà Líng) Lu9 (Tài Yuān); B. H7 (Shén Mén); P6 (Nèi Guān) Sp6 (Sān Yīn Jiāo); C. H7 (Shén Mén); P6 (Nèi Guān) Lv3 (Tài Chōng); D. Lv3 (Tài Chōng) Li4 (Hé Gǔ) Sp6 (Sān Yīn Jiāo).
2272	治疗湿热痢，除用主穴外，还可加用: A·脾俞 胃俞; B·中脘 胃俞; C·曲池 内庭; D·关元 中脘; E·以上都不是	In addition to needling major points, which group of points should be added in treating damp-hot dysentery? A. B20 (Pí Shū); B21 (Wèi Shū); B. R12 (Zhōng Wǎn) B21 (Wèi Shū); C. Li11 (Qū Chí); S44 (Nèi Tíng); D. R4 (Guān Yuán) R12 (Zhōng Wǎn); E. none of the above
2273	治疗湿热疝的主要处方是: A·关元 三角灸 大敦 中极; B·气冲 阳陵泉 太溪	Which group of points should be selected to treat damp-hot hernia?

	归来; C·关元 三阴交 大敦 三角灸; D·归来 中极 三阴交 太冲; E·以上均不是	A. R4 (Guān Yuán) Sān Jiǎo Jiǔ Lv1 (Dà Dūn) R3 (Zhōng Jí); B. S30 (Qì; Chōng) G34 (Yáng Líng Quán) K3 (Tài Xī) S29 (Guī Lái); C. R4 (Guān Yuán); Sp6 (Sān Yīn Jiāo) Lv1 (Dà Dūn) Sān Jiǎo Jiǔ; D. S29 (Guī Lái) R3 (Zhōng Jí) Sp6 (Sān Yīn Jiāo) Lv3 (Tài Chōng); E. None of the above
2274	治疗湿热下注型带下病，除针刺主穴外，还应加用：A·脾俞、太溪; B·中极、次髎; C·肾俞、上髎; D·中极、下髎; E·膻中、血海	What points may be added to the basic prescription of points to treat the damp heat flowing downward type of vaginal discharges? A. B20 / Pí Shū，K3 / Tài Xī; B. · R3 / Zhōng Jí，B32 / Cì Liáo; C. B23 / Shèn Shū，B31 / Shàng Liáo; D. · R3 / Zhōng Jí，B34 / Xià Liáo; E. · R17 / Shān Zhōng，Sp10 / Xuè Hǎi
2275	治疗湿热下注型带下病除主穴外可加用：A·太溪; B·足三里; C·太冲; D 行间; E·中极	What points may be added to the basic prescription of points to treat the damp heat flowing downward type of vaginal discharges? A. · K3 / Tài Xī; B. · S36 / Zú Sān Lǐ; C. · Lv3 / Tài Chōng; D. Lv2 / Xíng Jiān; E. · R3 / Zhōng Jí
2276	治疗湿热下注型癃闭，可在基本处方的基础上再加：A·中极、行间; B·太冲、支沟; C·血海、膈俞; D·肾俞、太溪; E·阳陵泉、太溪	What points may be added to the basic prescription of points to treat the damp heat flowing downward type of suppression of urination? A. · R3 / Zhōng Jí，Lv2 / Xíng Jiān; B. · Lv3 / Tài Chōng，Sj6 / Zhi Gōu; C. · Sp10 / Xuè Hǎi，B17 / Gé Shū; D. B23 / Shèn Shū，K3 / Tài Xī; E · G34 / Yáng Líng Quán，K3 / Tài Xī
2277	治疗湿浊困脾型失眠，可在基本处方的基础上再加：A·公孙、大包; B·脾俞、公孙 ·C:脾俞、大包; D 阴陵泉、脾俞; E·中脘、大包	What points may be added to the basic prescription of points to treat insomnia due to turbid dampness troubling the spleen? A. · Sp4 / Gōng Sūn，Sp21 / Dà Bāo; B. B20 / Pí Shū，Sp4 / Gōng Sūn; ·C. B20 / Pí Shū，Sp21 / Dà Bāo; D. Sp9 / Yīn Líng Quán，B20 / Pí Shū; E. · R12 / Zhōng Wǎn，Sp21 / Dà Bāo
2278	治疗石淋，可在基本处方的基础上再加：A·丰隆透承山; B·太冲透涌泉; C·秩边透水道; D·膀胱俞透小肠俞; E·阳陵泉透阴陵泉	What points may be added to the basic prescription of points to treat stony lin condition (urinary strains, strangury)? A. · S40 / Fēng Lóng inserted all the way through B57 / Chéng Shān; B. · Lv3 / Tài Chōng inserted all the way through K1 / Yǒng Quán; C. B54 / Zhì biān inserted all the way through S28 / Shuǐ Dào; D. B28 / Páng Guāng Shū inserted all the way through B27 / Xiǎo Cháng Shū; E. · G34 / Yáng Líng Quán inserted all the way through Sp9 / Yīn Líng Quán
2279	治疗实证崩漏应选用哪 · 经"井"穴 A.足厥阴肝经井穴，大敦; B 足太阴脾经井穴，隐白; C.足阳明胃经井穴，厉兑; D 足太阳膀胱经井穴，至阴	The well point (jing xue) of what meridian should be selected to treat the excess type of vaginal bleeding? A. well point of the liver meridian, Lv1 (Dà Dūn); B. well point of the spleen meridian Sp1 (Yīn Bái); C. well point of the stomach meridian S45 (Lì Duì); D. well point of the bladder meridian; B67 (Zhì Yīn)
2280	治疗实证的胃痛应选取 A.中脘内关足三里.B 中脘胃俞脾俞; C.中脘膻中天突;	Which group of points should be selected to treat the excess type of stomachache?

	D 中脘膻中足三里	A. R12 (Zhōng Wǎn) P6 (Nèi Guān) S36 (Zú Sān Lǐ); B. R12 (Zhōng Wǎn) B21 (Wèi Shū) B20 (Pí Shū); C. R12 (Zhōng Wǎn) R17 (Shān Zhōng) R22 (Tiān Tū); D. R12 (Zhōng Wǎn) R17 (Shān Zhōng) S36 (Zú Sān Lǐ).
2281	治疗实证腹痛应选用 A.中脘内关足三里; B.中脘天枢太冲; C.中脘天枢上巨虚; D 中脘神阙足三里	Which group of points should be selected to treat the excess type of abdominal pain? A. R12 (Zhōng Wǎn) P6 (Nèi Guān) S36 (Zú Sān Lǐ); B. R12 (Zhōng Wǎn) S25 (Tiān Shū) Lv3 (Tài Chōng); C. R12 (Zhōng Wǎn) S25 (Tiān Shū) S37 (Shàng Jù Xū); D. R12 (Zhōng Wǎn) R8 (Shén Què) S36 (Zú Sān Lǐ).
2282	治疗实证痛经的主方应是: A.中极次髎三阴交; B 中极血海三阴交; C.中极次髎地机; D 中极关元三阴交	Which group of points should be selected as the primary prescription to treat the excess type of period pain? A. R3 (Zhōng Jí) B32 (Cì Liáo), Sp6 (Sān Yīn Jiāo); B. R3 (Zhōng Jí); Sp10 (Xuè Hǎi) Sp6 (Sān Yīn Jiāo) Sp8 (Dì Jī); C. R3 (Zhōng Jí) B32 (Cì Liáo), Sp8 (Dì Jī); D. R3 (Zhōng Jí) R4 (Guān Yuán) Sp6 (Sān Yīn Jiāo).
2283	治疗实证哮喘，除取肺俞尺泽外，主穴还应选取 A.膻中气海; B 膻中关元; C.天突膻中; D，关元天突	Which group of points should be to treat excess type of asthma (xiao chuan) in addition to B13 (Fèi Shū) and Lu5 (Chǐ Zé)? A. R17 (Shān Zhōng) R6 (Qì Hǎi); B. R17 (Shān Zhōng) R4 (Guān Yuán); C. R22 (Tiān Tū), R17 (Shān Zhōng); D. R4 (Guān Yuán), R22 (Tiān Tū).
2284	治疗食积引起的呕吐，除主穴外还可加用: A·脾俞 章门; B 阳陵泉 太冲; C·下脘 璇玑; D·膻中 丰隆; E·上脘 胃俞	In addition to major points, which group of points should be added in treating vomiting due to food congestion? A. B20 (Pí Shū) Lv13 (Zhāng Mén); B. G34 (Yáng Líng Quán) Lv3 (Tài Chōng); C. R10 (Xià Wǎn) R21 (Xuán Jī); D. R17 (Shān Zhōng) S40 (Fēng Lóng); E. R13 (Shàng Wǎn) B21 (Wèi Shū).
2285	治疗暑湿感冒，可在基本处方的基础上再加: A·少商; B·尺泽; C·鱼际; D·风池; E·中脘	What points may be added to the basic prescription of points to treat the common cold of summer-heat dampness type? A. · Lu11 / Shǎo Shāng; B. · Lu5 / Chǐ Zé; C. · Lu10 / Yǔ Jì; D. · G20 / Fēng Chí; E. · R12 / Zhōng Wǎn
2286	治疗水肿以下列哪组穴位为佳? A. 水分.水沟 膀胱俞 小肠俞; B. 水分 气海.三焦俞 足三里; C. 温溜 肺俞 三焦俞三阴交; D. 肺俞 脾俞 足三里 阴陵泉; E. 肺俞 肾俞 三焦俞 水沟。	Which group of points should best be selected to treat edema? A. R9 [Shuǐ Fēn] D.26 [Shuǐ Gōu] B28 [Páng Guāng Shū] B27 [Xiǎo Cháng Shū]; B. R9 [Shuǐ Fēn] R6 [Qì Hǎi] B22 [Sān Jiāo Shū] S36 [Zú Sān Lǐ]; C. Li7 [Wēn Liū] B13 [Fèi Shū] B22 [Sān Jiāo Shū] Sp6 [Sān Yīn Jiāo]; D. B13 [Fèi Shū] B20 [Pí Shū] S36 [Zú Sān Lǐ] Sp9 [Yīn Líng Quán]; E. B13 [Fèi Shū] B23 [Shèn Shū] B22 [Sān Jiāo Shū]D26 [Shuǐ Gōu]。
2287	治疗胎位不正的要穴是: A·至阳; B 至阴; C·昆仑; D·少泽; E·太冲	Which is an important point to correct fetus in wrong position? A. · D9 / Zhì Yáng; B. B67 / Zhì Yīn; C. B60 / Kūn Lún; D. · Si1 / Shào Zé; E. · Lv3 / Tài Chōng
2288	治疗痰厥可在基础方上再加: A·肾俞; B·丰隆; C·风府; D·劳宫; E·气海 ·	What points may be added to the basic prescription of points to treat phlegm uprising (tan jue)? A. B23 / Shèn Shū; B. · S40 / Fēng Lóng; C. · D16 / Fēng

		Fǔ; D. · P8 / Láo Gōng; E. · R6 / Qì Hǎi ·
2289	治疗痰湿咳嗽，除背俞穴外还应该取: A·尺泽阳陵泉太冲; B·太白 章门 丰隆; C·列缺 尺泽 丰隆; D·合谷 外关 大椎; E·天突 足三里 膻中	In treating phlegm dampness cough, which group of points should be selected in addition to back shu points (bei shu xue)? A. Lu5 (Chǐ Zé) G34 (Yáng Líng Quán) Lv3 (Tài Chōng); B. Sp3 (Tài Bái) Lv13 (Zhāng Mén) S40 (Fēng Lóng); C. Lu7 (Liè Quē) Lu5 (Chǐ Zé) S40 (Fēng Lóng); D. Li4 (Hé Gǔ) Sj5 (Wài Guān) D14 (Dà Zhuī); E. R22 (Tiān Tū) S36 (Zú Sān Lǐ) R17 (Shān Zhōng).
2290	治疗痰湿咳嗽，除肺俞外，还可加用: A·列缺 合谷; B·大椎 少商; C·太渊 太白 丰隆; D·尺泽 太冲 阳陵泉; E·天突 膻中	In treating cough with phlegm dampness, which group of points should be selected in addition to B13 (Fèi Shū)? A. Lu7 (Liè Quē) Li4 (Hé Gǔ); B. D14 (Dà Zhuī) Lu11 (Shǎo Shāng); C. Lu9 (Tài Yuān), Sp3 (Tài Bái), S40 (Fēng Lóng); D. Lu5 (Chǐ Zé) Lv3 (Tài Chōng) G34 (Yáng Líng Quán); E. R22 (Tiān Tū), R17 (Shān Zhōng).
2291	治疗痰湿凝滞型痤疮，可在基本处方的基础上再加: A·尺泽; B·风门; C·血海; D 丰隆; E·攒竹	What point may be added to the basic prescription of points to treat the phlegm dampness congestion type of acne? A. · Lu5 / Chǐ Zé; B. ·B12 / Fēng Mén; C. · Sp10 / Xuè Hǎi; D. S40 / Fēng Lóng; E. B2 / Zǎn Zhú
2292	治疗痰湿壅盛型高血压，可在基本处方的基础上再加: A·风池、行间; B·太溪、肝俞; C·丰隆、足三里; D·血海、膈俞; E·关元、肾俞	What point may be added to the main prescription of points to treat hypertension due to phlegm dampness? A. · G20 / Fēng Chí， Lv2 / Xíng Jiān; B. · K3 / Tài Xī， B18 / Gān Shū; C. · S40 / Fēng Lóng， S36 / Zú Sān Lǐ; D. · Sp10 / Xuè Hǎi， B17 / Gé Shū; E. · R4 / Guān Yuán， B23 / Shèn Shū
2293	治疗痰湿中阻型眩晕的主要处方是: A·脾俞 肾俞 关元 足三里; B· 鸠尾 大椎 腰奇 间使 丰隆; C· 中脘 内关 丰隆 解溪 头维 D·大椎 水沟 风府 内关 丰隆 E·风池 肝俞 肾俞 行间 侠溪	Which group of points should be selected to treat vertigo due to middle obstruction of phlegm dampness? A. B20 (Pí Shū) B23 (Shèn Shū) R4 (Guān Yuán) S36 (Zú Sān Lǐ); B. R15 (Jiū Wěi) D14 (Dà Zhuī) Yāo Qí P5 (Jiān Shǐ) S40 (Fēng Lóng); C. R12 (Zhōng Wǎn) P6 (Nèi Guān) S40 (Fēng Lóng) S41 (Jiě Xī) S8 (Tóu Wěi); D. D14 (Dà Zhuī) D26 (Shuǐ Gōu, Rén Zhōng) D16 (Fēng Fǔ) P6 (Nèi Guān) S40 (Fēng Lóng); E. G20 (Fēng Chí)B18 (Gān Shū) B23 (Shèn Shū) Lv2 (Xíng Jiān) G43 (Xiá Xī)..
2294	治疗痰饮阻滞型妊娠呕吐，'·可在基本方基础上再加: A·三阴交、丰隆; B·百会、气海 ; C.脾俞、胃俞; D·神门、心俞; E·期门，太冲	What points may be added to the basic prescription of points to treat the watery phlegm obstruction and stagnation type of morning sickness? A. · Sp6 / Sān Yīn Jiāo， S40 / Fēng Lóng; B. · D20 / Bǎi Huì， R6 / Qì Hǎi; C. B20 / Pí Shū， B21 / Wèi Shū; D. · H7 / Shén Mén， B15 / Xīn Shū; E. · Lv14 / Qí Mén ，Lv3 / Tài Chōng
2295	治疗痰证首选: A·尺泽; B·足三里; C·条口; D·丰隆; E·天枢	What point should be selected as the primary point to treat phlegm syndrome? A. · Lu5 / Chǐ Zé; B. · S36 / Zú Sān Lǐ; C. · S38 / Tiáo Kǒu; D. · S40 / Fēng Lóng; E. · S25 / Tiān Shū
2296	治疗痰浊凝滞型痤疮，可在基本处方的基础上再加: A·丰隆; B·血海; C·足三里;	What point may be added to the basic prescription of points to treat the turbid phlegm congestion type of acne?

	D·命门; E，尺泽	A. · S40 / Fēng Lóng; B. · Sp10 / Xuè Hǎi; C. · S36 / Zú Sān Lǐ; D. · D4 / Mìng Mén; E.Lu5 / Chǐ Zé
2297	治疗痰浊上蒙型眩晕，可在基本处方的基础上再加：A·行间、太冲、太溪; B·内关、中脘、丰隆; C·气海、血海、足三里; D·肝俞、肾俞、太溪; E·合谷、曲池、太阳	What point may be added to the main prescription of points to treat vertigo due to turbid phlegm blocking upward? A. · Lv2 / Xíng Jiān，Lv3 / Tài Chōng，K3 / Tài Xī; B. · P6 / Nèi Guān，R12 / Zhōng Wǎn，S40 / Fēng Lóng; C. · R6 / Qì Hǎi，Sp10 / Xuè Hǎi，S36 / Zú Sān Lǐ; D. ·B18 / Gān Shū，B23 / Shèn Shū，K3 / Tài Xī; E. · Li4 / Hé Gǔ，Li11 / Qū Chí，Tài yáng / sun / temple
2298	治疗痰浊中阻型震颤麻痹可在基本处方上再加: A·丰隆、中脘; B·阴陵泉、足三里; C·中脘、太白; D·肝俞、肾俞; E·太冲、阳陵泉	What points may be added to the basic prescription of points to treat Parkinsonism due to turbid phlegm obstructing the middle region? · A. · S40 / Fēng Lóng，R12 / Zhōng Wǎn; B. · Sp9 / Yīn Líng Quán，S36 / Zú Sān Lǐ; C. · R12 / Zhōng Wǎn，Sp3 / Tài Bái; D. ·B18 / Gān Shū，B23 / Shèn Shū; E. · Lv3 / Tài Chōng，G34 / Yáng Líng Quán
2299	治疗痛经气血不足证加入为: A·足三里、脾俞; B·水道、脾俞; C·太冲、合谷; D·行间、地机; E·归来、命门	What point may be added to treat period pain due to deficient energy-blood? A. · S36 / Zú Sān Lǐ，B20 / Pí Shū; B. · S28 / Shuǐ Dào，B20 / Pí Shū; C. · Lv3 / Tài Chōng，Li4 / Hé Gǔ; D. · Lv2 / Xíng Jiān，Sp8 / Dì Jī; E. · S29 / Guī Lái，D4 / Mìng Mén
2300	治疗痛经气血瘀滞证加入为: A·足三里、脾俞; B·水道、脾俞; C·太冲、合谷; D·行间、地机; E·归来、命门	What point may be added to treat the energy-blood congestion type of period pain? A. · S36 / Zú Sān Lǐ，B20 / Pí Shū; B. · S28 / Shuǐ Dào，B20 / Pí Shū; C. · Lv3 / Tài Chōng，Li4 / Hé Gǔ; D. · Lv2 / Xíng Jiān，Sp8 / Dì Jī; E. · S29 / Guī Lái，D4 / Mìng Mén
2301	治疗脱肛，除取百会长强大肠俞外，还可加用: A·白环俞; B·会阴; C·二白; D·承山; E· 气海	In addition to D20 (Bǎi Huì), D1 (Cháng Qiáng), and B25 (Dà Cháng Shū), what point should be selected to treat prolapse of the anus? A. B30 (Bái Huán Shū); B. R1 (Huì Yīn); C. Èr Bái; D. B57 (Chéng Shān); E. R6 (Qì Hǎi).
2302	治疗脱肛病应取 A.百会长强气海; B.百会中极中脘; C.百会长强大肠俞; D 百会气海中极	Which group of points should be selected to treat prolapse of the anus? A. D20 (Bǎi Huì) D1 (Cháng Qiáng) R6 (Qì Hǎi); B. D20 (Bǎi Huì) R3 (Zhōng Jí) R12 (Zhōng Wǎn); C. D20 (Bǎi Huì) D1 (Cháng Qiáng) B25 (Dà Cháng Shū); D. D20 (Bǎi Huì) R6 (Qì Hǎi) R3 (Zhōng Jí).
2303	治疗外感头痛应选取经外奇穴是： A.印堂; B，太阳; C.四神聪; E 鱼腰	What extraordinary point should be selected to treat headache of external causes? A. Yìn Táng; B. Tài Yáng; C. Sì Shén Cōng; D. Yú Yāo.
2304	治疗外伤性截瘫，小便不通者可在基本处方的基础上再加: A·委中; B·三阴交; C·阴陵泉; D·悬钟; E·足三里	What point may be added to the basic prescription of points to treat traumatic paraplegia with suppression of urination? A. B40 / Wěi Zhōng; B. · Sp6 / Sān Yīn Jiāo; C. · Sp9 / Yīn Líng Quán; D. · G39 / Xuán Zhōng; E. · S36 / Zú Sān Lǐ
2305	治疗外伤性截瘫必取的穴位是：A·损伤脊柱上、下1~2个棘突的督脉穴及其	What points must be used to treat traumatic paraplegia? A·du mai points of 1-2 spinous processes above and below

	1~2个棘突的督脉穴及其夹脊穴; B·肝俞; C·肾俞; D·关元; E阴陵泉	the injuried spines, and related jiā jí / clippings of spine points; B. ·B18 / Gān Shū; C. B23 / Shèn Shū; D. · R4 / Guān Yuán; E. Sp9 / Yīn Líng Quán
2306	治疗痿证取穴的主要法则是取: A·足太阴经; B·足厥阴经; C·阳明经; D·少阳经; E·太阳经	Which meridian should be selected in treating paralysis? A. greater yin meridian of foot (zu tai yin jing); B.decreasing yin meridian of foot (zu jue yin jing); C. bright yang meridians (yang ming jing); D. lesser yang meridians (shao yang jing); E. greater yang meridians (tai yang jing).
2307	治疗痿证时应选取哪一经的腧穴？ A.足少阳胆经腧穴; B.足阳明胃经腧穴.C.足太阳膀胱经腧穴; D 手少阳三焦经腧穴	Which meridian of points should be selected to treat paralysis? A. points on lesser yang meridian of foot (gallbladder); B. points on bright yang of foot meridian (stomach); C. points on greater yang meridian of foot (bladder); D. points on lesser yang meridian of hand (san jiao).
2308	治疗胃肠疾病的首选穴位是:A·中脘; B·足三里; C·合谷; D.梁丘; E·天枢	Which point should be selected as the primary point to treat gastrointestinal diseases? A. · R12 / Zhōng Wǎn; B. · S36 / Zú Sān Lǐ; C. · Li4 / Hé Gǔ; D. S34 / Liáng Qiū; E. · S25 / Tiān Shū
2309	治疗胃火牙痛可在基本处方的基础上再加：A·翳风、风池; B·太溪、照海; C·尺泽、少商; D·厉兑、二间; E·足三里、三阴交	What points may be added to the basic prescription of points to treat the stomach fire type of toothache? A. · Sj17 / Yì Fēng，G20 / Fēng Chí; B. · K3 / Tài Xī，K6 / Zhào Hǎi; C. · Lu5 / Chǐ Zé，Lu11 / Shǎo Shāng; D. · S45 / Lì Duì，Li2 / Èr Jiān; E. · S36 / Zú Sān Lǐ，Sp6 / Sān Yīn Jiāo
2310	治疗胃痛，近部取穴应取: A·足三里; B·内庭; C·关元; D·中脘; E·以上均非	Which point may be selected to treat stomachache as a local point? A. S36 (Zú Sān Lǐ); B. S44 (Nèi Tíng); C. R4 (Guān Yuán); D. R12 (Zhōng Wǎn); E. none of the above.
2311	治疗胃心胸病症，公孙宜配: A·足三里; B·中脘; C·内关; D·神门; E·膻中	What point should be combined with Sp4 (Gōng Sūn) to treat the diseases of the stomach, heart, and chest? A. · S36 / Zú Sān Lǐ; B. · R12 / Zhōng Wǎn; C. · P6 / Nèi Guān; D. · H7 / Shén Mén; E. · R17 / Shān Zhōng.
2312	治疗温疟，可在基本处方的基础上再加：A·至阳、期门; B·脾俞、足三里; C·章门、太冲; D·曲池、外关; B 内关、十宣	What points may be added to the basic prescription of points to treat warm malaria? A · D9 / Zhì Yáng, Lv14 / Qí Mén; B. B20 / Pí Shū, S36 / Zú Sān Lǐ; C. · Lv13 / Zhāng Mén，Lv3 / Tài Chōng; D. · Li11 / Qū Chí，Sj5 / Wài Guān B P6 / Nèi Guān，Shí xuān / ten statements / ten expansions
2313	治疗下胞振跳，可在基本处方的基础上再加：A·心俞、脾俞; B·血海、肝俞; C·睛明、鱼腰; D·承泣、下关; E·下关、足三里	What points may be added to the basic prescription of points to treat flickering lower eyelid? A. ·B15 / Xīn Shū，B20 / Pí Shū; B. · Sp10 / Xuè Hǎi，B18 / Gān Shū; C. ·B1 / Jīng Míng，Yú yāo / fish waist; D. · S1 / Chéng Qì，S7 / Xià Guān; E. · S7 / Xià Guān，S36 / Zú Sān Lǐ
2314	治疗下列鼻出血各型中，针灸并用的是：A·脾虚气弱型; B·阴虚火旺型; C·胃热	What type of nosebleed may be treated by both acupuncture and moxibustion? A. ·spleen deficiency and weak energy type; B. · yin deficiency with abundant fire;

	炽盛型；D·肝火上逆型；E·肺经热盛型	weak energy type; B. · yin deficiency with abundant fire; C. ·stomach heat in abundance type; D. · liver fire uprising type; E. ·lungs meridian with abundant heat type
2315	治疗先天不足型眼睑下垂，可在基本处方的基础上再加：A·太溪、命门、肾俞；B·足三里、脾俞、尺泽；C·足三里、脾俞、百会；D·太溪、肾俞。·风门；E¨·合谷、风池	What points may be added to the basic prescription of points to treat the innate deficiency type of eyelid dropping? A. · K3 / Tài Xī, D4 / Mìng Mén, B23 / Shèn Shū; B. · S36 / Zú Sān Lǐ，B20 / Pí Shū，Lu5 / Chǐ Zé; C. · S36 / Zú Sān Lǐ，B20 / Pí Shū，D20 / Bǎi Huì; D. · K3 / Tài Xī, B23 / Shèn Shū 。·B12 / Fēng Mén; E.¨ · Li4 / Hé Gǔ，G20 / Fēng Chí
2316	治疗痫病的基本处方中具有交通任督、调整阴阳作用的穴位是：A·水沟，中脘；B·百会、气海；C·大椎、关元；D·长强、鸠尾；E·腰俞、天突	In the basic prescription of points to treat epilepsy, what points can connect the ren mai and du mai and regulate yin and yang? A. · D26 / Shuǐ Gōu / Rén Zhōng，R12 / Zhōng Wǎn; B. · D20 / Bǎi Huì，R6 / Qì Hǎi; C. ·D14 / Dà Zhuī、 R4 / Guān Yuán; D. · D1 / Cháng Qiáng，R15 / Jiū Wěi; E. · D2 / Yāo Shū，R22 / Tiān Tū
2317	治疗痫病的基本处方中具有舒缓筋肉、解痉止搐作用的穴位是：A·水沟；B·鸠尾；C·阳陵泉；D·申脉；E·丰隆	In the basic prescription of points to treat epilepsy, what point can relax tendons and muscles, relieve spasm and stop twitching? A. · D26 / Shuǐ Gōu / Rén Zhōng; B. · R15 / Jiū Wěi; C. · G34 / Yáng Líng Quán; D. B62 / Shēn Mài; E. · S40 / Fēng Lóng
2318	治疗痫病在白昼发作者可在基本处方上加：A·合谷；B·太冲；C·大椎；D·申脉；E·照海	What points may be added to the basic prescription of points to treat epilepsy that attacks during the daytime? · A. · Li4 / Hé Gǔ; B. · Lv3 / Tài Chōng; C. ·D14 / Dà Zhuī; D. B62 / Shēn Mài; E. · K6 / Zhào Hǎi
2319	治疗痫病在夜间发作者可在基本处方上加：A·肝俞；B.太冲；C·太溪；D·肾俞；E·照海	What points may be added to the basic prescription of points to treat epilepsy that attacks a night? A. ·B18 / Gān Shū; B. Lv3 / Tài Chōng; C. · K3 / Tài Xī; D. B23 / Shèn Shū; E. · K6 / Zhào Hǎi
2320	治疗小儿疳积不应取 A.中脘; B.合谷; C.四缝; D 足三里	What point should NOT be selected to treat malnutrition in children (xiao er gan ji)? A. R12 (Zhōng Wǎn); B. Li4 (Hé Gǔ); C. Sì Féng; D. S36 (Zú Sān Lǐ).
2321	治疗小儿疳积时，宜选何经经穴为主? A 任脉 足阳明经经穴;B 督脉足阳明经经穴; C.足太阴 足阳明经经穴; D. 足太阴 手阳明经经穴; E 手阳明 足阳明经经穴。	What meridian points should be selected as primary points to treat malnutrition in children? A. points on the ren mai and foot brightyang meridian; B points on the du mai and foot bright yang meridian; C. points on the foot greater yin and foot bright yang meridians; D. points on the foot greater yin and hand bright yang meridians; E. points on the hand bright yang and foot bright yang meridians.
2322	治疗小儿急惊风以选下列哪组穴位为佳? A 水沟百会百劳太冲十宣; B 水沟.印堂合谷太冲十宣; C 水沟太阳合谷太溪十宣; D. 水沟神庭劳宫.太溪十宣; E. 水沟	What group of points should best be selected to treat acute infantile convulsion? A. D26 / Shuǐ Gōu / Rén Zhōng D20 / Bǎi Huì; Bǎi láo / hundred labours Lv3 / Tài Chōng Shí xuān / ten statements / ten expansions; B. D26 / Shuǐ Gōu / Rén

	本神.劳宫太白，十宣.	Zhōng. Yìn táng / midpoint between eyebrows / seal hall Li4 / Hé Gǔ Lv3 / Tài Chōng Shí xuān / ten statements / ten expansions; C. D26 / Shuǐ Gōu / Rén Zhōng Tài yáng / sun / temple Li4 / Hé Gǔ K3 / Tài Xī Shí xuān / ten statements / ten expansions; D. D26 / Shuǐ Gōu / Rén Zhōng D24 / Shén Tíng P8 / Láo Gōng.K3 / Tài Xī Shí xuān / ten statements / ten expansions; E. D26 / Shuǐ Gōu / Rén ZhōngG13 / Běn Shén.P8 / Láo Gōng Sp3 / Tài Bái ， Shí xuān / ten statements / ten expansions
2323	治疗心、胸、胃的病症常选用：A.内关、公孙；B.列缺、照海；C·后溪、申脉；D·支沟、阳陵泉；E·合谷、太冲	What group of points should be selected to treat the diseases of the heart、chest、and stomach? A. · P6 / Nèi Guān，Sp4 / Gōng Sūn; B. Lu7 / Liè Quē、 K6 / Zhào Hǎi; C. · Si3 / Hòu Xī， B62 / Shēn Mài; D. · Sj6 / Zhi Gōu， G34 / Yáng Líng Quán; E. · Li4 / Hé Gǔ， Lv3 / Tài Chōng
2324	治疗心绞痛气滞血瘀者，可在基础方上再加：A·心俞、脾俞；B·太溪、肾俞；C·丰隆、中脘；D·劳宫、合谷；E·太冲、膈俞	What points may be added to the basic prescription of points to treat the energy congestion and blood coagulation type of angina pectoris? A. ·B15 / Xīn Shū，B20 / Pí Shū; B. · K3 / Tài Xī，B23 / Shèn Shū; C. · S40 / Fēng Lóng， R12 / Zhōng Wǎn; D. · P8 / Láo Gōng， Li4 / Hé Gǔ; E. · Lv3 / Tài Chōng， B17 / Gé Shū
2325	治疗心绞痛痰湿闭阻者，可在基础方上再加：A·心俞、脾俞；B·太溪、肾俞；C·丰隆、中脘；D·劳宫、合谷；E·太冲、膈俞	What points may be added to the basic prescription of points to treat the phlegm dampness closure and obstruction type of angina pectoris? A. ·B15 / Xīn Shū，B20 / Pí Shū; B. · K3 / Tài Xī，B23 / Shèn Shū; C. · S40 / Fēng Lóng， R12 / Zhōng Wǎn; D. · P8 / Láo Gōng， Li4 / Hé Gǔ; E. · Lv3 / Tài Chōng， B17 / Gé Shū
2326	治疗心绞痛心脾两虚者，可在基础方上再加：A·心俞、脾俞；B·太溪、肾俞；C·丰隆、中脘；D·劳宫、合谷；E·太冲、膈俞	What points may be added to the basic prescription of points to treat the heart and spleen deficiency type of angina pectoris? A. ·B15 / Xīn Shū，B20 / Pí Shū; B. · K3 / Tài Xī，B23 / Shèn Shū; C. · S40 / Fēng Lóng， R12 / Zhōng Wǎn; D. · P8 / Láo Gōng， Li4 / Hé Gǔ; E. · Lv3 / Tài Chōng， B17 / Gé Shū
2327	治疗心脾亏损型不寐，除用神门三阴交穴之外，还可加用：A·心俞 厥阴俞 脾俞；B·心俞 肾俞 太溪；C·心俞 胆俞 大陵；D·肝俞 间使 太冲；E·胃俞 足三里 脾俞	In addition to H7 (Shén Mén) and Sp6 (Sān Yīn Jiāo), which group of points may be selected to treat the heart-spleen deficiency type of insomnia? A. B15 (Xīn Shū)B14 (Jué Yīn Shū) B20 (Pí Shū); B. B15 (Xīn Shū) B23 (Shèn Shū) K3 (Tài Xī); C. B15 (Xīn Shū) B19 (Dǎn Shū) P7 (Dà Líng); D. B18 (Gān Shū) P5 (Jiān Shǐ) Lv3 (Tài Chōng); E. B21 (Wèi Shū) S36 (Zú Sān Lǐ); B20 (Pí Shū)
2328	治疗心脾两虚型痫病，可在基本处方的基础上再加：A·心俞、脾俞；B·脾俞、尺泽 C·心俞、足三里；D 脾俞、中脘；E·心俞、中脘	What points may be added to the basic prescription of points to treat epilepsy of heart and spleen deficiency? A. ·B15 / Xīn Shū，B20 / Pí Shū; B. B20 / Pí Shū，Lu5 / Chǐ Zé; ·C. ·B15 / Xīn Shū， S36 / Zú Sān Lǐ; D. B20 / Pí Shū，R12 / Zhōng Wǎn; E. ·B15 / Xīn Shū， R12 / Zhōng Wǎn
2329	治疗心脾两虚型眼睑瞤动，	What points may be added to the basic prescription of

	可在基本处方的基础上再加：A·心俞、脾俞；B·血海、肝俞；C·睛明、鱼腰；D·承泣、下关；E·下关、足三里	points to treat the simultaneous deficiency of heart and spleen type of flickering eyelid? A. ·B15 / Xīn Shū，B20 / Pí Shū; B. · Sp10 / Xuè Hǎi，B18 / Gān Shū; C. ·B1 / Jīng Míng，Yú yāo / fish waist; D. · S1 / Chéng Qì，S7 / Xià Guān; E. · S7 / Xià Guān，S36 / Zú Sān Lǐ
2330	治疗心虚胆怯型失眠，可在基本处方的基础上再加：A·隐白、至阳；B·尺泽，至阳；C·心俞、胆俞；D·风池、胆俞；E·中脘、胆俞	What points may be added to the basic prescription of points to treat insomnia due to deficient heart and timid gallbladder? A. · Sp1 / Yǐn Bái，D9 / Zhì Yáng; B. · Lu5 / Chǐ Zé ，D9 / Zhì Yáng; C. ·B15 / Xīn Shū，B19 / Dǎn Shū; D. · G20 / Fēng Chí, B19 / Dǎn Shū; E. · R12 / Zhōng Wǎn, B19 / Dǎn Shū
2331	治疗心血瘀阻型心悸，可在基本处方的基础上再加：A·神阙、中脘；B·曲泽、膈俞；C·气海、血海；D·关元、中脘；E·神阙、气海	What points may be added to the basic prescription of points to treat palpitation due to heart blood coagulation? · A. · R8 / Shén Què，R12 / Zhōng Wǎn; B. · P3 / Qū Zé，B17 / Gé Shū; C. · R6 / Qì Hǎi，Sp10 / Xuè Hǎi; D. · R4 / Guān Yuán，R12 / Zhōng Wǎn; E. · R8 / Shén Què，R6 / Qì Hǎi
2332	治疗心阳不振型心悸，可在基本处方的基础上再加：A·神阙、中脘；B·关元，足三里；C·气海、足三里；D·关元、中脘；E，神阙、气海	What points may be added to the basic prescription of points to treat palpitation due to heart yang in decline? A. · R8 / Shén Què，R12 / Zhōng Wǎn; B. · R4 / Guān Yuán ，S36 / Zú Sān Lǐ; C. · R6 / Qì Hǎi，S36 / Zú Sān Lǐ; D. · R4 / Guān Yuán，R12 / Zhōng Wǎn; E. R8 / Shén Què，R6 / Qì Hǎi
2333	治疗心阳不足型近视，可在基本处方的基础上再加：A·心俞、膈俞、足三里、三阴交；B·心俞、膈俞、内关、神门；C·脾俞、胃俞、内关、三阴交；D·脾俞、胃俞、足三里、三阴交；E·肝俞、肾俞、太冲、太溪	What points may be added to the basic prescription of points to treat the heart yang deficiency type of myopia? A. ·B15 / Xīn Shū, B17 / Gé Shū, S36 / Zú Sān Lǐ, Sp6 / Sān Yīn Jiāo; B. ·B15 / Xīn Shū，B17 / Gé Shū，P6 / Nèi Guān，H7 / Shén Mén; C. B20 / Pí Shū，B21 / Wèi Shū，P6 / Nèi Guān, Sp6 / Sān Yīn Jiāo; D. B20 / Pí Shū, B21 / Wèi Shū，S36 / Zú Sān Lǐ，Sp6 / Sān Yīn Jiāo; E. ·B18 / Gān Shū，B23 / Shèn Shū，Lv3 / Tài Chōng，K3 / Tài Xī
2334	治疗行痹，除取主穴外，宜加用：A·大椎 曲池 B·膈俞 血海 C·肾俞 三阴交 D. 曲池 阳陵泉 E· 风池 风门	In addition to major points, which group of points should be selected to treat migratory rheumatism (xing bi)? A. D14 (Dà Zhuī) Li11 (Qū Chí); B..B17 (Gé Shū); Sp10 (Xuè Hǎi); C. B23 (Shèn Shū); Sp6 (Sān Yīn Jiāo); D. Li11 (Qū Chí) G34 (Yáng Líng Quán); E. G20 (Fēng Chí).B12 (Fēng Mén)
2335	治疗虚火牙痛可在基本处方的基础上再加：A·翳风、风池；B·太溪、照海；C·尺泽、少商；D·厉兑、二间；E·足三里、三阴交	What points may be added to the basic prescription of points to treat the deficient fire type of toothache? A · Sj17 / Yì Fēng，G20 / Fēng Chí; B · K3 / Tài Xī，K6 / Zhào Hǎi; C · Lu5 / Chǐ Zé，Lu11 / Shǎo Shāng; D · S45 / Lì Duì，Li2 / Èr Jiān; E · S36 / Zú Sān Lǐ，Sp6 / Sān Yīn Jiāo
2336	治疗虚脱汗出多者，可在基础方上再加：A·复溜；B·太溪；C·风府；D:劳宫；E·气海	What points may be added to the basic prescription of points to treat deficient prostration with copious perspiration? A. · K7 / Fù Liū; B. · K3 / Tài Xī; C. · D16 /

	海	Fēng Fǔ; D. P8 / Láo Gōng; E. · R6 / Qì Hǎi
2337	治疗虚脱兼二便失禁，可在基础方上再加：A·肾俞·B·丰隆; C·风府; D·劳宫; E·气海	What points may be added to the basic prescription of points to treat deficient prostration with incontinence of urination and loss of control in bowel movements? A. B23 / Shèn Shū; B. · S40 / Fēng Lóng; C. · D16 / Fēng Fǔ; D. · P8 / Láo Gōng; E. · R6 / Qì Hǎi
2338	治疗虚证便秘除取支沟天枢穴外，还应取 A.大肠俞上巨虚; B.曲池内庭; C.曲池合谷 D 内关足三里	Which group of points should be selected to treat the deficiency type of constipation in addition to Sj6 (Zhi Gōu) and S25 (Tiān Shū)? A. B25 (Dà Cháng Shū) S37 (Shàng Jù Xū); B. Li11 (Qū Chí); S44 (Nèi Tíng); C. Li11 (Qū Chí); Li4 (Hé Gǔ); D. P6 (Nèi Guān) S36 (Zú Sān Lǐ).
2339	治疗虚证的癃闭除三焦俞肾俞脾俞穴外，还应选用 A.关元; B 气海; C.百会; D 三阴交	What point should be selected to treat the deficiency type of suppression of urination in addition to B22 (Sān Jiāo Shū);B23 (Shèn Shū);B20 (Pí Shū)? A. R4 (Guān Yuán); B. R6 (Qì Hǎi); C. D20 (Bǎi Huì); D. Sp6 (Sān Yīn Jiāo).
2340	治疗虚证的哮喘证应选取的背俞穴是： A.脾俞肾俞; B 肺俞膈俞; C，脾俞肝俞; D 肺俞 肾俞	What back shu points (bei shu xue) should be selected to treat the deficiency type of asthma? A. B20 (Pí Shū) B23 (Shèn Shū); B..B13 (Fèi Shū) B17 (Gé Shū); C. B20 (Pí Shū)B17 (Gé Shū); D. B13 (Fèi Shū).B23 (Shèn Shū).
2341	治疗虚证腹痛不应选用 A.中脘; B.胃俞; C.脾俞; D 阳陵泉	Which point should NOT be selected to treat the deficiency type of abdominal pain? A. R12 (Zhōng Wǎn); B. B21 (Wèi Shū); C. B20 (Pí Shū); D. G34 (Yáng Líng Quán)
2342	治疗虚证痛经除用关元气海外，还应取 A.足三里三阴交; B.血海三阴交; C.血海足三里; D 中极三阴交	Which group of points should be selected to treat the deficiency type of period. pain in addition to R4 (Guān Yuán) and R6 (Qì Hǎi)? A. S36 (Zú Sān Lǐ) Sp6 (Sān Yīn Jiāo); B. Sp10 (Xuè Hǎi) Sp6 (Sān Yīn Jiāo); C. Sp10 (Xuè Hǎi) S36 (Zú Sān Lǐ); D. R3 (Zhōng Jí) Sp6 (Sān Yīn Jiāo).
2343	治疗虛证肋痛除取三阴交、期门外，还应选取: A·足三里、三阴交; B·血海、足三里; C·肝俞、肾俞; D·脾俞、肝俞	What additional points should be selected beside Sp6 / Sān Yīn Jiāo，Lv14 / Qí Mén to treat the deficiency syndrome of pain in the costal region (hypochondriac region)? A. · S36 / Zú Sān Lǐ，Sp6 / Sān Yīn Jiāo; B. · Sp10 / Xuè Hǎi，S36 / Zú Sān Lǐ; C. B18 / Gān Shū，B23 / Shèn Shū; D. B20 / Pí Shū，B18 / Gān Shū
2344	治疗眩晕之实证以：A·胆经 督脉及手足厥阴经穴为主; B·肝经 心经 胆经 任脉经穴为主; C·任脉 脾经 心经 胆经穴为主; D·督脉 胆经 脾经 心经穴为主; E·心包经 督脉 胆经 胃经穴为主.	How to select points to treat excess syndrome of vertigo? A. · primarily points on the gallbladder meridian、du mai / governing meridian and hand and foot jue yin meridians; B. primarily points on the liver、heart、 gallbladder、conception meridians / ren mai; C. primarily points on the conception / ren mai 、spleen、heart、 gallbladder meridians; D. primarily points on the du mai / governing meridian、 gallbladder 、spleen、heart meridians; E. primarily points on the pericardium、du mai / governing meridian。 gallbladder 、stomach meridians.

2345	治疗血厥实证可在基础方上再加：A·行间；B·神阙；C·风府；D·丰隆；E·气海	What points may be added to the basic prescription of points to treat the excess type of blood uprising (xue jue)? A. · Lv2 / Xíng Jiān; B. · R8 / Shén Què; C. · D16 / Fēng Fǔ; D. · S40 / Fēng Lóng; E. · R6 / Qì Hǎi
2346	治疗血热内扰型崩漏，除针刺主穴外，还应加用：A·脾俞、足三里；B·行间、期门；C·肾俞、太溪；D·丰隆、阴陵泉；E·中脘、足三里	What points may be added to the basic prescription of points to treat bleeding from the uterus / metrorrhagia metrostaxis due to the internal disturbance of blood heat? A. B20 / Pí Shū, S36 / Zú Sān Lǐ; B. · Lv2 / Xíng Jiān, Lv14 / Qí Mén; C. B23 / Shèn Shū，K3 / Tài Xī; D. · S40 / Fēng Lóng, Sp9 / Yīn Líng Quán; E. · R12 / Zhōng Wǎn, S36 / Zú Sān Lǐ
2347	治疗血热生风引起的斑秃，可在基本处方的基础上再加：A·太冲··B·气海；C·申脉 ·D¨风池；E·太溪	What points may be added to the basic prescription of points to treat the blood heat generating wind type of alopecia areata? A. · Lv3 / Tài Chōng; ·B. · R6 / Qì Hǎi; C. B62 / Shēn Mài; ·D.¨ G20 / Fēng Chí; E. · K3 / Tài Xī
2348	治疗血热生风诱发的斑秃，可在基本处方的基础上再加：A气海；B.曲池；C·肾俞；D·血海；E·外关	What points may be added to the basic prescription of points to treat the blood heat generating wind type of alopecia areata? A. R6 / Qì Hǎi; B. Li11 / Qū Chí; C. B23 / Shèn Shū; D. · Sp10 / Xuè Hǎi; E. · Sj5 / Wài Guān
2349	治疗血虚风动的痫病，可在基本处方的基础上再加：A·血海、行间；B·三阴交、血海；C·行间、三阴交；D·中脘、血海；E·中脘、三阴交	What points may be added to the basic prescription of points to treat epilepsy due to blood deficiency and wind-disturbing? A. · Sp10 / Xuè Hǎi，Lv2 / Xíng Jiān; B. · Sp6 / Sān Yīn Jiāo，Sp10 / Xuè Hǎi; C. · Lv2 / Xíng Jiān，Sp6 / Sān Yīn Jiāo; D. · R12 / Zhōng Wǎn，Sp10 / Xuè Hǎi; E. · R12 / Zhōng Wǎn，Sp6 / Sān Yīn Jiāo
2350	治疗血虚风燥型eczema，可在基本处方的基础上再加：A·肝俞；B·胃俞；C·水道；D·十宣；E·命门	What points may be added to the basic prescription of points to treat the blood deficiency with wind dryness type of eczema? A. ·B18 / Gān Shū; B. B21 / Wèi Shū; C. · S28 / Shuǐ Dào; D. · Shí xuān / ten statements / ten expansions; E. · D4 / Mìng Mén
2351	治疗血虚风燥型神经性皮炎以针刺为主要用：A·补法；B·泻法；C·平补平泻；D.但补不泻；E·刺络出血	When acupuncture is used as the primary therapy to treat the blood deficiency and wind dryness type of neurodermatitis, what technique should be applied? A. · tonfication; B. · sedation; C. · neutral technique; D. tonification without sedation; E. ·bloodletting by inserting into linking meridians
2352	治疗血虚生风型眼睑瞤动，可在基本处方的基础上再加：A·心俞、脾俞；B·血海、肝俞；C·睛明、鱼腰；D·承泣、下关；E·下关、足三里	What points may be added to the basic prescription of points to treat the blood deficiency generating wind type of flickering eyelid? A. ·B15 / Xīn Shū，B20 / Pí Shū; B. · Sp10 / Xuè Hǎi，B18 / Gān Shū; C. ·B1 / Jīng Míng，Yú yāo / fish waist; D. · S1 /

		Chéng Qì，S7 / Xià Guān; E. · S7 / Xià Guān，S36 / Zú Sān Lǐ
2353	治疗血虚型月经不调，可在基本处方的基础上再加：A·中脘；B.太溪；C··膈俞 ·D·肾俞; E·太冲	What points may be added to the basic prescription of points to treat blood deficiency type of irregular menstruation? A. · R12 / Zhōng Wǎn; B. K3 / Tài Xī; C. ·B17 / Gé Shū ·D. B23 / Shèn Shū; E. · Lv3 / Tài Chōng
2354	治疗牙痛鼻鼽痢疾应选用：A·下巨虚; B·内庭; C·颊车; D·梁门; E·梁丘	Which point is frequently selected to treat toothache, allergic rhinitis, and dysentery? A. · S39 / Xià Jù Xū; B. · S44 / Nèi Tíng; C. · S6 / Jiá Chē; D. · S21 / Liáng Mén; E. · S34 / Liáng Qiū
2355	治疗牙痛可点刺何穴出血：A·少商；B·尺泽；C·鱼际；D·风门; E·内庭	What point may be treated by dotted-needling to let blood for toothache? A. · Lu11 / Shǎo Shāng; B. · Lu5 / Chǐ Zé; C. · Lu10 / Yǔ Jì; D. ·B12 / Fēng Mén; E. · S44 / Nèi Tíng
2356	治疗咽喉肿痛实证，主要处方是：A.合谷 颊车 内庭 下关 外关 风池; B·少商 尺泽 合谷 陷谷 关冲; C·合谷 颊车 内庭 下关 太溪 行间; D·太溪 照海 鱼际; E·以上都不是	Which group of points should be selected to treat the excess type of sore throat with swelling? A. Li4 (Hé Gǔ) S6 (Jiá Chē) S44 (Nèi Tíng) S7 (Xià Guān) Sj5 (Wài Guān) G20 (Fēng Chí); B. Lu11 (Shǎo Shāng) Lu5 (Chǐ Zé) Li4 (Hé Gǔ) S43 (Xiàn Gǔ); Sj1 (Guān Chōng); C. Li4 (Hé Gǔ); S6 (Jiá Chē); S44 (Nèi Tíng) S7 (Xià Guān) K3 (Tài Xī) Lv2 (Xíng Jiān); D. K3 (Tài Xī) K6 (Zhào Hǎi) Lu10 (Yǔ Jì); E. none of the above.
2357	治疗眼睑下垂针灸处方应以取( )为主：A·辨证取穴; B·远道穴; C·对侧穴; D·局部穴; E. 以上都是	What points should be selected to treat eyelid dropping by acupuncture and moxibustion? A. ·selecting points according to differential diagnosis; B. ·distal points; C. ·points on the opposite side; D. ·local points; E. none of the above
2358	治疗阳黄的主要处方是: A·胆俞 脾俞 中脘 足三里 至阳; B·胆俞 阳陵泉 阴陵泉 内庭 太冲; C·中脘 足三里 内关 天枢 三阴交; D·命门 气海 公孙 内关 内庭; E·胆俞 阳陵泉 三阴交 足三里 中脘	Which group of points should be selected to treat yang jaundice? A. B19 (Dǎn Shū);) B20 (Pí Shū) R12 (Zhōng Wǎn), S36 (Zú Sān Lǐ) D9 (Zhì Yáng); B. B19 (Dǎn Shū) G34 (Yáng Líng Quán) Sp9 (Yīn Líng Quán) S44 (Nèi Tíng) Lv3 (Tài Chōng); C. R12 (Zhōng Wǎn), S36 (Zú Sān Lǐ), P6 (Nèi Guān); S25 (Tiān Shū) Sp6 (Sān Yīn Jiāo); D. D4 (Mìng Mén) R6 (Qì Hǎi) Sp4 (Gōng Sūn) P6 (Nèi Guān) S44 (Nèi Tíng); E. B19 (Dǎn Shū); G34 (Yáng Líng Quán) Sp6 (Sān Yīn Jiāo) S36 (Zú Sān Lǐ), R12 (Zhōng Wǎn).
2359	治疗阳脱可在基础方上再加：A·复溜; B·太溪; C·风府; D:劳宫; E·气海	What points may be added to the basic prescription of points to treat yang prostration? A. · K7 / Fù Liū; B. · K3 / Tài Xī; C. · D16 / Fēng Fǔ; D. P8 / Láo Gōng; E. · R6 / Qì Hǎi
2360	治疗腰背部的疾病常取：A·至阴; B·会阳; C·肺俞; D·委中; E·天柱	What is the common point to treat diseases of the loins and the back? A. B67 / Zhì Yīn; B. · B35 / Huì Yáng; C. ·B13 / Fèi Shū; D. B40 / Wěi Zhōng; E. ·B10 / Tiān Zhù
2361	治疗腰痛的基本处方为：A·委中、阿是穴、大肠俞、	What is the basic prescription for lumbago? A. B40 / Wěi Zhōng 、Ouchi points / pressure points、B25

	肾俞、腰阳关; B·阳陵泉、肾俞、委中; C·照海、委中、阿是穴; D·秩边、环跳、委中、阿是穴; E. 大椎、环跳、委中、阿是穴	/ Dà Cháng Shū，B23 / Shèn Shū，D3 / Yāo Yáng Guān; B. · G34 / Yáng Líng Quán，B23 / Shèn Shū，B40 / Wěi Zhōng; C. · K6 / Zhào Hǎi，B40 / Wěi Zhōng 、Ouchi points / pressure points; D. B54 / Zhì biān，G30 / Huán Tiào、; B40 / Wěi Zhōng 、Ouchi points / pressure points; E. D14 / Dà Zhuī，G30 / Huán Tiào、; B40 / Wěi Zhōng 、Ouchi points / pressure points
2362	治疗腰痛的主穴不应取：A.足三里; B.肾俞; C.委中; D 腰眼	What point should NOT be used as the primary point to treat lumbago? A. S36 [Zú Sān Lǐ]; B. B23 [Shèn Shū]; C. B40 [Wěi Zhōng]; D YĀO YǍN (waist eyes).
2363	治疗夜盲症的主穴是: A·睛明 太阳 ; B·风池 上星 ; C·攒竹 合谷 ; D·肝俞 少商 ; E·肾俞 肝俞	Which group of points is the major points to treat night blindness? A. B1 (Jīng Míng). Tài Yáng; B. G20 (Fēng Chí) D23 (Shàng Xīng); C. B2 (Zǎn Zhú); Li4 (Hé Gǔ); D..B18 (Gān Shū) Lu11 (Shǎo Shāng); E. B23 (Shèn Shū) B18 (Gān Shū)
2364	治疗癔病的基本处方中"开四关"是指：A·太冲配合谷; B·太冲配期门·; C·太冲配心俞; D··太冲配神门; E·太冲配内关	In the basic prescription of points to treat hysteria, what do “opening four gates” mean? A. · Lv3 / Tài Chōng combined with Li4 / Hé Gǔ; B. · Lv3 / Tài Chōng combined with Lv14 / Qí Mén; C. · Lv3 / Tài Chōng combined with B15 / Xīn Shū; D. Lv3 / Tài Chōng combined with H7 / Shén Mén; E. · Lv3 / Tài Chōng combined with P6 / Nèi Guān.
2365	治疗阴·痒肝经湿热证的加穴是：A·行间、曲骨; B·行间、·地机·; C··太冲、期门; D·太溪、照海··E 归来、·命门	What is the prescription of points to treat the liver meridian damp heat type of yin itch (itch of female genitals)? A. · Lv2 / Xíng Jiān，R2 / Qū Gǔ; B. · Lv2 / Xíng Jiān 、· Sp8 / Dì Jī ·; C. · Lv3 / Tài Chōng，Lv14 / Qí Mén; D. · K3 / Tài Xī，K6 / Zhào Hǎi; ·E. S29 / Guī Lái 、 · D4 / Mìng Mén
2366	治疗阴黄的主要处方是: A·水分 气海 三焦俞 足三里 三阴交 脾俞 肾俞; B·胆俞 阳陵泉 阴陵泉 内庭 太冲; C·水分 气海 三焦俞 足三里 三阴交 肺俞 大杼 合谷; D·至阳 脾俞 胆俞 中脘 足三里 三阴交; E·以上都不是	Which group of points should be selected to treat yin jaundice? A. R9 (Shuǐ Fēn). R6 (Qì Hǎi) B22 (Sān Jiāo Shū) S36 (Zú Sān Lǐ) Sp6 (Sān Yīn Jiāo) B20 (Pí Shū) B23 (Shèn Shū); B. B19 (Dǎn Shū) G34 (Yáng Líng Quán) Sp9 (Yīn Líng Quán) S44 (Nèi Tíng) Lv3 (Tài Chōng); C. R9 (Shuǐ Fēn). R6 (Qì Hǎi) B22 (Sān Jiāo Shū) S36 (Zú Sān Lǐ) Sp6 (Sān Yīn Jiāo)B13 (Fèi Shū)B11 (Dà Zhù) Li4 (Hé Gǔ); D. D9 (Zhì Yáng);B20 (Pí Shū);B19 (Dǎn Shū), R12 (Zhōng Wǎn), S36 (Zú Sān Lǐ), Sp6 (Sān Yīn Jiāo); E. none of the above.
2367	治疗阴脱可在基础方上再加：A·足三里 ·B¨太白; C: 太冲; D·风府; E·太溪	What points may be added to the basic prescription of points to treat yin prostration (prolapse of genitala)? A. · S36 / Zú Sān Lǐ ·B.¨ Sp3 / Tài Bái; C. Lv3 / Tài Chōng; D. · D16 / Fēng Fǔ; E. · K3 / Tài Xī
2368	治疗阴虚火旺之咽喉肿痛宜：A·疏泄肝胆; B 清热化	How to treat the yin deficiency with abundant fire type of swollen and painful throat?

	痰; C 滋阴降火; D 疏风清热; E 清泻热邪	A. to disperse and sedate liver-gallbladder; B. clear heat, transform phlegm; C. · water yin and bring down fire; D. · disperse wind and clear heat; E. · clear and sedate pathogenic heat
2369	治疗阴虚血燥型神经性皮炎，可在基本处方的基础上再加: A·行间; B·太溪; C·脾俞; D·外关; E·委中.	What point may be added to the basic prescription of points to treat the yin deficiency and blood dryness type of neurodermatitis? A. · Lv2 / Xíng Jiān; B. · K3 / Tài Xī C. B20 / Pí Shū; D. · Sj5 / Wài Guān; E. B40 / Wěi Zhōng
2370	治疗阴虚血燥型神经性皮炎，可在基本处方上加: A·脾俞; B·血海; C·行间; D·侠溪; E·委中	What points may be added to the basic prescription of points to treat the yin deficiency and blood dryness type of neurodermatitis? A. B20 / Pí Shū; B. · Sp10 / Xuè Hǎi; C. · Lv2 / Xíng Jiān; D. · G43 / Xiá Xī; E. B40 / Wěi Zhōng
2371	治疗阴虚牙痛，除取主穴外还可加用: A. 风门 太溪; B. 太溪 行间; C. 照海 阳池; D. 风府 肾俞; E 合谷 下关	In addition to major points, which group of points should be selected to treat yin deficiency toothache? A. B12 (Fēng Mén); K3 (Tài Xī); B. K3 (Tài Xī) Lv2 (Xíng Jiān); C. K6 (Zhào Hǎi); Sj4 (Yáng Chí); D. D16 (Fēng Fǔ); B23 (Shèn Shū); E Li4 (Hé Gǔ) S7 (Xià Guān)
2372	治疗阴痒肝肾阴虚证的加穴是: A·行间、曲骨; B·行间、地机; C·太冲、期门; D·太溪、照海 · E 归来、命门	What points may be added to the basic prescription of points to treat the liver kidneys yin deficiency trype of yin itch (itch of female gentitals)? A. · Lv2 / Xíng Jiān，R2 / Qū Gǔ; B. · Lv2 / Xíng Jiān 、 · Sp8 / Dì Jī ·; C. Lv3 / Tài Chōng，Lv14 / Qí Mén; D. · K3 / Tài Xī，K6 / Zhào Hǎi; · ·E. S29 / Guī Lái 、 · D4 / Mìng Mén
2373	治疗饮食停滞引起的腹痛其主要处方是: A·中脘 足三里 内关 期门 阳陵泉; B，中脘 足三里 内关章门 脾俞 胃俞; C·中脘 足三里 章门 气海 脾俞 胃俞; D·中脘 足三里 神阙 内关 公孙; E·中脘 足三里 气海 天枢 里内庭	Which group of points should be selected to treat abdominal pain due to food. stoppage and stagnation? A. R12 (Zhōng Wǎn) S36 (Zú Sān Lǐ) P6 (Nèi Guān) Lv14 (Qí Mén) G34 (Yáng Líng Quán); B. R12 (Zhōng Wǎn); S36 (Zú Sān Lǐ). P6 (Nèi Guān)Lv13 (Zhāng Mén); B20 (Pí Shū)B21 (Wèi Shū); C. R12 (Zhōng Wǎn) S36 (Zú Sān Lǐ) Lv13 (Zhāng Mén) B20 (Pí Shū)B21 (Wèi Shū); D. R12 (Zhōng Wǎn) S36 (Zú Sān Lǐ) R8 (Shén Què) R4 (Guān Yuán) Sp4 (Gōng Sūn); E. R12 (Zhōng Wǎn); S36 (Zú Sān Lǐ) R6 (Qì Hǎi) S25 (Tiān Shū) Lǐ Nèi Tíng.
2374	治疗瘿病气滞痰凝证，可在基本处方的基础上再加: A·太冲、内关; B·尺泽、少商; C·复溜、阴郄; D·扶突、鱼际; E·关元、照海	What points may be added to the basic prescription of points to treat the energy and phlegm congestion type of goiter? A. · Lv3 / Tài Chōng，P6 / Nèi Guān; B. · Lu5 / Chǐ Zé，Lu11 / Shǎo Shāng; C. · K7 / Fù Liū，H6 / Yīn Xī; D. · Li18 / Fú Tū，Lu10 / Yǔ Jì; E. · R4 / Guān Yuán，K6 / Zhào Hǎi
2375	治疗瘿病阴虚火旺证，可在基本处方的基础上再加: A·太冲、内关; B·尺泽、少商; C·太溪、阴郄; D·扶突、鱼际; E·关元、照海	What points may be added to the basic prescription of points to treat the yin deficiency with abundant fire type of goiter? A. · Lv3 / Tài Chōng, P6 / Nèi Guān; B. · Lu5 / Chǐ Zé, Lu11

		/ Shǎo Shāng; C. · K3 / Tài Xī，H6 / Yīn Xī; D. · Li18 / Fú Tū，Lu10 / Yǔ Jì; E. · R4 / Guān Yuán，K6 / Zhào Hǎi
2376	治疗瘀血头痛应选用 A.太阳丰隆; B.脾俞足三里; C.肾俞太溪.D 血海足三里	What points should be selected to treat blood coagulation headache? A. Tài Yáng, S40 (Fēng Lóng); B. B20 (Pí Shū), S36 (Zú Sān Lǐ); C. B23 (Shèn Shū), K3 (Tài Xī); D. Sp10 (Xuè Hǎi), S36 (Zú Sān Lǐ).
2377	治疗瘀血阻络引起的斑秃，可在基本处方的基础上再加：A·太冲 ·B·气海; C·申脉 ·D·风池; E·太溪	What points may be added to the basic prescription of points to treat the blood coagulation obstructing linking meridians type of alopecia areata? A. · Lv3 / Tài Chōng; ·B. · R6 / Qì Hǎi; C. B62 / Shēn Mài; ·D. G20 / Fēng Chí; E. · K3 / Tài Xī
2378	治疗瘀血阻络诱发的斑秃，可在基本处方的基础上再加：A·膈俞 ·B·后溪; C·内庭; D·足临泣; E·大椎	What points may be added to the basic prescription of points to treat the blood coagulation obstructing linking meridians type of alopecia areata? A. ·B17 / Gé Shū; ·B. · Si3 / Hòu Xī; C. · S44 / Nèi Tíng; D. ·G41 / Zú Lín Qì / Lín Qì; E. ·D14 / Dà Zhuī
2379	治疗郁怒后耳鸣、耳聋加重，兼耳胀、耳痛，伴头痛面赤，心烦易怒，大便秘结，舌红，苔黄，脉弦数者治疗宜：A·疏风清热，通利耳窍; B·清泻肝胆，泻火开窍; C·豁痰泻火，通利耳窍; D·补肾填精，上荣耳窍; E·补益脾胃，濡养耳窍	What should be done in treating the following case? Tinnitus、deafness intensified after anger, accompanied by ear swelling, earache, headache with reddish complexion，mental depression prone to anger ，constipation，red tongue ，yellowish coating on the tongue ，wiry and rapid ? A. · to disperse wind and clear heat, connect and smooth out ear cavities; B. ·to clear and sedate liver and gallbladder，sedate fire and open cavities; C. ·expel phlegm and sedate fire，connect and smooth out ear cavities; D. ·tone the kidneys and fill essence，nourish ear cavities in the upper region; E. ·to tone and benefit spleen-stomach，soften up and nourish ear cavities.
2380	治疗月经不调的月经后期应选取 A.关元血海; B 关元三阴交; C.血海三阴交; D 气海三阴交	What group of points should be selected to treat overdue menstruation of irregular menstruation? A. R4 (Guān Yuán); Sp10 (Xuè Hǎi); B. R4 (Guān Yuán); Sp6 (Sān Yīn Jiāo); C. Sp10 (Xuè Hǎi); Sp6 (Sān Yīn Jiāo); D. R6 (Qì Hǎi), Sp6 (Sān Yīn Jiāo)
2381	治疗月经不调气虚证加：A·足三里、脾俞; B·肾俞、太溪; C·太冲、期门; D·行间、地机; E·归来、命门	What additional points may be added to treat irregular menstruation that belongs to energy deficiency syndrome? A. · S36 / Zú Sān Lǐ，B20 / Pí Shū; B. B23 / Shèn Shū，K3 / Tài Xī; C. · Lv3 / Tài Chōng，Lv14 / Qí Mén; D. · Lv2 / Xíng Jiān，Sp8 / Dì Jī; E. · S29 / Guī Lái，D4 / Mìng Mén
2382	治疗月经不调血热证加：A·足三里、脾俞; B·肾俞、太溪; C·太冲、期门; D·行间、地机; E·归来、命门	What additional points may be added to treat irregular menstruation that belongs to blood heat syndrome? A. · S36 / Zú Sān Lǐ，B20 / Pí Shū; B. B23 / Shèn Shū，K3 / Tài Xī; C. · Lv3 / Tài Chōng，Lv14 / Qí Mén; D. · Lv2 / Xíng Jiān，Sp8 / Dì Jī; E. · S29 / Guī Lái，D4 / Mìng Mén

2383	治疗痄腮针刺时应采用什么手法? A 灸法; B 补法; C 泻法; D 补法并灸; E 平补平泻。	What technique should be used in treating mumps by acupuncture? A. moxibustion; B. tonification; C. sedation; D. tonification and moxibustion; E.neutral technique.
2384	治疗痔疮，除取长强会阳次髎外，还可加用: A 大肠俞 上巨虚; B 小肠俞 下巨虚; C 承山 飞扬; D 二白 承山; E 二白 昆仑	Which group of points should be selected to treat hemorrhoids in addition to: D1 (Cháng Qiáng);B35 (Huì Yang);B32 (Cì Liáo)? A. B25 (Dà Cháng Shū) S37 (Shàng Jù Xū); B. B27 (Xiǎo Cháng Shū) S39 (Xià Jù Xū); C. B57 (Chéng Shān) B58 (Feī Yáng); D. Èr Bái;B57 (Chéng Shān); E. Èr Bái; B60 (Kūn Lún)
2385	治疗痔疮不宜选用: A 皮肤针; B 拔罐; C 电针; D 挑治; E 头针	Which is NOT to be applied to treat hemorrohids? A. skin needle; B. cupping; C. electro acupuncture; D. Pricking therapy; E. scalp acupuncture.
2386	治疗痔疮应选用的奇穴是: A, 太阳; B 定喘; C.四神聪; D 二白	Which extraordinary point should be selected to treat hemorrhoids? A.Tài yáng / sun / temple; B. Dìng chuǎn / fix panting / stop panting / panting tranquillizer; C. Sì shén cōng / four spiritual intelligences; D Èr Bái / two whites
2387	治疗滞产，针灸临床上一般选用: A 合谷 太冲 气海; B 合谷 三阴交 关元; C 合谷 至阴 神阙(灸); D 合谷 至阴 三阴交 独阴; E 以上都不是	Which group of points should be selected to treat long labor (over 30 hours)? A. Li4 (Hé Gŭ) Lv3 (Tài Chōng) R6 (Qì Hăi); B. Li4 (Hé Gŭ); Sp6 (Sān Yīn Jiāo); R4 (Guān Yuán); C. Li4 (Hé Gŭ); B67 (Zhì Yīn) R8 (Shén Què) by moxibustion; D. Li4 (Hé Gŭ) B67 (Zhì Yīn) Sp6 (Sān Yīn Jiāo) Dú Yīn; E. none of the above.
2388	治疗滞产时，宜取哪经经穴为主? A. 任脉和督脉; B. 任脉和足太阴经; C. 任脉和手太阳经; D. 手阳明经和足太阳经; E. 手阳明经和足太阴经;	The points on what meridian should be selected as primary points to treat long labor (over 30 hours)? A. ren mai and du mai (concneption meridian and governing meridians; B. ren mai (concneption meridian) and foot greater yin meridian; C..ren mai (concneption meridian) and hand greater yang meridian; D. hand bright yang meridian and foot greater yang meridian; E. hand bright yang meridian and foot greater yin meridian;.
2389	治疗中风半身不遂，其治法应以: A 太阳经穴为主，辅以阳明少阳经穴; B 厥阴经穴为主，辅以三阳经穴; C 少阳经穴为主，辅以阳明太阳经穴; D 阳明经穴为主，辅以太阳少阳经穴; E 少阴经穴为主，辅以阳明少阳经穴	How to treat wind stroke with hemiplegia? A. points on the greater yang meridians as primary points, points on the bright yang and lesser yang meridians as secondary points; B. points on the jue yin meridians as primary points, points on the three yang meridians as secondary points; C. points on the lesser yang meridians as primary points, points on the greater yang meridians as secondary points; D. points on the bright yang meridians as primary points, points on the greater yang and lesser yang meridians as secondary points; E. points on the lesser yin meridians as primary points, points on the bright yang and lesser yang meridians as secondary points.
2390	治疗中风脱证，宜取: A 督脉经穴为主; B 任脉	What points should be selected to treat the prolapsed. type of wind stroke?

	经穴为主; C·足三阴经穴为主; D·手三阴经穴为主; E·手三阳经穴为主	A. points on du mai as primary points; B. points on ren mai as primary points; C. points on three yin meridians of foot as primary points; D. points on three yin meridians of hand as primary points; E points on three yang meridians of hand as primary points.
2391	治疗中暑头晕头痛，可在基础方上再加：A·足三里；B·太白；C·太阳；D·三阴交；E·气海	What points may be added to the basic prescription of points to treat sunstroke with dizziness and headache? A. · S36 / Zú Sān Lǐ; B. · Sp3 / Tài Bái; C. · Tài yáng / sun / temple; D. · Sp6 / Sān Yīn Jiāo; E. · R6 / Qì Hǎi
2392	治疗子宫脱垂初期之脾气虚证，可在基本方基础上再加：A·中极、蠡沟；B·中脘、足三里；C·归来、足三里；D·肾俞、阴陵泉；E·中极、带脉	What points may be added to the basic prescription of points to treat the early stage of hysteroptosis / prolapse of uterus that belongs to spleen energy deficiency syndrome? A. · R3 / Zhōng Jí, Lv5 / Lí Gōu; B. · R12 / Zhōng Wǎn, S36 / Zú Sān Lǐ; C. · S29 / Guī Lái, S36 / Zú Sān Lǐ; D. B23 / Shèn Shū, Sp9 / Yīn Líng Quán; E. · R3 / Zhōng Jí, G26 / Dài Mài
2393	治疗子宫脱垂日久伴湿热下注者，可在基本方基础上再加：A·中极、蠡沟；B·中脘、足三里；C·肾俞、阴陵泉；D·三阴交、维道；E·归来、带脉	What points may be added to the basic prescription of points to treat chronic hysteroptosis / prolapse of uterus, accompanied by damp heat flowing downward? A. · R3 / Zhōng Jí, Lv5 / Lí Gōu; B. · R12 / Zhōng Wǎn, S36 / Zú Sān Lǐ; C. B23 / Shèn Shū, Sp9 / Yīn Líng Quán; D. · Sp6 / Sān Yīn Jiāo, G28 / Wéi Dào; E. · S29 / Guī Lái, G26 / Dài Mài
2394	治疗足跟痛肝肾不足者时可在基本处方的基础上选取穴位：A·肝俞、肾俞；B·厥阴俞、心俞；C·足三里、脾俞；D·太冲、膈俞；E·承山、阳陵泉	What points may be added to the basic prescription of points to treat the liver and kidney deficiency type of painful heels? A. ·B18 / Gān Shū, B23 / Shèn Shū; B. ·B14 / Jué Yīn Shū、B15 / Xīn Shū; C. · S36 / Zú Sān Lǐ, B20 / Pí Shū; D. · Lv3 / Tài Chōng, B17 / Gé Shū; E. B57 / Chéng Shān, G34 / Yáng Líng Quán
2395	治疗足跟痛痛及小腿者，可在基本处方的基础上加：A·太溪、委中；B·脾俞、承山；C·膻中、委中；D·承山、阳陵泉；E·太冲、委中	What points may be added to the basic prescription of points to treat painful heels with pain affecting lower legs? A. · K3 / Tài Xī, B40 / Wěi Zhōng; B. B20 / Pí Shū, B57 / Chéng Shān; C. · R17 / Shān Zhōng, B40 / Wěi Zhōng; D. B57 / Chéng Shān, G34 / Yáng Líng Quán; E. Lv3 / Tài Chōng, B40 / Wěi Zhōng
2396	治疗足跟痛血瘀型时可在基本处方的基础上选取穴位：A·肝俞、肾俞；B·厥阴俞、心俞；C·足三里、脾俞；D·太冲、膈俞；E·承山、阳陵泉	What points may be added to the basic prescription of points to treat the blood coagulation type of painful heels? A. ·B18 / Gān Shū, B23 / Shèn Shū; B. ·B14 / Jué Yīn Shū、B15 / Xīn Shū; C. · S36 / Zú Sān Lǐ, B20 / Pí Shū; D. · Lv3 / Tài Chōng, B17 / Gé Shū; E. B57 / Chéng Shān, G34 / Yáng Líng Quán
2397	治疗足跟痛宜：A·只针不灸；B·只灸不针；C·少针多灸；D·少灸多针；E·针灸并用	How to treat painful heels? A. · acupuncture without moxibustion; B. · moxibustion without acupuncture; C. ·less acupuncture and more moxibustion; D. ·less moxibustion and more acupuncture; E. · both acupuncture

		and moxibustion are applied
2398	治疗足跟痛因气虚者，可在基本处方的基础上加：A·太溪、足三里；B·脾俞，足三里；C·膻中、足三里；D·阳陵泉、膻中；E·太冲、侠溪	What points may be added to the basic prescription of points to treat the energy deficiency type of painful heels? A. · K3 / Tài Xī，S36 / Zú Sān Lǐ; B. B20 / Pí Shū ，S36 / Zú Sān Lǐ; C. · R17 / Shān Zhōng，S36 / Zú Sān Lǐ; D. · G34 / Yáng Líng Quán，R17 / Shān Zhōng; E. · Lv3 / Tài Chōng，G43 / Xiá Xī
2399	治疗足少阳经型坐骨神经痛的穴位 "处方为：A·环跳、风市、膝阳关、阳陵泉、**悬钟**、太溪；B·秩边、承扶，殷门、委中，承山，昆仑；C·秩边、承扶，殷门、委中，阳陵泉；D·环跳、风市，膝阳关、阳陵泉，阳辅、**悬钟**、足临泣；E，环跳、风市，膝阳关、阳陵泉、阳辅、昆仑	What is the prescription of points for sciatica of a foot lesser yang meridian type? A. · G30 / Huán Tiào、 G31 / Fēng Shì，G33 / Yáng Guān / Xī Yáng Guān，G34 / Yáng Líng Quán，G39 / Xuán Zhōng，K3 / Tài Xī; B. B54 / Zhì biān，B36 / Chéng Fú ，B37 / Yīn Mén，B40 / Wěi Zhōng ，B57 / Chéng Shān ，B60 / Kūn Lún; C. B54 / Zhì biān，B36 / Chéng Fú ，B37 / Yīn Mén，B40 / Wěi Zhōng ，G34 / Yáng Líng Quán; D. · G30 / Huán Tiào、 G31 / Fēng Shì ，G33 / Yáng Guān / Xī Yáng Guān，G34 / Yáng Líng Quán ，G38 / Yáng Fǔ，G39 / Xuán Zhōng 、G41 / Zú Lín Qì / Lín Qì; E. G30 / Huán Tiào、 G31 / Fēng Shì ，G33 / Yáng Guān / Xī Yáng Guān，G34 / Yáng Líng Quán，G38 / Yáng Fǔ，B60 / Kūn Lún
2400	治疗足太阳经型坐骨神经痛的穴位处方为：A·环跳、秩边、承扶、殷门、委中、阳陵泉、承山、昆仑；B·秩边、承扶、殷门、委中、足临泣；C·环跳、风市、阳陵泉、悬钟、足临泣；D·秩边、承扶、殷门、委中、丘墟；E·秩边、承扶、殷门、委中、光明	What is the prescription of points for sciatica of a foot greater yang meridian type? A. · G30 / Huán Tiào、B54 / Zhì biān，B36 / Chéng Fú，B37 / Yīn Mén，B40 / Wěi Zhōng，G34 / Yáng Líng Quán，B57 / Chéng Shān，B60 / Kūn Lún; B. B54 / Zhì biān，B36 / Chéng Fú，B37 / Yīn Mén，B40 / Wěi Zhōng 、G41 / Zú Lín Qì / Lín Qì /; C. · G30 / Huán Tiào、 G31 / Fēng Shì，G34 / Yáng Líng Quán，G39 / Xuán Zhōng 、G41 / Zú Lín Qì / Lín Qì /; D. B54 / Zhì biān，B36 / Chéng Fú，B37 / Yīn Mén，B40 / Wěi Zhōng，G40 / Qiū Xū; E. B54 / Zhì biān，B36 / Chéng Fú，B37 / Yīn Mén，B40 / Wěi Zhōng，G37 / Guāng Míng
2401	治疟疾应在发作前：A. 半小时左右针刺之；B. 1 小时左右针刺之；C. 2 小时左右针刺之；D. 3 小时左右针刺之；E. 4 小时左右针刺之。	In treating malaria, how far ahead of its onset should needle insertion begin? A. about half an hour; B. about 1 hour; C. about 2 hours; D. about 3 hours; E. about 4 hours.
2402	痔疮的治法，应以：A·足少阴经穴为主；B·足太阳经穴为主；C·足少阳经穴为主；D·足阳明经穴为主；E，任脉经穴为主	What meridian points should be selected as major points to treat hemorrhoids? A. points on the lesser yin meridian of foot; B. points on the greater yang meridian of foot; C. points on the lesser yang meridian of foot; D. points on the bright yang meridian of foot; E. points on the ren mai (conception meridian).
2403	中风闭证昏迷的主要处方是：A·地仓；B·颊车；C·合谷；	Which is the main prescription of treating the closed type of wind stroke with coma?

	D·足三里; E·丰隆	A. S4 (Dì Cāng); B. S6 (Jiá Chē); C. Li4 (Hé Gŭ); D. S36 (Zú Sān Lǐ); E. S40 (Fēng Lóng).
2404	中风脱证以取哪组配穴为佳? A 关元 足三里; B 人中 内关; C 关元 神阙; D 十二井 人中; E 命门 涌泉。	Which group of points is the best prescription to treat the prolapsed type of wind stroke? A. R4 [Guān Yuán] S36 [Zú Sān Lǐ]; B. Shuǐ Gōu [Rén Zhōng] P6 [Nèi Guān]; C. R4 [Guān Yuán] R8 [Shén Què]; D.十二井 Shuǐ Gōu [Rén Zhōng]; E. D4 [Mìng Mén] K1 [Yǒng Quán]。
2405	中风中经络的针灸基本处方为: A 内关, 极泉、尺泽、委中、三阴交, 足三里; B. 百会, 神阙、关元、足三里, 内关; C. 气海, 关元、丰隆、委中、三阴交; D. 神门, 内关、大陵、三阴交、足三里; E. 神阙、关元、委中、太溪、昆仑	What is the basic prescription of acupuncture-moxibustion to treat wind stroke attacking meridians? A. P6 / Nèi Guān, H1 / Jí Quán, Lu5 / Chǐ Zé, B40 / Wěi Zhōng, Sp6 / Sān Yīn Jiāo, S36 / Zú Sān Lǐ; B. D20 / Bǎi Huì , R8 / Shén Què, R4 / Guān Yuán, S36 / Zú Sān Lǐ , P6 / Nèi Guān; C. R6 / Qì Hǎi , R4 / Guān Yuán, S40 / Fēng Lóng, B40 / Wěi Zhōng, Sp6 / Sān Yīn Jiāo; D. H7 / Shén Mén , P6 / Nèi Guān, P7 / Dà Líng, Sp6 / Sān Yīn Jiāo, S36 / Zú Sān Lǐ; E. R8 / Shén Què, R4 / Guān Yuán, B40 / Wěi Zhōng, K3 / Tài Xī, B60 / Kūn Lún
2406	中极次髎地机三穴同用，多用于治疗: A·月经先期; B·月经后期; C·月经先后无定期; D·痛经实证; E·经闭虚证	Which symptom may be treated by the combination of three points: R3 (Zhōng Jí);B32 (Cì Liáo), Sp8 (Dì Jī)? A. premature menstruation; B. overdue menstruation; C. irregular menstruaiton; D. period pain due to excess; E. suppression of menstruation due to deficiency.
2407	中极关元治泌尿生殖系统疾病效果好的原因是: A.任脉冲脉之会; B. 足三阴任脉之会; C. 阴维任脉之会; D. 足太阴厥阴之会; E. 足少阴厥阴之会。	How do you account for the good results in treating the diseases of the urinary and reproductive systems by R3 (Zhōng Jí) and R4 (Guān Yuán)? A. meetinmg point between ren mai and chong mai; B. meetinmg point betweenfoot three yin meridians and ren mai; C. meetinmg point between yin wei mai and ren mai; D. meetinmg point between foot greater yin and jue yin meridians; E. meetinmg point between foot lesser yin and jue yin meridians。
2408	中暑病人突然面色苍白，汗出气短，四肢厥冷，神志不清，血压下降，气阴两脱，宜急以: A·百会人中以开窍醒脑; B·十宣刺血以开窍苏厥; C·曲泽委中以泻血分之热; D·阳陵泉承山以舒筋止痉; E·灸神阙关元以回阳救逆	What emergency measure should be taken when a sunstroke patient suddenly displays pale complexion, perspiration with short breath, cold four limbs, unclear consciousness, blood pressure going down, prolapse of energy and yin? A. needle D20 (Bǎi Huì) and D26 (Shuǐ Gōu, Rén Zhōng) to open cavities and wake up the brain; B. apply bloodletting at Shí Xuān to open cavities and wake up the patient; C. needle P3 (Qū Zé) and B40 (Wěi Zhōng) to sedate heat on blood level; D. needle G34 (Yáng Líng Quán) and B57 (Chéng Shān) to relax tendons and stop spasms; E. apply moxibusiton at R8 (Shén Què) and R4 (Guān Yuán) to restore yang

		and rescue uprising.
2409	中暑吐泻宜选: A·尺泽 B·孔最 C·列缺 D·太渊 E·鱼际	What point should be selected to treat sunstroke, vomiting, and diarrhea? A. · Lu5 / Chǐ Zé; B. · Lu6 / Kǒng Zuì; C. ·Lu7 / Liè Quē; D. · Lu9 / TàiYuān; E. · Lu10 / Yǔ Jì
2410	中脘内关足三里胃俞阳陵泉太冲诸穴组成处方，可以治疗哪种原因引起的呕吐? A·胃热; B·食积; C·痰饮; D·肝气; E·中虚	Which type of vomiting may be treated by the combination of the following points: R12 (Zhōng Wǎn), P6 (Nèi Guān), S36 (Zú Sān Lǐ);B21 (Wèi Shū), G34 (Yáng Líng Quán), Lv3 (Tài Chōng)? A. hot stomach; B. food accumulation; C. phlegm; D. liver energy; E. middle deficiency.
2411	中脏腑的脱证在治疗时应选用: A·太冲、关元; B·太冲、合谷; C·关元、神阙; D·天突、神阙	What point should be selected to treat viscera and bowels under attack to cause the collapse syndrome / prostration syndrome? A·. Lv3 / Tài Chōng，R4 / Guān Yuán; B. · Lv3 / Tài Chōng，Li4 / Hé Gǔ; C. · R4 / Guān Yuán，R8 / Shén Què; D. R22 / Tiān Tū，R8 / Shén Què
2412	主治舌体病，具有促进发音作用的穴是: A.廉泉; B.承浆; C.天突; D 地仓	What point can treat the disease of the body of the tongue and produce voice? A. R23 (Lián Quán); B. R24 (Chéng Jiàng); C. R22 (Tiān Tū); D. S4 (Dì Cāng).
2413	属督脉穴，针之可疏通项背部经气的是: A·风府; B·承山; C·风池; D·天柱; E·肩外俞·	What point on the du mai / governing meridian can facilitate meridian energy in the back of neck and the back? A. · Fēng Fǔ; B. Chéng Shān; C · Fēng Chí; D ·Tiān Zhù; E · Jiān Wài Shū ·
2414	属手阳明经，治疗肘劳旨在疏通经络气血的穴位是: A·曲池; B·曲泽; C·阿是穴; D·天井; E·支正	In treating elbow fatigue, what point on the hand bright yang / shou yang ming meridian can disperse and connect meridian energy and blood? A.. ·Qū Chí; B. · Qū Zé; C. ·Ouchi points / pressure points; D. · Tiān Jǐng; E. · Zhi Zhèng
2415	属于冬的天干是: A·甲; B·己; C·丙; D·丁; E·壬	What stem belongs to winter? A. ·Jiǎ; B. ·Jǐ; C. ·Bǐng; D. ·Dīng; E. ·Rén
2416	属于土的天干是: A·甲; B·己; C·丙; D·丁; E·壬	What stem belongs to earth? A. ·Jiǎ; B. ·Jǐ; C. ·Bǐng; D. ·Dīng; E. ·Rén
2417	属于针灸治疗视神经萎缩的基本处方的穴位是: A·行间，侠溪; B·肾俞、太溪; C·合谷、膈俞; D·风池、太冲; E·肝俞、合谷	What points belong to the basic prescription of points to treat optic atrophy? A. · Lv2 / Xíng Jiān ，G43 / Xiá Xī; B. B23 / Shèn Shū，K3 / Tài Xī; C. · Li4 / Hé Gǔ，B17 / Gé Shū; D. · G20 / Fēng Chí，Lv3 / Tài Chōng; E. ·B18 / Gān Shū，Li4 / Hé Gǔ
2418	子宫肌瘤全切术针麻应选用: A·足三里、中都; B·足三里、维道; C·足三里、上巨虚、D·足三里、带脉; E.足三里、合谷	What points should be selected to perform hysteromyomectomy by acupuncture anaesthesia? A. · S36 / Zú Sān Lǐ，Lv6 / Zhōng Dū; B. · S36 / Zú Sān Lǐ，G28 / Wéi Dào; C. · S36 / Zú Sān Lǐ，S37 / Shàng Jù Xū 、D. · S36 / Zú Sān Lǐ，G26 / Dài Mài; E. S36 / Zú Sān Lǐ，Li4 / Hé Gǔ
2419	足三阴经之交会穴，可养血活血、润燥止痒是: A·足三里; B·三阴交; C·肺俞;	What point is a meeting point of three yin meridians of foot, which can nourish blood and activate blood, lubricate dryness and stop itch?

	D·列缺; E肾俞	lubricate dryness and stop itch? A. · S36 / Zú Sān Lǐ; B. · Sp6 / Sān Yīn Jiāo; C. ·B13 / Fèi Shū; D. ·Lu7 / Liè Quē; E. B23 / Shèn Shū
2420	足太阴脾经的络穴是: A·通里; B·丰隆; C·公孙; D·脾俞; E·都不是	What is the linking point / luo point on the foot greater yin spleen meridian? A. H5 / Tōng Lǐ; B. S40 / Fēng Lóng; C. · Sp4 / Gōng Sūn; D. B20 / Pí Shū; E. · none of the above
2421	足阳明经的郄穴是: A·阳交; B·跗阳; C·飞扬; D·阳辅; E·梁丘	What is the fissural point / cleft point / xi point on the bright yang meridian of foot? A. · G35 / Yáng Jiāo; B. B59 / Fū Yáng; C. B58 / Feī Yáng; D. · G38 / Yáng Fǔ; E. · S34 / Liáng Qiū
2422	最能体现 "寒则 (温之)留之"治疗原则的是: A·埋针法; B·艾炷灸; C·拔罐; D·温针灸; E·火针法	Which of the following can best describe the treatment principle, "A cold disease should be treated by letting the needle stay in for a longer period of time for warming"? A. ·needle embedding therapy; B. · mugwort cone moxibustion; C. Cupping; D. ·warm acupuncture and moxibustion; E · method of inserting a fire needle
2423	在华陀夹脊穴中，治疗胸部疾患的是: A·胸1-7夹脊; B·胸1-8夹脊; C·胸1-9夹脊; D·胸1-10夹脊; E·胸1-12夹脊	Amopng Huá Tuó Jiā Jí [Dr Huatuo's clippings of spines], what cn treat disorders of the chest region? A. ·clipping of chest 1-7 spines; B. ·clipping of chest 1-8 spines; C. ·clipping of chest 1-9 spines; D. ·clipping ofcchest 1-10 spines; E. ·clipping of chest 1-12 spines
2424	用发泡法治疗疟疾，可用鲜毛茛或独蒜头适量捣烂为泥，在发作前1-2小时外敷于: A·大椎或身柱; B·陶道或合谷; C·后溪或阳池; D·鱼际或少商; E·内关或间使	Malaria may be treated by vesiculation with mashed herba et radix ranunculus and garlic in the mud form to apply to an acupuncture point 1-2 hour before onset; what point may be used? A. D14 (Dà Zhuī) or D12 (Shēn Zhù); B. D13 (Táo Dào) or Li4 (Hé Gǔ); C. Si3 (Hòu Xī) or Sj4 (Yáng Chí); D. Lu10 (Yǔ Jì) or Lu11 (Shǎo Shāng); E. P6 (Nèi Guān) or P5 (Jiān Shǐ).
2425	在华陀夹脊穴中，治疗上肢疾患的是: A·胸1-2夹脊; B·胸1-3夹脊; C·胸1-4夹脊; D·胸1-5夹脊; E·胸1-7夹脊	Amopng Huá Tuó Jiā Jí [Dr Huatuo's clippings of spines], what cn treat disorders of the upper limbs region? A. ·clipping of chest 1-2 spines; B. ·clipping of chest 1-3 spines; C. ·clipping of chest 1-4 spines; D. ·clipping of chest 1-5 spines; E. ·clipping of chest 1-7 spines
2426	在华陀夹脊穴中，治疗腹部疾患的是: A·胸1-12夹脊; B·胸1-腰4夹脊; C·胸6-12夹脊; D·胸12-腰4夹脊; E·胸6-腰4夹脊	Amopng Huá Tuó Jiā Jí [Dr Huatuo's clippings of spines], what cn treat disorders of the abdomen region? A. ·clipping of chest 1-12 spines; B. ·clipping of chest 1-lumbar 4 spines; C. ·clipping of chest 6-12 spines; D. ·chest 12- lumbar 4 spines; E. ·clipping of chest 6-lumbar 4 spines
2427	曲池可以治疗高血壓，是根据什么选穴原则？ A. 按經驗取穴; B. 辨证选穴; C. 远部取穴; D. 本经取穴法; E. 异经取穴法	What principle of selecting points is used when Li11 Qū Chí is used to treat hypertension? A. Principle of selecting experience points for treatment; B. Principles of selecting points according to syndrome; C. Principles of selecting distal points; D. Methods of pairing off points on affected meridians; E. Principles of selecting points on mother and child meridians.

2428	腰痛选委中是根据什么选穴原则？ A. 远部取穴; B. 按腧穴命名取穴; C. 上下配穴法; D. 表里经配穴法; E. 子母经配穴法	What principle of selecting points is used in selecting B40 weizhong to treat lumbago? A. Principles of selecting distal treatment points; B. Principles of selecting points according to their Chinese name; D. Methods of pairing off points on meridians forming a deep-superficial relationship; E. Methods of pairing off points on the meridians with child-mother relationship.
2429	虚劳咳嗽症伴有阴虚火旺者配以太溪、复溜、照海、涌泉，以滋阴降火、补水润肺，是根据什么选穴原则？ A. 原络配穴法; B.子母经配穴法; C. 同名经配穴法; D. 子母补泻法; E 表里经配穴法	What principle of selecting points is used when the syndrome of deficiency fatigue cough with yin deficiency and abundant fire is treated by K3, Tài Xī, K7, Fù Liū, K6, Zhào Hǎi, and K1, Yǒng Quán, to water yin and bring down fire? A. Methods of pairing off Yuán Xué and Luò Xué; B. Methods of pairing off points on the meridians with child-mother relationship; C. Methods of pairing off points on the meridians with identical yin-yang classification; D. Principles of selecting child and mother points for tonification and sedation; E. Methods of pairing off points on meridians forming a deep-superficial relationship.
2430	安眠可以治疗失眠是根据什么选穴原则？ A. 局部取穴; B. 按經驗取穴; C. 远部取穴; D. 本经取穴法; E. 异经取穴法	What principle of selecting points is used when Ān mián / good sleep is used to treat insomnia? A. Principles of selecting local points; B. Principle of selecting experience points for treatment; C. Principles of selecting distal points; D. Methods of pairing off points on affected meridians; E. Principles of selecting points on mother and child meridians.
2431	頸病选列缺是根据什么选穴原则？ A. 局部取穴; B. 按腧穴命名取穴; C. 上下配穴法; D. 表里经配穴法; E. 远部取穴	What principle of selecting points is used in selecting Lu7 / lieque to treat neck disorders? A. Principles of selecting local points; B. Principles of selecting points according to their Chinese name; D. Methods of pairing off points on meridians forming a deep-superficial relationship; E. Principles of selecting distal treatment points.
2432	肺经虛选太淵.,是根据什么选穴原则？ A. 子母经配穴法 B. 原络配穴法 C. 同名经配穴法 D. 子母补泻法 E 表里经配穴法	What principle of selecting points is used when lung meridian deficiency is treated by Taiyuan=Lu9? A. Methods of pairing off points on the meridians with child-mother relationship B. Methods of pairing off Yuán Xué and Luò Xué; C. Methods of pairing off points on the meridians with identical yin-yang classification; D. Principles of selecting child and mother points for tonification and sedation; E. Methods of pairing off points on meridians forming a deep-superficial relationship.
2433	至阴可以矫正胎位是根据什么选穴原则？ A. 局部取穴; B. 辨证选穴; C. 按經驗取穴; D. 本经取穴法; E. 异经取穴法	What principle of selecting points is used when B67 Zhì Yīn is used to correct improper position of the fetus? A. Principles of selecting local points; B. Principles of selecting points according to syndrome; C. Principle of selecting experience points for treatment; D. Methods of pairing off points on affected meridians; E. Principles of selecting points on mother and child meridians.
2434	牙痛选合谷是根据什么选穴原则？ A. 局部取穴; B. 远部取穴; C. 上下配穴法; D. 表里经配穴法; E. 子母经配穴法	What principle of selecting points is used in selecting Li4 / hegu for toothache? A. Principles of selecting local points; B. Principles of selecting distal treatment points; D. Methods of pairing off points on meridians forming a deep-superficial relationship; E. Methods of pairing off points on the meridians with child-mother relationship.
2435	肺经实选尺澤,是根据什么选穴原则？ A. 子母经配穴法 B. 原络配穴法 C. 同名经配穴法 D. 子母补泻法 E 表里经配穴法	What principle of selecting points is used when Chize=Lu5 is used to treat lung meridian excess? A. Methods of pairing off points on the meridians with child-mother relationship; B. Methods of pairing off Yuán Xué and Luò Xué; C. Methods of pairing off points on the meridians with identical yin-yang classification; D. Principles of selecting child and mother points for tonification and sedation; E. Methods of pairing off points on meridians forming a deep-superficial relationship.

2436	至阴可以催产下胎是根据什么选穴原则？ A. 局部取穴; B. 辨证选穴; C. 远部取穴; D. 按經驗取穴; E. 异经取穴法	What principle of selecting points is used when both B67 / Zhì Yīn and Dú Yīn are used to hasten parturition? A. Principles of selecting local points; B. Principles of selecting points according to syndrome; C. Principles of selecting distal points; D. Principle of selecting experience points for treatment; E. Principles of selecting points on mother and child meridians.
2437	项强选后溪是根据什么选穴原则？ A. 局部取穴; B. 按腧穴命名取穴; C. 上下配穴法; D. 表里经配穴法; E. 远部取穴	What principle of selecting points is used in selecting Si3 / houxi for stiffness of neck? A. Principles of selecting local points; B. Principles of selecting points according to their Chinese name; D. Methods of pairing off points on meridians forming a deep-superficial relationship; E. Principles of selecting distal treatment points.
2438	肝经虛选曲泉,是根据什么选穴原则？ A. 表里经配穴法 B. 原络配穴法 C. 同名经配穴法 D. 子母补泻法 E 子母经配穴法	What principle of selecting points is used when liver meridian deficiencty is treated by Ququan= Lv8 ? A. Methods of pairing off points on meridians forming a deep-superficial relationship;B. Methods of pairing off Yuán Xué and Luò Xué; C. Methods of pairing off points on the meridians with identical yin-yang classification; D. Principles of selecting child and mother points for tonification and sedation; E Methods of pairing off points on the meridians with child-mother relationship.
2439	身柱、灵台可以治疗疔疮是根据什么选穴原则？A. 局部取穴; B. 辨证选穴; C. 远部取穴; D. 本经取穴法; E. 按經驗取穴	What principle of selecting points is used when D12 Shēn Zhù and D10, Líng Tái are used to acute furuncle (pustule of the forefinger tip)? A. Principles of selecting local points; B. Principles of selecting points according to syndrome; C. Principles of selecting distal points; D. Methods of pairing off points on affected meridians; E. Principle of selecting experience points for treatment.
2440	腰痛选是根据什么选穴原则？ A. 局部取穴; B. 按腧穴命名取穴; C. 上下配穴法; D. 表里经配穴法; E. 远部取穴	What principle of selecting points is used in selecting B40 / Weizhong for lumbago? A. Principles of selecting local points; B. Principles of selecting points according to their Chinese name; D. Methods of pairing off points on meridians forming a deep-superficial relationship; E. Principles of selecting distal treatment points.
2441	肝经实选行間,是根据什么选穴原则？ A. 表里经配穴法 B. 原络配穴法 C. 同名经配穴法 D. 子母补泻法 E 子母经配穴法	What principle of selecting points is used when Liver meridian excess is treated by Xingjian= Lv2? A. Methods of pairing off points on meridians forming a deep-superficial relationship; B. Methods of pairing off Yuán Xué and Luò Xué; C. Methods of pairing off points on the meridians with identical yin-yang classification; D. Principles of selecting child and mother points for tonification and sedation; E Methods of pairing off points on the meridians with child-mother relationship.
2442	哑门、关冲可以治疗音瘖是根据什么选穴原则？,A. 按經驗取穴; B. 辨证选穴; C. 远部取穴; D. 本经取穴法; E. 异经取穴法	What principle of selecting points is used when D15 [Yă Mén], Sj1 Guān Chōng are used to treat hoarseness? A. Principle of selecting experience points for treatment; C. Principles of selecting distal points; D. Methods of pairing off points on affected meridians; E. Principles of selecting points on mother and child meridians.
2443	偏头痛选外關陽輔是根据什么选穴原则？ A. 远部取穴; B. 按腧穴命名取穴; C. 上下配穴法; D. 表里经配穴法; E. 子母经配穴法	What principle of selecting points is used in selecting Sj5 / Waiguan and G38 / Yangfu for migraine headache? A. Principles of selecting distal treatment points; B. Principles of selecting points according to their Chinese name; D. Methods of pairing off points on meridians forming a deep-superficial relationship; E. Methods of pairing off points on the meridians with child-mother relationship.
2444	偏正头痛可取头维、阳白、率谷、解溪、足临泣, 是根据什么选穴原则？	What principle of selecting points is used in treating headache in the forehead and migraine headache, by S8 / Tóu Wěi, G14 / Yáng Bái, G8 / Shuài Gŭ, S41 / Jiě Xī, G41 / Zú Lín Qì?

	A. 子母经配穴法 B. 原络配穴法 C. 同名经配穴法 D. 子母补泻法 E 表里经配穴法	A. Method of pairing off points on the meridians meeting with each other; B. Methods of pairing off Yuán Xué and Luò Xué; C. Methods of pairing off points on the meridians with identical yin-yang classification; D. Principles of selecting child and mother points for tonification and sedation; E. Methods of pairing off points on meridians forming a deep-superficial relationship.
2445	至阳可以治疗黄疸是根据什么选穴原则？A. 局部取穴; B 按經驗取穴; C. 远部取穴; D. 本经取穴法; E. 异经取穴法	What principle of selecting points is used when D9 Zhì Yáng is used to treat jaundice? A. Principles of selecting local points; B. Principle of selecting experience points for treatment; C. Principles of selecting distal points; D. Methods of pairing off points on affected meridians; E. Principles of selecting points on mother and child meridians.
2446	咳嗽选列缺是根据什么选穴原则？ A. 局部取穴; B. 远部取穴; C. 上下配穴法; D. 表里经配穴法; E. 子母经配穴法	What principle of selecting points is used in selecting lieque=Lu7 for cough? A. Principles of selecting local points; B. Principles of selecting distal treatment points; D. Methods of pairing off points on meridians forming a deep-superficial relationship; E. Methods of pairing off points on the meridians with child-mother relationship.
2447	髀枢部疼痛可取环跳配秩边、承扶、阳陵泉、承山; 是根据什么选穴原则？ A. 子母经配穴法 B. 原络配穴法 C. 同名经配穴法 D. 子母补泻法 E 表里经配穴法	What principle of selecting points is used in treating pain in the greater trochanter by G30 / Huán Tiào in combination with B54 / Zhì Biān, G34 / Yáng Líng Quán, and B57 / Chéng Shān? A. Methods of pairing off points on the meridians with child-mother relationship; B. Method of pairing off points on the meridians meeting with each other; C. Methods of pairing off points on the meridians with identical yin-yang classification; D. Principles of selecting child and mother points for tonification and sedation; E. Methods of pairing off points on meridians forming a deep-superficial relationship.
2448	定喘可以治疗哮喘是根据什么选穴原则？A. 局部取穴; B. 辨证选穴; C. 按經驗取穴; D. 本经取穴法; E. 异经取穴法	What principle of selecting points is used when Dìng chuǎn / fix panting is used to treat asthma with sputum noise in the throat? A. Principles of selecting local points; B. Principles of selecting points according to syndrome; C. Principle of selecting experience points for treatment; D. Methods of pairing off points on affected meridians; E. Principles of selecting points on mother and child meridians.
2449	头顶痛选太冲是根据什么选穴原则？ A. 局部取穴; B. 远部取穴; C. 上下配穴法; D. 表里经配穴法; E. 子母经配穴法	What principle of selecting points is used in selecting Taichong= Lv3 for headache in vertex. ? A. Principles of selecting local points; B. Principles of selecting distal treatment points; D. Methods of pairing off points on meridians forming a deep-superficial relationship; E. Methods of pairing off points on the meridians with child-mother relationship.
2450	泌尿、生殖系疾患和妇科病，取气海、关元、中极配太冲、太溪、三阴交治之,是根据什么选穴原则？ A. 子母经配穴法 B. 原络配穴法 C. 同名经配穴法 D. 子母补泻法 E 表里经配穴法	What principle of selecting points is used in treating the diseases of the reproductive system and diseases of women by R6 / Qì Hǎi, R4 / Guān Yuán, R3 / Zhōng Jí, in combination with Lv3 / Tài Chōng, K3 / Tài Xī, and Sp6 / Sān Yīn Jiāo? A. Methods of pairing off points on the meridians with child-mother relationship; B. Methods of pairing off Yuán Xué and Luò Xué; C. Methods of pairing off points on the meridians with identical yin-yang classification; D. Principles of selecting child and mother points for tonification and sedation; E. Methods of pairing off points on meridians forming a deep-superficial relationship.
2451	二白可以治疗治痔瘡，痔漏下血是根据什么选穴原则？ A. 局部取穴; B. 辨证选穴; C. 远部取穴; D. 按經驗取穴; E. 异经取穴法	What principle of selecting points is used when Èr bái / two whites is used to treat hemorrhoids, bleeding in hemorrhoids? A. Principles of selecting local points; B. Principles of selecting points according to syndrome; C. Principles of selecting distal points; D. Principle of selecting experience points for treatment; E. Principles of selecting points on mother and child meridians.
2452	胃病选左右足三里是根据什么选穴原则？ A. 双面对称取穴法 B. 按经配穴法	What principle of selecting points is used in selecting Zusanli S36, on both sides to treat stomach disease? A. Methods of selecting identical points on both sides in pairs to treat diseases; B. Methods of pairing off points according to meridian theory; C. Principles of selecting points on the affected meridians; D. Principle

	C. 本经取穴法 D. 按經驗取穴 E 辨证选穴	C. Principles of selecting points on the affected meridians; D. Principle of selecting experience points for treatment; E. Principles of selecting points according to syndrome.
2453	"井主心下满"是根据什么选穴原则？ A. 按五输主病对证选用 B.君臣佐使取穴法 C. 同名经配穴法 D. 子母补泻法 E 表里经配穴法	What principle of selecting points is used in treating viscera disease and fullness below the heart by well points / jing xue? A. Principles of selecting five command points according to their therapeutic effects; B. Methods of selecting king points, subject points, assistant points, and servant points combined to treat diseases; C. Methods of pairing off points on the meridians with identical yin-yang classification; D. Principles of selecting child and mother points for tonification and sedation; E. Methods of pairing off points on meridians forming a deep-superficial relationship.
2454	肩井可以治疗乳痈是根据什么选穴原则？A. 局部取穴; B. 辨证选穴; C. 远部取穴; D. 本经取穴法; E. 按經驗取穴	What principle of selecting points is used when G21 Jiān Jǐng is used to treat carbuncle in the breast? A. Principles of selecting local points; B. Principles of selecting points according to syndrome; C. Principles of selecting distal points; D. Methods of pairing off points on affected meridians; E. Principle of selecting experience points for treatment.
2455	女性疾患选左右三陰交是根据什么选穴原则？ A. 反面取穴法 B. 双面对称取穴法 C. 本经取穴法 D. 按經驗取穴 E 辨证选穴	What principle of selecting points is used in selecting Sanyinjiao Sp6 on both sides to treat diseases of women? A. Methods of selecting points on the opposite side of disease for treatment; B. Methods of selecting identical points on both sides in pairs to treat diseases; C. Principles of selecting points on the affected meridians; D. Principle of selecting experience points for treatment; E. Principles of selecting points according to syndrome.
2456	"荥主身热"是根据什么选穴原则？ A. 子母经配穴法 B.君臣佐使取穴法 C. 按五输主病对证选用 D. 子母补泻法 E 表里经配穴法	What principle of selecting points is used in treating hot sensations in th body by spring points / ying points? A. Methods of pairing off points on the meridians with child-mother relationship; B. Methods of selecting king points, , subject points, assistant points, and servant points combined to treat diseases; C. Methods of pairing off points on the meridians with identical yin-yang classification; D. Principles of selecting child and mother points for tonification and sedation; E. Methods of pairing off points on meridians forming a deep-superficial relationship.
2457	胆囊穴可以治疗胆系疾病是根据什么选穴原则？A. 按經驗取穴; B. 辨证选穴; C. 远部取穴; D. 本经取穴法; E. 异经取穴法	What principle of selecting points is used when gallbladder point / Dǎn Náng Xué is used to treat diseases in the system of gallbladder? A. Principle of selecting experience points for treatment; B. Principles of selecting points according to syndrome; C. Principles of selecting distal points; D. Methods of pairing off points on affected meridians; E. Principles of selecting points on mother and child meridians.
2458	前额头痛选左右頭維是根据什么选穴原则？ A. 反面取穴法 B. 按经配穴法 C. 双面对称取穴法 D. 按經驗取穴 E 辨证选穴	What principle of selecting points is used in selecting Touwei S8 on both sides may be used to treat headache involving the forehead? A. Methods of selecting points on the opposite side of disease for treatment; B. Methods of pairing off points according to meridian theory; C. Methods of selecting identical points on both sides in pairs to treat diseases; D. Principle of selecting experience points for treatment; E. Principles of selecting points according to syndrome.
2459	"病变于音者，取之经" 是根据什么选穴原则？ A. 子母经配穴法 B.君臣佐使取穴法 C. 同名经配穴法 D. 按五输主病对证选用 E 表里经配穴法	What principle of selecting points is used in treating voice disorders by river points / jing points? A. Methods of pairing off points on the meridians with child-mother relationship; B. Methods of selecting king points, , subject points, assistant points, and servant points combined to treat diseases; C. Methods of pairing off points on the meridians with identical yin-yang classification; D. Principles of selecting five command points according to their therapeutic effects; E. Methods of pairing off points on

		meridians forming a deep-superficial relationship.
2460	阑尾穴可以治疗肠痈是根据什么选穴原则？A. 局部取穴; B. 按經驗取穴; C. 远部取穴; D. 本经取穴法; E. 异经取穴法	What principle of selecting points is used when Lán Wěi is used to treat appendicitis? A. Principles of selecting local points; B. Principle of selecting experience points for treatment; C. Principles of selecting distal points; D. Methods of pairing off points on affected meridians; E. Principles of selecting points on mother and child meridians.
2461	咽喉疾患选左右少商是根据什么选穴原则？ A. 反面取穴法 B. 按经配穴法 C. 本经取穴法 D. 双面对称取穴法 E 辨证选穴	What principle of selecting points is used in selecting Shaoshang Lu11 on both sides to treat diseases of the throat? A. Methods of selecting points on the opposite side of disease for treatment; B. Methods of pairing off points according to meridian theory; C. Principles of selecting points on the affected meridians; D. Methods of selecting identical points on both sides in pairs to treat diseases; E. Principles of selecting points according to syndrome.
2462	"饮食不节得病者，取之于合" 是根据什么选穴原则？ A. 子母经配穴法 B.君臣佐使取穴法 C. 同名经配穴法 D. 子母补泻法 E 按五输主病对证选用	What principle of selecting points is used in treating diseases due to irregular eating by sea point / he points? A. Methods of pairing off points on the meridians with child-mother relationship; B. Methods of selecting king points, subject points, assistant points, and servant points combined to treat diseases; C. Methods of pairing off points on the meridians with identical yin-yang classification; D. Principles of selecting child and mother points for tonification and sedation; E. Principles of selecting five command points according to their therapeutic effects
2463	落枕穴可以治疗落枕是根据什么选穴原则？A. 局部取穴; B. 辨证选穴; C.按經驗取穴; D. 本经取穴法; E. 异经取穴法	What principle of selecting points is used when Luò Zhěn is used to treat neck pain with stiffness? A. Principles of selecting local points; B. Principles of selecting points according to syndrome; C. Principle of selecting experience points for treatment; D. Methods of pairing off points on affected meridians; E. Principles of selecting points on mother and child meridians.
2464	口眼歪斜选合谷内庭是根据什么选穴原则？ A. 上下配穴法 B. 前后配穴法 C. 本经取穴法 D. 按經驗取穴 E 辨证选穴	What principle of selecting points is used in selecting Hegu=Li4 and Neiting=S44 for the treatment of wry mouth and wry eyes ? A. Methods of selecting points on the opposite side of disease for treatment; B. Methods of pairing off anterior and posterior points; C. Principles of selecting points on the affected meridians; D. Principle of selecting experience points for treatment; E. Principles of selecting points according to syndrome.
2465	"合治内腑"是根据什么选穴原则？ A. 按五输主病对证选用 B.君臣佐使取穴法 C. 同名经配穴法 D. 子母补泻法 E 表里经配穴法	What principle of selecting points is used in treating the diseases of the internal bowels by the sea points / he points? A. Methods of pairing off points on the meridians with child-mother relationship; B. Methods of selecting king points, subject points, assistant points, and servant points combined to treat diseases; C. Methods of pairing off points on the meridians with identical yin-yang classification; D. Principles of selecting child and mother points for tonification and sedation; E. Methods of pairing off points on meridians forming a deep-superficial relationship.
2466	百劳可以治疗瘰癧是根据什么选穴原则？A. 局部取穴; B. 辨证选穴; C. 远部取穴; D. 按經驗取穴; E. 异经取穴法	What principle of selecting points is used when Bǎi Láo / hundred fatigue is used to treat scrofula? A. Principles of selecting local points; B. Principles of selecting points according to syndrome; C. Principles of selecting distal points; D. Principle of selecting experience points for treatment s; E. Principles of selecting points on mother and child meridians.
2467	眼疾选養老光明是根据什么选穴原则？ A. 上下配穴法 B. 前后配穴法	What principle of selecting points is used in selecting Yanglao=Si6 with Guangming=G37 for the treatment of eye diseases? A. Methods of pairing off upper and lower points; B. Methods of pairing off anterior and posterior points; C. Principles of selecting points on the affected meridians

	C. 本经取穴法 D. 按經驗取穴 E 辨证选穴	D. Principle of selecting experience points for treatment; E. Principles of selecting points according to syndrome.
2468	感冒以合谷配列缺,是根据什么选穴原则？ A. **原络**配穴法 B.俞募配穴法. C. 同名经配穴法 D. 郄会配穴法 E 表里经配穴法	What principle of selecting points is used when Li4 / Hé Gŭ and Lu7 / Liè Quē are combined to treat the common cold? A. Method of pairing off original points (Yuán Xué) and linking points, (Luò Xué); B. Methods of pairing off Bèi Shù Xué and Mù Xué; C. Methods of pairing off Xī Xué and Bā Huì Xué; E. Methods of pairing off points on meridians forming a deep-superficial relationship.
2469	十七椎下可以治疗痛经是根据什么选穴原则？A. 局部取穴; B. 辨证选穴; C. 远部取穴; D. 本经取穴法; E 按經驗取穴	What principle of selecting points is used when Shí Qī Zhuī Xià is used to treat period pain? A. Principles of selecting local points; B. Principles of selecting points according to syndrome; C. Principles of selecting distal points; D. Methods of pairing off points on affected meridians; E. Principle of selecting experience points for treatment.
2470	高热选合谷陷谷是根据什么选穴原则？ A. 反面取穴法 B. 上下配穴法 C. 本经取穴法 D. 按經驗取穴 E 辨证选穴	What principle of selecting points is used in selecting Hegu=Li4 with Xiangu=S43 for the treatment of high fever? A. Methods of selecting points on the opposite side of disease for treatment; B. Methods of pairing off upper and lower points; C. Principles of selecting points on the affected meridians; D. Principle of selecting experience points for treatment; E. Principles of selecting points according to syndrome.
2471	斜视以太冲配光明，是根据什么选穴原则？ A. 子母经配穴法 B.俞募配穴法. C. 同名经配穴法 D. 郄会配穴法 E**原络**配穴法	What principle of selecting points is used in treating strabismus by Lv3 / Tài Chōng and G37 / Guāng Míng? A. Methods of pairing off points on the meridians with child-mother relationship; B. Methods of pairing off Bèi Shù Xué and Mù Xué C. Methods of pairing off points on the meridians with identical yin-yang classification; D. Methods of pairing off Xī Xué and Bā Huì Xué; E. Method of pairing off original points (Yuán Xué) and linking points (Luò Xué).
2472	四缝可以治疗疳积是根据什么选穴原则？ A. 按經驗取穴; B. 辨证选穴; C. 远部取穴; D. 本经取穴法; E. 异经取穴法	What principle of selecting points is used when Sì Féng is used to treat malnutrition in children? A. Principle of selecting experience points for treatment; B. Principles of selecting points according to syndrome; C. Principles of selecting distal points; D. Methods of pairing off points on affected meridians; E. Principles of selecting points on mother and child meridians.
2473	胃痛选足三里太冲三陰交是根据什么选穴原则？ A. 反面取穴法 B. 前后配穴法 C. 上下配穴法 D. 按經驗取穴 E 辨证选穴	What principle of selecting points is used in selecting Zusanli=S36, Taichong= Lv3, and Sanyinjiao= Sp6 to treat stomachache? A. Methods of selecting points on the opposite side of disease for treatment; B. Methods of pairing off anterior and posterior points; C. Methods of pairing off upper and lower points; D. Principle of selecting experience points for treatment; E. Principles of selecting points according to syndrome.
2474	肺经疾病以太淵配偏歷，是根据什么选穴原则？ A. **原络**配穴法 B.俞募配穴法. C. 同名经配穴法 D. 郄会配穴法 E 表里经配穴法	What principle of selecting points is used in treating lung meridian disease by Lu9, Tài Yuān in combination with Li6, Piān Lì? A. Method of pairing off original points (Yuán Xué) and linking points, (Luò Xué); B. Methods of pairing off Bèi Shù Xué and Mù Xué; C. Methods of pairing off points on the meridians with identical yin-yang classification; D. Methods of pairing off Xī Xué and Bā Huì Xué; E. Methods of pairing off points on meridians forming a deep-superficial relationship.

2475	天宗配少泽可以治疗乳痈的经验穴，是根据什么选穴原则？A. 局部取穴; B 按經驗取穴; C. 远部取穴; D. 本经取穴法; E. 异经取穴法	What principle of selecting points is used when Si11 Tiān Zōng and Si1 Shào Zé are combined to treat carbuncle in the breast (acute mastitis)? A. Principles of selecting local points; B. Principle of selecting experience points for treatment; C. Principles of selecting distal points; D. Methods of pairing off points on affected meridians; E. Principles of selecting points on mother and child meridians.
2476	耳鸣耳聋选內關足三里是根据什么选穴原则？ A. 反面取穴法 B. 前后配穴法 C. 本经取穴法 D. 上下配穴法 E 辨证选穴	What principle of selecting points is used in selecting Neiguan=P6 with Zusanli=S36 to treat ringing in ears and deafness? A. Methods of selecting points on the opposite side of disease for treatment; B. Methods of pairing off anterior and posterior points; C. Principles of selecting points on the affected meridians; D. Methods of pairing off upper and lower points; E. Principles of selecting points according to syndrome.
2477	胃病以胃俞配中脘,是根据什么选穴原则？ A. 原络配穴法 B. 表里经配穴法 C. 同名经配穴法 D. 郄会配穴法 E 俞募配穴法	What principle of selecting points is used when B21 weishu and R12 zhongwan are combined to treat stomach disease? A. Method of pairing off original points (Yuán Xué) and linking points (Luò Xué); B. Methods of pairing off points on meridians forming a deep-superficial relationship; C. Methods of pairing off points on the meridians with identical yin-yang classification; D. Methods of pairing off Xī Xué and Bā Huì Xué; E. Methods of pairing off Bèi Shù Xué and Mù Xué.
2478	少泽可以生乳、下乳是根据什么选穴原则？A. 局部取穴; B. 辨证选穴; C. 按經驗取穴; D. 本经取穴法; E. 异经取穴法	What principle of selecting points is used when Si1 / Shào Zé is used to generate milk, and promote secretion? A. Principles of selecting local points; B. Principles of selecting points according to syndrome; C. Principle of selecting experience points for treatment; D. Methods of pairing off points on affected meridians; E. Principles of selecting points on mother and child meridians.
2479	耳鸣选聽宮聽會配太溪太沖是根据什么选穴原则？ A. 反面取穴法 B. 前后配穴法 C. 本经取穴法 D. 按經驗取穴 E. 辨证选穴	What principle of selecting points is used in selecting Tingong=Si19 and Tinghui=G2 combined with Taixi=K3 and Taichong= Lv3 to treat ringing in ears? A. Methods of selecting points on the opposite side of disease for treatment; B. Methods of pairing off anterior and posterior points; C. Principles of selecting points on the affected meridians; D. Principle of selecting experience points for treatment; E. Methods of pairing off upper and lower points.
2480	胃溃疡及十二指肠溃疡以上脘下脘，配懸樞，脊中，中樞，根据什么选穴原则？ A. 原络配穴法 B.. 表里经配穴法 C. 同名经配穴法 D. 郄会配穴法 E 俞募配穴法	What principle of selecting points is used when R13 shangwan, and R10 xiawan are combined with D5 xuanshu, D6 jizhong, and D7 zhongshu to treat gastric and duodenal ulcers? A. Method of pairing off original points (Yuán Xué) and linking points (Luò Xué); B. Methods of pairing off points on meridians forming a deep-superficial relationship; C. Methods of pairing off points on the meridians with identical yin-yang classification; D. Methods of pairing off Xī Xué and Bā Huì Xué; E. Methods of pairing off Bèi Shù Xué and Mù Xué.
2481	脾俞、气海， 二穴配伍可以治疗便秘是根据什么选穴原则？A. 局部取穴; B. 辨证选穴; C. 远部取穴; D. 按經驗取穴; E. 异经取穴法.	What principle of selecting points is used when B20 Pí Shū and R6 Qì Hăi are paired off to treat constipation? A. Principles of selecting local points; B. Principles of selecting points according to syndrome; C. Principles of selecting distal points; D. Principle of selecting experience points for treatment; E. Principles of selecting points on mother and child meridians.
2482	胃病选脾輸胃俞三焦輸配上脘中脘下脘是根据什么选穴原则？ A. 前后配穴法 B. 原络配穴法	What principle of selecting points is used in selecting Pishu=B20, Weishu=B21, Sanjiaoshu=B22, Weicnag=B50 in combination with Shangwan=13, Zhongwan=R12，Xiawan=R10, and Liangmen=S21 to treat stomach disease? A Methods of pairing off anterior and posterior points; B. Methods of

	C. 本经取穴法 D. 按經驗取穴 E 辨证选穴	pairing off Yuán Xué and Luò Xué; C. Principles of selecting points on the affected meridians; D. Principle of selecting experience points for treatment; E. Principles of selecting points according to syndrome.
2483	心脾两虛以陰郄配膈輸，是根据什么选穴原则？ A. 子母经配穴法 B.俞募配穴法. C. 原络配穴法 D. 表里经配穴法 E 郄会配穴法	What principle of selecting points is used when H6, Yīn Xī. is combined with B17, Gé Shū, to treat deficiency of both heart and spleen? A. Methods of pairing off points on the meridians with child-mother relationship; B. Methods of pairing off Bèi Shù Xué and Mù Xué; C. Methods of pairing off Yuán Xué and Luò Xué; D. Methods of pairing off points on meridians forming a deep-superficial relationship; E Methods of pairing off Xī Xué and Bā Huì Xué.
2484	胃管下俞可以治疗消渴是根据什么选穴原则？A. 局部取穴; B. 辨证选穴; C. 远部取穴; D. 本经取穴法; E. 按經驗取穴	What principle of selecting points is used when Wei Guan Xia Shu is used to treat diabetes (elimination and thirst)? A. Principles of selecting local points; B. Principles of selecting points according to syndrome; C. Principles of selecting distal points; D. Methods of pairing off points on affected meridians; E. Principle of selecting experience points for treatment.
2485	胃，十二指肠溃疡选上脘下脘配懸樞脊中中樞是根据什么选穴原则？ A. 反面取穴法 B. 前后配穴法 C. 本经取穴法 D. 按經驗取穴 E 辨证选穴	What principle of selecting points is used in selecting Shangwan=R13 and Xiawan=R10 in combination with Xuanshu=D5, Jizhong=D6, and Zhongshu=D7 to treat gastric and duodenal ulcers? A. Methods of selecting points on the opposite side of disease for treatment; B. Methods of pairing off anterior and posterior points; C. Principles of selecting points on the affected meridians; D. Principle of selecting experience points for treatment; E. Principles of selecting points according to syndrome.
2486	与胃有关的疾病以梁丘配中脘，是根据什么选穴原则？ A. 子母经配穴法 B.俞募配穴法. C.郄会配穴法 D. 原络配穴法 E 表里经配穴法	What principle of selecting points is used when S34, Liáng Qiū and R12, Zhōng Wǎn are combined to treat the causes associated with the stomach? A. Methods of pairing off points on the meridians with child-mother relationship; B. Methods of pairing off Bèi Shù Xué and Mù Xué; C. Methods of pairing off Xī Xué and Bā Huì Xué; D. Methods of pairing off Yuán Xué and Luò Xué; E. Methods of pairing off points on meridians forming a deep-superficial relationship.
2487	中平穴可以治疗肩周炎是根据什么选穴原则？A. 按經驗取穴; B. 辨证选穴; C. 远部取穴; D. 本经取穴法; E. 异经取穴法	What principle of selecting points is used when Zhōng pīng xué is used to treat scapulohumeral periarthritis? A. Principle of selecting experience points for treatment; B. Principles of selecting points according to syndrome; C. Principles of selecting distal points; D. Methods of pairing off points on affected meridians; E. Principles of selecting points on mother and child meridians.
2488	胃病选胃俞配中脘是根据什么选穴原则？ A. 反面取穴法 B. 原络配穴法 C. 前后配穴法 D. 按經驗取穴 E 辨证选穴	What principle of selecting points is used in selecting Weishu=B21 in combination with Zhongwan=R12 to treat stomach disease? A. Methods of selecting points on the opposite side of disease for treatment; B. Methods of pairing off Yuán Xué and Luò Xué; C. Methods of pairing off anterior and posterior points; D. Principle of selecting experience points for treatment; E. Principles of selecting points according to syndrome.
2489	与肺有关的疾病以孔最配膻中，是根据什么选穴原则？ A. 子母经配穴法 B.俞募配穴法. C. 原络配穴法 D. 郄会配穴法 E 表里经配穴法	What principle of selecting points is used when the cause associated with lungs is treated by Lu6, Kǒng Zuì in combination with R17, Shān Zhōng? A. Methods of pairing off points on the meridians with child-mother relationship; B. Methods of pairing off Bèi Shù Xué and Mù Xué; C. Methods of pairing off Yuán Xué and Luò Xué; D. Methods of pairing off Xī Xué and Bā Huì Xué; E. Methods of pairing off points on meridians forming a deep-superficial relationship.
2490	头痛选百會和太陽，是根据什么选穴原则？	What principle of selecting points is used when D20 Bǎi Huì and Tài Yáng are combined to treat headache?

	A. 远部取穴; B. **局部近取**; C. 上下配穴法; D. 表里经配穴法; E. 子母经配穴法	A. Principles of selecting distal points; B. Principles of selecting local points; C. Methods of pairing off upper and lower points; D. Methods of pairing off points on meridians forming a deep-superficial relationship; E. Methods of pairing off points on the meridians with child-mother relationship.
2491	右側偏头痛，取同侧太阳、维，配左侧外关、足临泣是据什么选穴原则？ A. 反面取穴法 B. 原络配穴法 C. 双面对称取穴法 D. 按經驗取穴 E 左右交叉配穴法	What principle of selecting points is used in selecting Tài Yáng (right side), S8 Tóu Wěi (right side) in combination with Sj5, Wài Guān (left side) and G41, Zú Lín Qì (left side) to treat migraine headache on the rig side of the head? A. Methods of selecting points on the opposite side of disease for treatment; B. Methods of pairing off Yuán Xué and Luò Xué; C. Methods of selecting identical points on both sides in pairs to treat diseases; D. Principle of selecting experience points for treatment; E. Methods of pairing off left and right crossing points.
2492	胃病以脾俞，胃俞，三焦俞，倉配上脘，中脘，下脘，是根什么选穴原则？ A. 原络配穴法 B.俞募配穴法. C. 同名经配穴法 D. 郄会配穴法 E 表里经配穴法	What principle of selecting points is used when B20 pishu, B21 weishu, B22 sanjiaoshu, B50 weicang, are combined with R13 shangwan, R12 zhongwan, R10 xiawan, and S21 liangmen to treat stomach disease? A. Method of pairing off original points (Yuán Xué) and linking points (Luò Xué); B. Methods of pairing off Bèi Shù Xué and Mù Xué; C. Methods of pairing off points on the meridians with identical yin-yang classification; D. Methods of pairing off Xī Xué and Bā Huì Xué; E. Methods of pairing off points on meridians forming a deep-superficial relationship.
2493	**眼疾**选 睛明，攢竹，四白，是根据什么选穴原则？ A. **局部近取**; B. 循经远取穴; C. 上下配穴法; D. 表里经配穴法; E. 子母经配穴法	What principle of selecting points is used when B1 jingming, B2 zanzhu, S2 Sibai, are selected to treat eye disease? A. Principles of selecting local points; B. Principles of selecting distal points along meridian; C. Methods of pairing off upper and lower points; D. Methods of pairing off points on meridians forming a deep-superficial relationship; E. Methods of pairing off points on the meridians with child-mother relationship.
2494	眼病以睛明，风池，光明相配是根据什么选穴原则？ A.三部配穴法 B. 原络配穴法 C. 双面对称取穴法 D. 按經驗取穴 E 辨证选穴	What principle of selecting points is used in selecting B1 / Jīng Míng, G20 / Fēng Chí, G37 / Guāng Míng to treat eye disease? A. Methods of pairing off points in three regions; B. Methods of pairing off Yuán Xué and Luò Xué; C. Methods of selecting identical points on both sides in pairs to treat diseases; D. Principle of selecting experience points for treatment; E. Principles of selecting points according to syndrome.
2495	肘痛选曲池.，天井是根据什么选穴原则？**局部近取** A. 远部取穴; B. 循经远取穴; C. 上下配穴法; D. 表里经配穴法; E. **局部近取**	What principle of selecting points is used when Li11 quchi, and Sj10 tianjing are selected for the treatment of pain in the elbow? A. Principles of selecting distal points; B. Principles of selecting distal points along meridian; C. Methods of pairing off upper and lower points; D. Methods of pairing off points on meridians forming a deep-superficial relationship; E. Principles of selecting local points.
2496	失语以廉泉，哑门，通里相是根据什么选穴原则？ A. 俞募配穴法 B. 三部配穴法 C. 双面对称取穴法 D. 按經驗取穴 E 辨证选穴	What principle of selecting points is used when aphasia is treated by R23 / Lián Quán, D15 / Yǎ Mén, and H5 / Tōng Lǐ? A. Methods of pairing off Bèi Shù Xué and Mù Xué; B. Methods of pairing off points in three regions; C. Methods of selecting identical points on both sides in pairs to treat diseases; D. Principle of selecting experience points for treatment; E. Principles of selecting points according to syndrome.
2497	膝痛选犢鼻.，陽陵泉是根据什么选穴原则？**局部近取** A. 远部取穴; B. 循经远取穴; C. 上下配穴法; D. **局部近取**; E. 子母经配穴法	What principle of selecting points is used when S35 dubi, and G34 yanglingquan are selected for the treatment of pain in the knee ? A. Principles of selecting distal points; B. Principles of selecting distal points along meridian; C. Methods of pairing off upper and lower points; D. Principles of selecting local points; E. Methods of pairing off points on the meridians with child-mother relationship.

2498	痔疮以长强，次聊，承山相配是根据什么选穴原则？ A. 俞募配穴法 B. 原络配穴法 C. 三部配穴法 D. 按經驗取穴 E 辨证选穴	What principle of selecting points is used when hemorrhoids is treated by D1, Cháng Qiáng, B32, Cì Liáo, and B57, Chéng Shān? A. Methods of pairing off Bèi Shù Xué and Mù Xué; B. Methods of pairing off Yuán Xué and Luò Xué; C. Methods of pairing off points in three regions; D. Principle of selecting experience points for treatment; E. Principles of selecting points according to syndrome.
2499	腕痛选陽池，外關是根据什么选穴原则？ A. 远部取穴; B. 循经远取穴; C. **局部近取**; D. 表里经配穴法; E. 子母经配穴法	What principle of selecting points is used when Sj4 yangchi and Sj5 waiguan are selected for the treatment of wrist pain? A. Principles of selecting distal points; B. Principles of selecting distal points along meridian; C. Principles of selecting local points; D. Methods of pairing off points on meridians forming a deep-superficial relationship; E. Methods of pairing off points on the meridians with child-mother relationship.
2500	肩周炎以肩顒，曲池，阳陵泉相配，是根据什么选穴原则？ A. 俞募配穴法 B. 原络配穴法 C. 双面对称取穴法 D. 三部配穴法 E 辨证选穴	What principle of selecting points is used when periarthritis of shoulder is treated by Li15, Jiān Yú，Li11, Qū Chí, and G34, Yáng Líng Quán? A. Methods of pairing off Bèi Shù Xué and Mù Xué B. Methods of pairing off Yuán Xué and Luò Xué; C. Methods of selecting identical points on both sides in pairs to treat diseases; D. Methods of pairing off points in three regions; E. Principles of selecting points according to syndrome.
2501	足痛选解溪昆崙是根据什么选穴原则？ A. **局部近取**; B. 循经远取穴; C. 上下配穴法; D. 表里经配穴法; E. 子母经配穴法	What principle of selecting points is used when S41 jiexi, and B60 kunlun are selected for the treatment of foot pain? A. Principles of selecting local points; B. Principles of selecting distal points along meridian; C. Methods of pairing off upper and lower points; D. Methods of pairing off points on meridians forming a deep-superficial relationship; E. Methods of pairing off points on the meridians with child-mother relationship.
2502	肝病以期门，肝俞，人中相配是根据什么选穴原则？ A. 俞募配穴法 B. 原络配穴法 C. 双面对称取穴法 D. 按經驗取穴 E 三部配穴法	What principle of selecting points is used when liver disease is treated by Lv14, Qí Mén, B18, Gān Shū, and D26, Shuǐ Gōu? A. Methods of pairing off Bèi Shù Xué and Mù Xué; B. Methods of pairing off Yuán Xué and Luò Xué; C. Methods of selecting identical points on both sides in pairs to treat diseases; D. Principle of selecting experience points for treatment; E. Methods of pairing off points in three regions.
2503	肩痛选肩顒是根据什么选穴原则？ A. **局部近取**; B. 循经远取穴; C. 上下配穴法; D. 表里经配穴法; E. 子母经配穴法	What principle of selecting points is used when Li15 jianyu on both sides are selected for treatment of pain in the shoulder? A. Principles of selecting local points;; B. Principles of selecting distal points along meridian; C. Methods of pairing off upper and lower points; D. Methods of pairing off points on meridians forming a deep-superficial relationship; E. Methods of pairing off points on the meridians with child-mother relationship.
2504	胃病以中脘、梁门，胃俞，内关、足三里相配是根据什么选穴原则？。 A. 三部配穴法 B. 原络配穴法 C. 双面对称取穴法 D. 按經驗取穴 E 辨证选穴	What principle of selecting points is used when stomach disease is treated by R12, Zhōng Wǎn and S21, Liáng Mén, and also B21, Wèi Shū, and P6, Nèi Guān and S36, Zú Sān Lǐ? A. Methods of pairing off points in three regions; B. Methods of pairing off Yuán Xué and Luò Xué; C. Methods of selecting identical points on both sides in pairs to treat diseases; D. Principle of selecting experience points for treatment; E. Principles of selecting points according to syndrome.
2505	鼻病选左右迎香是根据什么选穴原则？ A. 远部取穴; B. 循经远取穴; C. 上下配穴法; D. **局部近取**; E. 子母经配穴法	What principle of selecting points is used Li20 yingxiang on both sides are selected for the treatment of nose disease? A. Principles of selecting distal points; B. Principles of selecting distal points along meridian; C. Methods of pairing off upper and lower points; D. Principles of selecting local points; E. Methods of pairing off points on the meridians with child-mother relationship.

2506	心绞痛以内关配外关是根据什么选穴原则？ A. 表里经配穴法 B. 原络配穴法 C. 同名经配穴法 D. 按經驗取穴 E 辨证选穴	What principle of selecting points is used when P6, Nèi Guān and Sj5, W Guān are used as a pair to treat angina pectoris? A. Methods of pairing off points on meridians forming a deep-superficial relationship; B. Methods of pairing off Yuán Xué and Luò Xué; C. Methods of pairing off points on the meridians with Similar yin-yang classification; D. Principle of selecting experience points for treatment; E. Principles of selecting points according to syndrome.
2507	鼻血选巨髎. 口禾髎是根据什么选穴原则？ A. 远部取穴; B. 循经远取穴; C. 上下配穴法; D. **局部近取**; E. 子母经配穴法	What principle of selecting points is used when S3 juliao, and Li19 heliao are selected for the treatment of nosebleed? A. Principles of selecting distal points; B. Principles of selecting distal points along meridian; C. Methods of pairing off upper and lower points; D Principles of selecting local points; E. Methods of pairing off points on the meridians with child-mother relationship.
2508	胃痛以足三里配公孙是根据什么选穴原则？ A. 俞募配穴法 B. 表里经配穴法 C. 同名经配穴法 D. 按經驗取穴 E 辨证选穴	What principle of selecting points is used when S36 zusanli, and Sp4 gongsun, are selected as a pair to treat stomachache?. A. Methods of pairing off Bèi Shù Xué and Mù Xué; B Methods of pairing off points on meridians forming a deep-superficial relationship; C. Methods of pairing off points on the meridians with Similar yin-yang classification; D. Principle of selecting experience points for treatment; E. Principles of selecting points according to syndrome.
2509	胃疾选中脘梁門是根据什么选穴原则？**局部近取** A. 远部取穴; B. 循经远取穴; C. **局部近取**; D. 表里经配穴法; E. 子母经配穴法	What principle of selecting points is used when R12 zhongwan, and S21 liangmen, and B21 weishu, are selected for the treatment of stomach disease? A. Principles of selecting distal points; B. Principles of selecting distal points along meridian; C. Principles of selecting local points; D. Methods of pairing off points on meridians forming a deep-superficial relationship; E. Methods of pairing off points on the meridians with child-mother relationship.
2510	肝病以期门、太冲配阳陵泉，是根据什么选穴原则？ A. 俞募配穴法 B. 原络配穴法 C. 同名经配穴法 D 表里经配穴法 E 辨证选穴	What principle of selecting points is used when Lv14, Qí Mén and Lv3, T Chōng are combined with G34, Yáng Líng Quán to treat liver disease? A. Methods of pairing off Bèi Shù Xué and Mù Xué; B. Methods of pairing off Yuán Xué and Luò Xué; C. Methods of pairing off points on the meridians with Similar yin-yang classification; D. Methods of pairing off points on meridians forming a deep-superficial relationship; E. Principles of selecting points according to syndrome.
2511	腎腰痛选左右腎輸是根据什么选穴原则？ A. 远部取穴; B. 循经远取穴; C. 上下配穴法; D. **局部近取**; E. 子母经配穴法	What principle of selecting points is used when B23, Shèn Shū, on both sides are selected for the treatment of lumbago associated with the kidneys ? A. Principles of selecting distal points; B. Principles of selecting distal points along meridian; C. Methods of pairing off upper and lower points; D. Principles of selecting local points; E. Methods of pairing off points on the meridians with child-mother relationship.
2512	咳嗽以合谷配太淵，是根据什选穴原则？ A. 俞募配穴法 B. 原络配穴法 C. 同名经配穴法 D. 按經驗取穴 E 表里经配穴法	What principle of selecting points is used when Li4 hegu, and Lu9 taiyua are selected as a pair to treat cough? A. Methods of pairing off Bèi Shù Xué and Mù Xué; B. Methods of pairing off Yuán Xué and Luò Xué; C. Methods of pairing off points on the meridians with Similar yin-yang classification; D. Principle of selecting experience points for treatment; E. Methods of pairing off points on meridians forming a deep-superficial relationship.
2513	肋痛选左右章門是根据什么选穴原则？**局部近取** A. 远部取穴; B. 循经远取穴; C. 上下配穴法; D. 表里经配穴法; E. **局部近取**	What principle of selecting points is used when Lv13 zhangmen on both sides are selected for the treatment of pain in the ribs? A. Principles of selecting distal points; B. Principles of selecting distal points along meridian; C. Methods of pairing off upper and lower points; D. Methods of pairing off points on meridians forming a deep-superficial relationship; E. Principles of selecting local points.

2514	遗尿以委中、肾俞配太溪是根据什么选穴原则？ A. 表里经配穴法 B. 原络配穴法 C. 同名经配穴法 D. 按經驗取穴 E 辨证选穴	What principle of selecting points is used when B40, Wěi Zhōng and B23 Shèn Shū are combined with K3, Tài Xī to treat enuresis? A. Methods of pairing off points on meridians forming a deep-superficial relationship; B. Methods of pairing off Yuán Xué and Luò Xué; C. Methods of pairing off points on the meridians with Similar yin-yang classification; D. Principle of selecting experience points for treatment; E. Principles of selecting points according to syndrome.
2515	眼疾选睛明風池是根据什么选穴原则？ A. 远部取穴; B. 循经远取穴; C. **局部近取**; D. 表里经配穴法; E. 子母经配穴法	What principle of selecting points is used when B1 jingming, and G20 fengchi, are selected for the treatment of eye diseases? A. Principles of selecting distal points; B. Principles of selecting distal points along meridian; C. Principles of selecting local points; D. Methods of pairing off points on meridians forming a deep-superficial relationship; E. Methods of pairing off points on the meridians with child-mother relationship.
2516	胃经病以太淵配偏歷，是根据什么选穴原则？ A. 俞募配穴法 B. 表里经配穴法 C. 同名经配穴法 D. 按經驗取穴 E 辨证选穴	What principle of selecting points is used when the lungs meridian disease is treated by Lu9 taiyuan, and Li6 pianli?. A. Methods of pairing off Bèi Shù Xué and Mù Xué; B. Methods of pairing off points on meridians forming a deep-superficial relationship; C. Methods of pairing off points on the meridians with Similar yin-yang classification; D. Principle of selecting experience points for treatment; E. Principles of selecting points according to syndrome.
2517	牙痛选頰車下關是根据什么选穴原则？ A. 远部取穴; B. 循经远取穴; C. **局部近取**; D. 表里经配穴法; E. 子母经配穴法	What principle of selecting points is used when S6 jia che, and S7 xiaguan are selected for the treatment of toothache? A. Principles of selecting distal points; B. Principles of selecting distal points along meridian; C. Principles of selecting local points; D. Methods of pairing off points on meridians forming a deep-superficial relationship; E. Methods of pairing off points on the meridians with child-mother relationship.
2518	大肠经病以合谷. 配列缺， 是根据什么选穴原则？ A. 俞募配穴法 B. 原络配穴法 C. 同名经配穴法 D. 表里经配穴法 E 辨证选穴	What principle of selecting points is used when the large intestine meridian disease is treated by Li4 hegu and Lu7, Liè Quē? A. Methods of pairing off Bèi Shù Xué and Mù Xué B. Methods of pairing off Yuán Xué and Luò Xué C. Methods of pairing off points on the meridians with Similar yin-yang classification D. Methods of pairing off points on meridians forming a deep-superficial relationship E. Principles of selecting points according to syndrome.
2519	耳疾选翳風耳門是根据什么选穴原则？ A. **局部近取**; B. 循经远取穴; C. 上下配穴法; D. 表里经配穴法; E. 子母经配穴法	What principle of selecting points is used when Sj21 ermen, and Sj17 yifeng, are selected for the treatment of diseases of ears? A. Principles of selecting local points; B. Principles of selecting distal points along meridian; C. Methods of pairing off upper and lower points; D. Methods of pairing off points on meridians forming a deep-superficial relationship; E. Methods of pairing off points on the meridians with child-mother relationship.
2520	胃痛以梁门、足三里配公孙，是根据什么选穴原则？ A. 俞募配穴法 B. 原络配穴法 C. 同名经配穴法 D. 按經驗取穴 E 表里经配穴法	What principle of selecting points is used when S21, liáng mén, S36 zusanli, and Sp4 gongsun, are selected as a pair to treat stomachache? A. Methods of pairing off Bèi Shù Xué and Mù Xué; B. Methods of pairing off Yuán Xué and Luò Xué; C. Methods of pairing off points on the meridians with Similar yin-yang classification; D. Principle of selecting experience points for treatment; E. Methods of pairing off points on meridians forming a deep-superficial relationship.
2521	腹痛选天樞大腸輸是根据什么选穴原则？ A. 远部取穴; B. 循经远取穴; C. 上下配穴法; D. 表里经配穴法; E. 局部近取	What principle of selecting points is used when S25 tianshu and B25 dachangshu are selected for the treatment of abdominal pain ? A. Principles of selecting distal points; B. Principles of selecting distal points along meridian; C. Methods of pairing off upper and lower points; D. Methods of pairing off points on meridians forming a

	经配穴法; E. **局部近取**	deep-superficial relationship; E. Principles of selecting local points.
2522	牙痛、面瘫、阳明头痛取手阳明的合谷配足阳明经的内庭，是根据什么选穴原则？ A. 子母经配穴法 B. 原络配穴法 C. 同名经配穴法 D. 按經驗取穴 E 表里经配穴法	What principle of selecting points is used when toothache, facial paralysis, bright yang headache are treated by the pair of Li4 / Hé Gŭ and S44 / Nèi Tíng? A. Methods of pairing off points on the meridians with child-mother relationship; B. Methods of pairing off Yuán Xué and Luò Xué; C. Methods of pairing off points on the meridians with identical yin-yang classification; D. Principle of selecting experience points for treatment; E. Methods of pairing off points on meridians forming a deep-superficial relationship.
2523	膀胱疾病选中極關元是根据什么选穴原则？ A. 远部取穴; B. **局部近取**; C. 上下配穴法; D. 表里经配穴法; E. 子母经配穴法	What principle of selecting points is used when R3 zhongji, and R4 guanyuan, and B32 ciliao, are selected for the treatment of bladder diseases? A. Principles of selecting distal points; B. Principles of selecting local points;; C. Methods of pairing off upper and lower points; D. Methods of pairing off points on meridians forming a deep-superficial relationship; E. Methods of pairing off points on the meridians with child-mother relationship.
2524	落枕、急性腰扭伤、太阳头痛取后溪配昆仑，是根据什么选穴原则？ A. 子母经配穴法 B. 原络配穴法 C. 同名经配穴法 D. 按經驗取穴 E 表里经配穴法	What principle of selecting points is used when neck pain, acute twisting injury to the waist, and bright yang headache are treated by the pair of Si3 / Hòu Xī and B60 / Kūn Lún? A. Methods of pairing off points on the meridians with child-mother relationship; B. Methods of pairing off Yuán Xué and Luò Xué; C. Methods of pairing off points on the meridians with identical yin-yang classification; D. Principle of selecting experience points for treatment; E. Methods of pairing off points on meridians forming a deep-superficial relationship.
2525	脸和頭的疾病选合谷是根据什么选穴原则？ A. 局部取穴; B. 按腧穴命名取穴; C. 上下配穴法; D. 远部取穴; E. 子母经配穴法	What principle of selecting points is used when Li4 hegu is selected to treat face and head disorders? A. Principles of selecting local points; B. Principles of selecting points according to their Chinese name; D. Principles of selecting distal treatment points; E. Methods of pairing off points on the meridians with child-mother relationship.
2526	偏头痛、胸胁痛以支沟配阳陵泉是根据什么选穴原则？ A. 子母经配穴法 B. 原络配穴法 C. 同名经配穴法 D. 按經驗取穴 E 表里经配穴法	What principle of selecting points is used when migraine headache and pain in the chest and hypothoracic regions are treated by the pair of Sj6 / Zhi Gōu and G34 / Yáng Líng Quán? A. Methods of pairing off points on the meridians with child-mother relationship; B. Methods of pairing off Yuán Xué and Luò Xué; C. Methods of pairing off points on the meridians with identical yin-yang classification; D. Principle of selecting experience points for treatment; E. Methods of pairing off points on meridians forming a deep-superficial relationship.
2527	消化系統的疾病选足三里是根据什么选穴原则？ A. 局部取穴; B. 按腧穴命名取穴; C. 上下配穴法; D. 表里经配穴法; E. 远部取穴	What principle of selecting points is used in selecting S36 zusanli to treat digestive disorders? A. Principles of selecting local points; B. Principles of selecting points according to their Chinese name; D. Methods of pairing off points on meridians forming a deep-superficial relationship; E. Principles of selecting distal treatment points.
2528	虛劳咳嗽症见体弱羸瘦者配以血海、三阴交、足三里、脾俞、胃俞是根据什么选穴原则？ A. 同名经配穴法 B. 原络配穴法 C.子母经配穴法 D. 子母补泻法 E 表里经配穴法	What principle of selecting points is used when the syndrome of deficiency fatigue cough with body weakness is treated by Sp10, Xuè Hăi, Sp6, Sān Yīn Jiāo, S36, Zú Sān Lĭ, B20, Pí Shū, and B21, Wèi Shū? A. Methods of pairing off points on the meridians with identical yin-yang classification; B. Methods of pairing off Yuán Xué and Luò Xué; C. Methods of pairing off points on the meridians with child-mother relationship; D. Principles of selecting child and mother points for tonification and sedation; E. Methods of pairing off points on meridians forming a deep-superficial relationship.

2529	何谓上下配穴法？ A. "上"指上肢或腰部以上，"下"指下肢或腰部以下; B. "上"指上肢,"下"指下肢; C. "上"指腰部以上，"下"指腰部以下; D. "上"指头部，"下"指足部； E. 以上都不是.	What is the method of pairing off upper and lower points? A. The upper region means the upper limbs or the lumbar region, and the lower region means below the lumbar region or in the lower limbs; B. The upper region means the upper limbs, the lower region means the lower limbs; C. The upper region means above the lumbar region and the lower region means below the lumbar region; D. The upper region means the head, and the lower region means the feet; E. None of the above.
2530	何谓前后配穴法？ A. 前指面部后指头背部; B. 前指全身前面后指全身背后; C. 前指胸腹部，后指背部；D. 前指膝盖后指腘部; E 以上都不是.	What is the methods of pairing off anterior and posterior points? A. the anterior region means the face, and the posterior region means the back of head; B. the anterior region means the frontal region of the whole body, and the posterior region means the posterior region of the whole bod.; C. the anterior region means the chest and abdomen, and the posterior region means the back; D. the anterior region means the knee, and the posterior region means the popliteal fossa; E. None of the above.
2531	何谓左右配穴法？ 以右治左，以左治右 A. 以右治右，以左治左; B. 选左右对称穴位治疗；C. 以右手穴位治疗左边疾病，以左手穴位治疗右边疾病；D. 以右治左，以左治右; E. 以上都不是.	What is the methods of pairing off left and right points? A.. treat disease on the left side by the acupuncture points on the same side, and vice versa; B. selecting identical points on both sides in pairs to treat diseases; C.. treat diseases on the left side by the acupuncture points on the right hand, and vice versa; D. treat disease on the left side by the acupuncture points on the right side, and vice versa; E. none of the above.
2532	何谓三部配穴法？ A. 在头部，躯干，下肢同时选穴、配伍成方; B. 在病变的局部、邻近和远端同时选穴配伍成方; C. 在病变的局部选三穴、配伍成方; D. 在病变的邻近选三穴、配伍成方; E 在病变的远端选三穴、配伍成方.	What is the methods of pairing off points in three regions? The methods of pairing off points in three regions means to A. select points in the head, trunk, and lower limbs; B. select points in the local region, nearby region, and distal region of the disease; C. select three points in the local region of the diseases; D. select points in the nearby region of the disease; E select points in the distal region of the diseases
2533	何谓表里经配穴法？ A. 以经脉的上下关系为依据的配穴方法; B. 以经脉的左右关系为依据的配穴方法; C. 以经脉的内外关系为依据的配穴方法; D. 以经脉的交叉关系为依据的配穴方法; E. 以经脉的阴阳关系为依据的配穴方法.	What is the methods of pairing off points on meridians forming a deep-superficial relationship? A. Select points from meridians, which form a upper-lower relationship with each other; B. Select points from meridians, which form a right-left relationship with each other; C. Select points from meridians, which form an internal-external relationship with each other; D. Select points from meridians, which form a crossing relationship with each other; E. Select points from meridians, which form a yin-yang relationship with each other.
2534	何谓**原络**配穴法？ 主客配穴法"，是表里经配穴法的代表 A. 本经原穴与其表里经的络穴配合使用; B. 本经原穴与的络穴配合使用; C. 与表里经配穴法相同； D. 本经原穴与络穴配合使用; E. 本经络穴与其表里经的原穴配合使用;	What is the method of pairing off original points (Yuán Xué) and linking points (Luò Xué)? called host-guest combination, but such combination is confined to the meridians that form yin-yang relationship with each other,. The organ that is diseased first should have its original point (Yuán Xué) used in combination with the linking point (Luò Xué) of the organ that is diseased afterwards, because original points are host points while linking points are guest points. A. The organ that is diseased first should have its original point (Yuán Xué) used in combination with the linking point (Luò Xué) of the organ that is diseased afterwards; B. The organ that is diseased should be treated by its have its original point (Yuán Xué) and its linking point (Luò Xué); C. This method of selecting points is the same as the methods of pairing off points on meridians forming a deep-superficial relationship; D. the disease of an organ treated by its original point

		(Yuán Xué) and its linking point (Luò Xué); E. The organ that is diseased first should have its linking point (Luò Xué) used in combination with the original point (Yuán Xué) of the organ that is diseased afterwards.
2535	何谓俞募配穴法？ A. 以病变脏腑的背俞穴和募穴配合使用 B. 以病变脏的背俞穴和腑的募穴配合使用 C. 以病变腑的背俞穴和脏的募穴配合使用 D. 以病变脏腑的背俞穴或脏腑的募穴配合使用 E。以上都不是.	What is the method of pairing off Bèi Shù Xué and Mù Xué? A. pairing off Bèi Shù Xué (back shu point) and Mù Xué (gathering point) of the diseased organ; B. pairing off the Bèi Shù Xué of the diseased viscus and the Mù Xué of the diseased bowel; C. pairing off Bèi Shù Xué of the diseased bowel and the Mù Xué (gathering point) of the diseased viscus; D. pairing off Bèi Shù Xué or Mù Xué of the diseased organ; E. none of the above.
2536	真心痛选郄門膈輸是根据什么选穴原则？ A. **郄会**配穴法 B. 俞募配穴 C. **原络**配穴法 D. 表里经配穴 E, 上下配穴法	When P4, Xī Mén and B17 and Gé Shū, are used to treat angina pectoris, what is it called? A. the method of pairing off Xī Xué (fissural points) and Bā Huì Xué (eight influential points)? B. Methods pairing off Bèi Shù Xué and Mù Xué C. Methods of pairing off Yuán Xué and Luò Xué; D. the methods of pairing off points on meridians forming a deep-superficial relationship E. Methods of pairing off upper and lower points.
2537	胃痛吐酸选梁丘中脘是根据什么选穴原则？ A. 表里经配穴 B. 前后配穴 C. **郄会**配穴法 D. **原络**配穴法 E. 俞募配穴	S34, Liáng Qiū and R12, Zhōng Wǎn may be paired off to treat stomachache and acid regurgitation A. the methods of pairing off points on meridians forming a deep-superficial relationship B. Methods of pairing off anterior and posterior points C. the method of pairing off Xī Xué (fissural points) and Bā Huì Xué (eight influential points). D. Methods of pairing off Yuán Xué and Luò Xué; E. Methods pairing off Bèi Shù Xué and Mù Xué

13-6	医案	Clinical Cases	2538-2642

13-6 医案 / Clinical Cases (2538-2642)

[医案10] 昏倒 張xx，男，49歲. 患者午餐時，突然昏倒，即刻自醒，醒後呈現左側半偏癱，經當地醫生給安宮牛黃丸一粒未效，晚間，送來針灸科就診:觀患者體質一般，神志正常，語言清晰:追問病史，謂近幾個月來心情不快，常感頭昏，頭痛，全日由于在烈日下勞累過度，午間突然昏倒，即刻自醒，醒後左側半身不能活動，知覺尚可，右側活動自如，舌質紅，少苔，脈弦細數.	[Clinical case 10] fainting. Patient: Zhang, male, age 49. The patient suddenly fainted at lunch, and woke up right away, displaying hemiplegia on the left half of the body; a local doctor gave him 1 tablet of An Gong Niu Huang Wan without effect; the patient was sent to the acupuncture department in the evening. On observation, the patient displayed normal spirit, clear speech; on questioning about the history of illness, the patient related that in the past several months, he was not happy, and often felt dizzy, headache; and due to working all day under the strong sunlight, he fainted suddenly at noon, woke up right away, inability to move the left side of the body after waking up, with clear consciousness, free movements on the right side, red tongue, scanty coating, wiry and fine and rapid pulses.

2538	[医案10] 是何病機？ A 陰虛陽亢; B 阳虚阴盛； C 陰陽俱虛; D 陰陽俱盛	[Clinical case 10] what is the pathogenesis? A yin deficiency with uprising yang; B yang deficiency with abundant yin; C deficient yin and yang; D excessive yin and yang.
2539	[医案10]应用什么如何治则？ A 补陽泻陰; B 陰陽俱泻; C 陰陽俱补; D 育陰潛陽	[Clinical case 10] what treatment principle should be used? A toning yang and sedating yin; B sedating both yin and yang; C toning both yin and yang; D nuture yin and suppress yang.
2540	[医案10]应如何處方？ A 承山, 承扶; B 合谷、三陰交; C 大腸輸, 風市; D 后溪, 頰車.	[Clinical case 10] what points should be selected? A; B57;B36; B Li4, Sp6; C; B25, G31; D Si3, S6

[医案11] 昏倒 趙XX，女，68歲: 素有肝陽易亢，常頭痛眩暈:7 天前下午 4 時許，因情緒激動，突然昏倒，不省人事，喉有痰鳴，呼吸氣粗，面赤，牙關緊閉，握拳抽搐等:經及時急救治療後，神志已清，諸證均已好轉，惟左半身不遂，口角歪斜，語言蹇澀，牙關欠利，咳嗽痰粘, 納少，便結，尿利，夜臥尚安，脈右弦兼滑，左沉細軟，舌紅苔薄.	[Clinical case 11] fainting Patient: Zhao, female, age 68. The patient tends to display abundant liver yang, and she often suffers headache and dizziness. Seven days ago in the afternoon at about 4 pm, the patient suddenly fainted and lost consciousness due to emotional agitation, with sputum noise in the throat, rough breath, reddish complexion, lockjaw, closed fists, and twitching, etc. After first-aid, the patient regained consciousness, showing improvements in all symptoms, except hemiplegia, wry mouth, difficult speech, difficult movements of the jaws, coughing out sticky sputum, poor appetite, constipation, smooth urination, relatively secure sleep, wiry and sliding pulses in the right hand, deep and fine and soft pulses in the left arm, red tongue with thin coating.

2541	[医案 11]应如何處方？ A, 肩井配頰車; B解溪配金門; C厥陰輸配白環輸; D 頰車配合谷	[Clinical case 11] what points should be selected? A. G21(Jiān Jǐng) and S6 (Jiá; Chē) combined; B. S41 (Jiě Xī) and B63(Jīn Mén) combined; C. B14 (Jué Yīn Shū) and B30 (Bái Huán Shū) combined; D. S6 (Jiá; Chē) and Li4 (Hé Gǔ) combined.
2542	[医案 11] 为何要用廉泉、啞門？ A治口眼歪斜; B 治語言蹇澀; C 化痰; D增食欲	[Clinical case 11] why should R23 [Lián Quán] and D15 (Yǎ Mén) be used? A. to treat wry mouth and eyes; B. to treat speech difficulty; C. to transform sputum; D. to increase appetite.
2543	[医案11] 治療应如何操作？ A 强刺激; B 弱刺激; C 中等刺激; D 先强后弱	[Clinical case 11] what techniques should be applied? A. strong stimulation; B. weak stimulation; C. median stimulation; D. strong stimulation first, and then weak stimulation.

[医案12] 昏倒 卞XX，男，31歲， 十年前曾突然尖叫一聲，手足抽搐、神志不清而昏倒，繼口吐白沫，小便失禁，約 20 分鐘蘇醒:以後每隔一月發作一次，近年來發作次數增多，約每周一次，常	[Clinical case 12] fainting Patient: Ka, male, age 31. Ten years ago, the patient fell ill suddenly with a sharp cry, twitching of hands and feet, unclear consciousness with fainting, followed by vomiting of white bubbles, incontinence of urination. He woke up in 20 minutes. Afterwards, the

因疲勞、緊張引起，無發作先兆:未做腦電圖. [選自'針刺療法']	symptoms attacked every other month, the frequency increased in recent years, about once a week, often due to fatigue and tension, without advanced warning signs. No electro-encephalogram was done.

2544	[医案 12]应診斷为何病？A 中暑; B 头晕; C 中风; D 癲痫	[Clinical case 12] what is the correct diagnosis? A. sun stroke; B. dizziness; C. stroke; D. epilepsy

[医案 14] 中风中脏腑闭证 王某某，男，60 岁。素有高血压史。近日工作繁忙，休息较少。今在工作之时，突然昏仆，不省人事，口渴，半身不遂，牙关紧闭，两手握固，面赤气粗，喉中痰鸣，二便不通，脉弦滑而数。针灸学	[Clinical case 14] Wind stroke affecting viscera and bowels, closed type. Patient: Wang, male, age 60. A history of hypertension. The patient was busy with less rest recently. This day, the patient suddenly fainted at work, loss of consciousness, thirst, hemiplegia, lockjaw, closed hands, red complexion, rough breath, sputum noise in the throat, constipation and retention of urine, wiry and sliding and rapid pulses.

2545	[医案 14]应用何治则？A平肝熄风; B 补阴潜阳; C 发散风寒; D 补益阴阳	[Clinical case 14] what treatment principle should be used? A. to calm the liver and stop wind; B. to tone yin and suppress yang; C. to disperse wind cold; D. to tone and benefit yin and yang.
2546	[医案 14] 应診斷为何病？A中风中脏腑脱证; B中风中脏腑闭证; C中风中经络; D 癲痫发作	[Clinical case 14] what is the correct diagnosis? A. wind stroke attacking the viscera and bowels as the prolapsed type; B.wind stroke attacking the viscera and bowels as the closed type; C. wind stroke attacking the meridians; D. onset of epilepsy.
2547	[医案 14] 治療应如何操作？A 平補平瀉法; B 用補法; C 用泻法; D 補瀉兼用	[Clinical case 14] what techniques should be applied? A neutral technique; B tonifcation only; C sedation only; D simultaneous application of tonfication and sedation.

[医案 15] 中风中脏腑闭证 李 XX，男,68 岁。素患有高血压史，早晨起床时发现患者神志昏迷，牙关紧闭，两手紧握，面赤气粗，喉中痰鸣，二便不通，脉弦滑而数。针灸学	[Clinical case 15] Wind stroke affecting viscera and bowels, closed type Patient: Lee, male, age 68, with a history of hypertension. The patient displayed unclear consciousness when getting up from bed in the morning, with lockjaw, closed fists, red face, rought breath, sputum noise in the throat, constipation and retention of urine, wiry, sliding, and rapid pulse.

2548	[医案 15] 是何病機？A中风中脏腑脱证; B中风中脏腑闭证; C中风中经络; D 癲痫发作	[Clinical case 15] what is the pathogenesis? A. wind stroke attacking the viscera and bowels as the prolapsed type; B. wind stroke attacking the viscera and bowels as the closed type; C. wind stroke attacking the meridians; D onset of epilepsy.

2549	[医案 15] 用十二井穴点刺出血有何方义？ A 降肝经逆气以平熄肝阳; B以宣通脾胃二经之气机 ·蠲化浊痰; C 清心泄热，蠲化浊痰; D具开闭清热，醒脑开窍	[Clinical case 15] what is the rationale in using twelve well points with dotted insertion for bloodletting? A. to bring down uprising energy of the liver meridian, to calm and stop liver yang; B to expand and connect the energy mechanisms of the spleen and stomach meridians, to move and transform turbid sputum; C. to clear the heart and sedate heat, move and transform turbid sputum; D. to open up closure and clear heat, wake up the brain and open the cavities.

[医案 35] 胃痛 陈某某，男，17 岁。近日天气炎热，患者进食冷饮较多，午餐后，突然腹痛剧烈，得温则减，遇冷更甚，腹胀肠鸣，四肢欠温，口不渴，大便溏薄，小便清长。苔白，脉沉紧。针灸学	[Clinical case 35] stomachache Patient:; Chen, male, age 17. With an increased consumption of cold food and beverages due to hot weather in recent days, the patient suddenly displayed acute abdominal pain after lunch, the pain decreased on warmness and increased on cold, abdominal swelling with intestinal rumbling, four limbs not warm, no thirst, discharge of watery stools, clear and long streams of urine, white coating on the tongue, deep and tight pulse.

2550	[医案 35] 是何病機？ A胃痛（肝气犯胃）; B 胃痛（气血不足）; C 胃痛（脾胃虛寒）; D 胃痛（消化不良）	[Clinical case 35] what is the pathogenesis? A. stomachache (liver energy offending the stomach); B. stomachache (deficient energy and blood); C. stomachache (deficient and cold spleen and stomach); D. stomachache (indigestion).
2551	[医案 35] 治则如何？ A 温经散寒 ·理气止痛; B 除湿导滞，疏调肠胃; C 疏通瘀滞 ·和胃止痛; D 疏暢陽明經氣，通便導滯.	[Clinical case 35] what treatment principle should be used? A. to warm meridians and disperse cold, regulate energy and relieve pain; B. to remove dampness and direct the flow of congestion, disperse and regulate the intestines and stomach; C. to disperse and open up coaguation and congestion, harmonize the stomach and relieve pain; D to disperse and facilitate the energy of the bright yang meridians, promote bowel movements and direct the flow of congested energy.
2552	[医案 35] 应如何處方？ A 中庭, 筑賓, 照海; B, 攢竹, 云門, 淵液; C 涌泉, 内关, 陽陵泉; D 中脘、内关、足三里。	[Clinical case 35] what points should be selected? A. R16, Zhōng Tíng K9, Zhú Bīn K6, Zhào Hǎi; B. B2, Zǎn Zhú; Lu2, Yún Mén G22, Yuān Yè; C. K1, Yǒng Quán P6, Nèi Guān G34, Yáng Líng Quán; D. R12, Zhōng Wǎn P6, Nèi Guān S36, Zú Sān Lǐ

[医案 41] 腹痛 李某某，女，36 岁。患者平素性急，昨日因小事与家人发生口角，今晨突然出现上腹部近心窝处剧痛，且连及胁肋，服用止痛片效果不佳。现仍疼痛较剧，嗳气频频，心烦易怒，吐酸叹息，大便不畅，查	[Clinical case 41] abdominal pain Patient: Lee, female, age 36, with a history of impatience. The patient quarrelled with family members over a trivial matter. The patient got up this morning, displaying acute pain in the abdomen close to the pit of the stomach, affecting the costal region and ribs, and oral consumption of analgesic did not help much, with pain remaining acute at present, frequent bleching, depressed and prone to anger, vomiting of acid and sighing, difficult bowel movement, light-red tonge on observation, a thin layer of white coating, wiry pulse.

其舌质淡红。苔薄白，脉弦。针灸学	

2553	[医案 41]应如何處方？A中脘、神阙、足三里; B神阙, 少澤, 神門; C足三里,少澤, 神門; D 神阙, 手三里, 三陰交	[Clinical case 41] what points should be selected? A. R12, Zhōng Wǎn R8, Shén Què S36, Zú Sān Lǐ; B. R8, Shén Què; Si1, Shào Zé; H7, Shén Mén; C. S36, Zú Sān Lǐ Si1, Shào Zé H7, Shén Mén; D. R8, Shén Què Li10, Shǒu Sān Lǐ Sp6, Sān Yīn Jiāo
2554	[医案 41] 应診斷为何病？A腹痛寒证; B 腹痛虛证; C 腹痛实证 D 血瘀腹痛	[Clinical case 41] what is the correct diagnosis? Acold abdominal pain; Bdeficient abdominal pain; Cexcessive abdominal pain; Dabdominal pain due to blood coagulation.

[医案 47] 急性泄泻 王某，男，25 岁。昨晚因和客人一起就餐，夜深即腹痛泄泻，大便稀薄并有粘液，一天共 7 次，肛门有灼热感，口渴喜冷饮，小便赤。苔黄腻，脉濡数。针灸学	[Clinical case 47] acute diarrhea Patient: Wang, male, age 25. Last night the patient had a meal with guests, and then developed abdominal pain and diarrhea late at night, discharge of thin stools with pus, 7 times altogether, with burning sensations in the anus, thirst with craving for cold beverages, reddish urine, yellow and greasy coating on the tongue, soft and rapid pulse.

2555	[医案 47] 是何病機？A急性泄泻（热型）; B急性泄泻（湿型）; C急性泄泻（湿热型）; D急性泄泻（寒型）	[Clinical case 47] what is the pathogenesis? A. acute diarrhea (hot type); B. acute diarrhea (damp type); C. acute diarrhea (damp-heat type); D. acute diarrhea (cold type).
2556	[医案47] 应如何處方？A 天枢、阴陵泉、上巨虛; B 天枢、陽陵泉, 中樞; C 上巨虛, 陽陵泉, 陰市. D上巨虛, 陽陵泉, 中樞	[Clinical case 47] what points should be selected? A. S25, Tiān Shū; Sp9, Yīn Líng Quán S37, Shàng Jù; B. S25, Tiān Shū G34, Yáng Líng Quán D7, Zhōng Shū, S33, Yīn Shì; C. S37, Shàng Jù Xū G34, Yáng Líng Quán S33, Yīn Shì; D. S37, Shàng Jù Xū; Yáng Líng Quán; D7, Zhōng Shū

[医案42] 腹痛 患者: 王xx，性別 男，年齡 50歲. 主訴: 小腹痛一個月. 症狀: 臍下劇烈疼痛，每當腹痛時，患者在床上輾轉不安，大汗淋漓，曾多次急診注射阿托品，嗎啡，杜冷丁等均不能完全止痛: 檢查: 下腹部可觸及不規則之腫塊，有明顯壓痛，無明顯腹水. [選自'針灸配穴']	[Clinical case 42] abdominal pain Patient: Wang, male, age 50. [complaints] pain in the lower abdomen for a month. [symptoms] acute pain below the umbilicus, the patient had to toss about in bed with anxiety when abdominal pain occurred, with profuse perspiration. The patient had been given many injections of atrophine, morphine, dolantine, at the emergency unit, but the pain was not completely relieved. [examinations] uneven lumps of swelling may be touched in the lower abdomen, with obvious pressure pain, no signs of ascites.

2557	[医案 42] 用下巨虛治療有何方义？ A 因下巨虛是小腸經之下合穴; B 因下巨虛是小腸經之募穴; C 因下巨虛是治疗本病之经验穴 D 因下巨虛是交会穴	[Clinical case 42] what is the rationale for using S39 (Xià Jù Xū) in treatment? A. because S39 is the lower merging point (xia he xue) of the small intestine meridian; B. because S39 is the mu point (gathering point) point of the small intestine meridian; C. because S39 is an experience point in treating this disease. D. because S39 is a meeting point.

[医案43] 腹痛 高xx，男，54歲，1964年6月11日初診:門診號 011264, 主訴，腹痛三天. 現病史: 於三天前突然咳嗽引起左側腹直肌陣發性拘急抽痛，右側腹直肌·腰肌間斷性抽痛，時而腹直肌拘攣抽痛牽引腰部，腰腹活動受限，一晝夜拘攣抽痛約二十次左右，咳嗽、仰臥和起立時易於出現:四天未解大便，經服用蓖麻油後解便如羊屎，食欲不振，口味不佳:舌苔白膩微黃，脈沉弦數:按壓腰腹部無痛感. [選自'常用輸穴臨床發揮]	[Clinical case 43] abdominal pain Patient: Gao, male, age 54, first visit on June 11 1964, file 011264. [Chief complaints] abdominal pain for three days. [history of present illness] the patient suddenly developed cough three days ago, resulting in acute paroxysmal twitching pain in the left abdominal rectus muscle, interrupted twitching pain in the right abdominal rectus muscle and in the right lumbar muscle; spasmatic twitching pain in the abdominal rectus muscle sometimes affecting the lumbar region so that the lumbar and abdominal functions are restricted. About 20 times of spasmatic twitching pain lasting one whole day had occurred with cough. Such symptoms occur more easily when the patient lies on back or stands up. The patient had had no bowel movements for four days, discharging stools like dung of a sheep after oral administration of castor oil, with poor appetite, dislike of food, white and greasy and slightly yellowish coating, deep and wiry and rapid pulse, no pressure pain in the lumbar and abdominal region.

2558	[医案 43] 应如何處方？ A天樞; B天溪; C足通谷 D天宗	[Clinical case 43] what point should be selected? A. S25, Tiān Shū; B. Sp18, Tiān Xī; C. B66, Tōng Gŭ (Zú Tōng Gŭ); D. Si11, Tiān Zōng

[医案21] 喘症 王xx，女，31歲: 病者因患喘症前來針治，在治療中不慎感受風寒，於當日下午出現頭痛，惡寒，發熱，咳嗽吐白痰，鼻塞，全身酸痛，口淡無味，苔薄白，脈浮緊: [湖北省選拔中醫師針灸科臨床病例分析試題].	[Clinical case 21] asthma Patient: Wang, female, age 31 The patient came to clinic for asthma. She was accidentally exposed to the attack of wind and cold in the course of treatment; in the afternoon, she began to display headache, aversion to cold, fever, coughing out white sputum, nasal congestion, aching pain in the whole body, tasteless in the mouth, a thin and white layer of coating on the tongue, superficial and tight pulse.

2559	[医案21] 用大椎治療有何方义？ A 因大椎爲治疗本病之经验穴; B 因大椎爲陽經之交會穴，針之可振奮陽氣，驅風寒外出; C 因大椎位于本病之邻近处，此乃近部取穴; D. 因大椎可宣調肺氣，疏調太陽經氣而解表。	[Clinical case 21] what is the rationale for using D14 (Dà Zhuī) in treatment? A. because D14 is the experience point in treating this disease; B. because D14 is the meeting point of yang meridians, which can activate yang energy, drive out wind and cold; C. because D14 is located in the neighboring region of the present symptom, it is selected as a local point. D. because D14 can expand and regulate lung energy, disperse and regulate the energy of the greater yang meridians, and relax the superficial region.

[医案 22] 哮喘 丁某某，男，46 岁，患哮喘十余年。其发作不分季节，凡气候急剧变化和寒冷之时易反复发作。近日天气突变寒冷，患者即呼吸急促，喉中痰鸣，张口抬肩，不能平卧，咳嗽，咳吐稀痰，形寒无汗，头痛，口不渴。苔薄白，脉浮紧。针灸学	[Clinical case 22] Asthma with sputum noise in the throat Patient: Ding, male, age 46. The patient had suffered asthma for over a decade. Asthma may attack regardless of seasons; sudden change in weather and cold climate will increase the frequency of attack. Recently, cold weather set in suddenly, and the patient developed rapid breath, sputum noise in the throat, the mouth staying open with lifted shoulders, inability to lie flat, cough, cough and vomiting of thin sputum, shivering without perspiration, headache, no thirst, a thin and white layer of coating, superficial and tight pulse.

2560	[医案 22] 应診斷为何病？ A 肺热; B 肝气犯胃; C 风寒袭肺 D 肺肾阴虚	[Clinical case 22] what is the correct diagnosis? A. hot lungs; B. liver energy offending the stomach; C. wind cold attacking the lungs. D. yin deficiency of lungs and kidneys.
2561	[医案 22] 应如何處方？ A肝俞，脾俞，大肠俞，肾俞; B肾俞，耳門，復溜，光明，C 肝俞，會宗，脊中，急脈 D 肺俞、膻中、天突、尺泽。	[Clinical case 22] what points should be selected? A. B18 (Gān Shū) , B20 (Pí Shū) , B25 (Dà Cháng Shū) , B23 (Shèn Shū); B. B23 (Shèn Shū) ,Sj21 (Ěr Mén) ,K7 (Fù Liū) , G37 (Guāng Míng); C. B18 (Gān Shū) ,Sj7 (Huì Zōng) ,D6 (Jī Zhōng) , Lv12 (Jí Mài); D. B13 (Fèi Shū) , R17 (Shān Zhōng) R22 (Tiān Tū) , Lu5 (Chǐ Zé) 。

[医案23] 哮喘 XX，哮喘氣促，發熱惡寒，咳嗽痰鳴，脈浮，苔白. [福建省選拔中醫人員針灸、按摩科試題]	[Clinical case 23] Asthma with sputum noise in the throat Patient: XX Asthma with sputum noise in the throat, panting and short breath, acute breath, fever and aversion to cold, cough with sputum noise, superficial pulse, white coating.

2562	[医案 23] 应如何處方？ A 三陰交，膽輸; B 膻中，風池; C 復溜，伏兔; D 扶突，肝輸.	[Clinical case 23] what points should be selected? A. Sp6 (Sān Yīn Jiāo)B19 (Dǎn Shū); B. R17 (Shān Zhōng) ,G20 (Fēng; Chí); C. K7 (Fù Liū) ,S32 (Fú Tù); D. Li18 (Fú Tū) , B18 (Gān Shū).
2563	[医案23] 应診斷为何病？ A肺寒; B 肺热; C肺虛; D 肺阴虛.	[Clinical case 23] what is the correct diagnosis? A. cold lungs; B hot lungs; C. deficienty lungs; D.lung yin deficiency.

[医案24] 哮喘	[Clinical case 24] Asthma with sputum noise in the throat

牛xx，女，56歲，社員:I969年11月2日初診: 哮喘反復發作4年:經常口服麻黃素等藥:此次因突然呼吸困難，口唇紫紺6小時而來就診: 檢查: 痛苦表情，唇青面紫，張口抬肩，呼吸氣急，兩肺哮鳴音明顯:診斷爲支氣管哮喘: [選自'針灸臨証集驗']	Patient: Niu, female, age 56, staff, first visit on Nov. 2 1969. Recurrent asthma for 4 years, oral administration of ephedrine and others on a regular basis; this time, sudden attack of breathing difficulty, blueness of the lips for 6 hours, which made the patient visit the clinic. [Examination] looking in pain, blueness of the lips and face, with open mouth and lifted shoulders, rapid breath, apparent wheezing in both lungs, diagnosed as bronchial asthma.

2564	[医案 24] 应如何處方？ A 風門，厥陰俞; B昆崙，勞宮; C氣沖，氣海; D商丘，上巨虛.	[Clinical case 24] what points should be selected? A. B12 (Fēng Mén) B14 (Jué Yīn Shū); B. B60 (Kūn Lún), (P8 (Láo Gōng); C. S30 (Qì; Chōng), R6 (Qì Hǎi); D. Sp5 (Shāng Qiū), S37 (Shàng Jù Xū).

[医案 48] 泄泻 陆 XX，男，55 岁，工程师。，几个月来，每多在黎明前脐周微痛，入厕即泻，泻后痛止，大便稀薄，平时自觉腰膝肢冷。诊其面色晦暗，舌淡苔白，脉沉细。 针灸学	[Clinical case 48] diarrhea Patient: Lu, male, age 55, engineer. Mild pain surrounding the umbilicus mostly before dawn for a few months. Diarrhea occurs during each bowel movement, and pain is gone after diarrhea; discharge of watery and thin stools, with sensations of cold loins and knees and limbs. On observation, the complexion appears dark, pale tongue, white coating, deep and fine pulse.

2565	[医案 48] 应如何治疗？ A 针用补法，加以灸法; B 针用泻法，不用灸法; C 单用针法，以补为主; D 单用灸法	[Clinical case 48] how to treat it? A. needling with tonification, supplemented by moxibustion; B. needling with sedation without moxibustion; C. needling only, primarily by tonification; D moxibustion only.
2566	[医案 48] 应診斷为何病？ A 大肠湿热泄泻; B 寒湿泄泻; C 肾虚泄泻; D 消化不良泄泻	[Clinical case 48] what is the correct diagnosis? A. diarrhea due to large intestine damp heat; B. diarrhea due to cold and dampness; C. diarrhea due to kidney deficiency; D. diarrhea due to indgestion.

[医案50] 痢疾 一男學生，飲食生冷，夜半突然腹痛，晨起惡寒發熱 體溫38°C，心煩口渴，下痢赤白，肛門灼熱，裡急後重，小溲短赤，脈滑數，苔黃膩: [黑龍江省選拔中醫人員針灸科試題]	[Clinical case 50] dystery Patient: A male student who had a sudden onset of abdominal pain at midnight due to consumption of cold foods; symptoms in the morning include aversion to chills with fever, body temperature at 38°C, feeling depressed with thirst, diarrhea with red and white discharges, burning sensations in the anus, tenesmus, short and red streams of urine, sliding and rapid pulse, yellowish and greasy coating.

2567	[医案 50] 应用何治则？ A.清熱利濕,以清胃肠濕熱; B 清熱利濕,清少陽濕熱; C 清肝利胆，清肝胆濕熱; D 消食止泻，健脾和胃.	[Clinical case 50] what treatment principle should be applied? A. to clear heat and benefit dampness, regulate the functions of the stomach and intestines; B. to clear heat and benefit dampnes, clear damp heat in the lesser yang; C. to clear the liver and benefit the gallbladder, clear damp heat in the liver and gallbladder; D. to promote digestion and stop diarrhea, strengthen the spleen and harmonize the stomach.
2568	[医案 50] 应如何處方？ A 商丘, 三間, 少沖,天井; B 曲澤, 陰包, 陰谷, 涌泉; C合谷, 天樞, 大椎、曲池; D然谷,乳根, 商丘, 曲池.	[Clinical case 50] what points should be selected? A. Sp5 (Shāng Qiū), Li3 (Sān Jiān), H9 (Shào Chōng), Sj10 (Tiān Jǐng); B. P3 (Qū Zé), Lv9 (Yīn; Bāo), K10 (Yīn Gǔ), K1 (Yǒng Quán); C. Li4 (Hé Gǔ), S25 (Tiān Shū), D14 (Dà Zhuī), Li11 (Qū Chí); D. K2 (Rán Gǔ). S18 (Rǔ Gēn), Sp5 (Shāng Qiū) Li11 (Qū Chí)

[医案69] 癲痫 鄭xx，男，55歲，司機: 癲痫并發現高血壓已半年:檢查:血壓I80 / I00毫米汞柱，眼底無動脈硬化現象，心電圖正常，診斷爲高血壓病:[選自'針刺療法']	[Clinical case 69] epilepsy Patient: Zheng, male, age 55, driver; the patient suffered epilepsy with high blood pressure for six months. On examination, the patient's blood pressure was 180 / 100 mmHg, no signs of arteriosclerosis on fundus examination, normal electrocardiogram; diagnosed as hypertension.

2569	[医案 69] 应如何治法？ A 針刺治療癲痫只可用腕踝針; B針刺治療癲痫可用腕踝針及頭針兩種方法同時進行; C 針刺治療癲痫不可用腕踝針; D針刺治療癲痫不可用頭針，因为採用頭針療法，在電針儀通電時，病員可誘發癲痫的發作。	[Clinical case 69] what treatment method should be used? A. In treating epilepsy by acupuncture, only wrist and ankle acupuncture may be applied; B. in treating epilepsy, wrist and ankle acupuncture and scalp acupuncture may be administered simultaneously; C. In treating epilepsy by acupuncture, wrist and ankle acupuncture should not be applied; D. In treating epilepsy by acupuncture, scalp acupuncture should not be applied, because patients may be under attack when the apparatus of electro therapy is turned on.

[医案70] 癲痫 龔xx，男，8歲，兩月前突然昏倒，四肢抽搐，口吐白沫，繼之昏迷不醒，半小時後才蘇醒:以後每周約發作I-2次，兩個月來共發作I0多次.	[Clinical case 70] epilepsy Patient: Gong, male, age 8. The patient suddenly fainted two months earlier, with twitching of the four limbs, vomiting of white bubbles, followed by fainting and loss of consciousness, waking up in half an hour. Afterwards, 1-2 onsets every week, with a total of over 10 attacks in two months.

2570	[医案 70] 应如何處方？ A頭維、人中、內關、神門; B曲池, 強間, 偏歷, 三焦輸; C蠡溝, 昆崙, 歷兌, 居髎; D勞宮, 環跳, 肩貞, 魂門	[Clinical case 70] what points should be selected? A. S8 (Tóu Wěi), D26 (Shuǐ Gōu, Rén Zhōng), P6 (Nèi Guān), H7 (Shén Mén); B. Li11 (Qū Chí), D18 (Qiáng Jiān), Li6 (Piān Lì);B22 (Sān Jiāo Shū); C. Lv5 (Lí Gōu);B60 (Kūn Lún), S45 (Lì

		Duì) , G29 (Jū Liáo); D. P8 (Láo Gōng), G30 (Huán Tiào), Si9 (Jiān Zhēn;B47 (Hún Mén)

[医案105] 胃下垂 王xx，女，33歲，公社社員:一年前患胃下垂，胃小彎位置在髂脊線下6釐米，多方治療，效不明顯，乃採行針刺療法:患者訴頭暈、腹痛、腰酸、消瘦、納差，一年來常用胃托，否則不能直立，不能參加勞動: [選自'針刺療法']	[Clinical case 105] gastroptosis Patient: Wang, female, age 33, commune member. The patient suffered gastroptosis since a year earlier, with the lesser curvature of stomach situated 6 cm below the iliac-crest line. Multiple therapies had produced no apparent effect, which was why acupuncture therapy was used. The patient complained about dizziness, abdominal pain, a sore waist, skinniness, and poor appetitie. She was then treated by drugs, which seemed to be the only way to help her stand up and participate in labor.

2571	[医案 105] 应如何處方？ A 中脘，足三里，气海; **B中脘，太溪，委中;** C气海，委陽. 委中; D太溪, 水突, 外關,	[Clinical case 105] what points should be selected for treatment? A. R12 [Zhōng Wǎn], R6 [Qì Hǎi], S36 [Zú Sān Lǐ]; B. R12 [Zhōng Wǎn], K3 (Tài Xī); B40 (Wěi Zhōng); C. R6 [Qì Hǎi] ，B39 (Wěi Yáng) ，B40 (Wěi Zhōng); D. K3 (Tài Xī), S10 (Shuǐ Tū). Sj5 (Wài Guān).

[医案 73] 头痛 赵某某，女，43 岁。平素性情急躁，时有头痛发作。昨日因生气一夜未眠，晨起即头痛目眩，心烦易怒，面赤口苦，舌红苔黄，脉弦数。 针灸学	[Clinical case 73] headache Patient: Zhao, female, age 43, with an irritable and impatient personality, occasional headache. The patient did not sleep at all due to anger, she then developed headache and vertigo on getting up in the morning, with mental depression and prone to anger, red complexion, and bitter taste in the mouth. The patient also displayed red tongue with yellowish coating, wiry and rapid pulse.

2572	[医案 73] 应如何治法？ A 清肝利胆，滋阴降火; B 平肝潜阳，滋水涵木; C 平肝和胃，消积驱瘀; D 健脾和胃，消积止痛	[Clinical case 73] what treatment principle should be used? A. to clear the liver and benefit the gallbladder, water yin and bring down fire; B. to calm the liver and oppress yang, water yin and nourish wood; C. to calm the liver and harmonize the stomach, eliminate congestion and expel coagulation; D to strengthen the spleen and harmonize the stomach, eliminate congestion and relieve pain.
2573	[医案 73] 应如何處方？ A太溪, 太淵, 水道, 通里; B 太溪, 水突, 外關， 委陽； C 百会、风池、太冲、太溪; D太溪, 陽池, 委中,陽交,	[Clinical case 73] what points should be selected? A. K3 (Tài Xī), Lu9 (Tài Yuān). S28 (Shuǐ Dào) H5 (Tōng Lǐ); B. K3 (Tài Xī), S10 (Shuǐ Tū). Sj5 (Wài Guān), B39 (Wěi Yáng); C. D20 (Bǎi Huì), G20 (Fēng; Chí), Lv3 (Tài Chōng), K3 (Tài Xī); D. K3 (Tài Xī);B40 (Wěi Zhōng), Sj4 (Yáng Chí), G35 (Yáng Jiāo).

2574	[医案 73]用太溪穴位治療有何方义？ A清肝利胆，滋阴降火; B平肝和胃，消积驱瘀; C健脾和胃，消积止痛; D滋水涵木，育阴潜阳	[Clinical case 73] what is the rationale for using K3 (Tài Xī) in treatment? A. to clear the liver and benefit the gallbladder, water yin and bring down fire; B. to calm the liver and harmonize the stomach, eliminate congestion and expel coagulation; C. to strengthen the spleen and harmonize the stomach, eliminate congestion and relieve pain; D. to soften up water and nourish wood, nurture yin and suppress yang.

[医案33] 呃逆 周XX，女，23歲，1971年5月16日初診: 主訴，呃逆、太息月餘: 現病史: 因情志失和引起胃痛，內服中藥一劑胃痛停止，但隨即出現呃逆、太息交替頻作，影響言語和飲食，白天嚴重，平臥減緩，夜間較輕，熟睡停發: 伴有胃脘悶痛竄及肋肋·食欲不振、精神抑郁·腹直肌異常強直堅硬等症狀，舌苔薄白:因患者不合作，無法切脈: [選自 '常用輸穴臨床發揮']	[Clinical case 33] hiccups Patient: Zhou, female, age 23, first visit on May 16 1971. [Chief complaints] hiccups and sighing for over a month. [history of present illness] stomachache triggered by emotional disturbances, which was relieved by one dose of Chinese herbs, but followed by alternating hiccups and sighing, affecting speech and eating, severe during the day and improved on lying flat, lighter at night, no onset in deep sleep, accompanied by dull stomachache running through the costal and ribs regions, poor appetite, mental depression, abnormal stiffness and hardness of the abdominal rectus muscle, etc and thin and white coating. No pulse was felt due to her unwillingness to cooperate.

2575	[医案 33] 是何病機？ A肝氣犯胃; B 风寒胃痛; C风热胃痛; D 脾胃气虛	[Clinical case 33] what is the pathogenesis? A. liver energy offending the stomach; B. wind cold stomachache; C. wind heat stomachache; D. spleen-stomach energy deficiency.
2576	[医案 33] 应如何處方？ A 針瀉內關、足三里、公孫; B 針补內關、足三里、公孫; C 灸內關、足三里、公孫; D 針补中脘瀉梁門	[Clinical case 33] what points should be selected? A. apply acupuncture with sedation to P6 (Nèi Guān), S36 (Zú Sān Lǐ), Sp4 (Gōng Sūn); B. apply acupuncture with tonification to P6 (Nèi Guān), S36 (Zú Sān Lǐ), Sp4 (Gōng Sūn); C. apply moxibustion to P6 (Nèi Guān), S36 (Zú Sān Lǐ), Sp4 (Gōng Sūn); D. apply acupuncture with tonification to R12 (Zhōng Wǎn) and apply acupuncture with sedation to S21 (Liáng Mén).

[医案106] 高血壓 束 xX，男,49 歲，店員，患高血壓病已兩年，常感頭暈，有時惡心，血壓在 250 / IO0 毫米汞柱，用新針治療一個月，血壓一直穩定在 180 / 80~90 毫米汞柱之間. [選自'針刺療法']	[Clinical case 106] hypertension Patient: Shu, male, age 49, clerk. The patient had suffered hypertension for two years, with constant dizziness, occasional nausea, blood pressure 250 / 100 mm Hg. After treated by new acupuncture therapy, blood pressure became stabilized at 180 / 80-90 mm Hg.

2577	[医案 106] 应用何种疗法？ A 放血，留針; B 灸法不放血; C 針灸法 留針; D 放血，不留針	[Clinical case 106] what technique of treatment to use? A. bloodletting, retention of needle; B. moxibustion with no bloodletting; C. acupuncture and moxibustion with retention of needle; D. bloodletting with no retention of needle.

[医案86] 尿閉 尿閉不通，小腹脹滿，口渴，脈數，舌紅苔黃: [福建省選拔中醫人員針灸科、按摩試題]	[Clinical case 86] complete suppression of urine The patient suffered complete suppression of urine, abdominal swelling and fullness, thirst, rapid pulse, red tongue with yellowish coating.

2578	[医案 86]要采用何种治療原則？ A 补中益气; B 清熱利濕; C 温中散寒; D 温补下焦	[Clinical case 86] what should be the treatment principle? A. to tone the middle region and benefit energy; B. to clear heat and benefit dampness; C. to warm the middle reigon and disperse cold; D. to warm and tone the lower heater.
2579	[医案 86] 应用何种疗法？ A 放血，留針; B 灸法不放血; C 針灸法，留針; D 針用瀉法.	[Clinical case 86] what technique should be used? A. bloodletting, retention of needle; B. moxibustion with no bloodletting; C. acupuncture and moxibustion with retention of needle; D. acupuncture with sedation.

[医案58] 心悸 施Xx，男，23歲，工人. 曾於1966年體格檢查時發現心尖區有II-III級收縮期雜音，當時無任何症狀:1969年起心悸，勞累後加劇，心率爲105次 / 分，心律不齊:1970年心電圖示左心室肥厚，診爲二尖瓣關閉不全:經治療，效果不明顯:於1972年進行針刺治療. [選自'針刺療法']	[Clinical case 58] palpitation Patient: Shi, male, age 23, worker. The patient had undergone a physical examination in 1966, which found 2-3 degrees of systolic murmur in the apex region of the heart, but no symptoms occurred. Palpitation occurred in 1969, getting worse on labor, 105 heart beats per minute, and irregular heart beats. In 1970, electrocardiogram showed hypertrophy of left ventricle, diagnosed as mitral insufficiency. Treatment failed to produce apparent effects. Acupuntrue therapy was administered in 1972.

2580	[医案 58] 应如何處方？ A 胃俞、中脘、足三里; B 內關、心俞、俠白; C太溪, 水突, 外關; D 勞宮, 環跳, 肩貞.	[Clinical case 58] what points should be selected? A. B21 (Wèi Shū), R12 (Zhōng Wǎn), S36 (Zú Sān Lǐ); B. P6 (Nèi Guā_) B15 (Xīn Shū), Lu4 (Xiá Bái); C. K3 (Tài Xī), S10 (Shuǐ Tū), Sj5 (Wài Guān); D. P8 (Láo Gōng), G30 (Huán Tiào), Si9 (Jiān Zhēn).

[医案36] 胃脘痛 王xx，女，40歲，工人: 患者胃脘部隱痛，食後噯氣3年:服胃舒平後疼痛緩解，近來連續上夜班，飲食不節，胃脘疼痛加劇，脘部灼熱，偶有泛酸，曾服胃舒平疼痛不減，來針灸科治療:現症胃脘部疼痛較劇，痛有定處，拒按，飲減少，夜寐不安，大便軟，色黑，舌質黯紅，舌邊有瘀點，苔薄白，脈沉: [四川省選拔中醫人員針灸科試題].	[Clinical cas 36] stomachache Patient: Wang, female, age 40, worker. The patient had experienced mild stomachache with belching after eating in the past 3 years; relieved by oral administration of drug. Recently, the patient worked the night shift, with irregular eating, stomachache intensified with burning sensations in the stomach region and occasional acid regurgitation, which could not be relieved by drugs. And so the patient came to clinic for acupuncture treatment. [Present symptoms] more acute pain in the stomach in the fixed region, intensified by pressure, relieved by eating, insecure sleep at night, soft stools, black, dark-red tongue, blood spots on the sides of tongue, a

	thin layer of white coating, and deep pulse.

2581	[医案 36] 是何病機？ A 气虛型胃脘痛; B 瘀血型胃脘痛; C 肝郁型胃脘痛; D 风寒型胃脘痛	[Clinical case 36] what is the pathogenesis? A. stomachache due to energy deficiency; B. stomachache due to blood coagulation; C. stomachache due to liver congestion; D. stomachache due to wind cold.
2582	[医案36] 应如何治法？ A 毫針用瀉法; B 毫針用补法; C 毫針用补法，加灸法; D 毫針平补平泻，加灸法	[Clinical case 36] what technique to use? A. to sedate with a minute needle; B. to tone up with a minute needle; C. to tone up with a minute needle, accompanied by moxibustion; D. to apply the neutral technique with a minute needle, accompanied by moxibustion
2583	[医案 36] 用足三里治療有何方义？ A因为足三里是胃的募穴; B 因为足三里是血會穴; C 因为足三里是治療胃脘痛之要穴; D因为足三里是胃之合穴	[Clinical case 36] what is the rationale for using S36 (Zú Sān Lǐ) in treatment? A. because S36 is the mu point (gathering point) of the stomach; B. because S36 is the meeting of blood; C. because S36 is an important point for treating stomachache; D.because S36 is the lower merging point (xia he xue) of the stomach.

[医案37] 胃脘痞悶 刁xx，男，15歲 患者胸脘痞悶發涼，噯氣則舒，已有數載:伴有四肢乏力，納谷不香，大便稀溏. 曾在某醫院治療，其效不顯:終日感覺脘部發涼，時出冷汗，苔白潤，脈細弱. [湖北省選拔中醫師針灸科臨床病例分析試題].	[Clinical case 37] stomach lump and dullness Patient: Diao, male, age 15. In the past several years, the patient had displayed; congested chest with coolness which became better on belching, accompanied by fatigued four limbs, poor appetite, thin and watery stools, which were treated in a hospital with no apparent effect. Now the patient displayed congested chest with coolness all day long, cold sweats, white and moist coating, fine and weak pulse.

2584	[医案37] 应如何治法？ A 針刺施補法，同時加灸; B 針刺施泻法，同時加灸; C 針刺施泻法，不可 加灸; D 針刺施補法，不可 加灸。	[Clinical case 37] what technique should be used? A. acupuncture with tonification, plus moxibustion; B. acupuncture with sedation, plus moxibustion; C. acupuncture with sedation, no moxibustion; D. acupuncture with tonification, no moxibustion.
2585	[医案 37] 应診斷为何病？ A 肝气犯胃，肝胃不和; B 食滞停胃，胃气上逆; C脾陽虛衰，胃失和降; D 寒湿内阻，胃气不畅.	[Clinical case 37] what is the correct diagnosis? A. liver energy offending the stomach, disharmony between the liver and stomach; B. food stagnation in the stomach, stomach energy uprising; C. spleen yang in deficiency and decline, loss of harmony and descending function in the stomach; D. internal obstruction of cold dampness, stomach energy not flowing smoothly.

2586	[医案 37] 要采用何种治療原則？ A 溫中，健脾，和胃; B 溫中 ·散寒 ·降逆; C 养胃 ·降逆 ·安中; D和胃，理气，消食.	[Clinical case 37] what treatment principle should be used? A. to warm the middle region, strengthen the spleen, and harmonize the stomach; B. to warm the middle region, disperse cold, bring down uprising;.C to nourish the stomach, bring down uprising, and secure the middle region; D. to harmonize the stomach, regulate energy, and promtoe digestion.

[医案38] 胃痛 邢xx，男，26歲，1964年11月6日初診:門診號 0I3255. 主訴: 患胃痛已十年之久，因寒涼傷胃而得. 現病史: 十年前因吃甘蔗過多，寒涼傷胃所致，此後每因寒涼、郁怒或勞累過度即復發:其疼痛部位在中脘穴處及下、左上腹和臍周，時而劇痛、隱痛或脹痛. 痛甚時則竄及兩上肢，得暖則舒:食欲不振，暖氣吞酸，胃脘嘈雜，噫氣頻作，大便干秘，咳嗽則腹部及背部隱痛，語音低微，面色青黃，身體虛弱，脈象沉弦:中脘及左側梁門,天樞和肝俞、脾俞、胃俞、腎俞、氣海俞均有壓痛:胃腸貝餐检查無異常發現.	[Clinical case 38] stomachache Patient: Xing, male, age 26, 1st visit on Nov. 6 1964, File no. 0I3255. [Chief complaints] stomachache for ten years, due to cold and coolness causing harm to the stomach. [history of present illness] ten years earlier, due to an excessive consumption of sugarcanes, the stomach was damaged by cold and coolness; since then, the symptoms were often triggeredby cold and coolness, mental depression and anger or excessive fatigue. Pain occurred in the R12 (Zhōng Wǎn) area and the lower and left sides of the upper abdomen and the region surrounding the umbilicus, with acute pain or mild pain or pain with swelling, When pain becomes acute, it will become migratory to affect the upper limbs, relieved by warmness; poor appetite, bleching and acid regurgitation, gastric discomfort with acid regurgitation, frequent belching, constipation, cough causing mild pain in the abdomen and the back, low and feeble voice, green-yellowish complexion, weak body, deep and wiry pulse; pressure pain in the following regions: R12 (Zhōng Wǎn), left S21 (Liáng Mén), S25 (Tiān Shū) B18 (Gān Shū), B20 (Pí Shū), B21 (Wèi Shū); B23 (Shèn Shū), B24 (Qì Hǎi Shū). No abnormal findings during barium meal examination of gastro-intestinal tract.

2587	[医案 38] 应如何處方？ A 照海, 幽門, 下巨虛; B 上巨虛, 商丘, 手三里; C 梁門,間使、太衝; D陰陵泉, 中脘, 周榮.	[Clinical case 38] what points should be selected? A. K6 (Zhào Hǎi), K21 (Yōu Mén), S39 (Xià Jù Xū); B. S37 (Shàng Jù Xū), Sp5 (Shāng Qiū), Li10 (Shǒu Sān Lǐ); C. S21 (Liáng Mén), P5 (Jiān Shǐ), Lv3 (Tài Chōng); D. Sp9 (Yīn Líng Quán), R12 (Zhōng Wǎn), Sp20 (Zhōu Róng.
2588	[医案 38] 是何病機？ A 食滞型胃痛; B 肝氣犯胃型胃痛; C 寒湿型胃痛; D气虛型胃痛.	[Clinical case 38] what is the pathogenesis? A. stomachache due to food stagnation; B. stomachache due to liver energy offending the stomach; C. stomachache due to cold dampness; D. stomachache due to energy deficiency.

2589	[医案 38] 要采用何种治療原則？ A 散寒止痛，益气生津; B 清热化湿，驱瘀止痛; C 化瘀通络，导滞和胃; D 疏肝理氣，和胃調中.	[Clinical case 38] what treatment principle should be used? A. to disperse cold and relieve pain, benefit energy and produce fluids; B. to clear heat and transform dampness, expel coagulation and relieve pain; C. to transform coagulation and connect linking meridians, direct the flow of stagnated energy and harmonize the stomach; D. to disperse the liver and regulate energy, harmonize the stomach and regulate the middle region.

[医案 80] 眩晕 张某，男，42 岁，干部。 患者自诉近年来，时感头目眩晕、站立不稳、每次发作前，先感觉有热气自少腹上冲人头，随即头晕目眩，天旋地转，不能摇动头部，更不能启目，心烦，今晨发汗，口苦舌燥，便秘尿黄，查舌苔薄白，脉弦细数。针灸学.	[Clinical case 80] vertigo Patient: Zhang, male, age 42, officer. In recent years, the patient often displayed headache and vertigo, unable to stand up stably before onset, feeling hot energy ascending from the lower abdomen toward the head, followed by dizziness and vertigo, feeling the whole surroundings were moving and turning, unable to shake the head or open the eyes, mental depression, sweating this morning, bitter taste in the mouth, constipation, yellowish urine, a thin layer of white coating, wiry and fine and rapid pulse.

2590	[医案 80] 应診斷为何病？ A 中气不足型眩晕; B 肾精不足型眩晕; C 肝阳上亢型眩晕; D 痰浊中阻型眩晕.	[Clinical case 80] what is the correct diagnosis? A. vertigo due to insufficient middle energy; B. vertigo due to insufficient kidney essence; C. vertigo due to liver yang uprising; D. vertigo due to turbid phlegm obstructing the middle region.
2591	[医案80] 要采用何种治療原則？ A 清肝潜阳; B 清火息风; C 补气血; D 补肾填精.	[Clinical case 80] what treatment principle should be used? A. to clear the liver and suppress yang; B. to clear fire and stop wind; C. to tone energy and blood; D. to tone the kidney and fill essence.
2592	[医案 80] 应如何處方？ A 至陰，囟會，郗門; B风池、肝俞、肾俞; C 下關，下巨虛，曲泉; D 脾輸，胃俞，膀胱輸.	[Clinical case 80] what points should be selected? A. B67 (Zhì Yīn)，D22 (Xìn Huì)，P4 (Xī Mén); B. G20 (Fēng; Chí)，B18 (Gān Shū)，B23 (Shèn Shū); C. S7 (Xià Guān)，S39 (Xià Jù Xū)，Lv8 (Qū Quán); D. B20 (Pí Shū);B21 (Wèi Shū);B28 (Páng Guāng Shū).

[医案 79] 眩晕 刘某，男，56 岁，素体肥胖，喜食肥甘油腻，自述两天前晨起时突然感到头目牵眩，站立不稳，稍卧片刻后稍有好转。现自觉心烦，胸脘部痞满，不思饮食，恶心，时欲呕吐，四肢倦怠乏力，闭目不想睁眼。舌淡、苔白腻，脉滑。针灸学.	[Clinical case 79] vertigo Patient: Liu, male, age 56. The patient is usually overweight, enjoying fatty, sweet, and greasy food. The patient related that two days earlier, he suddenly felt dizzy on getting up in the morning, unable to stand stable, improving after lying down for a while. At present, he feels depressed, lumpy and full sensations in the chest and stomach, no appetite, nausea, a desire to vomit, fatigued four limbs, love of closing eyes with no desire to open the eyes, pale tongue, white and greasy coating, slippery pulse.

2593	[医案 79] 应診斷为何病？ A 中气不足型眩晕; B 肾精不足型眩晕; C 肝阳上亢型眩晕; D 痰浊中阻型眩晕.	[Clinical case 79] what is the correct diagnosis? A. vertigo due to insufficient middle energy; B. vertigo due to insufficient kidney essence; C. vertigo due to liver yang uprising; D. vertigo due to turbid phlegm obstructing the middle region.
2594	[医案79] 要采用何种治療原則？ A 清肝潜阳; B 运脾化痰; C 补气血; D 补肾填精	[Clinical case 79] what should be the treatment principle? A. to clear the liver and suppress yang; B. to clear fire and stop wind; C. to tone energy and blood; D. to tone the kidney and fill essence.
2595	[医案 79] 应如何處方？ A 至陰，囟會，郗門; B风池、肝俞、肾俞; C 丰隆、中脘、内关; D 脾輸，胃俞，膀胱輸.	[Clinical case 79] what points should be selected? A. B67 (Zhì Yīn)，D22 (Xìn Huì)，P4 (Xī Mén); B. G20 (Fēng; Chí)，B18 (Gān Shū)，B23 (Shèn Shū); C. S40 (Fēng Lóng), R12 (Zhōng Wǎn), P6 (Nèi Guān); D. B20 (Pí Shū);B21 (Wèi Shū);B28 (Páng Guāng Shū).

[医案30] 嘔吐，泄瀉 李xx·男, 45歲· 腹痛腹瀉嘔吐4小時:患者從今晨發生頭暈，惡心，腹部陣發性劇痛，瀉下淡紅色水樣便5次，嘔吐5天，均爲水和食物殘渣:檢查:面色蒼白，神志淡漠，四肢涼:脈細微，舌苔白膩質淡. [河南省選拔中醫人員針灸科臨床病例分析試題]	[Clinical case 30] vomiting, diarrhea Patient: Li, male, age 45. Abdominal pain and diarrhea and vomiting for four hours; this morning, the patient developed dizziness, nausea, paroxysmal abdominal pain, five times of diarrhea with discharges of light-red watery stools, vomiting for five days with mixture of food and dregs; on examination, the patient showed pale complexion, indifferent in spirit, cool four limbs, fine and feeble pulse, white and greasy coating, pale tongue.

2596	[医案 30] 是何病機？ A 寒湿型上吐下泻; B 虛寒型上吐下泻; C 暑湿型上吐下泻; D 食滞型上吐下泻.	[Clinical case 30] what is the pathogenesis? A. simultaneous or alternating vomiting and diarrhea due to cold dampness; B. simultaneous or alternating vomiting and diarrhea due to deficiency and cold; C. simultaneous or alternating vomiting and diarrhea due to summer heat and dampness; D. simultaneous or alternating vomiting and diarrhea due to food stagnation.
2597	[医案 30] 要采用何种治療原則？ A 調理脾胃; B 清暑利湿 C 温中燥湿; D 健脾利湿.	[Clinical case 30] what should be the treatment principle? A. to regulate the spleen and the stomach;.B to clear summer heat and benefit dampness; C. to warm the middle region and dry dampness; D. to strengthen the spleen and benefit dampness.
2598	[医案 30] 应如何處方？ A胃与大腸之募穴; B 胃经与大腸经之合穴; C胃经与大腸经之输穴; D 胃经与大腸经之井穴.	[Clinical case 30] what points should be selected? A. Gathering points (mu xue) of the stomach and large intestine; B. merging points (he xue) of the stomach and large intestine meridians; C. stream points (shu xue) of the stomach and large intestine meridians; D. well points (jing xue) of the stomach and large intestine meridians.

[医案116] 崩漏 王XX，女，29歲，1971年5月18日初診: 主訴: 患崩漏四十天: 現病史: 四十天前因性交後陰道出血至今末止，淋瀝不斷，小腹不痛，自覺口內有血腥氣味，頭暈惡心，氣短倦怠，脈象沉細:婦產科診斷爲慢性子宮頸炎，病理檢查鱗狀上皮增生:曾用中西藥效果不佳.	[Clinical case 116] metrorrhagia and metrostaxis (bleeding from the uterus) Patient; Wang, female, age 29, first visit on May 18 1971. [Chief complaint] bleeding from the uterus / metrorrhagia and metrostaxis for 40 days. [history of present illness] vaginal bleeding began 40 days earlier after sexual intercourse up to now, still continuing, no pain in the lower abdomen, bloody taste in the mouth, dizziness and nausea, short breath and fatigue, deep and fine pulse. Diagnosed in the Obstetrics and Gynecology Department as chronic cervicitis; pathological examination shows hyperplasia of squamous epithelium, treated by Western drugs and Chinese herbs without desired effects.

2599	[医案 116] 是何病機？ A 虛证; B 湿证; C 寒证; D 热证.	[Clinical case 116] what is the pathogenesis? A. deficiency syndrome; B. dampness syndrome; C. cold syndrome; D. hot syndrome.
2600	[医案 116] 要采用何种治療原則？ A 益氣; B 补血; C 塡精; D 升提.	[Clinical case 116] what should the treatment principle be? A. to benefit energy; B. to tone blood; C. to fill kidney essence; D to lift up.
2601	[医案 116] 应如何處方？ A 膀胱輸, 昆崙, 內庭; B 三陰交、合谷，內關; C 三陰交, 腎輸, 外關;. D委中, 溫溜, 下脘.	[Clinical case 116] what points should be selected? A. B28 (Páng Guāng Shū);B60 (Kūn Lún), S44 (Nèi Tíng); B. Sp6 (Sān Yīn Jiāo), Li4 (Hé Gŭ), P6 (Nèi Guān); C. Sp6 (Sān Yīn Jiāo);B23 (Shèn Shū) ,Sj5 (Wài Guān); D. B40 (Wĕi Zhōng), Li7 (Wēn Liū), R10 (Xià Wăn).

[医案 110] 痛经 李某，女，35岁，患者素体虚弱，每于月经过后出现腹痛，痛势绵绵不休，少腹柔软喜按，得热则減，经量少，色淡。并伴有腰酸肢倦，纳差，头晕心悸。舌质淡，脉弦细。针灸学	[Clinical case 110] period pain Patient: Li, female, age 35. The patient was physically weak, with abdominal pain after menstruation that dragged on and on, with tender and soft lower abdomen that craved for massage, which may be relieved by heat. The patient displayed scanty menstrual flow in pale color, accompanied by a sore waist and fatigued limbs, poor appetite, dizziness with palpitaiton, pale tongue, wiry and fine pulse.

2602	[医案 110] 是何病機？ A 虛证 /; B 湿证; C 寒证; D 热证.	[Clinical case 110] what is the pathogenesis? A. deficiency syndrome; B. dampness syndrome; C. cold syndrome; D. hot syndrome.
2603	[医案 110] 要采用何种治療原則？ A 理氣活血; B 温补氣血; C 塡精; D 升提.	[Clinical case 110] what should the treatment principle be? A. to regulate energy and activate blood; B. to warm and tone energy and blood; C. to fill kidney essence; D. to lift up.

2604	[医案110] 应如何治法？ A針刺施補法，同時加灸；B 針刺施泻法，同時加灸；C 針刺施泻法，不可加灸；D針刺施補法，不可 加灸.	[Clinical case 110] what technique should be used? A. acupuncture with tonification, plus moxibustion; B. acupuncture with sedation, plus moxibustion; C. acupuncture with sedation, no moxibustion; D. acupuncture with tonificatopm, no moxibustion.

[医案111] 經行腹痛 陳xx，女，35歲: 行經腹痛已數載:痛從小腹牽引胸，痛甚時需服止痛片方可緩解:但經期尚準，每次經期約3天，量少挾有瘀塊:苔薄白，脈弦細: [湖北省選拔中醫師針灸科臨床病例分析試題]	[Clinical case 111] abdominal pain during menstruation Patient:; Chen, female, age 35. The patient had suffered abdominal pain during menstruation for a number of years, with pain originated from the lower abdomen affecting the chest; the patient relied on pain killers when the pain became severe; however, menstruation was relatively punctual, lasting for 3 days each time, scanty flow mixed with blood clots, thin and white coating, wiry and fine pulse.

2605	[医案111] 是何病機？ A肝失疏泄 氣滯血瘀; B 脾胃失养，气血虚弱; C 肝肾亏损; D 湿热郁结.	[Clinical case 111] what is the pathogenesis? A. failure of the liver in performing the dispersing functions, energy congestion and blood coagulation; B. poor nourishment of the spleen and stomach, deficient energy and blood; C. impaired liver and kidney with poor nourishment; D. congestion of damp heat.
2606	[医案111] 应如何治法？ A 清热利湿止痛; B舒肝理氣，化瘀止痛; C 温经止痛; D 调补肝肾.	[Clinical case 111] what treatment method should be used? A. to clear heat, benefit dampness, and relieve pain; B. to disperse and regulate liver energy, transform coagulation and relieve pain; C. to warm meridians and relieve pain; D. to regulate and tone the liver and kidneys.
2607	[医案111] 应如何處方？ A 膀胱輸，昆崙，內庭; B 關元,三陰交、合谷; C 三陰交，腎輸，外關; D 委中，溫溜，下脘.	[Clinical case 111] what points should be selected? A. B28 (Páng Guāng Shū) B60 (Kūn Lún), S44 (Nèi Tíng); B. R4 (Guān Yuán), Sp6 (Sān Yīn Jiāo), Li4 (Hé Gǔ); C. Sp6 (Sān Yīn Jiāo) B23 (Shèn Shū) ,Sj5 (Wài Guān); D. B40 (Wěi Zhōng), Li7 (Wēn Liū), R10 (Xià Wǎn).

[医案114] 兩乳房痛 包xx，女，30歲，1969年9月17日初診: 主訴: 兩乳房痛，痛經年餘: 現病史:一年多前，因生氣後出現兩乳房脹痛，時覺刺痛，郁怒尤甚:經期腹痛，色黑量少，經期前錯:精神抑郁，心煩多怒，頭悶發沉，多夢少寐，潮熱身困，食欲不振，身體瘦弱，脈象沉澀: [選自‘常用輸穴臨床發揮']	[Clinical case 114] pain in both breasts Patient: Bao, female, age 30, first visit in Sept. 1969. [Chief complaints] pain in both breasts, and period pain for over a year. [history of present illness] over a year ago, the patient experienced swollen pain in both breasts after anger, with a feeling of pricking pain occasionally, intensified by inhibition and anger. The symptoms included: abdominal pain during menstruation, scanty menstrual flow in black, premature and irregular menstruation, mental depression, frequent anger, dull and heavy sensations in the head, many dreams and little sleep, tidal fever with body discomfort, poor appetite, skinny and weak, deep and retarded pulse.

2608	[医案 114] 是何病機？ A 肝氣郁結; B 气血虛弱; C 痰气阻闭; D 肝胆湿热.	[Clinical case 114] what is the pathogenesis? A. liver energy congestion; B. deficient energy and blood; C. obstruction and closure of phlegm energy; D. damp heat of the liver and gallbladder.
2609	[医案 114] 应如何治法？ A 針补三陰交、內關; B 針瀉歸來, 合谷; C針瀉三陰交、內關; D 針补歸來, 合谷.	[Clinical case 114] what treatment method should be used? A. needle the following points with tonifcation: Sp6 (Sān Yīn Jiāo), P6 (Nèi Guān). B. needle the following points with sedation: S29 (Guī Lái), Li4 (Hé Gŭ). C. needle the following points with sedation: Sp6 (Sān Yīn Jiāo), P6 (Nèi Guān). D. needle the following points with tonifcation: S29 (Guī Lái), Li4 (Hé Gŭ).

[医案131] 先兆流產 尙xx，女，37歲，1965年11月27日初診: 主訴: 陰道出血，小腹墜痛，腰痠隱痛已三天: 現病史: 近因當地水災，飲食欠佳，體質不好，復因三天前勞累過度，而致腰痠隱痛，小腹墜痛，漏血淋漓，血量不多:平素經常頭暈目眩，精神倦怠: 檢查: 面色不華，舌淡苔白，脈象細數而滑，語言低微，腹痛不安，觸及小腹有胎動感:此第四胎已五個月: 婦科檢查診斷爲先兆流產: [選自 '常用輸穴臨床發揮']	[Clinical case 131] threatened abortion Patient: Shang, female, age 37, first visit on Nov. 27 1965. [Chief complaints] vaginal bleeding, falling pain in the lower abdomen, a sore waist and mild pain for three days. [history of present illness] improper eating and poor physical condition due to recent flooding in the local region; and on top of that, her overworking and fatigue three days ago caused poor appetite, a sore waist and mild pain, falling pain in the lower abdomen, continual vaginal bleeding in small quantity, often feeling headache and vertigo, mental fatigue. [examinations] poor complexion, pale tongue with white coating, fine and rapid and slippery pulse, low voice, abdominal pain with insecure feeling, feeling of fetus motion on touching the lower abdomen. This is the fourth pregnancy already in the fifth month, a gynecologic examination diagnoses it as threatened abortion.

2610	[医案 131] 是何病機？ A血热之胎動不安 /; B 氣血虛虧，胎元不固之胎動不安 /; C 肾虛之胎動不安; D气郁之胎動不安.	[Clinical case 131] what is the pathogenesis? A. insecure fetus due to blood heat; B. insecure fetus due to energy and blood deficiency, unstable fetus essence; C. insecure fetus due to kidney deficiency; D. insecure fetus due to energy congestion.
2611	[医案131] 应如何治法？ A 針補三陰交、合谷、腎俞; B 針泻三陰交、合谷、腎俞 /; C 針補陰陵泉, 陽陵泉, 丰隆 / D 針泻陰陵泉, 陽陵泉, 丰隆.	[Clinical case 131] what treatment method should be used? A. needle with tonification: Sp6 Sān Yīn Jiāo），Li4 (Hé Gŭ)，B23 (Shèn Shū). B. needle with sedation: Sp6 （Sān Yīn Jiāo），Li4 （Hé Gŭ），B23 （Shèn Shū）. B. needle with tonification: Sp9 (Yīn Líng Quán), G34 (Yáng Líng Quán), S40 (Fēng Lóng). D. needle with sedation: Sp9 (Yīn Líng Quán). G34 (Yáng Líng Quán), S40 (Fēng Lóng).

[医案 136] 疳积 杨某，男，5 岁，患者经常饮食少，面色萎黄，手心和足心经常发热，近几天来，饮食欠佳，甚至不食，形体消瘦，皮肤干燥 毛发稀疏 腹大脐突。舌绛，苔黄。 针灸学	[Clinical case 136] malnutrition in children Patient: Yang, male, age 5. The patient normally suffers from poor appetite, withering and yellowish complexion, constant hot sensations in the center of palms and center of feet; in the past few days, the patient displayed poor appetite, or no appetite at all, skinny, dry skin, sparse hairs, enlarged abdomen and protruding umbilicus, deep-red tongue, yellowish coating.

2612	医案 136] 应診斷为何病？ A 消化不良; B 风寒感冒; C 蛔虫症; D. 疳积.	[Clinical case 136] what is the correct diagnosis? A. indigestion; B. common cold due to attack of wind and cold; C. roundworm; D malnutrition.
2613	[医案 136] 用四缝治療有何方义？ A 四缝是治疗小儿消化不良的经验有效穴; B 四缝是治疗小儿感冒的经验有效穴; C 四缝是治疗小儿疳积的经验有效穴; D 四缝是治疗小儿蛔虫症的经验有效穴.	[Clinical case 136] what is the rationale for using Sì Féng in treatment? A. from experience, Sì Féng is an effective point for indigesion in children; B. from experience, Sì Féng is an effective point for the common cold in children; C. from experience, Sì Féng is an effective point for malnutrition in children; D from experience, Sì Féng is an effective point for roundworm in children.

[医案 160] 乳痈 杨某，女，30 岁。患者 2 周前产一男孩，开始时乳汁分泌充足，2 天前因小事和家人生气突感乳房红肿胀痛，不可触摸，乳汁瘀积，排泄不畅。体温 39; C 以上，口渴纳減。舌红，苔薄，脉弦数。针灸学	[Clinical case 160] carbuncle in the breast (acute mastitis) Patient: Yang, female, age 30. The patient gave birth to a boy two weeks ago; she had sufficient milk secretion at the beginning; and due to an argument with family members over trivial matters two days ago, her breasts began to swell with pain, aversion to touching, retention of milk with obstruction, body temperature at over 39 degrees C, thirst and poor appetitie, red tongue, thin coating, wiry and rapid pulse.

2614	[医案 160] 应診斷为何病？ A 乳痈（血瘀）; B 乳痈（肝郁气滞）; C 乳痈（乳积）; D 乳痈（火毒）.	[Clinical case 160] what is the correct diagnosis? A. carbuncle in the breast (acute mastitis) due to blood coagulation; B. carbuncle in the breast (acute mastitis) due to liver inhibition; C. carbuncle in the breast (acute mastitis) due to milk accumulation; D. carbuncle in the breast (acute mastitis) due to toxic fire.
2615	[医案 160]處方中如何选用治疗乳痈的经验穴？ A 肩髎; B 肩髃; C 肩貞; D 肩井.	[Clinical case 160] what experience point for treating carbuncle in the breast (acute mastitis) should be selected? A. Sj14 (Jiān Liáo); B. Li15 (Jiān Yú); C. Si9 (Jiān Zhēn; D. G21 Jiān Jǐng)

2616	[医案 160] 应如何操作？ A毫针刺，用补法，留针; B毫针刺，用泻法，留针; C毫针刺，用泻法，不留针; D毫针刺，用泻法，及灸法.	[Clinical case 160] what techniques should be applied? A. acupuncture by tonification, with retention of needle; B acupuncture by sedation, with retention of needle; C. acupuncture by sedation, without retention of needle; D. acupuncture by sedation, with moxibustion also.

[医案176] 兩下肢拘急 王xx，女，40歲:1973年10月9日初診: 主訴: 兩下肢拘急不適已三年多: 現病史: 三年多來，每天晚上睡覺後兩小腿不適，不時伸屈，活動則舒，熟睡後兩下肢小腿突然抽搐而醒，冬天、陰雨感寒和勞動後加重，得暖或按壓則舒，伴有氣短頭暈、動則氣喘心跳、身困乏力. 站立或行走時下肢困痛·潮熱肢困、下肢無力等症狀:脈象沉弱: 既往史: 1972年9月患急性腎炎住院治愈已三個月: [選自‘常用輸穴臨床發揮']	[Clinical case 176] twitching of lower limbs Patient: Wang, female, age 40. First visit on Oct. 9 1973. [Chief complaints] twitching of lower limbs with discomfort for over three years. [history of present illness] over three years ago, the patient began to experience discomfort of lower limbs on sleep every night, constantly stretching and flexing to feel comfortable by movements, waking up from deep sleep due to sudden twitching of the lower legs; the symptoms were intensifed in winter after raining or cold or labor, but relieved by warmness and pressing, accompanied by short breath and dizziness, movements causing short breath and papitaiton. Her body felt in discomfort with low energy, with pain in the lower limbs caused by standing or walking, tidal fever with troubled legs, and weakness of the legs, etc. deep and weak pulse. [history] hospitalized in Sept. 1972 due to acute nephritis, recovered and discharged three months ago.

2617	[医案176] 应如何處方？ A 針泻三陰交、合谷; B 針補關元，歸來; C針補三陰交、合谷; D 針泻關元，歸來.	[Clinical case 176] what points should be selected? A. apply acupuncture by sedation to Sp6 （Sān Yīn Jiāo）, Li4 （Hé Gǔ）; B. apply acupuncture by tonification to R4 (Guān Yuán), S29 (Guī Lái); C. apply acupuncture by tonification to Sp6 （Sān Yīn Jiāo）, Li4 （Hé Gǔ）; D. apply acupuncture by sedation to: R4 (Guān Yuán), S29 (Guī Lái).

[医案179] 偏癱 孔 xx,男,7 歲. 一歲時因患腦炎後遺留左側偏癱,失語，經藥物治療無效,乃來行新針治療. [選自'針刺療法']	[Clinical case 179] hemiplegia Patient: Kong, male, age 7. The patient suffered aftereffects of encephalitis when one year old, with hemiplegia on the left side, and aphasia, which were treated by drugs without effect. The patient came for new acupuncture treatment, basically by scalp acupuncture.

2618	[医案 179] 治疗应用何穴？ A環中，經中，神門，極泉; B 上廉泉，金津玉液, 曲池, 合谷; C 外四滿，五虎，建里，間使; D下極輸，澤前，行間，下脘.	[Clinical case 179] what points should be selected for treatment? A. Huán Zhōng ,Jīng Zhōng ,H7 (Shén Mén) ,H1 (Jí Quán); B. Shàng Lián Quán ,Jīn Jīn Yù Yè , Li11 （Qū Chí）, Li4 （Hé Gǔ）; C. Wài Sì Mǎn, Wǔ Hǔ, R11 (Jiàn Lǐ). P5 (Jiān Shǐ); D. Xià Jí Shū , Zé Qián , Lv2 (Xíng Jiān), R10 (Xià Wǎn)。

[医案 175] 腰痛 刘某某，女，35 岁。近日出差，天气突变，被雨水所搏，现感腰部冷痛重着、酸麻，活动转侧不利，拘急不可俯仰。查其舌苔白腻，脉沉而迟缓。针灸学	[Clinical case 175] lumbago Patient: Liu, female, age 35. On a business trip recently, the patient was under the impact of sudden change in weather and rains; at present the symptoms include cold and pain in the loins, aching and numbness, difficulty in turning the body, spasms with inability to bend forward and backward; on examination, the patient displays white and greasy coating, deep and slow and relaxed pulse.

2619	[医案175] 应如何处方？ A太溪，腰奇，天井; B 肾俞、腰眼、委中; C 天冲，腰根，外關; D 膝關，腰宜，侠溪.	[Clinical case 175] what points should be used? A. K3 (Tài Xī)，Yāo Qí，Sj10 (Tiān Jǐng); B. B23 （Shèn Shū），Yāo Yǎn，B40 （Wěi Zhōng）; C. G9 (Tiān; Chōng) ，Yāo Gēn，Sj5 (Wài Guān); D. Lv7 (Xī Guān)，Yāo Yí，G43 (Xiá Xī)。

[医案180] 右半身麻木 哥台起·麥克溫，男，38歲，1979年4月10日初診. 主訴: 身痛無力，右半身麻木已四年: 現病史: 四年來全身無力尤以右半身爲甚，右側半身及兩踝關節痠痛，站立五至十分鐘即覺右下肢麻木，向右側躺臥時亦覺麻木，伴有尿頻尿急、排尿無力、尿液失禁、腰背痠痛、氣短、健忘、心悸、失眠、多汗等症狀，面色蒼白，舌苔薄白，脈象沉細無力:每聽到關門或拉笛聲音，頭部即脹痛發昏片刻: 既往史: 約在十五歲時患梅毒病，係父母遺傳，經過治療右腿留下一個疤痕: 內科以中樞性梅毒合并右半身不完全麻痺轉針灸治療: [選自 '常用輸穴臨床發揮']	[Clinical case 180] numbness on the right half of the body Patient: Ge Tai Qi Mai Ke Wen, male, age 38. First visit on April 10 1979. [chielf complaints] pain in the body with weakness, numbness on the right half of the body for four years. [history of present illness] in the past four years, the patient experienced the following symptoms: weakness of the whole body, the right half in particular, aching pain on the right half of the body and both ankle joints, numbness in the lower limbs, which may be felt after standing for five to ten minutes, and feeling of numbness while lying on the right side, accompanied by frequent and urgent urination, weak urination, incontinence of urination, lumbago and pain in the back, short breath, forgetfulness, palpitation, insomnia, profuse perspiration, pale complexion, thin and white coating, deep and fine and weak pulse, swollen headache and dizziness for a few minutes on hearing the noise produced by closing the door or a car sounding its horn. [history]; contracted syphilis at about the age of 15, an hereditary infection; and a scar was left on the right leg after treatment. Referred to acupuncture treatment by Internal Medicine Dept due to central syphilis combined incomplete paralysis on the right half of the body.

2620	[医案 180] 应如何處方？ A 針泻三陰交、合谷; B 針補關元, 歸來; C 針補三陰交、合谷; D 針泻關元, 歸來.	[Clinical case 180] what points should be selected? A. apply acupuncture by sedation to Sp6 (Sān Yīn Jiāo)，Li4 （Hé Gǔ）; B. apply acupuncture by tonification to R4 (Guān Yuán), S29 (Guī Lái); C. apply acupuncture by tonification to Sp6 （Sān Yīn Jiāo），Li4 （Hé Gǔ）; D.

		apply acupuncture by sedation to: R4 (Guān Yuán), S29 (Guī Lái).

[医案164] 腸癰 陶xx，男，30歲: 患者平素健康，于昨天上午在田間勞動時，感到臍周圍疼痛，陣發性加劇，低熱，惡心，嘔吐1次·今日腹痛轉移到右下腹，拒按，按之痛甚，大便干，尿黃，脈弦緊，舌苔薄膩黃: [河南省選拔中醫人員針灸科臨床病集分析試題]	[Clinical case 164] Acute appendicitis, periappendicular abscess Patient: Tao, male, age 30. The patient is normally healthy. While working in the field yesterday morning, he felt pain surrounding the umbilicus, becoming more intense periodically, with low fever, nausea, vomiting once; today, abdominal pain is moving to the right lower abdomen, with aversion to pressure, which intensifies the pain; other signs include dry stools, yellowish urine, wiry and tight pulse, thin and greasy and yellowish coating.

2621	[医案164] 应如何處方？ A 应取有关合穴募穴; B应取有关经穴井穴; C 应取有关背输穴郄穴; D应取有关母穴子穴.	[Clinical case 164] what points should be selected? A. pertinent he xue (merging points) and mu xue (gathering points) should be selected; B. pertinent jing xue (stream points) and jing xue (well points) should be selected; C. pertinent back shu points (posterior transport points) and xi xue (fissural points) should be selected; D. pertinent mother points and child points should be selected.

[医案177] 右側大腿內側疼痛 患者 沈xx，性別 女，年齡 45歲 主訴: 右側大腿內側疼痛已一個月: 症狀: 有大腿內側疼痛，右膝伸屈困難，經針灸治療十餘次，症狀無明顯好轉: 檢查: 右大腿內側沿大隱靜脈處I5釐米長有明顯壓痛，觸之局部靜脈血管較粗硬: 印象: 右側大隱靜脈炎: [選自 '針灸配穴']	[Clinical case 177] pain in the medial thigh on the right side Patient: Shen, female, age 45. [Chief complaints] pain in the medial thigh on the right side for a month. {symptoms} pain in the medial thigh, difficulty in stretching and flexing the right knee, treated by acupuncture and moxibustion for over ten times with no apparent improvement. [Examination] apparent pressure pain on the medial side of the right thigh along greate saphenous vein for 15 cm, relatively rough and hard of local venous blood vessels. [impression] inflammation of right greater saphenous vein.

2622	[医案 177] 应如何选用八会穴？ A 藏会：章門; B 脉会：太淵; C 骨会：大杼; D 髓会：懸鍾.。	[Clinical case 177] which of the eight meeting points (ba hui xue or influential points) should be selected? A. meeting point (ba hui xue or influential point) of viscera--- Lv13 (Zhāng Mén); B. meeting point (ba hui xue or influential point) of blood vessels ---Lu9 (Tài Yuān); C. meeting point (ba hui xue or influential point) of bones--- B11 (Dà Zhù); D. meeting point (ba hui xue or influential point) of marrow--- G39 (Xuán Zhōng)

[医案 168] 脱肛 张某某，男，54 岁。患者大便时有肛肠脱垂感 5 年余，曾患胃下垂，有大便秘结史，近期因大便干结致	[Clinical case 168] proctoptosis (prolapse of anus) Patient; Zhang, male, age 54. In the past five years, the patient had suffered prolapse of the anus and intestine while having a bowel

使脫肛加重，尤其是以劳累时加重，并伴有神疲乏力，面色苍白。舌淡，苔薄白，脉细无力。针灸学	movement. He had suffered gastroptosis before wth a history of constipation. Recently, the prolapse of anus intensified due to constipation, particularly after labor and fatigue, accompanied by fatigued spirit and weakness, pale complexion, pale tongue, thin white coating, fine and weak pulse.

2623	[医案168] 应如何處方？ A 陰陵泉，三陰交，曲泉；B 上關，合谷，昆崙；C百会、长强、大肠俞；D 足臨泣，足三里，中脘.	[Clinical case168] what points should be selected? A. Sp9 (Yīn Líng Quán), Sp6 (Sān Yīn Jiāo), Lv8 (Qū Quán); B. G3 (Shàng Guān Li4 (Hé Gǔ); B60 (Kūn Lún); C. D20 (Bǎi Huì), D1 (Cháng Qiáng);B25 (Dà Cháng Shū); D. G41 (Zú Lín Qì, Lín Qì), S36 (Zú Sān Lǐ), R12 (Zhōng Wǎn).

[医案92] 左腰腿痺證 周xx，男，36歲: 患者主訴左側腰腿痛已8年左右，起病於勞動出汗下冷水之後:曾經斷續地進行治療，時愈時發，每逢氣候較冷、潮濕，及疲勞時則易復發·近年由於疲勞，夜臥受寒，左腰連下肢后側疼痛加重，迄已旬日:今步履艱難，胃納亦減，大便時蹲下疼痛:檢查，左腰腿外形如常，環跳、殷門部壓之感痛，脈沉弦;舌苔薄白.[浙江省選拔中醫人員針灸科試題]	[Clinical case 92] rheumatism on the left side of waist and legs Patient: Zhou, male, age 36 [Chief complaints] the patient had suffered lumbago and leg pain on the right side for about 8 years; initially, the symptoms occurred after perspiration and washing with cold water after labor; since then treatment had continued on and off, symptoms come and go, but attack more often in cold and damp weather. In recent years, due to fatigue and working, under the attack of cold at night, the patient experienced more intensive pain on the left side of the waist extending to the posterior-lateral side of the lower limbs, for about ten days now. At present, the symptoms are walking difficulty, greatly decreased appetite, painful when squatting for bowel movements. [Examination] normal appearance on the left side of waist and legs, pressure pain in G30 (Huán Tiào) and B37 (Yīn Mén), with deep and wiry pulse, thin white coating.

2624	[医案92] 要采用何种治療原則？ A 补中益气; B 散寒祛濕; C 清热解毒; D 活血止痛.	[Clinical case 92] what should the treatment principle be? A. to tone the middle region and benefit energy; B. to disperse cold and expel dampness; C. to clear heat and detoxicate; D. to activate blood and relieve pain.
2625	[医案92] 应如何處方？ A 取手太陽經穴爲主; B 取足太陽經穴爲主; C 取足太阴經穴爲主; D 取手太阴經穴爲主.	[Clinical case 92] what points should be selected? A. select the points on the greater yang meridians of hand as the primary points; B. select the points on the greater yang meridians of foot as the primary points; C select the points on the greater yin meridians of foot as the primary points; D. select the points on the greater yin meridians of hand as the primary points.

2626	[医案 92] 应如何操作？ A 宜浅刺留針瀉法，重刺激，不可用溫針灸法; B宜深刺留針补法，轻刺激，可用溫針灸法; C 宜深刺留針瀉法，重刺激，不可用溫針灸法; D 宜深刺留針瀉法，重刺激，可用溫針灸法.	[Clinical case 92] what techniques should be applied? A. shallow insertion with retention of needle and by sedation, heavy stimulation, without warm needling or moxibustion; B. deep insertion with retention of needle and by tonfification, light stimulation, warm needling or moxibustion; C. deep insertion with retention of needle and by sedation, heavy stimulation, without warm needling or moxibustion; D. deep insertion with retention of needle and by sedation, heavy stimulation, using warm needling with moxibustion.

[医案93] 痺證 陳xx，男，47歲，工人，于8月某日就診· 患者素體虛弱，有身痛史，近因冒雨推車，腰關節疼痛加劇，重□無力，納少，腹瀉，自服小活絡丹等藥少效:但兩膝關節仍然沉重，麻木、疼痛,色微黃，舌苔薄白，脈沉緩無力，兩膝關節微腫，壓痛明顯;活動受限. [湖南省選拔中醫人員針灸科試題]	[Clinical case 93] rheumatism Patient:; Chen, male, age 47, worker, first visit in August. [Chief complaints] the patient is normally weak with a bodyache history; recently due to pushing a cart on rainy days, his pain in the lumbar joints was intensified and he felt too weak to hold heavy objects, with poor appetite and diarrhea. The patient decided to take xiao huo luo dan, etc by himself, but with little effect. He still felt heaviness in the knee joints, numbness, and pain, with slightly yellowish complexion, thin white coating, deep and relaxed and weak pulse, slight swelling in the knee joints, apparent pressure pain, restricted movements.

2627	[医案 93]根据辩证是何病機？ A 热痺; B着痺; C 寒痺; D 风痺.	[Clinical case 93] what is the pathogenesis according to differential diagnosis? A. hot rheumatism (re bi); B. fixed rheumatism (damp rheumatism or shi bi); C. cold rheumatism (han bi); D. wind rheumatism (feng bi).
2628	[医案 93] 要采用何种治療原則？ A 清热，凉血，止痛; B 溫經，散寒，止痛; C 溫經，燥濕，止痛; D 清热，利湿，止痛.	[Clinical case 93] what should the treatment principle be? A. to clear heat, cool blood, and relieve pain; B. to warm meridians, disperse cold, and relieve pain; C. to warm meridians, dry up dampness，and relieve pain; D. to clear heat, benefit dampness, and relieve pain.
2629	[医案 93] 应如何處方？ A 陽陵泉, 三陰交, 神庭; B太溪, 太淵, 太白; C 命門、腰陽關、足三里; D上巨虛, 昆崙, 足三里.	[Clinical case 93] what points should be selected? A. G34 (Yáng Líng Quán), Sp6 (Sān Yīn Jiāo), D24 (Shén Tíng); B. K3 (Tài Xī), Lu9 (Tài Yuān), Sp3 (Tài Bái); C. D4 (Mìng Mén), D3 (Yāo Yáng Guān), S36 (Zú Sān Lǐ); D. S37 (Shàng Jù Xū); B60 (Kūn Lún), S36 (Zú Sān Lǐ).

[医案94] 痺証周xx，女, 42歲，工人: 主訴:右側腰腿疼痛已半月之久:日輕夜重，不能翻身，近四天因疼痛不能睡眠，現在腰背不能伸直，行走時腿外側有觸電樣串痛，患者曾	[Clinical case 94] blockage condition, such as rheumatism Patient: Zhou, female, age 42, worker. [Chief complaints] the patient experienced pain on the right side of waist and legs for half a month; the pain became lighter during the day and more severe at night; she was unable to turn over the body. In the past four days, she could

針刺右側足少陽經環跳等穴，效果不明顯: 檢查: 痛苦病容，營養中等，右側直腿抬高試驗45度:右側環跳穴處有明顯壓痛，局部無紅腫，脈弦，舌苔薄白: [選自 '針灸配穴']	not sleep due to pain; at present, she is unable to stretch the waist and back, with running pain like electric shock on the lateral side of legs on walking. The patient received acupuncture treatment on the right side with the points on the lesser yang meridians of foot such as G30 (Huán Tiào) with no apparent effect. [Examination] the patient looks in pain, average nutrition, the test on lifting up the right stretched leg shows 45 degrees, apparent pressure pain at G30 (Huán Tiào) on the right side, no signs of local red swelling, wiry pulse, thin and white coating.

2630	[医案 94] 根据辩证是何病機？ A寒濕之邪，乘虛而侵襲肾經; B風寒濕之邪，侵襲膽經; C 風寒之邪，侵襲肝經; D風寒濕之邪，侵襲大肠經及膀胱經.	[Clinical case 94] what is the pathogenesis according to differential diagnosis? A. pathogenic cold and dampness penetrate into the kidney meridian; B. pathogenic wind cold and dampness penetrate into the gallbladder meridian; C. pathogenic wind cold penetrate into the liver meridian; D. pathogenic wind cold and dampness penetrate into the large intestine and bladder meridians.
2631	[医案 94] 应如何處方？ A 外關; B 足三里; C提托; D秩邊.	[Clinical case 94] what point should be selected? A. Sj5 (Wài Guān); B. S36 (Zú Sān Lǐ); C. Tí Tuō; D. B54 (Zhì biān).

[医案173] 兩肩疼痛 王xX，女，44歲，工人: 主訴:兩肩疼痛已七天，因受風寒所得:第二天發現兩肩關節及背部疼痛，不能活動，兩上肢前舉及背伸有困難，曾以循經取穴法，針刺肩貞，後溪諸穴，效果不明顯: 檢查: 痛苦病容，兩上肢上舉時疼痛難忍，舉右手僅與鼻同高，左側較右側稍高，但舉肘高也不能過頸，背屈兩手僅可觸至第二腰椎同高:脈緊，苔白: [選自 '針灸配穴']	[Clinical case 173] pain in the shoulders Patient: Wang, female, age 44, worker. [Chief complaints] pain in the shoulders for seven days, due to the attack of wind cold. On the following day, she developed pain in the shoulder joints and the back, unable to move, difficulty in lifting up upper limbs and in stretching the back. She was treated by the selected points along the meridians, by Si9 (Jiān Zhēn) and Si3 (Hòu Xī), etc with no apparent effect. [Examination] the patient looks in pain, with intolerable pain on lifting up the upper limbs; she can only lift up the right hand up to the nose, and lifting the left hand slightly higher, but unable to lift up the elbow to pass the neck. She can lift up both hands toward the back to reach only as high as the second lumbar vertebra; she displays tight pulse and whitish coating.

2632	[医案 173] 根据辩证是何病機？ A其疼痛部位正屬大腸經經脈所過之處; B 其疼痛部位正屬小腸經經脈所過之處; C其疼痛部位正屬膀胱經經脈所過之處; D其疼痛部位正屬胆經經脈所過之處.	[Clinical case 173] what is the pathogenesis according to differential diagnosis? A. The region in which pain takes place belongs to the distribution of the large intestine meridian; B. The region in which pain takes place falls within the distribution of the small intestine meridian; C. The region in which pain takes place belongs to the distribution of the bladder meridian; D. The region in which pain takes place belongs to the distribution of the gallbladder meridian.
2633	[医案 173] 用飛揚治療有何方义？ A 飛揚是治疗疼痛的经验有效穴; B 飛揚是下合穴; C 以下接經取穴法; D 以上接經取穴法.	[Clinical case 173] what is the rationale for using B58 (Feī Yáng) in treatment? A. from experience, B58 (Feī Yáng) is an effective point for pain relief; B. B58 (Feī Yáng) is a lower merging point (xia he xue); C. selecting point on the follow-up connecting meridian (xia jie jing qu xue fa); D. selecting point on the prior connecting meridian (shang jie jing qu xue fa).

[医案178] 右足跟疼痛 張xx，女 36歲，·工人: 主訴: 半月前由於受潮濕而致右足跟疼痛，走路障礙: 檢查，體胖，觸及右足跟部壓痛明顯:脈濡緩，苔薄白: [選自 '針灸配穴']	[Clinical case 178] pain in the right heel Patient: Zhang, female, age 36, worker. [Chief complaints] half a month ago, the ptient developed pain in the right heel due to the attack of dampness with difficulty in walking. [Examination] obese body type, apparent pressure pain in the right heel, soft and relaxed pulse, thin white coating.

2634	[医案 178] 用大陵治療有何方义？ A 大陵是治疗疼痛的经验有效穴; B 大陵是下合穴; C以下接經取穴法; D 以上接經取穴法.	[Clinical case 178] what is the rationale for using P7 (Dà Líng) in treatment? A. from experience, P7 (Dà Líng) is an effective point for pain relief; B. P7 (Dà Líng) is a lower merging point (xia he xue); C. selecting point on the follow-up connecting meridian (xia jie jing qu xue); D. selecting point on the prior connecting meridian (shang jie jing qu xue).

[医案147] 蕁麻疹 李xx，曾患蕁麻疹一年多，服用各種藥物，每日早晚仍常發作，未能控制，於1976年1月14日改用新針治療: [選自'針刺療法']	[Clinical case 147] urticaria Patient: Li. The patient had suffered urticaria for over one year; oral administraion of various drugs had failed to control the symptoms, which attacked every morning and evening. The patient changed to new acupuncture therapy on Jan. 14 1976.

2635	[医案 147] 治疗应如何處方？ A 曲池、血海、足三里; B 小腸輸，陽池，陽陵泉; C后溪，經渠,. 間使; D 通天，合谷，百會.	[Clinical case 147] what points should be selected? A. Li11 (Qū Chí), Sp10 (Xuè Hǎ), S36 (Zú Sān Lǐ); B. B27 (Xiǎo; Cháng Shū), Sj4 (Yáng Chí), G34 (Yáng Líng Quán); C. Si3 (Hòu Xī), Lu8 (Jīng Qú), P5 (Jiān Shǐ); D. B7 (Tōng Tiān), Li4 (Hé Gǔ), D20 (Bǎi Huì).

[医案 194] 目赤肿痛 马某，女，38 岁，患者今晨起床后，突感双眼灼热，羞明，流泪，眼睑肿痛，白睛红赤，眵多黄粘，且头痛、鼻塞。舌苔薄白，脉浮数。针灸学.	[Clinical case 194] pink eyes with swelling and pain in the eyes Patient: Ma, female, age 38. The patient suddenly felt burning sensations in both eyes after getting up this morning, with photophoia, watering of the eyes, swelling and edema of the eyelids, yellowish and sticky watering of eyes, and headache, nasal congestion, thin and whitish coating, superficial and rapid pulse.

2636	[医案 194] 根据辩证是何病機？ A 外感风寒; B 外感风热; C 肝气郁结; D 肝胆火盛.	[Clinical case 194] what is the pathogenesis according to differential diagnosis? A. external attack of wind cold; B. external attack of wind heat; C. liver energy congestion; D. excessive fire in the liver and gallbladder.
2637	[医案 194] 用太阳点刺出血治療有何方义？ A 消风去湿止痛; B 通络明目止痛; C 泄火疏肝止痛; D 泄热消肿止痛.	[Clinical case 194] what is the rationale for using Tài Yáng by dotted insertion for bloodletting in treatment? A. to eliminate wind, remove dampness, and relieve pain; B. to open up the reticular meridians, sharpen vision, and relieve pain; C. to sedate fire, disperse the liver, and relieve pain; D. to sedate heat, reduce swelling, and relieve pain.

[医案184] 眼瞼下垂 何xx，女，60歲，1970年10月17日初診: 主訴: 眼瞼下垂已兩個多月: 現在證: 兩上眼瞼下垂，睜眼和咀嚼無力，疲勞則重，休息則輕，伴有氣短、言語無力、身困乏力、嗜臥嗜睡、兩足不溫等症狀:半年來善飢，晨瀉便溏一日四至五次，脈象細弱: [選自 '常用輸穴臨床發揮']	[Clinical case 184] ptosis (dropping of the upper eyelids) Patient: He, female, age 60, first visit on Oct. 17 1970. [Chief complaints] ptosis (dropping of the upper eyelids) for over two months. [Present symptoms] dropping of the upper eyelids, lack of power to open the eyes and chew, particularly when fatigued, symptoms getting better while resting, accompanied by short breath, weak speech, discomfort and lack of power, love of lying down and sleepiness, two feet not warm, etc. Morbid hunger since half a year ago, diarrhea with discharge of watery stools in the morning, four to five times daily, with fine and weak pulse.

2638	[医案 184] 根据辩证是何病機？ A 脾氣不足; B 风邪入络; C 气滞血瘀; D 血虛生风.	[Clinical case 164] what is the pathogenesis according to differential diagnosis? A. insufficient spleen energy; B. pathogenic wind attacking the linking meridians; C. energy congestion and blood coagulation; D. deficient blood generating wind.
2639	[医案 184] 要采用何种治療原則？ A 补中益气; B 氣血雙補; C 补血驱风; D 补阳祛湿.	[Clinical case 184] what should the treatment principle be? A. to tone the middle region and benefit energy; B. to tone energy and blood simultaneously; C. to tone blood and expel wind; D. to tone yang and expel dampness.

2640	[医案 184] 应如何處方？ A 小腸輸，陽池，陽陵泉; B 后溪，經渠,. 間使; C 合谷，陽白,三陰交; D 通天，合谷，百會.	[Clinical case 184] what points should be selected? A. B27 (Xiǎo; Cháng Shū), Sj4 (Yáng Chí), G34 (Yáng Líng Quán); B. Si3 (Hòu Xī), Lu8 (Jīng Qú), P5 (Jiān Shǐ); C. Li4 (Hé Gǔ), G14 (Yáng; Bái), Sp6 (Sān Yīn Jiāo); D. B7 (Tōng Tiān), Li4 (Hé Gǔ), D20 (Bǎi Huì).

[医案67] 癔病性震顫 陳 xx，女性，因某種原因引起精神上不愉快而發生右手抖動，以致不能工作，拿筷，曾住院治療未見效果,乃試行針刺治療:患者右手不停地上下抖動，每分鐘在 120 次以上，精神憂郁,無病理征發現，診爲噫症性震顫，以頭針療法爲主.取左側舞蹈震顫控制區，加刺病肢 [選自'針刺療法']	[Clinical case 67] hysterical tremor Patient:; Chen, female. Tremor of the right hand started due to mental disturbances triggered by certain causes, leading to inability to work or hold chopsticks. The patient was hospitalized for treatment without effect and decided to try acupuncture therapy. The patient's right hand was shaking up and down continuously, over 120 times per minute, with mental depression, but no findings of any pathological causes, diagnosed as hysterical tremor, treated mainly by scalp acupuncture.

2641	[医案 67] 应如何處方？ A小腸輸，陽池，陽陵泉. 合谷; B 后溪，經渠,. 間使,曲池; C 曲池、手三里、外關、合谷; D 通天，合谷，百會，經渠.	[Clinical case 67] what points should be selected? A. B27 (Xiǎo; Cháng Shū), Sj4 (Yáng Chí), G34 (Yáng Líng Quán), Li4 (Hé Gǔ); B. Si3 (Hòu Xī), Lu8 (Jīng Qú), P5 (Jiān Shǐ), Li11 (Qū Chí); C. Li11 (Qū Chí), Li10 (Shǒu Sān Lǐ), Sj5 (Wài Guān), Li4 (Hé Gǔ); D. B7 (Tōng Tiān), Li4 (Hé Gǔ), D20 (Bǎi Huì), Lu8 (Jīng Qú).

[医案66] 精神分裂症 陳 xx，女，21 歲，四月前開始失眠，睡時多夢多語，逐步發展到有幻覺、妄想，以致驚恐、大哭、大吵、不睡，後送有關醫院，診爲精神分裂症，服用奮乃靜三個多月，未見效果，於是要求新針治療: [選自'針刺療法']	[Clinical case 66] schizophrenia Patient:; Chen, female, age 21. The patient displayed insomnia since four months ago, with many dreams and talking at sleep, gradually developing into hallucination, wishful thinking, causing shock and fear,; Crying out, refusing sleep; the patient was sent to hospital, diagnosed as schizophrenia, taking perphenaine for over three months without effect. New acupuncture therapy was requested.

2642	[医案 66] 应如何處方？ A 安眠一，安眠二; B 頸中，頰內; C脾熱穴，腎熱穴; D腦清，陰亢.	[Clinical case 66] what points should be selected? A. good sleep No 1 (an mian 1), good sleep No 2 (an mian 2); B. middle of neck, inside the cheek; C. spleen heat point, kidney heat point; D. clear brain (brain awareness), yin excitation (yin violence, yin excess).

13-7	医籍	Acupuncture Classics	2643-3062

2643	."十二刺"最早见于: A.《内经》B.《金针赋》C.《难经》D.《针灸甲乙经》E.《针灸问	What classic made mention of "twelve programs of needling" for the first time? A. 《Nèi Jīng》B. 《Jīn Zhēn Fù》C. 《Nàn Jīng》D.

	对》.	《Zhēn Jiǔ Jiá Yǐ Jīng》E. 《Zhēn Jiǔ Wèn Duì》.
2644	"治痿独取阳明"载于: A.《素问》B《灵枢》C,《难经》D. 《甲乙经》E. 《针灸大成》.	Which classic recorded the following passage? "Only bright yang should be treated in the treatment of paralysis." A. 《Sù Wèn》B《Líng Shū》C,《Nàn Jīng》D. 《Jiá Yǐ Jīng》E. 《Zhēn Jiǔ Dà Chéng》.
2645	《黄帝内经》称输穴有"365"个, 是指: A 与一年 365 天相应; B. 全身输穴实有 365 个; C. 全身双穴有 365 个; D. 经穴有 365 个 E, 奇穴有 365 个.	《Huáng Dì Nèi Jīng》The classic makes mention of "365 points", which refers to: A. corresponding to 365 days a year; B. it is true that the whole body has 365 points; C. it is true that the whole body has 365 double points; D. 365 points on the master meridians; E. 365 extraordinary points.
2646	《内经》中所记载的经穴数目约为: A. 160个; B. 200个; C. 309 个; D. 361 个; E. 以上均不是.	《Nèi Jīng》How many acupuncture points are recorded in 《Nèi Jīng》? A. 160 points; B. 200 points; C. 309 points; D. 361 points; E. None of the above.
2647	"九刺"最早见于: A.《内经》B. 《针灸大成》C. 《金针赋》D. 《神应经》E. 《针灸甲乙经》	What classic made mention of "nine ways of needling" for the first time? A. 《Nèi Jīng》; B. 《Zhēn Jiǔ Dà Chéng》; C. 《Jīn Zhēn Fù》; D. 《Shén Yìng Jīng》; E. 《Zhēn Jiǔ Jiá Yǐ Jīng》.
2648	骨度分寸定位法最早见于: A. 《内经》; B,《难经》; C. 《针灸甲乙经》; D. 《千金要方》; E. 《帛书》.	What Classic made mention of the bone measurements by Cun to locate points for the first time? A. 《Nèi Jīng》; B, 《Nàn Jīng》; C. 《Zhēn Jiǔ Jiá Yǐ Jīng》; D. 《Qiān Jīn Yào Fāng》; E. 《Bó Shū》.
2649	关于"标本"理论的论述, 下列哪一项是错误的: A. 与"根结"理论完全一样; B. 强调四肢末端与头面躯干部的联系; C. "本"在四肢肘膝关节以下; D. "标"部有赖于"本"部的滋养; E. "标"在头面躯干部	Which is incorrect regarding the theory of "primary and secondary conditions / biāo běn"? A. it is the same as the theory of " root (gen), and fruit (jie); B. it puts emphasis on the connection between tips of four limbs and the head and face and truck regions; C. " primary conditions / běn" are located below the elbow and knee joints; D. " secondary conditions / biāo" rely on primary conditions for nourishment; E. " secondary conditions / biāo" are located in the head and face and trunk regions.
2650	最早论述了灸法的适应证施灸顺序剂量补泻的是: A.《内经》; B. 《金针赋》; C. 《难经》; D. 《针灸甲乙经》; E. 《针灸问对》.	What classic discussed the indications of moxibustion and the sequences of its application as well as the quantity for tonification and sedation for the first time? A. 《Nèi Jīng》; B. 《Jīn Zhēn Fù》; C. 《Nàn Jīng》; D. 《Zhēn Jiǔ Jiá Yǐ Jīng》; E. 《Zhēn Jiǔ Wèn Duì》
2651	最早提出十四经脉的著作是: A.《十四经发挥》; B《黄帝内经》; C. 《针灸甲乙经》; D. 《铜人腧穴针灸图经》.	What classic made mention of fourteen meridians for the first time? A. 《Shí Sì Jīng Fā Huī 》; B《Huáng Dì Nèi Jīng》; C. 《Zhēn Jiǔ Jiá Yǐ Jīng》; D. 《Tóng Rù Shù Xuézhēn Jiǔ Tú Jīng》.
2652	"阿是穴"的取法和应用出自: A. (千金方) B.《外台秘要》C.《针	What classic presented the theory of locating and applying "ouch points / pressure points" for the frist time?

	经》D. 《针灸大全》	time? A. (Qiān Jīn Fāng》; B. 《Wài Tái Bì Yào》; C. 《Zhēn Jīng》; D. 《Zhēn Jiǔ Dà Quán》
2653	陈会提出的平补平泻法是：A. 先用泻法，后用补法; B. 小补小泻; C. 先用补法，后用泻法; D. 以泻为主，兼有补法; E. 进针后均匀提插、捻转、得气后 出针.	What is the neutral technique presented by Chén Hu? A. sedation first, followed by tonificaton; B. tonification and sedation on a small scale; C. tonification first, followed by sedation; D. sedation as the primary, accompanied by tonification; E. harmonious lifting and inserting the needle, twirl it, and withdraw it after energy response.
2654	古代最早的针具是: A. 砭石; B. 灸法 C·九针; D. 耳针; E. 头针	What was the earliest type of acupuncture needle in ancient China? A. stone needle; B. moxibustion; C. nine types of needles; D. ear needle; E. scalp needle.
2655	继《内经》，《甲已经》之后对针灸学的又一次总结是: A...《针灸大成》B. ·《针灸大全》··C《明堂孔穴针灸治要》D《十四经发挥》E《奇经八脉考》.	Following《Nèi Jīng》and《Zhēn Jiǔ Jiá Yǐ Jīng》, another important acupuncture classic was published; what is the title of this classic? A. 《Zhēn Jiǔ Dà Chéng》; B. ·《Zhēn Jiǔ Dà Quán》; ·C 《Míng Táng Kǒng XuéZhēn Jiǔ Zhì Yào》; D《Shí Sì Jīng Fā Huī》;E《Qí Jīng Bā Mài Kǎo.
2656	经脉属土，五行属水的输穴是: A. 阴陵泉; B. 少海; C. 曲泉; D. 尺泽; E. 曲泽	What point is on an earth meridian and belongs to water? A. Sp9, Yīn Líng Quán; B. H3, Shào Hǎi; C. Lv8, Qū Quán; D. Lu5, Chǐ Zé; E. P3, Qū Zé.
2657	灸法治病起源于: A. 原始社会; B. 战国以前; C. 新石器; D 魏晋; E. 秦汉	When was treatment by moxibustion originated? A. primitive society; B. before Warring Period; C. Neolithic Age; D. Wèi and Jìn period; E. Qín hàn period.
2658	据《内经》记载，针刺治病起源于我国的: A. 东方; B. 南方; C. 中部; D. 西方; E. 北方	From what region in China was acupuncture originated? A. East; B. West; C. South; D. North; E. Central.
2659	马王堆帛书《经脉》记载了十一条经脉，从名称上看缺少的是: A. 手厥阴心包经; B. 手太阴肺经; C. 手少阴心经; D. 足少阴肾经; E. 足厥阴肝经.	A total of eleven meridians are listed in Mǎ Wáng Duī Bó Shū 《Jīng Mài》, which meridian is missing? A. pericardium; B. lung; C. heart; D. kidney; E. liver.
2660	我国针灸最早传入的国家是: A. 朝鲜; B. 日本; C. 越南; D. 印度; E. 法国	To what country was Chinese acupuncture and moxibustion first exported? A. Korea; B. Japan; C. Vietnam; D. India; E. France.
2661	我国最早成立针灸专业教学的朝代: A. 唐朝; B. 宋朝; C. 元朝; D. 明朝; E. 清朝.	When did acupuncture and moxibustion become a teaching profession? A. Táng Dynasty; B. Sòng Dynasty; C. Yuán Dynasty; D. Míng Dynasty; E. Qīng Dynasty.
2662	我国最早论及输穴的部位名称主治的经典医籍是: A.《黄帝内经》: B. 《明堂孔穴针灸治要》	What Classic made mention of the locations, names, and indications of acupuncture points for the first time? A.《Huáng Dì Nèi Jīng》 : B.《Míng Táng Kǒng XuéZhēn

	C.《针灸甲乙经》; D.《黄帝八十一难经》E《帛书.脉法》或《五十二病方》.	Jiǔ Zhì Yào》; C.《Zhēn Jiǔ Jiá Yǐ Jīng》; D.《Huáng Dì Bā Shí Yī Nàn Jīng》; E.《Bó Shū. mài fǎ》or《Wǔ Shí Èr Bìng Fāng》.
2663	下列穴位，除……外都是马丹阳天星十二穴中的穴位: A. 内关; B. 列缺; C. 环跳; D. 通里; E. 承山.	Which of the following points is not contained in the classic, Mǎ Dān Yáng Tiān Xīngshí Èr Xué ? A. P6, Nèi Guān; B. Lu7, Liè Quē; C. G30, Huán Tiào; DH5, Tōng Lǐ; E. B57, Chéng Shān.
2664	徐凤所处的时代是; A. 明代 B宋代; C. 汉代 D元代 E清代	During what dynasty did Xú Fèng live? A. Míng Dynasty; B Sòng Dynasty; C. Hàn Dynasty; D Yuán Dynasty; E Qīng Dynasty.
2665	在明代我国针灸医学上的总结性著作是: A. (针灸大成); B. 《针灸大全》C. 《奇经八脉考》D. 《针灸问对》E. 《针灸聚英》.	What major comprehensive classic of acupuncture and moxibustion was written in the Míng Dynasty? A. (Zhēn Jiǔ Dà Chéng); B. 《Zhēn Jiǔ Dà Quán》; C. 《Qí Jīng Bā Mài Kǎo》; D. 《Zhēn Jiǔ Wèn Duì》E. 《zhēn jiǔ jù yīng》.
2666	针具是在何著作年代得到不断改进的: A. (内经》B. (难经》著作年代; C. (针灸甲乙经》著作年代; D. (针灸大成)著作年代; E. (资生经)著作年代.	What classic had continually improved the needle instruments? A. (Nèi Jīng》; B. (Nàn Jīng》; C. (Zhēn Jiǔ Jiá Yǐ Jīng》; D. (Zhēn Jiǔ Dà Chéng); E. (Zī Shēng Jīng).
2667	最早记载灸法的是: A. 《五十二病方》B. (《针灸大成》C. 《十四经发挥》D. 《阴阳十一脉灸经》E·《足臂十一脉灸经》.	What Classic recorded moxibustion for the first time? A. 《Wǔ Shí Èr Bìng Fāng》; B. 《Zhēn Jiǔ Dà Chéng》; C. 《Shí Sì Jīng Fā Huī》; D. 《Yīn Yang Shí Yī Mài Jiǔ Jīng》; E·《Zú Bì Shí Yī Mài Jiǔ Jīng》.
2668	"九针"最早被记述在哪部著作中 A.马王堆《帛书》B《内经》C.《甲乙经》D《针灸大成》	What TCM classic recorded "nine needles" for the first time? A. Mǎ Wáng Duī《Bó Shū》B《Nèi Jīng》C.《Jiá Yǐ Jīng》D《Zhēn Jiǔ Dà Chéng》.
2669	"轻滑慢而未来，沉涩紧而已至"。语出: A. 《灵枢·1九针十二原》B. 《标幽赋》C. 《金针赋》D. 《千金方》E. 《甲乙经》.	" If, after the needle is inserted, energy appears light, slippery, and slow, it means true energy has not arrived; if it appears deep, retarded, and tight, it means body energy has arrived. " The above statement was originated from: A. 《Líng Shū·1》B. 《Biāo Yōu Fù》C. 《Jīn Zhēn Fù》D. 《Qiān Jīn Fāng》E. 《Jiá Yǐ Jīng》.
2670	"一夫法。首见于: A. 《黄帝内经》B. 《肘后备急方》C. 《脉经》D.《千金要方》E.《千金翼方》.	What classic made mention of "mearsurement by width of four fingers closed together" for the first time? A. 《Huáng Dì Nèi Jīng》B. 《Zhǒu Hòu Bèi Jí Fāng》C. 《Mài Jīng》D. 《Qiān Jīn Yào Fāng》E. 《Qiān Jīn Yì Fāng》.
2671	"以痛为输。这一名词首载于: A. 《灵枢 经脉》B. 《灵枢 经筋》C. 《灵枢 经别》D. 《灵枢 经水》E. 《灵枢 背腧》.	What classic made mention of "taking pressure points as acupuncture points" for the firs time? A. 《Líng Shū·10》B. 《Líng Shū13》C. 《Líng Shū·11》D. 《Líng Shū·12》E. 《Líng Shū·51》.

2672	"针所不为，灸之所宜"出自：A·《灵枢·九针十二原》B. 《灵枢·官能》C. 《素问·异法方宜论》D. 《难经·二十九难》E. 《备急千金要方》.	Which classic contains this statement? "A disease that may not be treated by acupuncture may be treated by moxibustion." A·《Líng Shū·1》B. 《Líng Shū·73》C. 《Sù Wèn·12》D. 《Nàn Jīng·29th》E. 《Bèi Jí Qiān Jīn Yào Fāng, 652》.
2673	"知为针者信其左，不知为针信其右。"语出: A.·《内经》B.·《难经》C. 《甲乙经》D.·《标幽赋》E.·《针灸大成》.	What classic made mention of the following: "A skilful physician will trust the left hand more than the right hand, because the left hand is used to press the region surrounding the point to be needled; an unskillful physician will trust the right hand more than the left hand"? A.·《Nèi Jīng》;B.·《Nàn Jīng》;C. 《Jiá Yǐ Jīng》;D.·《Biāo Yōu Fù》;E.·《Zhēn Jiǔ Dà Chéng》.
2674	最早绘制彩色针灸图的 A. 皇甫谧; B. 孙思邈; C. 王惟一 D·杨继洲	Who created colorful diagrams of acupuncture and moxibustion for the first time? A. Huáng Fǔ Mì; B. Sūn Sī Miǎo; C. Wáng Wéi Yī; D. Yáng Jì Zhōu.
2675	八会穴首载于: A. 《内经》B. 《难经》C. 《肘后备急方》D. 《脉经》E·《针灸甲乙经》.	What Classic presented the eight influential points [bā huì xué] for the first time? A. 《Nèi Jīng》; B. 《Nàn Jīng》; C. 《Zhǒu Hòu Bèi Jí Fāng》; D. 《Mài Jīng》; E·《Zhēn Jiǔ Jiá Yǐ Jīng》.
2676	拔罐法的记载最早见于: A. 《内经》; B. 《五十二病方》; C. 《难经》; D. 《甲乙经》; E. 《千金要方》.	What Classic presented cupping for the first time? A. 《Nèi Jīng》; B. 《Wǔ Shí Èr Bìng Fāng》; C. 《Nàn Jīng》; D. 《Jiá Yǐ Jīng》; E. 《Qiān Jīn Yào Fāng》.
2677	陈会的著作是: A. 《脉经》; B. 《神应经》; C. 《针灸大全》; D. 《针灸问对》; E. 《针灸集成》.	What Classic was written by Chén Huì? A. 《Mài Jīng》; B. 《Shén Yìng Jīng》; C. 《Zhēn Jiǔ Dà Quán》; D. 《Zhēn Jiǔ Wèn Duì》; E. 《Zhēn Jiǔ Jí Chéng》.
2678	称为"四总穴"之一的穴位是： A. 丰隆; B. 委中; C. 委阳; D. 飞扬 E·合阳	Which point is listed in " Sì Zǒng Xué" as one of the four points? A. S40, Fēng Lóng; B. B40, Wěi Zhōng; C. B39, Wěi Yáng; D. B58, Feī Yáng E·B55, Hé Yáng.
2679	根据"四总穴歌"中的取穴原则，呕吐首选何穴: A. 中脘; B. 内关; C. 足三里; D. 人中; E. 以上均不是	According to the principle of selecting points presented in " Sì Zǒng Xué Gē", what point should be selected to treat vomiting? A. R12, Zhōng Wǎn; B. P6, Nèi Guān; C. S36, Zú Sān Lǐ; D. D26, Rén Zhōng; E. None of the above.
2680	灸治宜用陈艾的观点最早见于: A.左传;B. 孟子; C. 神农本草经 D 本草纲目; E. 本草从新.	Who first presented the concept that old moxa should be used in moxibustion? A. Zuǒ Zhuàn; B. Mencius; C. Shén Nóng Běn Cǎo Jīng; D Běn Cǎo Gāng Mù; E. Běn Cǎo Cóng Xīn.
2681	据 "辨证求经"原则，下列何穴可治喉中闭塞: A. 少商; B. 照海 C·合谷; D. 太冲; E. 鱼际	According to the principle of "selecting meridians in light of differential diagnosis", what point may be selected to treat blockage of the throat? A. Lu11, Shǎo Shāng; B. K6, Zhào Hǎi; C·Li4, Hé Gǔ; D. Lv3, Tài Chōng; E. Lu10, Yǔ Jì.

2682	首先记载募穴名称和位置的医学文献是: A.(难经》B. 《脉经》C.《甲乙经》D. 《铜人腧穴针灸图经》E.《针灸大成》	What Classic made mention of the names and locations of the anterior points [mù xué) for the first time? A. (Nàn Jīng》; B. 《Mài Jīng》; C. 《Jiá Yǐ Jīng》; D. 《Tóng Rén Shù Xué Zhēn Jiǔ Tú Jīng》; E. 《Zhēn Jiǔ Dà Chéng》.
2683	唐代王焘的《外台秘要》专门论述: A. 砭石; B. 灸法 C.九针; D. 耳针; E. 头针	In his book 《Wài Tái Bì Yào》, what was Wáng Shòu in Táng Dynasty specialized in? A. stone needle; B. moxibustion; C. nine needles; D. auricular acupucture; E. scalp acupuncture.
2684	我国最早流传到国外的针灸专著是:A. 《针灸大成》B《针灸甲乙经》C. 《针经》D. 《医宗金鉴》E. 《明堂图》.	What acupuncture classic was first exported to a foreign country? A. 《Zhēn Jiǔ Dà Chéng》; B《Zhēn Jiǔ Jiá Yǐ Jīng》; C. 《Zhēn Jīng》; D. 《Yī Zōng Jīn Jiàn》; E. 《Míng Táng Tú》.
2685	在清以前针灸文献中，记载经外奇穴最多的医籍是: A. (肘后备急方》; B. 《千金要方》; C. 《铜人腧穴针灸图经》; D. 《针灸资生经》; E. 《针灸大成》.	Before the Qīng Dynasty, what Classic recorded the greatest number of extraordinary points (jīng wài qí xué)? A. (Zhǒu Hòu Bèi Jí Fāng》; B. 《Qiān Jīn Yào Fāng》; C. 《Tóng Rén Shù Xué Zhēn Jiǔ Tú Jīng》; D. 《Zhēn Jiǔ Zī Shēng Jīng》; E. 《Zhēn Jiǔ Dà Chéng》.
2686	最早记载《角法》的是:A·《肘后备急方》B.《五十二病方》C. 《针灸大全》D·《针灸大成》E. 《阴阳十一脉灸经》.	Who made mention of horn cupping [jiǎo fǎ] for the first time? A·《Zhǒu Hòu Bèi Jí Fāng》; B. 《Wǔ Shí Èr Bìng Fāng》; C. 《Zhēn Jiǔ Dà Quán》; D·《Zhēn Jiǔ Dà Chéng》; E. 《Yīn Yángshí Yī Mài Jiǔ Jīng》.
2687	"刺之要，气至而有效。"语出: A，《灵枢·7》B. 《灵枢·3》C. 《灵枢·1》D. 《标幽赋》E. 《针灸大成》.	What classic contains the following statement, “Acupuncture therapy does not take effect until arrival of energy "? A，《Líng Shū·7》B. 《Líng Shū·3》C. 《Líng Shū·1》D. 《Biāo Yōu Fù》E. 《Zhēn Jiǔ Dà Chéng》.
2688	"窦氏八穴"是指: A. 八会穴; B. 八髎穴; C. 八脉交会穴; D. 八风穴; E. 八邪穴	" Eight points presented by Dòu Hàn Qīng” refer to: A. Eight Meeting Points / Eight Influential Points [Bā Huì Xué]; B. eight Liáo points; C. Eight Confluence Points [Bā Mài Bā Huì Xué]; D. Bā Fēng; E. Bā Xié.
2689	"合主逆气而泄“一语出自: A《灵枢》B.《素问》C.《难经》D.《脉经》E. 《甲乙经》	" Merging point is in charge of upstream energy and diarrhea “ is originated from: A《Líng Shū》B.《Sù Wèn》C. 《 Nàn Jīng》D. 《Mài Jīng》E. 《Jiá Yǐ Jīng》.
2690	《黄帝内经》指出经筋病症主要选用：A 肝经穴; B. 胆经穴; C 阿是穴; D. 特定穴; E. 经外奇穴.	《Huáng Dì Nèi Jīng》 What points should be used to treat tendon meridians (jing jin)? A. liver meridian points; B. gallbladder meridian points; C. ouch points / pressure points; D. specially designated points; E. extraordinary points.
2691	《左传》所载 "在肓之上，膏之下，攻之不可，达之不及" "攻"是指: A. 服药; B. 针刺; C. 艾灸; D. 推拿; E. 拔	《Zuǒ Zhuàn》“The disease that is located above the diaphragm and below the heart cannot be attacked, nor can it be reached”. What is meant by “attack”? A. treatment by herbs; B. treatment by needle

	艾灸; D. 推拿; E. 拔罐	insertion; C. treatment by moxibustion; D. treatment by tui na; E. treatment by cupping.
2692	复式补泻手法中的"烧山火""透天凉"见于: A. 《内经》B. 《针灸大成》C. 《金针赋》D. 《神应经》E. 《针灸甲乙经》.	What classic made mention of "forest fire" and "cooling the heaven" among the compound methods of needle insertion for the first time? A. 《Nèi Jīng》; B. 《Zhēn Jiǔ Dà Chéng》; C. 《Jīn Zhēn Fù》; D. 《Shén Yìng Jīng》; E. 《Zhēn Jiǔ Jiá Yī Jīng》.
2693	我国现存最早的一部针灸专著是: A. 《灵枢》; B. 《难经》; C. 《针灸甲乙经》; D. 《针灸大成》.	What is the earliest acupuncture classic in Chinese history? A. 《Líng Shū》; B. 《Nàn Jīng》; C. 《Zhēn Jiǔ Jiá Yī Jīng》; D. 《Zhēn Jiǔ Dà Chéng》.
2694	在家传《卫生针灸玄机秘要》的基础上，汇集历代诸家学说和实践经验，总结而成的针灸著作是: A.《医宗金鉴 刺灸心法》; B.《针灸甲乙经》; C. 《针灸大成》; D. 《铜人腧穴针灸图经》.	What acupuncture classic collected the practical experiences of various physicians in the past on the basis of《Wèi Shēng Zhēn Jiǔ Xuán Jī Bì Yào》? A.《Yī Zōng Jīn Jiàn · Cì Jiǔ Xīn Fǎ》; B.《Zhēn Jiǔ Jiá Yī Jīng》; C. 《Zhēn Jiǔ Dà Chéng》; D. 《Tóng Rù Shù Xuézhēn Jiǔ Tú Jīng》.
2695	反映经络学说早期面貌的著作是: A.《黄帝内经》; B《难经》; C. 《帛书》; D. 《灵枢经》.	What classic reflected the earlier system of meridians? A. 《Huáng Dì Nèi Jīng》; B《Nàn Jīng》; C. 《Bó Shū》 D. 《Líng Shū jīng》.
2696	汪机的针灸学术思想主要体现在何书中? A. 《医学起源》; B. 《外科理例》; C。《针灸问对》; D. 《石山医案》;. 《针灸资生经》	The acupuncrture and moxibustion theory by Wāng Jī (1463-1539) was reflected in the classic entitled: A. 《Yī Xué Qǐ Yuán》; B. 《Wài Kē Lǐ Lì》; C。《Zhēn Jiǔ Wèn Duì》; D. 《Shí Shān Yī Àn1519》; E. 《Zhēn Jiǔ Zī Shēng Jīng》.
2697	针灸学的理论核心是: A. 阴阳学说; B. 藏象学说; C. 经络学说; D. 五行学说.	What is the core of acupuncture-moxibustion? A. the theory of yin and yang; B. the theory of internal organs; C. the system of meridians; D. the theory of five elements.
2698	扁鹊治虢太子尸厥所用的"三阴五会"是指: A. 大椎穴; B ,命门穴; C. 百会穴; D. 神庭穴; E. 水沟穴.	What is the "three yins and five meetings" used by Biǎn Què to treat Prince Guó's corpse like syncope? A. D14, Dà Zhuī; B. D4, Mìng Mén; C. D20, Bǎi Huì; D. D24, Shén Tíng; E. D26, Shuǐ Gōu.
2699	第一个针灸铜人铸造于: A. 元朝; B. 金朝; C. 宋朝; D. 唐朝; E. 明朝	When was the first Bronze Statue of acupuncture built? A. Yuán Dynasty; B. Jīn Dynasty; C. Sòng Dynasty; D. Táng Dynasty; E. Míng Dynasty.
2700	《行针指要歌》，治疗水病的主要穴位是: A. 关元; B. 中极; C 水分; D. 中脘; E. 气海.	《Xíng Zhēn Zhǐ Yào Gē》 What should be selected as the primary point to treat water disease? A. R4, Guān Yuán; B. R3, Zhōng Jí; C. R9, Shuǐ Fēn; D. R12, Zhōng Wǎn; E. R6, Qì Hǎi.
2701	滑寿著： A. 《五十二病方》; B. (《针灸大成》; C. 《十四经发挥》; D. 《阴阳十一脉灸经》; E·《足臂十一脉灸经》.	Huá Shòu is the author of: A. 《Wǔ Shí Èr Bìng Fāng》; B. (《Zhēn Jiǔ Dà Chéng》; C. 《Shí Sì Jīng Fā Huī》; D. 《yīn yángshí yī mài jiǔ jīng》 ; E·《Zú Bì Shí Yī Mài Jiǔ Jīng》.

2702	灸法用于急救首见于: A 五十二病方; B 针灸甲乙经; C 肘后备急方; D (外台秘要); E 备急灸法.	What Classic advocated that emergencies may be rescued by moxibustion? A. Wǔ Shí Èr Bìng Fāng; B. Zhēn Jiǔ Jiá Yǐ Jīng; C. · Zhǒu Hòu Bèi Jí Fāng; D. · Wài Tái Bì Yào; E. · Bèi Jí Jiǔ Fǎ.
2703	起于内踝处照海穴的经脉是: A. 冲脉; B. 带脉; C. 阴跷脉; D. 阳跷脉; E. 阴维脉	What meridian is originated from the inner ankle at K6, Zhào Hǎi? A. Vigorous meridian [Chōng Mài]; B. Belt meridian [Dài Mài]; C. Heel meridian of yin [Yīn Qiāo Mài]; D. Heel meridian of yang [Yáng Qiāo Mài]; E. Fastener meridian of yin [Yīn Wéi Mài].
2704	世界卫生组织向全世界推荐 43 种病应用针灸治疗的时间是: A. 1977 年; B. 1978 年 C.1979 年; D. 1989 年 E 1990 年	When did WHO recommend acupuncture treatment of 43 diseases? A. 1977; B. 1978; C. 1979; D. 1989; E 1990.
2705	郄穴的名称和位置，首载于: A. 《灵枢》B. & 难经》C. 《针灸甲乙经》D. 《黄帝内经太素》E. 《千金方》	What Classic recorded the names and locations of fissural points / cleft points [xī xué] for the first time? A. 《Líng Shū》; B. & Nàn Jıng》; C. 《Zhēn Jiǔ Jiá Yǐ Jīng》; D. 《Huáng Dì Nèi Jīng Tài Sù》; E. 《Qiān Jīn Fāng》.
2706	下列穴位，除……外都是回阳九针穴: A. 哑门; B. 劳宫; C. 中冲 D，三阴交; E. 环跳.	Which of the following points is not contained in the classic, Huí Yáng Jiǔ Zhēn Xué? A. D15, Yǎ Mén; P8, Láo Gōng; C. P9, Zhōng Chōng; D，Sp6, Sān Yīn Jiāo; E. G30, Huán Tiào.
2707	夏商周时代出现的针具是：A 砭石 B 骨针; C. 青铜针; D. 不锈钢针; E. 金针	What kind of needle made its first appearance in Xia Shang Zhou dynasties? A. stone needle; B bone needle; C. bronze needle; D. needle of stainless steel; E. gold needle.
2708	现存医籍中，记载五输穴最完整的文献是: A. 《内经》; B. 《难经》; C，《针灸甲乙经》; D. 《肘后备急方》; E. 《千金要方》.	What existing Classic contained most complete information on the five command points [wǔ shū xué]? A. 《Nèi Jīng》;B. 《Nàn Jīng》;C.《Zhēn Jiǔ Jiá Yǐ Jīng》;D. 《Zhǒu Hòu Bèi Jí Fāng》;E. 《Qiān Jīn Yào Fāng》.
2709	现存最早、较完善的针灸学专著是： A《黄帝内经》;B. 《阴陽十于脉灸经》;C.《针灸甲乙经》;D.《针灸资生经》; E. 《明堂孔穴针灸治要》.	What existing Classic is the most complete publication specialized in acupuncture and moxibustion? A.《Huáng Dì Nèi Jīng》;B. 《Yīn Yang Shí Yú Mài Jiǔ Jīng》;C. 《Zhēn Jiǔ Jiá Yǐ Jīng》;D. 《Zhēn Jiǔ Zī Shēng Jīng》;E. 《Míng Táng Kǒng XuéZhēn Jiǔ Zhì Yào》.
2710	现存最早的经络学著作是: A. (针灸甲乙经); B. 《灵枢经》C. 《帛书》D. 《经络全书》E.《十四经发挥》.	What existing Classic is the earliest classic dealing with the system of meridians? A. (Zhēn Jiǔ Jiá Yǐ Jīng); B. 《Líng Shū jīng》C. 《Bó Shū》D.《Jīng Luò Quán Shū》E.《Shí Sì Jīng Fā Huī》.
2711	现存最早的腧穴学专著是: A. (黄帝内经明堂类成); B. 《明堂孔穴针灸治要》C. 《铜人腧穴针灸图经》D. 《金兰循经》E. 以上	What existing Classic is the earliest classic specialized in acupuncture points? A. 《Huáng Dì Nèi Jīng Míng Tang Lèi Chéng); B. 《Míng Táng Kǒng Xuézhēn Jiǔ Zhì Yào》; C. 《Tóng Rén Shù Xué Zhēn Jiǔ Tú Jīng》; D. 《Jīn Lán Xún

	都不是	Jīng》; E. None of the above.
2712	详细描述"阿是穴"取穴法的书籍首推: A. 《灵枢 经脉》B. 《针灸甲乙经》C. 《备急千金要方》D. 《十四经发挥》E. 《针灸大成》	What Classic described how to locate"ouch points / pressure poinst" in great detail? A. 《Líng Shū · Jīng Mài》; B. 《Zhēn Jiǔ Jiá Yī Jīng》; C. 《Bèi Jí Qiān Jīn Yào Fāng》; D. 《Shí Sì Jīng Fā Huī》; E. 《Zhēn Jiǔ Dà Chéng》.
2713	徐凤的著作是: A. 《脉经》B. 《神应经》C. 《针灸大全》D. 《针灸问对》E. 《针灸集成》.	What Classic did Xú Fèng write? A. 《Mài Jīng》; B. 《Shén Yìng Jīng》; C. 《Zhēn Jiǔ Dà Quán》; D. 《Zhēn Jiǔ Wèn Duì》; E. 《Zhēn Jiǔ Jí Chéng》.
2714	针刺疗法产生的时代是: A. 原始社会; B. 战国以前; C. 新石器; D 魏晋; E. 秦汉	When was acupuncture treatment originated? A. primitive society; B. before Warring Period; C. Neolithic Age; D. Wèi and Jìn period; E. Qín hàn period.
2715	针灸在太医院被禁止使用的时间是： A. 1828 年; B. 1826 年; C. 1822 年，; D. 1834 年:' E 1890 年	When was acupuncture and moxibustion banned in the Institute of Imperial Physicians? A. 1828; B. 1826; C. 1822 ; D. 1834: E. 1890.
2716	子午流注按时取穴的时间针法最早由谁提出 A.皇甫谧; B.孙思邈; C 何若愚; D 窦汉卿.	Who presented the theory of energy-flowing Acupuncture [Zǐ Wǔ Liú Zhù] for the first time? A. Huáng Fǔ Mì; B. Sūn Sī Miǎo; C. Hé Ruò Yú; D. Dòu Hàn Qīng.
2717	最早提出腧穴这个名词的是: A. ·皇甫谧; B. ·王执中; C. ·王惟一; D. ·高武; E. ·杨继洲	Who made mention of "acupuncture point" for the first time? A. · Huáng Fǔ Mì; B. · Wáng Zhí Zhōng; C. · Wáng Wéi Yī; D. · Gāo Wǔ; E. · Yáng Jì Zhōu.
2718	最早运用手指同身寸的一医家是：A ·淳于意; B. 张仲景。C 孙思邈 D 华佗; E. 葛洪。	Who applied digital measurements for the first time? A · Chún Yú Yì; B. Zhāng Zhòng Jǐng; C · Sūn Sī Miao; D. Huá Tuó; E. Gé Hóng.
2719	"艾味苦 微温 无毒 主灸百病"语出: A.(灵枢) B.(医学入门)。; C. 、本草从真、; D. (名医别录):; E. 《本草正》.	What classic contains this statement: "Mugwort tastes bitter, slightly warm, non-toxic, used in moxibustion to treat one hundred diseases"? A. (Líng Shū ·) B.(Yī Xué Rù Mén); C. Běn Cǎo Cóng Zhēn; D. (Míng Yī Bié Lù): E. 《Běn Cǎo Zhèng》.
2720	"不定穴"这个名称首见于: A. 《明堂孔穴针灸治要》B. 《子午流注针经》C. 《备急灸法》D. 《扁鹊神应针灸玉龙经》E. 《圣济总录》.	What Classic made mention of "points with no fixed location" for the first time? A. Míng Táng Kǒng XuéZhēn Jiǔ Zhì Yào》B. 《Zǐ Wǔ Liú Zhù Zhēn Jīng》C. 《Bèi Jí Jiǔ Fǎ》D. 《Biǎn Què Shén Yìng Zhēn Jiǔ Yù Lóng Jīng》E. 《Shèng Jì Zǒng Lù》.
2721	"脏寒生满病，其治宜灸焫"語出： A《左傳》, B《山海經》, C《灵枢˙脹論》,D·《素问˙異法方宜论》, E《灵枢。本藏》.	What classic contains the following statement? "Distention in the internal region due to cold accumulation in the viscera should be treated by moxibustion. " A《Zuǒ Zhuàn》B《Shān Hǎi Jīng》, C《Líng Shū˙35》D ·《Sù Wèn˙ ·12》 E《Líng Shū 47》.
2722	"左手重而多按欲令气散;右手轻而徐人，不	What classic contains the following statement? "Apply heavy pressure and press the skin more often with the

	痛之因"，语见: A. 《灵枢》B. 《素问》C. 《难经》D. 《标幽赋》E. 《通玄指要赋》.	left hand, in order to disperse energy; apply lighter pressure and insert the needle slowly with the right hand, which is why there is no pain." A. 《Líng Shū》B. 《Sù Wèn》C. 《Nàn Jīng》D. 《Biāo Yōu Fù》E. 《Tōng Xuán Zhǐ Yào Fù》.
2723	大力提倡针灸并用的是: A.《内经》;B.《金针赋》; C.《难经》; D.《针灸甲乙经》; E.《针灸问对》.	What Classic made it a point to stress the importance of combining acupuncture and moxibustion? A. 《Nèi Jīng》; B. 《Jīn Zhēn Fù》; C. 《Nàn Jīng》;D. 《Zhēn Jiǔ Jiá Yǐ Jīng》; E. 《Zhēn Jiǔ Wèn Duì》.
2724	明初陈会的"催气手法"见于: A. 《内经》; B. 《针灸大成》; C. 《金针赋》; D. 《神应经》; E. 《针灸甲乙经》.	What classic made mention of Chén Huì's method of "expediting arrival of energy" for the first time? A. 《Nèi Jīng》; B. 《Zhēn Jiǔ Dà Chéng》; C. 《Jīn Zhēn Fù》; D. 《Shén Yìng Jīng》; E. 《Zhēn Jiǔ Jiá Yǐ Jīng》.
2725	汪机在学术上，较多地继承了谁的思想？ A. 张子和; B. 李东垣; C. 刘完素; D. 朱丹溪; E. 张仲景.	What physician from whom Wāng Jīi inherited the greatest part of his theory? A. Zhāng Zǐ Hé; B. Lǐ Dōng Yuán; C. Liú Wán Sù; D. Zhū Dān Xı; E. Zhāng Zhòng Jǐng.
2726	"沉涩紧而已至"是指: A. 病人脉象的表现; B. 下针时的要求; C. 出针时的要求; D. 针下气至情况; E. 行针时的要求.	"Arrival of deep, retarded, and tight" refers to: A. the patient's pulses; B. requirements of needle insertion; C. requirements of needle withdrawal; D. conditions of energy arrival when the needle is inserted; E. requirements of needle manipulation.
2727	针灸铜人的设计者是: A. 孙思邈 B.杨继洲 C·王执中 D·王惟一.	Who designed the Bronze Statues for Acupuncture and Moxibusiton? A. Sūn Sī Miǎo; B. Yáng Jì Zhōu; C. Wáng Zhí Zhōng; D. Wáng Wéi Yī.
2728	根据"虚者补其母"的原则，胃经虚应补的经是: A. 肝; B. 心; C. 胆; D·小肠; E. 大肠.	What meridian should be toned up in case of stomach meridian deficiency according to the principle of "toning mother in case of deficiency"? A. liver; B. heart; C. gallbladder; D. small intestine; E. large intestine.□
2729	滑伯仁所处的时代是: A. 明代 B·宋代; C. 汉代 D·元代·E·清代	In what dynasty did Huá Bó Rén live? A. Míng Dynasty; B·Sòng Dynasty; C. Hàn Dynasty; D·Yuán Dynasty; ·E·Qīng Dynasty.
2730	将腧穴称为"砭灸处"的医家是: A.·医和; B.·医缓; C.·扁鹊; D.·仓公; E.·华伦	Who called acupuncture points the "places of acupuncture and moxibustion"? A.·Yī Hé; B.·Yī Huǎn; C.·Biǎn Què; D.·Cāng Gōng; E.·Huá Lún.
2731	《内经》记载，灸法治病起源于我国的: A. 东方; B. 西方; C. 南方; D. 北方; E. 中原	《Nèi Jīng》From what region in China was moxibustion originated? A. East; B. West; C. South; D. North; E. Central.
2732	灵龟八法首载于: A.·《扁鹊神应针灸玉龙经》B.·《针经指南》C.·《甲乙经》D.·《针灸大全》E.，《针灸大成》.	What Classic presented the "Eight Turtle Methods of Acupuncture" for the first time? A.·《Biǎn Què Shén Yìng Zhēn Jiǔ Yù Lóng Jīng》; B.·《Zhēn Jīng Zhǐ Nán》; C.·《Jiá Yǐ Jīng》; D.·《Zhēn Jiǔ Dà Quán》; E.，《Zhēn Jiǔ Dà Chéng》.

2733	马丹阳《十二穴主治杂病歌》中没有的穴位是: A，三里 太冲 承山; B. 列缺 环跳 通里; C. 内庭 昆仑 委中; D. 内关 阳池 太溪; E. 曲池 阳陵 合谷.	What points are not listed in Mǎ Dān Yáng《Shí Èr Xué Zhǔ Zhì Zá Bìng Gē》? A. S36, Zú Sān Lǐ, Lv3, Tài Chōng, B57, Chéng Shān; B. Lu7, Liè Quē G30, Huán Tiào, H5, Tōng Lǐ; C. S44, Nèi Tíng B60, Kūn Lún B40, Wěi Zhōng; D. P6, Nèi Guān, Sj4, Yáng Chí K3, Tài Xī; E. Li11, Qū Chí G34, Yáng Líng Quán, Li4, Hé Gǔ.
2734	全面介绍了灸法的著作是: A.《素问》B.《灵枢》C. 资生经; D. 外台秘要; E. 针灸聚英.	What Classic introduced moxibustion most comprehensively? A.《Sù Wèn》; B.《Líng Shū》; C. Zī Shēng Jīng; D. Wài Tái Bì Yào; E. Zhēn Jiǔ Jù Yīng.
2735	首次见到《难经》名称的书是指: A. (帛书); B.《脉经》; C.《甲乙经》; D.《伤寒杂病论》; E.《灵枢经》.	What Classic made mention of 《Nàn Jīng》for the first time? A. (Bó Shū); B. 《Mài Jīng》; C. 《Jiá Yī Jīng》; D. 《Shāng Hán Zá Bìng Lùn》; E. 《Líng Shū jīng》.
2736	我国现存最早针灸医案 (诊籍) 的作者是: A·杨上善; B. 孙思邈; C. 郭玉; D. 淳于意; E. 滑寿.	Who wrote the first classic of clinical cases of acupuncture entitled, (Zhěn Jí)? A · Yáng Shàng Shàn; B. Sūn Sī Miǎo; C. Guō Yù; D. Chún Yú Yì; E. Huá Shòu.
2737	下列各穴中，不属于四总穴的是: A. 列缺穴; B. 合谷穴; C. 委中穴; D. 三阴交穴; E. 足三里穴	Which point is not listed as one of the Sì Zǒng Xué? A. Lu7, Liè Quē; B. Li4, Hé Gǔ; C. B40, Wěi Zhōng; D. Sp6, Sān Yīn Jiāo; E. S36, Zú Sān Lǐ.
2738	下列诸法，除……外，在《伤寒论》中已有了记载。 A. 毫针刺法; B. 温针法; C. 烧针法; D. 拔罐法 E 熨法.	Which of the following is not listed in the classic, 《Shāng Hán Lùn》? A. inserting a minute needle; B. warm needling; C. heated needling; D. cupping; E. ironing.
2739	以下各穴中，除……穴外均是四总穴: A. 足三里; B. 委中; C. 列缺; D. 曲池; E. 合谷.	Which of the following points is not contained in 《Sì Zǒng Xué》? A. S36, Zú Sān Lǐ; B. B40, Wěi Zhōng; C. Lu7, Liè Quē; D. Li11, Qū Chí; E. Li4, Hé Gǔ.
2740	俞、募穴主要载于《脉经》，但还缺少: A. 肺俞 心俞 B 膈俞 肝俞; C. 胆俞 脾俞; D. 厥阴俞 三焦俞; E. 胃俞 肾俞.	Back shu points [bèi shù xué] and anterior points [mù xué] are mainly discussed in 《Mài Jīng》, but what points are missing in this classic? A. B13, Fèi Shū, B15, Xīn Shū; B. B17, Gé Shū B18, Gān Shū; C. B19, Dǎn Shū, B20, Pí Shū; D. B14, Jué Yīn Shū, B22, Sān Jiāo Shū; E. B21, Wèi Shū, B23, Shèn Shū.
2741	张子和临床应用针灸疗法的特点是: A，拔罐为主; B. 艾灸保健为主; C. 毫针刺法为主; D. 刺络放血为主; E. 按时取穴为主.	What is the most characteristic of clinical acupuncture and moxibustion presented by Zhāng Zǐ Hé? A，cupping as the primary therapy; B. moxibustion for health and prevention as the primary therapy; C. insertion of minute needles as the primary therapy; D. inserting into linking meridians for bloodletting as the primary therapy; E. selecting points according to periods of time as the primary therapy.

2742	针灸医学传到欧洲是: A. 公元 6 世纪; B. 公元 7 世纪; C. 公元 8 世纪; D. 公元 17 世纪 E 公元 9 世纪.	When was acupuncture and moxibustion exported to Europe for the first time? A. 6th century; B. 7th century; C. 8th century; D. 17th century; E. 9th century.
2743	针灸作为一门专科最早见于: A 宋代; B. 元代; C. 清代; D. 唐代 E 明代.	When did acupuncture and moxibustion become a specialized discipline? A Sòng Dynasty; B. Yuán Dynasty; C. Qīng Dynasty; D. Táng Dynasty; E Míng Dynasty.
2744	·《难经 66》既是输穴，又是原穴的是: A. 丘墟; B. 京骨; C. 腕骨 D 阳池; E. 陷谷	·《Nàn Jīng 66》What point is a stream point [shù xué] and also a source point (Yuán Xué)? A. G40, Qiū Xū; B. B64, Jīng Gǔ; C. Si4, Wàn Gǔ D ·Sj4, Yáng Chí; E. S43, Xiàn Gǔ.
2745	最早记载经穴数字为 361 穴的医家是:A ·皇甫谧; B 孫思邈; C. 王惟一; D. 杨继洲; E. 李学川.	Who made mention of 361 points for the first time? A ·Huáng Fǔ Mì; B. Sūn Sī Miǎo; C. Wáng Wéi Yī D. Yáng Jì Zhōu; E. Lǐ Xué Chuān.
2746	背俞穴中的厥阴俞 ,首见于 A《难经》; B ·《脉经》; C. 《甲乙经》; D ·《针灸资生经》; E. 《千金要方》.	What Classic presented B14, Jué Yīn Shū among the back shu points [bèi shù xué]? A. 《Nàn Jīng》; B ·《Mài Jīng》; C. 《Jiá Yǐ Jīng》; D ·《Zhēn Jiǔ Zī Shēng Jīng》; E. 《Qiān Jīn Yào Fāng》.
2747	隔盐灸法最早见于: A. 《灵枢》; B. 《素问》; C. 《五十二病方》; D. 《针灸甲乙经》; E. 《肘后备急方》.	What Classic presented the therapy of "moxibustion with salt in between moxa and skin" for the first time? A. 《Líng Shū》; B. 《Sù Wèn》; C. 《Wǔ Shí Èr Bìng Fāng》; D. 《Zhēn Jiǔ Jiá Yǐ Jīng》; E. 《Zhǒu Hòu Bèi Jí Fāng》.
2748	夹脊穴的创始人是: A. 张仲景; B. 扁鹊; C. 滑伯仁; D 王惟一; E 华佗.	Who invented the Jiā Jí point? A. Zhāng Zhòng Jǐng; B. Biǎn Què; C. Huá Bó Rén; D Wáng Wéi Yī; E Huá Tuó.
2749	李学川所处的时代是， A 明代 B 宋代; C. 汉代 D 元代 ·E ·清代	In what period of history did Lǐ Xué Chuān live? A. ·Míng Dynasty; B. ·Sòng Dynasty; C. Hàn Dynasty; D. ·Yuán Dynasty; ·E. ·Qīng Dynasty.
2750	首先提出"十四经"这一名称的医家是: A， 杨上善; B. 孙思邈; C. 王冰; D. 王壽 E 滑寿.	Who made mention of "fourteen meridians" for the first time? A. Yáng Shàng Shàn; B. Sūn Sī Miǎo; C. Wáng Bīng; D. Wáng Shòu; E ·Huá Shòu.
2751	我国出存最早的针灸学专著是: A. 《黄帝内经》; B.《帛书》; C. 《难经》; D. 《针经》; E. 《针灸甲乙经》.	What is the first acupuncture classic in Chinese history? A. 《Huáng Dì Nèi Jīng》; B. 《Bó Shū》; C. 《Nàn Jīng》; D. 《Zhēn Jīng》; E. 《Zhēn Jiǔ Jiá Yǐ Jīng》.
2752	我国最早主张废针重灸的医家是: A. 皇甫谧; B. 葛洪; C. 杨上善; D. 孫思邈; E. 王壽.	What physician advocated discontinuation of acupuncture with emphasis on moxibustion? A. Huáng Fǔ Mì; B. Gé Hóng; C. Yáng Shàng Shàn; D. SŪN SĪ MIǍO; E. Wáng Shòu.
2753	下列哪本书的出现说明经络学说已基本形成: A. 《阴阳十一脉灸经》B. 《足臂十于脉灸经》C.	What Classic signified the basic completion of the theory of meridians? A. 《Yīn Yang Shí Yī Mài Jiǔ Jīng》; B. 《Zú Bìshí Yú Mài

	《针灸甲乙经》D. 《针灸大成》E. 《黄帝内经》.	Jiǔ Jīng》; C. 《Zhēn Jiǔ Jiá Yǐ Jīng》; D. 《Zhēn Jiǔ Dà Chéng》; E. 《Huáng Dì Nèi Jīng》.
2754	下列哪一刺法不是:《黄帝内经》中提出的: A. 九刺 B:五刺 C 十二刺;，D·五节刺; E. 烧山火.	Which of the following techniques is not listed in《Huáng Dì Nèi Jīng》? A. Nine ways of needling; B: Five ways of needling; C twelve programs of needling; D · Five types of needling; E. forest fire.
2755	下列有关足三里在归属上的错误是: A. 四总穴之一; B. ·回阳九针穴之一; C. ·马丹阳天星十二穴之一; D. ·十二合穴之一; E. ·十五络穴之一	Which of the following is incorrect about S36, Zú Sān Lǐ? A. · it is one of the points in Sì Zǒng Xué; B. · it is one of the points in Huí Yáng Jiǔ Zhēn Xué; C. · it is one of the points in Mǎ Dān Yáng Tiān Xīng Shí Èr Xué; D. ·it is one of the twelve sea points [hé xué]; E. · it is one of the twelve linking points (Luò Xué).
2756	最早在政府医疗机构中专门设立针灸科的朝代是: A. 秦朝; B. 汉朝; C. 晋朝; D. 隋朝; E. 唐朝.	During what dynasty did acupuncture and moxibustion become a separate specialized unit within the government medical institute? A. Qín Dynasty; B. Hàn Dynasty; C · Jìn Dynasty; D. Suí Dynasty; E. Táng Dynasty.
2757	《十四经发挥》的作者是: A. 滑伯仁; B. 李学川; C. 杨继洲 已·皇甫謐; E. 王惟一.	《Shí Sì Jīng Fā Huī》 Who is the author of this classic? A. Huá Bó Rén; B. Lǐ Xué Chuān; C. Yáng Jì Zhōu; D. · Huáng Fǔ Mì; E. Wáng Wéi Yī.
2758	《针灸问对》是针灸史上第一部全面评议的专著: A. 刺灸法 B ·针刺手法; C. 子午流注针法 D 灸法; E. 针刺宜忌.	《Zhēn Jiǔ Wèn Duì》 On the whole, what therapy was this classic critical about in the history of acupuncture and moxibustion? A. acupuncture and moxibustion; B ·techniques of needle insertion; C. energy flowing and entering acupuncture therapy (zǐ wǔ liú zhù zhēn fǎ); D techniques of moxibustion; E. do's and don'ts in needle insertion.
2759	《针灸问对》中，(病)在血分的针刺取穴原则为: A. 随其血之所在，应病取之; B. 远道取穴; C. 上有病，下取之; D. 下有病，上取之; E. 在左取右，在右取左	《Zhēn Jiǔ Wèn Duì》 How to select point for treatment of the disease that attacks the blood level? A. it should be treated by the region in which the disease occurs; B. selecting distal points for treatment; C. it should be treated by the points in the lower region when it occurs in the upper region; D. it should be treated by the points in the upper region when it occurs in the lower region; E. it should be treated by the points in the left region when it occurs in the right region.
2760	《针灸问对》中，若病人形气不足，病来潮作之时病气亦不足，首选的治疗方法应为: A. 灸法· ·B 针刺; C. 针灸并用 D 以甘药补之; E. 针药并用.	《Zhēn Jiǔ Wèn Duì》 How to treat the disease in which body energy and the pathogen that causes the disease are both deficient? A. by moxibustion; B. by acupuncture; C. by acupuncture and moxibustion; D. by sweet toning herbs; E. by acupuncture and herbs.
2761	《针灸大成》中"非药饵不能以济"的病位在: A. 肠胃 B;血脉; C. 皮肤 D 腠理 E ·脏腑	《Zhēn Jiǔ Dà Chéng》 What diseases can only be treated by herbs? A. the intestines and the stomach; B blood vessels; C. skin; D. pores; E. viscera and bowels.

2762	《针灸大成 3-21-6》中"阴阳和，五气顺，荣卫固，脉络绥"中的"五气"是指: A:五脏之气；B. 怒喜思悲恐，C·风暑湿燥寒; D. 肝心脾肺肾; E. 呼笑歌哭呻	《Zhēn Jiǔ Dà Chéng 3-21-6》"Harmonious yin and yang, smooth five kinds of energy, solid nutritive and defense levels, protected linking meridians." What does "five kinds of energy" refer to? A: the energy of five viscera; B. anger, joy, thought, sad, fear; ·C·wind, summer heat, dampness, dryness, cold; D. liver, heart, spleen, lungs, kidneys; E. calling, laughing, singing, crying, groaning.
2763	《针灸大成 3-22-3》中，欲去腹中之病，则灸: A: 足三里; B. 合谷; C. 百会; D. 中脘; E. 内关	《Zhēn Jiǔ Dà Chéng 3-22-3》In order to treat the disease of the abdomen, what point should be treated by moxibustion? A. S36, Zú Sān Lǐ; B. Li4, Hé Gǔ; C. D20, Bǎi Huì; D. R12, Zhōng Wǎn; E. P6, Nèi Guān.
2764	《针灸大成 3-22-5》中静养以虚此心，观变以远此心，旁求博采以旷此心，使: A. 心与造化相通; B. 阴阳平衡; C. 扶正去邪 D。经络疏通; E. 气血和调	《Zhēn Jiǔ Dà Chéng 3-22-5》In order to be a good doctor, it is necessary to nourish the spirit of your heart calmly, alter the spirit of your heart according to circumstances, and expand the spirit of your heart by collecting data. By this way, what is to be achieved? A. the spirit of your heart will be in communication with natural phenomena; B. Balance of yin and yang; C. supporting body energy and expelling pathogen; D. opening of meridians; E. harmony and regulation of energy and blood.
2765	《针灸大成 3-23-1》中灸之疗疾也，有数有法，"法"是指: A. 针灸所立之规; B. 针灸所定之方; C. 针灸的经穴 D。针灸的奇穴; E. 针刺的手法	《Zhēn Jiǔ Dà Chéng 3-23-1》"Numbers and methods should be specified in acupuncture and moxibustion"; what does "methods" refer to? A. principles of acupuncture and moxibustion; B. prescription of acupuncture and moxibustion; C. points of acupuncture and moxibustion; D. extraordinary points of acupuncture and moxibustion; E. techniques of needle insertion.
2766	《针灸大成 3-22-3》中灸治下列何项而取诸风池、百会？ A. 风; B. 劳; C. 气; D. 水; E. 血.	《Zhēn Jiǔ Dà Chéng 3-22-3》 What disease may be treated by moxibustion at G20, Fēng Chí and D20, Bǎi Huì? A. wind; B. fatigue; C. energy; D. water; E. blood.
2767	《针灸大成 3-21-5》中评价 "或詆其不尽伤寒之数"的医书是: A. 《千金方》; B.《金兰循经》; C.《外台秘要》; D.《针灸杂集》; E. 《灵枢》.	《Zhēn Jiǔ Dà Chéng 3-21-5》Which classic was criticized as not being consistent with the principle of Shāng Hán? A. 《Qiān Jīn Fāng》; B. 《Jīn Lán Xún Jīng》; C. 《Wài Tái Bì Yào》; D. 《Zhēn Jiǔ Zá Jí》; E. 《Líng Shū》.
2768	《针灸大成 3-22-4》中下列哪一位医家灸中脘九壮不发，而渍以露水，熨以热履，熯以赤葱，即万无不发之理: A. 秋夫; B. 东垣 C·丹溪; D. 从正; E. 完素.	《Zhēn Jiǔ Dà Chéng 3-22-4》 What physician treated a patient with nine moxa cones at R12 (zhong wan), which did not induce lesions, he then moistened the patient with dew, ironed the patient with a hot shoe, and burned red onions over the skin. From that point on, he had never failed to induce lesions again? A. Qiu Fu; B. Dōng Yuán; C · Dān Xī; D. Cóng Zhèng; E. Wán Sù.
2769	《针灸大成 3-24-2》中先	《Zhēn Jiǔ Dà Chéng 3-24-2》 What disease mechanism

	寒后热者，其病机是: A. 阳隐于阴; B. 阴隐于阳; C. 本虚标实; D. 虚实夹杂; E. 气血两虚	accounts for chills preceding heat? A. yang concealed in yin; B. yin concealed in yang; C. deficient roots with excess symptoms; D. mixture of deficiency and excess; E. deficiency of both energy and blood.
2770	《针灸大成 3-24-4》中先寒后热者，须施以下列何法? A. 阳中隐阴 B. 阴中隐阳; C. 标本兼治; D. 急则治标; E. 缓则治本	《Zhēn Jiǔ Dà Chéng 3-24-4》 How to treat chills preceding heat? A. yin concealed in yang; B. yang concealed in yin; C. · treating both the roots and the symptoms; D. treating the symptoms in an acute disease; E. treating the roots in a chronic disease.
2771	《针灸大成 3-21-1》中杨氏强调药物与下列选项中的哪一条不可缺: A. 针灸; B. 推拿; C. 火罐; D，水针; E. 电针.	《Zhēn Jiǔ Dà Chéng 3-21-1》 Two types of therapy are indispensable to each other, one is herbs, what is the other? A. acupuncture-moxibusiton; B. tui na or manipulative therapy; C. cupping; D. hydro-acupuncture; E. electro-acupuncture.
2772	《针灸大成 3-23-6》中以下不是组穴约有: A. 中魁; B. 四关; C. 八风; D. 八邪; E. 四缝	《Zhēn Jiǔ Dà Chéng 3-23-6》 Which of the following is a single point? A. Zhōng Kuí; B. Sì Guān; C. Bā Fēng; D. Bā Xié; E Sì Féng.
2773	《针灸大成》中曰先曰后者，是指: A，邪气所中有荣有卫的区别; B. 邪气所中有阳经与阴经的区别; C. 邪气所中有气有血的区别; D. 邪气所中有经有络的区别; E. 邪气所中有深有浅的区别	《Zhēn Jiǔ Dà Chéng》 The so-called sequence of attack refers to: A. there is a difference between pathogen attacking nutritive energy and defense energy; B. there is a difference between pathogen attacking yang meridian and yin meridian; C. there is a difference between pathogen attacking energy and blood; D. there is a difference between pathogen attacking master meridians and linking meridians; E. there is a difference between pathogen attacking deep region and shallow region.
2774	《针灸大成 3-23-5》中指出腹部经穴宜多灸的原因是: A. 肌肉较为丰厚; B. 肌肉较为单薄; C. 气虚血少; D. 邪气不盛; E. 正气不足.	《Zhēn Jiǔ Dà Chéng 3-23-5》 Why should more moxibustion be applied to the points in the abdominal region? A. the muscles are thicker in the region; B. the muscles are thinner in the region; C. scanty energy and blood in the region; D. no abundant pathogen in the region; E. insufficient body energy.
2775	《针灸大成 3-22-4》中渍以露水，熨以热履，熯以赤葱，即万无不发之理，主要的机理是: A. 增强机体抗病能力; B. 扶正祛邪; C. 调整阴阳; D. 行气活血; E. 疏通经络	《Zhēn Jiǔ Dà Chéng 3-22-4》 The doctor moistened the patient with dew, ironed the patient with a hot shoe, burned red onions over the skin. From that point on, he had never failed to induce lesions again. What is the mechanism involved in the treatment? A. to reinforce the body's defense against disease; B. to support body energy and expel pathogen; C. to regulate yin and yang; D. to promote energy flow and activate blood; E. to disperse and connect meridians.
2776	《针灸大成》中"非针刺不能以及"的病位在： A. 肠胃; B. 血脉; C. 皮肤	《Zhēn Jiǔ Dà Chéng》 What diseases can only be treated by acupuncture?

	D 腠理; E. 脏腑	A. the intestines and the stomach; B. blood vessels; C. skin; D. pores; E. viscera and bowels.
2777	《针灸大成 4-21-1》中"圣人图设沟渠，通利水道，以备不虞，天雨降下，沟渠溢满，当此之时，雾霈妄行，圣人不能复图也，此络脉满溢，诸经不能复拘也"是指: A. 奇经八脉的名称 B，奇经八脉的作用; C. 奇经八脉的数量; D. 奇经八脉的病理; E. 奇经八脉与十二经脉的区别	《Zhēn Jiǔ Dà Chéng 4-21-1》"When the Sage drew a geographical map and designed waterways in order to facilitate the passages of water and to prepare for emergencies in case of heavy rains, he had no choice but leaving out the extraordinary meridians so that they might accommodate the extra amount of water which may overflow from the regular channels. This explains why the extraordinary meridians are beyond the scope of the twelve master meridians in the human body." Here, what is being discussed? A. names of eight extraordinary meridians; B functions of eight extraordinary meridians; C. numbers of eight extraordinary meridians; D. pathology of eight extraordinary meridians; E. distinction between eight extraordinary meridians and twelve master meridians.
2778	《针灸大成 3-22-4》中观下列哪一位医家灸三里七壮不发，而复灸以五壮即发: A. 秋夫; B. 东垣; C. 丹溪; D. 从正; E. 完素.	《Zhēn Jiǔ Dà Chéng 3-22-4》Who treated a patient with seven moxa cones at S36 (zu san li), which did not induce lesions, he then added another five moxa cones, which finally induced the lesions? A. Qiū Fū; B. Dōng Yuán; C. Dān Xī; D. Cóng Zhèng; E. Wán Sù.
2779	《针灸大成 3-22-3》中灸下列哪一项而取诸膏肓、百劳? A. 风; B. 劳; C. 气; D. 水; E. 血.	《Zhēn Jiǔ Dà Chéng 3-22-3》What disease may be treated by moxibustion at B43 [gao huang shu], Bai-Lao (hundred fatigue)? A. wind; B. fatigue; C. energy; D. water; E. blood.
2780	《针灸大成 3-21-5》中评价 "或嫌其太简而略"的医书是: A.《千金方》;B《金兰循经》; C.《外台秘要》; D.《针灸杂集》; E《灵枢》.	《Zhēn Jiǔ Dà Chéng 3-21-5》 Which classic was criticized as too simple and incomplete? A. 《Qiān Jīn Fāng》; B《Jīn Lán Xún Jīng》; C. 《Wài Tái Bì Yào》; D. 《Zhēn Jiǔ Zá Jí》; E《Líng Shū》.
2781	《针灸大成 3-24-2》中先热后寒者，其病机是: A. 阳隐于阴; B. 阴隐于阳; C. 本虚标实; D. 虚实夹杂; E. 气血两虚	《Zhēn Jiǔ Dà Chéng 3-24-2》 What disease mechanism accounts for heat preceding chills? A. yang concealed in yang; B. yin concealed in yang; C. deficient roots with excess symptoms; D. mixture of deficiency and excess; E. deficiency of both energy and blood.
2782	《针灸大成 3-22-3》中欲治头目之疾，则灸: A. 足三里; B. 合谷; C. 百会; D. 中脘; E. 内关.	《Zhēn Jiǔ Dà Chéng 3-22-3》 What point may be used to treat diseases of the head and eyes by moxibustion? A. S36, Zú Sān Lǐ; B. Li4, Hé Gǔ; C. D20, Bǎi Huì; D. R12, Zhōng Wǎn; E. P6, Nèi Guān.
2783	《针灸大成 3-24-4》中曰寒曰热者，是指: A. 邪气所中有荣有卫的区别; B. 邪气所中有阳经与阴经的区别; C. 邪气所中有气有血的区别; D. 邪气所中有经有络的区别; E.	《Zhēn Jiǔ Dà Chéng 3-24-4》The so-called cold and hot sensations refers to: A. there is a difference between pathogen attacking nutritive energy and defense energy; B. there is a difference between pathogen attacking yang meridian and yin meridian; C. there is a difference between

	邪气所中有深有浅的区别.	pathogen attacking energy and blood; D. there is a difference between pathogen attacking master meridians and linking meridians; E. there is a difference between pathogen attacking deep region and shallow region.
2784	《针灸大成 3-23-5》中指出手指末端井穴，不宜多灸的原因是: A. 肌肉较为丰厚; B. 肌肉较为单薄; C. 气虚血少; D. 邪气不盛; E. 正气不足.	《Zhēn Jiǔ Dà Chéng》 Why should limited moxibustion be applied to well points [jǐng xué] at the tips of fingers? A. the muscles are thicker in the region; B. the muscles are thinner in the region; C. scanty energy and blood in the region; D. no abundant pathogen in the region; E. insufficient body energy.
2785	杨继洲提出的平补平泻法是： A. 先用泻法，后用补法; B. 小补小泻; C. 以补为主，兼有泻法; D. 以泻为主，兼有补法; E. 进针后均匀提插、捻转、得气后出针	What is the neutral technique of acupuncture as presented by Yáng Jì Zhōu? A. sedation first, followed by tonificaton; B. tonification and sedation on a small scale; C. tonification first, followed by sedation; D. sedation as the primary, accompanied by tonification;; E. harmonious lifting and inserting the needle, twirl it, and withdraw it after energy response.
2786	《针灸大成》的作者是: A. 王寿B.李学川; C. 杨继州; D. 高武 E 李时珍:	《Zhēn Jiǔ Dà Chéng》 Who is the author of Zhēn Jiǔ Dà Chéng? A. Wáng Shòu b. Lǐ Xué Chuān; C. Yáng Jì Zhōu; D. Gāo Wǔ e Lǐ Shí Zhēn:
2787	《针灸大成 3-21-5》中"盖《素》、《难》者，医家之鼻祖，济生之心法"中的 "心法" 是指: A. 以心相传授的佛法; B. 传心养性的方法; C. 师徒授受心法; D. 用心体会的方法; E. 重要的方法	《Zhēn Jiǔ Dà Chéng 3-21-5》 Sù Wèn and Nàn Jīng are the earliest ancestors of physicians and the lifeline methodology"; what is meant by "the lifeline methodology"? A. the lifeline taught in Buddhism; B. the lifeline of the heart; C. the lifeline taught by teachers to disciples; D. methodology learned by heart; E. important methodology.
2788	《针灸大成 3-22-3》中灸治哪种病而取诸气海: A. 风 B。劳; C. 气; D. 水; E. 血.	《Zhēn Jiǔ Dà Chéng 3-22-3》 What disease may be treated by moxibustion at R6 (qi hai)? A. wind; B. fatigue; C. energy; D. water; E. blood.
2789	《针灸大成 3-21-5》中评价'"或议其为医之蔽"的医书是: A. 《千金方》 B. ·《金兰循经》·C··《外台秘要》; D.《针灸杂集》 E. (灵枢》.	《Zhēn Jiǔ Dà Chéng 3-21-5》Which classic was criticized as physicians' fault? A. 《Qiān Jīn Fāng》; B. ·《Jīn Lán Xún Jīng》; C·《Wài Tái Bì Yào》; D. 《Zhēn Jiǔ Zá Jí》; E. (Líng Shū》.
2790	《针灸大成 3-21-6》中在"诸家得决策:中"穷之以井、荣、俞、经、合之源"是指: A. 配穴补泻; B. 手法补泻 C，母子补泻 D 原络配穴; E. 迎随补泻.	《Zhēn Jiǔ Dà Chéng 3-21-6》 In "Answers to the questions about the merits and errors of various physicians", the text says that it is necessary to trace the source of the five command points, namely, well points [jǐng xué], spring points [yíng xué], stream points [shù xué], river points [jīng xué], and sea points [hé xué]"; what is that for? A. in order to pair off points for tonification and sedation; B. in order to apply the techniques of tonification and

		sedation; C, in order to apply mother-child tonification and sedation; D in order to pair off source point [yuán xué] and linking point (collateral points, luò xué); E. in order to apply the twirling technique of tonification and sedation according to energy streams of meridians.
2791	《针灸大成 3-21-6》中在"诸家得失策"中"究之以"迎随开合之机"是指: A. 进针手法; B. 行针手法; C 补泻手法; D. 留针; E. 出针.	《Zhēn Jiŭ Dà Chéng 3-21-6》In "Answers to the questions about the merits and errors of various physicians", the text says that it is necessary to investigate into the greeting and following as well as the pressing and non-pressing techniques: what are those techniques used for? A. techniques of needle insertion; B. techniques of manipulating the needle; C. techniques of tonification and sedation; D. retention of needle; E. withdrawal of needle.
2792	《针灸大成 3-22-3》中治疗哪一部位疾病，则取环跳、风市: A. 头目; B. 腹中 C 腰腿; D. 手臂; E. 颈项	《Zhēn Jiŭ Dà Chéng 3-22-3》 What diseases may be treated by moxibustion at G30, Huán Tiào and G31 (feng shi)? A. diseases of the head and eyes; B. abdominal diseases; C diseases of the waist and legs; D. diseases of hands and arms; E. diseases of neck and back of neck.
2793	《针灸大成》中"非熨焫不能以达" 的病位在：A. 肠胃; B. 血脉; C. 皮肤 D 腠理; E. 脏腑	《Zhēn Jiŭ Dà Chéng》What diseases can only be treated by ironing with herbs and stimulation therapy with warm needle? A. the intestines and the stomach; B. blood vessels; C. skin; D. pores; E. viscera and bowels.
2794	《针灸大成 3-21-6》中"究之以主客"中的"主客"是指: A 主次; B. 主气与客气; C. 主穴与配穴; D. 原络配穴法; E. 表经与里经	《Zhēn Jiŭ Dà Chéng 3-21-6》To study the treatment principle of host and guest; what does "host and guest" refer to? A. primary and secondary; B. host energy and guest energy; C. primary point and combined point; D.pairing off original points (Yuán Xué) and linking points (Luò Xué); E. superficial meridian and deep meridian.
2795	《针灸大成 3-22-3》中灸水分可治下列何病: A. 风; B. 劳; C. 气; D. 水; E. 血.	《Zhēn Jiŭ Dà Chéng 3-22-3》 What disease may be treated by moxibustion at R9 (shui fen)? A. wind; B. fatigue; C. energy; D. water; E. blood.
2796	《针灸大成 3-21-5》中评价 "或论其未尽针灸之妙"的医书是: A. 《千金方》B《金兰循经》"C《外台秘要》D. 《针灸杂集》E. 《灵枢》.	《Zhēn Jiŭ Dà Chéng 3-21-5》Which classic was criticized as not fully discussing about the ingenious theory of acupuncture and moxibustion? A. 《Qiān Jīn Fāng》; B·《Jīn Lán Xún Jīng》; C·《Wài Tái Bì Yào》; D. 《Zhēn Jiŭ Zá Jí》; E. 《Líng Shū》.
2797	《针灸大成 3-22-3》中治疗哪一部位疾病，则取肩髃、曲池: A. 头目; B. 腹中 C、腰腿 D、手臂 E、颈项	《Zhēn Jiŭ Dà Chéng 3-22-3》What diseases may be treated by moxibustion at Li15 (jian yu), Li11 (qu chi)? A. diseases of the head and eyes; B. abdominal diseases; C diseases of the waist and legs; D. diseases of hands and arms; E. diseases of neck and back of neck.
2798	《针灸大成 3-22-3》是百脉之皆归于头，如何治疗头部?	《Zhēn Jiŭ Dà Chéng 3-22-3》Hundred meridians are distributed in the head, how to treat the head region?

	A. 头部不可灸; B. 头部不可针灸; C 头部可针不可灸; D. 头部和其它部位一样; E. 头部不可多灸	A. no moxibustion in the head region; B. neither acupuncture nor moxibustion in the head region; C. no moxibustion in the head region; D. the head region should be treated like any other region of the body; E. moxibustion should not focus on the head.
2799	《针灸大成 3-21-6》中在"诸家得失策"中"施之以动，摇，进，退，搓，弹，摄、按之法"是指: A. 进针手法 ·B ·行针手法; C. 补泻手法 ·D 出针; E. 综合手法.	《Zhēn Jiǔ Dà Chéng 3-21-6》In "Answers to the questions about the merits and errors of various physicians", the text says that it is necessary to apply the vibrating technique, shaking technique, pushing-retreating technique, rolling technique, flicking technique, pushing-up technique, and pressing technique." What do those techniques refer to? A. techniques of needle insertion; ·B techniques of manipulating the needle; C. techniques of tonification and sedation; D. · techniques of withdrawing needle; E. comprehensive techniques.
2800	杨继洲在家传何书的基础上，编写成《针灸大成》? A.《难经》; B.《甲乙经》; C.《明堂孔穴针灸治要》; D.《铜人腧穴针灸图经》; E.《卫生针灸玄机秘要》.	What Classic handed down in family on the basis of which Yáng Jì Zhōu wrote his Classic, 《Zhēn Jiǔ Dà Chéng》? A.《Nàn Jīng》; B.《Jiá Yī Jīng》; C.《Míng Táng Kǒng XuéZhēn Jiǔ Zhì Yào》; D. 《Tóng Rén Shù Xuézhēn Jiǔ Tú Jīng》; E. 《Wèi Shēng Zhēn Jiǔ Xuán Jī Bì Yào》.
2801	針灸大成是谁的著作？ A. 皇甫謐(214-282); B. 孫思邈 (581-682);; C. 王惟一(987-1067); D. 杨继洲(1522-1620); E. 汪机(1463-1539).	Who is the author of Zhēn Jiǔ Dà Chéng ? ? A. Huáng Fǔ Mì (214-282); B. Sūn Sī Miǎo (581-682); C. Wáng Wéi Yī (987-1067); D. Yáng Jì Zhōu (1522-1620); E. Wāng Jī (1463-1539).
2802	《医宗金鉴》的作者是: A. 吴谦; B. 高武; C. 李学川; D. 汪机 E，吴昆	《Yī Zōng Jīn Jiàn》 Who is the author of this classic? A. Wú Qiān; B. Gāo Wǔ; C. Lǐ Xué Chuān; D. · Wāng Jī; E. Wú Kūn
2803	《百证赋》中，鼻内无闻之苦可选以下哪穴？ A. 通天; B. 迎香 C·上星，D·合谷; E. 列缺.	《Bǎi Zhèng Fù》What point should be selected to treat loss of the smell or nasal congestion? A. B7, Tōng Tiān; B. Li20, Yíng XiāngC ·D23, Shàng Xīng，D ·Li4, Hé Gǔ; E. Lu7, Liè Quē.
2804	《百证赋》中，悬颅、颔厌二穴，可以治： A. 偏头痛; B. 腿痛 C·头晕; D. 视力下降; E. 牙痛.	《Bǎi Zhèng Fù》 What can be treated by the two points G5, Xuán Lú and G4, Hàn Yàn? A. migraine headache; B. pain in leg; C. dizziness; D. decrease in vision; E. toothache.
2805	《百证赋》中，治疗厥寒厥热的穴是: A.涌泉; B. 复溜 · C. ·然谷; D. 承浆; E. 太冲	《Bǎi Zhèng Fù》What point should be selected to treat cold upstream diseases and hot upstream diseases? A.K1, Yǒng Quán; B. K7, Fù Liū · C. ·K2, Rán Gǔ; D. R24, Chéng Jiàng; E. Lv3, Tài Chōng.
2806	《百证赋》中，独泻太阳经治疗小便赤涩的穴是: A. 涌泉; B. 兑端; C. 然谷; D. 承浆; E. 太冲.	《Bǎi Zhèng Fù》What point should be selected to treat discharge of reddish urine with difficult urination? A. K1, Yǒng Quán; B. D27, Duì Duān; C. K2, Rán Gǔ; D. R24, Chéng Jiàng; E. Lv3, Tài Chōng.
2807	《百证赋》中，后溪、环跳二穴·相配可以治： A.	《Bǎi Zhèng Fù》What may be treated by pairing off Si3, Hòu Xī and G30, Huán Tiào?

	偏头痛; B. 腿痛 C·头晕; D. 视力下降; E. 牙痛	A. migraine headache; B. pain in the leg; C. dizziness; D. decreased vision; E. toothache.
2808	《百证赋》中，面上虫行有验，可取: A. 通天; B. 迎香; C·上星; D. 合谷; E·列缺	《Bǎi Zhèng Fù》 What point should be selected to treat the sensations of insects moving over the face? A. B7, Tōng Tiān; B. Li20, Yíng Xiāng; C. ·D23, Shàng Xīng; D. Li4, Hé Gǔ; E·Lu7, Liè Quē.
2809	《百证赋》中，舌干口燥可取： A. 通天; B. 复溜; C. 听会; D. 合谷; E. 列缺.	《Bǎi Zhèng Fù》 What point should be selected to treat dry tongue and dry mouth? A. B7, Tōng Tiān; B. K7, Fù Liū; C. G2, Tīng Huì; D. Li4, Hé Gǔ; E. Lu7, Liè Quē.
2810	《百证赋》中，主治积痢的穴是: A.涌泉; B. 中脘; C. 肩井; D. 商丘; E. 太冲，	《Bǎi Zhèng Fù》 What is the major point for treating dysentery? A. K1, Yǒng Quán; B. R12, Zhōng Wǎn; C. G21, Jiān Jǐng; D. Sp5, Shāng Qiū; E. Lv3, Tài Chōng.
2811	《百证赋》中，耳中蝉噪有声，可取: A. 通天 B·迎香 C，听会; D. 合谷; E. 列缺.	《Bǎi Zhèng Fù》 What point should be selected to treat ringing in the ears like the sound of a cicada? A. B7, Tōng Tiān; B. ·Li20, Yíng Xiāng; C. G2, Tīng Huì; D. Li4, Hé Gǔ; E. Lu7, Liè Quē.
2812	《百证赋》中，治疗乳痈效果很好的穴是: A. 涌泉; B. 兑端; C. 肩井; D. 承浆; E. 太冲.	《Bǎi Zhèng Fù》 What point should be selected to treat carbuncle in the breast with good results? A. K1, Yǒng Quán; B. D27, Duì Duān; C. G21, Jiān Jǐng; D. R24, Chéng Jiàng; E. Lv3, Tài Chōng.
2813	《百证赋》中，治疗小儿脐风的穴是: A. 通天; B. 复溜 C. 然谷 D. 承浆; E. 太冲.	《Bǎi Zhèng Fù》 What point should be selected to treat tetanus in infants? A. B7, Tōng Tiān; B. K7, Fù Liū; C. K2, Rán Gǔ; D. R24, Chéng Jiàng; E. Lv3, Tài Chōng.
2814	《百证赋》中，有治疗脱肛作用的穴是: A. 涌泉; B. 中脘 C·肩井 D 外丘 E·太冲	《Bǎi Zhèng Fù》 What point should be selected to treat prolapse of anus? A. K1, Yǒng Quán; B. R12, Zhōng Wǎn; C. ·G21, Jiān Jǐng; D. G36, Wài Qiū; E. Lv3, Tài Chōng.
2815	《百证赋》中，治疗牙疼的穴是: A. 通天; B. 复溜; C. 听会; D. 承浆; E. 太冲.	《Bǎi Zhèng Fù》 What point should be selected to treat toothache? A. B7, Tōng Tiān; B. K7, Fù Liū; C. G2, Tīng Huì; D. R24, Chéng Jiàng; E. Lv3, Tài Chōng.
2816	《百证赋》中，治疗痔瘤最佳的穴是: A 涌泉; B. 兑端; C. 肩井; D. 商丘; E. 太冲	《Bǎi Zhèng Fù》 What is the best point for treating hemorrhoid and anal fistula? A. K1, Yǒng Quán; B. D27, Duì Duān; C. G21, Jiān Jǐng; D. Sp5, Shāng Qiū; E. Lv3, Tài Chōng.
2817	《百证赋》中，能使唇喎速愈的穴是: A.通天; B. 复溜 C.听会; D. 合谷; E. 太冲	《Bǎi Zhèng Fù》 What point should be selected to speed up recovery of wry lips? A.B7, Tōng Tiān; B. K7, Fù Liū; C.G2, Tīng Huì; D. Li4, Hé Gǔ; E. Lv3, Tài Chōng.
2818	《标幽赋》中"住痛移疼，取相交相贯之迳"是取: A. 多经相交之穴; B. 阳经相交之穴; C. 表里经交接之穴 D、八脉交会穴; E. 阴经相交之穴	《Biāo Yōu Fù》" Make use of meridian-connecting points to relieve pain." What are meridian-connecting points? A. points connecting many meridians; B. points connecting yang meridians; C. points connecting superficial and deep meridians; D. eight confluence points

		[bā mài bā huì xué]; E. points connecting yin meridians.
2819	《标幽赋》中"阴交阳别而定血晕"是指: A. 鼻出血; B. 子宫出血; C. 便血; D. 胃出血; E. 吐血	《Biāo Yōu Fù》Which of the following can be treated by Sp6, Sān Yīn Jiāo? A. nosebleed; B. bleeding from uterus; C. discharge of blood from anus; D. stomach bleeding; E. vomiting of blood.
2820	《标幽赋》中"既至也，量寒热而留疾"的"寒热"是指: A. 皮肤温度; B. 疾病性质; C. 症状虚实; D. 自然界寒温; E. 寒热症状.	《Biāo Yōu Fù》"After energy arrives, whether the needle should be retained or it should be withdrawn quickly depends on cold and hot." What is meant by "cold and hot"? A. skin temperature; B. conditions of disease; C. deficiency and excess of symptoms; D. cold and warm of the environments; E. cold and hot symptoms.
2821	《标幽赋》中"筋挛骨痛而补魂门"的原理是: A. 魂门是背部穴; B. 魂门平肾俞 C. 魂门平肝俞穴; D. 魂门是筋会; E. 魂门是背俞穴	《Biāo Yōu Fù》How do you account for the statement that " tendon spasms and pain in bones should be treated by toning up B47, Hún Mén"? A. B47, Hún Mén is a point in the back; B. B47, Hún Mén is on a level with B23, Shèn Shū; C。B47, Hún Mén is on a level with B18, Gān Shū; D. B47, Hún Mén is meeting of tendons; E. B47, Hún Mén is Bèi Shù Xué (back shu point).
2822	《标幽赋》，眼痒眼疼泻: A. 申脉、金门; B. 大椎、风门; C. 太阳、丝竹空; D. 光明、地五会; E. 睛明、飞扬	《Biāo Yōu Fù》 What points should be sedated in the treatment of eye itch and eye pain? A. B62, Shēn Mài、 jīn mén; B. D14, Dà Zhuī、B12, Fēng Mén; C. tài yáng、Sj23, Sī Zhú Kōng; D. G37, Guāng Míng、G42, Dì Wǔ Huì; E. B1, Jīng Míng、B58, Feī Yáng.
2823	《标幽赋》的作者是: A. 王执中; B. 王惟一; C. 淳于意; D. 华佗; E. 窦汉卿	《Biāo Yōu Fù》Who is the author of this classic? A. Wáng Zhí Zhōng; B. Wáng Wéi Yī; C. Chún Yú Yì; D. Huá Tuó; E. Dòu Hàn Qīng.
2824	《标幽赋》中"寒热痹痛，开四关而已之"，四关是: A. 四肢关节 B 四肢末端; C. 合谷穴; D. 太冲穴; E. 合谷穴和太冲穴	《Biāo Yōu Fù》"Cold hot rheumatic pain may be treated by four gates", what do four gats refer to? A. joints of four limbs; B. tips of four limbs; C. Li4, Hé Gǔ; D. ·Lv3, Tài Chōng; E. Li4, Hé Gǔ and Lv3, Tài Chōng.
2825	《标幽赋》中"胁肋疼痛针飞虎"是指: A. 阳陵泉; B. 阴陵泉; C. 外关; D. 合谷; E. 支沟.	《Biāo Yōu Fù》" Pain in the hypochondriac region may be treated by acupuncture at flying tiger." What point is "flying tiger"? A. G34, Yáng Líng Quán; B. Sp9, Yīn Líng Quán; C. Sj5, Wài Guān; D. Li4, Hé Gǔ; E. Sj6, Zhi Gōu.
2826	《灵枢·7-3》中记载的赞刺络刺豹纹刺是指: A. 三棱针; B. 皮肤针; C. 皮内针; D. 穴位注射; E. 火针	《Líng Shū·7-3》What do supplemental needling, reticular needling, and leopard needling, refer to? A. three-edged needles; B. skin needles; C. intradermal needles; D. injection therapy; E. fire needles.
2827	《灵枢·71-17 邪客》篇说:肺心有邪，其气留于: A. 两肘; B. 两腋; C. 两髀; D. 两腘; E. 两踝	《Líng Shū 71-17》The pathogen that attacks the lungs and the heart will come to reside: A. in the elbows; B. in the armpits; C. in the greater trochanter; D. in the popliteal fossae; E. in the ankles.

2828	《靈樞 1-2》"知机之道了不可挂以发"是指: A. 应及时补泻 B，应及时出针 C·应及时进针; D. ·应手法轻巧 E·应轻微补泻	《Líng Shū 1-2》A physician with a mastery of the mechanism of the body will take action precisely at the right time without the slightest negligence; what does it mean? A. tonification and sedation should be administered on time; B. the needle should be withdrawn on time; C · the needle should be inserted on time; D. ·the technique should be used with precision; E. tonification and sedation should be moderate.
2829	《靈樞 19-3》"飧泄补三阴之上"主要是补: A. 足三阴; B. 手三阴; C. 足太阴; D. 手太阴; E. 阴陵泉.	《Líng Shū 19-3》Diarrhea with completely undigested foods due to spleen deficiency and coldness should be treated by toning up upper triple yin; what should be toned up? A. foot three yins; B. hand three yins; C. foot greater yin; D. hand greater yin; E. Sp9, Yīn Líng Quán.
2830	《靈樞 21-10》"暴瘅内逆，肝肺相搏，血溢鼻口"，治疗取穴为: A. 天府; B. 天牖; C. 人迎; D. 扶突; E. 天柱	《Líng Shū 21-10》What point should be used to treat "acute onset of diabetes-like disease with internal heat (xiao dan), internal upstream lung energy, a struggle between the lung and liver, nosebleed, and discharge of blood from the mouth"? A. Lu3, Tiān Fǔ; B. Sj16, Tiān Yǒu; C. S9, Rén Yíng; D. Li18, Fú Tū; E. B10, Tiān Zhù.
2831	《靈樞 24-11》肾心痛治疗用穴为: A. 京骨, 昆仑,然谷; B. 大都、太白 C;然谷、太溪; D. 行间、太冲; E. 鱼际、太渊	《Líng Shū 24-11》What points may be used to treat kidney heart pain? A. B64, Jīng Gǔ, B60, Kūn Lún, K2, Rán Gǔ; B. Sp2, Dà Dū、Sp3, Tài Bái; C. K2, Rán Gǔ、K3, Tài Xī; D. Lv2, Xíng Jiān 、Lv3, Tài Chōng; E. Lu10, Yǔ Jì 、Lu9, Tài Yuān.
2832	《靈樞 24-13》脾心痛治疗用穴为: A. 然谷、太溪; B. 京骨、昆仑、然谷; C. 大都、太白; D. 行间、太冲 E，鱼际、太渊.	《Líng Shū 24-13》What points may be used to treat spleen heart pain? A. K2, Rán Gǔ 、K3, Tài Xī; B. B64, Jīng Gǔ 、B60, Kūn Lún 、K2, Rán Gǔ; C. Sp2, Dà Dū 、Sp3, Tài Bái; D. Lv2, Xíng Jiān、Lv3, Tài Chōng E，Lu10, Yǔ Jì、Lu9, Tài Yuān.
2833	《靈樞 28-2》欠的治疗是: A. 泻足少阴, 补足太阳; B. 补足少阴 ·泻足太阳; C. 泻足少阴太阳; D. 补足少阴太阳; E. 补足少阴.	《Líng Shū 28-2》How to treat yawning? A. by applying sedation to the lesser yin of foot and tonification to the greater yang of foot; B. by applying tonification to the lesser yin of foot and sedation to the greater yang of foot; C. by applying sedation to the foot lesser yin and greater yang; D. by applying tonification to the foot lesser yin and greater yang; E. by applying tonification to the foot lesser yin.
2834	《靈樞 28-4》唏的治疗是: A. 补足太阳 ·泻足少阴; B. 补足少阴 ·泻足太阳; C. 补足少阴太阳; D 泻足少阴太阳; E. 补足少阴.	《Líng Shū 28-4》How to treat whimper? A. by applying tonification to the foot greater yang and sedation to the foot lesser yin; B. by applying tonification to the foot lesser yin and sedation to the foot greater yang; C. by applying tonification to the foot lesser yin and greater yang; D. by applying sedation to the foot lesser yin and greater yang; E. by applying tonification to the

		foot lesser yin.
2835	《靈樞 3-4》"所谓虚则实之者"是指: A. 气口虚而当补之也; B. 人迎虚而当补之者也; C. 三部九候虚而当补之也; D. 针下空虚而当补之也; E. 无针感而当补之也	《Líng Shū 3-4》What is meant by the assertion that "when energy is deficient it should be solidified"? A. When the mouth of energy appears deficient, tonification therapy should be applied; B. when the pulse at the wrist is deficient, it should be toned up; C. when the pulses in the three regions to indicate nine symptoms are deficient, they should be toned up; D. when inserted region is deficient, it should be toned up; E. lack of needling sensations should be toned up.
2836	《靈樞 34-2》气乱于肺的治疗取穴应是: A，手太阴荣 、足少阴输; B. 手太阴输 、足少阴荣; C. 唯取手太阴荣; D. 唯取手太阴输 E唯取足少阴输.	《Líng Shū 34-2》When the energy disorder occurs in the lungs, what points should be selected for treatment? A. the spring points [Yíng Xué] of the hand greater yin and the stream point [Shù Xué] of the foot lesser yin; B. the stream point [Shù Xué] of the hand greater yin and the spring point [Yíng Xué] of the foot lesser yin; C. only the spring point [Yíng Xué] of the hand greater yin; D. only the stream point [Shù Xué] of the hand greater yin; E only the stream point [Shù Xué] of the foot lesser yin.
2837	《靈樞 34-2》气乱于心的治疗取穴应是: A. 手少阴 、心主之输; B. 只取手少阴之输 C，只取手心主之输; D. 手少阴 、太阳之输，; E. 手太阳之输·	《Líng Shū 34-2》When the energy disorder occurs in the heart, what points should be selected for treatment? A. The stream points [Shù Xué] of the hand lesser yin and pericardium; B. only the stream point [Shù Xué] of the hand lesser yin; C. only the stream point [Shù Xué] of pericardium; D. the stream points [Shù Xué] of the hand lesser yin and greater yang; E. the stream points [Shù Xué] of the hand greater yang.·
2838	《靈樞 38-3》肥人的针刺要求是: A. 深而留之，多益其数; B. 深而疾之，多益其数; C. 浅而留之，多益其数; D. 浅而疾之，多益其数; E. 深而留之，少益其数	《Líng Shū 38-3》How to treat a fat person by acupuncture? A. A deep insertion and delayed withdrawal of needle, with increased number and frequency of needling; B. a deep insertion and quick withdrawal of needle, with increased number and frequency of needling.; C. a shallow insertion and delayed withdrawal of needle, with increased number and frequency of needling; D. a shallow insertion and quick withdrawal of needle, with increased number and frequency of needling; E.a deep insertion and delayed withdrawal of needle, with decreased number and frequency of needling.
2839	《靈樞 39-3》刺血络，出现仆倒现象的是: A. 气盛而血虚; B. 血气俱盛 C 阳气蓄积; D. 阴气积于阳; E. 阴阳俱脫	《Líng Shū 39-3》How do you account for needling that causes fainting in acupuncture treatment of blood clotting? A. Meridian energy is abundant while blood is deficient; B. both blood and energy are in abundance; C. yang energy has been accumulated for long; D. yin energy gets accumulated in the yang portion; E. a prostration of both yin and yang.
2840	《靈樞 4-13》刺六变之脉急者，宜: A. 深内而久留针 B 深内而不留针;	《Líng Shū 4-13》How should needling take place in response to the acute pulse?

	C. 浅内而久留针; D. 浅内而不留针; E. 疾发针而浅内之	A. A deep insertion and needle should stay in the body for longer; B a deep insertion and needle should be withdrawn right away; C. a shallow insertion and needle should stay in the body for longer; D. a shallow insertion and needle should be withdrawn right away; E. Rapid withdrawal of needle and shallow insertion.
2841	《靈樞 4-17》一病人肠中切痛，肠鸣，感寒即泻，当脐而痛，据 "合治内腑"原则，宜取 A. 巨虛上廉; B. 巨虛下廉; C. 足三里; D. 曲池; E. 委阳	《Líng Shū 4-17》A patient with sharp pain in the large intestine, intestinal rumbling as noisy as running water; diarrhea resulting from an additional attack of cold energy in winter; pain in the region around the umbilicus; what point should be used to treat it according to the principle of "Sea points [Hé Xué] can treat internal bowels"? A. S37, Shàng Jù Xū; B. S39, Xià Jù Xū; C. S36, Zú Sān Lǐ; D. Li11, Qū Chí; E. B39, Wěi Yáng.
2842	《靈樞 6-2》病在阴之阴者，当刺: A. 阴之荣输; B. 阳之合; C. 阴之经; D. 络脉; E. 阴之合.	《Líng Shū 6-2》When the disease strikes yin within yin (the disease of five viscera), what points should be needled? A. Five command points [wǔ shū xué] on yin meridians, such as spring points and stream points should be used to treat it; B the sea points [hé xué] on the yang meridians should be used to treat it; C. the river points [jīng xué,] on the yin meridians should be used to treat it; D. the points on linking meridians should be used to treat it; E. sea points [hé xué] on the yin meridians should be used to treat it.
2843	《靈樞 67-2》出现"神动而气先针行"的针刺反应见于: A. 重阳之人; B. 重阳之人有阴者 C，阴阳和调; D. 阴气多而阳气少; E. 粗之所败	《Líng Shū6 7-2》What kind of people react to needling with their spirits more easily moved and their energy more easily directed by needling? A. Yang-oriented type of people; B · Yang-oriented type of people with yin energy; C. yin and yang in harmony; D with more yin and less yang; E. · the poor skills of the physician.
2844	《靈樞 71-9》"焉至而徐，焉至而疾"是指: A. 经脉循行的屈折; B. 针刺的补泻 C，进针的快慢 D，出针的快慢; E. 治疗如何及时.	《Líng Shū71-9》"Where does it begin to slow down? Where does it begin to travel fast?" What do the above two questions refer to? A. the straight or crooked meridians; B. tonification and sedation of acupuncture; C. speed of needle inserton; D. speed of needle withdrawal;; E. Treatmmet should take place on time.
2845	《灵枢 · 1-12 九针十二原》说: 五脏有疾，应出于: A. 十二原; B. 十二俞; C. 十二募; D. 十二合; E. 十二井	《Líng Shū 1-12》What points should be used whenever five viscera are disordered? A. twelve source point [yuán xué]; B. twelve stream points [shù xué]; C. twelve anterior points [mù xué); D. twelve sea points [hé xué]; E. twelve well points [jǐng xué].
2846	《灵枢 1-12》所称 "肓之原"，指的是: A. 中极; B. 气海; C. 神[illegible]	《Líng Shū 1-12》Whatpoint is called, " the source point of the space in between the heart and the diaphragm"? A. R3, Zhōng Jí; B. R6, Qì Hǎi; C · R8, Shén Què; D.

	闕; D. 中脘; E. 鳩尾.	R12, Zhōng Wǎn; E. R15, Jiū Wěi.
2847	《灵枢·7-5 官针》中记载的半刺扬刺毛刺是指: A. 三棱针; B. 皮肤针; C. 皮内针; D. 穴位注射; E. 火针	《Líng Shū·7-5》What do halved needling, scattered needling, hairy-needling refer to? A. three-edged needles; B. skin needles; C. intradermal needles; D. injection therapy; E. fire needles.
2848	《灵枢·71 邪客》篇说: 肝有邪，其气留于 A. 两肘; B. 两腋; C. 两髀; D. 两膕; E. 两踝	《Líng Shū·71-17》The pathogen that attacks the liver will come to reside: A. in the elbows; B. in the armpits; C. in the greater trochanter; D. in the popliteal fossae; E. in the ankles.
2849	《靈樞 1-2》"空中之机，清静而微"是指: A. 进针要轻; 'B 经气变化; C. 出针要轻; D. 虚证病人针感小; E. 施用手法要轻	《Líng Shū 1-2》The phenomena of points are clear, quiet, and yet, very delicate; what does it mean? A. light insertion should be done; B · change in meridian energy; C. light withdrawal of needle should be done; D. milder needle sensations in weaker patients; E. light technique should be used.
2850	《靈樞 19-1》秋宜取: A. 经脉; B. 经腧; C. 分间; D. 血脉; E. 络脉	《Líng Shū 19-1》In autumn, what should be needled? A. master meridians; B. acupuncture points on various meridians; C. dividng muscles; D. blood vessels; E. linking meridians.
2851	《靈樞 19-14》"邪在三焦约，取太阳大络"，即: A. 委中; B. 委阳; C.飞扬; D. 养老; E. 承山.	《Líng Shū 19-14》Presence of pathogenic energy in the bladder should be treated by needling the greater link of the greater yang; what point should be needled? A. B40, Wěi Zhōng; B. B39, Wěi Yáng; C. B58, Feī Yáng; D. Si6, Yǎng Lǎo; E. B57, Chéng Shān.
2852	《靈樞 19-5》治疗"徒水"，下列哪种方式不正确 A. 束急; B. 束缓; C. 先取环谷下三寸; D. 间日一刺; E. 饮闭药	《Líng Shū 19-5》What kind of treatment of edematic diseases with swelling is incorrect? A. the quick draining process; B. slow draining process; C. the point located three cuns below Huangu; D. Draining should be done every other day; E. Herbs that can counteract retention should be administered.
2853	《靈樞 23-17》热病挟脐痛针刺取穴为: A. 太白、陷谷、内庭、厉兑 B. 涌泉、阴陵泉、廉泉 C. 鱼际、太渊、大都、太白; D. 三阴交、商阳 E十宣、涌泉.	《Líng Shū 23-17》What points may be used to treat "a hot disease that displays acute pain surrounding the umbilicus, congestion in the chest and costal regions"? A. Sp3, Tài Bái、S43, Xiàn Gǔ、S44, Nèi Tíng、S45, Lì Duì; B. K1, Yǒng Quán、Sp9, Yīn Líng Quán、R23, Lián Quán; C. Lu10, Yǔ Jì、Lu9, Tài Yuān、 Sp2, Dà Dū、Sp3, Tài Bái; D. Sp6, Sān Yīn Jiāo、Li1, Shāng Yáng; E. · Shí Xuān、K1, Yǒng Quán.
2854	《靈樞 23-3》以下哪种情況不可针刺: A. 热病三日，而气口静，人迎躁者 B. 身热甚，阴阳皆静者; C. 热病七日八日，脉打动喘而短者; D. 熱病頭痛顳顬，目瘈脈痛，善衄，厥熱病; E. 热病体重，肠中热.	《Líng Shū 23-3》Under what circumstances shouldn't acupuncture be used to treat hot diseases? A. When a hot disease has already lasted for three days, and the pulse at the wrist is quiet while the pulse at the Jenying point (neck) appears hasty; B. High fever and both yin and yang pulses are quiet; C. When a hot disease has already lasted for seven or eight days, and the mouth of pulse is in motion, with panting and

		shortness of breath; D. A hot disease with headache, pain in the temples, twitching pain in the meridians in the temples, frequent nosebleed, with upstream heat; E. A hot disease with heaviness of the body, and the heat in the intestines.
2855	《靈樞 24-14》肝心痛治疗用穴为: A. 京骨、昆仑、然谷; B 行间、太冲; C 鱼际、太渊; D 大都、太白; E. 然谷、太溪·	《Líng Shū 24-14》What points may be used to treat liver heart pain? A. B64, Jīng Gǔ、B60, Kūn Lún、K2, Rán Gǔ; B. ·Lv2, Xíng Jiān、Lv3, Tài Chōng; C. ·Lu10, Yǔ Jì、Lu9, Tài Yuān; D. · Sp2, Dà Dū、Sp3, Tài Bái; E. K2, Rán Gǔ、K3, Tài Xī.
2856	《靈樞 27-3》周痹和眾痹屬痹证分类中哪一类: A 痛痹; B 行痹; C 着痹;D 热痹;E 骨痹	《Líng Shū 27-3》What kind of rheumatism do sideways rheumatism and circular rheumatism belong to? A. painful rheumatism; B migratory rheumatism; C. fixed rheumatism; D ·hot rheumatism; E. bone rheumatism.
2857	《靈樞 28-3》噦的治疗是: A 补足少阴，补手太阴，B 补手太阴 泻手太阳 C 补手太阴足少阴 D 泻手太阴足少阴 E. 补手太阴.	《Líng Shū 28-3》How to treat hiccups? A. by applying tonification to the foot lesser yin and hand greater yin; B. by applying tonification to the hand greater yin and sedation to the hand greater yang; C. by applying tonification t the hand greater yin and foot lesser yin; D. by apling sedation to the hand greater in and foot lesser yin; E. by applying tonification to the hand greater yin.
2858	《靈樞 28-6》下列哪一项符合噫的治疗：A. 补手太阴阳明; B. 补足太阴阳明; C. 补手太阴足阳明; D. 补足太阴手阳明; E. 补手足太阴阳明	《Líng Shū 28-6》How to treat belching? A. by applying tonification to the hand greater yin and bright yang; B. by applying tonification to the foot greater yin and bright yang; C. by applying tonification to the hand greater yin and foot bright yang; D. by applying tonification to the foot greater yin and hand bright yang; E. by applying tonification to the hand and foot greater yin and bright yang.
2859	《靈樞 38-4》刺瘦人的针刺要求是: A. 深而留之 B 浅而疾之; C. 浅而留之; D. 深而疾之 E，不宜针刺	《Líng Shū 38-4》How to treat a thin person by acupuncture? A. A deep insertion with retention of needle; B · by a shallow insertion and quick withdrawal of needle; C. a shallow insertion with retention of needle; D. a deep insertion and quick withdrawal of needle; E. no acupuncture treatment should be done.
2860	《靈樞 38-6》气涩血浊的身体强壮之人的针刺要求是: A. 浅而疾之; B. 深而留之; C. 不深不浅; D. 深而疾之; E. 浅而留之	《Líng Shū 38-6》How to treat a strong person with retarded energy and turbid blood? A. a shallow insertion with quick withdrawal of needle; B. a deep insertion and delayed withdrawal of needle; C. neither deep nor shallow insertion; D. a deep insertion with quick withdrawal of needle; E. a shallow insertion and delayed withdrawal of needle.
2861	《靈樞 39-2》刺血络，出现脱色而苍苍然现象的是: A. 气盛而血虚; B. 阴阳之气新相得; C. 阳	《Líng Shū 39-2》How do you account for a pale complexion with light or heavy bleeding in acupuncture treatment of blood clotting?

	气蓄积，久留而不泻; D. 新饮而液渗于络; E. 阴阳俱脱	A. Meridian energy is abundant while blood is deficient; B. yin energy (nutritive energy and blood) and yang energy (defense energy and energy) have just met each other; C. yang energy has been accumulated for long without being sedated, and that is why there is no splashing of blood; D. the patient has just drunk some beverages with fluids penetrating into the superficial reticular meridians, not yet mixed with blood; E a prostration of both yin and yang.
2862	《靈樞 39-4》刺血络，出现刺之则射现象的是: A. 气盛而血虚; B. 血气俱盛; C. 阳气蓄积; D. 阴气积于阳; E. 阴阳俱脱:	《Líng Shū 39-4》How do you account for needling that causes the blood to splash in acupuncture treatment of blood clotting? A. Meridian energy is abundant while blood is deficient; B. both blood and energy are in abundance; C yang energy has been accumulated for long; D. yin energy gets accumulated in the yang portion; E. a prostration of both yin and yang.
2863	《靈樞 39-8》刺血络出现面色不变而烦悗现象的是: A. 气盛而血虚 B. 虚经之属阴者 ·C 阳气蓄积，久留而不泻 D¨新饮而液渗于络 E，阴阳俱脱 :	《Líng Shū 39-8》How do you account for unchqnged complexion with occurrence of congested chest and depression in acupuncture treatment of blood clotting? A. Meridian energy is abundant while blood is deficient; B. when major meridians are in deficiency, it will affect yin viscera; ·C. yang energy has been accumulated for long without being sedated, and that is why there is no splashing of blood; D¨ the patient has just drunk some beverages with fluids penetrating into the superficial reticular meridians; E. a prostration of both yin and yang.
2864	《靈樞 4-1》邪中于阳则溜于: A. 皮部; B. 经脉; C. 络脉; D. 府; E. 脏	《Líng Shū 4-1》When pathogens attack yang meridians, they will cause disease to: A. Skin zones; B. master meridians; C. linking meridians; D. bowels; E. viscera.
2865	《靈樞 4-13》六变之脉涩 ·治宜: A. 深内而久留针; B. 必中其脉 ·随逆顺而久留针; C. 浅内而久留针; D. 浅内而不留针; E. 疾发针而浅内之;.	《Líng Shū 4-13》How should needling take place in response to the retarded pulse? A. A deep insertion and needle should stay in the body for longer; B. Insertion into meridians along the direct or inverse energy stream with prolonged suspension of needle; C. a shallow insertion and needle should stay in the body for longer; D. a shallow insertion and needle should be withdrawn right away; E. Rapid withdrawal of needle and shallow insertion.
2866	《靈樞 4-22》一病人善太息 ·口苦 ·恐人将捕之，据 "合治内腑"原则，宜取: A. 足三里; B 阳陵泉; C ·委阳; D ·丘墟 E ·曲泉.	《Líng Shū 4-22》A patient with frequent belching, bitter tastes in the mouth, and fear as if being tracked; what point should be used to treat it according to the principle of "Sea points [Hé Xué] can treat internal bowels"? A. S36, Zú Sān Lǐ; B. G34, Yáng Líng Quán; C. ·B39, Wěi Yáng; D. ·G40, Qiū Xū; E. ·Lv8, Qū Quán.
2867	《靈樞 6》根据实者泻其子的原则 ·肺经实应泻的	《Líng Shū 6》According to the principle of "sedating the child in excess cases", what point should be sedated when

	经是: A. 胃 B，肾; C. 心; D. 肝; E. 脾	the lung meridian is in excess? A. stomach; B. kidney; C. heart; D. liver; E. spleen.
2868	《靈樞 71-12》手少阴之脉独无腧是指: A. 心经无输穴; B. 心经无治疗心脏病的腧穴; C. 心经无治外经病的输穴; D. 心经无原穴; E. 肾经无输穴	《Líng Shū 71-12》The lesser yin meridian of hand (heart meridian) alone has no acupuncture points below the elbow; what does it mean? A. no acupuncture points on the heart meridian; B. no acupuncture points on the heart meridian that can treat heart disease; C. no acupuncture points on the heart meridian that can treat the disease of the meridian traveling outside the heart; D. the heart meridian has no source points [Yuán Xué] on it; E. no acupuncture points on kidney meridian.
2869	《靈樞 71-13》"其外经病而藏不病。" "外经病"是指: A. 手太阳小肠经病; B. 手少阴经病; C. 手厥阴经病; D. 手太阴经病 E. 手少阳三焦经病	《Líng Shū 71-13》The meridian traveling outside the heart may be diseased; what is this meridian? A. small intestein meridian; B. heart meridian; C. pericardium meridian; D. lung meridian; E. triple heater meridian.
2870	《灵枢·1 九针十二原》篇记载，"菀陈"之证，应该采取什么原则 进行治疗? A. 补之; B. 除之; C. 疾之; D. 留之; E. 泻之.	《Líng Shū 1》What principle should be used to treat "decayed blood"? A. to tone up; B. to remove it; C. to treat it quickly; D. to retain the needle; E. to sedate it.
2871	《灵枢·10-45 经脉》篇所谓:"诸脉之浮而常见者"，指的是: A. 十五络脉; B. 十二皮部; C. 浮络; D. 十二络脉; E. 十四络脉.	《Líng Shū - 45》 What are the floating meridians that often remain visible to the naked eye? A. fifteen linking meridians; B. twelve skin zones; C. floating linking meridians; D. twelve linking meridians; E. fourteen linking meridians.
2872	《灵枢·71-17 邪客》篇说:脾有邪， 其气留于: A. 两肘; B. 两腋; C. 两髀; D. 两膕; E. 两踝	《Líng Shū ·71-17》The pathogen that attacks the spleen will come to reside: A. in the elbows; B. in the armpits; C. in the greater trochanter; D. in the popliteal fossae; E. in the ankles.
2873	《靈樞 1》关于十二原穴的论述，下列哪一项是错误的: A. 十二原穴属于五脏六腑; B. 十二原穴出于四关; C. 只有六腑有十二原穴; D. 十二原穴可治五脏病; E. 十二原穴可治六腑病	《Líng Shū1》Which of the following is incorrect regarding the twelve source points [yuán xué]? A. the twelve source points [yuán xué] belong to five viscera and six bowels; B. the twelve source points [yuán xué] are originated from four gates; C. only the six bowels have twelve source points [yuán xué]; D. the twelve source points [yuán xué] can treat the diseases of five viscera; E. the twelve source points [yuán xué] can treat the diseases of six bowels.
2874	《靈樞 1-2》"刺之微，在速迟"的"速迟"是:指: A. 进针的快慢; B. 出针的快慢; C. 用针有徐疾之意; D. 诊断的快慢; E. 针刺时间的长短	《Líng Shū 1-2》Rapid and slow insertions form the secret of applying a needle; what is the meaning of "rapid and slow"? A. speed of needle insertion; B. speed of withdrawing the needle; C. the needle may be inserted or withdrawn at different speeds; D. diagnosis may take place at different speeds; E. duration of acupuncture treatment.

2875	《靈樞 21-1》"三阳之络"指: A. 阳陵泉; B. 百会; C. 飞扬; D. 大椎; E. 肩井	《Líng Shū 21-1》What is "the linking point of the third yang"? A. G34, Yáng Líng Quán; B. D20, Bǎi Huì; C. B58, Feī Yáng; D. D14, Dà Zhuī; E. G21, Jiān Jǐng.
2876	《靈樞 21-9》暴挛癇眩，足不任身，治疗取穴为: A. 天井; B. 天府; C. 天柱; D. 扶突; E. 人迎.	《Líng Shū 21-9》What point should be used to treat "acute spasms with epilepsy and vertigo and inability to stand up due to weak legs"? A. Sj10, Tiān Jǐng; B. Lu3, Tiān Fǔ; C. B10, Tiān Zhù; D. Li18, Fú Tū; E. S9, Rén Yíng.
2877	《靈樞 23-1》热病能否针刺治疗的判别标准是: A. 身热的程度; B. 是否有汗; C. 证、脉相应与否; D. 脉象疾数与否; E. 脉象和缓与否	《Líng Shū 23-1》What are the criteria to determine whether a hot disease may be treated by acupuncture? A. degrees of body heat; B. presence of perspiration; C. whether symptoms and pulses corresponding to each other; D. whether the pulse is hurried and rapid; E. whether the pulse is harmonized and relaxed.
2878	《靈樞 23-1》以下哪项是热病的治疗总则: A. 上病下取，下病上取; B. 阴病取阳, 阳病取阴" C 益其不足，损其有余'; D. 病先起于阳、后人"于阴者，先取其阴，后取其阳，浮而取之 E.菀陈则除之	《Líng Shū 23-1》Which of the following is the treatment principle of hot diseases? A. upper diseases treated by lower points, lower diseases treated by upper points; B.yin diseases treated by yang points, yang diseases treated by yin points; C. to tone deficiency and sedate excess; D. If the disease attacks the yang portion first and then moves into the yin portion, then, select yang meridians first, followed by yin meridians, and shallow insertion should be applied to yang meridians; E. decayed blood should be removed.
2879	《靈樞 24-15》肺心痛治疗用穴为: A. 大都、太白; B. 京骨、昆仑、然谷; C 鱼际、太渊; D 然谷,太溪 E 行间、太冲.	《Líng Shū 24-15》What points may be used to treat lung heart pain? A. Sp2, Dà Dū、Sp3, Tài Bái; B. B64, Jīng Gǔ B60, Kūn Lún、K2, Rán Gǔ; C. Lu10, Yǔ Jì、Lu9, Tài Yuān; D. K2, Rán Gǔ, K3, Tài Xī; E. Lv2, Xíng Jiān、Lv3, Tài Chōng.
2880	《靈樞 26-7》篇喉痹以下列什么症状辨病变所属经脉: A. 喜恶冷热饮 压口中津液粘稠与否; C. 能言、不能言; D. 口渴与否; E. 疼痛与否	《Líng Shū 26-7》How to determine which meridian is involved in "throat rheumatism"? A. whether the patient likes or dislikes cold or hot drink; B. whether fluids in the mouth are sticky or not; C. whether the patient is able to speak or not; D. thirsty or not; E. painful or not.
2881	《靈樞 27-3》周痹的治疗上，按疼痛游走情况而定，痛从上向下沿脉走行者，先刺下部，后刺上部; 反之，痛从下向上沿脉走行者，先刺上部，后刺下部。这是遵循了什么治疗原则: A. 正治; B. 反治; C. 急则治其标，缓则治其本; D. 标本兼治; E. 扶正驱邪.	《Líng Shū 27-3》In circular rheumatism, treatment depends on the the conditions of migratory pain. If the pain shifts from the upper region to the lower region, needling should take place in the lower region first in order to head off the symptoms, to be followed by needling in the upper region in order to root out the disease. If the pain shifts from the lower region to the upper region, needling should take place in the upper region first in order to head off the symptoms, to be followed by needling in the lower region in order to root out the disease; what is the treatment principle used?

		A. Counteracting method of treatment; B. Head-on method; C. treat the symptom of an acute disease, and treat the roots of a chronic disease; D. symptyoms and roots of a disease treated simultaneously; E. support body energy and expel pathogen.
2882	《靈樞 27-4》"痛解则厥"，厥是指: A 厥病: B 厥证 C 气血逆乱 D 厥冷; E. 晕厥.	《Líng Shū 27-4》When the pain is relieved, energy may uprise; what is meant by "uprise"? A. uprising disease; B. uprising syndrome; C. abnormal and chaotic energy and blood; D. uprising cold; E. fainting.
2883	《靈樞 3-2》"上守机"是指: A. 守刺法; B. 守补泻; C. 守气; D. 守输穴 E，守关。	《Líng Shū 3-2》What is a good physician who really knows the mechanism of meridian energy? A. really knowing the method of needle insertion; B. really knowing tonification and sedation; C. really knowing about the condition of energy; D. really knowing acupuncture points; E. really knowing the points on the joints.
2884	《靈樞 38-5》五常人的针刺要求是: A. 深而留之 B.浅而疾之; C. 不深不浅; D. 深而疾之; E. 浅而留之	《Líng Shū 38-5》How to treat an average person by acupuncture? A. a deep insertion with retention of needle; B. a shallow insertion and quick withdrawal of needle; C. neither deep insertion nor shallow insertion; D. a deep insertion and quick withdrawal of needle; E. a shallow insertion with retention of needle.
2885	《靈樞 39-4》刺血络，出现血少黑而浊现象的是: A. 气盛而血虚; B. 血气俱虚 C 阳气蓄积，久留而不泻; D. 新饮液渗于络而未合于血; E. 阴阳俱脱	《Líng Shū 39-4》How do you account for needling that causes the blood to turn black and turbid in acupuncture treatment of blood clotting? A. Meridian energy is abundant while blood is deficient; B. both blood and energy are in abundance; C. yang energy has been accumulated for long without being sedated, and that is why there is no splashing of blood; D. the patient has just drunk some beverages with fluids penetrating into the superficial reticular meridians, not yet mixed with blood; E. a prostration of both yin and yang.
2886	《靈樞 4-2》邪中于面则: A. 下太阳; B. 下少阳; C. 下阳明; D. 下厥阴; E. 下任脉.	《Líng Shū 4-2》 When pathogens attack the face they will then travel downward toward: A. the greater yang meridian of foot; B. the lesser yang meridian of foot; C. the bright yang meridian of foot; D. the decreasing yin meridian of foot; E. the conception meridian.
2887	《靈樞 4-13》 六变之脉大治宜:下列哪一项适合刺六变之脉大？ A. 深内而久留针; B. 泻出其气与血; C. 泻气而不出血; D. 浅内而不留针 E，疾发针而浅内之·	《Líng Shū 4-13》How should needling take place in response to the big pulse? A. a deep insertion and needle should stay in the body for longer; B. sedation of energy and blood; C. Slight sedation of energy without causing bleeding should be applied; D. a shallow insertion and needle should be withdrawn right away E. Rapid withdrawal of needle and

		shallow insertion.
2888	《靈樞 67-4》出现气与针相逢的针刺反应见于: A. 重阳之人; B. 重阳之人有阴者; C. 阴阳和调; D. 阴气多而阳气少; E. 粗之所败	《Líng Shū 67-4》How to account for the fact that some people respond to needling at the right moment? A. Yang-oriented type of people; B · Yang-oriented type of people with yin energy; C. yin and yang in harmony; D ·with more yin and less yang; E. ·the poor skills of the physician.
2889	《灵枢 9-5》 下列哪一项是确定的治愈标准: A. 脉小如其故而不坚; B. 症状消失 C 气调; D. 脉大如其故 ·Eb 脉大小不变	《Líng Shū 9-5》What is the criterion of disease recovery? A. pulse remaining small and not hard; B. disappearance of symptoms; C. energy is brought into harmony; D. pulse remaining big; ·E. no change in the size of pulse, big or small.
2890	《灵枢 ·71-17 邪客》篇说:肾有邪，其气留于: A. 两肘; B. 两腋; C. 两髀; D. 两膕; E. 两踝	《Líng Shū ·71-17》. The pathogen that attacks the kidneys will come to reside: A. in the elbows; B. in the armpits; C. in the greater trochanter; D. in the popliteal fossae; E. in the ankles.
2891	《靈樞 19-1》"夏取盛经"，盛经是指: A. 阳明经; B. 少阳经; C. 心经; D. 阳经; E. 心包经	《Líng Shū 19-1》In summer, abundant meridians should be needled; what does "abundant meridians" refer to? A. bright yang meridian [yáng míng jīng]; B. lesser yang meridians [shào yáng jīng]; C. heart meridian; D. yang meridians [yáng jīng]; E. pericardium meridian.
2892	《靈樞 21-8》暴聋气蒙，耳目不明，治疗取穴为: A. 扶突; B. 天府; C. 人迎 D 天牖; E. 天柱.	《Líng Shū 21-8》What point should be used to treat "acute deafness with blurred vision as if obstructed by fog"? A. Li18, Fú Tū; B. Lu3, Tiān Fǔ; C. S9, Rén Yíng; D. Sj16, Tiān Yǒu; E. B10, Tiān Zhù.
2893	《靈樞 23-21》以下哪个穴位不属于本篇所提出的热病五十九穴: A. 神庭; B.、百会; C. 风府;D 大椎; E. 商阳.	《Líng Shū 23-21》 Which point is not included in the so-called fifty-nine points for hot disease? A. D24, Shén Tíng; B.、D20, Bǎi Huì; C. D16, Fēng Fǔ; D. D14, Dà Zhuī; E. Li1, Shāng Yáng.
2894	《靈樞 26-9》齿痛属下列何经病变: A. 太阳; B. 少阳 C.少阴; D. 阳明; E. 太阴.	《Líng Shū 26-9》What meridians account for toothache? A. greater yang; B. lesser yang; C. lesser yin; D. bright yang; E. greater yin.
2895	《靈樞 28-5》振寒的治疗是: A 泻诸阴 B·泻诸阳 C补阳明'; D. 补诸阳 E 补诸阴.	《Líng Shū 28-5》How to treat chills? A. by applying sedation to various yins; B. ·by applying sedation to various yangs; C. by applying tonification to bright yangs; D. by applying tonificaation to various yangs; E. by applying tonification to various yins.
2896	《靈樞 3-6》"气至而去之者"是指: A. 气至后邪气去; B. 气至而去针; C. 谷气至而去针; D. 补泻气调而去针; E. 针下气至而去针	《Líng Shū 3-6》The expression, 'do not leave until energy arrives' means: A. Pathogen will depart on the arrival of energy; B. withdrawal of needle on arrival of energy; C. withdrawal of needle on arrival of grains energy; D. tonification therapy or sedation therapy must continue until a response of energy has been elicited; E. withdrawal of needle on arrival of energy beneath the needle.

2897	《靈樞 38-7》婴儿的针刺要求是: A. 浅而留之 B 深而疾之; C. 不宜针刺; D. 浅而疾之; E. 不深不浅	《Líng Shū 38-7》How to treat an infant by acupuncture? A. with shallow insertion and retention of needle; B. with a deep insertion and quick action; C. no acupuncture treatment should be done; D. with a shallow insertion and quick withdrawal of needle; E. neither shallow insertion nor deep insertion.
2898	《靈樞 39-5》刺血络，出现血出而汁别现象的是: A. 气盛而血虚; B. 血气俱盛；C. 阳气蓄积，久留而不泻; D. 新饮液渗于络而未合于血; E. 阴阳俱脱	《Líng Shū 39-5》How do you account for needling that causes the blood to appear half-juicy when sent out in acupuncture treatment of blood clotting? A. Meridian energy is abundant while blood is deficient; B. both blood and energy are in abundance; C. yang energy has been accumulated for long without being sedated, and that is why there is no splashing of blood; D. the patient has just drunk some beverages with fluids penetrating into the superficial reticular meridians, not yet mixed with blood; E. a prostration of both yin and yang.
2899	《靈樞 4-13》刺六变之脉缓，宜: A. 深内而久留针; B. 深内而不留针; C. 浅内而久留针; D. 浅内而不留针; E. 疾发针而深内之	《Líng Shū 4-13》. How should needling take place in response to the slow pulse? A. A deep insertion with the needle staying in the body for longer; B. a deep insertion and needle should be withdrawn right away; C. a shallow insertion with the needle staying in the body for longer; D. Shallow insertion and rapid withdrawal of needle; E. Rapid withdrawal of needle and deep insertion.
2900	《靈樞 4-1》身半以上，何邪中之: A. 湿; B. 寒; C. 水; D. 风; E. 内邪	《Líng Shū 4-1》 What pathogen will attack the upper half of the body? A. dampness; B. cold; C. water; D. wind; E. internal pathogen.
2901	《靈樞 4-1》邪中于阴则溜于: A. 皮部; B. 络脉; C. 经脉; D. 府 E.脏.	《Líng Shū 4-1》When pathogens attack yin meridians, they will cause disease to: A. Skin zones; B. linking meridian; C. master meridians; D. bowels; E. viscera.
2902	《靈樞 4-13》治六变之脉小，宜: A，深内而久留针; B. 深内而不留针; C. 浅内而久留针; D. 以甘缓之药调之; E. 疾发针而浅内之	《Líng Shū 4-13》 How should needling take place in response to the small pulse? A. A deep insertion and needle should stay in the body for longer; B. a deep insertion and needle should be withdrawn right away; C. a shallow insertion and needle should stay in the body for longer; D. treat it by sweet and mild herbs; E. Rapid withdrawal of needle and shallow insertion.
2903	《靈樞 6-1》"人之生也，有刚有柔，有弱有强，有短有长，有阴有阳"，此处阴阳指: A. 刚柔之别; B. 弱强之别; C. 短长之别; D. 身形结构的内外; E. 形气偏盛	《Líng Shū 6-1》One is born to be robust or tender, weak or strong, short or tall, and yin or yang; what is meant by "yin or yang" here? A. the difference between robust and tender; B. the difference between weak and strong;; C. the difference between short and tall; D. yin body type or yang body type; E. excessive body or excessive energy.
2904	《靈樞 67-5》针已出而	《Líng Shū 67-5》: How do you account for the fact that

	气独行现象见于: A.重阳之人; B. 重阳之人有阴者; C. 阴阳和调; D. 阴气沉而阳气浮; E. 粗之所败	some people continue to respond to needling after the needle has been withdrawn? A. Yang-oriented type of people; B · Yang-oriented type of people with yin energy; C. yin and yang in harmony; D. yin energy stays deep down inside with yang energy floating in the superficial region; E. · the poor skills of the physician.
2905	《靈樞 67-6》数刺乃知现象见于: A. 重阳之人 B·重阳之人有阴者; C. 阴阳和调; D. 多阴而少阳; E. 粗之所败	《Líng Shū 67-6》 How do you account for the fact that some people respond to needling only after several times of needling? A. Yang-oriented type of people; B · Yang-oriented type of people with yin energy; C. yin and yang in harmony; D ·with more yin and less yang; E. ·the poor skills of the physician.
2906	《靈樞 71-13》"独取其经于掌后锐骨之端"的"掌后锐骨之端"指: A. 大陵; B. 间使 C·太渊; D. 神门; E. 腕骨	《Líng Shū 71-13》When the heart meridian is diseased, it may be treated by the tip of the head of the ulna behind the palm of the hand; what is the point involved? A. P7, Dà Líng; B. P5, Jiān Shǐ; C·Lu9, Tài Yuān; D. H7, Shén Mén; E. Si4, Wàn Gǔ.
2907	《针经》是指: A. 《阴阳十一脉灸经》B. 《足臂十一脉灸经》C. 《针灸甲乙经》D. 《灵枢》E、《素问》.	《Zhēn Jīng》 What classic is《Zhēn Jīng》 referring to? A.《Yīn Yang Shí Yī Mài Jiǔ Jīng》; B.《Zú Bì Shí Yī Mài Jiǔ Jīng》; C. 《Zhēn Jiǔ Jiá Yī Jīng》; D. 《Líng Shū》 E.《Sù Wèn》.
2908	《灵枢 34-3》五乱证的针刺宜: A. 补虚泻实; B. 浅不宜深; C. 深不宜浅; D. 徐入徐出; E. 不深不浅.	《Líng Shū 34-3》How to treat five disorders by acupuncture? A. to tone up deficiency and sedate excess; B. shallow, not deep, insertion; C. deep, not shallow, insertion; D slow insertion and slow withdrawal of needle; E. neither deep nor shallow.
2909	《灵枢 1-12》所称 "膏之原"，指的是: A. 会阴穴; B. 关元穴; C. 气海穴; D. 中脘穴; E. 鸠尾穴.	《Líng Shū 1-12》 What point is called, “the source point of fatty membranes below the heart” ? A. R1, Huì Yīn; B. R4, Guān Yuán; C. R6, Qì Hǎi; D. R12, Zhōng Wǎn; E. R15, Jiū Wěi.
2910	《靈樞 1-10》"凡将用针，必先诊脉"是指: A. 仅根据脉的变化针刺 B 针刺先于诊脉 C 据脉判定治内还是治外 D 针刺前一定要诊脉 E 针前要明确诊断	《Líng Shū1-10》"Prior to insertion of the needle, the patient's pulse must be taken in order to know about the excessive and deficient conditions of energy, so that a suitable treatment may be worked out. “What is meant by the statement? A. pulse diagnosis is the only basis for acupuncture treatment; B. acupuncture treatment should be followed by pulse diagnosis; C. treatment of internal or external regions must be based on pulse diagnosis; D. pulse diagnosis before acupuncture treatment; E. accurate diagnopsis before acupuncture treatment.
2911	《靈樞 21-6》"阳明头痛，胸满不得息，"治疗取穴为: A. 天柱; B. 天牖; C. 扶突; D. 天府; E. 人迎.	《Líng Shū 21-6》What point should be used to treat “headachc due to upstream yang energy in the yang meridians with congested chest and breathing difficulty”?

		A. B10, Tiān Zhù; B. Sj16, Tiān Yǒu; C. Li18, Fú Tū; D. Lu3, Tiān Fǔ; E. S9, Rén Yíng.
2912	《靈樞 24-12》胃心痛治疗用穴为: A. 京骨、昆仑、然谷; B. 鱼际、太渊; C. 然谷、太溪; D. 行间、太冲; E. 大都、太白.	《Líng Shū 24-12》What points may be used to treat stomach heart pain? A. B64, Jīng Gǔ、B60, Kūn Lún、K2, Rán Gǔ; B. Lu10, Yǔ Jì、Lu9, Tài Yuān; C. K2, Rán Gǔ、K3, Tài Xī; D. Lv2, Xíng Jiān、Lv3, Tài Chōng; E. Sp2, Dà Dū、Sp3, Tài Bái.
2913	《靈樞 3-3》关于"迎而夺之者"下列哪一个是正确的? A. 迎着经脉来的方向针刺; B. 迎着病位的方向针刺; C. 迎着气盛时针刺 D.逢气虚时针刺; E. 泻邪之义	《Líng Shū 3-3》To welcome and rob the coming energy means: A. to insert against the direction of meridians; B. to insert against the location of disease; C. to insert against the energy excess; D. to insert while energy is deficient; E. to apply sedation therapy.
2914	《靈樞 3-3》关于"追而济之者"下列哪一个是正确的: A. 顺着经脉的方向针刺; B. 顺着病位的方向针刺; C. 顺着气去的方向针刺; D. 在气实时针刺; E. 补虚之义.	《Líng Shū 3-3》To chase after energy and to assist it means: A. to insert along the direction of meridians; B. to insert along the location of disease; C. to insert along the energy excess; D. to insert while energy is in excess; E. to apply tonification therapy.
2915	《靈樞 39-2》刺血络，出现多出血而不动现象的是: A. 气盛而血虚; B. 血气俱盛; C. 阳气蓄积，久留而不泻; D. 新饮液渗于络而未合于血; E. 阴阳俱有余	《Líng Shū 39-2》How do you account for heavy bleeding which does not affect the patient in acupuncture treatment of blood clotting? A. Meridian energy is abundant while blood is deficient; B. both blood and energy are in abundance; C yang energy has been accumulated for long without being sedated, and that is why there is no splashing of blood; D. the patient has just drunk some beverages with fluids penetrating into the superficial reticular meridians, not yet mixed with blood; E both yin and yang are in excess.
2916	《靈樞 39-2》刺血络,出现发针而肿现象的是: A. 气盛而血虚; B. 血气俱盛; C. 阳气蓄积，久留而不泻; D. 新饮而液渗于络; E. 阴气积于阳，其气因于络	《Líng Shū 39-2》How do you account for the swelling of the skin after the needle has been withdrawn in acupuncture treatment of blood clotting? A. Meridian energy is abundant while blood is deficient; B. both blood and energy are in abundance; C. yang energy has been accumulated for long without being sedated, and that is why there is no splashing of blood; D. the patient has just drunk some beverages with fluids penetrating into the superficial reticular meridians, not yet mixed with blood; E. yin energy gets accumulated in the yang portion, and energy makes its exit through the reticular meridians.
2917	《靈樞 4-13》刺六变之脉滑，宜: A. 深内而久留针; B. 深内而不留针; C. 浅内而久留针; D. 浅针出气勿出血; E. 疾发针而浅内之	《Líng Shū 4-13》How should needling take place in response to the slippery pulse? A. A deep insertion and needle should stay in the body for longer; B. a deep insertion and needle should be withdrawn right away; C. a shallow insertion and needle should stay in the body for longer; D. Rapid withdrawal of needle and shallow insertion with no bleeding; E.

		Rapid withdrawal of needle and shallow insertion.
2918	《靈樞 5-7》"刺不知逆顺"之 "逆顺"指: A. 阴阳经脉循行方向; B. 经脉气血流注; C. 病情; D. 虚虚实实; E. 形气、病气之有余不足.	《Líng Shū 5-7》 the Classic says, "with knowledge of upstream and downstream"; what is meant by "upstream and downstream? A. Traveling direction of yin and yang merdians; B. flowing and entering direction of energy and blood; C. conditions of illness; D. sedate deficiency and tone up excess; E. excess and deficiency of body energy and the pathogen.
2919	《靈樞 67-7》针入而气逆现象见于: A. 重阳之人 B·重阳之人有阴者; C. 阴阳和调 D·多阴而少阳 E·粗之所败	《Líng Shū 67-7》Some people respond to needling negatively after they have been needled. What kind of people have such response? A. Yang-oriented type of people; B · Yang-oriented type of people with yin energy; C. yin and yang in harmony; D with more yin and less yang; E. the poor skills of the physician.
2920	《靈樞 9-6》"补则益实"之义是: A. 补法益于实证; B. 用补法使虚证转为实证; C. 用补法实之; D. 用补法则更实; E. 用补法则渐盛实	《Líng Shū 9-6》A deficient disease should be toned up to make it more excessive; what does it mean? A. tonification is good for an excess syndrome; B. use tonification to change a disease from deficiency to excess; C. use tonification to make it excessive; D. use tonification to make it even more excessive; E. tonfication will make a disease gradually become excessive.
2921	《靈樞 9-6》"泻则益虚"之义是: A. 泻法益于虚证; B. 用泻法使实证转为虚证; C. 用泻法虚之; D. 用泻法则更虚; E. 用泻法则渐虚衰	《Líng Shū 9-6》An excessive disease may be sedated so that it will become more deficient; what does it mean? A. sedation is good for a deficient syndrome; B. use sedation to change a disease from excess to deficiency; C. use sedation to make it deficient; D. use sedation to make it even more deficient; E. sedation will make a disease gradually become deficient.
2922	《通玄指要赋》中"牙齿痛，吕细堪治" "吕细"是指: A. 太溪穴 B·阳溪穴; C. 天溪穴; D. 解溪穴; E. 照海穴.	《Tōng Xuán Zhǐ Yào Fù》 "Lu Xi can treat toothache." What point does Lu Xi refr to? A. K3, Tài Xī; B. Li5, Yáng Xī; C. Sp18, Tiān Xī; D. S41, Jiě Xī; E. K6, Zhào Hǎi.
2923	《通玄指要赋》中"脊间心后者，针中渚而立痊"是指: A. 心痛; B. 脊柱痛 C，后背痛; D. 胃脘痛; E. 腹痛	《Tōng Xuán Zhǐ Yào Fù》 "Sj3, Zhōng Zhǔ may be used to treat the symptom in between spines and behind the heart." What symptom is being treated? A. heart pain; B. pain in the spinal column; C. backache; D. stomachache; E. abdominal pain.
2924	《通玄指要赋》中"髋骨将腿痛以祛残"，髋骨穴是指: A. 绝骨穴; B. 腕骨穴 C. 横骨穴; D. 然骨穴; E. 环跳穴.	《Tōng Xuán Zhǐ Yào Fù》 "Hip bone may be usd to treat leg pain so that the patient can walk." What point does hip bone refer to? A. G39, Jue Gu; B. Si4, Wàn Gǔ; C. K11, Heng Gu; D. K2, Rán Gǔ; E. G30, Huán Tiào.
2925	《通玄指要赋》中"冷痹肾余，取足阳明之土"是指: A. 取足阳明经 B·取足三里穴 C，取梁丘穴 D·取足少阴肾经 E·取土	《Tōng Xuán Zhǐ Yào Fù》"Cold rheumatism and hernia should be treated by the earth of the foot bright yang." What is "the earth of foot bright yang"? A. the foot bright yang meridian; B. S36, Zú Sān Lǐ; C.

	经之土穴	S34, Liáng Qiū; D. the foot lesser yin kidney meridian; E. the earth point of the earth meridian.
2926	《通玄指要赋》中"然骨泻肾"是指: A. 泻肾水; B. 泻肾气; C 泻肾阴; D. 泻肾阳 E，泻肾热.	《Tōng Xuán Zhǐ Yào Fù》 What does "K2, Rán Gǔ sedates the kidneys" mean? A. sedate kidney water; B. sedate kidney energy; C. sedate kidney yin; D. sedate kiney yang; E. sedate kidney heat.
2927	《席弘赋》中，"但患伤寒两耳聋，金门听会急如风"，其病属: A. 实证; B 虚证; C. 实中夹虚; D 虚中夹实; E. 先实后虚.	《Xí Hóng Fù》" Deafness of external causes may be treated by B63, Jīn Mén, and G2, Tīng Huì, with quick results." What is the syndrome of deafness being treated? A. excess syndrome; B. deficiency syndrome; C. deficiency within excess syndrome; D. excess within deficiency syndrome; E. excess syndrome followed by deficiency syndrome.
2928	《席弘赋》中，"肚疼须是公孙妙，内关相应必然廖"，是因为: A. 公孙通冲脉; B. 内关通阴维脉; C. 奇经八脉交会穴; D. 公孙是络穴; E. 内关是络穴	《Xí Hóng Fù》" Sp4, Gōng Sūn and P6, Nèi Guān are two effective points for treating abdominal pain." How do you account for their effectiveness? A. Sp4, Gōng Sūn is connected with vigorous meridian [Chōng Mài]; B. P6, Nèi Guān is connected with fastener meridian of yin [Yīn Wéi Mài]; C. eight confluence points [bā mài bā huì xué]; D. Sp4, Gōng Sūn is a linking point (Luò Xué); E. P6, Nèi Guān is a linking point (Luò Xué).
2929	《席弘赋》中，"耳内蝉鸣腰欲折，膝下明存三里穴"，其道理是: A. 三里调肠胃; B. 三里补肾; C. 三里补脾; D. 三里生气血; E. 上病下取.	《Xí Hóng Fù》" Ringing in the ears like the sound of a cicada and the sensation as if the waist were about to break should be treated by S36, Zú Sān Lǐ." What is the rationale for using S36, Zú Sān Lǐ? A. S36 regulates the instestines and the stomach; B. S36 tones up the kidneys; C. S36 tones up the spleen; D. S36 produces energy and blood; E. based on the principle that a disease in the upper region should be treated by points in the lower region.
2930	《席弘赋》中，"虚喘须寻三里中"的用穴道理是: A. 调节脾胃; B. 健脾化痰; C. 补肾纳气，D 扶正祛邪; E. 化生气血.	《Xí Hóng Fù》"Deficient panting / asthma may be treated by S36, Zú Sān Lǐ." What is the rationale for using S36, Zú Sān Lǐ? A. to regulate the spleen and stomach; B. to strengthen the spleen and transform phlegm; C. to tone up the kidneys and accommodate energy; D. to support body energy and expel pathogen; E. to transform and produce energy and blood.
2931	《席弘赋》中，"十三鬼穴"专门治疗： A. 五脏病，B 六腑病; C. 血病 D 气病; E. 神志病.	《Xí Hóng Fù》 What diseases are to be treated by the thirteen ghost points? A. diseases of five viscera; B. diseases of six bowels; C. blood diseases; D. energy diseases; E. mental illnesses.
2932	《席弘赋》中，"手连肩脊痛难忍，合谷针时要太冲"的配穴方法是: A. 循经局部取衣; B. 上病下取; C. 循经远端配穴; D. 表里经配穴; E. 四关穴.	《Xí Hóng Fù》"Intolerable pain in hands affecting the shoulders and spines may be treated by Li4, Hé Gǔ and Lv3, Tài Chōng." What is the rationale for selecting the two points in question? A. local points along the meridians; B. diseases in the upper region may be treated by points in the lower

		region; C. distal points along the meridians; D. points on the meridians forming a deep-superficial relationship with each other; E. points of four gates.
2933	《席弘赋》中，气刺两乳求太渊" 的用穴道理是什么? A. 循经局部取农; B. 上病下取; C. 循经远端配穴; D. 表里经配穴; E. 八會穴.	《Xí Hóng Fù》"Energy disease may be treated by the point in between two nipples (R17, Shān Zhōng) and Lu9, Tài Yuān." What is the rationale for selecting Lu9, Tài Yuān? A. local point along the meridians; B. diseases in the upper region may be treated by points in the lower region; C. distal point along the meridians; D. point on the meridians forming a deep-superficial relationship with each other; E. An influential point [bā huì xué].
2934	《行针指要歌》中的针灸配穴经验，强调下列哪一项为主: A，辨证取穴; B. 循经取穴; C. 前后取穴 D，原络取穴; E. 上下取穴	《Xíng Zhēn Zhǐ Yào Gē》 What method of pairing off points to treat diseases is emphasized in this classic? A. selecting points according to differential diagnosis; B. selecting points along the meridians; C. selecting anterior and posterior points; D. selecting source point [yuán xué] and linking point (collateral points, luò xué); E. selecting upper and lower points.
2935	《行针指要歌》中, 针灸治疗咳嗽肺俞、风门须用：A 针 B 灸 C 药 D 火罐 E 推拿	《Xíng Zhēn Zhǐ Yào Gē》How to use B13, Fèi Shū 、and B12, Fēng Mén to treat cough? A. acupuncture; B. moxibustion; C. herbs; D. cupping; E. tui na / manipulative therapy.
2936	《行针指要歌》中, 针灸治疗水肿，多取：A 大肠俞 B·二间; C. 水分 D 水道 E·上巨虛.	《Xíng Zhēn Zhǐ Yào Gē》What point is used to treat edema in most cases? A B25, Dà Cháng Shū; B · Li2, Èr Jiān; C. R9, Shuǐ Fēn; DS28, Shuǐ Dào; E. S37, Shàng Jù Xū.
2937	《行针指要歌》中, 中脘、三里主要治疗： A 风 B 气 C 虛 D 痰 E 吐	《Xíng Zhēn Zhǐ Yào Gē》What disease may be treated by R12, Zhōng Wǎn 、and S36, Zú Sān Lǐ? A. wind disease; B. energy disease; C. deficient disease; D. disease of phlegm; E. vomiting.
2938	《肘后歌》记载，腿脚有疾，应针: A. 人中; B. 百会; C. 风府; D. 腰阳关; E. 委中.	《Zhǒu Hòu Gē》What point should be selected to treat the disease of legs and feet? A. D26, Rén Zhōng; B. D20, Bǎi Huì; C. D16, Fēng Fǔ; D. D3, Yāo Yáng Guān; E. B40, Wěi Zhōng.
2939	《肘后歌》记载，头面之疾，应针: A. 列缺; B. 合谷; C. 内庭; D. 至阴; E. 太冲	《zhǒu hòu gē》 What point should be selected to treat the disease of the head and face? A. Lu7, Liè Quē; B. Li4, Hé Gǔ; C. S44, Nèi Tíng; D. B67, Zhì Yīn; E. Lv3, Tài Chōng
2940	《素问 43-2》风寒湿三气，风气胜者为: A. 行痹; B 痛痹;C 着痹; D 周痹; E 众痹.	《Sù Wèn 43-2》When rheumatism is caused by the predominant energy of wind among three energies, namely, wind, cold, and dampness, what kind of rheumatism does it belong to? A. migratory rheumatism; B. patinful rheumatism; C·. Fixed rheumatism; D. circular rheumatism; E. sideways rheumatism.
2941	《素问·12-10》:"藏寒生满病，其治宜灸焫." 是指灸法的何项功能: A.	《Sù Wèn ·12-10》 Cold accumulation in the viscera should be treated by moxibustion, what function of moxibustion is good for the treatment?

	温经散寒 B 活血通络 C 消瘀散结 D 扶阳固脱 E，防病保健	moxibustion is good for the treatment? A. to warm the meridians and disperse cold; B. to activate blood and connect linking meridians; C. to eliminate coagulation and disperse congestion; D. to support yang and solidify prolapse; E. to prevent disease and maintain health.
2942	《素问 26-14》下列什么情况可导致 "重实？ A·月满而补; B. 月生而泻 C，月生而治; D. 天温而刺; E. 天寒而刺.	《Sù Wèn 26-14》What will produce a double excess? A. When tonification is done while there is the full moon; B. When sedation is done while the moon begins to generate (the new moon); C When treatment is done while the moon begins to generate (the new moon); D. When acupuncture is done in warm weather; E. When acupuncture is done in cold weather.
2943	《素问 26-6》据 "得时而调之"原则天寒应: A. 无刺; B. 无疑; C. 无补 D·无泻; E. 无治	《Sù Wèn 26-6》What should be done in cold weather A. acupuncture treatment should not be administered; B. acupuncture treatment should be administered without doubt; C. no tonification should be done; D. no sedation should be done; E. no treatment should be done.
2944	《素问 32-36》热病始手臂痛者 ·应刺: A. 手阳明太阴; B. 手厥阴; C. 手少阴; D. 手少阳厥阴; E. 手太阳少阴	《Sù Wèn32-36》If a hot disease begins with pain in the arms, what meridians should be needled? A. the hand bright yang and greater yin meridians; B. the hand decreasing yin meridian; C. the hand lesser yin meridian; D. the hand lesser yang and decreasing yin merdiains; E. the hand greater yang and lesser yin meridians.
2945	《素问 51-2》"刺骨无伤筋"是指: A. 针至筋而去; B. 针至骨而去; C. 针刺时宜避开筋 D 针刺时应浅; E. 针刺时应深	《Sù Wèn 51-2》Needle insertion that should only reach bones should not cause harm to tendons. What does it mean? A. the needle should be withdrawn after it reaches tendons; B. the needle should be withdrawn after it reaches bones; C. the needle should avoid tendons; D. shallow insertion should be done; E. deep insertion should be done.
2946	《素问 54-17》"义无邪下者，欲端以正也"。"欲端以正"是指: A. 医生要心地坦荡，行为端正; B. 意念端正; C. 持针要端正; D. 病人体位端正; E. 垂直进针.	《Sù Wèn 54-17》What is meant by " Needle should be inserted without slanting"? A. the acupuncturist should remain in the straight position at the time of inserting the needle; B. thinking straight; C. holding the needle straight; D. the straight posture of the patient; E. perpendicular insertion.
2947	《素问 54-2》"刺虛则实之者"需: A，针下热; B. 针下凉; C. 浅刺之; D. 深刺之; E. 脉实.	《Sù Wèn 54-2》How to bring about excess in treating deficient symptoms? A. hot sensations under the needle; B. cool sensations under the needle; C. shallow insertion; D. deep insertion; E. excess pulse.
2948	《素问 54-14》"近遠如一者，深浅其候等也"。深浅是指: A. 进针深浅; B. 得气的部位深浅; C. 病位的深浅; D. 经气的深浅; E. 针的长短.	《Sù Wèn 54-14》Energy may be brought in from the neighborhood or from the far-off regions, which means that the common purpose of needle insertion, be it deep or superficial, is to wait for the arrival of energy. What is meant by "deep or superficial"?

		A. depth of needle insertion; B. depth of needling sensations; C. depth of disease location; D. depth of meridian energy; E. length of needle.
2949	《素问 60-4》"大风汗出，灸噫嘻，噫嘻在背下侠脊傍所"幾寸？... A. 三寸; B. 四寸; C. 五寸 D，六寸; E. 七寸.	《Sù Wèn60-4》If a gale causes perspiration, apply moxibustion to B45 [yi xi], which is located on the back, and how many cuns lateral to the spinal column? A. three cuns; B. four cuns; C. five cuns; D. six cuns; E. seven cuns.
2950	《素问 61-11》治取络脉分肉在什么季节: A. 春; B. 夏; C. 秋; D. 冬; E. 长夏.	《Sù Wèn 61-11》During what season should linking meridians and dividing muscles be needled? A. spring; B. summer; C. autumn; D. winter; E. prolonged summer.
2951	《素问 63-2》夫邪之客于形也，"必先舍于： A. 皮毛; B. 孙脉; C. 络脉; D. 经脉; E. 巨虛下廉.	《Sù Wèn 63-2》When pathogen comes to reside in the human body as guest, where does it reside first? A. the skin and hair; B. tiny meridians; C. reticular meridians; D. master meridians; E. S39, Xià Jù Xū.
2952	《素问 27-20》:"静以久留，以气至为故，如待所贵，不知曰暮。"是指: A. 得气 B 候气 C 催气 D 守气; E. 艾灸	《Sù Wèn 27-20》"Withdrawal of needle should be delayed quietly and for a prolonged period until energy arrives. The physician should remain calm and patient in the course of waiting for energy to arrive, just like someone waiting patiently for the guest of honor to arrive without knowing darkness is about to fall." What does the statement mean? A. Needling sensations have occurred; B. awaiting the arrival of energy; C. to speed up the arrival of energy; D. keeping the energy; E. moxibustion should be administered.
2953	《素问 12 异法方宜论》载，九针起源于我国的: A. 东方; B. 南方; C. 西方; D. 北方; E. 中央.	《Sù Wèn 12》Where were the nine needles originated from in China? A. east; B. south; C. west; D. north; E. Central region.
2954	《素问 25-18》关于"知毒药为真"，下列何者是正确的: A. 知道药物的真假; B. 了解药物的性能和作用; C. 针对不同医生习惯; D 针对病人要求; E. 医者明白针刺.	《Sù Wèn 25-18》How " to acquire true knowledge of medicinal herbs"? A. to learn about the truth or falsehood of herbs; B. to understand the actions and functions of herbs; C. to learn from the habits of different physicians; D. to learn from the demands of patients; E. a physician must understand acupuncture.
2955	《素问 26-10》据 "得时而调之"原则，月郭空应 A. 可刺; B. 无刺; C. 无补 D 无泻; E. 无灸	《Sù Wèn 26-10》When there is the crescent moon, what should be done in acupuncture treatment? A. Acupuncture should be done; B. no treatment should be done; C. no tonification should be done; D. no sedation

		should be done; E. no moxibustion should be done.
2956	《素问 26-13》下列什么情况可以导致 "脏虚"? A·月满而补; B. 月生而泻 C，月生而治; D. 天温而刺; E. 天寒而刺.	《Sù Wèn 26-13》What will intensify the deficient state of viscera? A. ·When tonification is done while there is the full moon; B. When sedation is done while the moon begins to generate (the new moon); C When treatment is done while the moon begins to generate (the new moon); D. When acupuncture is done in warm weather; E. When acupuncture is done in cold weather.
2957	《素问 26-7》据 "得时而调之"原则，天温应 A. 无刺; B. 无疑; C. 无补; D. 无泻; E. 无治	《Sù Wèn 26-7》 What should be done in warm weather? A. acupuncture treatment should not be administered; B. acupuncture treatment should be administered without doubt; C. no tonification should be done; D. no sedation should be done; E. no treatment should be done.
2958	《素问 32-17》肺热病刺手太阴阳明立已需要 A·大汗出;B·出血如大豆;C·面赤无汗 D·面赤大汗;E·数饮.	《Sù Wèn 32-16》 What must occur in order to cure the disease instantly by needling greater yin of hand (lung meridian) and bright yang meridian of hand (large intestine meridian) for bloodletting to remove blood clots? A · profuse perspiration; B · blood clots appear as big as a soy bean; C ·red complexion without perspiration; D · red complelxion with profuse perspiration; E ·drinking water frequently.
2959	《素问 47-17》肝者，取决于胆是指: A. 肝为将军之官; B. 无胆不断 C，胆为中正之官; D. 谋虑在肝; E. 肝胆相表里	《Sù Wèn 47-17》 The liver is the general with its functions directed by the gallbladder. What does it mean? A. the liver is the general; B. no judgement without gallbladder; C. the gallbladder as impartial judge; D. the liver in charge of strategy; E. the liver and gallbladder forming a deep-superficial relationship with each other.
2960	《素问 47-17》胆瘅的病机是: A. 数谋虑不决; B. 胆气上溢; C. 口为之苦; D. 肝木乘脾 巴肝胆气虚	《Sù Wèn 47-17》 What is the disease mechanism of gallbladder heat? A. indecisive; B. bile overflowing upstream; C. bitter taste in the mouth; D. liver wood attacking the spleen; E. energy deficiency of the liver and gallbladder.
2961	《素问 50-2》针刺不及会发生的病证是: A. 生大病 ·B·生外壅; C. 大贼 D 内伤 E·内动五脏	《Sù Wèn 50-2》 In treating a deep disease, a superficial insertion will cause: A. a severe disease; ·B · congestion and swelling of the affected region and also inducing the pathogen to move into that region; C. greatly harmed by pathogen; D. internal injury; E · five viscera shaken up internally.
2962	《素问 51-4》"刺筋无伤骨者，过筋中骨也"是说: A. 刺之过浅; B. 刺之过深; C. 刺之深浅适当; D. 刺用泻法; E. 以上都不是。	《Sù Wèn 51-4》 What is meant by “needle insertion that should only reach tendons should not cause harm to bones”? A. needle insertion too shallow; B. the needle should inserted past the tendons to reach bones; C. adequate depth of needle insertion; D. using the sedation

		technique; E. None of the above.
2963	《素问 54-2》"满而泄之者，针下寒也"。针下寒也指: A. 医生的感觉; B. 患者的感觉; C. 患者喜凉; D. 患者恶寒; E. 医生和病人的感觉.	《Sù Wèn 54-2》In sedating the excessive symptom, the patient should feel cold sensations in the region around the tip of needle; what is meant by " cold sensations in the region around the tip of needle"? A. Doctor's sensations; B. patient's sensations; C. the patient's love of coolness; D. the patient's aversion to chills; E. the senseations of the doctor and the patient.
2964	《素问 60-10》"取膝上外者使之拜，取足心者使之跪"的"膝上外者"指: A. 阳陵泉; B. 委中; C. 外膝眼; D. 肾俞; E. 伏兔.	《Sù Wèn 60-10》To locate the point on the side of the knee-cap, let the patient bow the head; to locate the point in the center of the sole of foot, let him stay on his knees; what point is on the side of the knee-cap? A. G34, Yáng Líng Quán; B. B40, Wěi Zhōng; C. Wài Xī Yǎn; D. B23, Shèn Shū; E. S32, Fú Tù.
2965	《素问 60-10》"鼠瘻寒热"，需要刺: 。A. 八髎; B. 寒府; C. 委中; D. 肾俞; E. 疼痛局部.	《Sù Wèn 60-10》What point should "cold and hot sensations in the disease named, rat fistula (shu□lou, fistula or scrofula or tuberculosis of lymph node) " be treated? A. eight Liáo points; B. the hanfu point (G33, yangguan); C. B40, Wěi Zhōng; D. B23, Shèn Shū; E. local pressure points.
2966	《素问 60-38》股际骨空在: A. 辅骨之上端; B. 在毛中动下; C. 外膝眼; D. 髀骨之后; E. 伏兔	《Sù Wèn 60-38》Where is the bone cavity at the thigh edge located?. A. above Femur; B. below the artery in pubic hairs; C. Wài Xī Yǎn; D. behind femur; E. S32, Fú Tù.
2967	《素问 61-19》 气冲、三里、巨虚上下廉，可泻: A. 四肢之热; B. 胃中之热; C. 脏之热; D. 胸中之热; E. 腹中之热.	《Sù Wèn 61》 What may be sedated by S30 [qi chong], S36 [zu san], S37 [shang ju xu], and S39 [xia ju xu]? A. heat of four limpbs; B. stomach heat; C. heat of viscera; D. chest heat; E. abdominal heat.
2968	《素问 61-13》治取盛经分腠在什么季节: A 春; B. 夏; C. 秋; D. 冬; E. 长夏.	《Sù Wèn 61-13》During what season should superficial meridians and dividing pores be needled? A. spring; B. summer; C. autumn; D. winter; E. prolonged summer.
2969	《素问 61-7》尻上五行行五者，此: A. 八髎; B 肾俞; C. 委中; D. 太冲; E. 疼痛局部.	《Sù Wèn 61-7》There are five planes above coccyx with five points on each plane; which of the following points is included? A. Eight Liáo points; B. B23, Shèn Shū; C. B40, Wěi Zhōng; D. Lv3, Tài Chōng; E. local pressure points.
2970	《素问 63-2》病邪在络脉时，病较: A 深 B 浅 C 高 D 低 E 前.	《Sù Wèn 63-2》If pathogen resides in reticular meridians, it means the disease is relatively: A. deep B. shallow; C. high; D. low; E in the front.
2971	《素问 63-6》左痛未已而右脉先病，如此者，必: A. 短刺，; B. 巨刺之	《Sù Wèn 63-6》Pathogen may cause a disease on the right side while pain on the left side has not yet recovered; what technique should be used?

	C，繆刺·D 半刺 E，巨虛上下廉.	recovered; what technique should be used? A. Slow paced needling; B. Opposite needling; C. reverse technique of acupuncture; D · Halved needling; E. needling the meridian.
2972	《素问 26-15》下列什么情况下可以导致 "乱经"? A. 月满而补; B. 月生而泻; C. 月郭空而治; D. 天温而刺; E. 天寒而刺	《Sù Wèn 26-15》What will cause energy to disturb the meridians? A. ·When tonification is done while there is the full moon; B. When sedation is done while the moon begins to generate (the new moon); C. treatment is done when there is the crescent moon; D. When acupuncture is done in warm weather; E. When acupuncture is done in cold weather.
2973	《素问 26-9》据 "得时而调之"原则，月满应 A. 无刺; B. 无疑; C. 无补 D.无泻; E. 无治.	《Sù Wèn 26-9》What should be done when there is the full moon? A. acupuncture treatment should not be administered; B. acupuncture treatment should be administered without doubt; C. tonification should not be done; D. sedation should not be done; E. no treatment should be done.
2974	《素问 41-32》腰痛上寒，应刺: A，足阳明; B. 足太阳 C·足太阳阳明 D·足少阳 E·足厥阴	《Sù Wèn 41-32》If lumbago is accompanied by chills in the upper half of the body, what meridians should be needled? A. the foot bright yang meridian; B. the foot greater yang meridian; C. the greater yang and bright yang meridians of foot; D · the foot lesser yang meridian; E. the foot decreasing yin meridian.
2975	《素问 47-17》胆瘅应取胆之: A. 原、络穴; B. 经 ·合穴; C. 募 ·俞穴; D. 经、俞穴; E. 合穴.	《Sù Wèn 47-17》What points on the gallbladder meridian may be used to treat gallbladder heat? A. source point (yuán Xué) and linking point (Luò Xué); B. river point (jīng xué) and hé xué / terminal-point / sea-point; C. the gallbladder gathering / anterior point [mù xué] and back shu points [bèi shù xué]; D. river point (jīng xué) and stream points [shù xué]; E. hé xué / terminal-point / sea-point.
2976	《素问 50-6》针刺过深而伤，导致腹胀烦不嗜食，伤及的是: A. 肝 B 心 C 脾 D 肺 E，肾	《Sù Wèn 50-6》what organ is harmed when the patient suffers abdominal swelling with depression and poor appetite due to excessively deep insertion? A. liver; B. heart; C. spleen; D. lungs; E. kidneys.
2977	《素问 60-2》一病人振寒 ·汗出头痛 ·身重恶寒，治在: A. 风门; B. 肺俞; C. 风府; D. 大椎; E. 风池.	《Sù Wèn 60-2》 Wind enters into the body from outside to cause a patient to display chills and perspiration, headache, heaviness of the body, aversion to cold; what point to treat it? A. B12, Fēng Mén; B. B13, Fèi Shū; C. D16, Fēng Fŭ; D. D14, Dà Zhuī; E. G20, Fēng Chí.
2978	《素问 61-14》,治取经俞在什么季节: A. 春; B.	《Sù Wèn 61-14》During what season should river point

	夏; C. 秋; D. 冬; E. 长夏	[jīng xué], and stream points [shù xué] be needled? A. spring; B. summer; C. autumn; D. winter; E. prolonged summer.
2979	《素问 63-29》有痛而经不病者，如何刺之: A. 短刺; B. 巨刺之; C. 繆刺 D 半刺; E. 经刺	《Sù Wèn 63-29》What technique of acupuncture should be applied if pain occurs, but master meridians are not diseased? A. Slow paced needling; B. Opposite needling; C. reverse technique of acupuncture; D · Halved needling; E needling the meridian.
2980	《素问 63-6》络病者、其痛与经脉繆处，故命曰: A，短刺; B. 巨刺之; C. 繆刺; D. 半刺; E. 巨虛上下廉	《Sù Wèn 63-6》When pain in the reticular meridians and the regular meridians occur in different regions, what technique of acupuncture should be applied to treat it? A. Slow paced needling; B. Opposite needling; C. reverse technique of acupuncture; D · Halved needling; E. needling the meridian.
2981	《素问 63-6》邪客于经，左盛则右病，右盛则：A. 上病 B;下病; C. 左病 D 右病; E. 经病	《Sù Wèn 63-6》When pathogen comes to reside in meridians as guest, it may cause a disease on the right side while the left side is excessive; what will happen when the right side is excessive? A. disease in the upper region; B. disease in the lower region; C. disease on the left side; D. disease on the right side; E. meridian disease.
2982	《素问 ·54-12》"经气已至，慎守勿失。"是指: A. 得气 B候气 C·催气 D **勿變更也**; E. 艾灸	《Sù Wèn ·54-12》" When meridian energy arrives, it should be guarded with great care" means: A. Needling sensations have occurred; B. awaiting the arrival of energy; C. to speed up the arrival of energy; D. no drastic measure should be taken unnecessarily; E. moxibustion should be administered.
2983	素问 ·60-13》记载的"男子内结七疝"是何经病症：· A·足厥阴肝经; ; B. 足少阴肾经; C. 足太阴脾经; D. 任脉; E. 冲脉.	Sù Wèn ·60-13》What meridian is diseased "when a man suffers from seven kinds of hernia of internal coagulation" ? · A · liver meridian; B. kidney meridian; C. spleen meridian; D. conception meridian; E. chong mai / rigorous meridian.
2984	《素问 25-17》关于"知养身"下列何者是不正确的: A. 懂得养生的道理 B;针刺取效的因素之一 C.与针刺作用相辅相成; D. 养生而不必针刺; E. 养生与针刺配合.	《Sù Wèn 25-17》Which is Not the proper way " to learn how to lead a healthy lifestyle"? A. to understand the way of nourishing life; B. to learn how acupuncture works effectively; C. acupuncture is consistent with leading a healthy lifestyle; D. to lead a healthy lifestyle without acupuncture; E. to lead a healthy lifestyle can be combined with acupuncture.
2985	《素问 26-8》据 "得时而调之"原则，月生应： A. 无刺; B. 无治; C. 无补; D. 无泻; E. 无灸	《Sù Wèn 26-8》When the moon generates (the new moon), what should be done in acupuncture treatment? A. No acupuncture should be done; B. no treatment

		should be done; C. no tonification should be done; D. no sedation should be done; E. no moxibustion should be done.
2986	《素问 26-8》据 "得时而调之。原则，下列什么情况下要求无泻: A. 天寒; B. 天温; C. 月郭空; D. 月生; E. 月满 '	《Sù Wèn 26-8》When sedation should not be done? A. cold weather; B. warm weather; C. there is the crescent moon; D. the moon generates (the new moon); E. when there is the full moon.
2987	《素问 41-35》腰痛如折不可挽仰，不可举,应刺 A. 手阳明太阴; B. 手厥阴; C. 手少阴; D. 足太阳; E. 手太阳少阴	《Sù Wèn 41-35》In case of pain as if the spine were about to break with an inability to bend forward or backward or inability to move around, what meridians should be needled? A. the hand bright yang and greater yin meridians; B. the hand decreasing yin meridian; C. the hand lesser yin meridian; D. the foot greater yang merdiain; E. the hand greater yang and lesser yin meridians.
2988	《素问 60-36》股骨上空在股阳 ,位于: A. 出上膝三寸; B. 出上膝五寸; C. 出上膝六寸; D. 出上膝四寸; E. 出上膝二寸.	《Sù Wèn 60-36》Where is the upper cavity of thighbone on the lateral side of the thigh located? A. three cuns above the knee; B. five cuns above the knee; C. six cuns above the knee; D. four cuns above the knee; E. two cuns above the knee.
2989	《素问 61-15》治取井荣在什么季节: A. 春 ';; B. 夏; C. 秋; D. 冬; E. 长夏	《Sù Wèn 61-15》During what season should well points (jing points) and spring points (ying points) be needled? A. spring; B. summer; C. autumn; D. winter; E. prolonged summer.
2990	《素问 61-9》踝上各一行行六者 ,此肾脉之下行也 ,名曰: A. 八髎; B. 肾俞; C. 委中; D. 太冲; E. 疼痛局部.	《Sù Wèn 61-9》There is one plane above medial malleolus with six points on the plane through which the kidney meridian travels downward; what are the points called? A. Eight Liáo points B. B23, Shèn Shū; C. B40, Wěi Zhōng; D. Lv3, Tài Chōng; E. local pressure points.
2991	《素问 32-19》 肾热病热争出现的症状是: A; 狂言及惊; B. 卒心痛; C. 喘咳 D，腰痛不可用俯仰; E. 项痛而强	《Sù Wèn 32-19》When heat begins to struggle in the hot disease of the kidney, what symptom may occur? A; talking as if insane and in shock; B. acute heart pain; C. panting and cough; D， lumbago and unable to bend forward and backward; E. pain and stiffness of the back of the neck.
2992	《素问 63-29》审其虚实而调之，不调者如何刺之： A. 短刺; B. 巨刺之; C. 繆刺 D 半刺; E. 经刺	《Sù Wèn 63-29》An acupuncturist should examine meridians to determine deficiency and excess, which should be regulated accordingly; what technique should be used? A. Slow paced needling; B. Opposite needling; C. reverse technique of acupuncture; D · Halved needling; E. needling the meridian.
2993	《针灸逢原》一书已载经穴: A 349 个; B 354 个; C 359 个; D. 361 个.	《Zhēn Jiǔ Féng Yuán》How many points are recorded in this Classic? A 349 points; B 354 points; C 359 points; D. 361 points.

2994	《肘后备急方》的作者是: A. 王惟一; B. 皇甫谧; C. 扁鹊; D. 滑伯仁; E 葛洪.	《Zhǒu Hòu Bèi Jí Fāng》Who is the author of this classic? A. Wáng Wéi Yī; B. Huáng Fǔ Mì; C. Biǎn Què; D. Huá Bó Rén; E. Gé Hóng.
2995	《难经·六十八难》指出"经"穴的主治症是: A. 喘咳寒热; B. 逆气而泄; C. 体重节痛; D. 心下满; E. 身热	《Nàn Jīng 68》What symptom can a flowing point (jing xue) treat? A. panting, cough, cold-hot sensations; B. upstream energy and diarrhea; C. heaviness of the body and pain in the joints; D. fullness below the heart; E. hot sensations in the body.
2996	《难经 62》三焦行诸阳，故置一俞日: A. 原; B. 俞; C. 输; D. 合; E. 经	《Nàn Jīng 62》The triple heater travels through the yang meridians which is why there is an additional point for each bowel, what is this additional point called? A. the starting point (yuán point or source point); B. Back Shu Points [Bèi Shù Xué]; C. Stream Points [Shù Xué]; D. hé xué / terminal-point / sea-point; E River Points [Jīng Xué].
2997	《难经 64》经脉属土，五行属水的输穴是: A 阴陵泉; B. 少海 C 曲泉; D，尺泽，E 曲择	《Nàn Jīng 64》 The meridian corresponds to earth, and its stream point [Shù Xué] also corresponds to Earth; what is the name of the stream point [Shù Xué]? A. Sp9, Yīn Líng Quán; B. H3, Shào Hǎi; C. Lv8, Qū Quán; D.Lu5, Chǐ Zé; E. P3, Qū Zé.
2998	《难经 74》春刺井是说: A 春天刺肝经井穴治疗肝病; B. 春天刺肝经井穴治疗内脏病; C. 春天刺井穴治疗肝病; D. 春天刺井穴治疗脏腑病; E. 春天刺井穴治疗腑病	《Nàn Jīng 74》In spring, well points [jǐng xué] should be needled; what does it mean? A. in spring, needle the well point [Jǐng Xué] of the liver meridian to treat liver diseases; B. in spring, needle the well point [Jǐng Xué] to treat the diseases of the internal organs; C. in spring, needle the well point [Jǐng Xué] to treat the liver diseases; D. in spring, needle the well point [Jǐng Xué] to treat the diseases of the viscera and bowels; E. in spring, needle the well point [Jǐng Xué] to treat the diseases of bowels.
2999	《难经 75》"母能令子虚"，在临床应用上是指: A. 母病及子; B. 子病累母; C. 肝病传脾; D. 子能令母实; E. 泻火补水	《Nàn Jīng 75》Mother can bring about the deficient state of child, what does it mean in clinical application? A. diseases of the mother will affect the child; B. diseases of the child will affect the mother; C. liver diseases will transmit to the spleen; D. child can bring about the excess state of mother; E. sedate fire and tone up water.
3000	《难经 75》泻南方补北方是针对: A. 肝实肺虚; B. 心实肾虚 C，肝实脾虚; D. 心虚肾实; E. 肺实肝虚	《Nàn Jīng 75》What is the target syndrome of " Sedate south and tone up north"? A. liver excess with lung deficiency; B. heart excess with kidney deficiency; C. liver excess with spleen deficiency; D. heart deficiency with kidney excess; E. lung excess with liver deficiency.
3001	《难经 79》根据 "随而济之者，补其母"的原则，胃虚应取的穴是: A. 解溪; B. 足三里 C·厉兑 D·少泽; E. 曲池.	《Nàn Jīng 79》To go along and assist means to tone up the mother; what point should be used in case of stomach deficiency according to the above principle? A. S41, Jiě Xī; B. S36, Zú Sān Lǐ; C·S45, Lì Duì; D·Si1 Shào Zé; E. Li11, Qū Chí.

3002	《难经 81》肝实肺虚治疗时应取的穴是: A 太渊、行间; B. 太敦、经渠; C. 曲泉、尺泽; D. 太冲、少商; E. 鱼际、中封	《Nàn Jīng 81》 What points should be used to treat liver excess and lung deficiency? A. Lu9, Tài Yuān、Lv2, Xíng Jiān; B. Lv1, Dà Dūn、 Lu8, Jīng Qú; C. Lv8, Qū Quán、Lu5, Chǐ Zé; D. Lv3, Tài Chōng、Lu11, Shǎo Shāng; E. Lu10, Yǔ Jì、Lv4, Zhōng Fēng.
3003	《难经 62》腑独有六者，指: A. 六腑; B. 五输加原穴 C，六个原穴; D. 三十个输穴; E. 三十六个输穴.	《Nàn Jīng 62》The bowels have six points, what are they? A. six bowels; B. five command points plus one source point (yuán xué); C. six source points (yuán xué); D. 30 command points (shu xué); E. 36 command points (shu xué).
3004	《难经 64》经脉属水，五行也属水的输穴是: A. 至阴 B 足通谷; C. 束骨 D 昆仑 E 涌泉	《Nàn Jīng 64》 The meridian corresponds to Water; and its stream point [Shù Xué] also corresponds to Water; what is the name of the stream point [Shù Xué]? A. B67, Zhì Yīn; B. B66, Zú Tōng Gǔ; C. B65, Shù Gǔ; D. B60, Kūn Lún; E. K1, Yǒng Quán.
3005	《难经 66》既是输穴，又是原穴的是: A. 足临泣; B. 太溪; C. 束骨; D. 中渚; E. 陷谷	《Nàn Jīng 66》What point is a stream point [Shù Xué] and also a source point [Yuán Xué]? A. G41, Zú Lín Qì; B. K3, Tài Xī; C. B65, Shù Gǔ; D. Sj3, Zhōng Zhǔ; E. S43, Xiàn Gǔ.
3006	《难经 69》据实者泻其子的原则，肺经实应泻的经是: A. 胃; B. 肾; C. 心; D. 肝; E. 脾	《Nàn Jīng 69》In applying the principle of sedating the child in case of excess, what meridian should be sedated in case of lung meridian excess? A. stomach meridian; B. kidney meridian; C. heart meridian; D. liver meridian; E. spleen meridian.
3007	《难经 70》應淺刺的情況爲: A 秋冬, B 春夏 C 寒冷 D 實證 E 裏証	《Nàn Jīng 70》Under what circumstances should a shallow insertion be administered? A. autumn and winter; B. spring and summer; C... cold weather; D. excess syndrome; E. deep syndrome.
3008	《难经 73》当刺井者，以荥泻之，应取的穴为: A. 大敦; B. 行间; C. 太冲; D. 中封; E. 曲泉	《Nàn Jīng 73》One may sedate the spring points [yíng xué] in lieu of the well points [jǐng xué]; what point should be sedated? A. Lv1, Dà Dūn; B. Lv2, Xíng Jiān; C. Lv3, Tài Chōng; D. Lv4, Zhōng Fēng; E. Lv8, Qū Quán
3009	《难经 77》中工治已病时，见肝之病，选择的针灸处方是: A. 窍阴、临泣、阴陵泉; B. 大敦、太冲、行间; C. 隐白、商丘、阴陵泉; D. 厉兑、内庭、足三里 E / 行间、大都、太白	《Nàn Jīng 77》A middle-class physician will concentrate on the treatment of the disease after it has occurred; which of the following prescription of points would be applied to treat the liver disease that has occurred?. A. G44, Zú Qiào Yīn、G41, Zú Lín Qì、Sp9, Yīn Líng Quán; B. Lv1, Dà Dūn、Lv3, Tài Chōng、Lv2, Xíng Jiān; C. Sp1, Yǐn Bái、Sp5, Shāng Qiū、Sp9, Yīn Líng Quán; D. S45, Lì Duì、S44, Nèi Tíng、S36, Zú Sān Lǐ E / Lv2, Xíng Jiān、Sp2, Dà Dū,Sp3, Tài Bái.
3010	《难经》书名的恰当解释应为: A. 刁难; B. 发难; C. 问难 D，非难; E. 论难	《Nàn Jīng》 What is the most appropriate meaning of the title of this classic? A. learning difficult questions; B. presenting difficult questions; C. asking difficult questions; D. critical and negative questions; E. on difficult questions.

3011	《难经·六十八难》指出"井" 穴的主治症是: A. 喘咳寒热; B. 体重节痛; C. 心下满; D. 逆气而泄; E. 身热	《Nàn Jīng 68》What symptom can a well point [jǐng xué] treat? A. panting, cough, cold-hot sensations; B. heaviness of the body and pain in the joints; C. fullness below the heart; D. upstream energy and diarrhea; E. hot sensations in the body.
3012	《难经·六十八难》指出"输"穴主治症是: A. 逆气而泄; B. 喘咳寒热; C. 体重节痛; D. 心下满; E. 身热	《Nàn Jīng 68》What symptom can a stream point [shù xué] treat? A. upstream energy and diarrhea; B. panting, cough, cold-hot sensations; C. heaviness of the body and pain in the joints; D. fullness below the heart; E. hot sensations in the body.
3013	《难经 67》指出在阴的穴: A. 肺俞; B. 肾俞 C 巨闕 D 肝俞 E 心俞	《Nàn Jīng 67》The gathering points of the five viscera are located in the yin region; which point is located in the yin region? A. B13, Fèi Shū; B. B23, Shèn Shū; C. R14, Jù Què; D. B18, Gān Shū; E. B15, Xīn Shū.
3014	《难经 68》下列输穴中是荣穴是: A. 太冲; B. 合谷; C. 二间; D. 三间 E 阳辅	《Nàn Jīng 68》Which point is a spring points [Yíng Xué]? A. Lv3, Tài Chōng; B. Li4, Hé Gǔ; C. Li2, Èr Jiān; D. Li3, Sān Jiān; E. G38, Yáng Fǔ.
3015	《难经 71》针刺阳部，应选用的进针方法是: A，直刺 B 斜刺 C 卧针 D 深刺 E 报刺	《Nàn Jīng 71》What technique should be used to needle the yang region? A. perpendicular insertion; B. slanting insertion; C. prone needling; D. deep insertion; E. retributive needling.
3016	《难经 72》"調气之方"的根本在于: A. 荣卫; B. 迎 随; C. 阴阳; D. 内外; E. 表里	《Nàn Jīng 72》What is the method of regulating energy? A. to regulate defense and nutritive levels; B. to twirl for tonification and sedation; C. to regulate yin and yang; D. to regulate internal and external; E. to regulate superficial and deep regions.
3017	《难经 74》五季针刺五输穴，下列哪项是错误的: A. 春刺井; B. 夏刺荣; C. 季夏刺原 D 秋刺经 E 冬刺合.	《Nàn Jīng 74》 According to the principle that in spring, well points [Jīng Xué] should be needled, which of the following is inconsistent with this principle? A. needle well points [Jīng Xué] in spring; B. needle spring points [Yíng Xué] in summer; C. needle source points [Yuán Xué] in prolonged summer; D. needle river points [Jīng Xué] in autumn; E. needle sea pints [Hé Xué] in winter.
3018	《难经 77》见肝之病，先实其脾气，应选择的针灸处方是: A. 大敦、曲池、列缺; B. 尺泽、阴陵泉、三阴交; C. 行间、大都 太白; D. 大敦 行间、曲泉; E. 隐白、太白、大都.	《Nàn Jīng 77》 When the liver is diseased, one should tone up the energy of the spleen first; which of the following prescription of points should be applied? A. Lv1, Dà Dūn、Li11, Qū Chí、Lu7, Liè Quē; B. Lu5, Chǐ Zé、Sp9, Yīn Líng Quán、Sp6, Sān Yīn Jiāo; C. Lv2, Xíng Jiān、Sp2, Dà Dū、Sp3, Tài Bái; D. Lv1, Dà Dūn、Lv2, Xíng Jiān、Lv8, Qū Quán; E. Sp1, Yǐn Bái、Sp3, Tài Bái、Sp2, Dà Dū.
3019	《难经 79》根据 "迎而	《Nàn Jīng 79》To greet and deprive means to sedate the

	夺之者，泻其子"的原则，肺实应取的穴是: A.少商; B. 鱼际; C. 尺泽; D.商丘 E 曲泉.	child; what point should be used in case of lung excess according to the above principle? A.Lu11, Shǎo Shāng; B. Lu10, Yǔ Jì; C. Lu5, Chǐ Zé; D. Sp5, Shāng Qiū; E. Lv8, Qū Quán.
3020	《难经，六十八难》指出"合"穴的主治症是: A. 身热 B 心下满; C. 喘咳寒热; D. 逆气而泄; E. 体重节痛	《Nàn Jīng 68》 What disease can a sea points [hé xué] treat? A. hot sensations in the body; B. fullness below the heart; C. the symptoms of panting, cough, cold-hot sensations; D. upstream energy and diarrhea; E. heaviness of the body and pain in the joints.
3021	《难经 29》记载 "阴维为病"是: A. 苦寒热; B. 苦咳逆; C. 阳缓而阴急; D. 苦心痛; E. 足痿不用	《Nàn Jīng 29》What symptom will occur when the fastener meridian of yin (yin wei mai) is diseased? A. chills and hot sensations; B. cough and uprising; C. a relaxation of yang side and tightening of yin side;; D. heart pain; E. foot paralysis.
3022	《难经 六十八难》指出"荥" 穴的主治症是: A. 体重节痛; B. 喘咳寒热; C. 逆气而泄; D. 身热 E 心下满	《Nàn Jīng 68》What symptom can a spring point [yíng xué] treat? A. heaviness of the body and pain in the joints; B. panting, cough, cold-hot sensations; C. upstream energy and diarrhea; D. hot sensations in the body; E. fullness below the heart.
3023	《难经 67》指出在阳的穴: A. 天枢 B 关元 C 中极 D 厥阴俞 E 中府	《Nàn Jīng 67》The posterior points of the five viscera are located in the yang region; which point is located in the yang region? A. S25, Tiān Shū; B. R4, Guān Yuán; C. R3, Zhōng Jí; D. B14, Jué Yīn Shū; E. Lu1, Zhōng Fǔ.
3024	《难经 69》根据虚者补其母的原则，胃经虚应补的经是: A. 肝; B. 心; C. 胆; D. 小肠; E. 大肠	《Nàn Jīng 69》In applying the principle of toning up the mother in case of deficiency, what meridian should be toned up in case of stomach meridian deficiency? A. liver meridian; B. heart meridian; C. gallbladder meridian; D. small intestine meridian; E. large intestine meridian.
3025	《难经 70》應深刺的情況爲: A 春夏 B 表証 C 風熱 D 秋冬，E 風寒	《Nàn Jīng 70》Under what circumstances should a deep insertion be administered? A. spring and summer; B. superficial syndrome; C. wind heat syndrome; D. autumn and winter; E. wind cold syndrome.
3026	《难经 71》针刺阴部，应选用的进针方法是:: A. 单手进针 B 左手进针 C 提捏进针 D 左右手配合进针 E 挟持进针	《Nàn Jīng 71》What technique should be used to needle the yin region? A. use one hand to insert the needle; B. use the left hand to insert the needle; C. Manipulating the inserted needle by lifting and pushing; D. Inserting the needle with both hands coordinating with each other; E. Needle insertion by holding the needle.
3027	《难经 74》肺病出现的五声变化为: A. 呼; B. 笑; C. 歌; D. 哭; E. 呻	《Nàn Jīng 74》What voice will the lung disease give rise to? A. Calling; B. Laughing; C. Singing; D. Crying; E. Groaning.

3028	《难经 76》当阴气不足、阳气有余时，采用的治疗原则是: A. 先补阳、后泻阴; B. 补阴; C. 先泻阳、后补阴; D. 先补阴、后泻阳; E. 先泻阴、后补阳	《Nàn Jīng 76》When yin energy is in deficiency while yang energy is in excess, what treatment principle should be applied? A. yang should be toned up first, and then yin should be sedated; B. yin should be toned up: C. yang should be sedated first, and then yin should be toned up; D. yin should be toned up first, and then yang should be sedated; E. yin should be sedated first, and then yang should be toned up.
3029	《难经 80》"有见如入，有见如出"中的 "见"意指: A. 看见 B.摸到 C.感到:; D. 显露; E. 想象.	《Nàn Jīng 80》Inserting the needle when something becomes evident; what does "evident" mean? A. when something has been seen; B. when something has been touched; ·C. when something has been felt; D. when something has been exposed; E. when something has been imagined.
3030	《难经·二十九难》记载的带脉病症是：A.带下; B. 疝气; C. 心痛; D. 寒热; E. 腹满	《Nàn Jīng · 29》What is the symptom of the belt meridian (dai mai)? A vaginal discharges; B. hernia; C. Heart pain; D. cold and hot sensations; E. abdominal swelling.
3031	《难经 63》"诸蚑行喘息"中 "喘息"是指: A. 咳喘; B. 哮喘; C. 喘病 D，咳嗽；E. 气息·	《Nàn Jīng 63》"All insects start walking with rough breathing", what is meant by "rough breathing"? A. cough and panting; B. asthma with sputum noise in the throat and short breath; C. asthma with short breath; D. cough; E. breathing with noise.
3032	《难经 68》下列输穴中是井穴是: A. 行间; B. 然谷; C. 足三里; D. 中封; E. 大敦.	《Nàn Jīng 68》Which point is a well point [Jīng Xué]? A. Lv2, Xíng Jiān; B. K2, Rán Gǔ; C. S36, Zú Sān Lǐ; D. Lv4, Zhōng Fēng; E. Lv1, Dà Dūn.
3033	《难经 73》刺井者，以荥泻之，应取的穴为: A. 厉兑; B. 足三里; C. 陷谷; D. 解溪; E. 内庭.	《Nàn Jīng 73》 One may sedate the spring points [yíng xué] in lieu of the well points [jǐng xué]; what point should be sedated? A. S45, Lì Duì; B. S36, Zú Sān Lǐ; C. S43, Xiàn Gǔ; D. S41, Jiě Xī; E. S44, Nèi Tíng.
3034	《难经 75》肝实肺虚之证，可应用的方法是: A. 虚者补其母; B. 实者泻其子; C. 子能令母实 D.母能令子虚; E. 泻南补北法.	《Nàn Jīng 75》The liver is in excess and the lungs are in deficiency; how to apply this principle in practice? A. tone up the mother in case of deficiency; B. sedate the child in case of excess; C. child can bring about the excess state of child; ·D mother can bring about the deficient state of child; E. Sedate the south and tone up the north.
3035	《难经 76》当阳气不足、阴气有余时，采用的治疗原则是: A. 补阳; B. 先泻阴，后补阳; C. 先补阴，后泻阳; D. 先泻阳，后补阴; E. 先补阳、后泻阴	《Nàn Jīng 76》 When yang energy is in deficiency while yin energy is in excess, what treatment principle should be applied? A. yang should be toned; B. yin should be sedated first, and then yang should be toned up; C. yin should be toned up first, and then yang should be sedated; D. yang should be sedated first, and then yin should be toned up; E. yang should be toned up first, and then yin should be sedated.
3036	《难经 78》"知为针者，	《Nàn Jīng 78》A skilful physician will trust the left hand

	信其左;不知为针者，信其右"中的"信"的含义是: A. 信息; B 确信; C. 诚实; D. 表明; E. 善用.	more than the right hand; an unskillful physician will trust the right hand more than the left hand; what does “trust” mean? A. using it to gather information; B. relying on it; C. honestly believing in it; D. using it to perform; E. skilful with the hand.
3037	《难经 80》"有见如入"是指: A. 见穴而刺; B. 针刺入得气; C. 刺络放血 D·见气尽; E. 候气至而进针.	《Nàn Jīng 80》Inserting the needle when something becomes evident; what does “something” refer to? A. acupuncture point; B. energy responses; C. linking meridian; D. complete departure of energy; E. inserting the needle on arrival of energy.
3038	《难经 81》肺实肝虚治疗时应取的穴是: A. 太冲、经渠; B. 太渊、大敦; C. 行间、鱼际 D、少商、中封; E. 尺泽、曲泉.	《Nàn Jīng81》What points should be used to treat lung excess and liver deficiency? A. Lv3, Tài Chōng、 Lu8, Jīng Qú; B. Lu9, Tài Yuān、Lv1, Dà Dūn; C. Lv2, Xíng Jiān、Lu10, Yǔ Jì; D. Lu11, Shǎo Shāng、Lv4, Zhōng Fēng; E. Lu5, Chǐ Zé、Lv8, Qū Quán.
3039	《针灸甲乙经》记载的腧穴名称共有: A·349 个; B. 354 个; C. 359 个; D. 361 个; E. 160 个左右.	《Zhēn Jiǔ Jiá Yǐ Jīng》How many points are named in this Classic? A·349 points; B. 354 points; C. 359 points; D. 361 points; E. about 160 points.
3040	《针灸甲乙经》发展和确定了多少个腧穴 A·345; B. 349; C. 354; D.361.	《Zhēn Jiǔ Jiá Yǐ Jīng》 How many acupuncture points are presented in this Classic? A·345; B. 349; C. 354; D.361.
3041	《针灸甲乙经》的作者是: A. 扁鹊; B. 葛洪; C. 皇甫谧; D. 孫思邈; E. 杨继洲	《Zhēn Jiǔ Jiá Yǐ Jīng》 Who wrote this Classic? A. Biǎn Què; B. Gé Hóng; C. Huáng Fǔ Mì; D. Sūn Sī Miǎo; E. Yáng Jì Zhōu
3042	《甲乙经》成书朝代及作者是: A. 唐代-孙思邈; B. 晋代-葛洪 C;宋代-王执中; ·D 晋代-皇甫謐; E·宋代-王惟一.	《Jiá Yǐ Jīng》 Name the dynasty in which this classic was published and its author. A. Táng Dynasty- Sūn Sī Miǎo; B. Jìn Dynasty- Gé Hóng; C. Sòng Dynasty- Wáng Zhí Zhōng; D Jìn Dynasty-Huáng Fǔ Mì; E·Sòng Dynasty- Wáng Wéi Yī.
3043	《针灸甲乙经》考证了腧穴： A. 354 个·B;359 个 :C.361 个 D·349 个; E. ··152 个'.	《Zhēn Jiǔ Jiá Yǐ Jīng》 How many points are verified by this Classic? A. 354 points; ·B. 359 points; C. 361 points; D·349 points; E. ·152 points.
3044	《针灸甲乙经》是将哪几本书汇集而成的? A. (素问) ·(灵枢)、《明堂孔穴》;B. 《明堂孔穴》;《针灸治要》、《黄帝内经》;C. 《针经》、《刺法》、《黄帝内经》;D. 《素问》、《灵枢》、·《明堂孔穴针灸治要》;E. 《刺法》、《经脉》、《黄帝内经》.	《Zhēn Jiǔ Jiá Yǐ Jīng》What classics are the sources of this Classic? A. (Sù Wèn)、(Líng Shū)、《Míng Táng Kǒng Xué》;B. 《Míng Táng Kǒng Xué》,《Zhēn Jiǔ Zhì Yào》, 《Huáng Dì Nèi Jīng》;C. 《Zhēn Jīng》、《Cì Fǎ》, 、《Huáng Dì Nèi Jīng》;D.《Sù Wèn》、《Líng Shū》·《Míng Táng Kǒng Xué Zhēn Jiǔ Zhì Yào》; E.《Cì Fǎ》,《Jīng Mài》,《Huáng Dì Nèi Jīng》.

3045	《针灸甲乙经》的作者是: A. 葛洪; B. 王叔和; C. 华伦; D. 孙思邈 E，皇甫谧.	《Zhēn Jiǔ Jiá Yī Jīng》Who wrote this Classic? A. Gé Hóng; B. Wáng Shū Hé; C. Huá Lún; D. Sūn Sī Miǎo E. Huáng Fǔ Mì.
3046	《千金要方 6-11》言不宜多灸的部位是: A. 头部; B. 脊背; C. 四肢; D. 腹部; E. 胸部	《Qiān Jīn Yào Fāng 6-11》 What region should not be treated by excessive moxibustion? A. head; B. spine and back; C. four limbs; D. abdominal region; E. chest region.
3047	《千金要方 6-14》言吴蜀地多灸是为了: A. 预防瘴厉温疟毒气 B 治疗温病; C. 预防蛇伤; D. 强身健体; E. 治疗湿病	《Qiān Jīn Yào Fāng 6-14》 More moxibusiton should be administered in the Wu Shu Di region; why is that? A. to prevent pestilential pathogen and warm malaria; B. to treat warm diseases; C. to prevent snake bites; D. to promote health and physical strength; E. to treat damp diseases.
3048	《奇经八脉考》的作者为: A. 杨继洲。B·李时珍; C. 孫思邈; D. 王惟一; E 汪机.	《Qí Jīng Bā Mài Kǎo》Who is the author of this classic?: A. Yáng Jì Zhōu。B. · Lǐ Shí Zhēn; C. Sūn Sī Miǎo; D. Wáng Wéi Yī; E. Wāng Jī.
3049	《千金要方》记载的经外奇穴约有: A. 70 多个 B ·150 多个 C ·190 多个; D. 120 多个; E. 200 多个.	《Qiān Jīn Yào Fāng》About how many extraordinary points are recorded in this classic? A. over 70 points; B. over 150 points; C. over ·190 points; D. over 120 points; E. over 200 points.
3050	《千金要方 6-1》言针刺补泻 "送坚付濡"的含义是: A. 除实邪，其脉变缓; B. 补助正气 ·去除虚邪气; C. 急去其邪 ·急脉变缓; D. 逐其实邪 ·补其濡弱; E. 脉由坚实变缓	《Qiān Jīn Yào Fāng 6-1》Tonification and sedation in acupuncture must expel hard pathgens and strengthen weak body energy. What does the statement mean? A. to remove excess pathogen so that the pulse may become relaxed; B. to assist body energy and expel deficient pathogen; C. to quickly remove the pathogen so that an acute pulse may become a relaxed one; D. to expel excess pathogen and tone up weak body energy; E. to make a hard and excess pulse become a relaxed one.
3051	《千金要方 6-10》灸法认为施灸的最佳时间是: A. 清晨; B. 上午 ·C 中午 D. 中午以后; E. 晚上.	《Qiān Jīn Yào Fāng 6-10》When is the best time to administer moxibustion? A. early in the morning; B. in the morning; ·C. · noon; D. late in the afternoon; E. evening.
3052	《千金要方 6-11》灸之尤宜大熟的部位是: A，四肢 B 脊背 C 腹部; D. 头部， E. ·胸部	《Qiān Jīn Yào Fāng 6-11》 What region should be treated by more moxibustion? A. head; B. spine and back; C. four limbs; D. abdominal region; E. chest region.
3053	《千金要方》言灸法认为不宜多灸的脉象是: A. 细弱之脉; B. 迟脉; C. 沉细脉; D. 弦脉; E. 微数之脉	《Qiān Jīn Yào Fāng》What pulse should not be treated by excessive moxibustion? A. fine and weak pulse; B. slow pulse; C. deep and fine pulse; D. ·wiry pulse; E. disappearing and rapid pulse.
3054	《千金要方》中特别强调: A. 针刺治疗 ·B 药物治疗; C. 灸法治疗; D. 针药并举; E. 针灸药并举	《Qiān Jīn Yào Fāng》What kind of treatment is particularly emphasized in this classic? A. acupuncture therapy; ·B. herbal therapy; C. moxibustion; D. combined acupuncture and herbal

		therapy; E. combined acupuncture and moxibustion and herbal therapy.
3055	《铜人输穴针灸图经》所载经穴数字为: A. 160 穴左右; B. 349 穴; C. 354 穴; D. 360 穴; E. 361 穴	《Tóng Rén Shù Xué Zhēn Jiǔ Tú Jīng》How many points are recorded in this classic? A. about 160 points;; B. 349 points; C. 354 points; D. 360 points; E. 361 points.
3056	《铜人腧穴针灸图经》的作者是: A. 王执中; B. 杨继洲; C. 王惟一; D. 李时珍; E. 滑寿	《Tóng Rén Shù Xué Zhēn Jiǔ Tú Jīng》Who is the author of this classic? A. Wáng Zhí Zhōng; B. Yáng Jì Zhōu; C. Wáng Wéi Yī; D. Lǐ Shí Zhēn; E. Huá Shòu
3057	《针灸资生经 5》中若治风则灸上星，前顶、百会，皆至: A. 二百壮; B 一百壮; C 五百壮; D 三百壮; E 四百壮.	《Zhēn Jiǔ Zī Shēng Jīng 5》How many sticks of moxibustion should a wind disease be treated at D23, Shàng Xīng, D21, Qián Dǐng, and 、D20, Bǎi Huì? A. 200 sticks; B. 100 sticks; C · 500 sticks; D ·300 sticks; E · 400 sticks.
3058	《针灸资生经》中占有绝大部分篇幅的内容是: A. 有关治疗学内容; B. 有关刺灸内容; C. 有关输穴内容; D. 有关经络内容; E. 有关内科内容. ·	《Zhēn Jiǔ Zī Shēng Jīng》What are the major contents of this classic? A. the contents of treatment methodology; B. the contents of needle insertion; C. the contents of acupuncture points; D.the contents of meridians; E. the contents of internal medicine.
3059	·《针灸资生经》中提倡针灸药物因证而施，但临床多用: A. 灸法; B. 刺法; C. 药物; D. 刺血法; E. 拔罐法.	·《Zhēn Jiǔ Zī Shēng Jīng》 The Classic advocated that treatment should take place according to syndromes, but in point of fact, it devoted most of its clinical practice to: A. moxibustion; B. acupuncture; C. herbs; D. bloodletting; E. cupping.
3060	《针灸资生经 1》称没有加热烧红的普通针具为: A. 冷针; B. 白针; C. 凉针; D. 黑针; E. 红针	《Zhēn Jiǔ Zī Shēng Jīng 1》 What is the name of the needle which is not heated? A. cold needle; B. white needle; C. cool needle; D. black needle; E. red needle.
3061	《针灸资生经》中用点灸的方法治疗腰背伛偻，所选穴位是: A. 委中; B. 阳陵泉; C. 肾俞; D. 悬钟; E. 大肠俞.	《Zhēn Jiǔ Zī Shēng Jīng》 What point should be selected to treat hunchback by dotted moxibustion? A. B40, Wěi Zhōng; B. G34, Yáng Líng Quán; C. B23, Shèn Shū; D. G39, Xuán Zhōng; E. B25, Dà Cháng Shū.
3062	《针灸资生经》中有脚气疾，遇春则足稍肿，夏中尤甚，至冬肿渐消，王氏的治疗选穴是: A. 委中; B. 阳陵泉; C. 足三里 D 悬钟; E. 大肠俞.	《Zhēn Jiǔ Zī Shēng Jīng》 What point should be selected to treat beriberi which displays slight swelling of foot in spring and gets worse in middle summer, with swelling gradually disappearing in winter? A. B40, Wěi Zhōng; B. G34, Yáng Líng Quán; C. S36, Zú Sān Lǐ; D ·G39, Xuán Zhōng; E. B25, Dà Cháng Shū.

13-8 Cautious Points (3063-3254)

(Select the item that best explains why the point requires caution / 选择一项最能解释为何该穴位要小心操作).

3063	B1, Jīng Míng, 睛明	A. Causing pneumatothorax / 误伤引起气胸; B. Forbidden point for women 女子禁针穴; C. Injury to eye, causing periorbital bleeding / 误伤眼睛, 眶周出血; D. Ancient Forbidden point 古传禁针穴; E. Injury to peroneal nerve, common peroneal nerve /

		误伤腓神经，腓总神经.
3064	B2, Zǎn Zhú, 攢竹	A. Injury to peroneal nerve, common peroneal nerve / 误伤腓神经，腓总神经; B. Injury to eye, causing periorbital bleeding / 误伤眼睛，眶周出血; C. often causing needle-sickness / 容易导致晕针; D. Ancient Forbidden point 古传禁针穴; E. Injury to ulnar nerve / 误伤尺神经.
3065	B8, Luò Què, 絡卻	A. Ancient Forbidden point 古传禁针穴; B. Injury to ulnar nerve / 误伤尺神经; C. often causing needle-sickness / 容易导致晕针; D. Causing pneumatothorax / 误伤引起气胸; E. Injury to peroneal nerve, common peroneal nerve / 误伤腓神经，腓总神经.
3066	B9, Yù Zhěn, 玉枕	A. Ancient Forbidden point 古传禁针穴; B. Injury to radial nerve / 误伤桡神经; C. Forbidden point during pregnancy 孕妇禁针穴; D. often causing needle-sickness / 容易导致晕针; E. Causing pneumatothorax / 误伤引起气胸.
3067	B11, Dà Zhù, 大杼	A. Causing pneumatothorax, hemathorax /误伤引起气胸，血胸; B. Forbidden point for women 女子禁针穴; C. Ancient Forbidden point 古传禁针穴; D. Injury to peroneal nerve, common peroneal nerve / 误伤腓神经，腓总神经; E. Injury to ulnar nerve / 误伤尺神经.
3068	B12, Fēng Mén, 風門	A. Injury to median nerve / 误伤正中神经; B. Causing pneumatothorax, hemathorax /误伤引起气胸，血胸; C. often causing needle-sickness / 容易导致晕针; D. Ancient Forbidden point 古传禁针穴; E. Injury to ulnar nerve / 误伤尺神经.
3069	B13, Fèi Shū, 肺輸	A. Injury to median nerve / 误伤正中神经; B. Injury to ulnar nerve / 误伤尺神经; C. Ancient Forbidden point 古传禁针穴; D. often causing needle-sickness / 容易导致晕针; E. Injury to organs/误伤内脏。Causing pneumatothorax, hemathorax /误伤引起气胸，血胸
3070	B14, Jué Yīn Shū, 厥陰輸	A. Injury to peroneal nerve, common peroneal nerve / 误伤腓神经，腓总神经; B. Ancient Forbidden point 古传禁针穴; C. Injury to organs/误伤内脏。Causing pneumatothorax, / 误伤引起气胸，血胸; D. often causing needle-sickness / 容易导致晕针; E. Injury to radial nerve / 误伤桡神经.
3071	B15, Xīn Shū, 心輸	A. Injury to peroneal nerve, common peroneal nerve / 误伤腓神经，腓总神经; B. Injury to median nerve / 误伤正中神经; C. Ancient Forbidden point 古传禁针穴; D. Injury to heart / 误伤心脏 / Causing pneumatothorax, hemathorax / 误伤引起气胸，血胸; E. often causing needle-sickness / 容易导致晕针.
3072	B16, Dū Shū, 督輸	A. Injury to radial nerve / 误伤桡神经; B. often causing needle-sickness / 容易导致晕针; C. Ancient Forbidden point 古传禁针穴; D. Injury to heart / 误伤心脏/ causing pneumatothorax, hemathorax / 误伤引起气胸，血胸; E. often causing hematoma / 容易导致血肿.
3073	B17, Gé Shū, 膈輸	A. Forbidden point for women 女子禁针穴; B. Causing pneumatothorax, hemathorax / 误伤引起气胸，血胸/ Injury to

		heart / 误伤心脏; C. Ancient Forbidden point 古传禁针穴; D. often causing needle-sickness / 容易导致晕针; E. Injury to peroneal nerve, common peroneal nerve / 误伤腓神经, 腓总神经.
3074	B18, Gān Shū, 肝輸	A. Injury to organs / 误伤内脏, causing pneumatothorax / 误伤引起气胸; B. Injury to radial nerve / 误伤桡神经; C. Ancient Forbidden point 古传禁针穴; D. Forbidden point for women 女子禁针穴 E. Injury to peroneal nerve, common peroneal nerve / 误伤腓神经, 腓总神经.
3075	B19, Dǎn Shū, 膽輸	A. Injury to ulnar nerve / 误伤尺神经; B. Ancient Forbidden point 古传禁针穴; C. Injury to organs / 误伤内脏, causing pneumatothorax / 误伤引起气胸; D. often causing needle-sickness / 容易导致晕针; E. often causing hematoma / 容易导致血肿.
3076	B20, Pí Shū, 脾輸	A. Injury to ulnar nerve / 误伤尺神经; B. Injury to median nerve / 误伤正中神经; C. Ancient Forbidden point 古传禁针穴; D. Injury to kidneys / 误伤肾脏, causing pneumatothorax / 误伤引起气胸; E. often causing needle-sickness / 容易导致晕针.
3077	B21, Wèi Shū, 胃俞	A. Injury to ulnar nerve / 误伤尺神经; B. Injury to peroneal nerve, common peroneal nerve / 误伤腓神经, 腓总神经; C. Ancient Forbidden point 古传禁针穴; D. often causing needle-sickness / 容易导致晕针; E. Injury to kidneys / 误伤肾脏, causing pneumatothorax / 误伤引起气胸
3078	B22, Sān Jiāo Shū, 三焦輸	A. Injury to median nerve / 误伤正中神经; B. Injury to kidneys / 误伤肾脏; C. Injury to ulnar nerve / 误伤尺神经; D. Injury to peroneal nerve, common peroneal nerve / 误伤腓神经, 腓总神经; E. Causing pneumatothorax / 误伤引起气胸.
3079	B23, Shèn Shū, 腎輸	A. Causing pneumatothorax / 误伤引起气胸; B. Ancient Forbidden point 古传禁针穴; C. Injury to kidneys / 误伤肾脏; D. often causing needle-sickness / 容易导致晕针; E. Injury to median nerve / 误伤正中神经.
3080	B24, Qì Hǎi Shū, 氣海輸	A. Injury to kidneys / 误伤肾脏; B. Injury to ulnar nerve / 误伤尺神经; C. Forbidden point for women 女子禁针穴; D. Ancient Forbidden point 古传禁针穴 E. Causing pneumatothorax / 误伤引起气胸.
3081	B25, Dà Cháng Shū, 大腸輸	A. Injury to median nerve / 误伤正中神经; B. Injury to ulnar nerve / 误伤尺神经; C. Ancient Forbidden point 古传禁针穴; D. Injury to organs / 误伤内脏; E. Injury to peroneal nerve, common peroneal nerve / 误伤腓神经, 腓总神经.
3082	B26, Guān Yuán Shū, 關元輸	A. Injury to ulnar nerve / 误伤尺神经; B. Ancient Forbidden point 古传禁针穴; C. often causing needle-sickness / 容易导致晕针; D. Injury to peroneal nerve, common peroneal nerve / 误伤腓神经, 腓总神经; E. Injury to organs / 误伤内脏
3083	B27, Xiǎo Cháng Shū, 小腸輸	A. Injury to ulnar nerve / 误伤尺神经; B. Ancient Forbidden point 古传禁针穴; C. often causing needle-sickness / 容易导致晕针; D. Injury to organs / 误伤内脏; E. often causing hematoma /

		容易导致血肿
3084	B36, Chéng Fú, 承扶	A. Ancient Forbidden point 古传禁针穴; B. Injury to sciatic nerve / 误伤坐骨神经; C. often causing needle-sickness / 容易导致晕针; D. Injury to radial nerve / 误伤桡神经; E. Injury to peroneal nerve, common peroneal nerve / 误伤腓神经, 腓总神经.
3085	B41, Fù Fēn, 附分	A. Injury to peroneal nerve, common peroneal nerve / 误伤腓神经, 腓总神经; B. Ancient Forbidden point 古传禁针穴; C. Causing pneumatothorax / 误伤引起气胸; D. Injury to median nerve / 误伤正中神经; E. Injury to ulnar nerve / 误伤尺神经.
3086	B42, Pò Hù, 魄戶	A. Causing pneumatothorax / 误伤引起气胸; B. often causing needle-sickness / 容易导致晕针; C. Ancient Forbidden point 古传禁针穴; D. Forbidden point for women 女子禁针穴 E. Injury to radial nerve / 误伤桡神经.
3087	B43, Gāo Huāng Shū, 膏肓輸	A. Injury to radial nerve / 误伤桡神经; B. Ancient Forbidden point 古传禁针穴; C. often causing needle-sickness / 容易导致晕针; D. Causing pneumatothorax, hemathorax /误伤引起气胸,血胸; E. often causing hematoma / 容易导致血肿.
3088	B44, Shén Táng, 神堂	A. Injury to median nerve / 误伤正中神经; B. Causing pneumatothorax / 误伤引起气胸; C. Ancient Forbidden point 古传禁针穴; D. Injury to peroneal nerve, common peroneal nerve / 误伤腓神经, 腓总神经; E. Injury to ulnar nerve / 误伤尺神经.
3089	B45, Yì Xī, 噫嘻	A. often causing hematoma / 容易导致血肿; B. Causing pneumatothorax/误伤引起气胸/ Injury to heart/误伤心脏; C. Ancient Forbidden point 古传禁针穴; D. Injury to radial nerve / 误伤桡神经; E. Injury to peroneal nerve, common peroneal nerve / 误伤腓神经, 腓总神经.
3090	B46, Gé Guān, 膈關	A. Ancient Forbidden point 古传禁针穴; B. Injury to ulnar nerve / 误伤尺神经; C. often causing hematoma / 容易导致血肿; D. often causing needle-sickness / 容易导致晕针; E. Causing pneumatothorax/误伤引起气胸/ Injury to heart/误伤心脏
3091	B47, Hún Mén, 魂門	A. Causing pneumatothorax / 误伤引起气胸; B. Forbidden point for women 女子禁针穴; C. Ancient Forbidden point 古传禁针穴; D. Injury to median nerve / 误伤正中神经; E. Injury to ulnar nerve / 误伤尺神经.
3092	B48, Yáng Gāng, 陽剛	A. Injury to median nerve / 误伤正中神经; B. Injury to radial nerve / 误伤桡神经; C. Ancient Forbidden point 古传禁针穴; D. often causing needle-sickness / 容易导致晕针; E. Causing pneumatothorax / 误伤引起气胸
3093	B49, Yì Shè, 意舍	A. Causing pneumatothorax/误伤引起气胸/ Injury to kidney/误伤肾脏; B. often causing needle-sickness / 容易导致晕针; C. Injury to peroneal nerve, common peroneal nerve / 误伤腓神经, 腓总神经; D. Injury to radial nerve / 误伤桡神经; E. Ancient Forbidden point 古传禁针穴.
3094	B50, Wèi Cāng, 胃倉	A. Injury to peroneal nerve, common peroneal nerve / 误伤腓神经, 腓总神经; B. Ancient Forbidden point 古传禁针穴; C. Injury

		to kidney/误伤肾脏; D. Injury to intestinal tract, ovary and uterus / 误伤肠道,卵巢及子宫; E. often causing hematoma / 容易导致血肿.
3095	B51, Huāng Mén, 肓門	A. often causing needle-sickness / 容易导致晕针; B. Injury to kidney/误伤肾脏; C. Injury to radial nerve / 误伤桡神经; D. Ancient Forbidden point 古传禁针穴; E. often causing hematoma / 容易导致血肿.
3096	B52, Zhì Shì, 志室	A. Injury to intestinal tract, bladder, ovary and uterus /误伤肠道, 膀胱, 卵巢及子宫; B. Causing pneumatothorax / 误伤引起气胸; C. Ancient Forbidden point 古传禁针穴; D. Injury to kidney/ 误伤肾脏; E. often causing needle-sickness / 容易导致晕针.
3097	B54, Zhì Biān, 秩邊	A. Injury to sciatic nerve，superior gluteal artery / 误伤坐骨神经, 臀上动脉; B. Ancient Forbidden point 古传禁针穴; C. often causing needle-sickness / 容易导致晕针; D. Injury to median nerve / 误伤正中神经; E. often causing hematoma / 容易导致血肿.
3098	B56, Chéng Jīn, 承筋	A. Injury to ulnar nerve / 误伤尺神经; B. Ancient Forbidden point 古传禁针穴; C. often causing needle-sickness / 容易导致晕针; D. often causing hematoma / 容易导致血肿; E. Injury to peroneal nerve, common peroneal nerve / 误伤腓神经, 腓总神经 Causing pneumatothorax / 误伤引起气胸.
3099	B60, Kūn Lún, 昆崙	A. Injury to radial nerve / 误伤桡神经; B. Injury to median nerve / 误伤正中神经; C. Ancient Forbidden point 古传禁针穴; D. Forbidden point during pregnancy 孕妇禁针穴; E. Injury to peroneal nerve, common peroneal nerve / 误伤腓神经, 腓总神经.
3100	B67, Zhì Yīn, 至陰	A. Injury to median nerve / 误伤正中神经; B. Causing pneumatothorax / 误伤引起气胸; C. often causing needle-sickness / 容易导致晕针; D. Ancient Forbidden point 古传禁针穴; E. Forbidden point during pregnancy 孕妇禁针穴
3101	D4, Mìng Mén, 命門	A. Injury to radial nerve / 误伤桡神经; B. Injury to peroneal nerve, common peroneal nerve / 误伤腓神经, 腓总神经; C. Injury to organs / 误伤内脏; D. Injury to median nerve / 误伤正中神经; E. Ancient Forbidden point 古传禁针穴.
3102	D5, Xuán Shū, 懸樞	A. Ancient Forbidden point 古传禁针穴; B. Injury to radial nerve / 误伤桡神经; C. often causing needle-sickness / 容易导致晕针; D. Injury to peroneal nerve, common peroneal nerve / 误伤腓神经, 腓总神经; E. Injury to organs / 误伤内脏
3103	D6, Jǐ Zhōng, 脊中	A. Injury to organs, spinal cord /误伤内脏, 脊髓; B. Injury to radial nerve / 误伤桡神经; C. Injury to median nerve / 误伤正中神经; D. Ancient Forbidden point 古传禁针穴; E. Causing pneumatothorax / 误伤引起气胸.
3104	D7, Zhōng Shū, 中樞	A. Injury to ulnar nerve / 误伤尺神经; B. Injury to organs, spinal cord /误伤内脏, 脊髓; C. Ancient Forbidden point 古传禁针穴; D. Injury to median nerve / 误伤正中神经; E. Injury to peroneal nerve, common peroneal nerve / 误伤腓神经, 腓总神经.

3105	D8, Jīn Suō, 筋縮	A. Injury to peroneal nerve, common peroneal nerve / 误伤腓神经，腓总神经; B. Injury to organs, spinal cord /误伤内脏，脊髓; C. Injury to median nerve / 误伤正中神经; D. Ancient Forbidden point 古传禁针穴; E. Injury to radial nerve / 误伤桡神经.
3106	D9, Zhì Yáng, 至陽	A. Injury to organs, spinal cord / 误伤内脏，脊髓; B. Causing pneumatothorax / 误伤引起气胸; C. Injury to peroneal nerve, common peroneal nerve / 误伤腓神经，腓总神经; D. Injury to median nerve / 误伤正中神经; E. Injury to ulnar nerve / 误伤尺神经.
3107	D10, Líng Tái, 靈台	A. Injury to gastric wall, bleeding or gastric perforation / 误伤胃壁， 出血， 胃穿孔; B. Causing pneumatothorax / 误伤引起气胸; C. Forbidden point during pregnancy 孕妇禁针穴; D. Traditional Forbidden point 传统禁针穴/ Injury to spinal cord / 误伤脊髓; E. often causing needle-sickness / 容易导致晕针.
3108	D11, Shén Dào, 神道	A. Forbidden point during pregnancy 孕妇禁针穴; B. Ancient Forbidden point 古传禁针穴; C. often causing needle-sickness / 容易导致晕针; D. often causing hematoma / 容易导致血肿; E. Causing pneumatothorax / 误伤引起气胸.
3109	D12, Shēn Zhù, 身柱	A. Injury to peroneal nerve, common peroneal nerve / 误伤腓神经，腓总神经; B. Ancient Forbidden point 古传禁针穴; C. often causing needle-sickness / 容易导致晕针; D. often causing hematoma / 容易导致血肿; E. Injury to spinal cord /误伤脊髓
3110	D13, Táo Dào, 陶道	A. Injury to radial nerve / 误伤桡神经; B. Ancient Forbidden point 古传禁针穴; C. often causing needle-sickness / 容易导致晕针; D. Injury to spinal cord ， arachnoid / 误伤脊髓，蛛网膜; E. Causing pneumatothorax / 误伤引起气胸.
3111	D14, Dà Zhuī 大椎	A. Injury to median nerve / 误伤正中神经; B. Causing pneumatothorax / 误伤引起气胸; C. often causing needle-sickness / 容易导致晕针; D. Ancient Forbidden point 古传禁针穴; E. Injury to spinal cord / 误伤脊髓
3112	D15, Yǎ Mén 啞門	A. Injury to medullary bulb, arachnoid / 误伤延髓，蛛网膜; B. Injury to ulnar nerve / 误伤尺神经; C. Injury to median nerve / 误伤正中神经; D. Injury to peroneal nerve, common peroneal nerve / 误伤腓神经，腓总神经; E. Causing pneumatothorax / 误伤引起气胸.
3113	D16, Fēng Fǔ 風府	A. Causing pneumatothorax / 误伤引起气胸; B. Injury to medullary bulb/误伤延髓/ Causing pneumatothorax/误伤引起气胸; C. Injury to peroneal nerve, common peroneal nerve / 误伤腓神经，腓总神经; D. Ancient Forbidden point 古传禁针穴; E. often causing needle-sickness / 容易导致晕针.
3114	D17, Nǎo Hù 腦戶	A. Causing pneumatothorax / 误伤引起气胸; B. Ancient Forbidden point 古传禁针穴; C. Injury to ulnar nerve / 误伤尺神经; D. Injury to median nerve / 误伤正中神经; E. Injury to peroneal nerve, common peroneal nerve / 误伤腓神经，腓总神经.
3115	D20, Bǎi Huì 百	A. Injury to brain / 误伤脑; B. Causing pneumatothorax / 误伤

	會	引起气胸; C. Injury to radial nerve / 误伤桡神经; D. Forbidden point for women 女子禁针穴; E. Injury to median nerve / 误伤正中神经.
3116	D22, Xìn Huì 囟會	A. Causing pneumatothorax / 误伤引起气胸; B. often causing hematoma / 容易导致血肿; C. Forbidden point during pregnancy 孕妇禁针穴; D. often causing needle-sickness / 容易导致晕针; E. Ancient Forbidden point 古传禁针穴
3117	D24, Shén Tíng 神庭	A. often causing needle-sickness / 容易导致晕针; B. often causing hematoma / 容易导致血肿; C. Ancient Forbidden point 古传禁针穴; D. Forbidden point during pregnancy 孕妇禁针穴; E. Causing pneumatothorax / 误伤引起气胸.
3118	G18, Chéng Líng 承靈	A. Injury to peroneal nerve, common peroneal nerve / 误伤腓神经，腓总神经; B. Injury to median nerve / 误伤正中神经; C. Ancient Forbidden point 古传禁针穴; D. Injury to ulnar nerve / 误伤尺神经; E. Causing pneumatothorax / 误伤引起气胸.
3119	G20, Fēng Chí 風池	A. Injury to median nerve / 误伤正中神经; B. Injury to gastric wall, bleeding or gastric perforation / 误伤胃壁， 出血， 胃穿孔; C. Injury to medullary bulb / 误伤延髓 / 脑出血; D. Ancient Forbidden point 古传禁针穴; E. Injury to median nerve / 误伤正中神经
3120	G21, Jiān Jǐng 肩井	A. Injury to peroneal nerve, common peroneal nerve / 误伤腓神经，腓总神经; B. Causing pneumatothorax, hemathorax / 误伤引起气胸,血胸; C. often causing hematoma / 容易导致血肿; D. often causing needle-sickness / 容易导致晕针; E. Injury to median nerve / 误伤正中神经.
3121	G22, Yuān Yè 淵液	A. Ancient Forbidden point 古传禁针穴; B. Causing hemathorax/ 误伤引起血胸; C. Injury to kidneys / 误伤肾脏; D. often causing needle-sickness / 容易导致晕针; E. Injury to median nerve / 误伤正中神经.
3122	G23, Zhé Jīn 輒筋	A. Injury to peroneal nerve, common peroneal nerve / 误伤腓神经，腓总神经; B. Ancient Forbidden point 古传禁针穴; C. Causing pneumatothorax, hemathorax /误伤引起气胸，血胸; D. Injury to intestinal tract, ovary and uterus / 误伤肠道,卵巢及子宫; E. often causing hematoma / 容易导致血肿.
3123	G24, Rì Yuè 日月	A. Injury to median nerve / 误伤正中神经; B. Injury to intestinal tract, bladder, ovary and uterus /误伤肠道，膀胱，卵巢及子宫/causing hemathorax/误伤引起血胸/ 误伤肠道; C. Injury to gastric wall, bleeding or gastric perforation / 误伤胃壁， 出血， 胃穿孔; D. Ancient Forbidden point 古传禁针穴; E. Injury to peroneal nerve, common peroneal nerve / 误伤腓神经，腓总神经.
3124	G25, Jīng Mén 京門	A. Injury to ulnar nerve / 误伤尺神经; B. Ancient Forbidden point 古传禁针穴; C. Injury to spleen, kidneys / 误伤脾，肾脏; D. often causing needle-sickness / 容易导致晕针; E. Injury to peroneal nerve, common peroneal nerve / 误伤腓神经，腓总神经.
3125	G26, Dài Mài 帶	A. Injury to ulnar nerve / 误伤尺神经; B. Injury to gastric wall,

	脈	bleeding or gastric perforation / 误伤胃壁，出血，胃穿孔; C. Injury to intestinal tract / 误伤肠道; D. Injury to peroneal nerve, common peroneal nerve / 误伤腓神经，腓总神经; E. Causing pneumatothorax / 误伤引起气胸.
3126	G27, Wǔ Shū 五樞	A. Injury to intestinal tract / 误伤肠道; B. Causing pneumatothorax / 误伤引起气胸; C. Injury to radial nerve / 误伤桡神经; D. Ancient Forbidden point 古传禁针穴; E. Injury to median nerve / 误伤正中神经.
3127	G28, Wéi Dào 維道	A. Ancient Forbidden point 古传禁针穴; B. Injury to ulnar nerve / 误伤尺神经; C. Injury to gastric wall, bleeding or gastric perforation / 误伤胃壁，出血，胃穿孔; D. Causing pneumatothorax / 误伤引起气胸; E. Injury to intestinal tract / 误伤肠道
3128	G30, Huán Tiào 環跳	A. often causing needle-sickness / 容易导致晕针; B. often causing hematoma / 容易导致血肿; C. Injury to radial nerve / 误伤桡神经; D. Injury to ulnar nerve / 误伤尺神经; E. Injury to sciatic nerve， superior gluteal artery / 误伤坐骨神经，臀上动脉。
3129	G34, Yáng Líng Quán 陽陵泉	A. often causing hematoma / 容易导致血肿; B. Injury to ulnar nerve / 误伤尺神经; C. Ancient Forbidden point 古传禁针穴; D. Injury to peroneal nerve, common peroneal nerve / 误伤腓神经，腓总神经; E. often causing needle-sickness / 容易导致晕针.
3130	H1, Jí Quán 極泉	A. Injury to peroneal nerve, common peroneal nerve / 误伤腓神经，腓总神经; B. Injury to median nerve / 误伤正中神经; C. often causing needle-sickness / 容易导致晕针; D. Injury to ulnar nerve / 误伤尺神经; E. Ancient Forbidden point 古传禁针穴.
3131	H2, Qīng Líng 青靈	A. Injury to median nerve / 误伤正中神经; B. Injury to peroneal nerve, common peroneal nerve / 误伤腓神经，腓总神经; C. Causing pneumatothorax / 误伤引起气胸; D. Forbidden point during pregnancy 孕妇禁针穴; E. Ancient Forbidden point 古传禁针穴 / Injury to ulnar nerve / 误伤尺神经
3132	H4, Líng Dào 靈道	A. Injury to peroneal nerve, common peroneal nerve / 误伤腓神经，腓总神经; B. Ancient Forbidden point 古传禁针穴; C. often causing hematoma / 容易导致血肿; D. often causing needle-sickness / 容易导致晕针; E. Injury to ulnar nerve / 误伤尺神经
3133	H5, Tōng Lǐ 通里	A. Injury to median nerve / 误伤正中神经; B. Ancient Forbidden point 古传禁针穴; C. Injury to ulnar nerve / 误伤尺神经; D. often causing needle-sickness / 容易导致晕针; E. Causing pneumatothorax / 误伤引起气胸.
3134	H6, Yīn Xī 陰郗	A. Injury to ulnar nerve / 误伤尺神经; B. Ancient Forbidden point 古传禁针穴; C. often causing needle-sickness / 容易导致晕针; D. often causing hematoma / 容易导致血肿; E. Causing pneumatothorax / 误伤引起气胸.
3135	H7, Shén Mén 神門	A. Ancient Forbidden point 古传禁针穴; B. Injury to ulnar nerve / 误伤尺神经; C. Causing pneumatothorax / 误伤引起气

		胸; D. often causing needle-sickness / 容易导致晕针; E. Injury to peroneal nerve, common peroneal nerve / 误伤腓神经，腓总神经.
3136	K11, Héng Gŭ 横骨	A. Injury to peroneal nerve, common peroneal nerve / 误伤腓神经，腓总神经; B. Causing pneumatothorax / 误伤引起气胸; C. often causing needle-sickness / 容易导致晕针; D. Traditional Forbidden point 传统禁针穴/ Injury to bladder/误伤膀胱; E. often causing hematoma / 容易导致血肿.
3137	K12, Dà Hè 大赫	A. Injury to intestinal tract, bladder, ovary and uterus /误伤肠道，膀胱，卵巢及子宫; B. Causing pneumatothorax / 误伤引起气胸; C. Ancient Forbidden point 古传禁针穴; D. often causing needle-sickness / 容易导致晕针; E. often causing hematoma / 容易导致血肿.
3138	K13, Qì Xué 氣穴	A. Injury to intestinal tract, bladder, ovary and uterus / 误伤肠道，膀胱，卵巢及子宫; B. Injury to radial nerve / 误伤桡神经; C. often causing needle-sickness / 容易导致晕针; D. Causing pneumatothorax / 误伤引起气胸; E. Ancient Forbidden point 古传禁针穴.
3139	K14, Sì Măn 四滿	A. Injury to intestinal tract, ovary and uterus / 误伤肠道,卵巢及子宫; B. Ancient Forbidden point 古传禁针穴; C. often causing needle-sickness / 容易导致晕针; D. Forbidden point for women 女子禁针穴; E. Causing pneumatothorax / 误伤引起气胸.
3140	K15, Zhōng Zhù 中注	A. Injury to peroneal nerve, common peroneal nerve / 误伤腓神经，腓总神经; B. Injury to gastric wall, bleeding or gastric perforation / 误伤胃壁， 出血， 胃穿孔; C. Ancient Forbidden point 古传禁针穴; D. Injury to ulnar nerve / 误伤尺神经; E. Injury to intestinal tract, ovary and uterus / 误伤肠道,卵巢及子宫
3141	K16, Huāng Shū 肓輸	A. often causing hematoma / 容易导致血肿; B. Ancient Forbidden point 古传禁针穴; C. often causing needle-sickness / 容易导致晕针; D. Injury to intestinal tract / 误伤肠道; E. Injury to radial nerve / 误伤桡神经.
3142	K17, Shāng Qŭ 商曲	A. Injury to peroneal nerve, common peroneal nerve / 误伤腓神经，腓总神经; B. Injury to median nerve / 误伤正中神经; C. Injury to intestinal tract, liver / 误伤肠道，肝脏; D. Injury to gastric wall, bleeding or gastric perforation / 误伤胃壁， 出血，胃穿孔; E. Injury to ulnar nerve / 误伤尺神经.
3143	K18, Shí Guān 石關	A. Injury to ulnar nerve / 误伤尺神经; B. Causing pneumatothorax / 误伤引起气胸; C. Injury to gastric wall, bleeding or gastric perforation / 误伤胃壁， 出血， 胃穿孔; D. Injury to intestinal tract, stomach, liver / 误伤肠道，胃脏，肝脏; E. Injury to peroneal nerve, common peroneal nerve / 误伤腓神经，腓总神经.
3144	K19, Yīn Dū 陰都	A. Injury to median nerve / 误伤正中神经; B. Injury to gastric wall, bleeding or gastric perforation，intestinal tract /误伤胃壁，出血， 胃穿孔，肠道 / Injury to liver / 误伤肝脏; C. Injury to

		radial nerve / 误伤桡神经; D. Injury to peroneal nerve, common peroneal nerve / 误伤腓神经，腓总神经; E. Causing pneumatothorax / 误伤引起气胸.
3145	K20, Fù Tōng Gǔ, Tōng Gǔ 腹通谷	A. Injury to gastric wall, bleeding or gastric perforation / 误伤胃壁，出血，胃穿孔 / Injury to liver, intestinal tract/误伤肝脏，肠道; B. Injury to median nerve / 误伤正中神经; C. Causing pneumatothorax / 误伤引起气胸; D. Forbidden point for women 女子禁针穴; E. Injury to ulnar nerve / 误伤尺神经.
3146	K21, Yōu Mén 幽門	A. Injury to peroneal nerve, common peroneal nerve / 误伤腓神经，腓总神经; B. Injury to median nerve / 误伤正中神经; C. Ancient Forbidden point 古传禁针穴; D. Injury to gastric wall, bleeding or gastric perforation/误伤胃壁，出血，胃穿孔 / Injury to liver / 误伤肝脏; E. Injury to ulnar nerve / 误伤尺神经.
3147	K22, Bù Láng 步廊	A. Injury to intestinal tract, bladder, ovary and uterus /误伤肠道，膀胱，卵巢及子宫; B. Causing pneumatothorax / 误伤引起气胸; C. Ancient Forbidden point 古传禁针穴; D. Causing hemathorax/误伤引起血胸/ Injury to heart/误伤心脏; E. often causing needle-sickness / 容易导致晕针.
3148	K23, Shén Fēng 神封	A. Causing pneumatothorax/误伤引起气胸/ hemathorax/误伤引起血胸/ Injury to heart/误伤心脏; B. Injury to median nerve / 误伤正中神经; C. Injury to gastric wall, bleeding or gastric perforation / 误伤胃壁，出血，胃穿孔; D. Ancient Forbidden point 古传禁针穴; E. Injury to intestinal tract / 误伤肠道.
3149	K24, Líng Xū 靈墟	A. often causing hematoma / 容易导致血肿; B. Injury to peroneal nerve, common peroneal nerve / 误伤腓神经，腓总神经; C. Ancient Forbidden point 古传禁针穴; D. often causing needle-sickness / 容易导致晕针; E. Causing hemathorax/误伤引起血胸/ Injury to heart/误伤心脏
3150	K25, Shén Cáng 神藏	A. often causing hematoma / 容易导致血肿; B. Injury to peroneal nerve, common peroneal nerve / 误伤腓神经，腓总神经; C. Ancient Forbidden point 古传禁针穴; D. often causing needle-sickness / 容易导致晕针; E. Causing pneumatothorax, hemathorax /误伤引起气胸，血胸/ Injury to heart/误伤心脏
3151	K26, Yù Zhōng 彧中	A. Causing hemathorax/误伤引起血胸; B. Injury to median nerve / 误伤正中神经; C. Injury to gastric wall, bleeding or gastric perforation / 误伤胃壁，出血，胃穿孔; D. Ancient Forbidden point 古传禁针穴; E. Injury to intestinal tract / 误伤肠道.
3152	K27, Shū Fǔ 俞府	A. Injury to median nerve / 误伤正中神经;B. Causing pneumatothorax, hemathorax /误伤引起气胸，血胸; C. Injury to radial nerve / 误伤桡神经; D. Ancient Forbidden point 古传禁针穴; E. often causing hematoma / 容易导致血肿.
3153	Li4, Hé Gǔ 合谷	A. Injury to median nerve / 误伤正中神经; B. Forbidden point during pregnancy 孕妇禁针穴 / Injury to radial nerve，vagus nerve / 误伤桡神经，迷走神经 / Injury to hand/误伤手部; C. Ancient Forbidden point 古传禁针穴; D. often causing needle-sickness / 容易导致晕针; E. Causing pneumatothorax / 误伤引起气胸.
3154	Li5, Yáng Xī 陽	A. Ancient Forbidden point 古传禁针穴; B. Injury to radial

	溪	nerve / 误伤桡神经; C. often causing needle-sickness / 容易导致晕针; D. Causing pneumatothorax / 误伤引起气胸; E. often causing hematoma / 容易导致血肿.
3155	Li6, Piān Lì 偏歷	A. Injury to radial nerve / 误伤桡神经; B. Injury to peroneal nerve, common peroneal nerve / 误伤腓神经, 腓总神经; C. often causing needle-sickness / 容易导致晕针; D. often causing hematoma / 容易导致血肿; E. Ancient Forbidden point 古传禁针穴.
3156	Li7, Wēn Liū 溫溜	A. Injury to radial nerve / 误伤桡神经; B. Causing pneumatothorax / 误伤引起气胸; C. Injury to peroneal nerve, common peroneal nerve / 误伤腓神经, 腓总神经; D. Ancient Forbidden point 古传禁针穴; E. Injury to median nerve / 误伤正中神经.
3157	Li10, Shǒu Sān Lǐ 手三里	A. Injury to median nerve / 误伤正中神经; B. often causing needle-sickness / 容易导致晕针; C. Injury to radial nerve / 误伤桡神经; D. Ancient Forbidden point 古传禁针穴; E. Injury to peroneal nerve, common peroneal nerve / 误伤腓神经, 腓总神经.
3158	Li11, Qū Chí 曲池	A. Ancient Forbidden point 古传禁针穴; B. Injury to radial nerve / 误伤桡神经; C. often causing needle-sickness / 容易导致晕针; D. often causing hematoma / 容易导致血肿; E. Injury to peroneal nerve, common peroneal nerve / 误伤腓神经, 腓总神经.
3159	Li13, Shǒu Wǔ Lǐ 手五里	A. Causing pneumatothorax / 误伤引起气胸; B. often causing needle-sickness / 容易导致晕针; C. Injury to radial nerve / 误伤桡神经; D. Ancient Forbidden point 古传禁针穴; E. Forbidden point during pregnancy 孕妇禁针穴.
3160	Lu1, Zhōng Fǔ 中府	A. Injury to ulnar nerve / 误伤尺神经; B. Ancient Forbidden point 古传禁针穴; C. Causing pneumatothorax, hemathorax / 误伤引起气胸, 血胸; D. often causing needle-sickness / 容易导致晕针; E. Injury to gastric wall, bleeding or gastric perforation / 误伤胃壁, 出血, 胃穿孔.
3161	Lu2, Yún Mén 云門	A. Injury to peroneal nerve, common peroneal nerve / 误伤腓神经, 腓总神经; B. Ancient Forbidden point 古传禁针穴; C. Causing hemathorax/误伤引起血胸; D. Injury to intestinal tract, ovary and uterus / 误伤肠道,卵巢及子宫; E. often causing hematoma / 容易导致血肿.
3162	Lu5, Chǐ Zé 尺澤	A. Injury to radial nerve / 误伤桡神经; B. Ancient Forbidden point 古传禁针穴; C. often causing hematoma / 容易导致血肿; D. Injury to peroneal nerve, common peroneal nerve / 误伤腓神经, 腓总神经; E. Causing pneumatothorax / 误伤引起气胸.
3163	Lu6, Kǒng Zuì 孔最	A. Injury to median nerve / 误伤正中神经; B. Causing pneumatothorax / 误伤引起气胸; C. Ancient Forbidden point 古传禁针穴; D. Injury to radial nerve / 误伤桡神经; E. often causing needle-sickness / 容易导致晕针
3164	Lu7, Liè Quē 列缺	A. often causing hematoma / 容易导致血肿; B. Causing pneumatothorax / 误伤引起气胸; C. often causing

		needle-sickness / 容易导致晕针; D. Ancient Forbidden point 古传禁针穴; E. Injury to radial nerve / 误伤桡神经
3165	Lu8, Jīng Qú 經渠	A. Injury to peroneal nerve, common peroneal nerve / 误伤腓神经，腓总神经; B. often causing needle-sickness / 容易导致晕针; C. Injury to radial nerve / 误伤桡神经; D. often causing hematoma / 容易导致血肿; E. Ancient Forbidden point 古传禁针穴.
3166	Lu9, Tài Yuān 太淵	A. Ancient Forbidden point 古传禁针穴; B. Injury to median nerve / 误伤正中神经; C. often causing needle-sickness / 容易导致晕针; D. Injury to radial nerve / 误伤桡神经; E. often causing hematoma / 容易导致血肿.
3167	Lu10, Yǔ Jì 魚際	A. Injury to median nerve / 误伤正中神经; B. Causing pneumatothorax / 误伤引起气胸; C. Injury to radial nerve / 误伤桡神经; D. Ancient Forbidden point 古传禁针穴; E. often causing hematoma / 容易导致血肿.
3168	Lv12, Jí Mài 急脈	A. Ancient Forbidden point 古传禁针穴; B. Injury to ulnar nerve / 误伤尺神经; C. Injury to median nerve / 误伤正中神经; D. often causing hematoma / 容易导致血肿; E. Injury to peroneal nerve, common peroneal nerve / 误伤腓神经，腓总神经.
3169	Lv13, Zhāng Mén 章門	A. Injury to spleen， intestinal tract, liver / 误伤脾， 肠道, 肝脏/ hemathorax / 误伤引起血胸; B. Injury to ulnar nerve / 误伤尺神经; C. often causing hematoma / 容易导致血肿; D. Ancient Forbidden point 古传禁针穴; E. Causing pneumatothorax / 误伤引起气胸.
3170	Lv14, Qí Mén 期門	A. Injury to peroneal nerve, common peroneal nerve / 误伤腓神经，腓总神经; B. Forbidden point for women 女子禁针穴; C. Injury to gastric wall, bleeding or gastric perforation / 误伤胃壁， 出血， 胃穿孔; D. Injury to radial nerve / 误伤桡神经; E. Injury to Aorta， intestinal tract, liver, gallbladder /误伤主动脉， 肠道, 肝脏, 胆囊 / hemathorax / 误伤引起血胸
3171	P1, Tiān Chí 天池	A. Injury to peroneal nerve, common peroneal nerve / 误伤腓神经，腓总神经; B. Ancient Forbidden point 古传禁针穴; C. Causing hemathorax/误伤引起血胸; D. Injury to intestinal tract, ovary and uterus / 误伤肠道,卵巢及子宫; E. often causing hematoma / 容易导致血肿..
3172	P3, Qū Zé 曲澤	A. often causing needle-sickness / 容易导致晕针; B. Injury to radial nerve / 误伤桡神经; C. Injury to peroneal nerve, common peroneal nerve / 误伤腓神经，腓总神经; D. Injury to median nerve / 误伤正中神经; E. Causing pneumatothorax / 误伤引起气胸.
3173	P4, Xī Mén 郄門	A. Injury to radial nerve / 误伤桡神经; B. Causing pneumatothorax / 误伤引起气胸; C. Injury to peroneal nerve, common peroneal nerve / 误伤腓神经，腓总神经; D. Ancient Forbidden point 古传禁针穴; E. Injury to median nerve / 误伤正中神经。
3174	P5, Jiān Shǐ 間	A. Injury to radial nerve / 误伤桡神经; B. Ancient Forbidden

	使	point 古传禁针穴; C. Injury to median nerve / 误伤正中神经; D. often causing needle-sickness / 容易导致晕针; E. Causing pneumatothorax / 误伤引起气胸.。
3175	P6, Nèi Guān 內關	A. Ancient Forbidden point 古传禁针穴; B. often causing hematoma / 容易导致血肿; C. Injury to vagus nerve reaction, median nerve / 误伤迷走神经反应， 正中神经损伤; D. Injury to radial nerve / 误伤桡神经; E. often causing needle-sickness / 容易导致晕针.
3176	P7, Dà Líng 大陵	A. Injury to peroneal nerve, common peroneal nerve / 误伤腓神经，腓总神经; B. Injury to median nerve / 误伤正中神经; C. Ancient Forbidden point 古传禁针穴; D. often causing needle-sickness / 容易导致晕针; E. Injury to radial nerve / 误伤桡神经.
3177	R1, Huì Yīn 會陰	A. Forbidden point for women 女子禁针穴; B. Forbidden point during pregnancy 孕妇禁针穴; C. Causing pneumatothorax / 误伤引起气胸; D. Injury to radial nerve / 误伤桡神经; E. Ancient Forbidden point 古传禁针穴
3178	R2, Qū Gǔ 曲骨	A. often causing hematoma / 容易导致血肿; B. Injury to peroneal nerve, common peroneal nerve / 误伤腓神经，腓总神经; C. Ancient Forbidden point 古传禁针穴;D. Injury to bladder/误伤膀胱; E. often causing needle-sickness / 容易导致晕针.
3179	R3, Zhōng Jí 中極	A. Ancient Forbidden point 古传禁针穴; B. Injury to radial nerve / 误伤桡神经; C. Causing pneumatothorax / 误伤引起气胸; D. Injury to intestinal tract, bladder, ovary and uterus / 误伤肠道，膀胱，卵巢及子宫; E. Injury to gastric wall, bleeding or gastric perforation / 误伤胃壁， 出血， 胃穿孔.
3180	R4, Guān Yuán 關元	A. Injury to intestinal tract, bladder, ovary and uterus / 误伤肠道，膀胱，卵巢及子宫; B. Ancient Forbidden point 古传禁针穴; C. often causing needle-sickness / 容易导致晕针; D. often causing hematoma / 容易导致血肿; E. Causing pneumatothorax / 误伤引起气胸.
3181	R5, Shí Mén 石門	A. Injury to median nerve / 误伤正中神经; B. Injury to ulnar nerve / 误伤尺神经; C. Causing pneumatothorax / 误伤引起气胸; D. Forbidden point for women 女子禁针穴。Injury to intestinal tract, ovary and uterus / 误伤肠道，卵巢及子宫; E. Forbidden point during pregnancy 孕妇禁针穴.
3182	R6, Qì Hǎi 氣海	A. Injury to peroneal nerve, common peroneal nerve / 误伤腓神经，腓总神经; B. Injury to gastric wall, bleeding or gastric perforation / 误伤胃壁， 出血， 胃穿孔; C. Ancient Forbidden point 古传禁针穴; D. Injury to radial nerve / 误伤桡神经; E. Injury to intestinal tract, ovary and uterus / 误伤肠道，卵巢及子宫
3183	R7, Yīn Jiāo 陰交	A. Injury to ulnar nerve / 误伤尺神经; B. Injury to gastric wall, bleeding or gastric perforation / 误伤胃壁， 出血， 胃穿孔; C. Injury to intestinal tract / 误伤肠道; D. Ancient Forbidden point 古传禁针穴; E. often causing hematoma / 容易导致血肿.
3184	R8, Shén Què	A. Injury to gastric wall, bleeding or gastric perforation / 误伤

	神闕	胃壁， 出血， 胃穿孔; B. often causing needle-sickness / 容易导致晕针; C. Ancient Forbidden point 古传禁针穴 / Injury to intestinal tract / 误伤肠道; D. Forbidden point during pregnancy 孕妇禁针穴; E. Ancient Forbidden point 古传禁针穴.
3185	R9, Shuǐ Fēn 水分	A. Injury to peroneal nerve, common peroneal nerve / 误伤腓神经, 腓总神经; B. Injury to gastric wall, bleeding or gastric perforation / 误伤胃壁， 出血， 胃穿孔; C. often causing needle-sickness / 容易导致晕针; D. Ancient Forbidden point 古传禁针穴 / Injury to intestinal tract / 误伤肠道; E. Forbidden point during pregnancy 孕妇禁针穴.
3186	R10, Xià Wǎn 下脘	A. Causing pneumatothorax / 误伤引起气胸; B. Injury to intestinal tract, stomach, liver / 误伤肠道, 胃脏, 肝脏; C. Injury to peroneal nerve, common peroneal nerve / 误伤腓神经, 腓总神经; D. Injury to gastric wall, bleeding or gastric perforation / 误伤胃壁， 出血， 胃穿孔; E. Injury to radial nerve / 误伤桡神经.
3187	R11, Jiàn Lǐ 建里	A. Injury to gastric wall, bleeding or gastric perforation, intestinal tract / 误伤胃壁， 出血， 胃穿孔， 肠道 / Injury to liver / 误伤肝脏; B. Ancient Forbidden point 古传禁针穴; C. often causing needle-sickness / 容易导致晕针; D. Injury to ulnar nerve / 误伤尺神经; E. Causing pneumatothorax / 误伤引起气胸.
3188	R12, Zhōng Wǎn 中脘	A. Injury to ulnar nerve / 误伤尺神经; B. Ancient Forbidden point 古传禁针穴; C. often causing needle-sickness / 容易导致晕针; D. Injury to gastric wall, bleeding or gastric perforation, intestinal tract / 误伤胃壁， 出血， 胃穿孔， 肠道 / Injury to liver / 误伤肝脏; E. Injury to peroneal nerve, common peroneal nerve / 误伤腓神经, 腓总神经.
3189	R13, Shàng Wǎn 上脘	A. Causing pneumatothorax / 误伤引起气胸; B. Forbidden point for women 女子禁针穴; C. Injury to gastric wall, bleeding or gastric perforation / 误伤胃壁， 出血， 胃穿孔 / Injury to liver/ 误伤肝脏; D. Ancient Forbidden point 古传禁针穴; E. Injury to peroneal nerve, common peroneal nerve / 误伤腓神经, 腓总神经.
3190	R14, Jù Què 巨闕	A. Injury to ulnar nerve / 误伤尺神经; B. Injury to gastric wall, bleeding or gastric perforation / 误伤胃壁， 出血， 胃穿孔 / Injury to liver/误伤肝脏; C. Ancient Forbidden point 古传禁针穴; D. Injury to median nerve / 误伤正中神经; E. Injury to peroneal nerve, common peroneal nerve / 误伤腓神经, 腓总神经.
3191	R15, Jiū Wěi 鳩尾	A. Injury to heart, liver /误伤心脏, 肝脏; B. Ancient Forbidden point 古传禁针穴; C. often causing needle-sickness / 容易导致晕针; D. often causing hematoma / 容易导致血肿; E. Injury to radial nerve / 误伤桡神经.
3192	R17, Shān Zhōng 膻中	A. Ancient Forbidden point 古传禁针穴; B. Forbidden point for women 女子禁针穴; C. often causing needle-sickness / 容易导致晕针; D. Causing pneumatothorax / 误伤引起气胸; E. often causing hematoma / 容易导致血肿.

3193	R22, Tiān Tū 天突	A. Ancient Forbidden point 古传禁针穴; B. often causing hematoma / 容易导致血肿; C. often causing needle-sickness / 容易导致晕针; D. Causing pneumatothorax / 误伤引起气胸; E. Injury to ulnar nerve / 误伤尺神经.
3194	S1, Chéng Qì 承泣	A. Forbidden point for women 女子禁针穴; B. Ancient Forbidden point 古传禁针穴 / Injury to eye / 误伤眼睛; C. Injury to radial nerve / 误伤桡神经; D. Injury to median nerve / 误伤正中神经; E. Forbidden point during pregnancy 孕妇禁针穴.
3195	S2, Sì Bái 四白	A. Injury to peroneal nerve, common peroneal nerve / 误伤腓神经, 腓总神经; B. Ancient Forbidden point 古传禁针穴; C. often causing needle-sickness / 容易导致晕针; D. often causing hematoma / 容易导致血肿; E. Injury to eye/误伤眼睛
3196	S6, Jiá Chē 頰車	A. Injury to vagus nerve / 误伤迷走神经; B. Injury to radial nerve / 误伤桡神经; C. Injury to peroneal nerve, common peroneal nerve / 误伤腓神经, 腓总神经; D. Ancient Forbidden point 古传禁针穴; E. Causing pneumatothorax / 误伤引起气胸.
3197	S7, Xià Guan 下關	A. Injury to mandibular branch of the trigeminus nerve (the third branch of the trigeminal nerve) / 误伤下頜神經; B. Causing pneumatothorax / 误伤引起气胸; C. Ancient Forbidden point 古传禁针穴; D. Injury to peroneal nerve, common peroneal nerve / 误伤腓神经, 腓总神经; E. Injury to radial nerve / 误伤桡神经.
3198	S9, Rén Yíng 人迎	A. Ancient Forbidden point 古传禁针穴; B. often causing needle-sickness / 容易导致晕针; C. often causing hematoma / 容易导致血肿; D. Injury to vagus nerve reaction / 误伤迷走神经反应; E. Injury to radial nerve / 误伤桡神经.
3199	S12, Quē Pén 缺盆	A. Forbidden point during pregnancy 孕妇禁针穴 / deep insertion may cause cough and panting / Causing pneumatothorax, hemathorax / 误伤引起气胸,血胸; B. Ancient Forbidden point 古传禁针穴; C. Injury to median nerve / 误伤正中神经; D. Injury to peroneal nerve, common peroneal nerve / 误伤腓神经, 腓总神经; E. Injury to radial nerve / 误伤桡神经.
3200	S13, Qì Hù 氣戶	A. Injury to median nerve / 误伤正中神经; B. Causing hemathorax/误伤引起血胸; C. Injury to radial nerve / 误伤桡神经; D. Ancient Forbidden point 古传禁针穴; E. often causing hematoma / 容易导致血肿.
3201	S14, Kù Fáng 庫房	A. often causing hematoma / 容易导致血肿; B. Injury to peroneal nerve, common peroneal nerve / 误伤腓神经, 腓总神经; C. Ancient Forbidden point 古传禁针穴; D. Causing pneumatothorax, hemathorax /误伤引起气胸, 血胸/ Injury to heart/误伤心脏; E. often causing needle-sickness / 容易导致晕针.
3202	S15, Wū Yì 屋翳	A. often causing needle-sickness / 容易导致晕针; B. Causing hemathorax/误伤引起血胸/ Injury to heart/误伤心脏; C. Injury to kidneys / 误伤肾脏; D. Ancient Forbidden point 古传禁针穴; E. Injury to median nerve / 误伤正中神经.
3203	S16, Yīng Chuāng 膺窗	A. Injury to peroneal nerve, common peroneal nerve / 误伤腓神经, 腓总神经; B. Ancient Forbidden point 古传禁针穴; C.

		Causing hemathorax/误伤引起血胸/ Injury to heart/误伤心脏; D. Injury to intestinal tract, ovary and uterus / 误伤肠道,卵巢及子宫; E. often causing hematoma / 容易导致血肿.
3204	S17, Rŭ Zhōng 乳中	A. Injury to median nerve / 误伤正中神经; B. Injury to gastric wall, bleeding or gastric perforation / 误伤胃壁， 出血， 胃穿孔; C. Injury to peroneal nerve, common peroneal nerve / 误伤腓神经, 腓总神经; D. Ancient Forbidden point 古传禁针穴; E. Forbidden point during pregnancy 孕妇禁针穴.
3205	S18, Rŭ Gēn 乳根	A. Causing hemathorax/误伤引起血胸/ Injury to heart/误伤心脏; B. Injury to median nerve / 误伤正中神经; C. Injury to gastric wall, bleeding or gastric perforation / 误伤胃壁， 出血， 胃穿孔; D. Ancient Forbidden point 古传禁针穴; E. Injury to intestinal tract / 误伤肠道.
3206	S19, Bù Róng 不容	A. Ancient Forbidden point 古传禁针穴; B. Injury to radial nerve / 误伤桡神经; C. often causing needle-sickness / 容易导致晕针; D. Injury to gastric wall, bleeding or gastric perforation / 误伤胃壁， 出血， 胃穿孔 / Injury to spleen, liver, gallbladder /误伤脾脏, 肝脏, 胆囊; E. often causing hematoma / 容易导致血肿.
3207	S20, Chéng Măn 承滿	A. Injury to radial nerve / 误伤桡神经; B. Ancient Forbidden point 古传禁针穴; C. often causing needle-sickness / 容易导致晕针; D. Injury to peroneal nerve, common peroneal nerve / 误伤腓神经, 腓总神经; E. Injury to gastric wall, bleeding or gastric perforation / 误伤胃壁， 出血， 胃穿孔/ Injury to spleen, liver, gallbladder /误伤脾脏, 肝脏, 胆囊
3208	S21, Liáng Mén 梁門	A. Injury to median nerve / 误伤正中神经; B. often causing needle-sickness / 容易导致晕针; C. Ancient Forbidden point 古传禁针穴; D. Injury to radial nerve / 误伤桡神经; E. Injury to gastric wall, bleeding or gastric perforation， spleen，intestinal tract / 误伤胃壁， 出血， 胃穿孔, 脾，肠道 / Injury to liver / 误伤肝脏, 胆囊
3209	S22, Guān Mén 關門	A. Injury to ulnar nerve / 误伤尺神经; B. Ancient Forbidden point 古传禁针穴; C. Injury to gastric wall, bleeding or gastric perforation，to intestinal tract / 误伤胃壁， 出血， 胃穿孔， 肠道 / Injury to spleen, liver / 误伤脾脏, 肝脏; D. often causing hematoma / 容易导致血肿; E. Injury to peroneal nerve, common peroneal nerve / 误伤腓神经, 腓总神经.
3210	S23, Tài Yĭ 太乙	A. Injury to peroneal nerve, common peroneal nerve / 误伤腓神经, 腓总神经; B. Injury to intestinal tract / 误伤肠道; C. Forbidden point for women 女子禁针穴; D. Ancient Forbidden point 古传禁针穴; E. Injury to ulnar nerve / 误伤尺神经.
3211	S24 Huá Ròu Mén 滑肉門	A. Causing pneumatothorax / 误伤引起气胸; B. Ancient Forbidden point 古传禁针穴; C. Injury to intestinal tract / 误伤肠道; D. Forbidden point during pregnancy 孕妇禁针穴; E. often causing hematoma / 容易导致血肿.
3212	S25, Tiān Shū 天樞	A. Injury to peroneal nerve, common peroneal nerve / 误伤腓神经, 腓总神经; B. Injury to gastric wall, bleeding or gastric

		perforation / 误伤胃壁，出血，胃穿孔; C. Injury to intestinal tract / 误伤肠道; D. Ancient Forbidden point 古传禁针穴; E. Causing pneumatothorax / 误伤引起气胸.
3213	S26, Wài Líng 外陵	A. Ancient Forbidden point 古传禁针穴; B. Injury to radial nerve / 误伤桡神经; C. often causing needle-sickness / 容易导致晕针; D. Injury to intestinal tract, ovary and uterus / 误伤肠道，卵巢及子宫; E. often causing hematoma / 容易导致血肿.
3214	S27, Dà Jù 大巨	A. Causing pneumatothorax / 误伤引起气胸; B. Injury to intestinal tract, ovary and uterus / 误伤肠道，卵巢及子宫; C. Injury to ulnar nerve / 误伤尺神经; D. Injury to peroneal nerve, common peroneal nerve / 误伤腓神经，腓总神经; E. Ancient Forbidden point 古传禁针穴.
3215	S28, Shuǐ Dào 水道	A. Ancient Forbidden point 古传禁针穴; B. Injury to ulnar nerve / 误伤尺神经; C. Forbidden point for women 女子禁针穴; D. Injury to peroneal nerve, common peroneal nerve / 误伤腓神经，腓总神经; E. Injury to intestinal tract, bladder, ovary and uterus / 误伤肠道，膀胱，卵巢及子宫
3216	S29, Guī Lái 歸來	A. Injury to peroneal nerve, common peroneal nerve / 误伤腓神经，腓总神经; B. Injury to intestinal tract, bladder, ovary and uterus / 误伤肠道，膀胱，卵巢及子宫; C. Injury to median nerve / 误伤正中神经; D. Ancient Forbidden point 古传禁针穴; E. Causing pneumatothorax / 误伤引起气胸.
3217	S30, Qì Chōng 氣沖	A. Forbidden point during pregnancy 孕妇禁针穴; B. often causing needle-sickness / 容易导致晕针; C. Ancient Forbidden point 古传禁针穴/ Injury to bladder / 误伤膀胱; D. often causing hematoma / 容易导致血肿; E. Injury to ulnar nerve / 误伤尺神经.
3218	S36, Zú Sān Lǐ 足三里	A. Injury to radial nerve / 误伤桡神经; B. often causing needle-sickness / 容易导致晕针; C. often causing hematoma / 容易导致血肿; D. Ancient Forbidden point 古传禁针穴; E. Injury to peroneal nerve, common peroneal nerve / 误伤腓神经，腓总神经
3219	S37, Shàng Jù Xū 上巨虛	A. Injury to peroneal nerve, common peroneal nerve / 误伤腓神经，腓总神经; B. Ancient Forbidden point 古传禁针穴; C. often causing needle-sickness / 容易导致晕针; D. often causing hematoma / 容易导致血肿; E. Injury to radial nerve / 误伤桡神经.
3220	S38, Tiáo Kǒu 條口	A. Ancient Forbidden point 古传禁针穴; B. Injury to peroneal nerve, common peroneal nerve / 误伤腓神经，腓总神经; C. Injury to radial nerve / 误伤桡神经; D. often causing needle-sickness / 容易导致晕针; E. Causing pneumatothorax / 误伤引起气胸.
3221	S39, Xià Jù Xū 下巨虛	A. Injury to radial nerve / 误伤桡神经; B. Ancient Forbidden point 古传禁针穴; C. Injury to peroneal nerve, common peroneal nerve / 误伤腓神经，腓总神经; D. often causing needle-sickness / 容易导致晕针; E. Causing pneumatothorax /

		误伤引起气胸.
3222	S41, Jiě Xī 解溪	A. Injury to radial nerve / 误伤桡神经; B. often causing needle-sickness / 容易导致晕针; C. often causing hematoma / 容易导致血肿; D. Ancient Forbidden point 古传禁针穴; E. Injury to peroneal nerve, common peroneal nerve / 误伤腓神经, 腓总神经.
3223	Si1 Shào Zé 少澤	A. Injury to ulnar nerve / 误伤尺神经; B. Injury to peroneal nerve, common peroneal nerve / 误伤腓神经, 腓总神经; C. Ancient Forbidden point 古传禁针穴; D. often causing needle-sickness / 容易导致晕针; E. Causing pneumatothorax / 误伤引起气胸.
3224	Si6, Yǎng Lǎo 養老	A. often causing needle-sickness / 容易导致晕针; B. Causing pneumatothorax / 误伤引起气胸; C. often causing hematoma / 容易导致血肿; D. Ancient Forbidden point 古传禁针穴; E. Injury to ulnar nerve / 误伤尺神经
3225	Si7, Zhi Zhèng 支正	A. Causing pneumatothorax / 误伤引起气胸; B. Injury to ulnar nerve / 误伤尺神经; C. Ancient Forbidden point 古传禁针穴; D. often causing needle-sickness / 容易导致晕针; E. Injury to median nerve / 误伤正中神经.
3226	Si8, Xiǎo Hǎi 小海	A. Injury to peroneal nerve, common peroneal nerve / 误伤腓神经, 腓总神经; B. Ancient Forbidden point 古传禁针穴; C. often causing needle-sickness / 容易导致晕针; D. Injury to ulnar nerve / 误伤尺神经; E. often causing hematoma / 容易导致血肿
3227	Si9, Jiān Zhēn 肩貞	A. often causing needle-sickness / 容易导致晕针; B. often causing hematoma / 容易导致血肿; C. Ancient Forbidden point 古传禁针穴; D. Causing pneumatothorax / 误伤引起气胸; E. Forbidden point during pregnancy 孕妇禁针穴.
3228	Si14, Jiān Wài Shū 肩外輸	A. Ancient Forbidden point 古传禁针穴; B. often causing needle-sickness / 容易导致晕针; C. Causing pneumatothorax / 误伤引起气胸; D. Injury to median nerve / 误伤正中神经; E. Injury to radial nerve / 误伤桡神经.
3229	Si15, Jiān Zhōng Shū 肩中輸	A. Injury to gastric wall, bleeding or gastric perforation / 误伤胃壁， 出血， 胃穿孔; B. Injury to median nerve / 误伤正中神经; C. Injury to peroneal nerve, common peroneal nerve / 误伤腓神经, 腓总神经; D. Ancient Forbidden point 古传禁针穴; E. Causing pneumatothorax, hemathorax / 误伤引起气胸, 血胸
3230	Sj2, Yè Mén 液門	A. Causing pneumatothorax / 误伤引起气胸; B. often causing hematoma / 容易导致血肿; C. Injury to sciatic nerve / 误伤坐骨神经; D. Ancient Forbidden point 古传禁针穴; E. Injury to peroneal nerve, common peroneal nerve / 误伤腓神经, 腓总神经.
3231	Sj15, Tiān Liáo 天髎	A. Injury to peroneal nerve, common peroneal nerve / 误伤腓神经, 腓总神经; B. Ancient Forbidden point 古传禁针穴; C. Causing pneumatothorax / 误伤引起气胸; D. often causing needle-sickness / 容易导致晕针; E. often causing hematoma / 容易导致血肿.

3232	Sj17, Yì Fēng 翳風	A. Injury to peroneal nerve, common peroneal nerve / 误伤腓神经，腓总神经; B. Ancient Forbidden point 古传禁针穴; C. often causing needle-sickness / 容易导致晕针; D. often causing hematoma / 容易导致血肿; E. Injury to vagus nerve reaction / 误伤迷走神经反应.
3233	Sj19, Lú Xī 顱息	A. often causing needle-sickness / 容易导致晕针; B. Forbidden point during pregnancy 孕妇禁针穴; C. Causing pneumatothorax / 误伤引起气胸; D. Injury to peroneal nerve, common peroneal nerve / 误伤腓神经，腓总神经; E. Ancient Forbidden point 古传禁针穴
3234	Sj20, Jiǎo Sūn 角孫	A. often causing needle-sickness / 容易导致晕针; B. often causing hematoma / 容易导致血肿; C. Ancient Forbidden point 古传禁针穴; D. Injury to radial nerve / 误伤桡神经; E. Injury to ulnar nerve / 误伤尺神经.
3235	Sj5, Wài Guān 外關	A. often causing hematoma / 容易导致血肿; B. Injury to peroneal nerve, common peroneal nerve / 误伤腓神经，腓总神经; C. Ancient Forbidden point 古传禁针穴; D. often causing needle-sickness / 容易导致晕针; E. Injury to radial nerve / 误伤桡神经
3236	Sj6, Zhi Gōu 支溝	A. often causing hematoma / 容易导致血肿; B. Causing pneumatothorax / 误伤引起气胸; C. often causing needle-sickness / 容易导致晕针; D. Injury to radial nerve / 误伤桡神经; E. Ancient Forbidden point 古传禁针穴.
3237	Sj7, Huì Zōng 會宗	A. Injury to peroneal nerve, common peroneal nerve / 误伤腓神经，腓总神经; B. Injury to radial nerve / 误伤桡神经; C. Ancient Forbidden point 古传禁针穴; D. Causing pneumatothorax / 误伤引起气胸; E. often causing needle-sickness / 容易导致晕针.
3238	Sj8, Sān Yáng Luò 三陽絡	A. Injury to peroneal nerve, common peroneal nerve / 误伤腓神经，腓总神经; B. Injury to radial nerve / 误伤桡神经; C. Causing pneumatothorax / 误伤引起气胸; D. Forbidden point during pregnancy 孕妇禁针穴; E. Ancient Forbidden point 古传禁针穴
3239	Sp11, Jī Mén 箕門	A. Injury to radial nerve / 误伤桡神经; B. Ancient Forbidden point 古传禁针穴; C. Injury to peroneal nerve, common peroneal nerve / 误伤腓神经，腓总神经; D. Injury to median nerve / 误伤正中神经; E. Causing pneumatothorax / 误伤引起气胸.
3240	Sp13, Fù Shě 府舍	A. Forbidden point for women 女子禁针穴; B. Injury to median nerve / 误伤正中神经; C. Injury to gastric wall, bleeding or gastric perforation / 误伤胃壁， 出血， 胃穿孔; D. Ancient Forbidden point 古传禁针穴; E. Injury to intestinal tract / 误伤肠道.
3241	Sp14, Fù Jié 腹結	A. Forbidden point for women 女子禁针穴; B. Injury to median nerve / 误伤正中神经; C. Injury to gastric wall, bleeding or gastric perforation / 误伤胃壁， 出血， 胃穿孔; D. Injury to intestinal tract / 误伤肠道; E. Injury to peroneal nerve, common peroneal nerve / 误伤腓神经，腓总神经.

3242	Sp15, Dà Héng 大横	A. Ancient Forbidden point 古传禁针穴; B. Causing pneumatothorax / 误伤引起气胸; C. often causing needle-sickness / 容易导致晕针; D. Injury to radial nerve / 误伤桡神经; E. Injury to intestinal tract / 误伤肠道
3243	Sp16, Fù Āi 腹哀	A. Injury to median nerve / 误伤正中神经; B. Injury to spleen, intestinal tract, stomach / 误伤脾，肠道，胃脏; C. Injury to peroneal nerve, common peroneal nerve / 误伤腓神经，腓总神经; D. Ancient Forbidden point 古传禁针穴; E. Injury to ulnar nerve / 误伤尺神经.
3244	Sp18, Tiān Xī 天溪	A. often causing hematoma / 容易导致血肿; B. Injury to peroneal nerve, common peroneal nerve / 误伤腓神经，腓总神经; C. Ancient Forbidden point 古传禁针穴; D. Causing hemathorax/误伤引起血胸; E. often causing needle-sickness / 容易导致晕针.
3245	Sp19, Xīong Xiāng 胸鄉	A. often causing hematoma / 容易导致血肿; B. Injury to peroneal nerve, common peroneal nerve / 误伤腓神经，腓总神经; C. Ancient Forbidden point 古传禁针穴; D. often causing needle-sickness / 容易导致晕针; E. Causing hemathorax/误伤引起血胸
3246	Sp21, Dà Bāo 大包	A. Causing pneumatothorax, hemathorax /误伤引起气胸，血胸; B. Injury to median nerve / 误伤正中神经; C. Injury to gastric wall, bleeding or gastric perforation / 误伤胃壁， 出血， 胃穿孔; D. Ancient Forbidden point 古传禁针穴; E. Injury to intestinal tract / 误伤肠道.
3247	Sp6, Sān Yīn Jiāo 三陰交	A. Injury to median nerve / 误伤正中神经; B. Injury to peroneal nerve, common peroneal nerve / 误伤腓神经，腓总神经; C. Forbidden point during pregnancy / 孕妇禁针穴. causing vaginal bleeding / 导致阴道出血; D. Injury to gastric wall, bleeding or gastric perforation / 误伤胃壁， 出血， 胃穿孔; E. Forbidden point during pregnancy 孕妇禁针穴.
3248	Dìng Chuǎn 定喘	A. Causing pneumatothorax/误伤引起气胸; B. Injury to ulnar nerve / 误伤尺神经; C. Injury to median nerve / 误伤正中神经; D. often causing hematoma / 容易导致血肿; E. Injury to peroneal nerve, common peroneal nerve / 误伤腓神经，腓总神经.
3249	Huá Tuó Jiā Jí 華佗夾脊	A. Injury to radial nerve / 误伤桡神经; B. often causing needle-sickness / 容易导致晕针; C. Ancient Forbidden point 古传禁针穴; D. Causing pneumatothorax/误伤引起气胸; E. often causing hematoma / 容易导致血肿.
3250	Nèi Jīng Míng 內睛明	A. Injury to median nerve / 误伤正中神经; B. often causing needle-sickness / 容易导致晕针; C. Ancient Forbidden point 古传禁针穴; D. Injury to radial nerve / 误伤桡神经; E. Injury to eye/误伤眼睛
3251	Qiú Hòu 球后	A. Injury to peroneal nerve, common peroneal nerve / 误伤腓神经，腓总神经; B. Injury to eye/误伤眼睛; C. Ancient Forbidden point 古传禁针穴; D. Injury to gastric wall, bleeding or gastric perforation/误伤胃壁， 出血， 胃穿孔 /Injury to liver / 误伤肝脏; E. Injury to ulnar nerve / 误伤尺神经.
3252	Shàng Jīng Míng 上睛明	A. Causing hemathorax/误伤引起血胸/ Injury to heart/误伤心脏; B. Injury to median nerve / 误伤正中神经; C. Injury to eye/误伤眼

		B. Injury to median nerve / 误伤正中神经; C. Injury to eye/误伤眼睛; D. Injury to peroneal nerve, common peroneal nerve / 误伤腓神经，腓总神经; E. Injury to radial nerve / 误伤桡神经.
3253	Sì Féng 四縫	A. Injury to radial nerve / 误伤桡神经; B. often causing needle-sickness / 容易导致晕针; C. Ancient Forbidden point 古传禁针穴; D. Injury to peroneal nerve, common peroneal nerve / 误伤腓神经，腓总神经; E. Injury to hand/误伤手部
3254	Yāo Yǎn 腰眼	A. Injury to kidney/误伤肾脏; B. Injury to ulnar nerve / 误伤尺神经; C. Injury to median nerve / 误伤正中神经; D. often causing hematoma / 容易导致血肿; E. Injury to peroneal nerve, common peroneal nerve / 误伤腓神经，腓总神经.

Part Three Suggested Answers to Questions

Test 1: Meridians

Test 1-1: Twelve master meridians

1	Lungs Meridian [Fèi Jīng, 肺經] (greater yin meridian of hand)
2	Large Intestine Meridian [Dà Cháng Jīng, 大腸經 (yang ming meridian of hand)
3	Stomach Meridian [Wèi Jīng, 胃經] (bright yang meridian of foot)
4	Small Intestine Meridian [Xiǎo Cháng Jīng, 小腸經] (greater yang meridian of hand)
5	Heart Meridian [Xīn Jīng, 心經] (lesser yin meridian of hand).
6	Spleen Meridian [Pí Jīng, 脾經] (greater yin meridian of foot)
7	Bladder Meridian [Páng Guāng Jīng, 膀胱經] (greater yang meridian of foot)
8	Kidneys Meridian [Shèn Jīng, 腎經] (lesser yin meridian of foot)
9	Liver Meridian [Gān Jīng, 肝經] (decreasing yin meridian of foot)
10	Pericardium Meridian [Xīn Bāo Jīng, 心包經] (decreasing yin meridian of hand)
11	Gall Meridian [Dǎn Jīng, 膽經] (lesser yang meridian of foot)
12	Triple Burning Space Meridian [Sān Jiāo Jīng, 三焦經] (lesser yang meridian of hand)

1-2 fourteen major meridians

	Governing Meridian [Dū Mài, 督脈].
	Bladder Meridian [Páng Guāng Jīng, 膀胱經] (greater yang meridian of foot)
	Gall Meridian [Dǎn Jīng, 膽經] (lesser yang meridian of foot)
	Gall Meridian [Dǎn Jīng, 膽經] (lesser yang meridian of foot)
	Spleen Meridian [Pí Jīng, 脾經] (greater yin meridian of foot)
	Stomach Meridian [Wèi Jīng, 胃經] (bright yang meridian of foot)
	Kidneys Meridian [Shèn Jīng, 腎經] (lesser yin meridian of foot)
	Conception Meridian [Rèn Mài, 任脈].
	Bladder Meridian [Páng Guāng Jīng, 膀胱經] (greater yang meridian of foot)
	Bladder Meridian [Páng Guāng Jīng, 膀胱經] (greater yang meridian of foot)
	Governing Meridian [Dū Mài, 督脈].
	Heart Meridian [Xīn Jīng, 心經] (lesser yin meridian of hand).
	Pericardium Meridian [Xīn Bāo Jīng, 心包經] (decreasing yin meridian of hand)
	Lungs Meridian [Fèi Jīng, 肺經] (greater yin meridian of hand)
	Large Intestine Meridian [Dà Cháng Jīng, 大腸經 (yang ming meridian of hand)
	Triple Burning Space Meridian [Sān Jiāo Jīng, 三焦經] (lesser yang meridian of hand)
	Small Intestine Meridian [Xiǎo Cháng Jīng, 小腸經] (greater yang meridian of hand)

Test 1-3: Extraordinary Meridians

71	
72	
73	
74	
75	
76	
77	
78	

Test 1-4: Separate Master Meridians Or Jing Bie

79	
80	
81	
82	
83	
84	
85	
[86]	
87	
88	
89	
90	
91	

Test 1-5: Linking Meridians Or Luo Mai

92	Lung collateral (reticular) meridian Shǒu Tài Yīn Jīng Bié Luò
93	Heart collateral (reticular) meridian Shǒu Shào Yīn Jīng Bié Luò
94	Stomach collateral (reticular) meridian Zú Yáng Míng Jīng Bié Luò
95	Spleen collateral (reticular) meridian Zú Tài Yīn Jīng Bié Luò
96	Large intestine collateral (reticular) meridian Shǒu Yáng Míng Jīng Bié Luò
97	Bladder collateral (reticular) meridian Zú Tài Yáng Jīng Bié Luò
98	Small intestine collateral (reticular) meridian Shǒu Tài Yáng Jīng Bié Luò
99	Kidney collateral (reticular) Zú Shào Yīn Jīng Jīn
100	Sanjiao collateral (reticular) meridian Shǒu Shào Yáng Jīng Bié Luò

101	Gallbladder collateral (reticular) meridian Zú Shào Yáng Jīng Bié Luǒ
102	Liver collateral (reticular) meridian Zú Jué Yīn Jīng Bié Luǒ
103	Pericardium collateral (reticular) meridian Shǒu Jué Yīn Jīng Bié Luǒ
104	Spleen greater collateral (reticular) meridian Pí Zhī Dà Luǒ
105	Ren mai collateral (reticular) meridian Ren Mai Bié Luǒ
106	Du mai collateral (reticular) meridian Du Mai Bié Luǒ

1-5A: Fifteen Linking Points (Collateral Points, Luò Xué)

92A	Lu7, Liè Quē
93A	H5, Tōng Lǐ
94A	S40, Fēng Lóng
95A	Sp4, Gōng Sūn
96A	Li6, Piān Lì
97A	B58, Feī Yáng
98A	Si7, Zhi Zhèng
99A	K4, Dà Zhōng
100A	Sj5, Wài Guān
101A	G37, Guāng Míng
102A	Lv5, Lí Gōu
103A	P6, Nèi Guān
104A	Sp21, Dà Bāo
105A	R15, Jiū Wěi
106A	D1, Cháng Qiáng

Test 1-6: Muscular Meridians 经筋

107	Lung muscular meridian Shǒu Tài Yīn Jīng Jīn
108	Large intestine muscular meridian Shǒu Yáng Míng Jīng Jīn
109	Stomach muscular meridian Zú Yáng Míng Jīng Jīn
110	Spleen muscular meridian Zú Tài Yīn Jīng Jīn
111	Heart muscular meridian Shǒu Shào Yīn Jīng Jīn
112	Small intestine muscular meridian Shǒu Tài Yáng Jīng Jīn
113	Bladder muscular meridian Zú Tài Yáng Jīng Jīn
114	Kidney muscular Zú Shào Yīn Jīng Jīn
115	Pericardium muscular meridian Shǒu Jué Yīn Jīng Jīn
116	Sanjiao muscular meridian Shǒu Shào Yáng Jīng Jīn
117	Gallbladder muscular meridian Zú Shào Yáng Jīng Jīn
118	Liver muscular meridian Zú Jué Yīn Jīng Jīn

Test 1-7: Skin Zones 皮部

119	Greater yang skin zone
120	Bright yang skin zone
121	Lesser yang skin zone
122	Greater yin skin zone
123	Lesser yin skin zone
124	Decreasing yin skin zone

1-8: 30 Points Of Branches (Biao) And Roots (Ben)

1	B2, Zăn Zhú, 攢竹
2	Yú Yāo, fish waist, 魚腰
3	Sj23, Sī Zhú Kōng 丝竹空
4	Li20, Yíng Xiāng 迎香
5	S4, Dì Cāng 地倉
6	R24, Chéng Jiàng 承漿
7	S9, Rén Yíng 人迎
8	Lu1, Zhōng Fŭ 中府
9	P1, Tiān Chí 天池
10	P6, Nèi Guān 內關
11	Lu9, Tài Yuān 太淵
12	K8, Jiāo Xìn 交信
13	K2, Rán Gŭ 然谷
14	S45, Lì Duì 歷兌
15	G44, Zú Qiào Yīn , Qiào Yīn 足竅陰
16	G43, Xiá Xī 俠溪
17	Lv4, Zhōng Fēng 中封
18	Sp6, Sān Yīn Jiāo 三陰交
19	Li11, Qū Chí 曲池
20	Li14, Bì Nào 臂臑
21	R23, Lián Quán 廉泉
22	G2, Tīng Huì 聽會
23	Si19, Tīng Gōng 聽宮
24	B1, Jīng Míng, 睛明
25	Jīn Jīn Yù Yè, 金津玉液
26	Sj19, Lú Xī 顱息
27	B15, Xīn Shū, 心輸
28	B18, Gān Shū, 肝輸
29	B20, Pí Shū, 脾輸
30	B23, Shèn Shū, 腎輸
31	Si6, Yăng Lăo 養老
32	Sj3, Zhōng Zhŭ 中渚
33	B59, Fū Yáng, 跗陽

Test 1-9: 9 Points in Four Seas (1-9)

1	D20, Băi Huì 百會
2	D16, Fēng Fŭ 風府
3	D15, Yă Mén 啞門
4	D14, Dà Zhuī 大椎
5	B11, Dà Zhù, 大杼
6	S36, Zú Sān Lĭ 足三里
7	S37, Shàng Jù Xū 上巨虛
8	S39, Xià Jù Xū 下巨虛
9	S30, Qì Chōng 氣沖

Test 1-10: 13 Points of Roots (Gen) and Fruits (Jie) on Six Meridians of Foot (1-13)

1	S8, Tóu Wĕi 頭維
2	B1, Jīng Míng, 睛明
3	Si19, Tīng Gōng 聽宮
4	R23, Lián Quán 廉泉
5	R18, Yù Táng 玉堂
6	R17, Shān Zhōng 膻中
7	R12, Zhōng Wăn 中脘
8	B67, Zhì Yīn, 至陰
9	G44, Zú Qiào Yīn , Qiào Yīn 足竅陰
10	S45, Lì Duì 歷兌
11	Sp1, Yīn Bái 隱白
12	Lv1, Dà Dūn 大敦
13	K1, Yŏng Quán 涌泉

Test 1-11: Four Energy Streets (1-4)

1	Tibia energy street, 胫气街
2	Abdomen energy street, 腹气街
3	Chest energy street, 胸气街
4	Head energy street, 头气街

Test 2: Bone Measurements / 骨度分寸

Q.	CUN	17	3	34	1.5	51	19
1	75	18	4	35	12	52	16
2	75	19	9	36	6	53	2
3	12	20	8	37	17	54	3
4	9	21	8	38	4	55	1
5	26	22	5	39	12	56	12
6	10	23	5	40	9	57	4.5
7	12	24	6.5	41	4	58	1
8	10	25	6.5	42	4.5	59	1
9	7	26	8	43	6.5	60	3
10	13	27	45	44	18	61	2
11	10	28	9	45	3.5	62	1.5
12	3	29	1.6	46	13	63	1
13	3	30	30	47	14	64	2
14	3	31	42	48	3	65	18
15	9	32	3	49	16	66	15
16	2.5	33	3	50	3	67	15

Test 3: Anatomy (1-140)

1	鎖骨上窩,	*supraclavicular fossa*
2	锁骨	*Clavicle*
3	三角肌	*Deltoid muscle*
4	肱三頭肌	*Brachial triceps muscle*
5	肱二頭肌	*biceps muscle of arm*
6	肱肌	*brachial muscle,*
7	肱骨外上髁	*lateral epicondylus of humerus*
8	鹰嘴	*olecranon*
9	拇短伸肌腱	*Short extensor muscle of thumb*
10	拇长伸肌腱	*Long extensor muscle of thumb*
11	髂嵴	*iliac-crest*
12	阔筋膜	*tensor fasciae latae*
	张肌	
13	股直肌	*rectus femoris*
14	股外肌	*Vastus lateralis (lateral great muscle)*
15	髌骨	*patella*
16	外膝眼	*Lateral knee eye*
17	髌韧带	*patella ligament*
18	胫骨前嵴	*crest of tibia*
19	外踝	*lateral malleolus*
20	内踝	*medial malleolus*
21	跟腱	*Achilles tendon*
22	胫骨内侧面	*medial side of tibia*
23	腓肠肌	*gastrocnemius muscle*
24	内膝眼	*Medial knee eye*

25	股内肌	*vastus medialis (medial great muscle)*
26	腹股沟韧带	*inguinal ligament*
27	髂前上嵴	*anterior superior iliac spine*
28	尺骨小头	*head of ulna*
29	肘窝	*antecubital fossa*
30	腋前皱襞	*anterior axillary fold*
31	胸大肌	*pectoralis major*
32	胸骨上窝	*suprasternal fossa*
33	斜方肌	*trapezius muscles*
34	胸锁乳突肌	*Sternocleidomastoid muscle*
35	喉结	*laryngeal prominence*
36	胸锁乳突肌	*Sternocleidomastoid muscle*
37	三角肌	*deltoid-muscle*
38	肱三头肌	*Brachial triceps muscle*
39	肱二头肌	*biceps muscle of arm*
40	肱骨外上髁	*lateral epicondylus of humerus*
41	尺骨小头	*head of ulna*
42	腓肠肌	*gastrocnemius muscle*
43	内踝	*medial malleolus*
44	跟腱	*Achilles tendon*
45	足跟	*Heel*
46	外踝	*lateral malleolus*
47	腓骨头	*head of fibula*
48	髌骨	*patella*
49	股外侧肌	*vastus lateralis*
50	肱二头肌	*biceps muscle of arm*
51	胸大肌	*pectoralis major*
52	锁骨	*Clavicle*
53	喉结	*laryngeal prominence*
54	肩胛冈	*spine of scapula*
55	斜方肌	*trapezius muscles*
56	鹰嘴	*olecranon*
57	肱骨内上髁	*medial epicondylus of humerus*
58	鱼际	*thenar eminence*
59	小鱼际	*hypothenar eminence*
60	肱二头肌	*biceps muscle of arm*
61	腘窝	*Popliteal Fossa*
62	腓肠肌	*gastrocnemius muscle*
63	跟腱	*Achilles tendon*
64	外踝	*lateral malleolus*
65	臀大肌	*gluteus maximus*
66	髂嵴	*iliac-crest*
67	背阔肌	*latissimus dorsi muscle*
68	大圆肌	*teres major.*
69	三角肌	*deltoid-muscle*
70	肱二头肌	*biceps muscle of arm*
71	尺骨小头	*head of ulna*
72	额骨	*frontal bone*
73	颞骨	*Temporal bone*
74	乳突	*Mastoid process*
75	肩峰	*acromion of scapula*

76	肱骨	*humerus*
77	尺骨	*ulna*
78	桡骨	*radius*
79	腕骨	*carpal bone*
80	掌骨	*metacarpal bones*
81	指骨	*phalanx*
82	髌骨	*patella*
83	胫骨粗隆	*tuberosity of tibia*
84	跗骨	*Tarsal bones*
85	跖骨	*Metatarsal bones*
86	趾骨	*phalanx*
87	内踝	*medial malleolus*
88	外踝	*lateral malleolus*
89	腓骨	*fibula*
90	胫骨	*tibia*
91	股骨	*femur (thighbone)*
92	大转子	*greater trochanter*
93	髂前上嵴	*anterior superior iliac spine*
94	腰椎	*Lumbar Vertebrae*
95	肋骨	*ribs*
96	锁骨	*Clavicle*
97	颈椎	*Cervical Vertebrae*
98	下颌骨	*mandible*
99	上颌骨	*Maxillary bone*
100	颧骨	*zygomatic bone (cheek-bone)*
101	颈总动脉	*common carotid artery*
102	颈内静脉	*internal jugular vein*
103	锁骨下动脉	*Subclavian artery*
104	锁骨下静脉	*Subclavian vein*
105	主动脉弓	*Aortic arch*
106	上腔静脉	*Superior vena cava*
107	肺动脉	*Pulmonary artery*
108	右肺	*Right lung*
109	横膈膜	*diaphragm*
110	肝脏	*liver*
111	胆	*gallbladder*
112	十二指肠	*Duodenum*
113	肾静脉	*Renal vein*
114	肾动脉	*Renal artery*
115	右肾	*Right kidney*
116	下腔静脉	*Inferior vena cava*
117	输尿管	*Ureter*
118	髂骨	*hip bone*
119	乙状结肠	*Sigmoid colon*
120	腹下动静脉	*Hypogastric artery and vein*
121	腹股沟韧带	*inguinal ligament*
122	膀胱	*bladder*
123	股骨	*femur (thighbone)*
124	股静脉	*Femoral vein*
125	股动脉	*Femoral artery*
126	髂外动脉	*External iliac artery*
127	髂总动脉	*Common iliac artery*
128	腹主动脉	*Abdominal aorta*
129	左肾	*Left kidney*
130	胰	*Pancreas*
131	脾	*Spleen*
132	胃	*Stomach*

133	左肺	*Left lung*
134	心脏	*Heart*
135	肺静脉	*Pulmonary veins*
136	肱骨	*humerus*
137	肩胛骨	*scapula*
138	锁骨	*Clavicle*
139	气管	*Trachea*
140	食管	*esophagus*
141	三角窝	*Triangular fossa*
142	对耳轮下脚	*Crus anthelicis inferior*
143	耳甲艇	*Cymba conchae*
144	耳轮脚	*Crus helicis*
145	屏上切迹	*Incisura supratragica*
146	外耳道口	*Orifice of external auditory canal*
147	耳屏	*Tragus*
148	屏间切迹	*Incisura intertragica*
149	耳垂	*Lobulu auriculae*
150	对耳屏	*antetragus*
151	耳轮尾	*Cauda helicis*
152	轮屏切迹	*Helix tragus notch*
153	耳甲腔	*Cavum conchae auriculae*
154	对耳轮	*anthelix*
155	耳轮	*Helix*
156	耳舟	*Scapha*

157	耳轮结节	*tuberculum auriculae*
158	对耳轮上脚	*Crus antihelices superior*
159	三角窝隆起	*Eminentia fossae triangularis*
160	耳轮背面	*Facies dorsalis helicis*
161	耳垂背面	*Facies dorsalis lobuli auriculae*
162	额骨隆起	*Prominence of frontal bone*
163	冠状缝	*Coronal suture*
164	冠矢点	*Bregema*
165	矢状缝	*Sagittal suture*
166	顶颞缝	*Parietotemporal suture*
167	顶骨隆起	*Parietal eminence*
168	人字缝尖	*Lambda*
169	人字缝	*Lambdoid suture*
170	枕外粗隆	*External occipital protuberance*
171	额骨	*Frontal bone*
172	顶骨	*Parietal bone*
173	枕骨	*occipital bone*
174	蝶骨	*Sphenoid bone*
175	*颞骨*	*Temporal bone*

Test 4 Acupuncture Points on the Fourteen Meridians (1-361)

1	Lu2	Yún Mén	云門
2	Lu1	Zhōng Fǔ	中府
3	Lu3	Tiān Fǔ	天府
4	Lu4	Xiá Bái	俠白
5	Lu5	Chǐ Zé	尺澤
6	Lu6	Kǒng Zuì	孔最
7	Lu7	Liè Quē	列缺
8	Lu8	Jīng Qú	經渠
9	Lu9	Tài Yuān	太淵
10	Lu10	Yǔ Jì	魚際
11	Lu11	Shǎo Shāng	少商
12	Li20	Yíng Xiāng	迎香
13	Li19	Kǒu Hé Liáo	口禾髎
14	Li18	Fú Tū	扶突
15	Li17	Tiān Dǐng	天鼎
16	Li15	Jiān Yú	肩髃
17	Li16	Jù Gǔ	巨骨
18	Li2	Èr Jiān	二間
19	Li3	Sān Jiān	三間
20	Li4	Hé Gǔ	合谷
21	Li1	Shāng Yáng	商陽
22	Li14	Bì Nào	臂臑
23	Li13	Shǒu Wǔ Lǐ	手五里
24	Li12	Zhǒu Liáo	肘髎
25	Li11	Qū Chí	曲池
26	Li10	Shǒu Sān Lǐ	手三里
27	Li9	Shàng Lián	上廉
28	Li8	Xià Lián	下廉
29	Li7	Wēn Liū	溫溜
30	Li6	Piān Lì	偏歷
31	Li5	Yáng Xī	陽溪
32	S1	Chéng Qì	承泣
33	S2	Sì Bái	四白
34	S3	Jù Liáo	巨髎
35	S4	Dì Cāng	地倉
36	S8	Tóu Wěi	頭維
37	S7	Xià Guān	下關
38	S6	Jiá Chē	頰車
39	S5	Dà Yíng	大迎
40	S9	Rén Yíng	人迎
41	S10	Shuǐ Tū	水突
42	S11	Qì Shě	氣舍
43	S31	Bì Guān	髀關
44	S32	Fú Tù	伏兔
45	S33	Yīn Shì	陰市
46	S34	Liáng Qiū	梁丘
47	S35	Dú Bí	犢鼻
48	S36	Zú Sān Lǐ	足三里
49	S37	Shàng Jù Xū	上巨虛
50	S38	Tiáo Kǒu	條口
51	S39	Xià Jù Xū	下巨虛
52	S40	Fēng Lóng	手隆
53	S41	Jiě Xī	解溪
54	S42	Chōng Yáng	冲陽
55	S43	Xiàn Gǔ	陷谷
56	S44	Nèi Tíng	內庭
57	S45	Lì Duì	歷兌
58	S12	Quē Pén	缺盆
59	S13	Qì Hù	氣戶
60	S14	Kù Fáng	庫房
61	S15	Wū Yì	屋翳
62	S16	Yīng Chuāng	膺窗
63	S17	Rǔ Zhōng	乳中
64	S18	Rǔ Gēn	乳根
65	S19	Bù Róng	不容
66	S20	Chéng Mǎn	承滿
67	S21	Liáng Mén	梁門
68	S22	Guān Mén	關門
69	S23	Tài Yǐ	太乙
70	S24	Huá Ròu Mén	滑肉門
71	S25	Tiān Shū	天樞
72	S26	Wài Líng	外陵
73	S27	Dà Jù	大巨
74	S28	Shuǐ Dào	水道
75	S29	Guī Lái	歸來
76	S30	Qì Chōng	氣冲
77	Sp20	Zhōu Róng	周榮
78	Sp19	Xīong Xiāng	胸鄉
79	Sp18	Tiān Xī	天溪
80	Sp17	Shí Dòu	食竇

81	Sp16	Fù Aī	腹哀
82	Sp15	Dà Héng	大横
83	Sp14	Fù Jié	腹結
84	Sp13	Fù Shě	府舍
85	Sp12	Chōng Mén	冲門
86	Sp21	Dà Bāo	大包
87	Sp11	Jī Mén	箕门
88	Sp10	Xuè Hǎi	血海
89	Sp9	Yīn Líng Quán	陰陵泉
90	Sp8	Dì Jī	地機
91	Sp7	Lòu Gǔ	漏谷
92	Sp6	Sān Yīn Jiāo	三陰交
93	Sp5	Shāng Qiū	商丘
94	Sp1	Yǐn Bái	隱白
95	Sp2	Dà Dū	大都
96	Sp3	Tài Bái	太白
97	Sp4	Gōng Sūn	公孫
98	H9	Shào Chōng	少冲
99	H8	Shào Fǔ	少府
100	H3	Shào Hǎi	少海
101	H2	Qīng Líng	青靈
102	H1	Jí Quán	極泉
103	H7	Shén Mén	神門
104	H6	Yīn Xī	陰郄
105	H5	Tōng Lǐ	通里
106	H4	Líng Dào	靈道
107	Si18	Quán Liáo	顴髎
108	Si12	Bǐng Fēng	秉風
109	Si10	Nào Shū	臑輸
110	Si11	Tiān Zōng	天宗
111	Si9	Jiān Zhēn	肩貞
112	Si19	Tīng Gōng	聽宮
113	Si17	Tiān Róng	天容
114	Si16	Tiān Chuāng	天窗
115	Si15	Jiān Zhōng Sh	肩中輸
116	Si14	Jiān Wài Shū	肩外輸
117	Si13	Qū Yuān	曲垣
118	Si6	Yǎng Lǎo	養老
119	Si7	Zhi Zhèng	支正
120	Si8	Xiǎo Hǎi	小海
121	Si5	Yáng Gǔ	陽谷

122	Si4	Wàn Gǔ	腕骨
123	Si3	Hòu Xī	后溪
124	Si2	Qián Gú	前谷
125	Si1	Shào Zé	少澤
126	B8	Luò Què	絡卻
127	B7	Tōng Tiān	通天
128	B6	Chéng Guāng	承光
129	B5	Wǔ Chù	五處
130	B3	Méi Chōng	眉冲
131	B4	Qū Chā	曲差
132	B2	Zǎn Zhú	攢竹
133	B1	Jīng Míng	睛明
134	B9	Yù Zhěn	玉枕
135	B10	Tiān Zhù	天柱
136	B11	Dà Zhù	大杼
137	B12	Fēng Mén	風門
138	B13	Fèi Shū	肺輸
139	B14	Jué Yīn Shū	厥陰輸
140	B15	Xīn Shū	心輸
141	B16	Dū Shū	督輸
142	B17	Gé Shū	膈輸
143	B18	Gān Shū	肝輸
144	B19	Dǎn Shū	膽輸
145	B20	Pí Shū	脾輸
146	B21	Wèi Shū	胃俞
147	B22	Sān Jiāo Shū	三焦輸
148	B23	Shèn Shū	腎輸
149	B24	Qì Hǎi Shū	氣海輸
150	B25	Dà Cháng Shū	大腸輸
151	B26	Guān Yuán Shū	關元輸
152	B27	Xiǎo Cháng Shū	小腸輸
153	B28	Páng Guāng Shū	膀胱輸
154	B29	Zhōng Lǚ Shū	中膂輸
155	B30	Bái Huán Shū	白環輸
156	B31	Shàng Liáo	上髎
157	B32	Cì Liáo	次髎
158	B33	Zhōng Liáo	中髎
159	B34	Xià Liáo	下髎

160	B35	Huì Yáng	會陽
161	B36	Chéng Fú	承扶
162	B37	Yīn Mén	殷門
163	B38	Fú Xī	浮郄
164	B39	Wěi Yáng	委陽
165	B40	Wěi Zhōng	委中
166	B41	Fù Fēn	附分
167	B42	Pò Hù	魄戶
168	B43	Gāo Huāng Shū	膏肓輸
169	B44	Shén Táng	神堂
170	B45	Yì Xī	噫嘻
171	B46	Gé Guān	膈關
172	B47	Hún Mén	魂門
173	B48	Yáng Gāng	陽剛
174	B49	Yì Shè	意舍
175	B50	Wèi Cāng	胃倉
176	B51	Huāng Mén	肓門
177	B52	Zhì Shì	志室
178	B53	Bāo Huāng	胞肓
179	B54	Zhì Biān	秩邊
180	B55	Hé Yáng	合陽
181	B56	Chéng Jīn	承筋
182	B57	Chéng Shān	承山
183	B58	Feī Yáng	飛揚
184	B59	Fū Yáng	跗陽
185	B60	Kūn Lún	昆崙
186	B61	Pū Cān	仆參
187	B62	Shēn Mài	申脈
188	B63	Jīn Mén	金門
189	B64	Jīng Gǔ	京骨
190	B65	Shù Gǔ	束骨
191	B66	Tōng Gǔ/Zú Tōng Gǔ	通谷/足通谷
192	B67	Zhì Yīn	至陰
193	K27	Shū Fǔ	俞府
194	K26	Yù Zhōng	彧中
195	K25	Shén Cáng	神藏
196	K24	Líng Xū	靈墟
197	K23	Shén Fēng	神封
198	K22	Bù Láng	步廊

199	K16	Huāng Shū	肓輸
200	K15	Zhōng Zhù	中注
201	K14	Sì Mǎn	四滿
202	K13	Qì Xué	氣穴
203	K12	Dà Hè	大赫
204	K11	Héng Gǔ	橫骨
205	K1	Yǒng Quán	涌泉
206	K10	Yīn Gǔ	陰谷
207	K21	Yōu Mén	幽門
208	K20	Fù Tōng Gǔ (Tōng Gǔ)	腹通谷
209	K19	Yīn Dū	陰都
210	K18	Shí Guān	石關
211	K17	Shāng Qǔ	商曲
212	K8	Jiāo Xìn	交信
213	K9	Zhú Bīn	筑賓
214	K7	Fù Liū	復溜
215	K3	Tài Xī	太溪
216	K4	Dà Zhōng	大鍾
217	K5	Shuǐ Quán	水泉
218	K2	Rán Gǔ	然谷
219	K6	Zhào Hǎi	照海
220	P1	Tiān Chí	天池
221	P2	Tiān Quán	天泉
222	P3	Qū Zé	曲澤
223	P9	Zhōng Chōng	中冲
224	P8	Láo Gōng	勞宮
225	P4	Xī Mén	郄門
226	P5	Jiān Shǐ	間使
227	P6	Nèi Guān	內關
228	P7	Dà Líng	大陵
229	Sj15	Tiān Liáo	天髎
230	Sj14	Jiān Liáo	肩髎
231	Sj13	Nǎo Huì	臑會
232	Sj12	Xiāo Luò	消濼
233	Sj11	Qīng Lěng Yuān	清冷淵
234	Sj10	Tiān Jǐng	天井
235	Sj1	Guān Chōng	關冲
236	Sj2	Yè Mén	液門
237	Sj3	Zhōng Zhǔ	中渚

238	Sj4	Yáng Chí	陽池
239	Sj20	Jiǎo Sūn	角孫
240	Sj19	Lú Xī	顱息
241	Sj18	Chì Mài	瘈脈
242	Sj17	Yì Fēng	翳風
243	Sj16	Tiān Yǒu	天牖
244	Sj7	Huì Zōng	會宗
245	Sj23	Sī Zhú Kōng	丝竹空
246	Sj22	Ěr Hé Liáo (H Liáo)	耳和髎
247	Sj21	Ěr Mén	耳門
248	Sj5	Wài Guān	外關
249	Sj6	Zhi Gōu	支溝
250	Sj8	Sān Yáng Luò	三陽絡
251	Sj9	Sì Dú	四瀆
252	G21	Jiān Jǐng	肩井
253	G7	Qū Bìn	曲鬢
254	G4	Hàn Yàn	頷厭
255	G5	Xuán Lú	懸顱
256	G6	Xuán Lí	懸厘
257	G1	Tóng Zǐ Liáo	童子髎
258	G3	Shàng Guān	上關
259	G2	Tīng Huì	聽會
260	G8	Shuài Gǔ	率谷
261	G9	Tiān Chōng	天冲
262	G10	Fú Bái	浮白
263	G11	Tóu Qiào Yīn (Qiào Yīn)	頭竅陰
264	G12	Wán Gǔ	完骨
265	G19	Nǎo Kōng	腦空
266	G20	Fēng Chí	風池
267	G15	Tóu Lín Qì/ (Lín Qì)	頭臨泣)
268	G13	Běn Shén	本神
269	G14	Yáng Bái	陽白
270	G22	Yuān Yè	淵液
271	G23	Zhé Jīn	輒筋
272	G24	Rì Yuè	日月
273	G25	Jīng Mén	京門
274	G26	Dài Mài	帶脈

275	G18	Chéng Líng	承靈
276	G17	Zhèng Yíng	正營
277	G16	Mù Chuāng	目窗
278	G29	Jū Liáo	居髎
279	G30	Huán Tiào	環跳
280	G27	Wǔ Shū	五樞
281	G28	Wéi Dà	維道
282	G31	Fēng Shì	風市
283	G32	Zhōng Dū	中瀆
284	G33	Yáng Guān/Xī Yáng Guān	膝陽關
285	G35	Yáng Jiāo	陽交
286	G34	Yáng Líng Quán	陽陵泉
287	G36	Wài Qiū	外丘
288	G37	Guāng Míng	光明
289	G38	Yáng Fǔ	陽輔
290	G39	Xuán Zhōng	懸鍾
291	G40	Qiū Xū	丘墟
292	G41	Zú Lín Qì/Lín Qì	足臨泣
293	G42	Dì Wǔ Huì	地五會
294	G43	Xiá Xī	俠溪
295	G44	Zú Qiào Yīn/Qiào Yīn	足竅陰
296	Lv9	Yīn Bāo	**陰包**
297	Lv8	Qū Quán	曲泉
298	Lv14	Qí Mén	期門
299	Lv13	Zhāng Mén	章門
300	Lv12	Jí Mài	急脈
301	Lv11	Yīn Lián	陰廉
302	Lv10	Zú Wǔ Lǐ/Wǔ Lǐ	足五里
303	Lv7	Xī Guān	膝關
304	Lv6	Zhōng Dū	中都
305	Lv5	Lí Gōu	蠡溝
306	Lv4	Zhōng Fēng	中封
307	Lv3	Tài Chōng	太冲
308	Lv2	Xíng Jiān	行間
309	Lv1	Dà Dūn	大敦
310	R24	Chéng Jiàng	承漿
311	R23	Lián Quán	廉泉

312	R15	Jiū Wěi	鳩尾
313	R14	Jù Què	巨闕
314	R13	Shàng Wǎn	上脘
315	R12	Zhōng Wǎn	中脘
316	R11	Jiàn Lǐ	建里
317	R10	Xià Wǎn	下脘
318	R9	Shuǐ Fēn	水分
319	R6	Qì Hǎi	氣海
320	R1	Huì Yīn	會陰
321	R22	Tiān Tū	天突
322	R21	Xuán Jī	琁璣
323	R20	Huá Gài	華蓋
324	R19	Zǐ Gōng	紫宮
325	R18	Yù Táng	玉堂
326	R17	Shān Zhōng	膻中
327	R16	Zhōng Tíng	中庭
328	R8	Shén Què	神闕
329	R7	Yīn Jiāo	陰交
330	R5	Shí Mén	石門
331	R4	Guān Yuán	關元
332	R3	Zhōng Jí	中極
333	R2	Qū Gǔ	曲骨
334	D18	Qiáng Jiān	強間
335	D17	Nǎo Hù	腦戶
336	D16	Fēng Fǔ	風府
337	D15	Yǎ Mén	啞門

338	D14	Dà Zhuī	大椎
339	D19	Hòu Dǐng	后頂
340	D20	Bǎi Huì	百會
341	D21	Qián Dǐng	前頂
342	D22	Xìn Huì	囟會
343	D23	Shàng Xīng	上星
344	D24	Shén Tíng	神庭
345	D25	Sù Liáo	素髎
346	D26	Shuǐ Gōu(Rén Zhōng	水溝 (人中)
347	D27	Duì Duān	兌端
348	D28	Yín Jiāo	齦交
349	D1	Cháng Qiáng	長強
350	D13	Táo Dào	陶道
351	D12	Shēn Zhù	身柱
352	D11	Shén Dào	神道
353	D10	Líng Tái	靈台
354	D9	Zhì Yáng	至陽
355	D8	Jīn Suō	筋縮
356	D7	Zhōng Shū	中樞
357	D6	Jǐ Zhōng	脊中
358	D5	Xuán Shū	懸樞
359	D4	Mìng Mén	命門
360	D3	Yāo Yáng Guā	腰陽關
361	D2	Yāo Shū	腰輸

Test 5: Extraordinary Points (1-48)

1	Sì shén cōng	四神聰	four spiritual intelligences
2	Dāng Yáng	当阳	Yang position
3	Yìn táng	印堂	midpoint between eyebrows/seal hall
4	Yú yāo	魚腰	fish waist
5	Qiú hòu	球后	behind the ball
6	Shàng yíng xiāng	上迎香	upper greeting the scent
7	Nèi yíng xiāng	內迎香	upper greeting the scent
8	Tài yáng	太陽	the sun, the temple
9	Ěr jiān	耳尖	tip of ear
10	Yì míng	翳明	shelter light
11	Jù quán	聚泉	Gathering fountain

12	Jīn jīn	金津	golden saliva
13	yù yè	玉液	jade liquid
14	Hǎi quán	海泉	Ocean fountain
15	Zǐ gōng	子宫	uterus
16	Jǐng Bǎi Láo	頸百勞	neck hundred labours
17	Dìng chuǎn	定喘	fix panting, stop panting, panting tranquillizer
18	Jiā jǐ	夾脊	clipping spines
19	Wèi wǎn xià shū	胃脘下俞	stomach
20	Pǐ gēn	痞根	abdominal lump root
21	Xià jí shū	下極輸	lower extreme transport
22	Yāo yǎn	腰眼	waist eyes
23	Yāo yí	腰宜	waist fitting
24	Shí qī zhuī	十七椎	17th vertebra
25	Yāo qí	腰奇	waist miracle
26	Zhǒu jiān	肘尖	elbow tip
27	Èr bái	二白	two whites
28	Sì féng	四縫	four stitches
29	Shí xuān	十宣	ten statements, ten expansions
30	Xiǎo gǔ kōng	小骨空	small bone cavity
31	Bā xié	八邪	eight evils
32	Yao tong dian	腰痛点	lumbago point
33	Zhōng kuí	中魁	middle head, middle leader
34	Wài láo gōng	外勞宮	lateral palace of labour
35	Dà gǔ kōng	大骨空	large bone cavity
36	Zhōng quán	中泉	middle fountain
37	Bǎi chóng wuō	百蟲窩	nest of hundred insects
38	Nèi xī yǎn	內膝眼	medial knee eye
39	Kuān gǔ	髖骨	hip bone
40	Hè dǐng	鶴頂	top of a crane
41	Xī yǎn	膝眼	knee eye
42	Dǎn náng	膽囊	gallbladder
43	Lán wěi	闌尾	appendix
44	Wài huái jiān	外踝尖	tip of the outer ankle, tip of the lateral malleolus
45	Nèi huái jiān	內踝尖	tip of the inner ankle, tip of the medial malleolus
47	Dú dīn	独陰	Solitary yin
47	Bā fēng	八風	eight winds
48	Qì chuǎn	氣喘	energy asthma, asthma

Test 6: Body Points (1-644)

1	D25, Sù Liáo 素髎.
2	Li20, Yíng Xiāng 迎香.
3	S3, Jù Liáo 巨髎.
4	Li19, Kǒu Hé Liáo 口禾髎.
5	D26, Shuǐ Gōu, Rén Zhōng，水溝. 人中
6	G14, Yáng Bái 陽白
7	B2, Zǎn Zhú, 攢竹
8	B1, Jīng Míng, 睛明
9	Sj23, Sī Zhú Kōng 丝竹空
10	G1, Tóng Zǐ Liáo 童子髎.
11	S1, Chéng Qì 承泣.
12	S2, Sì Bái 四白.
13	Jù Quán 聚泉.
14	B2, Zǎn Zhú, 攢竹
15	Yìn Táng 印堂.
16	B1, Jīng Míng, 睛明
17	Li20, Yíng Xiāng 迎香.
18	S4, Dì Cāng 地倉.
19	Tài Yáng 太陽.
20	Sj21, Ěr Mén 耳門.
21	S7, Xià Guān 下關.
22	D26, Shuǐ Gōu, Rén Zhōng，水溝. 人中
23	Jīn Jīn Yù Yè 金津玉液
24	Jing Bi 颈臂
25	Sì Shén Cōng 四神聰
26	S2, Sì Bái 四白.
27	S4, Dì Cāng 地倉.
28	Qiú Hòu 球后.
29	Li20, Yíng Xiāng 迎香.
30	D26, Shuǐ Gōu, Rén Zhōng，水溝. 人中
31	D20, Bǎi Huì 百會.
32	B1, Jīng Míng, 睛明
33	G1, Tóng Zǐ Liáo 童子髎.
34	S1, Chéng Qì 承泣.
35	G20, Fēng Chí 風池.
36	D20 (Bǎi Huì) 百會
37	Qiān Zhèng, 牵正
38	S8, Tóu Wěi 頭維.
39	S7, Xià Guān 下關.
40	Sj17, Yì Fēng 翳風.
41	Sj17, Yì Fēng 翳風.
42	Sj16, Tiān Yōu 天牖.
43	Si17, Tiān Róng 天容
44	Si16, Tiān Chuāng 天窗.
45	Li18, Fú Tū 扶突.
46	S9, Rén Yíng 人迎.
47	R23, Lián Quán 廉泉.
48	Li17, Tiān Dǐng 天鼎.
49	S10, Shuǐ Tū 水突.
50	S12, Quē Pén 缺盆.
51	S11, Qì Shè 氣舍.
52	R22, Tiān Tū 天突.
53	Tài Yáng 太陽.
54	S6, Jiá Chē 頰車.
55	S7, Xià Guān 下關.
56	S8, Tóu Wěi 頭維.
57	S12, Quē Pén 缺盆.
58	S11, Qì Shè 氣舍.
59	S9, Rén Yíng 人迎.
60	S10, Shuǐ Tū 水突.
61	Yì Míng 翳明.
62	R22, Tiān Tū 天突.
63	R23, Lián Quán 廉泉.
64	R24, Chéng Jiàng 承漿.
65	D20, Bǎi Huì 百會.
66	Sj23, Sī Zhú Kōng 丝竹空
67	Sj17, Yì Fēng 翳風.
68	S6, Jiá Chē 頰車.
69	S7, Xià Guān 下關.
70	Tài Yáng 太陽.
71	G1, Tóng Zǐ Liáo 童子髎.
72	Sj21, Ěr Mén 耳門.

73	Si19, Tīng Gōng 聽宫.
74	G2, Tīng Huì 聽會.
75	R23, Lián Quán 廉泉.
76	Sj20, Jiǎo Sūn 角孫.
77	Sj19, Lú Xī 顱息.
78	Sj18, Chì Mài 瘛脈.
79	Sj21, Ěr Mén 耳門.
80	Si19, Tīng Gōng 聽宫.
81	G2, Tīng Huì 聽會.
82	Sj17, Yì Fēng 翳風.
83	S6, Jiá Chē 頰車.
84	S8, Tóu Wěi 頭維.
85	S7, Xià Guān 下關.
86	S6, Jiá Chē 頰車.
87	S5, Dà Yíng 大迎.
88	Li20, Yíng Xiāng 迎香.
89	Sj20, Jiǎo Sūn 角孫.
90	Sj20, Jiǎo Sūn 角孫.
91	Shàng Lián Quán 上廉泉.
92	Ěr Jiān 耳尖.
93	Sj21, Ěr Mén 耳門.
94	S6, Jiá Chē 頰車.
95	D28, Yín Jiāo 齦交
96	G2, Tīng Huì 聽會.
97	Li18, Fú Tū 扶突.
98	Sj17, Yì Fēng 翳風.
99	G20, Fēng Chí 風池.
100	G20, Fēng Chí 風池.
101	Xīn Shè 新设
102	Sì Shén Cōng 四神聰
103	D20, Bǎi Huì 百會.
104	K12, Dà Hè 大赫.
105	Si9, Jiān Zhēn 肩貞.
106	Si11, Tiān Zōng 天宗.
107	G21, Jiān Jǐng 肩井.
108	D15, Yǎ Mén 啞門
109	B10, Tiān Zhù, 天柱
110	D16, Fēng Fǔ 風府.
111	D15, Yǎ Mén 啞門
112	Lu1, Zhōng Fǔ 中府.
113	Lv13, Zhāng Mén 章門.

114	Lv14, Qí Mén 期門.
115	G24, Rì Yuè 日月.
116	Lv13, Zhāng Mén 章門.
117	S13, Qì Hù 氣戶.
118	S14, Kù Fáng 庫房.
119	S15, Wū Yì 屋翳.
120	S16, Yīng Chuāng 膺窗.
121	S17, Rǔ Zhōng 乳中.
122	S18, Rǔ Gēn 乳根.
123	S25, Tiān Shū 天樞.
124	B18, Gān Shū, 肝輸
125	B27, Xiǎo Cháng Shū, 小陽輸
126	B31, Shàng Liáo, 上髎
127	B32, Cì Liáo, 次髎
128	B33, Zhōng Liáo, 中髎
129	B34, Xià Liáo, 下髎
130	G21, Jiān Jǐng 肩井.
131	D14, Dà Zhuī 大椎.
132	R12, Zhōng Wǎn 中脘.
133	R22, Tiān Tū 天突.
134	Bā Huá 八華
135	Lv12, Jí Mài 急脈.
136	Huán Zhōng 環中
137	D4, Mìng Mén, 命門
138	Wei Guan Xia Shu 胃管下输
139	Li15, Jiān Yú 肩髃.
140	Sj14, Jiān Liáo 肩髎.
141	D4, Mìng Mén, 命門.
142	D3, Yāo Yáng Guān, 腰陽關.
143	D2, Yāo Shū, 腰輸.
144	B27, Xiǎo Cháng Shū, 小陽輸
145	B31, Shàng Liáo, 上髎
146	B32, Cì Liáo, 次髎
147	B33, Zhōng Liáo, 中髎
148	B34, Xià Liáo, 下髎
149	G30, Huán Tiào 環跳.
150	Bā Liáo 八髎
151	R22, Tiān Tū 天突.
152	G21, Jiān Jǐng 肩井.
153	Sj15, Tiān Liáo 天髎.
154	Si13, Qū Yuān 曲垣.

155	Li15, Jiān Yú 肩髃.
156	Lv13, Zhāng Mén 章門.
157	R15, Jiū Wěi 鳩尾.
158	G26, Dài Mài 帶脈.
159	G21, Jiān Jǐng 肩井.
160	S18, Rǔ Gēn 乳根.
161	Lu2, Yún Mén 云門.
162	Lu1, Zhōng Fǔ 中府.
163	R4, Guān Yuán 關元.
164	Huán Zhōng 環中.
165	B43, Gāo Huāng Shū, 膏肓輸
166	G29, Jū Liáo 居髎.
167	Lu1, Zhōng Fǔ 中府.
168	Lu1, Zhōng Fǔ 中府.
169	S31, Bì Guān 髀關.
170	Sp15, Dà Héng 大橫.
171	Si15, Jiān Zhōng Shū 肩中輸.
172	Si12, Bǐng Fēng 秉風.
173	Si10, Nào Shū 臑輸.
174	Si11, Tiān Zōng 天宗.
175	Si9, Jiān Zhēn 肩貞.
176	Si14, Jiān Wài Shū 肩外輸.
177	G21, Jiān Jǐng 肩井.
178	B13, Fèi Shū, 肺輸
179	R15, Jiū Wěi 鳩尾.
180	K27, Shū Fǔ 俞府.
181	K26, Yù Zhōng 彧中.
182	K25, Shén Cáng 神藏.
183	K24, Líng Xū 靈墟.
184	K23, Shén Fēng 神封.
185	K22, Bù Láng 步廊.
186	Huá Tuó Jiā Jí 華佗夾脊.
187	R4, Guān Yuán 關元.
188	R3, Zhōng Jí 中極.
189	San Jiao Jiu 三角灸.
190	Wéi Gōng 維宮.
191	Zǐ Gōng 子宮.
192	H1, Jí Quán 極泉.
193	R1, Huì Yīn 會陰.
194	R17, Shān Zhōng 膻中.
195	Yāo Yǎn 腰眼.

196	Si12, Bǐng Fēng 秉風.
197	Si13, Qū Yuān 曲垣.
198	Si11, Tiān Zōng 天宗.
199	Si10, Nào Shū 臑輸.
200	Qí Zhōng Sì Biāng 脐中四边
201	B32, Cì Liáo. 次髎
202	Lu1, Zhōng Fǔ 中府.
203	Li16, Jù Gǔ 巨骨.
204	San Jiao Jiu 三角灸.
205	Si1 Shào Zé 少澤.
206	Si3, Hòu Xī 后溪.
207	Si4, Wàn Gǔ 腕骨.
208	Yāo Tuī Diǎn 腰腿点.
209	Luò Zhěn 落枕.
210	Sj3, Zhōng Zhǔ 中渚.
211	Sj4, Yáng Chí 陽池.
212	Si6, Yǎng Lǎo 養老.
213	Li15, Jiān Yú 肩髃.
214	Sj14, Jiān Liáo 肩髎.
215	Li14, Bì Nào 臂臑.
216	Li11, Qū Chí 曲池.
217	Sj14, Jiān Liáo 肩髎.
218	Lu5, Chǐ Zé 尺澤.
219	Sì Fèng 四縫.
220	Yá Tòng Diǎn 牙痛点.
221	Lu10, Yǔ Ji 魚際.
222	Lu11, Shǎo Shāng 少商.
223	B25, Dà Cháng Shū, 大腸輸
224	Sp20, Zhōu Róng 周榮.
225	Sp19, Xīong Xiāng 胸鄉.
226	Sp18, Tiān Xī 天溪.
227	Sp17, Shí Dòu 食竇.
228	Sp21, Dà Bāo 大包.
229	Si3, Hòu Xī 后溪.
230	Si1 Shào Zé 少澤.
231	H3, Shào Hǎi 少海.
232	Lu7, Liè Quē 列缺.
233	Shí Xuān 十宣.
234	Li15, Jiān Yú 肩髃.
235	Si8, Xiǎo Hǎi 小海.
236	P3, Qū Zé 曲澤.

237	Si6, Yǎng Lǎo 養老.
238	H1, Jí Quán 極泉.
239	H9, Shào Chōng 少沖.
240	H8, Shào Fǔ 少府.
241	Li15, Jiān Yú 肩髃.
242	Jīng Líng 精靈.
243	Wēi Líng 威靈.
244	Wài Láo Gōng 外勞宮.
245	Lu11, Shǎo Shāng 少商.
246	Li4, Hé Gǔ 合谷.
247	H3, Shào Hǎi 少海.
248	H8, Shào Fǔ 少府.
249	P8, Láo Gōng 勞宮.
250	Lu10, Yǔ Jì 魚際.
251	Li11, Qū Chí 曲池.
252	Shí Xuān 十宣.
253	Si1 Shào Zé 少澤.
254	Zhōng Kuí 中魁.
255	Shí Xuān 十宣.
256	P6, Nèi Guān 內關.
257	Lu9, Tài Yuān 太淵.
258	P7, Dà Líng 大陵.
259	H7, Shén Mén 神門.
260	Sj4, Yáng Chí 陽池.
261	G12, Wán Gǔ 完骨.
262	Sj6, Zhī Gōu 支溝.
263	Sj5, Wài Guān 外關.
264	Sì Féng 四縫.
265	Sj3, Zhōng Zhǔ 中渚.
266	Sj4, Yáng Chí 陽池.
267	Si6, Yǎng Lǎo 養老.
268	Bā Xié 八邪
269	Luò Zhěn 落枕.
270	Bā Xié 八邪
271	Yāo Tòng Xué 腰痛穴.
272	Zhōng Quán 中泉.
273	Li5, Yáng Xī 陽溪.
274	Li4, Hé Gǔ 合谷.
275	Li3, Sān Jiān 三間.
276	Li2, Èr Jiān 二間.
277	Li1, Shāng Yáng 商陽.
278	P8, Láo Gōng 勞宮.
279	Si6, Yǎng Lǎo 養老.
280	Si6, Yǎng Lǎo 養老.
281	Shǒu Nì Zhù 手逆注.
282	Sj5, Wài Guān 外關.
283	Quán Jiān 拳尖.
284	Wǔ Hǔ 五虎
285	Lu7, Liè Quē 列缺.
286	Zhǒu Jiān 肘尖
287	Li15, Jiān Yú 肩髃.
288	Sj14, Jiān Liáo 肩髎.
289	Li15, Jiān Yú 肩髃.
290	Sì Féng 四縫.
291	Yá Tòng Xué 牙痛穴.
292	Sj10, Tiān Jǐng 天井.
293	Sì Féng 四縫.
294	Li15, Jiān Yú 肩髃.
295	Duó Mìng 夺命
296	Lu5, Chǐ Zé 尺澤.
297	Si3, Hòu Xī 后溪.
298	Li4, Hé Gǔ 合谷.
299	Si5, Yáng Gǔ 陽谷.
300	Si7, Zhī Zhèng 支正.
301	Si8, Xiǎo Hǎi 小海.
302	Wài Láo Gōng 外勞宮.
303	Li11, Qū Chí 曲池.
304	Wēi Líng 威靈.
305	Jīng Líng 精靈.
306	Zhōng Quán 中泉.
307	Li1, Shāng Yáng 商陽.
308	Sj1, Guān Chōng 關沖.
309	Si1 Shào Zé 少澤.
310	Li2, Èr Jiān 二間.
311	Li3, Sān Jiān 三間.
312	Sj2, Yè Mén 液門.
313	Si2, Qián Gǔ 前谷.
314	Si3, Hòu Xī 后溪.
315	Sj3, Zhōng Zhǔ 中渚.
316	P9, Zhōng Chōng 中沖.
317	Zhōng Kuí 中魁.
318	Xiǎo Gǔ Kōng 小骨空.

319	Dà Gŭ Kōng 大骨空.
320	Shí Xuān 十宣.
321	Lu7, Liè Quē 列缺.
322	Li5, Yáng Xī 陽溪.
323	Sj4, Yáng Chí 陽池.
324	H8, Shào Fŭ 少府.
325	Sj10, Tiān Jĭng 天井.
326	Li11, Qū Chí 曲池.
327	H7, Shén Mén 神門.
328	Si8, Xiăo Hăi 小海.
329	Li4, Hé Gŭ 合谷.
330	Sp10, Xuè Hăi 血海.
331	Sj13, Năo Huì 臑會.
332	Li14, Bì Nào 臂臑.
333	P8, Láo Gōng 勞宮.
334	H8, Shào Fŭ 少府.
335	Li5, Yáng Xī 陽溪.
336	Si8, Xiăo Hăi 小海.
337	Li11, Qū Chí 曲池.
338	Lu5, Chĭ Zé 尺澤.
339	Si8, Xiăo Hăi 小海.
340	H3, Shào Hăi 少海.
341	Li11, Qū Chí 曲池.
342	Lu9, Tài Yuān 太淵.
343	Lu6, Kŏng Zuì 孔最.
344	Lu5, Chĭ Zé 尺澤.
345	Zhŏu Jiān 肘尖
346	Jian Qian 肩前
347	Bì Zhōng 臂中.
348	Èr Bái 二白.
349	Li11, Qū Chí 曲池.
350	Li1, Shāng Yáng 商陽.
351	Lu9, Tài Yuān 太淵.
352	P3, Qū Zé 曲澤.
353	Lu5, Chĭ Zé 尺澤.
354	H1, Jí Quán 極泉.
355	H8, Shào Fŭ 少府.
356	H7, Shén Mén 神門.
357	Lu11, Shăo Shāng 少商.
358	Sān Shāng 三商.
359	Shí Xuān 十宣.

360	Si8, Xiăo Hăi 小海.
361	P8, Láo Gōng 勞宮.
362	Sì Féng 四縫.
363	Bā Xié 八邪.
364	Lu5, Chĭ Zé 尺澤.
365	Lu11, Shăo Shāng 少商.
366	Li1, Shāng Yáng 商陽.
367	P9, Zhōng Chōng 中沖.
368	Sj1, Guān Chōng 關沖.
369	Si1 Shào Zé 少澤.
370	H9, Shào Chōng 少沖.
371	K1, Yŏng Quán 涌泉.
372	B67, Zhì Yīn. 至陰.
373	G44, Zú Qiào Yīn , Qiào Yīn 足竅陰.
374	S45, Lì Duì 歷兌.
375	Lv1, Dà Dūn 大敦.
376	Sp1, Yĭn Bái 隱白.
377	G34, Yáng Líng Quán 陽陵泉.
378	B40, Wĕi Zhōng, 委中.
379	B39, Wèi Yáng, 委陽.
380	S36, Zú Sān Lĭ 足三里.
381	S37, Shàng Jù Xū 上巨虛.
382	S39, Xià Jù Xū 下巨虛.
383	G34, Yáng Líng Quán 陽陵泉.
384	Dăn Náng Xué 膽囊穴.
385	G37, Guāng Míng 光明.
386	G39, Xuán Zhōng 懸鍾.
387	B60, Kūn Lún, 昆崙.
388	G40, Qiū Xū 丘墟.
389	B67, Zhì Yīn, 至陰.
390	Sì Qiáng 四強.
391	Hè Dĭng 鶴頂.
392	Xī Yăn 膝眼.
393	Dăn Náng Xué 膽囊穴.
394	Lán Wĕi Xué 闌尾穴.
395	Sp1, Yĭn Bái 隱白.
396	Sp4, Gōng Sūn 公孫.
397	Sp5, Shāng Qiū 商丘.
398	B36, Chéng Fú, 承扶.
399	B37, Yĭn Mén, 殷門.

400	B40, Wěi Zhōng, 委中.
401	B57, Chéng Shān, 承山.
402	B60, Kūn Lún, 昆崙.
403	B37, Yǐn Mén, 殷門.
404	B40, Wěi Zhōng, 委中.
405	B57, Chéng Shān, 承山.
406	B59, Fū Yáng, 跗陽.
407	B60, Kūn Lún, 昆崙.
408	B64, Jīng Gū, 京骨.
409	K1, Yǒng Quán 涌泉.
410	G31, Fēng Shì 風市.
411	G31, Fēng Shì 風市.
412	S31, Bì Guān 髀關.
413	Jiàn Xī 健膝 (Dǐng Shàng, 頂上)
414	S36, Zú Sān Lǐ 足三里.
415	Lán Wěi Xué 闌尾穴.
416	S37, Shàng Jù Xū 上巨虛.
417	S40, Fēng Lóng 丰隆.
418	S41, Jiě Xī 解溪.
419	S43, Xiàn Gū 陷谷.
420	S44, Nèi Tíng 內庭.
421	G30, Huán Tiào 環跳.
422	G31, Fēng Shì 風市.
423	G34, Yáng Líng Quán 陽陵泉.
424	Dǎn Náng Xué 膽囊穴.
425	G36, Wài Qiū 外丘.
426	G37, Guāng Míng 光明.
427	G38, Yáng Fǔ 陽輔.
428	G39, Xuán Zhōng 懸鍾.
429	G40, Qiū Xū 丘墟.
430	Bā Fēng 八風.
431	Qì Chuǎn 氣喘.
432	Sp6, Sān Yīn Jiāo 三陰交.
433	K3, Tài Xī 太溪.
434	K6, Zhào Hǎi 照海.
435	Lv4, Zhōng Fēng 中封.
436	Sp6, Sān Yīn Jiāo 三陰交.
437	B62, Shēn Mài, 申脈.
438	B67, Zhì Yīn, 至陰.
439	G44, Zú Qiào Yīn , Qiào Yīn 足竅陰.

440	S45, Lì Duì 厲兌.
441	B57, Chéng Shān, 承山.
442	K3, Tài Xī 太溪.
443	Lv3, Tài Chōng 太沖.
444	Sp3, Tài Bái 太白.
445	G40, Qiū Xū 丘墟.
446	S42, Chōng Yáng 沖陽.
447	B64, Jīng Gǔ, 京骨.
448	Lv5, Lí Gōu 蠡溝.
449	Lv3, Tài Chōng 太沖.
450	Sp3, Tài Bái 太白.
451	Sp2, Dà Dū 大都.
452	Lv2, Xíng Jiān 行間.
453	Dǎn Náng Xué 膽囊穴.
454	Lán Wěi Xué 闌尾穴.
455	Bǎi Chóng Wuō 百蟲窩.
456	Hè Dǐng 鶴頂.
457	Xī Yǎn 膝眼.
458	Bā Fēng 八風.
459	B57, Chéng Shān, 承山.
460	Sp2, Dà Dū 大都.
461	Sp3, Tài Bái 太白.
462	Lv1, Dà Dūn 大敦.
463	Sp1, Yǐn Bái 隱白.
464	K3, Tài Xī 太溪.
465	Nèi Huái Jiān 內踝尖.
466	Wài Huái Jiān 外踝尖.
467	B67, Zhì Yīn, 至陰.
468	Nǚ Xī 女膝.
469	Lv8, Qū Quán 曲泉.
470	Dú Yīn 独阴.
471	Lǐ Nèi Tíng 里内庭.
472	B40, Wěi Zhōng, 委中.
473	B39, Wěi Yáng, 委陽.
474	B57, Chéng Shān, 承山.
475	B60, Kūn Lún, 昆崙.
476	R1, Huì Yīn 會陰.
477	K1, Yǒng Quán 涌泉.
478	Sp10, Xuè Hǎi 血海.
479	Sp11, Jī Mén 箕門.
480	Lv8, Qū Quán 曲泉.

481	Lv9, Yīn Bāo 陰包.
482	Lv7, Xī Guān 膝關.
483	Sp9, Yīn Líng Quán 陰陵泉.
484	S41, Jiě Xī 解溪.
485	S43, Xiàn Gŭ 陷谷.
486	S44, Nèi Tíng 內庭.
487	S45, Lì Duì 厲兌.
488	K10, Yīn Gŭ 陰谷.
489	Líng Hòu 陵后.
490	B36, Chéng Fú, 承扶.
491	B37, Yīn Mén, 殷門.
492	B38, Fú Xī, 浮郗.
493	B39, Wĕi Yáng, 委陽.
494	B40, Wèi Zhōng, 委中.
495	G34, Yáng Líng Quán 陽陵泉.
496	S35, Dú Bí 犢鼻.
497	S36, Zú Sān Lĭ 足三里.
498	S35, Dú Bí 犢鼻.
499	S40, Fēng Lóng 丰隆.
500	Sp6, Sān Yīn Jiāo 三陰交.
501	G34, Yáng Líng Quán 陽陵泉.
502	S36, Zú Sān Lĭ 足三里.
503	Sp1, Yĭn Bái 隱白.
504	Sp4, Gōng Sūn 公孫.
505	Sp5, Shāng Qiū 商丘.
506	Sp6, Sān Yīn Jiāo 三陰交.
507	S32, Fú Tù 伏兔.
508	Lv4, Zhōng Fēng 中封.
509	Lv4, Zhōng Fēng 中封.
510	Lv3, Tài Chōng 太沖.
511	Lv2, Xíng Jiān 行間.
512	Lv1, Dà Dūn 大敦.
513	Sp10, Xuè Hăi 血海.
514	Lv4, Zhōng Fēng 中封.
515	Lv3, Tài Chōng 太沖.
516	Lv2, Xíng Jiān 行間.
517	S36, Zú Sān Lĭ 足三里.
518	S32, Fú Tù 伏兔.
519	K1, Yŏng Quán 涌泉.
520	G39, Xuán Zhōng 懸鍾.
521	Dú Yīn 独阴.

522	Lĭ Nèi Tíng 里內庭.
523	K6, Zhào Hăi 照海.
524	Lv3, Tài Chōng 太沖.
525	Lv3, Tài Chōng 太沖.
526	Lv2, Xíng Jiān 行間.
527	Bā Fēng 八風.
528	G31, Fēng Shì 風市.
529	Sp9, Yīn Líng Quán 陰陵泉.
530	Lv8, Qū Quán 曲泉.
531	G30, Huán Tiào 環跳.
532	G34, Yáng Líng Quán 陽陵泉.
533	S31, Bì Guān 髀關.
534	G29, Jū Liáo 居髎.
535	G30, Huán Tiào 環跳.
536	Xī Yăn 膝眼.
537	Lv8, Qū Quán 曲泉.
538	Lán Wĕi Xué 闌尾穴.
539	Dăn Náng Xué 膽囊穴.
540	Hè Dĭng 鶴頂.
541	K1, Yŏng Quán 涌泉.
542	Bā Fēng 八風.
543	Lv4, Zhōng Fēng 中封.
544	Bā Fēng 八風.
545	K3, Tài Xī 太溪.
546	B57, Chéng Shān, 承山.
547	B60, Kūn Lún, 昆崙.
548	B37, Yīn Mén, 殷門.
549	Lán Wèi Xué 闌尾穴.
550	G29, Jū Liáo 居髎.
551	Sp9, Yīn Líng Quán 陰陵泉.
552	S35, Dú Bí 犢鼻.
553	Qì Chuăn 氣喘.
554	G40, Qiū Xū 丘墟.
555	D1, Cháng Qiáng, 長強.
556	Băi Chóng Wuō 百蟲窩.
557	Sp10, Xuè Hăi 血海.
558	S41, Jiě Xī 解溪.
559	K10, Yīn Gŭ 陰谷.
560	Lv3, Tài Chōng 太沖.
561	Sì Shén Cōng 四神聰
562	Dāng Yáng 当阳.

563	Yú Yāo 魚腰.
564	Qiú Hòu 球后.
565	Shàng Yíng Xiāng 上迎香.
566	Yìn Táng 印堂.
567	Tài Yáng 太陽.
568	Ěr Jiān 耳尖.
569	Yì Míng 翳明.
570	Nèi Yíng Xiāng 內迎香.
571	Hǎi Quán 海泉.
572	Jīn Jīn Yù Yè 金津玉液.
573	Jǐng Bǎi Láo 颈百劳.
574	Wèi Guān Xià Shū 胃管下輸.
575	Pǐ Gēn 痞根.
576	Xià Jí Shū 下極輸.
577	Yāo Yǎn 腰眼.
578	Shí Qī Zhuī 十七椎.
579	Yāo Qí 腰奇.
580	Zǐ Gōng 子宮.
581	Dìng Chuǎn 定喘.
582	Huá Tuó Jiā Jí 華佗夾脊.
583	Zhōng Kuí 中魁.
584	Xiǎo Gǔ Kōng 小骨空.
585	Bā Xié 八邪.
586	Zhōng Quán 中泉.
587	Dà Gǔ Kōng 大骨空.
588	Wài Láo Gōng 外勞宫.
589	Yāo Tòng Xué 腰痛穴.
590	Kuān Gǔ 髖骨.
591	Hè Dǐng 鶴頂.
592	Xī Yǎn 膝眼.
593	Nèi Xī Yǎn 內膝眼.
594	Lán Wěi Xué 闌尾穴.
595	Dǎn Náng Xué 膽囊穴.
596	Wài Huái Jiān 外踝尖.
597	Bā Fēng 八風.
598	Qì Chuǎn 氣喘.
599	Nèi Xī Yǎn 內膝眼.
600	Nèi Huái Jiān 內踝尖.
601	Ěr Jiān 耳尖
602	Li11, Qū Chí 曲池.
603	G31, Fēng Shì 風市

604	Si8, Xiǎo Hǎi 小海
605	Si6, Yǎng Lǎo 養老
606	Si3, Hòu Xī 后溪
607	G2, Tīng Huì 聽會
608	Si3, Hòu Xī 后溪
609	Lv8, Qū Quán 曲泉
610	G30, Huán Tiào 環跳
611	G30, Huán Tiào 環跳
612	G31, Fēng Shì 風市
613	Li15, Jiān Yú 肩髃
614	Sj14, Jiān Liáo 肩髎.
615	H1, Jí Quán 極泉
616	Lu7, Liè Quē 列缺
617	Li5, Yáng Xī 陽溪
618	Li4, Hé Gǔ 合谷
619	Sp10, Xuè Hǎi 血海
620	Lv8, Qū Quán 曲泉
621	S6, Jiá Chē 頰車
622	S4, Dì Cāng 地倉
623	Sj23, Sī Zhú Kōng 丝竹空
624	G8, Shuài Gǔ 率谷
625	G14, Yáng Bái 陽白
626	Yú Yāo 魚腰
627	D20, Bǎi Huì 百會
628	B7, Tōng Tiān, 通天
629	R15, Jiū Wěi 鳩尾
630	R13, Shàng Wǎn 上脘
631	S21, Liáng Mén 梁門
632	R12, Zhōng Wǎn 中脘
633	D11, Shén Dào, 神道
634	D9, Zhì Yáng, 至陽
635	Sj14, Jiān Liáo 肩髎
636	H1, Jí Quán 極泉
637	S35, Dú Bí 犢鼻
638	Nèi Xī Yǎn 內膝眼
639	G34, Yáng Líng Quán 陽陵泉
640	Sp9, Yīn Líng Quán 陰陵泉
641	P5, Jiān Shǐ 間使
642	Sj6, Zhī Gōu 支溝

643	S38, Tiáo Kǒu 條口
644	B57, Chéng Shān, 承山

Test 7-1: Command Points or Shu Xue on Six Meridians of Hand (1-30)

1	Lu5, Chǐ Zé 尺澤
2	Lu8, Jīng Qú 經渠, ben
3	Lu9, Tài Yuān 太淵, mother
4	Lu10, Yǔ Jì 魚際
5	Lu11, Shǎo Shāng 少商
6	H3, Shào Hǎi 少海
7	H4, Líng Dào 靈道
8	H7, Shén Mén 神門, child
9	H8, Shào Fǔ 少府, ben
10	H9, Shào Chōng 少沖, mother
11	P9, Zhōng Chōng 中沖, mother
12	P8, Láo Gōng 勞宮
13	P7, Dà Líng 大陵
14	P5, Jiān Shǐ 間使
15	P3, Qū Zé 曲澤
16	Li11, Qū Chí 曲池, mother
17	Li5, Yáng Xī 陽溪
18	Li2, Èr Jiān 二間, child
19	Li3, Sān Jiān 三間
20	Li1, Shāng Yáng 商陽, ben
21	Sj1, Guān Chōng 關沖
22	Sj2, Yè Mén 液門
23	Sj3, Zhōng Zhǔ 中渚, mother
24	Sj6, Zhi Gōu 支溝, ben
25	Sj10, Tiān Jǐng 天井, child
26	Si8, Xiǎo Hǎi 小海, child
27	Si5, Yáng Gǔ 陽谷, ben
28	Si3, Hòu Xī 后溪, mother
29	Si2, Qián Gú 前谷
30	Si1 Shào Zé 少澤

Test 7-2 Command Points or Shu Xue on Six Meridians of Foot (1-30)

1	Sp9, Yīn Líng Quán 陰陵泉
2	Sp1, Yǐn Bái 隱白
3	Sp2, Dà Dū 大都, mother
4	Sp3, Tài Bái 太白, ben
5	Sp5, Shāng Qiū 商丘
6	S36, Zú Sān Lǐ 足三里
7	S41, Jiě Xī 解溪, mother
8	S43, Xiàn Gǔ 陷谷
9	S44, Nèi Tíng 內庭
10	S45, Lì Duì 厲兌, child
11	G43, Xiá Xī 俠溪
12	G44, Zú Qiào Yīn , Qiào Yīn 足竅陰
13	G41, Zú Lín Qì, Lín Qì 足臨泣
14	G38, Yáng Fǔ 陽輔, child
15	G34, Yáng Líng Quán 陽陵泉
16	Lv1, Dà Dūn 大敦, ben
17	Lv2, Xíng Jiān 行間, child
18	Lv3, Tài Chōng 太沖
19	Lv4, Zhōng Fēng 中封
20	Lv8, Qū Quán 曲泉, mother
21	K10, Yīn Gǔ 陰谷
22	K1, Yǒng Quán 涌泉
23	K7, Fù Liū 復溜, mother
24	K3, Tài Xī 太溪
25	K2, Rán Gǔ 然谷
26	B40, Wěi Zhōng, 委中

27	B60, Kūn Lún, 昆崙
28	B65, Shù Gǔ, 束骨, child
29	B66, Tōng Gǔ, Zú Tōng Gǔ, 通谷, 足通谷, ben
30	B67, Zhì Yīn, 至陰, mother

Test 7-3 Yuan Points or Source Points (1-12)

1	P7, Dà Líng 大陵
2	Lu9, Tài Yuān 太淵
3	H7, Shén Mén 神門
4	G40, Qiū Xū 丘墟
5	S42, Chōng Yáng 沖陽
6	B64, Jīng Gǔ, 京骨
7	Lv3, Tài Chōng 太沖
8	Sp3, Tài Bái 太白
9	K3, Tài Xī 太溪
10	Si4, Wàn Gǔ 腕骨
11	Sj4, Yáng Chí 陽池
12	Li4, Hé Gǔ 合谷

Test 7-4 Luo Points or Linking/Collateral Points (1-15)

1	P6, Nèi Guān 內關
2	Lu7, Liè Quē 列缺
3	H5, Tōng Lǐ 通里
4	Lv5, Lí Gōu 蠡溝
5	Sp4, Gōng Sūn 公孫
6	K4, Dà Zhōng 大鍾
7	G37, Guāng Míng 光明
8	S40, Fēng Lóng 丰隆
9	B58, Feī Yáng, 飛揚
10	Si7, Zhi Zhèng 支正
11	Li6, Piān Lì 偏歷
12	Sj5, Wài Guān 外關
13	R15, Jiū Wěi 鳩尾
14	Sp21, Dà Bāo 大包
15	D1, Cháng Qiáng, 長強

Test 7-5 Mu Points or Anterior Points (1-12)

1	R17, Shān Zhōng 膻中
2	Lv14, Qí Mén 期門
3	G24, Rì Yuè 日月
4	R12, Zhōng Wǎn 中脘
5	Lv13, Zhāng Mén 章門
6	G25, Jīng Mén 京門
7	R4, Guān Yuán 關元
8	R3, Zhōng Jí 中極
9	Lu1, Zhōng Fǔ 中府
10	R14, Jù Què 巨闕
11	S25, Tiān Shū 天樞
12	R5, Shí Mén 石門

Test 7-6 Bei Shu Points or Back Shu/Posterior Points (1-12)

1	B13, Fèi Shū, 肺輸
2	B14, Jué Yīn Shū, 厥陰輸
3	B15, Xīn Shū, 心輸
4	B18, Gān Shū, 肝輸
5	B19, Dǎn Shū, 膽輸
6	B20, Pí Shū, 脾輸
7	B21, Wèi Shū, 胃俞
8	B22, Sān Jiāo Shū, 三焦輸
9	B23, Shèn Shū, 腎輸
10	B25, Dà Cháng Shū, 大腸輸
11	B27, Xiǎo Cháng Shū, 小腸輸
12	B28, Páng Guāng Shū, 膀胱輸

Test 7-7 Meeting Points of Eight Extraordinary Meridians (1-8)

1	Lu7, Liè Quē 列缺
2	P6, Nèi Guān 內關
3	K6, Zhào Hǎi 照海
4	Sp4, Gōng Sūn 公孫
5	B62, Shēn Mài, 申脈
6	G41, Zú Lín Qì, Lín Qì 足臨泣
7	Si3, Hòu Xī 后溪
8	Sj5, Wài Guān 外關

Test 7-8 influential points (1-8).

1	G34, Yáng Líng Quán 陽陵泉, tendons

2	G39, Xuán Zhōng 懸鍾. ,marrow
3	Lu9, Tài Yuān 太淵, vessels
4	R17, Shān Zhōng 膻中, energy
5	R12, Zhōng Wǎn 中脘, bowels
6	B11, Dà Zhù, 大杼, bones
7	B17, Gé Shū, 膈輸, blood
8	Lv13, Zhāng Mén 章門, viscera

Test 7-9 xia he xue or Lower Sea Points (1-6)

1	S36, Zú Sān Lǐ 足三里
2	S37, Shàng Jù Xū 上巨虛
3	S39, Xià Jù Xū 下巨虛
4	G34, Yáng Líng Quán 陽陵泉
5	B39, Wěi Yáng, 委陽
6	B40, Wěi Zhōng, 委中

Test 7-10 Xi Xue or Fissural/Cleft Points (1-16)

1	Lu6, Kǒng Zuì 孔最
2	P4, Xī Mén 郄門
3	H6, Yīn Xī 陰郄
4	Sj7, Huì Zōng 會宗
5	Si6, Yǎng Lǎo 養老
6	Li7, Wēn Liū 溫溜
7	Sp8, Dì Jī 地機
8	Lv6, Zhōng Dū 中都
9	K9, Zhú Bīn 筑賓
10	K8, Jiāo Xìn 交信
11	K5, Shuǐ Quán 水泉
12	S34, Liáng Qiū 梁丘
13	G35, Yáng Jiāo 陽交
14	G36, Wài Qiū 外丘
15	B59, Fū Yáng, 跗陽
16	B63, Jīn Mén, 金門

Test 7-11 (1-12) write down the name of Mu Points / Anterior Points on the right column to pair off the Shu and Mu points / 根据俞幕配穴法在右栏写下幕穴名称.

	Bei Shu Points or Back Shu/Posterior Points	Mu Points or Anterior Points
1	B13, Fèi Shū, 肺輸	Lu1, Zhōng Fǔ 中府
2	B14, Jué Yīn Shū, 厥陰輸	R17, Shān Zhōng 膻中
3	B15, Xīn Shū, 心輸	R14, Jù Què 巨闕
4	B18, Gān Shū, 肝輸	Lv14, Qí Mén 期門
5	B19, Dǎn Shū, 膽輸	G24, Rì Yuè 日月
6	B20, Pí Shū, 脾輸	Lv13, Zhāng Mén 章門
7	B21, Wèi Shū, 胃俞	R12, Zhōng Wǎn 中脘
8	B22, Sān Jiāo Shū, 三焦輸	R5, Shí Mén 石門
9	B23, Shèn Shū, 腎輸	G25, Jīng Mén 京門
10	B25, Dà Cháng Shū, 大腸輸	S25, Tiān Shū 天樞
11	B27, Xiǎo Cháng Shū, 小腸輸	R4, Guān Yuán 關元
12	B28, Páng Guāng Shū, 膀胱輸	R3, Zhōng Jí 中極

Test 7-12 (1-12) write down the name of Luo Points / Linking / Collateral Points on the right column to pair off the Yuan points and Luo points / 根据原络配穴法在右栏写下络穴名称.

	Yuan Points or Source Points 原穴	Luo Points or Linking/Collateral Points 络穴

1	P7, Dà Líng 大陵	Sj5, Wài Guān 外關
2	Lu9, Tài Yuān 太淵	Li6, Piān Lì 偏歷
3	H7, Shén Mén 神門	Si7, Zhi Zhèng 支正
4	G40, Qiū Xū 丘墟	Lv5, Lí Gōu 蠡溝
5	S42, Chōng Yáng 沖陽	Sp4, Gōng Sūn 公孫
6	B64, Jīng Gŭ, 京骨	K4, Dà Zhōng 大鍾
7	Lv3, Tài Chōng 太沖	G37, Guāng Míng 光明
8	Sp3, Tài Bái 太白	S40, Fēng Lóng 丰隆
9	K3, Tài Xī 太溪	B58, Feī Yáng, 飛揚
10	Si4, Wàn Gŭ 腕骨	H5, Tōng Lǐ 通里
11	Sj4, Yáng Chí 陽池	P6, Nèi Guān 內關
12	Li4, Hé Gŭ 合谷	Lu7, Liè Quē 列缺

Test 7-13 (1-12) write down the name of Child Points on the right column to pair off the Mother points and Child points / 根据母子配穴法在右栏写下子穴名称.

	Mother points / 母穴	Child points / 子穴
1	B67, Zhì Yīn, 至陰	B65, Shù Gŭ, 束骨
2	Lv8, Qū Quán 曲泉	Lv2, Xíng Jiān 行間
3	K7, Fù Liū 復溜	K1, Yǒng Quán 涌泉
4	Sp2, Dà Dū 大都	Sp5, Shāng Qiū 商丘
5	S41, Jiě Xī 解溪	S45, Lì Duì 歷兌
6	Lu9, Tài Yuān 太淵	Lu5, Chǐ Zé 尺澤
7	H9, Shào Chōng 少沖	H7, Shén Mén 神門
8	P9, Zhōng Chōng 中沖	P7, Dà Líng 大陵
9	Li11, Qū Chí 曲池	Li2, Èr Jiān 二間
10	Sj3, Zhōng Zhŭ 中渚	Sj10, Tiān Jǐng 天井
11	Si3, Hòu Xī 后溪	Si8, Xiǎo Hǎi 小海
12	G43, Xiá Xī 俠溪	G38, Yáng Fŭ 陽輔

Test 7-14 (1-5) write down the name of northern points on the right column to pair off the southern points and northern points / 根据泻南补北配穴法在右栏写下北穴名称.

	Southern points for sedation / 南穴	Northern points for tonification / 北穴
1	H8, Shào Fŭ 少府	Lv8, Qū Quán 曲泉
2	Sp3, Tài Bái 太白	Lv1, Dà Dūn 大敦
3	Lv8, Qū Quán 曲泉	Sp3, Tài Bái 太白
4	Lu8, Jīng Qú 經渠	P8, Láo Gōng 勞宮
5	Lv1, Dà Dūn 大敦	Lu8, Jīng Qú 經渠

Test 7-15 (1-11) write down the name of well points [jǐng xué] on the right column, beginning with B67, Zhì Yīn, 至陰 to complete the cycle of twelve meridians in their connecting sequences in order to induce yang from yin / 根据接经从阴引阳配穴法在右栏写下井穴名称, 从至陰开始.

	Well points [jǐng xué] / 井穴
	B67, Zhì Yīn, 至陰
1	K1, Yǒng Quán 涌泉
2	P9, Zhōng Chōng 中沖
3	Sj1, Guān Chōng 關沖
4	G44, Zú Qiào Yīn , Qiào Yīn 足竅陰
5	Lv1, Dà Dūn 大敦
6	Lu11, Shǎo Shāng 少商
7	Li1, Shāng Yáng 商陽
8	S45, Lì Duì 歷兌
9	Sp1, Yǐn Bái 隱白
10	H9, Shào Chōng 少沖
11	Si1 Shào Zé 少澤

Test 7-16 (1-11) write down the name of well points [jǐng xué] on the right column, beginning with Lu11, Shǎo Shāng to complete the cycle of twelve meridians in their connecting sequences in order to induce yin from yang / 根据接经从阳引阴配穴法在右栏写下井穴名称,发从少商开始.

	Well points [jǐng xué] / 井穴
	Lu11, Shǎo Shāng 少商
1	Li1, Shāng Yáng 商陽
2	S45, Lì Duì 歷兌
3	Sp1, Yǐn Bái 隱白
4	H9, Shào Chōng 少沖
5	Si1 Shào Zé 少澤
6	B67, Zhì Yīn, 至陰
7	K1, Yǒng Quán 涌泉
8	P9, Zhōng Chōng 中沖
9	Sj1, Guān Chōng 關沖
10	G44, Zú Qiào Yīn , Qiào Yīn 足竅陰
11	Lv1, Dà Dūn 大敦

Test 7-17 (1-4) write down the name of confluence points [bā mài bā huì xué] on the right column to pair off the points on two columns / 根据交经八穴配穴法在右栏写下相配的八脈交會穴名称.

1	P6, Nèi Guān 內關	Sp4, Gōng Sūn 公孫
2	K6, Zhào Hǎi 照海	Lu7, Liè Quē 列缺
3	B62, Shēn Mài, 申脈	Si3, Hòu Xī 后溪
4	G41, Zú Lín Qì, Lín Qì 足臨泣	Sj5, Wài Guān 外關

Test 7-18 (1-4) write down the name of influential points [bā huì xué] on the right column to pair off fissural points and influential points / 根据交经八穴配穴法在右栏写下相配的八會穴名称.

	Diseases / 疾病	fissural points, cleft points [xī xué, 郄穴];	influential points [bā huì xué, 八會穴]
1	Asthma with panting / 喘逆气急	Lu6, Kǒng Zuì 孔最	R17, Shān Zhōng 膻中
2	Coughing out blood / 咳血	Lu6, Kǒng Zuì 孔最	B17, Gé Shū, 膈輸
3	Acute stomachache / 胃痛剧烈	S34, Liáng Qiū 梁丘	R12, Zhōng Wǎn 中脘

4	Angina pectoris / 真心痛	P4, Xī Mén 郄門	B17, Gé Shū, 膈輸

Test 8-1 Needles and Common Needling Techniques (1-33)

1	Big needle Da zhen 大針
2	Long needle Chang zhen 长針
3	Minute needle Hao zhen 毫針
4	Round-sharp needle Yuan li zhen 員利針
5	Sword-shaped needle Pi zhen 鈹針
6	Sharp-edged needle Feng zhen 鋒針
7	Key-shaped needle Ti zhen 鍉針
8	round needle yuan zhen 员针
9	Scooping needle Chan zhen 鑱針
10	Round-sharp needle Yuan li zhen 員利針
11	three-edged needles san leng zhen 三棱針
12	fire needle huo zhen 火針
13	Minute needle Hao zhen 毫針
14	Seven star needle qi xing zhen 七星針
15	Key-shaped needle Ti zhen 鍉針
16	Skin-Needle Pí Fū Zhēn 皮膚針.
17	awl-like long needle mang zhen 芒針
18	intradermal needle pi nei zhen 皮內針
19	Insertion with middle finger support zhong chi fu chi fa 中指扶持法
20	Insertion of needle tip by holding the needle Jia chi zhen jian fa 夾持針尖法
21	Rapid needle insertion Su ci fa 速刺法
22	Insertion with the needle from midair xuan kong fa 悬空法
23	Twirled pressing insertion nian ya fa 捻压法
24	lifting and pushing in technique ti cha fa 提插法
25	twirling the needle nian zhuan fa 捻轉法
26	Nail-cutting method zhi qie jin zhen fa 指切進針法
27	Needle insertion by pushing-up Ti nie jin zhen fa 提捏進針法
28	Needle insertion by holding the needle Jia chi jin zhen fa 夾持進針法
29	Needle insertion by spreading/spreading method Shu zhang jin zhen fa 舒張進針法
30	Needle insertion with a tube Guan zhen jin zhen fa 管針進針法
31	Technique of pressing with the ball of the thumb Chuai fa 揣法
32	Technique of pressing and pinching with the nail Zhao fa 爪法
33	Technique of cutting with the nail Qie fa 切法

Test 8-2 Techniques of Promoting Needling Sensations and Energy Circulation (1-25)

1	Technique of dragon and tiger taking turns in moving energy /long hu jiao teng fa 龍虎交腾法
2	technique of pushing and pinching along the point /she fa 摄法
3	Manipulating the inserted needle by tracing the meridian /Xun fa 循法
4	Manipulating the inserted needle by shaking the needle /Yao fa 搖法
5	Manipulating the inserted needle by flying the needle /Fei fa 飛法
6	mobilizing energy method /yun qi fa 運氣法
7	Technique of rolling the needle /cuo fa 搓法
8	vibrating the needle technique /dong fa 动法
9	Methods of directing energy /dao qi fa 导气法
10	white tiger shaking its head /bai hu yao tou 白虎搖頭
11	Red phoenix greeting the source /chi feng ying yuan 赤鳳迎源
12	holding the energy method /na qi fa/zhong qi fa 納氣法 (中氣法)
13	Green dragon wagging its tail /qing long bai wei fa 青龍擺尾
14	retaining energy /liu qi fa 留氣法
15	Technique of knocking the needle /qiao fa 敲法
16	Manipulating the inserted needle by circling/pen fa 盤法
17	method of pushing in energy /jin qi fa 进气法
18	Manipulating the inserted needle by scrapping the handle /gua fa 刮法
19	Dragon and tiger moving up and down /long hu sheng jiang fa 龍虎升降法
20	snapping-technique/Manipulating the inserted needle by flicking the needle /tan fa 彈法
21	Pressing and stopping the energy to direct its flow /an jie fa 按截法
22	Grey turtle scouting in the hole /cang gui tan xue fa 蒼龜探穴
23	Technique of pressing in the needle /an fa 按法
24	Technique of vibrating the needle /chan fa 颤法
25	Manipulating the inserted needle as if shooting an arrow/nu fa 弩法

Test 8-3 Techniques of Tonification and Sedation (1-18).

1	Tonification and sedation by lifting and pushing in /ti cha bu xie 提插補泄.
2	Tonification and sedation by twirling technique/nian zhuan bu xie 捻转補泄
3	Tonification sedation by twirling in two directions /ying sui bu xie 迎隨補瀉.
4	Slow-and-quick tonification and sedation /xu ji bu xie 徐急補瀉.
5	Breathing tonification sedation /hu xi bu xie 呼吸補瀉.
6	Opening and closing technique for tonification and sedation /kai he bu xie 开阖补泻
7	Neutral technique /ping bu ping xie 平補平瀉

8	Forest fire /shao shan huo 燒山火
9	Cooling the heaven /tou tian liang 透天涼
10	Yin hidden in yang /yang zhong yin yin fa 陽中隱陰法
11	Yang hidden in yin /yin zhong yin yang fa 陰中隱陽法
12	Technique of pushing in fire for tonification /jin huo bu fa 进火補法
13	Technique of pushing in water for sedation /jin shui xie fa 进水瀉法
14	Retaining energy /liu qi fa 留氣法
15	Lifting the energy /ti qi fa 提氣法
16	Lifting up and pressing down /chou tian fa 抽添法
17	First and middle branches pounding in a mortar /zi wu dao jiu fa 子午搗臼法
18	Fighting between dragon and tiger /long hu jiao zhan fa 龍虎交戰法

Test 9: Auricular Points (1-93)

1	Er jian	Tip of ear	耳尖
2	Gan yang	Liver yang	肝阳
3	Lun yi	Helix no.1	轮一
4	Lun er	Helix no.2	轮二
5	Lun san	Helix no.3	轮三
6	Lun si	Helix no.4	轮四
7	Suo gu	Clavicle	锁骨
8	Jian	Shoulders	肩
9	Zhou	Elbows	肘
10	Wan	Wrists	腕
11	Feng xi	Wind creek	风溪
12	Zhi	Fingers	指
13	Zhi	Toes	趾
14	Gen	Calcaneus (heel)	跟
15	Gang men	Anus	肛门
16	Huai guan jie	Ankle joints	踝关节
17	Xi	Knees	膝
18	Kuan guan jie	Hip joints	髋关节
19	Yao di zhui	Lumbar sacral vertebrae	腰骶椎

20	Xiong zhui	Thoracic vertebrae	胸椎
21	Jing zhui	Cervical vertebrae	颈椎
22	Jing	Neck	颈
23	Xiong	Chest	胸
24	Fu	Abdomen	腹
25	Tun	Buttocks	臀
26	Pen qiang	Pelvic cavity	盆腔
27	Shen men	Divine door (spiritual door)	神门
28	Jiao wo zhong	Middle triangular fossa	角窝中
29	Nei sheng zhi qi	Internal genital organs	内生殖器
30	Zuo gu shen jing	Sciatic nerve	坐骨神经
31	Ting jiao	Cymba angle	艇角
32	Pang guang	Bladder	膀胱
33	Shen	Kidney	肾
34	Yi dan	Pancreas and gall	胰胆

		bladder	
35	Gan	Liver	肝
36	Pi	Spleen	脾
37	Fei	Lung	肺
38	Wei	Stomach	胃
39	Shi er zhi chang	Duodenum	十二指肠
40	Xiao chang	Small intestine	小肠
41	Lan wei	Appendix vermiformis	阑尾
42	Ting zhong	Cymba center	艇中
43	Shu niao guan	Ureter	输尿管
44	Da chang	Large intestine	大肠
45	Niao dao	Urethra	尿道
46	Wai sheng zhi qi	External genital organs	外生殖器
47	Jiao gan	Sympathetic	交感
48	Jiao wo shang	Upper triangular fossa	角窝上
49	Zhi chang	Rectum	直肠
50	Wai er	External ear	外耳
51	Er zhong	Ear center	耳中
52	Bi men	Cardiac orifice	賁门
53	Shi dao	Esophagus	食道
54	Kou	Mouth	口
55	Ping jian	Tip of tragus	屏尖
56	Yan hou	Throat	咽喉
57	Wai bi	External nose	外鼻
58	Nei bi	Internal nose	内鼻
59	Qi guan	Trachea	气管
60	Xin	Heart	心
61	Yuan zhong	Mid-edge	缘中
62	Zhen	Occiput	枕
63	Nie	Temple	颞

64	San jiao	Triple burning (sanjiao)	三焦
65	Shen shang xian	Adrenal gland	肾上腺
66	Dui ping jian	Tip of antitragus	对屏尖
67	Pi zhi xia	Subcortex	皮脂下
68	Nei fen mi	Internal secretion, endocrine	内分泌
69	E	Forehead	额
70	Mu er	Eye no. 2	目二
71	Mu yi	Eye no. 1	目一
72	Han	Chin	颔
73	She	Tongue	舌
74	Ya	Tooth	牙
75	Lun wu	Helix 5	轮五
76	Nei er	Internal ear	内耳
77	Mian jia qu	Face bucca zone face cheek zone	面颊区
78	Yan	Eye	眼
79	Chui qian	Anterior lobe	垂前
80	Bian tao ti	Tonsil	扁桃体
81	Lun liu	Helix no.6	轮六
82	Nao gan	Brain stem	脑干
83	Shang ping	Upper tragus	上屏
84	Xia ping	Lower tragus	下屏
85	Er bei xin	Ear back heart	耳背心
86	Er bei gan	Ear back liver	耳背肝
87	Er bei pi	Ear back spleen	耳背脾
88	Er bei fei	Ear back lung	耳背肺
89	Er mi gen	Arnold's nerve root	耳迷根

90	Er bei gou	Ear back groove	耳背沟
91	Shang er gen	Upper ear root	上耳根

92	Xia er gen	Lower ear root	下耳根
93	Er bei shen	Ear back kidney	耳背肾

Test 10: Scalp Points (1-28)

1	Mid-forehead plane	额中线,
2	1st lateral plane on forehead	额旁一线
3	2nd lateral plane on forehead	额旁二线
4	3rd lateral plane on forehead	额旁三线
5	Mid-vertex plane	项中线
6	Vertex temporal anterior slanting plane	项颞前斜线
7	Vertex temporal posterior slanting plane	项颞后斜线
8	1st lateral vertex plane	项旁一线
9	2nd lateral vertex plane	项旁二线
10	Frontal temporal plane	颞前线
11	Posterior temporal plane	颞后线
12	Mid-occipital upper plane	枕上正中线
13	Mid-occipital lateral plane	枕上旁线
14	Mid-occipital lower plane	枕下旁线
15	Motor area	运动区
16	Sensory area	感觉区
17	Area of controlling St Vitus dance and tremor	舞蹈震颤控制区
18	Vasomotor area	血管舒缩区
19	Speech area No.2	言语二区
20	Vertigo-auditory area	晕听区
21	Speech area No. 3	言语三区
22	Intricate movements (application) area	运用区
23	Foot-motor sensory area	足运感区
24	Visual area	视区
25	Equilibrium area	平衡区
26	Stomach area	胃区
27	Thoracic cavity area	胸腔区
28	Reproduction area	生殖区

Test 11-1 Face Acupuncture (1-24)

1	Large intestine 大肠
2	Umbilicus 脐
3	Kneecap 膝膑
4	Foot 足
5	Spleen 脾
6	Gallbladder 胆
7	Liver 肝
8	Chest & nipple 膺乳
9	Medial thigh 股里
10	Throat 咽喉
11	Thigh 股
12	Mid-forehead 首面
13	Hand 手
14	Bladder (uterus) 膀胱(子宫)
15	Small intestine 小肠
16	Arm 臂
17	Lungs 肺
18	Kidney 肾
19	Heart 心
20	Knee 膝
21	Tibia 胫
22	Back 背
23	Stomach 胃
24	Shoulder 肩

Test 11-2 Eye Acupuncture with 8 zones and 13 Points (1-13)

1	Kidney 肾
2	Bladder 膀胱
3	Upper heater 上焦
4	Liver 肝
5	Gallbladder 胆
6	Middle hearter 中焦
7	Heart 心
8	Small intestine 小肠
9	Spleen 脾
10	Stomach 胃
11	Lower heater 下焦
12	Lung 肺
13	Large intestine 大肠

Test 11-3 Nose Acupuncture (1-29)

1	Mid-forehead 头面
2	Throat 咽喉
3	Ear 耳
4	Lung 肺
5	Heart 心
6	Liver 肝
7	Spleen 脾
8	Kidney 肾
9	Genitals 前阴
10	Chest 胸
11	Nipple 乳
12	Back of neck 颈项
13	Gallbladder 胆
14	Lumbar spine
15	Stomach 胃
16	Upper limbs 上肢
17	Small intestine 小肠
18	Thigh 股
19	Large intestine 大肠
20	Knee tibia 膝胫
21	Teste/ovary 睾丸/卵巢
22	Bladder 膀胱
23	Toes 足趾
24	Upper point of hypertension 高血压上点
25	Lumbar triangle 腰三角
26	Digestion triangle 消化三角
27	Lower point of hypertension 高血压下点
28	Innovative point 创新穴
29	Zibao point 子包穴

Test 11-4 Tongue Acupuncture (1-24)

1	Heart point 心穴
2	Lung point 肺穴
3	Stomach point 胃穴
4	Spleen point 脾穴
5	Gallbladder point 胆穴
6	Liver point 肝穴
7	Small intestine point 小肠穴
8	Bladder point 膀胱穴
9	Kidney point 肾穴
10	Large intestine point 大肠穴
11	Yin point, 阴穴
12	Gathering fountain 聚泉
13	Upper limb point 上肢穴
14	Lower limb point 下肢穴
15	Middle heater 中焦穴
16	Forehead point 额穴
17	Eye point 眼穴
18	Nose point 鼻穴
19	Ear point 耳穴
20	Throat 咽喉穴
21	Ocean fountain 海泉
22	Jīn jīn yù yè 金津玉液
23	Tongue pole 舌柱
24	Middle ruler 中矩

Test 11-5 Foot Acupuncture (1-44)

1	Head 头
2	Nose 鼻
3	Eye 眼
4	Ear 耳
5	Mouth 口
6	Throat 咽喉
7	Rebirth 再生
8	Heart 心
9	Lung 肺
10	Good sleep 安眠
11	Stomach 胃
12	Liver 肝
13	Spleen 脾
14	Gallbladder 胆
15	Small intestine 小肠
16	Anterior hidden pearl 前隐珠
17	Posterior hidden pearl 后隐珠
18	Kidney 肾
19	Cancer root no. 1 癌根一
20	Large intestine 大肠
21	Bladder 膀胱
22	Genitals 生殖器
23	Cancer root no. 2 癌根二
24	Anus 肛门
25	Small intestine 小肠
26	Midpoint on little toe crease 小趾横纹中点
27	Centre of sole of foot 足心
28	Cancer root no. 3 癌根三
29	Ischium no. 1 坐骨一
30	K1, yǒng quán 涌泉
31	Headache point 头痛点
32	Tonsil no. 1 扁桃一
33	Tonsil no. 2 扁桃二
34	Lumbago 腰痛
35	Ischium no. 2 坐骨二
36	Luò zhěn 落枕
37	Stomach intestine point 胃肠穴
38	Heart pain point 心痛穴
39	Waist thigh point 腰腿穴
40	Vertigo point 眩晕穴
41	Period pain no.1 痛经一
42	Period pain no.2 痛经二
43	Epilepsy point 巅痫穴
44	Hip 臀

Test 11-6 Mouth Acupuncture

(1-10)

1	Right upper limb zone 右上肢区
2	Right lower limb zone 右下肢区
3	Nerve zone 神经区
4	Head zone 头部区
5	Reproductive urinary zone 生殖泌尿区
6	Digestive zone 消化区
7	Viscera-bowels zone 脏腑区
8	Eye and blood pressure zone 眼及血压区
9	Lumbar zone 腰部区
10	Skin zone 皮肤区

Test 11-7 Wrist-Ankle Acupuncture (1-12)

1	Upper 1 上 1
2	Upper 2 上 2
3	Upper 3 上 3
4	Upper 4 上 4
5	Upper 5 上 5
6	Upper 6 上 6
7	Lower 1 下 1
8	Lower 2 下 2
9	Lower 3 下 3
10	Lower 4 下 4
11	Lower 5 下 5
12	Lower 6 下 6

Test 11-8 Hand Acupuncture (1-30)

19	Kidney, Bed wetting point 肾,夜尿点
1	Ankle 踝点
2	Chest point 胸点
3	Eye point 眼点
4	Shoulder point 肩点
5	Forehead point 前头点
6	Vertex point 头顶点
7	Side of head point 偏头点
8	Perineum point 会阴点
9	Back of head point 后头点
10	Spine point 脊柱点
11	Sciatic nerve point 坐骨神经点
12	Throat point 咽喉点
13	Back of neck point 颈项点
14	Lumbar-leg point 腰腿点
15	Neck pain point 落枕点
16	Stop itch point 止痒点
17	Gastrointestinal point 胃肠点
18	Cough asthma point 咳哮点
20	Heel point 足跟点
21	Spleen point 脾点
22	Small intestine point 小肠点
23	Large intestine point 大肠点
24	Triple heater point 三焦点
25	Heart point 心点
26	Liver point 肝点
27	Lung point 肺点
28	Life door point 命门点
29	Toothache point 牙痛
30	Asthma new point 哮喘新穴

Test 12-1 Five Wheels (1-5)

1	Water wheel 水轮
2	Wind wheel 风轮
3	Energy wheel 气轮
4	Blood wheel 血轮
5	Flesh wheel 肉轮

Test 12-2 eight contours (1-8)

1	Water contour 水廓
2	Wind contour 风廓
3	Heaven contour 天廓
4	Earth contour 地廓
5	Fire contour 火廓
6	Thunder contour 雷廓
7	Lake contour 泽廓
8	Mountain contour 山廓

Test 12-3 tongue and organs (1-4)

1	Kidney 肾
2	Spleen/ stomach 脾/胃
3	Liver/gallbladder 肝/胆
4	Heart/ lung 心/肺

Test 12-4 internal organs in the face (1-12)

1	Head and face
2	Throat
3	Lungs
4	Heart
5	Gallbladder
6	Liver
7	Small intestine
8	Large intestine
9	Stomach
10	Spleen
11	Bladder and uterus
12	kidneys

Test 12-5 five elements in four laws of (1-5)

1	Earth 地
2	Fire 火
3	Metal 金
4	Water 水
5	Wood 木

Test 12-6 six divisions of yin-yang (1-6)

1	Greater Yang [Tài Yáng, 太陽]
2	Bright Yang [Yáng Míng, 陽明].
3	Little Yang Or Lesser Yang [Shào Yáng, 少陽].
4	Greater Yin [Tài Yīn, 太陰].
5	Little Yin Or Lesser Yin [Shào Yīn, 少陰].
6	Decreasing Yin [Jué Yīn, 厥陰].

Test 12-7 changing patterns of yin and yang (1-14)

1	Yáng,陽
2	Yīn, 陰.
3	Greater Yang [Tài Yáng, 太陽]
4	Little Yin Or Lesser Yin [Shào Yīn, 少陰].
5	Little Yang Or Lesser Yang [Shào Yáng, 少陽].
6	Greater Yin [Tài Yīn, 太陰].
7	Qian, 乾,
8	Dui, 兌
9	Li, 離
10	Zhen, 震
11	Xun, 巽
12	Kan, 坎
13	Gen, 艮
14	Kun, 坤

Test 12-8 sections of pulses at wrist (1-6)

1	Heart 心

2	Diaphragm and liver 隔,肝
3	Abdomen and kidney 腹中, 肾
4	Chest and lungs 胸中,肺
5	Stomach and spleen 胃,气脾
6	Abdomen and kidney 腹中, 肾

Test 12-9 pulses in the three regions smptomatic of nine symptoms (1-9)

1	Energy of parietal eminence,头角之气
2	Energy of ears and eyes,耳目之气
3	Energy of mouth and teeth. 口齿之气
4	Chest energy 胸中之气
5	Lungs 肺
6	Heart 心
7	Liver 肝
8	Spleen and stomach 脾胃
9	Kidneys 肾

Test 12-10 nine numerals on a turtle in a square denote nine parts of the body (1-9)

1	Tail 尾
2	right shoulder 右肩
3	left back 左背
4	left shoulder 左肩
5	Center 中
6	right foot 右足
7	right back 右背
8	left foot 左足
9	Head 头

Test 12-11 nine numerals on a turtle in a square denote nine directions (1-9)

1	North 北方
2	Southwest 西南方
3	East 东方
4	southeast 东南
5	Centre 中
6	northwest 西北方
7	west 西方
8	northeast 东北方
9	south 南方

Test 12-12 nine numerals on a turtle in a square denote nine seasonal periods (1-9)

1	Winter 冬季
2	In between autumn and summer 夏秋之间
3	Spring 春秋
4	In between spring and summer 春夏之间
5	Late summer 夏秋
6	In between autumn and winter 秋冬之间
7	Autumn 秋秋
8	In between spring and winter 春冬之间
9	Summer 夏秋

Test 12-13 nine numerals on a turtle in a square denote nine periods in a day (1-9)

1	In between afternoon and dusk 下午傍晚之间
2	Midnight 半夜
3	In between morning and noon 请晨中午之间
4	Early morning 请晨
5	Noon 中午
6	Dusk 傍晚
7	In between dusk and midnight 傍晚半夜之间
8	Morning 上午
9	In between midnight and early morning 半夜请晨之间

Test 12-14 nine numerals on a turtle in a square denote nine internal organs (1-9)

1	Bladder 膀胱

2	Heart 心
3	Gall 胆
4	Lungs 肺
5	Spleen/ Stomach 脾胃
6	Kidneys 肾
7	S. intestine 小肠
8	Liver 肝
9	L. intestine 大肠

Test 12-15 nine numerals on a turtle in a square denote trigrams (1-9)

1	Kan,, 坎
2	Kun, 坤
3	Zhen, 震
4	Xun, 巽
5	-
6	Qian, 乾,
7	Dui, 兌
8	Gen, 艮
9	Li, 離

Test 12-16 nine numerals on a turtle in a square denote nine kinds of people (1-9)

1	-
2	Father 父
3	Guest 客
4	Host 主
5	Husband
6	Man 男
7	Mother 母
8	Wife 妻
9	Woman 女

Test 12-17 nine numerals on a turtle in a square denote eight acupuncture points (1-9)

1	B62 [shen mai, 申脈].
2	K6 [zhao hai, 照海].
3	Sj5 [wai guan, 外關].
4	G41 [zu lin qi, 足臨泣].
5	-
6	Sp4 [gong sun, 公孫].
7	Si3 [hou xi, 后溪].
8	P6 [nei guan, 內關].
9	Lu7 [lie que, 列缺].

Test 13: Multiple-Choice Questions 选择题库

Test 13: Answers to Multiple-Choice Questions/

13-1	经络	1-314	Meridians

No.	Ans.	No.	Ans.	No.	Ans.	No.	Ans.	No.	Ans.	No.	Ans.
1	B	40	B	79	B	118	A	157	A	196	C
2	A	41	C	80	B	119	D	158	B	197	C
3	E	42	A	81	D	120	B	159	A	198	C
4	B	43	C	82	C	121	B	160	D	199	E
5	D	44	A	83	D	122	A	161	A	200	D
6	C	45	E	84	B	123	C	162	B	201	E
7	E	46	B	85	C	124	C	163	B	202	D
8	A	47	E	86	A	125	B	164	E	203	C
9	B	48	A	87	B	126	D	165	E	204	D
10	D	49	B	88	B	127	C	166	D	205	A
11	A	50	C	89	A	128	A	167	B	206	E
12	C	51	D	90	A	129	B	168	A	207	C
13	E	52	A	91	A	130	C	169	E	208	D
14	E	53	B	92	C	131	A	170	E	209	D
15	D	54	D	93	D	132	D	171	D	210	D
16	C	55	C	94	A	133	B	172	E	211	C
17	C	56	E	95	D	134	B	173	E	212	C
18	A	57	B	96	C	135	B	174	C	213	A
19	D	58	B	97	A	136	D	175	D	214	A
20	D	59	E	98	A	137	B	176	D	215	C
21	B	60	B	99	C	138	C	177	A	216	B
22	B	61	C	100	D	139	C	178	B	217	E
23	E	62	C	101	B	140	C	179	C	218	C
24	C	63	B	102	B	141	A	180	A	219	B
25	D	64	C	103	C	142	A	181	B	220	C
26	D	65	B	104	D	143	B	182	A	221	D
27	C	66	B	105	B	144	D	183	C	222	C
28	C	67	A	106	B	145	B	184	B	223	D
29	A	68	C	107	A	146	C	185	E	224	E
30	B	69	D	108	B	147	D	186	B	225	A
31	A	70	A	109	B	148	C	187	C	226	C
32	D	71	A	110	C	149	E	188	A	227	D
33	E	72	A	111	B	150	A	189	E	228	D
34	D	73	C	112	C	151	D	190	C	229	B
35	E	74	D	113	B	152	D	191	C	230	A
36	D	75	C	114	B	153	E	192	D	231	B
37	D	76	A	115	A	154	B	193	C	232	C
38	B	77	C	116	B	155	B	194	A	233	A
39	C	78	C	117	D	156	B	195	A	234	B

235	A	249	C	263	D	277	A	291	A	305	C
236	D	250	C	264	C	278	D	292	D	306	A
237	C	251	C	265	E	279	D	293	B	307	B
238	A	252	C	266	A	280	A	294	B	308	E
239	D	253	B	267	C	281	D	295	B	309	C
240	C	254	B	268	A	282	C	296	E	310	C
241	B	255	A	269	B	283	E	297	D	311	D
242	A	256	A	270	C	284	E	298	C	312	B
243	C	257	D	271	C	285	D	299	D	313	A
244	B	258	C	272	C	286	A	300	A	314	A
245	B	259	E	273	C	287	A	301	D		
246	D	260	A	274	D	288	D	302	D		
247	B	261	C	275	C	289	D	303	D		
248	B	262	E	276	A	290	B	304	B		

13-2	腧穴	315-748	Acupuncture Points

315	E	341	B	367	B	393	D	419	E	445	D
316	A	342	B	368	E	394	B	420	B	446	D
317	B	343	C	369	E	395	E	421	A	447	A
318	E	344	E	370	C	396	A	422	A	448	B
319	D	345	E	371	D	397	A	423	B	449	A
320	E	346	D	372	B	398	B	424	D	450	E
321	E	347	E	373	C	399	C	425	E	451	B
322	E	348	C	374	C	400	D	426	E	452	C
323	D	349	A	375	B	401	A	427	E	453	B
324	A	350	A	376	C	402	B	428	A	454	B
325	A	351	C	377	C	403	B	429	C	455	B
326	C	352	C	378	D	404	D	430	D	456	E
327	C	353	C	379	A	405	E	431	D	457	B
328	D	354	C	380	B	406	B	432	B	458	D
329	D	355	D	381	E	407	D	433	B	459	C
330	C	356	B	382	E	408	B	434	E	460	D
331	B	357	C	383	D	409	B	435	D	461	B
332	B	358	C	384	B	410	A	436	C	462	A
333	A	359	D	385	A	411	B	437	E	463	A
334	D	360	D	386	B	412	D	438	C	464	C
335	D	361	C	387	B	413	D	439	E	465	A
336	B	362	D	388	B	414	B	440	B	466	B
337	C	363	B	389	B	415	B	441	E	467	D
338	D	364	B	390	B	416	A	442	E	468	C
339	A	365	B	391	A	417	D	443	D	469	D
340	A	366	D	392	D	418	D	444	D	470	C

Test 13: Multiple-Choice Questions 选择题库

471	B	514	B	557	D	600	C	643	E	686	E
472	B	515	B	558	C	601	D	644	E	687	E
473	C	516	B	559	D	602	D	645	E	688	B
474	B	517	B	560	B	603	C	646	D	689	B
475	B	518	D	561	C	604	B	647	E	690	B
476	B	519	E	562	D	605	D	648	C	691	D
477	E	520	D	563	B	606	E	649	D	692	B
478	D	521	B	564	C	607	B	650	D	693	B
479	D	522	E	565	C	608	E	651	B	694	D
480	D	523	A	566	C	609	A	652	C	695	B
481	A	524	D	567	C	610	A	653	A	696	D
482	C	525	C	568	E	611	D	654	C	697	E
483	A	526	A	569	A	612	A	655	E	698	D
484	C	527	B	570	A	613	C	656	E	699	E
485	D	528	E	571	D	614	C	657	B	700	C
486	B	529	E	572	C	615	D	658	A	701	C
487	D	530	C	573	C	616	E	659	C	702	B
488	D	531	D	574	A	617	D	660	A	703	C
489	C	532	D	575	D	618	C	661	B	704	C
490	D	533	C	576	C	619	C	662	A	705	E
491	C	534	D	577	C	620	B	663	B	706	B
492	D	535	E	578	A	621	A	664	C	707	D
493	A	536	C	579	D	622	D	665	E	708	B
494	C	537	D	580	E	623	B	666	C	709	D
495	B	538	A	581	B	624	B	667	E	710	D
496	D	539	B	582	A	625	C	668	C	711	C
497	C	540	C	583	A	626	B	669	B	712	A
498	C	541	C	584	E	627	D	670	D	713	B
499	C	542	A	585	D	628	B	671	E	714	B
500	C	543	B	586	D	629	D	672	E	715	B
501	C	544	A	587	B	630	D	673	B	716	D
502	E	545	B	588	A	631	C	674	A	717	C
503	A	546	C	589	E	632	E	675	E	718	E
504	B	547	A	590	B	633	A	676	D	719	A
505	C	548	E	591	A	634	B	677	B	720	D
506	B	549	B	592	D	635	C	678	C	721	E
507	D	550	B	593	D	636	E	679	B	722	B
508	B	551	D	594	B	637	C	680	E	723	A
509	C	552	C	595	C	638	A	681	A	724	E
510	C	553	D	596	E	639	D	682	A	725	D
511	A	554	C	597	E	640	B	683	A	726	D
512	B	555	C	598	C	641	D	684	B	727	B
513	D	556	A	599	E	642	C	685	E	728	D

729	E	733	C	737	D	741	A	745	D
730	E	734	B	738	C	742	D	746	D
731	A	735	C	739	C	743	B	747	C
732	B	736	C	740	C	744	E	748	C

13-3	表面解剖与针灸穴位	749-1066	Surface Anatomy and Acupuncture Points

749	E	783	C	817	B	851	C	885	E	919	C
750	B	784	D	818	A	852	D	886	D	920	C
751	B	785	C	819	B	853	D	887	E	921	B
752	D	786	C	820	E	854	E	888	D	922	A
753	E	787	D	821	C	855	D	889	B	923	D
754	E	788	C	822	A	856	C	890	C	924	B
755	E	789	C	823	C	857	A	891	B	925	A
756	E	790	B	824	B	858	B	892	A	926	C
757	A	791	C	825	B	859	E	893	C	927	C
758	B	792	A	826	B	860	D	894	E	928	C
759	D	793	C	827	B	861	A	895	B	929	E
760	A	794	B	828	E	862	C	896	D	930	D
761	B	795	B	829	A	863	C	897	A	931	A
762	A	796	D	830	B	864	B	898	A	932	D
763	C	797	C	831	E	865	D	899	D	933	A
764	D	798	E	832	E	866	C	900	C	934	C
765	B	799	C	833	B	867	C	901	E	935	B
766	D	800	B	834	E	868	B	902	A	936	E
767	A	801	A	835	D	869	E	903	B	937	D
768	D	802	A	836	A	870	C	904	D	938	B
769	B	803	C	837	A	871	D	905	C	939	B
770	A	804	E	838	D	872	B	906	A	940	C
771	A	805	D	839	C	873	B	907	B	941	D
772	E	806	A	840	D	874	B	908	D	942	D
773	B	807	B	841	B	875	A	909	D	943	E
774	B	808	E	842	A	876	B	910	C	944	A
775	E	809	B	843	B	877	A	911	D	945	D
776	E	810	E	844	A	878	D	912	A	946	A
777	A	811	B	845	C	879	B	913	A	947	D
778	A	812	E	846	B	880	E	914	D	948	D
779	D	813	E	847	B	881	A	915	C	949	A
780	C	814	A	848	A	882	B	916	D	950	E
781	B	815	C	849	E	883	C	917	E	951	A
782	B	816	A	850	A	884	D	918	E	952	A

Test 13: Multiple-Choice Questions 选择题库

953	C	972	E	991	B	1010	C	1029	D	1048	D
954	B	973	E	992	C	1011	B	1030	B	1049	C
955	E	974	E	993	B	1012	A	1031	E	1050	D
956	E	975	A	994	E	1013	D	1032	D	1051	E
957	D	976	C	995	C	1014	E	1033	A	1052	D
958	B	977	C	996	A	1015	B	1034	E	1053	A
959	B	978	C	997	D	1016	A	1035	E	1054	C
960	D	979	D	998	B	1017	D	1036	A	1055	C
961	C	980	D	999	B	1018	A	1037	D	1056	E
962	C	981	B	1000	B	1019	B	1038	C	1057	C
963	D	982	C	1001	B	1020	C	1039	D	1058	D
964	B	983	C	1002	D	1021	A	1040	B	1059	B
965	D	984	B	1003	A	1022	A	1041	B	1060	A
966	D	985	C	1004	C	1023	C	1042	B	1061	D
967	B	986	C	1005	D	1024	B	1043	E	1062	D
968	C	987	C	1006	C	1025	B	1044	A	1063	C
969	C	988	D	1007	D	1026	A	1045	D	1064	B
970	C	989	D	1008	E	1027	D	1046	A	1065	E
971	A	990	E	1009	C	1028	C	1047	A	1066	D

13-4	刺灸法	1067-1338	Techniques of Acupuncture-Moxibustion

1067	C	1086	E	1105	C	1124	C	1143	B	1162	E
1068	C	1087	B	1106	D	1125	B	1144	C	1163	C
1069	E	1088	C	1107	C	1126	B	1145	B	1164	C
1070	E	1089	A	1108	D	1127	A	1146	E	1165	C
1071	C	1090	B	1109	C	1128	A	1147	A	1166	D
1072	A	1091	A	1110	B	1129	D	1148	D	1167	E
1073	D	1092	B	1111	C	1130	A	1149	C	1168	A
1074	A	1093	A	1112	D	1131	D	1150	A	1169	C
1075	B	1094	A	1113	A	1132	B	1151	B	1170	D
1076	C	1095	E	1114	E	1133	A	1152	D	1171	A
1077	B	1096	D	1115	B	1134	B	1153	B	1172	E
1078	B	1097	B	1116	D	1135	A	1154	D	1173	C
1079	C	1098	C	1117	B	1136	E	1155	C	1174	E
1080	B	1099	D	1118	C	1137	A	1156	C	1175	D
1081	B	1100	B	1119	C	1138	C	1157	D	1176	C
1082	C	1101	D	1120	B	1139	B	1158	C	1177	E
1083	D	1102	D	1121	A	1140	B	1159	B	1178	D
1084	B	1103	C	1122	D	1141	A	1160	A	1179	C
1085	B	1104	B	1123	A	1142	D	1161	C	1180	D

1181	D	1208	D	1235	B	1262	A	1289	B	1316	A
1182	C	1209	B	1236	D	1263	B	1290	E	1317	C
1183	B	1210	D	1237	E	1264	C	1291	B	1318	A
1184	C	1211	D	1238	E	1265	D	1292	D	1319	A
1185	B	1212	C	1239	B	1266	D	1293	D	1320	C
1186	C	1213	A	1240	C	1267	B	1294	D	1321	B
1187	A	1214	D	1241	D	1268	B	1295	E	1322	C
1188	B	1215	B	1242	C	1269	B	1296	B	1323	D
1189	D	1216	C	1243	A	1270	A	1297	B	1324	E
1190	E	1217	D	1244	B	1271	E	1298	C	1325	D
1191	B	1218	D	1245	D	1272	B	1299	C	1326	A
1192	B	1219	C	1246	A	1273	B	1300	B	1327	C
1193	A	1220	C	1247	B	1274	A	1301	D	1328	C
1194	E	1221	C	1248	C	1275	D	1302	A	1329	A
1195	A	1222	D	1249	D	1276	D	1303	C	1330	D
1196	D	1223	B	1250	E	1277	C	1304	B	1331	D
1197	A	1224	B	1251	A	1278	D	1305	A	1332	A
1198	D	1225	A	1252	D	1279	A	1306	D	1333	D
1199	C	1226	E	1253	B	1280	A	1307	C	1334	B
1200	E	1227	B	1254	C	1281	C	1308	B	1335	C
1201	D	1228	C	1255	B	1282	D	1309	C	1336	E
1202	B	1229	C	1256	B	1283	C	1310	E	1337	C
1203	A	1230	E	1257	A	1284	B	1311	B	1338	B
1204	C	1231	E	1258	E	1285	D	1312	E		
1205	D	1232	A	1259	C	1286	B	1313	D		
1206	B	1233	C	1260	D	1287	A	1314	E		
1207	C	1234	E	1261	D	1288	D	1315	D		

13-5	针灸治疗学	Acupuncture Treatment, 1339-2537

1339	D	1350	C	1361	D	1372	C	1383	A	1394	A
1340	A	1351	E	1362	C	1373	A	1384	B	1395	A
1341	E	1352	D	1363	B	1374	E	1385	B	1396	C
1342	A	1353	B	1364	C	1375	A	1386	C	1397	D
1343	D	1354	A	1365	D	1376	B	1387	E	1398	C
1344	B	1355	C	1366	A	1377	D	1388	E	1399	D
1345	D	1356	B	1367	D	1378	C	1389	C	1400	B
1346	D	1357	C	1368	A	1379	A	1390	D	1401	A
1347	E	1358	E	1369	A	1380	E	1391	C	1402	B
1348	A	1359	D	1370	E	1381	B	1392	B	1403	B
1349	D	1360	D	1371	D	1382	C	1393	A	1404	D

Test 13: Multiple-Choice Questions 选择题库

1405	E	1448	D	1491	B	1534	E	1577	A	1620	C
1406	B	1449	D	1492	C	1535	B	1578	C	1621	B
1407	E	1450	A	1493	B	1536	D	1579	E	1622	B
1408	C	1451	D	1494	E	1537	B	1580	C	1623	A
1409	D	1452	C	1495	C	1538	B	1581	B	1624	D
1410	E	1453	A	1496	D	1539	C	1582	D	1625	C
1411	B	1454	C	1497	C	1540	C	1583	A	1626	B
1412	A	1455	E	1498	D	1541	B	1584	C	1627	C
1413	D	1456	B	1499	A	1542	C	1585	A	1628	B
1414	B	1457	D	1500	D	1543	C	1586	D	1629	B
1415	C	1458	C	1501	B	1544	C	1587	B	1630	C
1416	C	1459	D	1502	B	1545	A	1588	B	1631	E
1417	C	1460	A	1503	D	1546	D	1589	B	1632	A
1418	A	1461	C	1504	B	1547	C	1590	C	1633	D
1419	D	1462	A	1505	B	1548	C	1591	B	1634	B
1420	B	1463	B	1506	A	1549	D	1592	D	1635	D
1421	C	1464	C	1507	C	1550	E	1593	B	1636	D
1422	D	1465	D	1508	B	1551	D	1594	B	1637	B
1423	C	1466	B	1509	A	1552	D	1595	E	1638	B
1424	B	1467	B	1510	B	1553	C	1596	E	1639	A
1425	A	1468	D	1511	C	1554	C	1597	D	1640	C
1426	D	1469	B	1512	B	1555	A	1598	B	1641	D
1427	C	1470	D	1513	C	1556	E	1599	D	1642	D
1428	B	1471	B	1514	A	1557	B	1600	D	1643	B
1429	A	1472	D	1515	A	1558	C	1601	C	1644	D
1430	C	1473	D	1516	E	1559	C	1602	E	1645	C
1431	E	1474	A	1517	D	1560	A	1603	C	1646	D
1432	C	1475	E	1518	B	1561	D	1604	E	1647	D
1433	D	1476	C	1519	A	1562	B	1605	B	1648	C
1434	B	1477	D	1520	E	1563	E	1606	A	1649	E
1435	B	1478	C	1521	B	1564	C	1607	D	1650	B
1436	D	1479	B	1522	D	1565	D	1608	C	1651	D
1437	E	1480	C	1523	C	1566	E	1609	B	1652	D
1438	B	1481	C	1524	B	1567	C	1610	D	1653	A
1439	C	1482	E	1525	A	1568	C	1611	D	1654	B
1440	A	1483	C	1526	A	1569	C	1612	A	1655	A
1441	D	1484	E	1527	D	1570	A	1613	D	1656	B
1442	C	1485	E	1528	B	1571	B	1614	C	1657	B
1443	D	1486	B	1529	C	1572	D	1615	C	1658	E
1444	B	1487	E	1530	A	1573	D	1616	D	1659	C
1445	A	1488	E	1531	C	1574	D	1617	C	1660	E
1446	A	1489	D	1532	C	1575	B	1618	D	1661	E
1447	D	1490	B	1533	D	1576	C	1619	C	1662	D

1663	B
1664	B
1665	E
1666	A
1667	C
1668	C
1669	D
1670	C
1671	D
1672	D
1673	C
1674	E
1675	E
1676	D
1677	C
1678	E
1679	D
1680	A
1681	D
1682	E
1683	D
1684	E
1685	D
1686	A
1687	D
1688	B
1689	C
1690	C
1691	A
1692	A
1693	A
1694	D
1695	E
1696	E
1697	E
1698	C
1699	C
1700	B
1701	E
1702	E
1703	B
1704	E
1705	E

1706	D
1707	E
1708	C
1709	D
1710	C
1711	B
1712	E
1713	C
1714	A
1715	E
1716	E
1717	D
1718	D
1719	D
1720	D
1721	C
1722	D
1723	A
1724	A
1725	D
1726	E
1727	D
1728	B
1729	D
1730	A
1731	C
1732	B
1733	A
1734	B
1735	E
1736	C
1737	C
1738	D
1739	B
1740	E
1741	A
1742	B
1743	C
1744	C
1745	E
1746	C
1747	A
1748	C

1749	C
1750	B
1751	D
1752	D
1753	C
1754	A
1755	C
1756	D
1757	E
1758	D
1759	E
1760	E
1761	C
1762	D
1763	C
1764	A
1765	E
1766	E
1767	D
1768	A
1769	B
1770	B
1771	D
1772	E
1773	E
1774	C
1775	C
1776	C
1777	D
1778	B
1779	A
1780	B
1781	C
1782	D
1783	D
1784	B
1785	E
1786	B
1787	E
1788	A
1789	C
1790	E
1791	A

1792	D
1793	B
1794	C
1795	B
1796	C
1797	B
1798	E
1799	D
1800	E
1801	A
1802	D
1803	E
1804	C
1805	D
1806	B
1807	B
1808	A
1809	D
1810	B
1811	A
1812	A
1813	A
1814	C
1815	B
1816	B
1817	D
1818	E
1819	D
1820	C
1821	B
1822	C
1823	A
1824	C
1825	B
1826	A
1827	B
1828	D
1829	C
1830	C
1831	B
1832	B
1833	D

1834	A
1835	D
1836	B
1837	A
1838	C
1839	D
1840	B
1841	B
1842	A
1843	D
1844	C
1845	D
1846	A
1847	B
1848	E
1849	D
1850	A
1851	A
1852	E
1853	D
1854	B
1855	C.
1856	B
1857	C
1858	C
1859	C
1860	D
1861	A
1862	A
1863	B
1864	B
1865	A
1866	C
1867	C
1868	B
1869	C
1870	D
1871	C
1872	D
1873	C
1874	D
1875	E

1876	E
1877	C
1878	C
1879	C
1880	A
1881	B
1882	D
1883	A
1884	B
1885	A
1886	E
1887	C
1888	E
1889	C
1890	A
1891	A
1892	D
1893	C
1894	B
1895	D
1896	B
1897	B
1898	D
1899	D
1900	E
1901	C
1902	E
1903	E
1904	C
1905	D
1906	E
1907	D
1908	D
1909	E
1910	D
1911	C
1912	B
1913	B
1914	D
1915	E
1916	B
1917	B
1918	C

Test 13: Multiple-Choice Questions 选择题库

1919	C	1962	A	2005	D	2048	D	2091	C	2134	A
1920	C	1963	B	2006	C	2049	E	2092	B	2135	A
1921	C	1964	E	2007	C	2050	B	2093	A	2136	C
1922	A	1965	A	2008	B	2051	B	2094	D	2137	D
1923	C	1966	A	2009	A	2052	C	2095	B	2138	C
1924	B	1967	A	2010	D	2053	A	2096	E	2139	C
1925	B	1968	C	2011	B	2054	A	2097	D	2140	C
1926	C	1969	A	2012	C	2055	E	2098	D	2141	C
1927	B	1970	C	2013	D	2056	C	2099	E	2142	D
1928	D	1971	A	2014	E	2057	B	2100	E	2143	C
1929	B	1972	A	2015	B	2058	A	2101	A	2144	B
1930	C	1973	B	2016	C	2059	A	2102	C	2145	D
1931	D	1974	B	2017	B	2060	C	2103	C	2146	C
1932	E	1975	C	2018	C	2061	B	2104	D	2147	D
1933	C	1976	D	2019	B	2062	E	2105	B	2148	B
1934	A	1977	B	2020	D	2063		2106	A	2149	D
1935	B	1978	E	2021	D	2064	C	2107	E	2150	A
1936	D	1979	A	2022	A	2065	D	2108	E	2151	A
1937	C	1980	A	2023	A	2066	C	2109	E	2152	E
1938	B	1981	C	2024	A	2067	A	2110	B	2153	C
1939	B	1982	D	2025	C	2068	E	2111	E	2154	B
1940	E	1983	B	2026	E	2069	D	2112	A	2155	A
1941	D	1984	D	2027	B	2070	A	2113	A	2156	C
1942	D	1985	B	2028	A	2071	D	2114	A	2157	D
1943	B	1986	B	2029	A	2072	C	2115	C	2158	C
1944	C	1987	C	2030	C	2073	A	2116	E	2159	C
1945	C	1988	A	2031	D	2074	B	2117	D	2160	A
1946	B	1989	E	2032	D	2075	D	2118	B	2161	A
1947	E	1990	B	2033	D	2076	B	2119	D	2162	C
1948	D	1991	C	2034	A	2077	A	2120	B	2163	A
1949	C	1992	A	2035	B	2078	C	2121	D	2164	D
1950	B	1993	A	2036	A	2079	C	2122	D	2165	D
1951	D	1994	A	2037	A	2080	D	2123	D	2166	B
1952	D	1995	A	2038	D	2081	E	2124	A	2167	A
1953	B	1996	B	2039	C	2082	C	2125	B	2168	D
1954	A	1997	C	2040	A	2083	C	2126	C	2169	C
1955	D	1998	C	2041	D	2084	D	2127	E	2170	B
1956	A	1999	B	2042	B	2085	B	2128	D	2171	B
1957	C	2000	C	2043	B	2086	E	2129	D	2172	C
1958	B	2001	A	2044	C	2087	B	2130	A	2173	D
1959	C	2002	A	2045	C	2088	E	2131	E	2174	A
1960	A	2003	B	2046	A	2089	D	2132	B	2175	B
1961	E	2004	D	2047	C	2090	D	2133	A	2176	C

2177	B	2220	C	2263	C	2306	C	2349	B	2392	C
2178	B	2221	B	2264	B	2307	B	2350	A	2393	A
2179	C	2222	B	2265	A	2308	B	2351	C	2394	A
2180	C	2223	A	2266	C	2309	D	2352	B	2395	D
2181	C	2224	C	2267	A	2310	D	2353	C	2396	D
2182	B	2225	E	2268	E	2311	C	2354	B	2397	E
2183	C	2226	B	2269	C	2312	D	2355	E	2398	B
2184	D	2227	B	2270	D	2313	D	2356	B	2399	D
2185	B	2228	E	2271	B	2314	A	2357	D	2400	A
2186	B	2229	A	2272	C	2315	A	2358	B	2401	C
2187	C	2230	A	2273	E	2316	D	2359	E	2402	B
2188	E	2231	C	2274	B	2317	C	2360	D	2403	C
2189	E	2232	B	2275	A	2318	D	2361	A	2404	C
2190	C	2233	D	2276	A	2319	E	2362	A	2405	A
2191	C	2234	D	2277	C	2320	B	2363	E	2406	D
2192	E	2235	E	2278	C	2321	C	2364	A	2407	B
2193	A	2236	B	2279	B	2322	B	2365	A	2408	E
2194	D	2237	B	2280	A	2323	A	2366	D	2409	A
2195	A	2238	A	2281	B	2324	E	2367	E	2410	D
2196	B	2239	B	2282	C	2325	C	2368	C	2411	C
2197	C	2240	E	2283	C	2326	A	2369	B	2412	A
2198	D	2241	E	2284	C	2327	A	2370	B	2413	A
2199	A	2242	A	2285	E	2328	A	2371	B	2414	A
2200	C	2243	D	2286	B	2329	A	2372	D	2415	E
2201	B	2244	B	2287	B	2330	C	2373	E	2416	B
2202	D	2245	E	2288	B	2331	B	2374	A	2417	D
2203	C	2246	C	2289	B	2332	B	2375	C	2418	A
2204	C	2247	E	2290	C	2333	B	2376	D	2419	B
2205	C	2248	B	2291	D	2334	B	2377	A	2420	C
2206	B	2249	A	2292	C	2335	B	2378	A	2421	E
2207	A	2250	E	2293	C	2336	A	2379	B	2422	D
2208	C	2251	A	2294	A	2337	A	2380	D	2423	B
2209	B	2252	A	2295	D	2338	A	2381	A	2424	E
2210	B	2253	C	2296	A	2339	A	2382	D	2425	B
2211	D	2254	B	2297	B	2340	D	2383	C	2426	E
2212	E	2255	A	2298	A	2341	D	2384	D	2427	A
2213	C	2256	C	2299	A	2342	A	2385	D	2428	A
2214	D	2257	E	2300	C	2343	C	2386	D	2429	B
2215	D	2258	D	2301	E	2344	A	2387	D	2430	B
2216	C	2259	C	2302	C	2345	A	2388	E	2431	E
2217	B	2260	A	2303	B	2346	B	2389	D	2432	A
2218	A	2261	B	2304	C	2347	D	2390	B	2433	C
2219	B	2262	A	2305	A	2348	B	2391	C	2434	B

Test 13: Multiple-Choice Questions 选择题库

2435	A	2453	A	2471	E	2489	D	2507	D	2525	D
2436	D	2454	E	2472	A	2490	B	2508	B	2526	C
2437	E	2455	B	2473	C	2491	E	2509	C	2527	E
2438	E	2456	C	2474	A	2492	B	2510	D	2528	C
2439	E	2457	A	2475	B	2493	A	2511	D	2529	A.
2440	E	2458	C	2476	D	2494	A	2512	E	2530	C
2441	E	2459	D	2477	E	2495	E	2513	E	2531	D
2442	A	2460	B	2478	C	2496	B	2514	A	2532	B
2443	A	2461	D	2479	E	2497	D	2515	C	2533	E
2444	A	2462	E	2480	E	2498	C	2516	B	2534	A
2445	B	2463	C	2481	D	2499	C	2517	C	2535	A
2446	B	2464	A	2482	A	2500	D	2518	D	2536	A
2447	B	2465	A	2483	E	2501	A	2519	A	2537	C
2448	C	2466	D	2484	E	2502	E	2520	E		
2449	B	2467	A	2485	B	2503	A	2521	E		
2450	C	2468	A	2486	C	2504	A	2522	C		
2451	D	2469	E	2487	A	2505	D	2523	B		
2452	A	2470	B	2488	C	2506	A	2524	C		

13-6	医案	2538-2642	Clinical Cases

2538	A	2558	A	2578	B	2599	A
2539	D	2559	B	2579	D	2600	A
2540	B	2560	C	2580	B	2601	B
2541	D	2561	D	2581	B	2602	A
2542	B	2562	B	2582	A	2603	B
2543	C	2563	A	2583	D	2604	A
2544	D	2564	A	2584	A	2605	A
2545	A	2565	A	2585	C	2606	B
2546	B	2566	C	2586	A	2607	B
2547	C	2567	A	2587	C	2608	A
2548	B	2568	C	2588	B	2609	C
2549	D	2569	B	2589	D	2610	B
2550	A	2570	A	2590	C	2611	A
2551	C	2571	B	2591	A	2612	D
2552	D	2572	B	2592	B	2613	C
2553	A	2573	C	2593	D	2614	B
2554	A	2574	D	2594	B		
2555	C	2575	A	2595	C	2615	D
2556	A	2576	A	2596	D	2616	B
2557	A	2577	D	2597	A	2617	C
				2598	A	2618	B

2619	B
2620	C
2621	A
2622	B
2623	C
2624	B
2625	B
2626	D
2627	B
2628	C
2629	C
2630	B
2631	A
2632	B
2633	C
2634	C
2635	A
2636	B
2637	D
2638	A
2639	B
2640	C
2641	C
2642	A

Test 13: Multiple-Choice Questions

2643	B
2644	D
2645	B
2646	B
2647	C
2648	C
2649	D
2650	C
2651	D
2652	D
2653	B
2654	B
2655	A
2656	A
2657	D
2658	A
2659	A
2660	D
2661	A
2662	A
2663	E
2664	E
2665	C
2666	D
2667	D
2668	D
2669	A
2670	A
2671	B
2672	C
2673	A
2674	E
2675	D
2676	C
2677	D
2678	E
2679	E
2680	D
2681	A
2682	E
2683	C

2684	C
2685	E
2686	B
2687	E
2688	B
2689	E
2690	D
2691	C
2692	A
2693	C
2694	B
2695	A
2696	D
2697	C
2698	B
2699	A
2700	B
2701	D
2702	B
2703	B
2704	A
2705	D
2706	C
2707	A
2708	C
2709	D
2710	D
2711	B
2712	C
2713	E
2714	B
2715	B
2716	A
2717	A
2718	A
2719	B
2720	B
2721	D
2722	D
2723	B
2724	B

2725	B
2726	A
2727	C
2728	A
2729	B
2730	D
2731	D
2732	C
2733	B
2734	E
2735	A
2736	C
2737	D
2738	B
2739	B
2740	C
2741	B
2742	C
2743	A
2744	B
2745	A
2746	A
2747	A
2748	B
2749	B
2750	B
2751	C
2752	D
2753	B
2754	A
2755	A
2756	B
2757	C
2758	D
2759	B
2760	B
2761	D
2762	A
2763	B
2764	E
2765	C

2766	B
2767	C
2768	C
2769	E
2770	D
2771	C
2772	C
2773	D
2774	B
2775	C
2776	A
2777	E
2778	E
2779	A
2780	E
2781	A
2782	D
2783	A
2784	B
2785	A
2786	C
2787	A
2788	C
2789	B
2790	A
2791	D
2792	C
2793	D
2794	A
2795	C
2796	E
2797	C
2798	A
2799	B
2800	C
2801	D
2802	B
2803	D
2804	A
2805	C
2806	E

2807	A
2808	A
2809	B
2810	A
2811	A
2812	B
2813	A
2814	A
2815	A
2816	B
2817	A
2818	B
2819	B
2820	B
2821	D
2822	C
2823	E
2824	D
2825	A
2826	B
2827	A
2828	A
2829	C
2830	B
2831	D
2832	A
2833	D
2834	A
2835	D
2836	C
2837	C
2838	D
2839	D
2840	C
2841	E
2842	C
2843	A
2844	D
2845	C
2846	A
2847	B

No.	Answer
2848	E
2849	A
2850	B
2851	B
2852	D
2853	C
2854	E
2855	C
2856	B
2857	D
2858	D
2859	B
2860	C
2861	D
2862	C
2863	E
2864	B
2865	C
2866	A
2867	D
2868	A
2869	A
2870	E
2871	E
2872	D
2873	B
2874	C
2875	E
2876	C
2877	A
2878	E
2879	D
2880	A
2881	E
2882	C
2883	E
2884	C
2885	A
2886	B
2887	D
2888	B
2889	B
2890	A
2891	B
2892	C
2893	A
2894	E
2895	D
2896	C
2897	C
2898	C
2899	B
2900	D
2901	B
2902	A
2903	E
2904	A
2905	B
2906	C
2907	C
2908	D
2909	B
2910	C
2911	C
2912	A
2913	B
2914	A
2915	D
2916	B
2917	C
2918	E
2919	E
2920	A
2921	A
2922	A
2923	D
2924	A
2925	B
2926	C
2927	B
2928	D
2929	E
2930	E
2931	B
2932	A
2933	B
2934	C
2935	D
2936	B
2937	D
2938	B
2939	D
2940	C
2941	B
2942	A
2943	E
2944	D
2945	D
2946	A
2947	C
2948	B
2949	E
2950	B
2951	D
2952	A
2953	A
2954	C
2955	D
2956	D
2957	E
2958	B
2959	B
2960	D
2961	A
2962	E
2963	E
2964	C
2965	A
2966	A
2967	B
2968	A
2969	E
2970	D
2971	A
2972	D
2973	E
2974	E
2975	E
2976	C
2977	A
2978	D
2979	C
2980	D
2981	D
2982	D
2983	B
2984	A
2985	C
2986	A
2987	B
2988	C
2989	A
2990	B
2991	C
2992	C
2993	D
2994	E
2995	C
2996	D
2997	D
2998	A
2999	C
3000	E
3001	E
3002	A
3003	B
3004	A
3005	C
3006	D
3007	A
3008	C
3009	B
3010	B
3011	A
3012	E
3013	A
3014	C
3015	B

Test 13: Multiple-Choice Questions

3016	B
3017	A
3018	E
3019	C
3020	E
3021	E
3022	B
3023	D
3024	B
3025	D
3026	C
3027	D

3028	C
3029	D
3030	B
3031	A
3032	C
3033	C
3034	C
3035	C
3036	C
3037	B
3038	C
3039	D

3040	A
3041	A
3042	E
3043	C
3044	C
3045	C
3046	E
3047	A
3048	C
3049	D
3050	D
3051	C

3052	C
3053	D
3054	A
3055	B
3056	E
3057	E
3058	B
3059	D
3060	D
3061	A
3062	A

13-8 Cautious Points / 要小心操作的穴位 (3063-3222)

3063	C
3064	B
3065	A
3066	A
3067	A
3068	B
3069	E
3070	C
3071	D
3072	D
3073	B
3074	A
3075	C
3076	D
3077	E
3078	B
3079	C
3080	A
3081	D
3082	E
3083	D
3084	B
3085	C
3086	A
3087	D
3088	B
3089	B
3090	E
3091	A

3092	E
3093	A
3094	C
3095	B
3096	D
3097	A
3098	B
3099	D
3100	E
3101	C
3102	E
3103	A
3104	B
3105	B
3106	A
3107	D
3108	B
3109	E
3110	D
3111	E
3112	A
3113	B
3114	B
3115	A
3116	E
3117	C
3118	C
3119	C
3120	B

3121	B
3122	C
3123	B
3124	C
3125	C
3126	A
3127	E
3128	E
3129	D
3130	D
3131	E
3132	E
3133	C
3134	A
3135	B
3136	D
3137	A
3138	A
3139	A
3140	E
3141	D
3142	C
3143	D
3144	B
3145	A
3146	D
3147	D
3148	A
3149	E

3150	E
3151	A
3152	B
3153	B
3154	B
3155	A
3156	A
3157	C
3158	B
3159	D
3160	C
3161	C
3162	A
3163	D
3164	E
3165	C
3166	D
3167	C
3168	A
3169	A
3170	E
3171	C
3172	D
3173	E
3174	C
3175	C
3176	B
3177	E
3178	D

3179	D
3180	A
3181	D
3182	E
3183	C
3184	C
3185	D
3186	B
3187	A
3188	D
3189	C
3190	B
3191	A
3192	A
3193	D
3194	B
3195	E
3196	A
3197	A
3198	D
3199	A
3200	B
3201	D
3202	B
3203	C
3204	D
3205	A
3206	D
3207	E
3208	E
3209	C
3210	B
3211	C
3212	C
3213	D
3214	B
3215	E
3216	B
3217	C
3218	E
3219	A
3220	B
3221	C
3222	E
3223	A
3224	E
3225	B
3226	D
3227	D
3228	C
3229	E
3230	C
3231	C
3232	E
3233	E
3234	C
3235	E
3236	D
3237	B
3238	E
3239	B
3240	E
3241	D
3242	E
3243	B
3244	D
3245	E
3246	A
3247	C
3248	A
3249	D
3250	E
3251	B
3252	C
3253	E
3254	A

CPSIA information can be obtained at www.ICGtesting.com
Printed in the USA
LVOW091743260413

331153LV00019B/789/P